ISBN 978-0-332-69909-7
PIBN 11219034

For support please visit www.forgottenbooks.com

THE

AMERICAN

CATHOLIC QUARTERLY

REVIEW.

Bonum est homini ut eum veritas volentem, quia malum est homini ut eum veritas vincat
invitum.   Nam ipsa vincat necesse est, sive negantem sive confitentem.

S. AUG. EPIST. ccxxxviii. AD PASCENT.

VOLUME X.

FROM JANUARY TO OCTOBER, 1885.

PHILADELPHIA:

HARDY & MAHONY,

PUBLISHERS AND PROPRIETORS,

505 CHESTNUT STREET.

TABLE OF CONTENTS.

Table of Contents.

BOOK NOTICES.

THE

AMERICAN

CATHOLIC QUARTERLY

REVIEW.

Bonum est homini ut eum veritas vincat volentem, quia malum est homini ut eum veritas vincat invitum. Nam ipsa vincat necesse est, sive negantem sive confitentem.

S. AUG. EPIST. ccxxxviii. AD PASCENT.

PHILADELPHIA:

HARDY AND MAHONY, PUBLISHERS AND PROPRIETORS,

505 CHESTNUT ST.,—P. O. BOX 1044,

rk : D. & J. SADLIER & Co., F. PUSTET—*Boston :* THOS. B. NOONAN & Co., NICH. M. WILLIAM
ltimore : JOHN MURPHY & Co., JOHN B. PIET & Co.—*Cincinnati :* BENZIGER BROS., F. PUSTET—
St. Louis : P. FOX, BENZIGER BROS., B. HERDER—*San Francisco :* M. FLOOD—*New Orleans :*
CHARLES D. ELDER—*Montreal :* D. & J. SADLIER & Co.—*St. John, N. B.:* T. O'BRIEN
& Co.—*London :* BURNS & OATES—*Dublin :* W. H. SMITH & SON, M. H. GILL & SON.

NEWSDEALERS SUPPLIED BY THE AMERICAN NEWS COMPANY, NEW YORK—
NEWS CO., PHILADELPHIA—NEW ENGLAND NEWS CO., BOSTON—CINCINNATI NEWS CO.
CINCINNATI. OHIO—WESTERN NEWS CO.. CHICAGO, ILL.

Entered according to Act of Congress in   . 1879 by Hardy & Mahony in the Office of the

TENTH YEAR.

THE
AMERICAN CATHOLIC QUARTERLY REVIEW.

RIGHT REV. JAMES A. CORCORAN, D. D.,
EDITOR-IN-CHIEF.

$5.00 per Annum, in Advance.

Issued in January, April, July, and October. Each number contains 192 large octavo pages, printed from legible type, on fine white paper.

Subscriptions Respectfully Solicited.

Address,

HARDY & MAHONY,

No. 505 Chestnut Street.
Box 1044.

Publishers and Proprietors,

PHILADELPHIA.

THE AMERICAN CATHOLIC

QUARTERLY REVIEW.

VOL. X.—JANUARY, 1885.—No. 37.

THE PASTORAL LETTER OF THE THIRD PLENARY COUNCIL OF BALTIMORE.

THE grandest ecclesiastical body that ever met on the soil of America has closed its sessions, that lasted for more than a month, in the time-honored Cathedral of Baltimore, and Archbishops, Bishops, Superiors of religious Orders, and learned theologians have departed, each to the scene of his appointed ordinary labors in the Church. The solemnly enacted laws of this great Christian legislature will not be promulgated for some time, not till, like the laws of our national legislature, they receive their final sanction from the Supreme Ruler. But the Fathers of the Third Plenary Council did not disperse over the vast continent before they had issued to the Catholic clergy and laity of the United States words full of the spirit of faith, of wisdom, and of prudence, words which are full of lessons for every Catholic, and for every one who loves his country and its institutions, and hopes to see them maintained and upheld by citizens taking as their guide the highest principles of religion and morality.

The pastoral is not a repetition of ideas and words, used over and over again as a stereotyped charge to the people, droned out to drowsy ears. We stand on the brink of an abyss, the hundred years comprising the life of our Constitutional government marking, in Europe, the growth of elements that have steadily, persistently, and with

all the skill and adroitness of perverted ingenuity, aimed to destroy
all faith in Christianity, all social order, all sound political ideas.
Had the wide ocean that rolls between America and Europe kept
all this from our shores, the warning of the Plenary Council would
be needless.   But such is not the case; the principles of the
French Revolution, or rather those of which it was the first great
and fearful manifestation, have made literature, science, art, education, vehicles for corrupting mankind, and, under the specious
and insidious guise of liberalism, seduced men from the path of
right and light into the ways of wrong and obscurity.

The residue of Christianity retained in this country withstood,
for a time, the influence of these perverse ideas; but the barriers
have gradually broken away, and there is no longer a sound
Christian public opinion, no longer the former power in the bodies
still claiming to be Christian, either to teach the primary truths of
religion or to enforce the clearest rules of morality.

The Catholic Church has become the only one that can boldly
avow a belief in God and revelation, defend the integrity and authenticity of the Scriptures, or maintain the superiority of the supernatural over the material.   It must become daily more and more
distinctly the only institution in the land to which all who continue
to believe in God, in redemption through Christ, must gather, as
the only one which speaks authoritatively and unwaveringly.

In this view, a fearful responsibility rests on the Catholic Church
in this country.   Its mission is not only to save the souls actually
within the fold, and shield them from the deluge by retaining them
in the Ark of Safety, but also to withstand and oppose the torrents,
and rescue from their depths all who appeal for aid.

Eighteen years ago the Catholic hierarchy met before in Plenary
Council, and their wise and timely legislation has borne fruit.
There is nothing for the prelates just assembled to reverse, but in
that time, less than a generation, the designs of evil have become
clearer, its weapons are better known, and the rulers in the Church
of God, acting under His guidance, can take more decisive steps
to counteract it.

That the Church has been able to effect its organization over so
vast a territory, to develop, as it instinctively does, the great institutions and works that spring from the evangelical counsels, and
do this unchecked and almost unimpeded by civil government or
popular violence, amid a population imbued for centuries with
every form of heretical opinion and prejudice, is, in itself, one of
the most remarkable facts in the whole history of the Church.
What Cavour said in mockery, when he planned the subjugation
of the Church to the caprices of godless civil power—a Free
Church in a Free State—while it never has existed in Europe, is

here a reality. In no other country could seventy archbishops and bishops assemble with their theologians, with abbots of St. Benedict and Citeaux, with provincials of the orders founded by St. Augustine, St. Francis, St. Dominic, St. Ignatius, St. Vincent de Paul, St. Alphonsus Liguori, St. Paul of the Cross, with the Sons of Carmel and communities of more recent date, as well as superiors of theological seminaries, and deliberate freely. In many lands, to follow the rule of venerated Saints of God is regarded as a crime like those which consign men to a felon's cell, and the religious is punished by perpetual exile, while the malefactor loses his liberty but for a brief term.

Divine Providence, in thus constituting the Church in this country, like an army arrayed for battle, with the unseen legions of guardian angels of church and religious hall, and of Christian homes, gathered as auxiliaries near at hand, prepared it for some great work; and even among her enemies there must be Balaams who discern that the power of God is with her. Even on our soil the inscrutable ways of Providence have baffled, again and again, the designs and apparent triumphs of men. France, in her day of faith, planted Christianity in the valleys of the two great arteries of our northern continent. Her rulers, sunk in vice, lost to a Protestant power their fair American realm. The Catholic Church seemed doomed; but she was saved in Canada, and the very men who rose in indignation at that unexpected event opened almost all the rest of the Continent to the free action of the Church. Spain, that secured from the Pope such immense power in America for her sovereigns, lost her line of faith-inspired rulers: she lost her American possessions by the very irreligion she fostered. The paltry infidelity of the wretched parodies of our republic oppressed religion, and when provinces fell into the hands of the United States, with its dominant Catholicity-hating Protestantism, Catholicity seemed doomed; but from those very sections came Archbishops and Bishops, representing sees that still retain their Spanish names, to attend the Plenary Council. At the beginning of this century, when a Pope died a prisoner, pulpits in this country resounded with the eloquence of exultation. The Catholic Church was dead. Struck in its very head, it could never rise again. How little did the exulters dream that the closing years of the century would see their organizations powerless, and the Catholic Church pervading the land, greeting, by a means then unsuspected and unknown, a Pope in Rome, as it opened its solemn council, and receiving an instantaneous reply !

Thus has Providence, by a series of surprises, baffling human wisdom and human hopes, brought the Church to her actual condition in this country. And it is surely for a great purpose.

In the pastoral of the Fathers of the third Plenary Council, we are led to look into the future and divine their purpose and the duty incumbent upon all. Three years after the close of the previous Plenary Council, the illustrious Pope Pius IX., as the pastoral notes, assembled the Vatican Council; and many of those who had attended our national synod, with others succeeding them, and who are still alive, took part in the deliberations of that Council, which was the first that represented all quarters of the globe. " Its appointed task," says the pastoral, " was to condemn the most influential and insidious errors of the day, and to complete the legislation on weighty matters of discipline. . . . . During its short session of seven months, the Vatican Council gave solemn authoritative utterance to some great truths which the Church had unvaryingly held from the days of Christ and His apostles; but which she found at once more necessary to recall and inculcate against the widespread skepticism and unbelief of our day. Besides condemning the philosophy, no less wicked than false, and teeming with contradictions, of the last two centuries, and especially of our own times, she had to uphold (such is the lamentable downward course of those who rebelled against her Divine commission to teach all nations) the truth and divinity of the Sacred Books against the very children of those who once appealed to Scripture to disprove her teachings, and to maintain the dignity and value of human reason against the lineal descendants of those who once claimed reason as the supreme and only guide in picking out from her creed what mysteries they would retain, what mysteries they would reject."

The Fathers of the Council say to the flocks confided to their care : " We have no reason to fear that you, beloved brethren, are likely to be carried away by these or other false doctrines condemned by the Vatican Council, such as materialism or the denial of God's power to create, to reveal to mankind His hidden truths, to display by miracles His almighty power in this world, which is the work of His hands. But neither can we close our eyes to the fact that teachers of skepticism and irreligion are at work in our country. They have crept into the leading educational institutions of our non-Catholic fellow-citizens ; they have, though rarely, made their appearance in the public press, and even in the pulpit." " When we take into account the daily signs of growing unbelief, and see how its heralds not only seek to mould the youthful minds in our colleges and seats of learning, but are also actively working amongst the masses, we cannot but shudder at the dangers that threaten us in the future. When to this we add the rapid growth of that false civilization which hides its foulness under the name of enlightenment, involving as it does the undisguised worship of mammon; the anxious search after every ease, comfort, and luxury for man's physical well-being; the all-absorbing desire to promote his material interests; the unconcern or rather contempt for those of his higher and better nature,—we cannot but feel that out of all this must grow a heartless materialism, which is the best soil to receive the seeds of unbelief and irreligion, which threaten to desolate the country at no distant day. The first thing to perish will be our liberties. For men who know not God or religion can never respect the unalienable rights which man has received from his Creator. The State in such case must become a despotism, whether its power be lodged in the hands of one or many."

That the Fathers are taking no exaggerated view of the condition of the country will be admitted by every observant person. The foundation of our earlier political and educational system was Christianity, but the recognition of its truths is passing away. The exclusion of religion from the general teaching of the young has opened the door to the introduction of materialism and infidelity, for the exclusion of religion is practically infidelity. And where the great fundamental truths of Christianity are not inculcated as a basis and canon for the reasoning of man as he advances from youth to maturity, they never can become a controlling ele ment in the actions of life. The studies from the primary school to the university cannot be colorless; if not Christian, they are certain to be materialistic, naturalistic, or agnostic, if not openly infidel. The more recently established colleges, scientific publications, even the works issued at Washington by the general government, teem with theories and arguments directly at variance with the fundamental truths of the Christian religion; and writers on ethnology and antiquity seem to think that they cannot obtain European recognition except by warping facts and inferences to assail the existence of God and His providence. So indifferent has public opinion become, that this goes on unchecked. While a few were agitating to "put God into the Constitution," they and the rest beheld with indifference the Government Printing Office become the vehicle for disseminating arguments insidiously framed against revelation. In this weakening of the last remnant of faith, this growing indifference, vice and immorality find their fertile soil. Disregard of human life, profligacy, dishonesty in all commercial and fiduciary transactions, increase with a rapidity that is appalling.

The Church has a task of gigantic magnitude to save her flock in this country from the contamination of the world that surrounds it.

Earnestly, then, does the Pastoral exclaim to those who possess the treasure of Catholic faith: "Keep day and night before your eyes the law of God and His teachings through that Holy Church.

that He has appointed mother· and mistress of all men.   Fly the
reading of all infidel books, and keep them from your children, as
you would the poison of asp or basilisk.   Teach them that you
and they in listening to Holy Church have the guidance of Him
who said: ' I am the way, the truth, and the life.'   Let others
doubt or deny, but, with the Apostle, you know whom you' have
believed, and you are certain that He will make good the trust
you have reposed in Him."

But the works on every branch of human learning which are
insidiously made the vehicles of error are not so easily guarded
against, as the evil is not seen by all.   Hence the Church must,
in the training of her children, arm them to meet the enemies
whom they will have to encounter, and enable them to detect and
refute the soul-destroying errors that lurk in honeyed phrases.

All this flood of error sprang from the fundamental error of the
Reformers, that God revealed forms of words for men to seek amid
their mazes in translations for the truths by the light of private
judgment, when reason itself would show that God must reveal
truths, and must maintain an authority on earth to keep from mis-
construction the words of His inspired servants through whom He •
reveals them.   Starting from an erroneous standpoint, making the
Scriptures and their translations of them as understood by private
interpretation to be absolute truth, the Reformers and their followers have come at last to reject the truth and inspiration of the
Scriptures.   Their vagaries, from an almost idolatrous honor of
the material volume to the utter rejection of its letter and spirit,
attest the necessity of an infallible, ever-abiding authority on
earth, which could declare what was the truth revealed by God to
man.   In the designs of Providence it was ordained that when
this error of private judgment and denial of a teaching Church had
culminated in rejecting the Scriptures, the Infallibility of the Head
of the Church, in officially teaching the pastors and flocks confided
to him, should be distinctly and unequivocally asserted and maintained as the only safe guide for human reason seeking to know
the relations of man to his Maker.

The assertion of this great truth, which had always been practically recognized, excited " a storm of fierce obloquy and reckless
vituperation."   It is a curious fact, however, that the opposition to
it, and to the Church because of it, was greatest where civil liberty
was least known, and where governments were most despotic.   As
the luminous pastoral declares, " the governments by which, three
centuries ago, the new tenets of Luther, Zwingli, and Calvin had
been imposed on reluctant peoples by the sword, were the first,
indeed the only ones to unsheath it again against Catholic believers, and especially against bishops and clergy.   It was their

purpose to exterminate by degrees the Catholic hierarchy and replace it by a servile priesthood that would subordinate its preaching and ministry to the will of the State." While governments warred on the Church, striking in their folly at the most conservative element in human society, they closed their eyes to the dangers from the principles they had fostered and encouraged, but which the Church had strenuously condemned. Nations were found to be swarming with millions who had learned in secret societies to deny God and His Providence, to deny the authority of civil governments, the rights of property, and marriage as the basis of the family. One ruler assassinated, others constantly menanced, compelled monarchs to pause and consider. Like the handwriting on the wall came the words : " And now, O ye kings, understand, receive instruction, ye who judge the earth." The czar begins to see that the most loyal subjects of his empire are the Catholics whose portion has been Siberia, the knout, unheard-of cruelties. Prussia finds that her dangerous radicals learned their lessons from those most removed from Catholic teachings. France has no hope except in her deliverance from a nest of conspirators who even in power are ever plotting against each other and against the welfare and honor of the nation. Before it is too late, they have begun to cry, " Erravimus." Acknowledging their folly and injustice, " the rulers of Prussia have had to fall back on the patriotism of the Catholic body to stay the threatening march of socialism and revolution." England, which once denounced the Catholic clergy as surpliced ruffians, and loaded them with insult when she could no longer torture or slay, now seeks to aid them in their work, seeing in their beneficent action the safeguard of the constitution menaced by the widespread infidelity among the lower classes in England, but from which the Catholic Church has hitherto saved Ireland.

Men, of course, are slow to admit a truth which they have been trained from the cradle to impeach and deny, but every statesman, every thoughtful student of the political condition of the world is at least forced to admit, even if he has not the courage to avow it, that the safest element in every country is the body true to the teachings of the Catholic Church, with an unerring guide in its faith, its philosophy and its ethics, saving it from infidel and revolutionary tendencies, and guiding it by rules of such clearness and wisdom that they cannot be merely human. Our republic grew out of communities nursed in prejudice and error, and has not altogether thrown off the fetters of colonial days. Some look with fear and jealousy at the Church, but light is spreading even amid souls in the deepest mists and clouds of error. The pastoral puts a truth tersely. " A Catholic finds himself at home in the United

States; for the influence of his church has constantly been exercised in behalf of individual rights and popular liberties. And the right-minded American nowhere finds himself more at home than in the Catholic Church, for nowhere else can he breathe that atmosphere of divine truth which alone can make us free." "The Fathers wisely refute the idea that we Catholics need lay aside any of our love of our country's principles and institutions to be faithful Catholics.

"The spirit of American freedom is not one of anarchy or license." There is a striking proof of this in the apathy of our people at large in regard to the Bartholdi statue of "Liberty enlightening the world." The very conception shocks the mass of the American people. Liberty, as they understand it, is not the liberty of the French Republic, with its denial of God and its deification of reason; it is not the liberty of the Communist and the Nihilist; and the type of the statue is rather that liberty than the spirit of liberty which our fathers taught us to prize. Civil liberty is great in our eyes, but we look higher for the "Light of the World." Americans have not renounced Christ to look to such liberty as the statue typifies, and they do not take heartily to it. The spirit of American freedom "essentially involves love of order, respect for rightful authority and obedience to just laws. There is nothing in the character of the most liberty-loving American which could hinder his reverential submission to the divine authority of our Lord, or to the like authority delegated by Him to His apostles and His Church. Nor are there in the world more devoted adherents of the Catholic Church, the see of Peter and the Vicar of Christ, than the Catholics of the United States."

Passing from the general consideration of the Church in its head, the pastoral comes to the present condition of Pope Leo XIII. His condition as a virtual prisoner in the city which owes its modern life and importance to the care of the Sovereign Pontiff, is clearly stated, and the work of sacrilege in the capital of the Catholic world, where a horde of foreign adventurers have despoiled and scattered the central establishments of the great religious orders, so useful to the Church, and even the property contributed by the Christian world for foreign missions. His heroism in enduring the evils that surround him is equalled by the wisdom with which he has labored to disarm the hostilities of governments in other lands, which have been antagonistic to the Church, as well as to recall to the bosom of unity the ancient oriental churches, which, severed from the divine vine, preserved but a languishing life.

But in all the wide circle of his great responsibility, the progress of the Church in these United States forms in a special manner, both a source of joy and an object of solicitude to the Holy Father.

With loving care his predecessors watched and encouraged her first feeble beginnings. They cheered and fostered her development in the pure atmosphere of freedom, when the name of Carroll shone with equal lustre at the head of her new born hierarchy, and on the roll of our country's patriots. Step by step they directed her progress, as, with marvellous rapidity, the clergy and the dioceses have multiplied, the hundreds of the faithful have increased to thousands and to millions; her churches, schools, asylums, hospitals, academies, and colleges, have covered the land with homes of divine truth and Christian charity. Not yet a century has elapsed since the work was inaugurated by the appointment of the first Bishop of Baltimore in 1789; and as we gaze upon the results already reached, we must exclaim: " By the Lord hath this been done, and it is wonderful in our eyes."

In all this astonishing development, from the rude beginnings of pioneer missionary toil, along the nearer and nearer approaches to the beauteous symmetry of the Church's perfect organization, the advance so gradual, yet so rapid, has been safely guided in the lines of Catholic and Apostolic tradition, by the combined efforts and wisdom of our local hierarchy and of the successors of St. Peter. It was in order to take counsel with the representatives of the American hierarchy concerning the important interests of religion in this country, that the Holy Father, last year, invited the archbishops of the United States to Rome.

In the plenary council which has just held session after session in the Catholic capital of the country, the archbishops and bishops of the country, with the counsel of the most learned men in the secular and regular clergy, coming from seminary, college, and cloister, with priests grown gray in mission labors among the Catholics in all parts of the country, familiar with the wants, the difficulties, and the dangers of all, deliberated patiently and exhaustively to put into practical shape the means of religious improvement which had been suggested or resolved upon in the conferences at Rome.

One of the most serious points was the more thorough education of candidates for the priesthood. The great want of priests to meet the increase by immigration for a long time compelled the bishops to shorten the term of study and training, and to supply the want of regular seminaries as best they could. The multiplied duties devolving on the clergy gave little time to continue or even keep fresh in mind the detail of the teachings of the church in dogma, moral, or canon law. But the time has come when the young levite can go through a more extended course, and acquire the extended and thorough knowledge necessary to enable the priest of God " to show forth worthily the beauty, the superiority, the necessity of the Christian religion, and to prove that there is nothing in all that God has made to contradict anything that God has taught." The influence of such learned priests ought henceforward to be felt, not only in the church whose walls re-echo his voice, but throughout the land, in the literature, the science, the societies, and organizations of thoughtful men, where many would with thankful hearts receive the clear logical solution of the question before them from those whose superior training was based on the irrefragable principles of an unvarying faith.

To train priests who can thus acquire and thus exercise the learning which natural talents with long study and God's grace are to be acquired, seminaries must be maintained, and institutions created of a higher grade than any that the church yet possesses in this country. A great university is one of the necessities of the church. Canada has one; Mexico and Spanish America till the days of revolution had many. The fathers of the council appeal to the faithful to take to heart this great work of the training of the clergy. They remind those to whom God has been pleased to give wealth, "that it is their duty and their privilege to consider themselves the Lord's stewards, in the use of what his Providence has placed in their hands; that they should be foremost in helping on the work of the Church of Christ during life, and make sure to have God among their heirs when they die;" and the prelates especially recommend to the wealthy the founding of scholarships, either in their diocesan or provincial seminaries, or in the American college at Rome, and in time in our Catholic University. Such burses or foundations were one of the most ordinary pious uses favored by our Catholic ancestors, as the English, Scotch, and Irish colleges on the continent show; but unfortunately one of the rarest adopted in this country, where they are so much needed. The late Dr. Edmund B. O'Callaghan, and his wife who survived him, are among the notable exceptions. All the property of that Catholic historian of New York went to endow scholarships for the education of priests in the Provincial Seminary at Troy, and in the Society of Jesus. Year by year priests educated by the income of that fund will be ordained and begin to offer the holy sacrifice, and who can number the suffrages which these privileged souls will thus obtain? Surely such an example is worthy of imitation.

Reuben R. Springer, of Cincinnati, who has just passed away, remembered to make God his heir, and, among his numerous bequests to religion, gave one hundred thousand dollars, a sum somewhat exceeding that just mentioned, the income to be devoted to the education of priests at Mount St. Mary's of the West.

The due formation of the clergy is a topic that leads to the consideration of the position of the priest after he has been ordained and begun his labors among the flock of Christ. In Europe, after the time of Constantine, a system grew up, recognized in time by all Christian powers, by which the rights, immunities, and privileges of the clergy, their support, and all judicial matters relating to them, and to the church in general, were regulated. This was the canon law, which had its own ecclesiastical tribunals where it was enforced. The immunities secured by the church were the cradle of civil liberty, as from this point the people freed themselves from the rapacity of feudal lords. At times in the long struggle of the church against the attempt to enslave, some concessions would be made to save higher interests, and the whole system became a complex and difficult one.

Within the last hundred years, nearly everything of the earlier organization has been swept away in Europe. The great religious orders have been despoiled and banished; the property of the church has been seized; the tithes, that were once paid to the parish priest for his support, are replaced by a petty salary doled out by the state, subject to be delayed or stopped at any moment.

In Canada there is more of the old organization left than can be generally found in Europe. There the parishes remain as they were instituted in the seventeenth century, the parish priest still receives his tithes, and holds his appointment until a judicial tribunal declares that he has forfeited it by violation of law. It is a bit of old Catholic Europe preserved in our century.

But in this country none of this ever obtained. If there were regular parishes instituted at Detroit, Kaskaskia, Cahokia, St. Louis, Mobile, St. Augustine, and in Louisiana, most of these have lapsed; no tithes are paid, and throughout the country there have been simply missionary priests subject to the bishop of the diocese, who can transfer them from one mission to another, as in his judgment the good of the diocese requires. As the church has consolidated, this condition, temporary in its nature, and liable from hasty or ill-considered action to work injustice, was required to be superseded by one more in harmony with the general policy of the church. To adopt the whole body of canon law, which grew up during many centuries in countries existing under far different conditions, would entail endless confusion. To apply to the church in this country the spirit which underlies all the provisions of canon law, required the greatest wisdom, prudence, knowledge of the country and its needs, and freedom from any bias or prejudice prevailing among the Catholic clergy and people in this country; for, unfortunately, designing men are fanning hostility of Catholic priest and layman against Catholic priest and layman, because they saw the light in different lands.

The Fathers of the Council have endeavored to advance in applying to the Church here the wise fundamental laws which the Church has adopted by the experience of centuries, and which represent the perfection of Church organization. Steps have been taken to form a nucleus of priests in each diocese, who by long and blameless service on the mission shall be entitled to fixity of tenure in their charges, and similar steps to secure to all having care of souls inviolability of their pastoral authority within proper limits. These new regulations, adopted after the practical test of preliminary ordinances, and embodying the result of most serious counsel, cannot fail to benefit religion greatly by preventing to a considerable extent a class of contests which has increased within recent years, dividing the people and giving pain to all who have the real interests of the Church at heart.

The Council appeals to the laity to be loyal in upholding their pastors in the labors undertaken for the good of their souls, and of their children after them. " A grateful and pious flock is sure to make a happy pastor. But if the people do not respond to their pastor's zeal, if they are cold and ungrateful, or disedifying, then, indeed, is his lot sad and pitiable. Since, therefore, the priests of God leave all things to devote themselves to your spiritual welfare, show by your affection, by your co-operation with their efforts for your spiritual improvement, and even by your care for their physical comfort, that you appreciate their devotedness and the reciprocal obligation which it imposes."

One of the hardest and most thankless tasks of the priest in this country is the collecting of money for the parochial wants. A church to be built or enlarged, schools erected and maintained, asylum, cemetery, all require money. Few are the wealthy who ever assume any part, although the number is increasing. Generally the priest must collect, not dollar by dollar, but almost cent by cent, the thousands of dollars needed. He comes to the parish without means; and many a good priest, after by his exertions endowing a parish with a church and schools, departs as poor as he came, broken in health and spirits,—not even rewarded by the gratitude of the flock for whom he has unselfishly labored. The property remains, enabling the people to worship God in the awful sacrifice; to have their children trained for this world, and, what is far more, for heaven, by the doctrines of faith; the cemetery remains, where they can be laid in hallowed earth. What base ingratitude must there be in those who murmur against the poor priest who, uncheered but undaunted, secured these blessings to them! Well does the Council rouse the spirit of faith in the people to regard these things from a proper standpoint. And yet Catholics should hardly need urging and public entreaty to bring them to act heartily with their clergy in all that is for the common good.

The amount of work to be done to bring a parish to a normal condition often exceeded the means of the congregation, or the amount they chose to contribute. The pastor was forced to borrow, and where this was done, in the times of inflated prices, during and after the late civil war, the shrinkage of values has made these debts very onerous. In some parts, especially in the Southern States, where so much perished during the war, the condition is pitiable. Besides the current expenses of the Church, a vast load of debt, calling for annual interest, makes it necessary that heroic exertions should be made to diminish, if not extinguish, them.

Much debt has been incurred in establishing parochial schools, institutions of paramount necessity, as the public school system is controlled absolutely by Protestants, conducted on Protestant principles, and made an instrument for debauching the faith of Catholic children who enter the walls of State institutions. That they will in time become utterly unchristian seems almost inevitable.

" In days like ours, when error is so pretentious and aggressive, every one needs to be as fully armed as possible with sound knowledge,—not only the clergy, but the people, also,—that they may be able to withstand the noxious influences of the popularized irreligion. In the great coming combat between Faith and Agnosticism, an important part of the fray must be borne by the laity, and woe to them if they are not well-prepared." Religion is excluded from the State schools because a part of the people wish it; but no sound reason, no article of Constitution or law gives this part a right to say that those who wish their children's education imbued with religion shall not have them so trained. The advocates of secular education may ask it for their own children; they have no right to dictate to others in regard to the children of others. But as the public schools are, they are likely to remain; and every new demand of those who oppose religion will be granted, while the wishes of the religiously inclined portion of the community are to be treated as entitled to no respect whatever. Many zealous Protestants, guided only by prejudice against Catholics, gave strength and support to the opponents of all religion, and are now, in view of the fatal results of godless education, endeavoring to restore the old church-schools, once the prevailing ones in the country.

These men, having religion at heart, will read approvingly the words of the Council: " It cannot be desirable or advantageous that religion should be excluded from the school. On the contrary, it ought to be there, to be one of the chief agencies for moulding the young life to all that is true, and virtuous, and holy. To shut religion out of the school, and keep it for home and the church, is, logically, to train up a generation that will consider religion good for home and the church, but not for the practical business of real life. But a more false and pernicious notion could not be imagined. Religion, in order to elevate a people, should inspire their whole life, and rule their relations with one another."

"All religious denominations are now awaking to this great truth, which the Catholic Church has never ceased to maintain. Reason and experience are forcing them to recognize that the only practical way to secure a Christian people is to give the youth a Christian education." "Hence, the cry for Christian education is going up from all religious bodies throughout the land."

We need not wonder, then, that the great senate of Catholic Bishops urges the faithful to maintain and perfect the parochial schools, and supply them where they are still required. The due organization of the schools in each diocese, and the adapting of the course of study to our actual wants, is now a matter of serious consideration. Our schools have in many cases been modeled on the public schools, and the endeavor made to rival them. But we do not seem to have succeeded as well in imbuing our school children with attachment to the Church, with a dread of religious error, with the terrible consequences of a loss of faith, to the extent that Protestants succeed in imbuing their children with a fear and dread of our holy faith, and such an aversion to it, that they grow up to maturity full of a prejudice that makes them shrink from opening a Catholic book, or listening to a Catholic address.

Since our children meet, as soon as they leave school, those who attempt to seduce them, and destroy their faith in the Catholic Church, or in Christianity itself, it seems evident that they should go forth armed and prepared to meet this temptation, and not fall. That they are thus equipped in a majority of cases, it would be rash to assert.

When, a generation ago, the attacks on the faith of the Catholics in Ireland came from the Anglican Church, the peasant of that time, who could but read, as he was taught in a hedge school, had imbibed a stronger love of his faith, and was better able to answer objections to it, better able to retort arguments on his tempter or assailant, than the pupils of many of our schools are, although they are conducted on the most approved systems of pedagogics by teachers trained in normal schools. The young must be taught not in dull dry forms; they must be interested in their religion, and their enthusiasm awakened, so that their hearts shall be strong and their heads supplied with arguments to defend their faith and put the scoffers to flight. They should be trained never to be ashamed of their faith, but to confess and maintain it.

Christian marriage, as the world has known it, is the creation of the Catholic Church taught by her divine founder. Typifying the union of Christ and his Church, matrimony, raised to a sacrament, rose above the marriage of the Hebrews, and far above the ideas of marriage that prevailed among the most cultured of heathen nations. By Christian marriage woman was exalted from the position of a slave or a chattel to a higher and nobler sphere. One of the objects of the Reformation was to drag her down to the Pagan level, and we see this indicated only too clearly in their almost instantaneous change of the Ten Commandments, rejecting the ordinary and later form of Scripture, to make men learn one that made the wife less than her husband's house and little more than his ox. The Catholic indissolubility of marriage was rejected and divorces were allowed. At first, the causes were few, and restrictions were many; now, as irreligion and impiety advance, attempts are made to make marriage a merely temporary union, voidable at will. To the Catholic no divorce is possible; the union he contracts is indissoluble. Death alone can set either of a married pair free to marry again. No decree of court, no act of parliament or legislature, can justify a Catholic in re-marrying. It is a matter of consolation that, in the many works and articles, now called forth by the terrible license of divorce prevailing in this country, and the no less fearful immorality which must precede these divorces, writers unanimously acknowledge that divorces are almost unknown among Catholics. We have many of our people in this country who, led away by temptation, fall into evil courses, and neglect the worship of God, the sacraments, all religious acts; yet among even these there is a horror of divorce which will bring its reward.

It is one of the great dangers of mixed marriages, that the Catholic party may be abandoned by the non-Catholic, who goes through the form of procuring a State divorce, and re-marries. A sadder position can scarcely be conceived than that of the forsaken Catholic.

The Church always taught her children to love poverty, and by her religious orders, which specially professed it, preached constantly against the making haste to be rich, which is the absorbing passion of men in our time, and leads to a host of the daily crimes around us.

The Church, too, taught the necessity of mortification and self-control, and in her clergy and religious gave living lessons, while she blessed the holy union of man and wife as no other faith has ever done.

The breaking away from this salutary teaching in these two great points, even from the views of political economy, has been productive of so much sin and vice that the wisdom of the Church justifies itself.

Christian marriage leads to the Christian home, and the Council urges all Catholics to sanctify the home by family prayer, by pious reading, by the expulsion of all indelicate ornaments or pictures. A Catholic home should be recognized by all who enter it : the library should be stocked with good books, solid and popular works, to make the members of the family firm in their faith, and proof against the sophistries of the day. The Council especially encourages the cultivation, in families, of American history. "As we desire that the history of the United States should be carefully taught in all our Catholic schools, and have directed that it be especially dwelt upon in the education of the young ecclesiastical students in our preparatory seminaries, so, also, we desire that it form a favorite part of the home library and home reading. We must keep firm and solid the liberties of our country, by keeping fresh the noble memories of the past, and thus sending forth from our Catholic homes, into the arena of public life, not partisans but patriots."

The history of our country was first written by men too ignorant or too biassed to do full justice to the Catholic element; but the truth is becoming clearer, and our history is one that Catholics can read with patriotic pride. The organization of Catholic historical societies at this moment shows that the desire for cultivating the annals of our favored land was felt among the laity, as it was by the asembled Bishops and theologians.

The Council encourages the reading of the Holy Scriptures as translated and annotated by Bishop Challoner and Dr. Haydock ; and call upon Catholics to sustain a healthy Catholic press.

The Pastoral ends these exhortations with solemn words. "Beloved Brethren, a great social revolution is sweeping over the world. Its purpose, hidden or avowed, is to dethrone Christ and religion. The ripples of the movement have been observed in our country. God grant that its tidal-wave may not break over us.

"Upon you, Christian parents, it mainly depends whether it shall or not; for such as our homes are, such shall our people be. We beseech you, therefore, to ponder carefully all the various constituents of a true Christian home, and to the utmost of your ability to carry them into effect. And we entreat all pastors of souls to bear unceasingly in mind that upon the Christian school and the Christian homes in their parishes must mainly depend the fruit of their priestly labors. Let them concentrate their efforts on these two points—to make the schools and the homes what they ought to be ; then indeed will they carry to the Lord of the harvest, full and ripe sheaves, and the future generations will bless them for transmitting unimpaired the priceless gifts of faith and religion."

The Council raises its voice against the increasing disregard of the Lord's Day, and while discountenancing the gloomy, puritanical methods of regarding it, urges Catholics to sanctify the day, and to take no part in any movements tending to a relaxation of the observance of Sunday. It especially singles out the sale of liquors, and implores all Catholics never to take part in such Sunday traffic, nor to patronize or countenance it. The temperance cause, indeed, receives its warmest commendation.

The great question of authorized and forbidden societies is brought to a position where its solution is easy, and the words of the Pastoral ought to be at the head of the editorial page of every Catholic newspaper, and in every prayer book and catechism used by the faithful. Of societies not formally condemned by the Church it says:

"If any society's obligation be such as to bind its members to secrecy, even when rightly questioned by competent authority, then such a society puts itself outside the limits of approval; and no one can be a member of it, and at the same time be admitted to the sacraments of the Catholic Church. The same is true of any organization that binds its members to a promise of blind obedience to accept in advance, and to obey whatsoever orders, lawful or unlawful, may emanate from its chief authorities; because such a promise is contrary both to reason and to conscience. And if a society works or plots against the Church, or against lawful authorities, then to be a member of it is to be excluded from the membership of the Catholic Church." These authoritative rules, therefore, ought to be the guide of all Catholics in their relation with societies. No Catholic can conscientiously join, or continue in, a body in which he knows that any of these condemned features exist.

Every encouragement is given to Catholic societies, the pious sodalities and confraternities, the great missionary aid societies, "The Association for the Propagation of the Faith" and the "Holy Childhood," societies for works of charity and education, for encouraging temperance. And in order to acknowledge the great amount of good that the "Catholic Young Men's National Union" has already accomplished, to promote the growth of the Union, and to stimulate its members to greater efforts in the future, the Fathers of the Council cordially bless their aims and endeavors, and recommend the Union to all our Catholic young men.

The Pastoral closes with an appeal to the missionary spirit

among our people to elicit aid for foreign missions, and especially for the conversion of the Indians and Negroes in our own land.

This letter is worthy of the assembled Catholic hierarchy. It meets the great wants and dangers of our time, and especially those which beset the flock committed to their care. Its warnings and counsels are all inspired by faith, and should be pondered and kept by all, for we have fallen upon evil times, and, as the Pastoral truly says: The legislation of the Council is not intended to impose burdens or limitations on the faithful, but, on the contrary, to enlarge, and secure to them " the liberty of the children of God."

WHAT IS A LIBERAL EDUCATION?

THE faculty of Harvard has been the scene of some lively discussions within the last twelve months. The subject of dispute has been liberal education—what it means, and how it works. If its working effects were clearer, its meaning might be plain. Accordingly, the debate in the faculty has taken throughout this practical, every-day shape. What is the good of a liberal education? What does it do?

In the event of its doing less than it assumes, the proposal is made not to modify the name, but, retaining that, to modify the course which the name thus far has denoted. The study of the classics, which thus far have formed the staple of a liberal education, might be judiciously abridged, if not entirely excluded ; while a number of practical studies, which have been steadily asserting their claims to recognition, might forthwith be honored with the title of liberal studies, and take rank as elements in a polite education.

In January last the party favoring progress in this direction had made a lively onset upon Greek, which was the more obnoxious element in classical studies, when a new turn was given to the fortunes of the debate by an appeal to recent facts reported from Germany.

The data supplied by the German universities tended to support the cause of Greek and Latin in a manner quite forcible and new. We may have occasion to specify them further on. Meanwhile, the answers put forward to rebut the charges were, that the alleged

experience of the German universities in their ten years' trial of
the anti-classical programme was too insignificant an experiment
to be really a telling argument; that, even granting the force of
the argument for Germany, it held only there, not in America;
that in America learning is not worth much if it does not help one
to get money; that the classics are unpractical and therefore un-
American; and something else can be studied in our colleges at
the cost of the same time, but with a yield of more profit. Such
were the answers of the anti-Greek part, as we were informed by
the Boston *Globe* of that date. Professor Goodwin and John
Williams White were the warmest supporters of Greek, and most
of the classical instructors agreed with them. President Eliot and
Professor J. P. Cooke were strongest in opposition.

A little while afterwards a lecture was delivered by Charles W.
Eliot, president of Harvard, before the members of the Johns Hopkins University, Baltimore, an institution shaped exactly on the
programme advocated by the anti-classical party. And we need
scarcely add that the lecture put forward all the claims of the
scientists, with all the personal ability of the eminent chemist.

He does not distinguish any heads of argument; but after some
preliminaries, he advances the different studies which he should be
happy to see favored; he argues in their behalf; and thus establishes his first proposition, "that the number of school and college studies admissible with equal weight or rank," for the degree
of B.A., which completes a liberal education, "needs to be much
enlarged." From this first proposition two others are easily deduced. "Secondly, that among admissible subjects a considerable
range of choice should be allowed from an earlier age than that
at which choice is now generally permitted, and thirdly, that the
existing order of studies should be changed in important respects."

If we may be allowed to advance our views on the subject of a
liberal education, we shall naturally choose to begin with the essential idea conveyed in the term itself. And as this undertaking
calls to its aid the traditional support of history which records the
enlightened usage of mankind, we shall be quite willing, if space
allows, to follow the president into the arena of past history, when
he betakes himself thither to invalidate the arguments of the classicists. This, however, must lead us no farther than the state of the
question demands.

I.

The term education may be taken to cover two things, which
are quite distinct in themselves; but which, distinct as they are,
undergo an absolute fusion into one whenever the scientific school
uses the term. It means either a general education or a special
education; either general formative studies, or specializing profes-

sional studies ; either the roots and stem of a mind's complete formation, or the ramifications of specific energies ; finally, either the
bringing out of essential faculties in a boy's mind, or, letting essential faculties take care of themselves, the shaping of his thoughts
and his actions into a certain groove. In the one case, the former of
the two, we have a general result, a strengthening of fundamental
qualities, a solid sub-structure of the mind for any superstructure
of complementary science ; in the other case, which is the latter of
the two, we have a definite constraining, once for all, towards the
purposes of a narrow object. In the former, primary powers are
enlarged to receive all subsequent stores; in the latter, they are set at
once to gather what they may, in almost all the details of business.
A thousand fitnesses are conceived and developed, in the former
case, for all thought, labor and life; in the latter, all the potency
of the mind is fastened on and fixed, before being rightly unfolded.

> The spring is past, and yet it hath not sprung ;
> The fruit is dead, and yet the leaves are green.

If we mistake not, these ideas are pretty distinct; and a clear
discernment of the two goes far towards settling the question.
One is the general education, which sensitizes the powers for anything ; the other is the special training which fixes them for life.
The anti-classical school of scientists have heard of this distinction,
over and over again ; that is clear from the manner of their defence.
But it is just as clear that they fail to comprehend it. They use
the very words of the objection, showing that the words at least
have made an impression ; yet there seems to prevail a general
lack of intelligence as to the real distinctness of the distinction
alleged; as if the specializing studies might be made to do the
work of the general studies ; as if the defining work of a particular
science might be made to do service for an enlarging general education ; and, in short, as if, in the case of a boy, the same work
could be done by the same process as in the case of a man who,
being already mature, may develop specialities and generalities together. The boy, as being immature, must do one or other at a
time : he cannot do both. If he attempts both, he forfeits at least
the general education for life.

In the spirit of this confusion the following passage of the lecture was conceived : " We may be sure," says the president of Harvard, " that the controlling intellectual forces of the actual world,
century by century, penetrate educational processes, and that languages, literature, philosophies or sciences, which show themselves
fruitful and powerful, must win recognition as liberal arts and proper
means of mental discipline." The meaning, as determined by the
context, is that, because any language, literature, philosophy, or

science becomes fruitful and powerful, that is, professionally useful as a special branch, it has a right to win recognition as a true liberal study, as a proper means of mental discipline, as a genuine course of general education.

This is just the principle underlying the whole plea for admitting political economy, science, modern tongues, and other such elements, into the place and station thus far held by the classics. It is on the assumption that the classics on one side, and such branches on the other as political economy, are all on the same stage, all on the same level; and one set of scenes can be shifted off and another set moved on, without the least modification of the educational scaffolding, without the least fundamental difference to the boy's mind. But we shall undertake to show, after a while, what is meant by the classics; while, if we wish to know what is meant by political economy and the other candidates for office, we shall only have to consult the president's lecture, where he shows them off on their own merits. In the meantime, to dwell upon this point of the scientific confusion which the anti-classical party render singularly conspicuous, the president goes on to say with emphasis : " To my mind, the only justification of any kind of discipline, training, or drill, is the attainment of the appropriate end of that discipline. It is a waste for society, and an outrage upon the individual, to make a boy spend the years when he is most teachable, in a discipline the end of which he can never reach, when he might have spent them in a different discipline which would have been rewarded with achievement. Herein lies the fundamental reason for options." What does this mean ? It means simply that general education, which he styles " a discipline, the end of which the boy can never reach," does not yield the results of special studies, which he calls " a discipline that would have been rewarded with achievement;" and it means that if you wish to have the professional achievement resulting from professional studies, you must have professional training. In which passage, it is evident, he ignores any end or achievement except professional, special, partial success; and, naturally enough, since general studies, liberal formation, universal culture does not lead to such a partial end, the classics are put down as " a discipline, the end which the boy can never reach." But here we do not know what to deny, whether we should object to such a definition of the classics or should deprecate such a confusion of the two methods of training. Perhaps we had better do both, and proceed forthwith to set both points in their true and proper light.

We say, then, that the needs existing in a boy's mind call for general education, not for special training. His powers, unfolding in all directions, demand an instrument of development in all directions.   If this general unfolding be first secured, and the special training follow after, you will enjoy the results of both ; and, what is more, the results of the special training will be intensified in value, while the time and patience expended will be notably abridged, as the recent experiment of the German universities has abundantly proved.   But if the special training comes instead of the general culture, and not after it, you will enjoy only the special results, and those stunted, dwarfed, with no amplitude of organic growth, and fair-seeming symmetry of branches and foliage ; with no spreading out of roots, under a broad trunk, which then rami- fies as its vitality prompts and its surroundings invite.   In such a growth of the boy's mind thus unfairly curtailed, there is no sup- pleness of general powers—we might say, there are no general powers worth speaking of ;—no memory cultivated throughout its potential vastness, and capable of every kind of yield; no imagina- tion cultured with all the life and sentiments of humanity, in thought, action and history.   The capacious intellect energizes with but a small scattering of seed; though the seeds within reach, and sown in a truly liberal education, are as varied in kind as the lives and thoughts of other men have been manifold and instruc- tive ; and though the same seeds give promise of being at least as prolific in the boy's future as all the needs of his mature life can ever be widely exacting.   But there is to be none of all this, or very little.   Instead, a degree of compression is exerted on the struggling mind, a coercion is put upon it.   Its future is shipped as on the track of a railroad, from which it may never more be stirred except at the cost of some catastrophe,—that kind of catastrophe which now we witness every day when minds of the finest powers attempt to reason outside of their own little specialty, and, passing over from science, go floundering about in logic, or making an excursion from chemistry cut singular fig- ures in philosophy, or taking a recess in veterinary surgery utter pronouncements in Christian divinity, or, finally, looking up from political statistics deliver an opinion on classics and belles lettres. There is one mark and stamp about all their unprofessional efforts, and that is narrowness, no matter how unconscious ; ineffective- ness, albeit ever so self-sufficient; and conceited feebleness, except in the line of one exaggerated development.   We daily behold this only too palpably prominent in the cast of the scientific minds around us.   Their shape recalls to the mind a forest-tree, which, having been shut up in a state of duress vile, under the thick shade of its elders, protrudes violently upwards through the leafy canopy of darkness into some solitary hole of the sky.

Using, then, the elegant comparison of Père Cahour, we may say that, in the edifice of the sciences, as in physical constructions, the foundation is the same for all the orders of architecture. The special form of palaces and of temples, of fortresses and of churches, though intended from the first, does not in effect appear until the edifice rises; and, the higher it is intended to rise, the slower is the laying of that common foundation. Thus it is that the amplitude of science does not develop its characteristics of speciality, save as the result of advancing years. Neither in childhood nor in impressionable boyhood should the mind be constrained by anticipation to that which may yet be the spontaneous outgrowth of its further development. Nor, on the other hand, when nature and art are allowed to have their way, should this amplitude be expected too soon; for then it would fail to be spontaneous and healthy. D'Alembert and the Encyclopædists ran into this error of forcing on the young an encyclopædic vastness; the scientists run into the former error of sacrificing the integrity of a whole body to their fancy about some limb.

Mr. Matthew Arnold, moralizing on this topic in a somewhat pleasant vein, doubts whether his best impressions of history would have been notably improved by learning from distinguished scientists that his ancestors were of the biped kind, probably arboreal in their habits. Even the eminent president of the Royal Society betrays, with all his fixity of view on the physical basis of life and protoplasmic theories generally, that he is not quite dead to the æstheticism of a boy's life, and to the true meaning of culture and general education. Describing how the classics might be taught, he throws no little spirit into the description. He says: "If the classics were taught as they might be taught; if boys and girls were instructed in Latin and Greek not merely as languages, but as illustrations of philological science; if a vivid picture of life on the shores of the Mediterranean, two thousand years ago, were imprinted on the mind of scholars; if ancient history were taught, not as a weary series of feuds and fights, but traced to its causes in such men under such conditions; if, lastly, the study of the classical books were followed in such a manner as to impress boys with their beauties, and with the grand simplicity of their statement of the everlasting problems of human life, instead of with their verbal and grammatical peculiarities—." This, no doubt, is a vivid description from so declared an opponent as Professor Huxley; its shortcomings on the subject of philology and grammar we may touch on hereafter; in the meantime, let us hear the Professor out: these conditions being fulfilled, he still thinks the classics should not form the basis of a liberal education. What, then, should? Here the Professor is not distinct. He leaves it, however, to be understood from the context that commercial statistics and engineering interests would fill up the requirements of a liberal education.

But with a truer appreciation of the question, on its own proper merits, though with as false a philosophy of human life behind it as any of the scientific schools could propound, M. Taine discerns in the pursuit of classical studies some of those genuine elements which constitute their vitality, their actuality on the impressionable mind of youth. In the reading of a Greek tragedy, that frame of mind, he considers, will do justice to it, that liberal conception which realizes the men and the things, the place and the time— those men who lived under a glowing sky, face to face with the most noble landscapes, in sight of the Mediterranean, blue and lustrous as a silken tunic, with islands rising from it like masses of marble; and add to these, he says, "twenty select phrases from Plato and Aristophanes. Behold the Greeks within a lovely landscape, on a bright and laughing sea-coast, enticed to navigation and commerce, exempt from gross cravings of the stomach, inclined from the beginning to social ways, to a settled organization of the state, to feelings and dispositions such as develop the art of oratory, the talent for enjoyment, the inventions of science, letters and arts."

If this sketch, as far as it goes, is a correct literary estimate of certain elements in the study of Greek, we might borrow, in like manner, the exalted appreciation which a philosophical or a diplomatic spirit could form of the Grecian literature. Mr. Allies could explain to us why that little body of states, covering the ground of a modern county or two, described and analyzed in a few books of Thucydides and a few speeches of Demosthenes, have been found adequate to furnish future ages with a philosophy of society and politics, about broad enough to guide a modern president or premier. But, this not being the point before us, we shall pass on from the clear distinction between a general education and a special training; and we take up the discussion next in order. That shall be about the proper instrument wherewith to operate a general or liberal education; whether such instrument is to be a literature or a science; and, if a literature, whether it is to be any other than the Grecian and the Roman.

II.

Here some words of M. Taine may do us the service of introducing us into the question. He says: "Literary works are instructive because they are beautiful; their utility grows with their perfection, and, if they furnish documents, it is because they are monuments. The more a book represents visible sentiments, the more it is a work of literature; for the office of literature is to take note of sentiments. The more a book represents important sentiments, the higher is its place in literature; for it is by representing the mode of being of a whole nation and of a whole age, that a writer rallies round him the sympathies of an entire age and an entire nation. This is why, amid the writings that set before our eyes the sentiments of preceding generations, a literature, and notably a grand literature, is incomparably the best. It resembles that admirable apparatus of extraordinary sensibility by which physicians disentangle and measure the most recondite and delicate changes of a body."

For the sake of simplicity, we shall establish the two propositions together: that only a literature is the adequate instrument for general or liberal education, and that the classic literatures, notably the Greek, are the choicest amongst all.

A literature is to be distinguished from a language. If the description which is credited to Proudhon is correct, the language of a people is the sum total of its native ideas, the encyclopædia which Providence reveals to it from the first. There is a little anecdote, by the way, that the same atheist, Proudhon, expressed his regret at finding the idea of God so much a native in his own tongue; since he was compelled to use that idea to keep up his style. We say, now, that literature is more than language. To speak precisely, it means not only the language and all the native ways thereof, its turns of thought, idiom and the like, but also the whole product of thought and sentiment which has actually been gathered up in the course of time and vested in the garb of that tongue. To test the reality of this distinction, we have only to translate from one tongue into another. What remains of the former, out of which the translation is made? Nothing whatever of the tongue; but still a large amount of the literature. We say, only a large amount of the literature remains, and not all. For that which is finest and most delicate, that which is most individual, the features, shape, complexion of the thoughts expressed, is unavoidably lost in stripping it of its native garb. Slight as these elements are, they resemble mastertouches in a painting, most difficult to impart, most easy to lose. They are not copied. To be enjoyed they must be seized in the original. But, notwithstanding this loss, the literature is preserved in all that is solid. The process of translating hands over into another tongue all the solid contents of positive truth, proposition, proof. A translation of the finest literary piece may be about as good as the copy of a masterpiece, but no more.

Now all the generations have enjoyed a laugh at the expense of the Consul Mummius, who, on shipping the statues of Corinth to Rome, is reported to have stipulated with the merchantmen that, should any of the statues be injured in the way across the sea, the same should be replaced by others just as good. We do not know whether the generations shall not have a right to be amused at the wisdom of the scientific school, which now gravely informs us that "the English literature is beyond all comparison the amplest, most various and most splendid literature which the world has ever seen"; and why so? Because "to the original creations of English genius are to be added *translations* into English of all the masterpieces of other literatures, sacred and profane." That is one reason assigned. The other two are interesting; the next being, that the English literature is *immense*. "How does it stand now," asks the president, "with its immense array of poets, philosophers, historians, commentators, critics, satirists, dramatists, novelists, orators?" To our mind, the newspaper alone, especially in America, is superlatively immense. The third reason is that which has a right to cap any climax, a national and utilitarian argument: "It is the native tongue of nations which are preëminent in the world by force of character, enterprise and wealth."

Discarding English as the great lever for elevating the youthful mind, unless it have something more to say for itself than the president has advanced in its behalf, we beg to say a word now for Latin and Greek; which, unfortunately for the credit of our author's estimate on the subject, would seem to have no value whatever, to judge by all that he allows them. It is a presumption in their favor, that prejudice should so clearly be operating against them. And for any chemist or palæontologist, at this stage of the world, lightly to reverse the verdict of the ages in so very essential a matter, is a dangerous part to play—dangerous for his literary credit.

The ancient tongues of Greece and Italy come down to us charged with all the historic memories of antiquity, as well sacred as profane; with all the masterpieces of eloquence and poetry belonging to three great epochs, those of Pericles, Augustus, and the founding of Christianity; with all human philosophy, from Socrates, Plato, Aristotle, down to St. Thomas Aquinas, and further down to Leibnitz and Newton, both of them men of classical letters; in fine, these tongues come down to us with all the traditions, all the beliefs, all the divinity of Christendom. Under a literary aspect the eloquence and poetry of Greece were the mistress of Latin excellence. Under a philological aspect, the Latin tongue has been the principal base of our modern languages, as formed in the history of Christendom.

Now, what does education mean? Let us recall what we said above. If it consists in bringing out the undeveloped nature of a boy; in bringing him into contact with various elements of richest thought; in favoring his inquiring eyes with glimpses of human life, individual, social or political; if it is to make him feel the finest springs of human sentiment, as touched by the greatest masters of expression, and that in a language the most delicately organized and the most perfectly elaborated of all tongues living or extinct,—if this is education, endeavoring to unfold the little capacities of the boy's soul to the measure of mighty minds, and to feed his curious genius with the best product of great thinkers, who will designate an instrument for the purpose to be compared with the classic literature of Greece; or where will an arbiter of that boy's future be found to compare with the master, guiding and measuring, directing and controlling, correcting and supplementing the entire process?

Whether the literature be Latin or Greek, the deadness of the language is a distinct advantage. Even if it be spoken as if it were living, yet the advantage remains; for everything has to be learned by rule and formula. It is not the language of the nursery and of common life; and, therefore, it is not picked up without reflection, by dint of mere instinct. The relations of grammar and of logic must be attended to with deliberation. Thought and judgment are constantly exercised in assigning the exact equivalents in the vernacular for every phrase in the original. The coincidence of construction is too little, and the community of idiomatic thought too remote, for the boy's mind to catch at the idea by force of a preëstablished harmony. Only the law of thought and logic guides him, with a competent teacher to reassure his developing sense. Thus far, and farther still, the mere page of a dead language affords a distinct advantage; and if the lexicon has still to be used by an old professor, as C. F. Adams complained in his own case, that is no discredit either to the language or to him. But to have the dead language spoken is not to lessen the advantage; it is to expedite the work. It is not to make the dead tongue a living one, but to study the dead after the manner of the living, and to retain the advantages of the former without the drawbacks of the latter. This is to be thorough and expeditious together.

With grammar thus understood, or, as Professor Huxley expressed it, with "verbal and grammatical peculiarities" thus mastered, you may hope to have philologists. With the principles of great minds thus deliberately unearthed, you may hope to have philosophers. With so much rational labor expended, you may count on intellectual nerve and sinew. With the rays of all the fine arts streaming in through all the avenues of the finest literatures, you may hope to accomplish a liberal education.

From all this two consequences follow, relative to statements made by the anti-classical school; one with regard to the amount of labor expended; the other with regard to the permanence of any system adopted for conducting a liberal education.

In the first place, it is said, "If a language is to be learned, I would teach it in the easiest known method, and at the age when it can be easiest learned." To this remark of President Eliot we content ourselves with returning, by way of answer, an equally general observation of Père Daniel: "Easy methods ruin us. If we do not reëstablish the ancient system of teaching in its integrity, at all events let us not open the door to a general do-as-you-like (an American might be permitted to say "letting things slide"); let us not content ourselves in grammatical studies with results just so-so—results inevitable if we deprive these studies of their classical character."· We know there are persons amongst us who practically take the anti-classical view, while imagining they are classicists; they say, "How will you control this matter in practice, and prevent us from drifting into the utilitarian principle, or elevate us from the utilitarian practice, if we are lodged there? These theories are high." To which we answer: Never was practice lower than when it strove to bring theory down to itself; for then there is no resurrection. Moreover, we are discussing only theory now; the practice may be considered anon.

In the second place, it is thought that no system of liberal studies can be permanent, or fitted for all times, because, observes the President, "the educational value of any established study, far from being permanently fixed, is constantly changing, as new knowledge accumulates and new sciences come into being." And he considers those who differ from him to be "thoughtless and ignorant people," classing among such the quondam master of Trinity, W. Whewell, who "did not hesitate to apply to these three studies," Latin, Greek and the old mathematics, "the word *permanent.*" But, we reply, if the problem is always the same, the answer must be the same; if the one is permanent, so is the other. The problem is, how to develop a human mind. If the human mind is constant, and if its development has a fixed meaning, there must be, morally speaking, some best way, or some approximately best way, of developing that human mind.

III.

Having vindicated our own principles, we can now afford to review the special pleadings of the scientists. This we shall do; but it is worth while first to see their peculiar manner of pleading. The style of logic which they use is an important element, which we may criticise first. Then we shall take up the special subjects for which they plead.

Their style of logic is reduced to one set of principles, utility, money, convenience. Thus, when Whewell condemns, for many reasons, the modern analytical mathematics, and denies its claim to be a permanent study by which the reason of man is to be educated, and insists that the old geometrical forms of mathematics must be especially preserved and maintained, as essentially requisite for this office, the following brief answer is returned : " The modern analytical mathematics, thus condemned by Whewell, is practically the only mathematics now in common use in the United States." This answer is singularly wide of the mark, unless the question is to be determined by utility, by the mere practical argument, that the use of it is an accomplished fact, and there is an end of the question. What we want just now is something different; it is a rational account, a philosophical reason, an explanation from the "inwardness" of things, why analytical mathematics, if they hold a place, have a right to hold it. But the answer is, they hold it, and that is all. Certainly a practical view!

Such a method of logic explains why we meet with no very troublesome arguments to analyze in the opposition to the classics, nothing but assertion, repetition, and "practical utility." We distinguish practical from liberal utility, as the special from the general, the professional from the broad and fundamental utility, in which alone, as we have tried to show above, true liberal education consists.

That we make no mistake in the value of this distinction between the narrow utilitarianism and the broad utility of a wide fundamental education, is sufficiently evidenced by the unconscious admissions which we meet with here. The president of Harvard admits that to use such a staple of argument as mere practical utilitarianism, is derogatory to the dignity of such a discussion. Thus, when arguing for French and German, he says: " This claim rests not on the *usefulness* of these languages to couriers, tourists, or commercial travellers, but on the magnitude and worth of the literatures, and on the unquestionable fact that facility in reading these languages is absolutely *indispensable* to a scholar, whatever may be his department of study." Then, after dwelling at length on the manifold uses, possible and actual, of French and German, on their " indispensableness " to " philologists, archæologists, metaphysicians, physicians, physicists, naturalists, chemists, economists, engineers, architects, artists, and musicians," he proceeds thus: " I urge no utilitarian argument, but rest the claims of French and German, for admission to complete academic equality, on the copiousness and merit of the literatures, and the *indispensableness* of the languages to all scholars." In short, the eminent chemist urges no utilitarian argument, but he urges the argument of utilitarianism. For, as to the copiousness and merit of the literatures, he says not another word on either, though that were a legitimate ground on which to rest the question.

Further on, he argues for the introduction into a liberal education of political economy, or public economics. He describes it as being related to three distinct sciences, which, singularly enough, he seems to rank as coördinate—history, the accumulation of wealth, and ethics. This new science of political economy had better, he thinks, be called the science of the health of nations; it includes industrial, social, and political problems; and it is by far the most complex and difficult of the sciences of which modern education has to take account. Indeed, he goes on to say, it requires such exactness of statement, such accurate weighing of premises, and such closeness of reasoning, that many young men of twenty, who have been disciplined by the study of Greek, Latin, and mathematics for six or eight years, find that it tasks their utmost powers. Now, after this forcible description, the president continues: " Neither can it be justly called a material or utilitarian subject; for it is full of grave moral problems, and deals with many questions of public honor and duty." To this remark the most obvious rejoinder is: Neither can it be called anything but a utilitarian and material subject, for it deals with wealth, health, industry, population, and the like, as the writer abundantly shows. If it touches on anything. else, as public honor and duty, it is for the same reason that whatever deals with anything human remotely touches all things human, for human nature is always one. But that does not make all sciences one; nor raise a utilitarian statistician to the dignity of an ethical philosopher; nor exalt a New England farmer tilling his fields with great thought and judgment to the dignity of a metaphysician reasoning out a question with profound judgment and thought; nor make a science of public economics precisely the means to develop a boy's mind, cultivate his imagination, and ennoble his heart.

We might exhibit still farther the utilitarian vein of argument and thought, in which alone the members of this anti-classical school know how to indulge. But perhaps their apologetic sensitiveness, lest they be thought thus to indulge, may serve as a full confession that it is not a line of logic admissible on the present topic. This being established as to their style of argumentation, we may consider now what pleas they advance for their new and special branches.

Analytical mathematics comes first. This exact science is, as we have seen, already in possession of the ground; it is found in the curriculum of polite studies. But that need not prevent us from analyzing its merits, and seeing what claim it has to an educational value. We say, then, that a professor of the exact sciences, taken in general, need not be a man who educates. He may be eminent in his own science; but whether eminent or not, he does not, therefore, educate. If he is eminent, he has a special genius. If he is an ordinarily good professor, for instance in mathematics, he must have a certain sum of natural talents and acquired knowledge. But this sum of qualities, says Père Cahour, is not equal to the sum which makes a good professor of belles lettres. Eloquence and poetry demand a spirit accomplished in point of intelligence, sensibility, and imagination, and, besides, they call for literary, historical, and philosophical knowledge of no small extent. Algebra and geometry, in their ordinary courses, require, on the side of the professor, and impart to the pupil, only penetration and justness of perception; and whatever collateral knowledge is involved may be found within the limits of certain formulas and demonstrations which are contained, cut and dried, in the pages of mathematical books. This one fact shows the value of all that vaunted exactness which, as far as it is an exactness, is an excellence, but as far as it is nothing else, and has nothing to do with anything else, with probabilities for example,—and what is human life but a mass of probabilities and moral possibilities and uncertainties ?—is nothing but a narrowness, tending to beget a narrow and stiff habit of thought amid the ever-changing circumstances of life. The practical world has a horror of men who know how to reason only by abstract rules and scientific premises, and who despise with a lofty contempt the uncertain realities of poor human existence,—nay, not poor human existence, but beautiful human existence, with its yielding and obliging moral laws of public and private mutual deference. Only the eternal laws of essential morality are rigid in the anatomy of life. But the stereotyped exactness imparted and learnt in the scientific demonstration would make everything rigid—lines, minds, men, and all existence. There is no development of a boy's humanity about it. The gamut of a peal of bells might as well be taken to represent the thousand inflections and tones of a human voice, as that a mathematical training should be supposed to represent or to effect the education of a human soul. We are prone to compare it with the study of law; and we could imagine Cicero saying to a mathematician what he said to the lawyer Sulpicius, that, if he were provoked any more, he would learn the whole of that science in three days !

And, to say a word in particular of analytical mathematics, it may be that great minds understand the subject, and are educationally helped by its use. But, candidly, we doubt whether, educationally speaking, the minds of ordinary mortals are much assisted that way. They can follow the processes intellectually only a few paces from shore, through a few coefficients, a power or two, one or other factor, and then—one is beyond depth in a sea of manipulation, among high powers, multifarious factors, involved in a few larger brackets, and the whole wrapped up in a cube radical, with an imaginary or surd to sparkle somewhere in the trappings. What can save a man the credit of any intelligence but fidelity to a blind mechanical manipulation ? And only amid the last results may light begin to beam again, when we heave within sight of land, and within reach of some plain and simplified formulas, which we just find breath enough left us to interpret. It is capital work in its results. But, as a process, and an educational process, it reminds us only of those dull-looking compositions which, when rightly tipped and rightly mounted, are able, on the application of a spark, to shoot forth light, color, and brilliancy into the far-off skies of the night. The firmament itself can stand revealed in the final illumination of Kepler's laws. But the manufacture up to that point was anything but an illumination for the intelligence ; it was the manipulation of factory work. Now, is this an education for the young ? Either, therefore, as Whewell rightly observes, apply the geometry of Euclid, which step by step the boy understands, or let us at least have none of your modern mathematics vaunted as an educational power. It is a mechanism for making machines.

Whence it comes that anything like breadth or depth of view, such as mark profundity and genius, is very much out of place in the ordinary chairs of mathematics ; and those only are effective men for preparing students to pass examinations, who are methodical men, in the sense of being men who prefer to repeat the science of others, and are strictly devoted to accepted demonstrations and formulas. They are more successful in their teaching, according as they are more simple in their set of expressions, more unchanging in the proofs commonly employed, more circumscribed in keeping to the stereotyped propositions.

We proceed to the natural sciences. ' The plea put forward for them is on the ground that natural science investigation "spreads abroad the only spirit in which any kind of knowledge can be prosecuted to a result of lasting intellectual value." This is "the patient, cautious, sincere, self-directing spirit of natural science." We do not venture to deny this. We imagine that every branch of knowledge has something to recommend it, not only in its products, but in its method. And however much personally we might be enamored of a chorus in Æschylus, or a speech in Thucydides, we are still willing to admit that the patient, cautious, sincere, self-directing spirit necessary to guide one through the chorus or the speech, might quite possibly be improved still more by turning to the natural sciences, and exercising the same virtues on the back of a diatom under the microscope. There is no limit to the exercise of those precious virtues, patience, caution, perseverance. But just at present, in this educational question, we are inquiring whether natural science has anything else to recommend it; and whether boys have all the desirable time for it. Grave persons recommend it as a recreation to distract the minds of hard students. Cardinal Wiseman commended geological excursions for students to exercise themselves in the fresh air. But now we are not talking of recreation; rather of study and education. And this is the place to adduce the experience recently acquired in the German universities. The facts are briefly as follows:

The Prussian *realschulen* of the first rank differ from the *gymnasia* in this, that the realschule entirely dispenses with Greek in its course of study, and reduces the time devoted to Latin by about one-half. They differ besides in other minor respects. In 1869, the royal minister of public instruction issued a decree granting to subjects of Prussia, who had completed the full course of study in a realschule of the first rank, the right to enter the philosophical faculty of the academical department—that is to say, they were admitted into any Prussian university as having matriculated. This decree was issued in spite of general opinion called for by the minister, and communicated by the faculties interested. The faculties opposed the scheme, but they had to submit. Ten years later, in the year 1880, the philosophical faculty of the Royal Frederick William University sends in to the minister a report of such a nature as to be styled by a distinguished American scholar "the most powerful plea ever made on behalf of the classics." There is nothing vague about the testimony of the different professors. The representatives of the mathematical branches say "that the students of mathematics who have been prepared in the gymnasia, in spite of the fact that less time has been given in the gymnasium to this branch than in the realschule, are nevertheless, as a rule, superior to their fellow students from the realschule in scientific impulse and apprehension, and in capacity for a deeper understanding of their science."

Professor Kammelberg's testimony is entirely corroborative. In the study of English the realschuler are not apt, for their Latin is poor; they have no Greek, and they are almost entirely lacking in acuteness of apprehension and independence of judgment. Professor Mullenhoff, of the German department, judges that "it is simply impossible for one who has been prepared in the realschule to acquire a satisfactory scientific education." And Professor Zeller says that the realschuler are often a source of embarrassment to him, as many of his philosophical lectures are unintelligible to those who are not familiar with the Greek language.

Graduates of the realschulen are, almost without exception, found to be overtaken in the later semesters by students from the gymnasia. And the distinguished chemist, Dr. August W. Hofmann, on delivering his inaugural address as rector of the University of Berlin, cites it as his own experience, that he never heard a student from a gymnasium express a wish that he might have received his training at a realschule; but that he often meets young men prepared at a realschule who generally regret that they had never had part in the training of the gymnasium.

These are some of the facts relating to the German universities. And to speak of our own experience in the colleges of this country, the very same verdict must be given, and pretty nearly in all its particulars. The students of commercial courses are intellectually inferior to their compeers in the classical courses, though all other conditions may have been equally favorable. A graduate of a commercial course will lament his chances; or, if not yet finished, may pass over to the classical course. Post-graduate studies are unintelligible and uninviting to him. And, beyond this, there remains nothing to say in behalf of a scientific curriculum which has supplanted a classical formation.

We shall not dwell upon the other topics of the scientist's special pleading. We do but mention them. With respect to the English language, we say briefly that classical scholars are known as a rule to be the better masters of the vernacular. With respect to the English literature, if that is viewed on its utilitarian merits, it does not enter into this question; if it is viewed on its literary and educational merits, we have already seen that no claim is put forward in its behalf which would rank it anywhere near the classics. As to French and German, and other modern languages, we should venture an opinion that they are of such a formation, and such a relative bearing on the classical tongues, as to place them altogether within easy reach of any classical scholar. He can run over them, as surveyors run over a country, by a system of triangulation. Latin and English command French, and then more easily give a passport to Italian and Spanish. German can slip in readily, being remotely a mother tongue. As to political economy, it is, on the scientist's own showing, altogether unfit to be used as an educational power for boys. And yet, strange to say, a classical education will include it, in the way most fitted to boys. As a writer in *Blackwood* observes, commenting some years ago on Lord Lyttleton's letter to the University of Oxford regarding the study of Greek, "the laws of commerce lie in a classical education. Every great historian, as Thucydides, or orator, as Demosthenes, furnishes countless opportunities for entering into the commercial elements of human association." Finally, history is an every-day element in the classics. Nor should a certain amount of all that is useful, arithmetic, modern languages, geography, and physical science, be omitted from the course. But this belongs to the practical aspect of the question, and that we have not treated.

To conclude, then, we resume with the conclusion of the president's lecture. He says : " If history proves that the staples of education have in fact changed, reason says still more clearly that they must change." To this historical and philosophical appeal of the scientific mind, confident in the integrity of its motives, we answer, confident in the integrity of our demonstration, that, as we might go on to show, history can prove the staples of education never to have changed ; and as we have already shown, reason says more clearly still, that they never can change.

All the sciences are sisters, and there is amongst them a community of parentage and a community of resources. If justice is to be done to the sciences, as the means of ulterior progress, let a liberal education first do justice to the great literatures as a means of fundamental progress, and thereby do justice to the powers of the opening mind ; in order that, its sensibility and imagination with its reason and intelligence being well cultivated in the time of youth, the opening mind may expand early to the beauty of the ideal world, and breathe in the atmosphere of the infinite ; that in the early freshness which develops only in the sunshine of beautiful thought, the plastic soul may readily be formed to live from early years the life of truth. The noblest geometry and the sublimest astronomy will then find a congenial home in such a beautiful mind ; for the true science of the exact mind is not divorced from the æsthetic beauties of the liberal mind. This is the permanent law of human development, as the nature of the mind is permanent, as truth is permanent, and religion and morality—all are permanent. They are no functions of the passing hour. Nor is liberal education any function of the latest passing scheme.

ST. THOMAS'S LATEST CRITIC.

The Philosophical System of Antonio Rosmini-Serbati. Translated, with a Sketch of the Author's Life, Bibliography, Introduction, and Notes. By Thomas Davidson. London. 1882.

THE work here presented in an English dress is, the translator tells us in his preface, a "resumé of Rosmini's system, compiled by the author for Cantù's *Storia Universale,* accompanying it," he adds, "with explanations of my own and parallel passages from his longer works."

It is to that which is the translator's own, and mainly so much of it as touches upon St. Thomas's doctrine, that I desire to direct attention at present.

To those who, unlike Lessing and Sir William Hamilton, prize truth more than the search after truth, it must be a relief, after traversing the arid wastes of German transcendentalism, English agnosticism, and French positivism, to come into the fertile fields of Italian thought. The translator deserves well of the English reading public for having introduced to them even thus much of Rosmini's works, albeit Rosmini is far from the first of Italian philosophers. But as Dr. Pusey directed many to the pillar and ground of supernatural truth, while he himself was satisfied with a mere shadow, so may Mr. Davidson be instrumental in leading many an earnest inquirer after philosophic truth unto the luminous pages of the Angelic Doctor himself, the while berating scholasticism as a system of absurdities and contradictions.

Mr. Davidson may be a thorough classical scholar, a fair linguist, no mean philologist; but a philosopher he is not, and seems incapable of becoming, as may be seen by the reader anon.

Whoever cannot, from the existence of second causes, see the necessity of positing a first cause, can hardly lay claim to the slightest pretensions to philosophy. It is one thing to discourse glibly upon Greek literature, to give probable reasons for the possible origin and possible changes of words; but another and a very different thing to follow intelligently St. Thomas in his profound researches. St. Thomas deals not with possibilities or probabilities, but with certainties; not with mere words, but with truth.

An enthusiastic admirer of Rosmini, his translator is by no means prepared *jurare in verba magistri.* On page 246, Rosmini shows that, with the principle of causality, the mind cannot rest with second causes, which are all contingent, but must go back till it arrives at a first cause, a self-existent, necessary Being, in whose essence existence is included, viz., God, adding : " For this reason the existence of God has been admitted in all times and by all peoples of the world." The translator's note on this reads : " This is true, and yet the proof of the existence of God derived from the supposed necessity of positing a first cause is an extremely fallacious one." After proving to his entire satisfaction the palpable fallacy, he concludes : " An innumerable multitude of successive causes is therefore entirely possible, and there is no necessity in thought for positing a first cause."

There is and can be no innumerable multitude of causes or of any entities. Every multitude is numerable, for every multitude is made up of individuals, and every individual counts one, and any multitude of units can be counted or numbered. Again, if there is no necessity in thought for positing a first cause, neither is there in reality ; and if there is in reality, there is in thought. The thought cannot be true without a corresponding reality, and every reality is thinkable. It is only in German transcendentalism that ideas are *à priori* necessary forms of the mind, and that thought is merely subjective, the baseless figment of the thinker.

The above statement of Mr. Davidson is tantamount to saying that we may with all reason suppose a chain consisting of an " innumerable multitude " of links, enough, say, to reach to one of the fixed stars, to be suspended in space, without the need of having the topmost link attached to anything, it being quite sufficient for the support of the immense weight to have the lowest link supported by the next above it, and that by the next above, and so on till we come to the highest, this being able to support itself and all below it, because forsooth it is the first of the series and at such an immense distance from the lowest, though of the same nature with it. The link nearest the earth cannot support itself ; the farthest off can support the whole chain.

According to this manner of reasoning, if the world were to last an "innumerable multitude " of years, effects for which we are now forced to posit a cause would be to our very distant descendants perfectly intelligible without a cause. The oak would be believed to have sprung up without an acorn, the ship would have launched itself upon the deep without a maker, without the aid of any one. Indeed, Mr. Davidson maintains a more difficult position. For the oak would have had at least the earth to support it, the ship would have had trees from which to make itself ; but the case of the farthest back in the series of second causes, even though their multitude were " innumerable," would be far different. . That farthest back second cause, which we can certainly reach in thought, would have been absolutely alone, if there were no first cause, and therefore must have produced itself from nothing, it being, moreover, previous to its existence, itself nothing, as being a second cause, and therefore contingent. In a word, there was an absolute nothing first, if there be no first cause, and then either one entity made itself out of nothing, being itself nothing, and so became primogenitor to the whole race of second causes, call it protoplasm, proteine, or what you like; or an " innumerable multitude " of second causes made themselves out of nothing, themselves being nothing.

Here is how Mr. Davidson shows the fallacy of positing a first cause. " It is quite true that an infinite number is unthinkable, because all number, from its very nature, is finite. But number altogether is an intellective mode of grouping, and does not lie in things themselves. . . . . But it by no means follows that an infinite multitude, beyond any, and therefore beyond all, number, does not exist."

Without stopping to examine the logical validity of inferring all number from any number, this argument simply means that because our intellect is finite, and number is " an intellective mode of grouping," therefore an infinite number cannot be the object of our intellect, is unthinkable; but that there may still be an infinite multitude of things, an infinite succession of caused causes.

Now, it must be clear to every mind that this supposed infinite multitude is the aggregate of individual entities, for things exist in the real ontological order only as concrete individuals. Each individual is *one* entity, for unity is an essential mark of entity. Every entity is necessarily one; and any amount of units can be counted, and consequently are numerable. If, therefore, an infinite multitude of things is thinkable, an infinite number also is thinkable. An infinite number, Mr. Davidson says, is not thinkable, neither then is an infinite multitude thinkable, that is, it is impossible, for the unthinkable is intrinsically impossible. I can think a golden mountain reaching up to the moon. It is perfectly possible, therefore, and might exist, if a sufficiently powerful external cause so willed it. But think a square circle, think two mountains without a valley between, think two and two to be five, I cannot; for it is thinking an entity to be and not to be at the same time, thinking a square to be at once a square and not a square, four to be four and not four. I can in thought conjure up the " innumerable," no, but the perfectly numerable multitude that would be represented by a line of closely written digits, the value of each successive digit increasing tenfold, extending from here to the farthest fixed star, and back to earth as many times as there are stars in the firmament, and this number multiplied by itself as. many times as there are digits in the line. This number is thinkable, and the multitude of entities it would represent could exist, and, if the Almighty so willed it, would exist. But an infinite multitude of entities, be they what they may, equally as an infinite number, shocks my intellect, is unthinkable, and therefore impossible. Every multitude of things is numerable, every number is increasable, and therefore every multitude is finite, for the infinite can neither be increased nor diminished. God alone is infinite. Hence the absurdity of supposing any series of second causes, without positing a first cause, is " huge as Olympus."

I have given here the translator's argument in support of his doctrine that there can be second causes without a first cause, partly as proof of his originality and independent thought, partly because the Evolutionists must, as denying a first cause, hold this doctrine, and partly as showing what manner of reasoner he is who charges the Angelic Doctor with giving a handle to the Evolutionists and Darwinians. In his introduction, page 97, Mr. Davidson says: " It will be seen from this that St. Thomas attributes cognition to the senses! Indeed, he elsewhere says that ' Sensus est quædam deficiens participatio intellectus.' What a text for the Evolutionists and Darwinians! "

It were too much to expect Mr. Davidson's unmeasured praise of modern Italian philosophy and his undisguised contempt for the " philosophic romances of Germany," the sensism, subjectivism and skepticism of England, without a counter-balancing offset of some kind. And the Jesuits, of course, are equally available for statesman, politician, philosopher, and critic.

In his *Life of Rosmini*, page 33, Mr. Davidson says : " From that time (1834) until now the persecution of Rosmini and his followers, at the hands of the Jesuits, has never ceased even for a moment." Again : " The natural hostility of the Austrian Government to anything savoring of Ultramontanism was, in Rosmini's case, sharpened by the influence of the Jesuits and their friends, who saw in his enterprises possible dangers to their order."

This is more than strange. The Jesuits persecuted Rosmini for his Ultramontanism ! Why, all the world have been charging them with ultra-Ultramontanism ! What could they see in an Ultramontanist's " enterprises dangerous to their order " ? Where and how has the persecution against Rosmini and his followers been carried on until now by the Jesuits ? Perhaps he means that all who beg leave to differ with Rosmini's philosophy and to question its soundness, persecute him. If so, he has had, and is apt still to have, many a persecutor. The writer will count for one. And if his followers and defenders in philosophy are of a class with his translator, Rosmini would have reason to exclaim, " Save me from my friends ! " Whatever " universal principle of truth " Mr. David-

son has adopted from Rosmini, it certainly is not that of sufficient reason. Mr. Davidson would profit by practicing the advice
of Lord Mansfield to his ermined friend: "In all cases give your
judgment freely, but be chary of stating your reasons." Indeed,
"if reasons were as plenty as blackberries" with him, he should not
give one even "on compulsion."

In his introduction, page 89, Mr. Davidson, after censuring
modern thought, "inaugurated in the 17th century," for the mistake
it committed in having "revolted entirely from scholasticism,"
adds: "This revolt, indeed, was almost unavoidable; for a thorough-going temporary breach with scholasticism was necessary,
in order to deprive it of that tyrannical and morbid influence
which, as the handmaid of theology, it had gained over human intelligence."

Here is a palpable instance of the application of the principle,
that evil is to be done that good may come from it, that the end
justifies the means. The "mistake" of the revolt is acknowledged,
but strangely enough defended. Philosophy, in the hands of the
schoolmen, was made the handmaid of theology, was made to
minister to religion. This is the head and front of its offending,
and therefore any and every mistake or extravagance on the part
of the revolt, even to the extent of stultifying thought and dubbing
it philosophy, must be condoned, if shame prevents its being applauded.

But why, I would ask the learned translator, call the influence
scholasticism had gained over human intelligence "tyrannical"?
Nothing but truth can influence intelligence, for truth is the object
of intellect, just as color is the object of sight, sound of hearing.
You cannot influence the eye by sound, nor the ear by color, nor
the intellect by aught else than its object, truth. If there be no
colored object presented to the eye, it may be left inactive, but
cannot be influenced. In like manner does the intellect remain
uninfluenced till truth is presented to it. Error may indeed be
dressed up by sophistry in the semblance of truth, and under this
false color appeal to passion or prejudice or some low interest, and,
through the influence of one or more of these, inveigle the will and
thus prevail over man. This ascendency of error may be called
a species of tyranny, since it enslaves the noblest faculties in man
to animal instincts. And yet the will is always free to resist, and
hence its submission is voluntary and therefore criminal. But so
far is the intellect from being influenced, that, as soon as it is permitted in the silence of passion and prejudice to investigate the
error, it tears off the deceptive garb and casts away the unsightly
impostor. When intelligence, therefore, is influenced, it is by truth
it is influenced, and this influence, instead of being tyrannical, is

most legitimate; for truth possesses a just and natural right to sway that which it forms. It is truth that forms the intellect, develops, strengthens, and expands the intellect, enabling it to range at large throughout the broad fields of creation, and to mount through nature up to nature's God. Truth itself assures us: " The truth shall make you free." It follows that, since scholasticism, even as " the handmaid of theology," did influence human intelligence, philosophy contains a large share of truth, and to call its influence tyrannical is an appeal to prejudice or passion rather than to reason.

Indeed, the history of error, trace it as far back as we may, shows us on which side tyranny has invariably ranged itself. What final argument was brought against the adamantine logic of Socrates? Hemlock. What reasoning did the Roman Empire make use of to check the influence of early Christianity? Ten persecutions. How did Arianism meet the unanswerable arguments of the great Athanasius? By banishing him. What *novum organon* did Mohammedanism wield? The sword. What was Luther's culminating argument? *Pecca fortiter, sed fortius fide.* How did Henry the Eighth prove his spiritual supremacy? Ask Sir Thomas More and Bishop Fisher. And Queen Elizabeth? By every instrument of torture. And has tyranny changed its colors in our own day? The May Laws in Germany, the exiles from France, the Poles in Siberia, are the answer.

As to the term " morbid" applied to the influence of scholasticism, as the handmaid of theology, over human intelligence, it is no more than might be expected from one who, in his lectures at the Washington University, St. Louis, deplored most pathetically the " blighting and chilling influence of Christianity " upon Grecian civilization and Grecian refinement. When such moral turpitude, varnished though it be by towering genius, as reveals itself in Grecian literature, can fail to elicit a word of censure for pagan civilization and Grecian morals, we may not wonder to hear of the " morbid" influence of scholasticism as the handmaid of theology.

On page 93 of his introduction, Mr. Davidson states Aristotle's doctrine touching matter and form thus: " From all eternity there have existed matter and form in a state of combination. Matter is indeterminate and of itself unknowable," adding, in a foot-note: " According to St. Thomas, it (matter) has not even being, and is therefore a non-being. 'Materia secundum se neque esse habet neque cognoscibilis est.' "

He charges Aristotle's philosophy with having never risen above pantheistic materialism. " Since matter is non-being, the sum of being is God." From the above foot-note he gives us to understand that St. Thomas taught a still more pronounced pantheism.

St. Thomas has been already made to favor the evolutionists and Darwinians, now he is a downright pantheist.

Let us examine a little the doctrine of Aristotle and St. Thomas on matter and form. It is true that both Aristotle and Plato held that matter is eternal. This was the weak point in Aristotle's philosophy, and shows that, with all the ingenuity of his master-mind, he failed to attain to the knowledge of that grand truth—creation from nothing, which the little child, thanks to divine revelation, knows with absolute certainty as soon as it begins to learn its catechism. It shows, too, that peripateticism needed the superior mind of St Thomas to purge it of its errors, supply its deficiencies, and give it its full completion.

But, after all, it is not more unreasonable to hold that matter is eternal than to insist that it can exist without an eternal, self-existing first cause, as Mr. Davidson does. Matter cannot be eternal, for it is changeable, and therefore finite; whereas the eternal is infinite, for what is infinite in one attribute, duration, must be infinite in all its attributes, every way infinite. No attribute can be higher than its source, the essence. If, therefore, eternity be predicated of a being, it is essential to that being to be or exist. If essentially existing, it must be a necessary being, therefore unchangeable, therefore infinite, absolute, self-existing.

If the infinite were changeable, it would be no longer infinite; for every change implies two states, A and B, the state from which and the state to which. Now, A or B must be an actuality, for, leaving the possible state, we necessarily enter the actual state, and as, when A is lost, B is gained, therefore in every change there is an actuality either lost or gained. But the infinite cannot gain an actuality, since it has all; it cannot lose an actuality, since it necessarily has all. The infinite cannot leave the possible state, for it is already in the actual state; it cannot leave the actual state, because its essence is *actus purissimus,* and no entity can change its essence.

But to suppose contingent beings without a necessary being, the finite without the infinite, second causes without a first cause, is too absurd to contemplate. A boy who would dispense with number *one* in the science of arithmetic, an architect who would propose to build a castle without resting it upon the earth, the Hindoo who supports the earth upon the tortoise, leaving the support of the tortoise to foolish inquirers, would be just as reasonable as Mr. Davidson is in saying there can be second causes without a first cause.

According to Aristotle, Mr. Davidson tells us, " matter and form have always existed in a state of combination. Matter is indeterminate, and by itself unknowable."

From this he argues that the Stagirite taught that "matter is non-being, the sum of being is God." How he arrives at this conclusion were difficult to imagine. Aristotle says that matter and form exist in combination, that matter is indeterminate without form, is unknowable without form. Mr. Davidson makes him say that, therefore, it does not exist at all. One says it does not exist except under a certain condition, the other says this is equivalent to saying it does not exist at all. It might with equal reason be said that no house exists, no tree exists, because neither exists by itself independently of the earth which supports them.

When St. Thomas says: "Materia secundum se neque esse habet neque cognoscibilis est," he does not say that "matter has not even being, and is, therefore, a non-being." He only says, what every ordinary observer must see is true, that matter neither exists nor can exist without a substantial form of some kind, and is, therefore, by itself unknowable. Mr. Davidson would persuade us that no leaf exists, because no leaf exists by itself without the branch that supports it; that no color exists, because it does not exist without the object colored; that the image and inscription upon the coin do not exist, because they do not exist without the coin impressed.

If Mr. Davidson can find or name any one material entity existing without some form to *determine* it, I will abandon the contention, admit that he is right, and that Aristotle and St. Thomas spoke nonsense. But matter never did, never will, cannot, in its natural state, exist without form. Destroy one form, another is generated. "Corruptio unius, generatio alterius." If the form be taken from a statue, the statue no longer exists. The matter of it exists, but not without another form or forms, the form of a slab, of a log, of a lump, of wood, of stone, of metal, of something. Destroy the new form, another takes its place. Break the matter into fragments, each fragment has its form. The minutest grain of sand has its form. You can divest matter of form only by annihilating matter. How, then, is it not right to say with Aristotle: "Matter is indeterminate and by itself unknowable," or with St. Thomas: "Materia secundum se neque esse habet neque cognoscibilis est?" If it cannot exist by itself, it surely is indeterminate, unknowable by itself. The impossible is unknowable.

St. Thomas is speaking of *prima materia*, or primordial matter, not of what we sometimes understand by matter—a material entity constituted of matter and form united. Primordial matter can be considered apart abstractly, but cannot exist apart, any more than color can exist apart from the object colored, though we may consider it apart abstractly. But the order of existing is different from the order of our knowing. We know no entity more than in part, but every entity exists wholly.   According to St. Thomas, a material entity or body is made up of matter and form ; these constitute its essence, and essence cannot be divided.   Matter is the passive, indeterminate, merely perceptive part; form is the active, determining principle.   Of this matter, considered apart from its substantial form, St. Augustine says that it is " almost nothing."   It is a mere passive potentiality, a perceptivity.

Materia secunda is the material existing entity, the composite substance made up of primordial matter and its substantial form united.

Form is either substantial or accidental, according as it determines an entity in its essence and species, or modifies the entity already determined.   The soul is the substantial form of man, the body the matter informed ; both constitute man ; scientific knowledge is an accidental form of man.   The likeness of Washington is the form of his statue ; the white or brown color in which it has been painted is the accidental form.

Form again can be either intrinsic or extrinsic, according as it exists in the entity and perfects it, or exists beyond the entity as the exemplar idea according to which it is made.   Intrinsic form is either subsisting or non-subsisting, according as it can or cannot exist and act independently of matter.   Thus the soul of man is subsisting form, the *anima belluina* is non-subsisting form.

Finally, form is either informant or non-informant, according as it is naturally destined to be united with matter and to form with it a complete species, or is not so destined, but is a complete species in itself.   Forms of the latter kind are also called separate forms (formæ separatæ), of which the angels are examples.   Each angel, therefore, constitutes a species in itself, and there are as many species of angels as there are angels.   The highest form, and the most removed from matter, is God.

As to the vexed question regarding the constituent principles or elements of bodies, suffice it here to say that, however much the scholastic doctrine has been decried by some and ridiculed by others, no equally satisfactory explanation has yet been brought forward, notwithstanding the claim of increased enlightenment put forward by each successive age.

Pure atomism, originating with Leucippus, continued and elaborated by Democritus, Epicurus, and Lucretius, and, with hardly a modification save the denial of the eternity of atoms, reaching down through Gassendi, Descartes, and Malebranche, even to Newton, is now not even seriously thought of.   What has extension, gravity, motion, attraction, must be a material entity or body ; and we are looking for what constitutes body.

Chemical atomism is not substantially different from what we have just described. Be they atoms, molecules, simple elements, whatever you please to call them, they are still constituted material entities, endowed with cohesive, attractive, and repulsive qualities, that is, with the qualities of that whose principles we are in search of.

The dynamic system, however understood, is no less unsatisfactory. Leibnitz abandoned his favorite theory of *monads*, and adopted the scholastic doctrine of matter and form. Escaping, he tells us, from the yoke of Aristotle, as he thought, he found himself led on by imagination instead of reason. " There is no principle of unity in material entities left us," he further says, " unless we admit the doctrine of matter and form. Form is this unifying principle."

Neither Wolf, Boscovich, nor Tongiorgi has explained how unextended simple elements can generate extension, nor how that which is not already body can have attraction and repulsion. Besides, how can one and the same element be possessed of contrary qualities—repulsion and attraction ?

To return to Mr. Davidson. It would have been much more satisfactory to his readers to have given the very passages in Aristotle which St. Thomas " not unfrequently, partly from ignorance of Greek and partly from prejudice, misinterpreted," than his footnote, " Examples of such misinterpretation might easily be adduced."

It would be highly interesting to institute a comparison, and see how much more St. Thomas has misinterpreted Aristotle, whether from ignorance or prejudice, than Mr. Davidson has misinterpreted both authors, from one or both. It would be difficult to find any misinterpretation of any author go to the extreme of making him say there is no matter, that matter is a non-being, when he simply says that matter by itself, that is, without its substantial form, neither exists nor is knowable.

In his Introduction, p. 96, Mr. Davidson charges St. Thomas with adopting from Aristotle " principles which, if carried to their logical conclusions, are not only incompatible with each other, but fatal to Christian theology," affirming that his system is, " as a whole, without logical completeness," which statement he thinks is amply proved by adding " a fact which is at present only too apparent by the war which has been waging over his meaning, since the recent rehabilitation of his system in the Church through the Papal encyclical—*Æterni Fatris.*"

Strange proof of so grave a charge ! If St. Thomas's principles are contradictory, the whole system built upon them is absurd, and most certainly are they fatal to Christian theology ; for Christianity is preëminently reasonable. According to Mr. Davidson's strange

logic, Holy Scripture is full of contradictions, for wars have been
waging over its meaning for more than eighteen centuries.   What
will men not differ about?   How many various opinions about the
meaning of Tacitus, Thucydides, Horace, Homer, etc.?   Did these
authors, then, speak nonsense?   How many different interpretations of that luminous book of nature, in which some will see no
trace of a Creator, others nothing but Deity, or a development of
the Infinite, others the result of blind chance, and comparatively
few the handwriting of the living God, tracing in miniature some
of His infinite perfections?   Does nature contradict itself, or is
man's mind the measure of truth, the measure of reality?   St.
Thomas is misunderstood by those who read him to find proofs
for *à priori* theories and foregone conclusions; by progressionists,
who make novelty in thought the standard of perfection; by semi-
Cartesians, who hail singularity of views as a mark of advancement;
by Evolutionists, who imagine the magnitude of their pretensions
a guarantee of the survival of the fittest; by the various religious
sects, who fear the force of his logic will land them in the Catholic
Church; finally, by such shallow minds as cannot see the necessity
of positing a first cause from the existence of second causes.

No wonder, then, that we find Mr. Davidson, in his Introduction, p. 96, quoting from St. Thomas, as instances of the "palpably
false," and as proving that in his system "intelligence and sensation are both impossible," these passages: " The sensible in act is
the sense in act, and the intelligible in act is the intellect in act.
' *Sensibile in actu est sensus in actu, et intelligibile in actu est intellectus in actu.*'

" Knowledge is assimilation to the thing known, and the known
is also the perfection of the knower.   ' *Scientia est assimilatio ad
rem scitam, et scitum est etiam perfectio scientis.*'"

Here it is proper to remark that, as it does not follow that St.
Thomas contradicts himself, because of the " war which has been
waging over his meaning," so it is no proof that his doctrine here
is unintelligible and meaningless, if Mr. Davidson fails to detect
its meaning.   The short-sightedness of his readers cannot be imputed to the Angelic Doctor as a fault, nor is he to be censured for
investigating the profound depths of science, because some minds
cannot penetrate below the surface.

Let us analyze a little the process of sensible perception, or
sensation.   That a sense may be able to perceive its proper object,
it must in some way be joined to that object.   There is no action
on the distant without a medium connecting the agent with the
object.   The eye cannot see its object without the medium of light
connecting one with the other.   Now, every perception, whether
sensile or intellectual, as the name itself implies, denotes that the

object perceived is in the perceiver in some way. The known is in the knower. It is seized, taken, held by the knower, as the words *apprehension, comprehension, capacity, holding* in mind, *escaping* the memory, etc., signify. But evidently the object does not come itself to the sense, is not received in the sense. The tree you look upon is not in your eye. It must, then, send its representative, for your sense does not leave you to go to the object. This representative from the object is received by the sense, as everybody knows who has any acquaintance with optics. This representative is called *sensible species*, a sort of similitude or likeness of the object, and called *sensible* because received in sense, and also to distinguish it from *intelligible* species. The first act in sensible perception is from the object. This either immediately or through its proper medium impresses the sense, and calls it forth from the possible state into the actual state. This term of the object's action upon sense is called the species *impressa*. The sense so far is passive, merely receptive of the impression. But the sense, as being a vital organ, immediately on the reception of the species *impressa*, reacts upon it, and tending outward and in a manner stretching after the object whence the impression came, its effort to seize and retain it results in the formation of the species *expressa*, through which, as through a telescope, if I be allowed the comparison, it perceives the object.

We will examine this process more closely. Certainly the species *impressa* was nothing more than an affection, a modification of the sense produced by the action of the object. There was no entity there distinct from the sense affected. The sensible species *impressa* is distinguished from the sense only, as form is distinguished from the matter it informs, viz., abstractly or metaphysically, or even as the impression on wax is distinguished from the wax impressed. *A fortiori* was there no entity there distinct from sense in the species *expressa*, for this is merely the result of the action of the sense itself upon the species *impressa*, which was itself but an affection of sense.

Now the species *expressa* is the sense modified and in act, viz., the act of perceiving its object, that is, the sense in act; and the species *expressa* is the *sensible*, because it is in sense and representative of the object of sense. The species *impressa* is passive, as we have seen, on the part of the subject receiving it, being the effect of the action of the object. The species *expressa* is active, being the modification of the sense itself acting upon the species *impressa* and through the species *expressa* perceiving the object. This perception gives us sensible *cognition*, a name which will entitle us to be classed by Mr. Davidson among Evolutionists and Darwinians. Here we see that the "sensible in act," viz., the species *expressa*, is the " sense in act," viz., in the act of perceiving. "*Sensibile in actu est sensus in actu.*" In other words, the form informing is the substance informed. Mr. Davidson would do well to study St. Thomas before he undertakes to ridicule him.

From the above we see that in every cognition, sensile as well as intellectual, there is a conformity between the knowing and the known, not that the object known is changed, but its representative is so assimilated to the faculty receiving it that it is finally one with it, even as the impression or form of the dollar-piece is one with the dollar. If the learned critic can come so far as to understand the Angelic Doctor, which is, perhaps, taxing his intelligence overmuch, he may yet be able to see the impossibility of having second causes without positing a first cause.

We will now examine the process of intellection, and see if St. Thomas makes the " subject and object of intelligence one " when he says : " *Intelligibile in actu est intellectus in actu.* "

After sensation is completed, the sensible representation passes into the hands of memory and imagination. Imagination calls it up for intellect. Thus reproduced, it is called *phantasma*, and is the proper representative of the object of intellect at this stage of the process. But phantasma, as being the product of an organic faculty, is itself organic. It must, therefore, be sublimated or spiritualized, ere it can be received by intellect; for the received must be of the form of the receiver. The active intellect (*intellectus agens*) it is that effects this, viz., renders the phantasma intelligible or capable of reception by the intellect. The active intellect is an intellectual light, *lumen intelligibile, lumen rationis*, as St. Thomas calls it, corresponding to what some moderns prefer to call a power of abstraction, which abstracts the spiritual from the material in the phantasma, the universal nature or essence from the concrete particular, the intellectual from the sensible elements.

After the operation of the active intellect upon the phantasma, the result is the intelligible species, now ready for reception by the possible intellect, or intellect proper. It is called possible intellect, because it requires its proper object, the intelligible species, to call it into act, before which it is only in the power to act, just as the sense of sight requires a visible object to inform it, and render it actually seeing, before which it was only in the power of seeing. The intelligible species acts upon the possible intellect, impresses it, and calls it into act, as being its proper object. The intellect receives the intelligible species, and now, no longer in the possible but in the actual state, reacts upon that which brought it into act, and with it forms the conception, which is the term of intellection, the idea through which it perceives the object, the *verbum mentale* by which it affirms to itself that it knows the object.

The idea is not the object perceived in the direct or first act, but that through which the object is perceived, just as the telescope is not that which, but that through which, the eye sees directly. This concept, idea, notion, is the intellect's possession of the object, a true representative of the object, which object primarily, directly, and proportionately to the intellect's present state of union with the body, but not absolutely, is the essence of material entity. But for its present condition of dependence upon organic faculties, the proper object of man's intellect is all truth, every entity, not meaning by this that it could comprehend all truth, for the finite cannot grasp the infinite.

Now, every object known must be in the subject knowing according to the mode of the knowing, and accordingly, in this case, intellectually. For the receiver must contain the received according to the mode of the receiver. This is the reason that the object sends its representative, and the reason of the several transformations that take place between the first act of the external object and the final act of intellect by which it affirms that it knows. The sensible or material object puts on the form of the sensible species *impressa*, in order to be received by sense, not meaning by this that it loses its own form or ceases to be itself. The species *impressa* becomes the species *expressa* ere it can be received by imagination or memory. This again assumes the form of the phantasma before it is presented to the active intellect. After the operation of the active intellect upon the phantasma, there results the intelligible species *impressa*. Finally, the action of the intellect proper upon this latter gives us the idea or *verbum mentale*.

Now, what is the term of intellection? Is the act of intellection immanent or transient? Surely it is immanent. For my knowing an object does not change that object, does not affect or modify it in any way; but I am modified by it, my intellect is informed by it. What! Has the object parted with its form to give it to the intellect? No; there is nothing of the object in my intellect, as an entity distinct from intellect, any more than there is anything of the die on the coin impressed by it, as an entity distinct from the coin, though it is the form of the die that constitutes it such a coin. The act of intellection is therefore immanent, terminating upon the intellect itself in the idea, which is nothing else than a modification of the intellect in act, distinct from intellect only as modification from the thing modified, as accident from the substance which supports it, as the image on the coin from the coin.

Hence the "intelligible in act," that is, the intelligible species actually informing the intellect, "is the intellect in act." For the intellect in act so modified the intelligible species which called it into act, and so assimilated itself to this modification or intelligible species *expressa*, that finally it identified itself with it. Therefore "the intelligible in act" may well be called "the intellect in act." The intelligible in act is the form of the intellect in act, and the form and informed are one, even as the form and matter of the statue make one statue.

Let us now see how "palpably false," as Mr. Davidson has it, is St. Thomas's doctrine: "Knowledge is assimilation to the thing known, and the known is also the perfection of the knower," and whether it is the doctrine that "fails to render intelligible what it was intended to explain," or Mr. Davidson that fails to grasp its intelligibility.

Knowledge (*scientia*) is the acquisition or possession of truth, and truth is the conformity of the intellect knowing to the object known, the assimilation of the intellect to its object, their adequation. We have seen that this assimilation is effected through means of the intelligible species, which is the representative of the object. Now, the possession of this assimilation, which is knowledge, is assimilation to the thing known, since to be assimilated is to possess the assimilation. Furthermore, it is the intellect that is assimilated, and the assimilation is distinguished from the assimilated only as form from matter. Therefore the assimilated, the assimilation, and the possession of the assimilation, or knowledge, may rightly be called one, and hence "knowledge is assimilation to the thing known."

Again, since it is the intellect that is conformed or assimilated to the object, and not the object to the intellect, as is evident, the object (objective truth) develops and enlarges the intellect by informing it, and consequently perfects it. Therefore it is true that "the known is also the perfection of the knower."

Here we perceive how much we depend upon God's creatures around us for our perfection, and how these unintelligent beings present themselves to us, revealing their several perfections and calling upon us in their own eloquent language: "Know us, and knowing us, know Him that made both us and you; and knowing Him, praise Him for us." *Cœli enarrant gloriam Dei.*

Man cannot have a single thought of himself. How different this doctrine from German Transcendentalism, that baseless fabric of erring thought! Fichte would have each mind create itself and all things else by knowing them. "To-morrow," said he to his pupils, "we will create God." Hegel went a step farther, and affirmed that the absolute idea was the only reality.

To conclude, St. Thomas does not teach what Mr. Davidson says he teaches. He does not identify subject and object, when he says that the subject (intellect) is conformed or assimilated to the object, the thing known.

A man's photograph is a likeness of him, but it is not himself. The impression upon sealing-wax is not the seal, though it is assimilated to it. So also the assimilation of the intellect to the object known is not the object. In no other system of philosophy are subject and object so clearly distinguished, in no other has each its proper part so emphatically assigned to it in the act of intellection.

SOME ASPECTS OF MODERN UNBELIEF.

ALL who have read the Ethics of Aristotle will remember how he asserts the superior happiness of those who know as compared with those who are still engaged in the search after truth.[1] The assertion, at first sight, seems almost a truism. The perplexity of indecision, the intellectual struggle between conflicting opinions, the insecurity which accompanies a state of uncertainty, the practical difficulties which present themselves to him who is compelled to act without the possession of any fixed principles of action, all combine to convince us of the misery of doubt. " Wer hat die Wahl hat die Qual " must surely be true not only of the minor choices of daily life, but also, and to a far greater degree, of the choice of the dogmas—for dogmas of some kind we all must have—which are to be the governing principles of our whole moral and intellectual nature, to fashion for us our course through the world, to determine our relations to other men, to underlie that portion of the world's history which we call our life, and which is of supreme importance to ourselves, and, perhaps, of no small importance to a wider or narrower circle around us.

Yet, in spite of this, doubt has a certain attractiveness. To hurry into hastily formed opinions and to call them knowledge, is so common a danger that the wise man hesitates before he decides, and this hesitation is often, in certain fields of knowledge, lifelong. If, on the one side, it is painful to hesitate, there is yet a consolation in the thought that the long hesitation will, in the end, secure well-grounded opinions. He who confesses his ignorance and does not pretend to be as yet in possession of the facts necessary for decision, has a consciousness of superiority to him who, pos-

---

[1] Εὔλογον δὲ τοῖς εἰδόσι τῶν ζητούντων ἡδίω τὴν διαγωγὴν εἶναι.—Arist. Eth. X., viii., 3.

sessing the same or a smaller number of facts, finds in them a sufficient basis of authority, just as the man who declines to accept
some plausible tale of distress feels himself the superior of one who
listens with too ready a credence.   There is also a flavor of intellectual humility in the confession that he is still *in via*, and it implies that he intends to travel further along the Road of Truth than
his neighbor who is comfortably satisfied with the conviction that
he is already *in termino*.   To have already enlisted in one or other
of the many armies which claim the possession of truth, involves
a loss of liberty from which the free lance instinctively shrinks.
Even in matters intellectual there are many who would adopt the
well-known words of Horace :

> Nil admirari prope res est una, Numici,
> Solaque, quæ possit facere et servare beatum.

And though the lovers of doubt will always be in a minority,
they will, nevertheless, be a cultivated and intellectual minority;
and those who find themselves content to know or believe that
they can know nothing, have not such a bad time of it as might,
at first sight, be supposed.   If the man of firm convictions talks to
them of the misery of doubt, they will answer that doubt is not
half so miserable a thing as an obstinate adherence to opinions false
or unfounded.

That such men are acting on a principle sound and reasonable,
if kept within its due limits, none can deny.   There are subjects
without end where doubt, or rather the suspension of judgment
until a clearer light shall dawn, is a positive duty.   If I am asked
for an explanation of *thought-reading*, and answer at once that I am
convinced that it is the work of the devil, my hypothesis may be
a true one, or, at all events, it is not easy to disprove it.   But it is
rash, silly and superstitious to attribute the phenomena to a diabolical agency until I have some very solid ground for supposing that
there are no natural forces which can explain it.   The δαιμόνιον of
Socrates, the unseen companion of whose presence he was so strongly
convinced, and whose voice he used to hear warning, advising, directing him, *may* have been his guardian angel, or an evil spirit,
but I decline to adhere firmly to either the one or the other explanation as long as I can possibly account for it by the voice of his
practical reason, quick to discern what he ought to do or to shun,
and acting on a will prompt in its obedience to the call of duty.
In matters such as these I am content to know nothing of the
source of the phenomena, and if Aristotle's dictum about the superior happiness of those who know holds true in matters such as
these, it is because I am not in their respect a searcher after truth,
but deliberately acquiesce in my own ignorance.

But how far is this principle to extend? Is there to be no limit to the wise man's acquiescence in ignorance? Is there or is there not a field where knowledge is not only a privilege but a duty, where ignorance is death, and where contented ignorance is far worse than death? I think I can give an answer to this question to which every reader will yield a willing assent. I imagine that all will agree that this suspension of judgment, this satisfied acquiescence in ignorance, is inadmissible in certain cases which I now proceed to define.

1. No man can, without moral guilt, allow himself to rest in permanent doubt where that doubt affects the practical and immediate duties of life, or the happiness or virtue of himself or others.

2. No man can, without bartering away all pretence to be a lover of truth, allow himself to rest in permanent doubt respecting an hypothesis which embraces and explains all that is most important to the moral and intellectual welfare of mankind, but is bound either to accept that hypothesis or show clear grounds for rejecting it.

3. No man can, without forfeiting all claim to be listened to, assert the intellectual or moral superiority of doubt in any field of research, if the history of mankind shows on the one hand that those who have united in themselves the highest intellectual and moral qualities have invariably condemned any permanent contentment in doubt respecting this field of research; and if, on the other hand, doubt and disbelief in the possibility of attaining truth respecting it has generally been attended by some intellectual perversity or moral degradation.

4. No man can, without forfeiting all claim to be regarded as a lover of truth, as a reasoner whose arguments deserve consideration, or, indeed, as a man capable of any reasoning process at all, adopt any position which involves the simultaneous assertion of two contradictory premises. He who declares it possible that A and not A may be true of the same thing, in the same sense and in respect to the same part of it, excludes himself from the number of rational beings, and declares himself to be qualified only for intellectual intercourse with those who cannot discern between falsehood and truth.

My first proposition will, I think, be conceded by every reader as indisputable. I am going to apply it to the subject of the present article, to the question of the suspension of judgment advocated by many educated men in matters of faith or religious belief. Unfaith, whatever its deficiencies may be, professes to be directly practical. Its contentment in doubt results from its conviction that truth, as to the subjects of which it doubts, is unattainable, and it declines the rôle of the foolish child crying for the moon. They are as little its concern as the politics of Jupiter or Saturn (if Jupiter and Saturn contain living beings capable of political life). Its rule of life is to perform the duty lying immediately before it, without vain speculation about that which is and ever must remain beyond its ken.

But is this possible? Can it steer its course amid the troublous waters because, forsooth, the stars of heaven are far above our reach, and it is but waste of time to form hypotheses respecting them which may never be realized? Can the professor of unfaith find principles of action apart from the influence, direct or indirect, of the faith that he rejects? Can he supply the wants of human nature and the cravings of the human soul when, on almost every subject save those which concern material phenomena, he must, if he is to be consistent, proclaim that there is no means of satisfying the yearning, longing desire of the hungry spirit which cries out for food? Can he provide a sufficient motive to draw back from the dark gulf of vice or crime one whose feet are already on its slippery threshold? Let us take one or two instances which may bring the difficulty before us in concrete form.

A nurse is watching by the sick bed of a man who is hovering between life and death. For ten long years he has been the curse and bane of all around him; cruel, vicious, idle, unprincipled, a drunkard and a libertine, his cowardly brutality has made his poor wife's existence one protracted martyrdom during the period that she has been his slave rather than his wife. How often the nurse has listened with trembling horror to her poor mistress's cries for mercy! How often has she seen the marks of brutal violence on the fair form that she had fondly nursed in childhood, and in the dawning beauty of whose youth she had so often indulged in day-dreams of a happy, prosperous womanhood—all to be so cruelly disappointed! The love his wife once bore him has turned, if not to hatred, at least to abject terror and an unconquerable repugnance, an instinctive loathing of his presence. His little ones have already begun to look askance upon, and shrink in abject terror from, the vile brute who is their father. And now his coarse excesses have done their work, and he is lying between life and death. The doctor has just pronounced the flame of life to be flickering, and has expressed his opinion that before morning all will be over. There is just a hope that he may be saved if the remedies prescribed be administered almost without intermission; but even if he survives he will be a complete wreck, useless in the battle of life, powerless except as a source of misery to that little circle. As the nurse sits there, the thought occurs to her: Why try to save him? A few drops beyond the dose prescribed from the phial labeled "morphia," and the sleep he sleeps will be a sleep that knows no waking. In comfort and peaceful happiness the mother whom she fondly loves will be free from the black cloud which has made her life a living death. What does she herself owe him? What has she received from him? Oaths, and curses, and blows too, when she has ventured to say a word for her poor mistress. What motive is to hold her back? Egoism? There is not the faintest chance of detection—what a delicious thought to free her mistress from that cruel bondage! What a happy prospect to live in peace with her and her darlings in some quiet country home! Altruism? The sleep of death is for the sick man a preferable lot to the career of wretchedness and vice which may be prolonged for years; what an act of charity to relieve her mistress of the curse which blights her life! What a mercy for the poor children to be freed from the degrading influence of a villain and reckless libertine! Egoism and altruism combine to prompt her to pour into the glass the two or three extra drops—*just by mistake!* Are not the circumstances exceptional and the end to be gained a laudable and excellent one?

Now, I ask, what sufficient motive can unfaith put forward to prevent that poor woman from the crime of murder? I do not suppose that the professors of unfaith would go so far as to say that the deed she contemplated would be a praiseworthy or even a justifiable one. But if they are consistent, they would say that it was both one and the other. If no law descends from heaven, if there is no legislator who proclaims to us: "Thou shalt not kill," or if His voice cannot reach us from the throne where He sits far above out of our sight, then we must bid her consult her own happiness and the welfare of those little ones, and rid the earth of him who has been their curse. The limit which separates what is a crime from what is right and praiseworthy, the narrow limit, often wide only by a hair's breadth, has been wiped away; and who is to replace it when we have banished the legislator who alone can trace it again upon our hearts?

Or, let me take another and a very different instance. Let me place myself in the position of a professor of unfaith, a " moral, law-abiding, excellent man," whose children are just growing out of the years of early childhood. Fostered under a mother's care, they have as yet been kept safe from all that could taint their innocence. True, it is the innocence of ignorance, but innocence under any form is fair and beautiful to look upon. They have been brought up in the principles of unfaith ; once and again they have run to their father with the intelligent curiosity of children : " Father, who made the world?" And the answer, the cruel answer, has been: " We don't know, my boy; perhaps we shall know one day, but how we cannot tell." " Father, is there a God?"

and the answer again, the still more cruel and unnatural answer, has been : " We don't know, my boy; perhaps there is, but we cannot tell; perhaps we may be wiser some day." Yet in spite of this, they have never seriously offended against the law of the God whom they have been trained to ignore.

But at length the time comes when the shelter of the home must be quitted, and the youngsters must embark on the perilous waters of school life. What is to keep them safe, now that the innocence of ignorance soon will become impossible? Are there any influences in the public school which can ward off vice, or furnish the young warrior with an armor to defend him against its insidious attacks? Even the weapons which could aught avail have been torn from his hands by his father's teaching. However feeble the safeguards it provides for youthful purity, the average Protestant religion of our day at least teaches God ever present, and the cruel ingratitude of offending Him, and the need of a struggle against temptation, if God is to be our friend and Heaven our home. But all this the poor boy has been taught to regard as an empty fiction, or at all events a piece of mere vague guesswork ! Yet it may be true, even on the showing of the professor of unfaith ; and if it is true, then he allows that something more is true, that the whole Christian (and Catholic) system is true, and that its practical teaching, its elaborate care of youthful innocence, its heaven-taught safeguards for manly virtue, are in that case not only almost indispensable if his children are to be kept safe from vice, but rest upon a basis of truth, the acceptance or non-acceptance of which will affect their happiness to an almost unlimited extent, not in this world only, but in a future state of existence which will last to all eternity.

And if this is so, if there is a chance, a fair chance of these beliefs and these safeguards being a *sine quâ non* for the purity and happiness of his children, what can we think of one who is content to know nothing of those things which are essential, which at all events *may be* essential to the temporal and perhaps the eternal welfare of those he loves? What shall we think of him when he turns them out defenceless, knowing with an almost absolute certainty that their virtue is destined soon to perish under the malignant influences which threaten it? Is it that he cares not for their innocence, or recks not that his boys should return to their home scarred and stained with degrading and loathsome vice ? If he were a mere materialist, a denier of the existence of the supernatural, he might be content that they should eat of the tree of the knowledge of good and evil, as long as they did not injure body or mind by their debauch and avoided the disgrace of detection. But believing as he does that there *may be* a God, how can he be content to stand aloof from the two contending armies, when his professed neutrality exposes not only himself, but his young children to what may be the path to eternal death ? If there were some distant country on whose sanitary conditions men disputed, if some declared it to be healthy, others full of deadly miasma, would the man who could not gain any sure intelligence respecting it be content in emigrate thither ?

I might pile up instances of the guilt of resting content in practical doubt where immediate duties are affected by it. I might picture the professor of unfaith by the deathbed of one tormented by remorse. What would be his immediate duty to such a one ? He cannot tell the dying man he need not fear, since death is an eternal sleep, for he feels no certainty about it. He must, if he speaks at all, mock him with the ghastly hope that "*perhaps* there may be no God, no heaven, no hell ;" or if these things should unfortunately be realities, that they are out of our ken on earth, and we must wait until the light of another world breaks upon us; in other words, *until it is too late.*

Or I might picture him present in a Catholic church. The bell rings at the consecration, and the faithful adore their God present upon the altar. What is the logical position of him who is content to wait until science shall have settled whether faith or superstition is the mental attitude of those who worship there ? If he kneels to adore, it may be a degrading act of superstition ; if he refuses to bend the knee, it may be an insult to the King of kings. The sturdy Protestant may sit in peace and pity the poor idolaters around him ; but the atheist, he may view with supreme contempt the childish mummery ; but the agnostic, he who dares not pronounce Catholic dogma to be false, but only to be an hypothesis incapable of verification, what is his immediate duty in a case like this ?

But it is possible that here an escape from the difficulty may be found. It is in the crises of life, the scenes which decide human destiny, that there comes out most clearly the folly of resting content, not "to force the contest prematurely." It is easy in the midst of a busy, prosperous life, in the eager pursuit of a successful profession, when patients crowd the consulting-room, or clients strive for the advocacy of the rising barrister ; when fortune smiles and pleasure sparkles in the cup, to be content to postpone the solution of questions which perplex, to cease from crying after the moon. But in the tragic scences which from time to time diversify the lives of most, if not of all ; in times when some fierce battle is going on against passion and despair ; in times when the sky is black, and no ray of hope reaches through the darkness, unless it be the thought of God and of Heaven, then it is that these questions clamor for a solution, and not to solve them if we can involves the guilt of moral suicide or moral murder.

2. My second charge against unfaith is based on the characteristics of a tenable hypothesis. I need not remind my reader of the elements which must be combined to form a sound hypothesis; how it must explain all the facts of the case, how it must need no subsidiary hypotheses to back it up, how it must be capable of verification, how it must stand the test of a searching criticism. He who refuses assent to any hypothesis, the adoption or rejection of which intimately affects human well-being, must, if he is a wise man, show cause of his refusal. Until he can do this, he is bound to adhere to it, at least provisionally. He may fairly reject it because it pertains to some special department of knowledge which does not concern him, or because he has no manner of means enabling him to test its truth, or because it is not of any practical importance whether it is true or false, or because he is already in possession of some other hypothesis which satisfies him perfectly. If a scientific man puts before me some new theory respecting the Gulf Stream or the nature of electricity, I decline to give a decided assent, simply because I am not a scientific man and scientific theories do not immediately concern me. If a man of too credulous piety presses on me a theory respecting the intervention of the devil in all cases of magnetic influence, I dismiss his hypothesis as incapable of verification and therefore futile. If I am asked to accept the statement that the author of *Junius' Letters* was Sir Philip Francis, I decline to say yea or nay to what may be interesting as a literary curiosity, but seems utterly unimportant except to historians or lovers of antiquarian research. If I am told that a balloon filled with hydrogen rises into the air because there is an occult connection between the heavenly bodies and certain gases, I answer that I am already in possession of a thoroughly satisfactory theory to account for the fact, and that this imaginary connection is perfectly gratuitous and unnecessary.

But if none of these reasons can be alleged against a theory which is presented to me, if it appertains to a department of knowledge which intimately affects my interests; if I have within my reach means of verifying its claims to acceptance; if it is of the most intense practical importance to myself and to all mankind; and if I have no sort of satisfactory alternative to present, I cannot, if I am a sensible man, set aside the theory. I am bound, from every motive of reason and common sense and positive duty, to accept it, or, at all events, to adopt such means as my own intelligence and the suggestions of the friends or enemies of the theory may propose as tests for its positive acceptance or positive rejection. I cannot, without a grave dereliction of duty, without suicidal folly, remain neutral. Now, the teaching of Christianity affects not one department of knowledge, but all. It bears upon not only one of the interests most important to me, but all that are of any permanent character. It even affects my material interests, since my health of body, my mere physical activity, my position in the world, my conduct in business or in my profession, are continually influenced, directly or indirectly, by it. It is of the greatest practical importance to all mankind; happiness or unhappiness, content or uneasy disquiet, joyousness or melancholy, cheerfulness or depression, hope and glad expectation or despondency and unsatisfied sadness, are the prizes and penalties which are to be distributed as the results of a successful investigation into an acceptance or non-acceptance of its claims. There is no counter-theory which men agree upon as a tenable alternative—in fact, there is no alternative of even respectable pretensions. What folly, what madness, then, if I do not search and inquire with all diligence whether it be true!

But here, perhaps, I shall be told that I am ignoring the very point at issue. The professor of unfaith will allow all that I am saying, but will tell me that it does not apply to the case of those who hold themselves apart from any sort of religious belief or unbelief. Their case, he will remind me, is that of the inquirer who has a hypothesis presented to him incapable of verification. "You ask me," he will say, "to accept the Christian hypothesis, but you furnish me with no means of verifying it." He will allow that it is beautiful, picturesque, dignified, noble, elevating; but where, he asks, is the touchstone of its Truth? He will grant that it explains the facts of the case, perhaps even that the objections of Protestants to Catholic doctrine are futile, ignorant, unreasonable. He will concede that no other hypothesis ever proposed has superseded it. He allows its intense practical importance to himself and to every man who is born into the world. But he tells us that, all said and done, it is impossible for him to accept it simply because it *is* an hypothesis, and must, so far as we can see, ever remain so. It is up in the air, and, climb as high as we can, it is out of our reach, and so we must acquiesce in our inevitable destiny; we must be content to doubt.

To answer this objection would require a volume. But it is the central objection of all professors of unfaith, and I must bring them to look on a single point. No thoughtful, careful student of Christianity can fail to admire the character of Christ. No man of unbiassed intelligence can doubt that He was a real person and trod this earth and preached in the towns and villages of Palestine. No one who has not lost all sense of moral beauty can fail to admire, with an admiration passing all bounds, the exquisite, unap-

proachable loveliness of the teaching and character of Christ. No
one can. deny its power for good over the hearts of men. No
one can paint, in his wildest day-dreams, any possible doctrine
higher than the doctrine of Christ, or any person who ever presented to us, as He did, the ideal man. Now, if there is one thing
which Jesus Christ claimed, it was to be not only divine, but God.
He, humble and meek of heart, nevertheless claims to be King in
His own right of heaven and earth. What is the professor of
unfaith to assert respecting Him? That He was a deluded fanatic,
or a conscious impostor? It is not a happy alternative.

Nor is this all; in proof of His divine mission and consequent
credibility, He adduces His resurrection from the grave. It is on
the resurrection that the truth of Christianity takes its stand. It
is here that every possible hypothesis, except the true one, breaks
down and makes him who urges it ridiculous. The swoon-theory
and the theory of a pseudo-Christ after the resurrection are equally
futile and silly. To hold oneself aloof from any opinion about
it is a position untenable for one who loves the words and the
character of Christ. It involves an endless holding aloof on a
thousand matters of history which at last becomes impossible.
Are we to form no opinion about St. Paul and St. John and all the
other contemporaries of Christ whose teaching is the reflex of the
teaching of their Master? A man who is in his senses must have
some theory about Christ and Christianity and miracles, in order
to explain what are allowed as matters of history. Every other
theory but the true one leads to some puerile absurdity that no
one would ever admit unless he was hopelessly biassed beforehand.
Perhaps the most puerile of all absurd theories is Comte's assertion
that the Christ of the Gospels is an ideal whom His subsequent
followers constructed out of their own consciousness.

I say nothing here of miracles, ancient and modern, which are
practical and matter-of-fact tests within the reach of all who are
men of good will. If the only mode of egress for the professor
of unfaith, from facts which he cannot deny, is the childish hypothesis of powers of nature, hitherto latent, of which no hint or
sign has ever appeared since the beginning of the world even until
now, surely he will be pursuing a more scientific course in at least
investigating the claims of the Christian hypothesis than in inventing an explanation of the scientific absurdity of which none can be
more conscious than himself.

If Christianity, then, starts with these advantages (and I might
enumerate a thousand more, *e.g.*, its value as a practical rule of life;
its calm indifference to material prosperity; its joyousness amid
suffering and misfortune; its exclusive success in guarding innocence; its *admitted* power in raising the fallen; its doctrine of self-

sacrificing charity and practical altruism; the supreme, intense, inimitable cheerfulness and lightheartedness of those who throw themselves wholly and without reserve into the spirit of its teaching), if it possesses, I say, the sole right to these and other magnificent prizes, what folly to be satisfied to stand aloof from a contest in which the strife is about such high stakes as these! It does not ask for acceptance without trial; it offers as its credentials miracles, and the one great central miracle of the resurrection and the teaching and character of its Founder, the unity of its doctrine, the holiness of its saints, the continuity of its unbroken existence as a corporate body. At least you can verify these. They are historical facts. If Christ be not raised, says St. Paul, your faith is vain and our hope is also vain. Limiting myself merely to Christ and the resurrection, I challenge my opponents on historical grounds. If you find every explanation of a historical fact and of a historical character break down save one, and this one is consistent throughout, backed by incontrovertible evidence and explaining all the phenomena of the case, surely you are bound in common sense to accept that explanation, unless you can clearly show that in one way or other it leads to a positive contradiction. And this no one has ever shown and no one can ever show of Catholic Christianity.

3. My third proposition I need not linger over except for a moment. The respective characters of the adherents and adversaries of Christianity is again a matter of historical inquiry. I will not attempt to enumerate either the one or the other, either its friends or its foes. But this all must in fairness admit, that if they were looking for instances of all that is generous, noble, heroic in human nature, for self-sacrificing devotion, for self-denial without hope of earthly reward, for unflinching loyalty of heart, for innocence unstained and unspotted from the cradle to the grave, for singleness of purpose and purity of intention and life-long benevolence and patient, uncomplaining endurance of evil and all else that in our inmost souls we most admire and recognize as approximating to a perfect, a divine ideal—it would not be among the professors of unfaith ("moral, law-abiding, excellent" men though they be), nor among those who give in their allegiance to the various bungling, half-hearted, inconsistent forms of a spurious Christianity; nor yet among those who limit their beliefs to a deity who has set the world a-going and now leaves it to fufil its mechanical destiny; least of all among those who positively deny the existence of Him who created them and wage active war against Himself and all that is dear to Him—but in Catholic Christianity and nowhere else.

And on the other hand, if they were looking for instances of all that is proud, rebellious, independent, for instances of degraded morality, of antisocial theories, of an insidious teaching which undermines, or tends to undermine, all those virtues which appeal most strongly to our higher instincts, it would be among those who have for some reason or other thrown off all their allegiance to God, shrieked the shriek of liberty, proclaimed themselves apostles of free thought, made it the object of their lives to "*écraser l'Infâme.*" Many are the names which rise to my mind of men living and dead—it is needless to mention them. The saints of God need no praise—the names of the devil's heroes shall not disfigure my paper.

4. But my fourth and last proposition is the most important of all; I have discussed it from one and another point of view elsewhere.[1] But I am bound, in order that my present argument may be complete, at least to indicate the internal contradictions which I find in the theory of those who, " fearing to force the impending contest," hold themselves aloof alike from Christianity and from atheism.

The skeptic *putus et purus* needs no refutation. If he doubts of everything, he cannot be certain even that he doubts, and so puts himself out of court without delay. The professor of unfaith is not a skeptic *putus et purus*. But he is a modified skeptic; he declines to accept anything which goes by the name of the supernatural, anything which cannot possibly be matter as a function of matter. About the material as being subject to our senses, and about the material alone, does he feel certain; all else he declares to be pure speculation, a prying into that which is out of the sphere of human knowledge, an attempt after certainty where certainty is unattainable. You may frame, he says, beautiful hypotheses, but how can they be tested? You may build up a fair structure, but who is to know whether it is not a castle in the air. You may assert a Supreme, Omnipotent Ruler, Lord of heaven and earth, the God and Father of us all, but with what magic power have you risen from this poor world into the regions where you say God reigns supreme in ceaseless contemplation? You *may* be right; it may be that the theistic hypothesis, the Catholic hypothesis, is the true one; but I cannot see it, and, therefore, I cannot accept it. I think this is a not unfair statement of the position of the educated agnostic. It is plausible, and has that semblance of cultivated impartiality which allures the modern searcher after truth. But none the less does it contain an inherent contradiction.

---

[1] Vide the Month, November 1882, art. " Some more Agnostic Fallacies."

When the agnostic, or professor of unfaith (for I am using the two expressions as identical or almost identical), allows that the Christian hypothesis *may* be true, but cannot be verified in our present state of existence, he is asserting A and not A with the same breath. For if Christianity is true (and the same holds good if we limit our belief to theism), God, such as Christianity declares Him, is a really existent being. He is consequently God of truth, God who has revealed Himself to man, God who claims our obedience and our love, God who tells us in clear, plain, unmistakable terms, that in Him we live and move and have our being, that the invisible things of Him, His eternal power also and divinity, may be clearly seen by the things He has made, and, consequently, that those who refuse to acknowledge Him are inexcusable. When, therefore, a man says: God may possibly exist; of this I cannot form an opinion, it is altogether beyond my reach, he says in other words: It *may* be that there is a God who is a God of truth; who says, and therefore says with truth, that the knowledge of Him is within the reach of all His rational creatures; and He *may*, therefore, since I am one of His creatures, be within my reach. But at the same time I have tried in vain to find Him, and therefore I know He is not within my reach. The agnostic, inasmuch as he holds himself aloof from atheism, thereby admits the former proposition: *God is perhaps within my reach* (A). The agnostic, inasmuch as he holds himself aloof from theism, thereby asserts the latter proposition, which is clearly and directly contradictory of the former: *God is not within my reach* (not A). By his very profession of impartiality he declares implicitly: It may be that God is cognizable by man; by the very same profession he declares explicitly: It cannot be that God is cognizable by man. Could self-contradiction be more self-contradictory than this? We who are Christians and Catholics throw down the gauntlet before the modern agnostics, before the professors of unfaith. They are men of ability; let them, if they can, clear themselves of this very serious charge which we bring against them, not only against their logic, but against their very reason. We charge them with an implicit self-contradiction, which makes their position untenable and their arguments worthless; which vitiates all their fair professions of being lovers of truth. We charge them with blowing hot and cold with the same breath. We charge them with being intellectual charlatans, inasmuch as their whole system—if system it can be called—is based on a contradiction. At the root of the specious but poisonous tree of their philosophy, there is a cankerworm which warns, or ought to warn, away all earnest seekers after the tree of life. In spite of all their fancied liberty, no true

freedom is there for their soul, since they are unable or unwilling
to perceive that " perhaps there is a lie in their right hand." [1]

The reader who has followed my argument will, I imagine, now
perceive why I assert that theism and Christianity are not subjects
in which a continuance of suspended judgment is either lawful, wise,
or possible.   They enter so minutely into every detail of our life,
our motives and actions are so constantly influenced by our belief
or unbelief in them, that doubt never ceases to clamor for a speedy
solution.   Not only are we ourselves hampered and perplexed at
every step by the absence of fixed principles of action, but it tells
even more ruinously on the best interests of the young, the weak,
and the tempted.   In times of prosperity and good fortune we
may hush the craving of our souls, but in adversity, sickness,
physical or moral suffering, how cruel the lot of one who, as he
sinks beneath the waters, feels, and feels in vain, for some ground
beneath his feet! The interests concerned are so all-important, so
supreme, that we are madmen if we sit content to doubt, with our
hands folded, in guilty indecision.   We *must*, if we think at all,
form some hypothesis respecting virtue and vice, ethical and social
questions, the means of advancing the welfare of our fellows, and
in each and all of these the religious question must needs enter.
The opposing camps present to us their respective champions, and
to declare ourselves unable to choose our part is strange indeed,
when on the one side are assembled the chosen heroes of humanity,
and on the other the very scum and refuse of the moral world.
But strange above all is a hesitation which involves an inherent
contradiction and confesses itself to have no share or lot in truth.

---

[1] Non liberabit animam suam, neque dicet : Forte mendacium est in dextera mea.
Is. 44, 20.

THE CORRELATION OF AGNOSTICISM AND POSITIVISM.

Agnostic Metaphysics. By Fred. Harrison, Nineteenth Century, 1884.

Religion, a Retrospect and a Prospect. By Herbert Spencer, Nineteenth Century, 1884.

Creed of a Layman. By Fred. Harrison, Nineteenth Century, 1881.

Creeds, Old and New. By Fred. Harrison, Nineteenth Century, 1880.

The Ghost of Religion. By Fred. Harrison, Nineteenth Century, 1884.

Last Words about Agnosticism. By Herbert Spencer, Nineteenth Century, 1884.

THE two most prominent schools of modern English thought were for the first time directly arrayed against each other during the year which has just ended. In January, 1884, the first direct clashing of arms took place; and the controversy continued, with but short intervals, during the whole twelvemonth. The year closed with the respective positions apparently unchanged, an indication that this controversy had ended as most contests of that kind generally do, without having advanced the cause it was intended to advance. But this is not the case. I quite agree with Mr. Harrison, that in this instance controversy did not prove an unqualified evil; and I go further, even, because to my mind the crossing of swords between two men like Mr. Herbert Spencer, the great sociologist and leader of the Agnostic school of thought, and Mr. Fred. Harrison, the apostle of the creed of Humanity and acknowledged leader of Positivism, forms a most important, if not perhaps *the* most important event that the intellectual world was called upon to witness during the past year. It seems to me as if even the apparent loss of temper which colors more or less their controversial writings, and the very marked acerbity of feeling which both occasionally manifest, had served, this time, a good purpose. For, the use of weapons with keen edges helped to bring out their points of agreement as well as their points of disagreement, so that both speculative theories stand now in clear outlines before the world of thought. The real issues are no longer concealed; society can no longer plead a misunderstanding of Mr. Herbert Spencer's position, or of Mr. Fred. Harrison's creed of Humanity. The friction of diamond against diamond emitted some brilliant sparks, and removed, thereby, that most important of all problems of the day, religion, from the region of darkness; and since whatever tends to help towards a final solution of this, to many, so perplexing enigma deserves a hearty welcome at the hand of all thinking and reflecting minds; this intellectual struggle between the two schools possesses, I take it, great and unquestionable merit.

I do not attempt to deny that Agnostics and Positivists view the results of their labors as diametrically opposed to each other; for the one school of thought asserts as necessary elements of religious belief *what* the other strenuously denies as such. Each side has fortified its position by arguments which the other side in vain tried to override rough-shod. Nor can it be said that the narrow groove of strongly preconceived opinions, to the formation of which they have given years of arduous labor and incessant study, incapacitates the leaders from looking through other glasses than those turned out in their own laboratories; for it is not tenacity of purpose, nor an unwillingness to part with a cherished idol of years, that prevents them from abandoning their respective positions. Far from it. Their firmness rests upon much higher ground; it is based upon the consciousness that what each system postulates is true; and this consciousness grew into a conviction, this conviction gradually acquired full virility, and came thus to be turned into a stern belief. The unfailing courage, the earnestness, the force displayed in the defence of their respective attitudes, can only be accounted for as proceeding from a sincere belief that the only true and correct and possible basis of religion is furnished by their systems. To presume that less worthy motives actuated and vitalized their writings would be unjust in the highest degree. It must, moreover, be admitted that the postulates of both schools of thought contain a large share, though they do not contain the fulness, of truth. But, while all this is true, it is not less true that, though making for the same goal, they have worked on entirely different lines. Mr. Spencer, like Mr. Harrison, endeavored to penetrate the mystery of religion, and to discover its vital elements. Both made valuable discoveries; both have, indeed, unearthed some vital elements of religious belief; but neither have they discovered the same, nor have they unearthed all. They addressed themselves to certain aspects of the subject, rather than to its entirety; they took no pains to ascertain whether other elements besides those of their own discovery must not be taken into account before any final verdict can be rendered. They failed to perceive that the antagonism between their systems is not real, but apparent only, and disappears as soon as they are properly integrated in those grand and truly Catholic religious truths which no human theorizing will ever succeed in upsetting. For true religion, after all, covers, as they are bound to admit, only those truths which, having outlived the strife of ages in the past, will survive even the present confusion of thought, and serve to future generations as headlights, shining with the brilliancy of perennial youth to the very end of time. What is absolutely true is so only and solely on condition that it is eternally so. It is obvious, therefore, that whatever truth there is contained in the proposition of Agnosticism cannot collide with any truth uncovered by Positivism, and *vice versa.* Positivists and Agnostics wrestle, therefore, over a phantom which has no existence outside of their own chain of reasoning, and vanishes out of sight by assigning to their respective postulates their proper places in the domain of religion. And now that, thanks to the late controversy, the positions of both are clearly defined, it is possible to balance accounts and debit and credit the proper sides of the ledger without running the risk of having the accounts disputed afterwards. A sober analysis of the evidence of both sides, and a readiness to bid a gladsome welcome to truth wherever found, will readily establish how far they stand on solid ground.

The Agnostic school of thought, as is well known, follows the many winding footpaths of science, while the Positivists march on the broad highway of common sense and experience. It is well to keep this distinctive character of the two schools clearly before our mental vision. Now Mr. Herbert Spencer, after carefully travelling over the roads of science, endeavors to solve the enigma of religion by science, comes forward and announces that the only object of religion which he can discover is what he calls "the Unknowable." This Unknowable he defines as an "Infinite and Eternal Energy by which all things are created and sustained," making it thus the First as well as the Final Cause of the universe. This, he says, is the epitome of the philosophy of science, and the last word that can be spoken by a scientist about an intellectual basis of religion. He contends, moreover, that this is also the last dictum of philosophy. Mr. Fred. Harrison, on the other hand, maintains that a religion that begins and ends with the mystery of the Unknowable, is no religion at all, but "a mere logician's formula." He thinks that religion can not rest upon something that is "unknowable, inconceivable, and in no way to be understood," and claims for religion "an intelligible object of reverence, the field of feeling and of conduct as well as of awe." These are, briefly stated, the attitudes of Agnosticism and Positivism, attitudes, I am constrained to admit, that appear to me, with certain limitations which I shall presently point out, incontrovertibly true. The restriction with which I am prepared to accept Mr. Herbert Spencer's basis of religious belief is this, that I accept it as the result of science, and even of the philosophy of science, but not of philosophy proper. For I find it impossible to concede, as Mr. Harrison does, that the great sociologist is also the philosopher *par excellence* of our age. And the limitation with which I wish to surround Mr. Fred. Harrison's view, is simply this, that I am unable to accept Humanity, even if spelt with a big " H," as an adequate object of religion. And with these reservations, it seems to me, no candid-minded and thinking person can experience any difficulty in admitting both to be right, for the simple reason that the basis of religion furnished by science and the basis of religion furnished by life cannot be expected to be the same. Religion in the hand of Agnosticism is an entirely different instrument from religion in the hand of Positivism. Why, then, should these two different instruments produce only one, and that the identical sound?

Mr. Spencer is, beyond all question, right, in demanding, as the final result of all science, the recognition of an Allbeing which is at the same time Creative Power and First and Final Cause, and which is no fiction, but a reality. When he asserts that the recognition of this mysterious Power above and beyond the comprehension of science forms the cardinal point of every religious system, I find it quite impossible to differ with him, because the consciousness of such an infinite reality underlies, indeed, every sort of religious belief. That our vision of it through the glass of science alone remains dim and obscure, and that science is incapable of telling us more about it, is not in the least surprising. It is perfectly natural, and cannot well be otherwise, because the existence of the lesser of course postulates the greater, but beyond affirming its necessity it can say nothing. When Mr. Spencer ascribes to the Unknowable not a negative, but a positive character, he simply proves the consistency and soundness of his reasoning. So far, I contend, even the most orthodox theologian can follow the Agnostics, for so far they stand on perfectly unassailable ground.

As regards the Positivists, they claim that they, and in point of fact they do, concern themselves with religion only as it affects the lives of men and women and children in this world. They assert, and I think rightly so, that religion must be more than a mere intellectual speculation, that it must be able to furnish a basis for duty. They hold, with the late Mr. George H. Lewes, that " deeply as we may feel the mysteries of the universe, and the limitations of our faculties, the foundations of a creed can rest only on the Known and the Knowable." When Mr. Harrison insists that the " Unknowable " must needs remain a perfectly unintelligible quantity to the ordinary public, I find it impossible to disagree with him, and so far, again, I hold, orthodox theology can fall into line and say Amen. For, if the study of human nature and the contemplation of life compels us to give our unqualified assent to one proposition, it is this, that the object of religious worship must be a definite object, known as such to the worshipper, one towards which he may entertain feelings, and which, in turn, is able to generate in the worshipper sentiments that will issue forth in action,—an object, therefore, to which the terms personality, will, intelligence, can be applied without becoming, thereby, meaningless phrases. I quite agree with Mr. Harrison, that religion, in order to deserve that name, should take hold of human nature and become a law for the regulation of conduct; and he perceives that as an axiomatic truth.

From this very condensed synopsis of the two systems, the marked divergence of opinion, on nominally one and the same subject, by two men who deservedly rank amongst our foremost thinkers, and I am tempted to add, also amongst our foremost writers, is quite apparent. It is also apparent that their differences are not altogether attributable to the entirely different standpoints from which they view religion, but rather to the fact that they have entirely different ideals in their minds when they discuss that subject. To the one, religion presents itself as a purely scientific, as a mental, problem ; to the other, as a practical problem, a problem of life. The one understands by it the sum and substance of what abstract science can say about it, while the other consults life and experience, and draws from their study his conclusions. Now, if we view the situation in that light which I believe to be the only fair and equitable standpoint for judging the intrinsic merit of both attitudes, it ceases, of course, to be surprising that the results of these two sets of observations are not alike. Nor is this all. We are driven to further acknowledge that, inasmuch as the views of both schools are, in the main, true, they neither can nor do clash with each other; for truth, *ipsissima natura*, can never clash with, or contradict, truth. And this consideration forces upon us the conclusion that a way out of this perplexing dilemma does exist. In what direction, however, that road may lie, that is the question.

It has already been stated that " nature " (science) and " man " (life) form the chief objects of the investigations of Messrs. Spencer and Harrison, for the one moves along on the road of science, whose primary object consists in nature and natural facts, and the other moves along life, whose central figure is man. Nature, as well as man, stands out in all intellectual systems of the world as a main term of human knowledge. Both are recognized as such by Atheist and Pagan, by Catholic and Protestant, by Agnostic and Positivist, in fact, by every thinking mind of every age and every clime. But, let it be emphasized, nature and man, main terms of human knowledge though they be, are, nevertheless, not the only main terms of it.   There is one more, upon which both depend, to which both, of necessity, lead, and without which the great mystery of religion can never be satisfactorily understood, and that third, or, rather first, main term, is God.   I am well aware that Agnostics and Positivists alike deny that term, at least in the Christian acceptation of the word.   But what I insist upon is this : that Mr. Herbert Spencer and Mr. Fred. Harrison, clear-headed and powerful intellects as they are, each advancing on a well-defined though different line, inasmuch as they announce religion (I use here the word in the sense in which it is acceptable to both schools) to be a rational postulate of the study of science and of the study of life, have no right, on their own testimony, to deny the existence of that other term of knowledge upon which alone sound religion can rest, with which countless generations before us have dealt, with which, as a matter of fact, Positivists and Agnostics, all verbal protestations to the contrary notwithstanding, deal even now, and with which future generations will likewise deal.

To say that " God," in the Christian meaning of the word, is not an equivalent for this last and first term of knowledge, is one thing ; to deny its existence, is another.   Both have done the former ; neither has been foolhardy enough to do the latter.   It remains to be seen, however, whether their denial of the God of Christianity, as the proper equivalent of that disputed main term of knowledge, rests upon solid and unassailable ground ; it remains to be seen whether it does not amount to a mere play of words, a verbal assertion, without any weight ; it remains to be seen whether their own writings do not contain ample proofs that this personal triune Deity of Christianity offers, after all, the only rational solution of the religious problem ; it remains, lastly, to be seen whether their own definitions, and their own statements as regards necessary elements of religion, do not at least point to, if they do not proclaim, the necessity of a God-man, Christ, and whether, by integrating their systems in Christian theology, they do not lose their antagonism, become harmonious, and dispel forever the notion that they cannot be both correct.   All this remains to be seen, and whilst I have no hesitancy in asserting that Mr. Herbert Spencer's Unknowable and Mr. Fred. Harrison's personal object of reverence merge into one, and are completed and harmonized and perfected only in the God-man of Christianity, I assert also that only upon Him religion can be built, and that through relation to Him nature and life become not less intelligible than the very postulates of science and of life themselves.

I deem it quite unnecessary to enter upon any elaborate argument to support the statement I have made, that three great problems, namely, God, man, and nature, have confronted Humanity at all times. This is evident from the most superficial knowledge of the records of the past. They are found in all philosophies, in all theologies, in Virgil, in Homer, in the Bible, and in the sacred books of the east ; and I have no intention of insulting the intelligence of cultured society. Suffice it to say that, up to our own time, no systematized effort has ever been made to reduce these three main terms of knowledge to two. In our own days, however, this is being attempted, and modern advanced thought has deluded itself into the belief that there are but two, simply because only two, nature and man, fall under the direct observation of our senses. The elimination of the third, under the application of this narrow gauge, appeared, of course, not altogether irrational. Add to it the wonderful progress of science, which I am far from gainsaying, and the not less wonderful success crowning its efforts, and conditions are given well calculated to lead men to believe that science is the only really omnipotent goddess, fairer than Venus and mightier than Zeus, and abundantly able to throw the calcium-light of truth upon any and all objects, no matter how subtle or how deep. Thus it came to pass that the science of nature and the science of man were expected to illumine also the mystery of religion, and to render a final and infallible verdict in regard to it. And why not? Had not science pressed heretofore unknown forces into service ? had not every new-comer, after a careful analysis, been successfully subdued ? Why, then, should science fail in dealing with a force as old as religion ? Some such reasoning seems, no doubt, plausible enough, and may possess convincing power for those who are too lazy to think for themselves, and who are ever ready to assent, without any questioning, to any proposition that comes from the fashionable headquarters of the Agnostic or the Positivist school. Be that as it may, it is quite certain that the negation of a third term of knowledge, and particularly of the God of Christianity as its equivalent, is made in a summary and rather unceremonious way by Agnostics and Positivists. This being the case, the duty devolves upon us to examine Mr. Herbert Spencer's and Mr. Fred. Harrison's systems, and to see how far their own teaching and their own writing sustain their denial.

Well, the foremost philosophical intellect of the school of strictly scientific research tells us, to use his own words, " the nature of the Reality transcending appearances cannot be known, yet its existence is necessarily implied;" and, again, "this inscrutable Existence science, in the last resort, is compelled to recognize as unreached by its deepest analyses of matter, motion, thought, and feeling." He says, furthermore, that personality, will, and intelligence can neither be affirmed of nor denied to the Unknowable, which he defines as an " Infinite and Eternal Energy by which all things are created and sustained." Now this very clear, precise, and emphatic announcement of science invalidates, it seems to me, once for all any denial of the existence of what is generally understood by the term "God." If the quotations just given do not contain a pretty correct definition of what average minds understand under the word God, namely, a Power above us, the Creator and Sustainer of all, a Power both real and necessary, then I, for one, confess to having completely misunderstood every definition of God ever made by either philosopher or theologian. Nor do I think I stand alone. The vast majority of mankind, I imagine, if asked what word in any language is the equivalent for an " infinite and eternal energy, both real and necessary, by which all things are created and sustained," will return as reply the word " God." Thus, if I insist that science does not destroy, but establish, that first term of human knowledge which human short-sightedness and human pride tried to eliminate from the intellectual systems of the future, I simply defend common-sense, and refuse to be misled by an unmeaning play of words. I quite agree with Mr. Spencer that science proper can make no further admissions; science cannot furnish another or a better definition of God, nor another or a better basis for religious belief. When it has uttered that definition, it has uttered all it can utter. Its office ends by pointing out the reality and the necessity of a Power above, which established nature and all its wondrous laws all its marvellous harmony, and sustains all. This, let it be fully understood, is, indeed, the alpha and omega of science. Science should not give us less, but it can never give us more. So far, then, as Agnosticism is concerned, an unprejudiced examination of that system reveals to us that it does not abolish God, and that religion, based upon God, has not only nothing to fear from scientific investigations, but should, on the contrary, hail further explorations, because the more new ground is broken, the more new fields are brought under cultivation, the greater will be the cumulative evidence for the reality and necessity of a term outside of nature and of man, and the greater will also be the certainty that beyond the precincts of natural facts science remains forever silent. We have to go, however, one step further before dismissing Agnosticism. Science not only establishes God (I use here the word as the equivalent of the scientific equation: "Unknowable—Infinite and Eternal Energy, etc."); but it establishes, moreover, the *possibility* of the existence of the God of Christianity, with all the attributes with which that faith has equipped Him. For, while science admits that Personality, Will, Intelligence, etc., cannot be affirmed of the Unknowable, it also admits that these time-hallowed attributes of Deity cannot be denied. Thus, it is no stretching and straining to plainly assert that Agnosticism, as exposed by Mr. Herbert Spencer, furnishes mankind with the only correct scientific definition of God that science ever can make, is altogether impotent to deny the God of Christianity, and honest enough to tell us that the scientific definition is not full and exhaustive, since more may be predicated of the Unknowable than Agnostics feel warranted to predicate. And here I rest the case of Agnosticism for the present.

Turning now to Positivism, the attempt of this school consists in evolving by a careful study of man and of life in all its ramifications those highest ultimate truths of religion which force themselves upon the acceptance of every intelligent mind. I would be wanting in candor did I fail to state here that Mr. Harrison's ideas on the mission and functions of religion display an uncommonly keen sense of penetration and a really surprising appreciation and realization of the wants of human nature. When, therefore, he defines religion as " simply morality fused with social devotion, and enlightened by sound philosophy," and when he asserts that " Humanity is neither the shadow of God, nor the substitute for God, nor has it any analogy with God," he simply oversteps the boundaries of his own teaching and writing, and contradicts himself. He is much too clear-sighted not to perceive that these assertions in no way conform to the views which he develops and lays down with as much force as ability in " Creeds: Old and New," and in the " Creed of a Layman." These papers contain, besides, an irresistible refutation of the view, advanced by him lately, that an abstract notion can ever furnish an adequate object of religion. Thus I shall let Mr. Harrison refute Mr. Harrison, and shall be careful to use as far as possible his own words, so that no charge of misrepresenting him in any way can be lodged against me. In the Creed of a Layman Mr. Harrison explains what he understands by the true and real meaning of religion, and says "that meaning of religion is this. It is a scheme of thought and life whereby the whole nature of individual men and societies of men are concentrated in common and reciprocal activity with reference to a Superior Power which men and societies alike may serve. In popular use the latter phrase alone in the definition has survived, and that in a particular aspect only." " When various qualities of a man, and of masses of men, can be brought to work together to a great common object of Devotion—then you have religion." " The essence of the idea is that the faculties can all be brought by it into harmony and proper relation; that it binds up great multitudes in one feeling and one thought." " The nontheologial schools of the day are for the most part content to trust for this: either to some purely intellectual doctrine or doctrines, some say Science, some say Truth, some vaguely say Free Thought, some say the principle of Evolution or logical examination, the Spirit of Inquiry, the right of Private Judgment, some mystical gift for always being right of which we have never learned the secret." "Trusting to luck, or chance, or the ultimate triumph of what is called Truth, almost all the non-theological schools, Disciples of Science, of Free Thought, of Democracy, of Secularism, and the like, repudiate anything like an organized attempt to reduce life as a whole to harmony by a central principle of life; they reject systematic discipline of life; they start back from Worship, from any formal appeal to the Feelings, from the very idea of Devotion of spirit to a great Power—in a word, they turn with disgust or mockery from Religion." "Not, indeed, that they have ever proved this to be the sum of Philosophy, or the true teaching of history. Far from it, they assume it; they affect to know it by the light of Nature as an intuitive truth. Mention to them *worship, devotion, religion,* the discipline of heart and practice in the continuous service of the object of devotion—in a word, utter the word Religion, and they smile in a superior and satisfied way." On all this all rational and serious persons, at least, are, indeed, fully agreed. For, unless brain, heart, and will are taken hold of by religion, we have no religion at all.

It is further true that wherever around us to-day we see a beautiful character and a noble life, there we see something more than a set of opinions and implicit reliance on the principle of free inquiry. What is it that we do see? We always find a passionate resolve to make life answer in fact to some end that is deeply believed to be right. We have the three things—belief, enthusiasm, practice. Hence Mr. Harrison insists that belief, discipline, and worship constitute the very essence of religion, and in this assertion he announces merely what every human being instinctively feels to be true. Nor can anybody disagree with him when he says: "Man has a mind, and an enormous accumulation of knowledge. We have to satisfy that mind, and give order to that knowledge. Man has energies; we must give them full scope, and yet keep them in due bounds. Man has a soul, fitted for great devotion; we must fill that soul with a worthy object of devotion, strengthen it, purify it by constant exercise. If we leave out one of these sides, human nature is cramped, harmony destroyed. And, what is more, not only must all three sides be appealed to alike, but they must be appealed to by some great principle that can inspire them in one work." This, I fully agree with Mr. Harrison, forms, indeed, the true mission of religion, and, "since human nature calls out for religion, religion it must have or else die," and, "all else is of little moment till we have it." Further than this, Mr. Harrison is certainly not wrong when he says, "it is mockery to talk about science, enlightenment, progress, free thought, to the myriads of men and women, and to tell them that these ought to serve them." I believe with him that "the children, wandering forlorn and unkempt into rough life, cannot be comforted and sustained by science and enlightenment; that human nature is not a thing so docile and intellectual that it can be tamed by fine thoughts; and that society is not amenable to pure ideas." "It is playing with the question," as he says, "to offer us anything less than a systematic philosophy, a grand and overmastering object of reverence, a resolute scheme of social and personal practice." It is this clear perception of what religion should be, and should do, that leads him to the rejection of Agnosticism, and to emphasize that "we need something that we conceive able to reach our human sympathies, to be of nature akin to our own, something that we can really commune with in a moral union—something living, not dead." Yes, in all this Mr. Harrison is quite right, for only the Unknowable, as defined by science, that is to say, God, rendered human and personal by Christianity, can ever be the adequate object of a religion, satisfy human nature, appeal to brain, heart and will, and correlate society. "Humanity," separated from the Unknowable, is merely an empty phrase, a high-sounding abstract notion, but dead like all abstract notions, hence impotent to kindle enthusiasm. The Deity, foreshadowed by science, rendered "human," and hence an adequate object of religion, an object of worship, of discipline, and of belief, and nothing short of it, will ever harmonize Agnosticism and Positivism. But I anticipate here, somewhat, Mr. Harrison, and so I will retrace my steps, and follow closely his analysis of the necessary elements of religion. I shall also co-ordinate each element with those collateral truths to which he neither does nor can take exception, because, by doing so the necessity of integrating Agnosticism as well as Positivism in Christianity will be best brought out.

"First, of course," says Mr. Harrison, "religion implies belief. We always except the religion of Nature, and of the Unknowable, or the religion of the Infinite—which are mere phrases—meaning only that the supposed believer would like to believe something, if he could only make up his mind. But all serious religion implies belief." Quite right; there is no doubt about the necessity of belief as one, as, in fact, the central and most essential, element of religion. But I am compelled to take exception to Mr. Harrison's exception. And I do so because I hold that belief, whatever it may be, must be rational. Now, if science points with an irresistible force to the recognition of an Infinite and Eternal Energy by which all things are created and sustained, and if the recognition of that mysterious, though real and necessary Power, above the comprehension of science, must be conceded as the cardinal point of any creed whatever, then the scientific equation of God, as I call it for brevity's sake, must, at all events, be comprised in this belief. Mr. Harrison acknowledges this scientific equation as a correct result of the philosophy of science, and cannot, consequently, well dismiss it without forfeiting the claim to rational and logical reasoning. Religion implies belief, and belief implies, in turn, the recognition of that Infinite and Eternal Energy which is real as well as necessary. There is no getting round it. Mr. Harrison is free to say that, as yet, the object of religion of his conception is not brought out in such shape and form as to be that full and adequate object on which he insists, and on which he is quite right in insisting. But it will not do to say that the ultimate conclusion to which any intelligent search on the part of science must needs lead us, namely, that there is an Infinite, Real, and Necessary Being, is wrong, merely because that definition does not comprise all the elements which he believes it must contain. *That* knowledge, confirming as it does an innate human consciousness, forms, at all events, the cornerstone of any rational religious belief. Belief is recognized by Mr. Harrison as the fundamental essence of religion, and he has evidently no right to refuse to accept what light science is able to throw on that necessary cornerstone of belief. To be sure, the structure of religion is as yet far from being complete. But there is no gainsaying the fact that belief in the Unknowable, as defined by Mr. Spencer, instead of being in continual conflict with reason, is a rational postulate of reason itself. And since " man needs every shred of real knowledge attainable," as Mr. Harrison assures us, since this bit of knowledge cannot be disputed as real knowledge, and is, besides, attainable also, it seems to me entirely unwarranted to suppose that it can possibly be left out. As first element of religion, we have, then, a belief, which under all circumstances must cover all that Agnosticism uncovers to us as a rational, because strictly scientific basis of belief. Belief may cover more, it never can cover less. As the next element of religion, Mr. Harrison enumerates " Worship," some kind of external devotion; " the outward expression, the visible emotion of veneration, and of self-surrender to a power or being that we love and serve." I readily accept that definition, because worship is essential to religion, and is an " irrepressible appeal to emotion." He claims, rightly, the field of feeling for religion, for it is true that " man cannot forego the expression of noble feeling, if he is to have noble feeling at all." And for this reason does Mr. Harrison say : " Away, then, with the peevish paradox of pedants and cynics, that mankind has outgrown worship." When he holds that only a power, or a being, which we can love and serve, can form the object of worship, he is but one out of millions and millions who harbor that same belief. The analysis of the third element of religion brings out this point more fully still, as will be presently seen.

"Thought and feeling," says Mr. Harrison, "are not enough. We need practice—action. Hence, the elements of religion are not only belief, that is, an intellectual scheme, and worship, an appeal to the highest feeling, but Discipline (or scheme of life)." " How," he asks, " is the Unknowable, or Infinity, or the Universal Mind, to be made the basis of practical energy?" And how, I ask, can humanity become that basis if humanity has no real, intelligible equivalent; if it is merely a vague word like infinity, and, as such, unintelligible to the average mind of the masses? "Is anything at all worth trying, unless it can assert its power over the intellectual world, the moral world, and the practical world?" Quite so; and for that very reason I hold that " humanity," a " general term," as Mr. Harrison himself defines it, cannot fill the high office of serving as motive power for the threefold mission of religion. How, in all candor, can a general term be loved, and served, and exercise such tremendous power over brain, heart, and will? How can an indefinite, general term be the adequate object of religion, when the much more definite term " Unknowable " is debarred as not definite enough? Let us not deceive ourselves. The object of religion must, indeed, be "akin to our nature," but it must also partake of that nature with which the Unknowable can only be conceived. Sever humanity from Deity, sever personality from the First and Final Cause, and religious fervor is chilled into the stolid contemplation of an abstraction. Hence it is that humanity, divorced from Godhood, ceases to be a rational and a possible basis for any creed. It is true that " in humanity human life meets and rests at last," but, only in the humanity of the Unknowable; that is, in a God-man, in that Real, Infinite, and Eternal Energy become Man.

"What this age wants, what the deeper hearts are silently and sadly yearning for," so Mr. Harrison tells us, "is this—a key to man's whole complete being, entire history." This key he looks for in " Creeds, Old and New." Humanism he dismisses as a "toy." Of Protestantism he says "that it never returns, never revives, has no afterglow, no resurrection. In a philosophical survey of religion, Protestantism no longer exists. It is not in the field; it is a mere historical expression; it is no longer one of the competing creeds, any more than Judaism is or Arianism. It is neither a church, nor a creed, nor a religion." Deism he dismisses as "a form of metaphysics." For, "to have a vague hypothesis, not easily reduced to words, is certainly not to have a religion." "Any man," he says, "calls himself a Theist who thinks that on balance of probabilities as a philosophical problem, there is reason to assume that the Universe had some kind of First Cause." And, he goes on to question : "Is this to have a religion, a scheme of life and duty, of a supreme end ? In what sense this First Cause is a 'Person,' with what kind of qualities endowed, how formed, how related to man, demanding what of man, all this is left perfectly vague. Let who will, be it in piety, or in utter bewilderment, erect altars to the Unknown God. It may be a graceful thing to do ; it may be a soothing relief to the feelings. But let no man imagine that it is in any sense to have a religion." This, most assuredly, leaves no room for doubt as to "the intelligible object of reverence," having to be "personal" or a "Person." Then, he continues, "to have a religion resting on the belief in God, you must have a deep sense of the reality of His being, an inward consciousness that you can understand His will, and can rest in peace and love upon His heart ;" because, he says, "a grand 'Perhaps' is not God." Yes, a grand Perhaps is not God, nor, let me add, Humanity, even with a capital H. "The first and last business of religion," he assures us, "is to inspire men and women with a desire to do their duty, to show them what their duty is, to hold out a common end which harmonizes and sanctifies their efforts towards duty, and knits them together in close bonds as they struggle onward towards it." "That," he says, "is religion, the most abiding and the most fruitful of all the social forces." Again, "philosophy and science have given us priceless things, but they have given us no religion, no Providence, no Supreme Centre of our thoughts and our lives." "Man," he contends, "presents us not only with the phenomena of Law, but also with the phenomena of Will, Thought, Love, of sympathy and providence, and trust, and hope, phenomena that are not at all ultimately reducible to sequence and evolution." The human element in the complete synthesis of religion cannot, therefore, be left out. "A true synthesis," Mr. Harrison writes, "must, if it is to concentrate human life, be co-extensive with human nature ; it must needs be real ; it must perfectly submit to logical verification ; it must directly appeal to the whole range of thought, of affection, of energy ; it must harmonize all these to one end ; and, finally, that one end must be such as can inspire our noblest emotions of Love and Veneration. These tests and qualities are presented by one ideal alone, the ideal of a transfigured Humanity, in which the Past and the Future are bound up, in which the life of each one of us is incorporated and dignified, by which its fruits may be indefinitely continued." Does not this passage outline Christ, the centre of religious thought, religious enthusiasm, religious devotion? Or, does Mr. Harrison seriously pretend that this Power, human, real, demonstrable, and loveable, this object that can " stir all our intellectual efforts, and reduce them to a system," and which, at the same time, can " dignify and justify our best active exertions, transcending in perpetuity and power, in unimaginable proportions, the utmost duration and power of any single human life," is nothing else but a mere intellectual abstraction, like " Humanity"? Does he, in all earnestness, mean that the culture of that word can " appeal to our noblest affections and sympathies "? That we can look upon it " with Veneration, Attachment, Gratitude, so that our devotional instincts grow to be the dominant motives of our lives "? Does he really fail to perceive that only the " transfigured humanity" of the God-man of Christianity is that " real and beneficent Power which sheds throughout the complex scheme of human organizations harmony, complete and stable, and that gives, at length, peace, the child of harmony alone, to the spirit of the individual man, and to progress throughout the ages of human society "? What else but a God-man can " bind up thought and life into one centre of all ideas, and all activities, by presenting to us the image of one towards whom *all* thoughts can turn, and in serving whom *all* faculties can work "? Let us ask, honestly, who is humanity, what is humanity, and let us consider whether this abstract notion can " inspire men and women with a sense of duty, teach them their duty, and sustain their flagging hearts"; let us ask of humanity " the origin of moral evil, the sense of sin in man's heart, the conflict of self and not-self within us." " Humanity," the central force of Mr. Harrison's creed, is, according to his own words, " a collective notion "; it is " nothing but the sum and substance of all the forces of individual men and women," hence an abstract idea, a term, and as such, of course, unconscious, dead, inert, real, at best, only within the few who can rise to that abstract, collective notion, but forever unintelligible to the " millions in the rude plains of Asia and Africa, where the Hindoo struggles to rear an honest household in his plot of ricefield, and the Fellah yields to the will of heaven with sublime patience." Let it not be forgotten that " the majority of mankind," as Mr. Harrison admits with Sir James Stephen, cannot read, and that they devote their time to nothing but daily labor. How, then, can that " collective notion, Humanity," which " nothing will induce Mr. Harrison to address as a conscious being, or in any way whatever to treat as a Person," be an object of Veneration and Gratitude to these uncultured multitudes? Again, how does Mr. Harrison expect to instill into children " the idealized sum of those human feelings and

duties which all decent men acknowledge in detail and in fact,"
this being, in his own words, the equivalent of humanity? How,
after all Mr. Harrison has said about the indispensable characteristics of the central force of religion, can he expect us to be simple-
minded and credulous enough to entertain, for a moment, that
something which is neither real, nor a person, nor intelligible;
in short, "a collective notion," is able to be the very kernel of
religion? Humanity, he must concede, is a fabric woven by
imagination out of a correct perception of what the fundamental
element of religion should be; add on to humanity what the Unknowable is, give it Personality, Divinity, Omnipresence, and then
an adequate object of worship, discipline, and belief stands before
us, else it is bound to fade hopelessly out of sight. It is, indeed,
incomprehensible to me how so clear-headed an intellect as
Mr. Harrison, whose ideas about the very life-essence of religion
are so full, so precise, so correct, can fail to see that the truths of
Positivism, and the truths of Agnosticism, the postulates of nature
and man, of science and life, must be correlated before we can talk
about a satisfactory and rational basis of religion. Of course, the
moment we correlate these postulates of two entirely independent
sets of admirable observations, we are driven to recognize that
Christianity, instead of wearing the garb of impossibility any longer,
is rendered the one and the only means of harmonizing these otherwise irreconcilable truths, and of understanding the inherent yearning of human nature for religion, that is, for a complete synthesis of
life with an adequate object of belief, worship, and discipline. Then
church, sacraments, education, priesthood, sacrifice, become at once,
from incongruous, if not absurd appendages of any creed, the in-
strumentalities and channels through which alone religion can hope
to be the patrimony of all. Mr. Harrison truly remarks: "Common-
sense is too overwhelming to be resisted." And it is common-
sense which forbids me to accept, in the face of his lucid teaching,
a collective notion as corner-stone of any creed. With full and
unstinted measure do I endorse all that Mr. Harrison says religion
must be and religion must do. But, because I believe that he
outlines, with wondrous perspicuity, the genuine requirements of
religion; because his eloquent words bear the mark of truth on
their very face; because of all this do I find it utterly impossible
to subscribe to "Humanity" as either a rational or a possible
basis of religion. "Surely civilized society, with its complex
arrangements and involved processes, its multitudinous material
products and almost magical instruments, its language, science,
literature, art, must be credited to some agency or other," as Mr.
Spencer says. Did humanity, a collective notion, unconscious and
impersonal, act as that agency? Did this question never suggest

itself to the distinguished apostle of Positivism? So much about " Humanity " as the object of religion.

Leaving out, however, this error, and judging Mr. Harrison's writing only in reference to the practical side of religion, nobody can deny that his perspective discloses many, and these very valuable, truths. Religion, without the element of Humanity and Personality in its central object, appears, henceforth, as irrational as religion without a First and Final Cause, real and necessary, in its central object. Grouping these essentials together, recognizing the necessity of both, recognizing co-existence as a necessary relationship between them, we arrive at the conclusion that religion with a God-man alone comes up to the irrefutable postulates of science, as expounded by the leader of Agnosticism, and the irresistible postulates of life, as expounded by the apostle of Positivism, and this, of course, lands us at the door of that truly Catholic religion against which all forces of the earth, combined together for well-nigh two thousand years, proved absolutely powerless.

Agnosticism, by insisting upon the recognition of God, though piously shrinking from naming the Unknowable so, insists upon what is true, upon what is rational. Positivism, by insisting that the vitalizing force of religion must be human, and that the mission and function of religion lies mainly in the sphere of morality, insists likewise upon what is true, upon what is rational. Thus the postulates, unearthed as the ultimate result of the study of the two main terms of human knowledge, " nature " and " man," lead us to another term, not God simply and purely, as of old, but a God and Man, " Christ." God by Himself remains, indeed, unknowable; God remains too far removed from mankind; God is separated from man by an abyss which man can never cross. Alone by Himself, God, therefore, is not an adequate object of religion. " Humanity," as we have seen, calls out for religion, calls for belief in one of the reality of whose being we have a deep sense and an inward consciousness that we can understand his will and rest in peace and love upon his heart. Thus Positivism declares the adequate object must be human in the true sense of the word, must partake of our nature, etc. Thus, while the object must be Man, it must also be more than Man alone, it must be Christ, Real God and Real Man. Unless there is a God-man, true religion must forever remain a dream. Mr. Harrison does not hesitate to acknowledge that he cannot " speak with indifference, or coldness, much less with contempt," of what he calls " the magnificent conception of an Almighty, All-good, All-loving God." And he sees the dilemma, " How is that conception to be made the basis of a purely human and rational religion?" Certainly not by denying

Christianity's God-man, for without Christ no religious system can be erected that will command not only the respect and assent of cultured men, but also the fervent adhesion of the masses.

The correlation of undisputed truths puts us, then, in this position. Mr. Herbert Spencer, the philosopher of science, says: Science does not furnish an equivalent for "God" in the Christian acceptation of that word, but it establishes that the necessary basis of any rational belief consists in the recognition of an Infinite and Eternal Energy, which is Real and Necessary, and of which science is impotent to deny Personality, Will and Intelligence. As long as this postulate stands as true—I am inclined to think that its truth will outlast even the æons of time this globe may perhaps continue to exist—we have a perfect right to say that any creed which rests on belief in *less* than this scientific equation of the Unknowable is irrational. Agnosticism addresses us thus: "No religion is sound that stands on less than what we call the Unknowable; examine creeds by our definition, and wherever you find the God of a religion to be less than what Agnosticism says the Unknowable is, know that you are cruelly deceived. You must believe in the Unknowable to believe at all." This is all science pretends and claims to say about religion, and most assuredly science is right. On the other hand, Positivism accosts us, and says: "You must believe in much more than the Unknowable. Belief in the Unknowable does not suffice. You must believe in what can be a practical basis of religion, one that men and women and children can readily accept and assimilate." And, again, Positivism's postulates cannot be found fault with, for such an object alone can ever be a really vitalizing force of religion, and in these demands rests the strength of Positivism. Without a positive God, who is yet all human, religion ceases to be a possible structure. That much Mr. Harrison makes perfectly clear, and he has rendered a most signal service to society by lighting up hitherto obscure fields, by establishing with as much force as ability that our highest and noblest emotions, the whole field of action and the whole field of morality, can rest only upon a basis which satisfies heart, brain, and will alike, and can directly appeal to our nature, because akin in nature to our own. This essential basis of religion must, however, be added on to that other basis which reason on the part of science imperatively demands. And what, let us ask, is the result of this rational operation? We find Agnosticism and Positivism no longer out of joint; we find the postulates of both systems harmonized and correlated; we find science and life integrated in a higher order of knowledge, not obtainable by science or by life, but by revelation, by Christ. We find that Christianity, in offering us in the Person of Christ a perfect union of divine and human elements, offers us the one and only possible real and truly adequate object of religious belief. He is all that science predicates of the Unknowable; He is all that the study of life bids us seek in an adequate object of religion. Religion, from being irrational, becomes rational through revelation. For Christ has spoken, He has revealed Himself, His laws are not unknown; He is at once God, Infinite, Eternal, Omnipresent, All-powerful; an object of awe, of reverence, and also Man, loving fellow-man and beloved, living and the cause of life, and ever ready to listen to a heartfelt prayer for light.

Our age is not inclined to go back to superstition, its tendency is onward and forward. What is untrue is discarded along the whole line of thought, religious, moral, intellectual, scientific. And in this progress we must simply be candid and honest, conceding what must be conceded, and steadfastly denying what outrages our reason. Though Agnosticism cannot give us Christ, though Positivism likewise cannot give us Christ, both systems give us *truths*, and their correlation foreshadows the God-man. Beyond science looms up a faint vision of God; beyond life looms up a faint vision of a transfigured Humanity. The elements of Divinity and the elements of Humanity must be combined to give us an adequate basis of religion, and since they are only combined in Christ, the soundness, the solidity, the unshaken and unshakable firmness of Christianity is once for all established; for without Christ we cannot hope for a religion equally in accordance with science and with life, with " nature " and with " man," and yet centering and integrated in God.

MR. WEBB'S HISTORY OF CATHOLICITY IN KENTUCKY.

The Centenary of Catholicity in Kentucky. By Hon. Ben. J. Webb. One
vol. octavo, pp. 594. Louisville: Charles A Rogers. 1884.

WHATEVER the future may have in store for the Catholic
Church in the United States, it may be safely said that
the first chapter of its history, now drawing to a close, will ever
awaken the keenest interest of coming generations. It tells a glorious tale.

A century ago the Church had no organized existence in the
United States. The number of Catholics was exceedingly small;
they had but few churches, no schools, no colleges, no hierarchy;
in short, none of the elements that enter into the fabric of a religious body, except an earnest faith in God and in the divine
life and creative power of the Church. Now we count our numbers by millions; flourishing schools, colleges, and academies
abound in every State of the Union; our priesthood, ever zealous
and devoted, is daily developing its capabilities for its sublime
work by striving after a higher standard of ecclesiastical education.
Our hierarchy commands the admiration of the world. We are
to-day a power in the land, that cannot be ignored and will not
brook to be stayed in its progress. The divine vitality of the
Church was, of course, the primary cause of this magnificent
growth and development. Freedom from that bane of Catholic
life, state-interference, and immunity from questionable customs
to which, in other countries, a hoary antiquity gives the sanction
of law, had much to do with it. The spread of intelligence, the
fairmindedness of the American people, the increased facilities for
intercourse, come in for their share of credit. But, after all, we
must bow in lowly reverence to the heroic men of the olden time,
to the pioneers of the faith. They sowed the seed. They nurtured
it in its early growth; and now that the seed has grown into a
mighty tree, we who enjoy its shelter may well say of them:
"Going, they went and wept, casting their seeds; but coming,
they shall come with joyfulness, carrying their sheaves." Our
nineteenth century is often and deservedly berated for its materialistic tendencies, its frantic struggles to cast off the yoke of the
Lord, and its consequent hatred of the Church. It has been, all
in all, a very wicked century. But it is neither advisable nor
comforting to take too gloomy a view of one's own times. The

very fact that the uglier features of our age are continually paraded before our gaze, makes us sometimes grow despondent and weary. Yet this very century has given us examples of heroic devotion and self-sacrifice that recall the days of the Apostles. It has produced works that rival the brightest achievements of the " ages ot faith." For every blasphemy that was uttered, a prayer went up to Heaven. For every blow struck at the Church, brave men and women made ample reparation by countless acts of living faith and love. While this holds good of the Church in general, it is emphatically true of it in our own country.

All history, sacred and profane, opens with the heroic period. The philosophy of history requires that it should be so. The founders of society, the pioneers of faith and civilization, must be heroes. Weak, timid souls can have no part in the work. It requires too much self-denial, too much strength of heart and will, too much confidence in a brilliant future, as contrasted with present cheerlessness, for any but the bravest souls. Such were the men who laid the foundations of the Church in the United States. They laid them broad and deep. Verily may we say of them, and posterity will endorse our verdict : " There were giants in those days !"

It is, therefore, of the utmost importance that every portion of our early history should be carefully preserved. The time has not come to write a general history of the Church in this country. The causes that lie at the bottom of its splendid growth and development have not yet worked out all their legitimate effects. Until then we must perforce content ourselves with local histories, biographies, and kindred monographs. It is a healthy sign of the times that such publications are meeting with a fair measure of success. It is a proof that we hold our predecessors in grateful remembrance, and that we are trying, as far as we can, to follow in their footsteps. Much has already been done in the way of preserving our early history. The late Archbishop Spalding, in his *Sketches of the Early Missions in Kentucky*, and in his *Life of Bishop Flaget*, led the way in this work of love. The late Archbishop Bayley, in his *Life of Bishop Bruté*, and other writings, worked in the same field. It is needless to recall here the invaluable services of John Gilmary Shea, LL.D. Within the last few years Dr. Maes, the newly elected bishop of Covington, in his *Life of Father Charles Nerinckx*, Father Alerding, in his *History of the Diocese of Vincennes*, and Father Lambing, in his researches into the history of the diocese of Pittsburgh, have brought out very valuable contributions to our early Church History. In the *Centenary of Catholicity in Kentucky*, by the Hon. B. J. Webb, we welcome a fresh addition, of incalculable value to our historical literature.

With some authors the writing of history is an effort to marshal an array of facts in support of some preconceived theory ; with others it is a matter of love. To this latter class Mr. Webb belongs. He was eminently fitted for the work. It is safe to say that no other man, in or out of Kentucky, could have done it as well. IIe has been for half a century the veritable guardian of Catholic traditions in Kentucky. Born and brought up in that State, he was, in his youth and early manhood, on terms of intimate acquaintance with the mighty pioneers, the story of whose lives and labors he was destined to recall. As the publisher, and later as the editor, of the first Catholic paper published in Kentucky, he had exceptional means of acquiring knowledge not generally accessible to the public. His terms of service in the Senate of Kentucky threw him into contact with the brightest minds of the State, and widely enlarged the circle of his acquaintance. If we add to all this a thoroughly disciplined mind, a singularly retentive memory, and, above all, an ardent faith and love of the Church, we cannot but acknowledge the thorough fitness of the man for his work.

Mr. Webb is well and favorably known to the Catholic reading public of the country. As editor of the *Guardian* and *Catholic Advocate* newspapers, he secured for himself years ago an enviable position. During the dark days of Knownothingism, when it required both talent and courage to defend the Church, he boldly entered the lists against that brilliant but unscrupulous journalist, George D. Prentice, and in his " Letters of a Kentucky Catholic " dealt such telling blows as to discredit Knownothingism and its mouthpiece forever in Kentucky, and, we may add, throughout the country.

Mr. Webb wields a vigorous pen. His style is easy and graceful, equally free from any labored attempt at fine writing and from those unpleasant familiarities with language so common to old newspaper men. Whenever it is possible, he allows the actors in the scenes through which he leads his reader to tell their story in their own words. This agreeably diversifies the narrative, and relieves it of that dryness and monotony we meet with so often in historical writings. It may be objected by some that too much space is given to the mere recital of names of early Catholic settlers, names unimportant in themselves, and having no direct bearing upon noteworthy historical matters. The author anticipates this objection with the remark, that, as the descendants of men noted for wordly wisdom take pride in their ancestors, the children of Catholic pioneers have reason to be proud of forefathers " best known in their day and generation for their adherence to Catholic truth, and by their compliance with the precepts inculcated by their religion." (Pref., p. 10.) The numerous anecdotes with which the work is interspersed would, of course, ill befit the dignity of a general history; but as they invariably serve to illustrate the times or the characters of the men portrayed, they have, at least, a secondary value, and are no more out of place in a local history than in a biography. They throw a flood of light on the every-day home life of a hundred years ago, and to know something of the intimate social life of the rugged men and women struggling for existence amid the dangers of the wilderness is, if not solemnly instructive, at least charmingly interesting.

Had Mr. Webb dealt out unstinted praise to all the early Catholic settlers, and to all their spiritual guides, he would have thrown himself open to well-merited suspicion. It would be something bordering on the miraculous if every member of the various Catholic settlements had been a model of Christian perfection; it would be still more strange if every one of the early missionaries had been a type of heroic virtue. Among them there were some, happily very few, whose lives were unworthy of their sublime calling, and whose dark deeds and shameful falls were made more dark and hideous by the brilliant examples of holiness that surrounded them. The evil they wrought in their day survived them, and in tracing effects to their causes the historian is at times reluctantly compelled to drag them from the grave of oblivion. The worst historian is the panegyrist. Truth has its claims as well as charity. It is one thing to gloat over these deplorable deeds, another to set them down as historical facts and as the frightful causes of disaster. Mr. Webb has done the latter; nothing more. It is evident that he has even been at great pains to blend truth and charity together. Could the most fastidious reader demand more? Nor have we any fault to find with Mr. Webb's strictures on ecclesiastical financiering. His short but vigorous lay-sermon on the subject (pp. 310, 311) can give no offence to any one who knows and observes the stringent laws of the Church in this respect.

Serious objections may, however, be made to Mr. Webb's arrangement of his materials. He follows, indeed, the chronological order of events, particularly in the opening chapters of his work. But as noteworthy characters arise, and various institutions come into being, he interrupts too often, in our opinion, the general narrative, to give place to particular sketches, which carry the reader either too far back or too far in advance of the period then described. The result is that we meet at times a series of sketches and biographies, all well, and some of them admirably, written, but too much detached from the thread of the general narrative. But it must be borne in mind that Mr. Webb did not have well-appointed libraries at his disposal, in which to arrange and digest his materials. He had to gather them from far and

near, as best he could, often depending on the time and good will
of others. The mere work of collating these materials, and of
judging of their relative value, was of itself a heavy task. To make
them always dovetail easily into each other, would have been,
under the circumstances, well-nigh impossible. A historical work
must indeed bristle with facts; but must they invariably be presented in serried ranks of mathematical exactness? Young people,
to whom Mr. Webb's work deserves to be specially commended,
are usually averse to reading a severely dry chronological array of
facts. They want entertainment as well as instruction. They
require play for the lighter faculties of their minds, even in their
severer studies. The work before us affords them all this, together
·with those sterner lessons taught by history itself.

The material growth of the Church in Kentucky differs in many
points from its development in other States. The early settlers
brought with them the almost patriarchal habits of life in which
they had been brought up in Maryland and Virginia. They fought
manfully, and against fearful odds, to establish their homes in the
wilds of the "dark and bloody ground"; but the first hardships
once overcome, they settled down to a life of ease and comfort,
trusting to time and the natural increase of population for the further advancement of their State. That the system of slavery had
much to do with this wide-spread and totally un-American indifference to material progress, cannot be denied. It kept the more
energetic and wide-awake citizens of the free eastern and northern
States away from Kentucky. The mere fact of its existence was
enough to warn off European emigration. This comparative isolation did not, however, mar the happiness of the occupants of the
land. They recognized that their lives were cast in pleasant places,
and they were content. It led them to cling with something like
religious reverence to family histories and old traditions. While
in the States north of the Ohio river the waves of immigration
literally overwhelmed the descendants of the earlier settlers, and
almost blotted out their memory, the Kentuckian cherished in
peace, as something sacred, all that relates to the lives and times
of his pioneer forefathers. Hence spring that peculiar type of
character and that wealth of tradition and folk-lore of the native population, all as strongly marked and characteristic in its way as those
we meet with in the more remote localities of New England.
Hence, also, arises the fact at which strangers often wonder, that
the Catholic congregations in the rural districts of Kentucky are
almost exclusively composed of native Americans.

But if the material growth of the Church in Kentucky was slow,
its spiritual growth was rapid. It was marvellous. The first priest
that set foot on Kentucky soil, the Rev. W. Whelan, an Irish

Franciscan, commenced his labors in 1787. Six years later, the first priest ever ordained in the United States, the Apostle of Kentucky, the Rev. Stephen Theodore Badin, entered upon his missionary career. The first Bishop of Bardstown was appointed in 1808, and consecrated in 1810. An ecclesiastical seminary was at once established; two religious communities were founded; a college and a free school came into being; a stately Cathedral was built; churches sprang up in various parts of the State. Thus, within less than twenty-five years after the arrival of the first missionary, the Church of Kentucky,—the Mother Church of the West,—stood forth complete in its appointments, full of life and eager hope. What more striking proof of the faith and devotion of the early Catholic settlers need we seek? Without their co-operation the Bishop and his priests could not have attained such results. They might have labored, and suffered, and prayed; had not the hearts of their people beat in unison with their own, had the flock not taken pattern from its chief pastor, very little could have been accomplished.

We are convinced that it was the ready appreciation of the fact that he had to deal with a people endowed with sterling virtues, that led Bishop Flaget to establish the ecclesiastical seminary, immediately after his arrival in Kentucky. As a rule, we do not look for ecclesiastical vocations among a people struggling in a wilderness and hampered with the difficulties incident to the rudimentary stages of society. They usually manifest themselves in thoroughly organized communities where the beauties of God's house can be leisurely studied and taken to heart, and where the faint whispering of grace may not be drowned amid the all-engrossing cares of every-day life. Bishop Flaget had the keen insight of a saint. He understood his people. He felt sure that among the children of those whose faith, hope, and charity showed such wonderful life, he would surely find some called by God to the service of the altar. He was not mistaken. A band of sturdy young men came from the forests and fields of Kentucky, and gathered around their saintly Bishop. Hardship and toil had been their portion from childhood. They looked for nothing else in the seminary. The transition from the discipline of a Christian home to that of the seminary was to them natural and easy. To these first-fruits of Catholicity in Kentucky must, in justice, be added a number of young men who, like Abraham of old, went forth out of their country and from their kindred, to work for the salvation of souls in the distant wilds of Kentucky. France and Germany, Belgium and Ireland, sent thither some of their noblest sons. Under the watchful eye of their Bishop, and with his example continually before their eyes, these youthful Levites studied, and labored, and prayed. A good and holy man has said that the seminarian is the priest in embryo. Bishop Flaget's seminarians illustrated the truth of this saying. With but very few exceptions, they proved themselves men of unbounded devotion and self-sacrifice, men admirably suited for their times, men of God. The most pathetic pages in Mr. Webb's work are those which tell the story of Bishop Flaget's seminary.

In the establishment and conduct of his seminary Bishop Flaget was powerfully seconded by his intimate friend, Father David, who became his coadjutor in 1819. The following pen picture is given of him by Mr. Webb : " Father David was of average stature, possibly five and a half feet in height, of moderately full habit, deliberate in his speech, and retiring in his manners. He had little of the vivacity that is supposed to be a distinguishing characteristic of the French people, and in this particular he presented a strong contrast to his countryman and fellow-worker of the Kentucky mission, Rev. S. T. Badin. He rarely went into society, and never without a motive that had reference to the good of others, and not personal gratification. He could talk, and he could reason, eloquently and logically, but he gave his tongue no license except in the pulpit, in the class-room, and in the lecture-field. With the exception, possibly, of Rev. Charles Nerinckx, Father David showed more tendency to asceticism than any ecclesiastic that has appeared in Kentucky up to the present day. I have no remembrance of any occasion on which he was seen to laugh. He could smile, however, but his smiles were always for the encouragement of those who had previously laid open to him their spiritual or bodily miseries. Without being in any degree repulsive, his manners, so far as the general public were concerned, lacked the attractiveness that was so pleasing a characteristic in those of Bishop Flaget. To others than those with whom his intercourse was constant and intimate, he appeared as one who was too much occupied with serious matters to warrant interruptions, except for a better object than the pleasure to be derived from his conversations. It was not so with his seminarians, nor with his penitents. These feared not to approach him, because they were able to fathom the depths of his humility. To their eyes he presented an image of his Great Master, whose voice sounded in their ears as he spoke : ' Learn of me, because I am meek and humble of heart.' "

Bishop David was a man of commanding ability. He was often, though reluctantly, drawn into controversy with the Protestant preachers of his day. To defeat them was easy enough, for they were almost invariably densely ignorant, not only of Catholic doctrine and practice, but even of the tenets of their own sects. The reader of to-day is less astonished at the depth of learning displayed by the Bishop in his controversial writings than by the never-failing patience and boundless charity displayed towards his opponents. His Catechisms of Christian Doctrine have gone through innumerable editions, are still in general use, and are, in the opinion of many, the best we have in the United States. That he was a thorough master of the spiritual life is evinced in his eight-days' " Retreat," written for the Sisters of Charity of Nazareth, and edited and published about twenty years ago by the late Archbishop Spalding.

It is a wide-spread opinion that most of the early missionaries trained by Bishop David were wofully deficient in learning. It is true, indeed, that many a one among them could truthfully say with the poet of old : " I ken but little Latin and no Greek." But to be a good theologian one need not necessarily be an accomplished classical scholar. Because they dressed in homespun, despised social shams, cared little for the refinement and elegance of later days, and spoke the homely language of their people, it does not follow that they were deficient in theological lore. Some of the most profound theological arguments the writer ever listened to fell from the lips of some of the early missionaries of Kentucky. The very knowledge of the fact that their seminary career had been exceedingly short impelled them to earnest study in after years. Besides, they had for a long time in their midst such men as the late Archbishops Kenrick and Spalding, and the late Bishop McGill, of Richmond, Va., men whose profound learning exercised a most salutary influence on their less favored brethren. While on this subject we may note the singular fact that a considerable number of Bishop David's seminarians found their way into the Society of Jesus, into which as a rule none but men of marked ability are admitted.

The establishment of a diocesan seminary in the very earliest days of the church in Kentucky led to two noteworthy results. In the first place, it gave the clergy a homogeneity vainly looked for in places where the priests have not been brought up together, and have little in common, except the sacerdotal character and similarity of occupation. Their seminary career welded the priests of Kentucky into a band of brothers. This spirit of union and love was carefully fostered by Bishops Flaget and David. We find ample evidence of it on almost every page of Mr. Webb's work. Long after these good and holy men had gone to their reward, the fraternal spirit they had infused into their students survived. When the old theological seminary ceased to exist, it was transplanted to the preparatory seminary of St. Thomas. We do not hesitate to assert, and there are many priests in every part of the country who will bear us out in the statement, that the ties of

Christian union and charity were nowhere stronger or more tenderly cherished than at St. Thomas'. The students felt that no
other spirits could predominate in a place hallowed by Bishops
Flaget and David. They had much to endure, and were occasionally
loud in their complaints. But they never lost sight of the fact that,
however much they might have to suffer, they were infinitely
better off than their predecessors, better and holier men than themselves had ever been. This single thought was usually sufficient
to silence all complaints. Much credit is due to the late Very
Rev. Francis Chambige, for many years superior of St. Thomas',
and himself a worthy disciple of Bishop David, for his untiring
efforts to keep alive among his students the sacred spirit of the
olden time. It is to be regretted that Mr. Webb's biographical
sketch of this good man is so very brief and meagre. He probably
was unable to find the requisite materials, for Father Chambige
was as modest and retiring as he was learned and zealous.

To the establishment of the seminary is also due the rapid development of higher secular education in Kentucky. St. Joseph's
College, St. Mary's, and the whilom flourishing Institute of Mt.
Merino, owe their origin to it. For more than a quarter of a century after its foundation the Catholic Colleges of Kentucky were
almost the only centres of literary activity in the West. What Mt. St.
Mary's, near Emmittsburg, Maryland, did for the East, was done
for the West and Southwest by St. Mary's and St. Joseph's colleges.
Bishops Flaget and David, and in later years Bishop Spalding,
directed all their energies to this great work. It would indeed be
difficult to determine whether they labored more in the immediate
field of their high ministry, or in the spread of education. At an
early day they summoned to their assistance the Jesuit Fathers,
and their united efforts placed the Catholic educational establishments of the State in the very front rank of literary institutions—a
position which, we are happy to say, they hold even in our day.

The same spirit of ardent faith which built Bishop Flaget's seminary, also founded two religious female communities. The infant
Church of Kentucky was yet struggling for existence when a few
noble women, all native Kentuckians, conceived the thought of
consecrating themselves to God in the religious life. That a few
women, without resources, without experience, without powerful
friends, in short, without a single human prerequisite to success,
should dream, in an humble log hut, and in a society yet in its
formative stages, of establishing lasting and powerful communities,
may seem strange and absurd to the world. But nothing is impossible to faith. Of these devoted ladies not one had ever seen a
convent or a religious. God gave them, however, wise and prudent
guides. "The Friends of Mary at the Foot of the Cross," better

known as the Sisters of Loretto, were organized into a religious community by Father Nerinckx. In his admirable Life of that holy man, Bishop Maes gives the full history of this sisterhood. The Sisters of Charity of Nazareth were organized, the same year as those of Loretto (1812), by Bishop David. We would but mar the beauty of the story of these sisterhoods if we allowed ourselves to sketch an outline of it. Suffice it to say that they were the first religious communities founded west of the Allegheny mountains, that the humble log huts that first gave them shelter have grown into grand convents and academies, and that they have done, and are still doing, more good than tongue or pen can ever tell. Had Mr. Webb done nothing more than unfold the wondrous history of these two communities, he would have rendered an incalculable service to the Catholic history of our country.

Two among the early missionaries, Fathers Stephen T. Badin and Robert Abell, claim the special attention of Mr. Webb throughout his work. He dwells lovingly on every detail of their lives and labors. For this he gives a satisfactory reason in his preface. We may emphasize this reason by the single statement that he could not have written the history of the Church in Kentucky without giving them special prominence. They were grand and good men, typical pioneers of the Faith. Their zeal was boundless, their powers of endurance enormous. They loved the wilderness with all its hardships—one by the law of adaptation, the other by that of his very nature. Around them cluster nearly all the old Catholic traditions of Kentucky. The lonely life they were obliged to lead never made them morose or soured their temper. Father Abell was brimful of wit and good humor, even in his extreme old age. Though he was not a profound theologian, he could display to advantage all he knew. He was an orator by nature. It is even said that in his prime he fairly disputed the palm for popular eloquence with Kentucky's "Great Commoner"—Henry Clay. Father Badin, though genial and kind, had a less sunny temperament. He was a strict disciplinarian. He never failed to make the wayward of his flock feel that the way of the transgressor is hard. Strange tales are told of the penances he used to inflict in the confessional—penances which would make the hair of the penitents of our day stand on end. It has even been hinted that he was somewhat affected by that Jansenistic rigor, the remnants of which still lingered in the schools of France at the time he was a student. This is certainly untrue. We find the true explanation of his course in the fact that he suffered heroically for his Divine Master, and he therefore naturally concluded that those under his charge were also willing and able to suffer for His sake.

He was an accomplished scholar. His poem on the Blessed Trinity, which Mr. Webb gives in the appendix of his work, is a model of classical latinity. A metrical translation by one of Mr. Webb's clerical friends is appended. Though not devoid of merit, it is, in loftiness of sentiment and beauty of expression, far inferior to the original.

Nearly all the early missionaries of Kentucky have gone to their reward. Two or three, only, remain, providentially left us to be eye-witnesses of the glorious results of a century's work. Cardinal Newman, writing to a gentleman who had sent him a copy of Mr. Webb's book, says : " You could not give me a gift more interesting to me than the work of the Hon. B. J. Webb. I take the greatest pleasure in reading the accounts given by old priests here of the state of religion a century ago, when zealous and able missionaries saw in their lifetime no or little fruit of their labors ; and the same feelings of sympathy and triumph are excited by various parts of Mr. Webb's narrative." These sentiments of the great English Cardinal will no doubt be shared by thousands of Mr. Webb's readers. He undertook his task with diffidence, worked at it conscientiously, and, in spite of many difficulties and discouragements, has brought it to a successful close. He well deserves the thanks and practical encouragement of the Catholic public, not only in Kentucky, but throughout the country. His work will undoubtedly ever be one of the chief sources from which the material for the future general history of the Church in the United States will be drawn.

FREE THOUGHT IN NEW ENGLAND.

Life of Ralph Waldo Emerson. By Oliver Wendell Holmes. Boston: Houghton & Co. 1885.

Poems. By R. W. Emerson. Boston: Monroe & Co. 1847.

Proceedings at a Reception in Honor of Rev. O. B. Frothingham. New York: Putnam's Sons. 1879.

History of the People of the United States. By John Bach McMaster. New York: D. Appleton & Co. 1883.

The Blue Laws of Connecticut and New Haven, etc. By Trumbull. Hartford. 1876.

The Constitution of the Presbyterian Church in the United States of America, Containing the Confession of Faith, etc. Philadelphia: Haswell & Co. 1838.

Self-culture. By W. E. Channing. Boston. 1839.

Three Sermons of Lyman Beecher, on his Trial before the Presbytery and Synod of Cincinnati. Boston. 1852.

The Works of Jonathan Edwards. By S. E. Dwight. New York: Converse. 1829.

THE five millions or so of Americans who live in that part of the United States known as New England, and who are vulgarly called "Yankees," have probably the most interesting history in our great republic. Living in a cold, and not the most fertile, climate, their natural energy and astuteness have been stimulated by their physical environment. Their forefathers, exiles from England on account of stubborn hostility to the forms of its national creed and aristocracy, imparted to their posterity all the doggedness of the lower orders of the Saxon race. Sojourners for a time in clean, persistent, industrious, and Calvinistic Holland, they carried to Massachusetts the spirit and manners of the Dutch republic, and the theology of the Synod of Dort. Always unyielding when conscience prompted rebellion, the crop-haired Puritan showed the same stubbornness in his secular life that he manifested in his theological opinions. He fought well, whether against the king and church at home, or against the Indian in the colony; as he dug hard with the spade to force the reluctant soil to yield him sustenance, or as he studied deeply and applied his intellectual powers to industrial and mechanical pursuits, so, in course of time, he became a fierce and subtle polemist, a successful farmer, a good soldier, and a great inventor. That a character thus formed, by persecution at home and by hard labor abroad, should be somewhat narrow and intolerant was to be expected ; for none are so severe on others as they who spare no weakness of their own, unless an elevated charity should intervene. But no such charity pervaded the Puritan community. Their theology was essentially intolerant and vindictive, for it was the theology of John Calvin in its most unmitigated form. Stern, unrelenting, dark, and bloody was the theological system of the iron ruler of Geneva—the executioner of Michael Servetus. It brooded over the Puritan community like a bird of ill omen, whose sable wings kept the sunlight of true charity out of the Puritan heart. It was a re-establishment, after sixteen hundred years of broadening Christianity, of the strict literalism and exclusiveness of the Mosaic theocracy, necessitated once for the protection of the faith and morals of the people of God by the unnatural vices and degrading idolatry of the neighboring Moabite, Amalekite, and Philistine. The Puritan seemed to study the Old rather than the New Testament. His theology went back three thousand years—to Moses rather than to Christ. He leaped over the Gospels, and their spirit of Christian benevolence, to study Exodus, Leviticus, and Numbers; and these he perused by night and by day, until he became a Jew in religious spirit, although a Christian in name. " He seemed to worship God for spite," as Hudibras puts it. His commonwealth became a Mosaic theocracy, in its laws, ordinances, and customs, in everything except in its ritual and ceremonies. For these he had no mercy. They were identified in his mind with prelacy and persecution. They had driven him into exile from the green meadows and hawthorn hedges of pleasant England to the swamps and dykes of Holland, to the rugged rocks of Plymouth and the inhospitable banks of the Connecticut. Therefore did he hate a bishop as a child of the devil, lawn sleeves and a surplice as Moabitish idolatry, and Christian holidays as an invention of Satan; although he might have found in the same Mosaic law from which he drew his political inspiration and his respect for the Sabbath, a ceremonial as rich and holy days nearly as many as existed in the prelatical church of England or the Papal church of Rome. But logical as is the Calvinistic theology, if you once admit its premises, and logical as the old New Englander naturally was, and consequently narrow,—for all logic is rigid,—his hatred of the oppressing church got the better of his reason. He took, therefore, from Moses what pleased him, and ignored what was hostile to his prejudices. He united church and state in a strict alliance, allowed no one to vote in the state who was not in good standing in the church, enacted ordinances against heresy and blasphemy, adopted the penal code of the Pentateuch, and improved on it with a spirit worthy of Draco, while he rejected all ceremonies as heathenish no matter what might be the Bible warrant for their use :

> " For his religion it was fit
> To match his learning and his wit,
> 'Twas Presbyterian true blue."[1]

" He held it an abomination to read a novel, to see a play, to go to a dance, to make a jest, to sing a comic song, to eat a dinner cooked on Sunday, or to give a present on Christmas day."[2] Among these Puritans " religion and law were almost identical, and in their character both were so thoroughly infused that the mildest and the severest acts of public discipline were alike made venerable and awful. Meagre, indeed, and cold, was the sympathy that a transgressor might look for from such bystanders at the scaffold ; on the other hand, a penalty which, in our days, would infer a degree of mocking infamy and ridicule, might then be invested with almost as stern a dignity as the punishment of death itself."[3] To each of the laws of Massachusetts imposing the death penalty a text or texts of Scripture were appended in justification of the punishment.

Throughout the New England colonies this Mosaic severity pervaded the whole legislation. A burglar, for the first offence, was branded on the forehead with the letter B ; for the second, branded and whipped ; for the third offence, put to death. If the first offence were done on the Lord's day, he was condemned to have an ear cut off in addition to being branded. A child of sixteen years of age, or over, convicted of striking a parent, was put to death. It was death to practice idolatry. Witches, blasphemers, or those who cursed God or were guilty of bestiality, were punished with death. Sodomy, adultery,[4] rape, and perjury which resulted in taking away another's life, were also capital offences. In Connecticut, an incorrigible child, if sixteen years old, could be brought by his parents before the magistrate and, on conviction, be condemed to death.

An " open contemner " of the Gospel was obliged, on conviction, to stand two hours on a stool four feet high, on a lecture day, with a paper on his breast specifying his crime. A fine of five shillings was imposed on those who stayed away from church without just cause. If an Indian stole he had to pay double ; and if he com-

---

[1] Hudibras.

[2] A History, etc., John Bach McMaster, p. 20.

[3] The Scarlet Letter, Hawthorne, p. 60.

[4] The reader may remember the punishment for this crime inflicted on Hester Prynne, as described in Hawthorne's Scarlet Letter, probably the best of our American novels, and the best description of the habits of the early Puritans.

mitted some crime against the person, he was punished by the *lex talionis*, " an eye for an eye, and a tooth for a tooth." No one was allowed to remain in a liquor store or inn, after 9 P.M., or to drink more than half a pint of wine at once, or to stay more than half an hour in any inn or public house. Those who violated these laws were fined, or put in the stocks for three hours. A liar, if over fourteen years old, was fined ten shillings for the first lie, or condemned to stand three hours in the stocks ; for the second offence, he was whipped, or fined twenty shillings ; and for the third sin, he received thirty strokes of the lash on the bare back. A similar punishment was inflicted on slanderers; and female culprits were not exempted from the ignominy. Swearing was punished by the penalty of three hours' standing in the stocks; smoking publicly, by a fine of sixpence, and the habit was not permitted even privately to those under twenty years of age. This law was the same both in Massachusetts and in Connecticut.[1] It was even forbidden to play cards or dice in private families.

Philip Ratcliffe was fined forty pounds, whipped, and had his ears cut off for slandering the church of Salem. Robert Shorthouse, for swearing by the blood of God, was sentenced to have his tongue *put into a cleft stick* " and to stand so by the space of half an hour."[2] There were laws in Massachusetts against extravagance in dress, against the use of silver, gold, silk laces, girdles, and hatbands, and even against the wearing of long hair.

In the New Haven colony heresy was severely punished, and incest was punished with death. For sending a love-letter without the girl's parents' consent, the love-sick swain was fined forty shillings. In this colony, breaking the Sabbath " proudly and presumptuously" *was punished with death*, and the Scripture warrant, Numb. xv., from 30th to 36th verses, is given for the penalty.[3]

As late as the middle of the seventeenth century, A.D. 1638, Elizabeth, wife of Thomas Aplegate, was condemned to have her tongue put in a cleft stick, and "so to stand for half an hour," for swearing; and Robert Bartlet, for a similar crime, had to undergo a similar punishment. These evidences of early Puritan rigor are not taken from Peters's work on the *Blue Laws of New England*, which contains much that is fictitious, but from Trumbull's more recent book, written expressly to correct Peters's mistakes, and by one whose whole aim is to apologize for Puritan severity and extenuate the rigor of the early legislation of the New England colonists.

Yet, much as we may now condemn the harshness of these early laws, we must admire the deep religiosity and austere morality of the misguided lawgivers. Their very failings resulted from the

---

[1] Trumbull's Blue Laws, etc.　　　[2] Ibid., p. 334.　　　[3] Ibid., p. 343.

exaggeration of God's providence, before which they sacrificed human free will; from a superstitious extolling of grace, before which they immolated nature; and from a blind adoration of the Bible, whose plenary inspiration they extended to every letter and even comma in the vernacular version, and whose expressions they misinterpreted by the baldest and most rigorous verbalism.   They forgot that free will and reason are the works of God as well as grace and the Bible.   They sinned by excess rather than by defect. The Bible was their exclusive law, infallible in every word, inspired in every letter, and each Puritan was its high priest, sharing its inspiration and its infallibility by a communication which he believed he directly received from the Holy Spirit in its perusal. He conned it over and over.   He knew it by heart.   He forced his children to learn it by rote.   He named them after its names, and formed them after its ordinances.   He punished lying, unchastity, and swearing with great severity, and he strove to bring up a God-fearing and a Sabbath-respecting race.   "The discipline of the family in those days was of a far more rigid kind than now. The frown, the harsh rebuke, the frequent application of the rod, enjoined by Scriptural authority, were used not merely in the way of punishment for actual offences, but as a wholesome regimen for the growth and promotion of all childish virtues."[1]   The education of the children was essentially Christian.   The early New Englander was not a believer in godless education.   In the preamble of the colonial decrees, ordering the establishment of schools, the motive is always given, namely, that the children may learn the grounds of Christian faith and know how to read the Scriptures. This is true not only of the primary schools, but also of the colleges and universities.   In 1701, Yale College was incorporated for the "upholding and propagating of the Christian Protestant religion by a succession of learned and *orthodox* men."   The same spirit of religion pervaded their whole system.   No doubt, the system was too severe.   The Puritan's house, especially on the Sabbath, became a dungeon.   From sundown on Saturday to sundown on Sunday the children were tortured by their Puritan parents.   No romping, no play, no recreation; but gloom, religion, and study for the young culprits who had the misfortune to be born of parents who believed in "total depravity" and in Calvin's doctrine of election and reprobation.   Woe to the young maiden who dared to receive a love-letter without her parents' knowledge, and double woe to the youth who sent it, if he were found out. The Puritan protected the purity of his home.   He put the adulterer or the adulteress to death.   He insisted on the publication of the banns, for eight days before marriage, with a severity greater

---

[1] Scarlet Letter, p. 105. 15th edition. New York: Houghton.

than that of the Catholic Church; and although he did not believe that marriage is a sacrament, still he respected it as a holy ordinance, and, consequently, divorce was not frequent in the colonies so long as the old Puritan legislation and spirit held sway.

But this could not be for a long time. The severity was abnormal. Puritan cohesion had an essential element of dissolution in the principle of private interpretation of the Bible; and ultra-Calvinistic theology was too repugnant to reason and nature to be able long to hold its own against the army of liberals and skeptics who soon assailed it under the banner of liberalism and *free thought*. The children grew tired of the burdens imposed on them, especially on the Sabbath. They cursed the day, and the system that enforces its observance with such rigor. " Mother," pleaded a little Puritan boy, " since science tells us that the sun goes down eight minutes before its beams disappear in the horizon, the Sabbath ought to end eight minutes earlier than you make it." " In that case, my son," replied the pious Puritan lady, " we must begin the Sabbath eight minutes earlier on Saturday." " I cursed the day," said the boy, now a distinguished Catholic priest, " and made up my mind that when I became a man I would never go to church at all; and I resolved that, if ever I had children, I would not let them go to church." " How did the children spend Saturday evening ?" " In silence, reading Sunday-school lessons, and kicking one another's shins under the table." This excessive repression of the child's nature has driven many a man out of the Puritan church. Some, by the grace of God, have become Catholics; others, yielding to the spirit of doubt and the devil,—and alas! they are the most numerous class,—have gone into Unitarianism, rationalism, and infidelity.[1] Calvinism slowly dissolved in New England until at length only scattered fragments of it were left, like the patches of snow seen in the fields after a February thaw. The change in New England theology was by no means a sudden event. Even in the days of the most orthodox Puritanism, bickerings, dissensions, and quarrels were frequent. Even the great Jonathan Edwards was obliged to separate from his congregation at Northampton owing to theological disagreement with his flock, long before he wrote on "*free-will*" and "*original sin.*" It would be long and difficult to trace the various shades of opinion and of school into which the Congregational churches divided long before Whitefield preached in Massachusetts, or Taylor, Fitch, and Goodrich innovated in New Haven, or Lyman Beecher was tried for those anti-Calvinistic doctrines which Catharine Beecher taught with impunity. There is even now a variety of hue rivalling the chameleon among the opin-

---

[1] Ingersoll, in his lectures, publicly states one of the causes of his apostasy from Christianity to be the reaction from this Calvinistic rigor.

ions not only of New England Christians, but even of New England transcendentalists, from superstitious Cotton Mather to irreverent Henry Ward Beecher, from Theodore Parker to Emerson and O. B. Frothingham, from the Andover *Review* to the *New Englander* and the *Atlantic Monthly.* We may, however, consider this change in two stages of its development, the one represented by the giving up of the old Calvinistic doctrines regarding election and reprobation, free-will and total depravity ; the transition from the old to the new school Presbyterians ; the other marked by a complete negation of the supernatural, of the divinity of Christ, and of all revealed religion ; by a denial first proceeding to Socinianism or Unitarianism, and thence to " transcendentalism," which is but a polite name for skepticism, pantheism, and sheer atheism. In these two stages of religious, or rather irreligious, progress the prominent figures of Jonathan Edwards and Ralph Waldo Emerson loom up as coryphei, around whom lesser lights group, not in chronological order, but certainly in subordination of intelligence and leadership. " There were brave men before Agamemnon," but there were no abler exponents of new school Presbyterianism before Edwards, nor of New England transcendentalism before Emerson.

Jonathan Edwards was born at East Windsor, Connecticut, in A.D. 1703, at a time when John Calvin's theology was still the prevailing system of the New England Protestant churches. This system, in which Edwards was at first a bigoted believer, but which he afterwards considerably modified, contained the following fundamental principles.

According to Calvin, God created from all eternity some men for the purpose of making them eternally happy, and others for eternal damnation, irrespective of any personal merit or demerit. The elect show forth His goodness ; the reprobate glorify His justice. If it be objected to this harsh doctrine that God could not be glorified by creating men for the purpose of eternally torturing them, it is answered that the objection is impertinent. God is absolute Master, bound by no law, and can take out of the same tree one part to ornament His house and another to burn. God causes the reprobate to commit sin that He may show forth His justice in their punishment. He does not merely permit sin, as Catholics hold, but He really ordains and decrees its commission. But, although He is thus the author of sin, it is no sin for Him ; for, as He is above all law, He cannot be held responsible for what is a violation of law ! In other words, it is sin for man, although he is in it by a leaden necessity, and it is not for God, because He is bound by no law. A necessary consequence of this theory of election and predestination is that man has no free-will. Calvin, in his treatise on the *Slave Will*, distinctly teaches this. Man has no

power to act or not to act, to do good or to do evil, and everything in him proceeds necessarily from the decree of God, in whose
hand he is but potter's clay or a leaden mass.   Man is essentially
corrupt in all his faculties by Adam's sin.   He is totally depraved,
incapable of good; iniquity from the crown of his head to the sole
of his foot.   Salvation is not possible to all men, but to the elect
only; and, though others may be externally called, they cannot be
saved, because they have been foreordained to evil by God.   Christ
died, not for all, but only for the elect.   The reprobate receive
none of His grace whatsoever.   The elect receive it, and are necessitated by it to do good, for it would be impious to suppose that
men could resist divine grace.   The commandments of God are
in many cases impossible both for the just and for the wicked.
Men are not saved for keeping them, nor damned for breaking
them.   The elect are kept humble by God's causing them to fall
into sin; and the wicked, being destitute of all grace, and predestined to the eternal fires of hell, of course are unable to keep any
of God's ordinances.   Justification is purely an external act of
God, and man has neither act nor part in it.   It is a covering up
of his iniquities by the cloak of divine election, and not the washing out of sin by free human acts, prompted and aided by divine
grace.

A revolt against this doctrine was made as early as the latter
end of the sixteenth century, in Holland by Hermanzoon, or Arminius, the renowned preacher of Amsterdam; but even a slight
modification of it was slow in coming to the grim-visaged and
hard-hearted New England Puritans.   To this doctrine, more like
to pagan fatalism and Turkish predestination than to a teaching of
the merciful and just God of the Christians, even the great intellect
of Edwards paid early homage.   "From my childhood up," he
writes, "my mind had been full of objection against the doctrine
of God's sovereignty in choosing whom He would to eternal life,
and rejecting whom He pleased; leaving them eternally to perish
and be everlastingly tormented in hell.   It used to appear like a
horrible doctrine to me."[1]   He goes on to state, however, that at
last he found in this doctrine great consolation and even "delight,"
until maturer years had brought to him the convictions which he
gives in his treatise on "*Original Sin.*"   This work was published
in A.D. 1759, and although in it the author is far removed from the
liberal opinions of Arminius and from Catholic truth, yet there is
considerable change from the old and degrading theory of Calvin
on the same subject.   In it the author maintains that although
there is in human nature a prevailing and effectual tendency to
that sin which implies the utter ruin of all, and which comes from

---

[1] Life and works of Edwards, in ten volumes, S. E. Dwight, vol. i., p. 60.

Adam, yet that human appetites and passions are in themselves "innocent." He further denies the positive agency of God in producing sin. The innocent principles of nature are passions like love, hatred, fear, desire, joy, sorrow, etc., and are not sin, but only a propensity to it.[1] But in an earlier work, entitled "*A Careful and Strict Enquiry into the Modern Prevailing Notion of that Freedom of the Will which is Supposed to be Essential to Moral Agency, Virtue, Vice, Reward and Punishment, Praise and Blame*," published in 1754, Edwards came out boldly against the slavery of the will as maintained by Calvin, and strongly marked the line between the new and the old schools in New England Presbyterianism and Congregationalism. Edwards had evidently been studying Quesnel, Baius, and the Jansenists, and in fact his theology, still the prevailing one regarding free-will among Presbyterians, holds the same relationship to the old New England theology that Jansenism holds to Calvinism in the eyes of Catholic theologians. He teaches that the mere power of choosing or willing constitutes freedom, and that man has the *natural* ability to choose, but that accompanying it there is a *moral* inability to elect contrary to the predominant motive or sufficient reason. He says there is no necessity from without compelling a man to choose this rather than that; but there is a certainty from within that he will choose this rather than that, because he must choose for a sufficient cause. This teaching is far from the Arminian, and certainly far from that of the Council of Trent. The trite quotation, "*sic volo, sic jubeo, sit pro ratione voluntas*," aptly renders the true doctrine to be held on this subject. The will is free to act for a reason or for none at all, with or without a sufficient cause; and the inner consciousness of every sane and mature human being attests the existence of such a faculty. Nothing is clearer to man than that he can think or believe as he pleases. His freedom to act depends on external circumstances alone.

Nor was the logical New England intellect slow to push farther on than Edwards in this line of progress. The free-thinking Yankee began to investigate more closely the texts invoked by the Presbyterians for their theories of Total Depravity. His nature, essentially energetic and manly, revolted against this doctrine. He felt free-will throbbing in his bosom. He loved political freedom and free discussion. He was daily conquering the reluctant glebe and the dense forest with spade and axe. He felt in himself the force of nature and the force of will, certain natural good qualities which had no direct connection with the Church, the parson, or theology; and living in a climate which continually stimulated to labor and energy, fatalism and the fetich of Total Depravity gradu-

---

[1] Ibid., p. 557.

ally disappeared from his religious belief. He became in course of time an out-and-out Pelagian. He who felt how much the forces of nature and natural talent could do in secular life in reclaiming waste lands or producing new inventions, gradually came to judge that they could be equally efficacious in the domain of religion. So he gave up Calvin's theory of necessitating grace; gave up belief in grace altogether. A free man in politics, he could not brook to be a slave in theology; and so, step by step, he marched from Jonathan Edwards and liberal Presbyterianism to William Ellery Channing and Socinianism, to Theodore Parker, Ralph Waldo Emerson, and Transcendentalism. The heresy of Socinus kept pace with the opinions of Arminius in undermining New England orthodoxy. The spirit of Arius and Pelagius was abroad among the Puritans. Emerson, in an article published in the *Atlantic Monthly* for November, 1883, though written long before, speaking of Dr. Ripley, his grandfather, writes: "He was identified with the ideas and forms of the New England Church which expired about the same time with him, so that he and his coevals seemed the rear guard of the great camp and army of the Puritans, which, however, in its last days declining into formalism, in the heyday of its strength had planted and liberated America."[1] This was at the beginning of the present century; but long before it Unitarianism had made inroads on Calvinian orthodoxy. The Church of England, too, had increased in numbers. "The true high-caste religions of that day," the beginning of this century, "were white-handed Unitarianism and ruffled-shirt Episcopalianism."[2] Nothing better indicates the weakening of the hold of Puritanism on the New England mind than the introduction of the theatre and stage plays into New England cities. Yet it was "not till the close of Washington's first administration that a company of players dared to show themselves in the town" of Boston[3]; yet in A.D. 1804 Unitarian liberalism had so fermented in the Puritan mass that the "*Anthology*," a New England magazine, and the literary precursor of the *North American Review*, could publish with impunity a prospectus which stated that "the child," meaning the new periodical, "shall not be destitute of the manners of a gentleman, nor a stranger to genteel amusements. He shall attend Theatres, Museums, Balls, and whatever polite diversions the town shall furnish."[4] Unitarianism became in the early part of this century the ruling form of belief among the cultivated classes of both of the two great New England centres, the town of Boston and the University of Cambridge. Kirkland was head of the college, and the names of Ware,

---

[1] Life of Emerson, p. 15.
[2] Life of Emerson, p. 34.
[3] McMaster, p. 93.
[4] Life of Emerson, p. 30.

Norton, Palfrey, Freeman, Lowell, Buckminster, Everett, and above all William Ellery Channing, shine out as the most aggressive and the most able New England disciples of Arius and Socinus. But their Unitarianism was old-fashioned compared to what afterwards became the system of transcendentalists and the philosophers of the " Brook Farm." From Jonathan Edwards the descent was easy to Mayhew, from him to Channing, and then to Emerson, Theodore Parker, Thoreau, and O. B. Frothingham.

" The passage is like that which leads from the highest lock of a canal to the ocean level. It is impossible for human nature to remain permanently shut up in the highest lock of Calvinism. If the gates are not opened, the mere leakage of belief or unbelief will before long fill the next compartment, and the freight of doctrine finds itself on the lower level of Arminianism or Pelagianism, or even subsides to Arianism. From this level to that of Unitarianism the outlet is freer, and the subsidence more rapid. And from Unitarianism to Christian Theism the passage is largely open for such as cannot accept the evidence of the supernatural in the history of the Church."[1] Free thought in New England did not, however, stop at the mere denial of the supernatural. It denied the existence of God. It became pantheistic, socialistic, skeptical. It gave up the Bible for Spinosa, Plato, Porphyry, and Plotinus. It became a dreamy, watery metaphysicism, without dogma or purpose, and it has brought the New England mind to the verge of absolute atheism. No one has had more influence in this direction than Emerson. Theodore Parker is more aggressive, but, therefore, the less winning. O. B. Frothingham is, at best, only an echo of the great Transcendentalist prophet. Thoreau, of Walden Cottage fame, is but a savage of the school. Margaret Fuller, A. Bronson Alcott, George Ripley, James Freeman Clarke, Eliot Cabot, John S. Dwight, C. P. Cranch, and most of the other writers for the Transcendentalist organ, the *Dial*, are but Emerson's pupils or echoes, while George Ripley and the other Philansterians of " Brook Farm " were rather disciples of the Frenchmen, Le Roux and St. Simon, than of the Yankee poet and philosopher. In fact, he rather discouraged the project, and somewhat mocked it in his writings. " It was a noble and generous movement," he says, " in the projectors to try an experiment of better living. One would say that impulse was the rule in the society, without centripetal balance ; perhaps it would not be severe to say, intellectual sansculottism, an impatience of the formal, routinary character of our educational, religious, social, and economical life in

---

[1] Life of Emerson, by Holmes, p. 51, himself a fair specimen of the modern New England freethinker.

Massachusetts."[1]   And again, speaking of the opposition of the married women to the " Philanstery," he writes in his " *Historic Notes*": " It was to them like the brassy and lacquered life in hotels. The common school was well enough, but to the common nursery they had grave objections. Eggs might be hatched in ovens, but the hen, on her own account, much preferred the old way. A hen without her chickens was but half a hen."[2] Again: "The founders of the ' Brook Farm '[3] should have this praise, that they made what all people try to make, an agreeable place to live in. . . . . The art of letter-writing, it is said, was immensely cultivated. Letters were always flying, not only from house to house, but from room to room.   It was a perpetual pic-nic, a French Revolution in small, an Age of Reason in a patty-pan."[4] The " Philanstery," the only organization which New England freethinkers ever erected, was burned down in 1846, and never rebuilt.   From that date to the present New England free thought, true to history all over the world, has been engaged in destroying and not in building up.   It is ever iconoclastic or nothing.   It is simply a radical protest against everything religious, and social, and traditional.   Emerson, at first an "orthodox" Unitarian, like William Ellery Channing, and an associate preacher with Rev. Henry Ware, minister of the Second Church in Boston, adhered for a time to the old Socinian views. Although Christ's divinity was denied by them, still the " orthodox " Unitarians respected Him as a divinified man. They respected the Bible.   They were, like the Semi-Arians, believers in the *homoiousity*, in the similarity of Christ to God, although denying His identity of substance with the Eternal Father.   They even observed the forms of the Lord's Supper, and administered it like other Protestant sectaries.   But Emerson broke with them in 1832.   He then preached against the observance of these forms, and left the Unitarians to become a Transcendentalist.

What is meant by this he tells us in one of his lectures : " What is popularly called Transcendentalism among us, is Idealism ; Idealism as it appears in 1842."   This definition, however, is only a polite cover for what the system really is.   It rejects churches and dogmas, and all external authority of creeds and systems. It builds a system on the *Me*, and its very name is borrowed from Schelling's " *System of Transcendental Idealism*."   Emerson had travelled in Europe, where he made the acquaintance of Carlyle and Goethe, both of whom were impregnated with the philosophy of Kant and Fichte.   He became a convert to their system,

---

[1] Life by Holmes, p. 164.   [2] Ibid., p. 165.
[3] It was called, properly, " The West Roxbury Association," founded in 1840.
[4] Life, p. 166.

and dressed it up in Yankee clothes when he returned to his home. The identification of the subjective and the objective in the order of thought; the *me* producing the *not me;* the perfect identity of the external world with the thinking subject; these features of Fichte-ism are found all through Emerson's writings. The *absolute*, as the resultant identity of the subject and the object of the *me* and the *not me*, of the real and the ideal, of knowledge and existence, of unity and plurality of form and matter, which is the ruling principle of all Schelling's system, runs through the whole of Emerson's prose and verse. The German psychologists, who had captured Jouffroy and Cousin, easily captured the imaginative New Englander, full of an apostate's hate for Calvinism and formalism, and full of a convert's zeal for the new lights of a very old philosophy. For the German metaphysicians who won Emerson were simply Brah-mins and Buddhists, transplanting Oriental pantheism into the atmosphere of Europe; neo-Platonists, interpreting in Wittenberg, Jena, and Königsberg, in the eighteenth and nineteenth, what Porphyry and Plotinus taught at Rome and Alexandria in the third, or what the Dutch Jew, Spinosa, taught in the seventeenth century of the Christian era. In fact, the *me* of Fichte, which is identified with the *not me;* the *absolute* of Schelling, which is identical with the *relative;* and the *idea* of Hegel, which is the same in all things, and which is purely subjective, are but other expressions for Spinosa's universal substance, of which all things are but forms and modifications. That the views of these pan-theists were predominant in Emerson's mind, as they are to-day forming the intelligence of New England freethinkers, is evidenced by various passages in his and their writings. In " Each and All," an essay, he writes: "Truth and goodness and beauty are but different faces of the same All." In "Nature," another of his essays, he speaks of all as being nothing; he loses himself in nature in Universal Being, and becomes "a part or particle of God." This is Hegelian or Spinosan, as the reader may elect. In " Idealism," another essay, he says : " It is a sufficient account of that appear-ance we call the world, that God will teach a human mind, and so make it the receiver of a certain number of consequent sensations which we call sun and moon, man and woman, house and trade. In my utter impotence to test the authenticity of the report of my senses, to know whether the impressions they make on me corre-spond with outlying objects, what difference does it make whether Orion is up there in heaven or some god paints the image in the firmament of the soul ?"

This skepticism is as old as Pyrrho. There is no novelty in this doubting of the testimony of the senses, for George Berkeley, Bishop of Cloyne, held it, and the Hegelians preached it long before the European steamers carried it to Boston and Concord. Emerson reiterates the same Berkeleyism in an essay on "Spirit," with a strong infusion of Hegelian pantheism. "But when we come to inquire whence is matter, and whence so many truths arise to us out of the recesses of consciousness, we learn that the highest is present to the soul of man; that the dread universal essence, which is not wisdom, or love, or beauty, or power, but *all in one*, and *each entirely*, is that for which all things exist, and that by which they are." This is only an echo of Schelling. "It is one soul which animates all men," says Emerson, in an oration on the "American Scholar," thus borrowing a strain from Plato's muse. Seek the infinite in "the meal in the firkin; the milk in the pan," is his recommendation to the young men of Harvard College. "True Christianity," he says, "is faith in the infinitude of man."[1] Dr. Ware, his former colleague in the Unitarian ministry, attacked him for leaving out the idea of personality in his philosophy; and the charge was well founded, for Emerson wrote: "The great Pan of old, who was clothed in a leopard-skin, to signify the beautiful variety of things, and the firmament his coat of stars, was but the representative of thee, O rich and various man ;" and again: "Are there not moments in the history of heaven when the human race was not counted by individuals, but was only the influenced; was God in distribution, God rushing into manifold benefit ?"[2] In the same address we have a passage which is thoroughly Hegelian: "We can point nowhere to anything final but tendency; but tendency appears on all hands; planet, system, constellation, total nature is growing like a field of maize in July; is becoming something else; is in rapid metamorphosis. . . . . . There is in nature *no private will*, no rebel leaf or limb, but the whole is oppressed by one superincumbent *tendency*." This is the *to fieri* of Hegel; *le devenir, das ewige werden*, almost to the very letter. In fact, Emerson's philosophy was all plagiarized. Even his doctrine of the "*over-soul*" is borrowed from the neo-Platonists, and is the *sovra-intelligenza* of the ultra-Italian ontologists. His theory of the "*piu nell' uno*," the identification of plurality in unity, is Brahminism, which taught that the whole world is but a manifestation of Vishnu, who is identical with all things, and differs not from the wise, but is the same as themselves. "All is for the soul, and the soul is Vishnu; and animals and stars are transient paintings, and light is whitewash, and durations are deceptive, and form is imprisonment, and heaven itself a decoy." This doctrine is asserted in Emerson's poem, "Brahma ;" yet he often impresses Chris-

---

[1] Life of Edwards, p. 122.

[2] Address on the Method of Nature, delivered before the Society of the Adelphi in Waterville College, Maine, August 11th, 1841.

tian truths, and his teaching is often so contradictory and confused that it is impossible to get at his real meaning. Mr. Bowen, the Professor of Natural Theology and Moral Philosophy in Harvard University,[1] expresses our own judgment of the whole transcendental school in these words reviewing Emerson's "Nature" in the *Christian Examiner* in 1837: "On reviewing what we have already said of this singular work, the criticism seems to be couched in contradictory terms; we can only allege in excuse the fact that the book is a contradiction in itself." Carlyle, writing of the *Dial*, the organ of the Transcendentalists, says: "You seem to me in danger of dividing yourselves from the fact of this present universe, in which alone, ugly as it is, can I find any anchorage, and soaring away after ideas, beliefs, revelations, and such like, into perilous altitudes."[2] Indeed, they were and are dreamers, these same Transcendentalists. Margaret Fuller was their Priscilla, and Thoreau their Montanus. Their projects for reforming the world were as wild and varied as the dreams of an opium-eater. They paid no attention to facts, nor common sense, nor tradition. There was an utter absence of logic or method in all their plans, except in that of the "Brook Farm," which soon collapsed by the weight of its own impracticability. Logic and method were foreign to Emerson's mind. He tells us this himself in his answer to Henry Ward: "I have always been, from my very incapacity of methodical writing, a chartered 'libertine'—free to worship and free to rail—lucky when I could make myself understood, but never esteemed near enough to the institutions and mind of society to deserve the notice of the masters of literature and religion. . . . . . I could not give an account of myself if challenged. I could not possibly give you one of the arguments you cruelly hint at, on which any doctrine of mine stands, for I do not know what arguments are in reference to any expression of a thought. I delight in telling what I think; but if you ask me how I dare say so, or why it is so, I am the most helpless of mortal men."[3]

This is certainly a humiliating admission for a man to make who undertook to overthrow all the old systems of belief. A syllogism would have put him into convulsions. He was simply a prophet inspired by God, and must be accepted, as another Mahomet by New England advanced thinkers. Surely, some reason should be given for throwing away everything hitherto held sacred in New England—Bible, Christ, Church, and formulæ of belief. Any lunatic may rail thus against existing institutions; may thus throw

---

[1] He is the author of " Modern Philosophy, from Descartes to Schopenhauer and Hartmann." New York: Scribner's Sons, 1877.

[2] Life of Emerson, p. 163.

[3] Letter to Dr. Ware, his former colleague in the Unitarian ministry, Oct. 8th, 1838.

off his clothes and dance in his skin. But such conduct is neither rational nor decent. Nor were the followers of the Concord messiah more logical or consistent than the leader whom they worshipped. Emerson's description of them in his lecture on " New England Reformers," in 1844, is still applicable to their successors. " They defied each other like a congress of kings, each of whom had a realm to rule and a way of his own that made concert unprofitable. What a fertility of projects for the salvation of the world! One apostle thought all men should go to farming ; and another that no man should buy or sell, that the use of money was the cardinal evil; another, that the mischief was in our diet, that we eat and drink damnation. These made unleavened bread, and were foes to the death to fermentation. . . . . They wish the pure wheat, and will die, but it shall not ferment. . . . . Others attacked the system of agriculture, the use of animal manures in farming, and the tyranny of man over brute nature ; these abuses polluted his food. The ox must be taken from the plough, and the horse from the cart ; the hundred acres of the farm must be spaded, and the man must walk wherever boats and locomotives will not carry him. Even the insect world was to be defended ; that had been too long neglected, and a society for the protection of ground worms, slugs, and mosquitoes,[1] was to be incorporated without delay. With these appeared the adepts of homœopathy, of hydropathy, of mesmerism, of phrenology, and their wonderful theories of the Christian miracles!" Shade of Cotton Mather! are these the sons of the sturdy Puritans who, in thy days, burned witches, butchered Indians, sold slaves, and exiled Christians who would not believe in the rigid dogmas of John Calvin ? And is this the result of Calvinism in less than a century on the intelligence of New England? to make it a dreamer of absurdities, an analyzer of manures, a debater about bugs and mosquitoes, instead of an advocate of the Bible and of the divinity of the Redeemer of the world!

A false system of æstheticism is the natural outcome of this pantheistic New England philosophy. For the New England poet beauty is relative, not absolute. For him there is no absolute criterion of taste or standard of criticism. The beautiful is but the projection or creation of the human soul, just as religion is but the product of each man's individual consciousness. Emerson's poems show this

---

1 The New England sophists thus discussing bugs and mosquitoes remind us of their Athenian prototypes whom Aristophanes, in " The Clouds," ridicules for debating as an important question " whether gnats sing with their heads or with their tails."

> " 'Ανήρετ' αὐτὸς Χαιρεφῶν ὁ Σφήττιος
> 'Οπότερα τὴ γνωμην ἔχο·, τὰς ἐμπίδας
> Κατὰ τὸ στόμ' ᾄδειν ἢ κατα τοὐρροπύγιο."—Verses 168, κ. τ. λ.

subjectivism more strikingly even than his prose. While they are beautiful in form, often elevated in sentiment, and original in the manner of presenting old thoughts, they are frequently false and tainted with immorality in their tendencies; not with the coarse immorality of Whitman or Zola, but with an immorality that flows logically from the false in conception. Indeed, we cannot say of the leading New England freethinkers that they are immoral in their private lives, like the French, of one of whom, and "*ab uno disce omnes,*" the pungent Veuillot wrote in his "*Libres Penseurs,*" "*Monsieur ——, age de quatre-vingt ans et concubinaire.*" Of Emerson, his great contemporary and, for a time, fellow freethinker, Brownson wrote in 1847: "We know Mr. Emerson; we have shared his generous hospitality and enjoyed the charms of his conversation; as a friend and neighbor, in all the ordinary relations of social and domestic life, he is one it is not easy to help loving and admiring." Yet, in his poetry the same Emerson teaches devil worship, and degrades man as much as ever hated Calvinism had done:

> " But man crouches and blushes,
> Absconds and conceals;
> He creepeth and peepeth,
> He palters and steals;
> Infirm, melancholy,
> Jealous, glancing around,
> An oaf, an accomplice,
> He poisons the ground."[1]

Why, even the old pagan had a better opinion of human nature than this:

> " *Os homini sublime dedit erectos ad sidera tollere vultus cælumque tueri.*"
> " Pride ruined the angels,
> Their shame them restores,
> And the joy that is sweetest
> Lurks in stings of remorse."

Remorse is pleasure, pain is pleasure, joy is sorrow, and the devil is God; for all things are one, and each is in all! Such is the poetry of New England free thought.

> " The fiend that man harries
> Is love of the Best."

The aspiration for perfection is a vain desire; the Christian love of God, who is the all-perfect, truth, goodness, and beauty; the personal God Who created us and redeemed us, and Whom we long to see, and Who loves to unite Himself to us, is only " a fiend who harries us," and deceives us:

---

[1] " The Sphinx."

> " Thou art the unanswered question ;
> Couldst see thy proper eye,
> Alway it asketh, asketh,
> *And each answer is a lie.*
> So take thy quest through nature,
> It through thousand natures ply ;
> Ask on, thou clothed eternity ;
> Time is the false reply."

No dogma, no certainty, no truth. " Each answer is a lie ;" and the lie and the truth are one and the same. There is no rest for investigation. Man must always seek and never find. There is no ark upon which the poor bird can rest its wings wearied with flying over the desolate waste of waters. There is no Church, and no personal God :

> " Ask on, thou clothed eternity,
> Time is the false reply."

There is even no resurrection, no immortality in this new theology. Standing over the grave of his dead son, Emerson finds no consolation in the future. He will never meet again the boy whom he loved. His darling has been absorbed in the infinite, a particle in an immensity of dust :

> " What is excellent
> As God lives is permanent,
> Hearts are dust, heart's loves remain ;
> Heart's love will meet thee again."[1]

> " House and tenant go to ground,
> Lost in God, in Godhead found."

Remember, that in the Emersonian style god and godhead are only names for the *to pan* of the Brahmins, Giordano Bruno, and the Hegelians. No wonder that the sturdy Brownson, in commenting on these poems, calls them " hymns to the devil." " They are not sacred chants ; they are hymns to the devil. Not God, but Satan, do they praise, and they can be relished only by devil-worshippers."[2] Surely old Calvinism, with its vigorous code of morals and iron-clad dogma, was preferable to this watery and loose transcendentalism which has washed it out of the old home of the Pilgrim Fathers.

And yet, strange as it may seem, the New England rationalists revolted against Calvinism on ethical as well as on rational grounds. They wanted to reform the world and introduce a new system of ethics. They have even sent out colonies for the purpose. " Brook Farm " and the " Philansterians " of West Roxbury have their imitators, even in New York. The Rev. O. B. Frothingham, of the New England school, for twenty years tried to convert New York

---

[1] " Threnody."   [2] Brownson's Review, April, 1847.

from its wicked Christian ways, to abolish its churches and schools and its Trinitarian belief in order to put transcendental theology in their place. His system, indeed, would multiply the churches indefinitely; for, according to it every man's hat is his own church steeple. There would be as many churches as individuals in the world. Chadwick, in Brooklyn, and May, in Philadelphia, have been struggling with the same Quixotic purpose to make every man his own church and religious law. All the transcendental "birds," or "clouds" or "fogs," whichever of the Aristophanian choruses you may choose to name them by, assembled in 1879 to honor the New York Socrates of the sect. He was going on a vacation to Europe, and all flocked to bid him good-bye. Champions of women's rights led by Col. T. W. Higginson, haters of church organizations like George W. Curtis, and out-and out skeptics like Stedman, were there; and the *brekekex koax, koax* was loud and long. The name of God was hardly mentioned, and even when it was it had no meaning or a pantheistic one. In this chorus of birds Felix Adler played the leading part of *Epops*, and he still remains king of the feathered tribe in New York, although he is not a New Englander. But his philosophy is, and so he conducts a school of "ethical culture" on the principles of the Concord School of Philosophy; and after twenty-five years of reform, he and his followers have founded a "*kindergarten*" for the conversion of the world to transcendental principles! This "*kindergarten*" is the great substitute for Christian churches and schools. Whether it will last as long as the "Brook Farm" experiment remains to be seen; but so far these are the only institutions founded by the apostles of the new evangel of individualism and free thought in America. They are still behind the Mormons in zeal and productiveness; and in many respects their teaching has brought about consequences more injurious to public morals and the physical health of humanity than the doctrines of the deluded followers of Joe Smith. The Mormons at least have dogmas, and dogmas are the tonics of human intelligence. The Mormons do not destroy their children. Fœticide is almost unknown among them; and although they are fanatics, they are not hypocrites.

The moral and physical decadence of New England have been in proportion to the progress of free thought among the sons of the Puritans. Hawthorne, himself a New England freethinker, thus speaks of the deterioration, which has been growing worse and worse since the period which he is describing. "Morally, as well as materially, there was a coarser fibre in those wives and maidens of old English birth and breeding than in their fair descendants, separated from them by a series of six or seven genera·tions; for throughout that chain of ancestry, every successive

mother has transmitted to her child a fainter bloom, a more delicate and briefer beauty, and a slighter physical frame, if not a
character of less force and solidity, than her own."[1] To-day the
New Englanders are a race of invalids. They have become worn
and sapless. The vice of fœticide is notoriously common among
them. Physicians have been warning them that the Puritan stock
is dying out from free vice, the natural consequence of free
thought. "I see very few children in this village," remarked a
traveller recently to a resident of a New England town whose
brogue betrayed his origin. "Come with me, sir, and I'll show
you plenty of them," was the reply; and he brought the stranger
to a part of the town called "Dublin." There the children
swarmed. Their stout limbs were not well clothed, and there was
a sad need of pocket-handkerchiefs among them; but there was
plenty of bone, flesh, and pugnacity. At the rate of decay now
going on among the Puritans and the increase of foreign stock,
"New England" will soon become "New Ireland." The secularization of education, and the destruction of religious belief in God
or in rewards and punishments hereafter, have taken away all sanction to ethical training. It is vain to talk about duty and disin-
terestedness and self-sacrifice and love and justice when God and
heaven and hell have disappeared from the Catechism. A switch
is as necessary as the alphabet to train a child; a jail is as important as a magistrate for good order in society. But New England freethinkers, by abolishing God, Church, Bible, heaven and
hell, have undertaken the impracticable task of keeping discipline
without a sanction to enforce it. They are trying to do what
Emerson extravagantly describes, in one of his poems, as sowing
"the sun and moon for seeds." New England has been trying
"to hitch her wagon to a star," to borrow another Emersonian expression, but the star is Lucifer, and the wagon has become as
dilapidated as Oliver Wendell Holmes's "one-horse shay." Hypocrisy may endeavor to hide the true state of the case; but
statistics show the reality.

Take divorce in New England, for example. "Listen to some
statistics taken from the shameful record of the New England
States, which seem to be the centre of this moral cesspool. In the
State of Massachusetts in 1860 there were five causes for which
divorce could be obtained, and a ratio of one divorce to fifty-one
marriages. In 1878 the number of causes for which divorce was
allowed had advanced to nine, and the ratio to one divorce for
every twenty-one marriages. In other New England States the
case was even worse."[2] These are the words of a distinguished

---

[1] The Scarlet Letter, p. 60.

[2] "The Calling of a Christian Woman," by Rev. Dr. Dix. Appleton, New York,
1883, pp. 122 *et seq.*

Protestant clergyman. " In Vermont the ratio was one divorce to thirteen marriages ; in Rhode Island, one to ten ; in Connecticut the ratio was one to ten. New Hampshire showed about the same proportion, and in Maine it was even worse." [1]

" Crimes against chastity, morality, and decency have been steadily increasing. In Massachusetts from 1860 to 1870, during which time divorces have increased two and one-half times, while marriages have increased hardly four per cent. . . . . . those crimes known as being ' against chastity, morality, and decency,' filthy crimes, loathsome, infamous, nameless crimes, have increased three-fold." [2]

But let us cover the offensive picture. The twin sisters, free thought and free vice, are ruining what used to be the intellectual centre of our great republic. The native stock of New England is losing even its political power ; and even the Athenians and Transcendentalists of Boston are now governed by a foreign fellow with the Doric name of O'Brien. [3]

What is the remedy ? What will put a stop to this decadence? Not a return to Calvinism or early Puritanism, since its doctrines engendered the disease ; but a return to that Church which never misconstrues nor misinterprets the Bible ; that Church which tempers justice with mercy and love for sinners ; which asserts the necessity of grace, yet defends the power of free will ; which upholds the doctrine of original sin, yet denies total depravity and the innate wickedness of man ; which interprets the rigor of the old law by the benign charity of the new ; which guides the intellect from error and false lights by the staked, well-surveyed and illuminated road of dogmatic definition, and strengthens the will in its conflict with passion by the tonic graces of a divine sacramental system ; that Church which gives a definite answer to every question of the inquiring mind ; that Church which never tolerates divorce, nor the separation of Christian truth from the education of the child ; a Church which canonizes purity, protects morality, ennobles poverty, obedience, and chastity, which she houses in her convents and monasteries ; the Church which softened the manners of barbarians ruder and more cruel even than the Puritans, and converted Hindoo and Grecian sophists and poets wiser even than Emerson and Frothingham ; the Church whose beauty, ever ancient and ever new, needs only to be examined to be admired and loved ; the Church which Paul preached in Athens and a Catholic archbishop represents in Boston.

---

[1] Calling of a Christian Woman, p. 123.
[2] Ibidem, p. 124.
[3] The present mayor of Boston, an Irish-American.

THE SOCIALISTIC REVIVAL IN EUROPE.

Contemporary Socialism.   By John Rae, M.A.   New York :   Charles
   Scribner's Sons.   1884.

THIS century, of all others, has been disturbed by socialistic
   agitation.   Since the great outburst of the first French Revolution, the world has been in a chronic condition of unrest.   There
have been intervals of peace, alternating with intervals of turmoil
and violence.   Whatever may be said of the agitation, it is undeniable that it has been instrumental in accomplishing some good
for man.   The excesses committed by some of the agitators, and
the wild theories advanced by others, though they may stain and
retard a cause that is good in itself, do not alter the principles of
that cause, and should not be permitted to cloud the truth of it.
At all events, governments have been materially changed for the
better within the century by these great agitations.   The whole
complexion of the relations between governments and the governed has undergone a change.   That change may be summarized
as the insistence by the people on a proper representation in the
management of themselves, and in the shaping of the laws under
which they live, and in the national *acts*, as distinct from the mere
personal acts, of royalty or rulers.   Not all of this has been achieved,
but much has ; and liberties are placidly enjoyed to-day by most
peoples, the demand for which, at the beginning of the century,
was regarded, and naturally so, under the condition of things then
prevailing, as revolution.   And now, as the eventful century draws
toward its close, socialistic problems of the extremest radical nature are pressing impatiently for solution.

   The term Socialism has thus far been used in its broadest possible
sense ; in the sense defined by Webster (edition 1880), as " a theory of
Society which advocates a more precise, orderly, and harmonious
arrangement of the social relations of mankind, than that which
has hitherto prevailed."   In this sense, all honest men who wish
the advance and harmony of the race, the " peace on earth to men
of good will," that the angels sang at the coming of Christ, are
Socialists.

   There is, however, a secondary definition : " Communism ;" and
Communism is defined as " The reorganizing of society, or the
doctrine that it should be reorganized, by regulating property, industry, and the sources of livelihood, and also the domestic rela-

tions and social morals of mankind; socialism; especially the doctrine of a community of property, or the negation of individual rights in property. (J. H. Burton.)"

This latter comprehensive definition may be taken to cover the more general acceptation of the term Socialism to-day. Yet it should not be forgotten that there is, or may be, much of the first definition embraced in the second. The truest and greatest socialistic agency in the world is the Catholic Church. In attacking it, as is their habit, socialistic agitators attack, at once, their best friend and their invincible foe: their friend in all that is just, wise, and good in their demands; their foe in all that is false and foolish. As a matter of fact, the Catholic Church, in her peculiar institutions, carries out, and has carried out from the beginning, the practice of communism in property and worldly goods. In the great orders and societies, male and female, the benefits of property (as also the pressure of poverty) are shared alike by all the community, and distributed beyond to the people for whom they labor, in the spirit of Christian charity. The General of the Society of Jesus is, personally, no richer a man than the lay brother who waits at the door or washes the dishes. The monk or nun who dies, whether of princely or peasant origin, carries nothing to the grave but the shroud, and leaves nothing behind but the memory and the purity of a good life. It is needless to dilate on the fact, accepted by all thinking men, that the Church is the great Reformer. To her are owing the greatest reforms that have affected the general well-being of man; and to her is owing the structure and formation of civilized Christian society. The doctrine of human equality and fraternity, in the highest sense of children of God and brethren of the Son of Man, emanates from her. From this doctrine necessarily flowed the abolition of slavery, that wicked and cruel institution that converted free and immortal spirits into human chattels or cattle. To the Church woman owes her dignity and freedom, marriage its sacredness and indissolubility, and the family its safety and its pillar of strength. Hers is the doctrine that the laborer is worthy of his hire, and that to defraud him of it is one of the sins that cry to Heaven for vengeance.

The history of the world shows, the history of our own times shows, in many a horrid page, how often, through disregard of that doctrine, the cry for vengeance has gone up to Heaven, has been heard and answered under the free will of man. The Church was the great protector of the people's rights and liberties, when none other dared face the power of tyrants. She has ever been the teacher and the mother of the poor, the conservator of learning, the dispenser of knowledge, and the guide and guardian of enlightenment. Man cannot place his finger on any great reform within

the Christian era that is not traceable directly to the principles inculcated by and the influence of the Church. So that sincere Socialists, if the scales of prejudice and inherited misrepresentation could
only fall from their eyes, would see in the Church, not their enemy,
but their truest friend, well-wisher and guide, in all the real and
possible reforms that they would fain accomplish. Has she not
put up countless martyrs to die for the doctrines of truth and justice and Christian charity ? Is not her domain full of good works?
Is she not forever the preacher of peace among men? But the
difference between her and the others is this : that she is content
to work patiently in God's good time, by appeals to reason and
charity, and by the influence of .her own example. She believes
in no violent or immediate remedies for rooted wrongs. Evils that
are the growth of centuries must be slowly and laboriously abolished. To pluck them up by the roots is to destroy more than
them.

In the old days, Rome, that is to say, the Holy Father, was the
high court of appeal of subjects against rulers, and, at times, of
rulers against subjects. The Protestant Reformation cut off a
great portion of Christendom from that court, and thenceforth, in
the Protestant section of Christendom, there was no guiding voice
outside the State. If subjects rebelled, they rebelled. If princes
tyrannized, they tyrannized. There was no one who could cry
halt to either party. How much the people gained in individual
liberty, in piety, in prosperity, by the Reformation, may be seen
in the condition of European peoples at the beginning of this century, and may be seen to-day. That condition for the masses (to
use the most convenient term) was wretched in the extreme. In
Protestant countries, even more than in Catholic, there was tyranny
on the one side, and poverty, impiety, and ignorance on the other.
But not from Protestant lands alone was the power of the Church
shut off. The rulers and the statesmen of Catholic Christendom
entered into a conspiracy against the Church of Christ. In place of
Protestantism, they took up the cry of Liberalism, under the mask
of which was Atheism. Their pretence was that the Church chained
men's souls, and invaded the prerogatives of state-craft. They
professed Catholicity, but State Catholicity, rather than Christianity. So they chained the Church when they could, fettered
her limbs, choked her voice, broke up her good works, gave free
rein to the teachers of irreligion, and inoculated the minds of the
ignorant with the idea that the Church was the enemy of the
people and of the State, so that it came to be regarded as a badge
of servility and unpatriotism to be a sincere Catholic. Thus Protestantism on the one hand, and Liberalism or atheism on the
other, drew away from Christ great masses of people who ought

to be Christian, and educated them into impiety or indifference to religion. So that at the beginning of the present century Europe was to a very large extent atheist, and the one institution most hurtful to its eyes and hateful to its soul was the Roman Catholic Church.

Meanwhile social problems were secretly evolving themselves. On minds thus prepared to look into a godless future, the atheistic literature of the eighteenth century fell like sparks on powder magazines. The magazines flamed up, and the first explosion was the French Revolution. The cry for liberty, equality, and fraternity is a most noble one ; but the world with horror saw what it meant in mouths that pronounced the name of God only to blaspheme it. Within a short time not only government, but society, was disorganized. A dreader tyranny than France had ever known fell upon France. The cause of liberty was pushed back instead of forward ; but the rulers had received a startling shock.

This cry for an ideal liberty, equality, and fraternity, under impossible human conditions, is practically the cry of the Socialists to-day. Instead of being confined to one state or nation, they are now everywhere. They are regarded as a danger to the state, to the Church, and to society. Some of them openly proclaim their antagonism to these three necessary institutions of human life, and, with them, to property and to the family. Socialists carry on a vigorous propaganda, and it would be foolish to deny the fact that they are gaining numerous recruits. They go under different names in different lands ; but, under whatever names they go, their general purpose is the same. That purpose may be described, in brief, as the overthrow of the existing order of things, and the establishment on its ruins of a Socialistic Utopia, where property shall be common, where all shall be equal, where there shall be no poverty and no riches, no rulers and no ruled, no laws, no law-makers, no law-breakers, no nothing, in fact.

This would seem the idle dream of fools, were it not that the lot of the majority of mankind is a very hard one, that governments still are far from perfect, that the question of the laborer and his hire is forever pressing to the front, that many millions of people are weighed down under heavy grievances, not to say wrongs, and that the spirit of Christian charity, that would go far to regulate the questions between employer and employed, is dead over a great portion of the world. So, to-day, Socialism stands up as a menace in the face of nations, and all the bayonets and prohibitory laws in the universe will not and cannot put it down.

It is well, then, to scrutinize carefully this latest of the isms ; to see of what it is composed, and who compose it ; what it aims at, and what it is actually doing. For now Socialism, in some form or another, is a factor in every state; though this republic is at present freer from it than other states for the sole reason that here is liberty and that the conditions of life here are more favorable than in most lands. In Russia, Austria, and Germany, Socialism is treated as treason against the state; in the countries of the Latin race it is a constant fomenter of public disturbance; in England it is a daily growing power. It has become a name of dread in the councils of the nations, and all sorts of expedients are adopted, either to hush it up or to get rid of it. But there it stands, fast and firm and grim, gathering to its fold all the disturbing and distressed elements in human society. The only true safeguard against it is a return on the part of governments, and of those untitled governments of capital that control vast masses of labor, to Christian principles; to dealing just judgments, and to endeavoring to undo the work of the past three centuries that alienated the people from Christ and from His teachings.

Perhaps the completest study in English of this most important subject is that of Mr. John Rae, on *Contemporary Socialism.* The work is admirable in spirit; very close and logical in analysis; sufficiently full in detail; calm in temper and tone; and presenting the Socialist views in the clearest and most unbiassed manner, to refute them at the end. Socialists themselves could not find fault with Mr. Rae's exposition of their theories; and in its honesty of statement and comprehensive grasp of a most diversified subject, Mr. Rae's instructive and interesting volume finds its chief value. It is impossible within the limits of a review article to go into the minutiæ of the work, which is a large one. On such matters readers must satisfy themselves, and those who read Mr. Rae will be well rewarded. Only one or two salient points will be treated here, as illustrating what the Socialism of the day really is and means.

Mr. Rae confines himself to the broader phases of his subject; for, though there are many petty groups and coteries among revolutionary Socialists, " they differ only on minor points of future government or present policy." All adhere to one or other of the two main types, " the Centralist, which is usually known as Communism, Socialism, or Collectivism, and the Anarchist," which, though like in kind, " is generally known as Anarchism, or Nihilism." Mr. Rae calls attention to the wonderful spread of Socialism throughout Europe within the last twenty years. At the English International Exhibition of 1862, " it was a common topic of congratulation that the political atmosphere of Europe was then entirely free from the revolutionary alarms which overclouded the first Exhibition in 1851." This shows how little the course of events is turned by these international symposia, as they may be

called, or by the meetings of royalties to arrange among themselves the world's affairs. Treaties of Tilsit are out of date. "It
was in 1862 that Lassalle delivered to a club of workingmen in
Berlin his address on ' The Present Epoch of the World, and the
Idea of the Working Class.' " This was published shortly afterwards under the title of " The Working Man's Programme," and
has been called by Lassalle's friends " The Wittenberg Theses of
the New Socialist Movement." It was even at the same Exhibition
that the germ of the International was laid, in the mutual relations
established between delegates of the English and French trade
societies.

This latter movement started a new order of things, conducive
towards an international fraternity among workingmen. There
were many able men among those workmen-delegates, who met
from time to time in their own parliaments, not only to discuss
questions of mutual interest regarding their various trades, but
problems of a deeper kind, the relations of employers to employed,
of the unprivileged classes to governments, of all the demands
made by governments on those classes, of the money they earned,
the taxes they paid, the representation they had in their governments, the improvement of their homes and ways of life, the education of their children, and other such matters, that had hitherto
been placidly relegated to the chance good will of parliaments and
governments. This, and what came from it, was not at all like the
revolutionary movement of 1848 and the Socialistic schemes that
disappeared with that revolution. "The communities of Owenites,
St. Simonians, Fourierites, Icarians, which multiplied for a time
on both sides of the Atlantic, are extinct," says Mr Rae, with truth.
Those dreams and dreamers, more or less amiable in themselves,
but with the most unpractical and, sometimes unconsciously perhaps, immoral theories regarding the reform of society and the
regulation of the life of man, have passed away, laughed out of
very existence. " The Socialists of the present day have discarded
all belief in the possibility of effecting any social regeneration except by means of political authority; and the first object of their
endeavors is, therefore, the conquest of the powers of the state."

Here, indeed, is the whole case stated as far as the ultimate object of Socialism goes. The aim of the Socialists is no longer to
serve, to argue, to appeal, but to seize the power and rule. It was
said of Lord John Russell that, so great was his self-confidence,
he was prepared at a moment's notice to take command of her
British Majesty's fleet or to lead the government. Your dyed-in-
the-wool Socialist is ready at a moment to draw up laws for the
governance and the well-being of the world. Mr. Rae states a
truth worthy of attention when he says: " Out of the several sorts

and varieties of political Socialism, only one has revived in any strength, and that is the extremest and most revolutionary." Child's play is over. "It is the democratic communism of the Young Hegelians; and it scouts the very suggestion of state help, and will content itself with nothing short of state-transformation." This we see illustrated to-day in Germany. Prince Bismarck, who thinks "any stick good enough to beat a dog with," utilized the Socialists against the Catholics, when he entered on his anti-Catholic campaign. After having petted them, he found them growing dangerous. He tried to chain his hound; but the effort was useless. Socialism flourishes mightily under a rule of blood and iron, and despite all the efforts of the German Government to repress it, there were more Socialists returned to the Reichstag at the late elections than ever before. So the Government, wishing to steal their thunder, started a system of State-Socialism, in which the State plays the benevolent paternal part to the workingmen; but this, as was shown at the recent opening of the Reichstag, the Socialist deputies vehemently reject.

In France the working classes to-day hate the Republic more than they did the rule of Napoleon III., which at least gave them *panem et circenses.* "As a rule," says Mr. Rae, "the Socialists of France at the present day, like those of Germany, put their faith in iron rather than paper." In this the Socialists only take a leaf out of Prince Bismarck's own book.

"What they want is a democracy of labor, to use one of their own phrases—that is, a State in which power and property shall be based on labor; where citizenship shall depend on a labor qualification, instead of a qualification of birth or property; where there shall be no citizen who enjoys without laboring, and no citizen who labors without enjoying; where everyone who is able to work shall have employment, and everyone who has wrought shall retain the whole produce of his labor; and where accordingly, as the indispensable prerequisite of the whole scheme, the land of the country and all other instruments of production shall be made the joint property of the community, and the conduct of all industrial operations be placed under the direct administration of the State. Furthermore, all this is contended for as a matter of simple right and justice to the laboring classes, on the ground that the wealth of the nation belongs to the hands that made it; it is contended for as an obligation of the State, because the State is held to be merely the organized will of the people, and the people is the laboring class; and it is contended for as an object of immediate accomplishment—if possible, by ordinary constitutional means, but, if not, by revolution."

This presentation has a startling show, and yet it is only the other day that we heard many of these doctrines promulgated by a candidate for the Presidency of the United States, an able lawyer, a man who has occupied great positions of trust in his State and in the Congress of the United States, General Benjamin F. Butler. Not that he presented the new theory of government in this bald, simple, concrete form; but much of it was in his thought and in his theory as expressed. In other lands and at so exciting a time so able a man would have drawn to him a large following, and created vast disturbance. Here, in this nation of workers, he is laughed at and avoided by the workers, and his assumed candidacy was one of the ridiculous features of a most important and harassing political campaign. Some of what General Butler advocated under an American veneer, posing distinctly as the candidate of labor against capital, Mr. Rae calls " Revolutionary Socialist Democracy," which he divides into two main branches—German Socialism and Russian Nihilism, the difference between which he considers rather local than founded on matters of principle. There is a division of principle between modern democrats, that which classifies them as Centralists, and Federalists, titles which fairly well explain themselves. The Centralists wish the democratic republic to have a strongly centralized form of government, while the others would leave the local communes comparatively independent and sovereign and free, if they chose, to unite in convenient federations.

Bearing in mind that Socialism is the same substance in many forms and in many places, Germany may be taken as one of its strongest and most out-spoken centres to-day. And it is a fact not without significance that Socialism in its most dangerous forms is strongest under the two most despotic of European powers—Germany and Russia. German Socialism is set down by Mr. Rae as " the creation of Lassalle." He it was who gave the vague substance shape, coherency, and a voice, and changed it from a theoretic dream into a living and working organism.

Ferdinand Lassalle was the son of parents who were strict Jews. It is singular to note how many men of Jewish descent have allied themselves with the Socialists; for the Jews, as a race, are conservative. In Russia, for instance, there is scarcely a band of Nihilists captured that has not its Jewish members, men and women. Lassalle was possessed of great natural gifts, which he cultivated and developed in the universities of Breslau and Berlin. He was taken up and seems to have been made a pet of by the literary society in those cities. Humboldt called him a *Wunderkind*. He went to Paris, and there formed a close friendship with Heine. He began his public career by taking up the question of woman's rights, or woman's wrongs, with characteristic force and vehemence, and with some success. He was a strange mixture: at once full of noble and of ignoble passions; a man of thought, of intellect, of labor and of pleasure. " Lassalle," says Mr. Rae, " would have been a great man if he had had more of the ordinary restraining perceptions, but he had neither fear nor awe, nor even—in spite of his vein of satire—a wholesome sense of the ridiculous—in this last respect resembling, if we may believe Carlyle, all Jews." He was, he proclaimed, " revolutionary on principle,". explaining that by revolution he meant transformation, or a substitution of an entirely new principle for the existing state of things ; whereas reform merely meant a logical development of the principle of the existing state of things. Revolution might be carried out either peacefully or by force of arms. Like all Young Germany at the time, he was a pupil and admirer of Hegel, and was indoctrinated with the ideas of that philosopher. He took part in the revolutionary movement of 1848, and suffered on its collapse. He was brought to trial and imprisoned. He defended himself boldly, and the trial brought him fame. He was banished from Berlin, but was afterwards allowed to return. He was a strong advocate of the unity of Germany, with Prussia as the centre, and probably this may have first brought him in contact with Bismarck ; but the unity of Germany was to his mind a prime necessity for the establishment of freedom and democracy. In this he may not have been far wrong.

He wrote extensively, from tragedies to pamphlets on social and political subjects. He believed in power and not in paper, and ridiculed the constitutionalism of modern Liberals. Might was right to him. He was again prosecuted and imprisoned. He now (1863) turned his attention to the congresses of workingmen which were beginning to organize into a power. He sketched a political programme for them. To elevate their normal condition political agitation was needed rather than the establishment of savings banks, benefit societies, and so forth. Universal suffrage was requisite to enable them to achieve their elevation. Workingmen were ground down under the existing economical *régime*, and especially by " the iron and cruel law of necessary wages." Their only cure was in coöperative production, the substitution of associated labor for wage labor. But this system must be introduced by state help and on state credit. The state should do for the people what it does for the large and wealthy corporations and monopolists. Ninety-six and a half per cent. of the population are ground down by the " iron law " and cannot by their own power lift themselves above it. So the State, which is themselves, must step in and help them ; and universal suffrage alone can enforce State help.

Such was Lassalle's programme for the working classes. Strange to say, at the time it was received with indifference even by the workingmen, while it was universally condemned by the press. The Leipzig workmen alone received him with favor, and to Leipzig he proceeded and organized there (May 23, 1863) the General Workingmen's Association for the promotion of universal suffrage by peaceful agitation. He went on with the work ; lecturing, writing, agitating, moving from place to place. But in spite of his energy his success was small during his life-time. He was killed in a duel on August 31st, 1864.

His very death seemed to lend wings to the cause he advocated, though that death was owing to a purely personal quarrel. To-day the working classes of Germany are to a large extent impregnated with his doctrines. It is not necessary to go more deeply into them here. They had enough of surface plausibility and reasonable cause to appeal to crude intellects which could grasp rough facts and grievances, and see no serious attempt at reform on the part of the government, or of assistance on the part of the privileged classes. What is the fourth estate? asked Lassalle, and the answer was nothing. What ought it to be? Everything. The First French Revolution was a revolt of the third estate against the Crown and privileged classes. "The third estate, the *bourgeoisie*, conquered, and converted itself into a privileged class; plutocracy took the place of aristocracy. The revolution of 1848 was the beginning of the revolt of the fourth estate, the working classes, against the privileges of the third. "What is the State?" asked Lassalle of the workingmen. "You are the State," he told them. "You are ninety-six per cent. of the population. All political power ought to be of you, and through you, and for you; and your good and amelioration ought to be the aim of the State. It ought to be so, because your good is not a class interest, but is the national interest."

Of course, if right and wrong be a matter of count by noses, this argument is irresistible. The greater good of the greater number is a much-used but specious phrase, one of the multitudinous cants of the day that ignorance, whether lettered or unlettered, erects into a popular dogma. Good is absolute; and as has been nobly said, "one with God is a majority." Votes do not decide goodness or badness. The only standard of good is the law of God as given through His Divine Son, and guarded and expounded in His ever-living body, the Church. Morals are founded on the doctrines of Christ, the Prophet, the Priest, the King of God's human creatures. Either this is so or Lassalle's argument is true; and the only means of demolishing the force of his argument is to reconcile as far as possible the human with the divine law, bringing a wise Christian charity to bear on the development of the human race and the afflictions of various kinds that by its very nature and constitution it is bound to labor under. Adam, after the fall, with all the world before him, was compelled for very existence' sake to labor as severely as was the fictitious Robinson Crusoe on his solitary island. The old monk's saying that Carlyle loved—"labor is prayer"—sums up the life of any well-organized Christian. All that can be hoped from laws and human institutions is' not to create a universe of idlers and impossible communists, but to assist as far as is possible to insure man's living honorably and in security by the sweat of his brow or the sweat of his brain. Place Lassalle's ninety-six per cent. in power, give universal suffrage as in France and in the United States, and is the condition of things very materially altered as affects the general status of the ninety-six? Call them by what name you please, the other fraction will rule, if for no other reason, for convenience' sake.

There is no argument here for or against universal suffrage; simply a statement of indisputable facts as affecting the millennium expected by many from the carrying out of Lassalle's ideas and of all those who advocate similar plans for the reformation or regeneration of society. Adam had to delve, and Eve had to spin, and the answer to the question of that fourteenth century Socialist, John Ball, "Who was then the gentleman?" is that Adam was the gentleman and Eve the lady. Labor, though a burden, is an honorable one; the burden of human life, in fact, of which there is no evading. If there be what are called drones in the human hive, those drones have uses as well as abuses. The idea of reducing all human beings to a dead level is alike against nature, man, and God. Let any nation or people try the experiment and level itself to-day. The levelling would be simply a process of beheading and a social disruption and suicide. It is perfectly legitimate, and right, and wise for the ninety-six per cent. to labor with all honest effort for their own improvement and advancement and for necessary reforms in the State, for the curtailment of class privileges that oppress them and hinder their progress, and so forth; but it is simply foolish for them to call upon the State, by the issue of an edict, to work social miracles and change the purgatory of centuries into the paradise of a day. Moreover, are the working classes themselves wholly without blame, and do they set no obstacles in the way of their own advancement by lack of thrift, lack of industry, lack of obedience to the moral law, and drunkenness?

Lassalle's theories sufficiently illustrate whatever there is of logical scheme and common aim and purpose in Socialism. But Mr. Rae does not stop here. He follows up all the main branches of the system,—for a system it has now become,—getting at the heart of each, and dissecting it with the disimpassioned skill of a competent surgeon, exposing in the process the disease, and, as far as possible, its cause. To follow these branches in detail is impossible here. Mr. Rae has been most conscientious in his work, and seems not to have left a stone unturned that might help him in discovering the truth. He is familiar with all the chief writers on Socialism, and with the methods of the workers in their various geographical limits. After dealing with Lassalle, he proceeds to discuss Karl Marx, his labors and his writings. From London, that European headquarters of all kinds of international agitation, Marx exercised an immense influence by his publications alone. Marx was one of the leaders of the International, the chief aim of which was the concentration of associated labor. It had accomplished much in this direction when the Franco-German war broke out. The International was bitterly opposed to the war, for its leaders foresaw the divisions in its body that would inevitably result from that war. It will take many years, and an entire new order of the universe, to eradicate nationalism out of the heart of man. At the close of the war came the uprising of the Commune in Paris. "The leaders of the International," says Mr. Rae, "were undoubtedly heart and soul with the Commune." What became of the Commune we know. Its explosion killed the International. The English members at once fell away, and what was left of it was, later on (1872), rent by a schism at its congress at the Hague. As Mr. Rae well observes: "A Socialist organization always seems to contain two elements of internal disintegration. One is, the prevalence of a singular and almost pathetic mistrust of their leaders and of one another. The law of suspects is always in force among themselves. . . . . The other source of disintegration is the tendency to intestine divisions on points of doctrine. A reconstruction of society is necessarily a most extensive programme, and allows for the utmost variety of opinion and plan."

One of the most interesting of the chapters is that on Russian Nihilism, a branch of Socialism with which we are all familiar from the series of desperate deeds that have marked and continue to mark its course. Nihilism, perhaps, might be set down as the last development of Socialism; and wild, terrible, and hopeless as it is in its aims and methods, if such a lost cause, a cause that is lost in its very essence, could be ennobled, that has been in the barbaric sense ennobled by the marvellous devotion and self-sacrifice of so many of its adherents, women and men alike. It is barbarism fighting barbarism, and Mr. Rae's analysis of it is close and keen. Especially interesting, and to most of us novel, is his exposition of the part played by woman in Russian society. Just here it is well to remark that the decadence of the Russian priesthood has destroyed a potent influence for good among the people, more especially in an autocratic and bureaucratic government such as Russia—the state yoked the church to its car; the result, as invariably happens, was that the priesthood became a degraded profession, and religion fell into mere superstition, or into gross disrepute. Bakunine is one of the prophets and leaders of Nihilism. In 1857 he was condemned to exile for life in Siberia by the

Czar Alexander II. After twelve years he escaped, more devoted to the cause than ever. Pandestruction is his leading principle in revolution. " Admitting no other activity than that of destruction," he says, " we declare that the forms in which that activity ought to express itself may be extremely varied—poison, poniard, knout. The Revolution sanctifies all without distinction." And again : " Pandestruction is a series of assassinations and audacious, or even mad, enterprises, horrifying the powerful, and dazzling the people till they believe in the triumph of the Revolution." With what zeal and devotion the Nihilists have taken up these wicked and foolish doctrines, the world has seen. They were, also, the doctrines of Mazzini, at one time the pet of London drawing-rooms and society, and to whose memory a statue has been erected in the New York Central Park. As matters stand even to-day, Russia is staggering between two terrorisms—the terrorism from above and the terrorism from below.

But, as has been said, it is impossible to go into all these matters within the limits of an article. Each chapter in Mr. Rae's book is worthy of study by those who look at the later and, on the surface, more ominous movements of the age. The air is certainly clouded and charged with dangerous elements. There is a moral dynamite abroad that needs very careful watching. It should not be forgotten that deadly explosions are as often caused by the over-confidence or carelessness of the guards as by the attempts of miscreants. In either case, the wreck to the victims is the same. Sometimes, too, these disasters are caused by over-timidity or ignorant handling. It is for statesmen to deal with these problems, and deal with them in a wise and just spirit.

How to reconcile the malcontents, who are daily increasing in numbers, and who, it should not be forgotten, are being constantly wrought upon by the most evil agencies, is really the great social problem of the age,—greater than all your canal questions, colonizing questions, boundary questions, treaty questions, and other questions that come up for international arbitration in these days of much palaver. Mr. Rae devotes one chapter to " the Christian Socialists," and it ought to be suggestive to those who are vexed by the problem before us. " The Socialism of the present day," says Mr. Rae, " is not of a religious origin. On the contrary, there is some truth in the remark of a distinguished economist, M. Paul Leroy-Beaulieu, that the prevalence of socialistic ideas is largely due to the decline of religious faith among the working classes. If there is only the one life, they feel they must realize their ideal here ; and realize it quickly, or they will never realize it at all." This, of course, is essentially materialism, or that mode of mind that sees " the be-all and the end-all here," and that is preached by the favorite social scientists and philosophers of the day in all lands. How this mode of thought came to capture the minds of such multitudes has been shown in an earlier portion of this article. "The fact is certain," says Mr. Rae, "that most contemporary Socialists have turned their backs on religion." And just here it may be as well to dispose of a specious objection that is often put. It is said in substance: You Catholics are always talking of the Church and of her influence for good. Had she not all these people, or their forefathers, in her hand once, when, as you claim, all Christendom was one? Why did she not do better for them, then, and why should they desert her now?

Again, this objection has been partially met earlier in the article. These worthy objectors forget that even in Catholic days there was always a conflict, more or less stubborn, between the temporal and the spiritual powers. This conflict necessarily interfered materially with the work of the Church in the advancement and development of the human race. This was true up to the rupture at the Reformation. Since that date, as already shown, the Church has been conspired against and hampered by both Catholic and Protestant powers, and the people, as far as possible, educated into hostility to her influence and her teachings. They not only try to keep her out of the school, but also out of the land.

Thus governments to-day have to fight Socialism more or less single-handed, and they fight it with the only weapon they know,— the sword. The cross they have either deserted or rejected. This atheistic movement, says Mr. Rae, is looked upon by the Church "with a natural and justifiable suspicion." Nevertheless, he adds truly: "Some churchmen, however, scruple to assume this attitude; they recognize a soul of good in the agitation, if it could be stripped of the revolutionary and atheistic elements of its propaganda, which they hold to be, after all, merely accidental accompaniments of the system, at once foreign to its essence and pernicious to its purpose. It is in substance, they say, an economical movement, both in its origin and its objects, and so far as it stands on this ground they have no hesitation in declaring that, in their judgment, there is a great deal more Christianity in Socialism than in the existing industrial *régime*."

It is safe to say that this well describes the attitude towards Socialism of a large body of Christian believers. Indeed, had not Church and State and people been antagonized by infidel statesmen, it is highly probable that by this time governments and the governed, nations one with another, and class with class, would have been moving in fair harmony under the common bond of Christ. The rich would not have looked upon the poor, nor the poor upon the rich, as natural enemies, while secret societies would have known from the beginning that they were under the ban of the Church, and, consequently, of the whole Christian community. Thirty years ago the Christian Socialists were established in England under the lead of Frederick Maurice and other earnest men. They did excellent work, but the society finally fell through. In Germany a similar work has been taken up by Protestants and Catholics. "The Catholic group," says Mr. Rae, "deserves to be considered first, because it intervened in the discussion much sooner than the Evangelical, and because it originated a much more important movement, larger in its dimensions than the other, and invested with additional consequence from the circumstance that, being promoted under the countenance of dignitaries, it must be presumed to have received the sanction of the Roman Curia, and may, therefore, afford an index to the general attitude which the Catholic Church is disposed to assume towards continental Socialism." Germany is strong in Catholic clubs. In 1863, when the Socialist agitation assumed distinct and formidable form, Dr. Döllinger recommended the Catholic clubs to take the matter up. "These clubs," testifies Mr. Rae, "are societies for mutual improvement, recreation, and benefit, and are composed mainly of workingmen." Father Kölping's Society of Catholic Journeymen, founded as early as 1847, had in 1872 a membership of 70,000. There were affiliated clubs, numbering from fifty to four hundred members each, in various German towns. There were also Catholic clubs of apprentices, peasant clubs, benefit clubs, young men's clubs, credit clubs, literary clubs, and so forth. Indeed, the Germans, as is their fashion, seem to have converted the club business into a science, and the result of it is, to some extent, seen in the Catholic party in the Reichstag, which, under the pressure of persecution, sprang from nothing into the leading place. In 1864 the great Bishop Ketteler took up the matter and published to the world his views on the labor question and Christianity. In 1868 the Catholic bishops of Germany, in their conference at Fulda, discussed the relations of the Church to the labor question. They approved of the formation of associations of Catholic labor. In the same month there was a general meeting of the German Catholic clubs, and the result was the formation of the Christian Social Associations, or, as they are called from their patron, St. Joseph Associations. They are composed of and managed by workingmen, with clergymen and men of property and prominence as honorary members.

It would take a special article to go into the great practical work accomplished by these Catholic workingmen's clubs in Germany. Mr. Rae recognizes the worth of that work, and his general comment is, that "the Catholic movement goes a long way with the Socialists in their cries of wrong, but only a short way in their plans of redress." The idea is correction; not reconstruction, of the present industrial system. The aid of the State is called for to assist the workman against the overwhelming power of capital, but to assist him in reason. That cry is at our own doors, and must be heard sooner or later,—the sooner the better. Bismarck at one time seemed to fear what he termed "an alliance between the black International and the red." He is a great phrase-maker, as was Disraeli; but phrases are neither facts nor things. Mr. Rae's judgment is, that the Catholic sympathy is "not so much with the Socialists as with the laboring classes generally," and the Catholic labor movement, so far as it has gone, "is meant to take the wind from socialism, whether with the mere view of filling their own sails with it or no."

As for Protestant efforts in this direction, Catholics can have nothing but good-will towards them. And here is Mr. Rae, one of their own writers, telling us that in Germany "no voice was raised in the Protestant churches on the social question till 1878"; and he adds the grim comment: "They (the Protestant churches) suffer from their absolute dependence on the State, and have become churches of doctors and professors without effective practical interest or initiative, and without that strong popular sympathy of a certain kind which almost necessarily pervades the atmosphere of a church like the Catholic, which pits itself against States, and knows that its power of doing so rests, in the last analysis, on its hold over the hearts of the people."

What a world of unconsciously uttered truth and history lies in that sentence, ill-applied though it be! Surely, if we believe in anything at all, we must believe that the most potent agencies in promoting the moral well-being of man are the agencies of religion; and the moral well-being of man, in the broad sense, is the necessary adjunct of his physical well-being. Yet here is Protestantism enslaved to the State, or, where it is not enslaved, a matter of fashion rather than of principle. And here is Catholicity, that really touches and reaches the heart of the people, looked on with suspicion and hostile eyes by the governments of the day. And here is hunger, and thirst, and disease, and all the evils that afflict the mass of humankind, knocking at the doors of government for humanity, asking for bread and getting stones in answer to its prayer. It is these evils that give its life to Socialism, and lead those to despair of help from governments who have been taught to despair of help from God. And the remedy? That is a long question, hard to solve by those who have rejected Christ and His command to love God above all and our neighbor as ourselves.

CIVILIZATION, OLD AND NEW.

TO be interested in the poorer classes is in good taste. It is, also, comprehended in " civilization." In England there is a spasmodic impulse towards the poor. About a year ago there was an awakening to the fact that the poorer classes had no homes to live in. They had shelters, but no homes. Kind persons con-vened meetings and made speeches ; and royal princes paid visits to the " outcast poor." The result has been an increase of infor-mation in regard to the dire sufferings of " *les misérables.*" By and by there will be a systematizing of suggestions. New build-ings will be run up ; old hovels will be pulled down ; and then the committees will rest from their labors. It is a good movement, if spasmodic. That in the nineteenth century—and very close upon the end of it—English society should become interested in the very poor, is a hopeful sign that in the old age of the world civilization will not ignore charity.

A curious discussion is being raised by some philosophers as to whether civilization is the result of evolution or of wise and be-neficent legislation. Yet these philosophers have not told us—what should have been their first postulate—the real meaning, the whole meaning, of civilization. The movement just referred to, the new interest in the outcast poor, helps us to get at the high-class notion of civilization, as well as at the compass of its beneficence. We do not learn much from the illustration. Our philanthropists, like our philosophers, are not " thorough." Yet, at least, our philanthropists do something, which is more than can be said of our philosophers. These last gentlemen think and live up in the clouds. Upon all subjects they begin nowhere, and they stop there. In regard to civilization, as in regard to religion, they seem to have no postulates, no beginnings. It is not, therefore, to be wondered at that they have no endings. " What is civiliza-tion?" we may ask them ; but they will only answer us by telling us " how it grows." And even on this point they are as speculative as they are cold. Mere theories as to civilization—as to its causes or effects—may be interesting from the intellectual point of view, but the poorer classes are unable to dine off theories, or to pay rent out of speculative philosophy. It cannot matter one pin to the roofless outcast from all home, nor even to the half-clothed or half-hungry, whether civilization be a purely natural develop-ment, in accordance with the so-called laws of evolution,—brought about by the activity of individuals, and amplified by hereditary transmission,—or the result of legislation which secures liberty to the individual, and presents him with the opportunities of culture. What *does* matter to the poorer classes is the *nature* of that civilization which is assumed to be their true object of aspiration, and to afford to them blessings and enjoyments. Our philosophers will not define these things for us. Civilization is affirmed to have existence, and to be capable of still further development; but whether it includes anything higher than late dinners with silver plate, express trains, electric lights, standing armies, our modern theorists seem rather afraid to tell us.

If society be progressively self-civilizing—a statement which we should accept with distrust—it can only be so because the individuals who compose it are personally bent on "improving themselves." But does civilization mean self-improvement? It means popularly nothing of the sort. It means the arts of good harmony, which citizens, dwelling together, have learned from experience to be advantageous. Civilization means convenience. It means the calm and the ease which the observance of the proprieties secures to the most cultivated in good manners. To the rich classes it means luxury and repose; to the middle classes it means comfort and good behavior; and to the hardworking poor it means protection by the police and by the laws which prevent robbing and being robbed. As to the "inventions" of civilization, they are the result of business enterprise, *plus* the inherited gains of each age from the last age—that is, the gains from experience. The wonder is that, the world being so old, we have learned so very little in so long a time. The nonsense which is talked about our "enlightened age" is only to be accounted for by our vanity. Considering that we inherit all the knowledge and all the wisdom which half a dozen thousands of years have been heaping up, it is strange that the world is so full of mistakes; it is strange that no man has found out infallible politics; that, as to a religion, our newest philosophers are still searching for it; and, as to society, we have not yet housed our poor. We, accidentally, inherit the benefits which have come to us from the past industries of a very old world, and fancy ourselves a superior generation because we blunder over the uses of others' toil. But what has all this to do with civilization? Conventionally speaking, there is, unquestionably, *a* civilization; an external social refinement, or good-fellowship; there is a growing love of easiness in the material order, and of still greater easiness in freethinking. Is this, then, a true civilization? No more than money can be said to be personal merit, or good manners to be virtue or purity.

That the word civilization has different meanings—which it

would be absurd to confuse in critical estimate—is as obvious as that the highest kind of civilization is the least studied, the least cherished, in our own age. Let the Socialists have their way in sub-stituting state for individual action, or for corporate enterprise, and they would scarcely even touch upon the question of civilization—as a Catholic Christian should understand it. The Socialist is only thinking of abstract ideas of social blessedness, so far as labor and possessions are concerned. Or again, the Evolutionist, who views biologically the development of what he accounts to be civilization—just as he views the development of religion, as well as of the whole natural order—may indulge his theories without a thought as to that higher civilization which never was, never will be, *nationally* prized. How, then, is it possible, if the highest kind of civilization be ignored by the most cultivated societies—ignored as too sublime to be attainable—that the world, in its old age, can be asked with any hopefulness to leave off talking of civilization and to practice it?

There is a material, an intellectual, and a moral civilization. The most popular of these divisions is the material. There are many men who are superlatively silly, and many who are pro-foundly immoral, who would be shocked if an imputation were breathed against their civilization, or who would scorn the impu-tation as ridiculous. Who should say that any gentleman who rides in a brougham, and who knows how to take his hat off to a lady, can be wanting in the graces of civilization, any more than in the appreciation of its luxuries? The popular idea of civiliza-tion is the whitewashing of barbarism; and barbarism means rude-ness of toilet and of manner, with a contempt for the fine arts and for education. We say, arbitrarily, that a people is not civilized, because it cannot be trusted with civil liberties (some people say this of the Russians); but what we mean by " uncivilized," in com-mon parlance or apprehension, is the not having the appliances of modern comfort, or the not having the faculty to appreciate them. Now, in all such estimates, the ancient Greeks or ancient Romans (just as they were coming to their downfall) thought very much as we now think. Nay, in some things the ancient Persians or Carthaginians were, materially, quite as civilized as we are. They were our inferiors in but little save inventions. So that to say that civilization, materially, is anything to be proud of, or to aspire to, is really to lay claim to being barbarously self-indulgent; and this is most certainly to be uncivilized. No, civilization is not material; or, at the best, it should be so accidentally.

Pass we then to intellectual civilization. Now, here again we find it difficult to say that, intellectually (save only in the enjoy-ment of opportunities), the modern peoples of Europe are superior to the contemporaries of Socrates, Cicero, or Virgil. But let us come down to much later contrasts, to the contrast between the " Middle Ages " and our own age. Take away the art of printing out of the world, take away the *accidents* of invention, and are the peoples of modern Europe more appreciative of wisdom, of genius, of industry, of individuality, than they were in the days, say, of the Crusaders, or when Michel Angelo sketched an outline for St. Peter's? The boast of modern enlightenment—which, of course, means civilization—is the boast only of the *possession* of extraordinary means of education, not of the *using* them to the utmost advantage. A thousand newspapers, or the same number of public libraries, do not make a people intellectual. And here we come to the question : If to be civilized, intellectually, does *not* mean to possess vast opportunities, what is that spirit which should animate the intellect so as to justify the claim of civilization ?

Assuming that there is a material, an intellectual, a moral side to the just apprehension of being " civilized," what can be understood by the word " moral"? The answer may be found in Catholic history. All that has been grandly done in the last nineteen centuries has been done by the inspiration of faith. The history of the Church is the history of civilization. As Macaulay put it : " The history of the Catholic Church joins the two great ages of human civilization. No other institution is left standing which carries the mind back to the times when the smoke of sacrifice rose from the Pantheon, and when camelopards and tigers bounded in the Flavian amphitheatre. The proudest royal houses are but of yesterday when compared with the line of the Supreme Pontiffs." And this institution, the Catholic Church, has given the *motive*, or object, to intellect, which was precisely what was wanted for civilization. Take a most familiar example of the blending of a natural heroism with a supernatural. The mere mention of the Knights of the Temple, of St. John of Jerusalem, of the Teutonic Order, of St. Raymond, recall to us the union of the most robust martial spirit with the spirit of robust faith and robust virtue. Without exaggerating the merits of the Crusaders—which, doubtless, were often marred by a natural vanity—there is enough of " true zeal" in their chivalry to compel us to call their motive " ineffectual." Take a still grander illustration of the same motive —though acting in a different groove, and with different temper— the monastic life of learning and of piety. Now, here we have the intellect devoted to three agents, each of which is the highest of its kind: first, the cultivation of the highest learning ; next, the cultivation of the highest virtue ; and thirdly, the charitable protection of the weaker and poorer classes against the tyranny or the impiety of feudal lords. The abbeys and the priesthood were the homes and the pattern of the highest civilization possible to men ; just as, in a quite different groove, the spirit of Christian chivalry—in what we may call the second half of the Middle Ages—chose an object which, in faith and elevation, is proved to have been the noblest that was practical. The Crusaders did not know all the great things they were doing for the after history of both religious and civil life ; but this did not lessen the grandeur of the object, which, intellectually, was eternal and sublime. And just as chivalry and charity were blended—at least in purpose—in the spirit of the Catholic Crusaders, so let it be noted—for it is most appropriate to our subject—that the same blending was characteristic of monasteries. We are accustomed to pride ourselves at this end of the nineteenth century on the magnificent civilization of our public hospitals. The pride of the boast is quite justified. Yet, in the Middle Ages it was the exception for any monastery to be without a public hospital for all comers. " Public beneficence " was twin-born with the monastic life. Just as the Crusaders were both chivalrous and charitable, so the monks defended the weak against the strong, and nursed every wayfarer who fell sick. And here let a few features be noticed, very rapidly, of what may be called the true, as contrasted with the modern and spurious, civilization.

It was just at the time when the ages of faith were fully ripe in all parts of the Christian world, but when civil society was beginning to fall away from its old allegiance and chivalry and devotedness, that there broke over Germany and England, and subsequently over almost half of Europe, that most detestable revolution, the Reformation. Protestantism broke the unity of civilization. Civilization was at its height when Erasmus was examining into what he could find of all the sources of knowledge ; when Columbus was discovering a new world ; when Vasco da Gama was doubling the Cape ; when Ferdinand Cortez was penetrating a new continent ; when the standard of Castile was floating at Oran, and the Mussulman had been driven from Granada. In Italy philosophy was deeply studied. Spain was, perhaps, the queen of martial enterprise ; and the Pontiffs were blessing the ships that took out armies of missionaries to many a new country of the known world. And here let one great fact be noted. Centuries before these days the Catholic Church had crushed slavery ; for, having begun by improving the condition of slaves, and then gone on to obtain their enfranchisement, she ended by excommunicating all persons who indirectly took part in slave-traffic. The Council of Orleans, in 549 (a thousand years before the time of Paul III., who, like Urban VIII., and Benedict XIV., prohibited the practice of slavery), decreed that all slavery was anti-Christian. This was the true spirit of civilization. But, on every other point of civilization the Catholic Church had led the way. Women, by Catholicity alone, became socially the equals of men. The indissolubility of marriage, by Catholicity alone, became elevated into a Christian dogma. Education, as every writer of any eminence has confessed, was carried to its highest point by the Church. The individual, the family, society, were, by the Church alone, sanctified ; and all the world was included in one bond of brotherhood—the highest achievement of civilization. To the old world the exact opposite was civilization. To the Greek or to the Roman all strangers were barbarians ; to the Catholic all strangers were brothers. And one word must be said as to civil government, for it is but little apprehended by the majority of Protestants how the Church has fought the battle of "the people." The Catholic teaching was always this (and Suarez maintained it against a king of England), that princes received power "mediately " from God, but "immediately " from the people whom they governed. Rousseau's peevish saying, "Man is born free, and he is everywhere in fetters," might be rendered with perfect truth, "Every Catholic was always free, but heresy and schism destroyed freedom." Briefly, before the time of the Reformation civilization had made all the progress which, humanly speaking, was possible to it. Protestantism perverted its course. The progress which has been made in any sphere of civilization, during the last three hundred years, has been made in spite of, not by the aid of, Protestant ideas, and has been a heritage of the Catholic civilization.

Luther, Calvin, Melanchthon, and Beza,—so, too, Grotius, Papin, and Leibnitz,—all confessed that *after* the ruinous Reformation, learning, both in universities and outside them, fell down to a very common-place degree. And as to what we understand by "ideas," never, since the period of the Reformation, has philosophy soared as it did before it; never have painters, or architects, or poets, grasped the "supernatural idea." The spirit of faith, which touched with fire the old artists, has dwindled into compliments to "modern thought." In all the "religious" paintings of the Middle Ages, every one who has intuition must detect an "idea,"— which now seems quite lost to our best painters,—the "idea" of a supernatural purity. This idea was a realization by faith. Yet, not only did artists realize, they painted. They could not have painted had they not been able to realize ; and had they lived in Protestant England, they could not possibly have realized the "idea" of virgin purity, out of Protestantism. Could Murillo have thought out his Catholic subjects with the Thirty-nine Articles for his theology ? or could Dante have imagined his *Divine Comedy* in the atmosphere of a modern parsonage-house? or could Michel

Angelo have chiselled that exquisite " Agony," which is in St. Peter's, had he been "inspired " by heresy and schism ? And one word must be said as to Shakespeare. His Catholic genius ran riot in Protestant revels. Shakespeare was a " product of the ages of faith," though accidentally living under Protestant rule ; nor is it possible to conceive of his combination of greatnesses as having been fathered by " modern thought." He linked the old world with the new. Nor can modern civilization claim *him* for its son any more than it can claim St. Thomas Aquinas, or St. Augustine, or the mighty architects who built Catholic cathedrals. The motive, the object, was wanting to modern piety, modern talent, modern genius, modern " faith." *Waste* was begotten of that rebellion, which killed the motive, the object, of civilization. For ideas, men took up with speculations ; for profound study, they took up with controversy ; for divine faith, they took up with human caprice ; for Christendom, they took up with national churches. Protestantism contained the principle of dissolution, in that it shivered the unity of civilization ; so that, whereas, in the Middle Ages, a Spaniard or an Englishman, travelling to any Christian country, was certain to grip the hand of a brother Catholic, from the time of the Reformation he was timid in expecting sympathy from some new-born disciple of a new sect. Civilization stood still under such a shock. It has never recovered its deep purpose, and now we have to fall back on a fictitious philanthropy, and on the complacency and shallowness of philosophers, in the absence of the motive, the object, the intensity of a civilization which *began* in Catholic unity.

Yet there is one point on which modernism so prides itself that it is difficult to shake the delusion : " Liberty, religious and civil, was born," says a modern writer, " of the Reformation, which proves that the Reformation was civilizing." Civil liberty, on the contrary, was born of that protection which the Holy See always gave to suffering peoples, taking their part against half-civilized tyrants, whether kings, feudal lords, or heresiarchs. As to religious liberty, two reflections may be made. The first is, that in most of the struggles between professedly Christian princes, religion has been " used " (as it was used by the late Czar) as a pretext for robbery or injustice ; just as Cromwell used religion as a pretext for regicide, and Queen Elizabeth used religion as a pretext for hanging (and also for disemboweling and quartering) about forty Catholic priests and two hundred laity ; so, in all ages, ambitious princes have made religion responsible for crimes which necessitated a good excuse, and which the Pontiffs and the priesthood could not prevent. The closest student of history, who " reads everything on both sides," is often puzzled to assure himself which side was sincere; which side was telling lies to the Pontiff; which side was cloaking infamy with religion, which side was the more cruel, the most merciful. De Maistre, in his masterly treatise on the Inquisition, shows how absolutely necessary it is to know *everything* to form a judgment on all historical scandals. Meanwhile, this one remark must be hazarded: that Protestants are the last people in modern history who ought to presume to claim the title of "civilized" on the ground of granting others religious liberty; for, as Hallam and Macaulay and Guizot have stated,—and, indeed, every historian of any note,—it was persecution *alone* which established Protestantism; so that Protestant religious liberty is *not* civilized.

But, leaving the historic points to one side (since a whole book would not suffice for even a summary), has the new "liberty," it must be asked, made civilization more lovely, more generous, more heroic, more Christian? One word will suffice to sum up modern civilization, and this is that hateful word selfishness. Just as true civilization is all summed up in "charity," so false civilization is selfishness. A few words can demonstrate this truth. If most people were unselfish, it would be impossible that society should contain entire classes which are miserable; it would be impossible that whole classes should be driven to crime through the ignorance or the incentives which are preventable; it would be impossible that sectarianism and selfishism and atheism should be fomented by the *examples* in high places; in short, it would be impossible that this so-called civilized age should be, as it is in truth, so uncivilized. The whole philosophy of civilization was once summed up in the precept: "Thou shalt love thy neighbor as thyself." In obedience to that principle, all society would be civilized; whereas, society as a whole is uncivilized. So that it comes to this: that, in individual civilization must be found the civilization of communities; whereas, almost the whole world is so horribly selfish that civilization means the worship of self. Before the Reformation, the *principle* of unity, *plus* the sublime object of Catholic life, made civilization and charity to mean one thing; after the Reformation, the *principle* of disunion, *plus* the weakened objects of the human will, made civilization and selfishness to be inseparable. This is the general statement of the whole truth. It is only in general terms it can be stated. Individual exceptions prove nothing. The present age is an uncivilized age, because it makes materialism its chief good, while caring little for those who have *not* that good. In 1884 it suddenly occurs to English society that hundreds of thousands of the English poor are not housed. While esteeming material blessings above all other blessings, society esteems them chiefly for "Number One." Thus, both in principle and in practice, civilization has dropped to paganism, or, to what is much the same thing, living for self. Intellectually, civilization has lost its object, and, therefore, morally, has lost its grace and its heart.

THE CLASSICS IN MODERN HIGHER EDUCATION.

A College Fetich. An Address by Charles Francis Adams, Jr. Third Edition.

The Greek Question. "Popular Science Monthly," November and December, 1883.

The Question of a Division of the Philosophical Faculty. By Dr. A. W. Hoffman.

Ueber die Bedeutung der Sprache und des Sprachunterrichts für das geistige Leben. Von Professor E. Zeller.

ONE of the most striking characteristics of our age is its spirit of unrest. This spirit manifests itself everywhere and among all classes. It animates the inventor, the speculator, the reformer, the anarchist. It prescribes the changes of our bonnets and of our medicines. It inspires scientific progress and political revolutions. It has undermined the nobility of birth in Europe, and is now assailing the aristocracy of money. It has shaken thrones, threatens the long immovable foundations of the rights of property, and strikes at religion itself. Whilst it has called into life a thousand improvements, it respects nothing, however hallowed by age or authority. Where property, society, political institutions, and religion are daily made the subject of novel speculation, experiment, and attack, it would be strange if the old system of higher education alone escaped unassailed. Nor has it been an exception to the rule.

For thirty years back, voices have been heard demanding the partial or complete discarding of the classics in the gymnasia, the colleges and universities of the nineteenth century. At first few and feeble, these voices gradually grew in volume and strength until the modest petition swelled into a loud, in some cases a furious, chorus of demand. At the college commencement, at the society anniversary, among the doctors of science and the masters of the modern languages, in the weekly, the daily, and the monthly publications, in America and in Europe, we meet with denunciations of classic teaching. The study of the classics, so say its opponents, is a "great chronic scandalous failure, the one preeminent and historic failure of the so-called liberal education, in which there is more repulsiveness and more hatred than in any other kind of study, mathematics not excepted;" it is a "superstition" and a "college fetich." Strong language, this, and positive. Is it founded in fact? Is it true that the training under which the world has progressed for the past four hundred years, under which all, or nearly all, its great men were prepared for their life-work, was a failure, and that the world's advance in science and art was gained, not because of its system of education, but in spite of it? If strong assertion were proof, there could be no doubt, and we must root out the superstition and dethrone the fetich. But though in war it may sometimes be wise generalship to burn our ships, and trust to fortune and our good swords, this is not true in science and learning. To burn the ships which have carried us so far, and which have seemingly enabled us to achieve results so grand that not a few of our friends grow dizzy with self-admiration,—to burn these ships before reason and experiment have proven incontestably that the balloons and air-ships which are to replace them are safe and manageable, were midsummer madness. It is, therefore, the part of wisdom to examine the grounds of these charges, to see whether they are well founded or merely the visions of honest but misguided fanatics. We are not educational Bourbons; we do not shrink from change because it is change; but, on the other hand, we do not believe that all change is improvement. Before we disgrace a servant, who appears to have done his duty for many years, let us see whether he had really become useless, or rather an obstacle; let us examine whether there is any candidate for his place worthy of confidence, and able to perform the work he is supposed to have done. We shall approach this inquiry calmly and dispassionately, try to hear both sides fairly, and leave the reader to judge for himself.

It has been stated that this new crusade is directed against the classics, that is to say, against the study of both Latin and Greek. Let us be precise. The majority of the educational reformers, whose opinions we are examining, make little or no distinction between the two languages. Even those who for the present confine their attack to the Greek, use arguments which tell with equal force against both Greek and Latin, as will appear further on. Indeed, there is little reason why the non-Catholic of to-day should discriminate in favor of the Latin. Not so for the Catholic; to him the Latin is not a dead language, said to be admirably adapted to be the vehicle of mental discipline; it is the living language of his Church, and has to him a practical importance far exceeding that of French, German, or any other modern language. However, in the remarks which follow, we abstract wholly from this special character of the Latin, but base them solely on its availability as an educational instrument.

To inquire intelligently whether classics are entitled to a prominent place in the higher education of our day, we must first find the answer to another question. What is the aim or purpose of higher education, of a college course? Without knowing this, we have no standard by which to measure the value of the means employed. Fortunately there is practically no difference of opinion on this question. All, or nearly all, are agreed that its object is to prepare the student for life in a general way, to so unfold his faculties and powers as to make him not a specialist but a symmetrically developed man, to fit him not only to take up any profession with success, but to take the broadest views, to form the most intelligent opinions, to entertain the noblest aspirations, and to have the highest ideals. Listen to Mr. C. F. Adams, Jr.: "I am no believer in that narrow scientific and technological training which now and again we hear extolled. A practical and too often a mere vulgar money-making utility seems to be its natural outcome. On the contrary, the whole experience and observation of my life lead me to look with greater admiration, and an envy ever increasing, on the broadened culture which is the true aim of the university." According to this view, those studies are best suited to the college course which are best suited to bring out in the student the *power* to use his intellect, his reason, his imagination, his judgment, his taste, his powers of observation, his memory,—in short, all his faculties to the best advantage. The studies pursued need not, of necessity, be of practical application in after life. As the young gymnast, to secure the sound and symmetrical development of his body, does not swing the blacksmith's hammer, nor use the carpenter's saw, but has recourse to parallel lines, and cross-bars, and trapezes, which he will never use in after life, so the student, to bring out the powers of his mind, may, nay must, if needful, pursue studies which have no further practical aim. We say no "further practical aim," for we should carefully guard against the common error, that only such instruments are practical as show an immediate, visible effect. Hence, if the modernists, so we shall for brevity's sake call the opponents of Latin and Greek, denounce the classics as dead languages, which few do and few can learn to speak, this reproach, if true, would prove no more than if the classicists condemned astronomy because few persons in practical life calculate eclipses or transits of Venus, or analytical geometry, because, once an alumnus has his diploma, he never more dreams of the asymptotes. To convict of failure a study or an educational system, you must either prove that it has not and cannot have in it the means of drilling the learner's mental powers, or you must show that experience, correctly and honestly interpreted, convicts it as useless.

One more principle we must lay down. As the best tool, if ill-handled, is useless, so the best educational scheme, if badly carried out, must result in disappointment. A correct system should, therefore, not be made to answer for incompetent teachers or bad instruction.

Tested by these standards, have the modernists proved the study of the classics a failure? To do no injustice, let us consult, and, where possible, quote the very words of the advocates of modernism. Nothing that has been said or written during the past few years has so challenged public attention in this country as an address delivered by Mr. C. F. Adams, Jr., in July, 1883. It has been generally understood as an attack upon the study of the classics, and especially of the Greek. Hundreds of articles have been written on it from this point of view; and yet, after a careful perusal, it would be hazardous to say that Mr. Adams has really attacked classical training. He tells us, in so many words: " I have no wish to attack it (*i. e.*, the dead learning, or the study of the classics), except in its spirit of selfish exclusiveness."[1] " I have no light or disrespectful word to utter of the study of Latin or of Greek, much less of the classical literature. While recognizing fully the benefit to be derived from a severe training in these mother tongues, I fully appreciate the pleasure those must have who enjoy an easy familiarity with the authors who yet live in them." (P. 11.) "I object to no man's causing his children to approach the goal (*i. e.*, a true liberal education) by the old, the time-honored entrance (*i. e.*, the classics). On the contrary, I will admit that, for those who teach it well, it is the best entrance." (P. 10.) " I am not speaking at all of Greek, thoroughly studied and lovingly learned. Of that there cannot well be two opinions. I have already said that it is the basis of the finest scholarship." (P. 17.) " We are willing—at least I am willing—to concede a preference, and a great preference, to the dead over the living, to the classic over the modern." (P. 31.) Is this the language of an opponent of the classics? If so, what could an advocate say in their favor that would be stronger? Mr. Adams makes several of the above quoted remarks, "so that I (he) shall be misunderstood only by such as wilfully misunderstand, in order to misrepresent. With such I hold no argument." Surely, to rank Mr. Adams as an op-

---

[1] A College Fetich, p. 10.

ponent of the classics, or for that matter of Greek, is a delicate and a dangerous step. Moreover, much of what is said throughout his address is directed not against the study of the classics in itself, but against the manner in which he was made to study them at Harvard thirty years ago. If, as he assures us, the Harvard men of his day "were compelled to acquire a confessedly superficial knowledge of two dead languages, if they passed examinations in Latin and Greek that did not set at defiance the science of cramming, if they were made to neglect their mother tongue, if the slipshod methods accepted in Latin and Greek were also accepted in other studies, if a prominent feature of the instruction in the classics was unintelligent meaning," then, indeed, Mr. Adams and his fellow-students are entitled to our deepest sympathy. If the facts were as he states, we should not wonder at his demanding reform, radical reform, in the methods of instruction, so that future generations may have opened to them "the best entrance" to the "goal of a liberal education." But Mr. Adams will have none of the bests. Like Medea, he sees and approves what is better; but he chooses the worse. Side by side with the unstinted eulogy measured out to the classics in the passages given above, we read as follows: "I cannot myself profess to have any great admiration for Latin literature." (P. 16.) John Adams's endowment of an academy, where Latin, Greek, and Hebrew were to be *thoroughly* studied, was "fetich worship, pure and simple." "In these days of repeating-rifles she (Harvard College) sent me and my classmates out into the strife equipped with shields and swords and javelins. We were to grapple with living questions, through the medium of a dead language. It seems to me I have heard somewhere else of a child-cry for bread being answered with a stone." (Pp. 28, 29.) "But are those transcendent beauties really there (in Greek and Latin literature)? I greatly doubt it. I shall never be able to judge." "I am free to say that, whether viewed as a thing of use or as an accomplishment, as a source of pleasure or as a mental training, I would rather be familiar with the German tongue and its literature than be equally familiar with the Greek. . . . . . What I have said of German as compared with Greek, I will say of French as compared with Latin." (Pp. 37-8.) After digesting this anthology, let the reader say under what flag the speaker sails. To us he furnishes one of the most marvellous instances of mental bipolarity which it has been our fortune to meet. It is hard to say whether, like Balaam, he went forth to curse and broke out into blessing, or whether, unlike that noted prophet, he set out to bless and ended in cursing. On the one hand, the study of Greek is the best basis of the finest scholarship; on the other hand, it is a fetich and a stone. Are we to infer that a fetich and a stone are the best basis of the finest scholarship? We confess that, so far from misunderstanding Mr. Adams, in his duplex attitude towards the classics, we have not even understood him.

So much is certain, however, that, whether Mr. Adams really thinks Latin and Greek the best entrance to a true liberal education, or whether he really prefers German and French to Greek and Latin, he wants no classics, or at least as little classics as possible, for himself and his children. Most people prefer the best wine, Mr. Adams the inferior quality ; and why ?

Mr. Adams himself tells us that his preference is based on his own experience and that of his family for the past century and a half. As one swallow does not make a summer, so the experience of one man, or of one family, out of thousands, nay millions, cannot furnish the ground-work of a valid indiction. Mr. Adams is too frank and too well-trained a man not to suggest this himself. So this experience, whatever it consists in, by itself can prove neither one thing nor the other. Such as it is, however, it seems to prove to us the contrary of Mr. Adams's inferences. We will state it. Mr. Adams's grandfather, John Adams, received a classical education. The training he received at college enabled him to become a successful teacher and lawyer ; he espoused his country's cause in the Revolution, and rendered it distinguished service, both at home and abroad, as envoy to France. He ranked so high as a statesman that he was found a worthy successor of the Father of his Country. All this he achieved in virtue of his talents and his education. But his education did not enable him to appreciate Isocrates and Dionysius of Halicarnassus, at the age of seventy years, after long neglect, nor to speak French, at forty-two, as the diplomatic representative of America. No doubt it would have been pleasanter to the elder Mr. Adams had he been a French scholar. That he would have been a better diplomatist with French and without the classics, it is easy to assert, but as impossible to prove as it is to prove the contrary. On the whole, if a man's success is at all due to his education—and both classicists and moderns hold this—Mr. Adams certainly had no fault to find with his classical training.

Mr. John Quincy Adams's case comes next. He was no less successful as a diplomatist and a statesman than his father ; he, also, had studied Latin and Greek at Harvard, but then he had also picked up some living languages in Europe as a boy. As his father made his mark as a diplomatist without French, it is not self-evident that Mr. John Quincy Adams would have failed without it. Men speaking French have been unsuccessful diplomatists, and the same can be said of men who have had a classical education. We modestly suggest that an able man with a good training would succeed with or without French, as experience has proved more than once. No doubt a knowledge of French is a decided advantage in a diplomatic career ; but that, without it, his grandfather would have been tongue-tied at St. Petersburg, as Mr. C. F. Adams, Jr., hints, does not follow. What inference, for or against classical training, can be drawn from a career like that of Mr. J. Q. Adams, would puzzle the ordinary mortal. Still, even he is made to point a moral ; for his education is criticised, on the one hand because he did not read Greek in after life, and on the other hand because he did read Latin. This knowledge of Latin, it seems, and not the prevailing taste, led the old gentleman to indulge in an affectation which he seems to have transmitted, in some faint degree, to his grandson—the affectation of, at times, airing his knowledge of Latin quotations.

Whilst Mr. J. Q. Adams enables his grandson to have a fling at the classics, because he did not "keep up" his Greek, Mr. C. F. Adams, Sr., did keep up his Greek, but the Greek fares no better at the hands of our critic. The Greek caused him "to lose the step of his own time"; it prevented him from becoming "a wiser, a happier, and a more useful man." Such is the language of the son, who is President of the Union Pacific R.R., we believe, concerning the father, whose services, as the representative of the United States at the Court of St. James during the civil war, have met with unanimous and hearty commendation. If success be the criterion, then C. F. Adams, Sr., with his love of Greek, need not shun comparison with his son. His career as a whole is an honor to his Alma Mater, and certainly does not countenance the charge that his education unfitted him, or fitted him ill, to play his part in the drama of life.

Even the younger Charles Francis Adams, despite his own opinion to the contrary, seems to us to show that the time-honored classical training has not lost its virtue. It may seem presumptuous to set up our opinion on this point against Mr. Adams's, but we are told that no one is a judge in his own case. Here is the story of Mr. Adams's experience. With the exception of some independent reading in English literature, he owes his intellectual training to the college course established at Harvard thirty years ago—a course largely made up of the classics and mathematics. How did this training serve him ? He first studied law ; as appears, successfully. Being called to fight for his country's cause in the field, he made an honorable record for himself during the civil war. When, at the close of the war, he returned to civil life, he changed his profession, and devoted himself to what he calls "a specialty in connection with the development of the railroad system,"—some scientific pursuit, we infer. A course of training that prepares a man to become, successively, lawyer, soldier, and railroad scientist, certainly does not fossilize the mind; it seems to have rendered Mr. Adams's mind remarkably elastic. It must have unfolded, drilled, and strengthened all its faculties; for, to pursue successfully the three avocations mentioned would, ordinarily, be beyond the powers of a mind that had not been so developed and invigorated. Mr. Adams has not a word of recognition for the services thus rendered to him, which he includes, it must be presumed, among the "impalpable essence" effects of classic training. He only remembers that it did not teach him French, or rather, that it did not enable him to speak that language fluently in a public assembly. "Representing American educated men in the world's industrial gathering," he wails, "I have occupied a position of confessed inferiority." We have read of German and English, and we are proud to say it, American *savans*, who, though not masters of French, did not occupy a position of confessed inferiority at the world's scientific gatherings.

A more serious and, if well founded, more damaging charge against his classical education, is the rhetorical assertion made by Mr. Adams that Harvard sent forth most of her graduates unable to follow out a close, sustained line of thought, and to express themselves in clear, concise terms. To determine the validity of this accusation, we must be certain, first, that the facts are accurately stated, and next, that they are correctly explained. Far be it from us to suggest that Mr. Adams would wilfully mis-state any fact. But when we study his mental habits, and find that in one place (p. 4) he assures us that "the college course was a pleasant sort of vacation, which he would be very sorry not to have enjoyed," and, on another (p. 28), that he studied Greek (which elsewhere he informs us was a nightmare to him) with patient fidelity, we must either infer that the patient, faithful study of Greek was a pleasant vacation, or suspect that facts unconsciously shape themselves to his mental ken according to the needs of his argument. But allowing that, in the present instance, there is no delusion (and students of his pamphlets will, perhaps, concede this in Mr. Adams's own case), why blame the classics, which, we are told, were only superficially studied, especially when every other branch of study was learned no more thoroughly?

So much for the experience of the Adams family. We hold that it is an argument in favor of classical training, as far as the experience of a few individuals can be called an argument. In reality it only supports the experience of thousands of others, to whom the mental strength and elasticity acquired by the study of Latin and Greek proved the means of becoming successful men, and sometimes of attaining fame. Let the reader review the roll of honor in England, and where were her greatest statesmen, scholars, and scientists trained? At her great classical schools. What education prepared the political and intellectual heroes of Germany—a Stein, a Scharnhorst, a Metternich, a Bismarck, a Gœthe, a Lessing, a Schlegel, a Humboldt, a Liebig, a Ganss, a Kant, and a thousand others,—to achieve fame? The classical education of the Gymnasium. Who, aside from her military heroes, are the intellectual leaders of France? Ask her Bossuets, her Racines, her Corneilles, her Descartes, her La Places, her Mirabeaus, her Talleyrands, her Guizots, her Thiers, her Montalemberts, and her Lacordaires; they will tell you, the alumni of her classical schools. And here, in our country, most of those whom we honor as national benefactors, most of those in whose intellectual achievements we glory, grew up under like educational influences. Beginning with John Adams, we name Hamilton, Jefferson, Madison, John Quincy Adams, Webster, Calhoun, Van Buren, Sumner, Benton, Irving, Longfellow, Emerson, Hawthorne, Holmes. To-day, the American people, untrammeled as it is by traditions, and unfettered by prejudice in this regard, strong though be its leaning to the self-made candidates for political honors, numbers among its senators, its representatives, and its governors, an overwhelming proportion of college-bred men; that is to say, of men trained for their present positions by the study of Latin and Greek. Here, then, we have the experience of four nations, all tending to establish the same thesis, all bearing witness to the value of classical training.

For Greek, especially, we have another argument, also based on experience. Towards the end of the Middle Ages, Manuel Chrysoloras, at the invitation of the Signory of Florence, in 1396, introduced true Greek learning in Italy. The foremost Italian minds of that day, lay and clerical, flocked in swarms to become his scholars. They, in turn, became enthusiastic apostles of the newly-recovered learning, and thus greatly contributed to the intellectual movement called the Renaissance.

Now, in the opinion of those best fitted to judge in our age,— of men, too, of whom it would be presumptuous to say that they are not in sympathy with it,—what was the influence of the study of Greek in Italy and, through Italy, in Europe? Listen to Mr. J. Addison Symonds (" *Renaissance in Italy*," ii., p. 112): "The study of Greek implied the birth of criticism, comparison, research. . . . It stimulated the germs of science, suggested new astronomical hypotheses, and indirectly led to the discovery of America. The study of Greek resuscitated a sense of the beautiful in art and literature." Burckhardt, in his work on the " *Renaissance in Italy*," after insisting "that it was not the revival of antiquity alone, but its union with the genius of the Italian people, which achieved the conquest of the Western World" (vol. i., p. 239), remarks that "it is idle to ask if this cause (*i. e.*, humanism) ought not to have stopped short in its career of victory, to have restrained itself deliberately, and conceded the first place to purely national elements of culture." In his opinion, therefore, the national movement, the beginning of which was marked by the powerful genius of Dante, was not only modified, but to a certain extent overborne, by the new influence exerted by the study of classic literature, and especially by Greek. Lastly, Dr. Draper, in his "*Intellectual Development of Europe*" (p. 469), tells us that "Greek literature, forced into Italy by Turkish arms, worked wonders." Though, as a historian, Draper is far from being a model, yet we have cited his judgment as being that of a scientist, whom the modernists will certainly not charge with being behind the age. The study of Greek, consequently, was a powerful force, shaping the current of men's thoughts, developing their intellectual powers, and opening up new and correct views in literature and art. If it be true that the greatest works of man's genius in every branch of literature and science are undying in their influence, then Greek and its literature, though not to us a new revelation, as it was to the Italians of the fourteenth and fifteenth centuries, must still be endowed with potent mind-fashioning power.

So far Mr. Adams's argument from experience; his proposal to substitute for the study of the classics a practical command of the modern languages we shall say a word about later on. For the present, we shall turn to consider the objections made to the study of the classics by many scientific men. We say "many," because in Germany, in particular, some of the most distinguished representatives of science have raised their voices in favor of the old-time training. Nor does this surprise us. On the contrary, we are amazed at the attitude of a school of scientific men, of whom Professor Youmans, of the *Popular Science Monthly*, is a good type,—men who condemn not only the study of the classical language, but inform us that "no kind of culture degenerates so readily into stupid mechanical routine as that of language." (" *College Fetich,*" p. 70.) We are amazed at them, because, even as men of science, they, above all, should be the ardent champions of the study of language. They pose as the devoted students of nature, as the ardent advocates of all that familiarizes us with its phenomena. Of course, the higher something stands in the order of nature, the more claim it should have on their attention and to their enthusiastic study. Now, these gentlemen tell us that man stands at the head of all nature. They may be evolutionists, and trace man's pedigree through never-found links to the mere cell-beings, that differ but little from the slime of the earth,—all the same do they recognize man as nature's greatest and crowning achievement. Surely they should advocate, above all, the study of him who is the crown of nature and re-echo the poet's line:

"The proper study of mankind is man."

Above all, they should plead for the thorough, the loving study of that which, according to their own teaching, is the characteristic that distinguishes man from the brute, that which makes man a human being, namely, language. Where, then, should we look for stronger, warmer champions of the study of language than among the men of science? And, of course, among all languages they should single out that one as especially worthy of the most careful study which is acknowledged on all sides to be the most perfect in its structure,—the Greek. But the unexpected, we are told, always happens, and so we behold the very men denounce the study of language whom right logic would lead to recommend it above all others.

But what are the grounds of this opposition? the reader will naturally ask. Of course, those physicists who are broad-minded and clear-minded enough to see that nature does not end where it refuses to submit to the test of the balance, the microscope, and chemical reaction, cannot share in this opposition, for it is based largely upon the idea that language is something apart from, nay, almost opposed to, natural science. Only this explanation can account for such assertions as: "The old method (of education) occupied itself mainly with the study of language; the new method passed beyond language to the study of the phenomena of nature." As if language were an "unnatural" phenomenon. But let us hear the pundits of the *Popular Science Monthly.* "Professor Cooke," says Mr. Youmans, "struck the keynote of this discussion when he remarked in his article on the 'Greek Question' in the last *Monthly*: 'A half century has wholly changed the relations of human knowledge, and the natural sciences have become the chief factors of our modern civilization.'" "*Le roi est mort, vive le roi,*" is the shout of these gentlemen; and if lusty lungs and loud assurance could create facts, the reign of religion, of morality, and of law would be replaced by the reign of science, and the decalogue by dietetic prescriptions. We yield to no one in just and sincere admiration of the achievements of modern science. No one appreciates more fully the grand discoveries in astronomy made by means of the spectroscope and telescope, the wonderful revelations of the microscope, the striking progress in the philosophy of physics, and the remarkable engineering feats of our days. They have unveiled new marvels of the power and wisdom of God;

they have extended man's mental horizon; they have added new grandeur to his conceptions. But that, in consequence of these discoveries, law, morality, and religion have ceased to be the chief factors in our civilization, is a discovery far ahead of our age, and, we think, of any age. For we fail to see how the social fabric, or the political fabric, can ever be made to rest chiefly on the laws of natural science. Indeed, if we compare our civilization with that of fifty, or, to oblige the learned gentlemen of the *Popular Science Monthly*, of a hundred years ago, we fail to see any warrant for their proclamations. What was right then is looked upon as right now; and what was wrong then is still held to be wrong. Our ideas of property, of the rights of government and of the governed, are but little modified, and the changes again can neither be debited nor credited to natural science. Law and theology are studied very much as of yore, and even in medicine we see little, if any, change in the method of study. Above all, man's passions and feelings, his faith, hope, love, fear, envy, hate, and greed, are the same as of yore. It is true that we use lucifer matches, whereas our great-grandfathers used the flint, and that among us gas or electricity takes the place of sperm-oil and candle. It is true that, owing to the advance of agricultural chemistry and the progress of mechanical discovery, we reap fifty-fold where our grandfathers reaped ten-fold. It is true, in fine, that we move with a rapidity rivalling the winds, and dispatch our thoughts to great distances in a few instants. But all these things do not constitute human life, or human society; they influence human life and society in little more than their externals. And so with the grand assertion falls the grand inference, and the classics are safe, if Professor Cooke has struck the keynote of the "Greek Question."

Before dismissing Dr. Youmans we must, however, look into some few assertions with which he seeks to bolster up his cause. It seems extraordinary that an evolutionist should tell us that the new knowledge (natural science) came, not by the old method of study, but by new exercises of the mind, contracted with previous habits, when it is the cardinal principle of the evolutionists that the new is but the development of the old, and when it is a fact that long before Bacon of Verulam, and long before Youmans of New York, experiments and observations were made, verifications, inductions, and classifications worked out, and physical hypotheses constructed. It is not true that any absolutely new exercise of the mind gave rise to the new knowledge; but, as time rolled on, practice made perfect; there were more observations and experiments to be utilized, and new experiments were made in greater number; where one man cultivated the field of science before, a hundred do so now, and such drudgery is now spared to the really great man, and delegated to underlings. Hence the great and successful advance of modern science; the " brand-new " exercises of the mind exist in the cerebral convolutions of Professor Youmans.

Nor is it true, as Dr. Youmans says, that " the old method has for its end lingual (*sic*) accomplishments;" it is an unfounded assertion, and those who are acquainted with the course of history know well that no system, the end of which is even the prettiest and most skillful prattle and babble, and whose " results are barrenness," could last for four centuries. In further contrasting the old and the new method, Mr. Youmans implies that a scientific training especially, and far more than the classical education, fits the student for dealing with the problem of life. At first sight this appears plausible. The common mind, largely soaked in the material tendencies of the day, thinks at once of steam engines, artificial manure, new methods of lighting, of heating, of assaying, improvements in all kinds of manufactures. Science rises before him at once as the genie of fortune-making. And surely it would be the greatest rashness to deny that it has made—and, we may add, unmade—the fortunes of many. The effects it has produced are visible to the eye of the senses. But on the other hand, because they strike the eye of the senses they are likely to appear magnified and exaggerated, and this seems true also of the training acquired by natural science; its results are visible and material, and therefore impress the imagination far more vividly than the results of a classical or philosophical training, the results of which appear only to the eye of the intellect. Yet, after all, the activity which constitutes by far the greatest and most important portion of our lives, the actions on which depend the welfare and happiness of our family, our social and our political relations, lie almost wholly outside of the sphere of natural science. We love, and woo, and wed, and are not influenced in the slightest by considerations of brachycephalism or dolichocephalism; we choose our friends and never ask how much nitrogenous and how much albuminous food enters into their constitution; we choose our presidents and are astonished when their weight in avoirdupois is made a matter of discussion. In all these things what determines our selection are qualities beyond the reach of balance and microscope, and surely a mistake in the choice of a wife or of a friend is as likely to be serious as a lack of skill in determining plants, or insects, or minerals. Even to the business man, scientific knowledge is generally not of primary importance. No doubt, the brewer and sugar-refiner depend for their success largely on correct scientific methods, but when they manufacture, and above all when they sell their goods, much also depends on the right selection of their agents, and a correct judgment of the character of their customers. Indeed, it may be said without too much risk, that even to the sugar-refiner the knowledge of sugar is hardly more important than the knowledge of men. How to acquire this knowledge of men—what is the best means ? No doubt it is useful by means of scientific training to learn to make a skillful use of our eyes, our ears, our touch, our senses, in short. It is well to observe the physical phenomena about us, to notice the form, and color, and size, and weight of the plants and stones and animals around us. It is useful to group them by their resemblances and differences. But, after all, men do not act like sticks and stones, and the only way to learn to know man is to study man, and to study what is specially and characteristically human ; and here we are again led to the study of language and of the thoughts it embodies.

We see, then, that the study of natural science, which Professor Youmans and other no doubt well-meaning enthusiasts recommend as a substitute for the classical training, instead of developing all the student's faculties completely, develops only some of them, and those only inasmuch as they deal with the material world. The far more important world of mind and spirit this method neglects. Indeed, "natural science," says E. du Bois Reymond, a distinguished German scientific professor, "like every other activity so pursued, narrows the field of view. . . . . . Where it is exclusively dominant, the mind is apt to grow poor in ideas, the imagination in pictures, the soul in sensitiveness, and the result is a narrow, dry, and hard mode of thought deserted by the muses and the graces." Our friends of the *Popular Science Monthly* are themselves capital instances of this narrowing tendency of natural science when too exclusively pursued. All that is good they see in natural science, and outside of science nothing that is good. In their eyes not only the study of the classics, but the study of all language, degenerates into stupid mechanical routine. Contrast with this the broad, liberal spirit of the classicists. They were in sole undisputed possession of the academic field, when natural science first lifted up its head. They did not regard it as an enemy, nor as a rival, but as a fellow-laborer in the field of culture. They recognized that it developed a side of our mental activity untrained by classic studies, the power of observation by the senses; and, many years back, they gave to natural science a place beside the classic learning.

But it is time to see what the advocates of the old classic training have to say in its behalf, and to examine whether or what there is in the study of Latin or Greek that makes it an efficient instrument of mental training. By way of introduction, let us see

what is language, and of what service it is to the human mind.
Language, as all know, consists of words, and words are signs.
Signs of what? Of things? No; but of our ideas or conceptions
of those things. You may speak of "red," and I may speak of
"red," and yet we may speak of very different colors. To the
rude farmer a "scholar" is one thing, to the college professor another. To understand each other correctly, therefore, "men must
not only hear the sounds called words, but know what they represent in each other's minds, and, as much as possible, how far they
correspond to the things outside of their minds. Now, these words
with this double relation are most important to us all. By their
means we communicate with each other, and, if we observe the
workings of our minds, it will be found that by their means we
communicate with ourselves; that is to say, we think and judge
and reason mentally. Many ideas are almost begotten of their
word-signs, and most ideas are made clearer by them. We shall
not go so far as to say that we cannot think and reason at all without
words, but as a matter of fact we seldom do so. Without language
our mental activity would be exceedingly limited. Whether in
theology or philosophy, in science or art, or even in business,
words play an all-important role. In truth, to know precisely
what ideas correspond, and to know well the things which words
designate outside of the mind, would be to banish half of our mis-
understandings, and to accumulate vast stores of most solid and
practical knowledge. But it is not only the crude words that thus
reflect the workings of men's minds, but even their modifications,
their declensions and conjugations, their very position. All these
contribute to express our mental operations; not only our perceptions, but our judgments and our reasoning. Terminations and
prefixes are often marvellously subtle means to express certain conceptions. Take, for instance, the comparative suffix, *er*. To what
shifts must we resort to say, "James is taller than John," without
using the suffix, *er*, or the word, *more*, which contains that suffix.
In short, these words, with their grammatical modifications of
all sorts, are, so to say, audible photographs of the action of our
mind, that mind which is our intellectual life, the treasure-casket
of all our acquirements and enjoyments, and the God-given instrument whereby we are to support and defend ourselves. To
study language, then, is to study the science of the mind and its
intellectual operations; in other words, to study logic, and at the
same time to acquire mastery over an instrument absolutely necessary to success in our intercourse with our fellow-men.

There are two ways of learning a language,—1st, mechanically
and almost unconsciously, as the child does, and as some adults
learn foreign languages; and, 2d, scientifically or grammatically,

as we learn Latin and Greek at school. How much even the first method helps to unfold the mind, no one can fail to have noticed who has seen a child learn to prattle its mother-tongue. Every new word gained is an idea cleared up and stored away ready for use when needed. What was in a state of flux becomes fixed, and dreamy visions become well-defined knowledge. Then the first sentence becomes the stimulus to hundreds of others, each quickening and strengthening the budding power of judgment. But the child learns to speak by imitation and almost unconsciously. Because by this first method we learn languages unconsciously and by imitation, it has not a like stimulating power for elder children, or adults, in whom the first mental awakening has already taken place. No doubt even so it reveals new features in their mother-tongue, clearing up, limiting, and defining much that was blurred and indistinct. But, after all, the mechanical method of learning languages has, as chief result, the power to handle a new means of intercourse with others. Hence, too, we do not find that populations who have acquired this power—such as certain districts of Germany and Switzerland, on the French border—are noted for exceptional mental power or adroitness.

It is far different with the second or scientific method of acquiring a language. Show us a man who has learned not only to understand or speak a second language, but also to know why every word and every form are used, and we will show you a man with an active, open-eyed mind, who perceives rapidly, judges correctly, and reasons quickly. Why is this so? We have only to analyze his training to grasp the reason. Place before a student a moderately hard sentence in Latin or Greek. What will he do? Firstly, he observes the words composing it and notices their forms, picking out nouns and verbs and adjectives, identifying the cases and other accidents. What is this but cultivating the mind's powers of observation? Having finished his inspection, he addresses himself to the solution of the problem before him; for every sentence to be translated is a problem to be solved, in which the meaning is the unknown quantity. By reasoning on their forms, he infers that certain words belong together; he has recourse to the dictionary, and balances the *pros* and *cons* of the meanings there set down, and thus exercises his judgment. Next he proceeds to combine the subjects and predicates and the various clauses, until he arrives at the meaning sought for. But the end is not yet. He must now go back to the preceding sentence and look forward to the following one, in order to verify his translation. Thus the mere translation according to grammatical rule has called into play his powers of observation, of reasoning, of combination or invention, of judgment, and taught him that even then his results must be verified. In his reasoning, too, he will have occasions both for deductive argument and for induction; for every rule of grammar is the conclusion of an induction, and the proper way to teach the beginner the more common rules is to lead the pupil to notice the examples and to draw the rule as the inference. Again, by selecting his English words carefully, he gains a nicer and fuller insight into the power of his mother-tongue and its vocables; nay, at times, when he comes across words for which his own language has no equivalent, he has found an idea foreign to the genius of his own people, and thus he enlarges the field of his conceptions. As the sentences increase in difficulty, higher and higher powers of combination and invention, more delicate insight, more skillful reasoning, are called into play, and, moreover, the student's moral qualities are drawn upon. If he be made of the true metal, increasing difficulties will call forth not only subtler reasoning, greater versatility, and more ingenious combinations, but increasing determination, until, having triumphed over every obstacle, he tastes the sweets of intellectual conquests. To this add the power of expression gained by a faithful, close, idiomatic reproduction in the vernacular of the thoughts and language of the original; for, surely, if we can express the thoughts of others suitably and well, we will not fail in the expression of our own ideas. Finally, a really intelligent and complete translation of the original includes, of necessity, a reproduction of its literary beauties. Emphasis must be matched by emphasis, figure by figure, always having due regard to the genius of the mother-tongue. Adroitness of expression, logical force, pathetic power, sublimity,—all must be brought home to the translator's mind and copied in the version. Surely, such a course of drill repeated again and again on different subject-matter cannot fail to nurture the student's literary taste, to enliven his imagination, to vivify and brace his logical faculty. All these advantages are derived from a mere careful and intelligent translation. But to master fully his author, the student must understand all the allusions which he meets with, be they in the domain of history, geography, archæology, ethnology, customs, laws, religion, art, or science. A loving study of all these features will confer new interest on the writer, will enable the scholar really to understand the people whose literature he peruses, broaden his mind and widen his sympathies, so that even when, in later life, he becomes a specialist, he will not be a narrow-minded one, but will always feel that, though to him his profession goes above every other, there is no profession, no branch of human knowledge, that has not its attractions, that does not render service to mankind.

And here it may be well to state that of late more and more

stress has been laid on these historical features of classic study. Look at a Latin or Greek text-book of to-day, and you will be struck at once with the wealth of illustrations that adorn it. Works of ancient art, homely tools, musical instruments, portraits of old heroes, arms, plans of battle, all contribute to clear up the text, to interest the scholar, to inspire him with a taste for art and history, and to store his mind with a living knowledge that will leaven his intellectual life, and be a source of enjoyment and advantage for the rest of his days.

Such, then, are some of the benefits to be reaped from a thorough, loving study of the classics. But, it may be asked: Could not like benefits be derived from a study of modern languages? For ourselves, we have a high estimate of the practical value of the modern languages to the man of letters as well as to the business man. Nor is this wonderful; it may be said to be a tradition among educated Catholics. For as long back as thirty years ago there was hardly a Catholic college in the land in which a course of French or German was not an integral part of the academic curriculum. Still, if, as is admitted on all sides, the training and drill of the mental powers be the end of higher education, it must be confessed that, in this respect, the modern languages are not the peers of the classical languages. Why not? If, as Mr. Adams wishes, they are to be learned so as to be spoken fluently, then they must be learned mostly on the imitative plan, and that, as we have shown above, does not, and cannot, develop our mental faculties as the scientific study of language does. But even if studied on the same plan as the classics are taught, they are far inferior to the latter for purposes of intellectual drill. For, in the first place, they are far easier. Their constructions, and their accidence, or rather lack of accidence, are largely cut after the same pattern. Rarely, very rarely, will the student be called upon to invent and try combination after combination in order to find the meaning of a sentence, rarely to cultivate that intellectual dash, determination, and perseverance that are such admirable means of shaping the character. A great number of the forms having died out in the modern languages, words belonging together are always placed near each other, and hence the scholar need not be constantly on the alert to discover the endings that show which words go together. Besides, the very fact that these languages are close to ours in time, in degree, character of culture, and often, to a great extent, in vocabulary, leave them less to teach us than a language remote from ours in all these respects. We must, therefore, conclude that their very difficulty makes the classic tongues more powerful means of drilling the mind, more fitting instruments of education. We may, indeed, never learn to read Greek as fluently

as German, and yet derive more profit therefrom.   But the greater
ease with which we read modern languages is often only apparent.
Thousands hear Shakespeare performed at the theatre, and go
away convinced that they have understood him throughout.
Thousands read the bard of Avon in their closet, they pass from
page to page, and seldom or never meet with a stumbling-block.
And yet how many passages have not puzzled, and do not to this
day, after centuries of research and volumes of commentaries,
puzzle the Shakespeare scholar.   In like manner, in reading French
or German, the general parallelism of construction in these languages with the English construction makes it needless to be too
precise in looking up words and forms; we quickly catch the
general meaning, and often make conjecture take the place of
scientific study.   Thus is generated in us gradually a sense that
we understand when we do not understand, that we know when
we know not.   A dangerous, unscientific, self-inflating, self-deceiving
state of mind.   To this temptation the student of the classics is
rarely exposed; even in later life there is no danger of such self-
deception, as appears so clearly from Mr. Adams's account of
his grandfather's Greek experiment in old age.   In reading the
classics, any scholar of average intelligence will be in no doubt
whether he knows or does not know.   The Delphic Apollo declared Socrates the wisest of the Greeks because he knew that he
did not know; to know that they do not know is denied to many
modern oracles, who would do well to have recourse to the
classics.

We cannot do better than to reinforce these remarks by citing
the opinion of one of the foremost scholars and thinkers of Germany, Professor Zeller, of Berlin, on the educational value of Latin
and Greek.   "Latin grammar," says Zeller, "by its strictness and
logical correctness, is as excellent a means for the general training
of the mind as Roman law is for its juridical training, and, in this
respect, it can no more be replaced by any modern language than
the pandects can be replaced by the *Code Napoléon.*   The Greek
language combines, with the transparency of its logico-grammatical
structure, wealth of words, mobility of construction, the power to
accommodate itself to every need of expression, a full and clear
formation of its sentences, and a euphony, which is as unique as is
the classic perfection of Greek art.   All the mental faculties and
powers, which the formation of language demands and the study
of language develops, are equally stimulated by the Greek tongue."
And here we may suggest the answer to a riddle that greatly
puzzles Professor Youmans and his friends: "How could the
Greeks, who studied no foreign language, arrive at such perfection
in almost every branch of literature and thought?"   Because they

learned and spoke and studied the Greek language. Were the modern languages as perfect images of all that is logical in the human mind as the Greek, were they as rich in inflections, had they the same subtle means of expressing the most refined shades of thoughts and the nicest modes of action, the same capacity to form compounds, the same mobility of construction and adaptability,—qualities which, while adding to the power of expression, demand close attention, logic and precision of mind, insight into the relations of the various thoughts composing a sentence, a fine sense of their relative importance, and an ear sensitive to the most delicate harmonies of language,—then, indeed, we might achieve what the Greeks accomplished without having recourse to any language but our own mother tongue.

That the classics are superior for mind-training purposes to natural science and the modern languages, does not lack the support of practical experience. Many years back there were established in Germany, along-side of the old-time *gymnasium*, the curriculum which consists mainly of classical and mathematical studies, a new kind of high-schools called *Realschulen*, destined to prepare young men for commercial pursuits or the polytechnic schools. Their course was gradually enlarged until it occupied the same length of time as that of the gymnasium. The chief differences between the two classes of schools was that the *Realschulen* discarded the study of Greek wholly and lessened the Latin instruction, these branches being replaced by additional time given to mathematics, natural science, and the modern languages. The graduates of the *Realschulen* were at first debarred from entrance to the university. About 1870, in spite of protests from several sources, the Prussian government ordered that these graduates be admitted to the philosophical department of the universities. Henceforth the graduates of both classes of schools worked side by side, and afforded an excellent opportunity to compare the relative merits of the classical and the modern training. In 1880, after a ten years' trial, the philosophical faculty of the University of Berlin reported to the minister of Public instruction its opinion on the question whether the graduates of the *Realschulen* were fitted to pursue a university course with the *gymnasium*-graduates. It was decidedly adverse to the efficiency of the modern training in developing and drilling the mind and its powers. Even the representatives of science and the modern languages in the Faculty joined heartily in this judgment. The science professors reported that the *Realschulen*, though starting with more extensive knowledge of their subjects than their classically trained fellow students, soon fell behind the latter. In specifying the deficiencies of the students trained by the modern system, the various instructors complain of their dulness of comprehension, their lack of independent judgment, of a clear consciousness of their own scientific capacity and of sure insight into the growth of man's mental life, their want of self-knowledge and their defective power of expression; the very results we should expect from our analysis of the two systems. Attempts have not been wanting to belittle this experiment. It has been said that the experiment, being concrete, did not affect the abstract question of the superiority of classics or science; but all experiments are concrete, and their concreteness does not destroy their value; it only requires us to be careful in interpreting their results. The honesty, or rather the impartiality, of the respective professors has been questioned; though it seems strange that thirty-six gentlemen of various pursuits, which would naturally lead them to take different views on the question submitted, gentlemen famed for their insight and their integrity, should all be stricken by the same prejudice. And if it be true that the *gymnasia* have the advantage of greater age, the upholders of the *Realschulen*, as well as their chosen instructors, should naturally shine by their greater enthusiasm in a new cause. Certainly this experiment, as well as the experience of the past three centuries, totally subverts the position of the anti-classical radicals of the Youmans type, confirms the arguments that have been presented above, and warns us not to give up what, tested by experience, has proved useful, and fly to ills we know not of.

We have sought above to convey an imperfect idea of the peerless qualities of the Latin and especially the Greek, as instruments of training the faculties of the mind. But the study of the classics bestows advantages of a different kind on the scholar. We all know the great educational benefit derived from travel, how it opens and stimulates the mind, how it broadens our views and removes prejudice, and finally how, whilst it excites our admiration of what is good in foreign lands, it also confirms our love of home and country. A classical course is in reality an excursion into a different world, the world of the ancients, and affords us most of the educational advantages which intercourse with the best and wisest people in foreign lands would confer. This consideration alone will explain why men with a classic training are so much less narrow minded than those without this advantage. Besides, we must not forget that our travels are most productive of intellectual fruit, if they take us, not to lands and nations most like our own, but among peoples as unlike ourselves as possible, provided, of course, that they are bright and cultivated and enlightened. Hence, we shall gather more fruit from the study of Latin and Greek than we could reap from the study of modern literature; for whilst more remote from us in time and place, the Greeks were superior to modern nations in brightness and culture, and above all in freshness of intellect.

One more argument, and a weighty one, must be presented in favor of the maintenance of the classical studies. No man, it will be allowed on all hands, can truly lay claim to be educated unless he understands, if not perfectly, at least measurably well, the nature, the source, the rise, and the development of our present civilization. To such an understanding it is of great importance that the student should have investigated with especial care and minuteness the sources and early course of that stream of culture which has come down to us so wonderfully widened and deepened. As the direction and force and character of our rivers is largely determined by the physical peculiarities of the land in which is their source, so the current of human civilization greatly depends for its power, tendency, and results, on the places and peoples where they rise. Now, aside from religion, which, heaven-sent, came to us from the East, all the other elements of our culture must be traced back to the Greeks and Romans. To the latter, of whose national mind their language, with its strict rules, is the perfect image, we moderns owe the basis and principles of our law; for, without the Roman law, neither the German law, which is its direct offspring, nor the common law of England, nor yet the *Code Napoléon*, would be possible. From the Greeks, on the other hand, we have received an almost controlling impulse in philosophy, in the plastic arts and in literature, as well as the beginnings of our science, our medicine, and our music. Of most of these varied branches of human learning this wonderful people laid the foundation, at least in their literary and artistic form; many they carried to a marvellous degree of perfection. In philosophy, for instance, many of the latest modern schools are, after all, nothing but revivals of long-abandoned Greek systems, and in the belles-lettres, and in art, it would be rash to say that the nineteenth century, with the example of Greece, and the experience of two thousand years to guide it, has equalled, much less surpassed, old Hellas. But it is useless to dilate on what all men of culture know and admit. It may be asked: Cannot we acquaint ourselves with these masterpieces of Greek genius, and thus understand the sources of our culture, by means of translations? We might almost as well ask: Can marble, even if carved by the hands of Phidias or Michel Angelo, can any material but flesh and blood, give us an adequate, or, for that matter, an approximate idea of the living, breathing human being? Our modern hard, mechanical forms of speech can never reproduce the original, or convey to one unacquainted with the Greek, even a faint idea of what Homer, and Sophocles, and Aristophanes really are. Moreover, in the translation we have the ancient author filtered through a modern mind, a process that must inevitably destroy much of the ancient fragrance, and give to the product an incongruous flavor of modernism. No; the only way really to understand the ancients is to go to the ancients themselves, to study the classic languages and literature. If we do so, Rome will reveal to us the genius which made her the lawgiver of the civilized world; and Greece bestow on us what she bestowed on victorious Rome when the latter sat down at the feet of conquered Hellas, and what she bestowed a second time on the modern world in the fifteenth and sixteenth centuries. The Catholic Church has always rated the classic learning, Greek no less than Latin, at its true value. In the days of the revival of learning, under such Pontiffs as Nicholas V. and Leo X., the Church was the foremost patron of the classics. To-day, whilst with the elasticity given to her by her divine Founder she urges upon her bishops and priests the cultivation of true science, true to her usual conservatism when there is question of what is right and good, she stands forth the champion of classic learning. Disappointed railroad men may join with too enthusiastic advocates of science in denouncing the study of the Greek. American bishops recommend the study of science, but at the same time decree that their theological students shall prove that they have enjoyed the advantages of a thorough training in Greek classics. The reason is not far to seek. The Church alone, in the nineteenth century, free from its spirit of unrest, judges old and new alike, according to their merits.

THE HOLY FACE OF LUCCA.

FEW things are more remarkable in the Italy of the present day than the difference between the government and the mass of the people in their attitude towards religion. To judge by the Parliamentary debates at Monte Citorio or the common course of the higher officials, one would be inclined to think that hostility to the Church was the dominant feeling of the nation. To mix with the people, more especially in the country districts, and observe the hold which religion has on every part of their daily life, and how their feelings and faith alike cling to its observances, one would say that devotion to Catholicity was their most marked national characteristic. In Italy, as in some other countries, the politicians are one thing and the people another. How it happens, in countries possessing representative institutions, that an active minority, often insignificant in its numbers, should be able to shape the policy of the government in opposition to the feelings and wishes of the people, we do not propose to discuss here. That it often does so happen in other countries as well as in Italy, is an undoubted fact. Even American communities, with which the charge of indifference to their own interests is not usually connected, have found themselves fleeced with impunity by small gangs of audacious politicians, whom they were powerless to shake off. We might as fairly charge the New York taxpayers with sympathy for the extortion inflicted on them by political rings, as assume that the Italian people sympathize with the anti-Catholic policy of their government. At the present day, as in former times, it is round the Church that the popular national life of Italy really centres. Her shrines are still the chief centres of art; her festivals are celebrated with an enthusiastic devotion in striking contrast with the popular indifference towards the official public displays, or the noisy demonstrations of political partisans, and her influence is willingly recognized in all the events of the popular daily life. Thus it may often happen that a deputy is denouncing the Church as the national enemy in the Assembly at Monte Citorio, while the district he is supposed to represent is solemnizing a Church festival with the most enthusiastic devotion. Such demonstrations are a prominent feature of Italian life at the present day as in the past. A striking instance was the centenary of the Holy Face celebrated in the September of 1882 in the ancient city of Lucca.

Among the many shrines of Catholic devotion in Italy, few,

except Loreto itself, are more honored than that which is known as of the Holy Face (Santo Volto) of Lucca. The crucifix which bears that name is a work of the earliest times of Christianity, if it is not, indeed, the very first work of Christian art. In its present abode its history goes back almost to the beginning of the Middle Ages, before most of the modern nations of Europe had come into existence, or Charlemagne had been crowned Emperor of the West. From Palestine, where it had been made, it was transported to Italy in 782, and thus, in September, 1882, it was the eleventh centenary of its installment that was celebrated in Lucca. What the fountain of Lourdes is to our own times, the crucifix of Lucca was to mediæval Europe during many centuries. From every part of Italy, as well as from the countries beyond the Alps, pilgrims flocked thither in thousands, and its fame was spread throughout Christendom. Popes and emperors came to pay their devotions before it. Its name was honored by chapels and altars in the most distant countries, France, Spain, Germany, Bohemia, Flanders; and even the distant regions of Northern · Europe, Poland and Lithuania, thus testified their veneration through a long series of ages. The Abbey of St. Denis, the first of the great Gothic buildings of France, contained an altar dedicated to the Holy Face of Lucca in the early Middle Ages, and similar shrines yet exist in Vienna, Madrid, Bruges, and many other cities of Catholic Europe. Students of English history may recall that it was "by the Holy Face of Lucca" that the half infidel king, William Rufus, gave the most solemn attestation of his often-doubted pledges, during his bitter quarrel with St. Anselm. In Italy, its own seat, the veneration for the miraculous crucifix was almost unbounded. Its name was a household word in daily devotion, and Lucca and its crucifix were inseparably united in the public mind. Dante in his great poem speaks of it as familiarly as he does of the baptistery of his native Florence, and St. Catherine of Sienna records her deep devotion to it in the most heartfelt terms. The Republic of Lucca, from the eleventh century, stamped its representation on its coinage, which continued to bear it long after the independence of the city had passed away, and it was only removed by the late government of Tuscany the year before its own downfall.

At the present day, though the " Holy Face " has been removed from the ensigns of government, it has lost nothing of the veneration with which it has ever been regarded by the people. Twice in the year, in May and September, it is exposed to the public gaze, and each time it receives fresh demonstrations of the popular devotion. During the rest of the year it is closely veiled, and even its chapel is locked and carefully guarded; but the occasions of its opening are the most cherished festivals of the whole population of the province as well as of the city. In the approach of danger, or the pressure of misfortune, it is the centre to which individuals and the public alike come to seek the divine protection. A massive gold lamp, hanging before the door of its shrine, testifies to the faith of the city which, in our own times, offered it as a public expiation to avert the visitation of cholera with which Lucca was threatened. But a proof more striking by far than any material offerings, however rich, of the veneration in which the sacred crucifix is held by all classes of the population, even after the changes of more than a thousand years, was given by the wide enthusiasm and intense devotion displayed at the festival of September, 1882.

The fourteenth of September, the day known in the Calendar as the Exaltation of the Cross, is the great festival of the year in the sanctuary at Lucca. On the late occasion, however, a single day was wholly too little for the popular celebration, which extended over five days, from the Sunday preceding the anniversary. To a stranger, the scene all through was most remarkable. On the Saturday evening the preparations began through the province. Every village and hill-top around the ancient city was brilliantly illuminated as far as could be seen from the city walls, which now serve the peaceful purpose of a popular promenade. The varied effects produced by the fires, which, in some places, wound up the sides of the hills like glittering serpents, in others blazed up in masses of such dimensions as to suggest a great conflagration; while each village was marked by peculiar arrangements of its own illuminations, and the colors of its lights were wonderful. The church bells were vigorously sounded everywhere, and were mingled with the discharge of muskets and small cannon and the constant display of rockets and other fireworks to break the silence of the night. Every one seemed awake and on foot, both in city and country, and no American Fourth of July could surpass the enthusiasm everywhere displayed. At an early hour of the following morning, bands of pilgrims from the country round began to pour into the city on their way to the Cathedral, where the sacred image was to be exposed to the public veneration. Confraternities of both men and women, representatives of trades and factories, and parochial and village deputations, each numbering from fifty or sixty up to three or four hundred, continued to arrive in succession, all walking in regular order, and chanting hymns or else reciting the rosary aloud. The Cathedral, in spite of its size, was soon densely filled, and all the other churches of the city were called into requisition to contain the numerous worshippers both from town and country. The High Mass at the Cathedral, which was celebrated by the Archbishop, commenced at seven o'clock, and was followed by a general Communion. So great was the number approaching the rails that the Archbishop and two assistants were engaged in administering the Holy Sacrament for fully an hour and a half, though many had already received without waiting for the conclusion of the mass. The crowds in the various parochial churches were, in proportion, scarcely less dense than in the Cathedral, and in all the spirit of devotion on the part of the congregations was equally well marked. After the close of the Communion the sacred image was unveiled to the popular view; and from that time until late in the afternoon, its chapel was constantly filled by bands of pilgrims succeeding one another in orderly rotation and all displaying the strongest marks of devotion. Each deputation made an offering at the shrine, which usually took the form of a quantity of wax candles for use in the ceremonial, though offerings in money were made by some parishes. Chalices, medals, and other votive gifts in gold or silver, to be used or suspended in the sanctuary, were also presented by some of the pilgrims. Amongst others, the operatives of a woollen factory in the city presented a frame containing a golden crucifix and two medals, the employees of the tobacco manufactory a frame containing the letters Alpha and Omega in gold relief, and a village deputation offered two silver lamps. Shortly after five in the afternoon, the Coadjutor Bishop of San Miniato, near Florence, mounted the pulpit and preached at length on the subject of the Holy Face and its relations to Christian art, to history, and to religion. The ordinary prayers of the Triduo were recited at half-past six, after which the crucifix was covered, and the religious ceremonies closed for the night. The whole proceedings were marked by the utmost order and solemnity, and it was impossible not to recognize the thoroughly religious spirit which pervaded the crowds engaged in them all through the day. Clergy and laity, city and country alike, seemed wholly engrossed in the religious exercises.

On Monday, instead of lessening, the throng of pilgrims seemed to increase. Their bands were arriving incessantly, with chanting of hymns and recitation of prayers, and taking their way to the Cathedral. Nor was the pilgrimage for many of these villagers by any means a mere pleasure promenade. Some deputations were travelling the whole night on foot, and that, too, while the rain came down in torrents. But wet or dry, tired or fresh, the newcomers bent their way towards the Cathedral, and there, sometimes, had to wait long for the time of their admission to the oratory of the sacred crucifix. There was no uncertainty about the earnestness of devotion of these Luccese countrymen and women. They came to perform a solemn religious act, not as a matter of recreation however innocent, and they cheerfully faced the troubles that awaited them. The confessionals were thronged in all the churches of the city. The crowds coming in from the country to the festival filled all the hotels and private lodgings, and many were unable to obtain beds at any price. Still, the following days showed no falling off in the number of the visitors, which was greatest on the final day of the celebration.

The order observed on the three days between the opening Sunday and the concluding day of the festival, was much the same throughout. The image was uncovered at an early hour of the morning, and each succeeding half hour was set apart during the day for particular villages or parishes. However, the number of the pilgrim bands was too large to be all thus provided for; so, occasionally, two deputations entered the chapel together. The number of delegations that arrived was little short of forty a day, often numbering three or four hundred persons each. All brought offerings, most commonly wax lights and flowers, with occasional votive gifts of gold or silver, and also money at times, though rarely. On each day a pontifical high mass was sung at half-past ten by one of the neighboring bishops, and vespers were chanted at four in the afternoon, after which followed a sermon and subsequently the prayers of the Triduo, after which the crucifix was covered for the night.

The villages around had been the most prominent actors in the outdoor rejoicings on the first day; but on the eve of the great day the citizens of Lucca itself began their display. Public illuminations of the walls and streets were ordered by the municipality, and many of the private citizens prepared to take part in the work by decorations of an elaborate character. Transparencies of the sacred image were to be seen everywhere, and devices of various kinds in gas, colored lanterns, and electric lights were brought into requisition to do honor to the occasion. Unfortunately, the weather was awfully bad. Incessant rains and high winds, though they did not prevent the influx of the country visitors, compelled a postponement of the municipal illuminations and also diminished considerably the private displays. After vespers on Wednesday a public procession was organized in the Church of San Frediano, which proceeded to the Cathedral to offer the homages of the city to the Almighty at the sacred shrine. Cardinal Martinelli, three archbishops, and five bishops, with the canons of the Cathedral and the members of the other collegiate chapters of the city, took part in the procession. The decorations of the Cathedral itself were of the most elaborate kind. In Italian fashion the walls and the fronts of galleries were covered with hangings of rich materials, and the ordinary lights were increased by numerous chandeliers and lamps.

The chapel in which the crucifix hung was a perfect sea of light, as the procession approached it through the densely packed congregation.   The sacred music all through the festival, though somewhat florid to a northern taste, was of a high order of excellence, as might, indeed, be expected in Italy.

The chapel in which the sacred crucifix is preserved is erected within the Cathedral in the northern aisle.   Its form is octagonal, with columns of the composite order wrought of the purest white marble at each angle.   The columns stand on a plinth of the same material, inlaid with a band of red porphyry.   Three doorways, filled with iron gates of an elaborate pattern, and two windows occupy five of the eight sides.   Two of the remainder are filled with slabs of red marble covered with inscriptions, but on the exterior of the side behind the crucifix is a marble statue of the marytr St. Sebastian attached to the trunk of a tree.   Above the columns runs a cornice of classical outline, having its friezes richly decorated with festoons and masks of marble.   The parapets above the cornice are in the form of semicircular shells, behind and above which the roof rises in a dome surmounted by a tall lantern of octagonal shape.   The sides of the lantern are occupied by long windows, and the top is crowned by a ball and cross.   Though rich and varied, there is nothing of the rococo style of ornament to mar the beauty of this graceful edifice.   The latter part of the fifteenth century, in which it was built, was perhaps the best period of modern Italian architecture, alike removed from the slavish adherence to purely classical forms of Renaissance art, and from the extravagance that marked the work of its immediate successors.   The richness of the materials used throughout is peculiarly Italian, and gives the whole the appearance of a giant reliquary.   The dome is covered with plates of majolica of various colors and designs. The shell-shaped lunettes above the cornice, and the moulded ribs of the dome are richly gilt, as well as the volutes in the composite capitals of the columns and the mouldings of the cornice, their metallic lustre contrasting with the pure white and deep red of the marbles below.   The interior of the chapel is even richer than the outside, especially in the variety of its marble lining.   The sense of beauty in color, and the skill to apply it harmoniously to building, has alway been common in Italy to a much greater extent than in the other countries of Europe. It finds abundant play in this shrine. The pavement is tessellated with marbles whose names are scarcely known to northern builders, as the green marble of Genoa, the yellow of Surina, and red porphyry.   Gold is abundatly used on the walls, yet not so as to hide the beauty of the marble panellings. The altar is a table of Silician jasper, upheld at the sides by kneeling angels in gilt bronze. The steps above the altar table are of the purest oriental alabaster.

The popular enthusiasm reached its height on the anniversary day. The high mass was sung by Cardinal Martinelli, and the vespers in the afternoon by the bishop of Massa Carrara. The country deputations continued to arrive after the high mass, as on the former days, in spite of the rain. The festival was closed at half-past seven by a *Te Deum*, chanted by alternate choirs; but even after this the illuminations, which had been abandoned the day before, prolonged the excitement to a late hour of the evening. Nothing occurred to mar the harmony of the proceedings throughout the festival, which showed so strikingly the hold which Catholicity has on the Italian people, even amid the revolutions that have agitated their land in recent years.

The celebrated crucifix, the anniversary of whose arrival in Lucca so many centuries ago was thus honored by the entire population, is indeed a most striking object even apart from its historical associations. Its form is altogether peculiar, and bears no resemblance to any known school of art, yet its singular beauty leaves a deep impression on every beholder. The figure of our Lord is life-size and clothed with a tunic of eastern fashion reaching to the ankles and wrists, the whole carved of cedar wood, and fastened with nails to a cross of planks not much higher or wider in the arms than the figure. The ends of the top and arms of the cross are widened into circles, and the feet, instead of being crossed, as in most modern examples, are nailed separately to the shaft. There is no inscription above the head, but a circular band is attached to the back of the cross, almost in the form of the well-known Celtic crosses of Ireland. The circle, however, in this case, is not complete, but the lower ends of the band are terminated in the form of fleurs de lis near the sides of the figure. In some other details the execution of the crucifixion is also peculiar. The arms are extended at full length at right angles to the body, and, what is more remarkable, the head is not encircled with the crown of thorns, which are never absent from the crucifixes of modern patterns. It may be remembered that though the Gospel speaks of the crowning with thorns of our Lord and of his going forth so crowned to be shown to the people, it makes no mention of his having continued to wear the thorny crown during his agony on the cross. The most ancient crucifixes were without it, although a later custom has made it appear almost essential. The hair of the crucifix of Lucca flows down in long waves on the shoulders and on the cheeks, the separated locks meeting below the chin. But it is, above all, the face which rivets the attention and commands an involuntary reverence by its strange and awful beauty.

The eyes are partly open, the lips closed, but not compressed, and the whole expression so full of life and of a wonderful combination of sorrow and suffering with divine power as to be perfectly startling. We know of nothing to compare with it in the whole of sacred art, and as we gaze on it we perceive the full fitness of the feeling which gave to the sacred image its name of the Holy Face.

Such as has been described is the crucifix of Lucca in its original condition; but as it appears in its shrine at present, it is covered with ornaments offered by the devotion of successive ages. The head is encircled with a gold crown, richly jewelled, which was solemnly put on in 1655, and a collar of similar design was, at a later period, placed around the neck with a breast-plate thickly set with diamonds dependent from it. The figure is, moreover, covered with a close-fitting dress of black velvet, richly plated with gold ornaments which form a girdle round the waist and a heavy fringe at the bottom. The feet, in which the color of the wood is still preserved with wonderful freshness, are cased in silver slippers having crosses on top, which are kissed by the pilgrims on solemn occasions, as the cross is during the devotions of Good Friday, in all Catholic churches. A silver cup or chalice is placed on the step of the altar below the feet. Maniples, richly embroidered with gold, have been placed on the arms. The workmanship of all these ornaments is of the most artistic kind, and they are valuable as evidences of the popular devotion; but it may be open to question whether the effect produced by the beauty of the statue itself is in any way enhanced by its extrinsic decorations.

Great, however, as is the interest which attaches to this crucifix, for its strange form and extraordinary beauty, it is as nothing in comparison to the historical associations which surround it and connect its origin with the very foundations of Christianity. According to the general belief, the Holy Face is no merely artistic conception, however grand, but a faithful representation of the lineaments of our Lord as He hung on the Cross on Calvary. The hand which carved it was guided by actual recollections of the most familiar kind, and was, indeed, that of one who actually aided in taking down our Lord's body and laying it in the tomb from which He was to rise triumphant on the Third Day. Its reputed artist is no other than that Nicodemus who, with Joseph of Arimathea, obtained the privilege of giving burial to our Lord's body from Pilate, and whose interview by night with our Saviour, at an early time of His mission, is recorded by St. John. After the Resurrection, Nicodemus, having incurred the hostility of his fellow-countrymen on account of his adherence to our Lord, retired to the village of Ramleh, in Palestine, and, during his residence there, he was inspired to preserve in wood the features of his Master as they had been indelibly stamped on his memory on Calvary. The hostility of the Jewish population, alike to Christianity and to art, naturally suggested a considerable degree of secrecy, both in the execution and subsequent preservation of such a work. Accordingly, though the belief in its existence was widely spread among the Christians of Syria, its place of concealment, during many ages, was known only to a very few guardians. The custody of the sacred relic was handed down from generation to generation without enlarging the circle of those in the secret. The long continued persecutions of the Roman emperors and the subsequent Arian hostility to the Catholic Christians, as well as the invasions of the Persians and the Saracen conquest of Palestine, in the seventh century, all contributed to maintain the concealment of this earliest work of Christian art down to the close of the eighth century.

Such is the early history of the famous crucifix as preserved by tradition. Containing much that is strange, it offers nothing inconsistent with the natural course of human events, and the amount of credibility which attaches to it must be determined by external evidence. It is different with the evidence itself, which involves events of a wholly supernatural character connected with its arrival at the place, so far removed from its origin, where it has now been enshrined for eleven centuries. The degree of credit to be attached to its early history, thus shrouded in eight centuries of concealment, must of course depend on the miraculous character of those events which in its case take the place of the ordinary historical proofs. In the same way as the miracles that are now being performed at Lourdes are fairly regarded as proofs of the vision of the Blessed Virgin to the peasant girl of the Pyrenees, which preceded and foretold their occurrence, so the truth of the visions which revealed the origin of the crucifix of Lucca, as it has been just told, must rest on the evidence of the miracles which followed in direct connection with them. At this point again the ordinary rules of human evidence are called in. An undoubted supernatural manifestation of the divine power is the strongest proof that can be offered of the truth of any statement, but the fact that such a manifestation has been actually made in a past age, or in a distant place, can only be established by the common laws of human evidence. That an occurrence is an extraordinary one, warrants a stricter inquiry into the evidence on which it rests; but if that is found satisfactory, it furnishes no reason for rejecting it. On this principle, conformable alike to Catholic faith and common sense, we shall first describe the events which accompanied the arrival of the celebrated image in Italy, and afterwards examine the evidence of their actual occurrence supplied us by history.

The history of the removal of the crucifix from Palestine to Lucca is told by Leboin, a writer of the eighth century, who himself took part in it during a pilgrimage to the Holy Land, whither he accompanied the Piedmontese Bishop Gualfrid, in 782. Leboin was archdeacon of the diocese, and his work, of which copies exist in numerous libraries at Rome, Paris, Padua, and elsewhere, was written at the time when the occurrences were before the public mind, in a manner which precluded the possibility of a false statement of facts. According to Leboin, Gualfrid, during his visit to Jerusalem, was directed by an angel to go to the house of a Christian there, and obtain the image long concealed in a grotto beneath. At the same time he was informed of its history and origin such as has already been told. Gualfrid accordingly went to the place indicated, accompanied by his companions in the pilgrimage, and with much difficulty was admitted to the hidden crypt by its guardian. The Bishop and his companions finally induced the latter to resign its charge to them that it might be exposed to public veneration in a safer place. The difficulty of transporting it in safety was, however, so great that after long and anxious consultation, its new possessors took the resolution of placing it in a covered boat, and sending it adrift on the Mediterranean in the confident hope that the same power which had made its existence known to them would guide it to the place chosen by Providence for its reception. The crucifix was accordingly carried down to the small port of Jaffa, where the bishop procured a boat, within which the precious relic was placed, amid numerous lights and ornaments. The hatches were then planked over, and the whole exterior covered with pitch in imitation of the ark of Noah. The boat was set adrift, amid the prayers of the pilgrims. It at once took a rapid course, as if guided by a superhuman power, and was soon lost to the view of the Bishop and his companions.

Unguided by human means, the boat with its freight passed in safety from Jaffa to the shores of Tuscany, where it appeared before the port of Luni, a now ruined town. There it halted as strangely as it had arrived, and made no approach to the port, though both wind and tide combined to carry it in. The fishermen of Luni put off to board the strange craft, but during two days it baffled their approach as if by instinct. The Lombard governor of the town was soon informed of the extraordinary vessel on which no person appeared, and which yet seemed to move self-guided in utter indifference to the force of wind or waves; but neither he nor the municipality could form any idea of its meaning. They were suddenly surprised by the arrival of the Bishop of Lucca, accompanied by a large number of the clergy and citizens of that place. The Bishop had received a supernatural warning of the arrival of the hitherto unknown image, and a description of its character and origin similar to that previously given to the pilgrims in Palestine. The Lunese were still engaged in their fruitless efforts to seize the vessel, but either in despair of success, or out of respect for the words of the Bishop of Lucca, they gave up the attempt, and allowed the Bishop and his companions to advance in procession to the edge of the sea. The vessel, which had hitherto kept off in spite of the power of the elements, now immediately approached the shore. The deck, when opened, showed the sacred crucifix and some other relics, such as the Bishop of Lucca had been informed of them by his previous vision. One of these relics, a vase, containing the sacred blood of our Lord, was presented to the Bishop of Luni. The crucifix itself was borne in solemn procession to Lucca, and there installed in the church of St. Martin, on the northern side of the basilica, in the year 782.

The account given by Leboin, from which the foregoing history of the arrival of the crucifix in Lucca has been drawn, bears in itself strong evidences of truth. He carefully distinguishes between the facts which he had himself seen, and those which he had learned by hearsay from the Syrians, and he hides nothing of certain occurrences which were likely to excite considerable animadversion at the time. The piratical habits of the Lunese, who, like the Cornish fishermen of a century ago, were wont to regard wrecked vessels as lawful booty, and also the threats used by some of Bishop Gualfrid's companions towards the Syrian guardian of the sacred image, when he first refused to admit them to its hiding-place, are facts of this kind which would scarcely have been introduced into a fiction devised to mask an imposition on the public. The publicity attendant on the arrival of the crucifix itself in Luni, and the rivalry for its possession between the people of that town and Lucca, were such as to defy imposture, had such been attempted. Moreover, in place of being contradicted, the detailed statement of the Lombard archdeacon, who, it will be observed, had no personal connection with the city which thus acquired the celebrated crucifix, is corroborated by contemporary legal documents attesting the veneration which was attached to it immediately on its installation. Donations of lands and monasteries, made to the church in which it was placed, are still preserved in the Luccan archives, with the dates of 797, 798, 800, and subsequent years. Moreover, the veneration which attached to the Holy Face, and the publicity given to all the facts connected with its arrival in Italy, far from decreasing as the novelty wore off, increased enormously with the passage of time. Lucca became the centre of pilgrimages from all parts of Europe during the following centuries. The fame of the miracles wrought at its shrine, in constant succession, contributed to this result no less than the sacred character of the image itself. Such was the influx of pilgrims to Lucca during the ninth, tenth, and eleventh centuries, that no less than thirteen hospices were founded within its walls for their free accommodation, according to the custom of the Middle Ages, when travelling was far from being the matter of merely time and money that it is at present. Nor were these all, for similar erections were raised in the villages around, and on the roads leading to the city where rich and poor were sheltered alike by the charity of the founders.

Among the pilgrims who, in succession, came to pay their homage to the Holy Face of Lucca, it is remarkable to find several of the German emperors who were bitter political foes of the Holy See. Henry the Second, Henry the Third, and Frederick Barbarossa were amongst those·who thus testified their veneration for the sacred image. The list of Imperial visitors commences with Louis the Third in 901, and closes with Charles the Fifth more than six centuries later. For Catholics the reverence paid to it by successive Popes is the strongest testimony to the historic authenticity of the facts connected with the sacred image. The Holy See is proverbially cautious in giving its public approval to miraculous events. Yet no less than eight Pontiffs have come on pilgrimage to the shrine of Lucca. Alexander the Second, in the eleventh century, was the first who thus stamped it with his approbation, and his example was followed in subsequent ages by Pascal the Second, Calistus the Second, Eugenius the Third (the pupil of St. Bernard) Urban the Sixth, Gregory the Twelfth, Paul the Third, and, finally, our late Holy Father Pius the Ninth. That a devotion of so peculiar a character should have received so general an approbation during a long course of ages is, even in a purely human point of view, one of the most remarkable facts in history. "Time destroys fiction while it confirms the judgments of truth," was the maxim of pagan philosophy. That eleven centuries have passed over the shrine of Lucca, without lessening the veneration with which it has been regarded from the first, is a striking illustration of the axiom as applied to the history of its origin.

The miracles connected with the Holy Face of Lucca are not, however, confined to those immediately relating to its first appearance in Italy. Through the whole course of its history it has been, like the fountain of Lourdes at the present time, the centre of almost countless supernatural manifestations. Its chapel is filled with the memorials of such events. Votive offerings of the most varied kind, and often accompanied by the strongest attestations, testify to the numberless cures of diseases and deliverances from dangers of every kind that have been wrought through its instrumentality. One of these is of so strange a kind as to deserve being recorded, even in our limited space. Attached to an iron grating hangs an executioner's axe, whose history is given by an inscription attached to it. In 1334 a citizen of a neighboring town, unjustly condemned to die, was miraculously preserved on the scaffold itself. The headman's axe refused to perform its deadly office, and fell with all its force on his neck three times in vain. It rebounded from the flesh without leaving even a mark. The execution thus suspended was afterwards followed by a pardon, and the escaped victim attributed the miracle to having vowed a pilgrimage to the shrine of the Holy Face in case of his deliverance. The axe which had failed to do its work was presented to the shrine and has remained there since. A similar event is told by another inscription as having occurred in the seventeenth century to a native of Marsiglia. But to enumerate the miracles recorded here would require volumes. Many favors acknowledged by votive offerings cannot be regarded as miracles in any public sense, but the number that actually have a public, and, evidently, superhuman character, is enormous. Comparatively few, even of well-informed Catholics among us, ever reflect on the number of distinctly miraculous events that have been constantly occurring within the Church at every period of her history. We are far from attributing faith lightly to such events. Rumor, as we all know, far outstrips fact in the production of miracles; but no unprejudiced investigator can fail to be struck by the number of events, inexplicable except by supernatural interference, that are attested by the clearest evidence. Why such events should occur more numerously in particular places, or in connection with particular persons or objects of devotion, it is beyond the province of human reason to explain. The fact is, that they do so occur. The evidence of it is irresistible in such places as Lourdes or the shrine of the crucifix of Lucca.

BOOK NOTICES.

THE WORKS OF ORESTES A. BROWNSON. Collected and Arranged by *Henry F. Brownson.* Volume XIV. Containing the Writings on Development and on Morals, and Some Miscellaneous Essays. Detroit: Thorndike Nourse, Publisher. 1884.

The nearer the republication of Dr. Brownson's works, collected and arranged by his son, Henry F. Brownson, approaches completion, the more evident their very great value becomes. Orestes A. Brownson was a "born" critic and essayist. His native intellectual gifts were strengthened and developed through a course of Providential circumstances which eminently qualified him for the task he undertook, or which, rather, was Providentially devolved upon him. Naturally honest and sincere, closely observing, reflective, acute, and logical, in spite of early disadvantages, or, perhaps, as is often the case with minds of unusual strength, because of them, he thought and studied profoundly and acquired a knowledge accurate and exact of prevailing lines of thought, and of metaphysical and philosophical ideas and theories, which few scholars of far higher pretensions to erudition have attained.

His knowledge, too, was not simply speculative or theoretical. It was personal and practical. He knew schemes of philosophy and metaphysical systems, not merely by studying them at a distance and from the outside, but by entering into them, adopting them, and testing them exhaustively. Of nearly all of those which he has analyzed and criticised, he might have truly said:

> . . . "Quæquæ ipse miserima vidi
> Et quorum pars magna fui." . . .

By the providence of God he was led in his earnest quest for truth successively through Presbyterianism, Methodism, Unitarianism, and various forms of pure Rationalism and Socialism, to the very verge of Atheism, trying and testing practically and experimentally their interior spirit and fundamental principles. Then he was brought back, step by step, through various systems of thought and belief until he found the truth, and with it rest and peace, in the Catholic faith.

There was scarcely any form of modern heresy and error with which he was not personally and experimentally familiar. He first examined and scrutinized them, not as an opponent and enemy, but as a believer and a friend. Only when he found them delusive and false he abandoned and denounced them. His writings furnish constant evidence of this. And this alone, and apart from his genius, would give value to his analysis of those false systems of thought and strength to his testimony against them.

But, along with all this, Orestes A. Brownson carried to his work a degree of straightforward, heroic (we can call it nothing else) sincerity and honesty, as well as a keenness and precision of analysis, that qualified him beyond anyone else, of the present century in Europe or America, whose name we can recall for the special and important work he set himself to perform.

This comes out much more clearly in Brownson's writings, as they are now collected, arranged, and republished, than it did in the pages of his *Review*, powerful as it was in its day. Persons who have an unbroken, complete series of the successive numbers of *Brownson's Quarterly Review* are greatly mistaken if they suppose that in it they have a full collection of Brownson's writings. Many of his most important papers were given to the public through other channels and in other ways. Those, too, that appeared in his *Review* follow each other in the order of time and as various circumstances suggested. But his son and posthumous editor, Henry F. Brownson, has collected *all* his most important writings, and has arranged them rather in a logical than a historical order. This gives an additional value to *Dr. Brownson's Works*, as now republished, through the strength which one article, following another in the order of thought, gives to that which succeeds it.

Of this the volume now before us, the fourteenth, is a fair example. The twenty or more papers of which it consists were written and published at different times, and as various occasions called them forth. Yet throughout the greater number of them there runs a close connection of ideas; so that each succeeding paper in the volume might be regarded as the logical sequence of that which precedes it.

Thus the first eight articles, taken together, form a very able and profound criticism and refutation of the theory of development, as attempted to be applied to Christain doctrine and morals. Of these the first six deal immediately with the theory which was formulated by Newman in his once famous "Essay on the Development of Christian Doctrine." The work itself has in great degree passed out of notice, but its fundamental thought has found lodgment in many minds and helped to give vogue and prestige to very pernicious errors. Though written, at least in greatest part, when Mr. Newman was still a Protestant, though in transition, consciously or unconsciously, to Catholicity; and though it is an attempt to defend Catholic doctrines on grounds which no Catholic can consistently accept, so far as we can see; yet it found great favor, not only among Protestants of a "Romanizing" turn of mind, that is, Protestants who wished to find excuses for holding Catholic doctrines and yet remaining Protestants, but was also held as a convenient theory for defending the Catholic religion, by a large number of very able men who became zealous converts from Puseyism. It was defended, too, if not advocated, by the *Dublin Review* as a theory that was not, at least, forbidden to Catholics to hold, and which might smooth the way for Anglicans to enter the Church.

Dr. Brownson took alarm at once. In a paper, which is the first in the present volume, he thoroughly analyzes and dissects Mr. Newman's theory, pointing out the fundamental fallacies on which it is built up. Mr. Newman assumes, at the commencement of his Essay, that *Christianity "may legitimately be made the subject matter of theories."* But Dr. Brownson conclusively shows that this is a false assumption. Whether Christianity is divine or human is not a question of opinion or of theory, but of fact. And so of all the other questions Newman raises, to illustrate and support his assumption. Christianity, itself, is a fact not only in the world's history, but in itself. Consequently, if received at all it must be received not as a theory, but as a *revealed* fact. Brownson further shows that in his "Essay on Development" Mr. Newman was misled by adopting the method of the so-called "Inductive Philosophy," and is guilty of the logical sin of stating as conclusions what his premises do not contain; and that it is impossible by any logic to conclude the unknown from the known.

He then points out a still more serious fault of the *Essay.* It assumes that there *have been real variations in Christian doctrine;* that *the Church at first received no formal* revelation ; that as the Israelites went forth from Egypt into the desert " in haste," so, too, the Church went forth into the world with her "dough unleavened," her creed incomplete, her understanding of her faith imperfect ; ignorant, at least in part, of the precise truth she was to teach respecting every article of faith she was authorized to teach ; that new definitions of faith are new developments, and that thus the Church grows in her belief and apprehension of the truth ; that before she defines an article of faith the Church herself does not clearly and distinctly apprehend what, on the point defined, is the revelation she originally received.

To point out that no Catholic can consistently hold this theory is needless. It differs but slightly and as to the form in which it is worked out from that of Neander and other German rationalists.

Dr. Brownson further shows that Newman, when he speaks of the recipients of the divine revelation, seems always to have in his mind the *ecclesia credens,* and to forget the *ecclesia docens.* He appears to have never heard that Almighty God gave His revelation to pastors and teachers qualified from the first to teach it in its purity and integrity ; but that he threw it upon the great concourse of believers for them to receive and make the most of, as well as they could. "The time at last came," said Newman, "when these recipients ceased to be inspired ; and on these recipients the revealed truths would fall, at first vaguely and generally, and would afterwards be completed by developments." But this view, if followed out, would suppress entirely the proper teaching authority of the Church, competent at any time to declare infallibly what is the precise truth revealed ; or, at least, would raise the *ecclesia credens* above the *ecclesia docens.* It would reduce the office of the *ecclesia docens* to that of defining from time to time the dogmatic truth, which the *ecclesia credens* has gradually worked out from her implicit feelings or belief. The supernatural assistance would then attach to the *ecclesia credens* and superintend the elaboration by it of doctrine, rather than to the *ecclesia docens;* and if it attached to the *ecclesia docens* at all, it would be only so far as would enable it faithfully to collect and truly to define what the *ecclesia credens* elaborates.

Again, Mr. Newman in his *Essay* proceeds on the assumption that Christianity can be abstracted from the Church, and considered apart from it, as if the Church were accidental, and not essential in our holy religion. "Christianity," he says, "though spoken of in prophecy as a Kingdom, came into the world as an *idea,* rather than an institution, and has had to wrap itself in clothing, and fit itself with an armor of its own providing, and form the instruments and methods of its own prosperity and warfare."

Dr. Brownson dissects this fallacy and shows that it is not only theologically and historically false, but that it rests on the assumption that ideas, in themselves considered, are active and potent, and may "take unto themselves hands, build the temple, erect the altar, and instaurate the worship of God." He proves that ideas, not concreted, not instituted, are not potencies, not active, but are really to us as if they were not, and that the ideal must become actual before it can become operative. Moreover, if it be assumed that Christianity came as an idea and was developed only by the action of the human mind on it, " the institutions with which it is clothed, the authorities established in its name, the precepts enjoined, and the rites prescribed, are all really products of the human mind ; and instead of governing the mind, may be governed, modified, enlarged, or contracted by it at its pleasure. The Church, then, would be divine only in the sense that philosophy or civil government is divine.

Following up this branch of his subject; Dr. Brownson says that Mr. Newman's own definition of *idea*—a habitual judgment which the mind forms of that which comes before it—strips Christianity of its essential divine character and makes it purely human; and resolves it, in its last analysis, into naked deism, or, at best, mere Quakerism.

Regard for space prevents us following Dr. Brownson further through his criticisms of the "Essay on the Development of Christian Doctrine." What we have already given is sufficient to show the keenness and exhaustiveness of their analysis of Newman's learned but dangerous *Essay*.

This paper a few months afterwards was followed by another, equally able, on the same general subject, elicited by an American reprint of Northcote's "Difficulties of Anglicanism." It is a work which measurably refutes the pretensions of Anglicanism to possessing any of the "notes" of Unity, Sanctity, Catholicity, and Apostolicity, by which the Church proves her divine origin and character. But as a defence of the Catholic religion it is open to the objection of following the same line of thought Newman adopted in his theory of the development of Christain Doctrine.

In his criticism Dr. Brownson does full justice to the learning and piety of the author, and the admirable style and spirit in which he wrote, but points out the defects of his work, growing out of the un-Catholic theory which underlies it. He then again adverts to Newman's theory of development, and, on still other grounds than those stated in his first paper, he proves that it is irreconcilable with the Catholic faith.

The *Dublin Review* opened its pages to defenders of the development theory, who undertook to show that Dr. Brownson had misunderstood the *Essay*, and to refute him on other grounds. In the three papers immediately following the one we have last referred to, Dr. Brownson answered their attempted refutations. These papers are as remarkable for their perfect candor and manly honesty as for the learning, logical ability, and clearness of thought which they display.

In the next paper—"Morris on the Incarnation"—Dr. Brownson, after pointing out the leading defects of the book, examines and criticises the general method of disputation and discussion adopted by the Oxford converts. He regards their writings as wanting in aggressiveness, and seemingly constructed too much on the idea that the Catholic religion needs defence or apology. This brings Dr. Brownson again to a consideration and criticism of the general mental posture, logic, and philosophy of the school, if such we may call it, that was formed in England, by converts to Catholicity from Puseyism or Tractarianism. Doing full justice to the learning and ability, the zeal and piety of English converts, he regards their writings as faulty; well intentioned, evincing unquestionable learning and ability, and an earnest zeal and piety that cannot fail to command respect, yet wanting in sound logic, in true philosophy and in a clear apprehension of the fact that conversion from Protestantism to the Faith involves not only "a putting on" but also a "putting off"; an abandonment of previously held errors as well as embracing their new-found faith. The paper is a very able and acute disquisition upon the errors of judgment which cling to converts from Protestantism, and especially to those from English Tractarianism long after they have, with entire honesty, accepted and embraced the true faith.

The six papers we have thus far noticed, taken together, form the keenest and profoundest analysis both of Newman's theory of development of doctrine, and of the general mental posture of the Oxford or Tractarian school of English converts that has ever been made, so far as our knowledge extends. It thus, too, has more than a historical interest and value. For the questions involved in the development theory of Newman are still raised and agitated; and the theory itself, under changed forms, is employed in defending many erroneous opinions respecting religion and morals, and the fundamental principles of society.

Having thoroughly discussed the development theory as it obtained vogue in England, Dr. Brownson next turned his attention to a form of the same theory that was formulated in this country, chiefly by the Rev. John W. Nevin, D.D., then President of a Protestant Theological Seminary at Mercersburg, Pa. It started from a different point of beginning and differed in form and substance materially from Newman's, yet it involved the same fundamental false principle. It scouted Newman's notion that Christianity started merely as an *idea.* It insisted that Christianity, from its very beginning, was a *fact,* a *living, supernatural,* DIVINE FACT in the world. But it held that what that fact *involved* was *evolved* in the course of time, by a process of historical development. It held that the doctrines of Christianity, the articles of the Christian faith, as well as discipline and ritual, were all, and in their entirety, comprehended in the revelation of Christ, but undeveloped. They were *involved* in it, included in it in germ and possibility, as the germ of the acorn includes within itself the possibility of becoming the oak, by following the law of its growth and assimilating to itself the elements necessary to its growth. It regarded the Church of the Middle Ages, not as Protestants commonly regard it, as a corruption of "Primitive Christianity," but as a "legitimate development" of it, and insisted that the only possible ground on which Protestantism could defend itself from the charges of novelty, heresy and schism, was to show that it was a genuine continuation of the Church of Christ evolved from the Church of the Middle Ages by a process of legitimate historical development. The idea, common to the English Tractarians and the non-Episcopalian Evangelicals (though held by them in very different ways), that "Primitive Christianity" was the type of Christianity for all time, was scouted by the formulators of the Mercersburg "Historical Development" theory as an empty dream, a "fond delusion." They held that what each age needed and required was not "a repristination of Primitive Christianity,"—which was an absurdity and impossibility—but a continued development of new truths or at least of new aspects of truths, which Christianity indeed included from its commencement but to the clear apprehension of which it could only arrive through a process of evolution or development.

This theory met with violent general opposition from the Protestant sects of our country. They regarded it as essentially "Romanizing." At the same time it rallied around the leading promulgator of the theory a little band of zealous followers and defenders, who gradually became known as the "Mercersburg School," now almost forgotten. They insisted that it was the only basis on which Protestantism could be successfully defended; that the Church as a visible fact in the world's history must be continuous and indefectible, or else Christ's promise has failed —a thought too impious to be entertained even for a moment—and that Protestantism, to maintain its claims, must prove itself to be a genuine historical development of what "Primitive Christianity" contained in germ and partially developed, and of what was still further, but only partially and under other aspects, developed in Mediæval Christianity;

and that Protestantism itself was but one aspect of Christianity and that a temporary one, yet by further developments visible Christianity would still further evolve itself into higher and more perfect forms.

The theory in the particular form in which it was put forth by its chief formulator is almost forgotten, but it is easy to trace many of its leading ideas in the rationalistic speculations of various Protestant writers of to-day, who dissolve Christianity into mere naturalism.

Brownson saw the inherent fallacies of the theory from the first, and ably refuted it in several papers. The article in the volume before us deals mainly with it as logically and historically non-consecutive. It meets Dr. Nevin on his own chosen ground. Over against his Protestant opponents, Dr. Nevin strenuously declared :

"The Christianity of the second, third, and fourth centuries, we say, was progressively of the same general order throughout the entire Christian world, and in this character it differed altogether from modern Protestantism, and led fairly and directly towards the Roman Catholic system of the Middle Ages. In proof of this simple historical assertion, we point to facts. It is purely a question of history in the first place, to be either granted or denied as the truth of the facts may seem to require. Is the general proposition true as a historical fact, or is it not? If not, let this be shown by proper evidence. But if it be true, what then? . . . . We are bound to look it firmly in the face ; and when the question is then asked, *How is this fact to be construed against the claims of Protestantism ?* it should be felt to be one that is entitled to some bold and manly answer. . . . . Protestantism *must* be historical, to be true. To say that it is not the continuation of the previous life of the Church, of one substance, though not of one form with what this was *in all past ages*, is at once to pronounce it anti-Christian and false."

But what Dr. Nevin signally failed to do, and what it was necessary for him to do, to make his argument historically complete, was to show that Protestantism was such a continuation. With a wealth of learning he proved the substantial identity, and historical continuity of the Church of the Middle Ages with that of the first centuries. But there he stopped short. He made no effort to prove that Protestantism was the historical continuation of Mediæval Christianity. He insisted that it must be, or else it was a schism and heresy. But he made no effort to resolve the dilemma in which his argument placed himself and all other Protestants. He simply *assumed* that Protestantism *must* be such a continuation, but made no attempt to prove that, in fact, it was.

Brownson, in the article to which we are referring, exposes with consummate ability this fatal defect in Dr. Nevin's argument.

"Saint-Bonnet on Social Restoration" forms the subject of the eighth and last paper, in the volume before us, on development theories. The work Dr. Brownson criticises was very able and interesting. It probed to the bottom our social, moral and economical wounds, traced them to their origin, and prescribed the only possible remedy—a hearty return to Christian faith and the practical observance in every department of life of Christian principles and maxims. But some of the author's premises were unsound, and in the development of his subject and the application of his principles he pursued to a great extent a line of thought similar to that of the "Essay on the Developmant of Christian Doctrine." These defects in the work Dr. Brownson exposes, and in their exposure gives an exceedingly able and lucid disquisition upon the origin of human society and the principles and laws of its progress.

The space we have already occupied forbids our noticing in particular the many remaining articles contained in the volume. They are on

subjects of profound importance and are immediately and directly related questions of deep practical concern to-day respecting the fundamental principles of morality. of society, and kindred subjects, as their
respective titles indicate: "Hildreth's Theory of Morals;" "Jouffroy's Ethical System;" "Rights and Duties;" "Ward's Philosophical
Introduction;" "Lecky on Morals;" "Madness of Anti-Christians;"
"Charity and Philanthropy;" "The Reformation not Conservative;"
etc.

Following these critical articles, are four admirable papers; severally,
on Bishop Fenwick, Archbishop Hughes, Archbishop Spalding, and
Count de Montalembert. They are not biographical sketches or memoirs, but careful and profound analytical studies of the distinctive
characteristics of the subjects of the several papers, the influence they
exerted, the special work they did, and the manner in which they did it.
As giving an interior view of the characters and work of the three Prelates named and of Count de Montalembert, we know of nothing more
interesting or valuable.

The last three papers of the volume are critical studies respectively of
the "Questions of the Soul," and "Aspirations of Nature," by Rev.
Father Hecker; and of the "Meditations of St. Ignatius."

Volume XV. contains the first part of Dr. Brownson's political writings. From a statement in the editor's Preface to this volume, we infer
that the collection now in process of republication will extend through
three more volumes. These writings cover a period of nearly forty
years, from 1837 to 1875. When the earliest articles were written, Dr.
Brownson was a radical both in religion and in politics. Consequently
there are many erroneous ideas in these early articles, which the author
afterwards repudiated and earnestly combated. Yet even along with
the errors there are important truths clearly stated and ably defended.
The political theories of Locke, Rousseau, Hobbes, etc., are critically
examined and thoroughly refuted. Dr. Brownson establishes the divine
right of government, and the providential constitution of the State as
anterior to the written constitution. He shows that the divine right of
government is the real basis of individual freedom and of lawful authority; that the unrestrained will of the sovereign, whether the sovereign be one or many, and whether the government be monarchial, aristocratic, or democratic, is despotism; and that there is freedom only
where this will is limited and restrained.

The papers on the "Origin, Ground, and Constitution of Government," and on "Political Constitutions" are profound studies of their
respective subjects. Other papers in volume XV. are able discussions of
public measures closely connected with the history of our country. The
volume concludes with a very interesting article on Ireland and Daniel
O'Connell.

LIFE OF RIGHT REV. JOHN N. NEUMANN, D.D., OF THE CONGREGATION OF THE
    MOST HOLY REDEEMER, Fourth Bishop of Philadelphia. From the German of
    Rev. John N. Berger, C. SS R., by *Rev. Eugene Gramm, C. SS. R.* New
    York, Cincinnati & St. Louis: Benziger Brothers, 1884.

The opportunity of possessing a biography of Bishop Neumann, afforded by the publication of a second edition of the work before us, will
be gladly availed of by very many who personally knew that saintly
Prelate or knew of him by the testimony of others. Twenty-two years
have passed since his death, but he still lives in the hearts of thousands,
and his name and memory are held in benediction. Indeed as time rolls
on the conviction of his holiness seems to strengthen and the estimate

of his attainments in Christian virtue to become higher. And this, too, though, as far as was possible and consistent with his Episcopal office, his life was a hidden one and, in his great humility, he concealed his deeds from the eyes of all save God alone.

The diocesan archives, according to the testimony of the writer of his Life, contain little calculated to throw light upon the subject. The missionaries who labored with him, comparatively few in number, were too much occupied with the care of souls to record their own trials and labors or what they knew that he endured and accomplished. Yet God, when in His wisdom he sees that it is well to preserve the memory of one of His faithful servants, provides for this. Consequently sufficient material has been collected from which the Life of this Holy Bishop can be clearly portrayed. From the members of his immediate family, his brother and sisters, from those who knew him in his childhood and early manhood, from his fellow class-mates and the Professors who instructed him in the Theological Seminary at Prague, and from other sources of krowledge abundant reliable information has been obtained, showing his intellectual brightness, his rapid progress in knowledge, as well as his deep piety and shining Christian virtue while yet a youthful aspirant for the priesthood. His letters, too (comprising a large correspondence), and his journal, in which his most secret thoughts and spiritual experiences are faithfully recorded, throw a clear light upon his labors, his trials and his interior character.

The work before us, plainly was not intended to be a Life of Bishop Neumann, merely as Bishop of Philadelphia and during the few years he labored there with eminent fidelity to the trust committed to him. It was, evidently, written with the purpose of bringing clearly into the view the entire life and character of its subject. It commences with a sketch of the surroundings of Bishop Neumann at his birth and in his childhood, records the Christian virtues of his parents—for the divine blessing frequently descends visibly from parents to children—and the Christian lives of his brother and sisters, several of whom entered the religious state, and one of whom for many years held the office of Superior-General of the Sisters of Charity of St. Charles Borromeo, and discharged the duties of that office with distinguished fidelity and efficiency.

The work then describes the youthful student-life of Neumann in the elementary school and at the Seminary, his exemplary piety and consistency of conduct, his diligence in study, his devout performance of religious duties ; the trials and sufferings which even at that early period of his life he was called to endure. It then vividly depicts the difficulties which arose against his ordination to the priesthood, and his emigration to the United States where he had aspired from early youth to labor as a missionary. These difficulties grew partly out of the peculiar ecclesiastical rules and laws of his native country, and partly out of Neumann's family circumstances. They seemed for a time insurmountable, and were a severe trial to faith and patience. But Neumann's faith and conviction as to where duty called him never wavered, even when the obstacles seemed insurmountable. He persevered, and God providentially opened the way, when it appeared to be entirely closed.

Then, the work before us describes young Neumann, not having received sacred orders in his native land, landing in New York, virtually penniless, finding his way to St. Nicholas' Church, kindly received by its Pastor, and charged with the duty of giving regular instructions in Christian Doctrine, then ordained by Bishop Dubois, and then at his entrance upon the duties of his sacred office met with questions as to the *licitness* of his ordination (though its validity was admitted), which questions, however, were soon happily solved. Almost immediately on his ordination, the young Priest was sent by Bishop Dubois to labor among the German Catholics of Western New York.

. The field of labor assigned to him was, at that time, almost a wilderness materially, and spiritually. The country was sparsely settled, and the Catholics were separated from each other at great distances and with roads scarcely passable except on foot in winter and spring, and in summer on horseback. The condition of the German Catholics was even still more deplorable than that of the English-speaking Catholics. They were isolated from the others by their language, were far fewer in numbers, and even poorer as respects their material resources. The non-Catholics of this region were far more numerous than the Catholics, and were rude, ignorant, superstitious, and bitterly prejudiced against Catholics. In this missionary field Father Neumann labored for four years in poverty, and with apostolic zeal. The history of his labors, his self-denial, his intense desire to save souls and guide them in the right way, as narrated in the work before us would be incredible, did we not know how the love of Christ constrains His chosen servants to endure all things for His sake.

After four years of faithful, zealous, self denying labor, bearing abundant spiritual fruit, though amidst countless difficulties, Father Neumann's health broke down. At the same time his previous convictions that he ought to enter a religious society ripened into a certainty. Accordingly he applied to be received into the Congregation of the Most Holy Redeemer, and on the 16th of September, 1840, received permission from its Superior to enter the Order. The Right Rev. Bishop Hughes, then Administrator of the Diocese of New York, after repeated refusals, being reluctant to lose the services of so faithful a missionary priest, gave him his discharge. As incidentally yet closely connected with the main purpose of his work—to depict Father Neumann's apostolic zeal—his biographer here devotes a chapter to describing the special mission and labors of the "Redemptorists" in the United States. He then follows Father Neumann for the space of twelve years, first through the term of his novitiate, then as a simple missionary priest, then as one of the two Consultors to the Superior of the Redemptorist Order in America, and then as Vice-Provincial of the Order. In all these positions he was alike humble, mortified and obedient to the rules of the Order, and consumed with a desire to win souls to Christ.

. Father Neumann loved obscurity. But "he that humbleth himself shall be exalted." The Divine purpose sought him out. He was appointed Bishop of Philadelphia by the Holy See, that diocese having become vacant by the translation of Bishop Francis Patrick Kenrick to the Archiepiscopal See of Baltimore. With tears and earnest entreaties Father Neumann endeavored to escape from the responsibilities of a Bishop. But it was not to be. Obedience was laid upon him, and he obeyed.

The next eight years of his life—the term of his Episcopate—are well described in the work before us. His zeal for religion, his unsparing labor; his solicitude for his Clergy and the Religious Orders in his Diocese, his introduction of still other Religious Orders; his fervent Pastoral Letters and discourses ; his special love for children ; his meekness, humility and ardent piety are vividly depicted.

Bishop Neumann, as described by his biographer, was not only indefatigable in his labors, but also systematic in their performance. He drew out a map of his vast diocese on which each parish was accurately marked

·out. He visited the hospitals, asylums, and convents and personally acquainted himself with their temporal and spiritual condition. He visited regularly every parish throughout his diocese. His custom was to visit the larger annually, the smaller and more remote once in two years. When making these visits he spent several days in each parish, instituting a minute inquiry into their actual condition, and endeavoring to remedy as far as he could any abuses or evils that existed. These visits partook, too, somewhat of the nature of a Mission. He catechised and preached and gave special instructions to the children. Wherever there was no church edifice and it was possible to erect one, he encouraged the people to undertake it. During the five years of his Episcopate more than fifty new churches were opened and blessed.

The completion of the Cathedral, commenced by his predecessor, was a subject of earnest desire and he labored earnestly to accomplish it. A few weeks after his installation he issued a circular soliciting contributions in aid of the continuance of the work of erection, and from time to time he so pressed the subject upon the attention of the faithful, that in 1859 he had the satisfaction of seeing the keystone of the dome placed in position and the cross erected upon its summit.

Bishop Neumann was ardently interested in the subject of Christian education. In his first Pastoral letter he says: "Our Catholic youth can be saved only by Catholic schools." The same sentiment and in almost the same words was repeated in his first sermon after his installation. Nor were these declarations mere words devoid of earnest intention.

Within a month he invited the Pastors of the several congregations and several prominent laymen to meet at the Episcopalresidence for a conference on the subject of Catholic schools. In opening the conference he expressed his firm conviction that "for Catholic children Catholic schools are an absolute necessity in order to educate them in the faith, form them into good and useful members of the Church and of society, and secure their eternal salvation." The Bishop's sentiments were warmly approved by the assembly. Resolutions looking towards the establishment of parochial schools were adopted, a committee was appointed to consult on the best means to employ; and the Secretary of the meeting was directed to notify all absent Pastors and request them to attend the next meeting. This meeting was held a few days later and was a full one. A "Central Committee for the education of Catholic Youth" was appointed, of which the Bishop was President. It was the business of this committee to deliberate upon a practical method of instruction, and by the collection of monthly contributions to assist in the maintenance of schools in parishes that were unable to support them. Meetings were held every month at the Bishop's residence, and the proceedings were forwarded to every Priest in the diocese. The Bishop was invariably present at these meetings unless other imperative duties prevented it. In such cases he was careful to notify his Vicar-General to attend in his place and preside over the meeting.

But Bishop Neumann not only thus promoted in a general way the establishment of parochial schools. He interested himself in their details, frequently visited them, and endeavored to secure thoroughness of system in them, as regards instruction and discipline. The result was that a healthy emulation arose among the several schools, the teachers and pupils of each striving to be able to furnish the Bishop with solid proofs of its excellence.

This work was not carried forward without encountering difficulties and opposition, open or covert. But Bishop Neumann was not discouraged by them. He knew how to pray and labor and how to wait. If the difficulties in the way of immediately accomplishing his object seemed to be insurmountable, he waited patiently till a change of circumstances arose. If they consisted simply in a dread of labor and expense, his prudence and energy discovered means to overcome both. His biographer narrates an example of this; he had repeatedly enjoined the Pastor of one of the largest parishes in Philadelphia to establish a Parochial school, and was as often met with the reply, "It is impossible just now." At last the Bishop rejoined, "If it is indeed impossible for *you* to establish a school, I shall have to look for another to fill your place, who willfind it possible to secure a Christian education for the children of that parish." The Rev. Pastor promised to make the effort himself. He set to work, built a large school-house, and opened it with an attendance of a thousand children on the very first day.

The result of Bishop Neumann's holy persistent zeal in promoting the establishment of Parochial schools became quickly visible. The number of schools, and attendance upon them increased rapidly, so that a few months before his death Bishop Neumann could say : Almighty God has so blessed the work of Catholic education that nearly every church in my diocese has now its school. The falling off in attendance at the public schools became so noticeable that it attracted the attention of the public press. The following appeared in one of the daily papers of the time : "We regret to see that the most esteemed denomination in this city has withdrawn its confidence from the public schools," etc.

Besides the parochial schools Bishop Neumann gave earnest attention to the industrial schools and the academies and colleges that were already in existence, and encouraged the creation of new ones. Under his fostering care, St. Joseph's College was established in Susquehanna County ; and three new academies for girls, one in the above mentioned county, one in Reading and one in Philadelphia ; also an industrial school for girls ; St. Vincent's Home ; St. Vincent's Orphan Asylum ; and a Hospital, under the care of the Franciscan Sisters.

The orphans were dear objects of Bishop Neumann's solicitude. He was a true father to them. He delighted, too, in visiting the hospitals and alleviating the sufferings of the poor sick by loving words and tender sympathy.

Nor did he neglect institutions for the promotion of higher education. He was interested with his whole heart in the work of training candidates for the Sacred Ministry. He strove with holy zeal to sustain and increase the resources and efficiency of the diocesan Theological Seminary, previously established. Seeing, too, that it was important that young candidates for the priesthood should pursue their studies and receive their training under ecclesiastical rule in the diocese in which they were to labor, he entertained the desire and idea, from the very beginning of his Episcopate, of establishing a diocesan Preparatory Seminary. He had to wait for seven years before his plan became practicable. But at the year before his death he had the happiness of seeing its realization commenced by the purchase of an eligible property for that purpose. He had a high estimate of the holy office of the priesthood, and believed that most thorough preparation was necessary before entering on its functions. In one of his Pastoral Letters he insists that to properly qualify a Priest "to instruct the ignorant, strengthen the doubting and wavering, guide the faithful, preach and defend fearlessly the truths of our holy faith," a period of "ten or twelve years" is necessary, "devoted to scientific branches, especially ecclesiastical science."

The latter part of the work before us is occupied with an account of

Bishop Neumann's private Christian life and virtues, his death, and obsequies, his reputation for sanctity, and the many cures and other special favors piously believed to have been obtained from God by prayers at Bishop Neumann's grave, and by invoking his intercession.

———

THE FAITH OF CATHOLICS CONFIRMED BY SCRIPTURE, AND ATTESTED BY THE FATHERS OF THE FIRST FIVE CENTURIES OF THE CHURCH. With Preface by *Right Rev. Monsignor Capel, D.D.*, Domestic Prelate of His Holiness, Leo XIII., Member of the Congregation of the Segnatura, Priest of the Archdiocese of Westminster. In three volumes. New York and Cincinnati: Fr. Pustet & Co. 1885.

Monsignor Capel has done great service to the cause of truth in presenting the public in this country with an American reprint of Rev. Father Waterworth's renowned work. It takes up and conclusively disposes of the accusation that the "Roman Church" has departed in her belief and doctrine, from the faith and teaching of the Apostles and their immediate successors. This is a charge which High Church Episcopalians, Evangelical Protestants, and those of the various schools of rationalism unitedly make against the Holy Catholic Church. For, though Evangelical Protestants professedly uphold private interpretation of the Sacred Scriptures as their only authoritative rule of faith, and professedly discard all other means, except as secondary and subordinate, to arriving at a knowledge of divine revelation, yet in practice they find it impossible to follow out their professed rule. Nor can they deny that Christians, in the first centuries of the Christians taught by the Apostles and their immediate successors, must have known what the Apostolic doctrines were, and that the writings of those Christians, many of which have been preserved to us, must be accepted as evidence of their faith and practice.

And even rationalistic Protestants who do not deny even the naked fact that Christianity is a divine revelation, are compelled to admit that Christians of the early ages of the Church must have known what doctrines and practices the Apostles taught.

The question, "What was the belief of Christians in the first centuries of the Christian era?" is a crucial one to all who professedly regard Christianity as a divine religion. Indeed, if the true answer to it is proved to be, "It is the same that Catholics now hold and ever have held," it constitutes a challenge which even deists and atheists cannot ignore or evade. It calls upon them to explain consistently with their unbelief, how it comes that this faith, unchanged and unchanging, is to-day, as it quickly became immediately after its first promulgation, the most active, all-pervading, potent fact in the world's life; not in one country only, among the people of one language or race, or in one age only, but in all ages and amongst all peoples; all else constantly changing, it alone remaining unchanged.

And the question answered in the work before us is one, too, which has a special interest in our own country and at this particular time. Nowhere else in the world is the Catholic Church more free to carry out its mission. It is not recognized, it is true, by either our Federal or our State governments. But it is unhampered by Concordats and other limitations of secular governments. Prejudices exist against it, and its members are a minority of our population. But prejudice may be overcome by constant exhibition of the truth, and even a minority may be allowed its proper degree of liberty, if sound reasons can be shown for its existence; and this minority is increasing in numbers and in power more rapidly than the population of our country.

Moreover, there never was a time nor a country—at least not since the close of the Middle Ages, and the revolt in Europe against authority, spiritual and temporal, miscalled "The Reformation"—when and where such attention is given to the action of the Church, and its position in relation to questions of vital importance to society and good morals, as is now given in our own country and at the present time. We need only specify as examples of this the references constantly made in secular newspapers, and even in Protestant pulpits, to the position occupied by the Church with respect to the subjects of marriage and divorce, the proper observance of Sunday, the true nature of civil authority as exercised by the State, of civil liberty as claimed and enjoyed by the individual, the relation of Christianity to public and private morals, etc.

The pronouncements of the assemblies and synods of various Protestant sects and the personal speculations of different Protestant ministers on these subjects, are published as matters of news by our leading daily newspapers, and are forgotten in a week. But the Encyclical Letters of the Sovereign Pontiff of the Church, the Acts and Decrees of its Councils, their Pastoral Letters, and those of Archbishops and Bishops receive yet wider publication, and are referred to and commented upon, and their bearing upon different subjects vitally connected with religion and morals and the interests of civil society, are felt to demand most serious consideration, not only by Catholics, but by all classes of non-Catholics.

The question, too, constantly mooted by the non-Catholics of our country is: Are these utterances—so just, so wise, so timely in their relation to religious belief and disbelief, to good morals, to the evils which afflict society and their effectual remedy—the outcome and practical application of what has always been the belief and teaching of the Catholic Church? Or may they be attributed to a wonderful superior shrewdness of the rulers of the Church, changing their doctrine, and adapting their utterances to the religious, moral, and social wants and needs of our time and country?

The answer to these questions is found in the work before us. The faith of Catholics to-day and in the United States, as elsewhere, is the same that it was always and in all ages from the days of the Apostles until now, and will be in all subsequent time.

For these reasons, we regard the American reprint of the "Faith of Catholics," one of the most valuable and important contributions to Catholic literature in the United States, that has been made for many years, or, we may say, well could be made.

Nor is its value confined to the reasons we have given above. It should find a place in the libraries of all intelligent Catholics, not merely for controversial purposes, and as furnishing an answer to those who ask them for "a reason of that hope" they entertain, but also for the purpose of confirming their faith, by having at hand the evidences that their belief is identically the same which the Christians of the first ages of the Church, who were instructed by the Apostles, held and testified to despite of cruel persecution, and sealed with their blood.

Of the intrinsic merits of the work it is scarcely necessary for us to speak. The task of gathering the body of evidence it presents was undertaken by the Rev. Fathers Berington and Kirk in the early part of this century. Their book found such favor that. after it was out of print, the Rev. Father Waterworth undertook to republish it. In order, however, more fully to accomplish the objects comprehended in this design, "it was thought necessary to read the entire works of the Fathers and ecclesiastical writers of the first five centuries, to give an entirely new translation of nearly all the extracts—especially those from the Greek writers, and to use such other aids as numerous authors have furnished towards distinguishing the genuine from the spurious or doubtful works of those early ages of the Church. To that labor four years of severe study were devoted." The original work was also considerably enlarged, and instead of a mere selection of passages from the writings of the Fathers of the first five centuries, a digest of their evidence was made, by arranging the extracts from their writings under distinct titles. Taken collectively, these extracts comprise almost every passage in the early Church Fathers that touch on the controversies of the present age between Catholics and non-Catholics.

In carrying out his purpose, Father Waterworth adopted the following plan : First, he states in distinct proposition, as briefly but comprehensively as possible, the articles of Catholic belief. Each proposition is then followed by passages of Scripture (chiefly from the New Testament) that confirm it ; and then the authorities from Scripture are followed by copious extracts from the Fathers of the first five centuries of the Church.

The editor of the reprint before us—Monsignor Capel—has now given Father Waterworth's work to the American public with a number of corrections, and has added a chapter from the admirable work of the learned Bishop Ullathorne on the Immaculate Conception, a translation of the First Dogmatic Constitution of the General Council of the Vatican, and a chronological list of the Popes of the first five centuries.

HISTORY OF THE CATHOLIC CHURCH ; For Use in Seminaries and Colleges. By *Dr. Heinrich Brueck*, Professor of Theology in the Ecclesiastical Seminary of Mentz. With Additions from the Writings of His Eminence Cardinal Hergenröther. Translated by Rev. E. Pruente. With an Introduction by Right Rev. Mgr. James A. Corcoran, S. T. D., Professor of Sacred Scripture, Moral Theology, etc., etc. Vol. I. Einsiedeln, New York, Cincinnati, and St. Louis : Benziger Brothers, Printers to the Apostolic See. 1885.

The diligent careful study of the history of the Church necessarily forms an important part of the course of instruction and training which those who are to enter upon the office of the Sacred Ministry of Christ and discharge its functions, should receive. For in the "History of the Church" are displayed the unfolding of the divine intention in establishing His Kingdom on earth, and the manner and way in which that Kingdom has spread itself in all previous ages and among all peoples ; its relations to all those various peoples, to secular governments, philosophy, literature, art, science, human industry, and all the multifarious concerns of civil society ; and also the interior development of the Church in regard to its constitution, doctrine, worship, etc.

The need, therefore, in the English language, of such a work as this, of which the first volume is before us, has been widely and deeply felt. Nearly all the manuals of Church History that up to this time have been published in English fail to meet the want, from one cause or another. Some of them are entirely too voluminous. Others are defective in method and arrangement, breaking the continuity of the narrative by discursive treatment of particular topics, or treating at too great length, and with too much minuteness, subjects which, however interesting to advanced scholars as subjects for special investigation, would consume too much of the time of students of seminaries and colleges, and divert their attention from the general course of Church History. Still others are intended for popular use rather than for students.

Owing to these causes an English text-book on church history for use in theological seminaries, combining sufficient conciseness with sufficient clearness, accuracy, and precision, has been up to this time a great desideratum.

The want, we believe, will be supplied by the translation of Dr. Brueck's work. Its author is Professor of Theology in the Ecclesiastical Seminary at Mentz, and has attained high distinction as an accurate and profound scholar. His work has received favorable recognition from learned reviewers in Germany and other European countries, and has already been introduced into a number of Catholic Seminaries. An eminent European critic and scholar characterizes it " as uniting historic accuracy and scientific keenness, and an incomparable clearness, and a conciseness that avoids everything superfluous, with a thoroughly ecclesiastical spirit and great precision when treating of doctrine."

In endeavoring to give a concise yet truthful representation of the principal events in the history of the Church and their relations, the author bestows his chief attention upon subjects of greater importance, treating more briefly questions which, though interesting to historical critics or others engaged in special researches, are yet of minor importance. Thus the work is an admirable compendium, in which the several topics receive consideration proportionate to their relative importance.

As English-speaking Catholics naturally require a fuller consideration of Church History connected with their own countries, the translator has introduced such changes and additions as would satisfy this demand. In so doing he has made judicious use of the valuable historical researches of Cardinal Hergenröther and other distinguished Catholic Church Historians, and has also made such other changes as would better adapt the work for use by English-speaking students.

Numerous notes at the bottom of the pages furnish the reader with the historical sources and authorities, which confirm the statements of the text, and also direct him to the works through which he may prosecute his studies of particular subjects more extensively and minutely. Vol. I., which is before us, brings the "History of the Church" down to the death of Pope Boniface VIII.—1303. It divides the times of which it treats into two epochs. The first epoch extends from the Birth of Christ to the Sixth Œcumenical Council, the third at Constantinople, in 680. This Epoch is divided into two Periods, the first of which comes down to the time of Constantine the Great, and the second to the year 680. The Second Epoch extends to the death of Boniface VIII., and is also divided into two Periods, the first extending to the Pontificate of Gregory VII. (1073); the second to the death of Boniface VIII., in 1303.

The chief events in the history of the Church during these epochs and periods are considered and exhibited, first, with reference to the exterior condition of the Church, and secondly, with reference to its interior condition. The subjects treated of in each period are further subdivided under the several general heads of the "Spread of Christianity," "Church and State," "Constitution of the Church," "Development of Doctrine" (with a statement of the chief heresies and schisms opposing each doctrine), "Worship and Discipline." Added to the body of the work, as appendices, are a chronological list of the Popes, a chronological list of the Œcumenical Councils of the Church, and a chronological table, exhibiting the contemporaneous Popes, Emperors, and important events.

Preceding the body of the work is an "Introduction," by Right Rev. Monsignor James A. Corcoran, S. T. D., which is a model of conciseness and clearness, and which compresses into brief compass an immense amount of information respecting the sources of Church History and the works that have been published upon it. This "Introduction," as we learn from the publishers, is as yet unfinished, its completion having been prevented by the demands upon Monsignor Corcoran's time, made by the Third Plenary Council of Baltimore and the work of preparation for it. The remainder of the "Introduction," we presume, will appear in the second volume of the History.

The work is published with the *Imprimatur* of the Most Rev. Peter Richard Kenrick, Archbishop of St. Louis, and is dedicated (presumably by permission) to the Most Rev. P. J. Ryan, Archbishop of Philadelphia. The fact of its thus having the threefold approval, express or implied, of the two distinguished Prelates just named, and of Monsignor Corcoran, distinguished in Europe as well as in America for his extensive, accurate, and profound erudition, and whose long and varied experience as teacher of Church History, as well as of other branches of Sacred Science, eminently qualify him to decide upon the merits of text books, are a sufficient guaranty of the excellencies of this work.

ANCIENT RELIGIONS AND MODERN THOUGHT, by *William Samuel Lilly.* London: Chapman & Hall. 1884.

W. S. Lilly's "Ancient Religions and Modern Thought" richly deserves the encomium of praise which has been freely accorded to it by critics. It displays a very extensive erudition, considerable scholarship, and unquestioned literary ability. Nor is this all. These gifts, whenever found in an unstinted measure combined in one writer, suffice by themselves to make his productions well worthy the careful attention of the reading public. But there is in this volume that which displays at once a great familiarity with the subject, a clear perception of the drift of the tendency of the age, and of the relationship true religion holds towards this current. Mr. Lilly correctly observes that the existence of the supernatural forms the keynote of the whole problem of unbelief, and, of course, a world, denying the reality of all that is supersensible, necessarily denies also the soul's existence, and hence its immortality. Correct perceptions are so rarely met with in discussions of this momentous issue of our days, that the clear and perspicuous mode of presenting this phase of modern cultured thought strikes the reader with unalloyed pleasure and not less great force. An excellent synopsis of the Eastern religious systems and a careful noting of the true positions these creeds occupy in the history of the world, go far towards convincing the reader that the author has succeeded in discharging a difficult task in the spirit of real and not feigned impartiality.

But, in spite of the many and great excellencies of this work, and in spite of our honest belief that it stands in the front rank of books on this grave topic of our times, there are some points on which it seems to us the author is neither clear to himself nor, on that account, able to clarify the reader's notions. In the first place, the existence of God is not a thesis open to doubt, as the physicists themselves furnish abundant proofs of the reality of an order above and beyond nature, and as, moreover, a cogent philosophical and irrefragable argument on that point exists, apart from any assumptions of theology. In the second place, the immortality of the soul, a necessary sequence of the preceding fact, admits of a much stronger proof than has been furnished by Mr. Lilly. It seems to us that his statements of the negative side are fuller, and cover more ground, than the replies he makes for the positive side. And, as these are precisely the points on which light is so much need.d for a proper understanding of true religion, it is much to be regretted that this remarkable work does not enter more fully upon them.

Again, while reading the remarks called forth by the analysis of Eastern creeds, and the very well selected quotations from the documents by the unearthing of which our times have gained much insight into the religious life of the major part of this globe's population, some inferences, which strongly suggested themselves to our mind, have either been overlooked or else not made as irrelevant to the subject. Buddhism, it seems to us, should be considered as the very strongest confirmation of Christianity. The fact of a primordial revelation is the one upon which Christianity and Judaism rest alike. In the course of time these truths became corrupted, but then, where the second revelation in the person of Christ was not made, it seems the fundamental ideas were preserved in greater purity and held with greater tenacity than in the world which proved the first field of true religious expansion.

Again, Mohammedanism, far from being an original creed, presents to us merely a strange mixture of Christian tenets and Eastern fantastic ideas, welded together under the magnetic influence of a really great man aided by the unrelenting power of the sword. True, the estimate society is in the habit of bestowing upon Mohammed and Islamism is quite erroneous in the majority of cases. But the view held by Mr. Lilly corrects only some misconceptions in regard to it, and leaves it to be inferred that Islamism stands forth as an original creed of the world on the same level as Christianity, Buddhism, etc., which, as Mr. Lilly himself best knows, is an altogether erroneous belief.

These critical remarks may, perhaps, seem too severe, but a work which discusses the most vital subject of all, one that is of paramount import to every human being, must be criticised on every weak point, if subject to criticism at all. Nor do these suggestions impair in any way the high value which this volume deserves in contemporary literature. They purpose merely to indicate shortcomings which, in an undertaking of this kind, appear almost unavoidable, because the minds of no two men run exactly in the same line.

LIFE OF ST. CLARE OF MONTEFALCO, PROFESSED NUN OF THE ORDER OF HERMITS OF ST. AUGUSTINE. Translated from the Italian of the Most Rev. Lawrence Tardy, formerly Vicar-General of the Augustinian Order, by *Rev. Joseph Locke, O. S. A., permissu superiorum.* New York, Cincinnati, and St. Louis: Benziger Brothers.

The subject of this biography died in the odor of sanctity in the year 1308, and within eighteen years afterwards the entire tedious process of her canonization was completed. Nothing remained but for the Sovereign Pontiff of the Church to issue his declaration. This he had determined to do, but circumstances, not his will, prevented him. The cause then lay unnoticed for more than four centuries, when it was taken up, and again laid aside for no apparent reason, as Benedict XIV. himself remarked. Finally, and after the lapse of six centuries, it was brought to a successful issue under our present gloriously reigning Pontiff, Leo XIII., who canonized St. Clare on September 11th, 1881.

Clearly, this was Providential. God, in His far-reaching wisdom, saw that the spirit of mortification and the love for the Cross of Christ, which were the leading characteristics of St. Clare's life, were just what are now needed to remedy the evils of our times. Knowing, as He does, "the times and the seasons," He chose to reserve her canonization till the moment when her example would do most good.

We heartily commend the work. Its perusal will tend to inspire, what is so much needed, a spirit of detachment from the world, and of charity and self-mortification.

THE AMERICAN CATHOLIC

QUARTERLY REVIEW.

THE AMERICAN CATHOLIC QUARTERLY REVIEW is issued regularly in January, April, July, and October.

EACH NUMBER CONTAINS 192 pages, large octavo, printed from legible type, on fine white paper.

SUBSCRIPTION, $5.00 per annum, payable in advance, or $1.25 a single copy. Postage free to all parts of the U. S.

The Editorial Department is conducted by Right Rev. James A. Corcoran, D.D.

It is DESIGNED that the *American Catholic Quarterly Review* shall be of the highest character that can be given it by the educated Catholic mind of the United States and of Europe.

It is NOT PROPOSED that it shall be confined to the discussion of theological subjects, but that it shall embrace within its scope all subjects of interest to educated Catholics, whether philosophical, historical, scientific, literary, or political—using the latter term in its original and proper meaning. Partisan politics, or politics in the popular sense of the word, it is scarcely necessary to say, will be rigidly excluded.

THE MOST LEARNED and scholarly writers that can be secured will be enlisted in support of the *Review* as regular and occasional contributors; and every effort will be made by its conductors to render it an able and efficient auxiliary to the Church in her warfare against modern error.

Subscriptions respectfully solicited.

Address,   **HARDY & MAHONY,**

505 CHESTNUT STREET,

POST-OFFICE BOX, 1044,   **PHILADELPHIA.**

THE

AMERICAN

CATHOLIC QUARTERLY

REVIEW.

Bonum est homini ut eum veritas vincat volentem, quia malum est homini ut eum veritas vincat
invitum. Nam ipsa vincat necesse est, sive negantem sive confitentem.
S. AUG. EPIST. ccxxxviii. AD PASCENT.

PHILADELPHIA:

HARDY AND MAHONY, PUBLISHERS AND PROPRIETORS,

505 CHESTNUT ST.,—P. O. BOX 1044,

York: D. & J. SADLIER & Co., F. PUSTET—Boston: THOS. B. NOONAN & Co., NICH. M. WILLIA
more: JOHN MURPHY & Co., JOHN B. PIET & Co.—Cincinnati: BENZIGER BROS., F. PUSTET
't Louis: P. FOX, BENZIGER BROS., B. HERDER—San Francisco: A. WALDTEUFEL—New Orleans:
CHARLES D. ELDER—Montreal: D. & J. SADLIER & Co.—St. John, N. B.: T. O'BRIEN &
Co.—London: BURNS & OATES—Dublin: W. H. SMITH & SON, M. H. GILL & SON.

NEWSDEALERS SUPPLIED BY THE AMERICAN NEWS COMPANY, NEW YORK—
NEWS CO., PHILADELPHIA—NEW ENGLAND NEWS CO., BOSTON—CINCINNATI NEWS CO
CINCINNATI, OHIO—WESTERN NEWS CO., CHICAGO, ILL.

TENTH YEAR.

THE

AMERICAN CATHOLIC QUARTERLY REVIEW.

RIGHT REV. JAMES A. CORCORAN, D. D.,
EDITOR-IN-CHIEF.

$5.00 per Annum, in Advance.

Issued in January, April, July, and October. Each number contains 192 large octavo pages, printed from legible type, on fine white paper.

REGULAR AND OCCASIONAL CONTRIBUTORS.

Subscriptions Respectfully Solicited.

Address,

HARDY & MAHONY,
Publishers and Proprietors,

PHILADELPHIA.

No. 505 Chestnut Street.
Box 1044.

THE AMERICAN CATHOLIC
QUARTERLY REVIEW.

VOL. X.—APRIL, 1885.—No. 38.

THE CATHOLIC CHURCH AND CIVILIZATION.

The Encyclical Letter, "Humanum Genus," of Our Holy Father Pope Leo XIII., on the Sect of the Freemasons.

IN his great and instructive Encyclical Letter, *Humanum genus,* our Holy Father Leo XIII. traces out with a master hand the evils that afflict modern society, exposes its wounds and sores, and points out the destructive forces that are arrayed in wicked warfare against the Church of Christ and the Christian civilization which she has created and fostered. This magnificent document is so luminous in style, so irresistible in argument, so irrefutable in its deductions and statements of facts, that any words of ours would add nothing to its power or to the salutary and lasting impressions its perusal must make on all candid and unbiassed minds. Naturalism, which is the denial of the supernatural, and, therefore, of all revealed religion, is the curse of the age and the canker worm that is gnawing at the very vitals of society. Its doctrines are most destructive of public and private virtue, and aim at the overthrow of the whole Christian order.

The fundamental doctrine of the Naturalists, says the Holy Father, "is that human nature and human reason ought in all things to be mistress and guide." Laying this down, they care little for duties to God, or pervert them by erroneous and vague opinions. For they deny that anything has been taught by God; they allow no dogma of religion or truth which cannot be understood by the human intelligence, nor any teacher who ought to be believed by reason of his authority. And since it is the special and exclusive duty of the Catholic Church fully to set forth, in words, truths divinely received, to teach, besides other divine helps to salvation, the authority of its office, and to defend the same with perfect purity, it is against the Church that the rage and attack of the enemies are principally directed. According to the gospel of the flesh, the existence of God and the immortality of the soul, which the light of unaided reason points out as certain and fundamental truths, are to be regarded as questionable and uncertain; and consequently the foundations of law and order, of all justice and morality, are shaken and undermined. God, the Creator and provident Ruler of the world, is outlawed from His own creation. Law is stripped of all divine sanctions. The political order is supreme and independent of all responsibility to a higher law. Man in society is the source of supreme civil power, and therefore can appoint or displace the chief magistrate according to his good pleasure. The education of youth must be Godless, and marriage, the bond of domestic life and the basis of society, must be reduced to the genus of commercial contracts. Says the Holy Father: What refers to domestic life in the teaching of the Naturalists is almost all contained in the following declarations: That marriage belongs to the genus of commercial contracts, which can rightly be revoked by the will of those who made them, and that the civil rulers of the State have power over the matrimonial bond; that, in the education of youth, nothing is to be taught in the matter of religion as of certain and fixed opinion; and each one must be left at liberty to follow, when he comes of age, whatever he may prefer. To these things the Freemasons fully assent; and not only assent, but have long endeavored to make them into a law and institution.

For in many countries, and in some nominally Catholic, it is enacted that no marriages shall be considered lawful except those contracted by the civil rite; in other places the law permits divorce; and in others every effort is used to make it lawful as soon as may be. Thus the time is quickly coming when marriages will be turned into another kind of contract—that is, into changeable and uncertain unions which fancy may join together, and which the same, when changed, may disunite. With the greatest unanimity the sect of the Freemasons also endeavors to take to itself the education of youth. They think that they can easily mould to their opinions that soft and pliant age and bend it whither they will; and that nothing can be more fitted than this to enable them to bring up the youth of the State after their own plan. Therefore, in the education and instruction of children, they allow no share, either of teaching or of discipline, to the ministers of the Church; and in many places they have procured that the education of youth shall be exclusively in the hands of laymen, and that nothing which treats of the important and most holy duties of men to God shall be introduced into the instruction on morals.

Then come their doctrines of politics, in which the Naturalists lay down that all men have the same right, and are, in every respect, of equal and like condition; that each one is naturally free; that no one has the right to command another; that it is an act of violence to require men to obey any authority other than that which is obtained from themselves. According to this, therefore, all things belong to the free people; power is held by the command or the permission of the people, so that, when the popular will changes, rulers may lawfully be deposed; and the source of all rights, and civil duties, is either in the multitude or in the governing authority, when this is constituted according to the latest doctrines. It is held also that the State should be without God; that in the various forms of religion there is no reason why one should have precedence of another; and that they are all to occupy the same place.

Such are the destructive doctrines and forces that are now in active operation in the world, and which have for aim the destruction of civil society as at present constituted, the ruin of Christian civilization and the overthrow of the Catholic Church, which is the firm prop of the one and the fruitful mother of the other. These terrible anti-Christian doctrines, if put into successful operation, would result in Communism, Socialism, and Anarchy, in desecrated homes, in faithless peoples and Godless states; in other words, Christian society and Christian civilization would be utterly destroyed, the work of Christ and of His Church in the world would be undone, and the devil, the world and the flesh would once more reign in Paganism, revived, restored and triumphant. Now, the great aim of Freemasonry and of cognate societies is to bring these doctrines and principles to a successful and triumphant issue; and therefore they wage a fierce and unrelenting war against the holy Catholic Church, which is the great obstacle to the realization of their wicked and diabolical purposes. Hence it is that the Holy Father raises his voice in warning against these wicked anti-Christian confederations, and from the chair of Peter calls upon the Christian world to rally around the banner of the Cross and to hold fast to the saving truths and holy laws which it symbolizes.

The many evils that afflict modern society and menace it with ruin, are the logical consequences of the Protestant " Reformation," and of the action of its principles and teachings. Naturalism and its allies are the progeny of Protestantism. The Catholic Church, on the other hand, is the foster-mother and saviour of Christian society and Christian civilization, and she alone has the divine remedies for the healing of the nations and for the removal of the moral and social evils that, like a wasting plague, ravage and threaten them with death. This it is proposed to prove to some extent in this article; but, it would, of course, be impossible within the space at our disposal to do full justice to the subject in all its bearings. There are no moral evils for which the Church has not a remedy, no human sorrows for which she has not a heavenly consolation, no wounded, broken hearts for which she has not a healing balm; there are no dark problems of life for which she has not a solution, no questionings of the human soul for which she has not satisfactory answers, no dark despair for which she has not the blessed light of assured and immortal hopes. In her the sick and afflicted have a mother of consolation, the poor a friend and benefactor with an ever open hand, the oppressed a powerful protector that in all ages has never failed to shield them with the power of her influence and laws, whilst she smote with her banns and anathemas the tyrants and enslavers of their fellow-men. To the king and his subjects, to the master and his servants, to the employers and the employed she teaches the just relations that should exist between them, the reciprocal rights and duties which, like the nicely adjusted works of a clock, should in their harmonious action and reaction regulate all social grades and interdependencies, and bind all members of society in the golden bonds of justice, charity, good rule and friendly offices, thus establishing in this fallen world the reign of law and order, and of peace and good will to all men. Were the voice of the Church listened to and obeyed, and her teachings reduced to practice in individual and social life, the world would have been spared the existence of those organizations which, under the pretence of exercising philanthropy and benevolence, have been the fruitful source of innumerable evils, and modern civilization would not be forced to shudder with fear at the apparition of such associations as Communism, Socialism and Nihilism, which desperate men in their despair have framed to right their political and social wrongs, whether real or imaginary, and which threaten civil society and christian civilization with ruin and overthrow. Within the Church's pale all rights are protected, all duties enforced, and the just relations and subordinations of the social hierarchy are based on true and firm foundations. She is the friend of the poor, the protector of the orphan, the defender of the weak and the oppressed. She is the firm support of legitimate authority and the promoter of civil liberty. Hers is, in fine, the fruitful womb whence has sprung Christian civilization, with its unnumbered blessings and sweet and tender charities.

The poor have been at all times the object of her special solicitude and affection, following in this the example and the precepts of her divine founder.

A considerable portion of Church revenues was by her direction to be set aside for the maintenance of the poor, and in various councils laws were passed making provision for their support. Thus, the Council of Tours, held in 566, by its fifth canon orders every town to maintain its poor; and the priests in the country as well as the faithful were required to maintain their own poor in order to prevent the abuses of unrestricted mendicancy. The Church had a register of the poor for the purpose of ascertaining their wants and of regulating the distribution which was made to them of a portion of the ecclesiastical property.

No form of human misery and suffering was a stranger to the all-embracing charity and Christ-like compassion of the Church. The lepers, excommunicated from the society of their fellow men, were embraced by her with a mother's affection; the ordinary sick poor were tenderly nursed and cared for; and even prisoners were visited and consoled, and their physical as well as their spiritual well-being was carefully considered and looked after.

It would, in fact, be too long to enumerate in detail even a small part of the laws and provisions which prove the Church's holy zeal for the comfort and consolation of the unfortunate. Amongst her canons may be found one directing that priests should refuse to accept the gifts of those who oppress the poor.

In the midst of the awful solemnities of his consecration, the bishop-elect, standing in the presence of God's altar, is made to promise that he will be affable, kind, and compassionate to the poor for the sake of God's holy name. The Church, like her divine Founder, respects and dignifies, whilst she compassionates, poverty, and she impresses her children with reverence for what the Fathers call "the Sacrament of the Poor," that is, recognizing Christ under the rags of the poor man as faith recognizes Him under the sacramental species. She exclaims with Bossuet: "Let no one any longer scorn poverty or treat it as a vulgar thing." True, it was once of the dregs of the population, but the King of Glory, having espoused it, He has ennobled it with His alliance, and henceforth He grants to the poor all the privileges of His empire. We therefore in very deed may say of the holy Church,

> " For she is still the poor man's friend,
> The poor man's heart, the poor man's hand,
> And all the oppressed who have no strength
> Have her at their command."

Veronica-like, she has never ceased to wipe the blood and sweat and tears from the face of suffering humanity; nor has she ever failed to act as an angel of consolation in every Gethsemane of human sorrows. In every centre of population she has raised hospitals and institutions of charity like blessed probaticas for the relief and comfort of the sick, the suffering and the poor, and she has entrusted the care and administration of these institutions to holy men and women who have embraced the virginal life, and who have renounced all property and all rights to property in order to live for the poor and suffering, to expend themselves in their service, and to bestow upon them their undivided care, their tender commiserations and their unselfish and Christ-like charities. We may, therefore, say of the Church what Solomon said of the mother of the disputed child, " Haec est vera mater." She is the true mother of suffering humanity. It would exceed the limits of this article to dwell on all that the Church has done to alleviate human sorrows, to relieve distress, and to care for the sick and suffering. We venture, however, to quote the following striking testimony on the subject from a Protestant journal, the *Saturday Review*, written apropos of the Pope's intention to establish a hospital for cholera patients, should that dread plague visit the Eternal City :

" The proverb about ' an ill wind ' appears to have been illustrated by the terrible visitation of cholera in Italy, even more fully than was known last week, and in the same sense which we then pointed out. The Pope himself has openly come forward, not to thwart, but to praise and to second, the efforts of ' those at the head of public affairs ' in Rome, as is testified by his letter to Cardinal Jacobini on ' the dreadful scourge of the Asiatic malady' which has attacked Italy. His Holiness is not content with commending ' the zeal and prudence ' of the Government; he finds it impossible to remain an indifferent spectator, and announces his intention of himself co-operating in this work of charity by founding a hospital at a cost of a million francs, in the close neighborhood of the Vatican, so that he may himself be able to visit and console those attacked by the malady. That such a step is a very fitting, as well as a politic and a gracious one on his part, is obvious enough, and it appears to be generally appreciated as such on the spot, except by ' Liberals ' of the irreconcilable class. But it is also the course which might have been expected from the antecedents and general character of Leo XIII., who has all along manifested a special anxiety both to emphasize and, so far as circumstances permit, to emulate the nobler historical traditions of the Papacy. The name and notion of a hospital is to us so trite, and so much a matter of course, that we are sometimes apt to forget how comparatively new in the world's history such institutions are. There are probably some who will even be surprised to learn that the idea and the fact are alike of purely Christian origin, and form part of our large indebtedness to the early and mediæval Church. Milman is quite within the mark when he says that, ' in institutions for the poor, hospitals, leper houses, charity was not only reckoned as a duty specially incumbent on churchmen, but was a duty ostentatiously discharged.' He adds that Latin Christianity may point to her hospitals and brotherhoods, as well as to her universities, schools, and churches, ' as in great part owing to the munificence or the active agency of her universal hierarchy.' But we must go further back than the date of distinctively ' Latin Christianity ' for the origin of hospitals. It is really one aspect of the striking contrast which challenges attention in many different ways, whether in art, in literature, or in life, between the civilizations of the Pagan and of the Christian era. And it may be said without exaggeration to reveal the radical nature of that contrast. A modern writer has justly observed that 'there is no feature of the old (Pagan) civilization so repulsive as its indifference to suffering.'

"The weaklings of mankind could neither contribute to the joyousness of life nor bear its burdens; they were out of place equally in court or camp, and were better out of the world altogether, seeing that they were not of it. And therefore, as was only natural, charitable institutions were absolutely unknown. The almost entire ignoring of all sympathetic reference to childhood in classical poetry, as compared with the prominent place it occupies in the poetry of every Christian age—which is somewhere dwelt on by Dr. Farrar—illustrates one side of this contrast. It finds a more ghastly illustration in the fact, noted by Mr. Lecky, that 'the infant was entirely unprotected, and infanticide was regarded by no one as a crime.' But the sacredness of human life and the sentiment of compassion so conspicuous in Christian ethics speedily produced a marvellous change. Even during the ages of persecution the hospital and the refuge (*Xenodochion*) had already come into existence, and the catacomb epitaphs bear abundant witness to the multitude of foundlings supported by Christian charity. After the conversion of the Emperor, one of the first changes in the law was to provide for the care of infants, and under Justinian we find mention of public *brephotrophia*. . . . . If we pass on to the Middle Ages, Innocent III., one of the ablest and most representative of the Popes, founded both the Hospital of Santo Spirito at Rome, for patients of all nationalities, and a Foundling Hospital, and Gregory IX. not long afterwards founded the Lateran Hospital, which is still kept up. Every monastery, moreover, as a rule, had its infirmary, not only for the use of its own members, but for the care of invalids and convalescents generally, and the nursing of the weak, the blind, and the aged; and these infirmaries were in fact the originals and patterns of our modern hospitals. The earliest record of the establishment of a separate hospital in England is in the time of Lanfranc, Archbishop of Canterbury, who founded two in 1080, one for leprosy, and one for general purposes. St. Bartholomew's, Smithfield, founded in 1102; St. Thomas's, in the Borough, in 1213; and Bethlehem, in 1247—converted under Henry VIII. into a receptacle for lunatics—were all originally connected with religious houses.

"The curious fact, which has been noticed by historians, that so few names comparatively have come down to us signalized for what yet was from the first so widely spread a work of Christian philanthropy, is in itself significant. And hence it comes to pass that the men who, at a later date, covered Europe with a network of hospitals after the Crusades, have passed from recollection, though in another and most important sense the good they did 'lives after them.' But this really shows how entirely that has become a matter of course, a necessary and universal incident of Christian civilization, which under the previous *régime* had been altogether unknown. If, to cite Milman's words, 'the haughtiest Popes condescend to imitate the Lord in washing the feet of poor men,' the ceremony, however perfunctorily it may sometimes have been performed, had a background of meaning which was never lost sight of in the Church. It is no doubt a satisfaction at once to the piety and the historical sense of Leo XIII. to know that, in his proposed foundation of a cholera hospital at Rome, he is emulating the best example of some of the grandest of his predecessors in a matter where they—to use his own phrase—trod most closely in the steps of their divine Master. Rome, Athens, Alexandria, in their old heathen days, took no heed of suffering, or only recognized it as an eyesore to be concealed or even a crime to be suppressed. The question has been debated from various points of view in our own day, whether Christian morality can be maintained in the absence of Christian belief. A Pope may at all events be pardoned for the amiable weakness of adhering in this respect to the old-fashioned ethics of Christendom.

It is in this way the Church has solved the problem of poverty as a social question. She has ever treated poverty as our Lord prescribed, with reverential respect, kindly sympathy, and tender compassion.

Let us now briefly consider the beneficent action and influence of the Church on the condition of the laboring and artisan classes. At the time of the advent of our Blessed Lord, the civilization of the pagan world had reached its height, but it was a cold, heartless civilization ; it was like a marble statue by Phidias, exquisitely beautiful, and seeming to breathe and palpitate with life, but yet hard, cold, unfeeling, and pitiless. There was then no pity for the poor, and no consideration for the toiling masses. Labor had fallen into contempt, was a badge of degradation, and considered as only fit for slaves. Workingmen were deprived of the rights of manhood, were robbed of their liberties and civil rights, and were reduced to the position of slaves. Both in Greek and Roman civilization work had been made servile, and workingmen slaves. At the time of Augustus Cæsar there were upwards of sixty millions of slaves in the vast empire over which he ruled. And those slaves were not men on whose brows an Indian or an African sun had burnt the brand of slavery ; they were, in blood and race, the equals of their masters. In Roman law a slave was not a person, but a thing ; he had, of course, no civil or political rights ; he had no power to receive a legacy, no power of civil action, and was entirely beyond the pale and protection of law ; he had not even religious duties or hopes. He was in everything absolutely subject to his master's will, who had the power of life and death over him. Such is the frightful condition to which millions of workingmen were reduced in ancient civilization, when they were described by Seneca as having " fettered feet, bound hands, and branded faces."

Our divine Saviour became a workingman, was a carpenter, and the reputed son of a carpenter, and for years labored and toiled with St. Joseph for his daily bread.

He thus made labor sacred, He exalted it in human estimation, and gave it a dignity in the eyes of men and a power of merit in the eyes of God. In the Christian system, labor having become ennobled by the action and example of Christ, the workingman rose in the scale of human estimation ; he ceased to be regarded as a thing, and was looked upon as a man possessing human rights and liberties and duties. Men, whether free or bond, were taught the doctrines of equality before God, who was their common father ; they were taught the doctrine of human and Christian brotherhood, that, in the language of St. Paul, " in one spirit they were all baptized into one body, whether Jews or Gentiles, whether *bond* or *free* " (1 Corinthians xii., 13) ; " that they were all children of God by faith in Jesus Christ, that there was neither Jew nor Greek, neither bond nor free, but that they were all *one* in Christ Jesus "

and at the same time safeguarding the interests of his employer or patron, thus establishing the harmonious play of rights and duties, of reciprocal claims and interests. We proceed to quote some of those enactments and rules that governed the trade-associations of the Middle Ages as we find them cited by Digby, from a curious old book, called *Livre des Métiers*, which contains the registry of the trades of Paris in the 13th century and the rules enacted for their government. The simplicity of some of these rules is combined with a most useful discretion.

But let us hear them as they are delivered. "Any person," says one of them, " can exercise this trade in tin vèssels at Paris freely—" pour tant qu'il face bon œuvre et loial."[1] He must never work at night, on pain of a fine to the king, "quar la clartez de la nuit n'est mie si suffisant que il peussent faire bone œuvre et loial de leur mestier. Nus cordiers ne puet œuvrer de nuit pour les fausses œuvres que on i puet faire."[2] The bucklemakers ordain "que nus mestre ne doit souffrir entour li vallet qui ne soit bons et loiaus, ne réveur ne mauvès garçon de quelque lieu qu'il soit, soit de Paris ou d'ailleurs."[3] The lacemakers ordain that no one shall work by night "pour les fauses œuvres que en i feit, et pour ce que la clartez de la chandoile ne suffist mie à leur mestier."[4] The general condition required in all the trades is expressed thus : "pour tant que il face bone œuvre et loial."[5] The silk-mercers ordain "que nul ouvrier soit vallet ou mestre qui soit blasmés de houlerie ou de mauvése renommée, ou qui auroit esté banis d'aucun mestier ou d'aucun pays, ne puist ouvrer ou dit mestier,"[6] before being punished. Generally, in all trades, masters could employ their sons as apprentices, but " seulement nez de loial mariage."[7] Of stonemasons, Master Guillaume swore, " que il le mestier garderait bien et loiaument à son pooir ausi pour le poure come pour le riche, et pour le foible come pour le fort."[8] Every mason and plasterer swore that he would himself loyally observe the rules,

---

[1] " As far as he makes good work and lawful."

[2] " For the light of the night is not by half so sufficient that they can make good work and lawful of their trade. No rope-makers may work by night, on account of the false works one may then make."

[3] " That no master must suffer around him workmen who are not good and loyal, nor idler, nor bad boy, from whatever place, whether from Paris or elsewhere."

[4] " On account of the false works one does in it, and because the light of the candle is not half sufficient for their trade."

[5] " As far as he makes good work and loyal."

[6] " That no workman, whether apprentice or master, who is blamed for irregularity or bad fame, or has been banished from any trade or country, can work at the said trade."

[7] " Only born of lawful marriage."

[8] " That he, the tradesman, should care well and lawfully, according to his power, as well for the poor as for the rich, and for the weak as for the strong."

but that he would inform the master if he should ever find any
one in fault in anything.   The stonemasons and plasterers must
swear that they will put nothing in the plaster but the best materials and that they will give good and loyal measure, that the mor-
tar shall be made of good lime and that if it be made of other
stone they shall pay a fine.   The linen-draper swears that he cannot have an apprentice " se il n'est si fil de léal espouse, ou ses
frères ou ses niès nès de léal mariage."[1]

No draper should suffer near him, or near any other of the trade,
any workman who lives immorally; and if any workman should
be discovered, having a vicious connection in the suburbs, the
provost of Paris should be informed, and he will make him leave
the city or have him chastised for his folly.   In the trade of " tapiz
nostrez," or coarse carpeting, no one shall employ any thread,
" fors que de file de laine bon et loial. Et ce ont establi li preudomes
du mestier pour le commun profit de touz et pour léauté."[2]   Of the
foulons (fullers), if any workman in the trade should discover that
there is any fellow-servant who has been a bad character, he should
make it known to the master under pain of a fine.   The stocking
makers swear that they will use strong thread, which has not been
rotted by the dye; for, if the thread should be thus rotted, the stock-
ings shall be burned, and the maker must pay a fine of five sous;
four to the king, and the rest to the guardians of the trade for their
trouble.   No glover shall work by night, " à clartez de feu ne de
lumière, quar l'uevre qui est fête par nuit n'est ne bone ne léal."[3]   In
the bridle trade, if any old work be painted over and regilt, or
mended and exposed for sale, the work must be burned, and the
seller fined.   Of linen drapers, " nule qui soit eslongiés de son
paiis por mauvès cas l'en ne le doit recevoir on dit mestier."[4]   In the
trade of " tapiz Sarrassin " no one shall employ a strange workman
until he knows that he is a " preudome et loial."   Tailors were
obliged to cut their cloth in an open shop, " à la veue du peuple,"[5]
to prevent any suspicion of fraud.

It is in this admirable manner that the Church, in the days of
an undivided Christendom, regulated the relations between capital
and labor, between the employers and the employed.   The rights
of both were well defined and secured.   The artisan was awarded

---

[1] " If he is not son of lawful spouse, or his brothers or kindred born of lawful marriage."
[2] " Except woollen thread good and lawful.   And this the inspectors of the trade
have established for the common profit of all and for loyalty."
[3] " By light of fire nor of torch, for work made by night is neither good nor lawful."
[4] " None banished from his country for bad causes may be received into the said
trade."
[5] " In the sight of the people."

just compensation for his labor and skill, and his patron was certain to obtain good work and just value for his money. There were no harsh separations, no exasperating inequalities, no heart burnings between class and class, but on the contrary there prevailed peace, harmony and good-will. The Church, to a great extent, reigned supreme over men's consciences; her teachings were, on the whole, listened to and obeyed; her authority as the divinely appointed teacher and guide was generally acknowledged, and the result was the reign of justice, of right and order amongst the various classes of society. Of course, in this fallen world the Church will be always the Church militant and not the Church triumphant; and hence, even in the Middle Ages there were several dark spots which she was unable to remove, in consequence of the opposition of human passions and self-interests; but from all that she accomplished in the teeth of the tremendous difficulties created by the exceptional social and political circumstances of the period, we can easily picture to ourselves the glorious reign of " peace on earth and good-will to men " she would have established, had she not been impeded and thwarted in the perfect fulfilment of her divine mission to mankind by the events of the sixteenth century.

In the ages of faith the spectral hand of " Proletariat " had not yet appeared on the walls of the social fabric writing the sentence of its doom, and making kings' faces change and grow pale with affright. Such a dread apparition was reserved for our days, when the principles and teachings of the so-called Reformation are working out to the bitter end their logical but destructive consequences. If the ripe fruit of the Protestant revolt is bitterness and ashes to the taste, it is because the tree that produced it is radically bad, from root to branch, and is in very deed the wild olive of Scripture that has not been grafted on the good olive which is Jesus Christ living in His Church.

Another peril of our times pointed out and deplored by the Holy Father in his Encyclical letter, *Humanum genus*, is the pernicious and subversive doctrine now in vogue regarding civil authority, its origin and rights, and the rights and duties of subjects. Says the Sovereign Pontiff:

" From the disturbing errors which we have described the greatest dangers to States are to be feared. For the fear of God and reverence for divine laws being taken away, the authority of rulers despised, sedition permitted and approved, and the popular passions urged on to lawlessness, with no restraint save that of punishment, a change and overthrow of all things will necessarily follow. Yea, this change and overthrow is deliberately planned and put forward by many associations of *Communists* and *Socialists;* and to their undertakings the sect of Freemasons is not hostile, but greatly favors their designs, and holds in common with them their chief opinions. And if these men do not at once and everywhere endeavor to carry out their extreme views, it is not to be attributed to their teaching and their will, but to the virtue of that divine religion which cannot be destroyed."

It will be in order here to consider briefly Catholic teaching and action as regards the question of civil power and the duties and rights of subjects. It will be seen that she holds the scales equally poised between the correlative rights and duties of authority and allegiance, that whilst she protects and upholds the just rights of kings and rulers, she at the same time provides for the largest measure of rational liberty for subjects.

She has ever taught the divine origin of civil power. She anointed her kings and made their persons and their office sacred in the eyes of their subjects, and inculcated the duty and obligation of obedience to them for the reason that they were God's ministers. With St. Paul she said: " Let every soul be subject to the higher powers, for there is no power but from God, and those that are, are ordained of God. Therefore, he that resisteth the power resisteth the ordinance of God, and they that resist purchase to themselves damnation. Wherefore, be subject of necessity, not only for wrath but also for conscience' sake " (Romans, xiii.).

She condemns disobedience, disloyalty, and rebellion to just laws and legitimate government, as most grievous sins, and she bans and excommunicates from her pale all members of secret societies that have for aim the overthrow of governmental authority and the destruction of the State. Hence, the Holy Father in his Encyclical Letter teaches : " As men are by the will of God born for civil union and society, and as the power to rule is so necessary a bond of society that, if it be taken away, society must at once be broken up, it follows that from Him who is the Author of society has come also the authority to rule ; so that whosoever rules, he is the minister of God. Wherefore, as the end and nature of human society so requires, it is right to obey the just commands of lawful authority, as it is right to obey God, who ruleth all things ; and it is most untrue that the people have it in their power to cast aside their obedience whensoever they please." On the other hand, the Church has not failed to impress on kings and rulers the duty of governing with justice and for the welfare and happiness of their subjects. With St. Thomas, she told them that the people were not for the kings, but the kings for the people. Liberty of the subject, mild government, economy in regard to public revenue, maintenance of justice, peace and order, the responsibility of kings, were the lessons she constantly inculcated.

In this connection it will be useful to call attention to the teachings of some of the most eminent and representative Catholic theologians on the origin of civil power and on forms of government. St. Thomas Aquinas teaches that civil governments are not " jure divino," but " jure humano," and that to " ordain anything for the common good is the right of the people, or of some one representing the people."

Bellarmine says : " It is false that political princes (civil rulers) have their power from God only ; for they have it from God only so far as He has planted a natural instinct in the minds of men that they should wish to be governed by some one. But whether men should wish to be governed by kings or by consuls, by one or by many, by a perpetual or a temporary magistrate, depends on their own wishes ; as also it is not the special command of God, but the wish of men which determines that this person should be king rather than that. Wherefore St. Thomas, in the cited passage 22, quaes. x., art. 10, and quaes. xii., art. 2, lays it down as a matter certain and decided that political governments and kingdoms are not founded on divine, but on human, law,—a proposition which no scholar would contradict." (*De Potestate Sum. Pontif.*, cap. 21, p. 203.) This doctrine of the delegation of civil authority from the people, Suarez states, was the common opinion of his day, and he goes on to say " that the civil power, whenever it is found in a man or in a prince, has emanated, according to usual and legitimate law, from the people and the community, either directly or remotely, and that it cannot otherwise be justly possessed " (*De Leg.*, lib. iii., cap. 4.) And the same illustrious theologian, in his work against James I. of England, declares that the opinion of Bellarmine, cited above, was " *ancient, received, true and necessary.*" And this has continued to be the doctrine of Catholic theologians down to the present day. The king or supreme magistrate is, in Catholic teaching, but the executor of the will of the nation or people whom he governs ; and should he abuse his trust, or employ the supreme power with which he has been invested to the public detriment ; should he, in other words, rule his people with injustice and tyranny, and trample on their rights and liberties, he could be lawfully dethroned and torn down from his place of power.

The following is a synopsis of Catholic teaching on this subject :

1st. Civil society is a divine appointment.

2d. In all societies there must be a governing power.

3d. This power, in all its just laws, must be obeyed, not only for fear but for conscience' sake, for it is an ordinance of God, and they who resist purchase to themselves damnation.

4th. The form of human government is founded on human and not on divine right.

5th. The king or chief magistrate must rule for the common weal and not for his personal interest or gratification.

6th. The subjects cannot obey the civil power when its commands are opposed to the divine law.

7th. When laws are unjust they are not binding in conscience. It may, however, become necessary to obey such laws from motives of prudence, that is, in order to avoid scandals and commotions.

8th. Laws are unjust from some one of the following causes:

(1.) When they are opposed to the common weal.

(2.) When the laws have not for aim the good of the common weal.

(3.) When the legislator outsteps the limits of his powers.

At the coronation of a Catholic king, the bishop, after admonishing him to defend the Christian religion, says to him: " Justice, without which no society can last long, thou shalt unwaveringly exercise towards all. Widows, orphans, the poor and the weak thou shalt defend from all oppression.

" According to thy royal dignity thou shalt show thyself benignant, mild, and affable to all approaching thee.

" And thou shalt so carry thyself that thou mayest appear to reign not for thine own utility, but for that of all thy people, and to expect the rewards of thy good deeds not on earth, but in heaven."

For the cause of justice and peace, says Digby, the Holy See was invoked by all nations in common until the sixteenth century; and no power was too secure of its own sufficiency to set the Pope's counsels at defiance. Its great judgment when censuring the unjust seemed to long ages like Heaven's dreadful thunder. "The stones heard the voice and the trees of the wood trembled."

It is in this way the Church of God sought to establish the just equilibrium between responsibilities and duties, between rights and obligations, between the authority and responsibility of supreme power and the rights and duties of subjects, thus ensuring as far as in her lay the reign of liberty without license and of authority without despotism.

On the subject of the respective influences of the doctrines of Catholicity and Protestantism on civil liberty, a Protestant writer, in the *Christian Examiner* for January, 1865, makes the following acute and, for the most part, correct observations:

" That the Catholic dogma is more congenial with democratic institutions than the Protestant dogma, is a fact too clear to be disputed; and if this consideration were of any vital moment, we might leave the case here on the threshold. The principle that lies at the foundation of democratic institutions is *man's capability for self-government.* This principle implies the essential rectitude of human nature, in all its spheres of faculty. It implies that man is possessed of reason and of free-will; that he knows what is wise, just, orderly, beneficial, that he is at liberty to elect it, and that he has power to enact it. It implies that his natural ideas of what is right, equitable and obligatory are correct, or may be made so by suitable study, care and attention. All this the Catholic theology asserts; all this the Protestant theology denies. The Catholic dogma maintains that human nature preserved its essential goodness after the fall of Adam. The Protestant dogma contends that human nature, in consequence of the fall of Adam, became totally depraved. The Catholic dogma accommodates itself to human reason, assuming its capacity to receive truths presented to it; the Protestant dogma almost vilifies reason in its jealousy for faith, and allows it no power of judgment in matters of moral truth. The Catholic dogma acknowledges man's moral freedom; the Protestant doctrine affirms predestination. The Catholic ought, therefore, to be a democrat; the Protestant ought to be a monarchist. Neither can logically be anything else.

"This logical necessity is confirmed by other peculiarities of the two systems. The Protestant Church makes a radical distinction between different orders of mankind, by classifying them as regenerate and unregenerate, elect and non-elect, children of God and children of the world. It divides by palpable barriers the sheep from the goats. The church member is a person set apart from the general congregation, as an object of peculiar consideration in the sight of God and man,—a sacred person specially illuminated, guided, upheld by the Holy Spirit. Here, it would seem, is a basis something more than speculative,—a basis actually laid in institutions,—for the most absolute of all governments, a theocracy,—a government of priests ruling in the name of God—a spiritual oligarchy. The Catholic Church, on the contrary, puts all mankind in the bosom of the Church on an equality. The sacraments and the symbols are for all on the same terms; the same articles of faith satisfy the wise and the simple. All social distinctions disappear at the foot of her altar. Her priesthood is not a caste; no one of the faithful is disqualified by his obscurity for the office of Supreme Pontiff. Side by side, the rich and the poor, the noble and the plebeian, the lord and the serf, bend in worship and kneel on the pavement to receive the consecrated elements."

Whilst it is undeniably true, as this writer affirms, that many of the doctrines of Protestantism tend to absolutism in civil government, it is equally true that its radical principle of private judgment leads to anarchy and revolution.

With the "Reformation" there came into play a new philosophy of life and new doctrines and principles of action that aimed at the removal of the landmarks of Catholic civilization. In proportion as the influence and authority of the Church were diminished, the balancing power of her laws and teachings was removed, and history tells the result. Voluntary poverty for Christ's dear sake was denounced as a mean superstition; Dives was reëstablished in his place of honor, and poor Lazarus, with his sores and rags, was left begging and scorned at the door. Alms-houses and charitable institutions were suppressed, monasteries were destroyed, the abbey-lands—the patrimony of the poor—were confiscated, and religious orders of holy men and women, Christ-consecrated, were themselves reduced to beggary. Poverty had lost all its sacredness and became an object of scorn and contempt, and was treated as a crime; and the old pagan adage of Juvenal was again verified, viz.,

" that poverty has nothing so repugnant as this, that it makes men objects of ridicule and scorn."

Poverty was regarded as a crime, and mendicants were punished as criminals. When the Catholic monasteries were suppressed in England, the poor wandered in hungry crowds over the country. To suppress this nuisance, so condemnatory of the teachings and policy of the "Reformers," the first parliament that assembled under Edward VI. enacted "that whosoever lived idly and loiteringly for the space of three days came under the description of a vagabond, and was liable to the following punishment: Two justices of the peace might order the letter V to be burned on his breast, and to adjudge him to serve the informer two years as his slave. His master was bound to provide him with bread and water, but not meat; might fix an iron round his neck, arm or leg, and was authorized to compel him to labor at any work, however vile it might be, by beating, chaining, or otherwise. If the slave absented himself for a fortnight, the letter S was burned on his cheek or forehead, and he became a slave for life; and, if he offended a second time in like manner, his flight subjected him to the penalties of felony."

Let us listen to the testimony of a Protestant historian, Cobbett, regarding the misery and ruin brought on the poorer classes of England by the so-called Reformation:

"330. Returning, now, to paragraphs 50, 51 and 52, just mentioned; it is there seen, that the Catholic Church rendered all municipal laws about the *poor* wholly unnecessary; but, when that Church had been plundered and destroyed; when the greedy leading ' Reformers ' had sacked the convents and the churches; when those great estates, which *of right belonged* to the poorer classes, had been taken from them; when the parsonages had been first well pillaged, and the remnant of their revenues given to *married men;* then the *poor* (for poor there will and must be in every community) were left destitute of the means of existence, other than the fruits of beggary, theft, and robbery. Accordingly, when '*good* Queen Bess ' had put the finishing hand to the plundering of the Church and poor, once happy and free and hospitable England became a den of famishing robbers and slaves. STRYPE, a Protestant, and an authority to whom HUME appeals and refers many hundreds of times, tells us of a letter from a Justice of the Peace in Somersetshire, to the Lord Chief Justice, saying: ' I may justly say, that the *able men* that are abroad, seeking the spoil and confusion of the land, are able, if they were reduced to good subjection, to give the greatest enemy her majesty hath a strong battle, and, as they are now, are so much strength to the enemy. Besides, the generation that daily springeth from them *is likely to be most wicked.* These spare neither rich nor poor; but, whether it be large or small, all is fish that cometh to net with them; and yet I say, both they and the rest are trussed up a-pace.' The same Justice says : ' In default of justice, many wicked thieves escape. For most commonly the most simple countrymen and women, looking no farther than to the loss of their own goods, are of opinion that they would not procure any man's death for all the goods in the world.' And while the '*good* Bess ' complained bitterly of the *non-execution* of her laws, the same Protestant historian tells us that '*she executed more than five hundred criminals in a year,*' and was so little satisfied with that number, that she threatened to send private persons to see her penal laws executed '*for profit and gain's sake.*' It appears that she did not threaten in vain; for, soon after this, a complaint was made in Parliament that the stipendiary magistrate of that day was 'a kind of living creature, who, for half a dozen of chickens, would dispense with a dozen of penal statutes.' She did not, however, stop, with this '*liberal*' use of the gallows. Such was the degree of beggary, of vagabondage, and of thievishness and robbery, that she resorted, particularly in London and its neighborhood, to *martial law*. This fact is so complete a proof of the horrible effects of the ' Reformation ' upon the moral state of the people, and it is so fully characteristic of the government, which the people of England had, in consequence of that Reformation, become so debased as to submit to, that I must take the statement as it stands in HUME, who gives the very words of '*good* and *glorious* Bess's ' commission to her head murderer upon this occasion. ' The streets of London were very much infested with *idle vagabonds* and *riotous persons ;* the Lord Mayor had endeavored to repress this disorder; the Star-chamber had exerted its authority, and inflicted punishment on these *rioters.* But the Queen, finding these remedies ineffectual, revived ' [*revived ?* What does he mean by REVIVED ?] '*martial law,* and gave Sir THOMAS WILFORD a commisson as Provost-martial ; ' Granting him authority, and commanding him, upon *signification* given by the justices of the peace in London or the neighboring counties, of such offenders, *worthy to be speedily executed by martial law,* to take them, and, *according to the justice of martial law,* to execute them *upon the gallows or gibbet.*' And yet, this is she whom we have been taught to call '*good* Queen Bess;' this is she, of the '*glories*' of whose reign there are men of learning base enough to talk, even to this day !

" 331. But, such were the natural consequences of the destruction of the Catholic Church, and of the plundering of the poor, which accompanied that destruction, and particularly of lodging all power, ecclesiastical and civil, in the same hands. However, though this terrible she tyrant spared neither racks nor halters, though she was continually reproving the executors of her bloody laws, for their *remissness* while they were strewing the country with the carcasses of malefactors or alleged malefactors, all would not do ; that hunger, which breaks through stone walls, set even *her* terrors and torments at defiance : at last, it was found to be absolutely necessary to make some general and permanent and solid *provision for the poor ;* and, in the forty-third year of her reign, was passed that Act, which is in force to this day, and which provides a maintenance for indigent persons, which maintenance is to come from the land, assessed and collected by overseers, and the payment enforced by process the most effectual and most summary. And here we have the great, the prominent, the staring, the horrible and ever-durable consequence of the ' Reformation,' that is to say, *pauperism established by law.*"

The teachings and principles, in relation to poverty and wealth respectively, brought into play by the " Reformation," have been in operation in the world for the last three hundred years, and have borne bitter fruit, and leave the question of pauperism one of the most difficult problems of political economy. Protestantism has stripped poverty of the sacredness given it by Christ and recognized by his Church, and exalted wealth in human estimation. It has, in fact, constituted temporal prosperity as the test of Gospel truth. Through the mouths of its theologians and apologists it has again and again pointed to the alleged prosperity and wealth of Protestant nations as an irrefutable proof of the heavenly origin and truth, as well as the elevating influences, of Protestant teachings, and it has pointed the finger of contemptuous scorn at the alleged unprogressiveness and comparative poverty of Catholic States as the most undeniable proof of the corrupting and degrading influences of the Catholic faith.

The Gospel of Protestantism is not that of Him who said: "Blessed are the poor," and who denounced woes against the rich. It has covered poverty with contempt; it has belauded wealth; it has thereby served to intensify into fierce activity the desire for riches and love of gain inherent in the human breast, and consequently it has directly tended to beget that intense selfishness, that rage for money, which characterize modern society, and which have created those wealthy monopolies that under the wheels of the juggernaut of commerce are grinding and crushing the poor and toiling masses, and are more. or less responsible for the heartburnings and fierce discontent of the lower orders with society as at present constituted, and which find their expression and embodiment in Socialism, Communism and kindred associations that threaten to rend asunder the body politic, and tear it into shreds.

The principles of the "Reformation" had two opposite tendencies in relation to government and civil liberty—that is, towards absolutism on the one hand, and revolution on the other. In Protestant countries the state subjected the spiritual order to the temporal or secular, and sought to govern the souls and consciences as well as the bodies of its subjects. It became a despotic Cæsarism and attempted to reduce to practice the false and tyrannous doctrine expressed in the formula: "*Cujus regio illius et religio;*" the people of the country must be of the same religion as are the rulers. The absolutism of Protestant states was on the one hand the result of their revolt against the authority of the Church, which asserted and maintained the independence of the spiritual order and the subjection of the governing power to the laws of eternal justice; and on the other hand it was the effect of their recoil from the logical tendencies of the licentious and anarchical principle of private judgment which constituted private opinion and individual reason the judge of religious and civil authority, and which, as it created revolution in the spiritual order, tended also to beget revolt and rebellion against the State. Government in England became a tyranny of the most pronounced type; for one hundred and fifty years after the "Reformation" in that country the liberties of the people were crushed, the privileges secured by the Catholic *Magna Charta* were trampled under foot, and the royal prerogative swallowed up almost every other element of government. It was only at the Revolution of 1688 that the principles of the great charter were partially asserted and revived. Political freedom shared the same fate in the other Protestant countries.

"In the Roman Catholic religion," says a Protestant writer, "there is a resisting principle to absolute civil power from the division of authority with the head of the Church of Rome, but in the north of Europe the Lutheran church is entirely subservient to the civil power, and the whole of the northern peoples of Protestant countries have lost their liberties ever since they changed their religion." On the other hand, it is undeniable that the logical tendencies of the principle of private judgment are necessarily in the direction of revolt and anarchy. The most striking effect of the first preaching of the " Reformation," says Hallam, was that it appealed to the ignorant; and though political liberty cannot be reckoned the aim of those who introduced it, yet there predominated that revolutionary spirit which loves to witness destruction for its own sake, and that intoxicated self-confidence which renders folly mischievous.

Macaulay institutes a comparison between the " Reformation " and the French Revolution—the one was a revolution in religion, the other in politics, but both were the outcome of the Protestant principle of private judgment.

" The only event," he says, " of modern times which can be properly compared with the Reformation is the French Revolution ; or to speak more accurately, that great revolution of political feeling which took place in almost every part of the civilized world during the eighteenth century, and which obtained in France its most terrible and signal triumph. Each of these memorable events may be described as a rising up of human reason against a caste." —(Review of Nares's Memoirs of Lord Burghley, Miscell., p. 173). It is, then, the Protestant principle of private judgment, not the Catholic principle of authority, that begets revolutions, overturns thrones, and sends kings into exile or to the scaffold. Revolution and Communism are political Protestantism, for they are the application of the principle of private judgment to civil government, social order, and the rights of property. It may be said that Communism has invaded Catholic countries, and has therein more fully displayed its diabolical character. Granted ; but it has invaded and flourished in those countries in spite of the Catholic principle which condemns it, and not because of it. The flood of burning lava that flows from the crater of a volcano is the direct issue of the volcano which vomits it forth; but should it flow down to the underlying villages and destroy them, those villages will be its victims and not its generating cause. And so it is with the Catholic countries that are cursed by the presence of Communism : they are its only victims, but the volcano from which it has burst forth in a wasting burning flood is the Protestant principle of private judgment. We gladly admit that Protestants have no sympathy with the wickedness of Communism, but that is because they are better than their principle.

It may be objected that the most equitable laws and the best regulated liberty obtain in England and America—Protestant na-

tions.   The answer is that these nations inherit their just laws and
their broad and ennobling liberties from their Catholic forefathers,
and that the great charter of their rights and liberties was won for
the English speaking races by the Catholic bishops and Catholic
barons assembled on the field of Runnymede.   Besides, the natural
and political qualities and characteristics of a people count for
much in the matter of self-government and political liberty.   We
find, therefore, that Protestantism has been by turns the friend and
flatterer of despotic rulers, and the ally and associate of rebellious
mobs.   Janus-like, it has had two faces, one of which smiled approvingly on absolutism and the other on revolution and civil war.
It has, therefore, been in principle neither the support of just government nor the friend of civil and rational liberty.   It has powerfully
contributed to destroy the just equilibrium established by the
Church between the reciprocal rights and duties of rulers and their
subjects, and must, therefore, be rightly held responsible for the
present unsettled state of civil society, where kings rule, not by
the grace of God, but by the power of " big battalions;" and subjects grudgingly obey, not for the love of God, but because they
cannot help themselves, and are habitually ripe for the work of
revolution and social anarchy.

Another pernicious and destructive evil which is eating at the
very vitals of modern society, and which the Holy Father, in his
Encyclical Letter, so earnestly condemns and deplores, is the doctrine and practice of divorce.   The respective teachings of Catholicity and Protestantism on this fundamental question are too well
known to require to be here detailed at any length.   In her teaching and action in this matter, the Church has been the saviour of the
family and the bulwark of civil and religious society.   The family
is the germ and matrix of all other societies.   The state is but a collection of a certain number of families organized under the authority
of a common chief for the protection of life, liberty, and property, and
the pursuit of happiness; and the Church is in a certain sense but
the organization of a certain number of Christian families under the
guidance and authority of a common father for the protection and
development of their spiritual life.   Hence, what the root is to the
tree that grows from it, what the foundation is to the house that rests
upon it, what the well-spring in mountain solitudes is to the river
that rises and flows from it, that the family is to the State and to
the Church.   From it the former receives its citizens, and the latter her children. It follows, therefore, that whatever tends to break
up and desecrate the family inflicts the same injury on society as
he who poisons the river-head inflicts on the healthfulness and
purity of its waters, or as he who gashes and hacks the roots of a
tree would inflict on the trunk and branches.   Now, as society rests

on the family, so the family rests upon marriage and draws from it the character and purity of its life. The Church, then, by insisting on the unity of marriage and its indissoluble character, has guarded and protected the honor and integrity, the purity and sacredness of family life, and has thereby guarded and secured the best and most sacred interests of society at large. Even her enemies admit and extol the saving action of the Church in relation to this matter. In order to obtain some idea of the immense benefits and blessings for which society is indebted to her for her holy and inviolable guardianship of the sanctities of marriage, let us glance for a moment at the effects of divorce. Divorce is a violation of the sacredness of home, it is a desecration of the sanctities and purity of family life, and a wicked invasion of the inalienable rights of the family and children. It is a rending asunder of the unity of marriage, and it establishes successive polygamy. It destroys the indissolubility of marriage by dissolving the bond of matrimony; it desecrates the sanctity of home, for it encourages conjugal infidelity, and puts a premium on adultery. It breaks down the barriers raised up by Christ and His Church against the headlong tide of human passions, and lets this impure tide loose in a destructive flood on society. It is a violation of the dignity of Christian womanhood, and pulls it down into that state of shame and degradation to which it was reduced in Paganism. It is, for the most part, a conspiracy against the rights of woman both as wife and mother, and robs the children of such broken marriages of that moral training and home education to which they are entitled, and makes them practically orphans even during the lifetime of their parents.

Now, what has been the attitude of Protestantism on this momentous question? Has it been true to the teachings of Christ? Has it been loyal to the highest interests of the family and to the sacred cause of Christian morality and civilization? History emphatically answers—No. It is an undoubted historical fact that Luther, Melanchthon, and the other leaders of the " Reformation " officially permitted Philip, Landgrave of Hesse, to have two wives at once. It is an undoubted historical fact that Henry VIII. of England broke with the Holy See because of its stern refusal to allow him to discard his legitimate wife, and during her lifetime to take to himself another. It was on this account, and on this account alone, that Henry VIII. became the head of the " Reformation " in England. Thus it may truly be said that the doctrine and practice of divorce have been the parents of the Protestant revolt. Protestantism has been wittily defined as the emancipation of the flesh ; and the definition is certainly true of it in its relation to the marriage question, for it has emancipated the flesh and its lusts from the holy and salutary restraints put upon them by the doctrine of the unity and indissolubility of marriage. Accordingly, it is found that the practice of divorce is, under certain conditions, sanctioned by the civil laws of every Protestant state with the most destructive results to the best interests of the family and society as well as to the sacred cause of Christian morality. So widespread has this evil become in the United States, and so detrimental to public morality and to social well-being, that several State legislatures have had under consideration the necessity of passing more stringent laws in regulation and restriction of it.

But it is time to conclude. The Holy Father, towards the end of his memorable Encyclical on Freemasonry, exhorts the clergy and laity " to strive by their united efforts to make men thoroughly love the Church; for, the greater their knowledge and love of the Church, the more will they be turned away from clandestine societies." It is in compliance with this exhortation, which comes with such force to all true and loyal Catholic hearts, that this article has been written. Would that we could do full justice to the inspiring theme. Enough, however, has been written to show that the Catholic Church is the mother of Christian civilization and the friend and saviour of society ; whereas, Protestantism, in its teachings and influences, is principally the cause of the terrible evils that afflict modern society and menace it with ruin. Other evil agencies, such as Freemasonry and kindred associations, have taken up the destructive forces brought into life and action by Protestant principles, and are energetically carrying them out to their sad and fatal consequences.

If, then, Christian society is to be saved, and Christian civilization is to be awakened into a new life and given a new power for the welfare and happiness of mankind, the world must return to the teachings of the Catholic Church, and must embody its divine principles in its life and conduct. Protestantism cannot undo its destructive work. It has been able to pull down, but it is not able to build up again. Freemasonry has neither the power nor the will to save Christian society and social order; it would rather surround itself with the ruins and the wrecks of both. Communism, Socialism, and other human organizations serve but to aggravate the evils which they have been ostensibly established to remove. God has made the nations of the earth curable, " sanabiles fecit nationes orbis terrarum " (*Wisdom I.*, 14), but He has given the healing power to but one institution here below, and that is the Church—Catholic, Apostolic and Roman ; and she is, indeed, like her divine Founder, and by virtue of His indwelling presence and power, the healer of the sick nations and the saviour of society. May God hasten the day of the universal triumph of the Church for His greater glory and for the salvation and happiness of the human race, which He has redeemed in the Precious Blood of His

Adorable Son—Christ our Saviour. "*O Emmanuel, rex et legifer noster, expectatio gentium, et salvator earum ; veni ad salvandum nos, Domine Deus noster!*" "O Emmanuel, our King and our Law-giver, the longing of the nations, yea and the salvation thereof, come to save us, O Lord our God!"

LITERARY AND SCIENTIFIC HABITS OF THOUGHT.

THE philosophical problems that come up for solution at the present day are very ancient. We find them all debated in Plato; and in the light of modern issues his pages become instinct with life. Whether we sit with Socrates in the forum and listen to him discussing with Theætetus the limits of science and the relativity of knowledge; whether we recline with him under the lofty and widespreading plane-tree by the cool fountain, whilst he talks with Phædrus of love, and art, and beauty, and the soul in its relations to these things; whether we laugh at the inimitable irony with which he brings Gorgias and his disciples to confusion; or, whether with bated breath we listen to his sublime discourse on immortality, delivered to his devoted followers in the prison in which he is about to drink the poisoned cup; be the occasion when it may, we still meet with the same questions that face us to-day. Then as now, it is the human intellect beating against the bars of its limitations and seeking to compass the unattainable. It is the ever-recurring problem of knowing, in which men forget the very circumscribed limits within which thought moves. And after traversing a dreary waste of controversy with wrecks of systems scattered through the pages of Plato and the schoolmen, of Locke, and Hume, and Berkeley, and Kant, and of Herbert Spencer in our day, we inquire, what is the outcome of it all? We have gotten no nearer to the solution. And in all earnestness we ask, is there a solution at all, or rather, is there a problem to be solved? We know; and after we shall have known how we know, we still only know. There is no going back of this. The mental labor of five and twenty centuries has been expended on that one problem of knowing; ought this not suffice? How long, maelstrom-like, will it continue to whirl within its eddy all issues? To our mind, the only practical solution to this problem—if problem there be—is, as has been hinted at in the following paper, to accept things as they are, to take upon trust our faculties with all their shortcomings, and to recognize both shortcomings and limitations in all our thinking.

I.

There is a wide difference between the habits of thought engendered by literary pursuits and those begotten of scientific studies. The difference is as marked as are the diverse objects of thought. Literature we know to be personal in its nature, in its method, and to a great extent in its object. Science is impersonal, both in its subject-matter and in its treatment. Literature deals with persons and things, so far as they affect our humanity; every piece of written composition that appeals to the emotional element in our nature may be regarded as literature. Science deals with persons and things as they are in themselves, or in coördinated relations. It examines, investigates, discusses from an impersonal point of view; utterly regardless of individual bias, it gropes its way through the entanglements and environments of a subject-matter, and cautiously passes from the known to the unknown. Science, in a word, is concerned with the true as true. Its object is truth. Literature, on the other hand, ranges over a wider field. It may be personal and impersonal, subjective and objective, as best suits its inclinations. It accepts the true and the false, the good and the evil, the beautiful and the deformed, and moulds them all to its own purposes, ultimately with the view of acting upon man's feelings—now arousing his curiosity, now exciting his wonder and admiration, again working upon his sympathies and stirring his soul. Its object is the ideal of all that is sublime and beautiful in nature.

Entering the interior of the thinking-subject, we may note the process the mind goes through in developing a definite course of thought upon some object. Is the object one of a scientific nature? See how cautiously the mind proceeds. It lays down its postulates; it runs over the principles that it holds within its grasp; it casts about among the laws and facts already demonstrated and recognized as certain truth; these it groups together into classes and sub-classes; it compares them with one another; it considers their various properties; it views the modes and properties and behavior of other facts, or groups of facts, in the light of those well-known and well-understood; it applies to them its demonstrated formula, and draws its conclusions. Throughout this process the scientific mind remains unimpassioned, and regards persons and things as labelled abstractions, rather than concrete realities. It works within narrow and closely defined lines. It grows impatient of all that does not bear upon the question under consideration, and rejects it as a distraction. The habit of mind thus developed is rigid and exclusive, and unfits its possessor for grasping and treating with facility other subjects than those upon which it has had life-long practice.[1] It lacks in extension what it gains in comprehension.

Is the object of thought one of a literary nature? Here the mind follows a process the reverse of that employed in a scientific pursuit. Its first effort is to grasp the conclusions and work backward to the starting principles. Nothing comes amiss to it. The thought apparently farthest removed from the main idea may throw upon it additional light. All that science, or art, or nature can contribute, the literary mind makes its own, not for the sake of science, or art, or nature, nor by way of determining some unknown truth, or reaching some scientific discovery, but as so many illustrations drawing out, exemplifying, clearing up more vividly the ideal which it has grasped, and which it labors to express. To every literary mind may be made, and made as little to the purpose, the reproach that the sophist Callicles addressed to Socrates: "By the gods, you never stop talking about shoemakers, fullers, cooks, and physicians, as though our discourse were of these."[2] All such illustrations are the material out of which the literary mind constructs a body for its conception. Literature is an art, and the process of literature is the process of all art. Note that process. The soul conceives a thought. The thought grows into a central idea, around which group other subordinate ones. It becomes for the soul an ideal. That ideal is nourished by reading, or reflection, or study, or experience, or all of these combined, and quickens into life, and waxes strong, and takes possession not only of the intellect, but of the whole man, and gives him no rest till he finds for it an adequate expression according to the bent of his genius, be it that of a poem, a novel, or a historical study, a painting, a statue, or a musical composition.

In all this the literary mind experiences, with a thoughtful writer, "how hard it is to think oneself into a thing and to think its central thought out of it."[3] It is not the work of a few days or a few weeks. It is a slow and elaborate process. At the age of four Goethe first witnessed the puppet-show of Faust. He was still a child when he read the legend.[4] From the start, the idea enters

---

[1] Since writing the above, we find a striking confirmation of its truth by the experience of Professor Tyndall. Speaking of his student-life in Germany, about the year 1851, he thus describes the state of his mind: "In those days I not unfrequently found it necessary to subject myself to a process which I called depolarization. My brain, intent on its subjects, used to acquire a set resembling the rigid polarity of a steel magnet. It lost the pliancy needful for free conversation, and to recover this I used to walk occasionally to Charlottenburg, or elsewhere. From my experiences at that time I derived the notion that hard-thinking and fleet-talking do not run together." ("My Schools and Schoolmasters," in the *Popular Science Monthly* for January, 1885.)

[2] Plato, "Gorgias," cap. xlv.   [3] Hare, "Guesses at Truth," p. 275.

[4] In an abridgment of Wedemann's "Faust-Book."

his soul, and takes possession of it, and grows into a thing of life; and forthwith it becomes the ruling idea of his life, and he makes it the inspiration of his activity, and moulds upon it in many respects both thought and conduct, and picking up all the traits and characteristics of his age, he weaves them into this legend, not hastily, but slowly, studiously, in the spirit of true art, till, finally, in his eighty-second year he pens the last line of his great Faust-poem. The first conception in his fourth, the last line in his eighty-second year; this is a lesson that who runs may read. The example of Goethe illustrates the spirit of artistic genius. It takes the old and remodels it into a new artistic whole. The scientific genius builds upon the foundations already laid. A Newton or a Descartes may add to the sum of mathematical knowledge; he may give new methods of demonstration and calculation; but he leaves untouched every principle and every proposition that science had previously established. Even when such a scientific genius grasps by anticipation a new law or a new truth, he co-ordinates it with other known laws, and corrects his first impressions accordingly. Not so the literary genius; for, whilst both have this in common, that the terms they use possess a recognized value, still he of the literary habit makes not—nor does he seek to make— a connection or a continuity with aught of the past; having grasped the ideal, he labors to give it full and adequate expression independently of any other ideal, past or present. He lives and breathes in an atmosphere of opinion and assumption that permeates his thinking, and colors both thought and language; he takes it all for granted; he draws from it the material with which to shape and strengthen his own creation. Richter, in contemplating this literary habit of thought, is filled with admiration: " I fear and wonder," he says, " at the latent almightiness with which man orders—that is, creates his range of ideas. I know no better symbol of creation."[1] It is, indeed, the process of moulding something entirely new and distinct out of material hitherto used for other purposes. It is a creation because it is a launching into existence of an artistic type that pre-existed only as an ideal in the author's mind. It is an imitation—as indeed is all art—in a finite manner, and within the limits belonging to finiteness, of the creative act by which the Infinite First Cause drew all things from nothingness.[2]

But there are certain habits of thought in which literary and scientific methods interlace and overlap to the detriment of both letters and science. Here is a case in point. Science pretends,

---

[1] " Wit, Wisdom and Philosophy of Jean Paul Friederich Richter," ∤ xi., p. 129.

[2] See Gioberti, " Del Bello," cap. vi. Del Modo in cui la Fantasia Estetica si può dire Creatrice del Bello, p. 105.

and even seriously undertakes, in the study of things, to discover the laws according to which they are, and move, and act. But does science always succeed? Are the laws it claims to have discovered really and indeed in the things themselves, or in the mind of the observer? Let us see. In the natural sciences, a law is a generalized experience. Its validity depends upon the range of experience or observation which it covers. Now, that range is frequently very limited. Not unfrequently is it inadequate. Oftener still is it confined not so much to things themselves as to certain aspects of things. Imagination, at a single leap, transcends the facts within the range of observation and experience, and under the same generalization includes all possible facts and all possible experiences. Sometimes imagination hits the truth, and discerns the order governing a certain number of phenomena. Sometimes, also, it misses reality; and, after establishing so-called laws, and erecting theories upon a plausible hypothesis, some unexplained phenomenon reveals the underlying fallacy, and science reconstructs another theory, and announces another law, that may or may not be more correct. And sometimes again, the explanation is inadequate. A wider range of experience informs us that the so-called law is only a half-truth, or one aspect of a larger law regulating the order and harmony of things. A glance at the history of chemical, physical and geological theories will suffice to bear us out as to these various modes in which so-called laws of nature proved to be only false translations of nature's language. Instance Newton's law of gravitation in physics;[1] the phlogiston and atomic theories in chemistry; and in geology the revelations made by the deep-sea dredgings of Carpenter and Thomson.[2] This issue leads to many interesting lines of thought; but the point we would here make is this: That scientists are apt to forget that what they call the laws of nature may be really such only to a very limited extent; that some of them may be simply their interpretation of certain aspects of certain sets of phenomena falling within the narrow range of their experience; that these interpretations may, as likely as not, be fabrications of their imagination; that, therefore, it ill-becomes them, in the name of science, to be intolerantly dogmatic concerning them; and that such dogmatism is opposed to the scientific spirit. They are no longer following the scientific method. They are simply misapplying the literary method. The intellectual structure of their theories is of a piece with the construction of a parable or a fable.

On the other hand, scientific habits of thinking cause the sci-

---

[1] See Faraday on this law in his paper on the " Conservation of Forces." Youmans' ed., pp. 359–383.

[2] With H. M. S. *The Challenger.*

entist to look upon persons and things no longer in their concrete nature, but rather as so many abstractions, or, at most, as concrete specimens of an abstract principle. His very feelings and emotions he learns to classify and, as far as possible, separate from himself. He measures the worth of things accordingly. They possess value in proportion as they explain a difficult problem, or contribute a new truth to the sum of knowledge. It has been well remarked: " Even the feelings of speculative men become speculative. They care about the notions of things and their abstractions, and their relations, far more than about the realities." [1] So that, whilst the scientist may unwittingly bring literary habits to bear upon scientific issues, to the detriment of science, unwittingly also may he bring his scientific habits into affairs of everyday life, and measure persons and things by a false criterion. So, also, may the man of a literary way of thinking use false weights and measures in forming his estimates. " An author's blood will turn to ink. Words enter into him and take possession of him, and nothing can obtain admission except through the passport of words." [2] And, because words do not always represent the full measure of things, or are at times totally inadequate to express them, the mind living in words becomes guilty of blunders no less egregious than the mind living in abstractions. What, then, is the normal state of the mind?

II.

The normal function of the human intellect is to apprehend truth. Its activity feeds upon truth, and by truth is nourished. For truth it was created; by the light and warmth of truth it develops in strength and grasp; without the truth, it gropes in darkness, restless, yearning, in misery, hungering and thirsting for that which alone can satiate its desires. There may be barriers in the way; it may require enduring labor to remove the barriers; opposition only sharpens the eagerness with which the quest is pursued. In this life, subject to the present order of things, with body and sense standing between the soul and the apprehension of all knowledge, it is not easy to determine which is the true and which the false. The gratuitous and unquestioned notions acquired in early training; the habits of thought in which the intellect works; natural likes and dislikes; feeling, sentiment, inclination; prejudices of the age and the race; assumptions and opinions that are the outcome of one's environments,—are all so many hindrances in the way of the clear and simple apprehension of truth. But they are not insuperable barriers. The human intellect, acting in its normal state, and according to the laws of its nature, may with time and patience,

---

[1] Hare, " Guesses at Truth," p. 495.   [2] Ibid.

and without deceiving itself in the process, attain to the knowledge of certain truth. It cannot accept error as error; and if error does, as error will, enter into its calculations, it first assumes the garb of truth, and as such alone is it admitted. Thoughtful study, comparison, careful reasoning upon evident principles, truths and facts, will furnish sufficient light to penetrate the mask and reveal the underlying falsity, if falsity there be.

It is within the province of the human mind not only to apprehend the truth, but also to recognize it as truth. In this recognition consists the mind's certainty. It is with absolute certainty that we know and distinguish that two and two make four, and not five or three. There is nothing relative either in my knowing this truth or in my being certain of it. The Hottentot and the Indian are equally certain. The Agnostic who denies this absolute certainty is also equally certain. It is an ultimate fact of consciousness. If you would inquire how we know that we are certain with an absolute certainty, we can give you no further reason than that, being constructed as we are, we cannot think differently. It is of the very essence of our reason so to think. Nor could it be otherwise. God could not create a reason whose normal condition of thinking would be such as to make two and two equal to any other number than four, without annihilating Himself. Such an act were to destroy the very essence of reason; it would, therefore, be an infinite contradiction of God's Infinite Nature. The one is as unthinkable as the other. We are what we are. We find ourselves to be what we are as thinking beings independently of ourselves. We take ourselves on trust. We take on trust all the faculties of our souls. We use them as we find them. What they report to our consciousness—our inner selves—as true, we accept as true. We cannot do otherwise. The attitude of our mind towards all knowledge is the same to this extent: that in all it seeks to discern the true from the false, to reject the false and to accept the true.

For this reason we cannot agree with Mr. Herbert Spencer when he tells us that "we are not permitted to know—nay, we are not even permitted to conceive—that Reality which is behind the veil of Appearance."[1] Why not? Where is the hindrance? Since we recognize this reality, do we not conceive it? It seems to us that the knowing and thinking of Mr. Herbert Spencer is not the knowing and thinking of the normal intellect. If we are not permitted to know or conceive this reality back of appearance, how come we to know that it exists? And yet Mr. Spencer is sure of its existence and recognizes it as essential to our thinking. Recently he has explained himself more fully in these words: "Phenomenon without noumenon is unthinkable; and yet noumenon cannot be

---

[1] "First Principles, p. 110."

thought of in the true sense of thinking. We are at once obliged to be conscious of a reality behind appearance, and yet can neither bring this consciousness of reality into any shape, nor can bring into any shape its connection with appearance. The forms of our thought, moulded on experiences of phenomena, as well as the connotations of our words formed to express the relations of phenomena, involve us in contradictions when we try to think of that which is beyond phenomena; *and yet the existence of that which is beyond phenomena is a necessary datum alike of our thoughts and our words.*" [1] Underlying this assertion is an important fact, ill-apprehended, we fear, by Mr. Herbert Spencer. It is the fact that thought is always more than its expression. But why quarrel on this account with either thought or expression, so long as each is evolved according to the law of our intelligence? That intelligence is limited in its operations; but it is not we who have defined the limits, or set the boundaries. We find ourselves with those limitations; we cannot change them. Our consciousness reports to us the phenomenon; our reason infers that there is no meaning in phenomenon without noumenon. The one connotes the other in our thinking. What substance is to accident; what the ideal is to the actual; what essence is to existence—the noumenon is to the phenomenon. We perceive the one in the other. We perceive it and we know it. We accept the vouchment of our intellect on the subject. True, we cannot pass beyond this vouchment and give this noumenon a local habitation and a name. What then? At this point we discern the fallacy of Mr. Herbert Spencer's conclusions. He seems to forget that the ultimate analysis of any and every thought brings home to us the fact that the clearly-defined image of the thought does not represent the whole thought; that that image is only a symbol; that the word in which that image is expressed is also a symbol; and that in this manner every expression is only a symbol symbolizing a symbol of the thing expressed. And it may happen, and it does happen, that we think correctly in terms of things of which we know nothing beyond their existence and relations. Such is the case with space and time. The great intellect of an Augustine wrestled with the problems of these two ideas; the more he sought to fathom them, the greater was his awe. And his verdict on the problem of time is that in which all thinkers must rest. "If nobody questions me, I know; if I should attempt an explanation, I know not." [2] In other words, we know these things to use them rightly in our thinking; but we cannot grasp at a sufficiently clear image of them to explain them to others.

---

[1] "Last Words about Agnosticism." *Nineteenth Century*, December, 1884.

[2] Quid ergo est tempus? Si nemo ex me quaerat scio, si quaerenti explicare velim nescio. (*Conf. Lib.* II., cap. xiv.)

Therefore, in opposition to Mr. Spencer, we may lay down the proposition that we not only think the noumenon, but we know it and conceive it back of the phenomenon—not indeed as an image distinct from the phenomenon—but as an element in the existence of the phenomenon without which the phenomenon would be unthinkable. Furthermore, whilst our thinking is circumscribed, words and images are not the measure of its limits.[1]

Nor can we agree with Pascal when he tells us: "It is a natural disease of man to believe that he possesses truth directly; whence it comes that he is always disposed to deny whatever he does not understand; whereas in reality he naturally knows only falsehood, and he should take for true only those things whose opposites seem false."[2] Why call that conviction of direct knowedge of the truth a malady? What would become of reasoning and inferring, of all indirect knowledge, if that which we hold directly is not valid? It is all based upon this very conviction. Man is born for the truth; how comes it that falsehood should be more acceptable? "If our intellect," says Mivart, "is to be trusted at all, it must be trusted in what it declares to be the most certain of all—namely, necessary truths."[3] But our intellect is to be trusted even as we trust the reality of our own existence; and necessary truths do not come to us by a process of indirection, but are directly and immediately self-evident. We have no other vouchment than that we take upon trust our whole nature, and with it the normal workings of our intellect. You may call it an assumption or any other name you choose to give, but it is none the less a fact the most primary of all facts, underlying all action, be it physical, moral, or intellectual. Universal skepticism is an absurdity; the very act of doubting all things is a positive mental act. Therefore the habit of confidingness is the healthier habit of mind. Speaking of these two habits, Cardinal Newman, with that keenness and practical grasp of his subject for which he is pre-eminent, says: "Of the two, I would rather have to maintain that we ought to begin with believing everything that is offered to our acceptance, than that it is our duty to doubt of everything. The former, indeed, seems the true way of learning. In that case, we soon discover and discard what is contradictory to itself; and error having always some portion of truth in it, and the truth having a reality which error has not, we may expect that when there is an honest purpose and fair tal-

---

[1] Were this the place, it might be shown that this fallacy runs through all of Mr. Spencer's reasoning regarding personality and all the elements of Christian philosophy.

[2] "Pensées," t. i., 1re partie, art. ii., p. 154.

[3] "A Philosophical Catechism for Beginners," p. 25. This is indeed a marvel of clearness and condensation.

ents, we shall somehow make our way forward, the error falling off from the mind, and the truth developing and occupying it."[1]

When, therefore, we are told that "error is inextricably bound up with the spirit of man," we may interpret it in the sense that it is with difficulty, and after long search, man is enabled to discover truth, and disentangle it from the errors with which it not unfrequently is bound up. But we must keep this fact distinct from the no less palpable fact that in itself and by the light of reason man's intellect recognizes at sight, and accepts with a certainty beyond cavil, all necessary, self-evident truths as truths necessary and self-evident. Be it remembered that it is the truth that is necessary, and not the error. Truth is of things. Truth is reality. Error is only accidental. And when the writer whom we have just quoted, making error necessary, adds the following remarks, we feel bound not only to dissent from him, but to disengage the truth from the sophism in which he has enveloped it. "This necessary error," he tells us, "is the ideal. Man has an innate tendency to form ideals. It would be blocking the way to every deeper insight into things, did we hesitate to consider the first stirrings of religion in man as the first emergence of the ideal."[2] It is to be borne in mind that Herr von Hellwald takes care to tell us that all religion is based upon error and illusion. So he makes the ideal the outcome of necessary error. This is the latest word of the philosophy of negation. Certainly it is a remarkable intellectual feat that bases that which represents whatever is perfect in man's conception, and positive in the order of things—as the outcome of mere negation. Art has its ideal; life has its ideal; religion has its ideal; civilization has its ideal. Are these ideals the outcome of error and illusion? Has it indeed come to this, that men gather grapes of thorns? that the seeds of error grow up and give forth the ripe and luscious fruit of truth? that deception may be sown and confidence reaped? No; error exists but as the excrescence cast off by truth. There could be no wrong if there were not first a right; there could be no error if truth did not have a prior existence; there could be no ideal if there were not a foundation of absolute truth, absolute goodness, and absolute beauty upon which to build it up. Surely literature and art cannot be the outcome of error. Think you the ideals after which Shakespeare and Dante, Beethoven and Haydn, Rafael and Murillo, and Michael Angelo, worked and constructed their masterpieces, are the growth of error? We defy pessimism to come forward and say as much. Error and mistake may enter into every human

---

[1] "Grammar of Assent," 2d ed., p. 377.

[2] F. von Hellwald, "Culturgeschichte." See *Dublin Review*, art. "The Battle of Theism," by Rev. W. Barry, D.D., Oct. 1884.

expression of the ideal; but the error and the mistake are not of the ideal. It is rather because human hands are unskilled, and human expression is stammering, and human judgment is feeble. Let us dwell a moment on the nature, the origin, and the functions of the ideal, and we will be in better position to understand how it is that genius is not a living in error, nor art a groping after illusions.

III.

A genius conceives and expresses a great thought. The conception so expressed delights. It enters men's souls; it compels their admiration. They applaud and are rejoiced that another masterpiece has been brought into existence to grace the world of art or letters. The genius alone is dissatisfied. Where others see perfection, he perceives something unexpressed beyond the reach of his art. Try as best he may, he cannot attain that indefinable something. Deep in his inner consciousness, he sees a type so grand and perfect that his beautiful production appears to him but a faint and marred copy of that original. That original is the ideal; and the ideal it is that calls forth men's admiration.

An analysis of this admiration will lead us to an understanding of the ideal. It is universal. It is a sense as innate to man as is his sense of taste or touch. Savage and civilized admire whatever appeals to their admiration. Now, not everything does so appeal. The trivial, the contemptible, the weak, the inferior, are all beneath man's sense of admiration. The virtuous, the noble, the heroic; whatever expresses strength or power; whatever is beautiful or sublime; in a word, whatever raises man's thoughts and aspirations to a superior plane—that is for him an object of admiration. Man has within him two opposing elements. One seeks to raise him up into a spiritual and spiritualizing sphere of thought and action; the other tends to drag him down to things earthly and debasing. They are the two steeds that Plato represents the soul as driving, likening it to a charioteer; one steed "leans and presses heavily towards the earth, if he be not well-trained by his charioteer;" the other, "beautiful and noble and of a godlike character."[1] They are the opposing elements—the law in his members fighting against the law of his mind—of which St. Paul speaks in language less allegorical.[2] Now, it is the function of this sense of admiration to raise up and spiritualize the inferior parts of man's nature, so that they grovel not in things earthly, and to strengthen and improve his nobler aspirations. Where man may not imitate, where he may not even love, he can still admire. Wherever an ideal is expressed, there is an object for his admira-

---

[1] Plato, "Phaedrus," cap. xxv., p. 712, t. i., ed. Hirschigii.
[2] Romans, vii., 23.

tion. We may not explain this mysterious correspondence, but we all have the experience of it. Our souls are so attuned as to give out a music responsive to the chords that are touched. This we know and feel. Let us study the impression.

Take a Rafael or a Murillo. We gaze upon the painted canvas till its beauty has entered our soul. The splendor of that beauty lights up within it depths unrevealed, and far down in our inner consciousness we discover a something that responds to the beauty on which we have been gazing. It is as though a former friend revealed himself to us. There is here a recognition. The more careful has been our sense-culture, the more delicately have our feelings been attuned to respond to a thing of beauty and find in it a joy forever, all the sooner and the more intensely do we experience this recognition. And therewith comes a vague yearning, a longing as for something. What does it all mean? The recognition is of the ideal. "The memory," says Plato, "on beholding the beautiful object, is carried back to the nature of absolute beauty."[1] Thus, there is not only a recognition; there is also a reminiscence of a higher spiritual order of things of which the soul has had occasional glimpses; there is a yearning for the home to which it belongs. Cavil as men may, the artistic ideal is a reality, and speaks to something higher than the material sense. There are moments when, beneath the spell of some great masterpiece, man feels the nearness of the Godhead, and his soul is thrilled with emotions that vibrate beneath the Divine touch. There is no denying it. A year ago, a newly elected member of the French Academy, amid the applause of his fellow-members, quoted these words of Charles Blanc: "The ideal is the primitive divine exemplar of all things; it is, so to speak, a reminiscence of having already witnessed perfection, and the hope of seeing it once again."[2] Charles Blanc was only repeating the magnificent definition of the ideal which has come home to every soul not buried in the inert material, and which has been echoed down the ages ever since Plato gave it expression: "It is," says this wonderful seer, "a recollection of those things our soul formerly beheld when in company with God, despising the things that we now say are, and looking upward towards that which really is."[3] Without admitting the Pythagorean doctrine of a pre-existent state, here implied,[4]

---

[1] "Phaedrus," cap. xxxv., p 718.

[2] M. Edouard Pailleron, "Discours sur Charles Blanc dans l'Académie," *Le Temps,* 18 Janvier, 1884.

[3] "Phaedrus," cap. xxix., p. 714.

[4] In another work of mine may be found additional remarks on this doctrine: "Philosophy of Literature," part ii., chap. i., p. 124.

we may go farther, and say that without the ideal there is no reality.

Nature recognizes the ideal. She has her types, and works by them. Each of her products is a specific realization of a separate type. As genus is a reality, distinct from, and causative of, the species, so is each of nature's types a reality, distinct from the concrete thing fashioned after it and causative thereof. Hence it is that, in the animal and even the vegetable world, we daily witness reversions to older types and the reproduction of ancestral traits of character. Nor is this all. Ascending higher still

> " Upon the great world's altar-stairs
> That slope thro' darkness up to God,"

we come to the prototype of all created types, and find it existing in the Word. Here is the source and fountain-head of the ideal. In the Word—from the beginning—before there was a beginning of time, and the voice of God caused created things to leap forth from nothingness—throughout the cycles of eternity—God contemplated those types. And by the Word were they made real in the order of created things. Were the eternal type not in the Word, the actual existences fashioned after it would not be. And this is why we say that without the ideal there is no reality. We have at last found the origin and source of the ideal. In all earnestness have we sought it; and, hushed in holy awe before the Godhead, in a loving reverence do we contemplate its splendor. The Word is not only the source of all created existences; the Word is also the light that enlightens this world. Its glory is reflected, now dimly, now clearly, in every created thing. As the reason is illuminated with a light above and beyond the sparks that it throws out in its workings, that light giving it all necessary and self-evident truths; as the spiritual sense is nurtured and strengthened by that mysterious energy called grace, so the created ideal in each individual mind is enlightened and vivified by the uncreated ideal dwelling in the Word. This illumination of the ideal is the expression of the beautiful.

We now know whence it comes that a thing of beauty becomes for each of us a joy forever. It is the mission of the artist to rend the veil of accidents and accessories in which the ideal is shrouded and present it to us in all its beauty and loveliness. And the beauty reflected therefrom lights up the folds and inner caverns of our souls, and reveals therein a recognition of this ideal, and reflected from our inmost souls is the image of Him from whom we come, and who is our Home—His image and a pale reflex of the splendor of His glory : on beholding which reflection we are moved; our souls are stirred to their very centre ; a yearning takes possession of us—a longing for the home whence we came—a groping after the Invisible Ideal—and we feel our souls vibrate beneath the touch of the Infinite. God is in us and we are in God, and the sense of our nearness to Him grows upon us. This is the experience that passes over us in the presence of the ideal. It is the experience that Plato has grandly recorded in his wonderful allegory.[1]

IV.

We are now in position to understand the importance of an ideal in literary habits of thought. It is essential to them. Literature is the form of art the most varied and complicated. Plato hath well and aptly said of a literary structure : " Every speech ought to be put together like a living creature, with. a body of its own, so as neither to be without head, nor without hands, nor without feet ; but to have both a beginning, a middle and an end, described proportionately to one another and to the whole."[2] So to construct a literary masterpiece that part fits to part and each is subordinate to the whole, requires a central idea. As the parts in the animal organism are determined by the vital principle animating them, in such manner that all unconsciously develop into fitness and harmony, even so is it with the literary production. When the central thought, the animating principle—the ideal—is clearly grasped, it shapes the form in which it would be expressed. This teaching is clear and simple and as ancient as art. It is the teaching on which all the masterpieces throughout the ages have been constructed. You may wonder why we lay stress upon what seems to be an elementary and incontrovertible principle. We will tell you.

It is because Agnostic science rejects this beautiful and ennobling doctrine of the ideal, and regards what we have here advanced as a play of fancy. The Agnostic can neither weigh nor measure this ideal ; he therefore relegates it to the regions of the impossible. And yet, even the Agnostic knows and feels, and, so to speak, touches the ideal. By what right does he regard as an illusion a thing so intimate to him ? He has no more reason for rejecting the ideal than he has for accepting some of the most positive conclusions of science. In his last analysis he would resolve the whole universe into an ultimate atom. But why should he ? He has never seen, nor weighed, nor measured that atom. You say that he infers it. But what right has he to infer anything? Why should he deal in inferences ? He does not accept the vouchments of his consciousness, or his reason, or his memory. He does not take himself for granted. The evident brings no evidence

---

[1] In the " Phaedrus," cap. xxxiii.–xxxviii.
[2] " Phaedrus," cap. xlvii., p. 726.

to him. Vouchers for error are to him equally convincing with vouchers for truth.[1] His knowledge is merely subjective impressions. He is himself but an impression. He recognizes only phenomenon. You will bear witness that we are not inventing; we are simply, almost in the Agnostic's own words, describing the habitual state of mind in which he lives and thinks. Are not the words of Plato as fresh and of as direct application to the Agnostic of to-day as they were to the sophist of his age? " Let us not admit into our souls," he says, "the notion that there appears to be nothing sound in reasoning, but much rather that we are not yet in a sound condition, and that we ought vigorously and strenuously to endeavor to become sound."[2]

Moreover, it never occurs to the Agnostic that, if there is nothing beyond phenomenon and phenomenal impressions, there is no true science; for, in order that a science exist, there must needs be more than the mere cataloguing of facts and observations. But this is all that is warranted, on the assumption that all knowledge is made up of phenomenal impressions. Thus does the Agnostic contradict the primary facts of his nature, and the elementary workings of his intellect. Consider the scientific method. Facts are observed, then classified and methodized; principles are stated; laws are inferred or asserted; a reasoning process based upon known truths and facts is gone through, and leads up to other truths and other laws hitherto unknown. But all this implies an order of things above and beyond mere phenomena. It implies a world of ideas, and therefore the existence of an ideal. And in ignoring this world of ideas and of necessary truths the Agnostic, in all logic, is compelled to abandon science and deny even the existence of the external world. The true scientist admits both the internal and external orders upon the same plane of evidence; and this is the criterion of true science, that it rejects no fact, accepts things as it finds them, and seeks for all an adequate explanation.

Plato, in one of those sublime passages that light up a whole world of thought, thus shows how our knowledge of things is not simply of the transient and the phenomenal, but of essences and eternal principles: " Essence," he says, " which really exists colorless, formless, and intangible "—which, therefore, let me remark, is above the conditions of time and space—" is visible only to intelligence that guides the soul, and around this essence the family of true science take up their abode. And, as the divine Mind is nourished by intelligence and pure science, so the mind of every soul that is about to receive what properly belongs to it, when it sees after a long time that which is, is delighted, and by con-

---

[1] See Kant's " Paralogisms and Antinomies," " Critique of Pure Reason," bk. ii.
[2] " Phaedo," cap. xi., p. 76.

templating the truth is nourished and thrives. . . . And it beholds justice herself, and temperance, and science, not that to which creation—γενεσις—is annexed, nor that which is different in different things of those we call real,[1] *but that which is science in what really is.*"[2] This is the only science to think in. It is, indeed, the only true science. Agnostic science loses its claim to the title of science by placing itself in a habit of thinking inconsistent with itself and derogatory to the intellect, to thought, and to real knowledge. It is unscientific in another direction. All science worthy of the name confines itself to its subject-matter, and acknowledges itself incompetent to pronounce upon issues outside of its clearly defined limits. This rule Agnosticism does not observe. Pretending to deal exclusively with the visible, the material, the phenomenal, it passes judgment upon the invisible and supersensible, the spiritual and supernatural. Finally, Agnosticism, in regarding the ideal as an illusion and the outcome of error, is thereby, so far as in it lies, the death of the ideal and the bane of all literary excellence,—indeed of all artistic excellence whatever. In what manner and how far it remains for us to note.

V.

The shadow of Agnostic science has crept over the spirit of art and letters. Now, we have seen that there is no real art without the ideal, and that it is the function of art to appeal to our admiration by the presentation of the ideal in all possible beauty and vividness. But, whilst the artist disentangles the ideal from such accidents and accessories as tend to conceal it, he still clothes it in nature. Out of the materials that nature furnishes he fashions for it a body, and breathes into that body the ideal as its living soul, and forthwith the masterpiece stands out a thing of life and beauty and artistic excellence for undying admiration. Defects of detail may enter into its execution ; but they are lost, forgotten, absorbed in the general effect produced. It is the *Transfiguration* of Rafael. Who, in presence of that noble scene, would cavil about the posing of limbs or the laws of perspective ?[3] It is the *Hamlet* of Shakespeare. Surely, he who overlooks the power, the depth, the philosophy, the dramatic greatness of that tragedy, and quarrels with grammatical structure or obscure expression, has yet to learn the elements of true criticism. Or, it is the *Phaedo* of Plato, whose sublime thoughts so frequently recur throughout

---

[1] Or as Jowett more strongly translates it, " Not in the form of generation or of relation, which men call existence, but knowledge absolute, in existence absolute." Jowett's " Plato," vol. ii., p. 581.

[2] " Phaedrus," cap. xxvii., p. 713.

[3] For an instance of such cavilling, see Taine's " Italy," Eng. tr., pp. 142, 143.

the sentences that are repeated here. He who should stop at the hard metaphysic or the apparently pointless questions and obscure answers, and not soar with Socrates in his dying song into the pure regions of truth, proves that he lacks the sympathy and knowledge to appreciate Grecian thought in the days of Plato, and is, therefore, unable to place at its worth one of the sublimest pieces of writing ever penned by human hand.[1] Or, it is the *Divina Commedia*. What boots it that Dante's estimates of men and measures are not those of the historian? It detracts naught from the wonderful poem. Men are lost in admiration when they note the care with which word is built upon word, each having a special significance, and all made into a grand allegory wrought out of the politics and the philosophy, the strife and struggle, the fierce hates and the strong loves, in which the author lived and moved and fought. Or, it is Mozart's *Requiem*. The critic who would quarrel with that grand composition because in its intricate and complicated structure, speaking of a life's hopes and fears, and the more awful hopes and fears beyond the grave, he misses the sweeter strains of other days, would fail to grasp the sublime conception of the piece as a whole. Or, it is the Gothic Cathedral. Who thinks of making faces at gargoyle or statued niche, where all is emblem and significancy, the stone embodiment of a nation's aspirations? We read in it thought, satire, censure, desire, pathos, passion.[2] In all these instances, back of the mechanical structure, looking out upon us, and peering into our souls, is the ideal.

Now, Agnostic science would promulgate theories calculated to paralyze art, and render it incapable of producing such masterpieces as we have instanced. One is the theory that claims that all art has no other aim than to construct the form for the form's sake. Much that is done to-day, whether in words, or on the canvas, or in marble, is done for the simple pleasure of producing. Now, the art that has only itself for its aim may amuse, may please, may even cause admiration on account of the mechanical skill exhibited; but it is not the art that endures for all time. I will grant you that a Shakespeare or a Goethe may sing as the blackbird sings; but I deny that their art is without purpose. Distinguish between the art that is conscious and that which is uncon-

---

[1] It is this lack of sympathy that makes the reading of Plato so laborious. Perhaps it is a failing to distinguish between the mental habits of the ancient Athenians and those of modern thinkers that has led Mr. Mahaffy, in his admirable " History of Greek Literature " (vol. ii., p. 173), to make the criticism noticed above as regards part of the dialogue.

[2] This idea has been grandly drawn out by Victor Hugo, in " Notre Dame de Paris," liv. iii., chap. 1.

scious.　The Æsopian fable is conscious in purpose; it is written
for a definite aim.　But, of the great masterpieces that we have
been contemplating, can you say that they are purposeless, or that
their end is simply this or that?　In each of them one may read
as many purposes as one takes aspects of them.　Their authors
may have had no other intention than that of unburthening themselves of the great thought that oppressed their souls, but as surely
as their work expresses an ideal, so surely does it embody a purpose.
For the ideal, in calling forth our admiration and raising up our
thoughts to things higher and beyond the scene of every-day life, or
in purifying the incidents of ordinary duties, is educating our better
nature; it is working with a purpose.　And ideal and purpose combined determine the form.　"To act with a purpose," says Lessing,
"is what raises man above the brutes; to invent with a purpose, to
imitate with a purpose, is that which distinguishes genius from the
petty artists who invent to invent, imitate to imitate." [1]　Be it remembered that nothing outside of the Godhead exists for its own sake.
The art produced in this spirit is sheer pettiness.　Nowhere is this
more evident than in the world of letters.　Just as a word has value
only inasmuch as it expresses an idea, so any number of words
strung together is meaningless and inane, unless it expresses a
thought, not for the expression's sake, but for that of the thought.
The sophists of Plato's day attempted to teach expression for the
form's sake.　He refuses the very name of art to such expression.
"She lies," he tells us in his own scathing words, "and is not an
art, but an inartistic trick." [2]　And, in the domain of fiction, it hath
well been said that one can no more conceive a great novel without a purpose than one can conceive an arch without a keystone.[3]
All art worthy of the name is imbued with the earnestness of life.
Consciously or unconsciously, the artist's is a mission to crystal-
lize in his work the spirit of the age; it is, also, his mission to educate his age, to raise it above itself, and to sustain its aspirations
upward and onward—

> " *Artistry being battle with the age*
> *It lives in!* Half life,—silence, while you learn
> What has been done; the other half,—attempt
> At speech, amid world's wail of wonderment—
> ' Here's something done was never done before!'
> *To be the very breath that moves the age,*
> *Means not to have breath drive you bubble-like*
> *Before it—but yourself to blow: that's strain;*
> *Strain's worry through the life-time, till there's peace;*
> We know where peace expects the artist-soul."[4]

[1] Prose works, Bohn ed., Dramatic Notes, No. 34, p. 327.
[2] καὶ οὐκ ἔστι τέχνη, ἀλλ' ἄτεχνος τριβή.　" Phaedrus," cap. xliii.
[3] This remark was made to the author by one of the most successful of living American novelists, Mr. W. D. Howells.
[4] Robert Browning: " Red Cotton Night-Cap Country," p. 110.

VI.

Another theory fostered and developed by Agnostic science is the so called Realism in literature and art. It is the outcome of ignoring the ideal or regarding it as the product of error. If there is no ideal, or if the ideal is only an illusion, then there is nothing beyond the nature we behold and live in ; then the supreme effort of all art is to delineate that nature in detail with the greatest fidelity ; then the sole rule of art is, " Copy, describe, imitate, express minutely whatever you see or hear: the more accurately you follow your model the greater artist you are." There is in this doctrine a mixture of truth and error. True it is that art cannot ignore nature. The world we live in is the material upon which it works. Therefore the artist observes men and things ; he studies the nature without him and the nature within him ; he experiments ; he compares, judges, discriminates ; in this way does he gather up and select the subject-matter upon which he afterwards labors for artistic purposes. But there is in all this more than mere imitation. It is a wholesome realism, and does not exclude the ideal. It is the realism that Millet paints and Ruskin commends. The art that merely imitates can only produce a corpse ; it lacks the vital spark, the soul, which is the ideal, and which is necessary in order to create a living organic reality that will quicken genius and arouse enthusiasm throughout the ages. Let us make the distinction ; it is a vital one : Art is not imitation ; art is interpretation.

This distinction the realistic school in art and letters loses sight of. Accordingly, it abandons all attempt at an ideal ; it makes no effort to read the lessons of nature ; it sees nothing in nature to read beyond the cold, hard lines that it traces. Here Agnostic science steps in, and directs this school in the ways it must walk. It teaches that as the only knowledge is the knowledge of observation and experiment, upon these two lines must art work. And, as the novel is the most potent literary influence of the day, it would especially make the novel a mere study in nature and character, in which naught is to be set down save what has fallen under the eye or has been experienced in actual life. On the face of it, this theory is sound enough. By all means, let us have observation and experiment. But distinguish between the observation that takes in all the elements of nature and the observation that regards only its material side. The latter alone falls under the scope of the realistic school. It has no other field for development. In consequence, it deals only with man living and acting out his brute nature in all its cunning and sensuality. The writers of this school give us observations indeed ; but they are of the street and the tavern. They picture human nature; but it is diseased human nature. They paint us life episodes; but what lives! Now it is the drunkard's; now it is that of the fallen woman; now it is that of actors and authors of bohemian ways; again it is that of notorious criminals; invariably it is passion wallowing in the mire of depravity. This is no freak. It is a systematic procedure, and the logical outcome of the realistic school as inspired by Agnostic science. Believing only in the animal man, naught else remains for the members of this school to depict. Not saintliness of life; for saintliness of life means to them only hypocrisy, or, at most, warped character. Not nobility of thought or word; for weak, erring, human nature is the only nature that the Agnostic recognizes. In his last word he is a pessimist. The conclusions of Schopenhauer on the misery of life, its worthlessness, its crime, its helplessness in the great machine of the universe, are those to which every logical Agnostic must come.[1] The only poetry he can weave is that which, with Ackerman, cries out in an agony of despair and rebellion worthy of Satan.[2]

But this is not the world in which we live and move. This is not the human nature that we are cognizant of. The circle of our acquaintance includes—we know intimately—men and women of a far different stamp; men and women who are true and faithful in their love and friendship; grand and generous souls, who are self-sacrificing whenever good is to be accomplished or duty to be fulfilled; who think and say the sweetest and sublimest thoughts; whose lives are pure and disinterested; whose intentions and aspirations are elevated and ennobling; who, in the daily round of their beautiful lives, shed around them loveliness and peace and joy and gladness of heart. These are the men and women that surround us, and beneath whose influence for good our own hearts and souls strive to rise in the scale of perfection. Here is the reality that we know. Here is the reality that even the Agnostic knows. It is only in his library that humanity is to him such a monster. The lowliest life has its sublime passages. It has wherewith to inspire the poet, for it has its ideal. In this thought we place our consolation and our hope for the future of art and letters. "Realism," said an eloquent French preacher, "is a chronic disease; it is the leprosy of art; it is the epidemic of literature in the nineteenth century."[3] This is the proper diagnosis of the case. Let it be treated as a leprosy or an epidemic.

---

[1] See Schopenhauer's "Essay on the Misery of Life."

[2] "Poésies Philosophiques," par L. Ackerman, Paris, 1877.

[3] R. Père Felix, Conferences, 1867, Conf. v., p. 251.

If realistic works are left untouched and the home atmosphere is kept purified, both leprosy and epidemic will soon die out.[1]

VII.

Such are the relations that exist between the literary and the scientific spirit. Each has a distinct sphere. Each may aid the other. But when one assumes the functions of the other or attempts to dictate to the other, collision and confusion are the result. We have noticed an interlacing and overlapping of literary and scientific habits of thought greatly to the detriment of both literature and science. We may trace this cause to the present intellectual state of our own day. Every age may, in a sense, be said to be in a state of transition, for all time is a becoming. But there are influences hovering over epochs and peoples that give them a characteristic coloring, and place upon them a distinctive impress. Our age is pre-eminently a transition period. New discoveries, new industries and new sciences are calling for new terms, new habits of thought, and new methods of work. And yet, much of our thinking runs in old grooves. We are groping in mist and darkness, with new and complex problems pressing upon us harder and faster than we can solve them. Each decade brings its riddle. The conjectures of one decade become the conclusions of the next, and are made the elementary truths of the third. Hence it is that the books of the day are so many fleeting records of impressions as fleeting. Hence the mental entanglements and inconsistencies that beset men's thoughts and actions; their reasoning and their sentiments; their formal expressions and their inner convictions.

Now every age and every people whose spirit became crystallized in a literature that may be called classic, was possessed of a central thought, an all-absorbing idea—in a word, an ideal—

---

[1] There is an awakening to the danger all along the line. In Denmark, the poet Drachman, to the surprise of many, in his last volume of poems—" Deep Chords "—has entered protest against the realistic spirit, and proclaimed himself the poet of "heart and home." (Viggo Petersen in *Athenæum*, No. 2983, Dec. 27, 1884.) Speaking of this school in Italy, Signor Bonghi writes in the same number of this journal: "But while in the past years there was a great array of poets following this path, and one saw lying about in every bookseller's shop their elegant volumes of every k nd o shape and type, but especially the Elzevir, *this year there is not one to be seen,* an l their principal publisher, Zanichelli of Bologna, *tells me he no longer publishes any on his own account.*" The fact is significant. M. de Pressensè writes words no less encouraging from the parent-soil of this school. " If it is true that in literature, as in everything else, the demand in the long run regulates the supply, it is indubitable—and this is a consoling prospect of which we have need—that a reaction will, before long, set in throughout France, and that our country will not endure to all eternity the debasement of the level of the imagination and the corruption of art." (*Athenæum*, Ibid., p. 833.)

that fired genius and laid its impress upon the form of expression. Thus, the Hindu literature teems throughout with the illusory and passing nature of all things earthly; the inmost feeling that this life is only a preparation for another form of existence, pervades its poetry and philosophy and in a great measure moulds the Hindu life. So with the literature and art of ancient Greece. The one absorbing idea that became a passion for her, was beauty of form and corresponding harmony of expression and action—a beauty and harmony everywhere reflected from her sculpture, her architecture, her poetry and her life. So it was with ancient Rome. All Rome's greatness, all her conquests, all her jurisprudence, her public and domestic life, her art, her worships, her literature, were centred in, and became the outcome of, the one idea of Rome. To be a Roman citizen was the supreme badge of honor; to live for Rome was the sole aim of life; to die for Rome was the most heroic of deaths; to sing Rome's glories, to record her deeds, or to perpetuate the names of her heroes, was the highest ambition of her greatest poets and historians. The literature of Mediæval days has also its distinct mark. It reflects throughout the spirit of chivalry and feudalism. This is the one idea into which all thought is translated. Even the popular religious writings of the day represent the soul as standing towards its Maker in the relation of serf or yeoman to his baronial lord, and as going through life in a spiritual combat with the powers of darkness.

But the idea of chivalry and feudalism is for us a matter of history; it no longer comes home to us as a living reality; we are outgrowing the forms of thought into which it so largely entered. Our modern life has little or nothing in common with those days of adventure-seeking and wonderful feat-performing. Commerce and the industries and sciences are the absorbing occupations of the present. But we lack, or we fail to see, a distinctive centralizing thought predominating over our lives and moulding action and expression into a harmonious whole. Our business affairs are one thing; our literature and its topics are another thing. Agnosticism is making strenuous efforts to impress its spirit upon life and thought. It has enlisted under its banner genius, culture, learning and passion. But the underlying principle of Agnosticism is negation and a reversion to what is brutal and debasing in the pagan ideal; and the age is not prepared to accept such a principle. The leaven of Christianity permeates too intimately the world's thinking.[1] There is profound truth in the sublime expres-

---

[1] I am glad to present this corroboration from one whom all will regard as a not over-partial witness: "To deny that Christianity in its various forms has been, and still is, one of the greatest powers in the world, or to deny that its leading doctrines have, in fact, been associated in many ways with all that we commonly recognize as

sion of Tertullian, that the human soul is naturally Christian. It loves positive, wholesome truth; it pines in bondage till it possesses truth; but holding the truth, the truth shall make it free. Too long has it fed upon the nourishing meats of Christian truth to be content with the winnowed husks of negation' that Agnosticism would impart. Through long and dreary ages, the world fed upon all that Agnosticism has to offer it, and souls became starved, and civilizations went down and were buried in the grave of materialism. Agnosticism cannot harmonize the clashing elements of the age.

In the meantime it is the life-work of each of us to harmonize, in his own nature, all the elements that go to make it up. Socrates, on that memorable day when he drank the hemlock cup, told the faithful followers who were gathered around him, how at different times a dream visited him in diverse forms, exhorting him to apply himself to the cultivation of music.[1] By music Socrates meant not simply that combination of sounds that catches up a few fragments of this world's harmonies, and with them moves our souls. There is another and a higher music. It is the music of a soul in which dwell order and method; which co-ordinates all knowledge; which recognizes the ideal; in which the good, the true, and the beautiful are cultivated, each according to its own nature, and by its own method. It is the rhythm of a thoroughly-disciplined intellect and a well-regulated life. That dream comes to us all. In its fulfilment will we find the reconciliation of literary with scientific habits of thought.

---

virtue, is like denying the agency of the sun in the physical world." (James Fitzjames Stephen in the *Nineteenth Century* for June, 1884). The admission is a remarkable one, coming from Mr. Stephen.

[1] " Phaedo," cap. iv., ed. Hirschigii, t. i., p. 46.

THE TREATY OF PARIS, 1763, AND THE CATHOLICS IN AMERICAN COLONIES.

I.

ON the 10th of February, 1763, there was signed at Paris the definitive Treaty, of Peace between France, Spain, and England. This treaty besides terminating the Seven Years' War, contains an adjustment of the North American possessions of these three nations. Prior to this, the English ruled over the Atlantic seaboard provinces—Acadia, afterwards divided so as to comprise New Brunswick and Nova Scotia, and the territory lying to the south of it, running westward from the Atlantic Ocean, north of Florida, to Louisiana and the Mississippi River. The French possessions were Canada, along the banks of the River St. Lawrence (except the Gulf Islands) and the country north of the Great Lakes and westward, including part of the present State of Michigan, to the wilderness beyond. Northward they held sway to the limits of the Hudson Bay Territory. Besides these northern possessions, named New France, the French held a chain of forts running south from Canada to New Orleans; and whether or not these corresponded to the Mississippi, they claimed to own all westward—all to the rear—of the English colonies. They owned the substantial province of Louisiana, extending east to Georgia and Florida, and northward about a third or more of the distance between the Gulf of Mexico and the Great Lakes of Canada.

Florida under this treaty was given up to England by the Spaniards, and Canada by the French, leaving the western territory and its forts undetermined; subsequently the French reasserted their claim to these ; but, by the Peace of Versailles, 1783, the French and English, as is well known, lost the entire territory south of Canada.

The fall of Quebec, the stronghold of the French, was in the year 1759, and in the following year the capitulation at Montreal surrendered the whole of Canada to the English. It is true that the effort of Pontiac was made subsequently (but before the Treaty), yet the cession was complete in 1760 as a military, though not as a diplomatic, fact. A rupture having occurred between England and Spain, a period of over three years passed before all parties agreed to settle their then impending difficulties. Canada, in the meantime, lived under a military rule—the " reign of the soldiery ;" and the law, if any, in all matters, was to be found in the terms of capitulation between General Amherst and Vaudreuil made at Montreal, in 1760.

The terms of capitulation at Quebec and at Montreal are not now of any real value, except in so, far as they throw light upon a similar question in the Treaty of Paris. It is much to the credit of the French in Canada, and correspondingly uncomplimentary to their enemy, the English, that in every treaty between these two powers in this country, the French stipulated for the free exercise of their own—the Roman Catholic religion. About 130 years before the date we are now considering, the French surrendered Canada to Sir David Kirk, the English commander, and stipulated for these terms. The same was done, in Quebec, between De Ramezay and the English commanders, and in Montreal the matter was gone into more fully. The contracting or negotiating parties were not on very good terms, and the French commander complained bitterly of the want of courtesy shown him and his troops by his opponents. The demands and replies have been used a good deal by those who wish to minimize the power of the Church in Canada, yet it could not be argued but that these terms became *merged*, as the lawyers say, in the subsequent treaty.

The following articles and the replies thereto are useful on other than historical grounds :

Article 27. " The free exercise of the Catholic, Apostolic; and Roman religion shall subsist entire, in such manner that all the States and people of the towns and country places and distant posts, shall continue to assemble in the churches, and to frequent the sacraments as heretofore, without being molested in any manner, directly or indirectly. These people shall be obliged, by the English Government, to pay to the priests the tithes, and all the taxes they were used to pay, under the Government of His Most Christian Majesty.

Answer. " *Granted,* as to the free exercise of their religion. The obligation of paying the tithes to the priests will depend on the King's pleasure.

Article 28. " The chapter, priests, cures, and missionaries shall continue, with an entire liberty, the exercise and functions in the parishes of the towns and country.

Answer. " Granted.

Article 29. " The grand vicars named by the chapter to administer the diocese during the vacancy of the episcopal see shall have liberty to dwell in the towns or country parishes, as they shall think proper. They shall at all times be free to visit in different parishes of the diocese, with the ordinary ceremonies, and exercise all the jurisdiction they exercised under the French dominion. They shall enjoy the same rights in case of death of the future bishop, of which mention will be made in the following article.

Answer. " Granted, except what regards the following article.

. *Article* 30. " If, by the treaty of peace, Canada should remain in the power of His Britannic Majesty, His Most Christian Majesty shall continue to name the bishop of the colony, who shall always be of the Roman communion, and under whose authority the people shall exercise the Roman religion.

Answer. " Refused.

Article 32. " The communities of nuns shall be preserved in their constitution and privileges. They shall continue to observe their rules. They shall be exempted from lodging any military, and it shall be forbid to trouble them in their religious exercises, or to enter their monasteries; safeguards shall even be given them if they desire them.

Answer. " Granted.

Article 34. " All the communities, and all the priests, shall preserve their movables, the property and revenues of the seignories, and other estates which they possess in the colony, of what nature soever they may be. And the same estates shall be preserved in their privileges, rights, honors, and exemptions.

Answer. " Granted."

After the capitulation at Montreal, the English ruled New France for the next three years under a martial system. In Quebec, at all events, the decencies were observed towards Bishop Pontbriant and the clergy. No one expected the then state of things to continue, and perhaps, under all the circumstances, the rule might have been less objectionable. The people looked forward to the treaty, and faith was expected to be kept under the provisions of the capitulation. These are not within our present purpose to consider, but the reader will bear in mind that under the French régime the Catholic Church was part of the law of the land—the established Church of Canada—or New France, as it was called. No one was ignorant of the absence of toleration in the British laws towards that Church, so that both parties knew what their position was, and what each wanted to secure.

II.

The negotiations for the treaty begun in 1761 were mainly intrusted to two representatives from France and England who exchanged protocols, etc., as is the custom in such formal proceedings. Mr. Pitt represented the English nation—the French side was intrusted to the Duke de Choiseul.

Mr. Garneau, in his History of Canada, states that the Clergy of Quebec drew up two memorials on ecclesiastical affairs in Canada, one for the Duke de Nivernois, the other to the Duke of Bedford— these nobles being the two chief diplomatists employed in settling terms of pacification between France and Great Britain. He refers also to one of the Canadian agents, Etienne Charrest, who was charged to negotiate in the article of religion as expressed in the treaty of Paris, and who wrote several times on that subject to Lord Halifax, Secretary of State.

It cannot be supposed, therefore, that each party did not minutely understand the business in hand, or what was meant by the free exercise of religion ; nor was any one ignorant of the fact that the laws of Great Britain—the penal laws—were aimed directly at the Roman Catholic religion, and in fact that there was no toleration of it in England at the time. The first memorial from the English contained no reference to this question of religion. Subsequently a French memorial of Propositions was submitted of which the second clause is as follows:

> "The King, in making over his full right of sovereignty over Canada to the King of England, annexes four conditions to the cession.
> "1st. That the free exercise of the Roman Catholic religion shall be maintained there, and that the King of England will give the most precise and effectual orders that his new Roman Catholic subjects may as heretofore make public profession of their religion according to the rites of the Roman Church."[1]

To this, so far as religion is concerned, Mr. Pitt made no objection, and in the ultimatum of France in reply to England, 5th August, 1761, it is reasserted that his majesty "will not recede from the conditions he has annexed to the same memorial relative to the Catholic religion."

An answer to this ultimatum came on the 16th August. *Inter alia* it says : "As to what concerns the public profession and exercise of the Roman Catholic religion in Canada, the new subjects of his Britannic Majesty shall be maintained in that privilege without interruption or molestation."

The rupture with Spain, and some differences in other articles of the treaty, delayed its conclusion during the following year.

In November, 1762, the preliminary articles of peace were signed at Fontainebleau between Great Britain, France and Spain, and in the 2d article "his Britannic Majesty on his side agrees to grant to the inhabitants of Canada the liberty of the Catholic religion. He will in consequence give the most exact and effectual orders that his new Roman Catholic subjects may profess the worship of their religion according to the rites of the Roman Church as far as the laws of Great Britain permit."

The same words in Article XIX. are used for the cession of the Spanish possessions.

Mr. Fox rose in the House and moved the adoption of an address recommending the treaty.

Mr. Pitt violently opposed almost every part, but made no reference to the change of the words added after he himself had ceased negotiations respecting it some months before. That would not have been a popular argument. The House accepted the address, 319 being for and 65 against it.

The words of the treaty, as finally agreed upon, do not differ from the foregoing, except that the word "precise" is used for "exact" in the official reports.

The last article, XXVI., reads:

> "Their Sacred Britannic, Most Christian and Catholic, and Most Faithful Majesties promise to observe sincerely and *bona fide* all the articles contained and settled in the

---

[1] The other conditions have no reference to the subject here discussed.

present treaty; and they will not suffer the same to be infringed directly or indirectly by their respective subjects; and the same High Contracting parties generally and reciprocally guarantee to each other all the stipulations of the present treaty."

Attorney-General Maseres, writing about ten years after the treaty, says:

"Two senses may be put upon these words, 'as far as the laws of Great Britain permit.' They may either be supposed to mean that the Canadians shall be at liberty to profess the worship of the Roman Catholic religion as far as the laws of Great Britain permit that worship to be professed in England itself, or that they shall be at liberty to profess that worship as far as the laws of England permit it to be professed in the outlying Dominions of the Crown of Great Britain that are not parcel of the realm, such as Minorca, Senegal, the West India Islands, and the colonies of North America. The former of these senses I acknowledge to be too narrow to be put upon these words, because it would in a great measure destroy the grant of the liberty of professing the worship of the Romish religion which these words were only intended to qualify and restrain; because in England itself the laws do not permit the worship of the Romish religion to be professed in any degree.

"We must therefore have recourse to the latter sense above mentioned and suppose these words to mean that the Canadians should have the liberty of professing the worship of their religion as far as the laws of England permit it to be professed in the outlying dominions of the crown that lie without the realm. . . .

"Now, upon making this enquiry we shall find that though most of the penal and disqualifying statutes passed against the professors of the Romish religion relate only to England and Wales, yet the Act of the first of Queen Elizabeth, cap. i., which is entitled ' *An Act to restore to the Crown the ancient jurisdiction over the state ecclesiastical and spiritual and abolishing all foreign powers repugnant to the same,*' which is commonly called the Act of Supremacy, does expressly relate to all the Queen's dominions as well as to the realm of England, and is even extended by positive words to such countries and places as should at any future time become subject to the crown of England."

He then sets out the effect of this statute of Elizabeth, and adds in conclusion that "the British Nation is bound by that article to grant to the Canadians the liberty of professing the worship of the Roman Catholic religion only so far as is consistent with that statute."

The statute, however, imposes no insuperable difficulty; it requires all priests and other ecclesiastical persons to take the oath of supremacy, but, in the event of their refusing, it annexes no penalty beyond the deprivation of their benefices or other spiritual promotions. The question therefore would not arise until the state held the property of the Church, and in Lower Canada, at all events, this question did not arise. The Quebec Act, as will be seen presently, provided an oath in lieu of the one in the Act of Elizabeth,[1] and though many difficulties arose under the Quebec Act, they terminated in favor of the Church.

Besides the construction put upon the words of the treaty by

---

[1] By an act passed in the first year of the reign of William and Mary, the *Bill of Rights*, the oath of supremacy as provided in the Act of Elizabeth was taken away and another of a milder character substituted. It is, however, much more objectionable than the one in the Quebec Act, which is indeed no more than an oath of allegiance.

the English Parliament, which is substantially that of Mr. Maseres, eminent lawyers in England have given opinions thereon.

In reference to it Attorney-General Wedderburne, afterwards a Lord Chancellor of England, says : " True policy dictates, then, that the inhabitants of Canada should be permitted freely to profess the worship of their religion ; and it follows of course that the ministers of that worship should be protected, and a maintenance secured for them."

And Attorney-General, afterwards Lord, Thurlow says : " The free exercise of their religion by the laity and of their function by their clergy was also reserved."

As a matter of fact it would be of little account, after the Quebec Act was passed, what any legal opinion might have been as to the meaning of these words—the Act thenceforth was the guide. The Act, it is true, could not abridge the effect of the treaty so far as the new British subjects were concerned—the subjects who were the subject of the treaty; but the act could, and probably did, enlarge the meaning of the words for the benefit of these subjects. For instance, it might have been a condition that each of the three religious orders then in Canada should receive one thousand acres of land. No act could be passed, without setting at naught the law of nations, giving them only five hundred acres, but an act giving them two thousand would be valid. And so the Quebec Act took the sting out of the objectionable words in the treaty and apparently established in Canada the Roman Catholic Church. It gives probably the most favorable construction that could be put on the treaty, and indeed a much less equitable interpretation would have suited the English party in Canada and in some of the other American provinces.

III.

Thus stands the treaty, and in the fall of the same year, 1763, a proclamation was issued by George III. referring to the valuable possessions secured by this treaty, and under it were erected four governments under the names of Quebec, East and West Florida, and Grenada. The governments of Newfoundland and Nova Scotia were also referred to, and a general promise given that the colonists could confide in the royal protection for the enjoyment and benefit of the laws of England, until assemblies of the people could be summoned.

There were at this period about seventy thousand inhabitants in Canada, and less than five hundred of these were English and Protestant. The remainder were French and Roman Catholic. The Catholic religion had been the law of the land, and in Quebec at least the British soldiers were ordered to be respectful to the clergy and to the religious processions in the streets. It will be remembered that after Cardinal Richelieu founded the royal government in New France, the governor, the bishop, and the royal intendant practically ruled the province. It is, therefore, to be expected that the Church and its ministers in their time would be respected. Under the comparatively mild rule of Sir Guy Carleton the Catholics had little to complain of on this score.

The people complained somewhat that the terms of the capitulation were not observed, the French as to innovations, the English that everything was not expressly made to suit their wants. However, the ministers in England urged that their case would be considered as soon as the war—the Seven Years' War— would be at an end, and it came to an end by the treaty which we are now discussing.   •

Before the treaty, the military rule depended much on the temper of the governor, who, all things considered, was better vastly than those of his countrymen who formed his staff.

The question of the status of the Roman Catholic Church in Canada arose at once as to a successor to Bishop Pontbriant. In 1763 the governor sent M. Cramahé to London to sustain an application in this matter. In 1765 the attorney and solicitor general, Norton and Grey, expressed their opinion regarding the ·Church of Canada, that the Catholics of that (now British) colony were not liable to the operation of the disabilities imposed by statutory law on their co-religionists in Great Britain. In 1768 ·the king issued three mandates to the governor for the appointment of a rector for each of the towns of Quebec, Three Rivers ·and Montreal. Governor Carleton directed Mr. Maseres, the ·attorney-general, to prepare a draft commission, which that zealous ·official did with all promptitude. On consideration of " the peculiar and delicate situation of the province with respect to the article of religion," as Mr. Maseres put it, " his excellency did not think it expedient to grant these gentlemen commissions of this form under the seal of the province, but in lieu thereof gave them licenses to preach and perform divine service according to the ceremonies of the Church of England in the respective parishes of Quebec, Three Rivers and Montreal, under his hand and private seal." The draft was never availed of, and Mr. Maseres in about a year afterwards calls attention to this in certain other papers preserved at the time.

The Proclamation of 1763 promised the people that as soon as it was convenient an assembly would be given the Canadians—the new subjects—and that in the meantime they could rely on the regard of the sovereign for the solution of any difficulties that might arise. This *meantime* lasted for ten years, greatly to the annoyance of the old subjects, who regarded the colony as a place to make money in and regain their shattered fortunes while their past history in England might be forgotten. There is little room for doubt as to the character generally of these noble five hundred; but it is not with them we are concerned, though they made themselves heard more clamorously than the whole French population.

In this interval a chief justice, an attorney-general and some other officials were sent out from England. The attorney-general, Francis Maseres, lived in Quebec for about three years, up to 1769, and retired apparently in disgust to England, where he was appointed to an inferior judgeship. He is the author of certain papers—and violent papers they are—regarding the colony and its laws. These are called the " Maseres papers," and from them a good deal of inspiration can always be drawn against the French people and their religion.

He and Sir Guy were not of one mind as to the manner of ruling the new possession, but the governor had not only the more sensible plan, but also the one that recommended itself to the home government. Maseres became the spokesman for the English in Canada—he represented their grievances and formulated reports. He even drafted a bill for the better government of Quebec. Under this model document the five hundred colonists referred to were to have full control of Canada, to the exclusion of every Frenchman and Catholic.

In the "draught of an act . . . ." for the good government of Quebec, prepared by Mr. Maseres, the members of the assembly would be required to take an obnoxious oath passed in the reign of George II :

" And likewise to make and subscribe the declaration against the Romish doctrine of transubstantiation mentioned in an act of Parliament made in the twenty-fifth year of the reign of King Charles II. entitled ' *An Act for preventing dangers which may happen from Popish recusants,*' before they are permitted to sit in said assemblies."

Another recital, in the spirit of this one, stated :

" That hitherto it was not practicable, by reason of the general prevalence of the Romish superstition among his Majesty's ' new ' Canadian subjects, to summon and call a general assembly."

The draught goes on to enact that in view of these and other things an assembly be called, each member of which should take the oath referred to, and so exclude any Roman Catholics.

" If it should be approved and carried into execution," wrote Mr. Maseres, " I confess I should think the inhabitants of the province would be likely to be governed more happily under it for seven or eight years to come, than under the influence of an assembly into which the Papists should be admitted. As to an assembly of Protestants only, I see no objection to the establishment of one, but the danger of disobliging the Catholics of the province, who are so much superior in number."

Mr. Maseres's plan of a legislative council was so good as to merit the approval of " Mr. Thomas Walker, of Montreal, and Mr. John Paterson, of Quebec, English merchants of eminence settled in those towns," but it did not commend itself to the governor nor to the British ministers. The council was to consist of thirty-one members, all Protestants and thirty years old:

" Because if Roman Catholics are admitted into the council, there is no good pretence for not having an assembly agreeably to the King's proclamation and commissions to General Murray and General Carleton."

The council afterwards established, it may be remarked, was comprised of seventeen members, seven of whom were Catholics.

The ordinance appointing them is as follows :

" To consist either of seventeen members or of twenty-three members, or of any intermediate number of members at the King's pleasure. And they may be all papists or even popish priests if the King shall so please, and of any age the King shall please above twenty-one years."

Mr Maseres might be pardoned for writing, as he did, a " remark " of ten pages upon this.

The petitions of the London Board of Trade and of the English at Quebec were entrusted to him, and in 1773, after a ponderous mass of materials from French and English petitioners were in the hands of the home ministry, the government set to work to frame an act for their new and old subjects of Canada.

IV.

The Earl of Dartmouth introduced the bill into the Lords, and Lord North assumed the task of defending it in the Commons. It may save some speculation here if we anticipate and say that in almost every particular, and certainly in every important one, the British Ministry disregarded the clamor of the now Baron Maseres and his requisitionists, and passed an act much more in the spirit of justice to the French than might have been expected. There were reasons for this outside of pleasing the French, as the coming events of 1775 were shadowing the whole continent.

Indeed, the cause of the difficulties at Boston, in 1773, was an error admitted in English councils. Whatever may have been the motive, the English government certainly desired to deal fairly with the French.

The English emigrants, once in America, were intolerant and revolutionary to a great degree, and in Canada they were, at the time about which we are writing, and later, in 1791, the most troublesome and unreasonable of subjects.

The Quebec Act of 1774 was an important measure, and so much so that although anything approaching a Hansard or parliamentary reporter was then in its infancy, we have, thanks to the industry of the then member from Lostwithiel, a very full report of the whole measure—the debates, the evidence taken, and the reports before the committee. These form a volume of 300 pages and are called Sir Henry Cavendish's reports. The fact that such a thing was done is good reason for believing how great an interest was taken in the act itself. Sir Guy Carleton was examined, Chief Justice Hey, a touchy and bigoted Doctor of Laws named Mariott, and many others of less note. Edmund Burke made several good speeches, and we can read the names of Attorney-General Thurlow, Colonel Barré, Mr. Wedderburne, Charles Fox, and others.

The bill defined the boundaries of the new British province which was thereafter to be known as " Quebec," containing :

"All the territories, islands, and countries in North America, belonging to the crown of Great Britain, bounded on the south by a line from the bay of Chaleurs, along the high lands which divide the rivers that empty themselves into the river St. Lawrence from those which fall into the sea, to a point in forty-five degrees of northern latitude, on the eastern bank of the river Connecticut, keeping the same latitude directly west, through the lake Champlain, until, in the same latitude, it meets the river St. Lawrence; from thence up the eastern bank of the said river to the lake Ontario; thence through the lake Ontario, and the river commonly called Niagara; and thence along by the eastern and southeastern bank of lake Erie, following the said bank, until the same shall be intersected by the northern boundary, granted by the charter of the province of Pennsylvania, in case the same shall be so intersected; and from thence along the said northern and western boundaries of the said province, until the said western boundary strike the Ohio; but in case the said bank of the said lake shall not be found to be so intersected, then following the said bank until it shall arrive at that point of the said bank which shall be nearest to the northwestern angle of the said province of Pennsylvania, and thence, by a right line, to the said northwestern angle of the said province; and thence along the western boundary of the said province, until it strike the river Ohio; and along the bank of the said river westward, to the banks of the Mississippi, and northward to the southern boundary of the territory granted to the merchants-adventurers of England, trading to Hudson's Bay; and also all such territories, islands, and countries, which have, since the 10th of February, 1763, been made part of the government of Newfoundland, be, and they are hereby, during his majesty's pleasure, annexed to, and made part and parcel of the province of Quebec, as created and established by the said royal proclamation of the 7th of October, 1763."

This boundary has been given in full because it will be seen to what extent the Quebec Act stretched across the continent the protection of the law in regard to the Roman Catholics. Part of this old province is now in the United States, part in several provinces of the Dominion of Canada other than the present province of Quebec, which, after an interval of 93 years, resumed its old name. It would, therefore, include Ontario, Manitoba in part at least, and part of the Northeast and Northwest Territories. But it might not include Nova Scotia and New Brunswick, as these became British provinces by the treaty of Utrecht, 1713, and were then undivided and known by the name of Acadia. The English owned Prince Edward Island since 1758. Although the treaty confirmed these provinces to Great Britain, it could scarcely be said that the inhabitants were " new " subjects. But this and the matters adverted to at the end of this article may be referred to on another occasion. However, any one with a map before him can see the extent of the old Province of Quebec; and this much is certain, that for so much of that as had been wrested from the French by the capitulation of 1760, its inhabitants came within the relief given by the Quebec Act.

Attention will now be called to the clause as to religion, which is as follows :

" And for the more perfect security and ease of the minds of the inhabitants of the said province, it is hereby declared that his majesty's subjects, professing the religion of the Church of Rome of and in the said province of Quebec, may have, hold, and enjoy the free exercise of the religion of the Church of Rome, subject to the King's supremacy, declared and established by an act, made in the first year of the reign of Queen Elizabeth, over all the dominions and countries which then did, or thereafter should belong to the imperial crown of this realm ; and that the clergy of the said church may hold, receive, and enjoy their accustomed dues and rights, with respect to such persons only as shall profess the said religion.

" Provided, nevertheless, that it shall be lawful for his majesty, his heirs or successors, to make such provision out of the rest of the said accustomed dues and rights, for the encouragement of the Protestant religion, and for the maintenance and support of a Protestant clergy within the said province, as he or they shall, from time to time, think necessary and expedient.

" Provided always, and be it enacted, that no person, professing the religion of the Church of Rome, and residing in the said province, shall be obliged to take the oath required by the said statute passed in the first year of the reign of Queen Elizabeth, or any other oaths substituted by any other act in the place thereof; but that every such person, who, by the said statute is required to take the oath therein mentioned, shall be obliged, and is hereby required, to take and subscribe the following oath before the governor or such other person in such court of record as his majesty shall appoint, who are hereby authorized to administer the same ; *videlicet.*

" I, A. B., do sincerely promise and swear, that I will be faithful, and bear true allegiance to his majesty King *George*, and him will defend to the utmost of my power, against all traitorous conspiracies and attempts whatsoever, which shall be made against his person, crown, and dignity ; and I will do my utmost endeavor to disclose and make known to his majesty, his heirs and successors, all treasons and traitorous conspiracies and attempts, which I shall know to be against him, or any of them, and all this I do swear without any equivocation, mental evasion, or secret reservation, and renouncing all pardons and dispensations from any power or person whomsoever to the contrary.

So· Help Me God." [1]

---

[1] When this clause was open for debate Mr. William Burke, a kinsman of Edmund Burke, said, " I do not remember that I ever saw the House of Commons in so sick a situation as it is at present (cry of order! order! order!). I say Sir, that the parliament of Great Britain is in an unfortunate situation. This is the worst bill that ever engaged the attention of the British Council. It is a bill to establish the Popish religion—to establish despotism. There have been instances in human affairs in which for purposes of commerce we have established freedom as far as we could in a certain locality ; but to establish Popery—to establish despotism in a conquered province is what we have never done before. . . . . The gentlemen who opposed the bill, knowing it was impossible to defeat it, have almost worked themselves to death to make it, as

V.

This bill created a great sensation in England, and the debates are instructive and interesting. As the reports are very scarce, the important references are given here.

"THE SOLICITOR-GENERAL (afterwards Lord Chancellor Loughborough) said: 'I will state in a few words the intention of the proviso, with respect to the establishment of a provision for the clergy in Canada. First, I agree that the Roman Catholic religion ought to be the established religion of that country in its present state; the clergymen of which are paid by the landed revenue of that country. I do not mean to assert that this should be perpetually the state of Canada, or that we are by law to enact that the people are not to be converted, or that the tithe shall remain in the Popish clergy, or that the tithe shall sink. I would not hold out the temptation that if you are a convert you shall not pay tithe. If the majority of a parish are Popish, there ought to be a Popish clergy in that parish; that Popish clergy ought to be maintained by such as are Papists; but the money of the Protestants ought to be applied for the encouragement of Protestants, and for the maintenance of Protestant clergy. In proportion as the scale, with regard to numbers, shall turn to the Protestant side, the clergymen ought to be Protestant. The amendment points rather more definitely to this object than the clause. There is no harm in leaving the discretion open. I would leave it so large that if they were to be converted to the Protestant religion, I should hold it to be absolutely necessary to adopt the mode of Protestant worship; and then all tithes should be paid by Popish inhabitants and others to the Protestant clergy. The bill waits events.'

"MR. CHARLES FOX.—'I perfectly agree that no Protestant ought to pay tithe to the Romish clergy. That is provided for in the clause. It could not be better stated for that purpose. But the learned gentleman has not absolutely said how far this proviso goes. The noble lord's amendment points to a more definite purpose. Am I to understand the tithe to be absolute so that you are not to alter it, and that it is contemplated to give to his Majesty the power of applying that tithe to the support of which clergy he pleases?'

"THE SOLICITOR-GENERAL.—'Though I wish to tolerate the Popish religion, I do not wish to encourage it. When we tell the Roman Catholics of Canada that we will not oppress them, we, at the same time, tell the followers of the Church of England that whenever their faith shall prevail, it will have a right to its establishment. As soon as the majority of a parish shall be Protestant inhabitants, then I think the ministers of the Crown are bound to make the minister of that parish a Protestant clergyman; then, I think, it could not be felt by any man an act of injustice to say that the whole revenue of that parish shall be paid to the Protestant clergyman.'

"LORD NORTH.—'Sir, as you have pointed to me, I presume to offer my sentiments, to explain the views I had when I made this amendment. I was in hopes of meeting the objections which had been made against the bill as it stood before. Those objections are two: one, that no care was taken of the Protestant clergy; that no establishment had been thought of for them; that, in the course of this bill, we had not only tolerated, but established the Roman Catholic religion, and that nothing had been thought of for the Protestant clergy. I am persuaded, in the present state of that country, the Protestant religion does not call much for support; but the hope of greater encouragement should be held out to it. A small establishment, however, will be sufficient at present. The question then is asked, what is to become of the tithe which will be paid to the Protestant clergy at a future period? Are the people in the meantime to pay no tithe? And do you hold out to persons that they may, for the sake of

far as they could, consonant to English liberty and the principles of the English Constitution." After much more in the same strain the clause was carried, no other member speaking on it.

saving the tithe, disclaim the Roman Catholic religion and not embrace any other? I thought, by the alteration of this clause, that both those questions would be answered, and I proposed it, by way of pointing out the method in which the tithe which would otherwise be paid by the Protestants to the Popish clergy, should be applied by the king to the Protestant clergy. The words I offered would, I thought, have answered that purpose. If gentlemen do not approve of them—I proposed them to remove particular objections,—but if they encounter greater objections I shall withdraw them. I will read my amendment:

"' The king will not be able to raise any tithe not now payable; but may dispose of that which is payable. There will be an extent of power given to the king in that circumstance.'

"MR. DUNNING.—' My opinion of religious toleration goes to all who stand in need of it, in all parts of the globe. It is a natural right of mankind that men should judge for themselves, and offer up to the Creator that worship which they conceive likely to be most acceptable to Him. It is neither competent, wise, nor just for society to restrain them further than is necessary. I should think the Roman Catholics would consider themselves well treated if they were put in the same situation the Protestant subjects are put in by this bill; at least, the preference ought not to be given against them. I am anxious to know from the learned gentleman what the extent is understood to be of those laws which we are going, by this bill, to give to the Catholic Church. Will they include all ranks now in that province? Will it include the bishop? I should be glad to know how he came there; what power he has there; from whom he derives that power, whether by Papal authority or whether by royal authority? In my apprehension, these questions deserve a serious answer. The dues and tithes, whatever they are, which may belong to this bishop and which he has thought fit to appropriate to himself by his own authority, will go to his successor to the end of time without any interposition of royal authority. Whether the bishop has exercised the power of nomination I do not know. Upon that fact I wish to be informed. Is it the intention of ministers that he shall, for the future, name to vacant churches, or that the king shall so name? If they think that the king only should name thereto they will take care not blindly to give the power to the bishop; nor will they give him the power of suspension, if they are, as they ought to be, ministers of peace, anxious to promote good will and good fellowship among men. To establish, in the judgment of the learned gentlemen, is not to encourage; in my judgment it is to encourage; and especially if this is to be the predominant religion. I do not like domineering in religion. I do not think the religion of the many ought to be the religion of the few. According to my apprehension those few have as good a right to judge for themselves as those many. Every man has a right to pursue his own opinion; no man ought to be permitted to control that of another.'

"MR. STANLEY.—' There is no inconvenience in supposing two religions established in the same country. For example, the establishment of the Roman Catholic religion has by no means excluded the Protestant.'

"MR. THOMAS TOWNSEND, JR.—' I want to see some specific provision immediately made in Canada for the Protestant religion. I was concerned to hear that nine or ten years ago there was not a single place of worship for the Protestant, which I consider to have been a great disgrace to the English governor. I was surprised at an expression dropped by the noble lord, 'that the Protestant religion in Canada at present was hardly an object worthy of consideration.' During the whole of these discussions, pains have been taken by the Prime Minister of this country, and Chancellor of the University of Oxford, to rank the Protestants in Canada as low as possible in number, consequence and character.'

"LORD NORTH.—' The honorable gentleman is word-catching. I certainly did say that the Protestant inhabitants were so few that they were hardly worthy of attention; but I explained it at the time. What I meant was that they were not sufficiently numerous at present to make it necessary for the legislature to provide establishments and a revenue for them. With regard to the bishop, it is my opinion—an opinion founded in law—that if a Roman Catholic bishop is professedly subject to the king's supremacy, under the act of Queen Elizabeth, none of those powers can be exercised from which dangers are to be apprehended '

"MR. EDMUND BURKE.—'The noble lord says he makes the proposition contained in the amendment in order to make the clause palatable; but if not liked, he has no objection to withdraw that amendment. Are they then mere nugatory words, since they are drawn with such extreme levity? Then I promise mine as a better candidate for the consideration of the committee. But before I proceed, allow me to state, in a few words, my opinion with regard to the principle of toleration. There is but one healing Catholic principle of toleration which ought to find favor in this House. It is wanted, not only in our colonies, but here. The thirsty earth of our own country is gasping and gaping, and crying out for that healing shower from heaven. The noble lord has told you of the right of those people by the treaty; but I consider the right of conquest so little, and the right of human nature so much, that the former has very little consideration with me. I look upon the people of Canada as coming, by the dispensation of God, under the British government. I would have us govern it in the same manner as the all-wise disposition of Providence would govern it. We know He suffers the sun to shine upon the righteous and unrighteous; and we ought to suffer all classes, without distinction, to enjoy equally the right of worshipping God according to the light He has been pleased to give them. The word "established" has been made use of; it is not only a crime, but something unnatural to establish a religion, the tenets of which you do not believe. Applying it to the ancient inhabitants of Canada, how does the question stand? It stands thus: You have got a people professing the Roman Catholic religion, and in possession of a maintenance, legally appropriated to its clergy. Will you deprive them of that? Now that is not a question of " establishment"; the establishment was not made by you; it existed before the treaty; it took nothing from the treaty; no legislature has a right to take it away; no governor has a right to suspend it. This principle is confirmed by the usage of every civilized nation of Europe. In all our conquered colonies, the established religion was confirmed to them; by which I understand that religion should receive the protection of the state in those colonies; and I should not consider that it had received such protection, if their clergy were not protected. I do say that a Protestant clergyman going into that country does not receive the protection of the laws, if he is not allowed to worship God according to his own creed. Is this removing the sacred landmark? What I desire is that every one should contribute towards the maintenance of the religion he professes; and if this is proper to be done, why not do it immediately? . . . .'

"THE ATTORNEY-GENERAL.—' The present question turns upon the merits of two propositions. The one moved by the noble lord stands in a very small compass—" let those inhabitants who profess the Popish religion continue under the obligation of paying tithes for the maintenance of the Popish clergy." But as there are a certain number of persons in the province who do not profess the Popish religion, some regulation ought to be entered into with regard to their tithe. The noble lord proposes a clause referring it to the king, to appoint the payment of their tithe, in such course and order as his Majesty's wisdom shall suggest, for the support of the Protestant clergy. Another plan which has been proposed is that instead of the tithes of the Protestants being paid as circumstances may require, they shall all be paid to the receiver-general. They are not even then to be disposed of, even by his Majesty, as the exigency requires, but to be paid to the Society for the Propagation of the Gospel in foreign parts; so that, instead of the disposal of the tithe being committed to the king, we are called upon to declare by our vote, that it is a fitter thing to place greater confidence in the wisdom and discretion of a religious corporation. I should never have thought of 're-ferring this to the opinion of the House. I have no difficulty in saying that the first proposition is infinitely the better of the two.' "

This is substantially all there is preserved of the debates on the clause as to religion, though there was considerable discussion on the second reading of the bill, when its principle was discussed.

The clause was carried by a very large majority, and in a few days afterwards the bill passed into the act of Parliament.

VI.

Whatever success the French regarded as falling to their side, the English—the old subjects—were sorely disappointed. They were defeated and they knew it. The act, besides what we have referred to, established the French municipal law in Canada as it was formerly—at least for all civil cases. The criminal law of England was in use since the capitulation and was only formally introduced. The bill produced something like a panic at Quebec among the English colonists. All his Majesty's ancient subjects settled in the province of Quebec petitioned against it, and in the following year Lord Çamden endeavored to get the act repealed, but the motion was defeated. Mr. Maseres finally gave expression to his feelings by declaring that in his opinion " it had not only offended the inhabitants of the province itself in a degree that could hardly be conceived, but had alarmed all the English provinces in America and contributed more, perhaps, than any other means whatsoever to drive them into rebellion against their Sovereign."

For the next fifteen years, of course, the influx of English speaking citizens was very great, not only by the natural emigration from the British soil, but also by the hegira of those superior souls, the United Empire Loyalists. These came chiefly to the western part of the province of Quebec—what was later called Upper or Western Canada and now the Province of Ontario. In 1790 a dead set was made by all those on the Quebec Act, and a worthy man from Montreal went to England on a like mission as was previously intrusted to Baron Maseres.

This was Mr. Lymburger, who made a long speech in the Commons against the proposed constitutional act brought in by Mr. Pitt. Mr. Fox thundered against the new bill and its provisions, but all chiefly because it did not repeal the old act—the Quebec Act. Mr. Lymburger and his friends met with no better reception than the agents of the British colonists did in 1774. They wanted the province to remain as one province—the English laws to be the law in all cases, and the obnoxious act repealed.

The Pitt ministry divided Quebec into Upper and Lower Canada —they did not touch the Quebec Act except in so far as the new act expressly altered it, and the only concession was a clause for the Protestant clergy. This gave rise to what was called the Clergy Reserve, which, after disturbing the country for over fifty years, was finally wiped out of the statute book.

The Quebec Act has, since the constitutional act of 1791, been recognized in a score of statutes by the provincial and imperial authorities.

As late as the year 1880 a leading judge in Quebec, in giving judgment in a case involving what elsewhere would be a conflict of municipal and ecclesiastical law, says :

> " Inutile d'établir ici que la religion catholique romaine et son plein, entier et libre exercice ont été reconnus dans ce pays et garantis par la foi des traités confirmés par l'acte imperial de 1774 si souvent cité devant nos tribunaux sous le nom ‹ d'Acte de Québec.' La plus forte partie de notre législation civile se rattache à ce fait et en est la conséquence nécessaire."

The writer of this paper has no intention of discussing *coram non judicibus* nice points of law. The exact *status* of the Church may be referred to hereafter. Enough has been given to form an estimate of what at all events was intended by the Treaty of Cession and by the subsequent legislation down to the division of Quebec into two provinces. Authoritative opinions and the weight of interpretation of the English parliaments and its legal lights, have been referred to in discussing the position of the Church generally. The opinion of eminent judges of the Privy Council of England at the present day could be given to show that no subsequent legislation has effected the general *status* referred to. In a court of law several other circumstances would have to be considered—what was the exact *status* of the Church in Canada before the cession, under the French king? Was the law of the Church modified, and to what extent, by " *les libertés de l'Eglise Gallicane* " ? What relations have actually subsisted between the Church and state in Canada since the treaty? Was the Roman Catholic Church established by law by the act of 1774 subject to whatever may be meant by the supremacy of the Sovereign of Great Britain? Did the sovereign of Great Britain succeed to all the rights of the French king in his relations to the Church in France or in Canada ?

Exactly one hundred years after the Quebec Act was passed the Privy Council of England heard and decided a celebrated case from Montreal known as the Guibord case.

It may be said to have decided no point of importance, and it appears to have been argued in a remarkable way—those upholding the *Fabrique* at Montreal and the action of the *Curé* in refusing ecclesiastical burial to the member of a condemned *Institut*, arguing that the Church in Canada was not established by law, and their opponents asserting that it was an established Church. Their Lordships decided on a narrow ground—(the extent of an *et cetera* in an ordinance as construed *ejusdem generis* with other terms)—and avoided every important point, conceding, however, the difficulty and importance of the questions raised in the argument.

WHAT IS THE MOTIVE POWER OF MAN?

The Physiology and Pathology of the Mind.   By Henry Maudsley, M.D.,
    London, Physician to the West London Hospital, Honorary Mem-
    ber of the Medico-Psychological Society of Paris, formerly Resident
    Physician of the Manchester Royal Lunatic Hospital, etc.   New
    York.   D. Appleton & Co., 1871.

The Brain and its Functions.   By J. Luys, Physician to the Hospice de
    la Salpétrière.   With illustrations.   London.   Kegan Paul, Trench
    & Co., No. 1 Paternoster Square, 1881.   International Scientific
    Series, vol. xxxvii.

Body and Will; being an Essay concerning Will in its Metaphysical,
    Physiological, and Pathological aspects.   By Henry Maudsley, M.D.
    London.   Kegan Paul, Trench & Co., No. 1 Paternoster Square,
    1883.

THE fundamental idea in modern philosophical discussion lies
in the question, whether the human intellect is a manifestation of physical force on matter, or the brain the instrument of a
something superphysical, called mind.

That man is largely automatic in his brain processes and in his
bodily actions is amply demonstrated by the facts which are here
set forth and generally known.   Let us frankly concede that man
is largely automatic.   Let us, at the same time, however, try to
see if his automatism may not hold the secondary place in his
being; whether that is not the fairest induction from all we know.
The things—the mysteries—that surround him interest him deeply,
because, ulteriorly, they are related to his being.   This has always
been so, and it is doubly so now, because, whereas only a few
years ago, comparatively, nothing had been effectively done,
impugning the spirituality of man, now a powerful, materialistic
school, armed with the latest results of science, has arisen, ready
to do battle against all comers.   It contends that there is naught
in man, non-physical, non-dynamical, ethical, spiritual; nothing
that can justify the ascription to him of that which is termed soul.
It contends that man is of the earth, earthy, an evolution of matter
directed in certain grooves of action by physical forces.   It finds
itself as unable to conceive of a psychic force—soul, emanating
from a supreme psychic force—God, as to conceive of a cloud-
compelling Jove.

Let us first proceed to the consideration of automatic man, to
that in him which has been demonstrated by physiology to be automatic, and then, proceeding beyond, see if we do not find a resi-

duum for which the theory of his essential automatism in everything is utterly unable to account.

It is a part of popular misconception regarding man, that his every act is the result of an exercise of will, and this in face of daily evidence to the contrary. A man has, let us say, the habit of winding his watch as he takes it from his pocket on retiring for the night. Many times he withdraws it, winds, and lays it in a safe place, without any conscious perception or will whatever having been concerned. Or he has, we will say, lived for many years in a certain house, and moves away from it to one a few doors off. Shortly afterwards he passes his own door unknowingly, his steps not arrested until he finds himself in front of his former residence, when he is aroused suddenly to his mistake. Will certainly does not enter into these acts. Whence are they then derived? They are clearly ideo-motor, as contradistinguished from volitional acts. They are as somnambulistic acts, compared with ordinary waking acts. Just as, waking, it is possible to see without perceiving, so it is possible to act without willing.

Man's few first simple movements as an infant are either inherited or automatic. Thenceforward, as the adjustment of his life with reference to his environment proceeds through the nervous centres and the machinery which they actuate, which gradually learn the lesson of greater or less adaptation to his needs, he becomes endowed with manifold secondary automatic movements, which serve in the commonplace actions of life, that call for no exercise of the powers vested in the supremacy of the brain. The brain, it would seem, like a chief of state, can withdraw itself into the seclusion of the closet, having relegated to well-instructed ministers the petty details to which it is below its dignity to attend.

That it is not the brain only which, so to speak, possesses memory and will and executive powers is readily perceived upon slight consideration of some facts open to daily observation. Recollect how slowly and laboriously many movements are acquired, and it will be seen how little conception and will are competent in these to insure success. Recollect, further, how easily, from want of practice, a movement which has reached perfection is imperfectly executed or lost entirely, without any diminution of the appropriate conception or of the will to execute. With regard to some movements, it is only in the general immaturity of youth, at a time when, of course, the brain also is immature, that certain movements can be thoroughly acquired, and this apart from any question of flexibility of muscles and joints. The difficulty of acquiring the manual of arms, dancing (in the rhythmical, not in the agile sense), instrumental music, and the succeeding diminution in facility in proportion to want of practice, are examples of the slowly acquired action, and the gradually lost action of co-ōrdinative nervous centres possessing capacity independent of conception and so-called memory and will. The brain's mandate may or may not issue for a particular action. Its sway, in proportion to the individual's elevation in the scale of being, and the consequent training which it has imparted to his life-work, is not exercised save in a supervisory capacity, which generally takes in the whole situation represented by the actions to be performed, and the greater or less degree of excellence with which they are performed.

Having now considered in this cursory, but sufficient, manner, the automatism of man in his waking life, let us consider it in the other aspect of his existence, the sleeping life. In sleep the response of simple reflex action and of sensori-motor reaction to external stimulus is plainly to be observed. The tickling of a sensitive part of the body, as of the nostril, with a feather, or the application of cold or heat, will bring about the same reactions that would be produced by the same causes during waking. Everyone knows that, in sleep, sound is readily taken up and appropriated by the dreamer, and assimilated with the subject of his dream, or may initiate a dream; that it may give a new direction to a dream, or a modification to a theme proceeding quietly to its *dénoûment;* or that, reaching the climax of an explosion or·a roar, it may cause a sudden awakening. This last effect is produced by sensori-motor reaction. On the other hand, a noise may not cause awakening, even when violent. It may not cause an expenditure of outward energy. It may, even although violent, be accommodated by the dream; so that a violent concussion shall appear, in a dream of battle, the report of a cannon, the springing of a mine, or a signal-gun from a rocky coast. Or, so accommodating are dreams, a battle, or something else where noise would be a concomitant, lends itself at once to the imagination of the dreamer, solely for the purpose of accounting rationally for the noise. A dream, to a sound sleeper, can accommodate much, for all things that the sleeper has experienced are, fundamentally at least, memories recombined, lending themselves in profusion to his phantasy. Why should a sound, or a touch, or a smell, refuse to assimilate itself with the manifestations of a life in which the laws are but amplifications of the laws among which, awake, he has lived and moved and had his being? Amid dream-perceptions, whether derived from inward or outward impulse, or from them combined, the sleeper is thinking, under the limitations of dream-life.

Having thus afforded a rapid but well-balanced survey of the two lives of man, the waking life and the dream-life, turn we for a moment away from both (to recur later to some of their phenomena in detail), in order that, upon the basis of what has been already said as to automatic man, whether awake or asleep, we can proceed with discussion from this point, beyond which he, as he seems to us, whether awake or asleep, ceases, at least mainly, to be automatic. The exception to which we refer in saying "mainly" is that relating to "unconscious cerebration," the very terms of which, admitted, concede automatism in action. We admit formally, however, that there is no question in our mind, that "unconscious cerebration" exists, and is, moreover, as active in waking as in sleeping moments. In the first, it is coupled with other cerebration ; in the second, it is almost alone.

When we consider, from the psychological point of view, the processes constituting the law of thought, we find that related sequence is the first in importance. A man cannot have a single thought. One thought engenders another—not another entirely diverse, for if it were, there would be no related sequence, but another which in turn transmits its ancestral attributes, and bears the same relation to it as parent to child, however at the first glance seemingly dissimilar. If this be not so, it is impossible to conceive of individuality, or of variety in individuality. Individuality consists far less in features, form, and other bodily attributes (these change greatly merely from the advance of age) than in character, of which we possess no other manifestation besides expressed thoughts and acts, which, through all disguises, in the long run always correspond; and character, which is only another term for individuality, is regarded by modern science as being as persistent as anything in nature. It certainly would not be regarded as persistent, if thought in the individual were not so related to thought as to cause him to be best known through his mind. If we experience a difference in a friend's expressed ideas, we say with surprise that he is changed. If his ideas, although coherent, are utterly different from those with which we are familiar as emanating from him, we are alarmed lest he may be verging on insanity. So strongly as this do we confess our faith in the persistence of individuality. At the same time, however, that the law of related thought, through heredity, is not to be disputed, it is only a general law of sequence, conservative of individuality, and is immeasurably far from involving the narrow limitations enunciated by Lord Kames in his *Elements of Criticism*, who makes thoughts, through generations of thought from the cradle to the grave of every man, one long line of generations, each linked indissolubly to its predecessor, of necessity its progenitor. To hold this is certainly to admit that man has no control over his action, is to make of man the merest automaton passing over the stage of life.

From outward experience, and from self consciousness, one must concede the existence of the law of related sequence in ideas, but consideration of the evidence deducible from both proves that the law is no more than general in its binding force. It is true that we should refute ourselves if, by way of showing that an existing thought is not the parent of the succeeding one, we were to say, "we shall prove our position by conceiving here and now a thought that shall be utterly unlike what the succeeding thought would, without the intervention of our act of will, have been," and were then, in pursuance of our intention, to leap instantaneously in mind from this essay to some idea foreign to all our surroundings, as, for instance, to the conception of the frosty Caucasus, or to the perforation in manufacture of the eye of the needle. For these conceptions are merely drawn from the storehouse of memory, and the thought, of which they are the form, was born of the thought of avoidance of parentage, and therefore is the veritable child of the first thought.

But no regular sequence can be proved of many evolutions in the mind, especially in the mind actively and multifariously engaged. There are to be discerned other laws, by virtue of which the memory and the will, sometimes in conjunction, sometimes separately, assert their claims. It is a matter of daily observation to the man earnestly employed, that he has other things to attend to, besides those represented by the thoughts which are for the moment in a determinate direction passing through his brain. He is often, without individualizing one of them, conscious that many things are awaiting his attention. Some one or more of these may obtrude themselves upon him, but many more may still await in the antechamber of his mind the pleasure of his memory to introduce them, or of his will to summon the memory to introduce them to his presence. What is of commoner occurrence than that, when his preoccupation slackens, he invites them one by one to appear before him? Was his last thought, in the previous absorption of his mind, in any wise the parent of the next thought, directed to an entirely different quarter? Assuredly not—he merely became at leisure to entertain thoughts which, previously, he had not had leisure to entertain. If his preoccupation continues inordinately long, we find him often losing all hold upon the circumstance that something had required his attention; he has forgotten something, often to the point of never knowing of it, except, perhaps, through "mechanical memory," over which he can, of course, exercise no control.

Notwithstanding this, M. Luys, the French physiologist, says:

"I imagine that I think of an object by a spontaneous effort of my mind; it is an illusion—it is because the cell-territory where that object resides has been previously set vibrating in my brain. I obey when I think I am commanding, merely turning in a direction towards which I am unconsciously drawn. A phenomenon quite analogous to the conjuring trick of forcing a card takes place in this instance; the conjurer forcing us unconsciously to take a card, while letting us imagine we have liberty of choice."[1]

Can this be the process always, seeing that memory sometimes calls a man's attention to a subject dormant in his mind, in regard to which consciousness admits the importance (presumably associated with energetic cell-activity)? and that, although he strives to convert the warning as to the existence of a something important, to be attended to, into a recollection of the subject-matter, he may or may not succeed; for he sometimes does and sometimes does not? If he does, can the rescued idea possibly be physically represented by a previous specific cell-vibration? Is it also, of necessity, the lineal descendant of the last one of his preoccupation, or of an intermediate phase of thought? If it had been, it would not have required to be dragged forth into the light. If he does not succeed in rescuing it from oblivion, its lineage is, of course, disproved by the fact of its eluding observation. In point of fact, not only are volition and memory capable of instituting as well as breaking trains of thought, but circumstances in the outward world are continually engaged in instituting and breaking them. On the one hand, an episode of any sort, great or small, may institute a new train, and on the other, the thought that would have been born, but for the interposition of an exterior force, in the voice of a friend or an enemy, in a sudden accident or a catastrophe, may never come into being.

The truth is, that when the power, called will, enters, the automatic man does not end, but the higher man begins. Certain of man's brain-processes do not cease to be automatic then; they continue to act for themselves, but they then begin to act also under the mandate of the higher man. "Unconscious cerebration" will often have taken place on a theme in which there has been conscious interest, but no intention of proceeding with reason to the ultimate point; but again, the higher man may consciously think upon a subject which he wishes to elucidate, and may also, at the same time, commit to "unconscious cerebration" the task of doing its part towards placing him in the mental frame in which he can best devote himself to the subject, when his will decides to

---

[1] J. Luys, "The Brain and its Functions." "The International Series"—translation. Kegan Paul, Trench & Co., London, p. 254.

attack it with his whole vigor. The higher man, in a word, can utilize the automatism of his being, as a machine, to grind out a portion of his work. But it does not follow that the higher man (and higher he is, in the supreme function assumed, without our begging the question by that term) is therefore no more than the machine. On the contrary, if he can use the machine, he must be a something separate and apart from it. Every man, who, from the beginning of the world, has thought or said, " I will take some time to think over this question," has to some degree, whether he knew it or not, committed his subject to his " unconscious cerebration," as well as to prospective, conscious thought. He has, whether knowingly or unknowingly, used the automatism of his being as a machine which he knew would yield him product which he could further shape through intending will.

Dr. Maudsley, in his *Physiology and Pathology of the Mind,* contends that character is not determined in the particular act by the will, but determines the will. That is true if sufficiently qualified. Unqualified, it will not stand the test of experience. Dr. Maudsley himself expressly says in the same treatise, " The way in which the will does operate upon the character, or affect the *ego,* is indirectly, by determining the circumstances which subsequently gradually modify it." These two propositions are irreconcilable. If character must always determine the will in the particular act, it must also determine the circumstances in accordance with its own bent. It is impossible to conceive of its determining an act in one direction and circumstances (which are to control acts) in the opposite direction. And yet, it is just these two propositions that Dr. Maudsley calls upon us to accept. The idea, that the process of which he speaks shall be gradual, is misleading; it could never be initiated. The propositions amount to saying, in sum, that it is in man, through character, to determine to act in a particular direction, and at the same time, or later, to act otherwise in future. The terms " circumstances " and " acts " are, in this connection, equivalent. The character (upon the assumption) must needs determine circumstances for the future, that would result in acts precisely like those which it, in the present, decrees. The well-known effect, too, of taking a direction is to strengthen a tendency. That fact also is irreconcilable with the statement that the same character can determine circumstances—virtually acts—conflicting with its acts. The whole difficulty is resolved, if we regard will as capable of determining against desire, and therefore, against character at a given point of time.

This is the true theory. We cannot accept Dr. Maudsley's theory that, in the individual act, one must, for " will," read " character." His answer would perhaps be, that we know what the will is by knowing what the act is, but that we do not know what the character is, for that is not directly knowable ; that, in a word, this unknown character determines, in strict accordance with itself, the known act.   But we must assume that we can know character. All discussion of the question must cease if we cannot make that assumption.   Dr. Maudsley's own conclusions are based upon that assumption.   We therefore say emphatically, that we find in experience the individual act often in opposition to the character.

It is only upon the theory of the reciprocal action and reaction of will and character, that improvement or degradation in the individual is comprehensible.   It is only upon this, the true theory, that Dr. Maudsley's own description of the efficacy of the will can be justified, and never has it been more brilliantly described.   He says, " Without doubt the will is the highest force in nature, the last consummate blossom of all her marvellous efforts. . . . By the power of a well-fashioned will man re-acts with intelligent success upon the external world, brings himself into a complete harmony with his surroundings, assimilates and incorporates nature, and thus carries forward its organic evolution.   The highest action of will is therefore truly *creative*."

Even in dreams, to which we will now revert, to show that even in that life where the mental powers are most in abeyance, the intelligence and the will of the individual man still bear witness by their persistence to the identity and the will of the man.

Problems that have eluded the thinker in his waking hours have sometimes been solved by him during sleep ; perhaps because the synthetical process is then less embarrassed by the commonplace surroundings of the waking life.   Sometimes, as though by intuition, is grasped by the sleeper what had been denied him when awake.   As if by intuition it must be, for deliberation is impossible to the dreamer.   But what, after all, is intuition at any time, awake, but the synthetical faculty unconscious of acting ?   It, like the best brain product of other kinds, is from the mind at the time unconscious of its processes, working with the maximum of power, because with the minimum of friction.   In the case described, the ideation may be held to be automatic just because of its rapidity. We have a right to reply that that adverse criticism is not applied to rapid waking thought.

Considering that Newton struggled to bring to the surface a thought which seemed to him great, and succeeding, found it unutterable nonsense, it may be inferred by some persons, unaware of very different cases, that dreams must always be of such stuff, for what could be expected of lesser men ?   But appeal to some experience of every one, and principally to that of certain great men who have told of their dreams—Condorcet, Franklin, and others,—proves that true thought is sometimes evolved in dreams. Even Sir Humphry Davy's experience when experimenting with nitrous-oxide gas, and under its influence conceiving that the universe resolves itself into thought, cannot be held nonsensical. His thought was a beautiful abstraction, but another form of the conception that Goethe makes the Earth-Spirit utter, when he says:

> " 'Tis thus at the roaring Loom of Time I ply
> And weave for God the Garment thou seest Him by."

How defenceless the sleeper lies, open to all potentialities! Well may Shakespeare speak of dreams abusing the curtained sleeper! His brain, with all its accumulated treasure of ideas, is ready to respond to an impulse from within itself, ready to respond to an impulse initiated in the sensory system, or to one due to that system's communicating with the outer world. Ideas, abstract and concrete, roll onward, directing and directed by ceaseless phantasmagoria—the sensible images that people this special world invisible to all but himself, visible to him as if he saw them with his bodily eyes. Probably the molecular changes in the sensory ganglia, which would accompany actual sight, are the same in kind as they would be if the images were received upon the retina, and thus excited vision. Sight, which, as Dr. Johnson says, can, of all the senses, occupy itself longest without satiety, asserts its predominance over the other senses in our sleeping as well as in our waking moments. These phenomena are, of course, for the most part automatic, but much thought is mingled with them, however evanescent, and it is not always evanescent.

Dreams are as various in character as the men who dream them; but one essential quality underlies them all—that they are, as one ought to know they must be, wrought out of the nature of the individual sleeper. There are men and women who lead humdrum lives within the same lights and shadows from the cradle to the grave; and they, perhaps, as the father of Robinson Crusoe said to him of the middle estate, are the happiest of mortals. Others there are who have lived lives within lives, which, viewed from their present standpoint, seem eras distantly related. To the people and places associated with these, the dream-visits from the last period have often more than the ordinary reality of dreams, and present truthful scenes more vividly than their counterpart real prototypes appear in waking hours. The dreamer bears with him, as the ordinary traveller does, the thoughts and feelings of his present home, and sits in melancholy musing near the ashes of his former hearths. He even sees people, not as they were when he lived among them, but as they ought to look from the actual lapse of time, regarding which he is often wonderfully accurate.

One man, as intimated, does not dream as another dreams. A man is no other than himself when he dreams; he never loses his identity. The dreams of each person are the resolution of the whole person, plus or minus something—a variable quantity for each person, when asleep, as compared with awake, but a different and constant quantity in comparing one person with another. It is as the *ego*, not the *eidolon*, that one threads the labyrinth of dreams. High or low as he may rise or sink in fortune, as he occupies the stage of his fancy's creation, where he has furnished every actor's part and the whole *mise en scène*, he never loses his identity. If he should be then asked his name, he may not know it, but he is in some subtle sense himself, and knows that.

It will be apparent to any one who may choose to investigate the subject, that, although man shows much automatism in sleep, yet the higher man, the intellectual, ratiocinative man, capable not only of reasoning, but of what is called intuition, is not always absent in sleep. It remains to consider whether the highest part in man—the will (without which the whole man is neutralized) is absent in sleep. We think that to a certain degree the will is not absent, Miss Frances Power Cobbe to the contrary notwithstanding. Released as all mankind are by the fact of sleep from moral obligation, the will, nevertheless, asserts and effects in sleep a certain restraining influence.

The most marked characteristic of dreaming, however, is the weakening of morality in the dreamer. The consciousness which accompanies the *ego* of the dreamer is the same consciousness in kind, but not in degree, as that which accompanies him as a man awake. He commits or allows certain actions impossible for him to commit or allow if he were awake. And yet, if he be at all a moral man, there are bounds beyond which his weakness never passes, by which his individuality is still preserved. If, awake, he be a man incapable of fraud, he cannot, asleep, conceive himself guilty of fraud. If, awake, he cannot lie, neither can he when asleep. With self-consciousness, which we have said exists in the dreamer, must be associated conscience. In a superficial sort of way the terms consciousness and unconsciousness serve to distinguish between the states of waking and sleeping; but not otherwise. Self-consciousness—the presence of the *ego*—belongs to both waking and sleeping thought, and the most essential difference between waking and sleeping thought is in the diminution of the power of will. Physiologically speaking, a man's mental and moral condition in sleep is owing to loss of coördination of the nervous centres; psychologically speaking, that involves the diminution of reflection and will. Asleep, a man's intellect for single, isolated ideas is often as brilliant as in his waking moments. Tested by comparison, under the different conditions of sleeping and waking, as the Persians, according to Herodotus, and the ancient Germans, according to Tacitus, tested an important question, drunk and sober, they often stand the ordeal. They sometimes add a happy conception which had failed to offer itself under the noonday sun. The memory is not dulled; it unlocks its treasures and pours them forth in reckless profusion, but so blended and transfused that the owner cannot always recognize them as his own. The imagination does not lack wings, and the mind is seldom unequal to accepting its flights as realities. We say " seldom," advisedly, because there are cases where the mind refuses its assent. But memory in profusion, without order, imagination almost without bounds, affords no resting place for any but the most transient reflection—deliberation in the true sense is impossible, so that real thought in dreaming comes in flashes, and the moral force and will-function suffer from the absence of deliberation. The sleeping adult becomes in a measure like the child, which possesses but little of either reflection or will.

The true test to apply, after all, to the solution of the problem that has been set before us is to try to ascertain whether or not the manifestation of thought—mind—is not in some particulars, and indeed the chief, so unlike, as far as we know them, other manifestations of force upon matter, as to lead to a definite conclusion, either that they are like or unlike. We think that it will be found that the manifestations are so little alike as not to be analogous. Mingled with and dominating the physical aspect of the case is a superphysical one, just as plainly as the other, by painstaking observation, to be perceived. Granting all that has preceded regarding the automatism of man, we may still dissent from the view that his brain-product is mere manifestation of physical force in matter.

What right is there to infer, when we consider that discrete intelligence acts upon discrete intelligence, that the physical force and matter which, associated, seem to make man, represent in sum his intelligence? We find intelligence present even when the body is being renovated through the process of sleep. We find in that state the individual man duly represented in the character of his mind, even to its most distinctive trait—his will. Is it not rationally deducible from all we know, that the brain is the instrument of the mind?—the machine for all directive life purposes,—and that its synchronous response to the mind depends upon whether or not the master is at the keys? In the opposite view, it would seem that the fallacy of the *post hoc, propter hoc* argument is apparent. It seems to us as irrational to hold that mere numerals and algebraic signs, which are but the symbols of computation, contain in themselves all the possibilities of mathematics, as to hold that it is through a synthesis from the revelations of the senses, that we reach abstract ideas. All that is included in man—body, sensorial apparatus and brain proper, however they may have acted in the beginning of life, when they were informing and educating each other; later, when the education is completed to the possible extent in the individual, are dominated by the brain, for which term read *mind*. This to some physiologists would seem hyperbole, rather than a scientific conception; but ought not, consistently, to one who, like Dr. Maudsley, can say, as-already quoted, "Without doubt the will is the highest force in nature" and that its highest action is "truly creative." Unless it be creative, it is not the highest force in nature, but is merely on a par with other forces; and if it be not creative, it has not, as Dr. Maudsley also says, power to affect the *ego* indirectly, "by determining the circumstances which subsequently gradually modify it." [1]

If it be true that the mind is exercised upon the basis of life experience, internal and external; that it makes laws of conduct, subject to its own revision, amendment and abrogation, it is evident that, trammelled though it be by its corporeal entanglement and its environment, it is the most independent of all agents in nature, enjoying legislative, executive, and judicial functions. In an analogous manner to that in which a man's conduct is modified by his environment in the world, by what is imposed upon him, so the brain, as the organ of the mind, entangled with internal forces, has its product modified by them. Although this is inseparable from the constitution of man, yet, in sanity and health, his mind is master of all else in his composition, originating and developing thoughts never received, excepting in the form of signs and symbols with which, according to greater or less capacity, to work out the problem of life.

Yet there are those, as intimated, who would have us believe, from analogy and experiment, that, whether waking or sleeping, mental phenomena are merely modes of motion; who seem to forget that the integrated entity which we call mind communicates with exterior force and matter by the determination of what kind, of what complexity, and of what amount the communicated energy shall be. The modes of motion belonging to the brain end there, unless man chooses to let them proceed beyond. There, in the brain—in the mind—they, unlike other modes of motion, reach conclusions, which may or may not, in accordance with, and in proportion to, the individual man's knowledge and will, affect external force and matter.

If it be affirmed, as is true and conceded, that in following their

---

[1] Dr. Maudsley has recently published a volume entitled "Body and Will," in which his views are even more explicitly adverse to those herein set forth than they are in his "Physiology and Pathology of the Mind."

transitions, the modes of motion whose existence and action have been demonstrated, and that matter also, implicitly obey their own laws, unless when sometimes interfered with and utilized by man, how can it possibly be held that in creating, say, a great poem, the steamship, the telephone, exterior force and matter are directly acted upon only through physical forces by which he is himself actuated? Unless that view be held, the notion of his mental manifestations being merely modes of motion is inconsistent with our knowledge of the correlation and conservation of force, the theory of which is that the chain is unbroken. There can be no correlation and conservation of physical forces involved in the transmutation of the idea of the poem, the steamship, the telephone, into the concrete creation of these and a thousand other things. If the truth of this be granted, it follows, of course, that what we call mind acts upon internal and external physical force and matter through something superphysical, is, in a word, superphysical.

Nature, however we may choose to formulate our idea of her, is certainly intelligent. So far as experience goes, she does not palter with the truth, but is, so to speak, brutally straightforward, even to the point, to our limited vision, of cruelty. She does not divulge, nay even, to appearance, sometimes jealously guards her secrets; while at other times it seems marvelous, when one is discovered, that we have not seen what she was clearly pointing out. We may or may not understand the lines which she puts before us to read, but in them is never found, if at last interpreted, any evidence of deceit or subterfuge. The great majority of men cannot believe, with M. Luys, in her juggling with the consciousness of her highest type. Beginning with the *Cogito, ergo sum*, there are other axiomatic postulates of life, rendering inconceivable to most men the proposition that freedom of action within the limits defined (limitation encompassing all nature) can be a visionary concept.

Some forty years ago we had not reached further than knowledge of the indestructibility of matter. Since then, Helmholtz, Mayer, Grove, and others, have demonstrated the indestructibility of force. May we not rationally conclude, although unable to demonstrate it, that, as we know force, and what we call mind, only through matter, and both force and matter (through ever extending bounds) as directed and ruled by mind, that it too is indestructible? The vast majority of men have held, and will continue to hold, if for no other reason than that man is creative, that a scintillation of a Great Intelligence shines on earth. If, as Mr. Herbert Spencer says, "Force, as we know it, can be regarded only as a certain conditioned effect of the Unconditioned Cause," must not what we call mind, with its limited creative power and dominion over both force and matter, be regarded as a conditioned effect, but none the less as a conditioned cause, and, like force and matter, indestructible?

THE FIRST CENTURY OF RELIGIOUS PERSECUTION
IN IRELAND.

T HE history of nations, like the history of individuals, is made
up of trials and of triumphs. As the centuries of the world's
life roll on, one race after another rises to prominence and power
only to fall again, so that the successes of one age are balanced by
the disasters of another. In its day of power each thinks itself all
but eternal, unmindful of the fate of its predecessors, and regards
its national policy as the supreme effort of human wisdom. The
courtly poet of Rome could find no more fitting expression of endless fame than " while Pontiff and Vestal should ascend the Capitol "
of the Emperors. To Dante the fate of the world was forever
bound in the fortunes of the German Empire; and the Spanish conquerors of America in their time held that the occupation of a New
World was the seal of the lasting supremacy of Spain. We need
only open a newspaper to-day to see how complacently similar
ideas are held as self-evident truths. Bismarck's victory over
France is accepted readily as proof of the innate superiority of the
race which he rules, as if there had never been a Thirty Years' War,
a Louis the Fourteenth, or a Jena. Gladstone sees in the growth of
English wealth convincing proof that the power of England must
still increase through unknown ages. The decay of the once
powerful Spanish empire is constantly taken as a proof of her
ignorance of the true principles of government, as if the building
up of that empire had not in its day commanded the same admiration that is now given to the work of Bismarck or of England. So
wide-spread is the worship of present success that ages of past
misfortune are looked on as fully compensated for by a few years
of prosperity, when that prosperity happens in the present century.
Leading writers to-day, men like Green and Freeman, speak of the
long centuries of devastation which England underwent at the
hands of Saxon and Dane, through Norman conquest and civil
war, as absolute blessings to humanity, because from them has
resulted two generations of prosperous Englishmen in the nineteenth century, to be succeeded, it well may be, by other unpros-
perous generations in the coming years. In the eyes of Carlyle and
his school, the miseries inflicted on Germany by the so-called
Reformation and the century of wars that followed are more than
compensated for by the fact that a hundred years later the Prussian Frederick had the best drilled army in Europe. That indeed

was a compensation to humanity compared with which three or four generations filled with the ravages of war and famine, the uprooting of the most cherished beliefs, and the wreck of old popular liberties, were as nothing.

To such a view of history we cannot assent. The prosperity of one generation cannot really compensate for the sufferings of another in this world. It would have afforded no relief to the Saxon serfs in the days of the Norman Conqueror to learn that their life-long slavery was necessary if England was to control the commerce of Europe six centuries later. In point of fact every generation has its appointed work, and the individuals that make it up receive their rewards as that work is done, apart from the fate of future times. The work may be different in different cases. A people may be called to make right prevail by victory, or to spread civilization by its intellect, or it may be its allotted task to maintain the eternal principles of truth and justice by patient resistance to superior brute force and heroic self-sacrifice. Even humanly considered, the last is as noble a work as the former, if not nobler. Thermopylæ is a more glorious page in history than Salamis. Washington was as great amid the hardships of the Valley Forge winter as when triumphant at Yorktown.

The full value to human nature of suffering for justice' sake is nowhere so fully brought out as in the history of the Catholic Church. During the first three centuries of its existence the power of the Roman Empire was arrayed against it, and all through succeeding ages it never has lacked occasions of holding its faith against hostile force. The persecutions of Pagan Rome had hardly ceased when the Arian war on Catholic faith began ; and scarcely had Arianism passed away, when the sword of Mohammed raised up an anti-Christian empire mightier than that of Rome itself. The Saracen invasion had been but just checked by the sword of Charles Martel in the centre of France, when the pagan Vikings of Scandinavia began their raids on Western Europe. Christianity was almost destroyed in the north of England and in Ireland. France and Flanders during a century and a half had to bear the almost constant attacks of the pirates whose hatred to the " White Christ " was scarcely less violent than their love of plunder. In the end the Church prevailed, the Norsemen became Christians, and with the general adoption of Christianity the piracy of Scandinavia disappeared. But almost simultaneously with the conversion of the Norsemen, a new anti-Christian invasion poured in from Asia. The Mongols overran Russia and Poland, and penetrated to the heart of Germany, in the days of St. Louis, and they did not relax their hold on Russia till the middle of the sixteenth century. The kindred tribe of the Ottomans commenced its career of conquest in the thirteenth century, and never halted until its banners waved supreme from the Indian Ocean to the Danube, and from the Atlantic to the Persian Gulf. We often hear of the time when the Church was supreme in Europe, as if she had exercised undisputed sway over its destinies during many centuries. As a matter of fact, however, there has never been a time since the fall of the Roman Empire when large Catholic populations were not forced to hold their faith at the cost of the dearest temporal interests. "No cross, no crown," is the law of human nature within the Church as well as in other spheres.

The history of Ireland, since the so-called Reformation, is a striking instance of the vitality of the Catholic Church under persecution From the days of Elizabeth to the close of the last century all the power of English Government was steadily bent to the task of uprooting the Catholic religion in Ireland. The deprivation of civil rights, the all but total confiscation of their property, the suppression of their schools, the proscription of their clergy, the breaking-up of families, and at times the exile or enslavement of thousands of Catholics, were the means employed during over two centuries to stamp out Catholicity among the Irish people. How utterly they have failed, the state of the Church in the English speaking lands to-day attests. "Where the Parliament of England has power, the Mass shall never be allowed of," wrote Cromwell, in the middle of the seventeenth century, when Ireland lay crushed under his armies; and for more than a hundred years Parliament rigidly adhered to the same policy. In 1660 a single Bishop, worn down by age and infirmities and hidden away from sight among the poorest peasants of Ireland, was the only representative of the Catholic hierarchy within the British dominions. To-day more than fifty Bishops find ample work among the Catholics of Ireland and Great Britain alone, apart from the still larger churches of the United States, Australia and New Zealand which are mainly sprung from the descendants of the few hundred thousand Irish Catholics of the seventeenth century. No victorious revolution, no foreign invasion, has come to bring about the result. It is simply the supernatural power of divine Faith which has overcome the efforts of man. The way in which the contest was carried on can best be gathered from the records of Catholic life in Ireland under the Penal Laws.

It is not a part of our task to speak of the rise of the "Reformed" doctrines in Europe. The Irish people took no part in them, and it was only when Henry VIII. had established himself as Head of the English Church that any religious question arose in Ireland. In England, the worldliness of the episcopacy and the lately acquired power of the throne enabled him to accomplish his purpose changing the outward organization of the Church without much difficulty. It was confidently expected that even less would be found in Ireland, whose people were far more remote from the centre of Catholic unity, and were besides almost destitute of any general national organization. Henry assumed the title of King of Ireland, which had never before been borne by the English sovereigns, and in virtue of this title he further had himself proclaimed head of the Church. The assumption of royal authority was not especially unpopular in Ireland. The Norman nobles of the Pale had been daunted by the wholesale execution of the Kildare Geraldines, long the chief family of the Anglo-Norman colony. The Celtic chieftains through the rest of the island had small scruple about accepting a nominal kingship, when coupled with the full recognition of their local independence and laws. The headship of the Church claimed by Henry seems to have been scarcely distinguished from the right of presentation to the bishoprics long enjoyed by the crown in the English Pale. The monasteries, indeed, were partially suppressed, and a royal commission was appointed to plunder the churches of their "superfluous" plate and ornaments; but the people in general could hardly distinguish such action from the ordinary policy of the government whenever it found itself strong enough to make English law "respected" in Ireland. Henry's religious policy in fact seems to have been regarded merely as a new act of legal robbery, and not as a new form of Christian faith.

The fate of the monastic establishments in Ireland under the new regime, is a striking illustration of the attitude of the people towards the new doctrines. Henry had secured supporters in England to his religious changes by lavish gifts of the property of the suppressed monasteries. The politicians of his court for the most part were as ready to change their creed for a share in the stolen property of the monasteries as a modern adventurer is to sell his reputation for a share in the profits of a swindling speculation. On the proclamation of Henry as King of Ireland, the same policy was tried to bring the Irish people over to the royal modification of Christianity. The abbeys and benefices of Thomond, or North Munster, were granted as a free gift to O'Brien, the newly-made Earl of Thomond, those of Clanrickard in Connaught to McWilliam Burke, the monasteries of Aghadoe and Aghmacart to Fitzpatrick of Ossory, and various similar donations made to the different other nobles and to the corporations of the towns of the Pale. Through a large part of the country those "gifts" were accepted, but the grantees made no use of the privilege to plunder. The corporation of Clonmel continued the Franciscans in the possession of their church and convent, which had been formally suppressed and handed over to the town by law. The convents of the same order continued to exist in a similar manner in Drogheda and Galway, in spite of their legal suppression. The convent of Multifernan, in Westmeath, remained in possession of its occupants under the protection of the Barons of Delvin, those of Kilcrea and Timoleague under that of the McCarthys of Muskerry. Muckross, in Killarney, continued to shelter Franciscans under the ownership of the O'Sullivans, as did Moyne and Kilconnell, in Connaught, under that of the Burkes and O'Kellys. In Ulster, the royal decrees remained in complete abeyance, and even the bishops continued to be nominated by the Pope directly all through Henry's reign. In other dioceses the priests nominated by the crown often remained Catholics and applied to Rome for confirmation, like the Primate Dowdall. At the close of Henry's reign, only seven bishops were even claimed as adherents to the royal supremacy, and five of these were Englishmen sent over specially to occupy Irish sees. One of the other two resigned in the early part of Edward VI.'s reign, and the other, Bishop Tirrey of Cork, appears as a Catholic in the following reign. Altogether it was pretty clear that the change in the faith proposed by Henry met no approval among any class of the Irish people.

The adventurers who controlled the English government during the reign of Henry's son speedily pushed the work of changing the national religion to a point which left no doubt of its true nature. The sacrifice of the mass was forbidden, and a new form of service, devised by Cranmer and his confederates, ordered to be substituted for it in all the churches of Ireland. To carry out this sweeping change, the Deputy called a convocation of the bishops and clergy in Dublin in 1551, and communicated to them the royal orders. Five of Henry's episcopal nominees, of whom only one, Coyne of Limerick, was an Irishman, accepted the new rule of faith; all the others refused, and the struggle was thus formally opened between Catholicity and Protestantism in Ireland three hundred and thirty years ago. The rulers of the land had decided that their belief should be regulated by their temporal interest (Northumberland himself, the Regent, it will be remembered, professed Catholicity at his execution after persecuting its professors during his power); the people of Ireland refused to do likewise. Their constancy had to be soon and terribly tested.

The government of Edward VI. had freely employed German and Swiss mercenaries to force their new doctrines on the English people, who showed no inclination to receive them. The same policy was adopted in Ireland. Sir Edward Bellingham brought over a large body of disciplined troops, such as in the sixteenth century were taking the place of the old militia in war everywhere through Europe, and the work of "converting" the Irish was vigorously commenced. The hitherto almost independent Celtic chieftains of Leinster were attacked and reduced to subjection, and the famed monastic university of Clonmacnoise, on the Shannon, which had survived the changes of nine centuries, was mercilessly sacked and burned by the garrison of Athlone. In the north, however, the invaders were repulsed by Shane O'Neill, and in Kilkenny the citizens put a summary stop by force to the Protestant Bishop Bayle's attempt to destroy their altars. In spite of the " hobillers and mounted bowmen," the " Reformation " made scanty progress in Ireland during the reign of Edward; and with the accession of Mary its missioners either fled the country or, like the deputy St. Leger, again professed themselves Catholics, like the majority of their colleagues in England.

The accession of Elizabeth soon renewed the briefly interrupted struggle. The Queen and her counselors after some hesitation decided to separate from the Church, whose faith they had so solemnly professed belief in during the last few years. The chief inducement was the increase of the royal power, expected from the supreme control of religious worship among the Queen's subjects. However, Burghley and Elizabeth, on mature reflection, concluded to go further than Henry, and prepare a new form of belief, suited to the politics of the time, for the use of all the Queen's subjects. How that creed was established in England is foreign to our subject. It is enough to say that it was ratified by Parliament as the only one which it was lawful for Englishmen to hold. Lord Sussex was sent over to Ireland as Lord Deputy, with orders to settle the religion of the people there on the same footing as in England. A Parliament was called for that purpose in the second year of Elizabeth. The system of representation in the Anglo-Irish government was of a peculiar character, and its complexion depended mainly on the will of the deputy. Deputies were only invited from ten counties, less than a third of the island, and by a liberal construction of the forms of Parliament members were freely returned for villages without the formalities of previous residence, election, or even the existence of electors. In this manner a considerable number of English officers and adventurers found place among the representatives of Ireland, and by some dexterous management, such as holding a session on a holyday in the absence of the Catholic natives, the Act of Uniformity was passed. The Church in Ireland was ordered to conform to the creed of Elizabeth, all public officers were ordered to swear to their belief in it; the sacrifice of the Mass was forbidden, all Catholic priests ordered to conform or leave the country, and the laity in general directed to attend the churches at the new worship, when-

ever her majesty could provide ministers to teach in them, under
penalty of fines for every absence. The churches were pretty
generally seized at once, but the other penalties were suffered to
lie dormant for a time. A system somewhat like that of the Cul-
turkampf recently tried in Germany was inaugurated. The bishops
and priests were to be driven off in detail,'official favor was to be
extended exclusively to the professors of the new doctrine, and the
Catholics of note were to be made to feel the power of the government whose religion they dared to reject. Meanwhile the Penal
Laws remained in force, and any part of them might be executed at
the will of the deputy or even his subordinate officers in remote
districts. Such was the nature of the pressure applied to separate
the Irish people from the Catholic Church, more than three centuries ago; and which has resulted as the world knows. "Unstable
as water," regretfully writes Mr. Froude, the Irish temperament
lacked cohesiveness to receive permanent impressions. The impression of the Catholic faith on the heart and mind of the Irish
people is the same to-day as it was when Elizabeth knelt at mass
in the royal chapel.

The English officials made no secret of the want of success
which attended their attempt to force a new creed on the Catholic
people. "I assure your Lordship," wrote Loftus, the Protestant
Archbishop of Dublin, to Burghley, in 1589, nearly thirty years
after the Act of Uniformity had been made the law of the land,

> "That unless they (the people of this realm) be forced, they will not ever come to
> hear the Word preached, as by experience we observed at the time appointed by the
> Lord Deputy for a general assembly of all the noblemen and gentlemen of every county,
> after her majesty's good success against the Spaniard to give God thanks for the same,
> at which time, though the sheriffs did their duties with all diligence, yet very few, or
> none almost, resorted thereto; but in Dublin itself the *lawyers in term time* took occa-
> sion to leave the town, on purpose to absent themselves from that goodly exercise."

In the other towns the same story was told. In 1585 the Protestant Primate was informed by an English schoolmaster, who
had been established in Waterford under government protection to
instruct the children of the citizens,

> "That it was not for any man that feareth God (after the Queen's fashion) to dwell
> among them; for although they cannot martyr his body, yet will they trouble his
> mind. First, there is not one couple among twenty married according to her majesty's
> injunctions, but hand-fasted only, *or else* married at home, with a mass; then they
> never christen their children, but in their houses, either with a mass priest, or for want
> of him the women themselves christen. Their dead they bury not (*i. e.*, not in legal
> fashion), but tumble them into the graves like swine, without any service (Protestant),
> or any minister; and as for the Word, altogether, they either abuse the Word or absent
> themselves from the church, or when they come they walk round about, like mill
> horses, chopping and changing and making merchandise; and these be not small
> fools, but even the chief of the city. The ministers cry out that they are abused,

deceived, despised, and almost discomfited, and *for this especially*, that they being constrained to send up a true certificate (for legal punishment) of such as frequented not the church nor received the communion; this certificate was presently shown to their enemies and such comfortable and friendly speeches given to them that they returned home again with open mouths and foaming jaws, and reviled the ministers with such opprobrious terms that they, poor shepherds, for fear of those brutish and savage lions are almost afeard to come near the sheepfold."

The strong family resemblance of this last document to recent letters of English special correspondents from Ireland makes it all the more valuable evidence of the reception given to the new doctrines in the teeth of the English power in Ireland.

It is not to be thought that the authorities contented themselves with the mere seizure of the churches and levying fines, in their policy of uprooting Catholicity. The clergy had to keep carefully out of the way of the royal troops, and where occasion offered there was no lack of executions. Bishop O'Haly, of Mayo, and a friar named O'Rorke had landed at Dingle, in 1579, and were arrested by Sir William Drury, who, on discovering their character, had them put on the rack, sharp needles thrust under their finger nails, their legs and hands broken with hammers, and finally hanged outside Limerick and their bodies used as targets. Archbishop O'Hurley, who fell into the hands of Loftus, was detained nearly a year in prison, and had his feet toasted at the fire before he was hanged at the gates of Dublin. The Bishop of Kilmore was three times arrested and escaped twice by his friends bribing the guards, and on the third time, in 1602, as he was unable to walk, he was stripped and thrown into a brake of thorns and left for dead. The Primate Creagh died in prison in London for his faith, and these are only a few examples of the fate of Catholic bishops in Elizabeth's reign. The priests, and especially the regulars, were equally at the mercy of ill-disposed officials. It was not very often, perhaps, that like Father Stephens, they were hanged by plain sentence for having celebrated mass; but they were practically outlaws, whose lives might be, and on favorable occasions were, taken with impunity by officious judges or a ferocious soldiery. The friars still clung around many of their suppressed convents under protection of the public feeling, and a favorite display of "vigor" on the part of the government was to dispatch parties to raid such settlements. Multifernan, Kilcrea, Timoleague, Moyne, Donegal, and numerous other convents were thus sacked at various times, and such of the inmates as fell into the hands of the soldiers were murdered, carried off prisoners, or released according to the whim of the commanding officers. Still the friars refused to abandon their old homes, and the courage with which they returned again and again to their abodes is astonishing. Multifernan was burned to the ground and its prior carried off in 1601. Yet a community was there again, to be again dispersed, in 1602, and again in 1607. Timoleague and Donegal have similar histories, and around some of the old monasteries communities continued to dwell all through the next two centuries.

But it was not on the clergy alone that the hand of the government fell. A third refusal to take the oath of supremacy was treason in a layman, and thus the lives of the population lay virtually at the mercy of the deputy. In the corporate towns the municipal privileges, indeed, gave protection in general against the enforcement of this law; but the lives of the country people were absolutely at the mercy of the judges. Thirty-six were hanged in one session at Kilkenny, in 1578, by the same Drury who tortured and executed the Bishop of Mayo, and twenty-two more at Limerick. "Down they go on every side," wrote the Deputy, Sir Henry Sidney, describing his progress through the country (not then in war, be it remembered), "and down they shall go." When it is remembered that the ill-will of a judge could thus at any time send a score of Irish peasants to their death on any charge, or none, and that the power was freely used, we can appreciate what the holding of the faith meant to the Irish people in the sixteenth century.

A still more terrible proof, however, of what resistance to the will of the "authorities" meant was to be given to the recusant Catholics. Among the nobles of Norman descent, the Geraldines of Desmond were conspicuous for their attachment to the ancient creed. The Earls of Kildare and Ormond, the other two heads of the Anglo-Norman aristocracy, had bowed to the Queen's will, and accepted the decree of Parliament as the revelation of the Almighty. The Earl of Desmond, whose authority extended all through the south of Munster, steadily refused apostasy. In the first parliament he had stoutly opposed the proposed change of religion, and shortly afterwards he had given shelter to the Bishop of Kildare, Leverous, when driven from his diocese by the government. Sir Henry Sidney bided his time, and suddenly descended on Kilmallock, where Desmond resided, and carried him off a prisoner of state, or, as in modern English usage in Ireland it would be called, a suspect, on no special charge. The earl and his brother, who had been invited to Dublin and similarly arrested, were transferred from Dublin to the Tower of London, and again returned to Dublin in custody. Their relatives and clansmen rose in arms under Sir James Fitzmaurice, and, after a couple of vigorous campaigns, Desmond himself escaped from Dublin, and Fitzmaurice submitted. Four years passed in apparent peace, until an English army was available, and then the attack on the devoted

Geraldine was renewed.   Driven to desperation, he took the field in 1580, and the raw levies of his clansmen, as might have been expected, were overpowered by the disciplined troops of the crown. For three years the horrors of war, such as no pirate raid had ever inflicted in civilized history, were let loose on the Catholic "rebels" of Desmond.   Edmund Spenser, the poet, who himself was an eye-witness, and whose zeal for the new-made religion of the Queen urged the application of similar treatment to the other Irish Papists, tells us how the growing crops and cattle were destroyed, and the hapless peasants driven to the woods by the scattered parties of soldiers, " so that in all that war there perished not many by the sword but all by extremity of famine."   Old men, women, and children were driven in crowds into their dwellings, and burned with them, and women were found hanging on trees, with their infants strangled in their mothers' hair.   The poet himself tells how, through the once fertile fields, a few wretched fugitives might be seen "crawling forth like anatomies on hands and knees " for utter weakness to walk ; how they " did eat the carrion if they found it," and that, if by any chance a plot of water-cress or of sorrel was found, " thither they flocked as to a feast."   Finally, even the "anatomies" disappeared, and "a most populous and plentiful country was suddenly left void of man and beast," so that, as Holinshed, another English authority, tells, "the very wolves and foxes, many of them, lay dead, being famished."   For sixscore miles, from Limerick to Cashel, no human being was left to question the queen's supremacy through all the open country of Munster.   The land was partitioned out among English undertakers on the condition that none of the native Irish should be admitted. Spenser himself received a grant of three thousand acres in Cork, where he wrote the *Faërie Queen*, in glorification of Elizabeth, and warmly urged on Government the wisdom of applying the system of famine, which had worked so thoroughly in Munster, to the rest of Catholic Ireland.

The advice was not neglected.   Twenty years later, when the struggle of Ulster for liberty had been broken down by the power of England, Mountjoy repeated in Tyrone and Donegal the horrors which had been already experienced in Munster.   " No spectacle," says Moryson, " was more frequent in the ditches of towns than to see multitudes of the poor people dead, with their mouths all colored green by eating nettles, docks, and all things they could rend up above ground."   Ghastly trial was this, surely, of a people's faith, yet neither in Desmond nor in Ulster would the remnant that had escaped the sword and famine accept the new religion so sternly urged on them.   Fifteen years after the desolation of Desmond, when O'Neill was threatening the English power, the son of the last earl, who had been kept a prisoner in England and brought up a Protestant, was sent back to his country. The awful miseries of the war were forgotten in the enthusiasm of his still-devoted people on his arrival in Kilmallock, so that a military guard had to open a way for him through the crowd. The next day, however, the young lord attended the Protestant church, and immediately he was deserted by the whole population. The sword of Drury and Mally might make the land a desert, but it could not force the Irish people to accept the will of queen and parliament as the truth of God. Nearly three hundred years have since come and gone, but still the Catholic Church holds its sway unchanged over the hearts and minds of the Irish people, even as it did in the days of Elizabeth.

The story of Hugh O'Neill's family is a stranger tale than novelist could invent of fortune's changes and unconquerable tenacity. When O'Neill took up arms against the Government of Elizabeth in 1594, he demanded liberty of conscience through Ireland, and five years later, in a stirring address to the Anglo-Irish towns, he declared: " I have already protested, and do now protest, that, if I had to be King of Ireland, without having the Catholic religion, I would not the same accept." The English officials were unable to comprehend such language in any other sense than a partisan cry. They had adopted the new religion, and were ready to forswear it if Parliament should so decide, and it was beyond their ken why an Irish chief should risk a principality for his faith. " You talk of religion," said the Earl of Essex to O'Neill at a conference between them ; " why, you have no more religion than your horse." English historians have since repeated the charge on the word of Essex, whose authority as a moralist they accept unquestioned in this instance. The Prince of Ulster was still, however, obstinate in refusing to abandon his faith. The war went on, the battle of Kinsale was lost, and O'Neill with a few hundred men still held out, while thousands of corpses lay unburied in the track of his victorious foes. Nor did he submit until Mountjoy had promised that his religion should not be interfered with. The same promise was renewed by James I., when O'Neill was received at his court and confirmed in his possession of Tyrone and Londonderry as an Anglo-Irish earl. A few years later the promise was broken, and the earl was told he must conform. Had he been as careless of his belief as Essex thought, it would have been easy for him to have become the most powerful man in Ireland. The earls of Ormond, Kildare and Inchiquin had conformed and were high in favor and power. The man who " had no more religion than his horse " abandoned the widest estates in Ireland and his native land, when nearing his seventieth year, rather than betray his conscience. The English Court seized his lands, and parcelled them out among Scotch adventurers. His sons won distinction in the Spanish service, but still cherished hopes of returning to Ireland. Thirty years after the great O'Neill had gone to his rest, a grandson of his returned to serve in the war between Charles I. and the Puritans. He won high honors on various fields of battle, and was created a baronet for distinguished services during the struggle. Following the fortunes of Charles I., he returned to Ireland after the downfall of the Protectorate, and recovered some part of his family's property under the act of settlement. But the baronet held his faith as his grandfather had done, and he transmitted it to his successors. William and his foreign soldiery once more conquered Ireland, and the Protestant Parliaments were determined to pauperize, if they could not pervert, the Catholics of Ireland. Sir Bryan O'Neill's family were gradually stripped of all, and the fourth baronet was reduced to support himself by keeping a little meal-store in a country village. The title was abandoned, but still the Catholic faith was held, and little more than twenty years ago the lineal heir died in a back street of Dublin, so poor that a subscription had to be raised to defray his burial. He had served in the army as a sergeant, and afterwards had earned his living as a cabinet-maker in one of the poorest quarters of Dublin; but the pressure of hard times had reduced him to absolute want. If we think for a moment on what is involved in the slow, grinding reduction of a family from wealth to the hardest poverty, with the means of arresting that reduction within easy reach by the sacrifice of conscience, and bear in mind that the temptation was steadily withstood through private misery and national calamity for nine successive generations, we will more fully appreciate the quiet heroism of the resistance to persecution which has left Ireland to-day essentially a Catholic nation.

The story of Spenser's career and family was widely different. As we have seen, he had recommended starvation as the surest means for bringing the Irish into due subjection and establishing the new-made "divine faith" according to the English politicians of the day among them. As secretary of Lord Grey, he was rewarded with three thousand acres of Munster lands, whose inhabitants had been, in his own language, "forced to devour one another" by the means which he afterwards recommended should be used towards the rest of their countrymen. The latter resisted the process, and under Hugh O'Neill they not only swept back the invaders from Ulster, but descended in triumph on the southern provinces. Spenser and his fellow "undertakers" who had been settled on the confiscated lands were driven from their stolen property, and the poet himself fled to England. His friends had scanty sympathy for a ruined man, and in the heart of London the lot which he had himself recommended for the Irish Catholics fell on the courtly poet. Ben Johnson wrote to Drummond of Hawthornden that the author of the *Faërie Queen* died for "lack of bread" in the English capital. His son afterwards returned to Ireland, and seems to have obtained some share in the lands before granted to his father. Sixty years later, the grandson of the poet appears again in history as an Irish Papist, whose lands had been seized by the Cromwellian soldiers, but who was ready to abjure his religion for their restoration. Cromwell himself, then Lord Protector, in a letter dated 27th March, 1657, wrote in his behalf to the Commissioners for Affairs in Ireland, urging the restoratian of his estate, on the grounds of his professed apostasy, and his grand-father's "eminent deserts and services to the Commonwealth." But even Cromwell's recommendation failed of effect, and the lands passed away forever from the family of the poet, whose grand-son had so strangely been found among the ranks of the Irish Catholics, though lacking the courage to hold his faith as they did, when his interests were involved in abandoning it.

The long, and for some years successful, struggle of the North-ern Irish, under Hugh O'Neill, against Elizabeth's government brought about some relaxation of the government's war on the Church. The penalties prescribed by law for rejecting the State worship were not enforced in the southern part of the island, though the laws themselves were left unrepealed. After a seven years' war O'Neill's resistance was finally broken down, but the government was so exhausted in the effort that he was willingly received into submission. His lands were all confirmed to him and his allies in Ulster, and James I. promised personally that the Catholic religion should be tolerated in Ireland. The corporate towns of the south restored the open practice of the Catholic wor-ship on the death of Elizabeth, and though the Deputy Lord Mountjoy, at the head of an army, speedily forbade such proceed-ings, he granted for a while permission for the private exercise of religion. Vice-regal or even royal promises were, however, a short-lived security. James decided, after a short delay, that the religion invented by Elizabeth's council was the best adapted to maintain royal power, and he abandoned the Presbyterian creed, in which he had been reared, for it in consequence. That subjects should be more tender of their beliefs than their monarch appeared absurd to his majesty, and accordingly, in 1605, the old decrees against Catholicity were renewed by public proclamation of the vice-roy, Sir Arthur Chichester. The Catholic bishops and regulars were ordered to leave the country at once, under penalty of being arrested wherever found. All celebration of Catholic worship was strictly forbidden, and every one was ordered to attend the Protestant churches on Sundays under pain of a fine for each absence. Heavier penalties were proclaimed against all parents who should neglect to present their children for baptism in the State churches, and against persons who should marry without the presence of a Protestant minister. The proclamation in which these measures were announced concluded by informing his majesty's Irish subjects that he never would grant toleration in any shape to any form of divine worship except that established by the law of England.

The conditions of the struggle between the Irish people and their rulers were very different from what they had been in the former reigns. The local independence of the Celtic chieftains had been finally broken down by the defeat of Hugh O'Neill, and for the first time in history the law of the English monarch was supreme in every part of Ireland. The whole country was mapped out into counties, and the law administered by English judges and enforced by English sheriffs, supported at need by the whole military force at the disposal of the crown. The surviving monasteries were successively raided by armed bodies of men, and their inmates seized or scattered. The homes of prominent Catholics were suddenly searched for priests, and amongst others those of O'Neill, in Dungannon, in spite of the royal promise of toleration given to him on his surrender. The aldermen and mayors of the towns were successively summoned before the judges and required to abjure the Catholic faith on oath. Almost to a man they refused, and in consequence they were subjected to heavy fines and sometimes to imprisonment in a body. In some cases, as in Waterford, the charter of the town was suspended in consequence of the refusal of the corporation to conform their belief to that of the king. By the peculiar system of administration in Ireland, the viceroy and judges appointed by the court had absolute power over the lives and liberty of the people. The Catholic members of Parliament were as liable to the penalties of treason for refusing to accept the State religion as the rest of the population, and from time to time they received significant proofs of the fact. A still more formidable engine of persecution was devised for punishing the Catholics who possessed any property, by means of blackmail titles. A class of discoverers, needy lawyers, and adventurers were employed to hunt up flaws in the titles of the Catholic proprietors of lands, and technicalities of the flimsiest character were held by the English judges a sufficient warrant for stripping them of their property. The flight of the Earls of Tyrone and Tyrconnell from Ireland was thus held sufficient ground for confiscating the greater part of Ulster, and similar measures, on a smaller scale, were carried out in the other provinces. The lands thus seized were granted to English and Scotch adventurers on the condition of planting them exclusively with Protestants. The system of eviction, with all its horrors, was introduced as a legal consequence of the refusal of the people to accept the religion of the king. Chichester swept Innishowen, in Donegal, of six thousand of its inhabitants in this way, and sent the able-bodied men to serve in the armies of the Protestant kings of Sweden and Denmark. Where the means to collect the fines for non-attendance at church were available, they were unsparingly levied on the Catholic farmers. Thus, in one year, eight thousand pounds, probably equivalent to nearly four hundred thousand dollars in our days, was thus levied off the small county of Cavan alone. The capriciousness of these enforcements of the "law" made them even more terrible. The arrival of each new viceroy or judge might be the signal for a fresh outburst of persecution. Year after year the Catholic proprietors saw themselves stripped of their lands; the cultivators of the soil found themselves liable to fresh exactions, and the merchants of the towns had to meet new and indefinite fines, at the discretion of the legal officials. For each class the remedy for this state of things was an easy one. To accept the State religion and abjure the Catholic faith was a ready road to relief. But no body of the Irish people was found to sacrifice their consciences to their interests; and after three generations had passed away, and when four-fifths of the land of Ireland had been torn away from its native owners, a free-thinking writer, Sir William Petty, thus summed up the religious elements of Ireland: "The Scotch settlers are Presbyterians, the English half Protestants (Episcopalians) half Anabaptists and other sects, the Irish *all Catholics.*"

One class was specially marked out for punishment by the goverment. Whatever hesitation there might be in applying the rigors of the law to an entire population, there was none with regard to the clergy. We have seen that the Catholic Episcopacy and the regulars, Jesuits, Franciscans, and Dominicans, had been ordered to leave the country by royal proclamation, and the arrest of any of them was a gainful object to the minor officials. In spite of this fact, both bishops and regulars continued to discharge their duties in Ireland. The friars often clung around their suppressed monasteries, and in some cases even continued to inhabit them under the protection of a few Catholic nobles, whose influence was capable of keeping off in general the official priest-hunters. Multifernan in Westmeath thus continued to shelter a little community all through the reigns of James and Charles; the old convents of Rosserilly and Clare Galway, in Connaught, held together under the protection of the powerful Earl of Clanrickard; and in Clonmel the municipality, in spite of pains and penalties, still allowed the Franciscans to possess the ancient church of their monastery. In other places, as at Moyne and Crevelea, in Leitrim, the Protestant settlers themselves allowed the friars to use their ancient churches for rent, and, stranger still, in Galway a wealthy apostate protected their convent as his private property while allowing the friars to occupy it unmolested. Elsewhere, the proscribed Franciscans and Dominicans lived in cabins near their former convents, and continued their work among the people. The government, from time to time, renewed its edicts against their presence in the country, and sheriff's posses or military detachments swooped down on their abodes; but the vigilance of the people usually gave the intended victims warning, and it was found almost impossible to seize them unless by accident.

At Drogheda, in 1616, a raid was made on the house occupied by the Franciscans, and a priest, Father Holan, was seized at the foot of the altar; but the women of the town assailed his captors so vigorously that they were forced to take refuge in a neighboring house. Multifernan was raided in 1607, and again in 1608 and 1614, in spite of the powerful protection of the Nugents, and on each occasion several of the friars were carried off to prison. Such captives often had to spend months in jail, as the authorities cared little for bringing them to trial, and bribes were usually efficacious in obtaining their ultimate release. The law which identified Catholicity with treason left the viceroy and the English officials virtual masters of the lives and liberties of individual Catholics, and they usually employed their power like Turkish pashas in squeezing as much as possible out of the Catholic population. A letter of the viceroy to some of his friends engaged on a tour of official inspection of the churches of Ireland gives a ludicrous specimen of these petty vexations in the advice to " cess themselves on the Papists for chickens and bacon." But the administrators of the law were not without giving more significant proofs of their hatred to Catholicity and their power over its professors. Lord Falkland, in 1627, had organized a state emigration scheme to remove some thousand Ulster Catholics from their country as soldiers for the Kings of Sweden and Denmark. The project was unpopular, and as the best he could think for its encouragement the viceroy wrote to the English Privy Council for permission " to rack one Glassney O'Cullenan, a priest," who dissuaded the idle swordsmen of Ulster from joining the mercenaries of Gustavus Adolphus. The answer of the Council was prompt. " You ought to rack and hang the priest if you find reason for doing so, for such is the opinion of the Council and his Majesty's pleasure." Whatever toleration was allowed to the Irish Catholics was thus dependent on the humor of their rulers, and liable to suspension at any moment.

The execution of Bishop O'Devany, of Down and Connor, in 1611, under the administration of Chichester, was a still more striking proof of what punishments awaited obnoxious Catholics. The bishops in general were too well watched by their people to be easily taken. " We are full," wrote the viceroy in 1613 (speaking of his want of success in catching a certain Father Meagh just returned from Rome), " of priests of this man's condition, practicers of sedition and insurrection, of which there is not a greater worker than Owen MacMahon, the titular Archbishop of Dublin. Albeit I cannot get any draught, though I have offered largely for it." The year after Archbishop MacMahon's arrival, however, chance threw Bishop O'Devany into his hands as he was administering confirmation in his diocese. The captive was eighty years of age, and high in the esteem of the people for his courageous labors during the former reign. Him accordingly Chichester resolved to make an example of. He and his chaplain were charged with high treason on general principles, and a packed jury at once found them guilty. It may be necessary to explain to those unfamiliar with the course of English law in Ireland that there was at the time no resistance anywhere in Ireland to the royal authority, nor was it assumed that the octogenarian bishop was about to take up arms. The charge of treason was simply a general formula for sending an obnoxious individual to death, and as soon as the conviction was obtained from the jury, eleven of whom were English or Scotch settlers, the viceroy offered to release the prisoner if he would take the oath of supremacy, in other words, declare himself a Protestant. The Bishop, of course, refused, and on the following Saturday he and his chaplain were publicly executed with all the horrors of the English law of treason. The executioner had run away, and an English volunteer had to be obtained for the purpose. The hanging and cutting down before life was extinct, in order that the sufferer might be disembowelled while still living, the beheading of the body and hacking it into quarters, were all performed on the old Bishop and his chaplain in the sight of nearly the whole Catholic population of Dublin, who, in the words of an English eye-witness, Rich, " made such a dole and lamentation after him as the heavens themselves resounded the echoes of their outcries." The same writer adds the strange information that the following night a crowd surrounded the gallows, and after midnight, " having their priests in readiness, they had Mass after Mass till daylight." It is pretty evident that the butchery of O'Devany had utterly failed in striking terror into either the laity or the priests of Ireland.

One of the most striking points about the Irish resistance to the religion which it was sought for over two hundred years to force on them is the manner in which the hierarchy and priesthood was kept up.   In the ordinary affairs of the world, it would be absurd to expect that any number of men should freely choose a life such as that led by the Irish clergy in the seventeenth century, except in the excitement of some thrilling and doubtful struggle.   To live apart from all public assemblies of men, and debarred even of the solemn celebration of their religious functions, to be constantly on the watch for prowling enemies armed with the full powers of the law against Popish priests, to have to fly again and again to the woods and caves for shelter, and it might well be to spend occasionally months in the loathsome jails of the period (no improved modern penitentiaries, be it borne in mind, but ill-lighted fireless dungeons); such was the ordinary career of the Irish Catholic priest at the time we are speaking of.   To celebrate Mass in private houses or often in the shade of woods and mountains, to instruct a flock, to whom it was forbidden to assemble in any numbers, or to open schools for them, to avoid, as far as might be, giving any umbrage to the local magnates whose acceptance of the state religion made them masters to a certain extent of their Catholic neighbors, to subsist on the alms of an impoverished people, was the course of the priest's or bishop's life in more than usually favorable times. Yet all through the long years from Elizabeth to George the Fourth, the persecuted clergy continued to recruit its ranks in Ireland.   In some shape or other schools were maintained, now in one place, now in another, where young Catholics managed to acquire education. Colleges were established abroad in Rome, Spain, Flanders and France for the education of Irish ecclesiastics who bound themselves to return to the dangerous mission of their native land when qualified for it by due training.   In the reign of Elizabeth, Spenser had marvelled how the Catholic priests " spared not to come from Rome and Rheims and other places with long toyles and travails for no reward of richesse," to uphold the Catholic doctrines in Ireland.   For more than two centuries the same spectacle continued to bewilder the minds of the foreign rulers of Ireland.

The accession of Charles Stuart made little difference in the condition of the Catholics of Ireland.   The raids on " Mass houses " were still made from time to time, and the young heirs of Catholic families were carried off in large numbers to be educated by the Court of Wards in England as Protestants.   Still the marriage of Charles to a Catholic princess was supposed to show that he was less bigoted than the former sovereigns, and through Parliament, which was still nearly half composed of Catholics, an appeal was made for the full freedom of worship and the cessation of the legal confiscations which were constantly being made under pretext of flaws in titles. A large subsidy was offered to the king as the price of those concessions which were promised, and the money paid. We have not room here to tell how the royal promise was broken, and how Lord Strafford attempted to seize the whole of Connaught, and generally ruled as absolute monarch in Ireland. In justice, however, it must be said that although he refused to grant legal toleration to the Catholics, Strafford refrained from persecuting them himself. Catholic chapels and schools were allowed even in Dublin. In other respects the condition of the people, however, was so nearly intolerable that a crisis was evidently at hand. It was not slow in arriving, and with it a fiercer storm of persecution than had yet been experienced in Ireland.

Elizabeth and her ministers had, as we have seen, formed a religion of their own, which they and their successors had been in vain trying to force on the Irish. The opposition to it, as might be expected, had been strong in England, but it had been put down remorselessly, and during the following reigns an ultra Protestant party, the Puritans, had grown into a power. Charles was what would be called to-day a High-Church Episcopalian. As king, he claimed the headship of the three churches of England, Ireland and Scotland, and in each he was confronted by a separate political and religious hostility. The Scotch Calvinists had very reluctantly accepted bishops into their church organization, under James, and the majority of the nation, with the Parliament of Scotland, rose in arms for the overthrow of Episcopacy, and the English Parliament, in which the Puritans had a majority, openly sympathized. The Puritan faction in England had a grievance of their own. They held that the Catholic Church was not being persecuted enough, and they charged the king with being a secret favorer of the Catholics. The matter was a little complicated by the fact that it was the refusal to accept the king's own creed that legally made Catholicity a crime, as the king was officially regarded as the infallible head of the Protestant Church. The Puritans, however, were not the men to stand on trifles in such points. Their Protestantism had grown into fanaticism, and its distinctive form was clear on one point, and one only,—hatred to the Catholic Church and its children. Puritanism under its first form was Episcopalian, of the Low Church type, and such was the creed of Hampden and the earlier leaders of the great rebellion. Presbyterianism appeared to be the prevalent creed during the triumph of the Parliament properly so-called. The army, in the hands of Cromwell, adopted Congregationalism, and ejected Parliament and Presbyterianism from State and Church, and finally the socialists of the day were busily preparing for a new upheaval at the close of Cromwell's reign, when Monk suddenly recalled Charles II., and the whole English nation went wild with delight over the event. The Puritan fanaticism was " like light straw on flame," " a fierce but fading fire," but for its time it had to burn fiercely in the already sorely-tried Ireland.

On the downfall and execution of Strafford, Charles appeared to yield to the demands of his Puritan Parliament. No Lord Lieutenant was appointed for a time, but two Puritans, Borlase and Parsons, were appointed Lords Justices, with virtual control of the country. The newcomers loudly denounced the toleration granted by their predecessor, and made no secret of the intention of their friends in the English Parliament to utterly crush out Catholicity. The same body was evidently on the eve of a death struggle with the king, and the leaders of the Irish Catholics decided to seize the opportunity of securing civil and religious freedom for their own country. The Catholic members of Parliament, both Lords and Commons, withdrew from Dublin, and established a national government at Kilkenny, which for several years virtually controlled the greater part of the country. It would far exceed our limits to go into the details of the succeeding wars, nor is it essential to our object, which is to point out the conditions under which the Catholic faith was preserved in Ireland, in despite of the attempts made so persistently by the rulers to suppress it. It is enough to state that, in 1652, the last stronghold of Irish freedom—Galway—was forced to surrender to the forces of the English Parliament after a resistance of nine months, more than double that of the boasted siege of Derry, nearly forty years afterwards. The English Puritans, who had already executed Charles, and reduced the hitherto independent kingdom of Scotland, were now, by force of arms, absolute masters in Ireland.

The conquerors resolved to use their power without mercy. The population was probably about a million at this period, and, as a first step, between thirty and forty thousand of the able-bodied men who had borne arms during the war were transported to the European continent to serve as soldiers in the armies of the various powers at peace with the new government of England. Pestilence and famine had already fearfully decimated the Irish population during the two preceding years. In Dublin alone thirty thousand persons had been swept away by plague in 1650 and 1651, and the garrison of Waterford had been reduced by the same cause from twelve to four hundred men in a few months. The Parliamentary troops, during the same time, had regularly followed the traditional English plan of cutting down the growing crops and destroying the cattle wherever their forces extended, so that their parties often travelled thirty miles through lately populous districts, without meeting a living creature. Dean Bernard tells how, around Newry and Dundalk, the dogs of the exterminated peasantry had grown as ferocious as tigers from feeding on the unburied bodies left by the English soldiers. The wolves increased so fast that hunts were organized for their destruction around the suburbs of Dublin, and state leases were made of lands for keeping up packs of wolf-hounds. It is only when we read such things as these that we can appreciate the resistance of the Irish people to the foreign conquest, and how utterly powerless they must have been when the thirty-four thousand " swordsmen " had been swept off to fill the ranks of any power in Europe.

For the rest of the Catholic population it was ordered by the Parliament that all proprietors and all who had served in the war against their forces should remove by a fixed day beyond the Shannon. The province of Connaught, the wildest and most barren, as well as the smallest, of the four divisions of Ireland, was assigned as the abode for the entire nation, except whatever laborers might be needed for the service of the new English settlers. Even those laborers were not allowed to remain in the cities, from which all Catholics had to remove under pain of death. The whole Catholic population of Dublin was ordered to present themselves in the Puritan Churches on the day after Christmas in 1651, or leave the city. Similar decrees were published in Cork, Galway, and Waterford. In the capital, by the statement of the Puritan authorities, only a few hundred were found to accept apostasy even on such conditions, and a still smaller number in the other cities. In 1655 Sir Charles Coote received the thanks of the English Government for having cleared Galway of all its Catholic inhabitants except the sick and bed-ridden, whom he was requested to remove, too, as soon as the weather would permit. In Wexford, after its capture, Cromwell informed the Parliament that not one in twenty of its former population remained, and in 1654 it was stated by the clerk of the Council, Herbert, that in a whole barony of Tipperary no inhabitant of Irish race remained, so that a few families had to be brought back to inform the government surveyors of the boundaries of the confiscated estates.

The land thus swept of its Irish owners was divided among the soldiers of Cromwell and English adventurers who had taken shares in the expenses of the war. The national hatred of the English Puritans might have been supposed satisfied by so wholesale a despoiling of the Irish race; but, so long as the latter retained their religion, the conquest seemed incomplete. Henry Cromwell, the son of the Protector, in 1655, urged on Secretary Thurloe the policy of sending a couple of thousand Irish boys, from twelve to fourteen, as slaves to Jamaica, on the ground that " we could well spare them, and it might be the means of making them Englishmen, I mean Christians." Pym had declared in Parliament that they would not leave a priest in Ireland, and Cromwell himself had declared that " where the English Parliament had power no Popish Mass would be endured." It had now full power, and the Protector set himself in earnest to make good his words. The Catholic clergy were hunted down by armed parties. During the continuance of hostilities the priests who fell into the hands of the soldiers were, for the most part, at once executed, and even after the submission of the country the same practice was occasionally followed. Three bishops, O'Brien of Emly, MacMahon of Clogher, and MacEgan of Elphin, with about three hundred priests, were thus put to death by the Parliamentary soldiery, and all the remaining bishops save one, the aged and nearly helpless Bishop of Kilmore, were driven from the country. The remaining priests were keenly pursued everywhere.

" We have in Ireland three beasts to destroy that lay burden on us," said Major Morgan, the member for Wicklow in Cromwell's Parliament at Westminster, in 1657. "The first is the wolf, on whose head we lay five pounds a head if a dog, and ten if a bitch. The second beast is a priest, on whose head we lay ten pounds, and if eminent, more. The third beast is a Tory (rápparee), on whose head, if he be a public Tory, we lay twenty pounds, and forty shillings if a private Tory." With garrisons in every town, with the old landmarks of Irish owners broken down and a population guarded within the limits of a small province like prisoners at large, it may be realized how hard it was for the Catholic priests to escape capture. At times the jails were full of them. In 1656 orders were given to transmit all captive priests to Carrickfergus, thence to be shipped by the first ship to Barbadoes. It was, however, directed that any who would renounce the Pope's supremacy, and frequent the Protestant meetings, and no others, should be allowed to remain. Scarcely any could be found to accept such terms, and the majority had to find their graves in the slave quarters of the West Indian plantations. In spite of all, however, over three hundred continued to elude capture, and maintain the Catholic faith in Ireland all through the reign of the Protector, whose boast, that "the Popish mass should not be endured," was thus baffled by the constancy of its undaunted ministers.

The laity were not allowed to profess their faith without further trials. With the cant which was so characteristic of the Puritan declarations, Cromwell, at the same time that he declared the mass should not be endured, said, " he meddled not with the internal conscience of any man." To show what value was to be attached to these words, an oath was drawn up, in which the leading Catholic doctrines were declared to be false and damnable, and all Catholics were required by law to solemnly invoke the name of the Divinity to a denial of their internal faith. The oath might be tendered by any magistrate, and the penalty was the forfeiture of one-third of all property for a first refusal to take it, and of life imprisonment for a third. The Catholics who had received lands in Connaught, or still retained some movables, were summoned frequently to take this oath; but we are told it was almost generally refused. For the laborers and others who could not be fined, for the simple reason that they had nothing, another means of punishment was invented. Contracts were made with the Bristol merchants for the supply of Irish slaves for the West Indies, and the military governors of various posts, as Carlow, Kilkenny, Clonmel, Ross, and Waterford, got orders in 1654 to arrest "all such Irish within their precincts as could not prove they had a settled course of industry enough to maintain them," and deliver them and all children in hospitals and work-houses to Captain Morgan, Mr. North, and John Johnson, English merchants, who were empowered to transport them as slaves to the West Indies. Six thousand four hundred were thus carried into slavery before May, 1655, when the orders were repealed, because the slave hunters were found to be carrying off English children as well as Irish when occasion offered. The difficulty which has so constantly beset the English administration of Ireland, namely, how to have robbery and rapine honestly carried into execution, thus put a stop to the Cromwellian slave trade in Irish Catholics.

Nine years had passed since Cromwell had emphasized his declaration that "the Mass should not be endured," by the massacre of Drogheda, and still there was no sign of Catholicity dying out in Ireland. Confiscation, slavery, and wholesale slaughter had all been tried, and tried in vain. The Puritan fanaticism had well-nigh burned itself out in England, and on the death of Cromwell the popular feeling there turned irresistibly against its professors. Charles II. was recalled to the throne amid a delirium of public rejoicing. The body of the late ruler was dragged from its grave and shamefully hung up to public insult by the very people who had a few years before raised him to supreme power. The creed which he had established was swept away. The Irish Puritans, who had been so loud in their outcry against Popery and prelacy while seizing the lands of Ireland, were among the first to pay homage to the new monarch, on whose head a price had been set by their party a few years before. Henry Cromwell himself was among the foremost of the new loyalists, and while his father's dishonored corpse was still rotting at Tyburn, the late Lord Lieutenant was humbly begging the favor of Lord Ormond to enable him to retain Lord Clanrickarde's estate of Portumna, which had been granted him by that father's government as a reward for his services. Coote and Broghill, the executioners respectively of Bishops MacMahon and MacEgan, and the merciless leaders of the Parliamentarians against the Irish royalists, were prompt to follow Henry Cromwell. As Lords Justice, they presided at the formal restoration of the royal authority, and in the words of their address quoted by their apologist, Froude, they could not " conceal the unspeakable joy " with which they welcomed the revival of " the true worship of God " among them and pronounced the Protectorate which had enriched them with Irish spoil " a wicked, traitorous and abominable usurpation."

The body of Cromwellian settlers, in the words of the same author, " so long as they lived retained their own beliefs, but deprived as they were of school or chapel, they were unable to perpetuate them, and thus their children were swept into the Irish stream and became Catholics." A hundred years had passed since school and chapel were taken from the Irish Catholics, as far as the power of English law could take them; yet after that hundred years, with its sad story of war, famine, confiscation and executions, the old Irish Nation was Catholic still. The contrast speaks for itself.

FREEDOM OF WORSHIP IN THE UNITED STATES.

W HEN, on September 25th, 1789, the first amendments to the Constitution of the United States were proposed by Congress, and afterwards ratified by eleven of the thirteen original States, the Catholics thanked God, because, by the first article of these amendments, it was enacted that " Congress should make no law respecting an establishment of religion, and prohibiting the free exercise thereof." The third section of the first article of the Constitution of New York reads as follows: " The free exercise and enjoyment of religious profession and worship, without discrimination or preference, shall forever be allowed in this State to all mankind."

The influence of the wiser and more farseeing statesmen of that day tended towards an almost universal repeal of all the disabilities under which the Catholics had groaned in the previous colonial days. The States that refused to sign this treaty of religious peace were sure soon to follow an example which the spirit of the age rendered, as it were, necessary in the new republic.

But the prejudices existing still in the great mass of the nation against " papal power " could not be instantly removed, and in many public institutions of the new States the superintendents thought themselves authorized to exclude from the premises any Catholic clergyman who had been called by a sick person living at the time in the house. We remember that in 1847 no priest could enter the poor-house of Westchester county, at the gates of New York city, and the faculty of St. John's College, Fordham, obtained that permission only after a discussion before the Board of Supervisors of the county.

A happy change has taken place since then. In the charitable and reformatory establishments founded by the municipal government of New York, and situated in the beautiful islands of the East River, there is now, and there has been for a number of years, a perfect freedom of action for the ministers of the Catholic faith. They are allowed to perform their duties whenever they are called, night and day, to the bed of the sick, or for the consolation of the afflicted. All citizens, whatever may be their creed, concur in saying that the former disabilities were the deplorable remains of a brutality, yea, a savageness, whose past records, chiefly in England, strike the reader with amazement and horror.

Still this country is not yet entirely free from those excesses of bigotry. The doctrine of perfect equality of all religions before the law, though it has been now accepted or enacted by all the States, remains, as it were, an affair of theory rather than of universal practice.   We meet occasionally with facts which can scarcely tally with the renowned principles of civil toleration prevalent at this day in all free States.   The abnormal exceptions introduced by European agnosticism on the other side of the Atlantic, which bring back again despotism under the garb of liberty, are, it is true, scarcely perceptible in this happy country ; still there are yet some symptoms of it, and the sooner they disappear the better it will be for us.

The spirit of the new political institutions created in this country at the period of the Revolution was that of civil and religious liberty, but in many of the colonies the penal laws of England against Catholics had been copied in their legislation, and prejudice and suspicion against them had been fostered by the enactments of assemblies and the prevailing tone of the pulpits.

The prejudices, pervading as they did the mass of the nation against "papal power," could not be instantly removed, and it required time to carry out in fact the beneficent and reasonable provisions of the National and State constitutions.   People who had been brought up to regard adherents of the primitive Christian Church as entitled to no civil rights, but as beings who could claim only such rights as any man in position might for the moment see fit to grant them, could scarcely be expected to give a generous and hearty interpretation to the constitutional guarantee of religious freedom.   Nursed in ideas of intolerance many were, unconsciously to themselves, grossly intolerant and acted accordingly. The mass of the American people ultimately entered heartily into the spirit and practice of religious liberty, accepting as a fundamental principle that every man in the land should be free to attend the worship of the denomination to which he belonged, and that no man could be compelled to attend, or be bound directly or indirectly to support any other.

As Catholics increase in numbers Catholic inmates of prisons, reformatories, and asylums for the homeless and unfortunate increase.   That these people have a right to attend the worship of their own church, and ought not to be compelled to attend the service of another faith, all would admit as an abstract proposition ; but it unfortuately has happened that in isolated cases and institutions a few set themselves against the sound American principle of religious freedom and equal rights, and seize any opportunity afforded by the absence of express laws to prevent Catholics from being allowed to hear mass on Sunday, and to force them to attend some Protestant form of service, either that of some denomination, or one framed for the institution, which thus has a religion of its own.

The ingenuity of perverted reason is shown in the fertility of arguments put forward to defend this course and make the unreflecting think that they are advocating American and liberal principles against a grasping ecclesiastical body. Whenever they are called to account for their illiberal and oppressive course they make the discipline of the house a pretext, as though the assembling of Catholics for half-an-hour apart, to attend services by a clergyman of their own faith, could endanger discipline. That it is a mere pretext, and a shallow one, is clear from the experience of the English government, which ever since 1862, now nearly a quarter of a century, has carried out this separate worship in all institutions on the British Isles, and in this period of twenty-three years has found it an aid, and not an obstacle to discipline.

Another pretext is that the service enforced suits all; that it is not that of any particular denomination, and is unobjectionable. It is essentially Protestant, however, and even if it were acceptable to all Protestants, which can seldom be shown to be the case, it cannot be made by the State compulsory on any one, Protestant or Catholic. The State cannot by law institute a form of worship and compel any class of citizens to attend it, and the State cannot delegate a greater power than it possesses.

Every sophistry and trick of false reasoning is resorted to when the question arises of depriving officials of the un-American power they assume of violating the rights of conscience. Catholics are accused of claiming special privileges; of attempting to interfere with Protestants and to deprive them of their religious rights; of seeking to proselytize. Yet, with singular inconsistency, they will maintain that their so-called non-sectarian service suits everybody, and in the next breath say that if every denomination is allowed to come in it will lead to general confusion. If all Protestants accept the non-sectarian form they will not seek to introduce anything else. If they do seek this it is clear that the non-sectarian form does not suit them. As to the other charge, that allowing Catholics to hear mass will interfere with Protestant inmates and deprive them of rights, it is merely absurd, as the priest will officiate only for those of his own faith, and not come in contact with others at all.

Catholics never have sought in any country to force Protestants to attend mass, and certainly do not ask it in any institution in this country. The mass, in the Catholic Church is the essential act of worship, in which every member of the Church is required to join on Sunday, and it is the great act of sanctifying that day. It is not an optional service with him. It binds him in conscience, and if he is free he must hear mass. If he is confined the privation is to him the greatest of evils. The Protestant system has nothing analogous. No service of his appeals to a Protestant conscience as one that he must attend under pain of sin. As the mass has this claim on the Catholic conscience, the denial of it has a character of especial cruelty, and wantonly to deprive a Catholic of the privilege shows a heart insensible to every fine feeling of love for our neighbor which should ever mark a true Christian character.

That we in no degree exaggerate this will be clear to every one living out of cities who wishes to secure Catholics as servants or for farm work. If Catholics thus employed cannot get to mass on Sundays, they give up situations where the recompense and the treatment are all they can desire, because all these weigh as nothing compared to the loss of the great sacrifice of their religion. In numerous places aid is given to the erection of Catholic churches by residents who wish in this way to put the minds of those whom they employ at rest on this to them important and essential point.

It would be impossible to enumerate and discuss the pretexts raised by the few institutions which array themselves against true American liberal feelings. They pretend that those in eleemosynary and reformatory institutions are criminals, and that criminals have no rights, reviving in their worst features the old laws of attainder, and setting up the most dangerous theories, making poverty itself a crime, in defiance of all the teachings of our Lord. They claim to be private institutions while asking for public money; they declare that they belong to some particular denomination at the very time that they earnestly aver themselves to be non-sectarian and open to all; they retain Catholic children and force them to attend Protestant service, and complain that the State unjustly compels them to receive Catholic children. No good or sound cause can possibly require in this free country such absurdly inconsistent defences.

The necessity for legislative action is not general. In many States the institutions, on a fair presentation of the case, have freely adopted the English rule, and recording the religion of each inmate on entering, enabled him to receive the ministrations of a duly appointed clergyman of that creed in the full extent.

In Ohio, Kentucky, New York, New Jersey, Rhode Island, and Pennsylvania, it has been necessary for Catholics to ask specific laws in order to prevent officials from infringing a clear provision of the Constitutions of those several States. In Ohio, a law was passed, but, before its salutary provisions could be tested and their advantage shown by experience, it was repealed in deference to the outcry of a few fanatical opponents of religious liberty. In Kentucky, the struggle was a long one, before even in that State the inalienable rights of men were secured. In New Jersey, under the impulse given by the present liberal governor of that State, Catholics in reformatories are able to attend the Catholic service, the mass, as Protestants are to attend their own services. Yet, the New Jersey Methodist Conference, in March, 1885, protested against this act of justice, as giving " pre-eminent and peculiar privileges to a particular denomination," insisting that Catholics must be prevented from hearing mass. In Pennsylvania, application has frequently been made to the Board of Managers of the House of Correction at Philadelphia, and, though the grand jury has recommended it, liberty is constantly refused to Catholics to have mass said for them. The Board say : " The Board has no doubt that the good order, discipline of the house, and cleanliness of the inmates are greatly promoted by these general services at fixed times at which all the inmates are obliged to attend." They admit and defend " a compulsory attendance " on services held by a Methodist minister and Protestant in character. In the words of the managers, the usual shallow pretexts for a great wrong are put forward, perhaps in their most ridiculous form. How order, cleanliness and discipline could suffer by allowing a Catholic priest, either before or after the Protestant service, to offer mass for the Catholic inmates, the only service which for Catholics constitutes divine worship, no man in his sound reason could explain. The long experience under the English law shows that men are more disposed to reform and to respect the law when it acknowledges their religious rights, than when they have to brood over a great and shameful wrong done them by the strong arm of the State.

In New York there is at least one example of this anomaly in one of the " beautiful islands of the East River," where everybody can contemplate an establishment supported in great part by the public money of the city, in which it must be said that " the free exercise of the Catholic religion is prohibited." This is the House of Refuge, so called, in Randall's Island, which this year has called up long debates in the Legislature, and unless redress is granted, will make the subject one of the State issues for a long time.

During more than ten years the Catholics have meekly taken all the legitimate means of coming back into possession of their rights. These rights have been several times acknowledged by the Legislature of the State. Large majorities in both the Senate and the House of Assembly have enacted laws for this purpose ; but delays due to some proposed amendments to those bills were followed by the blunt veto of a Governor of the State, Mr. Cornell.

The reasons he gave for his action appeared so unsatisfactory to the legislative body that the following year the same bill in a stronger form was presented. The new Governor, Mr. Cleveland, counselled a private settlement of the matter between the Church authorities and the managers of the House of Refuge, and an informal understanding was reached. But the faithless directors at Randall's Island refuse to fulfil their promise, and come again before the public with their arbitrary conditions, which would render the ministry of a priest absolutely futile and of no effect. It is time to speak plainly, so as to open the eyes of all, Protestants as well as Catholics. It must be made clear to all Christians of any denomination whatever, that the system followed in this and similar cases is the most anti-Christian and sectarian that can well be imagined.

The bill having been lately introduced again at Albany, the managers of the House of Refuge have given a new form to their pretensions, and at this moment they publish in the most extensively spread papers of the State the long list of their reasons for setting aside those of the Catholics; though they take good care not to allude to the best and most peremptory of those reasons, the one derived from the Constitution of the United States incorporated into that of New York. Of this anon.

Anti-sectarianism is the fortress behind which they have intrenched themselves. In a series of resolutions passed among them on April 5th, 1883, and reproduced in the New York *Tribune* of January 26th, 1885, they declare:

"That the House of Refuge is, in every sense of the word, an unsectarian institution;

"That all the inmates have entire freedom of conscience, and from all religious restraint;

"That no sacrament of any particular church or creed is used or allowed in the institution;

"That services of a purely non-sectarian character are held in the chapel on Sundays as part of the discipline of the house;

"That clergymen of all denominations can hold service according to the rule of non-sectarianism," etc.

This is sufficient for their absolute condemnation; and it is proper to consider first the meaning of the words *sect* and *Church*. The word sectarianism comes from *sect*, and the Church is not a sect, no more than a sect can be the Church. A word on the foundation of Christianity is absolutely necessary here. Our Lord Jesus Christ was the Founder, and is forever the Head of the Church. He knew what He meant when He commissioned His apostles to preach; when He told them, as recorded by St. Matthew (xxviii., 18, etc.): "All power is given to Me in heaven and in earth. Going, therefore, teach ye all nations, baptizing them in the name of the Father, and of the Son, and of the Holy Ghost; teaching them to observe all things whatsoever I have commanded you ; and behold, I am with you all days, even to the consummation of the world." This is the solid foundation of Christianity.

The Saviour himself has described His Church as an institution coextensive with the world *in space*, and destined to subsist until the end of the world *in time*. The world, therefore, must allow people to receive from the apostles and their successors—*usque ad consummationem sæculi*—all the doctrine He had during His public career communicated to them ; with the express promise, besides, that He would remain invisibly with them, to guide them in their decisions, and support them in their trials.

That the apostles felt the full weight of responsibility imposed upon them by these words, and the high dignity to which they had thus been raised, is proved by the meeting they held, as a body, at Jerusalem, to decide on the first question proposed to them by Jewish proselytes, who wanted to impose on Gentile converts the prescriptions of the Jewish law. After a proper discussion, in which Peter spoke first, the apostles issued together their decree in the following terms (Acts xv., 28) : " It hath seemed good to the Holy Ghost and to us, to lay no farther burden upon you (Gentiles) than these necessary things," etc. Their decision, they knew from Christ, was that of the Holy Ghost Himself. Many Jewish proselytes preferred their personal opinion to that of the apostles, and thus they formed the first *sect*—the Ebionites. For, owing to the constitution of the human mind, it was *necessary* there should be heresies and schisms, as St. Paul declared (1 Cor. xi., 19). Those who cut themselves off from the Church are properly called a sect ; but it would be absurd to call the Church a sect when she is in fact the main stem of the Christian tree.

The reader, whatever may be his belief, is no doubt aware that this is not a mere conjecture derived from a doubtful text. It is simply history, attested not only by the New Testament, but also by the subsequent events of the Jewish race in Palestine. For the Ebionites had their own short-lived existence, ending at the destruction of Jerusalem. Every author who has spoken of them avoids confounding them with the Church, but has given them the character of a true sect separated from the main body.

This main body meanwhile had its organs, which have continued to speak until our own day. The voice of pontiff and of councils has constantly been heard during nearly nineteen hundred years, since the first council at Jerusalem, holding forth the doctrine communicated by the God-man to the primitive apostles, and speaking at this day with the same authority and the same assurance. The advocates of the Protestant ascendency which hypocritically hides its schemes under the pretext of non-sectarianism ought to be afraid of making themselves ridiculous by calling sectarian such a body as the Catholic Church, which has good reasons to claim an antiquity coeval with Christ, and to promise to itself a continuance of life until the day of judgment. It shall be seen anon on which side the true sectarians are likely to be found.

But the pretensions of these men go straight to the ruin of Christianity itself, and it is important to bring this immediately forward. Christianity is eminently a positive religion. Its dogmas are all highly supernatural, and its moral precepts always perspicuous and forcible. There is nothing shadowy in its history, nothing hesitating in its commands. From the time it was first preached man found at last he could rely on his conscience, because it was not the voice of reason alone, but above all the voice of God speaking to the reason of man; Christianity is nothing if it is not supernatural. It comes from God, and cannot be a shadow.

On this account chiefly heresies and schisms have abounded, because the pride of many could not brook a *superior* control, namely, that of God himself. But at the same time heresies and schisms have universally been called sects; being evidently cut off from the main stem, and unable to claim a higher origin than private reason. To apply the epithet sectarian to the stem itself is thus to set aside all ecclesiastical history.

There are, however, various degrees in the system of sects; and it will not be difficult to prove that the worst of all is precisely that which a certain class in institutions, legislatures, and the press hold up as eminently non-sectarian. Their attempt consists in suppressing altogether the supernatural, and consequently Christianity; they forbid Christian ministers to preach positive Christian doctrine to their spiritual children, and they call this practice un-sectarian.

To deny or wilfully ignore *a single* dogma is heresy, and is sufficient to constitute a sect, by denying a supernatural fact or doctrine pertaining to the deposit of faith as handed down from the time of the apostles to our own. To reject, or refuse to admit, *several* articles of the creed, is a concentration of sects in a single religious body. Consequently the act of expunging the whole creed at once cannot but be the supreme degree of sectarianism; and it is exactly what those gentlemen boast of securing under the pretext of non-sectarianism. What becomes of the religion of Christ in such a system as this? In the absence of all dogmas there cannot be but skepticism in the mind; in the absence of a divine sanction given to moral precepts, a sickly sentimentality is the only guide of the human conscience. Can, then, the voice of duty be heard, and temptation be warded off? It is puerile to speak of "the broad principles of Christianity being composed of what all sects teach together." Since all Christian truths have been denied or doubted by some sect or other, there is no *common ground* among them to stand upon. In any institution based on these theories, do they teach " on Sundays in their chapel " the belief in the Holy Trinity? They cannot according to their principles, since the Unitarians deny it. · Do they teach the necessity of baptism, which was formerly the common rite of all Christians? I am sure they would rather discourage it, as a matter controverted in our days. What do they, what can they teach of the Christian religion to the unfortunate children confided to their care?

It is, indeed, painful to see, in this age and country, many men animated with the best intentions, listening with a sort of approbation to such paltry sophisms and plausible nonsense as are contained in the " resolutions " quoted above. Still, it is a consoling fact that few of those men who feel inclined to apply the word sectarian to the Catholic Church, have ever gone so far as to discard altogether the doctrines of Christianity. They would feel insulted if they were openly accused of it. Some raving maniac may occasionally bring many to hear his denunciations of the belief in Christ, and even of God; but among his listeners a great number, I hope, would reject with scorn the imputation of not being Christians.

Let, however, people understand that it is not only those who blaspheme God, and throw their venom on the pages of Holy Writ who can be said to have abjured their religion. Those also who refuse to the ministers of God the faculty of addressing children in public institutions, and telling them that there is in heaven one God in Three Persons; that the Son became incarnate in the bosom of the Virgin Mary, in order to atone for our sins on the cross; that the Holy Ghost speaks both to the individual human heart who invokes Him with sincerity, and also to the whole Church through its pastors, in order to establish the kingdom of God on earth; that, finally, the soul is immortal and there shall be a day of judgment, etc., etc.; yea, those who insist on preventing all positive Christian doctrine from reaching the mind and heart of children, are as dangerous adversaries of truth as Tom Paine was in his day and Ingersoll is in ours.

In case this much-vaunted non-sectarianism were finally considered a condition to be enforced in all our houses of education, public and private, what would become of religion in this country? It has been attempted twice in France, with the most appalling results—we can conjecture how it would turn out among us. The public worship of the Christian to his God would gradually disappear, and in its place would be substituted a senseless performance without substance or form. Nevertheless, public worship is necessary in a nation unless godlessness can be the foundation of society; and in all ages this has been denied by all profound thinkers. What is the use of citizens meeting together in a public edifice on some appointed day of the week, unless they have some common and positive doctrine relating to the attributes of the Deity, and to what God may have revealed to mankind? If either the Deity is not known in its attributes, or no revelation has come from that heavenly source, religion is a mockery; and the most solemn act of human life—the worship of God—turns out to be the most flippant and meaningless. Look around you and examine whether this has not been so far the clear expression of our ancestors' wisdom. Can you see in this country, where sects are so numerous, a single temple or church in which there is not some profession of positive faith publicly avowed by the worshippers? I know there are men who pretend that henceforth creeds must disappear, and a broad Christianity without dogmas and rites is the only thing acceptable to human reason. But did they ever dare to reduce to practice their bold assertion? Can any one point out in the vast extent of this continent a single meeting-house devoted to non-sectarianism in the sense of our adversaries? It has not been attempted, because all are aware that the project would soon end in the establishment of practical atheism. Not one of those who advocate non-sectarianism in public institutions belongs to a non-sectarian church, for no such thing can exist, for as soon as it became a church, it became a new sect ; that is, must be sectarian. And this is true of the religious position of the institutions in question. Where there is a set of moral and religious doctrines, a form of worship and a ministry, it belongs to some old sect, or is a new sect.

The greatest error, perhaps, of non-sectarians consists in believing that by the adoption of their system there will be unity among Christians; and Jesus Christ certainly prayed that His disciples should be *one*, as He Himself was one with His Father (John xvii., 21). The Church has always insisted on this great prerogative of the Christian religion—unity—which is the first mark—*nota*—of true religion. It has just been seen that by rejecting all creeds and all visible authority in point of morals, the non-sectarians are reduced to fall upon "the common *feelings* of our Christianity," as if this could form a bond between brethren, and unite them together in the worship of the same God. We said that a *positive* creed was required to form this bond, and that the moral precepts required also a *positive* sanction; otherwise they cannot be taught, but only proposed as probable suggestions. This point we feel it necessary to examine more at length, and state clearly and explicitly, because the greatest error of non-sectarianism—that of claiming unity—must be thoroughly confuted, and the mock dress of Christianity, they assume, must be stripped from their shoulders.

All Christians must admit that the relation of man toward God—religion—affects him both in the order of nature and in the order of grace. This second one supposes the first; but the first does not suppose the second. And as the order of grace is in general little understood by the men of the present age, this must be more fully explained. All know, however, that man, created at first in holiness and in the image of God, fell from his high estate by the disobedience of Adam and lost all claim to heaven and union with God. This was restored by the Author of grace—the Son of God made man, who redeemed us by dying for us on the cross. This new dispensation must be as far above the first as grace is above nature. Hence the supernatural destiny of man was far better expressed by the doctrine of redemption than by the religion of the patriarchs who expected a redeemer, but knew that He had not come and would delay His coming. As soon as He appeared, all the circumstances of His advent proclaimed a new kingdom of God of a totally supernatural character. He was eternal, yet appeared in time. He had an All-powerful Father in heaven, and chose for His human mother a Virgin of the race of Eve. Angels sang at his birth, and kings adored him. It is not necessary here to follow in detail His public career when He revealed us His origin, and His intention of making us His brethren and His co-heirs in eternity. His power over nature, His superhuman wisdom, His very sufferings and death proclaimed that He was truly the Son of God. The religion He founded was destined to unite intimately the order of nature and that of grace. Nature was not totally depraved by Adam's fall, but it is to be raised by redemption to a higher plane by its union with the divine. Hence natural elements must be used in the highest mysteries of grace, and bread and wine are changed into the body and blood of Christ. All sacraments—and there are seven—partake of this union between earth and heaven; and—as it was meet it should be—man becomes a different being from what he was; and he is raised far above even the high state which Adam and Eve enjoyed in Eden.

Unless this statement is admitted as the true one, nobody can know what Christianity is. From one of the "resolutions" quoted above as a condition for entering the House of Refuge, a type of these pretendedly non-sectarian systems, no one can administer any sacrament, nor enforce any creed when allowed to deal with the children of the establishment. The necessary consequence of this declaration is that the order of grace is totally denied by these gentlemen, and nothing but pure philosophy can be inculcated within the precincts of the house. This was already seen in what was said previously; but it is much more clear at this moment by their very words that Christianity is excluded from their pretended unsectarian system. If no minister of religion can teach any "creed," any summary of truth, necessary to salvation, he cannot preach Christianity; if he cannot administer any sacrament, he cannot obey the express commands of Christ to the body of teachers instituted by Him. Such a regulation literally forbids Christianity. If these gentlemen were more familiar than they are with the classics of Greece and Rome, they might propose to burn incense before the statues of Pythagoras, Socrates, Aristotle, and even-Cicero in some of his pious moods. For by these great men the highest philosophy was taught. But as probably their culture is not so far advanced as this would suppose, we must consider a moment the philosophy they themselves teach, since they cannot teach Christianity, of which they repudiate all possible notion. It will thence become evident that there can be no unity in their system, and the prayer of Christ for His disciples that "they should be one as He is one with the Father," is everlastingly for them of no effect. Since among them the order of nature is not ennobled by that of grace, their teaching must be confined to the averments of human reason. But it would be preposterous to imagine that their lessons are in any way systematic, and that they can enter into the discussion of the various philosophical systems. Should they do so, the poor boys and girls whom they teach would find themselves in a Babel of the most contradictory problems. Has there ever been any unity among the followers of pure reason? Have the philosophers of even our age settled the innumerable questions they have always been discussing? But this consideration does not deserve to be insisted upon, as there can be no question of such philosophy among them. In what does their teaching really consist? When the inmates of such an institution come out of their prison, after seven or eight years of a strict confinement, the best among them may remember having heard their masters speak sternly against lying, gambling, drinking, etc. Had the same poor boys and girls remained rambling in the streets, instead of being sent to the institution, they would have known as much; for we speak here *of the best among them,* and the inward light which all men receive at their birth is at least as good a monitor for the well-disposed as the utterances of a superintendent.

As to the multitude of those boys and girls who naturally during their imprisonment rebelled against their confinement, the first thought of all of them, on coming out, must be that of " dear liberty," and the only meaning they can attach to the word is precisely to do what they have been forbidden to do. Yes, they rush out like proud *philosophers;* and it would be sad indeed to disclose in detail the foul anticipations and desires towards which they feel an irresistible attraction.

Thus all the money spent by the city to give those unfortunate waifs of society a *moral* education, is absolutely thrown away. In spite of what may be said to the contrary, the evil is known by its fruits. But the chief objection the Catholics have against the continuance of the system is that their own children, who are immured within the walls of such institutions, are prevented by bigoted officials from being reached by the very influences—those of their own religion—most powerful to reform their hearts, and not only that, but these Catholic inmates invariably lose all Christian faith in the institution, and come out under no check of supernatural truths, but entirely deprived of Christian faith. This has been proved by too many instances to be at all put in question; and the Catholics think that the loss of faith by their own children is the loss of their soul. The constitution gives them the right of claiming that their offspring shall be educated in their own faith. The constitution is a more important thing to preserve than the regulations adopted from time to time by boards of management, superintendents, and keepers, which certainly cannot be superior to constitutional rules. Many papers and periodicals that oppose the broad claim of religious liberty which Catholics contend for, pretend that no religious question can be discussed in the legislature. Under our constitution the State cannot certainly discuss the doctrines taught by any denomination, unless they are subversive of peace and morality, but as the constitution guarantees the right of free worship to every citizen, it is eminently proper for the legislature to discuss and pass a bill whose only object is to enforce an article of the constitution.

Some men insinuate to the public that if Catholics are allowed to have their own worship in public institutions as Protestants have, they will in time suppress Protestant worship there and everywhere. Absurd as this idea is, it may not be idle to examine it coolly and thoroughly; because, though it is perfectly groundless, it might make an impression on some otherwise impartial minds. Arguments still more flimsy than this have sometimes produced an immense amount of mischief; and in the present case it is most important to clear up every thing calculated to throw a shade of doubt on the debate.

In the first place, let us consider the fear just expressed, that Catholics may be wishing to make their Church established by law in this country. We will confine ourselves to the remark that Catholics have uniformly in this country favored religious freedom; that they heartily accepted the amendment to the constitution which declares that " congress shall make no law respecting an establishment of religion, or prohibiting the free exercise thereof." It is from the day of the passage of this amendment to the constitution and of the acceptance of it by the states that their emancipation is dated. The load of disabilities which weighed on them suddenly disappeared in theory and have gradually continued to vanish in practice one after another, so that at this moment few remain. The first Catholic periodical established in this country, by Bishop England of Charleston, bore every day at the head of its columns the text of this amendment as the proud basis of our religious liberty ; and we are sure that in case it was proposed to blot it out of the constitution, every Catholic in the land would oppose the intended outrage with all means in his power. In the whole history of the country there is no instance where Catholics destroyed the religious institutions or churches of Protestants, or attempted to interfere with their religious rights. Catholics have suffered, but never, even in retaliation, made others suffer.

Our chief pastors, besides, are not unintelligent ; yet they would appear to be lacking in wisdom, should they make such an attempt at a time remarkable indeed by the gradual disappearance everywhere of state churches. Are they ignorant of the fact that already in Ireland the state church has been disestablished, as it will soon be in England and Scotland ? Is this the time to court the favor of states ? The very idea of it is silly, and it would be simply loss of time to discuss it any longer. As to the notion that the Catholics, in the present instance, aim at claiming a share at least of the public money, nobody has heard them express such an intention as this. When they do, it will be time to examine whether they have a right to it or not.

These apprehensions of those opposed to the bill being answered, another argument may be stated in the following words. " The Catholic Church maintains that out of her there is no salvation ; infallibility is her exclusive prerogative ; all members of the Christian flock who wander out of her visible sheepfold cannot have any share in Christ's redemption." This doctrine, they pretend, must necessarily produce a stubborn spirit of intolerance ; and intolerance, we know, is the bugbear of modern liberals. To this intolerance they attribute the darkest designs, particularly that of enslaving others ; and in order to obtain this nefarious object they first try to procure the support of the state, of its money, of its influence, of its laws, in order to acquire everywhere the pre-eminence. It has been said in particular that this is the purport we have in view when we insist on the freedom of worship in any state or city institution, that is, on the liberty of teaching Catholic children the dogmas and precepts of their religion. Yet whenever liberty has been granted, not one of the supposed consequences of this liberty has yet given the least alarm to the city authorities either in England or in this country.

In order to come to a more direct answer to all those attacks, it is proper to see first whether intolerance is the necessary consequence of the Catholic tenets on exclusive salvation and infallibility.

In point of fact, Catholics have always been, and are chiefly at this moment, less intolerant than their adversaries. Balmez, in his *Protestantism and Catholicity Compared,* has written some admirable pages on this question of toleration, particularly in his chapter xxxiv. We can only select a few of his remarks. "Toleration," he says, "strictly speaking, means the patience with which we suffer a thing we judge to be bad, and which we think desirable not to punish. Thus some kinds of scandals are tolerated. . . . . The idea of toleration is always accompanied with the idea of evil. . . . . To respect opinions (contrary to our own) sometimes means to respect those who hold them, on account of their good faith or their good intentions. A man is called *tolerant* when he is able to bear opinions contrary to his own without irritation or disturbance. . . . . St. Francis de Sales was tolerant, Voltaire excessively intolerant." Balmez might have added that Voltaire, nevertheless, was a great preacher of tolerance, though he practiced it but little. "The tolerance of a religious man," Balmez continues, "arises not from want of faith; it may coexist with a burning zeal for the spread and preservation of the truth. It is born of two principles, charity and humility." And the noble Spanish writer develops at length this last idea, which the reader can easily peruse in his great work.

But who in this country can say that Catholic priests are intolerant toward persons of another creed? In former times they have been violently attacked and often deprived of their most sacred rights. Did they ever show a spirit of retaliation wherever they gained some influence owing to what Balmez calls "their charity and humility"? They at this moment occupy situations of trust in many public establishments of states or cities; and it is but proper to ask whether the freedom they enjoy as to the practice of their ministry has ever given reason to accuse them of an undue proselytism towards the non-Catholics with whom they come in contact in those houses. The fact that never a whisper of this kind has been uttered against them is a proof of the groundlessness of the contrary supposition.

And this is not in the Catholic Church a peculiarity of our time and country. If the defenders of our faith have always in their controversies with opponents displayed an ardent zeal against *errors,* they invariably spoke courteously of *persons.* We do not allude here to state prosecutions against heresy—a principle of jurisprudence adopted formerly by all Christian nations, and indulged in by Protestants as well as by orthodox canonists. But in theological encounters, either in writing or in oral discussions, it is a remarkable fact that during the Middle Ages, particularly, it was extremely rare to hear any opprobrious epithet hurled by a Catholic theologian against an opponent. This may surprise many people, but it is nevertheless true. The works of St. Thomas Aquinas would suffice to prove it. He was undoubtedly the best type of that much-abused period. He undertook the task of confuting all philosophical and theological errors of previous times, and in his *Summa contra Gentiles* he not only refuted the old theories of Greek, Jewish and Mohammedan writers, but he anticipated the follies of our own times and gave the proper answer to the sensualistic, materialistic and agnostic ravings in the midst of which we now are living. He did it with a perfect composure and almost superhuman patience, without a single word which could offend his adversaries. No contrary way of speaking can be found in all his works.

All the great mediæval schoolmen have been remarkable for the same peculiarity; and in modern times St. Francis de Sales, Bellarmine, Bossuet and many others, can be quoted to the same purpose.

And there is nothing surprising in all this, because the Church requires of her champions that such should always be their conduct. Error they must prosecute without flinching; for the persons, they must follow the law of charity. Balmez has sufficiently proved it in the passage hinted at on a previous page.

The Catholics, it is true, believe that their Church is infallible, and that out of her there is no salvation. Does it follow that theological adversaries on earth must be considered and treated by them like reprobates, altogether out of the pale of Christ's redemption? Far otherwise, since the Church teaches that invincible ignorance exempts from sin, and that among the elect in heaven many will be found who never belonged to the visible fold of Christ, namely, to the exterior pale of His Church on earth; and because this is most important in the present question, it must be treated of with sufficient explanations and details.

Cardinal Hergenröther, in his *Church and State* (Essay xvii., on Liberty of Conscience), declares that "the Church has always recognized that people might be in error of faith and yet might be saved; that they might be in unconscious communion with the true Church, although through invincible ignorance they were not in external communion with her; that condemnation regarded false *principles,* not the *persons* in error; that towards these all the duties of brotherly love were to be exercised; and that no Catholic had the smallest right to impute guilt to them."

This is not the private opinion of this learned cardinal. It is the common teaching of all theologians; and if in a public dispute the Catholic champion were to impute to his adversary the guilt of mortal sin for supporting his erroneous opinions, he certainly would be reproved by his superiors, because he would have taken on himself to pronounce a sentence which must come from God alone, since God alone knows the conscience of the disputant.

And this is not a matter of theory only; I wish all non-Catholics should know that it is often reduced to practice among us. We can and do pray for our friends living and dead, Protestants or not. Every one is aware that on Good Friday the Church, even in her public liturgy, prays for heretics, Jews, infidels, etc. Nay, more; the Catholic relative or friend of a deceased Protestant can apply to any clergyman of his communion (chiefly in case the dead person has given signs of earnest endeavors to know the truth) for offering the holy sacrifice of the Mass in his behalf. This charitable office is based on the common opinion among theologians, that there are persons who, though not belonging to the visible organization of the Church, are in *unconscious* communion with her (according to the expressions of Cardinal Hergenröther). The communion of saints (one of the articles of our Creed) includes them, and gives them a right to participate in our glorious privileges. Thus, because even a private Mass is always a public office in the Church, and is the highest of all Catholic rites, it can be maintained that the Church does not deny the highest prerogatives of her communion even to those who have lived and died out of her jurisdiction. The only thing she cannot grant in this case is a public display of any kind. The objects of prayer in the present case have never *publicly* belonged to her; and besides, it might be wrongly interpreted by those who constantly reproach her with a grasping spirit, and a desire of enlisting into her ranks even those who have *protested* against her. Thus Catholics follow on all occasions and with due prudence the precept inculcated by the eminent author of *Church and State*, namely, "the duty of practicing brotherly love toward those of other communions. They are not, in fact, considered as members of another communion; they belong to the Church in spirit, though foreign to her organization."

The same doctrine has been maintained by a still higher authority than Cardinal Hergenröther—by Pius IX. himself, to quote only one of our Supreme Pontiffs. All are fully aware how strongly he insisted on answering *non possumus* to all those potentates and proud statesmen who required of him anything he felt bound not to grant. To the knowledge of all he openly declared that " there

is only one true Church " and that " out of her there is no salvation." He consequently protested against all attempts at withdraw-
ing from the pale of this Church—as they do at Randall's Island—
any of those who were born Catholics. He exposed in the *Syllabus*
the modern errors invented for undermining the Church's action
on society at large, and particularly on Catholic commonwealths.
These measures and axioms of the Sovereign Pontiff are precisely
those against which the strongest arguments of our pretended unsectarian managers are based. It is but fair to examine the explanations Pius IX. gave of them on a most solemn occasion.

In an allocution to the Cardinals assembled at Rome on December 9th, 1854—ten years before the publication of the *Syllabus*—
the Pope had occasion to speak of a new sect just appearing in
Germany, whose members took the name of Old Catholics and became thenceforth notorious in Germany and Switzerland. Among
the propositions they already advocated there was one which the
Pontiff at that time condemned, and which was afterwards reprobated again in the *Syllabus*. Its purpose was to maintain that
" there is *good* hope of the eternal salvation of *all* those who are
not in the Church of God." This certainly was opposed to Catholic doctrine, and the Pope could not but condemn it. But what he
said on this occasion and on this subject deserves a serious consideration, because the supposed consequences derived by Protestants from the condemnation of this proposition were precisely had
in view by the Pontiff, and his decision on the subject must be acknowledged as perfectly satisfactory by all men of good faith.

" Far be it from us," he said, " to dare to set bounds to the
boundless mercy of God ; far be it from us to desire to search into
the depths of the hidden counsels and judgments of God, an abyss
that the mind of man cannot fathom. . . . . We must hold as of
faith that out of the Apostolic Roman Church there is no salvation ; that she is the only ark of safety, and whosoever is not in
her perishes in the deluge. We must also on the other hand recognize with certainty that those who are in invincible ignorance
of the true religion are not guilty on this account in the eyes of
the Lord. And who will presume to mark out the limits of this
ignorance according to the character and diversity of peoples,
countries, minds, and the rest ? "

On another occasion (in his Encyclical to the Italian bishops,
14th August, 1863), Pius IX. used the following words, which cannot leave the smallest loophole to the blame of the caviller. " It is
known to us and to you that those who are in invincible ignorance
of our holy religion, but who observe carefully the natural law and
the precepts engraved by God into the hearts of all men, who feel
disposed to obey God and lead an honest and upright life, may,

aided by divine grace, attain to eternal life. God, who sees clearly, searches and knows the heart, the dispositions, the thoughts and intentions of each, by no means permits in His supreme mercy and goodness that any one suffer eternal punishment who has not of his own free will fallen into sin."

In point of fact, would it not be absurd that the Church should indorse the proposition of the "Old Catholics," namely, " that there is *good* hope of the salvation of *all* those who do not belong to the Church," since she teaches even her best children that their salvation is uncertain ? Was not St. Paul himself " afraid of becoming a castaway " ?

To the Catholic reader the previous discussions must appear mere commonplace : but they are necessary for those who have never gone deep into Catholic teaching. Moreover, it must be said that the considerations which have been so much insisted upon are simply side issues. Even should we not be able to answer a word to the difficulties raised by our adversaries, the *main* issue of the question is sufficient for all purposes. This, namely, is the clear text of the constitution both of the United States and of the several states. The *non-sectarian* party might go so far as to call for a change in this fundamental law of the nation. It must be done in order to deprive us of our rights. The liberty of conscience for the citizen, however, is written not only on parchment countersigned with the seal of a state, it is besides deeply engraved in the hearts of all Americans ; and what is more, the public peace and safety require it, owing to the multitude of denominations in this country.

The state legislature cannot enter into the discussion of those questions which have just been called *side* issues, because religious topics are out of its competence. Some men have lately pretended that on account of this want of power in the field of religion, the legislature's duty is to leave the whole affair in *statu quo*, and allow fanatical managers to have their own way. This would be a gross sophism ; and the question must rest on its *main* issue in which the legislature is perfectly competent. Is not the state of things such as it exists in many places an open violation of the fundamental law of the country ? and is not the legislature competent to pass bills whose object is simply to secure the execution of this fundamental law ? What has the good order and discipline, and cleanliness of any establishment to do with the true safeguard of the whole country ? Any board whose ideas of discipline, cleanliness, and order are in contravention of the fundamental law, must either change its discipline or disappear. The liberty of the citizen is not to be sacrificed to the petty spirit of routine set up by any set of men. This is but strict justice, and the claim of justice in this country is always heard sooner or later.

Why should a few institutions be the only ones where peace cannot exist together with one of the supreme laws of the nation? The answer to this simple question is left to the right-minded American reader.

THE PROPOSED AMERICAN CATHOLIC UNIVERSITY.

THIS country is practically without a great university. Spanish America boasted of some in other days, but they are gone, or exist only as a shadow of former greatness. The recently established University at Quebec is still struggling with the obstacles that prevent its entering upon its expected career of usefulness.

The collegiate institutions in the English colonies, out of which our Republic has grown, were all based on the plan of the universities at Oxford and Cambridge, as those seats of learning came forth dwarfed and crippled from the destroying and study-despising epoch of the " Reformation." As the universities lost with Catholicity the very idea of their creation, the copies were indeed far removed from the true ideal. The narrowness and insular character of the training and knowledge imparted by the universities in the seventeenth and eighteenth centuries was strikingly seen in the vast difference between the cultured Catholic gentleman who had been trained in a continental university, and the Protestant squire whose education was limited to Oxford or Cambridge. One was versed in the schools of philosophy, science and mathematics of the day, versed in ancient and modern literature, familiar with art and architecture, in its history and best examples, the other was tolerably familiar with a certain range of Latin and Greek authors, and could occasionally make passable Latin verses, but that summed up for most their whole stock of acquirements.[1]

The great universities of Europe were the creations of the Catholic Church and an outgrowth of her life; where that life was sapped, that Church proscribed, the university lost much of its real

---

[1] That this may not be supposed to be an exaggeration, we need but read what Cardinal Newman wrote : "About fifty years since, the English university, of which I was so long a member, after a century of inactivity, at length was roused, at a time when (as I may say) it was giving no education at all to the youth committed to its keeping, to a sense of the responsibilities which its profession and its station involved."

motive for existence and much of its real effectiveness. In the intellectual and scientific development in England, the universities, since the " Reformation," have contributed but little. The progress has been not within their walls or effected by their scholars, but from without, and they took part tardily, if at all, in movements whose spring and origin were found in vigorous and untrained minds, under no obligation to those institutions for their fostering care. In philosophy the English universities are inferior to the Scotch schools in power and influence ; in mathematical sciences, England was so far behind in the last century, that when she at last adopted the Gregorian Calendar, one of the best mathematicians she could find to take the necessary steps was not one who had won honors at Oxford or Cambridge, but a proscribed Catholic bishop whose very presence in his native land was almost high treason.[1] In the study of language the universities have followed an old routine, while the general study of the subject, certainly a fit subject for university training, was ignored, ignored even in its application to the tongues spoken in the British isles. Indeed, this study has been so strangely neglected, that not only the best works on the Anglo-Saxon, but even on Celtic grammar, are the work not of Englishmen, but of Germans ; and the development given to Aryan studies is due not to the universities in England, but to the studies of scholars encouraged by a company of shopkeepers.

The Church, an active living body, an army set in array, created the universities as her auxiliaries, and, age by age, equips them to meet the foe before her. The Catholic university, to carry out the real design and justify its existence, must grasp all forms of knowledge and intellectual activity, and guide men through all by the unerring standards of a faith that has the God of truth Himself for its source. The distinguishing vice of scientific men in all times is self-conceit ; religion is a yoke which chafes many of them, and as a rule they make light of it ; but, while they denounce religion, they have the heartiest disdain for the scientific views as held half a century before their own day, and for anything called science of an earlier period they have nothing but the most withering contempt. Each glides down the stream of time to meet the treatment he has given his predecessors, and the Church, with her deposit of supernatural truths irradiating the whole scheme of human knowledge, looks serenely on, beholding blindfold science condemning error, but dexterously avoiding the truth to which she would willingly guide them.

The Church from her infancy fostered learning. No religious system of the older time ever made such efforts to instruct man-

---

[1] Bishop Walmesley (Signor Pastorini).

kind in human and heavenly knowledge. The old world had its schools; the learned philosophers, rhetoricians and sophists had their schools, but they were without uniformity or system; they did not spring from religion or uphold it. The Church was from the outset a comprehensive teacher; but, though instruction was general, the great object was the training of the men who were to minister at her altars, and who were to be the guides of the people. Cathedral and monastic schools arose with the trivium and quadrivium; courses of study directed rather to the practical wants of parochial clergy than to the mere acquisition of learning for its own sake. A sufficient mastery of theology, to insure correct instruction, especially on dogmas which had been assailed by recent heresies; rhetoric, to fit them to announce the word with efficiency; dialectics, to enable them to bring propounders of heresy to definite issues and refute them; music, for forming choirs to the Church service; astronomy, to regulate the calendar, and the movable feasts of the year; arithmetic and geometry, to fit men to become the architects, engineers and artists of the structures which the Church created in all parts of Europe,—monuments that a century of dense ignorance destroyed, but which our more enlightened ones are fain to copy. Our modern diocesan theological seminaries, in the same spirit as the old cathedral schools, aim to fit priests for parochial work; and the monastic schools still live, training religious for their especial work.

As the state of Europe became settled after the fall of the Roman Empire and the submission to the Church of the conquering barbarians, there were many scholars in cathedral school and monastic cloister whose taste and leisure prompted them to a wider range of study than the course usually pursued. Monasteries became depositories of the laws and adjudications of sovereigns, as well as of treaties between monarchs. Their force and bearing were sought at the hands of the learned men in whose custody they were, who became legists, jurisconsults, diplomatists. Men, who had no vocation for the priesthood, acquired learning to benefit by the legal knowledge of the monasteries which, to temper the savage legislation of the northern tribes, introduced the civil law of Rome and the wise canons of the Church. England, alone, clung obstinately to her old system, and retains to-day many of the barbarous elements which Germany, and other continental states, rejected centuries ago; and English and American judges have more than once had occasion to pay tribute to the wise and equitable influence exerted by the Church in favor of human rights. As it was with law, so it was with other branches. The ancient works on diseases, their nature and treatment, were in the hands of learned priests and monks, with no competitors but men, chiefly Jews, who had been trained in the Saracen schools where the works of Greece were translated and studied. Men studied medicine under the clergy. As the number of the isolated scholars, pursuing special studies, increased, there came the sense of the need of a general institution of a higher grade where the great objects of study could be pursued. To meet the want, the Church created the University, for to her alone is due the honor of establishing and directing that form of educational institution. The faculties embraced were mainly four, and each university, as one after another sprang up, acquired renown for a special faculty, as Salerno for medicine, Bologna for law, Paris claiming a primacy in all. The general course embraced theology and philosophy as (essential and primary), jurisprudence, and medicine. Latin was cultivated rather as a vehicle than a study. Literature as distinct from the classic authors was yet almost unknown, and mathematical and scientific studies had not yet so developed as to claim an equal state with jurisprudence and medicine, but were still left to individual study and special schools.

Once universities were founded, they increased in number, in influence, in scholars, till they became like cities of learning. This continued for several centuries; and with them grew up the close reasoning, the scholastic forms, the methodical and comprehensive treatment of each department of knowledge. The "Reformation" was a revolt against learning as much as it was against the Church and its doctrines. The fickle and illogical Luther exhausted his power of vituperation in abusing the schoolmen, whose logical reasoning left him no chance of escape. The success which he and his imitators obtained by pandering to the greed and ambition of princes, to the lusts and self-indulgence of all, closed many universities and stripped others of all usefulness. Theology and philosophy sank in Protestant countries to be mere forms. Where religion depended on the will of the sovereign or a variable private interpretation of Scripture, it could not assume a form that would bear a close philosophical analysis. Each sect could live only by denouncing Rome and its rivals, and averting close scrutiny of its own claims. A summary of Protestant doctrine, like the Summa of St. Thomas Aquinas for Catholic doctrine, is impossible. The logical part would lie in a nutshell; the illogical would require libraries to state and refute. Though Protestantism began by declaring the Bible to be the religion of Protestants, it at once began by suppressing part; of course, the Maccabees, which denied the power of the state as against the Church, and maintained the independence of the Church, could not remain in the Bible of those who made all religion depend on the will of the monarch. It formed its canon and text of Scripture at random and without regard to the general teaching of Christendom for centuries, and without any critical study of the original Hebrew and Greek texts. The Protestant universities of England to this day have never contributed the least to Biblical criticism, and as they incline to revealed religion or atheism, adopt either Catholic or German rationalistic critical theories in the slight attention they pay to what, in their theory, constitutes their religion. . Nor have they ever treated the sacred books as literary productions, studied them as classics. Religion was practically excluded from the universities, and theology came to be regarded as a science that had no place there at all. Hence, when the Catholic University of Ireland was founded, Cardinal Newman deemed it necessary to show at length to those biassed by the English university idea, that theology had properly a place in university training.

Civil and canon law were, with the " Reformation," banished from the English universities, although the former held its own in the great German institutions. Thus, in the idea of English speaking people, the idea of jurisprudence as part of a university course was lost. Unfortunately, too, in England and the United States, the bench is recruited from the bar, and the judicial and legal professions, which ought to be distinct, are confounded; and no schools exist for training men for the minor and more exalted positions as magistrates. Jurisprudence, as a science, can scarcely be said to be recognized in English-speaking countries. The faculty of medicine retired to special schools, and science founded its own for the study of its various branches. Of course, it is not the province of the university to stimulate invention or discovery, to open the way to the study of hitherto unrecognized or misunderstood powers in nature ; but where knowledge has been acquired and systematically treated, a university which professes to treat all knowledge cannot ignore it. The study of the nature of man and of the universe from the standpoint of science, is fully within the scope of university training. Ignored by universities, this study has grown up outside of universities and their influence, and as these studies tended to sap Christian faith, the universities, by ignoring them, afforded no corrective, but sent forth their students cultivated men in a certain sense, but not strong men ; in fact, men who, meeting at the onset theories they had never learned to grapple, were more likely to adopt than refute them.

The English universities, the type of early American institutions, are certainly inadequate. This is now felt generally in the United States by the institutions founded here. They have hitherto followed to some extent the classical training of England, but the tendency is now general to abandon it and make Greek and Latin, with their literature, merely optional studies. The collegiate institutions in this country seem destined to die away into special schools. Philosophy is out of the question. Religion is to be eliminated, and, as Dr. McCosh recently reproached the President of Harvard, most of the American colleges have become or are becoming infidel, Harvard keeping up a divinity course with almost as many professors as it has pupils.

The time has come in American life when a university is imperatively needed, a real university, not in name but in fact; and a real university can be created only by the Catholic Church. The Catholic University of Ireland came into existence at the call of the Venerable Pontiff, Pius IX. He suggested its establishment to the Catholic hierarchy of Ireland, and surely he deemed that the cause of religion required it. The suggestion came from no passing fancy of a wayward ruler. Cardinal Newman, called upon to aid in organizing the great work, said: "It is the decision of the Holy See; St. Peter has spoken; it is he who has enjoined that which seems to us so unpromising. He has spoken and has a claim on us to trust him. He is no recluse, no solitary student, no dreamer about the past, no doter upon the dead and gone, no projector of the visionary. He for eighteen hundred years has lived in this world; he has seen all fortunes, he has encountered all adversaries, he has shaped himself for all emergencies. If ever there was a power on earth who had an eye for the times, who has confined himself to the practicable and has been happy in his anticipations, whose words have been facts and whose commands prophecies, such is he, in the history of ages, who sits from generation to generation in the chair of the apostles, as the Vicar of Christ and the Doctor of his Church."

What was the position of the Catholics in Ireland at that time? There were about half as many bishops, half as many priests, half as many Catholics in Ireland then as there are this day in the United States. The resources of Catholics there must have been in even greater disproportion compared to those of our body in this country, and the poverty more widespread. If the Sovereign Pontiff deemed it necessary that Ireland should then have its Catholic university, there seems to be no ground for denying the fact that one is needed in this country. Canada, a mere colony of Great Britain, lying on our northern frontier, took to heart the words of Pius IX. as a general recommendation, and created the Laval University. We have moved more slowly; yet the idea of a Catholic university in the United States is older than the project of that in Ireland; and it has required only the active zeal and energy of some member of the hierarchy to induce the Catholics of this country to do what the late Sovereign Pontiff called upon Ireland to establish. The Rt. Rev. Bishop of Peoria, John Lancaster Spalding, trained in university life in- Europe, and fully conversant with its advantages, has been earnestly attracting the attention of the Catholic body to his great work; and the Fathers of the Third Plenary Council gave it their warm approval and indorsement. Rome has not spoken, indeed, but who can doubt that a learned Pontiff like Leo XIII. will encourage and commend it? There are difficulties, doubtless, in the way. At first the want of means to erect suitable buildings was made an objection. In reality this was unnecessary; a university could be organized in leased as well as in purchased houses. But that there will be no lack of means is evident from the spontaneous offerings made by wealthy Catholics, led by the generous Misses Caldwell, whose names will remain for all time as the foundresses of the great Catholic work.

Again, it has been objected that we have none fitted for a university course. It is not easy to understand this fully. If the Laval University and the Catholic University of Ireland can find students able to follow their courses of study, and each institution has American pupils, as other European universities have, why cannot a similar institution in the United States obtain scholars? There are nearly sixteen hundred ecclesiastical students in the diocesan seminaries of the country and the colleges and houses of study in the United States. Some of these will certainly, in the natural course of things, seek a higher divinity training than· the short term of the usual theological seminary; if not members of a religious order having a higher theological school, they will seek what they desire in some European university. Were there a Catholic university here, with its professors of theology, holy scripture, ecclesiastical history, and canon law, surely there would be at the very lowest one hundred who, after passing through a seminary, would gladly avail themselves of the opportunity of pursuing a higher course in the halls of a university. The selection of professors for dogmatic and moral theology, patristics, holy scripture, canon law, ecclesiastical history and rites, can entail no difficulty. The professors of the advanced theological school at Woodstock College, men already known far and wide by their close and accurate theological learning and reasoning, the Sulpitians of St. Mary's, the Redemptorist professors who have made Ilchester famous, the studious Benedictines, the Lazarists, the faculties of the seminaries at Overbrook, Milwaukee, Troy, and elsewhere, give men not only safe and learned, but suited to the class of minds whom they are to guide; and, moreover, the great universities abroad can, if need be, send able men for the work. In the school of theological learning there need be no lack of students able to follow the course with advantage, and no lack of learned men to impart the knowledge. Few of the young men of our time and country, who are not destined to the priesthood, will follow a course of theology, it is true; but the time may come when many will see the importance and value of such study. Indeed, many a Catholic, in the busy walks of life, trained at a Catholic college in youth, now regrets that he had not gone through a course to make him familiar with the doctrines of the Church, its polity, its influence on nations and government, social and political life, as well as its government, religious orders, discipline, ritual. And he finds no book at hand to which he can recur, where he can find all these treated in a form that he can read with satisfaction and pleasure. For the knowledge that he can acquire for use in daily intercourse with intelligent men who really wish to obtain information on these points, he must depend on desultory reading in papers and periodicals, occasional lectures and incidental passages met with in the books he reads. It is no exaggeration to say that ere long, in a country of thought like this, there would soon be men following the course of theology, to acquire knowledge for its own sake, not feeling themselves called to the priesthood.

That a university can scarcely deserve the name unless the faculty of theology is strong and comprehensive, Cardinal Newman showed ably when combating the idea that had grown up in the British Isles from the forced and unnatural exclusion of that science from the great English universities. But here we are free to follow out the true Catholic idea, unbiassed by the example of any so-called university hoary with age, which has made its errors and follies a precedent for others to follow at their cost.

In the proposed university there will be no difficulty in regard to the faculty of theology. All will admit that it is essential to the idea of a university, as the exposition of truth by the teachings of a divinely guided Church. The professors are to be obtained, we may say, in our own country, and eminent men of other lands will not refuse chairs if we go abroad for them; the pupils, in number sufficient for a nucleus, can also be obtained, men preparing for the higher work in the ranks of the secular and regular clergy, and even occasionally men who expect to take their place among the laity.

The next faculty, that of philosophy, will be attended by many aspirants to the priesthood, but by a far larger body of young men who will justly regard a more thorough course of metaphysics and ethics as of high importance in their training for future professional and political life. The active minds of our countrymen are tending to philosophical studies here as they long have tended in Scotland. There, narrowed to insular and erroneous schools, the study has borne but poor and scanty fruit. Here a university, giving to the world in its lectures a sound course of philosophy, would attract general attention, lead to discussion, and ultimately acquire an enviable position. It is the course which, perhaps, more than any other, will give the university its standing in the minds of thinking Americans. What Dr. Brownson effected as a single individual, will be effected in a degree that we can now hardly realize by the philosophical faculty of a Catholic university. The course of study, we know, will be conducted in Latin, but its whole substance, the discussion of particular topics and heads, will in English reach readers in all parts of the country, be weighed, examined, challenged perhaps, doubted, and ultimately accepted by many.

The faculty of philosophy presents, therefore, no difficulties, but has a most promising field; for while there is abundant unreasoning prejudice against Catholic theology, as it is seen distorted in a warped mirror, there is no settled unreason to which men have sworn allegiance that will prevent them from yielding to the dictates of reason. Men may follow the *Encomium Moriæ* as their religious guide; they will not accept it as their standard of sound reason.

The faculty of jurisprudence will be new, but its fitness will not be questioned by thinking Americans. In a land of states, each with a constitution where men really sought to embody the soundest principles of right and justice, and from time to time seek to remedy defects in a similar spirit, with a national government binding all together, and framed in a spirit of concession, all will recognize that the study of the essential principles of human government, of individual rights, of the extent of the powers of rulers, of the divine sanction, must be, for all who take part in public life, one that deserves the highest attention. That we have had no institution where the great principles underlying all governments, the powers of the ruler and the governed, the responsibility of the lawmaker, and then ultimately of the force of law, its execution, its definition, the rules to guide the decision of courts, the rights of the citizen in the various capacities and their consequent duties to the government and to his fellow-men, are made the matter of thorough and exact study, is certainly a misfortune. The faculty of jurisprudence in universities like that of Bologna often became the arbiter between prince and people, between rival cities and states. The faculty of the proposed university may never attain that rank, but it will find scholars and exert an influence. If it does no more than give courses on civil law, it would meet a want felt in all parts; for that law, the basis of the law in Louisiana and the States in the southwest, underlies, too, all the equity and chancery courts, as well as those affecting admiralty cases, and is intimately connected with international law. The faculty of jurisprudence will be timely; it may be slower of growth, but its necessity will be admitted, and there can be little fear that it will not command enough scholars to justify its existence.

The faculty of jurisprudence ought to be a real one, and not a mere adoption nominally of some existing law school; nor should that of medicine be made by affiliating a school of anatomy and medicine, even though all the members were Catholics. They would be mere barnacles or excrescences on the institution, and as has been sadly demonstrated in Canada, will draw the university from its proper work and involve it in dissentions and disputes from which the real faculties of the university must feel to keep aloof. It would be far better to make no attempt to establish such faculties, unless they grow out of the university idea, are in harmony with the other faculties, actuated by the same spirit, and aim at the same results. The attempt to elevate schools founded independently, with a life and spirit of their own, into component parts of the university will be fraught with mischief. The university should be homogeneous in all its parts, actuated by one spirit and one consensus of ideas, not a mere collection or association of independent schools.

The faculties of arts and sciences are more easily understood, and are those which in the popular sense many consider the real and active part of the university, as being that to which the English universities dwindled when they no longer possessed the animating vital spirit of Catholicity. We need something of a higher grade than any institution we now possess, and if these have not always attained the success expected from them, it may well be that they did not aim at the highest and most effective course, and failed to give satisfaction, or deemed it better to meet the wants of the many rather than of a select few, who might elsewhere or by their own exertions supply the deficiency. That the collegiate training in this country is inadequate is conceded on all sides, and heads of colleges from Maine to California meet to discuss the situation and its remedy.

With the declining taste for classic literature and the languages of Greece and Rome, came the passion for athletic exercises, carried to such an extent that they seem to be the main and essential element of university life in many non-Catholic institutions.

Some, strangely criticising the project of a university, sanctioned as it has been by the hierarchy of the United States assembled in Plenary Council, tell us flippantly that we need parochial schools rather than a university. It is not possible that those who say this really mean that those who have passed through Georgetown, or Notre Dame, or Fordham, or St. Louis university, or Rock Hill, or Mount St. Mary's, or Woodstock, or Troy, or North East, ought to go through a parochial school in order to acquire a completeness for their education. Yet when we speak of a university, we speak of something for young men of this class.

In regard to parochial schools, considering all that Catholics have been called upon to accomplish, much has been done both in regard to the numbers taught and the nature of the instruction afforded, although equal exertion has not been made in all parts of the country.

The question of a university is one entirely distinct from that of the gratuitous education of the poor, and the steps to be taken to save them from influences hostile to their faith, by so training them that as they must by God's providence grow up Americans, it shall be as Catholic Americans.

The question of a university is an entirely different one, and the Sovereign Pontiffs, while encouraging parochial schools, have been as explicit in regard to the necessity of universities.

Why did Pope Pius IX. advise the Irish hierarchy to establish a university? " Has the Supreme Pontiff," asked Dr. Newman, " done so, for the sake of the sciences, which are to be the matter, or rather of the students, who are to be the subjects of its teaching? Has he any obligation or duty at all toward secular knowledge as such? Would it become his Apostolical Ministry and his descent from the Fisherman to have a zeal for the Baconian or other philosophy of man for its own sake? Is the Vicar of Christ bound by office or by vow to be the preacher of the theory of gravitation or a martyr for electro-magnetism? Would he be acquitting himself of the dispensation committed to him if he were smitten with an abstract love of these matters, however true or beautiful or ingenious or useful? Or rather, does he not contemplate such achievements of the intellect, as far as he contemplates them, solely and simply in their relation to the interests of revealed truth? Surely what he does, he does for the sake of religion. . . . . And if he encourages and patronizes art and sciences, it is for the sake of religion. He rejoices in the widest and most philosophical systems of intellectual education from an intimate conviction that truth is his real ally, as it is his profession, and that knowledge and reason are sure ministers to faith."

The faculty of arts takes the range of classic literature and the studies connected with it, and in the history of literature comparing modern with ancient works of renown. The study of history and its underlying principles, the conflicting elements, which ultimately bring all human governments to an end; with the history of the gradual discovery of the parts of the world unknown to the ancients, and the occupation and colonization, by civilized Europe, of far distant lands where it planted Christianity and civilization.

Our civilization, with its literature, art, science, laws, and government, is an outgrowth of the civilization of Greece and Rome, springing mainly from tribes which were in a comparatively barbarous phase when Greece had venerated for centuries the masterpieces of poetry, eloquence, sculpture, architecture, painting, metalwork, in which utility was combined with the graces of art. To this fountain we naturally turn, for though the models were long since adopted, they are, by the common consent of mankind, still unsurpassed. The masterpieces of Greece, approached most nearly by those of Rome, are still immeasurably in advance of all that we can boast. But our civilization, though drawn from these nations, is modified by the heaven-guided civilization of Palestine, the civilization of a people comparatively children in all but their higher and clearer knowledge of the relation of man to God and of the Creator to his creatures. Its literature modifies that of Greece and Rome to form our actual civilization. But the faculty of arts is blended with that of science, and Cardinal Newman well distinguishes the two. " Science has to do with things, literature with thought; science is universal, literature is personal; science uses words merely as symbols, but literature uses language in its full compass as including phraseology, idiom, style, composition, rhythm, eloquence, and whatever other properties are included in it."

The faculty of science, embracing mathematics, does not, in a university, seek to rival technical schools, or to make its scholars chemists, mining, civil, or military engineers, architects, painters, or sculptors ; but it takes these sciences in their present condition, reduces their phenomena to system, and shows their relation to theology and other branches of knowledge—their compatibility with the teaching of faith. So in mathematics, while in previous courses of study the practical application was more especially the aim, the professor in the university takes the whole subject as a matter of intellectual study to consider its meaning and bearing rather than to seek out in what way this knowledge is to be made advantageous to man.

If political economy is treated in such a university, it will be on Christian and Catholic principles. As generally understood, it is the science of wealth. The seeking, within due bounds, of a competence for the support of the individual and those whom he is bound to care for, is just and lawful; but the grasping of wealth, merely for itself, is dangerous and too often the occasion of sin. Wealth, as it accumulates, seems to fascinate men as the serpent does the bird, and, as a spiritual writer remarks, we speak of men of wealth, because men seem to belong to wealth rather than wealth to men; they become its slaves instead of being its masters. Political economy is a science of which it has been wisely said "that if studied apart from the control of revealed truth it is sure to conduct the speculator to unchristian conclusions." From the chair of a Catholic university this science would be treated in harmony with the teachings of our Lord, and with the teachings of the Church, which honors evangelical poverty, and singling out the resistance to the promptings of avarice as a representative virtue, portrays in her office the Confessor as one "who hath not gone after gold, nor put his trust in money nor in treasures."

This is a brief and imperfect attempt to convey a correct idea of the work of a university as distinguished from inferior educational institutes, and of a Catholic university as distinguished from those with which English readers are most familiar. In the detail of the treatment of the various faculties, its scope will be extremely wide. Wherever a science, or even a question, becomes the subject of erroneous teaching either in the school or through the press, the university can and ought to counteract it by a sound teaching based on solid and recognized principles.

But, it may be asked, what has the Catholic Church and her doctrines to do with the thousand questions of the day? Would it not be better for the Church to confine herself, to confine her ministry, to the altar, the pulpit, and the catechist's chair? The answer is found in the very writings in which the questions of the day are discussed. Why do arbitrary governments, or liberal governments as they are called, but acting the tyrant as they too often do,—why do these governments and the anarchists, the systematized sansculottism of our century, alike regard the Church as their enemy, and make her the object of their unremitting hostility and assaults? Why do the scientific men, who treat the mind as a mere outgrowth of matter and man as a mere animal developed from irrational stock,—why do these men regard the Church as an enemy, and lose no opportunity to impugn her? Why cannot a school of astronomy discuss the nature and relations of the planets and stars without introducing accusations against the Church? Why must works on the origin of the American Indians and the structure of their language enliven the dulness of their topics by malicious innuendos and accusations against the doctrines and practices of the Church? Why do men, who hold themselves as truthful and honorable in the ordinary affairs of life, resort to falsehood and to every possible stratagem and trick to prevent Catholic ideas from influencing public opinion and legislative action? Why has history, as generally written, become, as Cardinal Wiseman truly said, a conspiracy against Catholic truth?

It is not difficult to answer. These men, all acting from different points, on different lines, recognize the Church as a great living fact, a great institution, a power, with a fixed set of doctrines, clear, distinct, logical, all interdependent, all mutually supporting each other, an institution which upholds some system they seek to destroy. They find its influence surrounding them like the atmosphere, pressing on them, penetrating into their very being, and they rebel against the Church. They acknowledge that the Church at all times can and must examine their theories.

There is, indeed, not a question, political, scientific, social, which can be treated fully without at some point reaching a position accepted or condemned by the Church, as it harmonizes or conflicts with revealed truth. And she meets the multiform error by her multiform presentation of the truth. Surely there can be no greater tribute to the majesty, the serenity, the wide-reaching power and influence of the Church than this consensus of the fallible, the fallacious and the false. While they recognize her as the universal teacher, can we question her right, her duty of showing herself clearly in the university form the reasserter of impugned truths, and their expounder in the clearest light by human intellect, to mankind?

Our country pullulates with strange theories on every possible subject, which show a mental activity, but they are in the main wild, not from innate evil, but from the fact that men have been trained with false ideas and false systems, and whether following them or breaking from them, can reach no safe conclusion while their premises are false. The Catholic university will save the next generations of Catholics from being drawn into any of these schemes, and will send out its envoys of truth fitted to enlighten and save many who are groping in darkness and would be thankful for light. Men everywhere are breaking away from Protestantism, satisfied of its hollowness; and we should have and must have master minds, fully imbued with the spirit and teaching of the Church of God, who can show these active, logical minds where the real basis of truth is, expose the weakness of the theories that attract them, and bid them render the homage of their intellect to that God whose spouse the Church is, and who illuminates her to do His work.

The Catholic university must come. The present generation seems ready to undertake it. Means are not wanting, professors and pupils will not be wanting. We may not live to see it, like Alcalá, number its thirty thousand students, or, like Paris, have all civilized nations represented; but if it is not cramped and thwarted by half-hearted assent and real opposition, we shall see an institution producing a host of intellectually trained priests and laymen whose influence will be felt in every department of thought, who can make the American contributions to literature, science and the arts instinct with the life and the light that can come from but one source, Divine Truth.

ST. CHARLES BORROMEO AND HIS BIOGRAPHERS.

Histoire de Saint Charles Borromée, Cardinal Archevêque de Milan,
   d'après sa correspondance et de documents inédits.   Par l'abbé Ch.
   Sylvain, Chan. honoraire, membre de plusieurs sociétés.   Collection historique.   Société de Saint Augustin.   Desclée, de Brouwer
   & Cie.   Lille, 1884.

The Life of St. Charles Borromeo. Cardinal Archbishop of Milan.   From
   the Italian of John Peter Giussano, priest and Oblate of St. Ambrose.   With Preface by Henry Edward Cardinal Manning,
   Archbishop of Westminster.   Burns and Oates.   1884.

ON the eve of the tercentenary of St. Charles, a new Life of the
      Saint appeared in French.   Almost simultaneously with it
the Oblate Fathers published, under the auspices of Cardinal Manning, a translation in English of the old and well-known biography
by Giussano.   The two works are distinct types of their kind;
the one, a sort of autobiography, inasmuch as it consists in the
main of data furnished from the vast correspondence of the saint,
the other, originally written by an intimate friend, a daily witness
to the truth of what he writes some fifteen or eighteen years after
the death of the saintly cardinal.

   Apart from the relative value of the two lives thus written from
different standpoints, the Abbé Sylvain has been the first to give
pointed expression of—and in a manner to supply—a want which
must have been felt heretofore by many admirers of the great
saint.   And so far the latter work constitutes a criticism upon that
of Giussano and his followers.   Its author shows how the conception we form of St. Charles from the older existing biographies
must needs be partial and incomplete, and he leads us to a height
whence we may view him differently and more to advantage.
From that elevation, too, he points out mines hitherto in great
part unexplored, whence we may gather precious material wherewith to raise a monument at once worthy of the saint and useful
to posterity.   He himself has collected some stones from these
hidden treasuries, and offers them, fit tribute of love and gratitude,
to his holy patron, in the hope that they might serve some master-
hand in future days to rear the edifice, which he modestly, yet
withal justly, confesses he has not attempted.

   And, in truth, the more we examine the subject, the more must
we become convinced how inadequately the ground really occupied

by the great archbishop has been covered by his historians, numerous and singularly favored in their tasks though they were. We see in him the austere and humble cardinal, friend of the poor and of plague-stricken Milan; the priest of God, consumed with burning zeal, to whom the honor of His Church was dearer than all other glory, and who defended her rights with a courage proportionate to that zeal. But we know hardly anything of his early boyhood; of the influences that were at work in forming his mind and heart, particularly during his years of study at Pavia. We can form no proper estimate of his qualifications as a statesman, vindicating the action of Pius IV., if not wholly from the charge of nepotism, certainly from that of imprudence, in making the young Count Borromeo Cardinal Secretary of State at the early age of twenty-two. Giussano and his co-laborers give us no true idea of how far the saint deserves to be accounted one of the most influential patrons of letters both ecclesiastical and secular, and in some respect of Christian art. Yet, it is true that, in those troubled times of political and social upheaval, it was St. Charles, above all other men, who raised the moral and intellectual level not simply of Italy, but of the greater part of Europe, by his direct interference in the action of foreign courts. These are subjects that have hitherto received but the most passing and unsatisfactory attention; unsatisfactory all the more when we consider the vast material which is actually at the command of the writer who, with adequate ability, might undertake the task of utilizing it. Canon Sylvain has, as we have said, pointed out the most important sources. He has searched the correspondence of St. Charles, together with other pertinent documents, and, as the result of his labor, he places before us letter upon letter, making a united whole that lays open to us the thoughts, feelings and motives which guided and accompanied the actions of the saint. Yet all this, whilst it gives us a more correct outline of St. Charles than we have had hitherto, is still but a small part of his history. Oltrocchi had drawn, long years before, from several of those sources to which our attention is newly called; and his excellent notes to the Latin edition of Giussano's work are in many instances, as Sylvain himself attests, precious chronicles and full of profound and rare erudition. The English translators have availed themselves in many instances of these notes.

But, when we remember that the history of St. Charles is perhaps more the history of his times than that of any of his contemporaries; when we see the vast amount of authentic manuscript-matter that offers itself to elucidate much of that history which was hitherto doubtful or wholly unknown, we can hardly content ourselves with what has been actually put before us in the form of biography, even though it were given us in a manner and in a spirit that could satisfy our actual needs. Yet, herein also we lack. If the history of all great men, but especially that of the saints, be given to posterity for its instruction and emulation, account must assuredly be taken, not only of the time in which they lived, but of our own time and selves. Not, indeed, as if the present offered always, or even generally, a proper balance by which to determine the motives of the past ; but the present cannot receive the lessons of the past, unless in its own language, interpreting the meaning of the old characters. Enough is being constantly said of the ceaseless and rapid growth of the human mind ; of its swiftly changing attitude towards absolute standards of morality and truth, to dispense us from entering on the subject here. It will not be denied that, whatever flaws and sophisms this tendency of changing thought has been employed to cloak, it forces upon all teachers of truth the necessity of casting a different, hitherto unused, light upon old-standing facts ; of taking emphatic notice of all the countless microcosms which arouse the eager zeal of impatient students ; nor to be slow and hesitating in doing so, for the art grows daily longer, and life with its opportunities in all much shorter.

The life of St. Charles is of course in an especial manner the pattern of the priestly life. " The character of that saint," says Cardinal Manning in his Introduction,[1] " will be best understood by reading his life." And he singles out what might be termed the prominent feature of that life. " The work of St. Charles was the renewal of the pastoral fervor of the Good Shepherd." His model is in this respect of more than ordinary importance to us, because ours " is the age of pastors, and to every pastor's heart St. Charles is dear."[2] And as if to emphasize this characteristic view of the saint, he adds that " he was not a great theologian, or a great orator, or a great statesman. But he was a great pastor," etc.[3] Such is in reality the impression we receive from reading Giussano's book. But when we take up Sylvain, our estimate of the great saint gradually changes.

> Tum partes auctus in omnes
> Crescit in immensum.

Even if his published works or his connection with the council of Trent, which was not confined to an activity of a merely executive or pastoral nature, does not in our eyes entitle him to the name of a great theologian, the voice of his contemporaries seems to yield him that right abundantly. His knowledge in every branch of theology was, we are told, simply extraordinary. He

---

[1] Preface, page xxii.   [2] Ibid., xix.   [3] Ibid., xxii.

never gave an opinion—and the wisest heads, both clerical and lay, in Europe often sought it—without citing at once the authority of councils, or canonists, or theologians, and this with a marvellous correctness and precision.[1] " His library," says Carlo Canneta, " was one of the richest and most precious in Italy." [2] We know how incessantly he used it at night and on his travels. Truly, he had asked God and wisdom came upon him, " the spirit of understanding, holy, one, manifold, subtile."[3] (Wisd., chap. vii.) Not all his writings in which that gift is manifested are published. Besides, many of the best theological works of that day were written under his inspiration and at his suggestion, by disciples and friends, as we shall have occasion to notice. Whether he was a great orator is difficult to say. He was assuredly a great preacher. The defect of enunciation which had hampered his speech in earlier years yielded to his unwearying efforts, and so well did he succeed in this that, says Sylvain, " like a new Demosthenes " he began to exercise a singular fascination by his sermons upon all who heard him. As for his written discourses, they are models of lucidity, elegance of expression, and full of erudition.[4] There are some eight volumes of his sermons in the Ambrosian library at Milan, still unpublished. Some of them are written in a different hand from that of St. Charles, most likely Possevino's, who himself relates in his account of the saint[5] how he used to take down the sermons whilst they were being preached. In order to form some estimate of the talents of St. Charles as a statesman, one need but read Bascapé's account of his political connections, of the correspondence that passed between the cardinal and the Roman pontiffs, or the chapters in Sylvain's book entitled " St. Charles and France " and " St. Charles and the Princes of Europe." [6] If Giussano did not bring out sufficiently all these traits, it was, no doubt, because his own bias leaned—as all his still extant works show—towards the pastoral virtues of St. Charles, which he himself had learned so well to imitate. No wonder, then, that this should constitute the all-pervading feature of his book. Yet it is plain, at the same time, that however edifying or otherwise useful that life may prove to the average reader, we are not enabled to obtain from it a sufficiently correct and complete view of the saint, so that it is no exaggeration to admit, with Sylvain, that

---

[1] Sylvain, vol. iii., pp. 277–280.   [2] Ibid.   [3] Ibid., p. 266.

[4] A modern critic says of these sermons : " Des sermons . . . . . l'on remarque de l'élégance, de la methode, un style simple et naturel, et un ton de douceur et de piété qui attache et touche singulièrement. Le style des discours au clergé a plus de noblesse et d'élévation." (Bibliographie univers., art. Charl. Borr.)

[5] Discorsi della vita ed attioni di Carlo Borr. (Roma, 1591, page 46.)

[6] Sylvain, vol. ii., chaps. 35 and 36.

"the holy archbishop of Milan has not as yet found his proper historian."[1]

It may be opportune, then, to consider the question of what would constitute such a history and how far the elements of it are already given and within our reach. Accordingly, it is not so much our purpose to review the two above-mentioned biographies,[2] as rather to make them the occasion of passing a general glance over the entire biographical field of St. Charles Borromeo. Or, to state our object more precisely, it touches three points. First, to ascertain in some measure the real value of the written lives of St. Charles Borromeo and to see how far they are of service in the composition of a history at once worthy of the subject and equal in importance to the material offered for use. This will be partly done by noticing in brief the leading intellectual and moral qualities of the writers, as well as the opportunities with which they entered upon their work. In the second place, we shall point out some of the sources whence the principal material may be drawn, and particularly those to which Canon Sylvain directs our attention. Lastly, we shall ask ourselves in what spirit a history of St. Charles should be properly conceived, considering the nature and extent of the above-mentioned resources on the one hand, and the high order of the subject, together with the just aim of such a work for our times and conditions, on the other.

When Giussano, still in the mid-vigor of his life, retired to the fertile and lovely district of Monza, there to mourn the loss of his dear master, and to devote himself to a life of pastoral charity and literary labor in the same spirit, he had, apparently, no thought of writing a life of St. Charles. Before a few years had elapsed after the death of the saint, other men had done so, and their works bore the stamp of ability and love. When, therefore, on the eve of the canonization of the holy cardinal, Giussano took up the task at the request of Frederico Borromeo, he was able to avail himself of the collected labors and judgments of several writers of acknowledged ability and trustworthiness. These latter did not,

---

[1] Sylvain, avant-propos, page ix.

[2] We might here say that the English translation requires a careful revision. If Sylvain's work, which was evidently in the hands of the translator, was made use of in correcting Giussano's text, it has not been done consistently throughout. Notice, for example, the statement on page 465, vol. ii., as contradicting page 8, vol. i. There are other material errors not warned against in the *errata*, as vol. i., 347; vol. ii., 185, 417, etc., besides some annoying inaccuracies in the paging of the Index.

It is to be regretted that the otherwise superbly gotten-up edition of Sylvain should contain any disfiguring misprints, such as *amorte* for *amore* in the illuminated frontispage, and elsewhere. Why the author prefers throughout to write Bescapé for Bascapé we are at a loss to know. If some Italian writers have followed that spelling, it is evidently a local corruption for the originally adopted name Bascapé, a contraction for "Basilica S. Petri."

of course, contain the detailed testimony of the heroic virtue of St. Charles, brought out in the process of canonization, but they summed up as much in brief from their own experience. Giussano makes mention of the work of Cardinal Valerio, who published a life of St. Charles[1] as early as 1586, that is, two years after the saint's death. Two other noteworthy publications which he occasionally cites are *The Life and Actions of St. Charles*, etc., by Possevino,[2] which appears to have been the first written in the Italian vernacular; and *The Life of St. Charles*, by Bascapé,[3] which had been printed in two editions before Giussano began his work. In fact, there must have been a great deal in the form of biographical attempts of more or less importance before that time, as Giussano himself says: " Many of the cardinals of Holy Church have written in praise of St. Charles."[4] Among those written in foreign tongues he mentions an English life, of which there appears, howeve:, no remaining trace.[5] Botero, another of the saint's secretaries, had already published a collection of the letters of St. Charles.[6]

All this, together with the papers belonging to the Ambrosian library, the documents of the process of canonization, and, in fact, the bulk of the material lately re-examined by Sylvain, was placed at Giussano's disposal, who was requested by Cardinal Frederico, nephew of the saint and his second successor in the See of Milan, to write a life of him, in order to give fit expression to the celebration of his canonization. It appears from the circumstances that not very much time was allowed him. But he was the only one of the illustrious household of the late cardinal who enjoyed the privilege of literary leisure,[7] and had the necessary qualifications for the task which the intents and purposes then required. Yet, looking at the matter from our own standpoint, and at the character of the men who could have been induced to take up the work, we regret almost that it was not intrusted to other hands. There is every reason to believe from what we know of Valeria and Bascapé, of whom we have the earliest biographies above mentioned, that they would have brought to the work, at this stage of its history, not simply ability of a far higher order, but a more comprehensive view

---

[1] Vita Caroli Borromei, Verona, 1586.

[2] Discorsi della vita et azioni di Carlo Borr., Roma, 1591.

[3] De vita et rebus gestis Caroli card. archiep. Mediol., Ingolstadt, 1592; Brescia, 1602.

[4] Vol. ii., p. 273.

[5] Vol. ii., 280. A note suggests that the life here alluded to was probably written by Father Campion, S. J., who had known the saint personally.

[6] Preserved in the library San Sepolcro, Milan.

[7] Almost all the private secretaries and other superior officers of St. Charles' household had, at this time, been chosen to fill important positions as bishops, papal legates, or ambassadors to foreign courts. See Sylvain, vol. i., p. 337.

of the entire subject than did Giussano. The latter's character was marked by a singular devotion to St. Charles, a burning pastoral zeal, and, as we judge from his occupations during the life of the saint, a certain talent for finance and economical administration. But both Cardinal Valeria and Monsignor Bascapé, and we might even add Possevino and Botero, were men no less remarkable for their saintly lives, whilst they joined to this a consummate knowledge of the world, superior literary tastes, and, what above all we miss in Giussano, a keen appreciation of those subtler qualities which made the saint incessantly active in creating that under-current of moral purification in the political stream of his day, wherein these very men had served him as instruments in raising the tone of European court society. They would, in short, have given us a more historical, more influential, whilst no less attractive and edifying, work. They were, in fact, the principal historians, both ecclesiastical and civil, of Milan at that time. As secretaries of St. Charles, they, with the exception of Valerio, acted as his diplomatic agents and legates in foreign lands. They knew him fully as intimately as, and loved him no less than, Giussano. As for Valerio, he could bear ample testimony to the worth of St. Charles in the sphere of theology, philosophy, science, and the arts ; for he had been one of the first who gathered around the young Cardinal Borromeo at those brilliant evening coteries in the Vatican palace, where the genius and culture of the best society, clerical and lay, of Rome assembled for the purpose of mutual intellectual and moral improvement. And later St. Charles had, out of Rome and Milan, no dearer friend, no wiser counsellor, nor more generous colaborer in his furtherance of learning and of social beneficence. What these different biographers of St. Charles wrote about him may by all these accounts be supposed to have its value. Still, there is only one of the number, besides Giussano, whose work has really survived to our day, having been repeatedly published both in Latin and Italian, and that is Carlo Bascapé. This fact of itself sufficiently indicates that his history of St. Charles differs in some respect from that of Giussano, which has been hitherto most popular, and, especially with important additions by Oltrocchi, justly so. How far later writers, as Godeau[1] and Touron,[2] have adhered to the texts of their predecessors we cannot say,[3] both being, we believe, more than a century out of print.

Comparing Giussano and Bascapé, we shall probably obtain some estimate, sufficient for our purpose, of the entire body of biogra-

---

[1] Vie de S. Charles Borromée, Paris, 1747; 2 vol.

[2] La vie et l'esprit de Saint Charles Borr., Paris, 1761; 3 vol.

[3] The writer of art. S. Ch. in Michaud's Biogr. Univ. says of these: "G. avait composé une vie de St. Ch. qui est trop succinte. Celle de P. Touron est trop diffuse."

phers, which they may be said to represent. Both resemble each other in many points. They labored together, side by side; accompanied the saint at all times and in all sorts of affairs; they enjoyed in an equal degree his fullest confidence, and neither of them yielded to the other in devoted and affectionate attachment to him. Almost equal in age, of the best families in Milan, their tastes were high and of a cultivated character, they having received the best advantages of the education of that time. The tone in which Giussano habitually speaks of his friend assures us how highly he esteemed him. Indeed, there is a certain romantic parallelism in the circumstances which brought them under the influence and into the service of St. Charles, as we shall presently see. Like brother spirits in all things, they differ only in the particular bent of their genius—and in this differ, like the subjects of all their writings, their histories of the saint.

Giussano, a young Milanese nobleman, we find spoken of in the annals of his native city as a successful and highly promising physician at the early age of 19. Almost at the same time the aula of the Pavian University rings with the applause from an admiring assembly of dignitaries and students upon the first brilliant defence of a young lawyer, a patrician by birth, Giovanni Francesco.[1] At once he is appointed to his native city of Milan and entered upon the list of noble jurisconsults. But the world of cabal and intrigue ill suits his discerning love of justice, and the frank and noble youth turns with lofty disdain from the tortuous ways of high-born associates. Unwilling to prostitute his genius or his eloquence to low designs, he seeks St. Charles for advice. The result is that he forsakes the world, dons the ecclesiastical garb, and places himself at the service of the saintly cardinal. In the episcopa palace he meets Giussano, who, too, having recognized the vanity of earthly pursuits, had denied the beck of ambition and entered the community of Oblates of St. Ambrose. Both youths had yearned, indeed, after retirement, but St. Charles, whilst he permitted them to give their vows to religion,[2] reserved to himself the right to employ them in his service. He felt how valuable both their talents and the pure ardor of their zeal would prove to him; for the son of Margherita de' Medici had inherited not only the magnificent appreciation of culture which had distinguished his illustrious relatives, Cosmo and Lorenzo de' Medici, but, as the living historian of Milan, Cesare Cantù, assures us,[3] he possessed that singular gift, the supreme art of administrative power, which

---

[1] He assumed the name of Bascapé later on entering religion.

[2] Bascapé joined the Clercs Regular of St. Paul.

[3] Storia di Milano del Cav. Cesare Cantù; p. 184, vol. i. of Grande Illustrazione del Lombardo-Veneto, 1857, Milano.

quickly recognizes the symptoms of true worth and sterling ability. And he knew how to single out and gather around him,[1] as well as most fitly to employ, the men who would prove useful to the Church in its then crisis of reform. "And about him was the ring of his brethren, and as the cedar planted in Mount Libanus. As branches of palm trees they stood round about him, and all the sons of Aaron in their glory."[2]

This is one of the most striking features in the economic activity of St. Charles. We distinctly trace in the labors of his many secretaries and officials, long years after his death, the direct influence which he inspired for some line of work. He had marked out, as it were, the field to each, suitable to their peculiar talent, and when his word and cheering look were no longer there, his spirit still hovered over them, and under the charming spell of that stewardship they kept on laboring until they would meet him beyond the tomb to give him their account. Certainly, the persons who occupied positions of trust in his palace were not, in any case, simply well-trained or highly competent officials who obtained a natural and ready insight into his affairs and were pledged to the customary bond of diplomatic secrecy. They were his most intimate friends, bound to him by a sincere and reverent affection, which arose from his disinterested care for his subjects and the daily example of his virtue. Thus they did not merely copy for him, but from him. They labored in his spirit and carried out his every suggestion with a readiness which made it, in effect, a command. And whether we view him as the priest or the statesman, as the missionary toiling along the narrow pathways of the Alps, or as the munificent patron of science and of art, as the ecclesiastical reformer knowing no mercy but the mercy of God, or as the adviser of kings and of princes—in each case these men whom he held around him were but so many copies of himself, doubling his work in an undivided spirit. Thus we find the young Bascapé exercising his legal and diplomatic skill in arranging the affairs of St. Charles in the latter's capacity as grand protector of the several kingdoms, as adviser and representative of the princely houses of Italy, with most of whom the Borromeo family was connected by marriage or descent. We see him principal agent in adjusting the tangled difficulties between the Spanish government and the see of Milan. In 1581 he is actu-

---

[1] In Rome, among the literary circles, St. Charles was well known as a "rapacissimo ladro di savj," for he never went there without carrying away to Milan some of the best talent. He had in his household not only members of the various religious communities, but men of almost every nationality. There is a curious letter of St. Philip Neri to the Saint, wherein he refuses to allow the illustrious Cesar Baronius, of the Oratory, to join St. Charles's household at Milan. Vid. Vita St. Phil. Neri (Boll., 26 Maii).

[2] Eccli, l., 13, 14.

ally on his way to Portugal to find the king, on precisely such a mission, of which he himself gives a detailed account in his Life of the Saint. When the latter breathes his last, Bascapé is at his bedside. He closes those dear eyes which had, thus far, been the light unto his own. Now, at length, weary with sorrow and the ceaseless toil of the past years, which had made him encounter through loving obedience the very intrigues from which once he had fled, he shall find rest in the solitude of his cloister. But no! He is only half-way on the path of life and not yet to lay down the burden of responsibility. His brethren elect him superior-general of his congregation. Here, during the scant hours of repose, when mind and heart revert to St. Charles, his first true love, he writes down his recollections of him to whom his hand would point as the form by excellence according to which the youth, now in his own care, might shape and bind their missionary zeal. The work was published for the use of ecclesiastics mainly, in seven parts and in Latin. It appeared first at Ingolstadt and soon after at Brescia. About this time Clement VIII. accidentally meets Bascapé. Charmed with his talent and humility, the pontiff sends him as bishop to Novarra. Henceforth his activity is absorbed in carrying out the lessons he had learned in the administration of the diocese of Milan, so faithfully, indeed, that, as we are told in the traditions preserved by local writers, the people commonly called him " un altro san Carlo."[1] And the recollections that had been to him his joy and strength, the breath, as it were, of his nostrils when at eventide he rested from his labors in his cloistral home at Milan during those eight years which he had spent there, were to become, in the latter end, the solace of his reflecting old age. During the last years of his life he himself published a beautiful translation in Italian of his *Vita S. Caroli* under the name of Luca Vandoni.[2] This was two years after Giussano's life had appeared, which in its turn was translated into Latin two years later by Bart. di Rossi.[3] We have, therefore, both Latin and Italian versions of the two biographies made during the lifetime[4] of these two men intimately connected with the saint. That there was no thought of rivalry is evident from the circumstances. From what we have said regarding the bent of mind in these two friends of St. Charles some idea may be formed of the different character of their writings. Bascapé

[1] Vid. Raff. Notari—Storia della letteratura Italiana.

[2] Bologna, 1614. It appears that a translation had actually been made by a certain Luca Vandoni (Vanione) who died before its publication. The MSS. were sent to Bascapé, and he, not being pleased with the work, re-translated it entirely under the original author's name. This we gather from one of his letters. (Ibid.)

[3] Bart. Rubeus, 1615.

[4] According to the writer in the Bibl. Univers., Giussano died in 1615, but this must be an error. Argellati, " Bibl. Script. Mediol.," assigns it to the year 1623.

is probably superior in style and critical quality, but less exhaustive and naturally less read than Giussano. The writings of the latter are all more or less of a pastoral theological temper; and this tone predominates accordingly in his view of the saint.

We said that Bascapé would, had he been commissioned to do so, have probably given us a more complete picture of St. Charles, a truer and in every way more excellent history of his life. It might be justly asked, why then did he not do so, since he wrote that life and afterwards even translated it? It will not be difficult to explain this, however, if we remember the time at and the object for which the latter composed his work. His charge at the time when he wrote was such as to induce him to give only a particular view of our saint. He never meant to write his history. It was rather a panegyric or a meditation on the life and deeds of St. Charles which he contemplated. He wished, for the purpose of imbuing his clerics with the spirit of their saintly patron, to leave them a memorandum of what he had seen, thus to perpetuate among them that inspiring presence which had often visited those very halls with young Bascapé by his side. In all else it was labor of the heart much more than of the intellect. But had he been given the leisure, had the purpose and scope of the work been set before him, together with all the material for a complete history, as was done in the case of Giussano, we can hardly doubt that a man of his mould would have reared an edifice which it was, perhaps, not in the nature of Giussano to conceive.

But we have laid special stress upon the character and activity of these two intimate associates of the life of the holy archbishop for a further reason beyond that of comparison between them. It was because we are thus enabled to judge to some degree of the value of their remaining works as a contributing source to the desired history of St. Charles. Both writers have left behind them considerable works reflecting the state of the Church and duchy of Milan in their day.

To Bascapé, above all, are we indebted for much original research. A beautiful style, vast and varied erudition and critical power, are marked characteristics of his writings and lend them considerable prominence in Italian literature.[1] Yet, like the letters of St. Charles, the bulk of his literary labors is far from being known or accessible to the public.[2] The same might be said of

---

[1] "Ingegno, dottrina, critica, lingua propria, stile vago e senza delicatezza ornato rendono preziose tutte le scritture del Bascapè." Raff. Notari—Storia della letteratura Italiana.

[2] His manuscripts, of which there are over forty volumes, are preserved in the Collegio San Marco at Novarra (Michaud. Bibl. Univ.).

Valerio[1] and other contemporary writers. Ripamonte, too, furnishes much lore on the subject of those times, which, however, is to be used cautiously, as he has been convicted of many material errors in his history.

Looking at the biographers of St. Charles, irrespective of their individual characteristics and differences, there appears in them one aspect common to all, and which has been brought out in the publication of some of St. Charles' earliest correspondence. The friends of the holy archbishop exhibit to us the saint, but in their affectionate regard they forget the man. As one of them, Gagliardi,[2] expressly says: " He attained to so high a degree of perfection that it is not so much to be imitated as rather to be held up for admiration." Whatever they saw in him bore the stamp of the supernatural. Nor need we wonder that they, who in the chivalrous ardor of their early years had fled to him for refuge, should behold in him the object of that loving admiration which not only realizes all the actions of its hero, but avoids with the instinctive caution of a lover whatever may be out of harmony with the sweet music of its worship.

> Specto cultum faciemque gradumque;
> Nil ibi, quod credi posset mortale, videbam.[3]

And yet it would be so much more encouraging to our poor aspiring nature to know how all came to be gradually supernaturalized. Giussano seems not to have realized this need. He does not even care to inform himself correctly concerning certain facts of the saint's earlier life, because they bear not with them the evidence of his sanctity. Hence arise errors, such, for instance, as the age at which the young Count Borromeo entered the University of Pavia. But it is a pleasant thought withal that this fault of the saint's biographers lay in their personal virtue. We, of course, account it more valuable, in our own struggle towards life eternal, to know that St. Charles once had faults, that he went much the ways of human prudence ere he recognized their feeble stay, that by essaying and finding wanting the world he renounced it gradually, struggling with common faults; whilst of a truth he always hated evil and was endowed with noble instincts, as many a man to-day who yet falls short of sanctity.

However, we cannot ignore that, though this attitude of devoted attachment was naturally an impediment to furnishing a history of

---

[1] Valerio's writings are of so exquisitely beautiful a style and merit that Card. Mai exclaims: " Invidiamo a un secolo che diede alla chiesa un tale vescovo e cardinale " (ibid., art. Ag. Val.).

[2] P. Achille Gagliardi, S. J. Documents of the Process of Canonization. Giuss., vol. ii., 277.

[3] Ov., Metam., iii., 610.

St. Charles such as we might require in these days of wanton skepticism on the one hand and slow and low aspirations to sanctity on the other, the time and circumstances of the earlier writers did not, perhaps, call for so complete a history. This appears corroborated by the fact, already mentioned, that the two lives by Giussano and Bascapé, written in days when the memory of the saint was still fresh in the minds of every one, went through many editions and translations up to our own day.[1] Later writers could hardly have changed anything in this respect; and an atmosphere of pure faith among the people where these lives were read prevented any realization of other wants. But of late there has been a momentous change in the world's psychical attitude. The universal spirit of investigation suddenly confronts us with problems in the concrete which not only were hitherto unknown, but never existed before. The real agencies, for example, that brought about and shaped the religious revolution of the sixteenth century have but of late had turned upon them a new and stronger light. And that this new knowledge, coming to us from old forgotten documents, is of real worth in this age of novelties, is amply attested by the unwearied activity among the archives of the Vatican library. Is Providence thus renewing the flagging interest to combat old and ever-recurring errors? Then it is well that we equip ourselves afresh, burnish and whet the old weapons, since their steel is the true Damascene and serves its purpose of striking down error better still than the new-fashioned sword of gilded brass and tinkling sound. At the same time, the development of the body requires a refitting of the garb. On this account, no less than because he has uncovered many dusty boxes of parchment and manuscript, owe we thanks to Sylvain. Botero, who had made his selection of the letters of St. Charles with a view to show the esteem and influence which the saint had enjoyed at foreign courts, played precisely the same part of secretary to the holy cardinal as Bascapé had done, and acted, in fact, as substitute of the latter during his absence in Spain. Soon after the saint's death, he was appointed ambassador to the Court of France by Carlo Emmanuele I., Duke of Savoy. In 1599 he went to Spain, acting a decided part in the administration of that kingdom whilst having in charge the education of the Princes of Savoy. These facts give evidence of his ability and so far of the value of his works, a considerable portion of which remains still unpublished.[2] He was the first writer who successfully refuted

---

[1] An edition of Bascapé's work—the latest we know of—was published at Lodi in 1858.

[2] Preserved in the library of Turin and said to be of much value (Mich., Bibl. Univers.).

the political theories of Machiavelli.[1] His works on social politics
are said to be equal to the best written on the subject.[2] Some of
those treating of ecclesiastical subjects were composed at the request of St. Charles.[3] Nor was he averse to the muses, for Vallauri
praises his poetry.[4]

During the last century a choice collection of letters was
printed in French by the advocate Pineault,[5] with notes and the
Italian original by the side of the translation. These letters are
said, however, to be of less importance and less numerous than
those of a similar edition which had previously appeared in
Lugano.[6]

Of decided importance are the documents, drawn from the
archiepiscopal archives, which the Abbé Aristide Sala has published.[7]

We must not leave out of sight the annotations that have been
made from time to time to the lives of St. Charles, and which in
some cases exceed in importance the works to which they belong.
Among them stands foremost Oltrocchi,[8] who annotated, as has
already been said, the elegant Latin version of Giussano's book.
Whether the Abbé Sépher's notes to Godeau's life[9] of St. Charles
have any specific value, we are not able to ascertain. It may
suffice to have pointed them out. We might here mention Sassi's
notes to the saint's own works.[10]

Leaving aside the ordinary sources with which a historian of the
time of St. Charles must and would naturally make himself
acquainted, we come to those more direct ones to which Sylvain
calls our attention. The letters he has examined and from which
he has culled to make up his biography, amount to some 30,000.
They are drawn from the secret archives of the Holy See, from
the registers of the various nuntiatures of France, Germany, Spain,
etc. In the city of Milan he has examined the archiepiscopal
archives, the treasures of the Ambrosian library, the library of the
Oblate Fathers, containing, besides thirty-one volumes of letters

---

[1] " Della Ragione di Stato," 10 vol. The work has been many times republished and
translated into almost all the modern languages and even into Latin. Bossuet has
modelled his " Politique de l'Ecriture Sainte " after it (ibid., art. Botero).

[2] Vide " Vite degl' illustri Piemontesi "—Conte Giamb. Napione.

[3] As titles like " De praedicatione verbi Dei, lib. v., jussu Caroli Cardin. Borr. editi,"
indicated.

[4] Storia della Poesia in Piemonte. Thom. Vallauri (ex R. Notari).

[5] Paris and Venice, 1762.

[6] Michaud, Bibl. Univers., art. Borr Charles.

[7] Documenti circa la vita e le geste di San Carlo Borr., publicati per cura del Ca-
nonico Aristide Sala. 4 vol., c. suppl. Milano, 1857–1863.

[8] Edit. Mediol., 1751.

[9] Vie de S. Charles B., corrigée, augmentée et ornées de notes. Paris, 1748.

[10] Opera omnia S. C. B., cum notis. J. A. Saxii. Mediol., 1717.

written by the saint to eminent persons, a detailed digest of the process of canonization. At the Barnabite convent " ai Catinari," in Rome, he found a large collection of authentic copies of letters made evidently a short time after the saint's death. He seems, moreover, to have had access to some private libraries containing original documents, such as that of the Marchese Trivulzi. Over and beyond all this, he has wisely inquired into the traditions religiously handed down in the convents and among the people of Milan. And before presenting the fruit of his gleanings to the public, he submitted it, in the main, to the superior-general of the Oblates of St. Charles at Milan.

We ask, in passing, whether there be nothing in the library of Vercelli, which is said to be rich in valuable manuscripts, since we know that St. Charles left his MSS. by testament to the Bishop of that see? It is noteworthy, too, that in those times the city of Milan had its regularly appointed historiographer, kept by the municipal government.[1] A certain Bugati[2] is mentioned about this time. A few years later we read of Ottavio Ferrari, who has left much of local history. Less known, but perhaps more serviceable in this connection, may prove the writings of Francesco Bernardo Ferrari, uncle of the last mentioned, who was one of the first directors of the Ambrosian library,[3] and went to Spain for the purpose of collecting material for the same. He had seen the saint and was greatly devoted to the interests of the Borromean family. Some effort might also be made—we should think successfully—to recover part of St. Charles's library, from which, according to the extant catalogue, the most rare MSS. are missing, said[4] to have been carried off by the French, who were lodged in the library of the cathedral chapter during the days of the Republic.

We have repeatedly, in the course of these notes, alluded to the desirability of having all this heterogeneous mass of lore concerning the history of St. Charles placed in a certain order and light which would be more true to the memory of the saint, and probably more acceptable to his lovers and imitators. What most impresses the modern reader of the old lives is the careful avoidance of all that might tend to destroy the beautiful ideal image to which in truth St. Charles corresponded only in the latter end. Aside from this, we are constantly kept in mind of the predominance of what was supernatural in his life, and that frequently by the relation of

---

[1] Cantù remarks, rather sardonically: " La città aveva allora una istituzione che la cianciera vanteriò del nostro tempa non oso rinnovare, cioè uno storiographo." (Storia di Mil., p. 216.)

[2] Gaspardo Bugati, † 1588.   [3] Opened formally in 1609.

[4] Vid. Archivio Storico Lombardo. September, 1882. (Cited by Sylvain.)

facts unquestionably true, yet which of themselves and as related bear the interpretation of most obvious and natural occurrences. Both features are easily explained. They accorded at once with the personal attachments of the writers and the mental attitude of the people for whom they wrote, possessed of a spirit of simple faith, with the living monuments, created by that faith and serving as an ever fresh impulse to act according to its dictates, around them. For the people of Milan do not believe that St. Charles is dead: " Mortuus est pater ejus et quasi non est mortuus." Yet, however satisfactory this mode of writing the saint's history may have been to a generation no more, it is tellingly insufficient for the present. Not that we would or could consider the manner of the old writers as in any real sense a fault. They simply do not cover the space which our eyes can take in now that we stand on different ground. On the other hand, we should in some cases have to shade our sight, grown unaccustomed to certain strong lights from our habitual bending towards the earth. The lives of great men are much like paintings. The artist, however grand his subject, however great his own inborn genius, may fail from want of attention to *technique,* to what is called the proper pronunciation, the bringing out into sufficient contrast his lights and shades. His picture may be all neutral tint or *sepia ;* and then our first impression would be that it is a study merely. No matter, then, how otherwise perfectly finished, it does not appeal, as works of lesser merit might do, to certain predominant sentiments within us. Or even supposing that there were no such deficiency of accentuation in the work, that, moreover, we who look at it were possessed of all the requisite knowledge which would make an appeal to our æsthetic faculties possible, still, in order that the picture should speak to us, it would be necessary to take a certain distance between it and ourselves, to get a certain light upon it without which it could be seen but partly or distorted or blurred. Nay, not the light alone that falls upon the picture, but the light that falls upon ourselves is of importance. A picture seems different when we view it with the broad reflection of noontide upon us, or from the dark corner of a gallery. So is it precisely with our view of the history of St. Charles. We have a grand subject. But they who delineated it for us failed to give it that becoming *claro-oscuro,* that interesting piquancy, which has become a kind of necessity to us, who are much influenced, whether we will or not, by the wares offered in our marts of taste and intelligence by Doré, Wagner or Marian Evans. It might be a symptom of a generous soul to clamor for the staid old honest faith of bygone times, or to avow that truth, above all truth about God's saints, should not be tempered because of a simpering society that derides what it cannot estimate the value of; but it would hardly be in accordance with the tactics of prudent charity to alienate the weak and lose our chances of profiting a society to whom we owe a duty. A doubtful champion of ancient prowess in sooth were he who first puts Richard's armor on our youth, and bids them fight as did of old their sire! To kill is not at all times to conquer. So, in the lives of the saints there are phases which the devout must admire and most of us will rightly understand and reverence, but which to the great body even of Catholics will have no meaning and create in some a skeptical and aggressive spirit. Many of the saints are simply miracles of God's holiness and omnipotence. They are to us like sudden lights revealing the simple fact of the supernatural in tangible form, so as to set us thinking of that fact and of our destiny in consequence. But this is not the case of all, nor even of the majority of canonized saints. It is not so, we are quite sure from the facts before us, of St. Charles Borromeo, who seemed raised not merely as a stupendous luminary to rouse us into energy of admiring submission to God's holy law, but who is to serve as a beacon-light in our narrow way, passed over before, step by step, by one who differed from us only in this, that he had to grope his path with more care, and did not lose his courage till he reached the end of it.

Cardinal Newman tells us that when he had read the life of St. Antony written by the holy anchorite's friend, St. Athanasius, he felt convinced of his extraordinary greatness.[1] Nevertheless, he seems to have felt it incumbent upon him to defend that saint in the eyes of believing men from the charge of having been an exaggerated visionary. Indeed, even the average reader in good faith of that life of a saint, pictured by another saint who knew him personally, and whose veracity and intelligence are alike above suspicion, would experience something of that feeling. " Had St. Antony lived in this day, and in this country, he would have been exposed to a considerable—though of course not insuperable— temptation to become a sectarian."[2] It is obviously wise, then, to anticipate the necessity of repelling analogous charges. This can be done by giving to such works that cast which would produce views and feelings harmonious and congenial to our own, without abating in the slightest the truth, but without at the same time placing, with no sufficient reason, in the foreground facts, however true of themselves, yet not likely to be rightly and quickly apprehended by the general reader. St. Paul himself calls the attention of the Corinthian preachers to this manner of setting forth truth. He draws the distinction between " speaking in tongues " and

---

[1] Miscellanies. Hist. Studies, VI.
[2] Ibid., page 74. Edit. 1872.

"prophesying." By tongues he means the mysteries of faith as set forth by the word of God; by prophesying he means the interpreting of them so as to rouse others to piety. " I would have you all to speak with tongues," that is, to study and meditate the holy law, "but rather to prophesy. He that speaketh in a tongue edifieth himself; but he that prophesieth edifieth the Church. Unless you utter by the tongue plain[1] speech, how shall it be known what is spoken ?"

As to recognizing that the saints had their faults—and that this was not only the case with such as St. M. Magdalen or St. Augustin, who were suddenly converted by some miracle of divine grace, but with the great body of those who struggled onward with unwearied zeal until habit overcame habit and begot that " inward character" which necessarily follows from frequently repeated acts of virtue—it will hardly weaken our admiration for them. The heroism is only the greater whereby action begets sanctity than if it were the reverse. " The lingering imperfections of the saints surely make us love them more without leading us to reverence them less and act as a relief to the discouragement and despondency which comes over those who, in the midst of much error and sin, are striving to imitate them."[2] And this is in accordance with the general meaning of the term sanctity as applied in ascetical theology. St. Isidore[3] interprets the term *sanctus* as *sanguine tinctus*, that is, having undergone that process of purification by which a person or thing, before in a manner unclean, is rendered a pure and acceptable instrument for the service of God. Hence, sanctity is that quality of the human soul by which the latter disposes itself and its actions towards God, in order to the proper worship of Him.[4] " Let us remember," says St. Ambrose,[5] " that the saints were not of a superior nature from our own, but rather more observant of the law ; they were not without faults, but they amended them." " Is not holiness the result of many patient, repeated efforts after obedience, gradually working on us, and first modifying and then changing our hearts ? Thus the separate acts of virtue are of service to us, as gradually severing us from this world of sense, and impressing our hearts with a heavenly character."[6]

And surely this element duly observed in modern hagiography

---

[1] Εὔσημον, *i. e.* bene significantem, intelligibilem.   Corn. a Lapide ad 1 Cor. xiv., 5 *sq.*
[2] Histor. Sketches, J. H. Newman, vol. i., p. 13.
[3] Lib. Etymol.
[4] St Thom., Summa, Sec. sec., quæst. 81, art. 8.
[5] " Discamus ergo et sanctorum invidiam, ut imitemur patientiam ; et cognoscamus, illos non naturæ præstantioris fuisse, sed observantioris ; nec vitia nescisse, sed emendasse."—Lib. de S. Joseph, in Off. Dom. III. Quadrg.
[6] Miscell., Holiness and Fut. Blessedness.—J. H. Newman.

will serve all the better the purpose for which the Church holds out to our veneration and imitation the saints whom she places in honor upon her altars. If she claims their intercession in her militant state, she also wishes to inspire her battling children by their heroic example : " Be followers of me, brethren, and observe them who walk so as you have our model."[1]

In this sense, no less than in view of the different special avocations in the priesthood, all of which St. Charles united, as it were, within himself, may his life be considered as an eminently practical pattern of the priestly life to-day. Its attentive study will not only show to us what it is under the grace of God within our ready reach to accomplish for the kingdom of heaven without and within us, but it will also mark with a peculiarly apt emphasis for us what it is needful in these times for us to do. So did we understand our Holy Father Leo XIII. when, lately in the assembly of ecclesiastical students gathered from every quarter of the globe, to do honor to St. Charles, he recommended urgently the imitation of the saint. Keen in the penetration of the needs as of society so of the priesthood, he lays emphatic stress on the pursuit of science and letters. St. Charles, he said, was a priest not simply of signal charity and apostolic zeal, but he was a man possessed of extraordinary and extensive knowledge. And so he was. A devoted student of the ancient philosophers, he began at Rome, in the midst of the countless distractions of an intensely severe official life, to give a new impulse to these studies in their proper direction, and thus he counteracted that excessive leaning towards the Pagan element brought on by the Humanists. He placed himself silently, but withal effectively, at the very head of secular progress. At a time when but few printing presses were to be found in Italy, we see him establish one in his diocesan seminary for the use of professors and students. And the persons whom he raised and inspired incessantly to labor in confuting errors, religious, social, or scientific, are the glory of their day. The most able men, whether in science, law, or theology, were the constant companions of his labor and his leisure, if indeed he can be said to have had leisure. The learned doctor, Ludovico Settala, a layman, is by his side during those dreadful days of the pestilence, never leaving him, whether in the haunts of the plague-stricken city or in the rough mountain-passes around the Lago Maggiore. All Europe tempts this man to accept its honors,[2] but he prefers the company of the humble cardinal.

---

[1] Phil., iii., 17.

[2] St. Charles had met him at Pavia in 1568. When Settala had passed his doctorate, at twenty-one years of age, he was at once appointed first lecturer of practical medicine at the university. Two years later, the saint called him to Milan, and made him

And what in all this is of importance to us is that the knowledge of the life and character of St. Charles will contribute to a revival and perpetuation of his spirit in our priesthood so as to exert its legitimate influence upon society at large. For, whilst every lover of that sublime calling must be anxious to see in its ministers the full growth of a spirit of prayer, of a habit of self-denial, of a pure and single-hearted faith, and an ever-ready charity, yet have we not found that these gifts alone are insufficient to check the wanton infidelity or to rouse into animation the drooping indifference of our present society? Nay, we want the very keenest apprehension of all the special needs of our time. The study of the world and of mankind is gained, indeed, by the study of our own hearts, with prayer guarding against self-absorption ; but no man has ever successfully studied his heart in the dark. We can arrive at no knowledge of ourselves, and consequently of the world of human hearts, without recognizing our surroundings, without making the world, as it were, the basis which somehow by its very existence will shape the angle of our introspection.

" The priest of our day," says a modern writer,[1] whose special task it was to know, " is cast amid a population partly hostile to his teaching, often mistrustful of his intention, but ever merciless to his weakness. That world it is impossible for us to win unless by a genuine ascendancy of our own superior character combined with an indefatigable self-devotion and the tenderest charity. Henceforth we shall have to prove even our right to be believed. Thus it becomes essentially necessary that we should recognize in its colors the social system of which we are a part ; we must become acquainted with its dangers and with its resources, its weakness and its strength, so as to be able rightly to use the one, nor be disheartened by the other." The life of St. Charles covers this ground much more than we would at first suspect, and this not only in principle, but in fact. Did he live to-day, he need hardly—as in the case of St. Antony—be other than he was three centuries ago, in order to command the same influence and achieve similar results. If the people of Milan are said to be the most religious people in the world, it is probably because its religious life is so intimately interwoven with the traditions of St. Charles. Wherever you turn, not only in Milan and Arona,[2] but

---

protomedico of the duchy. Shortly, Philip of Spain appointed him historiographer to the kingdom, but he declined. The Elector of Bavaria offered him the directorship of the University of Ingolstadt. Bologna, Pisa and the Senate of Venice made him similar offers, all of which he declined in favor of the laborious life with St. Charles. His works are all of a scientific and philosophical character, full of original research and observation. They were published both in Italy and Germany.

[1] Oratoire de France.—Ad. Perraud, in " H. Perreyve," by P. Gratry, p. 114.
[2] The birthplace of St. Charles.

all along the Lago, that tradition confronts you, in all its attractive vividness, to this day.   How the contadine, old and young, cling to that memory, uttering with lovely reverence the name of him

Di cui dolente ancor Melan ragiona,[1]

whose charities to their fathers long centuries ago are fresh upon them as if of yesterday.   And so far as ecclesiastical legislation is concerned in all its branches, the rules and discipline of the see of Milan, as instituted by St. Charles, are still the norm of nearly every episcopal see in the Western Church.   Sylvain makes us realize this and much more that casts new light upon the mental constitution of the saint.   He leads him to tell himself what he thinks and feels.   " Loquere, adolescens," he says, with Socrates, " ut te videam," and a new life,

ut sol, qui tectus aquosis
Nubibus ante fuit, victis ubi nubibus exit,

rises up before us.

Assuredly it is a great help to our knowledge of any man to have him explain expressly or unawares of himself, in his own words, the motives of action and the circumstances which prompted them.   Nor is there in this case any danger of lessening the saint's greatness.   But few persons in public life would willingly endure the indiscriminate publishing of their private correspondence. One can understand and appreciate the prudence of men like Sydney Smith, who called in all his letters before he died, because, as Chorley says, " he was averse to the misuse which could be made, according to the flagrant fashion of our time, of every scrap of written paper by literary ghouls who fatten ther purses in the guise of biographers."[2]   But it is very different with men like St. Charles. His aim had been, what precisely constitutes his merit in the eyes of the Church, not to do great things merely, but to do them singly and solely for the love of God.   Free from the bias of human censure and applause alike, what judgment need he fear who sought approval only in the eyes of heaven ?

Nevertheless, there might be an objection to an autobiography made up entirely of letters, even if we aimed merely at a complete picture of the person of the saint, without measuring the impulse of his activity by its results.   Just as we see the traveller in his true size when he begins to ascend the mountain, but gradually lose sight of him as he nears the summit, discerning no longer his proportions and only estimating his height by the very fact

---

[1] " That name never uttered without tears in Milan."—(Carey), Purg., xviii. 120.

[2] Autobiography, Memoirs and Letters of Henry F. Chorley.

that we see him no longer—so with the saints. We lose accurate measure of them as they near the summit of their heavenly Father's perfection. They become more and more impersonal as they go on. To our gaze they are no longer discernible in the same way as when they commenced their earthly pilgrimage up the mountain of God, where their self is gradually lost in Him who is their highest aim and end. Accordingly, their letters and words about themselves would really tell us less of them than we would like to know. At such a period it is a real advantage to have an estimate of them by men who were their friends and associates. This we have, as has been seen, in the life by Giussano and others. Sylvain has not entirely ignored them. He could hardly have done so without creating much useless labor for himself. But to complete a history, this may be done to a much greater extent, and many of the facts given us by Bascapé, Valerio, and others, may be wrought into the general plan by which a proper picture of the saint would be formed with its right historical background, so as to make it a true portrait and at the same time a genuine piece of art.

Beyond this it is a real advantage that three centuries have elapsed, allowing us an unbiassed judgment upon all there is of ripe and substantial fruit, giving forth the original seed. An ingenious woman [1] has aptly compared the work of contemporary history to that of the celebrated Arras tapestries. Looking over the shoulder of the skillful workman, each thread appears distinct as wrought into the composition. Still the whole is but a confused surface giving us no idea of the design, for we see as yet only the back of the carpet. But when, after years of labor, all is done, when the first assorted thread has found its match in the last, as cause and effect in history, then we come to form some judgment of the whole and may estimate the value of expended labor of brain and hand.

It may be our privilege to recur to the subject another time, giving some faint illustration of what can be gleaned from the material history of St. Charles, to which we have referred in these notes. Perhaps no one would be more capable of undertaking the grateful work of writing that history than the Oblate Fathers themselves. There is an obvious advantage in a number of persons engaging in such a task under the guidance of one controlling intellect. The Dominican Fathers have long ago given the example in their history of Dom Bartolomew de Martyribus,[2] one of

---

[1] Countess Ida Hahn-Hahn; Reisebriefe I. 102.

[2] " *La vie de Dom Barthélemy des Martyrs* etc. Tirée de son Histoire écrite en Espagnol et en Portugais par cinq Auteurs dont le premier est le Pere Louis de Grenade. Avec son esprit et ses sentiments pris de ses propres écrits." Paris, 1664.—

the most intimate friends of St. Charles.   But we need hardly point
to a model where we have a subject that of itself is so suggestive
as this great servant of God who was " commended for the gift
of discipline and understanding—eloquent, active, undefiled, sure,
sweet, loving that which is good—beneficent, gentle, kind, steadfast,
assured, secure, having all power, overseeing all things." [1]

————————

THEISM AND THE VISIBLE UNIVERSE.

Walks in the Regions of Science and Faith.   By Harvey Goodwin, D.D.,
      Lord Bishop of Carlisle.   Murray, 1883.

IT will have been observed by those who follow the current of
      popular literature, that a sharp dispute has arisen recently
between two agnostic philosophers as to whether an unknowable
God, an " Infinite and Eternal Energy, by which all things are
created and sustained," is or is not a fitting object of religious
veneration.   Into the merits of that controversy, which, from the
appearance in the lists of two other able combatants, has been
styled a quadrangular duel, it is not our purpose to enter; but we
avail ourselves of the lesson that is taught us by the fact of such a
discussion being continued month after month in the pages of a
widely-circulated magazine, and thus brought prominently before
the public eye, to suggest to educated Catholics the desirability
of acquainting themselves more and more with the solid grounds
on which their faith rests, and not only their faith in revealed
religion as taught by the Church, but also in natural religion,
or, to use the words of the Vatican Council (in its first canon), in
" one true God, of things visible and invisible the Creator and
Lord."   Modern sophistry calls in question the existence of such
a Being, and not merely in books such as are read chiefly by
thoughtful and studious men; but in miscellaneous periodicals, in
ephemeral publications, that meet us at every turn, and sometimes, though more rarely, in casual conversation.   It is well, then,
that Christians, exposed to so many incidental dangers of this

———————————————

This is in scope, of course, less pretentious than a life of St. Charles would be, owing
to the more extended influence of the latter saint.
   [1] Wisdom, VII.

description, should know something of the strength of their case, lest casual remarks, heard or read, should weaken their grasp on the vital truths they hold.

There are, of course, several valid arguments, such as man's natural reason can apprehend, for the being of a personal God. It is said by those who converse with the literary agnostics of the day, that they are little moved by the proofs drawn from design in creation, less so by moral considerations. Be this as it may, the recognition of God from His works in the visible universe is one that Catholics are not at liberty to disregard, as is manifest from another canon of the Vatican Council,[1] and indeed from the words of St. Paul in the Epistle to the Romans, where those who cannot read this lesson are said to be inexcusable. It is, therefore, well worth our while to inquire whether this time-honored argument can be presented in a really cogent form. It is sometimes said that it has been overthrown by the Darwinian theory of evolution; but that is probably because the *imagination* of men, more easily affected than their reason, is excited by a plausible hypothesis, which, without denying a Creator, tends to put Him as much as possible in the background. No doctrine of evolution accounts for the first commencement of organic life, or for the laws which every particle of matter obeys.

We ought, then, to welcome any contribution that tends to strengthen our position as to design in creation, even when it proceeds from one who is a stranger to our faith; and we think a special welcome is due to an excellent little volume from the pen of Dr. Harvey Goodwin, the Anglican Bishop of Carlisle, which deals very ably with this question. It is a collection of essays, reprinted with modifications and additions, which had previously been published in magazines, or delivered in the shape of lectures. Bishop Goodwin is a great mathematician; he was second wrangler of his year at Cambridge, and has since then been mathematical examiner in the University. We mention this to show that he is no mere novice in science, but on the contrary well acquainted with at least those branches of physical science which are based upon mathematics. In a religious point of view, he writes, with some slight exceptions, almost like a Catholic; in answering the sneer of an infidel writer about the morality of certain Popes, he lets us see that his sympathies are on the right side; and his tone is invariably reverent.

He explains in his preface that his book contains "the record of wanderings through that land which belongs exclusively neither

---

[1] " Si quis dixerit Deum unum et verum, Creatorem et Dominum nostrum, per ea quæ facta sunt naturali rationis humanæ lumine certo cognosci non posse, anathema sit." (De Revelatione, I.).

to science nor to faith, but appertains more or less to both." And he gives a caution (which some of our newspaper controversialists might well lay to heart), that the protection of the territory of morals and religion—a protection the necessity of which he fully recognizes—" if it is to be wise, righteous and successful, must take account of the nature of the attacks made upon it, and must not expend itself in charging windmills, nor court defeat by the use of antiquated or worn-out weapons."

The essays, though not entirely disconnected, yet to a certain extent have a fragmentary character which is slightly embarrassing to one who is endeavoring to state their substance concisely and without repetition. One cannot always avoid being brought back upon the same ground. We hope, however, to be able to convey a fair idea of their purport, or at least of the more important among them. There is also another difficulty, so far as the general reader is concerned: the author in several places introduces mathematical reasoning and uses technical phraseology, intelligible only to those acquainted with that science. We shall endeavor to give a sketch of the argument employed in those passages (so far as is necessary) in popular language, and insert in notes the strict mathematical details, which are, after all, of an elementary character.

We ought to observe that the first essay has but little to do with the main purport of the book; its subject is: "The Connection between Mechanics and Geometry," and it is a modified reprint of a memoir read before the Cambridge Philosophical Society many years ago. It will well repay the attentive perusal of any one familiar with the subject, showing as it does the close relation that geometry and mechanics bear to one another, and how the same symbols are applicable to both.[1]

The essay closes with the following words, after a prediction that the elementary truths of mechanics will gradually present themselves with axiomatic clearness: "It cannot, I think, be doubted by any one who has reflected on the foundations of truth, that this is the natural course, that all demonstrations tend to merge in intuition, and that human knowledge, as it becomes more dear and is more thoroughly apprehended, converges towards that absolute intuition which is the attribute of the Divine mind."

This is followed by an essay on "The Unity of Nature; a

---

[1] Those readers who know the principles on which the Calculus of Quaternions is based will at once see how it illustrates this connection; a point moving with infinite velocity along two sides of a triangle (taken in their proper consecutive order), arriving at the same position and at the same moment as another point moving (also with infinite velocity), along the third side; which side is therefore said to be *equal* to the two others.

Speculation,"—which, in fact, is one of the most important in the volume.

Bishop Goodwin lays down, as an indubitable fact, that there is a certain unity pervading nature. Theists, whether Jews, Christians, or Mahometans, virtually assume the existence of it. To them "the oneness of the creating mind implies a corresponding oneness in the created work;" phenomena apparently pointing in a contrary direction are treated as the almost necessary results of the partial understanding of a complicated system.

Now, he does not propose to discuss this theological aspect of the subject, but passes on to that which is scientific and experimental; and here the presidential address delivered by Dr. Allman to the British Association in Sheffield in 1879, furnishes him with a theme. "The ground-tone of that discourse, if I rightly understand it, is the unity of the principle of physical life, whatever that principle may be. Dr. Allman traces life up from the simplest form of protoplasm to its highest exhibition in the bodily systems of mammals and men." Again, "the life of the animal and the life of the plant," Dr. Allman remarks, "are, like their protoplasm, in all essential points identical." He illustrates this by stating that plants are capable of being acted upon by anæsthetics,—and the sensitive plant, when under the influence of ether, loses its peculiar properties.

The bishop, however, feels that the real difficulty of conception is this: Suppose all this to be true, grant protoplasm as the prime form of universal life, take the hypothesis of evolution to assist you, and still you find strangely different results; there is, as he says, "an enormous difference between a squirrel and a codfish, between a dog and a cabbage;" that is to say, the real difficulty is, that there should be so much *diversity* in nature, assuming it to rest upon one all-pervading principle. He thinks this combination of unity with diversity will never admit of a complete solution. Mr. Darwin's hypotheses and investigations may be described as an attempt to solve the problem; he waives the question whether the attempt has been successful, and suggests, as his own speculation, that there may be a law from which the existing order of physical life, with all its apparent anomalies, flows as a necessary result; and the knowledge of this principle or law, if attainable, might exhibit the order of nature to us as one consistent system. There must have been what he terms a "delicate adjustment of the initial circumstances"; in other words, the phenomena of the universe, including the existence of man, are easy to account for if you suppose an intelligent First Cause, but difficult otherwise.

He illustrates this view at some length by mathematical considerations. After alluding to the story that the acute mind of

Sir Isaac Newton regarded the propositions of Euclid as necessary truths requiring no demonstration, he speculates on the extent to which the intuition of geometrical truth, as also of mechanical science, can be carried. He suggests that the law of gravitation, as we now know it, that is, the attraction of every particle of matter by every other in the inverse proportion of the square of the distance between them, may be possibly reduced hereafter to a necessary truth,—meaning, apparently, not the fact of such attraction itself, but the law that regulates it—just as some other such laws are seen to be simple mathematical results which could not be otherwise than what they are.

Continuing his mathematical speculations, the bishop endeavors to account for the anomalies that seem to present themselves in animal life, by showing that there are also in astronomy certain things strange and unaccountable if astronomy were merely a science of observation like botany or biology ; that there are movements of the heavenly bodies which, to a person viewing them and judging of them *under such conditions only*, would doubtless appear to be utterly anomalous ; the great difference being that we happen to know the law that regulates the orbits of the heavenly bodies, and we do not know the law which has governed the many varied phenomena of biology.

May not, he asks, certain parts of the vegetable and animal kingdoms, though apparently useless, hold a place similar to that of comets or meteoric stones, which latter are really inseparable in connection from the more orderly planets ?[1]

---

[1] We know that if particles were projected with different velocities about a centre of force, the law of attraction being the inverse square of the distance, they would describe conic sections of one or another kind. We see in nature that the earth and other planets describe ellipses of small eccentricity, nearly circular in fact, and that comets move in orbits frequently resembling parabolas, sometimes, however, in hyperbolas ; in which latter case they use only *one* branch of the curve, which, nevertheless, consists of *two* branches mathematically inseparable. We happen to be acquainted with the law to which all this is due, but if we were not so, we should regard all these bodies as *anomalous*, much as we now regard some things in biology,—the existence of noxious snakes, mischievous insects, etc. Bishop Goodwin suggests that the nipples and lacteal vessels of male animals, the rudimentary feet of certain snakes and other unused organs of sundry living things, may possibly be like " branches of a hyperbola, involved in the definition of the creature, inseparable from its existence, and yet forming no part of its active life." And soaring to still loftier heights of imagination, he suggests that, as the variety of planetary motion corresponds precisely to the variety of the locus of the equation of the second degree, some other development of natural forces may correspond in variety to the locus of the equation of the third, fourth, or higher degrees, and that we may gain from our knowledge of the complications of such curves some notion of the variety of phenomena corresponding to the same development of natural force. Again, taking another illustration from pure mathematics, he alludes to an argument drawn by Babbage (in the Ninth Bridgewater Treatise) from the *conjugate points* of certain curves, to show the relation in which miracles may stand to the ordinary course of nature. Conjugate points stand absolutely separated

The object of this reasoning is to counteract the arguments employed against design in creation by the infidel school among the evolutionists, such as, for instance, the German biologist Ernst Haeckel, who denies the existence of " purpose in nature " and of the supposed "beneficence of the Creator "; the bishop's argument cannot be quite apprehended in all its force excepting by those who are acquainted with the technical phraseology of mathematics (and it is for such readers that I have given it in fuller detail in a note); but the drift of it is to show that the seeming anomalies, which cross us in our study of natural history, might vanish if we did but know the *law* to which they owe their origin. The orbits of the heavenly bodies do not depend *only* on that law of attraction which we term gravitation, but also on the conditions under which they were first set in motion; and if these conditions had been different from what they were actually in the case of the earth, if its orbit, in fact, had been similar to that of many comets, then the earth would not have been fitted to be the home of the highest form of life; this looks like the working of design, and we may infer in a similar way the " necessity of original delicate adjustment in the process of the evolution of a highly organized creature from a protoplastic germ."

A passage from a work of the late Professor Jevons is quoted which confirms this view : " The general tendency is, I think, to suggest that neither gravitation nor evolution carries us up to the prime cause of existing nature, or renders the hypothesis of such a cause unnecessary."—(*Principles of Science*, by Professor Stanley Jevons.)

The argument of Bishop Goodwin does not proceed, as we have already intimated, in regular logical order, from chapter to chapter; nor could it under the circumstances have done so. Thus the essay following the one last mentioned, entitled " God and Nature," is partly devoted to an examination of the position a scientific

---

from the curve's continuous branches, and to a mere ocular observer seem to have nothing whatever to do with them ; but their coördinates satisfy the equation of the curve, and they are then shown to be truly a part of it, algebraically speaking He proposes, therefore, to substitute the words *apparently anomalous* for miraculous in Babbage's argument, and thus to utilize it against the deniers of a Divine purpose in creation. If nature is the work of a beneficent Creator, the law expressing the action of that beneficence must be of a very complicated kind; certain anomalies may be like conjugate points, truly a part of the curve to the mathematician who knows the equation, though not to the casual observer; and these apparently useless excrescences cannot be removed without destroying the system of which they form a part. Besides which, it has been shown by an able writer that conjugate points probably belong to branches of the curve that lie *out of the plane of reference*, but *cross that plane* in these very points. We, as observers of nature, are compelled to move in one plane ; but if we were free from the ordinary trammels of human experience, we might discover the " anomalies " to be parts of a continuous law.

investigator ought to hold towards God. The bishop coins the word *atheous*, in contradistinction to atheistic, to express his idea of the attitude that a student of pure mathematics or astronomy would for the moment occupy; for he concerns himself, for the time being, with results, without sounding the depths where the origin of existence is to be found, or entering into any speculative questions whatever. The phraseology he uses is not, I think, what any Catholic theologian would fully approve; but his meaning is to draw a very real and legitimate distinction; thus, in combating the views of Haeckel, who denies the moral order of the universe and the fact of a beneficent Creator, he condemns them as not merely *atheous* but *atheistic*.

On the other hand, he gives a salutary caution for the benefit of inexperienced persons who, in their zeal for theism, do not always discriminate between things which are really indications of a Divine purpose and things necessary in themselves, such as those which are the simple results of an arithmetical or mathematical law.

There is one curious point that our author mentions: some people have fancied that the moon would be much more useful if it were always at the full; and even so great an astronomer as Laplace has lent the weight of his name to some idea of this kind, and pointed out an arrangement by which the earth would have received much more light than it actually does.

It has, however, since then been shown that Laplace's arrangement would be dynamically *unstable*,—no more to be relied on than the balancing of a pin on its point; and if such an unstable system had existed, the moon might have flown off into the regions of space and the earth have been left without a satellite to give light at all.

Several of the essays contained in this little volume, though full of interest in themselves, must receive but a passing notice, because of the more important matter treated of in the other essays, and because space does not suffice to do justice to them all. This remark applies to the one on the " Philosophy of Crayfishes," which is a review of Professor Huxley's book on that subject; also to the essay on " Man's Place in Nature," which, however, well deserves attentive perusal, relating, as it does, in great measure, to the distinction that exists between the mental powers of man and those of the lower animals. Again, there is one on " Evolutism and Evolution," on which I do not propose to dwell at any great length; yet, like the rest, it is quite worthy of study; the author, while believing, in some sense, in evolution, such as that to which the geological strata with the fossils they contain bear testimony, guards himself from expressing an opinion upon it in its more extensive signification; and as to Mr. Darwin's hypothesis of " Natural Selection," he deems it "entirely inadequate to explain the facts of the case." If we consider the material universe and assume the truth of the nebular hypothesis, if we contemplate the forces in action,—light, heat, electricity,—also the order pervading the whole system, as well as the phenomena of life upon this earth, we still cannot account for the results; we cannot conceive of nebulous evolution as taking the place of the fundamental idea of a creative mind. And in the organic world we do not get life out of evolution; "life has never yet been evolved in any material substance which had not in it the element of life already." Nor can we believe that man was produced by a mere natural and necessary process without any volition. The subject is too extensive, perhaps, for treatment in so small a compass; but the essay contains a powerful protest against the atheistic notion of a blind evolution regulated by no creative power and devoid of all unity of design.

There is one production in the work before us which, we think, appeals less to our sympathies than the rest; it stands last in the volume, and is a sermon preached in Westminster Abbey on the Sunday after Mr. Darwin's funeral. There is much in it that is good and true; and, moreover, whatever we may think of Mr. Darwin's opinions, it is fair to say that he had the refinement and good taste to abstain from all direct assaults on religion; indeed, Bishop Goodwin goes so far as to say that he has "every reason to believe that such attacks had not his sympathy, but were contrary to his most solemn convictions." There is some conflict of testimony as to what Mr. Darwin's convictions or opinions on the subject of God and of religion really were; and we may gladly adopt the more favorable hypothesis; but we have always felt that there was something incongruous in the interment of the author of such a work as the *Descent of Man* in a building which is, nominally, at any rate, a Christian Church, which is hallowed by many sacred associations of the past, and in which the body of St. Edward the Confessor still rests.

To return to the more important portion of Bishop Goodwin's book: His essay on "Law, Physical and Moral," merits considerable attention. He commences by a quotation from the Duke of Argyll's *Reign of Law*, showing the different senses in which the word *law* is used, one of them being simply "an observed order of facts," though the true signification of the word is (as the Duke of Argyll holds) the expressions of a will enforcing itself by power. The ambiguous use of so important a word being injurious, the bishop, after giving what he conceives to be a better definition from Hooker, "that which doth assign unto each thing its kind, that which doth appoint the form and measure of working, the same we term a law," proposes to get over the difficulty with regard to the word law by distinguishing between what he would call *objective* and *subjective* law.[1] In the one case we are concerned with orders of facts, in the other with that which lies beneath such orders. The subjective laws that lie beneath the objective may be indefinitely numerous, one depending on that immediately below it, and the objective law may be the result of several coöperating subjective laws. He illustrates this by supposing that you notice that the houses in some street are almost uniform in height and pattern, etc.; this seems to be an objective law, the order of things as you observe them; you probably, however, find that there is something else beneath, some conditions as to plan and pattern prescribed by the owner of the soil, and this may be called the subjective law; but the analogy is more complete if you take in the intermediate chain and consider the builder's contract and the architect's instructions, and so forth, as links, until, at last, you come to the volition of the owner of the ground.

On the other hand, there may be a class of facts resting on no subjective law at all, but complete in themselves. This is the case with the facts of space and number; and it may be illustrated by reference to geometrical laws such as we find proved in Euclid, as, for instance, that the tangent of a circle is at right angles to the diameter; and to arithmetical laws, such as that the sum of any two numbers multiplied into the difference between them, is equal to the difference between their respective squares.[2] These are simply objective laws. Other illustrations may be given from the higher branches of mathematics and from the fundamental propositions of mechanics.

When we come, however, to physical laws, properly so called, the case is different; we have the objective law as expressed in an observed order of facts, and the subjective law or laws that lie below it. If we take the well-known astronomical laws called Kepler's, we find that to Kepler himself they were simply objective; but in the hands of Newton they ceased to be so, and the subjective laws beneath them appeared. The first and third of these laws (for the case of the second is somewhat different) involve the law of gravitation as we now know it to exist. The question then arises, can we push our law further still? Is this law of gravitation something which, like those of space and

---

[1] The distinction, he says, is analogous to that between plane and physical astronomy, or between geometrical and physical optics.

[2] This is expressed algebraically by the simple expression $(a + b)(a - b) = a^2 - b^2$. Take as an example the two numbers 3 and 7; their sum is 10, their difference is 4; multiply these together, and you have 40. Subtract their respective squares from one another, take 9 from 49, and the result is 40.

number, could not have been otherwise? Or does it carry us up to the expression of a Supreme Will? It may be difficult to answer these questions confidently. It is possible that the particular law by which gravity acts (the inverse square of the distance) may be hereafter proved to be a sort of physical necessity; but why need you have such a force at all? Why attraction rather than repulsion? Why need any force exist? Why need matter itself exist? If its existence is necessary it must be so " in consequence of some other law, the nature of which it puzzles the mind even to imagine." I shall return later on to this question of gravitation, which is evidently a profound mystery. But, the bishop says, " the result of this discussion, and probably of all similar discussions, is to point to a supreme will as the mainspring of all." .

To illustrate the difficulty that a mere observer has in detecting the law which underlies certain arrangements if it happens that he has not the true key,—the case is supposed of a person endeavoring to find out by inspection of the calendar the law (unknown to him) by which Easter is regulated,—he might make some curious guesses,—and a chart is given in the book marked with dots following some apparent order,—but no rule could be discovered that would not eventually fail. A similar table is given of lines indicating the length each year of the Epiphany season, to which the same remark applies. And yet how simple the subjective law of Easter is, when you once know it, depending as it does on the date of the Paschal full moon (not necessarily the astronomical full moon, but an ecclesiastical and conventional one), and how complicated an order of facts flows from this simple law, in itself merely the result of an act of human volition! The inference is that if such be the case in a matter involving human will, there *may be* something similar, unknown though it be to us, that would unravel the causes of those phenomena of the material world that have been such a puzzle to the mind of man. There is one more curious point about the calendar; it was reformed by Pope Gregory XIII., and the change then made is now a part of the law of Easter. It is possible that natural laws (though from a scientific point of view we can quote no such thing) are sometimes also changed by an act of the Supreme Will?[1]

---

[1] To give clearness to the conception, we may " denote these successive strata of law by a series such as the following:

$$L^0, L^1, L^2, L^3 \ldots \ldots L^\infty.$$

In this series L^0 represents an observed order of facts and nothing more. L^1 represents a subjective law upon which L^0 depends. L^2 is a law which underlies L^1, and so on. Following this series, we may conceive of it as tending ultimately to L^∞, which would represent the volition of an infinite mind." Some writers confuse law and cause, and seem to think that when the law has been discovered and defined the whole mystery is explained, which is far from being the case.

One word may be added on the subject of moral laws, which differ from physical laws on account of the interference of other volitions, that is, of the free will of man, which disturbs the chain of consequences ; still, we conclude that the basis of both is the same, and both may be resolved into the ultimate conception of an Omnipotent Will.

The essay following the last one, and having for its theme " Science, Human and Divine," is full of information as to certain modern discoveries, which however do not bear immediately on the subject before us. There are one or two things worthy of notice ; as for instance Sir William Thompson's opinion, to which allusion is made, to the effect that the present state of things on the earth, with all the results to which geology bears witness, has not existed for more than about 10,000,000 years ; this depends " upon considerations of heat or of energy," and if true is somewhat embarrassing to a certain important school of geologists, and not less so to evolutionists of the Darwinian type.

There is also an important remark in answer to the unwise argument of the agnostics that God cannot be known; which is met by the following forcible reply : " Grant that in a certain sense God must be unknowable, and how foolish it is to regard this admission as at all equivalent to this other assertion, that nothing can be known about God. Once more I take the analogy of physical science, and I say that matter is unknowable; but I ask whether this admission proves that no knowledge of matter is due to the discoveries of Newton." That is to say, we know little indeed of the ultimate constitution and origin of matter, but we do know something of the laws that it obeys and the attributes which belong to it.

Before going on to other subjects, we take the opportunity here of observing, that some modern writers have disputed the generally accepted doctrine that geometrical axioms and theorems, which we find, for instance, in Euclid, are *necessary truths ;* and have attempted to show that they are merely the results of experience, an experience which is limited by our existing circumstances and which we presume they would say might conceivably be reversed by a more extended knowledge of nature. These imaginary difficulties, for such we hold them to be, are not touched upon in the volume we are reviewing, and it would be impossible to discuss them at length on the present occasion ; those, however, who are curious on such matters may refer to Professor Cayley's Presidential address to the British Association in 1883, where some questions of this kind are skilfully sifted by a master hand.

There are some points well deserving of record in an essay on " Pessimism," which is defined to be " the doctrine of a hopeless predominance of evil, against which it is of no use to contend; of a fundamental blunder which can only be cured by the extinction of the human race," and against such a doctrine (as held by Schopenhauer, Von Hartmann, and others) we must protest, though it does not necessarily involve atheism. The following hypotheses, it appears, can be held consistently with the assumption of pessimism. " I. That there is no God. II. That there is a God, who is (1) evil and therefore desiring pessimism; or (2) weak, and therefore unable to check it; or (3) good and powerful, but for some inscrutable reason permitting it." Now, the physical aspect of the universe is an irresistible argument against both atheism and pessimism; if that be so, we may dismiss the first supposition. Then taking the first head of the alternative hypothesis—the principal reply to it is that if it were true, the world would have been *purposely* made much worse than it really is. Bad as the world is, there is too much good in it to admit of " the horrible conception of a Creator who desires and designs pessimism."

Taking in the next place the second head, we come to the supposition, which was that of the late Mr. J. S. Mill, that there is a weak God unable successfully to oppose pessimism; this resembles the old doctrine of the Manicheans, and is, of course, antagonistic to monotheism, and therefore to the true conception of God as held by Christians and even by Mahometans. It leads, in fact, to polytheism, for if you have one weak God, why not more than one? Most persons will indorse the bishop's observation: " With regard to the Divine Nature, it seems to me to be true that there is no resting-place between zero and infinity." The remaining head is the doctrine (held by Christians and other theists) of a good and powerful God, permitting evil to exist for some *inscrutable* reason; and this, though it may have its difficulties, is the one satisfactory solution. We must not assume that our faculties are adequate to comprehending all the elements of the system. There are things physical that we cannot well conceive; take, for instance, the totality of material existence; " there must be a total, and, therefore, you can conceive an envelope which shall contain the universe; but what will there be outside the envelope? You cannot say. Again, think of the ether which fills all stellar space, and to the vibrations of which light is due; has it a limit? What can it be? What exists beyond? The intellect simply breaks down." Now, we may fairly speculate that the highest act of a Creator would probably be the production of a creature having an independent will. We may easily imagine that any creation not including this would fall short of what the Divine will and the Divine perfections require. But it is this introduction of an independent will that is at the root of the evil existing in this world. Then an independent will cannot be tried without some opportunity of choosing between right and wrong, and if this be so, we see at once that any amount of evil may occur ; and this may well be the key to the whole difficulty. We have given a brief sketch of the bishop's able reasoning on this point, but we forbear to enter on a full dissertation upon a subject that would require a treatise to itself.

There remains an essay on " Natural Theology," which, though not standing last in the volume, we have left till the last because we consider that the others lead up to it, and it may be more conveniently taken in this order. It is the substance of an address delivered to the " Carlisle Scientific Society and Field Naturalists' Club " in 1878, and the place where it was delivered, the city of Carlisle, suggested, not unreasonably, the name of Paley and his well-known work on this same subject as a topic for the lecturer to handle ; for Paley held the office of Archdeacon of Carlisle, and appears to have resided there for several years. After defining natural theology to be the knowledge of God as it can be obtained from the knowledge of nature, and after some other preliminary observations, Bishop Goodwin introduces Paley's remarkable treatise, as he justly calls it ; he admits that the work may be said to be, in a certain sense, out of date, for whole sciences have come into existence since the time when it was written. Science is more extended and more accurate ; difficulties have been raised which were then unknown ; and, on the other hand, some of the objections against a belief in God which were then prominent have mainly vanished and given place to others. Yet the principle of the argument is solid, and " perhaps there will never be a book more permanent in its character."

Paley's *Natural Theology* opens with the celebrated argument drawn from the supposed finding of a watch, upon the ground, by a casual traveller, presumably ignorant of watches and their mechanism ; and it is shown that such a person, after a thorough examination of it, would, inevitably, draw the inference that the watch had had a maker, and " that there must have existed, at some time and at some place or other, an artificer or artificers who formed it for the purpose which we find it actually to answer, who comprehended its construction and designed its use." The writer's object, then, is to prove that " the material universe, like the watch, has a purpose and had a maker ; " he adduces a variety of instances and a multitude of details to demonstrate this, but his first and best instance is that of the human eye, and he takes great pains to show that it presents the same unmistakable proofs of design on the part of a Divine Creator that the watch does of a human artificer.

A great part of Paley's arguments, however sound intrinsically and confirmatory of the faith of a man who already believes in God, cannot be used with effect against modern agnostics, who would appeal to Darwin's theory of natural selection in reply. Not that such theories were unheard of in Paley's time; in fact he expressly notices the hypothesis now known as " the survival of the fittest," which had probably reached him in some crude form, and to which he attaches no great weight. At the date when he wrote (A. D. 1802), when the doctrine of evolution was, if not unknown, almost unheeded, it was not unnatural that while expatiating on the marks of design in the organic world, he should treat astronomy as a good but subordinate topic in proving the agency of an intelligent Creator; some time previously—so we are informed in one of these essays—an outbreak of infidelity had been caused by the first reduction of the mechanism of the heavens to mathematical rules and formulæ, as was done by Laplace, a result which, to us at the present day, seems almost grotesquely absurd, accustomed, as we are, to the idea of astronomical laws acting with inflexible regularity and reducible to mathematical expressions; and it is a curious instance of what we have already mentioned—that it is the imagination rather than the reason that in the case of the generality of men is acted upon by scientific theories or discoveries.

To return, however, to the essay before us: Bishop Goodwin holds that Paley's principal instance, that of the human eye, is a forcible one. " Much progress," he says, " has been made in the science of optics since Paley's time; and in one recent book, at least, the eye is described as an instrument having defects of which a modern optician would be ashamed; nevertheless, I cannot perceive that Paley's fundamental argument is weakened."

The passage to which he alludes is from the *Popular Scientific Lectures* of Helmholtz (translated into English, 1873), and it runs as follows : " It is not too much to say that if an optician wanted to sell me an instrument which had all these defects, I should think myself quite justified in blaming his carelessness in the strongest terms, and giving him back his instrument. Of course, I shall not do this with my eyes, and shall be only too glad to keep them as long as I can—defects and all. Still the fact that, however bad they may be, I can get no others, does not at all diminish their defects, so long as I maintain the narrow but indisputable position of a critic on purely optical grounds." This quotation, however, which has a strange and unpleasant tone about it, does not give a fair impression of the very interesting lecture on " The Eye as an Optical Instrument " from which it is extracted. It is necessary to read the whole lecture, and not to confine one's attention to extracts, that it may be properly understood and appreciated. There is nothing to show that the writer opposes the idea of design and of providence in treating of the construction of the eye; thus, he says, " the adaptation of the eye to its function is therefore most complete, and is seen in the very limits which are set to its defects. Here the result which may be reached by innumerable generations working under the Darwinian law of inheritance, *coincides with what the wisest wisdom may have devised beforehand.*" And in another place, after stating that actual examination of the performances of the eye had revealed its imperfections, he goes on to say: " But, as again in similar cases, reasonable admiration rather increases than diminishes when really important functions are more clearly understood and their object better estimated, so it may well be with our more exact knowledge of the eye." Helmholtz also explains that the defects of the eye are so counteracted, chiefly by the continual and rapid movement of the organ, that some of them were very difficult to discover, and it was only by careful observation that they were shown to exist at all; the principal one, perhaps, being that the image of an illuminated point is not accurately formed by the human eye, owing to the construction of the crystalline lens; there is an irregularity about it, as may be noticed in the rays that we see around stars and other distant lights. This is obviously a very slight inconvenience.

The bishop goes on to explain Paley's argument, and, without dwelling on the imperfections (whatever they may be) of the eye, shows what a marvellous optical instrument it is; how easily it adapts itself to the reception of a greater or less amount of light under different circumstances; how it adjusts its focus according to the greater or less distance of the object; again, how there is a wash that lubricates it; an eyelid that protects it, even as a case protects an artificial instrument; also a drain opening into the nostril to carry off the superfluous brine; and the eyebrow above, in the form of an arch, to prevent the moisture that runs down the forehead from entering. It is well worth the trouble to read Paley's reasoning *in extenso*, as also that which he founds upon the structure of the ear.

To illustrate the difficulty of believing that this world, or the whole universe, can be a mere piece of mechanism, having no moral purpose connected with it, the bishop supposes some one to visit a modern iron-clad vessel, to inspect the machinery, and the enormous guns, capable as they are of throwing shells to a considerable distance; assuming for a moment that the visitor stops there and ignores any ulterior purpose, such an expenditure of money and mechanical skill must appear to be simply wasteful extravagance. On the other hand, if he is told that there is a purpose in all this, that vessels of this description can, by their movements, affect the whole policy of Europe and the interests of mankind, an entirely new light is thrown on the machinery and the guns, and the mind is satisfied. So in a similar way "we need the hypothesis of some great moral or spiritual design to justify the existence (as it were) both of the world and of ourselves."

Now all this, true though it be, is not inconsistent with the position laid down by some persons to the effect that "the being of God, regarded as a bare intellectual proposition, may be incapable of strict logical proof." . . . . "There is great danger of the want of perfect logical demonstration of a positive proposition being regarded as proof that the negative of that proposition is true. No greater mistake can be made."

The bishop, after exemplifying this fallacy in the case of a recent atheistic work, illustrates his own position by alluding to the well-known difficulty, raised by some philosophers, of demonstrating the existence of an external world ; also by the question as to the certainty of one's own personal existence, which has exercised the minds of some of the most profound thinkers that the world has ever seen ; again, by the controversy about man's free will, a thing we all know that we possess, notwithstanding the materialistic argument to the contrary. In all these points it is evidently almost impossible to frame a demonstration so cogent as to convince a determined opponent.

Returning however to the main subject of his essay, our author says : "The great argument of natural theology is this : that look where you will, either in small things or great, whether it be the construction of a fly's foot, or the high intellect of man, or the movement of the heavenly bodies, or the universe taken in its completeness, you see everywhere the suggestion of purpose." And before concluding he thus expresses himself: "I feel convinced that by refusing to acknowledge a living creating God, we fall into a greater difficulty than any which belief in God involves."

It strikes us that this last remark of the Bishop of Carlisle is very much to the point, and may assist us greatly in summing up the case (if we may venture to use such an expression) for theism. It is not pretended that the argument can be put into that compulsory form which would *force* belief even on the most reluctant. Cardinal Newman tells us in a passage in the *Apologia* that he finds it difficult to put the proof of the existence of God into strict logical mode and figure, though his whole being is penetrated with the conviction of its truth. If it could be demonstrated like a proposition of Euclid, atheism and agnosticism would be almost impossible amongst men of intelligence. But though this is not so, there are abundant proofs, even in the phenomena of visible creation, on which to found a belief amounting to moral certainty. We have specified the phenomena of *visible creation,* because moral considerations, and the powerful argument that may be drawn from the working of the human conscience (as done in such masterly language by Cardinal Newman in the *Grammar of Assent*) are, strictly speaking, no part of our present subject; they must not, however, be omitted if we wish to exhibit the *convergent* proof arising from various indications of the creative hand of God, no one in itself absolutely conclusive, yet strong in the cumulative force of the united whole. This reasoning is to some minds more satisfactory than anything else; it proceeds on the same principle as other inductive reasoning, upon which, in fact, so many scientific theories are based. In applying it we must bear in mind Bishop Goodwin's suggestions, which we have quoted above, that the apparent anomalies we observe in animal life (as well as in other things) may probably be explained by the existence of some law, to us unknown, or at least imperfectly apprehended. We may then be able to say that a belief in theism is the only solution of the problem of the universe, to which everything points; and that the denial of it would only land us in greater difficulties than any we now perceive. But there is another and we think most valuable method of stating the case, by selecting what may be termed *crucial* instances, where there seems to be irrefragable proof of design. Of these we will take three, which approve themselves to our own mind, though there may be many others—the human eye, the human intellect, the law of universal gravitation. They have all been touched upon in the volume before us. To begin with the human eye (and we suppose that most of what we say respecting it is applicable also to the eyes of animals)—it seems that the attempt to account for such an organ on the principle of natural selection alone involves such violent improbabilities that we may safely reject it as untenable. If Paley's opinion is less trustworthy because he wrote before the birth of Darwin, let us refer to an author who is still living and well acquainted with the advances of modern science, and, in fact, wrote with the *Origin of Species* before him : we allude to the Rev. C. Pritchard, now Professor of Astronomy at Oxford. And here we would observe that it is possible for a man to be a great biologist, well versed in all the details of natural history, and yet to know very little of certain other sciences, as, for example, of optics. Now, Professor Pritchard, in an appendix to a volume of sermons preached before the university of Cambridge and also before the British Association (*Analogies of Nature and Grace,* 1868), selects the structure of the human eye as a critical instance of the failure of the Darwinian hypothesis. He tells us that optics is a branch of physics with which it is his lot to be most familiar, so he takes his instance from it. " From the cornea to the retina " he says " the eye is an optical instrument " (it is in fact a natural camera obscura); " but," he continues, " what an instrument ! The computation of the curves and distances of the refracting surfaces in this instrument, and the assigning of the proper law of density for the several layers in its principal lens, would require the application of a mathematical analysis, such as I hesitate not to say was never yet possessed by a human geometer. The mechanism required for instantaneously changing the forms and distances, and in one instance the magnitude of its component parts, would require a handicraft such as never yet was possessed by a human mechanic." Professor Pritchard had not apparently read Helmholtz's work, which, indeed, was not published (at least in English) until the year 1873, or he would perhaps have modified his language ; but we do not think he would have been at all shaken in his conclusion. He quotes Mr. Darwin's imaginary history of the formation of the eye, and points out with great force the unreasonableness of supposing that "natural selection (as this author suggests) has converted the simple apparatus of an optic nerve, merely coated with pigment and invested by transparent membranes, into an optical instrument as perfect as is possessed by any member of the great articulate class." He then takes Mr. Darwin's theory of successive improvements in the structure of the eye by *accidental* variations extending over millions on millions of years, and shows how utterly incredible it is that so complex an instrument could have been optically improved by any such process ; " not less improbable, than if all the letters in the *Origin of Species* were placed in a box, and on being shaken and poured out millions on millions of times, they should at last come out together in the order in which they occur in that fascinating and, in general, highly philosophical work." Professor Pritchard, whose remarks well deserve to be quoted in *extenso* if space permitted, concludes that nothing but a *constantly exerted* intelligent will could have caused such a succession of circumstances as have resulted in the formation of the human eye.

There is, of course, considerable reason to doubt, upon astronomical grounds, as to these " millions on millions of years " which Mr. Darwin imagined to have elapsed while the eye was being gradually elaborated ; but without entering upon that question, we may, we think, safely say this much : the hypothesis which regards the eye as having assumed its present form merely by the operation of natural selection is so unlikely that it may be dismissed ;

and we must adopt the alternative supposition of the workmanship of a Divine Being. If this be so, the first crucial instance is a successful one.

The second is one upon which we must not here enlarge ; the mental powers of man, as compared with all other creatures on earth, have been discussed fully by many learned writers, and it would be simply impossible to do justice in a small space to so great a subject ; a few remarks, however, may be permitted. Now, it must always be remembered that the real question is not whether the lower animals have *any intelligence at all*, not strictly referable to instinct ; but whether such intelligence as they have does or does not differ *in kind* from the intellect of man. Every one, of course, admits the enormous difference in degree ; the controversy hinges upon the other and far more important distinction. As to the reality of this difference in kind, we think there is no reasonable doubt. Those who are interested in the subject should consult Professor Mivart's work on *The Cat*, in which there is a chapter bearing upon it ; also an article by the same author in the AMERICAN CATHOLIC QUARTERLY REVIEW (April, 1883), where there occurs the very forcible remark that " if animals had capacities similar to our higher mental powers, they would quickly make us unmistakably aware that such was the case." Mr. Mivart holds that the so-called intelligence of animals is but a " sensuous simulation " of true human intelligence. Indeed, there is good ground for saying that as plants in some way *simulate* the consciousness of animals, so do animals occasionally *simulate* the reasoning faculties of man. A book has been quite recently published with the strange title of *The Sagacity and Morality of Plants* (by J. E. Taylor, Ph.D., etc.). This author actually leans to the opinion that plants are possessed of some sort of consciousness. Allowance must be made for a certain amount of figurative language, but such seems to be really the view to which he inclines. He is an evolutionist of the school of Darwin, and yet apparently a theist ; his book contains several statements about plants scarcely intelligible excepting on the supposition of design in nature, and the concluding paragraph expresses his conviction that " underneath and behind all are the untiring purposes of divine wisdom and love." To return, however, to animals, we must be on our guard against the numerous stories (often very foolish stories) that are published under the head of animal intelligence. In a work entitled *Ten Years Among the Wild Beasts of India* (by Sanderson), the author, who has had some experience in the matter, states that the popular belief as to the extraordinary sagacity of the elephant is wholly unfounded ; moreover, that the natives of India, who know the elephant well, who catch him, train him, and make him what he is, do not consider him to be at all exceptionally intelligent. The popular error has arisen partly from apocryphal stories, the absurdity of which he points out, and partly from the real docility and obedience of the animal, which cause him to respond to the least touch of the driver who guides him.

If, then, we are right in holding that the human mind differs altogether, and in kind, from any faculties possessed by the animals, we must conclude that that was something of the nature of a separate creation ; something that evolution cannot account for, where man, such as we see him to be, first appeared on the earth. Now the advocates of natural selection admit, we think, that if you could show cases of separate creation, the inference in favor of Providential design would be irresistible. Here, then, is a case in point, and the second crucial instance is a sound one. We may mention, before quitting this subject, that there is in the September number of the *Nineteenth Century* an article by Mr. Romanes on "Instinct" from the Darwinian point of view, in which some curious examples of instinct are given, which seem almost inexplicable unless on the hypothesis of design. Mr. Romanes does not draw this inference, but his article is written with ability and moderation.

We now come to our third instance, the force of which we regard as very great indeed. We must premise that there are two things to consider, the fact of universal gravitation and the law by which it acts. And a word must be said, too, about that law before we proceed further ; we are sufficiently certain that everything in the solar system, great and small, is under the well-known law already enunciated, that every particle attracts every other particle with a force that varies jointly as their masses and inversely as the square of the distance between them. But we are not equally certain that this same law holds good for the whole universe, and that all the stars are subject to it. We cannot doubt that *some* law of attraction exists even in those distant regions, and, indeed, one which insures stability, but it is not physically certain that it is the same as our own. Still, there is some good evidence to show that it is so, and the probability in favor of it is so great that, for the purpose of our present inquiry, we may safely assume it to be true, and we shall consequently make that assumption.

Now we have seen that Bishop Goodwin is half inclined to think that this law of the square of the distance may be shown hereafter to be a kind of mathematical necessity, as is the case with light, which varies in its intensity inversely as the square of the distance between the object that receives and the object that gives out the light ; this, however, depends on the fact that the greater the diffusion of light, the less in exact proportion is its intensity, from whence it follows mathematically that we have the law just men-

tioned.[1] But gravity does not act in this way; it is equally powerful whether it has a large surface to deal with or a small one, and
loses nothing of its intensity; it varies as the *mass* of the bodies
concerned, but not either one way or the other according to the
extent of their surfaces. Moreover, it requires no time to travel
(as light does); it acts instantaneously, as if by a magical touch.
Newton himself seems to have struggled with questions of this
kind, and to have investigated the possibility of gravitation being
a case of some wider law, underlying it; but he struggled in vain,
and the question was never solved either by him or by subsequent
thinkers. It has all the appearance of an unfathomable mystery.

Supposing, however, it should hereafter be shown to be the
result of some more general law, which, as Bishop Goodwin would
express it, is the *subjective* law,—that law in its turn must have
something within it that involves the principle of order and stability, and so carries one back to the volition of the Creator. Mathematicians have occupied themselves in making suppositions as to
the effects of imaginary laws of gravity, some of which would no
doubt lead to sufficient order and regularity for the sustenance of
the universe, while others would cause hopeless confusion; and the
remarkable thing is that the present law, as we now know it, perfectly answers its purpose.

Indeed the case may be put more strongly; modern writers have
maintained that, besides the law of attraction, there must be a subordinate one of repulsion, for otherwise the particles of matter
would be dashed against each other with an *infinite* velocity, with
results that we can scarcely conceive.[2] Now, if this be so, and if a
repulsive force exists of *less* intensity, but sufficient to avoid such
destructive collision,—surely this is the work of intelligent design,
or it resembles it so closely that we cannot detect the difference.
It ought, however, to be remarked that no less an authority than
Sir William Thompson has, on a recent occasion, expressed a doubt
as to the existence of any repulsive force in nature, and proposes
to account for existing facts in another way. Be all this as it may,
we can, at any rate, say that this law of gravitation, as it now stands,
is one to which the whole stability of the universe is due, and which,
in a word, brings order out of chaos. Only let us imagine no law of

---

[1] Light may be considered as being diffused over the surface of concave spheres, the
respective radii of which are the various distances from the centre whence the light
emanates; then the surface of a sphere varies as the square of its radius.

[2] If the ordinary expression for attraction be taken in this shape, $m\,m'\,\frac{c}{r^2}$, where m
and m' are the masses of the bodies, c the attraction between two bodies of unit mass
at unit distance, and r the actual distance; then if $r = 0$, the attractive force becomes
infinite; so it has been suggested that the true expression is $m\,m'\left(\frac{c}{r^2} - \frac{c^1}{r^4 + n}\right)$.

attraction to exist at all, neither a force of repulsion, nor a force of any kind, there would simply be no coherence, no fit abode for human or animal life, but universal reign of anarchy. And what a contrast to all this is the physical universe as we now contemplate it, under the action of this mighty law! Here, if anywhere, we must acknowledge the agency of a Creator, of a real and personal God; and if so, our third crucial instance is a successful one.

We have enlarged upon this argument because the Bishop of Carlisle has, we will not say undervalued, but slightly understated its cogency. How highly we respect his work has already been stated, and we would venture to take leave of him in the trite and well-known phrase, originally applied to a clever, bold, bad man, but more fittingly addressed to one in whom high moral and intellectual qualities are combined: "Dum talis sis, utinam noster esses."

BOOK NOTICES.

THE LIFE AND MARTYRDOM OF ST. THOMAS BECKET, ARCHBISHOP OF CANTERBURY. Second and enlarged edition. By *John Morris, Priest of the Society of Jesus.* London: Burns and Oates. New York: The Catholic Publication Society Company, 1885.

The republication of this work in a new and enlarged edition is eminently timely. St. Thomas's long-continued struggle, culminating in his martyrdom, in defence of the rights and liberties of the Church, involved the same questions and issues which now, after a lapse of seven hundred years, form the subjects of contention between the Sovereign Pontiff of the Church and the temporal rulers of nearly every Christian country. Then, as now, the Church asserted her right to be supreme within her own sphere, and free from all state interference in the administration of her own affairs. And then, too, as now, temporal rulers enforced their pretensions to supremacy over the Church, and to interference in and control over her government and administration. The enforcement of these pretensions by temporal rulers and their resistance by the Church cause her, to-day, to be persecuted in Russia and Germany and France, to be restricted and hampered in Austria, Spain, Portugal, South America, Central America, and Mexico, and have led to the Church's despoliation, the suppression of her religious orders, and the imprisonment in the Vatican of her Sovereign Pontiff.

The contention of St. Thomas of Canterbury with Henry II. of England involved precisely this issue. It was not, and it was felt and clearly understood both by St. Thomas and by the Norman tyrant that it was not, a dispute merely over Church revenues or the filling of certain vacant episcopal sees, or any other matters of detail, but a struggle in which the latter and the former refused to concede the supremacy of temporal rulers over the Church, and its right of free action as regards its own affairs.

This is confessed even by James Anthony Froude. He endeavors to confuse the issue by representing the principle at stake as involving consequences which it does not involve; but he acknowledges that if the principle upon which the Church bases her claims to freedom and supremacy in her own sphere be true, then St. Thomas was right. His language is: "If it be true that the clergy are possessed in any real sense of supernatural powers; if 'the keys.' as they are called, have been actually granted to them; if, through them as the ordinary and appointed channel, the will of God is alone made known to mankind, Becket was right and the High Churchmen are right. . . . If, on the other hand, the clergy are but like other orders of priesthoods in other ages and countries—mere human beings set apart for peculiar functions, and tempted by the nature of those functions into fantastic notions of their own consequence—then these recurring conflicts between Church and state resolve themselves into phenomena of social evolution, the common sense of mankind exerting itself to control a groundless assumption."

The underlying thought of this is plain, though skilfully wrapped up by the specious writer in phrases adroitly adapted to conceal its naked hideousness. "*If* the clergy (of the Christian Church) are but like *other* orders of priesthoods in other ages and countries"—such as those of ancient Greece and Rome and Egypt, or of China and Hindostan, to-day—then it is right that "the common sense of mankind" should "control the *groundless* assumption."

This is the true meaning of Mr. Froude's alternative, put into plain English. *His* notion is that the claim of Christianity to being of divine origin, and to its possessing and exercising divinely-given powers and authority through its own divinely-constituted ministers, is a "*groundless* assumption," and hence that Henry II. in his day, and temporal rulers in our times, only exercise common sense in "controlling" and seeking to crush out the "fantastic notions" of the Church's priests and hierarchy.

This, too, is the underlying idea of all the efforts made to-day by temporal rulers to limit and fetter the Church, and deprive her of her rights and liberties. It has its roots and ground in a real though unexpressed disbelief in the divine origin of the Christian religion.

On this account, the life of St. Thomas of Canterbury and the history of his contentions with Henry II. have a special interest to every one who wishes to understand the real and primary reason why, in all ages, since the commencement of her existence, the Church has been involved in almost constant conflicts with temporal rulers. And, because these conflicts have increased of late years both in number and intensity, it is all the more important that this be understood.

The work before us clearly sets forth the truth we have referred to. It is strictly a biography of St. Thomas of Canterbury, and simply states the successive occasions of controversy between him and Henry II., and the issues that were involved, with but little of comment upon those issues. Yet, still, they are brought clearly and prominently, though incidentally, into view.

The first edition of the work was published in 1859. The demand for it was such that the edition was soon exhausted, and for twenty years it has been out of print. In the interval much valuable historical material, throwing fuller light upon the life and character of St. Thomas, and upon obscure and disputed facts in his life, has been discovered and made accessible. Of these the author has industriously availed himself, and incorporated them into the present enlarged edition. Among these are six volumes which have appeared in the "Rolls' Series," entitled *Materials for the History of Thomas Becket, Archbishop of Canterbury,* edited by the late Baron James Craigie Robertson.

The work bears evidence on its every page of most careful and painstaking study and research. Nothing is taken for granted or asserted at random. Legends are sifted thoroughly, and separated from authentic history. Disputed points are carefully examined, and the evidence for and against them impartially stated. Incidentally, yet very clearly, the lives and characters are brought into view of those of the bishops in England and France who took prominent parts in the controversy between St. Thomas and Henry II. In copious notes at the end of the volume, explanatory statements and extracts from many ancient documents elucidate the text of the work itself and add to its interest. The illustrations, showing the plan and structure of the Cathedral at Canterbury, both before and after the saint's martyrdom and canonization, add to the value of the book.

To those who look at the subject superficially, it may seem that St. Thomas, in giving his life for the rights and liberty of the Church in England, died in vain. But it is not so. True, Henry II., false to the promises he made to prevent his own excommunication and the placing of England under a Papal interdict, and false as well to his short-lived contrition and penitence—perhaps at the time sincere, and perhaps entirely insincere—renewed his tyranny over the Church, and his successors followed his example in various ways, and with different degrees of audacity. Yet, still, St. Thomas, by his life and death, delayed for four centuries, till the time of Henry VIII., the day when the king of England would dare to assert in unqualified terms his pretended spiritual and temporal supremacy.

By this long delay, the act was, when it was consummated, indelibly stamped by historical evidence, as well as by the principles of religion and sound reason, with the plain marks of usurpation and tyranny.

THE LIFE OF ST. CHARLES BORROMEO, CARDINAL ARCHBISHOP OF MILAN. From the Italian of John Peter Giussano, Priest and Oblate of St. Ambrose. With Preface by Henry Edward Cardinal Manning, Archbishop of Westminster. In two volumes. London: Burns & Oates. New York: The Catholic Publication Society Co., 1884.

John Peter Giussano, the author of this Life of St. Charles Borromeo, was closely associated with the Saint for twenty-one years. At the age of nineteen, after a course of study, he took the degree of Doctor of Medicine. This profession he followed only a few years, when he devoted himself to the office of the sacred ministry. He was received by St. Charles into his immediate household, and became Priest and Oblate of St. Ambrose. On the death of the Saint, he retired to Monza to write this work, being appointed a conservator of the Ambrosian library. He died at Monza in 1623.

Thus Giussano had ample opportunities for acquainting himself accurately not only with the events of St. Charles's life, his labors, and their results, but also with his private personal habits and character. His work is thus both a biography and a history. The text of Giussano's work is supplemented in the translation before us by notes taken from additions made to it by Bartholomew De Rossi, of the Congregation of Oblates, in 1751. The translation was made by the Oblates in the diocese of Westminster, and was published in England a short time before the Tercentenary of St. Charles's death.

The work is made more convenient for reference by a very full table of contents and a minute chronological table of all the important acts of Saint Charles, in the order of their occurrence, month by month and day by day. His Eminence Cardinal Manning has contributed a very valuable Preface, describing the special work which St Charles did, particularly in his relation to the Sovereign Pontiffs of the Church, to the reforms inaugurated by the Council of Trent, and his influence in giving effect to the decrees of that Council, and incorporating them permanently into the life and action of the Church. Without a knowledge of what St. Charles did in these respects, it would be impossible to clearly understand the interior history of that great Council, or the way in which, after many interruptions, sometimes for months and sometimes for years, it was re-assembled in January, 1562, and closed in December, 1563. Appointed a member of the Sacred College in 1560, at the age of twenty-two, and made Secretary of State by Pius IV., the Sovereign Pontiff consulted him on all important affairs, and the whole guidance of the Council of Trent by the Holy See passed through his hands. In an archivium fitted up for the purpose at his residence, all the documents and correspondence of the Council were deposited and carefully preserved. The couriers who brought letters from Trent were admitted at any moment day or night, and he gave strict orders that he should be immediately awakened up if they arrived when he was asleep in the night. When it is remembered that the proposition of all matters to be discussed in an Œcumenical Council belongs to the Sovereign Pontiff of the Church, and that no new matter can be introduced and none withdrawn without his authority, it becomes obvious how close an oversight this implies.

Indeed it was chiefly through the advice and influence of St. Charles that, despite formidable obstacles, the Council was re-opened for the last time; and it was his firm and vigilant will that pressed it to its conclusion, so that no accident, such as the death of Pius IV., of which at one period of the sessions of the Council there seemed to be serious danger, might prevent the confirmation of its decrees, and thus the fruit of all its labors might be lost.

Immediately upon the termination of the Council, which was quickly followed by the confirmation of its action by Pius IV., St. Charles put forth all his energies to secure the execution of its holy decrees. He classified them according to subjects, and studied their minutest details. In the first Consistory held after the return of the Apostolic Legates from Trent, he proposed that a Congregation of eight Cardinals should be formed for the purpose of deciding upon controversies that might arise in the interpretation of the decrees. This Congregation was soon afterwards appointed by Pius IV. He also obtained from the Holy Father various provisions and constitutions concerning the residence of Bishops and Archbishops in their Sees, and of Canons and other ecclesiastics in their proper fields of labor, and had the time fixed for commencing to carry the decrees and constitutions into execution. He presided over the compilation of the "Catechism of the Council of Trent," and the revision of the Roman Breviary and Missal.

But while St. Charles was thus abundant in labors at Rome for the reformation of abuses in the entire Church and its edification, he was constantly mindful of his immediate episcopal flock. When he was consecrated Archbishop of Milan, in 1563, no one of its Prelates, for eighty years previous, had resided in his See ; but in spite of all efforts to detain him at Rome, St. Charles was resolved to live in the midst of his flock. Accordingly, within less than two years afterwards, having concluded his work at Rome, he obtained by his importunities from Pius IV., who reluctantly consented to part with him, permission to proceed to Milan. There for nineteen years he wore out his life amongst his people, never leaving the city, except on short visits to Rome or to make visitations of different places over which his jurisdiction extended. The record of his Episcopate, as found in the *Acta Ecclesiæ Mediolanensis*, is a model of diocesan legislation. They consist of the decrees of six Provinicial Councils and eleven Diocesan Synods held by St. Charles; of the rules and constitutions of various confraternities of devotion, and especially of the Oblates of St. Ambrose, Patron of the Church of Milan. Cardinal Manning in his admirable preface says: "There is no part of a bishop's diocesan administration which is not to be found in these Acts reduced to the most precise order and system. . . . . It is a whole of great proportions, complete in outline and finished in the minutest details. Next to the collection of the Œcumenical Councils, there is no work of ecclesiastical and spiritual legislation so perfect as the Acts of the Church of Milan. In them the Council of Trent is to be seen translated into provincial and diocesan administration for the reform of all orders of the Church."

St. Charles was one of the three men who, by Divine Providence, were the chief leaders in the Church's special work in the sixteenth century. They were warm friends. Possessed of very different gifts and inspirations, and working with great diversity of operations, they yet were of one will and labored with perfect unanimity of purpose for the one great end. To St. Ignatius was given the work of combating the intellectual errors and heresies engendered by Protestantism, and of adapting the way of life of the regular orders of the Church to the needs of the modern world. To St. Philip was given the work of recalling Rome from worldliness and the fascinations of a revived heathenism. To St. Charles was committed the office of raising the Priesthood from the condition into which it had fallen, and restoring it to the state of perfection in which its Divine Founder had created it and left it.

Each of these Saints shines in the Church of Christ with a lustre different from the others. They each represent different aspects or perfections of Him who is the sum of all perfections. St. Charles Borromeo represents the Good Shepherd. He is peculiarly the Saint of the Episcopate and the Priesthood ; the Saint for bishops and the clergy to study and imitate.

The volumes before us clearly exhibit this. They contain full details of the manner in which he carried on the work of a shepherd of souls; his methods for reforming the clergy, and for raising them to a higher degree of perfection ; his being the first to set an example of executing the decrees of the Council of Trent with regard to establishing diocesan theological seminaries, and training in knowledge and virtue candidates for the sacred office of the priesthood ; the manner in which he regulated his own episcopal household, and in which he vigilantly acquainted himself with the character and habits, the competency and degree of faithfulness of every priest in his vast diocese; his abounding charity, austerities, and self-mortification ; his holy life and happy death ; his beatification and canonization.

THE WORKS OF THE RIGHT REV. JOHN ENGLAND, Bishop of Charleston, S. C. With Memoir, Memorials, Notes, and Full Index. By *Hugh P. McElrone.* In two volumes. Vol. I. Baltimore: The Baltimore Publishing Company.

The collecting and republishing of the most important writings of Bishop England was a happy and timely thought. The previous editions have long ago been exhausted. Nor was it desirable to reprint them in the form in which they issued from the press. They contained much matter, some from the pen of Bishop England, and some too from the pens of others, that was then undoubtedly interesting from its relation to circumstances then still existing, or still clearly remembered. But those circumstances have now entirely passed away, and are forgotten except by a very few. The papers of Bishop England on those subjects, therefore, and the copious references to them in papers from other pens included in the previous editions of Bishop England's works, are properly omitted in the present collection.

Yet many of his writings are of great and permanent value. He was learned, eloquent, acute and strictly logical. In controversy he had no superior and perhaps no equal—unless it be Archbishop Hughes—among the Prelates of the Church in the United States, who are now living, or who have forever ceased from their labors. His zeal for the interests of religion, his personal piety, devotion, humility, self-mortification and abundance of labors in the discharge of the duties of his exalted office, were even greater than his natural gifts and his acquirements by study. He was a perfect and polished Christian gentleman. By his urbanity and geniality, his evident consideration for others, his abounding charity, he won all hearts, even of those who were bitterly opposed to the Catholic religion, and exerted an influence for good upon public opinion in the Carolinas and Georgia, all of which were then included in his diocese, that is felt to this day. He understood perfectly the value of the press as an auxiliary in the defence of truth. He established the *United States Catholic Miscellany,* which was practically the first Catholic journal established in the United States. But, recognizing the fact that through it he could hope to reach, at most, only a few Protestants, he had recourse also to the secular press. In it articles from his pen constantly appeared, correcting misrepresentations of Catholic doctrines and practice, refuting fallacious arguments against the Catholic religion, castigating malicious enemies of the Church, and defending the truth. It was no easy matter for him to gain admission to the columns of the secular press. At first it refused to publish his letters as communications. He persevered, and had them inserted as advertisements, for which he paid the regular price. At last, however, the secular press, recognizing the avidity with which the public read whatever emanated from his pen, opened their columns to him. He was "a born" controvertist, fitted for it by natural gifts; and those gifts were developed by educational training and assiduous study. Yet the controversies in which he engaged were not needless, nor the outcome of a naturally combative disposition. There was an earnest practical purpose in them; and he engaged in them from no mere fondness for disputation, but from a desire to dispel error, to extend knowledge of the truth, and to promote the greater glory of God.

Hence, even his controversial writings have a positive value, independent of the time and circumstances that elicited them. But Bishop England has left many other writings besides those of a controversial character. His fruitful cultured mind was ever active, and employed itself on a variety of subjects, literary, historical and theological; and it may be said of him without the least exaggeration that he touched upon nothing that he did not elucidate.

The volume before us well illustrates this. His address on *Epochs of Irish History* has a solid historical value, while his paper on the *Irish Franchise* may be studied with profit by those who desire to thoroughly understand the political state of Ireland to-day. The *Pleasures of the Scholar, Classical Education,* the *Descent of Æneas into Hell,* are productions of a thoroughly cultured and scholarly mind, and will be read with pleasure by all who appreciate those qualities. His discourse on *Duelling* is a convincing argument against that barbarous and senseless practice, and tended greatly to influence public opinion in the right direction. His address on the *Character of Washington* and his *Discourse before Congress* were, each of them, masterly disquisitions on the subjects which they respectively treated. The *Pen-Pictures of Rome* are graphic descriptions of the chief objects of interest the Capital of the Christian world presents to the observing Christian visitor. The *Waldenses, Historical Sketches* of Denmark, Sweden, Russia, European Turkey, and the Greek Schism are models of concise, lucid, historical articles. *St. Peter's Roman Pontificate* is a complete exhibit of the historical proof that St. Peter was the first Bishop of Rome and suffered martyrdom there.

These papers make up the first volume. The second, we presume, will contain the writings of Bishop England that are of a more strictly theological character, and will be of even higher value, though not of greater interest, than those which the first volume contains.

Prefixed to the first volume is a memoir by the editor. It is concise, and delineates the character of the deceased prelate in strong lines. Yet we regret that the writer has not incorporated into it copious extracts from the "Memoir of Bishop England" written by his successor in office, Bishop Reynolds. This, if not necessary to the completeness of the editor's sketch, would, at least, have given it greater fulness of detail. It would also have placed Bishop England more clearly before the reader's mind, in his relation to the Church in this country and the work which he did in building it up, almost creating it, we may say, in the region over which his labors as a Bishop and Christian missionary extended.

REGISTER OF FORT DU QUESNE; Translated from the French, with an Introductory Essay and Notes. By *Rev. A. A. Lambing, A.M.,* author of " A History of the Catholic Church in the Dioceses of Pittsburgh and Allegheny," etc., President of the Ohio Valley Catholic Historical Society. 4to, 97 pp. Pittsburgh, Pa. 1885.

Pittsburgh, grimy beneath the murky cloud always settling above it, with the din of anvil and the glare of furnace, gives not the faintest clue of French origin, suggests in nothing the gay, light-hearted, adventurous sons of Gaul. Yet, its earliest civilized record, dated beyond the day when it received its present name in honor of an English statesman, attests that it once owed allegiance to France, and was a shrine of Catholicity. It was a bold and decisive step to seize the point where the northern and southern streams united to form the Beautiful River ; and it was held so brilliantly and gloriously as to make Fort Du Quesne one of the most interesting points in colonial history. Where the French monarch planted a military post, he reared a chapel and maintained a chaplain, generally a priest of the Recollect or reformed branch of the Franciscan Order. The registers kept at such posts have in many cases been preserved, and that where the friars who sang mass in the chapel of the Assumption of the Blessed Virgin on the Beautiful River is preserved to this day in the prothonotary's office, Montreal. From a copy which he had made for the illustrious Bishop Michael O'Connor of Pittsburgh, Mr. Shea printed a hundred copies of this early record in a quaint series, antique in form and type, which he issued for amateurs. Scholars received it with interest, as it led to new and more accurate knowledge of the French commander and officers who with a few gallant men routed Braddock's well appointed force. Rev. Mr. Lambing, successor in a measure of the French Franciscans who ministered at the point, is filled with true and reverent antiquarian taste. His church revives the memory of the early chapel of the Assumption, and he has written the history of the two dioceses which, in our time, have grown up in Western Pennsylvania, and founding an Historical Society, over which he presides, seeks to perpetuate his own antiquarian spirit and taste, and imbue others with a love for recording and preserving the early annals of the struggles of the pioneers of the Faith. In the same spirit he has issued, in a very well printed quarto, an edition *de luxe* of the *Register of Fort Du Quesne*, reproducing the French, and giving, what was by no means an easy task, a correct rendering into English, and notes in which his local knowledge enables him to afford the student valuable aid. The notes show extensive research, and cover a multitude of topics, on some of which. like his adopting the old story of La Salle's descending the Ohio, cautious scholars will be reluctant to follow him. These are but slight points. The *Register*, in its attractive shape, is now made accessible and intelligible to all, and takes us back vividly to the French post where the chaplain, looking on the unbroken forest, said his mass, confessed officers and men going forth to battle, and gave Christian burial to those who fell fighting nobly for their king and country. There was no village of French settlers, no farms of men who had held the plough in Canada or France, with mothers bringing children to the sacred font ; yet, Father Baron records baptisms of some children born in the fort, of Indians at the point of death, of white children carried off by Indians from the English frontiers. The most interesting entries are those of Daniel Lienard de Beaujeu, who commanded the fort, and set out to engage Braddock, falling gloriously in the hour of victory, and of Lieutenant Carqueville, Ensign La Pérade, Cadets Sennonville and Hertel, who all met their death on that famous field.

THE MIRACULOUS EPISODES OF LOURDES. By *Henry Lasserre*. Continuation and Second volume of "Our Lady of Lourdes." Translated from the Seventeenth Edition with the express permission of the author, by *M. E. Martin*. London : Burns & Oates. New York : The Catholic Publication Society Co. 1884.

This book is a continuation of the one written fourteen years before by Henri Lasserre. The first work gave an account of the apparition of the Blessed Virgin to Bernadette Soubirous, at Lourdes, of the spring that was there miraculously opened in the solid rock floor of a dry cavern, and of miraculous cures wrought through employment of its water and devout invocation of the Blessed Virgin. The work, of which an English translation is now before us, is a continuation of the history of the wonderful work of God there performed.

Since then the miraculous cures of all manner of diseases and physical infirmities, wrought at Lourdes, and elsewhere by the use of its water, have multiplied, until it has become a shrine to which pious pilgrimages are made from every land.

The volume before us recounts a number of these miraculous cures,

It recounts them, too, not in a hurried or superficial manner, but gathers all the facts connected with them, all the threads of testimony which converge upon the miraculous event, and weaves them into a body of irrefragable proof.

The writer's motives for writing this sequel to his first work on the subject—written after an interval of fifteen years, during which he has watched and studied the continual series of miracles at Lourdes—and his plan are stated in his preface.

"It is not our intention," he says, "to offer to our readers, in a compact series of short accounts, a hurried narrative of each and all of the innumerable miracles that have been accomplished at Lourdes. We think, and we have always thought, that such accumulations of superficial facts can only produce a superficial effect on those who read them. . . . . . To examine the supernatural event on all sides, and in all its details; consider its course; study its causes and its most distant preparations; penetrate, so to speak, to its very essence; determine its real character; and bring its chief features into relief:—such is . . . . . what we have tried to do."

The miracles, of which the writer gives a full and detailed account, and a history of all important preceding and subsequent circumstances connected with them, were accomplished in the healing of persons whose infirmities were pronounced incurable by natural means, by the most eminent medical authorities in France. In each case recounted, the miraculous cure was wrought upon a person so well known that the knowledge both of the affliction and of the cure was wide-spread.

The latter part of the work is occupied with a fuller account than was given in his previous work of the writer's own miraculous cure. His first account was confined to a bare statement of the case as connected with himself. The recital contained in the volume before us gives the names of those whom God made the chief instruments to induce him, contrary to his own intentions, to employ the water of Lourdes. Prominent among them, the first to advise and most persistent in urging recourse to the water of the miraculous spring, and also his amanuensis in writing the letter addressed to Mgr. Peyramale, Curé of Lourdes, requesting a package of the water to be sent to Henri Lassere, was *M. Charles de Freycinet*, Lasserre's intimate friend, then director of works on the Southern Railway of France, and subsequently carried by the revolutionary storm to the highest offices of the French Government; first as Minister of War, then of Public Works, then of Foreign Affairs, and then President of the Council.

In an appendix, photograph copies of letters—M. de Freycinet's among them—and other evidences of the miracles are furnished.

THE SACRED BOOKS OF THE EAST. Translated by various Oriental scholars and edited by *Max Müller.* Vols. XX and XXI. Oxford: At the Clarendon Press. 1884.

The first mentioned of these volumes contains translations by Max Müller of seven of the oldest and most important of the Upanishads of the Vedic philosophy, viz.: The KATHA, MUNDAKA, TAITTIRIYAKA, BRIHADARANYAKA, SVETASVATARA, PRASNA, and the MAITRAYANA-BRAMANA. The second contains the SADDHARMA-PUNDARIKA, or "the Lotus of the True Law," translated by H. Stern.

The enthusiastic industry with which oriental scholars prosecute their studies of ancient Hindoo literature is not at all surprising. They find themselves in a world of ideas entirely different in its forms of thought, its philosophy and logic from those which European nations have appropriated from the Latins and Greeks.   And the farther they go back, the more elevated and purer, the more closely approaching the truths of Christian revelation, they find those ancient Sanskrit writings are.   In those which bear evidences of the most remote antiquity, the ideas of God are purely those of monotheism, and not of monotheism in a pantheistic sense, as many modern skeptics now use the word, but of Christian monotheism.

Max Müller and other skeptical orientalists contend that these ideas were arrived at by a system of gradual development or evolution ; that at first the notions of deity were crude and low, but that gradually, by eliminating the grosser elements, they became more refined and elevated.   The simple fact, however, that the oldest remains of ancient Hindoo literature are incontestably the purest and most sublime, completely overturns this rationalistic theory.   The steps can be clearly traced of a process not of advancement and elevation in the Hindoo mind, in the lapse of ages, but of retrogradation and debasement.   First there was belief in the one God, supreme, uncreated, self-existent, the Creator and Preserver of the Universe.   Then this belief gave way to a vague and broad pantheism, and that by gradual corruption was supplanted at last by atheism and the doctrine of total annihilation, or, as it is called, *nirvana.*

The study, therefore, of the ancient Hindoo theology and philosophy is important, as furnishing incontestable evidence of the existence of a primitive revelation to man in the earliest ages, a revelation which embraced the same fundamental ideas of God which Christianity has again made known ; and as showing how men, from worshipping the one true God, fell first into worshipping His works in the natural world, then into gross idolatry and atheism

Thus Max Müller and his co-laborers are doing a work of high importance in furnishing the means for a more general and accurate knowledge of the most ancient literature extant, and, contrary to their own intentions, or, at least, their own theories, are furnishing Christian philosophers with proofs and arguments to overthrow the popular doctrine of man's starting in existence as an ignorant brutal savage, devoid of all ideas of deity, and gradually developing or creating those ideas for himself.

HISTORY OF THE CHURCH, FROM ITS FIRST ESTABLISHMENT TO OUR OWN TIMES. Designed for the Use of Ecclesiastical Seminaries and Colleges. By *Rev. J. A. Birkhauser*, Professor of Church History and Canon Law in the Provincial Seminary of St. Francis de Sales, near Milwaukee, Wis. New York : Fr. Pustet & Co. 1884.

There is manifest need of a good English text-book on Church history for the use of students in colleges and theological seminaries. Such a text-book, however, it is not easy to prepare. On the one hand, there is the danger of making it too lengthy and voluminous, and on the other that of excluding important matter, and obscuring the significance of important events in their relation and consequences, by too great condensation and conciseness. Most of our present English histories of the Church are either for popular use, and, therefore, to some extent, superficial, or else are too extensive to be used as text-books.

Judging from the volume before us, the undertaking of Prof. Birkhauser promises to be fairly successful in striking the happy medium. In the course of 252 pages he has given a reasonably clear and sufficiently full exhibit, for the use of students, of the leading events and movements of the period intervening between the nativity of our Blessed Redeemer and the year A.D. 313.

This period in the history of the Church, it seems to us, is insufficiently studied, and, we were going to say, too lightly passed over in many of our theological seminaries. It was a period when the Church was in the formative process of her external organization; and was intensely active not only in diffusing the faith, but also in resisting both the external opposition of heathenism in its efforts to oppose her progress, and in combating the outcroppings of heathen errors among her own members, in the form of false philosophy and subtile heretical opinions.

The careful study, therefore, of that period, cannot be prosecuted too earnestly. For " there were giants in those days "—giants among the leaders of the Gnostic and other heretical sects, who sought to corrupt the Faith, and giants among the Christian Fathers who, with equal learning and intellectual gifts sharpened and developed by the Faith itself, opposed those heretical leaders. The fundamental ideas and principles of all modern heresies are found in the false opinions of heathen and heretical sophists of those early ages of the Church. A study, therefore, of the refutations of those errors by the early Christian writers cannot well fail to arm our college and theological students with answers to all the heresies, scientific and philosophical, of modern times.

THE VIRGIN MOTHER OF GOOD COUNSEL. A History of the Ancient Sanctuary of Our Lady of Good Counsel in Gennazano, and of the Wonderful Apparition and Miraculous Translation of her Sacred Image from Scutari in Albania to Gennazano in 1467. With an Appendix on the Miraculous Crucifix, San Pio, Roman Ecclesiastical Education, etc. By *Monsignor George F. Dillon, D.D.*, Missionary Apostolic. Rome: Printed at the Offices of the Sacred Congregation of the Propaganda Fide. London: Burns & Oates. New York: Catholic Publication Society Co. 1884.

Among the many beautiful devotions to Mary, the Immaculate Mother of God, there is one that has very long been practiced in Italy, and which has spread into different regions of Continental Europe, but as yet has not made much progress in English-speaking countries. It is the devotion to " Our Lady of Good Counsel." The volume before us has been prepared for the purpose of making this devotion more fully known and propagating its observance. In the prosecution of this design the author has carefully traced the history of the venerable shrine at Gennazano in Italy, and of the miraculous picture of which it has been for. four centuries the resting place. In order to make this clearer and to elucidate the reasons on which this special devotion is based, he has also described the physical features of the locality, the magnificent scenery with which it is surrounded, and its previous history both in Christian and in antecedent pagan times. He also recounts the evidence of the existence of the sacred picture in Scutari, Albania, on the other side of the Adriatic Sea, previous to its miraculous translation to Gennazano.

Thus the scope of the work has been extended so that it embraces a very large amount of valuable information respecting the special history of famous localities in Italy, in both Christian and pagan times, its shrines and churches, the habits and sentiments of the people, the extent of their devotion, their firmness of faith, etc.

The work is written in charming style, narrative rather than didactic, and cannot fail to interest those who read it.

CATHOLIC BELIEF, or a Short and Simple Exposition of Catholic Doctrine. By the *Very Rev. Joseph Faà Di Bruno, D.D.*, Rector-General of the Pious Society of Missions, Church of SSmo Salvatore, in Orda, Ponte Sisto, Rome, and St. Peter's Italian Church, Hatton Garden, London. Fifth Edition. London: Burns & Oates. New York: Catholic Publication Society.

CATHOLIC BELIEF, etc. (same work as above). Author's American Edition, edited by *Rev. Louis A. Lambert*, author of *Notes on Ingersoll*, etc. Fifteenth Edition. New York, Cincinnati, and St. Louis: Benziger Brothers.

These are two different editions of the same work, severally brought out by the publishing houses named above. The latter, as we learn from the introduction to it, by the Right Rev. S. V. Ryan, D.D., Bishop of Buffalo, has been " revised and accommodated to the wants of our country."

The motive of the work is explained by the author as having its ground in his thirty years' experience as a missionary priest in England. In the course of his long-continued labors in that capacity, he found that nearly all the objections so often repeated against the faith and practice of the Roman Catholic Church, come from misunderstanding the true teaching of our holy religion. Influenced by this conviction, he set himself to the work of preparing an exposition of the Catholic faith, in which the doctrines of the Church are concisely and plainly expressed, and the common objections to them are answered. In the performance of his work, the author has aimed at simplicity and plainness, and has succeeded admirably well. He has avoided using technical expressions and language that might give even seemingly just cause of offence to any one. Yet, at the same time, he has never compromised or disguised the truth.

This book evinces rare ability and tact in " setting forth Catholic principles in few words, and with winning simplicity, yet at the same time with scholastic accuracy." It is pervaded, too, by a spirit of the warmest charity. While lucidly explaining and logically proving all the chief doctrines and practices of the Catholic Church. it is entirely free from polemical acerbity. It shows a delicate consideration and a just appreciation of the difficulties, intellectual, social, and moral, which converts to the faith must encounter and overcome, and endeavors, in the kindest manner, to remove misconceptions and deep-rooted prejudices from the minds of persons who are otherwise well-disposed, by instructing and edifying them, and thus leading them to the truth.

Another admirable feature of the book is, that the learned and able author, though thoroughly familiar with the principles, arguments, and facts involved in the subjects discussed, does not rely entirely on them. He fully realizes that the salvation of souls is the work of God. Hence he treats also of grace and the means of obtaining it, and the spirit of prayer pervades his whole work. Indeed, the latter part of his book is specially devoted to this subject.

The work is well calculated to benefit every one who reads it. Catholics will acquire clearer knowledge and deeper love for their holy faith. Protestants will have their misconceptions dispelled and their anti-Catholic prejudices softened and removed.

THE ROMAN HYMNAL. A Complete Manual of English Hymns and Latin Chants for the use of congregations, schools, colleges, and choirs. Compiled and arranged by *Rev. J. B. Young, S.J.*, choir master of St. Francis Xavier's Church, New York. Fr. Pustet & Co.: New York and Cincinnati.

One of the chief difficulties in the way of congregational singing is the scarcity of English hymns suited to large numbers of voices and intended for use in the Church. Attention seems of late to be earnestly directed to this fact, and very praiseworthy efforts have been made by several different compilers to supply the deficiency. Among these the author of the work before us seems to us to have been one of the most successful. Without in the least detracting from the merits of other publications having the same or a kindred object in view, we think that the work before us will aid largely in supplying the deficiency already referred to.

The compiler has very properly drawn largely upon the grand old hymns of Catholic ages, which are full of devotion, and impress themselves on the mind as well by their own interior spirit as by the pious associations which are inseparably connected with them. He has supplemented them with a careful selection of the best modern English Catholic hymns diligently gathered from various sources.

His work, therefore, if not complete, is certainly very full and comprehensive, and carefully discriminating. It contains the melodies and words of 194 English and Latin hymns, all the music of the Gradual and the Vespers for every Sunday and holyday in the year, with the Psalms written out under the music of all tones and endings; and also a number of choice prayers and meditations.

Additional value is given to the work by its first pages being occupied with matter which adapts it to use as a Manual of Devotion; consisting of Morning and Evening Prayers, Devotions for Mass, Manner of Serving Mass, Devotions for Confession, Prayers before Communion, Prayers after Communion, Prayers for Various Occasions, Pious Reflections and Meditations for every day of the Month, the Little Office of the Immaculate Conception, and the Little Office of the Holy Angels.

CATHOLIC CHRISTIANITY AND MODERN UNBELIEF. A Plain and Brief Statement of the Real Doctrines of the Roman Catholic Church, as Opposed to those Falsely Attributed to her by Christians who Reject her Authority, and by Unbelievers in Revelation. By the *Right Rev J. D. Ricards, D.D.*, Bishop of Retimo, and Vicar Apostolic of the Eastern Vicariate of the Cape Colony. New York, Cincinnati, and St. Louis: Benziger Brothers, Printers to the Apostolic See. 1884.

It seems rather strange that a book which deals with fiercely debated questions in Europe and America, and treats them, too, with far more than ordinary ability, and far more than ordinary insight into the interior meaning of those questions and their practical consequences, should come to us from South Africa, written by a missionary bishop, whose time is necessarily occupied with the duties of his office. It reminds us of a pen-picture we once read, describing the followers of St. Benedict in ancient times. Secluded from men, taking no part in their pursuits, their plans, and their conflicts, they looked down from their mountain top upon the world beneath them and understood, better than the active participants themselves, the motives and causes, the results and consequences of all their movements. So it seems to us with the author of this work. A bishop, engrossed in missionary labors, in a country only partly civilized, separated from the civilized world by a dreary waste of waters and a distance compared with which that of Europe from us is short, he yet finds time to write a book which exhibits a familiarity that is extraordinary with the questions around which, to-day, in Europe and America, the hottest polemical contests are waged. He is as well acquainted as a resident of France, or Germany, or England, or of the United States, with the various forms disbelief assumes in all those countries; their fallacies, their self-contradictions, and their irreconcilable hostility to Christianity.

In refuting these various forms of unbelief the author casts his statements and arguments in popular form and style, discarding all resort to
metaphysical technicalities.   Yet, at the same time, he states the objections of infidels to the doctrines of Christianity with precision and
clearness ; and the answers to these objections, though discursive and
popular in form, are strictly logical, direct, and conclusive.

The work immediately on its publication obtained the warm commendations of the South African press, and on its reception in England
it at once elicited favorable critical notices.   We warmly commend it
as both useful and interesting to all who desire to acquaint themselves
with conclusive answers to the current infidelity of our country and
times.

REASONS WHY WE SHOULD BELIEVE IN GOD, LOVE GOD, AND OBEY GOD.   By
Peter H Burnett, Author of "The Path that Led a Protestant Lawyer to the
Catholic Church," and "Recollections and Opinions of an Old Pioneer."   New
York : The Catholic Publication Society Co.   London : Burns & Oates.   1884.

In the first part of this work the author brings forward the evidences
of the existence of God that are furnished by the natural world, and
points to the proofs of divine purpose that are found in the structure of
various plants and animals.   He then answers various objections to the
line of argument he adopts.

In the second part of the work the subject of Evolution is discussed
and with much fulness of detail.   The theory of Natural Selection
is examined and the gratuitous character of many of its assumed premises—as well as the inconsequence of its conclusions—are pointed out.
It is shown that many of its alleged facts are unproved, and that others
lead to conclusions just the opposite of those which evolutionists deduce
from them.   Numerous citations, too, are made from naturalists of the
evolutionary school, showing that they are at direct variance with each
other, as regards their premises in some cases, and that in others, where
they agree upon common premises, they differ as regards the conclusions to be deduced from them.

In the third part of his work the author considers and exhibits the
evidences furnished by the Old Testament Dispensation of God's existence and of His having revealed Himself.   In distinct chapters the
Mosaic Record of Creation, the giving of the Divine Law through
Moses and the Pentateuch, are examined, and the evidences, both internal and external, to their having been inspired, are adduced.   Various
objections of infidels and rationalists are then taken up seriatim and
refuted.

In the fourth and last part of the work the external and internal evidences of the divine origin of the Christian religion are exhibited under
several different heads, and the leading objections are separately considered and their falsity exposed.

ANNUS SANCTUS: Hymns of the Church for the Ecclesiastical year.   Translated
from the Sacred Offices by various authors, with modern, original and other
hymns and an Appendix of Earlier Versions.   Selected and arranged by Orby
Shipley, M.A.   Volume I., Seasons of the Church ; Canonical Hours ; and
Hymns on Our Lord.   London and New York : Burns & Oates.   1884.

The compiler of this work says in his preface, that two main objects
are proposed to be promoted by its publication.   One of these is devotional ; the other is literary.   *Annus Sanctus* is intended, in the first
place, to be used as a book for spiritual reading, the contents of which

have been compiled from the sacred Offices, or authorized sources, and arranged according to the sequence of the seasons of the Church. It is intended, in the second place, to be "made a store-house for the in-gathering and preservation of much valuable hymnological labor, which, from the lapse of time, is in danger of being forgotten, and, from the decay of books, of being entirely lost."

At the same time other important objects are incidentally yet effec-tively promoted. The work is a valuable contribution towards the study of English Catholic hymnology. It is a collection, and is intended to be a very complete collection, of the efforts of English Catholics in this direction, so as to furnish the materials whence could be drawn the com-ponent parts of a Catholic hymn-book of the future.

The hymns in the volume before us are confined to general hymns for the seasons of the Church and their subdivisions, to a selection of hymns for the Canonical Hours, and to hymns specially addressed to our Divine Lord. The materials from which *Annus Sanctus* has been com-piled consist, first, of hymns which are already well known and highly prized by English Catholics; secondly, comparatively recent hymns that are little known; and thirdly, earlier hymns that, once popular and widely used, are almost forgotten and are in danger of being entirely lost to the Church.

The compiler has diligently devoted several years to the compilation of his book, ably assisted by many friends, who have generously placed at his disposal manuscripts and rare books not within reach of the general public. Should the present work secure a favorable reception, which it certainly merits, the compiler will supplement it with another volume.

LIFE OF SISTER ST. PIERRE, A CARMELITE OF TOURS, FRANCE. Written by her-self. Collated and Completed by Means of her Letters and the Annals of the Monastery, by the *Rev. P. Janvier*, Dean of the Chapter of the Metropolitan Church of Tours, Director of the Priests of the Holy Face. With the approba-tion of the Most Rev. Charles Colet, Archbishop of Tours. Translated from the French by Henri Le Mercier de Pombiray. Baltimore and New York: John Murphy & Co. 1884.

The name of the holy Carmelite of Tours has become so familiar in Religious Communities, and among devout persons in the world, that all are eager to know more of her, and especially of her communica-tions with our Divine Lord. This desire the volume before us will gratify. The seal once placed by ecclesiastical authority upon her writings and letters, has been removed by the same authority, and the holy Sister is allowed to speak for herself to the pious Christian public.

The special object of the biography now published is to promote de-votion to the Holy Face, and reparation for the blasphemies constantly uttered against our Blessed Redeemer. Nor could any purpose be more opportune or more urgent in its present necessity. Never was blasphemy more prevalent, and never was reparation for it more needed.

The work before us is a clear and graphic portrait of the virtues of Sister Saint-Pierre, her interior struggles and sufferings, and of the special revelations made to her; and especially of those by which the devotion to the Holy Face is encouraged and enjoined.

The book is a very interesting one, and that it is eminently calculated to excite to devout and pious thoughts and practices the high commen-dations it has received from numerous holy ecclesiastics are a sufficient guarantee.

MEDITATIONS FOR EVERY DAY IN THE YEAR. Collected from Different Spiritual Writers and suited to the Practice called a *Quarter of an Hour's Solitude.* Edited by *Rev. Roger Baxter, S. J.,* of Georgetown College. New York, Cincinnati, and St. Louis: Benziger Brothers. 1884.

"This precious book," to use the language of the Most Rev. Archbishop of Baltimore, was first written in Latin, in the year 1639. Manuscript copies of it were made and handed around among holy persons in the days of persecution in England. In 1669 it was translated into English, and in 1822 it was revised and modernized by Rev. Roger Baxter, S. J., of Georgetown College. It is now revised afresh and republished by Rev. P. Neale, S. J., of St. Inigo's, Md.

The work consists of short selections from the best ascetical writers of his period. The ordinary Christian, as well as the devout contemplative, may use its Meditations with great advantage.

HISTORY OF THE SODALITIES OF THE BLESSED VIRGIN MARY. A Memorial of the Tercentenary Jubilee; 1584—1884. Boston: Thomas B. Noonan & Company. 1885.

This little work, the title of which sufficiently suggests its scope and contents was first written and published in French by Father Louis Delplace, S. J. The translation into English was made by several ladies who are members of a Sodality of Children of Mary. The work contains matter that will be specially interesting to members of sodalities.

WILD FLOWERS FROM "THE MOUNTAIN-SIDE." Poems and Dramas by *Mercedes.* Press of J. B. Lippincott & Co., Philadelphia. 1885.

A volume of poems and verses, which, though put forth with a very modest and apologetic preface, yet, to use the words of the Most Rev. Archbishop Ryan, "exhale a true poetic fragrance." The latter part of the volume consists of dramas, which were written for actual performance at Commencements, and like occasions, in Catholic female academies. They are brief, spirited, and full of action—as dramas written for such purposes should be.

The spirit which pervades them, as well as all the poems, is an admirable one. We heartily commend the volume to our readers. The author is a lady originally from Philadelphia, and a Religious. The proceeds of the volume are devoted to the support of a hospital in one of our western cities.

RITUS CELEBRANDI MATRIMONII SACRAMENTUM, cum Formula impertiendi Benedictionem Nuptialem; accedunt versiones vulgares omnium Orationum, Anglice, Germanice, et Gallice conscriptæ. New York and Cincinnati: Fr. Pustet & Co.

Nothing more useful for the priest has, for a long time, appeared than is this separate publication of the marriage ceremonial. It will enable the reverend clergy to officiate without using either the Missal or the Ritual, as all the instructions and prayers are given in full, on four pages of convenient size (6½ by 9½ inches), and in four languages, Latin, English, French, and German. It is printed in large type, with red and black ink, and bound in strong leather cover. The price is only $1.

TO CLERG MEN.

PLEASE READ.

It may seem a small matter, but it is nevertheless one of the most important, and at the same time most difficult questions for a clergyman to determine, How shall I dress? A wide latitude is allowed to the laity on this subject, who may, if they please, indulge their own peculiar taste in the matter of dress, whether it accords with the prevailing style or not. But not so with the clergy. They must dress in a manner distinctive from other men, and in keeping with their sacred calling. And how to do this successfully, how to strike the happy medium between the secular and the ultra clerical in this matter of their dress, is where the difficulty lies.

Three things are necessary to a good clerical garment. First, the material should always be plain black goods of fine quality. Second, it should be cut in a style, modest, unpretentious, and gentlemanly, with just sufficient fulness in front, and length in the skirts, to indicate the wearer's profession. And Third, the fit should always be close and as near perfect as possible, for no matter how fine the goods, or how clerical the cut, if the garment is not a good fit it is an eyesore, and a cause of constant discomfiture to the wearer.

Now many years of experience in this branch of our business have given us a familiarity with the wants of clergymen in this matter of dress that has proved of great service to our patrons; and we shall be pleased to give to all who may favor us in the future the benefit of our best judgment on the subject.

Our large experience and extensive facilities enable us to give entire satisfaction, not only as regards the style and quality of the garments themselves, but also as to the reasonableness of the prices.

On application a set of samples will be forwarded to any Clergyman in the U. S., with full instructions for self-measurement. The samples will be of goods which will cost, when made up, from $20 to $50.

Address,

WANAMAKER & BROWN,

OAK HALL, SIXTH AND MARKET STREETS,

PHILADELPHIA.

The Largest Retail Clothing House in America.

P. S.—Samples also sent and orders received for all kinds of Gentlemen's Clothing at the lowest possible prices.

THE AMERICAN CATHOLIC

QUARTERLY REVIEW.

THE AMERICAN CATHOLIC QUARTERLY REVIEW is issued regularly in January, April, July, and October.

EACH NUMBER CONTAINS 192 pages, large octavo, printed from legible type, on fine white paper.

SUBSCRIPTION, $5.00 per annum, payable in advance, or $1.25 a single copy. Postage free to all parts of the U. S.

The Editorial Department is conducted by Right Rev. James A. Corcoran, D.D.

It is DESIGNED that the *American Catholic Quarterly Review* shall be of the highest character that can be given it by the educated Catholic mind of the United States and of Europe.

It is NOT PROPOSED that it shall be confined to the discussion of theological subjects, but that it shall embrace within its scope all subjects of interest to educated Catholics, whether philosophical, historical, scientific, literary, or political—using the latter term in its original and proper meaning. Partisan politics, or politics in the popular sense of the word, it is scarcely necessary to say, will be rigidly excluded.

THE MOST LEARNED and scholarly writers that can be secured will be enlisted in support of the *Review* as regular and occasional contributors; and every effort will be made by its conductors to render it an able and efficient auxiliary to the Church in her warfare against modern error.

Subscriptions respectfully solicited.

Address, 		*HARDY & MAHONY,*

505 CHESTNUT STREET,

POST-OFFICE BOX, 1044, 		PHILADELPHIA.

THE

AMERICAN

CATHOLIC QUARTERLY

REVIEW.

Bonum est homini ut eum veritas vincat volentem, quia malum est homini ut eum veritas vincat
invitum. Nam ipsa vincat necesse est, sive negantem sive confitentem.
S. AUG. EPIST. ccxxxviii. AD PASCENT.

PHILADELPHIA:

HARDY AND MAHONY, PUBLISHERS AND PROPRIETORS,

505 CHESTNUT ST.,—P. O. BOX 1044,

York: D. & J. SADLIER & CO., F. PUSTET—*Boston:* THOS. B. NOONAN & CO., NICH. M. WILLI
altimore: JOHN MURPHY & CO., JOHN B. PIET & Co.—*Cincinnati:* BENZIGER BROS., F. PUSTE
St. Louis: P. FOX, BENZIGER BROS., B. HERDER—*San Francisco:* A. WALDTEUFEL—*New Orleans.*
CHARLES D. ELDER—*Montreal:* D. & J. SADLIER & CO.—*St. John, N. B.:* T. O'BRIEN &
Co.—*London:* BURNS & OATES—*Dublin:* W. H. SMITH & SON, M. H. GILL & SON.

THE AMERICAN CATHOLIC

QUARTERLY REVIEW.

VOL. X.—JULY, 1885.—No. 39.

THE SYNTHETIC PHILOSOPHY OF HERBERT SPENCER.

A System of Synthetic Philosophy. Vol. I. First Principles. By Herbert Spencer. New York: 1883.

A GNOSTICISM is, in our age, deemed by many the best and most solid philosophical system. It is thought at once to embody the most comprehensive knowledge of nature, the mysteries of which modern researches have so wonderfully succeeded in bringing to light, and to open for us the only rational view that can be taken of the things beyond experience. It is praised as the wisdom of the learned, since it affords them an insight into all knowable truth, and the enlightenment of the masses, because it frees them from inveterate prejudices and leads them to true happiness upon earth. It spreads among all classes of society, being taught and expounded from the chairs of the universities and in the lecture-halls of the cities, in the erudite works of philosophers and in popular monthlies and other magazines. Centuries may pass away, and agnosticism, with its twin sister, materialism, will still be in power; not so much because it has been clothed with all the splendor of modern science, as because it pampers a strong and indelible tendency of human nature, the love for the sensible and material.

Among the agnostics of our days none is more prominent than

Herbert Spencer. What praises are not lavished on him? He has, it is said, reduced agnosticism to a perfect system. All its conclusions have been drawn by him from first principles and united under one general aspect; by him all its tenets are shown to be in full agreement, to illustrate and uphold one another. In his writings the whole positive knowledge thus far attained by mankind seems to be enlisted for the defence of the agnostic view. Nay, all philosophical systems contrived by modern thought, if purified of misconceptions, if considered in their general tendency, are proved by him to result in the one philosophy of the unknowable. He is, on this account, admired as the greatest and clearest thinker of the age, as the apostle of the understanding, as the restorer of true philosophy, and the champion of universal truth.

Such being his renown, who would not be desirous of becoming acquainted with Mr. Spencer's ideas? Enhanced must this desire be if we not seldom hear that his speculation is not hostile to Christianity, but rather, if well understood, leads back to God, the First Cause; being, in reality, as it purports to be, a reconciliation of science and religion. The outlines of his entire system are laid down in " The First Principles. " From this first volume of his work on synthetic philosophy we may both obtain an insight into the foundations and the intrinsic connection of this extensive structure, and observe the whole in all its bearings and consequences. To attain this end by the shortest way, we put the following questions: I. What, in Mr. Spencer's opinion, can we know, and what can we not know? II. What is the nature of the unknowable? III. What is the nature of the knowable? IV. In what does the whole system result, and by what method is that result reached?

I.

The first and most fundamental position held by Mr. Spencer is, that we cannot know but what manifests itself to us by experience, and that this itself we do not know as to its essence or nature, but only as to its relation; not as to the entity it has without us, but as to the impressions it produces within us. He did not start that idea. It had already been conceived by the Grecian philosophers; it had been wrought into a whole philosophical system by David Hume; it is adopted by all agnostics and positivists as the basis of all their assertions. Mr. Spencer is but one of the many interpreters of the relativity of knowledge, as this theory is termed. The object of our direct perceptions, he says, is not the thing without us, but the impression produced on our faculties, namely, the sensation of heat or pressure, and not the body that is hot or hard. But impressions are relative. Into thought and consciousness the various impressions enter only by being compared as to their likeness and unlikeness. Relative, therefore, is the form under which anything is apprehended and known by us. Take away the relations from the object, and it becomes by that very fact *unthinkable;* just as a body, as soon as its color has vanished away, is rendered invisible. The relative, consequently, is the knowable; the absolute, the unknowable.[1] Not even science can give us a higher or a deeper knowledge; for its task is but to compare the phenomena or impressions, and, by discovering the traits in which they resemble one another, to reduce them to common laws and classes. Beyond the highest generalizations thus attained it cannot go. By no scientific researches can we grasp the origin or nature of things outside us; nor can we form universal notions by conceiving the essence of objects, and derive from them universal principles .from which to reason *a priori*. For universals are nothing but images that faintly resemble the average of the objects of a certain class; they are, therefore, but symbols of the latter, and have no validity unless verified by experience (§ 9).

That such is the nature of our cognition Mr. Spencer attempts to prove, chiefly from two reasons : First, from what he takes for an undeniable fact, that our ultimate ideas concerning the causes of things, both intrinsic and extrinsic, are self-contradictory (§ 11). A self-existent being is inconceivable; for it would be necessary to think of its existence as endless and beginningless. But this would imply a past time of infinite length, which is an evident impossibility. Hence the self-existence of the world, as well as its creation by a self-existent being distinct from it, is *unthinkable*, because both involve marks no less contradictory than those of a square fluid. The theistic, pantheistic and atheistic hypotheses are, therefore, alike absurd, all being based on the same illegitimate and illusive conception. To the same impossibilities we find ourselves reduced, when we inquire into the causes of our impressions. A cause, he grants, and even a first cause of them, we are compelled to assume. But how conceive of it ? Is it limited ? Then it supposes the infinite which surrounds it. Is it unlimited ? Then we give up the principle of causality, admitting an existence without a cause. Is it dependent ? Then it is not first. Is it absolute and independent ? Then nothing can be besides it, nothing can exist by it, because by action the absolute would undergo a change and would become relative. Nay, these three conceptions, as he imagines he proves from Mansel, imply contradiction to one another, if considered as attributes of one and the self-same being. The passage he approvingly quotes from the late

---

[1] See " First Principles," Part I., Chapter IV.

Dean ends with the following words: " The conception of the Absolute and Infinite, from whatever side we view it, appears encompassed with contradictions.   There is a contradiction in supposing such an object to exist, whether alone or in conjunction with others; and there is a contradiction in supposing it not to exist. There is a contradiction in conceiving it as one; and there is a contradiction in conceiving it as many.   There is a contradiction in conceiving it as personal; and there is a contradiction in conceiving it as impersonal.   It cannot, without a contradiction, be represented as active; nor, without an equal contradiction, be represented as inactive.   It cannot be conceived as the sum of all existence; nor yet can it be conceived as a part only of that sum."[1]

No less self-destructive are the proximate causes reached by science.   Time, space, matter, motion, action, the *ego*, which we are compelled to regard as existing without our conception in themselves, are, if analyzed, all found to teem with contradictions (§§ 15–22).

To show that we know nothing but relations, Mr. Spencer advances a still deeper reason; he resorts to the very nature of the cognitive act.   Our vital faculties he considers as not distinct from the material forces.   Life, in general, he says, consists in counteraction on exterior impressions or influences, in a correspondence between outer and inner actions, in an adjustment between internal and external relations in order to keep the being in balance.   Intellection falls under the same notion.   Is not intellectual truth guiding us to successful action and to the consequent maintenance of life, and, according to its very definition, simply the active correspondence between subjective and objective relations?   What conclusion is to be drawn from this is apparent. " If every act of knowing is the formation of a relation in consciousness parallel to a relation in the environment, then the relativity of knowledge is self-evident—becomes, indeed, a truism.   Thinking being *relationing*, no thought can ever express more than relations" (§ 25).

Thus far Mr. Spencer is in harmony with all other agnostics. Neither the principles from which he reasons nor the conclusions which he draws are unlike to theirs.   But, having arrived at this point, he begins to frame a structure of his own.   The relativity of knowledge, he maintains, whilst it excludes a definite conception of the absolute, necessarily implies an indefinite one of it.   The noumenon, everywhere named as the antithesis of the phenomenon, is throughout necessarily thought of as an actuality.   It is altogether impossible to conceive that our knowledge is a knowledge of

---

[1] Page 42.

appearances only, without conceiving, at the same time, a reality of which they are appearances, a knowledge of impressions without conceiving a power or cause by which they are produced. Nor can we conceive of the relative without something to which it is opposed, or something in which the relations are and from which they can be abstracted. Now this something is evidently the absolute. The thought, however, of the absolute is altogether vague and indeterminate. We conceive some cause of the impressions, some reality under the relations. Yet what and how that cause or that reality is in itself, we cannot at all conceive. Accordingly we call the absolute the unknowable; the phenomena or impressions, both singly and reduced to classes, the knowable, understanding by knowledge a clear and definite perception (§ 26).

The unknowable is the object of religion, the knowable the object of science. Religion is concerned with the ultimate verity, the inscrutable origin of the visible universe; or rather, it consists in the consciousness and awe of that mystery. Herein all religions agree, and that into which they all converge must be their nature and their common soul of truth. Religion, therefore, in general, is based on a true foundation. Yet, in particular, every religion has become erroneous and irreligious by attempting to represent the incomprehensible in a comprehensible manner, and to render the ultimate cause knowable, the mysterious unmysterious. It was science that showed the inconsistency of the arguments made use of by religion, in order to unravel the nature of the absolute. Science has purified religion. But science, in its turn, has become unscientific by adopting untenable hypotheses and substituting for the agencies and causes which it proved to be absurdly believed in by religion, others not less absurd and self-contradictory. Both science and religion, however, have always been progressing in the pursuit of their real object; religion has become ever more conscious of the incomprehensibility of the absolute; science has ever more cleaved to experience and ceased to consider causes and forces as knowable. All conflicts between science and religion were the consequence of either one's outstepping its own sphere in contravention to its own end and interest. Perfect reconciliation between them will be obtained, if science will confine itself to the knowable, the relative; religion to the unknowable, the absolute.

Nor is it to be feared that religion will suffer by the division. For the confession of the unknowableness of the absolute is the true religion, the acknowledgment of the limitation of our intellect the true religious position. " May we not," says Mr. Spencer, " without hesitation affirm that a sincere recognition of the truth that our own and all other existence is a mystery absolutely and forever beyond our comprehension, contains more of true religion than all the dogmatic theology ever written ?"[1] (§ 27–35).

The line of distinction being drawn between that which we can know and that which we cannot know, let us now at once proceed to examine the nature of the unknowable.

II.

As we have seen above, the unknowable is the absolute, the unconditioned, the ultimate cause of all impressions and phenomena, and is, for this reason, frequently termed the eternal, universal, infinite creative power or energy. But how shall we reconcile all these appellations with the very name of the unknowable ? How can eternity, infinity, omnipresence, causation be predicated of it at the same time that any definite notion of it is emphatically denied to be possible, and that all those attributes are regarded as inconceivable? Mr. F. Harrison, indeed, charges Mr. Spencer, on that account, with palpable self-contradiction. It will be necessary carefully to reconsider the respective notions and definitions. In Mr. Spencer's opinion, the irrelative or absolute is that which is clothed with relations ; and the infinite is that which underlies the limits, that from which limits may be abstracted, but not that which positively excludes all limits. The universal power or eternal energy is that which is always in our mind whenever we think of impressions as produced. So conceived, the absolute is a generalization or abstraction, it is universal being, not distinct from particular existence, but common and intrinsic to all that exists and is conceived, not determinate, but altogether undetermined. If such, of course, the absolute is apprehended only by a vague and indefinite conception. To convince the reader that this is Mr. Spencer's train of thought, we shall let him speak for himself. " We are conscious," he says, " of the Relative as existence under conditions and limits ; it is impossible that these conditions and limits can be thought of apart from something to which they give the form ; the abstraction of these conditions and limits is, by the hypothesis, the abstraction of them *only ;* consequently there must be a residuary consciousness of something that filled up their outlines; and this indefinite something constitutes our consciousness of the Non-relative or Absolute. Impossible though it is to give to this consciousness any qualitative or quantitative expression whatever, it is not the less certain that it remains with us a positive and indestructible element of thought."[2]

" When we are taught that a piece of matter, regarded by us as existing externally, cannot be really known, but that we can know only impressions produced on us, we are yet by the relativity of our

---

thought compelled to think of these in relation to a positive cause —the notion of a real existence, which generated these impressions, becomes nascent. If it be proved to us that every notion of a real existence which we can frame is utterly inconsistent with itself— that matter, however conceived by us, cannot be matter as it actually is, our conception, though transfigured, is not destroyed : there remains the sense of reality, dissociated as far as possible from those special forms under which it was before represented in thought. Though philosophy condemns successively each attempted conception of the Absolute—though it proves to us that the Absolute is not this, nor that,—though in obedience to it we negative, one after another, each idea as it arises ; yet as we cannot expel the entire contents of consciousness, there ever remains behind an element which passes into new shapes. The continual negation of each particular form and limit simply results in the more or less complete abstraction of all forms and limits, and so ends in an indefinite consciousness of the unformed and unlimited." [1] " By fusing a series of states of consciousness, in each of which, as it arises, the limitations and conditions are abolished, there is produced a consciousness of something unconditioned. To speak more rigorously —this consciousness is not the abstract of any one group of thoughts, ideas, or conceptions; but it is the abstract of *all* thoughts, ideas, or conceptions. That which is common to them all, and cannot be got rid of, is what we predicate by the word existence. Dissociated as this becomes from each of its modes by the perpetual changes of those modes, it remains as an indefinite consciousness of something constant under all modes—of being apart from its appearances. The distinction we feel between special and general existence is the distinction between that which is changeable in us and that which is unchangeable." [2]

After this we ought not to be astonished if Mr. Spencer most energetically refuses to attribute to the absolute personality, intelligence, and will (§ 31). For attributes of that kind suppose the Supreme Being to be distinct from the visible universe, and to be of a determinate nature; whereas the absolute he speaks of is quite indeterminate, common and intrinsic to all things that exist, being only their highest generalization and abstraction.

However, though Mr. Spencer's absolute being is indefinite and void of all determination, he has learned from the German idealists to look upon it as self-determining. It so becomes the universal cause, immanent in its effects. It thus develops out of itself the whole existing world, and manifests itself by the phenomena of the universe. That this is the view he takes is evident from his reply

---

[1] Page 93. [2] Page 95.

to Mr. Harrison in the *Nineteenth Century*,[1] where he repudiates causation by which the creating power is separated from the created thing, and from his scornfully styling the Christian idea of creation "the carpenter's theory."

Viewed in this light, the absolute at once changes its character. Being the source and root of all, it appears superior in perfection to any other thing, and is the summit of all reality. Hence it is that Mr. Spencer in several places considers it as higher than nature, and as too great to be comprehended by us. "Is it not just possible," he says, "that there is a mode of being as much transcending Intelligence and Will as these transcend mechanical motion? It is true that we are totally unable to conceive any such higher mode of being. But this is not a reason for questioning its existence; it is rather the reverse. Have we not seen how utterly incompetent our minds are to form even an approach to a conception of that which underlies all phenomena? Is it not proved that this incompetency is the incompetency of the conditioned to grasp the Unconditioned? Does it not follow that the Ultimate Cause cannot in any great respect be conceived by us because it is in every respect greater than can be conceived? And may we not therefore rightly refrain from assigning to it any attributes whatever, on the ground that such attributes, derived as they must be from our own natures, are not elevations, but degradations?"[2]

From all we have said thus far it is to be inferred that the absolute in Mr. Spencer's philosophy is not God. The absolute he speaks of is not infinite, but indefinite; not being or existence itself, but abstract, indeterminate, universal being, intrinsic to the world and indistinct from it.[3] So he himself has unmistakably defined it at the very outset of his speculation. Whenever later on he elevates it to the supreme degree of perfection, he does so only by a strange confusion of the indeterminate and the infinite, borrowed from idealistic pantheism. At most, therefore, his absolute being may be a pantheistic divinity. Nobody is, in fact, louder than he in protesting against the one personal God adored by the Christians. Why should we say that he, in reality, does not hold what he constantly asserts and attempts to prove? We have no reason not to believe him; it is, on the contrary, to be acknowledged that in denying a personal Deity he is altogether consistent. Not to see this only those can fail who have not yet succeeded in distinguishing the infinite from the abstract and indefinite, the being on the supreme grade of perfection from that on the lowest, nearest to nothingness.

The judgment we have pronounced on the real value and in-

---

[1] 1884, page 832.　　[2] Page 109.

[3] See St. Thom., Sum. c. Gent., lib. I., p. 26.

wardness of the unknowable or absolute will be greatly confirmed by the examination of the knowable, which is now to follow.

III.

The knowable consists of the phenomena or impressions. It concerns, of course, philosophy, but not under the same aspect as it does experience or even as it does science. Science, if we are to believe Mr. Spencer, reduces the phenomena to certain classes, philosopy reduces all the divers classes to one supreme idea; it is the unification of all sciences, the fusion of them into a whole by the integration of truth or by the highest generalization. Science is partly unified knowledge, philosophy is completely unified knowledge (§ 37). By such unification, it is thought, the true nature of the phenomena will, as far as it is possible, be revealed to us. Let us follow the renowned agnostic in his pursuit of unity; we shall then know at least what the knowable is in his opinion, and what has become of the universe under his magic wand.

Unification, we are first told, may be obtained in two ways; either by ascending from the particular to the universal by induction, or by descending from the universal to the particular by deduction. The latter way is taken in General Philosophy. But here at once a difficulty presents itself. How can agnostic philosophy, relying exclusively on experience, get into possession of universal truths from which to deduce its conclusions? There are, indeed, it is answered, no *a priori* truths known independently of experience, but there are certain intuitions forced on us by the very structure of our organs, a structure which is nothing else but the registered and accumulated experience of ourselves and much more of our ancestors from whom we have inherited the nervous system.[1] Such intuitions or fundamental views, without which we cannot think at all, are not really self-evident, they are data or postulates assumed questionably and as *provisionally* true. Yet they themselves, as well as the conclusions drawn from them, may be compared with experience, and if throughout congruity is perceived, both their truth is proved and the unification of the phenomena accomplished. "Debarred," says Mr. Spencer, "as we are from everything beyond the relative, truth, raised to its highest form, can be for us nothing more than perfect agreement throughout the whole range of our experience, between those representations of things which we distinguish as ideal and those presentations of things which we distinguish as real. If, by discovering a proposition to be untrue, we mean nothing more than discovering a difference between a thing expected and a thing per-

---

[1] See the foot-note of page 179.

ceived, then a body of conclusions, in which no difference any-where occurs, must be what we mean by an entirely true body of conclusions. And here, indeed, it becomes also obvious that, setting out with these fundamental intuitions provisionally assumed to be true—that is, provisionally assumed to be congruous with all other dicta of consciousness—the process of proving or disproving the congruity becomes the business of Philosophy ; and the complete establishment of the congruity becomes the same thing as the complete unification of knowledge in which Philosophy reaches its goal."[1]

What, then, are the data required by agnostic philosophy? They are three in number : an unknowable power, the existence of knowable likenesses and differences among the manifestations of that power, and a resulting segregation of the manifestations into those of the subject and object, the *ego* and *non-ego*.[2] For each of them a few words of explanation are necessary. To begin with the second, consciousness mainly consists in the comparison of our mental states, the perception of likeness or unlikeness, of congruity or incongruity between them. This being the process that constitutes reasoned knowledge, philosophy, if it is not to destroy itself, must postulate the truth of consciousness in affirming the existence of such likeness or unlikeness. Nay, we must even take the evidence of likeness or unlikeness as identical with the permanent consciousness of it. "To say that a given congruity or incongruity exists, is simply our way of saying that we invariably have a consciousness of it along with the consciousness of the compared things. We know nothing more of existence than a continued manifestation."[3] But, manifestations which make up our mental states suppose something that is manifested, and impressions something that is impressed. That something, manifested to us and impressed on us whenever we have some cognizance, is the absolute unknowable power. Being the ultimate ground and cause of all, it is the first fundamental datum, and must, at the same time, be the most universal principle of unification. But these manifold manifestations, which are at once our cognitions and the existence we know, are reduced to order by classification. They are first segregated spontaneously, that is, by the very law of thought, into two great classes, the vivid ones, called also perceptions or impressions, and the faint ones, generally termed ideas, the latter being but copies or repetitions of the former. "The faint manifestations forming a continuous whole we call the *ego ;* the vivid manifestations indissolubly bound together we call the *non-ego.* Or, rather, each order of manifestations carries with it the irresistible implication of some power that mani-

---

[1] Page 139.   [2] Page 157.   [3] Page 142.

fests itself; and by the words *ego* and *non-ego*, respectively, we mean the power that manifests itself in the faint forms, and the power that manifests itself in the vivid forms "[1] (§§ 39–46).

So much about the origin of the three first data. On them we may base others, if we continue to classify the manifestations. For these, separated into the two divisions of self and not-self, are re-divisible, and next into the ultimate scientific ideas, time, space, matter, motion, and force. Yet, as above these ideas were proved to be self-contradictory, if considered as existing without us, a doubt may rise whether it is possible to base any truth on them. The difficulty will be solved, as soon as the genuine notion of reality is established. Reality is not a thing that is outside us, but corre-sponds to our impressions or ideas as their cause or object. This is the view taken only by the peasant and the metaphysician; reality is nothing else but the persistence of a manifestation in con-sciousness. Now, impressions or manifestations are in our con-sciousness as effects of the unknowable that underlies them as their immanent cause. Hence we distinguish a twofold reality, a relative one, which is the persistence in thought of relations under some definite form, and an absolute one, which is the persistence in thought of the common substratum of all relations, surviving them under all changes and under any form whatever (§ 46). The ultimate scientific ideas, as they persist in consciousness, no doubt have reality, but a relative one only. For that they are but relations is evident both *a priori* and from experience.

As relations are the form of all our thoughts, it is easily under-stood that the ultimate ideas must all be derived from them by division and analysis. Now relations are of two orders, of sequence and of co-existence. The abstract of all sequence is time; the abstract of all co-existence is space. So, in fact, this latter is ex-perienced; we are conscious of it as of co-existent positions. It is not strictly an entity, a sensible existence, but the blank form left behind when the realities are taken away. Matter is the exist-ence that keeps the position by resistance to our touch. "Our conception of matter," says Mr. Spencer, "reduced to its simplest stage, is that of co-existent positions that offer resistance, as con-trasted with our conception of space, in which the co-existent positions offer no resistance. We think of Body as bounded by surfaces that resist; and as made up throughout of parts that resist. Mentally abstract the co-existent resistances, and the conscious-ness of Body disappears, leaving behind it the consciousness of space. And since the group of co-existing resistant positions con-stituting a portion of matter is uniformly capable of giving us

---

impressions of resistance in combination with various muscular adjustments, according as we touch its near, its remote, its right or its left side, it results that as different muscular adjustments habitually indicate different co-existence, we are obliged to conceive every portion of matter as containing more than one resistant position,—that is, as occupying space.   Hence the necessity we are under of representing to ourselves the ultimate elements of Matter as being at once extended and resistant."[1]

The conception of motion arises from that of space, time, and matter. "A something that moves ; a series of positions occupied in succession; and a group of co-existent positions united in thought with the successive ones—these are the constituents of the idea" (§ 49).   Matter is thus prior to space, time, and motion, but it is not primary, being itself built up from the experience of force.[2] A single impression of force is receivable by the senses ; a multiplication of such impressions, differing in kind and degree and differently combined, gives the material of manifold relations; and these, as they are diverse in their forms, as well as their contents, make up a body moving in space and time.   Force, therefore, as impressed on our senses, is the ultimate element of matter. Being, as such, no more capable of being classified according to likeness and difference, it is inscrutable.   Still it is not the absolute cause, but only its immediate effect, inherent in it, and not separated from it (§ 50).

The ultimate scientific ideas being explained, and their reality being evinced, we deduce from them seven primary truths, which so serve philosophy as further data that they also prove to be conformable to experience.   The first truth is the indestructibility of matter ; it means that matter cannot be called out of non-existence, or be made non-existent.   The *a priori* reason is, that did matter not at any time exist, we should not have the elements necessary to form a thought.   Its non-existence, therefore, is *unthinkable.* Experience, too, shows that phenomena do not arise out of nothing, or vanish away into nothing, but are simply changes or transformations of substances.   Such experimental perception, however, amounts merely to this, that the force which in a given quantity of matter exercises resistance remains always the same ; for it is by resistance that we become cognizant of matter (§§ 52–55).

The second truth is the continuity of motion. Motion, like matter, is never destroyed, but only transformed, the principle of activity implied by it always continuing the same.   This property of motion is proved *a posteriori* by scientists, yet so that their estima-

---

[1] Page 166.

[2] In the Appendix (page 578) Mr. Spencer calls matter a localized manifestation of force.

tion is based on the indestructibility of force; and is demonstrated *a priori* by philosophers from our incapacity of suppressing in thought force, the cause of motion (§§ 55–60).

The third truth is the persistence of force. The indestructibility of matter and the continuity of motion rest on the unchangeableness or constancy of the units of force, and this, again, supposes the persistence of force, not of that which we are immediately conscious of in our muscular efforts, for this does not persist, but of that which we are always indefinitely conscious of as the ultimate, but immanent cause of all impressions and all phenomena. Thus the unknowable, in which religion and science coalesce, the ground underlying all experience, the eternal energy, the supreme principle which is the basis of all scientific unification, turns out to be the persistence of force.

From it the four other truths are deduced. Two of them regard force. According to the one, the relations among forces always persist the same, there being an invariable connection between every antecedent and consequent; according to the other, any force displayed in each surrounding change does, in that act of expenditure, undergo a metamorphosis into an equivalent amount of some other force. The two last truths refer to motion. All motion is rhythmical or periodical, and all motion follows the line of the greatest attraction or least resistance[1] (Part ii., Chap. iv.–xi.).

These seven laws, for such are the primary truths above expounded, Mr. Spencer finds everywhere in nature at work so as to see them throughout verified by experience. Not only in inorganic matter, in the formation of the universe out of a nebulous mass, and in the geological changes are they followed; they govern, likewise, the organic realms, the mind, the will, and society. Life, whether sensitive, intellectual, or moral, is nothing but the play of attractive and repulsive forces, transformed, exchanged, and tending to equilibrium. All mental phenomena are a transformation of physical impressions. "Various classes of facts," Mr. Spencer remarks, "unite to prove that the law of metamorphosis, which holds among the physical forces, holds equally

---

[1] For the two forces themselves from which the direction of motion results, Mr. Spencer accounts by the form of our experience. "Matter," he says, "cannot be conceived except as manifesting forces of attraction and repulsion. Body is distinguished in our consciousness from space, by its opposition to our muscular energies; and this opposition we feel under the twofold form of a cohesion that hinders our efforts to rend, and a resistance that hinders our efforts to compress. Without resistance there can be merely empty extension. Without cohesion there can be no resistance. Probably this conception of antagonistic forces is originally derived from the antagonism of our flexor and extensor muscles. But be this as it may, we are obliged to think of all objects as made up of parts that attract and repel each other, since this is the form of our experience of all objects." Page 224.

between them and the mental forces. Those modes of the Unknowable which we call motion, heat, light, chemical affinity, etc., are alike transformable into each other and into those modes of the Unknowable which we distinguish as sensation, motion, thought; these, in their turn, being directly or indirectly re-transformable into the original shapes."[1] Again, vital actions, even thought and volition, are motions along the line of greatest attraction, or least resistance, which, when, by frequent repetition, they have become movements set up in certain directions, widen the channels of operation within the organism. Social movements start, population increases, commerce is developed where the least resistance is met with, where the greatest result is to be obtained with the least labor. Undulation is nowhere more striking than in the organic processes both of individual living beings and of species, in consciousness, in feelings and emotions, in national developments, in religion, and in science.

Important as the results thus far attained may seem to be for agnostic speculation, Mr. Spencer is conscious of not yet having solved the problem set before him. The ultimate scientific ideas have been considered but singly, each in its peculiar sphere. But force, matter, motion, do not stand apart; they form one well-connected whole. What law do they follow in their joint action? What rule, common to all the single agents, regulates their co-operation throughout the universe? Only by answering this question will philosophy accomplish the unification of all knowledge.

The idea which thus completely explains and unifies all phenomena of the world as a whole is, in Mr. Spencer's opinion, that of evolution and dissolution. These two processes include all changes ever observed, and make up the entire history of the world, comprising as they do its appearance out of the perceptible into the imperceptible, and its disappearance out of the perceptible into the imperceptible; though we ought not to imagine that first the one and then the other takes place, because every transformation implies both of them, yet so that either of the two is predominant. Evolution, in its general aspect, is concentration, or rather condensation of matter with concomitant dissipation of motion, whereas dissolution is the absorption of motion with concomitant disintegration or diffusion of matter. However, evolution is scarcely ever seen in that single and primary form. It is, in general, not single, but compound; such at least it is in a slowly condensing body, which, during concentration, is exposed to many external influences and so undergoes many secondary changes,

---

[1] Page 217.

particularly if it retains a great deal of molecular motion. Hence in compound evolution there is, together with the transition from the less coherent to the more coherent form, a passage also from the uniform to the multiform, or from the homogeneous to the heterogeneous. For while there is a progressive concentration of the aggregate, the parts into which the whole divides and subdivides are also condensed and become unlike. So the same process is exhibited by the whole and by its members; as the mass is *integrating* (condensing) and at the same time *differentiating* (being rendered different) from other masses, so each part of it is *integrating* and simultaneously *differentiating* from other parts.

Consequent on differentiation is a change from the indefinite to the definite, or in other words, an increase of the distinctness of its parts. For as the whole gains density, it becomes sharply marked off from the space or matter lying outside of it; and as each separated division draws by concentration into its mass the first imperfectly disunited segments from other divisions, it acquires a precise outline. But matter is condensed only as far as motion is dissipated. Accordingly, as there is, besides the primary redistribution, a secondary redistribution of matter, so there must be both a primary and a secondary redistribution of motion; and as the material parts of the whole become more unlike and definite so also motion is rendered more multiform and distinct. If concrete matter arises by aggregation of diffused matter, then concrete motion arises by the aggregation of diffused motion. The formula, therefore, of the whole process stands thus: *Evolution is an integration of matter and concomitant dissipation of motion; during which matter passes from an indefinite, incoherent homogeneity to a definite coherent heterogeneity; and during which the retained motion undergoes a parallel transformation*[1] (P. ii. Chapt. xii., xvii).

It remains still to reduce evolution itself, so manifold in its partial processes, to one common cause. For that purpose it will be retraced to four *factors*, and each *factor* will be retraced to the persistence of force, which so becomes the absolutely ultimate principle that transcends all experience by underlying it, and furnishes a common basis for the widest generalizations. The first factor of evolution is the instability of the homogeneous. Any finite aggregate must, owing to unequal exposure of its parts to incidental forces, soon lose its homogeneity. The relations of inside and outside and of comparative nearness to neighboring agencies imply the reception of unlike influences, which must necessarily produce unlike changes in the parts dissimilarly acted upon. Nor does this hold true only of the whole; the process must, for the

---

[1] Page 396.

same reason, repeat itself in each of the subordinate groups of units. Hence another factor is inferred, the multiplication of effects. "Every differentiated unit is not only a seat, but also a cause of further differentiation, since, in growing unlike to other parts, it becomes a centre of unlike reactions on incident forces, and by so adding to the diversity of forces at work, adds to the diversity of effects produced," because each differentiated force must produce, throughout the aggregate, a further series of differentiations. Whilst the two factors just mentioned account for differentiation, segregation is the factor that works the increasing distinctness of parts which accompanies homogeneity. Mixed units or unlike groups of units of which the aggregate consists, if under the influence of a force acting indiscriminately on them all, part from each other and segregate into minor aggregates. Mixed units of the same kind must be moved differently by different forces, and consequently separate from one another. Units of the same kind, if impressed with the same movement, will cluster together in the same place. After such segregation the several groups of unity must of necessity be sharply marked off. The fourth factor is the tendency to equilibrium. Forces, being counteracted, continually divided and subdivided, are at last stopped. Motion then ceases. In all stages and in all cases of evolution there is a progress to equilibrium ever more perfect. First the various motions which an aggregate possesses are separately equilibrated; then, when the aggregate has a movement of its parts with respect to each other that encounters but little resistance, an *equilibrium mobile* is established; and this at last will lapse into complete equilibrium.

That of these four factors each one is deducible from the persistence of force, Mr. Spencer thinks to have shown to evidence. If forces are not destroyed, but always persist in their equivalents, the homogeneous cannot be stable; its parts must be differently acted upon, because either they themselves or the surrounding agencies are different. Forces, if indestructible, must, when differently counteracted and divided, become differentiated causes of ever more different effects. The elements or units diversely moved and modified must separate and reunite according as they have become like or unlike in kind, unless we are to say that the effect produced is not equivalent to the amount of power expended. Lastly, forces encountering and resisting each other, yet not destroyed, will work an arrest of motion in which as in their effect they continue to exist (P. ii. Chapt. xvii.–xxiii).

Evolution, therefore, with all its laws, is inferable from one supreme principle, the persistence of force. But does experience verify it? Is it universal as in theory, so also in fact? Is the history of the universe but a realization of it? Only then its truth is proved, and the unification of all science is based on a solid foundation. Mr. Spencer, in treating of the several processes and laws of evolution, every time goes through all the realms of nature, to evidence the congruity between theory and experience. It is chiefly in this attempt that the real tendency of his speculation manifests itself. Space does not allow us to follow him into details; we can reproduce his ideas only in their general outlines.

Attraction and repulsion, the two constituents of matter, never destroyed, yet always transformed, differentiated, subdivided, and balanced, are, in his opinion, the only cause of the passage of the universe from the nebulous form into its present state so wonderful in its order and beauty. Organic development is but a highly compound evolution, an organism being a combination of matter under a form embodying an enormous amount of molecular motion (§§ 103, 110). To ever progressing differentiation and distinction of matter is due the division of species and varieties, as well as the growth of a perfect organism consisting of many different and precise parts out of the uniform mass of an ovum (§§ 119, 120, 121, 132, 133). To the differentiation of motion are to be attributed the different, though integrated functions which are performed in any organic system (§ 142). From the instability of the homogeneous and the multiplication of effects by the subdivision of the forces result the perpetual changes of structure and activity, the destruction of an organism by seemingly insignificant causes, the different development of specifically the same germ, the rising of organization out of unorganized seed, the distinction of sexes, the extinction of the existing and the origin of new and higher species, and divergence of the human races (§§ 159, 166). By segregation the various species of plants and brutes are formed and preserved. Life, in general, is a tendency to establish equilibrium between external and internal relations, a moving equilibrium, fitted to preserve itself during a certain period. "Every living body exhibits in a fourfold form the process of equilibration, from moment to moment in the balancing of mechanical forces, from hour to hour in the balancing of functions, from year to year in the changes of state that compensate the changes of condition, and finally in the complete arrest of vital movements at death"[1] (§ 173).

Mental activity is derived from no other laws and forces. "The phenomena," says Mr. Spencer, "subjectively known as changes in consciousness, are objectively known as nervous excitations and discharges, which science now interprets into modes of motion. Hence, in following up organic evolution, the advance of retained

[1] Page 498.

motion in integration, in heterogeneity, and in definiteness, may be expected to show itself alike in the visible nervo-muscular actions and in the correlative mental changes."[1] Consequently, the redistribution of motion, too, accompanying the redistribution of matter, may be supposed to be exhibited in the divers muscular and nervous actions, and in the transformations of the same, the mental changes. In confirmation of all these assertions, he recalls to the mind of the reader how both in man and in *brutes* intelligence is developed by degrees, and how objects are perceived and judgments formed, first confusedly, and only at a later period with clearness and distinction (§ 143). Later on, he ascribes this gradual evolution also to the instability of the heterogeneous. " In every infant might be traced the analogous transformation of a confused aggregate of impressions of surrounding objects, not recognized as differing in their distances, sizes, and shapes, into separate classes of objects unlike each other in these and various other respects. And it might be shown that the change from this first indefinite, incoherent, and comparatively homogeneous consciousness, to a definite, coherent, and heterogeneous one, is due to differences in the actions of incident forces on the organism"[2] (§ 153).

To exemplify the multiplication of effects in intellectual life, Mr. Spencer reminds us how differently one and the self-same exterior object, for instance, an unusual bird, acts on minds differently developed, on that of a shepherd or of a cow-herd, on that of the village bird-stuffer, of a naturalist of the old school, and of a comparative anatomist. The same is observed in emotions. Quite different feelings are produced by the anger of the father in the younger and in the elder child, and in the wife. The difference of the effects is owing to the greater or lesser difference of structure in the respective persons, and the different structures themselves are slowly accumulated results of the functional changes, of thoughts, and of emotions (§ 160). Segregation accounts for the establishment of classifications. Sensations are molecular modifications in some part of the organism. By like things similar groups of impressions and sensations are produced, which are combined and superposed. From unlike things divers groups of forces or impressions pass through the organs, and they must be decomposed, like being separated from unlike. Hence species and genera result, which, as often repeated actions work structural changes, are registered and embodied in the organs. In a similar manner are connections of sequence and co-existence grouped in the mind simultaneously with the impressions. When

---

[1] Page 391.   [2] Page 421.

several phenomena that have been experienced in a given order are repeated in the same order, those nerves which before were affected by the transition are again affected; and such molecular modification as they received from the first motion propagated through them, is increased by this second motion along the same route. Every such motion works a structural alteration, which involves a diminution of the resistance to all such motions that afterwards occur. Meanwhile, phenomena that are recognized as different from these, and hence affect different nervous elements, will have their connections severally represented by motions along other routes, and along each of those other routes the nervous discharges will take place with a readiness proportionate to the frequency with which experience repeats the connection of phenomena. This sorting and grouping together of changes or motions, whilst it gradually forms our nervous structure, is the cause and the measure of the mental connection between impressions (§ 167). The moving equilibrium to be maintained between internal and external relations is the cause of the never stopping flow of thoughts and emotions in the mind, of the alternation of mental activity and rest, of facility or difficulty in thinking, of the rapidity or slowness of feelings, of the oscillation of emotions, of joy and grief, of excitement and paroxysm. On account of the same equilibrium, each outer connection of phenomena which we perceive generates, through accumulated experience, an inner connection of mental states. The result in which the process ends is the formation of a mental connection having a relative strength that answers to the relative constancy of the physical connection represented. Such equilibration between the two orders of relations is ever progressing, and will reach its end only when each relation of things has generated in us a relation of thought, so that on the occurrence of conditions the relation in thought arises as certainly as the relation in things. No doubt, the whole is intended to be a theory on reasoning (§ 174).

In the continual approach to equilibrium between the emotions and the kinds of conduct necessitated by surrounding conditions moral adaptation consists. To render this definition of morality intelligible, and to convince us that moral equilibration is as truly physical as any other, Mr. Spencer thinks it sufficient to point out " that what we know subjectively as states of consciousness are, objectively, modes of force; that so much feeling is the correlate of so much motion; that the performance of any bodily action is the transformation of a certain amount of feeling into its equivalent amount of motion; that this bodily action is met by forces which it is expended in overcoming; and that the necessity for the frequent repetition of this action implies the frequent recurrence of forces to be so overcome. Hence, the existence in any individual of an emotional stimulus that is in equilibrium with certain external requirements, is literally the habitual production of a certain specialized portion of nervous energy, equivalent in amount to a certain order of external resistances that are habitually met."[1] Morality or perfect moral adaptation is thus the limit towards which evolution carries us; for it is a state " in which the kinds and qualities of mental energy daily generated and transformed into motions are equivalent to, or in equilibrium with, the various orders and degrees of surrounding forces which antagonize such motions." It should, however, not be forgotten, that such a state of perfection is tended to and attained not so much individually, as by the joint action of the whole human race; since the habits acquired, or, rather, the structural changes effected by repeated actions are transmitted from one generation to another together with the organism. In this sense, Mr. Spencer, like many other agnostics, speaks of organic morality, just as above he treated of experience registered in our organs. He concedes to the different religions, though false in their views and irreligious, a necessary influence on the formation of these habits and organic structures, particularly among the lower and less cultivated classes of the people and in earlier stages of civilization, and he finds therein a reason for religious toleration (§ 32).

Nobody will now wonder, if he hears that arts and languages have come into existence and are perfected by the process of integration, differentiation, and distinction (§§ 113, 124, 125, 126, 136, 137), that society in all its classes and functions is the necessary outcome of redistribution of matter and motion according to the physical laws observed in all other realms, that it is a moving equilibrium of forces opposed and under constant oscillation ever more perfectly balanced, until at last complete rest will ensue. In this ideal state the individual will have no desires but those which may be satisfied without exceeding his proper sphere of action, while society maintains no restraints but those which the individual voluntarily respects (§§ 111, 122, 134, 144, 154, 161, 168, 175).

Yet if the process of evolution is going on everywhere, and necessarily ends in equilibrium, " are we not manifestly progressing to a state of universal quiescence, of omnipresent death ?" Mr. Spencer, without any hesitation, answers in the affirmative. But death is not the end of all. After evolution comes dissolution. All molar motion having been arrested by equilibrium, and having been converted into molecular motion, the opposite process begins to predominate. When the whole is, when all the parts of

---

[1] Page 506.

the mass are, reduced to rest, any influence from the environment is sufficient, by causing an excess of motion, to disturb the equilibrium between the molecules. The latter, then, must needs disperse. So dissolution is caused in civil society by the contact with other states or nations; so organisms fall victims to corruption. So, too, at a period beyond the stretch of imagination, the earth will be reduced to a gaseous state, when, in consequence of the resistance of the ether, it will collide with the sun, and intense heat will be produced by the shock. Nay, a time will come when the whole solar system, when all heavenly bodies, will be dissolved, and the entire universe will return to a nebulous form. The molecules will be dispersed as widely as they were before the evolution, owing to the persistence of force and the equivalence of action and reaction. However, from the state of diffusion they will again be condensed as before, and for the same reasons, and go again through the same process of evolution. So the universe undergoes the same changes which are observed in particular bodies; consisting of matter that never came into existence, and will never go out of existence, it is in a perpetual transition from the imperceptible to the perceptible, and from the perceptible to the imperceptible, from evolution to dissolution and vice versa, in a perpetual rhythm of motion and transformation, produced, not by an external, but an immanent, cause, the absolute persistent force, which, different in its modes of manifestation, ever remains the same in quantity, and being at the root of all and intrinsic to all, becomes all that exists (P. II., chapt. xxiii.).

Summing up, at the end, his system, Mr. Spencer gives utterance to the confidence he has in the solidity of this system. The conclusions he drew from the first data he sees irrefragably confirmed by experience. The process of evolution and dissolution was understood to be a necessary consequence of the persistence of force, and nature exhibits it everywhere and always, invariably and according to the same laws. All *a priori* deductions flow from the necessity under which we are of conceiving the unknowable as the ground of the knowable; and, indeed, the reality and the persistence of the unknowable and absolute is manifested by the universal order and succession of all phenomena. Can a demonstration be more convincing? Can ever a more solid unification of knowledge and a more natural reconciliation of religion and science be attained? (P. II., chapt. xxiv.).

After we have heard what conclusion Mr. Spencer draws at last from all his reasonings, and what unity he is confident of having given to philosophy, it is now time for us also to review his theories and pass judgment on their merits. In what, then, does his system result, and by what method is it built up?

IV.

Shall we, considering his doctrine, admire in Mr. Spencer the greatest thinker of the age? Shall we, with so many of his followers, say that by him philosophy and civilization have been marvellously advanced, and the human understanding has been wonderfully developed? Can we agree with those who say that he has led science back to God, or has, at least, begun to reconcile it with religion? Is it true, as was said of late, that he and Mr. F. Harrison embrace each a part of truth, and that both united teach the worship of the God-man, our Saviour? Is his teaching, as the *Christian Spectator*[1] maintained, so profoundly, so intensely, so overwhelmingly religious, nay, so utterly and entirely CHRISTIAN, that its true meaning cannot be seen for its very glory? Let us briefly recapitulate the foregoing statements.

What is the knowable? Nothing but phenomena, impressions, and ideas copied after them. What are reality and existence? Manifestations persistent in consciousness; all we think of as being beyond them is self-contradictory and self-destructive. The world we imagine to see without us consists of sensations within us. There is no matter in which, as in their subject, qualities inhere; matter is posterior to forces, made up of them as of its components; and forces themselves, the ultimate elements reached by experience, are impressions on our touch. The world within us is distinct from that without us, only by its lower degree of vividness since it is the order of faint manifestations reproduced by transformation from the vivid ones in which things seem to be outside us. Both worlds, the outer and the inner, are a mechanical play of attraction and repulsion, a balance kept up between the one and the other, a division and exchange of them. Sensation, the first impression on our organs, is mechanically turned into thought, thought into emotion, and the discharge of this, that is, its conversion into muscular movement, is action and conduct. True and perfect knowledge is correspondence between impressions and ideas, congruity among the relations of vivid and of faint manifestations; morality is equilibrium between emotion and conduct. The normal state of social life is equipoise established between the actions of several individuals, of which each one strives to attain the greatest advantage by the least labor. Nor is there in all that any essential difference between man and brute; intelligence being in one, as well as in the other, both being but a complicated redistribution of matter and motion. The ultimate ground on which all these forces rest, or the ultimate cause from which all these phenomena proceed, is the absolute, the eternal power and energy.

---

[1] See Appendix, page 589.

But what is the absolute itself? A generalization or abstraction. It is the quantity of force that always remains, though variously transformed and manifested; force, therefore, as it is abstracted from its modes and particular relations; force, which is intrinsic to every energy impressed on our organs, immanent to every concrete existence, and identical with the impressions themselves; it is not a cause separated from its effects, nor a subject distinct from qualities, nor a soul different from thoughts and volitions. The reality of the absolute, too, consists in manifestation.

What name shall we give to a system ending in such a result? It is atheistical, inasmuch as it denies or ignores a personal Deity, a Supreme Being above the material universe and distinct from the same; it is pantheistical, inasmuch as it considers the abstract or universal as the absolute, eternal, and infinite cause or power; it is materialistic, inasmuch as it admits nothing besides material forces, and regards life as an evolution of matter; it is idealistic, inasmuch as in it all existence is manifestation in consciousness, a manifestation which has not an object distinct from itself which it represents, nor a subject or substance in which it inheres, and is, therefore, like Hegel's impersonal thought, identical with being; it is skeptical, inasmuch as, according to it, we can never know what the things or objects are in themselves, and can never grasp the ground or reality that underlies them; it is pessimistic, not unlike Buddhism, inasmuch as the highest degree of evolution it admits is omnipresent death, and inasmuch as the universe is perpetually tending to, and returning from, dissolution. Mr. Spencer's "Synthetic Philosophy" is a pantheon, not of truth, but of falsehood. As once into the temple built by Agrippa in Rome all false divinities were gathered, so in his system all idols of modern thought, all philosophical tenets of unbelief, doubt, and negation are embodied and united. Being of a chameleon-like nature, it does not professedly or exclusively teach the views of any particular modern school, but it contains them all, and glitters in the colors of every one of them.

The ultimate result is of itself an infallible test of the intrinsic value of the Spencerian philosophy. Judging by it, we are necessitated to condemn that system as erroneous and destructive, and are convinced beforehand of the unreality of the basis on which it rests, and the unsoundness of the method by which it is built up. Directly to prove the latter charge, we must restrict ourselves to few remarks, but they will suffice to unmask many a fundamental untruth.

First of all, the relativity of knowledge, the starting-point of Mr. Spencer's speculation, is not only assumed without any solid reason, but is also in open contradiction with his own principles and method.   The only sure and reliable knowledge, as he thinks, is experience.   Now, if we consult our consciousness, what do we in reality experience ?   What do we directly and immediately perceive ?   Not, indeed, impressions within us, but the objects outside us as they are in themselves, qualities that act on us from without, and are inherent in material subjects.   Nay, our own impressions, thoughts, and volitions we perceive as existing in ourselves, that is, in our self or substance, which is not a mere relation, but an absolute reality that stands in itself.   And of these objects within us and without us we apprehend the nature and intrinsic constitution.   True, we compare things according to their likeness or difference ; but we do not rest content with the comparison as such ; comparing them, we intend to know their very constituents, the marks which, in part common to all, in part peculiar to each one, are the roots, the intimate sources of their properties.   By all means we want to know the real causes and principiants of their actions, of their origin, their growth and extinction.   So Mr. Spencer himself reasons throughout his work.   Everywhere he is inquiring into cause and nature, everywhere he assigns for effects sufficient reasons and proper agents, trying to give, not an indefinite, but a determinate notice of them.   Nor is he unaware of all this.   He grants that we are compelled to conceive of the ultimate realities as existing in themselves beyond the phenomena, yet maintains that the objects as thus viewed are delusions in which only peasants and metaphysicians believe.   But if this be so, Mr. Spencer adopts a fundamental tenet certainly not upheld, but rather contradicted, by experience.   And besides, by such an assertion is not experience itself declared to be false and illusive as to its main and substantial element ?   Are not our cognitive faculties thus stultified and rendered untrue ?   Mr. Spencer goes even farther ; he positively denies our capacity of knowing an object as it is.   For that reason he defines truth as, not conformity of the mind with the object, but congruity between mental states, or correspondence between the two orders of impressions and ideas.[1]   Yea, he destroys cognition itself.   For what has become of it in his system ? Impression, or a faint copy of it, without a real object, which they represent, and without a subject in which they inhere.   Mr. Spencer, then, not merely transcending, but rather altogether falsifying experience, begins, like Kant, his speculation with denying the truth of that very faculty of which he is constantly to make use, and with condemning that very method which he is to follow.

Of all the reasons he alleges for the relativity of knowledge, not

---

[1] Page 86.

one has any validity. They are nearly all based on a false conception of the infinite, which he supposes to consist of numberless finite parts, and on the confusion of incomprehensibility and inconceivability, as if anything which we cannot thoroughly and in every regard understand and explain were altogether *unthinkable* and self-contradictory; a confusion, indeed, which would disgrace even a beginner in philosophy. If from his definition of life he infers that all *thinking is relationing*, he simply moves in a vicious circle; for that life is, as he imagines, but an adjustment of the interior to the exterior relations, is just as questionable as the relativity of knowledge itself.

What shall we think of his first and supreme principle, out of which, in the ontological order, the whole universe is developed, from which, in the logical order, he deduces all conclusions by demonstration *a priori*, and to which he reduces all experience, all phenomena by induction? We have here touched the very soul of his theory. Nothing can be weaker, nothing more self-destructive than this ultimate foundation of synthetic philosophy. Considered in the ontological order, the first principle, which was shown to be the persistence of force, is the first cause of all existence by evolution. And yet Mr. Spencer cannot say whether it exists or not. For if it exists objectively, it is either self-existent or produced. It cannot be self-existent, for self-existence is, in his opinion, a self-contradiction; nor can it be produced, for then it would not be the first cause. Again, this absolute force or energy is altogether formless and indeterminate, a mere abstraction. Nevertheless, it develops from itself all forms, and manifests itself in all possible modes and shapes. It is, therefore, at once no determinate reality, and all reality whatever. Furthermore, this persistent force, being the generalization of all forces, is not really distinct from them, and is, consequently, as forces are but impressions, only impression in general, without any determinate mode. It is not the cause of impressions distinct from them and existent in itself, for such a transient cause is an abomination to Mr. Spencer; nor is it the subject in which impressions exist, for it is ultimate and prior to matter. Impression, then, vague and indeterminate, without a cause from which it is, without a subject in which it is, impression which is neither self-existent nor produced, is the ultimate principiant, the ultimate sufficient reason of all. We challenge any one to show a more startling self-contradiction uttered by any other philosopher. Such a chimera Mr. Spencer would like to be put in place of a personal self-existent, infinitely wise and perfect God, in whom he cannot see anything but absurdity; with such speculation he thinks to supplant theistic or Christian philosophy, at which he sneers on every occasion with sovereign contempt.

No better does he fare with his first principle in the logical order, where he is to unify by it all knowledge, by deducing from it, and retracing to it, all our cognitions. From the very outset Mr. Spencer constantly repeats that the absolute is unknowable, and he is in the highest degree scandalized at the impious piety of those who dare predicate of it any determinate attribute. He even adds that the manifestations also of the absolute, at least the primary ones, are unfathomable mysteries. His entire "Synthetic Philosophy" is, therefore, a deduction of the knowable from the unknowable, and a reduction of the knowable to the unknowable. Ancient philosophy proceeded by the opposite way; it deduced the unknown from the known, and illustrated that which was not clear by that which was self-evident. And in that, no doubt, it harmonized with common sense, which will never understand how darkness may illume light. Yet, be it as it may, we must confess, and therein we agree with many of his critics,[1] that Mr. Spencer has carried out his plan. His entire synthesis is indeed a deduction of laws and phenomena, which we know very well by experience, from reasons which prove absolutely nothing, and a tracing back of well-known facts to principles which render them absolutely unintelligible. He begins with the absolute persistent force, the existence of which cannot be definitely conceived, and is only postulated by our organs, the living records of experience. Being without form, it manifests itself under two forms, that of attraction and that of repulsion. How these originate, Mr. Spencer cannot tell us; he but knows that they are postulates of our senses or our constitution. Nor can he say of what intensity they are, how far extended their existence is, and how they come to be combined; for force is itself inscrutable. This alone he knows, that they must be eternal and indestructible; for else we had not even the material or the terms necessary to think; and that they cannot annihilate each other, because else the absolute would not be persistent. From these two relative forces, attraction and repulsion, everything is to be understood. Hence the division of the outer and the inner world, of nature and mind, all laws of physics, of chemistry, of astronomy, of life, of morality, are to be derived. Hence results the formation of the universe; hence all the changes that ever have taken place or will take place in the whole sidereal system; hence arts, sciences, languages, political institutions; hence follow the regularity and constancy of the mundane order, the beauty, harmony, variety, and unity of nature. In a word, attraction and

---

[1] See the excellent criticism on the Spencerian Philosophy in the *Edinburgh Review*, January, 1884.

repulsion, of which we do not know anything at all but that they impress themselves on our sense of touch, have effected everything and account for all.   This is in brief Mr. Spencer's demonstration *a priori*, as lucid and orderly as the nebulous mass out of which, in his opinion, the universe rose by itself into its present condition.

It might be expected that at least his *a posteriori* proof, his inductions, would be more solid and convincing.   But in vain are such hopes entertained.   Not one law, whether physical, mechanical, or chemical, has he legitimately inferred.   That the universe was brought into its present shape according to his theory, he imagines to have sufficiently proved *a posteriori* by the mere possibility he can conceive that it was so.   For the particular processes and laws implied in evolution as taught by him he alleges a few examples, and then at once leaps to the conclusion that they are in existence absolutely everywhere, and always, in times past, present, and future.   He stands in no need of mathematical proofs, he is not embarrassed by intricate calculations; the first and most superficial observation is sufficient for him.   That sometimes instances of the opposite kind could be put forth matters not.   And still Mr. Spencer admits no universal notions that have objective validity, no self-evident *a priori* principles, by means of which he might from many and various instances infer a general law.   By right, therefore, in order to attain a certain and unquestionable conclusion of universal truth, he is bound to make a careful inquisition into all individual cases; a task which no scientist can ever perform, and which he least of all has attempted to perform.

And what are the general laws to which he even so ascends?   Do they explain the phenomena?   Are they, perhaps, mathematical formulæ? or physical axioms, exact and well defined?   Not in the least.   They are vague, scarcely, if at all, intelligible, or truisms mystified by extravagantly abstract language.

Most offensive, however, is the manner in which he disposes of the gravest subjects that concern mankind, of life, mind, religion, morality, society.   Who would not expect that Mr. Spencer, here at least, would carefully examine facts?   That he does not will be at once evident.   He lays it down as an axiom, that the element common to all religions must be true, and then goes on to say that the awe of the unknowable and mysterious is that which they all have in common.   But soon after, when speaking of the reconciliation between science and religion, he very gravely remarks that all religions have become irreligious by endeavoring to render the unknowable known.   Ought he, then, relying on experience, not to have inferred that the element common to all of them is the tendency to know the Supreme Being?   This is in reality the truth. Except him and his admirers, no one is willing to worship an absolutely unknowable being; men become religious in proportion as they progress in the definite and certain knowledge of a personal, infinitely wise, good, and perfect Deity. By such superficial reasoning, Mr. Spencer would like to overturn religion based on a solid and enlightened conviction,—a principle so important for the welfare of man, and productive of so much in the course of history,—and to replace it by the blind and inactive awe of an abstraction, or rather, to speak plainly, of an absurdity. Is such a religion not a hundred times worse and more irrational than any idolatry or fetichism ever practiced?

As to life, it is to Mr. Spencer *a priori* evident, though he elsewhere rejects any evidence *a priori*, that there are no spiritual beings. Life, in general, is for him but a play of attraction and repulsion, a tendency to equilibrium between the two orders of external and internal relations. Does this definition hold, at least of organic living beings? Of course, when there are material forces at work, some equilibrium must be established. But is this the essence, the distinctive characteristic of life? Equilibrium exists also in inorganic bodies, between their molecules, between their masses and their environments, and one that is much more perfect and more stable than that of organic bodies. If, therefore, the tendency of a being to keep itself in balance with the surroundings constitutes life, the bodies that are termed lifeless have life in a much higher degree than those which are considered as living. Does Mr. Spencer see no essential difference between a tube containing heated gas, in which, too, there is much retained heat, and man, between an artificial mechanism and himself? Is it not worth while for him to inquire whether, besides equilibration, there is any other activity, any other active principle in living beings? Whether they are governed by peculiar laws or not? Whence is that unity in them that strikes so forcibly every observer, that apparent design with which they work and develop themselves? It is not apparent. Living and not living beings have something in common, and, therefore, he concludes, they are all the same, notwithstanding all the discoveries of physiology, notwithstanding the mysteriousness of vital processes acknowledged by all scientists. He might have reasoned with the same right: A stone is heavy, and a watch is heavy; therefore they are one and the self-same thing.

The human mind, inventive of all arts, thirsty of truth and knowledge, uniting in its ideas the past, the present, and the future, and searching, with incessant activity, into the ground and foundation of all, extending far beyond experience to the eternal and necessary, satisfied only with the infinite, is but a complication of attractive and repulsive forces. The rational will, with its inborn tendency to good, to unlimited good, free, generous, apt to sacrifice all self-interest for a higher end, aspiring to the highest perfection, is material emotion conformable to mechanical laws. For Mr. Spencer has observed that external or vivid impressions are followed by faint ones, and that these latter produce emotions, and emotions again muscular exertions. He has further seen that in the activity of mind and will there is some analysis and division of the objects thought of, some segregation of dissimilar conceptions and grouping together of similar ones, some connection between ideas and affections; hence, upon the whole, some slight resemblance to chemical and physical processes. No other reason does the greatest thinker of the age adduce for the identity of spirit and matter. Of freedom or power of choice he does not seem to know anything; it does not enter at all into his accounts. If morality is but equilibrium between feeling and conduct, as necessitated by the exterior circumstances, the holy, the charitable, the just, the merciful, the temperate man is a well-balanced mechanism; he that is unjust, lustful, intemperate, is a mechanism deranged owing to some complication; the order of the one as well as the disorder of the other being the consequence, not of any free action, but of a mere combination of forces and motions commenced already in our ancestors. The only difference will be that the moral mechanism will run smoothly, the immoral one like a rusty engine with many painful disturbances; yet both will alike, after a certain period of time, reach the same end, dissolution. This view of morality Mr. Spencer does not think necessary to support by any reasons; it follows, evidently, from his theory on the human mind. The same or similar reasons he puts forth when he says that the course of human history, of states, of nations, cultivated under the influence of science and Christianity, is a moving equilibrium, the constituent parts of which are set in motion along the line of the greatest attraction or least resistance.

Nobody, he tells us at last, ought to feel offended by these speculations, and think human nature to be lowered. Such sensitiveness is based on the underrating of matter, an error no less injurious to the Creator than the undervaluing of the spirit. His system is not a degradation of the so-called higher, but an elevation of the so-called lower. To console us fully, he adds that the controversy between the materialist and the spiritualist is a mere war of words, in which the disputants are equally absurd.[1]

Not to mention how destructive of the social and moral order such ideas must be, particularly if instilled into the mind of youth, we simply ask: Is this method of inquiry solid? Is it in keep-

[1] Page 556.

ing with the importance of the questions discussed? Is it worthy of a philosopher? Does it justify, or even in the least excuse, the utmost contempt shown by agnosticism towards the philosophy of former ages, towards theism and Christianity?

What final issue may we expect, and what mental development may be attained, if Spencer is to become the highest authority in philosophy, from which it is not allowed to appeal, and if, as the American editor says in the preface, among the young men of our country he is to find the largest and the fittest audience? Certainly the gravest fears should awake in any thinking mind and in any friend of youth, were the remark true which the same preface adds, that "there is something in the bold handling of his questions, and in the earnest and fearless appeal to first principles, and in the practical availability of his conclusions, which is eminently suited to the genius of our people."

When Mr. Spencer's synthetic philosophy is recommended in such terms, when the ideas developed in it begin to spread in all directions, and to pervade a great many literary productions, it is time to lay open not only its impiety, but also its absurdity.

MODERN USES OF WEALTH.

SOME men are born to wealth, some men "come into" wealth, and some men make wealth for themselves. How a man may use his wealth will depend, not a little, on the ideas he imbibed in early youth. It will depend on his family traditions. It will depend on his surroundings and friends. It will depend on the needs of his relations. It will depend on the accident of any particular sympathy being awakened by this or that cause. Yet over and above all such influences there will be one supreme autocrat, and that will be the natural temperament. Let us say that there are three things which mould a man: his temperament, education, and circumstances. His education may be varied from his fifth to his twentieth year; his circumstances may be varied through seventy years; but his temperament will not be varied, save only in degree; it will never be varied in kind. And therefore it is that in considering the. question: "How will this rich man use his riches?" the answer must be looked for in his natural temperament, far more than in his education or circumstances. There are men in whom temperament is so marked that nothing which is external much affects them. Thus the intensely generous man will remain the intensely generous man, though he be crushed by hard poverty or even want; and the intensely mean man will remain the intensely mean, though he might put the Bank of England into his pockets. In the same way, there are prudent men whose prudence is so superlative that it is lord and master of all their graces of character; while there are other men who are so reckless that the "hospital for incurables" would be the best home for themselves and their fortunes. It may be replied that such examples are extreme. Yet, who will not admit that what is born in the nature is lord paramount through life over habit?

Obviously, the way a man *spends* his wealth must depend very largely on how he *got* it. Perhaps we may hazard these three *principia:* "traditions" will govern the man who was born to wealth; thought-out principles will govern the man who has made his wealth; and temptations will govern the man who has come into wealth. Yet such assertions are necessarily too general; they contain truth, but they are far from being all truth. Sometimes a man who was born to wealth will strike out new grooves of expenditure; sometimes a man who has made his wealth can never make up his mind how to spend it; and sometimes a man who has come into wealth will resist all temptations, and live rigidly. Yet no matter *how* a man may spend his wealth, his "temperament," as we have said, will be his master. It will also be *felt* by all who know him. A man's temperament colors all that he does. His principles may direct him as to grooves, but his temperament makes him disliked or liked. We put disliked before liked, because rich men, as a rule, are personally, because socially, disliked. They are courted, from vanity or from interest, but the homage they receive is not personal. It is to their bankers that the world raises its hat. The same truth holds good in regard to noblemen. They are not liked by the general public, they are wondered at. It is the exception when a big man is liked. And the reason is, that temperament is what is liked in those we know; and the temperament of grandees is but little felt. Yet so wonderful is this influence of the temperament, that even as to the mighty few whom we know but by repute, or with whom we have superficial relations, we are conscious of attributing to them a "type." We do not know, but we strongly suspect, their "type." "I do not think he is a sort of man who would do that," is not said in regard to a man's principles, but in regard to his dispositions or bent. This bent may be roundly called "temperament." And just as it colors a man's actions all through life, so does it color our sense of them. Since we are attributing vast importance to this temperament—call it bent, call it type, or what you will—it will be instructive to view it closely in its twofold operation of influencing a rich man and his "circle." Every man has a circle, no matter what his caste, from the king down to the meanest of his subjects. But the circle of a rich man has a necessarily big circumference, unless he be a miser or a recluse. Now the temperament of a rich man will make every inch of his circle to respond more or less to his own pulses. His virtues, if he have any, will live all round it; and his vices, if he have any, will be felt everywhere. And this is a fact of grave importance. "The modern uses of wealth" are not ordinarily taken to include the pulsations of a man's character all over his sphere. That they do include them, and must include them, is that fact of primary moment which it may be useful to consider for all our sakes.

As to religion,—or its influences,—we will speak by and by; but for the present we will say only this much: Religion will, no doubt, have a good deal to do with the uses or misuses of wealth, but even religion will not much affect the "temperament." There are some severely religious men whose temperaments are most offensive, and most detractive from all the good which they try to do. And there are some few religious men, who, by the charm of their temperament, double all the good they do, and even sanctify it. Let us speak of that wonderful word "gentleman."

How many rich men are gentlemen? How many big men are gentlemen? Most rich men are educated, and have the veneer of politeness—the aspect of conventional good breeding. But a man is like a horse, in the sense that his " points " are born in him, and cannot be altered. You may as well try to make an aquiline nose a Roman nose as to make a man who is born vulgar become refined. You may veneer him, but you cannot get at his bones. A man is what he is and no more. Instinct is somehow germed by nature's will. It matters not one pin whether a man is born a duke, or born to the counter of a ham and beef shop; his mother instinct will be as impregnable to change as will the color of his eyes or his hair. Religion, if rightly learned, may direct him ; and infused graces may soften his character; yet the man will remain the man in all the toilet of his nature, just as the flower remains the flower in all its tints and its perfume, or the sea remains deep, the puddle shallow. What then, it may be objected, is the use of treating of temperament, if we take away the owner's power of improving it ? Nothing of the kind has yet been hazarded.

A man is necessarily a hot-house plant. He is not a wild weed on the prairies. He is subjected to certain atmospheres, from his cradle to his grave—the social, the religious, the domestic. His gardeners dig him, train him, and lop his twigs. It is in the hot-house of social career that he must live. And therefore, though he will never change his nature, it is perfectly marvellous if, in contact with a thousand thoughts, he does not modify a good many of his ideas. Yet a rich man, as a rule, has two difficulties to contend with in the endeavor to rise to the highest standard. He has the difficulty of living always artificially, and the difficulty of a comparative ignorance of worlds of care. The first difficulty makes him, personally, unreal. He adopts principles which are simply grooved in his own surroundings. And his second difficulty—his comparative ignorance of worlds of care—makes him, judicially, quite incompetent to feel with others.

In the word " sympathy " lie a thousand delicate secrets of the influence of every heart on every other heart, and of the influence of the rich classes on the poor classes. Sympathy is the very soul of a fine temperament. What is sympathy ? Some persons speak of sympathy as if it were the giving of a bun to a person who is obviously in want of a bun ; and it is certain that to do this is sound, practical sympathy, and entitles the bun-giver to our esteem. Some persons speak of sympathy as if it were a sensible realization of the extreme unpleasantness of the misfortunes of others ; so that when they hear of such misfortunes, they heave a deep sigh, and try to look as though they were themselves suffering pain. Some persons fancy that sympathy must be demonstrative ;

as when a man spouts benevolently on a platform, or "throws open his suite of rooms" to public philanthropists, or advertises a big cheque for some good purpose, or writes letters to the news-papers to plead a cause, or gets up a benefit concert for a fallen artist—or as in a thousand other ways of doing kindnesses. Nor can any one dispute that all such practical sympathies are meas-urably truthful and admirable. The defect in them all is—that they cost us nothing. The doers have their reward in cash homage. The sympathy, so far as it goes, brings honor to the sympathizer at least as great as is the benefit to the recipient. So that, just as "civility is the desire of being esteemed," such sympathy may be the desire of being praised. Shall we say that sympathy's merit is in the suppression of our own selves for the exaltation of the heart of those we benefit? Such suppression may be too delicate to be defined. Yet the absence of it is sufficiently sensible to be assured. Let us confess at once that the most exquisite of all pleasures—to the man of real refinement and generosity—is the constant giving of happiness to those who suffer, no matter in what groove, from what cause. If this be so, where is the merit of being sympathetic? Obviously in the suppression of the *egomet*. And how should we be sure of this suppression? It may be said of it that its true test, on the part of the sympathizer, is that he feels only the privilege of doing a service; while, on the part of the benefited one, he is treated with such grace that he does not feel himself to be humbled in the least. The highest test of a gentleman is, that he can confer a benefit in such a manner as to imply that he himself is the hon-ored one. But what an instinct a man must have to do this; what a modesty and refinement of the temperament! You could never *teach* such an instinct to any person. You could never put into a man what is not there. You may train, you may direct, you may infuse, you may pitch precepts by the bundle into a man's head, but if nature has not made a man "an exquisite," Eton, Oxford, and a dukedom cannot do so.

Now relatively to our subject, "the modern uses of wealth," these uses depend, first, on the natural instinct; and since it is certain that most men misuse their wealth, or use it mainly for spasmodical gratification, it follows that most men's instincts guide them wrongly, or that they do not care a pin on the sub-ject.

The uses of wealth must *begin* with the possessor; but, the be-ginning, like a river's source, may be a trickling, and the issue, twenty miles down, a roar. We may stride a river, without effort, in particular inches of its course, which river, in some reaches, is miles across. So, the uses of a man's wealth, most modest in their beginning, may grow into national benefit—long after. That

such results must depend chiefly on the " uses," as distinct from
the mind or temper of the users, it would be totally impossible to
deny. Of such " uses " we will speak as we go on : for the moment, let us linger on the " mind and temper "—yet only so as to
sum up what has been said. Our argument is, that the spirit of a
rich man, his own character or features of disposition, will be impressed on every one of his good works. It may be easier to trace
this in private kindnesses than in the magnificent outlay of public
deeds ; yet no man can separate himself from his public deeds in
such way as not to impress himself upon them. The impress of
the founder will last forever. In the delicacy of the forethought,
or in the roughness of the outline, as in the general scope or mental
grasp of the plan, there will be a certain felt perfectness, or a
certain felt want of it, which will elevate or which will lower the
in memoriam. So that a rich man will teach perpetually by his own
temperament. Not only the good thing which he does, but the
" soul " with which he does it, will last as long as his memorial
shall last. Just as a shilling given to a beggar may be given in
such a way as to create an impression which shall never fade
through his whole lifetime, so " endowed charities " may be made
to teach lessons of tender grace, which shall be eloquent from
generation to generation.

A rich man may make a choice between two grooves of outlay :
the groove in which, bestowing his wealth, he ceases to interfere
with its use, and the groove in which the management of his
investment remains with himself all his days. We would consider *all* uses with reference to a man's relations to his own
" circle," to society, and to the poor. As to a man's uses of wealth
for his own personal enjoyment, the subject is not worthy of consideration. And yet, since *most* men who are wealthy think first of
their own enjoyment,—or of their own " position " or grandeeism,
which is the same thing,—it would be unreal to ignore what the
whole world knows for certain—that wealth *makes* a man egotistic.
It also has a tendency to make men lazy. We will assume that a
man is his own master, or can spend his money in any way most
agreeable to him. Will he cherish "sublime ideas and aspirations," or will he cherish what he likes best or values most ? If
his natural temperament dispose him to a career of pleasure, will
he take up with travelling or horseracing, or will he devote himself assiduously to laziness ? For, laziness, if pursued as a career,
may take all a man's thought, all his time ; and, even if it be pursued only as one grand object of life, it may make demands on
health, strength, and even brains. Indeed, laziness is a profession
of such magnitude, among a section of the children of fortune, that
it is probable that more time is spent over it than would suffice to

build cities or conquer kingdoms. It is an approved, high vocation
of some cultured classes. " He is a man of independence" means,
relatively to a certain type, " he has no motive for working and he
does not work." It is true that this " fashion " of wealthy indolence
is, happily, passing away from good society; so that it is now thought
bad form for a man to " do nothing "—to rise at ten, and then not
rise any more. Laziness is now more formulated than it used to be,
say, in the days of our grandfathers or great-grandfathers. It is
pursued more artistically, with more method. Shall we say that
there are three kinds of laziness,—that is, with a certain class of
rich men,—that of the mind, which refuses to take the trouble to
consider what are the best ways of spending money ; that of the
heart, which is too dull in its affections to care for the pains or the
wants of other people ; and a sort of physical laziness, which will
not carry out the promptings of head and heart when in their sun-
niest mood ? To this laziness is due the fact that many rich men
spend their money as they smoke a cigar, step into a brougham,
or sip claret. The grand object is to avoid everything that might
" bore " one. Just as some rich men keep a secretary to write
their letters for them, because they would be saved the trouble of
personal relations with mere nobodies, so most rich men would be
saved the trouble of thinking out anything, working out anything
—unless it be the plans for a new house or a county ball. This
disposition leads most rich men to prefer using their money-mar-
gins in such way as shall bring themselves least fatigue. And,
happily, there are the most exquisite ways of doing this. What
can be more beautiful, more enviable, than the power of giving a
cheque to a public hospital ? As we pass by the doors of those
glorious institutions, do we feel most with the sufferers who are
tended so tenderly, or do we long most to cart bank-notes into
the treasury ? And so of other institutions, less touching in their
tenderness, but admirably designed and worked up; such, for example, as orphanges or refuges, or even workingmen's reading-
rooms or concert-halls, or industrial schools, thrift societies, friendly
societies ; the rich man who devotes his margins to multiplying
such blessings has a happy and an enviable vocation. Nor is it
possible not to approve the wisdom of those who devote themselves to any of the grooves of real philanthropy ; such as emigration, or the spread of temperance, or the lessening of labor-hours,
or the enjoyment of the best art galleries by the humblest classes.
It is a grand thing even to draw a cheque for any such purpose.
Sitting in a cozy library, and ringing the bell for the butler, who
may be intrusted with the lazy dignity of posting a cheque, is a
happy task, after breakfast, for the rich man—and for the butler—
and one that not a few of us would like to realize. It is more than

a happy task, it is a grand duty. It may not make any demand on the inventive powers; but there is no need to invent what is invented. To build a church, to build a market-place, to build a drinking fountain, are right things, deserving thanks, if not homage. A rich man who has got so far as to contribute largely to " the public good," is a " capital fellow," and deserves to be toasted at public dinners.

It must be remembered that there are two distinct classes of rich men,—the landed proprietors and the mere magnates of finance, —and that the duties of the two classes are quite distinct. Even the social position of the two classes is not identical. It is true that, in these days, money *is* position; it is worshipped more than is rank or official dignity. But money does not create those fixed spheres of social duties which are inalienable from landed proprietorship. In England, more perhaps than in any other country, these exceptional duties are exacting. The landed proprietor is compelled by his position to " keep up " every bit of property on his estate, whether it be the church, schools, parsonage-house, model farms, or the peasants' cottages, private roadways, gates or palings. So that most of the income from any estate must be returned to it. Then the landed proprietor, having a position in his county, is appealed to in every need of a public kind; the neighboring towns and nestling hamlets naturally looking to him for subscriptions, as well as for indirect, expensive aid. Add to such public demands all his private obligations, with the possibility that he is an M. P., or wishes to be one; that he is at the least a politician and leader of men ; and it must be owned that, with a class of property which pays but two or three per cent.—three per cent. is very good interest for land—the landed proprietor has his expenditure "cut out" for him. It is true that a landed proprietor may have many sources of income besides farms, tenements, preserves, cattle, timber; but so far as land is concerned, he is a poor man. Possibly in many instances this is his own fault. He might farm his land to better account. And here we touch on a very delicate subject, and one which in England is of growing moment. Setting aside the rubbish talked by " social democrats " about "landed property being theft," or "all landowners being public robbers," it must be admitted that there are huge wastes of pleasure land, or land not even devoted to pleasure. This is not the place to enter into even an analysis of the arguments pro and con large estates. It is only relevant to observe that, in the event of a revolution, such arguments would come to the very forefront. It was the fashion before the great French Revolution to mock the popular sophistries about land; and Rousseau was much derided in the Paris drawing-rooms and in gay writings for his mild estimate of what socialism *might* demand. His *contrat social* offended the landowners. True, the French landowners were mostly tyrants, who bled their tenants through the middle-men or speculators; whereas in England there is scarcely a tyrant among the landholders, though there are a good many selfish men or men of pleasure. The chief misuse of land, from a public-benefit point of view, is that landowners love it for pomp, not for service; preferring to increase their social dignity by countless acres of waste pleasure ground to benefiting themselves or their poor neighbors.

Yet in doing this they stand only on their rights. And so does the moneyed man stand only on his rights when he gives banquets night after night to rich people, who would be all the better for going without their dinners once a week; or spends a thousand guineas on ropes of pearls for a young lady who has got so many ornaments that her cabinets can scarcely hold them; or buys more carriages for his wife and daughters to loll their souls in, though they would be all the better for being made to walk or hoe the garden; or gives a cheque, that sounds like a thunder-clap, for some old china, while refusing the price of an earthenware teapot to a beggar. Who doubts that all such magnates are within their rights? or who doubts that when a man rents an opera-box, for which he pays perhaps the price of a good house, he is encouraging fine art, supporting elegant industry, besides helping the gas companies and the stage carpenters? or who doubts that if a man gives ten guineas for a bouquet, though its beauty is meant to charm only for one evening, he is encouraging the florists, paying the wages of honest gardeners, supporting many an early rising family? or who doubts that many a trade interest is advanced by selfish luxury; that the carriage builders live on laziness and on pomp; that the crest-painters, panelling carriages with pretty heraldry, earn an honest as well as a charmingly made livelihood; that countless milliners—no, we will not even allude to the ladies; that ten thousand journeymen live honorably by making trinkets, though perhaps the jewellers cannot boast much of their honorableness; that glovers thrive by making pretty gloves, and that the more gloves a dandy wears the more they thrive; that cigars —most sweet effacement of troubled hours—bring as much money to the tills of a thousand tobacconists as they bring smoke and easy chat to a thousand coteries, and are a positive " necessity " to the happy slaves who have learned their charms; that good wine and bad wine—but especially bad wine—are a source of revenue to both wine merchants and the exchequer; the "duty" which is paid on them helping the State to remit taxes, and the "duty" which *we* pay on them poisoning our system; but still both "duties" being compensated by the obvious gain of the wine merchants, as well as by a certain winging of our own temperaments; that lordly mansions, big enough for half a parish, bring grist to architects, builders, painters, and upholsterers; in short, that all luxuries deserve the patronage of the philanthropist, on the ground that they are sources of profit to the working classes? Most exquisitely subtle dilemma of a rich man's conscience: " ought a rich man to be luxurious—to support trade?" The pagan Romans were not such hypocrites as to affirm this; they simply said " carpe diem," and lived sumptuously. Our modernists are Christian apologists for their own paganism. " Be luxurious on the ground of active charity, and self-indulgent that you may support the working classes," is the profound Christian philosophy of many an egotist. Yet that there are legitimate uses of luxuries, and that some luxuries ought to be patronized, is a principle which no moralist can dispute. Nor is any mind sufficiently acute, or analytical, or comprehensive, to say precisely what those luxuries *are;* or in what proportion they should be relatively cultivated. It is safe to say of *some* luxuries that they should be shunned; but it is difficult to say of *most* luxuries that they are evil. Such luxuries as are implied by gluttony and extravagance are mostly luxuries in degree, not in kind. To give a dinner party implies luxuries, at least abundance; yet hospitality has been always regarded as a virtue. To dress well is a natural instinct of a gentleman, but to have a new suit once a week would be disgraceful. It is the degree which makes the luxury or the—moderation. Juvenal's description of the entertainments of pagan Rome shows that luxury, not only in degree but in kind, had attained to the proportions of crime. Science and art, thought and labor, were lavished on the invention of whatever could be titillating to the senses, or effeminately deteriorating to the manhood. This was crime, both in kind and degree. Shall we compare our modern dinners—full dress, at a quarter to nine—with the pagan suppers mocked by Juvenal or by Terence? In some details we surpass our pagan ancestors. A few weeks ago a poor Londoner—in fact a man of such nobodiness that he was said occasionally to " dine off fried fish and potatoes "—slipped on a crimson carpet that had been laid down across a pavement, for the tender care of dress boots and ladies' shoes. He was hideously injured by the fall. A grand gentleman in Grosvenor Square was giving a banquet, and he expected "the public" to "clear off" from the public pavement. The poor gentleman, who was injured for life by his fall, brought an action to recover damages from the banquet-giver. The *Times* newspaper sneered at the poor position of the plaintiff, though happily the Lord Chief Justice approved the "damages." Here we have civilization carried to a degree of selfish tenderness

which has not a little in it of the spirit of Roman effeminacy.
With some slight modification we might apply Juvenal's ridicule:

> " Who, proud of impious gains,
> Choke up the streets, too narrow for their trains."

Nor is there much difference between Juvenal's description of
the Roman "supper" and the supper which we prefer to call
"dinner." Even the dishes which he speaks of are our own.
The chief difference between the two fashions is that our guests sit
at table, whereas the chief guests used to recline at Roman banquets. Then, too, gambling was the fashion after the Roman
supper. We also have adopted card-playing as an institution. Is
it not in Juvenal we read:

> " Is it simple madness, I would know,
> To venture costly thousands on a throw ;
> Yet want the soul a single piece to spare,
> To clothe the slave, that shivering stands and bare ?"

There is not much to choose between the epochs.

It has been gravely urged by a modern apologist, that " no
luxury which is productive, that is, that helps to support a class
of workmen, can be mischievous to the community that encourages it." Such a theory is, to say the least of it, superficial. We
could name luxuries which support workmen, but which are hateful.
We must be safe in affirming the principle that the excessive indulgence in any luxury must have a deteriorating effect on the
individual ; and what deteriorates the individual must deteriorate
the community, in the proportion of the number which indulges
in it. The luxuriousness of our rich classes deteriorates those
(whole) classes, in making them selfish, cold-hearted, and worldly.
Riches are deteriorating, unless a man have a strong character, a
fine heart, or some active religious principle. Selfishness and vul-
garity being one and the same thing, and most rich persons being
intensely selfish in their use of wealth, it follows that most rich
persons are intensely vulgar ; whereas poor persons, as a rule, are
refined.

Assuming that wealth, like capacity, or muscular power, or like
any rare gift of head or heart, is a " talent " not to be " laid up in
a napkin," we may well pity its possessors in their terrible responsibility, which, however, it must be said that they feel lightly.
The number of wealthy men who lie awake half the night in fear
of having misused " that thousand pounds," or whose consciences
are disturbed, even in the day-time, lest they should have given
pain where they might have given infinite solace, is not a large
proportion of the plutocracy. And this leads us to consider the

question : How far does religious principle,—nay, good principle which does not affect to be religious,—influence the majority of golden men ? It is a difficult question, because one that cannot be answered ; yet we may " diagnose " the symptoms of this sensibility, and ask what would appearances indicate ?

When a man boasts of " doing everything by principle," we may put him down as "a man who has no soul." It goes without saying that a man should be principled; but intuition is far above principle. As a matter of principle, if you owe a man five shillings, and have no hope of paying him more than four, you are not justified in giving away one shilling. As a matter of intuition, if you see a man in great need, and give him one shilling out of the four you should give to the other man (we must assume that the man you owe the money to is quite above the bitter need of the one shilling), you act as an angel, and bless your own soul and the poor man's soul, and leave it to God to make it up to the comfortable man. We call this intuition, not principle; it is the divine touch we have, most of us, on our natures. Let the materialists say what they may, there is an instinct of the pure intellect which is divine. It would be out of place in this kind of essay to even touch on moral theology, or to speak about the " spiritual " man. Let laymen keep to their measure, which is to write as men of the world who know the Christian catechisms and read everything.

Now our rich friends, who " do everything by principle,"—taking care to construct their principles to their own taste,—are usually men who are full of platitudes or trite sayings, which are as false as they are pretentiously sagacious. For example, it is very common to hear a rich man make the remark : " There is much harm done by giving to the undeserving." Very possibly. We could imagine that a man who pretends to be maimed or sickly, or who has a preference for a leisurely life to an industrious one, would not be benefited, morally or financially, by having a sovereign given to him every time he wanted it. In the same way we could imagine—if we may take the side of the " undeserving," and act as counsel for the prisoner at the bar—that many a rich man *would be* benefited, morally and in every other sense, by being compelled once a week to go dinnerless. As counsel for the defendant—that prejudged wretch, the undeserving—we retort that his accusers are, as a rule, *less* deserving that even the habitually lazy pauper or the sometimes lazy. The poor man has not magnificent opportunities. He has no independence—scarcely a dependence. He does not know the taste of the rich man's luxuries; probably he knows the names of but a few of them; and as to a banker—he may have several, but they are pawnbrokers. Now, as counsel for the undeserving, we urge that it is not usual to refuse the invitations of a rich man to his banquets on the ground that "the rich man is undeserving." "Mr. de Consols does not deserve his vast income, and therefore I really cannot dine with him," is not a protest we often hear in Vanity Fair. Yet it is obvious that if the rich man is to argue with any consistency, that it is wrong to help a poor man who is undeserving, it must be equally wrong to give dinners, or to eat dinners, which are paid for by money that is not deserved. If all our interchanges, for our own good or for others', were to be done solely on the ground of personal merit, we should be obliged to refuse many a " my lording," many a hat-lifting, which accident, not desert, renders customary. How many rich men "deserve" their riches? How many dukes "deserve" their dukedoms? You say: "We ought not to give that mendicant a shilling, because he will spend the whole of it on whiskey, or because, by whiskey, he has come to feel the need of it." As counsel for defendant we admit the whiskey; but we ask: Does not the plaintiff drink Lafitte? And since you, my Lord Broadacres, live comfortably every day, without the excuse of seeking oblivion of your biting cares, would it not be in better taste,—and would it not show a bigger mind,—were you to take account of the incitements to a poor man's folly? You have plenty,—perhaps by the accident of your birth, perhaps by speculation, perhaps by "cuteness,"—yet you do not make the best use of your plenty, nor do you deny yourself "the pomps and vanities of this wicked world." Ought you not then to speak modestly of the "undeservingness" of a class of men who may have their faults,—just as you have,—but who have not your means; or who, if they had your means, might use them better? You are very discriminating as to the vices of the poorer classes; but is it not in Phædrus that we read such lines as these :

> "Great Jove, in his paternal care,
> Has given a man two bags to bear;
> That which his own pet vice contains
> Behind his back, unseen, remains;
> But that which others' vice attests
> Swags full in view before our breasts."

"Oh, but it is principle," you say, "high principle, which makes me profoundly discriminating in my charities." This is a very satisfactory state of things. We are so glad you are discriminating; and we feel that your own virtues and your own graces entitle you to be judicial towards others. The discrimination shown by nature in making *you* a rich man, while leaving the industrious, the ingenious, and the imaginative poor, is a warranty, to begin with, that you are the right man in the right place, and that no one else could top your pinnacle with such fitness. Yet—banter aside— how much trouble do rich men give themselves to find out the whole truth of a suggested need ; how many personal calls or visits do they make ; with what solicitude do they set themselves the angelic task of anticipating all unnecessary pain or humiliation ; or with what modesty, with what justice, do they believe only what is good of those they know little about—and care less ? If it be difficult for a rich man to enter the kingdom of Heaven,—a difficulty which does not seem to oppress most rich men,—it must be so, not because he keeps a brougham, not because he gives diamonds to rich people, not because he lets the poor sit behind him in church, while he occupies a paid-for, cushioned pew ; but because of the indolence or selfishness, and therefore the cruelty, which lead him to misapprehend others' sorrows.

In England it is customary, when some one dies whom we respect, to send our empty carriage to follow the hearse. Perfect symbol of the hypocrisy of sympathy ! We do our sympathy by proxy ; just as secretaries write our letters, or our clergy distribute our cheques, to save ourselves the trouble of active charity. We shut our eyes to grooves of sympathy which might bore us. Let us take a recent example of this truism—of English *natural* neglect and *fashionable* charity. During the past few months there has been an awakening of public sympathy in regard to the unkempt tenements of the poor ; royal princes and fine gentlemen having suddenly come to be conscious that they have been living within stone's throw of styed humanity. The sympathy is a sound one, but it would not have been awakened had not a dissenting minister published " The Bitter Cry." That " Bitter Cry " set a thousand tongues wagging, and set some scores of persons writing to the newspapers ; hence " the fashion " of becoming interested in a national infamy which had been in full bloom for scores of years.

If, instead of mere suffering, mere mortal destitution, there had been a thousand cases of plague or of cholera, the fashionable community would have realized " the danger " much sooner than it has realized the suffering. If a cock crows in the early morning, and wakes the neighbors, the public-nuisance act is speedily invoked to stop the nuisance ; but if it is only a case of starving or of overcrowding,—or only a thousand or two of such cases within one district,—the peaceful slumbers of the comfortable classes are not in the smallest degree disturbed—unless royal princes make the new sympathy to be fashionable. This does not say much for " modern uses of wealth." It does not speak volumes for our " men of principle." It does not imply that those tender consciences which are so afraid of " helping the undeserving " have used their vaunted discrimination as to the " deserving." Perhaps they have fancied, during the last hundred years, that one-eighth of London, living as pigs—without the sweet assurance of two meals a day, which pigs have—was every body's business except their own. Shall we put it in this way—that the neglect of public duties comes from the want of combination among the powerful classes, while the neglect of private duties comes from the want of personal interest in anything that is troublesome or humiliating? We all know the hopeless difficulty of trying to work out "political economy," or fine theories about the "improvement of the masses." The "natural rights of man," like the "greatest happiness of the greatest number," are logically mere theories, full of fallacy. The solution of all such puzzles is probably this: You will never get any one class to act improvingly on another class, unless the one class first improves *its own* character. And since character is not form, or feature, or manner, but the influence of our own qualities upon others—every character necessarily influencing other characters—the self-respect of the powerful classes begets the self respect of the lower orders, just as immorality in high places poisons the commonalty.

Platitude as all this is, the whole gist lies in character—that is, in the moral sense of relative duties. Theoretically every man admires virtue, praises industry, imagines that he detects one man's superiority, another man's culpable emergency. Man is a judicial animal. He judges everybody except himself. The result is, that he generally judges wrongly. This is as true of whole classes as of individuals. The discontented classes as utterly mistake the rich classes as the rich classes mistake themselves and the discontented classes. And the reason is that they never come into personal contact. Just as the word "Catholic," which might be supposed to imply brotherhood, really means nothing but a common creed, so the word "sympathy," which might be supposed to imply interchange, really means nothing but "sorry for you." Now, the primary use of wealth,—to a man who apprehended it with intellect, heart, soul, and all earnestness,—would be to link all classes together in one common aspiration—by an example of the highest aims in the higher classes. But this is the last use of wealth which is dreamed of. It is a good thing that Lord Carnarvon, with the dukes of Argyle and Westminster, should have just discovered that "a peasant proprietary of small lands would be beneficial to both the poorer classes and to agriculture"; it is a good thing that the universities should establish "settlements" in East London,—nay, it is the best thing of the kind that has yet been done,—for lifting the standard of local thought or education; it is a good thing that Lord Folkstone and other gentlemen have interested themselves in organizing cheap concerts for the enjoyment of the working classes in poor neighborhoods, just as Lord Bute and other gentlemen have shown a liberal disposition in lending their best works of art to provincial galleries; yet *the* barrier between the rich and the poor classes is, that the rich classes mistake their acts for themselves, or imagine that deeds of kindness, in the cold abstraction of " philanthropy," can take the place of a class sympathy which would be enduring. That hateful word " philanthropy," newspapered, platformed, cheque-booked imposture,—like the empty carriage sent by a rich man to a funeral,—has usurped the place, in social canons as in religion, of the sympathy which is personal, and therefore real. A " great philanthropist " means little more than a poor-law guardian in high position; a sort of man who, in evolving schemes for the improvement of everybody, talks himself and his listeners out of improving anybody. A rich man who, in his own " circle," sets the highest example of modesty, of delicacy, of forethought, of graceful kindness, while at the same time distributing his wealth with a generosity which is equalled by his own simplicity and self-denial, is a philanthropist who improves every one's tone and character, at the same time that he helps their material estate.

It is a funny delusion of the mind that whatever it possesses is, in some mysterious way, part of its own self. The rich mind which possesses wealth—for it is the mind which possesses wealth, in the sense that it is conscious of the possession—somehow imagines that the wealth, which is but " possessed," is part and parcel of the identity of the mind. Why is any man vain of wealth, but because he imagines it is himself—that £. *s. d.* is, somehow, brain, character, personality? Just as a man who is well coated fancies that *he* is a superior man to even himself when he is ill-coated (or ill-hatted), so a man who is well " balanced " fancies that he and his banker's account—he and his landed estate, he and his big title, or he and his position in the neighborhood—are somehow a unity of identity. Probably no man ever lived who could wholly separate his *egomet* from the accidents of his surroundings or worldly toilet. A man walks the street with a tacit conviction that he is respected because he *is* twenty thousand a year. It is not only that he thinks that others think more of him, but he really thinks more of himself. Money being power, and money being his, he and the power are one. It is so true, and yet so false. You might as well try to separate a river from its bed as to separate a man from his fortune; and yet, to say that the river is its bed would be as grotesque as to say a man is his money. Now, it would not much matter that, when we meet Sir Million de Consols, we raise our hat to his securities or to his sweet dividends, if only Sir Million did not raise his hat in return, fully impressed that he *is* his own million. Let us take the most familiar of illustrations : Why is the king the greatest man? Is it because he is the chief magistrate of the nation? No ; it is because he is surrounded by the most pomp. Pass a law that the king shall have fifty pounds a year, and shall live in a garret without servants, and the king might walk the streets without any one looking round, or so much as remarking, " There is the king." The same truth holds good of the nobility. If a duke were only allowed to have one pound a week, and were obliged to live within the measure of that allowance, the opulent tradesman or mechanic or the parish curate would run him close in point of " social consideration." Now, playful as all this seems, the " philosophy " of it lies in this: That the highest effort of a rich man is to learn reality ; to know that riches can only be used but not assimilated ; that a man's use of all he has is in purely probationary stewardship, but cannot affect *himself*, save in character. Pure philosophy, but utterly hopeless impossibility! Vanity is so interwoven with every fibre of the constitution of every man who lives upon the earth, that, of the three levers of human life—vanity, love, interest—vanity is the only one which *always* rules. Love is an incidental operation ; interest is cold, calculating office-work ; but vanity begins in the morning when we are brushing the hair, and ends at night after the bed-candle is put out. To tell a rich man not to be vain of his riches, but to fear himself for a misuse of God's loan, is like telling a man not to be human, not to be sensitive about appearance, not to be conscious that his " six feet high " are more than four feet. A man is what he is ; and he can only modify his misfortunes—of vanity, selfishness, feebleness.

So that, when we hear a man boasting of his " high principles," in regard to the distribution of his wealth, we suspect that he has not realized these three facts : the first, that *all* men, being full of faults, are to be charitably judged, charitably treated ; the second, that such sympathies as are to avail for personal happiness must be personally rendered, and with modesty ; the third, that it is the privilege, just as much as it is the duty, of every rich man to try to bless others.

Privilege is a relative possession. A privilege is a central point which must have a circumference of the same size as a man's opportunities. Now, the ordinary idea of the privilege of being wealthy is, first, that it makes a man independent—that is, *not* dependent on other men ; next, that it gives immunity from vulgar contact, enabling a man to avoid his inferiors ; thirdly, that, in conferring status, it is itself to be respected, without reference to uses, to duties ; and, lastly, that it gives the power of enjoyment, and, with this power, the right. Even the " man of principle " does not forget any of these privileges, though there are some few men who rise above weakness. Happily, in England, the obligations of position are now much more recognized than they used to be. No man can now presume on his position. But the duties of wealth are not recognized, proportionately, as are the duties of rank or of office. Why is this? Because wealth is regarded as a man's own—not as " God's loan for life's span "—rights of property including rights of use. Is this true? Legally, and also morally, it is true; but is there no ideal beyond morals? Conceive of a world in which the Catholic Ideal should be carried out in perfect practice and fruition! Imagine a nation in which all members of all classes positively acted on St. Paul's beautiful belief, that " we are every one members one of another," and that, " if one member suffer, all the members suffer with him." St. Paul's assurance, that Christian society is equally integral with the human body—every one person being to every other person as a nerve or a bloodvessel of the same body, and, therefore, by sympathy, of the same mind—sounds fantastically ironical, in the face of the *fact* that most persons feel complete in their own selves. Thus, the privilege of wealth is esteemed to be the privilege of monumenting one's self above one's fellows; not—to use St. Paul's similitude—the privilege of tenderly caring for every poor or sorrowing member of the social body, but the privilege of being so tall that the extremities of the social figure—or even the anatomy which is just below one's *tête montée*—are in quite another world of being to our own apex. " Temperament" and " principle " play their parts in this estimate; but selfishness and vanity are at the bottom of it.

VAGARIES OF PROTESTANT RELIGIOUS BELIEF.

UNCHECKED by civil or ecclesiastical authority, and imbued with no awe for public opinion, the mind of man in this country has, found its action unfettered for the announcement and promulgation of the most extraordinary theories in regard to the nature of God, and man's relation to Him; the channel by which God makes known His will, the special and peculiar public honor which God requires from His creatures. The right of private judgment claimed by the " Reformers " has been put in practical form, and Protestants cannot logically condemn those who act under it, and seek to induce others to accept their judgment. The result has been the rise of an incalculable number of religions and schools of thought in the denominations which still adhere together from force of association rather than from any fidelity to the symbols or creeds adopted originally as their standard of divine truth. For, as no denomination or body cutting itself away or assuming a new name, can arrogate to itself infallibility in the conception of God, of His law and of His worship, which it holds for the time being, so none can exact obedience or condemn those who refuse to accept its dictation.

On the other hand stands the Catholic Church, recognizing a personal God, revealing His will to man, making the Church the guardian of His truth, the channel of His graces, the teacher entitled to obedience, and holding, as its great act of worship, the sacrifice of Christ completed by the consuming of the divine victim in the Holy Eucharist.

While the Catholic theory is thus clear, distinct and comprehensible, resting entirely on God, objective; the moment her teaching authority is denied, every religious idea becomes subjective, a conception of the human mind, which may approach the truth or diverge from it most grossly.

Absolutely, none of these conceptions corresponds to God; so that, in a certain sense all who adopt them worship a false god, and in some forms, as the Shakers, the Mormons, the Leatherwood, the idea of the deity has become as gross and sensual as ever existed in the mind of a pagan, before he embodied it in stone or metal.

It is not easy to draw the line, and say where the idea of the true God, resulting from the teaching of the Catholic Church and traditionally held, often unconsciously, has been so effaced by the erroneous conceptions of the mind as to be virtually lost. For, though the rejection of the true theoretically implied necessarily the acceptance of the false, the Catholic tradition of God and the correct habit of thought proved, for a long time, stronger than the abstract teachings of error. In this country, unfortunately, in all the Protestant denominations the residuum of Catholic truth is fading away, and men, falling back on mere reason, wish to acknowledge only what they think they can understand, and refuse to understand everything that militates against prejudice, temperament or pride.

The church of England set out by endeavoring to retain many truths, and has, since its origin, exhibited a strange spectacle, one portion grasping at rejected truths and graces, the other endeavoring to cast aside what it had retained. The Lutheran church still retains in its books of devotion the Augsburg confession, in which Lutherans indignantly deny that they wish to cast aside the Mass and the confessional; yet they would not tolerate either for a moment. Hence, an English bishop can deny the authenticity of the books of Moses, the inspiration of scriptures, the apostolicity of the Church, and retain his position against cavillers. A Lutheran professor in a German university can, without compromising his salary, treat the existence of God or of revelation as something to be as little respected as the Mass or the confessional. The teachings of Calvin are nowhere distinct and clear in regard to the doctrines of the Holy Trinity; that dogma was never prominently put forward in the Presbyterian or Congregational systems, and as soon as men dared express their opinions in New England, people began to reject the doctrine, till Unitarianism became the leading belief in those States. A sect, losing a divine truth, never regains it, and the effort produced in the minds of a few by the loss seems in most cases to carry them not back to what had been lost, but into some new form of error.

Yet, as dogmas and doctrinal truths faded and religion became an aching void, men sought to delude themselves by forms and ceremonies. These, as the outgrowths of a doctrine, or clung to as hallowed outworks, have a value and a significance; but when introduced afresh to revive a dying creed and re-animate it, are like decorations of a corpse; they only serve to make death itself more ghastly.

But, while every truth seems to become evanescent and perishable in the keeping of the sects that have fallen away, seems to lose all vivifying sap, a hatred, prejudice and bitter antagonism against the Church as the guardian of the principle of divine truth and its appointed definer seems never to weaken, but to increase in intensity even when the peculiar ideas that led to schism and heresy have lost their hold and been practically superseded by new forms of error. No philosophical analysis of this strange phase in human thought, this enduring and potent hatred of the Catholic Church, has ever been attempted. It darkens the understanding, making it, in otherwise clear-headed men, unable to use the ordinary rules of reason; in an age when men demand reasons and proofs for every allegation, it makes men accept unhesitatingly the most absurd statements without a shadow of proof and in defiance of common sense. It seems really to manifest a character of diabolical possession. Take up a newspaper of the day. A falsehood against the Church will be started—as that Pope Pius IX. was a free-mason in Philadelphia, that he sent Riel, as a relic, one of the nails of the true cross to reward his rebellion, that some Catholic bishop is leading a revolt in Spanish America; and not an editor will stop to examine whether it is not preposterously false on its face, when he would regard it as trash if told of some one not connected with the Church. It is at once accepted, and the penny-a-liners are set to pad it out, and extend it by " it is said " and " it is well known," till a paragraph grows into a column, to be cited gravely in some legislative hall, not by an idiot escaped from an asylum for mental imbeciles, but by a man of ordinary good sense, while controlled by this demon which suspends the exercise of his habitual good faith, judgment and honesty. It is this spirit which compels men who profess to be religious, and earnestly so, to make public education godless or irreligious, to aim deliberately at a system that will prevent their own children from being imbued from the cradle with religious thought, rather than allow Catholic children to enjoy that advantage, to make the young unreligious, though they themselves, impelled by exaggerated religious feelings, ought naturally to seek to make them religious. It is this strange phase of the human mind that makes so many ready to assist in sapping and weakening the faith of Catholics, to pervert them, and to applaud and encourage all efforts of atheism in Catholic countries, without the slightest care as to results or to the horrors which they are preparing for the social and civil order by this extirpating of all Christian check on millions, who become the blind tools of atheistic demagogues. A sample of this was seen recently in the general approval by our press of the French government in expelling the ministers of religion from the Church of St. Genevieve to make it a National Pantheon, not that the State needed means to erect a suitable edifice for that purpose, but simply to show its power. Had the State of New York seized the new Cathedral at Garden City for a Walhalla, what paper in the land would have denied the right of Bishop Littlejohn, as a citizen and a bishop representing thousands of fellow-citizens, to protest against the act and invoke the aid of the courts to protect the rights of religion?

Thus we see the human mind, after discarding the gift of faith, become enslaved by a hatred of the Church as the guardian of truth, and produce the most strange and wild conceptions in the place of lost truths, and induce others to accept them.

Thus in early times in this country Roger Williams was so imbued with hatred of the Church that he raised a turmoil in Massachusetts by inducing people to believe it idolatrous to have a cross in the English flag, so that they actually cut it out; yet he was soon driven out of that colony for his ideas in regard to religion, and in Rhode Island set up a new community, stoutly holding that " there is no visible Church in the Bay, nor in the world, nor any true Ministerie ;" or, as Hanbury puts it more explicitly, " no church, no sacraments, no pastors, no church officers or ordinance in the world, nor has been since a few years after the Apostles."[1] He swayed from excessive views of the authority of the Protestant church to a denial of all church authority, doctrines, sacraments.

The religious vagaries in this country show no case more astounding than that of Joseph C. Dilks, who, appearing suddenly at a camp-meeting near Galesville, Ohio, in August, 1828, startled the assembly by shouting " salvation," and giving a prodigious snort. In a few days he impressed several people with the belief that he was the Messiah.   One of his proselytes soon told of the heavenly light that surrounded him, and described a contest with Satan in which Dilks defeated the enemy of mankind with his breath.   The next Sunday this man took possession of the log meeting-house of the place and proclaimed himself God.   " I am God, and there is none else."   One of his adherents cried out : " Behold our God ! " and the people fell on their knees and worshipped him.   A Moravian minister became a convert, and though other ministers endeavored to withstand the delusion, the people shouted, " He is my God."   A party was at last formed against Dilks, he was seized, ill-treated, and dragged before magistrates, who released him. After remaining concealed for a time, he again appeared in public, asserting his claims, and finally left the place to go and establish the New Jerusalem in Philadelphia.   Though he never returned, men lived and died recognizing him as the living God.

This monstrous case would seem to be incredible, and we should not venture to state that men in this country could be found so ignorant of the first principles of natural, not to say revealed, religion, as to fall down and worship an ordinary man on his mere assertion that he was the Deity ; but the history of the whole affair has been carefully traced and gathered, and remains undisputed.[2]

If Dilks stands pre-eminent in his fearful blasphemy as claim-

---

[1] Lechford's " Plain Dealing," p. 96.

[2] The Leatherwood God. By R. H. Taneyhill. Cincinnati. 1870.

ing to be God, there have been many "false Christs and false prophets." At the head of these stands the celebrated author of the "Book of Mormon." The length of time that his imposture has gained credence, and the numbers who have been led to recognize him as the prophet of a new dispensation, make the history of Mormonism one of the most curious and extraordinary studies in the religious history of the nineteenth century. Joseph Smith, born at Sharon, Vermont, in 1805, and removing with his parents as a child to Palmyra, New York, grew up idle and unguided. That he had some religious yearnings may be possible, and that he found in the systems around him nothing to satisfy any one, is no less probable. That he saw the field open for a bold religious adventurer, who, by a show of earnestness and enthusiasm, might promise himself success, is pretty evident. As he approached manhood he began to claim that he was visited by angels, and in September, 1823, he boldly averred that a heavenly messenger had appeared to him announcing that he was to be the instrument of a new dispensation. Four years after that he produced a set of en-graved brazen plates which he asserted had been placed in his hands by an angel with a Urim and Thummim to enable him to translate them. The result was the Book of Mormon, alleged by some to have been a work of fiction composed in Biblical style by a Mr. Spalding, and pretending to give the history of the earliest inhab-itants of America. This Book of Mormon became, together with the Bible, the basis of a new religion founded by Smith at Manchester, New York, to which he gave the name of "the Church of Jesus Christ of the Latter Day Saints." He found followers, and soon gathered many proselytes; but as the State of New York seemed a place where his imposture could grow but slowly, he moved to the West, and made many converts in Illinois and Missouri. In the latter State, however, the people generally did not view the religious extravagance and pretensions of Smith with any favor. The Mor-mons were persecuted in every way and driven from their farms. After enduring all this for several years, they finally made Nauvoo in Illinois their chief settlement, founding that city in 1837, and beginning a grand temple. Here their troubles were renewed, the people rose against them, and Smith was at last murdered by a mob, but not before he had established or paved the way for polygamy and other horrors among his deluded followers. Led by Brigham Young, who had joined the body in 1832, the Mormons made their way to the neighborhood of the Great Salt Lake, where, under the supineness and at times actual encouragement of the Federal Gov-ernment, they have increased to a community of more than one hundred thousand, completely controlling the territory of Utah, practising polygamy, and murdering with impunity any whom they condemn in their secret councils. They form at this day one of the most perplexing difficulties in the country. They are heathens as much and as completely as the Chinese, although they assume the name of our Lord in the title of their church, for the god whom they profess to worship in their obscene rites is not the true God, but a being with material body, with flesh, and limbs, and members, and human passions, and the holy spirit is, they assert, simply a fluid![1] This horrible enormity has grown up, drawing its votaries from Protestant sects, none of which have attempted to withstand it. In that new Sodom by that American Dead Sea, Catholicity alone has dared to raise an altar to the Living God, and preach Christ and him crucified.

Second only to Joseph Smith, in the extent and permanence of his religious imposture, was Mrs. Ann Standley, usually known as Mother Ann Lee, the foundress of the Shaker community, which grew up in the woods of New York during the stormy period of the American revolution. She was born in England about 1735, the daughter of a blacksmith, and, when still young, married Abraham Standley, who followed her father's trade. She soon after joined a community of what were called the French Prophets, a wild and visionary sect founded by John Cavelier who, beginning as a religious enthusiast in France, died an English colonel. She became in time the spiritual mother of the little sect, which denounced marriage and looked upon her as the incarnate word. In obedience to a pretended revelation she came to America in 1772, and with a few companions settled at Niskayunà near Watervliet. The enthusiasm and industry of the new-comers attracted attention, and during the period of religious exaltation caused by some Baptist revivals in that part of the country, hundreds flocked to the Shakers, where Mother Ann Lee received them warmly, declaring that their coming was announced to her, that she was the woman clothed with the sun, and daily judged the dead. Many became her proselytes, and her community grew, her wild dreams being received as revelations. The body subsists to this day, and has spread to Massachusetts and the West. Celibacy is enjoined on all, the Brothers and Sisters living in separate houses, and meeting to conduct religious services, in which dancing forms a striking feature. She asserted that she was not subject to death, and that she would ascend to heaven in the twinkling of an eye. Even her death in September, 1784, did not dispel the delusion of her followers, and the sect, with its idolatrous honor of Mother Ann Lee, its strange doctrines and services, lingers on amid the busy population that has grown up around its original settlement. The

---

[1] This is the teaching of the catechism used to instil their religion into the minds of the young.

Shakers, gaining only by accessions of adults from without or poor waifs whom they adopt in childhood, have never increased greatly in numbers; and as the census of 1885 returns only 25,000 for the whole country, the body seems destined to early extinction. Of course, their ideas of God have become so perverted that it would be rash to assert that the object of their devotion is the true God.

What are called the Pagan Onondagas and Senecas, on the other hand, who still linger by their old camp-fires in New York, are really more advanced than Mormon or Shaker or Dilksite. They rejected two centuries ago the Agreskoué or Thoronhiawagon of their ancestors, to worship Dieu or Niio, the God whose nature was explained to them by the Catholic missionaries.

Prophets claiming to be the recipients of special revelations from the Almighty have constantly appeared in this country, and never fail to obtain credulous followers. To the ordinary Protestant they say: You admit that the Catholic Church has fallen into error; but your ministers all disagree. There is no one to teach the people truth. Open your bibles. How did God act in such cases? Did he not raise up his prophets to announce his will to the people and lead them back to him? Even such am I.

As early as 1724, there arose a prophet among the French emigrants to South Carolina, one Peter Rombert, who obtained complete authority over the family into which he had married, and many others in the neighborhood. As in most similar cases, the prophet took to himself a new wife. Refusing all submission to the laws of the colony, his followers would not work on the roads, and defied the officers of the law. When the prophet's immorality called for the action of the authorities, it became necessary to send a body of armed men. The prophet and his followers stubbornly defended the houses, killing one of the officers, but were all at last secured, save one woman, who was killed during the affray. Rombert and two of the men were tried, when they pleaded their authority from God, and insisted that they had done nothing but by His express command, and they maintained that they would rise again on the third day. Their failure to do so seemed to disabuse the rest of their community; yet, not long after, one of these who had been spared killed an innocent person without provocation, maintaining that he acted by the command of God. He paid the penalty of his crime.

Pennsylvania in the last century teemed with prophets and men who claimed commissions from on high to frame new ways of salvation for mankind. A writer in the *Lutheran*, who undertook to treat of the extinct sects in Pennsylvania, carried his series of articles through several years, so extensive did he find the field which he had undertaken to treat.

In later days several prophets rose in various parts, winning local adherents and flourishing for a time, to vanish at last from the page of history. It is not easy to trace all these, and the current histories, either of the country or of local divisions, and even the works which pretend to treat of all the religious denominations in the country, seem ashamed of these vagaries, and seek to consign their record to oblivion. A broken-down country storekeeper in Washington County, New York, excited by the preaching of some rhapsodical revivalists, began to have revelations and held forth in the streets of Albany, but, being rejected there, went to New York city. There he assumed a strange garb, and soon obtained influence enough to gather a band of disciples. Over these his influence was supreme; their houses, their property, their wives were at the disposal of the prophet. But Mathias seemed to be in haste to secure all, and the death of one of his older followers was ascribed to poison administered by the false prophet. He escaped the gallows, but soon disappeared from public view.

More recently a woman in Philadelphia, Myra Mitta, assumed the role of prophetess or Messiah, and was almost worshipped by a few deluded followers, from whom she took care to obtain the deed of a house, which was used as her residence and church. But though, like Ann Lee, she had proclaimed herself immortal, death took her from her votaries, leaving the courts to settle the title to the sacred edifice.

In these cases all will admit that the true idea of God, as handed down in the Church, has been lost to such an extent that these blind leaders of the blind can no longer be regarded as worshipping Him in common with Jews and Christians, but as distinctly heathen.

Most of these cases of false prophets are directly traceable to the mad and extravagant preaching of itinerant ministers, from the days of Whitefield and the first Moravian and Methodist preachers. The wild appeals, the excitement which they caused, always dangerous, inflamed the worst passions, unsettled reason, caused the most aggravated forms of mania, often resulting in permanent insanity. The camp-meetings were prolific sources of all these evils. The first of these was an outgrowth of the Kentucky Revival of 1800, and was held at Cane Ridge. There not only ministers, but men and women, and even children, took part.

"At no time," says a recent writer, "was the 'falling exercise' so prevalent as at night. Nothing was then wanting that could strike terror into minds, weak, timid and harassed. The red glare of the camp-fires reflected from hundreds of tents and wagons; the dense blackness of the flickering shadows, the darkness of the surrounding forest, made still more terrible by the groans and screams of the 'spiritually wounded' who had fled to it for comfort; the entreaty of the preachers; the sobs and shrieks of the downcast still walking through the dark valley of the Shadow of Death ; the shouts and songs of praise from the happy ones who had crossed the Delectable Mountains, had gone on through the fogs of the Enchanted Ground and entered the land of Beulah, were too much for those over whose minds and bodies lively imaginations held full sway. The heart swelled, the nerves gave way, the hands and feet grew cold, and they fell headlong to the ground speechless and motionless. In a moment crowds gathered about them to pray and shout. Some lay still as death. Some passed through frightful twitchings of face and limb."

" As the meetings grew more and more frequent, this nervous excitement assumed new and more terrible forms. One was known as jerking ; another as the barking exercise; a third as the Holy Laugh." The community seemed demented. From the nerves and muscles the disorder passed to the mind. Men dreamed dreams and saw visions, nay, fancied themselves dogs, went down on all fours, and barked till they grew hoarse. It was no uncommon sight to behold numbers of them gathered about a tree, barking, yelping, " treeing the Devil." " The Holy Laugh became a recognized part of worship."

And all this was the outgrowth of what was and is paraded as pure Evangelical Christianity! Men claimed that Catholic doctrines and Catholic rites were incompatible with a due exercise of human reason, and their attempt to display human reason duly exercised resulted in wild unreason.

It is sad to follow these wanderings of the human mind and see what extravagances the revolt from the authority established of God entailed on the unfortunate nations which took the fatal step.

The development of what is called Spiritualism seems to indicate that men are worshipping not a mere subjective god, the conception of their own brain, but Satan himself.

The oscillations of error are curious. The whole tendency of New England Puritanism was to relegate from thought the humanity of our Lord, prompted apparently by the desire to avoid honoring the real mother of one really man. This led to confusion of thought as to the Father and the Son, and paved the way for Unitarianism, which so largely supplanted the earlier Christian doctrine of the Trinity even in the feeble form in which New England held it. Unitarianism exalted the humanity of our Lord, and, Sadducee-like, spread disbelief in all things spiritual. Science came with its gross materialism.

Then came the reaction in favor of spiritual existences. Instead of yielding to the clear, intelligent teachings of the Church, the minds of men sought to hold intercourse with the unseen world. They did not bow before God in humility, with sorrow for sin, with a desire for His love, a dependence on His graces and mercies.

They became the sport of evil spirits and more frequently of charlatans. The influence of the Spirit of God or spirits sent by God would be seen in peace, in greater love for God and man, in desire to advance in virtue. But in the vagaries of Spiritualism we can see nothing of this. Pride, insanity, hardness of heart, are much more likely to meet our inquiries.

So far as any effects are seen that are above natural powers, we find nothing to induce us to ascribe them to God. If not from God but yet supernatural, they are diabolic, and the whole affair is a service of demons. Men fall lower than Mormon or Shaker, they become worshippers of Satan. In fact, in all this system of Spiritualism there is no real active recognition of the true God; He is utterly ignored. The whole honor of the votaries is paid to the spirit working to delude them, who can be Satan only.

While Mormonism and Shakerism are mainly local, Spiritualism pervades the country, and without church or minister is sapping the last remnant of Christian faith and leading thousands who are scarcely aware of their lapse from Christianity to a real and distinct worship of the Evil Spirit. New England in its early days, while formally denying that the saints and angels, in the order of God's providence, could be aware of the prayers emanating from the hearts of the faithful or could aid them in soul and body,—though our Lord portrayed Dives as praying from hell itself to Abraham in behalf of his brethren,—admitted and maintained that evil spirits could hear men, make compacts with them, and render service for their temporal benefit or the injury of their neighbors. With little scientific knowledge even for their own day, with no criteria for judging the supernatural, the people of New England undoubtedly condemned many innocent persons to death; but in modern Spiritualism they might have found clearer cases than any that came before their tribunals.

The Protestant sects themselves, where they have retained the traditional teaching of the true God, have not been able to check extravagance. Protestantism is not a religion, although many of our early statute-books required people to swear to a belief in the truths of the Protestant religion. It is merely a phase of thought, and has no real characteristics of a religion, since it rejects authority, has no infallible creed, no priesthood, no essential act of divine worship. Its one vital principle, hatred of Catholicity, cannot satisfy the wants of the human soul. Man feels that there must be an authority from God to guide him, that there must be an authority to speak infallibly in God's name, that there must be some distinct act of divine worship, and a priesthood to offer it. All this his Bible tells him distinctly, constantly; but in practice he finds none of it, and the prejudice against the Church in which he has been trained from the cradle, in his meeting-house, in public school and general literature, keeps him from turning to it to seek relief. The death of our Lord on the cross is represented to him as the only sacrifice, but it is not brought home to him, and is made a mere fact of history. Yet the death of our Lord on the cross, though decreed by the high-priest, and carried out under his will by the Romans, was not in itself a sacrifice. Nowhere in or out of the Bible is there a case where a victim was slain on the wood of the altar, and then taken away and buried. The victim must be consumed by fire or by eating. This is essential. The Holy Eucharist "fills up those things that are wanting of the sufferings of Christ," and makes His death a real sacrifice, complete and perfect, enabling each one to partake of the victim and join in the great act of adoration as well as enjoy the blessings it procures. What to the Protestant is only a fact of history, is to the Catholic an ever-existing sacrifice, " showing the death of the Lord from generation to generation, till He come."

Cut off from this, with no guide and no chart that he can feel absolutely certain in following, the Protestant seeks constantly something to rouse and excite him. From time to time we see movements tending in this direction. Like Wesley, some attempt to copy Catholic methods, and apply them; but as the error of justification by faith only makes each one judge in his own case, he considers himself justified whenever the thought comes to him that he is; and as he is taught that he is thus one of the elect, there is no precaution against relapse, no purpose of amendment based on contrition for the past, no looking to our Lord for help through the channels He has appointed. The momentary fervor passes, and the last state becomes worse than the first, often to be a mere jest and scoff. The Moravian and Methodist systems, with the camp-meetings which grew up in this country in days when settlements were sparse, and rough, untutored, but earnest ministers were the only ones to reach many of the people, gradually declined as population increased, and have taken a new phase, combining commercial thrift with summer relaxation at the seaside or the mountain. The camp-meeting, in becoming more decorous, has become less earnest; there is less of scripture and more of human oratory, The great revivals among the Congregationalists have, in a similar way, lost all their supposed efficiency. The Lorenzo Dow of former days re-appears in a singing Phillips, or Moody and Sankey, or in some rough outspoken man like a Sam Jones. But the regular ministrations of Protestantism fail to gather people within the walls of their meeting-houses, except where some preacher suits himself to the popular taste, and discusses questions of the day rather than the tenets of religion or the teaching of morality. In the Church of England, and the Episcopal Church in this country, the largest congregations are those drawn by the saddening imitation of Catholic rites and Catholic thoughts, sad because they are but a figure without the substance.

Outside of that body, the only exhibition of a real spirit of reaching the people, and rousing them to a sense of the importance of religion, is the strange creation of our times, the Salvation Army. This is entirely outside of the Protestant ministry. The actors are not ministers, claim no rights or privileges as such; in fact, attest the uselessness and inefficiency of any ministry in the Protestant system; they take their titles, not from any ecclesiastical offices, but from the military nomenclature. Their leader is General Booth; the superintendents of their bands of home missionaries, as they would, in other terms, be called, are captains. They go about with noisy music, singing and declaiming their exhortations. They are earnest, and gather crowds. While the earnestness lasts, their sincere endeavor to reform the sinful may excite some sympathy for their misdirected zeal; but the earnestness flags, and unworthy motives appear, and the whole affair becomes a public nuisance, often leaving no result but an unhealthy religious excitement, which leads to the overthrow of all rational equilibrium in weak minds, producing insanity, sometimes attended with most terrible results, as it points to lust or murder, developing into acts like those of the Newark Adamites, gathering naked in their prayer-meetings, or like the case in Massachusetts, where a father, impelled by religious fanaticism, murdered his own children, reviving the sanguinary worship of Moloch to honor the Almighty.

As the knowledge of the true God is so rapidly disappearing, and false gods are gradually obtaining the honor due to Him alone, ought we not to make some exertion to rescue the country from a return to heathenism? The Council of the Vatican is the first ever held by the Church in which it became necessary to define the existence, personality, and nature of God. This seems to indicate clearly the importance of inculcating these truths as against the errors condemned. Our great theological school at Woodstock has, in the same spirit, given a grand treatise, *De Deo Uno et Trino*, suited to the wants of our day. If learned priests in our great cities were, on Sundays in some hired hall, and with nothing to suggest church ceremonies, to give conferences on God, Revelation, Redemption, the End of Man, on topics such as were propounded by the Apostles to the Gentiles of the Roman Empire, many would be saved who are now losing all trace of Christianity. The very fundamentals of religion are so obscured in many minds that it is necessary to begin at them, and so clearly exhibit the whole scheme of Redemption that thousands with clear minds and willing hearts will, when they hear the word of truth, correspond to the grace of God, and believe.

MORALITY AND LIFE.

W HEN we consider the dishonesty and fraud of our times, the vices and crimes destructive of all confidence of man in man and almost of society itself, we must acknowledge that life is out of jóint with morality in this nineteenth century. The pomp and parade of wealth, the deference it commands, the honors paid to it, the influence it exerts, if they mean anything at all, mean certainly the worship of mammon, which renders the poor discontented with their lot and creates a universal desire and a universal scramble to get rich, honestly if possible, but to get rich at any rate. Public opinion is but slightly scrupulous as to the means employed to gain wealth or to obtain control of it. Offences against the person which spring from heated blood or untamed passion are bad enongh, but they are not nearly as bad as the cool, deliberate offences against the rights of property which constitute the chief characteristics of modern society, and so numerous and gigantic have these become that the strongest governments are impotent to redress or to restrain them. The moral sense of society appears stunted and suffering from a radical defect.

That life should be moral, and that the degree to which genuine moral principles penetrate thought, will and action, determines the greater or lesser value of life, both as regards the individual and as regards society, are propositions just as clearly recognized now as of old. The absolute necessity of a moral code for the regulation of conduct is not in the least contested. But the notions as to what constitutes morality, on what basis ethics must rest, and what office they have to perform, have undergone material changes. The issues of life are now being viewed from entirely different standpoints, so much so that the reasoning which thoroughly satisfied the tenor of mind of the mediæval period, and of our more immediate ancestors, though it has lost neither its force nor its correctness, is no longer applicable in our times. Large numbers nowadays believe that our age is a great movement in behalf of intelligence against ignorance, of reason against blind authority, of mental freedom against mental bondage, of rational scientific belief against bigotry and superstition. The world, which once held that morality is inseparably bound up with religion because of the direct influence which religious belief exercises upon human actions, no longer thinks so. Religion is now superseded, so people try to persuade themselves, by " enlightenment," " the culture of the nineteenth century," "the creed of science." This view resulted quite logically in the secularization of the schools, that is to say, in a system of education which carefully avoids engrafting any religious principles upon the juvenile mind. The fruits of this system confront us in the present moral condition of society, for it has now been long enough in existence to show what fruits it can bear. Its success, as a Protestant divine tersely states, ought to be apparent in politics and upon the bench, upon boys and girls, men and women, and upon the statistics of crime. In all these respects, however, a decided deterioration has taken place wherever "advanced ideas" and "modern cultured thought" appear in the foreground. In the most civilized countries we behold corruption in the legislative bodies, bribery at elections, juries equally deficient in learning and integrity, politics a regular and rather disreputable business, repudiation of debts, betrayal of financial trusts, crookedness in mercantile life, adroit embezzlements of public funds. Nor is this all. We behold, moreover, the magnificent offenders flaunt their crimes with impunity in the face of a helpless community, divorce legalize concubinage, and free-love administer the death-blow to the family. This sad picture of the moral condition of our times resembles only too closely the period of the decadence of the Roman Empire, and yet it is by no means overdrawn. As has already been stated, the rueful deficiency of the ethical code, construed by the leaders of thought of this age, offers the only explanation. The code of morality, based solely upon scientific truths, no matter how admirable a structure it may be in its way, no matter what a wonderful evidence of the keenness of human intellect, has proven an ignominious failure in its effects upon the life of mankind.

Strong suspicions begin to arise now in the minds of many that these systems, after all, present to us nothing but the achievements of fanciful mental gymnastics; the impotency and the hopeless incapability of appealing by science to more than the intellect is being more and more understood; society gradually awakens to a proper realization of the fact that these modern systems of morality are far from furnishing a basis upon which society could rest without most serious misgivings for the "morrow"; and in proportion as this recognition grows, in the same proportion grows the desire in earnestness and intensity to find the one vital force by virtue of which society may be reconstructed on the basis of true morality. The great question, then, is this: how can the re-acceptance of the true code of morality be brought about, and how can the world be taught where the same is to be found?

There is, it is true, the Church of Rome, which says to mankind, with the same unalterable firmness as in the days of the apostles,

"Turn to my form of Christianity for genuine morality." She presses her claim of being sole possessor of an ethical code by which life is rendered worth living, and all incongruities of time and place and circumstances harmonized. But let us not deceive ourselves. To outsiders this apodictic statement appears as an arrogant assertion, entitled to no more weight than that of any other religious belief. Add to it the fact that there are but too many who, though nominally at least belonging to the Catholic Church, belie by their lives the purity of the moral code they profess as their own, and it is easily understood that the situation is not much improved by the attitude of Catholicity. It is idle to hope that dogmatic assertions, no matter how strongly emphasized, will change the tenor of mind of our age, and whoever indulges in such belief betokens only a gross misunderstanding of the intellectual attitude of society. The only road which, to our mind at least, promises a fair share of success, consists in a careful re-examination of the true meaning of morality, and in evolving by such a study what basis ethical principles demand in order to hold humanity with the grip of omnipotence. Such inquiry will soon convince us that true morality does not float in the air, but can be generated and sustained only by the true teachings of Christianity. By following this road we are at once free from all objections that might be raised against any other method of inquiry, for we adopt then the very line of thought of our times and keep thus abreast of the tendency of the age.

Now, "life," that dire fact, staring us in the face with a tale of crime, of misery, of suffering, of wretchedness; life, exhibiting to us the unceasing struggle of human passions, the victories and, alas! the defeats also of virtue; life, this conglomeration of volition, reasoning, and sentiment, issuing forth in energy and activity; this great enigma, life,—shall we, can we, believe it to be unable to tell us wherein true morality consists, and what its origin, its sustenance, if we attentively read the lessons of that stupendous drama? Ah, it would be the extreme height of sadness if life could make no answer. To feel that reason imposes an obligation which it cannot instruct us how to fulfil; to find ourselves with broad conceptions which we know not how to realize, with a sense of duty hanging over us which we cannot practically discharge—to hesitate between probabilities, to balance between uncertainties, to find the darkness increasing as we advance, and finally to lose ourselves in doubt and bewilderment, this would be our cruel fate if life had to remain silent. But though, engrossed with the world, with its cares, its follies, its gayeties, its dissipations, we may for a time silence the voice within and disregard the admonitions of conscience, the day must come in each individual life, for it comes to all men, when all of a sudden we realize the true inwardness of morality, and at that time conscience imparts a knowledge to us which we feel and know by intuition to be true, irresistibly true knowledge. But for conscience morals would be an idle phantom, ethical codes superfluous brain-speculations. This conclusion, to which the introspection of life in individuals drives us, is also corroborated by the study of the lives of nations; that is to say, by inquiry into the true meaning of public morality.

Before proceeding further, it may not be superfluous to make some few remarks, or rather statements of facts on morality itself, because most of the errors into which men fall generally arise from the attempt to solve questions without the necessary preparatory knowledge and discipline. Now, morality means a set of first principles which, by taking hold of thought, will, and action, regulate our conduct in life. First principles in ethics, as well as in anything else, must, of course, possess the character of universal applicability, that is, the character of truth. And if absolutely true, they are necessarily so irrespective of time and place. If we do not insist upon what is strictly true, independently of our notions of truth and justice, but insist merely upon what appears to the actor to be so, we make right and wrong vary with the varying notions of each individual, and deny all invariable standard of right and wrong. Morality would then depend solely upon the private notions, caprice, or idiosyncrasies of each separate individual. The same thing might be right for one and wrong for the other, which is obviously preposterous and absurd. We know very well by natural reason that the distinction between right and wrong is not arbitrary, accidental, and variable, but immutable, independent, and eternal. The moral law is consequently the same at all times, in all places, and under all circumstances, and, instead of being the creature of our notions and convictions, is independent of and unaffected by them. For, the moment we substitute our views of truth for the truth itself, we deny virtually all truth and all falsehood, all right and all wrong, make them relative matters, one or the other, according to one's mode of seeing, feeling, or thinking. The laws of logic and of reason forbid us, if we think at all, to think otherwise. Consequently there can be but one absolute and invariable standard of morals which is not subject to change, but remains, all the wide world over, the same.

Again, all morality necessarily pre-supposes an objective law— a law out of man, above man, to which he is accountable, which he is under obligation to obey, obedience to which constitutes virtue, and disobedience to which constitutes vice. This conception, let it be emphasized, is essential to the very idea of morality. If there be no such law, or if it is not and cannot be known to us, then man would simply cease to be a moral being. Nor is this all. From the necessity of a moral law out of and above man springs also the necessity of a moral lawgiver, who has the sovereign right to impose the law. "Duty," that which a man is *bound* to perform, is conceivable only if there is an absolute sovereign law which binds us. There is no use trying to smooth over these very plain facts or to invent fine phrases for covering up an intolerable and unjustifiable ignorance on this subject. If we do not recognize the existence of the supernatural, we cannot, consistently, recognize any moral law whatsoever. The attempt to separate religion and morals, and to obtain a solid foundation for our moral superstructure independent of religion, has for this reason proved and always will prove disastrous. The men who propound in our times theories and systems of ethics, which in reality are far from being in accord with true morality, do not profess to break with Christian civilization, or to reject religion and morals; but they strive to assert a morality without God and a Christianity without Christ. It is but a little while and all their works need recasting, because their systems are giving way. Sincerity or firmness of conviction on the part of those who dish up the modern vague theories of morality, does not render what they announce true and of moral obligation. Uncertain opinions, unproved theories, unverified hypotheses, have no claim to be listened to in the moral sphere. From a moral point of view, from a rigidly ethical standard, the codes of Darwin, Sir John Lubbock, Taine, Buchner, Schopenhauer, Huxley, Tyndall, and Herbert Spencer are simply opinions, theories, hypotheses, which are, at best, plausible conjectures under the imposing name of science, and which, being nothing more, should not unsettle men's minds, bewilder the half-learned, mislead the ignorant, undermine the very bases of society, and assail the whole moral order of the universe. It will not do to arraign the faith and the convictions of enlightened and living mankind and try to overrule them by science which is not proved with apodictic certainty to be science, and by truth which is not demonstrated to be truth. Yet this principle of ethics and of logic is disregarded by the whole tribe of contemporary moralists. Let us not deceive ourselves. The merit or the demerit of earthly career is measured only by the absolute and invariable standard of morality; that alone determines the individual, the intrinsic, as well as the sociological, the extrinsic, value of our morality. People are not moral because they frame their lives in accordance with an essentially deficient standard of morality; else all we would have to do to be truly moral would be to adopt a code in harmony with our propensities, whatever these may be. Relative morality does not count in life; unless we are moral in the true sense of the word, we possess no right to call ourselves so, nor does the world call us so.

We are now prepared to go one step farther. We will inquire first what does morality embrace in the surging ebb and flow tide of life, and what is the principle upon which it can rationally rest. Individual morality is twofold; it is negative and it is positive. It is negative in so far as it enjoins us not to perform any inherently immoral acts; and it is positive in so far as it bids us to exercise and practice virtue. For the shunning of vice is by no means the practice of virtue. The groundwork on which the regard and esteem of our fellow-men does rest, comprises hardly more than negative morality. Our social intercourse is conditioned upon certain civic virtues; our actions are constantly watched by those around us; the laws of every land impose certain restraints upon us. To steer clear of the criminal code does not consequently imply a really moral character. It is not enough to be honest, straightforward and truthful, because the thief is imprisoned, the liar dishonored, and the murderer hanged. Fear is, then, our motive power rather than love, and such morality is hardly worthy of the name. To be truly moral requires a subduing of our passions, a curbing of every inordinate appetite, a checking of undue ambition; but it requires much more still. It is not action alone, but will and thought likewise that must be governed by our moral principles. Licentiousness of thought, though less reprehensible than licentiousness of word and deed, remains nevertheless a criminal offence against the moral code, and differs from immoral actions not in kind, but only in degree. Consequently, the inward disposition, the habit of the mind, the principles we cherish and live up to, these are essential elements of any truly moral character. Morality, therefore, is not put on like a garment from without, but issues forth from within. And these principles adopted for the guidance of conduct must prevail to such an extent that we would part with life itself rather than forfeit one iota of these principles. And not only that, but all moral virtues, as for instance, chastity, temperance, charity, must not remain passive, but become active in us: they must inspire our thoughts, fill our hearts and bring tangible fruits during our lives. Now, if this has to be conceded, as it must needs be conceded, we perceive at once that a stronger motive than the world must impart life-giving power to those principles which are to produce all that. Let us consider a few striking examples. The virgin, who prefers cruel death to the loss of virtue, displays a conduct which remains utterly inexplicable by any moral code which makes the " here-below " the all of life. We must reach higher than science, higher even than this world, to realize what can and does prompt this preference of cold, pitiless death to a life of luxurious ease, if conditioned upon the loss of virginity. And as with chastity so with all other virtues. Social upheavals may from time to time induce the amasser of wealth to disgorge some of his ill-gotten gain; but this is not charity, no matter how often it may be misnamed such. In order to behold true charity, we must seek the principle which teaches self-sacrifice, bids us forego pleasures in order to sit at the bedside of the sick and watch their feverish brow, and not until we reach the immolation of self in the service of fellow-man do the noblest and highest examples of charity stand before us. We may single out all typical figures of unquestioned morality, those that have received the unanimous plaudits of all succeeding ages, and we will find that the fundamental principles which actuated them to do what re-echoes to their praise from century to century, proceeded not from the senses, but from the soul, not from this world, but from belief in another world presided over by a sovereign lawgiver. True morality presupposes, thus, for a rational basis a common relation to a supreme lawgiver by which all distinctions of sex, of rank, of wealth, of age, of time and place are abolished. Only by perceiving in fellow-man the image of Him towards whom we have to discharge a duty, can we rise to an actual discharge towards that fellow-man of the debt we owe to the Creator. Thus belief in a supernatural life which centres in and revolves around God offers the only possible and real basis of morality. The law of love, the law of freedom, the law of equality by means of which mankind not only rose from the low plane of brute animalism, but recovered its own dignity and breathed again the pure atmosphere of genuine morality, these laws do not result from a contemplation of physical facts, nor can they be evolved from science. They are due, it must be acknowledged, to the all-embracing love of that transfigured Humanity, the God-Man crucified, who shed from the foot of the cross the life blood of all true morality, and bade us believe and hope and practice the moral law. As the love given of free accord by man to that central figure of the whole human race, proceeds not from the senses, but from the soul, so also do the affectionate devotion and observance of the moral code taught by Him proceed not from any mundane, but from supernatural motives. Let human nature act according to its present laws, give to each faculty its natural exercise, to each tendency its natural gratification, to the whole the natural objects craved for, and it is never further from having attained its goal. With all that nature can give, man remains infinitely below his destiny—a mere inchoate creature, wanting an object that can fill the deep void within; for though man, he is not as yet a moral being. It is both a remarkable and an undeniable fact that all who take reason alone for their

guide and disown conscience, fail to grasp the one essential principle of all ethics. It is an undeniable fact, for it is the standing
reproach of all speculative systems, from Plato down to our own
times, and it is remarkable because it is invariably reproduced in
every department of life, if we trust ourselves in practical matters
to the guidance of reason rather than of conscience, because it runs
through all human life, when abandoned to simple nature. True
morality, then, as far as the inquiry into individual life reveals,
consists in the practical worship of those highest and purest
virtues that are embodied in a real person, living and acting, the
God-man, Christ, out of an affectionate devotion. The recognition
of the relationship of man to God, and of God to man, and of man
to man through and on account of the common relation to God, is,
then, the very essence and substance of all morality. Only by
referring all our actions back to God do we obtain rational, acceptable motives. Life, as we have seen, asks us to do a great many
things which neither civic nor social relations can ever impose
upon us, and these very acts, whose performance sometimes seems
almost to defy reason and every law of nature, are those which
secure to the performers the character of exalted and unquestionable morality. Sociologists and agnostics, together with all Christendom, point out, as prototypes of the highest ethics, acts which,
without a supernatural motive, refuse altogether to be comprehensible, and thus, in point of fact, acknowledge that without a belief
in God, an accounting for our deeds and a retribution in accord
with their merit or demerit, the individual is bereft of, is *minus* that
one motive power which alone can stir up his sluggish energies to
overcome the low promptings of human nature.

Apart, however, from the consideration of morality in the individual, an inquiry into the moral aspect of nations and ages forces
us to precisely the same conclusion, for history is by no means a
silent book on this very point. Let us confine ourselves, first of
all, to those three principal virtues or perfections which are most
wanting in heathen society and most characteristic of true civilization, namely, humility, regard for maternity, and lastly, chastity.

The whole philosophical and moral system of the Stoic school,
which must be acknowledged as the least discreditable of all ancient systems, is founded on pride. The Stoic, to be sure, taught
self-denial, detachment from the world, contempt of riches and
honors, and superiority to all accidents of fortune. But he taught
so because a man should have too high an opinion of himself to
be affected by such trifles. Very different is the view taken by
Christian moralists. The truly moral man rises with them above
the world, not by his pride but by his humility. He proves his
superiority to the world and to fortune by proving that his capacity

to suffer pain, disgrace, and even death, is much stronger than the power of the world to inflict them. The Christian observes the moral law, not like the Stoic, from a contempt of the weakness that could violate it, but from love of the law itself, from a profound sense of its sacredness and justice, engendered by the love of its Author. The Stoic found himself not unfrequently compelled to lay hands on his own life, while the Christian triumphs in his weakness by relying on a greater strength than his own. The Greek, as well as the Roman, civilization, was founded on pride and respect for success, and exhibits, consequently, no trace of compassion and sympathy for the poor, the friendless, the helpless, and the aged. " *Væ victis!*" was a maxim most scrupulously observed. Not until we go back to the nations of old, and make ourselves acquainted with their manners and customs, usages and laws, prior to their conversion to Christianity, do we see their real deformity, or can we in any degree appreciate the immense change, as regards humility, wrought by the ethics of Christianity.

Coming next to the holy function of maternity, nowhere do we find in heathendom any conception of its true significance, its sacred character. It is well known that in Sparta all malformed children were put to death as soon as born, and, in Rome, also, the mother had no right over the child. The father had to say, when the nurse brought the child to him, whether it was to be reared or strangled. The prevalence of child murder, and the exposure of children in China and India, result likewise from the low estimate in which maternity is held. By placing maternity on the level of a mere animal function, society leads not only to the toleration and authorization of infanticide, but it degrades also womanhood, by making her a mere accomplice with man in sensual gratification. On the other hand, we observe that in proportion as the Christian view of woman and motherhood gains way, in like proportion child murder ceases.

As to chastity, suffice it to say that voluptuousness was worshipped as a goddess through nearly all polished heathendom, and, if what grave historians have recorded is to be believed, nothing can exceed the corruption of the moral atmosphere of Rome with a Julia and a Messalina. We cannot speak of really moral notions on any of these three virtues prior to the advent of Christ.

If we consider next the social position of woman, we arrive at the same result. The sale of women to the highest bidder for the gratification of lust was customary among the Babylonians, and if we mistrust Herodotus and turn to Strabo, we learn of still more revolting practices among other nations. Woman's position in Greece was hardly less degrading. She was the instrument of lust, and the bearer of children, but not man's equal ; on the contrary, his inferior, whom it was no crime to treat with contempt. Beauty of form constituted her main worth even at the time when the civilization of Greece had reached its summit. If we turn to savage tribes, we learn that men went wife-hunting as they went bear-hunting, and the captives were slaves. Judging by the foregoing crucial tests the morality of any age or nation, we are constrained to admit that except in Christendom none can be found. The normal current of human morals has flowed, and never ceased to flow, from the foot of the cross. Whatever real progress has been made during the last nineteen hundred years, came from the influence of Christianity upon society. No one can hold otherwise without confounding change with progress. Changes, very great changes, have been wrought outside of that current, but no real progress. Fortunately, the world is pretty well agreed that the Christian code of ethics is so far superior to anything preceding it as to offer no longer debatable ground. Unfortunately, the world is not yet agreed that there is but one code of Christian morality extant, and that all others, whether sailing under the disguise of Christianity or not, are spurious fabrications. And here again, we take it, the questioning of life enables us to discern the genuine from the sham code.

Society, as is well known, depends upon the family, and the family, in turn, depends upon a sacred and sanctified relationship, marriage. Now, if we withdraw from marriage the moral principle by and through which it acquires a sacred character, the only supports left to virtue are the natural sentiments, instincts, and inclinations which lead invariably to crime, vice, and immorality. The moment we look upon marriage merely as a civil institution, the moment we remove from it the moral element, we leave, practically, the relation of the sexes to the concupiscence of human nature. Divorce is, in reality, nothing but successive polygamy or successive polyandry, as the case may be, and wherever divorce is not tabooed, there we need not look for the true code of ethics. Nor is this all. If marriage consists only in the operation of the unrestrained sensual appetites of men and women, it can have no regard to the birth and education of children, but must look solely to the self-indulgence and pleasure of the couple to which children would be a great encumbrance. Thus divorce and free-love are not only incompatible with true morality, but wherever they are, the atmosphere is far from pure.

But this is not all. A more careful investigation tells us more still. As morality in the individual must needs begin with a habit of thought, a belief in the authority of the moral law, and must next influence will, and finally issue forth in action ; so morality begins in society with the social unit, the family. And since the family is constituted by marriage, the morality of society depends entirely and solely upon the correct moral view in regard to marriage. Now marriage, in order to be in full accord with the true moral code, demands, or rather presupposes, three things : sanctity, unity, and indissolubility, three things which it lacked in the pagan world, and which it lacks even in the modern world in proportion as it ceases to be truly Christian. Social corruption, whether ancient or modern, begins always with the family; and to destroy the family means, then, to destroy society and all that deserves the name of civilization. Whatever moral greatness modern nations possess, as compared with pagans, proceeds from the moral view of marriage, from the Christian view of the family. Let this be clearly understood, for it is the most important lesson history teaches us in order to find where true morality is now to be found in the world. Now, the "reformers" of the sixteenth century began by first denying the indissolubility of marriage; and by next denying its religious character, viz., its sanctity, they entirely cut loose from true morality. To permit polygamy, not simultaneous polygamy, but successive, actual polygamy, by permitting the divorced man or woman to marry while wife or husband is still alive, is to proclaim a moral code, not on a higher, but on precisely the same plane with that of antiquity. It is strange, indeed, with what blind tenacity would-be Christianity clings to a shadow after having discarded the substance. It is sheer mockery to talk about morality alongside of divorce ; it is a mere play of words to acknowledge divorce, but to disown polygamy. Yet Protestantism could not help itself. The two cardinal principles underlying all its countless forms of belief, that of negation and that of private judgment, once admitted into ethics, destroy with deadly certainty. It needs but a denial of an absolute, invariable standard of morality ; it needs but an application of private judgment as to what is and what is not moral, in order to have, not only divorce, but free-love. Private judgment, guided on one hand by our rebellious inclinations, and on the other hand by our disinclination to morally reproach ourselves, easily coins a code by which the semblance of moral conduct, at least, may be preserved, by which that which is repulsive to truly moral notions may be seemingly moral by being in accord with a loose ethical code. Again, denying, as Protestantism does, that an infallible interpretation of God's law exists here below outside of human reason, the ultimate tribunal pronouncing upon right and wrong is transferred to that selfsame *Ego* which hates so much self-accusation. The repugnance within us to offend our own sinful propensities predisposes us to cling to every straw, if, by holding on to it, we appear a trifle less sinful in our eyes. If we are immoral, we hate to so consider ourselves, èven in the secrecy of our chambers, so strong is our innate desire to escape the censorship of conscience, and for this reason are people so ready to subscribe to ethical codes which apparently remove, or at least lessen, that odium.   The old lines,

> Video meliora proboque,
> Deteriora sequor,

have lost none of their force.   They apply even to our unwillingness to see after we are no longer blindfolded; for to own up that the truth is perceived, and yet not to embrace the same at once, requires a moral courage much greater than to pretend to not having seen the truth, an avowal of moral cowardice with which, alas, our times are surfeited.   Let it not be forgotten that we are responsible, morally responsible for our convictions, our belief, our actions, for all in which the *will is brought directly into play*.   Great heroism is not required to plead ignorance, when ignorance suits our purposes; but to see and embrace truth, requires a complete attachment to truth, and very few in a period of laxity such as ours have the courage to do it.   " Morality without foundation in the belief in God and the soul's immortality," so M. Emile de Laveleye, a Protestant, writes, " the vague sentiment which wavers between good and evil, without any exertion on our own part to awaken in us the consciousness of our imperfection and the aspirations after an ideal of the true and the just; in a word, human nature totally delivered up to its earthly instincts, how is it to follow the right path and accomplish its high destiny ?   Without doubt the animal species, directed by its instincts, subsists and perpetuates itself by gratifying the appetites.   Savages live pretty much in the same way, without the ideas of duty and of another life exercising great influence over their actions; but their existence also is that of brutes; without ceasing, they fight over the prey, and the strongest comes off the best.   What would become of our societies, which rest upon respect paid to law, were the duty and the very idea of justice to disappear ?   Atheism, conscious, universal, publicly avowed and everywhere taught, would it not inevitably lead us back to the barbarity of prehistoric times ?"   Evidently, M. de Laveleye recognizes the necessity of a supernatural belief as the only basis of morality, and hence of society.   Whether the inability to believe in God proceeds from the cherished and unchallenged bias of atheistic education, or from a violent recoil from religious training, or from a habitual disregard of the voice of conscience, or from a too exclusive addiction to the methods and teachings of physical science, or to the combined action of these influences, it is quite certain that man is none the less morally responsible for his convictions.   It is, therefore, not the relative, but the absolute standard of ethics which alone applies universally. Of course, in the limited space of a review article, it is impossible exhaustively to treat as vast a subject as morality and life even in any one respect. The mere attempt would at once show a fatal delusion on the part of him who would venture upon so bold a task. Yet from the few outlines which we have jotted down, from the line of thought which we have tried to point out, certain conclusions are already inevitable, and it seems to us that more thorough inquiries into the aspects of the question on which we threw out merely a few suggestions, can not fail further to confirm these conclusions.

To sum up: We hold that the introspection of morality, as far as individuals are concerned, reveals to us the imperative necessity of belief in an omnipotent law-giver as a first and indispensable condition of morality. To render suffering meritorious; to impart contentment with our lot, no matter how humble and miserable it may be; to awaken in us a life-giving consciousness of our duties to our fellow man and to society; to make us consider ourselves not owners, but trustees simply, of what is given to us, stewards who have to render account; to render charity, compassion, love, chastity and all ennobling and elevating sentiments as active forces in life the priceless treasures which these virtues are acknowledged to be; in short, to put mankind above the level of the brute and prevent humanity from crawling along with gaze bent downward upon the crust of the earth, we need God, we need His moral law. But we need one thing more; and that is, we need an infallible interpretation of that law by the observance of which we rise to the heights of true moral beings. We must consider ourselves moral beings, for without a higher central force impelling us to forsake and overcome our corruption, the victory of our animalism is certain; we must believe ourselves moral, for without belief our intuitive consciousness of responsibility for all we do and leave undone would be fatal mockery; but we must believe, finally, also in an infallible interpretation, else the knowledge of the moral law would be wanting, and it would not be our inheritance, our birthright, our privilege to stand upon the elevation of the moral ground. And all this, let it be well understood, we must believe, not because the Catholic Church and the Pope in Rome say so, but because life bids us see that only upon the co-existence of these conditions can morality be predicated. Every truth taught by life is a truly Catholic truth, a dogmatic truth, not because the See of St. Peter proclaims it so, but because of its being a truth; and as Catholicity can hold only truths, it is then, *ipsissima natura*, a Catholic truth. This road we take, is the one best adapted in our times to lead society back to the re-acceptance of that incorruptible moral code of Christ which we must live up to, if we hope for true life as the reward of a truly moral earthly career.

THE LATEST PHASE OF THE GREAT PYRAMID DISCUSSION.

Life and Work at the Great Pyramid during the months of January, February, March, and April, A.D. 1865. In three volumes. By C. Piazzi Smyth, Professor of Practical Astronomy in the University of Edinburgh, and Astronomer Royal for Scotland, etc. Edmonston & Douglas. Edinburgh. 1867.

Our Inheritance in the Great Pyramid. New and enlarged edition, including all the most important discoveries up to the present time. By Piazzi Smyth, Astronomer Royal for Scotland, etc. W. Isbister & Co. London. 1874.

A Miracle in Stone; or, the Great Pyramid of Egypt. By Joseph A. Seiss, D.D. Thirteenth edition, enlarged. Porter & Coates. Philadelphia. No date, but the preface to the fourth edition is dated September, 1878.

The Pyramids and Temples of Gizeh. By W. M. Flinders Petrie. Field & Tuer; Simpkin, Marshall & Co.; Hamilton, Adams & Co. London. Scribner & Welford. New York. 1883.

The International Standard. A Magazine Devoted to the Preservation and Perfection of the Anglo-Saxon Weights and Measures, and the Discussion and Dissemination of the Wisdom contained in the Great Pyramid of Jeezeh, in Egypt. Article by the Rev. H. G. Wood, in the January number of 1884.

The Imaginary Metrological System of the Great Pyramid of Gizeh. By F. A. P. Barnard, President of Columbia College. From the Proceedings of the American Metrological Society. Presented to the Society December 29th, 1883. Reprinted from School of Mines' Quarterly of January, March, and May, 1884. John Wiley & Sons. New York. 1884.

WHAT may fairly be termed the vagaries of the Pyramidists might be passed by in silence, were it not that one form of them presents itself as obstructive, both in this country and Great Britain, to the general introduction and use of the metric system. When we say "metric system," we have in mind much more the idea of a decimal system, based on some convenient unit, than the idea of the particular metric system, based on the French metre. The value of the "metric system" depends less upon its initial unit than upon its decimal and correlated character. But, in opposing the metric system, as based upon the metre, pyramidists, some of whom favor a decimal system, do more than this.

They advocate without alternative the inch as the base of their system. They establish no relations, such as exist in the metric system, between standards of capacity and weight, and make no adequate suggestion as to whence to derive the unit of weight. Therefore, as the case stands now, the metric system having been largely adopted by civilized countries, it were best to give it our cordial support, and to regard as of little force an objection to it which would obstruct its final general adoption, because of a far from insuperable difficulty, inherent in its derivation from a truly standarded metre. Nevertheless, this system is called, at least by some pyramidists, atheistical, upon the rather vague ground that it originated about the time of the French Revolution, and that it is antagonistic to the measures which pyramidists regard as prescribed by divine authority, deduced by them from indications in the Great Pyramid of Gizeh.

One of the latest prominent incidents of the Great Pyramid controversy is the publication in book form of President F. A. P. Barnard's essay on the Pyramid, which had appeared serially in the Columbia College *School of Mines' Quarterly*, and which has been adversely reviewed by believers in the authenticity of the Pyramid's metrological and religious record. The wide difference of opinion regarding the significance of the Great Pyramid could not be better exemplified than by the title of President Barnard's book, as contrasted with that of the Rev. Dr. Seiss, published a few years ago, President Barnard calling his work " The Imaginary Metrological System of the Great Pyramid of Gizeh," and the Rev. Dr. Seiss, his " A Miracle in Stone, or The Great Pyramid of Egypt."

The literature of the subject is voluminous, originating before Professor C. Piazzi Smyth's large contribution to it, but only from that date acquiring momentum, until now, when belief in the religious significance of the Great Pyramid includes in the list of its promoters several men of ability combined with certain scientific attainment, is represented by a society called the International Institute, and by a magazine devoted wholly to the discussion and elucidation of discoveries in regard to the Great Pyramid, and to the promulgation of faith in its divine origin. From our point of view, it is strange that such men as we find among the membership of the International Institute can credit certain things which they affirm upon what has, to them, seemed sufficient evidence derived from the Great Pyramid. But while, on the one hand, it must be remembered that acceptance of truth has not always or generally followed immediately upon its promulgation, it must, on the other, be conceded that the finding of certain names of mark ranged on one side of a given question is no infallible criterion to which men may pin their faith in assent. So, the misery of it in this world is that every one must, in the long run, judge for himself, while, at the same time, few are capable of judging wisely.

We do not understand President Barnard as altogether denying the metrological (measuring) significance of the Great Pyramid, but as denying the peculiar metrological significance ascribed to it by some persons. We understand him as denying what we, according to the best lights obtainable by us, ourselves deny, that from the Great Pyramid is deducible a sacred cubit, from which, in turn, was originally deduced the British inch, now degenerated by the loss of one one-thousandth part; that this sacred cubit, in contradistinction to the profane cubits (profane, in this connection, meaning merely secular), was used by the inspiration of God in the construction of the Great Pyramid, and that certain pyramid dimensions are inspired teachings, or indeed any teachings at all, with reference to earth-dimensions, and to the earth's astronomical relations, in time to certain constellations, and in distance to the sun. We do not deny that metrological knowledge is embodied in the Great Pyramid. We hold merely that its degree is undemonstrated; and that, as to the question of whatever there exists being there placed by divine wisdom for the instruction of future generations, it must remain forever undemonstrable and unknown. There have been deduced from certain interior portions of the Great Pyramid even prophetic details of the "Reformation." Undoubtedly, President Barnard goes too far in the opposite direction from pyramidists, in designating the Great Pyramid "that huge and senseless pile;" for it has been clearly shown that, both exteriorly and interiorly, the relation of the radius to the circumference of the circle is expressed in its proportions, and that, in many other particulars, it is wonderful in design and execution. That President Barnard has used the expression quoted, only goes to show, nothing more, that the controversy has led as usual to extreme statement, to meet exaggeration on the other side.

It seems to us that the exaggeration of the other side is immeasurably greater. Considering that exaggeration, it is strange to us, for one thing, that President Barnard's critics deny that the believers in the Pyramid metrological-religious theory have rendered themselves liable to the ascription to them of having instituted a new religion. New religion, strictly speaking, it certainly is not; but when these persons acclaim as inspired of God a work in which they find so much significance as they do at every step in the Pyramid, in physical teaching and in prophecy, their belief is surely sufficiently defined in popular parlance by the statement originally made by Professor Proctor, that they had instituted a new religion. In strict accuracy, the Great Pyramid is to them another Bible, antedating even the Old Testament. It is, according to their view, one of the only two inspired records on earth. It may be said, on the other hand, that many pyramidists probably repudiate the extreme views which others entertain. Probably they do ; outside pressure has hitherto been too strong for the potentially existing sects to break out into open schism. The Rev. Dr. Seiss took occasion, in a foot-note to page 248 of the thirteenth edition, enlarged, of his work on the Great Pyramid, to reprove some zealous writers, who, going far beyond his own belief that it was possibly Melchizedec or some similar personage who was the founder of the Pyramid, had put forth and were upholding the doctrine that its founder was none other than " the Son of God in human form." If such views, however, as those expressed by Mr. John Taylor, Mr. William Petrie, Professor C. Piazzi Smyth, and the Rev. Dr. Seiss, represent the general sense of believers, they should not object to the tenor of President Barnard's essay. It must be regarded as fairly summarizing the general sense, as published, of believers regarding the metrological-religious significance of the Great Pyramid.

We are all disposed at the present day to examine and judge of everything upon its own merits as far as we can learn them, and not, as of old, to decide by snap-judgment as to credibility and incredibility in any given case. Thus viewing this matter, we, for our part, find in the Great Pyramid much that is extraordinary, much of even what might be called marvelous in design and execution. That it has metrological significance, in the sense that it was constructed by most competent architects and workmen, and that it has in its design, seen through its construction, geometrical and astronomical knowledge, we have not a shadow of doubt. But that it has, incorporated in its structure, indication of earth-dimensions and solar distance, and time commensuration, and other things attributed to it, there is no evidence whatever, except in arbitrarily derived numerical values which modern science has reached as approximate determinations. The length of the polar axis of the earth, for instance, being known to modern science only approximately, and being a quantity, too, which never can be determined with precision, the assumed length of it, derived from the Great Pyramid, while having a close agreement with the approximate length deduced from observations by modern science, is held by pyramidists to be exactly correct, and the error, supposing it to be represented by the difference between the two determinations, to reside in the modern scientific determination. Thus, the Pyramid arbitrarily-derived length of the polar axis of the earth is first proved to be right by the fact of its coming near to the value assigned to it approximately by modern scientific determination, and having been in this way proved virtually right, is regarded as therefore absolutely right, and rules the modern scientific determination out entirely, as comparatively of no weight. According to Pyramidists, the uttermost refinements of modern scientific work are far below the accuracy discovered in the Great Pyramid. Naturally this must be the true view, if the points be conceded that, first of all, its revelation is as to the particular subject-matter alleged, and then that it is inspired. Pyramidists have over scientists a great apparent and real advantage in the argument, from the circumstance that whenever a number, however derived from the Great Pyramid, nearly coincides with the number which modern science has shown to be an approximation to the truth, they are enabled through their theory to claim that their figures are confirmed by the scientific approximation. How unfortunate it would have been for pyramidists if there had been no such thing as the approximations of modern science. Without them the revelations of the Great Pyramid would not have been revealed. Perhaps the whole function of modern science is to suggest revelations to the Great Pyramid, by offering approximations that draw forth the exact truth, lying otherwise buried for all time! How, if astronomers had not suggested within a half million or so of miles, the mean distance of the earth from the sun, could the Great Pyramid have ever been able to give up the secret of the exact distance!

A crucial test of the truth of the theory of believers in the extraordinary significance of the Great Pyramid should lie in their conclusions drawn from the length of the sides of the Pyramid, measured at the base. It so happens that there had been no satisfactory measurements of the base-sides until those made between 1880–1882, by Mr. W. M. Flinders Petrie. The Royal Engineers, it is true, and Mr. Gill, and Professor Watson had made, respectively, measurements of the base-sides of the Pyramid, which are good; but the discrepancy which those measurements showed with previous results brought it about that no confidence, generally, existed, as to the base-side lengths, until Mr. Petrie determined them and published his methods in full. The French Academicians, commissioned to make investigations by Napoleon I., when in Egypt, had long previously found the northeast and northwest corner-sockets of the base of the Pyramid, and, of course, could measure the line only between them, which they did. Theirs, and other measurements, however, were not deemed conclusive, although all four corner-sockets were eventually discovered and utilized. The French measure proves to be utterly bad. But good, bad, or indifferent, as the measurements of any or of all the base-sides may have been, even including Mr. Petric's, if one choose to think so, the fact remains, that not until Mr. Petrie's

measurements was it taken into consideration that the length of·
a base-side of the Pyramid is not to be regarded as the line between the outside corners of any two sockets, taken around the
Pyramid's perimeter. The corner-sockets, cut in the living rock,
represent merely the Pyramid's foundation on the side of the hill.
The real lengths of the base-sides of the Pyramid are to be regarded
as the lengths of the four lines as projected above, with the Pyramid angles, on the horizontal pavement that originally surrounded
the structure, vestiges of which remain to this day. Consequently,
as the Pyramid (sacred) cubit is in one case, and that the most
important, derived by pyramidists from the base-side as originally
measured between any two corner-sockets on the slope of the hill,
divided by the number of days and the fractional part-thereof, in
the solar tropical year, the same cubit cannot now be obtained by
dividing the shorter line, proved by Mr. Petrie to be the true
length of the base-side, by the same number as before. In other
words, the Pyramid (sacred) cubit length, deduced by Professor C.
Piazzi Smyth, from the formerly assumed length of the base-side
of the Pyramid, divided by the number of days and the fractional
part in the solar tropical year, being alleged by him to be one ten
millionth part of half of the earth's polar axis, what becomes of the
Pyramid (sacred) cubit, now that the base-side of the Pyramid is
known to be of a different length from that which it was thought
to be, and what becomes of the determination of the length of the
earth's polar axis? Not only is what we have mentioned the
fact,—that the base heretofore taken by pyramidists is not the true
base of the Pyramid,—but their theoretical length of the base-
side of the base adopted by them has been proved by Mr. Petrie's
measurements to be incorrect.

As remarked, not until the advent of Mr. Petrie upon the scene
were all the base-sides of the Pyramid measured satisfactorily, and
the question disposed of as to which is the true base. He found
that lines connecting the Pyramid's corner-sockets on the base-
sides did not represent a true square; consequently, that the lowest sockets on the hill-side were farthest from, and the highest
sockets nearest to the centre of the Pyramid. The base of the
Pyramid had been so long assumed to be the ground-plan on the
hill-side, that Mr. Petrie must have been startled at coming unex-
pectedly upon what is the contrary fact. Back of this lay a reason
for it, and he proceeded to find that reason. That the Pyramid
should be square at the base was involved in the conception of the
architecture. He was soon rewarded by discovering the cause of
the absence of symmetry in the ground-plan. It had been formerly
assumed that, from the corner-sockets, the Pyramid had been built
vertically until it cut, at a short distance above, the horizontal

plane that was eventually represented by the pavement around it; so that a base-side of the Pyramid measured on the ground between the corner-sockets would be of the same length as a base-side measured between the corners of the Pyramid as projected vertically on the pavement. Both of these original assumptions, one of which depends upon the other, Mr. Petrie found to be untrue. He found that the angle of the Pyramid started at once from the four corner-sockets on the hill-side, and consequently, that the length of a base-side of the Pyramid, measured on the ground between the corner-sockets, was longer than if measured on the level of the pavement between the Pyramid corners. The difference, which is about five feet, was easily ascertained by him, with the aid of levelling, by reducing to figures the length of the lines actually measured between the corner-sockets, to the length that they would be if projected by the corner-angles of the Pyramid upon the horizontal plane above, represented by the now fragmentary pavement.

Despite the fact that the ground-plan of the Pyramid has been found by Mr. Petrie to be askew, and not horizontal, and that the horizontal pavement, now discovered on all four sides of the structure, exhibits the Pyramid as there equilateral, if the plane of the pavement be constructively extended to the Pyramid's sides; and that it is therefore proved that the pavement-base of the Pyramid is, architecturally, to be considered the true base, there are still dissentient voices harping on the other base, when even by it the theoretical measure has been disproved. To reconcile discrepancies, pointed out through the labors of Mr. Petrie, his book had not long been published when the Rev. H. G. Wood, in an article in the *International Standard*, of January, 1884, started out with the assertion that there had always been doubt as to what to consider as the true base of the Pyramid, whether the pavement-plane or some other plane below it. Then, by the ingenious method of assuming the level of the floor of the southeast corner-socket (the lowest of the corner-sockets) as the datum of levels, and by hypothetically carrying down the Pyramid angle of the northeast corner through the rock on which it rests, until it reached the same level as the floor of the southeast corner-socket, the length of the east base-side of the Pyramid was made to conform nearly to the theoretical base-side length. By the process of thus arbitrarily projecting the northeast corner of the Pyramid, and correspondingly projecting the northwest corner, the north base-side length became theoretically nearly correct. Finally, by supposing the west and south base-sides respectively conformable to the other sides thus established, we have, ready-built, a theoretical pyramid on a theoretical base. After having established this imaginary pyramid on this imaginary base, by imaginarily thrusting three extended corners of the real Pyramid through the rock until the base-lines had attained a length theoretically needed, a process which the writer informed us is according to the principles of geometry, he proceeded. He took up the question of the base-sides between the corner-sockets, as they actually are, according to Mr. Petrie, and imaginarily girdling the Pyramid with four links, represented by lines whose length was arbitrarily derived from astronomical considerations (lengths fortified by their approximation to Mr. Petrie's actual measures), he found in his results all that he had put there. But a little balance of adjustment still appearing to him desirable, an earthquake sufficed to set things nearly right. A genie, Slave of the Lamp, accomplished, like a skilful waiter, the task of tilting the Pyramid without leaving any record of his earth-tray having been lifted; for the ample floors of the corner-sockets remain level to this day.

The thoroughgoing pyramidist will stick to the ground-plan for his base, askew or not askew, horizontal or not horizontal, because the ground-plan supports, with the least apparent imperfection, his theoretical measures upon which other theoretical things rest. If actual measures be found not to agree with theory, it is easy enough to imagine a modified Pyramid, and an earthquake of a few thousand years ago can hurt no one of that time and may much benefit living men. There are certain dislocations in the interior of the Pyramid, which are certainly from settling, and which were probably produced by the shock or shocks of an earthquake. But that earthquake shocks could have affected the mass of the Pyramid to the degree ascribed to them by the writer in question is disproved by the fact that the floors of the four corner-sockets have retained their level so well that they stand the test of a levelling instrument. If the earth had permanently settled in one place, enough to satisfy the needs of this writer,—that is, settled four inches, so as appreciably to change the statical height of the floor of even a single corner-socket, neither it nor the floor of any other corner-socket would have remained level. The evidence as to the direction of the earthquake shock, adduced by this writer from the fact of the pavement in the middle of the west and on the middle of the south side of the Pyramid being slightly lower than the level of the pavement elsewhere, producing, as he claimed, a settling of the Pyramid towards the southwest, will not stand for a moment against the evidence existing on the ground, that the four corner-sockets are now, at the present day, as truly level as they were in the day when they were hewn to a perfect horizontal plane. The occurrence of earthquake shocks is not disputed. There can hardly be any question that there have been earthquake shocks at the Pyramid, perhaps many and severe shocks; the evidence in favor of the supposition, in the wrecked condition of the interior about the King's Chamber, seems overwhelming in support of the theory. But shocks that would shatter with their wrench the integrity of interior, hollow spaces, pressed upon by enormous superincumbent weight, would not necessarily affect the integrity of the foundation of the Pyramid. That the foundation has not been affected has been amply proved.

It has not been doubtful, as this writer stated, where the base, architecturally considered, ought to lie. Pyramidists have always claimed the ground-plan base to be the true base, because that nearly agrees with theoretical measures, and no other base was much thought of; anti-pyramidists contenting themselves with showing that the measures of it presented by their opponents were unsatisfactory. Every one believed the base on the hill-side to be essentially square, the discordance of its proffered base-side lengths being supposed to be chiefly owing to imperfect measurements. When, not only was it found to be not square, but, on the contrary, the pavement-base was discovered, and found to be square, the requirement in every one's mind ought to have been satisfied; but this pyramidists now seem to wish to evade. Every one was unaware, not long since, that the Pyramid did not rise vertically from the ground-plan until it passed through the pavement, and at that point take the pyramid slopes. Many persons did not even know that there had probably once been a continuous pavement around the Pyramid. Mr. Petrie it is who has for the first time certified to the existence of pavement on all four sides. If the Pyramid had ascended vertically until it passed through the pavement, and if the ground-plan had been square, then, of course, the base-sides measured on the pavement or on the ground-plan would have been identical in length. But the fact being, as already set forth, that the Pyramid at the ground-plan is askew and not horizontal, but, on the contrary, at the level of the pavement is essentially equiangular and equilateral, taken in connection with the other fact that the pyramid slopes start from the corner-sockets and pass with those slopes through the pavement; the base-sides of the Pyramid, measured on the pavement, are considerably shorter than the base-sides measured on the ground-plan. Architecturally speaking, a pyramid's base must be square. As the earth is not formed primarily to support pyramids, in a spot in which the design is to place a pyramid the ground must generally be levelled to insure that the pyramid's earth base and its architectural base shall be horizontally of the same dimensions. In fact, in this case the earth base and the architectural base would be one and the same thing. But the ground was not levelled at the Great

Pyramid ; hence, the earth base, which is merely the condition *sine quâ non* of the Pyramid's standing, is not the architectural, therefore not the true base. One should therefore say, it would seem, that as the base of the Great Pyramid on the level of the pavement is square, and the base on the ground-plan askew and not equilateral, there could be no question as to which base is to be regarded as the true one. But, unfortunately, pyramidists have a theoretical base-side measure (to which measurement does not conform), and, upon the faith that the theoretical measure is true, they still maintain a stout fight in defence of their theories. Now that an undeniable, actual measure has entered into the question, the theoretical measure must be upheld by some means; one of which, as we have shown, is by assuming the southeast corner-socket floor as the datum of levels, and at all the other corners the Pyramid as piercing the ground to such depths as will make the ground-plan sides accord with the theoretical measure. Let us not be misconstrued. We have no intention of stating or implying that these gentlemen wittingly manufacture and discard evidence at pleasure. All that we think and are responsible for stating, and frankly say, is, that we believe them to be so imbued, through long meditation on the mysteries of the Great Pyramid, with the truth of their theories, that now, when new lights have been thrown upon the subject, they are unable to overcome the force of their prepossessions.

All sorts of things have been supposed of the Great Pyramid's base. One, the wildest, is that there was originally a plinth extending all around the Pyramid, on which astronomers sat in rows, contemplating the stars. But the fact remains, nevertheless, that the Pyramid slopes up, with the pyramid angles, from the ground-plan, through the pavement ; that the base on the pavement is, architecturally, the true base ; that the ground-plan always was and is now askew ; that it must needs have been askew to render it possible for the horizontal plane of the pavement to make the Pyramid square as it rose through that surface ; that the ground-plan measures of the base-sides between corner-sockets have never been, through an earthquake or any other cause, other than they are now, for the all-sufficient reason that the floors of the corner-sockets remain perfectly level.

Even Professor C. Piazzi Smyth, although he lived for months on the ground, had very vague notions about the relations to each other of the pyramid slopes, the ground-plan, and the pavement-base, for he says (pages 139 and 140, vol. iii., of " Life and Work at the Great Pyramid "), referring to the casing-stones discovered by Colonel Howard Vyse (and the reader will please observe that the italics are Professor Smyth's) : " These remarkable stones, according to his [Colonel Vyse's] testimony, spring at once, with their oblique exterior slopes of 51° 51' 14", from the upper surface of a broad, flat, level area of exquisite masonry, known as the 'pavement;' which, in *that* part of the Pyramid, passes under it to some extent, is twenty-one inches thick, and four hundred and two inches broad from the outer line of the casing-stones. Hence, the extensive assumption has been made by some persons, that a pavement of the same breadth and thickness completely surrounds the Pyramid ; but, so far as thickness is concerned, a portion of the pavement is shown in one of our stereo-photographs, taken near the northwest socket, and is found to be barely more than ten inches thick. By examining, however, the angles and positions of the joints of this fragment, the inference may be pretty safely made, that the lower part of the *corner-stone* of the oblique casing-stone sheet there must have been of rectangular figure, though pyramidally bevelled above, and that it did, by the depth of such rectangular part or base, go through the whole thickness of the pavement there, whatever that was, and into the socket-hole cut for it in the rock below. Hence, the horizontal distance from the outer corner of one, to outer corner of another, adjacent socket-hole,— measured *on* the pavement and by means of the rectangular edges of the holes worked therein,—is, or should be, the true measure of the length of the ancient maximum bevelled side of the Pyramid ; and may be considered equal to either 9140 or 9142 British inches, as already indicated. But whether that number would be extended to 9159,—by the slope being carried symbolically through the pavement, and then measured on the level of its under side, or at a thickness nearly similar to that which obtains at the northwest corner,—is a residual problem that must be left, notwithstanding its importance, for future excavations to settle ; seeing that the earth, and the earth only, still retains the secret."

Noting, as we pass, the incorrect statement that Colonel Vyse had made the angle of the casing stones, discovered by him, 51° 51' 14", for Professor Smyth himself says (page 23 of "Our Inheritance in the Great Pyramid ") that Colonel Vyse had determined their angle as 51° 50', we have only to add that 51° 51' 14.3" is the *ideal* angle of the Pyramid (of which we shall have more to say presently), and then proceed to discuss the gist of Professor Smyth's statement. From it several things are apparent as to his belief. He was inclined to think that, including the northwest corner of the Pyramid, about which he incorrectly thought he knew, wherever there was question of pavement, the plane of the pavement passed under the Pyramid instead of the Pyramid's passing angularly through the pavement. He believed, however, that, notwithstanding pavement might have existed all around the structure, if it in any or all cases proved to be the fact, the measures of the base-sides on the pavement would prove to be the same as the measures of the base-sides on the ground-plan; which is only as much as to say that the Pyramid would be found to have ascended vertically through the pavement, and to have thence taken its slopes. He was inclined to doubt (although from other evidence we know that he suspected) the existence of pavement all around the Pyramid. It is a corollary of his belief that the base-side measures above and below would be found to be the same, that he supposed the northwest corner of the angle of the Pyramid to be cut away vertically, so as not to go over greater space below than above. In all these points he was wrong. The corner-angles of the Pyramid might, he granted, have been symbolically carried below the level of the pavement there. The Rev. Mr. Wood, without hesitation, after the earth had given up its secret, carried three corners of the Pyramid symbolically through the rock. We do not say solid rock, because symbolical work makes no account of material. Were it adamant, it must yield. Such is the pertinacity with which preconceived ideas sometimes assert their authority in the face of the most contradictory established facts!

In view of the facts heretofore recited, regarding the mere facts, omitting the precision with which they have been established by Mr. Petrie, how President Barnard's critics can maintain that Mr. Petrie's results confirm the assertions of Pyramidists, and that his work is a cherished contribution to their literature, is a mystery! President Barnard, on the contrary, says that if Mr. Petrie's book had come out in time for him, it would have saved him the trouble of writing his essay. The fact stares us in the face that the ground-plan length of the base-sides of the Pyramid, upon the incorrect assumption of whose length so much has been founded, are not of the length assumed, and, to cap the climax, that the ground-plan of the Pyramid is not its architectural base. Can the ground-plan base-sides be known to be of a different length from that formerly believed to be their length, and the conclusions which depended upon the error be allowed to stand?

With this pavement-length of the base-side of the Pyramid, what becomes, we ask, of the pyramid (sacred) cubit, at least as derived from the former base-side measurements of the Pyramid? What becomes of the determination of the earth's polar axis as twenty million pyramid (sacred) cubits in length? What becomes of the three hundred and sixty-five days, plus, of the solar tropical year being represented by a base-side's measuring three hundred and sixty-five, plus, pyramid (sacred) cubits? What becomes, too, of the length of the diagonals of the base, and with change in their length, what becomes of the belief that, divided into pyramid-

(sacred) inches, they indicate the number of years ·in the great precessional cycle? As not directly related to the foregoing questions, but interesting as within the general topic, one should like to inquire, also, upon what principle pyramidists multiply. Why do they consider the ninth power of ten indicated as the power to which the height of the Pyramid is to be raised to represent the mean distance from the earth to the sun? There is no reason for it. The cause of it was that Mr. William Petrie, the father of Mr. W. M. Flinders Petrie, who has so notably departed from the Pyramid faith, jumped to the conclusion, that the base-side of the Pyramid referring to the number of days of the solar tropical year, and its height in relation to its perimeter, referring to the relation of radius to the circumference of the circle, its height must represent the radius of the earth's mean orbit around the sun, as one is to one thousand million, or, in other words, to the height of the Pyramid raised to the ninth power of ten. But why the *ninth* power of ten? Mr. William Petrie's reason was that the angle of the Pyramid at the corners is ten parts of base to nine of height. It will occur to the reader that, given a unit at discretion, and unrestricted liberty to raise it arbitrarily to any degree, by any power, one can produce, within inappreciable differences, any dimension—height, length, width, distance—known or assumed. Professor Smyth, according to Mr. Petrie, having, by mistake, made the pavement too low by twenty inches, these twenty inches deducted from the height of the Pyramid, and raised to the ninth power of ten, make it necessary to reduce, by over three hundred thousand miles, the original pyramid indication of the earth's distance from the sun. The amount is small, according to scientific views, as a margin of uncertainty regarding the earth's distance, but from the pyramidist's point of view, it must be excessive.

President Barnard goes so far as to deny that the Great Pyramid was probably intended to indicate in its main proportions the relation of radius to circumference of the circle, ascribing to the adoption, without that intention, of the slope of ten to nine for the corner-angles of the Pyramid, the fact of the proportions actually found seeming to indicate reference to that relation. This view is not borne out by the measurements in certain portions of the interior of the Pyramid where there is no question of angle. President Barnard also remarks, that Mr. W. M. Flinders Petrie's work "demolishes completely the pretensions of the pyramid religion, and buries, beyond all hope of resurrection, the ingenious theories of Mr. John Taylor and Professor Piazzi Smyth." It has buried, fathoms deep, the religious, and the exaggerated metrological significance of the Great Pyramid, but it has not buried its real, legitimate wonders. Much remains outstanding, when the miraculous about the Pyramid is removed. It is not nearly so great as the pyramidist, nor quite so little as President Barnard believes.

The account of the labors of Mr. W. M. Flinders Petrie on the site of the Pyramid, in two winters, 1880–1882, published in 1883, in quarto form, with the aid of a subvention of one hundred pounds from the Royal Society, says the last word possible regarding the exterior and interior dimensions of the Pyramid. Knowing how averse the general reader is to figures, we do not attempt to give from the mass of material at disposal, for which we are indebted to his labors and those of Professor Smyth, Colonel Howard Vyse, and others, any tabulated statement of angles, dimensions, or any minute statistics of the perfection of its masonry. No adequate notion, however, can be formed of the stupendous character of this monument, both as to size and workmanship, unless some details be given relating to those features of the structure. We do not say that it may not be amiss to give them; it is positively necessary to a comprehension of the subject, that they should be given. The workmanship of something that may be held in a casket does not astonish, for smallness itself suggests to the artificer elaboration, and the mind of the beholder equally demands it. But when we find, as the work of man, elaboration conjoined with colossal size, giving an idea of immensity, we contemplate the work with almost stupefaction.

One mention by Mr. Petrie (many similar details will be found in Professor Smyth's volumes) will give an idea of the character of the workmanship of the Great Pyramid. Speaking of the final adjustment of the Pyramid angles, by inference from some of the few casing-stones still remaining *in situ* (casing-stones originally made of the whole of the outside of the Pyramid a smooth surface) to the steps of the core-masonry, he says: " Several measures were taken of the thickness of the joints of the casing-stones. The eastern joint of the northern casing-stones is, on the top [in inches], .020, .002, .045 wide; and on the face, .012, .022, .013, and .040 wide. The next joint is on the face, .011 and .014 wide. Hence the mean thickness of the joints there is .020; and, therefore, the mean variation of the cutting of the stone from a straight line, and from a true square, is but .01 on length of 75 inches up the face, an amount of accuracy equal to most modern opticians' straight-edges of such a length. These joints, with an area of some thirty-five square feet, each, were not only worked as finely as this, but cemented throughout. Though the stones were brought as close as one five-hundredth inch, or, in fact, into contact, and the mean opening of the joint was but one-fiftieth inch, yet the builders managed to fill the joint with cement, despite the great area of it, and the weight of the stone to be moved—some sixteen tons. To merely place such stones in exact contact at the sides would be careful work; but to do so with cement in the joint, seems almost impossible."

Mr. Petrie found the length of the base-sides of the Pyramid, on the pavement, to be, in inches, as follows: north, 9069.4; east, 9067.7; south, 9069.5; west, 9068.6. The mean is 9068.8 inches, the maximum difference from the mean of all the measurements being only about an inch. The original height of the Pyramid, as determined by Mr. Petrie, is 5776.0 inches, plus 'or minus seven inches. These measurements give the ratio of radius to circumference of the circle to within three units in the third place of decimals. What mere mason-work could reach a result like this, in attempting to carry out in an edifice of four hundred and eighty-one feet in height, the slope of so many parts of base to so many of perpendicular?

What has been mentioned regarding the mere exterior of the Great Pyramid, leaving untouched the wonders of its interior passages and chambers, will suffice for the purpose in view. Let us summarize the original dimensions and angles of the Great Pyramid and perceive its pristine grandeur. It rested on a square base, at the level of the original pavement, of nearly seven hundred and fifty-six feet to the side, and rose above the pavement vertically to the height of a little over four hundred and eighty-one feet, its sides looking skyward from the pavement to the apex, nearly six hundred and twelve feet, and its diagonal slopes a little over seven hundred and nineteen feet. That this monument, adjusted on a hill-side so accurately that when it cropped out of the horizontal plane of the eventual, but then prospective, pavement should have been exactly square, is wonderful. But that such a mass, ascending equiangularly to such a height, had not, as has been suggested, for the construction of its determining diagonal slopes, something more for guidance than the "rule of thumb," of 10 to 9; that it had not in its design and execution comprehensive mathematical knowledge, as largely inclusive of the mechanical rules of its construction, is more wonderful still, too wonderful to believe. It may be said that we are not certain that the builders succeeded in making it perfectly equiangular in the slopes of its sides, for we find at the now truncated top, about thirty-one feet below the original apex, that the platform is not exactly square, differing from a square by a little less than eight inches. But Mr. Petrie leaves it scarcely doubtful, from his instrumental angular measurements from the platform down the sides of the masonry, and from his discussion of the thickness of casing-stones, of hollowing and grooving of core-masonry, and from other considerations, that the defect in the symmetry of the core-masonry was made up by the casing-stones.

As the final result of all his measurements, linear and angular, Mr. Petrie gives the mean angle of the Pyramid at 51° 52', plus or minus two minutes. Let us assume, for a moment, that it was perfectly equiangular in its slopes, and then see how nearly the angle computed from the ratio of the radius to the circumference of the circle, upon the supposition that the Pyramid was intended to have reference to that relation, will come to the angle found by Mr. Petrie. The ideal angle so computed is 51° 51' 14.3".

When we consider what number of parts of base to what of perpendicular are represented by this ideal angle of 51° 51' 14.3" for the side slope, that they are as 7.8539 + to 10, we shall see, independently of other considerations, that the masons' work could not have been constructed to that batter. Taking, on the contrary, the diagonal slope, we find that, whether angularly measured as nearly as possible on the Pyramid, or derived from the relation of the ancient height to ancient perimeter of the Pyramid, or from the computation of the ideal diagonal of the Pyramid, from the ratio of radius to circumference of the circle, the approximation is so close to the ratio of 10 to 9 that we can say, with reasonable certainty, that it must have been so intended, if not as a primary object, yet as one involved in the general design. We can say, with reasonable certainty, putting out of question any other mode of nicer inclusive adjustment, that in laying the masonry of the Pyramid, it was built along the diagonal slopes to the batter of 10 to 9; for the ideal angle of the side slope gives for the diagonal slope in parts of base to perpendicular 10 to 9.0032, and the diagonal slope, derived from computation from measures of ancient height and ancient perimeter, is 10 to 9.0073. The difference from each other, and from the ratio of 10 to 9, is so trifling as to bring conviction to the mind that it was intended that the diagonal slope should be 10 parts of base to 9 of perpendicular. That would bring it out sufficiently close to the ratio of radius to circumference of the circle, which is indeterminate.

The ideal angle of the diagonal slope of the Pyramid, upon the assumption that the Pyramid had reference to the ratio of radius to circumference, is 41° 59' 50.0". The angle of the same slope computed from the ratio of 10 parts of base to 9 of perpendicular, is 41° 59' 14.0". The angle of the same slope computed from measures of height and perimeter, is 42° 00' 36.6". The greatest difference between any two is one minute, twenty-two and six-tenths seconds, and the least difference thirty-six seconds. Finally, deducing the angle for the side slope from the ratio of 10 to 9 for the diagonal slope, it is found to be 51° 50' 39.1". The difference is only thirty-five and two-tenths seconds from the ideal angle for the side slope, as already given, namely, 51° 51' 14.3".

The masonry ought to have been adjusted by the diagonal slopes, with the help, as Mr. Petrie suggests as having been actually employed (a suggestion whose correctness is justified by the fact of the horizontal inward general hollowing and central grooves of the core-masonry sides), of a finely-set line of casing-stones down the middle of the sides. Undoubtedly that would be the true way of adjusting the work in its details. But the question remains as to what kept up the rigid refinement of angle in the four diagonal slopes of over seven hundred feet long, so that they, in all probability, came out exactly at the apex of the Pyramid. Certainly not the 10 to 9 rule. The adjustment of the Pyramid on the hill-side, with its ground-plan there made with exactly the amount of irregularity to insure, as it did, that when the Pyramid passed through the horizontal plane of the eventual pavement, it should be equilateral and equiangular at the pavement-base, that, in other words, it should be square on the pavement, as it was, shows that its architect could deal with figures; and the precision of its slopes argues with equal force that this refinement was secured by adjustment with an instrument, of some sort, capable of taking vertical angles.

Considering the fact, which has now been dwelt upon with such particularity as to warrant the belief of its being impressed upon the reader, that the socket-sides' base was made unsymmetrical to just the degree necessary to insure that the Pyramid slopes, as they cut the pavement, would represent a square, the use of two things is strongly implied, one as a certainty, the other as a strong probability. The certainty implied is that, in laying out the ground-plan, the builders used a levelling instrument of some sort, whether spirit-level or water-level (*niveau d'eau*), to determine the relative heights of the floors of the corner-sockets. The probability implied is that they used, for laying out the angles of the ground-plan, an instrument capable of taking horizontal angles. Although it would be possible, upon a piece of ground similar to that on which the Pyramid stands, of slight eccentricity of surface, to lay out by direct measurements, tied together, a ground-plan representing that of the Pyramid, to fulfil the condition of a pyramid there being square as it rose through a horizontal plane; yet it would be difficult, without an instrument for horizontal angles, to do it with the nicety with which the operation was performed at the Great Pyramid.

The lengths of the socket-line sides of the Pyramid are, in inches, respectively: north 9129.8, east 9130.8, south 9123.9, west 9119.2. The greatest difference in any two sides is 11.6 inches, and the least, 1 inch. The relative heights of the corner-socket floors, taking the southeast corner-socket floor as zero, are, in inches, as follows: northeast 11.4, northwest 7.1, southwest 16.9. The reader has now the opportunity to compare critically the unsymmetrical ground-plan base with the symmetrical pavement-base, previously given, and will perceive how nice must have been the adjustment to insure that the pavement-base should be exactly square; the levels of the socket-floors, taking the pavement as zero, being, in inches, below the pavement, respectively: northeast 28.5, southeast 39.9, southwest 23.0, northwest 32.8.

There is, then, so far none but presumptive proof that the builders had means of taking horizontal angles; but when we consider, as has been said, the extreme accuracy of angle of the diagonal slopes of the Pyramid, it is hard to believe that the builders had not means of taking vertical angles. One probability supports the other, and each gains force. We know positively, by finding it, that they used iron. We know, too, that in ancient times lenses were used, for one has been found at Kouyunjik, a precinct, which, with Nimroud, Khorsabad, and Karamles, formed the *enceinte* of Nineveh. We cannot say that they were used telescopically, but the fact that they were known is worth taking cognizance of in this connection.[1] Godfrey Higgins, the great antiquarian writer, asserts that the telescope was known to some Egyptian priests, and the use of it permitted only to those admitted to, the arcana of mysteries.

We have seen that, whether or not the Great Pyramid was built by the process of its diagonal slopes being laid out by ten parts of base to nine of height, or these slopes were controlled in the nicety of their adjustment by an observed angle of 41° 59′ 14.0″, corresponding to ten parts of base to nine of perpendicular, or by the ideal diagonal angle of 41° 59′ 50.0″,—at least the relation of the Pyramid proportions of height to perimeter of base is so close to the ratio of the radius to the circumference of the circle, that if the Pyramid had been designed with that as one of the ends in view, it is mechanically impossible for it to have been closer to that ratio; for the difference of 36″ of arc in the last mentioned

---

[1] In this same connection, it will interest the reader to see Professor Sayce's account of the lens found at Nineveh, contained in the following letter to the writer:

QUEEN'S COLLEGE, OXFORD, April 12th, 1885.

MY DEAR SIR: Owing to absence in Egypt, I have been unable to send an earlier reply to your question.

A crystal lens was found by Sir A. H. Layard on the site of Assur-bani-pal's Library at Kouyunjik, and is now in the British Museum. It was examined about a year ago by two experts, who came to the conclusion that the lens had been ground. I fancy it was used (or rather intended to have been used, for it is not completely finished) in writing the cuneiform tablets, some of which are inscribed with such minute characters as to imply the use of a magnifying glass.

Yours faithfully,
A. H. SAYCE.

angles would, for the diagonal slope of 719 feet of the Pyramid make only 2.0256 inches. Are its proportions, then, accidental? All that can be said in reply, if one take the isolated fact of its main proportions, is that they might have been accidental, so far as intention of including reference to the ratio of the radius to the circumference of the circle is concerned. We should have to rest content with this doubt, if it were not in our power to go beyond this isolated fact. But the Pyramid has an interior as well as an exterior, and there are some dimensions as well established with regard to that as others are to the exterior, and these repeat the ratio of the exterior dimensions. Accidents repeat themselves, but, when things repeat themselves very many times, the conception of accident is violated, and men think and say this is design. Because literature does not record mankind's knowledge of the ratio of the radius to the circumference of the circle, at the period of pyramid building, it is not necessarily to be concluded that mankind did not possess that knowledge. Deciphered inscriptions on terra-cotta tablets have brought down to us astronomical information of the times, much more recondite than that knowledge. On those very tablets, or in some other form, inscription of that knowledge may still be lying buried, or it may have been destroyed. Again, it may have been so common as not to have been recorded in so lasting a form as inscription on clay or stone; but if, in one sense, it is not recorded in the Great Pyramid, then all record is in vain.

Mr. Petrie does not believe in the existence of the Pyramid (sacred) cubit. From many comparisons in several ancient structures, and from cubit-rods found, he has deduced the Egyptian cubit as 20.62 plus or minus one one-hundredth of an inch, and employs it as 20.62 inches. He remarks that, with the Egyptian cubit theory, the outside dimensions of the Pyramid exactly agree, the height being 280 even cubits, and the semi-perimeter, 440 cubits. This, he grants, agrees with the theory of reference to the relation of radius to the circumference of the circle. With the Egyptian cubit theory, he adds, the proportions of the Pyramid's passages, chambers, and other parts, also agree. By the theory of areas, he says, the outside form of the Pyramid, and several other things which he mentions, are given, such as that the level of the King's Chamber is where the Pyramid's diagonal equals its base-side. These, and other things not mentioned here, do not conflict with each other. If they do not show design, then it is impossible to discover design; it will never be understood whenever men do not give direct testimony, written or oral, as to their intentions. Mr. Petrie frankly says: " That, in a building whose design appears on good evidence to include the π proportion (reference of radius to

circumference) and the use of areas, some design of cubic quanti-
ties might be followed in the principal object of the structure, is
not at all improbable. But any claim to even respectable accuracy
and regularity in the coffer is decidedly disallowed by its roughness of work."

It is unfortunate that, in all controversy, credit for sincerity
should not be accorded to each other by the disputants on the
opposing sides. For a long time this discussion has waxed hotter
and hotter, not failing, as usual, to beget a certain amount of acri-
mony. Yet there is really no reason for offence to either side.
Both sides are striving for the truth. Even ridicule, for using
which President Barnard's critics take him to task, is perfectly
legitimate as one weapon. It is wrongfully used only when it is
employed in serious matters as the sole weapon. . It is used only
as an auxiliary by President Barnard, who does not mainly rely
upon it, but upon the solid array of facts and conclusions which he
has previously marshalled to the front. In his final charge of
raillery, he does but bring up reserves to share the triumph of
seeing the enemy in full rout, and contributing to their discomfiture.
That, at least, is evidently his view at the point of time; that the
conflict of reason is over, that the enemy is routed. If, in the
hypothetical case with which he concludes his essay, he has not
succeeded in presenting a *résumé* of his preceding argument,
clothed in facetious guise, we are much mistaken. If he has not
succeeded, the ridicule recoils upon himself. If, on the contrary,
he has succeeded, he has merely presented afresh his argument,
condensed, in the attractive form of appeal to the imagination as
well as to the intelligence.

Both parties to this controversy are perfectly sincere. Let them,
then, formally concede to each other the merit of sincerity, and
the consideration that ought to go with the concession. Men
must believe what they believe; they cannot help it; the contrary
proposition would be absurd; and yet how little is this truism
recognized in practice! There are those who have remained unbelievers, who, in approaching this subject, did so with a certain
awe. It would be awful, they felt, to read divine teaching graven
on the rock, standing almost in the presence of the Most High.
Yet to one who thought it might be that such a revelation existed
for eyes willing to see, it must be duty to learn, if it were so,
whereof the Presence spake. The bounds of credibility are not
established; it is no more irrational to believe that, by special inspiration, God had chosen to communicate with mankind through
a record in stone, than that He had inspired the Bible, or given
the intuition by which men know of His existence. The evidence
adduced in the case of the Great Pyramid was startling. If what

was alleged to be there actually existed there, insusceptible of other explanation than the supernatural, then the supernatural there was to be accepted ; there could be no option, one must believe in it as the supernatural. It was in this spirit that many who do not believe in the record of the Great Pyramid as divine, approached the subject, and with the newest as well as the oldest light that has been shed upon it by researches. We, among many others, have reached the conclusion, that whatever ulterior significance, astronomical, astrological, metrological, the Great Pyramid may have, it has no relation to the New and the Old Law.

If, to a zealous pyramidist, it seems lamentable that any set of men, approaching the subject in the spirit described, should reach so lame and impotent a conclusion, all we can say is, what was before remarked, that one cannot help thinking what one thinks, and that we hope to be credited with the sincerity which we are willing to accord. Nothing more heinous can be attributed to us than invincible ignorance. Our opponents ought to remember that, if their belief has been sometimes ridiculed, they, on the other hand, have called the hard name of atheist. It seems to us perfectly consonant with belief in the convenience of the metric, or of some similar system, for a man to believe in the existence of God ; to reject the teachings of the Great Pyramid as divine, and yet to believe in God. The question is whether they are divine. The attempt is made to prove them by their character to be divine, and at the same time, to assume their character, to prove the Pyramid divine. The truth will not suffer by contending for it; it is in danger only when men cease contending for it, having reached the condition of easy indifference to it and passivity. We recognize the worthiness of the conscientious conviction of the divine teaching of the Great Pyramid, and have the kindest feeling towards believers in the sacredness of the record, regretting that we cannot be with them one in faith.

THE POLITICAL ASPECTS OF CHRISTIANITY.

" CHRISTIANITY is a fundamental condition of modern civilization." The design of these pages is to bring into view its influence upon the State. It has been done before, and done ably; but a wholesome truth can bear repetition, even if the changes emerging from the current course of events did not furnish fresh illustrations and applications.

These influences properly are indirect and pure, not those flowing from the union of Church and State. Such a union may appear under one of three forms.

A theocracy—where the Church dominates the State—is to-day unknown, at least among a people of any name. A government of this kind God enjoined upon His ancient people, under circumstances that cannot reappear; and we are to distinguish between the supernatural order of their polity and the natural order of the polity of other nations. From the Israelites was to arise a spiritual Prince, to whom the history of the nation was to bear witness. A theocratic regime, that better answered this extraordinary and singularly exceptional end, is not a precedent for the same form of government under ordinary and totally changed conditions; and the bearing of the new law seems altogether another way.

In Russia, the State rules the Church; for the Czar nominates the members of the Holy Synod, over whose deliberations he presides, and whose decrees he ratifies. The centre of spiritual and political authority, he is theoretically the most august sovereign in Europe, yet the outlook is promising neither for the throne nor the altar. Nowhere is treason so thoroughly intrenched. The reigning emperor, a prisoner within his own realms, is ceaselessly guarded against the hand of the political assassin, by which his father fell. As for the Church, her attitude is neither spiritual nor aggressive. Despoiled of her wealth by Peter I. and Catherine II., her clergy, outside of a few centres, barely subsist. Serfdom, indeed, no longer exists, yet ignorance and idleness abound, and there is not a feature to recommend the existing form of rule.

The union between Church and State, which is more usual in modern history, is regulated by a Concordat. It is a treaty in regard to the administration of ecclesiastical affairs, between a temporal ruler and the head of a Church; and supposed to be necessary when the former finds himself confronted by a powerful religious organization. Under the most favorable circumstances— where the people are a practical unit in religious belief—the *à priori* grounds against its utility are sustained by experience. To governments the administration of ecclesiastical affairs has been vast and vexatious; but the balance of disadvantage has been greatly on the Church's side. Support for the clergy, which is her consideration in the pact, is very dearly bought. A State Church, especially to those in authority, tempts to formalism and hypocrisy, and " chills the life in her breast." A State Church so far forth surrenders her independence, is compelled often to sacrifice to state exigencies the better interests of religion, and retards development according to her true genius.

Hence, as the political world is now consolidated, either in fact or in its tendencies, which seem growing daily in intensity and loud utterance, the Church is not unwilling to accept the situation, and to allow the State to go free from what men call the " compulsory authority of religion." But she has a right to demand that this new polity must be founded in honesty and truth; and that if the State cease to be religious and Christian, it must not thereby become irreligious and anti-Christian. If it choose to devote itself solely to the development and promotion of material wealth and earthly advantages, it must not interfere with the Church, whose duty it is to make use of spiritual means to further man's best interests and eternal warfare.

So, it would appear, our Lord Himself taught. We speak here of His teachings as bearing upon the political order in His day. The subject of human law, it has been observed, and the relation of His mission to the State, must have been often in His consciousness. The immense pressure brought to bear upon Him, to declare Himself a temporal prince, is the ground of Renan's theory of the Temptation. In resisting the national aspirations of His countrymen, so profound and universal, He drew upon Himself complete isolation, and sympathy for His loneliness and admiration for His calm, heroic courage, mingle in the tribute to His unparalleled character. Yet, with these environments, He not even suggested a single State law. He disclosed the pith of moral and religious truth with a simplicity, depth, and precision "that leave nothing more to be said," but is silent upon human law and politics. For righting wrongs, reforming abuses, and the general discharge of political duty He sought to fit men by ennobling the interior motives. The independence of Church and State He expressly intimates: " Render to Cæsar the things that are Cæsar's, and to God the things that are God's "—a memorable sentiment, that statesmen may still profitably ponder. Such are His teachings, and our own great and growing country, where religion flourishes but forms no alliance with the State, illustrates their wisdom.

The indirect and pure influences of Christianity upon the State are as valuable as they are powerful and far-reaching. These are gathered under two heads: (1) The ideal of character which the example of Christ has originated; (2) The bearing of the doctrine of a Future Life upon social order.

A people cannot rise above their ideals. Religious ideas have been the dominant ideas in nations; and, as these ideas have created their ideals, we find nations standing, in the order of advancement, in strict accordance with their conception of religion. Where the religious intuition has received an earthy development, as among pagan nations, the ideas are of the earth. The ultra-fierce temper of the ancient Scandinavians, for example, accords with their belief, that those who enter heaven—their ideal characters—engage in perpetual war, and, after daily combat, repair to a spacious hall, to eat plentifully of the flesh of the wild boar, and drink beer from the skulls of their enemies.

The superiority of European civilization to that of the East has been properly attributed to a superiority in respect to religious ideas; and for this, it may be said in passing, Europe may be remotely indebted to a poet's pen. To the Homeric poems, sung throughout Greece, must be chiefly traced that martial spirit which enabled so small a state to repel, from the gateway to Europe, the colossal invasions of Persia, and save that continent from an oriental civilization, and an obstruction to the entrance of Christianity. Mark the difference in material development, and every advanced characteristic of a nation, between Turkey and those neighboring Christian powers, whose mutual jealousies are the sole guarantee for her existence. No cause is found either in the age or character of the Turks. In times comparatively recent they issued forth from that fruitful source of ethnic inundation, central Asia, and, before the faith of which they became the representative had time to bear permanent national fruit, won, as Saracens in the East and Moors in the West, a brilliant record in war and in literature. The decadence is due to an inferior religion and a low ideal.

Mahometanism teaches that slaying an unbeliever is an act of piety—that all knowledge is despicable save that found in the Koran—that polygamy is lawful—that heaven is a paradise of voluptuous joys, where the gross pleasures of earth are but enlarged and intensified. The necessary issue for the Turk has been a cruel, sensual, unlettered characteristic, and national decay.

Christianity offers the highest possible ideal; since, unlike a human science elaborated from crude beginnings, it came at once perfect from the hand of God. The founder of Christianity we adore as divine, not by way of mission or authority merely, but in His essential nature. His religion has received no earthly or national elaboration. In anticipation, perhaps, of such a cavil, it was decreed that the political destruction of the people among whom it arose should be contemporaneous with its origin. Its teachings, traced by the very finger of God, remain unchanged and unchangeable. Some of these teachings (such as the essential brotherhood of men), taught by the Church from the first, the state is beginning slowly to recognize—an evidence that Christianity has led, not followed, civilization. Others (as the precepts respecting charity) the best school of modern criticism, while commending them as sublime illustrations of Christian virtue, puts aside as wholly impracticable within the domain of the State—an evidence that political science is to receive further accessions from Christian ethics. Preserved throughout its course by the divine agency that created it, Christianity maintains an integral existence in the world as the visible and complete manifestation of God, and furnishes a pre-eminent ideal—an ideal which, diffused through its sacred writings, gathers with unequaled splendor in the character of its Founder.

The perfection of character stands in the exhibition of contrasted virtues. Pascal, therefore, rates Epaminondas first among ancient heroes, because he combined the extremes of gentleness and valor. Jesus Christ, appearing at a point where three strongly marked peoples met, excludes the peculiarities of each, the spiritual pride of the Jew, the intellectual pride of the Greek, the political pride of the Roman, and reveals a character unequaled in its poise and sublimity. He touched at every point the circle of virtue, embracing all its contrasts. His purity and self-abnegation, His fortitude and composure, the strange reserve of power displayed by His ease in discomfiting the premeditated assaults of the subtlest adversaries, the simplicity, tenderness, and penetration of His teachings, which a child may understand, yet philosophers explore without finding their depths—are the vestibule of a temple within whose courts dwells God. His Person, wherein human nature is allied with the divine, reveals man's essential worth and dignity. In His mediatorial office we behold the essential brotherhood of the race, where, in the necessary elements of being, all are equals, and where, therefore, there is liberty, under guidance of law. His example is humility, moderation, self-restraint.

The ideal, therefore, which Christ has originated, is that of a freeman, conscious of a noble nature and a noble heritage, guided by the sympathies of a universal brotherhood, with passion restrained, appetite subdued.

Towards this ideal, within the pale of a divine society endowed with spiritual means, His followers consciously tend. But without the Church, upon the mass of men in a Christian state, the Christian ideal powerfully impresses itself. Character turns upon environments. The infant of a savage, transferred to an enlightened home, will lose the traces of savagery, and assume the hue of the surroundings. In a Christian state—where Christianity is generally . recognized, where Christian sentiments, issuing from custom, law, literature, and religious institutions, glide into the common thought of the people—in such a state skeptic and anti-Christian unwillingly yield to the environments. They unconsciously take on the enveloping atmosphere, and become fashioned on a Christian model, more or less realized, and by whatever name called.

The influence of this ideal, entering everywhere, consciously or unconsciously, into the details of public and private life, has been powerfully felt by the State. By teaching princes and magistrates a sense of accountability, it has greatly lessened personal rule. It has humanized the action of governments and turned legislation towards the needs of the multitude. It has raised the subject and liberated the slave, not by abruptly breaking legal relations, but by a constant upward pressure—by creating a humane public opinion, the prelude to law.

Whatever good has been effected by infidel advocates of human rights, we freely own. That their teachings have been commonly associated with violent agencies, cannot be denied. To those whose eyes are clear to see the movement of the forces that form and sustain society, what these turbulent reformers have done for real liberty and sound government, is insignificant by the side of the political benefits which the spirit of Christianity has gradually achieved. The French Revolution (for example), conducted in the name of liberty, was a state of insanity, and dates, it is thought, a downward course in Gallic tendencies. Voltaire began the work, followed up by Rousseau in his "Contrat Social," "Nouvelle Heloise," and "Confessions." "Seduced by their sophisms, enchanted by the magic of the style, the higher classes of society, followed by all France, went madly astray. Two souvenirs remain of that period, the goddess Reason enthroned on the altar of Notre Dame, the scaffold dripping with blood in the public squares." The teachings of these apostles of liberty penetrated Hayti, the fairest colony France ever owned. The negro slaves, indeed, became free —but alas! how? Through scenes of uproar, butchery, and beastly outrage, unparalleled in the annals of the world. What a contrast between the course of affairs in this island and that in Jamaica, where, under the ripened Christian sentiment of England, the slaves, without material disturbance, were gradually emancipated through a term of apprenticeship, and an award made to the owners of more than six millions of pounds! The subsequent histories of the islands are parallel with these methods of emancipation.

In closing this section, we call attention to two facts, emphasized by one of the best minds of the age : (1) that the sensible advance made in the religious character of Europe within the past hundred years is in correspondence with an improved political condition— with a more refined moral sense in individuals and nations—with a more humane conduct of war—with less open bribery in legislative bodies—and with less dissimulation in diplomatic intercourse; (2) that the course of Christianity in history is, after all, one of victory and glory—that the most powerful states now profess it— that the feeblest European state is the anti-Christian one—and that, should the Christian powers combine their physical forces, they could speedily subdue the world. It is the rise of nations towards a grand ideal.

The discussion of the remaining point—the bearing of the doctrine of a future state upon social order—brings into view those forces which, under divers names, are menacing the present structure of society.

Nihilism, by which Russian radicalism is commonly designated, is refused as a name by its adherents, who style themselves " revolutionists." Originating in the ideas brought to the front by the French Revolution, it is ambitious to excel its parent. For years it has found favor among the young men and " short-haired " girls in the schools and universities of Russia. The attempt upon the life of Alexander II. in 1879, and his assassination two years later, rendered it notorious. It is a species of religion—its god being the " suffering people "; and its followers, in spreading the doctrines, show the zeal of devotees. To gain the vantage-ground of sympathy, Russians of birth and education, under assumed names, will take menial positions, as cooks and workmen, and descend with their mission to the side of the laborer and mechanic. In philosophy, it is materialism; in politics, radicalism, advanced to frightful extremes. In one aspect it is idealistic; for the visions of the Nihilists, founded upon the reorganization of society, discount the utopias. The details of this reorganization, however, they will not enter upon. Nothing (whence the name *Nihilism*) is to be done prior to the destruction of the present order, and this destruction the Nihilist proposes to make complete. A supreme pessimist, he sees only evil everywhere, and his doctrine is—down with the State, the Church, the King, and God, even to the ground.

Nihilism, as a whole, is peculiar to the Russian mind, which is given to extremes, and to the despotic character of Russian politics, and a monster so odious could scarcely appear elsewhere. It may not be too late for political liberty to arrest it. The Russians, as a whole—especially the lower orders—are, or at least have been, distinguished for religious and political veneration; and had Alexander III. signalized his accession to the throne by granting a constitutional government, the back of this hideous conspiracy would in all likelihood have been broken.

Socialism is too vague a word for accurate definition. As a modified form of Communism, it assigns land and the implements of production to associations or the State; the fruits of labor, to the individual. Communism embodies a definite idea. It is wrong, it says, for one to possess wealth and live in jovial splendor merely by taking the trouble to be born, while others around him beg. It, therefore, takes from him who has, to give to him who has not, maintaining a perfect equality in the distribution of the means of living. The logical sequence is the universality of the idea. For to have things in common, men must labor in common—do tasks authoritatively imposed—lest individual freedom create an excess of production in this or that direction. Lest, too, the individual secretly use that portion of his product belonging to others, men must consume in common; and the family, as one writer expresses it, becomes transferred to the public square. In a word, under an enforced equality, pressing every thing to a level, all—goods, persons, education, love, religion—must be in common.

To effect this, the State is the necessary agent, armed with extreme authority, and furnished with an immense capital, to be drawn from no other source than the unprofitable spirit of coercive fraternity. Such, essentially, is the plan of society presented by Robert Owen, Saint-Simon, Fourier, Louis Blanc, Leroux, and others.

Successful organizations, founded on the " in common " principle, have existed. But these have been either voluntary associations, with free ingress and egress; or religious communities, distinguished by the spirit of discipline and self-denial; and neither has force as a precedent for the State.

The fundamental error of Communism is the attempt to reach equality by suppressing liberty. The sole equality among men resides in liberty. Equality in the state is regulated liberty. Outside of liberty there are only inequalities in the individual. These will be recognized by sound statecraft, and given free play, creating here and there *those* surpluses of wealth, essential to industry, commerce, science, and art. Communism, starting from a capital fallacy, finds its end in the slavery of the individual and destruction of natural rights, under the artificial regime of a limitless despotism. Of late years, it has been assuming, more and more, the form of political conspiracy.

Under a supposable oppressive state of affairs it might acquire a temporary ascendency; but such a monster can never permanently influence the social order. A meeting in one of our cities, presided over by a negro woman, the wife of a white communist, and met to laud the London explosions, and glorify "a few cents' worth of a little hog's grease and a little nitric acid," as the avenging agent for the "fourth estate"—is the glimpse of a picture that ordinary human nature cannot be made to fancy. Unless the entire history of morals and of political thought is without a lesson, the instincts of the heart, and the deductions of reason, confirmed by the widest experience, will rouse the average public conscience to reject the communistic doctrine in any of its essential forms.

The advocates of revolutionary Communism are comparatively few, yet admit it we must, that among the working classes generally there is unrest, great and growing—a fact which has procured a hearing for those ultra plans of human society which, in modern times, have been drawn from Plato's "Republic"; and it requires wise recognition to avoid outbreaks and infinite trouble. Popular education has roused, among the masses, an ambitious spirit, and multiplied artificial wants, while, under the current conditions of labor, the poor have become relatively poorer. The working classes were told, in the pinching days of the past, that the application of steam would so increase production as to put the industrious man beyond a reasonable fear of want. The result has been bitterly disappointing.

It appears that as nations advance in wealth, the space between rich and poor widens. The profitable use of steam requires expensive machinery. Competition and narrow margins extend individual operations and outlay; and the benefits of steam force have been concentrating, more and more, in the hands of capitalists. No blame can attach to capital. At the peril of existence, it has been impelled towards such an issue. It is the outcome of its own powers and antagonisms.

The superior intelligence usually found associated with wealth, stimulated by the keen emulation of the age, has naturally won from this powerful steam agent disproportionate results for the moneyed class; and labor unions became necessary to save workingmen from being ground to powder between the unavoidable rivalries of wealth. Confessedly, the richest among nations, where laws have been modified in every way to cheapen food, and where steam has wrought its best work, is England. Yet the late Postmaster-General of that country, an authority on labor questions, thus speaks of the condition of workingmen : " A majority of the people of England have a severe struggle for existence, and no inconsiderable minority live in abject misery and in degrading poverty. One out of every twenty is a pauper. To a great proportion of our loboring classes a life of incessant toil yields no other result than an old age of dependent mendicancy. In many rural districts horses are stabled far more comfortably than laborers are housed ; and in cities the poor are so crowded and huddled together that in countless cases families herd together in a single room." The statement is true, in the main, respecting the condition of workingmen throughout Europe and in America.

Sympathy, too, between employer and employed has almost disappeared. In times past the manufacturer dwelt near his workmen, and was, so to speak, the head of a family among them. He now commonly lives far away, seldom sees his men, is personally unknown to most of them,—" the relation between them is commercial only, and labor is bought and sold like merchandise."

The workman broods over his social position. He finds himself stationary, or relatively losing ground, in the midst of the manifold inventions of the age, which wealth appropriates to augment wealth, and build up vast corporations, whose heads are hedged about with antechambers and ushers, after the manner of kings. The feeling is deep-set that the logical development of society is against him ; and while he may own that there must be material inequality, yet he cannot be persuaded that the actual inequality is not disproportionate, and that, through State agency, ways should not be provided to make some of the redundance of the super-rich ease his lot.

In this sense " Socialism " has ground to rest on ; its aims are pure and lofty ; and its adherents are the multitude. It presents the problem of the age, and, unless wise measures of betterment are devised, the fear is that this vast body may, in a moment of despair and madness, go over to the ultra-Socialists, and seek relief through the violent overthrow of existing order.

This is a question, primarily, for the State. Let us point out, briefly, how Christianity comes to its aid.

If Christianity, in advancing the estimate of personal worth, advances sensitiveness to wrong and injustice, it applies the palliative in the Future Life it reveals.

The heaven of the Christians is a final home, which God has made worthy of Himself, where His throne is fixed and His unveiled glory displayed. The individual will remain himself, but himself wonderfully expanded—life unfolding under conditions as far superior to the present as these are to those of life before birth. Made possible by the Blood of the Cross, its attainment is due to no accident of wealth or station, but to the presence of certain in-

terior affections—as love, joy, peace, long-suffering—which constitute the spiritual life, and whose cultivation is alike within the
reach of all.

The vivid apprehension of this truth finds expression in the con-
fessors and martyrs. From such spirits the faith descends, with
diminishing effect, through the various grades of Christians, and
passes out, as an impression, into the general mass in a Christian
State, unconsciously influencing character.

Its total effect upon social order is prodigious. The absence of
all thought in respect to a future state and its dread sanctions,
would be the harbinger of "political disintegration, and rise of individual passion and anarchy." It would render the rule of life
utterly of the world, exacting towards others, indulgent towards
self. It would retire the nobler tendencies, and make the animal
emphatic, stimulating those tendencies towards brute force that
only brute force can keep subdued.

The general presence of the thought sheds a calming, quieting
influence upon society. The body of conscious Christians have a
share in shaping public opinion far exceeding their proportion of
the population, and their faith must here be taken fully into account.
Not only does it promise an offset to the inequalities and ills of
life, but sees in the endurance of these ills an enrichment of the
reward. Hence, suffering is the expression of religion; and the
union of the individual streams of Christian sentiment sends a
powerful and preserving current through society.

But beyond a conscious personal faith, the general impression of
a future life, entering into the habitual thought of a people has a
material political bearing. It strengthens a principle which England illustrates more, perhaps, than any other modern nation—the
organizing principle, or patience to work out reforms in a circum-
spect and orderly way, rather than resort to violent methods.
When reforms are effected in this manner, they promise to be
sound as well as abiding. Time and discussion test their merits,
and settle them in the popular consciousness.

In fine, the influence of Christianity upon the State lies in
general lifting tendencies, whose action is gradual, yet, acting continuously, aggregate vast results. Necessarily it is a movement
toward reforms. Where reforms become practicable, the tendencies
are towards rational and pacific means. Otherwise, the tendencies
are to suffer. The conclusion, therefore, is fairly warrantable that,
if a social crisis be near—such as the logical course of affairs apparently threatens—the wisdom of the solution will largely turn upon
the prevalence and purity of the Christian element.

Let the discussion close with the following reflections from
Bluntschli: That Christianity is a force which, at the end of two
thousand years we find still spreading, and with to-day more vitality

than ever before to extend itself; that the opponents of Christianity speak of it now with more respect than they did a hundred years ago; that the assaults of criticism have revealed an unexpected wealth of spiritual and moral force; that Christianity has fairly kept abreast of intellectual progress; that it was a deceptive thought that modern civilization has so far gone ahead of Christianity as to be able to do without it; that in its essential idea there is a wealth and power which has not yet attained its highest development; and that its opponents should learn to respect a system which has guided them in their intellectual advance, and infinitely promoted their civilization.

THE CRISIS IN ENGLAND.

WHEN all is said and done, no doubt remains on the mind of any reasonable and impartial man in England that the recent defeat of the Liberals was a godsend to the Gladstone government. It seems to be a law of English administrations that they shall, when the fifth year of their existence comes, have fallen so low in the estimate of the English nation that any change is regarded as an improvement. The Gladstone government, instead of being an exception, was a striking exemplification of this law. It would scarcely be possible to mention an administration which in modern times had committed mistakes more disastrous, had met fortunes so stormy, had violated all the promises and pledges of its inauguration so absolutely. The loss of its prestige without had had the usual effect of provoking dissension within. It is the universal experience of political parties that while success brings union, defeat brings division. So it was with the Gladstone government. For several months past no people have been more disgusted with the government of Mr. Gladstone than many of the members of that government itself. Composed of heterogeneous elements, it required but small cause to bring about collision of principle and still more of temper. Between men like Mr. Chamberlain, on the one side, and Sir William Harcourt and Lord Spencer, on the other, there are differences of opinion almost as complete as those that separate the ordinary Liberal from the ordinary Conservative. Then Mr. Chamberlain is not a man to conciliate political opponents by personal demeanor. He is a man of open, avowed, pushing ambition. He has not concealed for a moment since he entered the office the fact that he regarded his present position in the Cabinet as a temporary stepping-stone to the highest position in the country; and he has pursued his purpose with relentless steadiness; it might almost be said with ostentatious and aggravating steadiness. The great object, said a cynical member of the Liberal party, with Chamberlain is, having got into the Cabinet, to get out of it as soon and with as much flourish of trumpets as possible. On every occasion on which the principles of moderate and extreme Liberalism have come into contact, Mr. Chamberlain has taken care to let the public know that if Radical principles did not prevail, the fault was with the Whigs and not with the Radical members of the Cabinet. He has denounced the feudal tenure in land, which has representatives as wealthy, and to some extent as stubborn, in the Gladstone Cabinet as in any government that could be formed by a Conservative Prime Minister. At least half the prominent members of the Gladstone Cabinet are large landed proprietors; the Marquis of Hartington, the second in command to Mr. Gladstone, is the son of one of the three or four richest landlords of England. Nor has Mr. Chamberlain spared even the financial doctrines of Mr. Gladstone himself. Mr. Gladstone's fame—however assailed on other points—is admitted on finance; and one fine day his subordinate informed the world that the finance of Mr. Gladstone was all one great mistake. Sitting side by side with men trained in the most rigid school of political economy, Mr. Chamberlain has preached doctrines which, in spite of all explanations, have a dangerous resemblance to some of the utopian schemes that are associated with the name of Mr. Henry George. He has likewise on all occasions had his fling at the Established Church and at the aristocracy; amid wild cheers he on one occasion reminded an audience that he was a Dissenter, and had the memory of a Dissenter for the wrongs his fathers had suffered; and during the struggle with the House of Lords he almost implied that if the nobility did not give way, the democracy must resort to force. To sum up: member of a Cabinet composed in the main of landed aristocrats, churchmen, and economists, he has since assailed the aristocracy, the land, the Church, and orthodoxy, political economy.

The result has been even more exasperating. For beyond all question he is the one man who has made great and enormous strides in popular favor since he took office. To-day he has a firmer sway over the masses than any man of the Ministry except Mr. Gladstone. Sir Charles Dilke has also greatly advanced his reputation by his tenure of office; but his success has been a social and a Parliamentary rather than a popular success. In the drawing-rooms of London, from which he was rigidly excluded in the hot days of his early republicanism, he has become one of the most welcome guests in clubs; he is voted a good fellow; and in the House of Commons a quiet, smooth, and apparently frank and kindly manner has made him the friend of all men. But he has lost rather than gained hold upon the masses; to some of them his silence and something like an apology for his earlier and fiercer utterances have produced a feeling of distrust. It is known that Dilke, like Chamberlain, has sworn to be Prime Minister of England; but he is not so popular; if he reach his ambition, it will be by a Parliamentary or a social cabal, and not through his hold upon the masses.

Mr. Chamberlain, then, is the man; and it requires little acquaintance with English politics to know how galling his prospect must be to many of his colleagues. He is but eight or nine years in Parliamentary life; most of his colleagues have been members for twenty or thirty years. He is a manufacturer; and in England still the manufacturer occupies a social position far inferior to that of the landed aristocrat. And then there is something about him personally that suggests smallness—and smallness aspiring to greatness is especially obnoxious. In strength of will, tenacity of purpose, cool self-possession, and bold, unscrupulous strategy, he is a born politician, and must extort respect. He speaks, too, with great vigor; strikes home; and has much command over those commonplaces of political vituperation which influence the masses. But there is something that suggests thinness in his mind, as he has a sectarian and venomous narrowness that repels rather than attracts; and his physical appearance and general air are not attractive. He has one of those smooth faces that make men look not much more than half their age. There is a story, of course not true, of his being called "the boy" during a recent excursion in Spain. Then this gives him a certain pettiness, something of that pettiness of air that is associated with the dry-goods clerk in all countries of the world. The only word that can describe it is the word "perky"; he seems to be filled with self-admiration; pauses between his sentences—which, it must be admitted, are delivered in a fine, musical, penetrating voice and with excellent intonation—as though to admire the sound of his own voice and the roundness of his own periods; and when you add that he has a nose with the fatal tendency to turn up which belongs rather to the Irish than the English face; that he wears the single eye-glass which has made the stony stare of the British the hatred and the abomination of all other nations—it will be seen that his exterior is not one to attract. His pretensions are those of a gigantic leader of men; his stage presence is that of the aspiring and self-complacent "super."

And his colleagues? The Marquis of Hartington, though a man nearer Captain Hawtree—the proverbially apathetic and un-emotional Englishman—is by no means so devoid of ambition as he looks, or would make believe. And he has every thing, too, to entitle him to the leading place in a British administration; enormous wealth, lofty position, a line of ancestors going back to infinite lengths, and long parliamentary experience and great parliamentary talents. When he succeeded Mr. Gladstone in the Liberal leadership some years ago, he had a heritage as difficult as any that ever fell to a political leader; yet he acquitted himself of the task in a manner that gained the approval of all men; and he developed a power of parliamentary debating that was not hitherto even suspected. He is hard to rouse; but when he is roused he can strike blows as hard and as straight as any debater in the House of Commons; he has that frank, downright manner that commends itself to Englishmen. Less loose-tongued and more self-controlled than Gladstone, he avoids making so many enemies or provoking so much animosity; and often, when he has been leading the House in the absence of the Prime Minister, he has suggested comparisons that were not altogether unfavorable. To the Marquis of Hartington Mr. Chamberlain must appear nothing but an upstart, more remarkable than other men simply in the amount of his gush and self-conceit. Then Sir William Harcourt is a man who, at one period of his career, fell foul of Mr. Gladstone himself, in the silly hope that he might thus climb to the first place on the ruins of his former chief. Of all the men in the House, there is not one of a vain ambition more vain and more unscrupulous. Then he loathes Radicalism almost as much as though he sat on the Conservative benchès; and to him Mr. Chamberlain must be an object of even fiercer and more bitter hate than to the Marquis of Hartington.

Such was the general state of affairs among the men who formed the Gladstone Cabinet when a match was applied to the magazine of irreconcilable ambitions and fierce personal hatreds with the question of coercion for Ireland. The forces in favor of coercion within the Cabinet are well known. The leader of the coercionists was, of course, Lord Spencer. With him it was a matter of life and death. Unless coercion were a necessary agent of governing Ireland, then the verdict of the Irish people upon him was just; he murdered innocent men through packed juries and partisan judges; and his regime was that of a reign of legalized terror, not of restored order. His position was certainly a peculiar one; a position that led him to back his opinions by strong personal appeals. He had risked his life to govern Ireland at a moment of unprecedented difficulty and danger; he was the friend and the associate of the men who had fallen victims to the knives of the Invincibles; and above all things, he had a hold upon large masses of Englishmen that gave him a strong leverage against the Ministry. If he did not get coercion, they would not have him; and his resignation, just on the eve of a general election, would supply the Tories with a new and a more dangerous cry in the announcement that another Kilmainham Treaty had been made, that the· Ministry were in league with Mr. Parnell. The views of Lord Spencer were backed up fiercely by Sir William Harcourt and by the Marquis of Hartington, brother of one of the men who were assassinated in Phœnix Park; and the combination was, therefore, very powerful.

The attitude taken up by Mr. Chamberlain and Sir Charles Dilke was mainly regulated by the consideration of the altered state of parties that must come after the next general election. Neither they nor any other intelligent observers have the least doubt that Mr. Parnell will return with at least eighty followers; and that any political leader who has eighty followers can immensely influence —if he cannot entirely control—the fortunes of the two parties. It is this dread and inevitable portent of a great Irish party that commands all the considerations, and negotiations, and combinations of the present situation. It enters into everything; but more of that by-and-by. For the present suffice it to say that Mr. Chamberlain and Sir Charles Dilke have always preached and believed in·the advent of the day when they could use the Irish vote to precipitate reform in England; and their own prepossessions are favorable to moderate concessions on the Home Rule question. Their calculation was that if they could defeat coercion they would gain the Irish vote in the English constituencies, and so secure a great Liberal majority; and, secondly, that they would gain for themselves the Irish vote in Parliament, and in that way break down, if necessary, the dominance of the Whig families, and compel the Liberal party to accept a Radical premier, either of themselves, and a thorough-going Radical policy. They accordingly resolved to oppose coercion. The conditions which they proposed are not of any great concern just now; the great fact is that they opposed coercion, and opposed it bitterly and obstinately. Here, then, was a difficulty that no Prime Minister, however dexterous, could patch up; it seemed as if Mr. Gladstone had no choice but a choice of evils; he must abandon coercion, and with coercion abandon all the Whig members of his Cabinet, or he must adopt coercion and lose all the Radical members of his Cabinet. The sacrifice of so many personal and political ties, moreover, brought no promised compensation. If, by driving out the Whigs, he had a Cabinet entirely Radical, the Whigs would probably soon bring his Cabinet to an end; and the expulsion of the Radicals, by getting free of Chamberlain and Dilke, would insure the defeat of coercion, and the break-up of the government.

On the other hand, the position of Chamberlain and Dilke was not without difficulty. They were quite willing to go out, having had as much of office as they cared for, and the break-up of the administration was not a matter about which they would have had any particular qualms. But the break-up of a Ministry on the eve of a general election meant, in all probability, the break-up of the Liberal party also; and this was a serious responsibility, especially on the part of a man like Mr. Chamberlain, who has done so much to introduce into English life that rigor of party discipline which in America is comprehensively called " machine politics."

All through, the cynic observers of so many successive abandonments of principles by the Radicals thought that the quarrel would be patched up, and that Mr. Chamberlain and Sir Charles Dilke would be spared. But this view of the situation has not been confirmed by the information with regard to the state of things in the Cabinet which has oozed out since the ministerial defeat. On the Monday on which the fatal division on the budget took place, there was a Cabinet council. It was one of a whole series that had been held for the purpose of finding some compromise between the two contending sections. The attempt, like all those which had preceded it, was a failure ; and it looked more than ever as if a break-up was inevitable. It was when things had reached this lamentable and perilous pass that the Opposition came to the rescue of the Government by defeating them on the budget. Never was a defeat more welcome. The ministers themselves made no attempt at concealing their satisfaction. The faces of Mr. Chamberlain and Sir Charles Dilke, especially, beamed with joy. And, naturally ; they had been released from an intolerable dilemma.

Since the downfall of the Government this has been felt to be so much the case that a new and strange controversy has been added to those already existing in English history. The question most hotly disputed is whether the Government avoided or sought defeat. The Ministers hotly take up one side ; the Conservatives as vehemently the other. There is certainly some explanation necessary when, on a great and vital division, there are no less than seventy absentees on the Ministerial side. The enterprising news agency has sent to the absentees for their explanation of their absence, and the whole political world has been laughing ever since at the grotesqueness of these different excuses. One man could not come because he had to be by the side of his wife "invalided"; another was suddenly indisposed; a third got a wetting and did not care to risk a cold; no less than three missed their trains; one was in Switzerland, another in Egypt; two were on their honeymoon; a whole host protest that they did not know the division was important. The inevitable conclusion is, either that the party managers bungled their business, or allowed the incautious enemy to snatch a Pyrrhian victory.

The part the followers of Mr. Parnell took in the matter is of great significance. It was they who won the victory for the Conservatives. This is a fact that one can gather, not merely from the exultant comments in the Irish National press, but from the remarks in the speeches of the leaders of the fallen party. It is the favorite charge now in the speeches of Liberals that the Conservatives snatched their victory by means of the Parnellite vote, which is, of course, a confession that it was the Parnellite vote that defeated the Government. It did not require the excited shouts that came from the Parnellite benches on that night of "Coercion," "Buckshot," "Spencer," "Myles Joyce," to accentuate the meaning of the action of the Irish members. Mr. Parnell, and other leaders of the party, declared, when first coercion was spoken of, that coercion would in the end kill the Government; and the promise has been kept. And now, short as is the time which has elapsed since the overthrow of the Ministry, it has sufficed to justify the action of the Irish party, not only in this division, but their attitude for some time past to the Ministry.

There are many persons at some distance from the scene of conflict—in America their number is particularly large—who fail to understand the attitude of the Irish members towards the present Ministry,—and especially towards Mr. Gladstone. Such critics point out that the Liberals, as a body, are more friendly to the Irish people than the Conservatives; that the Liberals favor democratic government, the rights of the masses, the claim of the tenant to the fruits of his labors, the Irish householder to the same vote as the householder in England and Scotland. The Conservatives, on the other hand, it is pointed out, are allied with the Irish Tory party, the party of landlords, and rackrenting and evicting landlords; of bigots, who loathe the name and, if possible, would still persecute the religion of the Irish Catholic. And, after this, attention is called to the friendship which Mr. Gladstone has always professed for Ireland; to his constant kindliness of tone; and, above all, to the gigantic reforms which he has carried for the Irish people, —the ballot, the disestablishment of the Church, and the two Land Acts. How then, it is asked, frequently in surprise, can an Irish Nationalist reconcile it with his duty to his country to help in expelling from office the party that is friendly and the man who has proved his affectionate interest in the advance of the Irish people?

The events since the crisis are alone sufficient to supply the answer to these objections. What is the very first effect of the fall of the Gladstone government? Its first and most important effect is that coercion for Ireland is killed; it is dead, as though beyond all recall or revival. If the Liberals be the friends of Ireland, the continuance of whose power is certainly beneficial to Ireland, is it not a somewhat curious circumstance that the very first effect of the expulsion of the Liberals from office is to prevent the introduction of coercive legislation for the Irish people? And the full significance of this change is only understood by a comparison of the prospects of Ireland on this question of coercion before and after the fall of the Gladstone government. The state of affairs in the Gladstone Cabinet on coercion has already been described; it has been shown that on the very day of their fall the Ministers themselves were divided in opinion upon the question. It is possible, nay, it is probable—or lest we should put the case one hair's breadth more strongly than facts justify—it is certainly possible that the coercion section would have carried the day; that Mr. Gladstone would have continued to hold office, and would have introduced a coercion bill. Thus the case, put in the most moderate form, stands thus : as long as there was a Liberal ministry in power, there was a possibility of coercion ; the moment the Liberals were powerless, coercion became impossible.

This paradoxical state of things is easily understood by anybody acquainted with the English political parties. Let us try to explain it to our readers; the point is well worthy of being thoroughly understood, because it lies at the root and foundation of the policy of the Parnellite party, both in the past and the immediate future. The *Times* newspaper, speaking with its characteristically shameless cynicism, explains the whole situation in a sentence : " To carry the Crimes Act, however mutilated, in the teeth of Parnellite and Radical resistance, and with no disposition to afford active help on the part of the retiring Ministers, would be impossible." In other words, the coercion which the Radicals and the Liberal leaders generally would have been ready to pass themselves they would most resolutely oppose if brought in by their political opponents. And that is just what the Irish leaders have always been saying. Their answer always has been to those who found fault with their hostility to the Liberals, that when the Liberals were in power they were friends, when they were in opposition they were enemies of coercion.

The chief cause of the fallacy so prevalent with regard to the effect of the two English parties on Irish affairs, is mistaking will for power. So far as will to do injury to the Irish popular cause is concerned, the Tories are infinitely worse than the Liberals. It is quite true that between the English Liberal and the Irish Nationalist there are many points of agreement; and it is true that between the Irish Nationalist and the English Tory there spreads an impassable chasm on almost every subject under the sun. Nor is it to be denied, that if the Tories could have their way, they would treat all Irish national movements with the humane methods of martial law and drum-head courts-martial. But, then, where is the harm of an enemy who, while he may have all the venom of the most malignant and murderous hatred, is perfectly powerless? And that is the position of the English Tory; his power to do harm to Ireland is gone, and gone for ever. Here is how the English parties work with regard to Ireland. If a Conservative government be in office, it has no power of passing severe coercive laws for Ireland, because the Liberals in opposition always combine with the Irish party, and oppose almost as vigorously every repressive proposal of a Conservative administration. On the other hand, if a Liberal administration exist, and it proposes coercive legislation, its adoption of a Tory policy is, of course, hailed with delight by the Tory party; and the Tory opposition, instead of being a drag, and a critic, and an enemy, cheers, and helps, and stimulates the Liberal administration. And thus, while coercion bills brought in by a Conservative administration are certain to be watered by a Liberal administration, or a coercion bill brought in by a Liberal administration is the more welcome to the Conservative opposition in proportion to its stringency. Thus the statement is literally true, that a Liberal government is much more potent for evil to Ireland than a Conservative government could possibly be.

And this further is true, that a Liberal administration is often less potent for good than a Conservative administration—that is, if the Conservative administration be not more powerful than the Liberals and Irish Nationalists combined. When a Conservative administration brings in a measure of reform, the converse position is established to that of the Liberal government bringing in a coercion bill. The Conservative administration introducing reform is stimulated and encouraged instead of being obstructed and opposed by the Liberal opposition. On the other hand, when a measure of reform is introduced by a Liberal administration, it is opposed obstinately and at every step and by all the forms and expedients of filibustering and obstruction by the Conservative opposition in the House of Commons; and if the Conservative opposition fail to defeat or reduce the measure in the House of Commons, there is the permanent Conservative majority, at once irremovable and irresponsible, in the House of Lords, and that majority can only be got to swallow reform when reform comes backed by the ugly spectres of terror and force. But the Conservative Ministry has nothing to fear from the House of Lords; what the Conservative Prime Minister orders, the House of Lords will obey. And if a Conservative Minister order that there shall be a regime of reform in Ireland, the House of Lords will swallow reform without a gulp. Thus, then, reform proposed by a Conservative administration would pass rapidly and easily through the House of Commons, would be fortified, not weaked, by the opposition in that body; while in the House of Lords the sanction of a Conservative Premier would be more potent than a cyclone of popular passion, an epidemic of wild crime, or the surly roar of enraged masses. To end this part of the subject as it began, a Liberal government is more potent for ill, and a Conservative government is more potent for good to the Irish cause.

All this reasoning, as will have been observed, is guarded by an important proviso; that proviso is, that the Conservative administration is not so powerful as to be independent alike of the Liberals and the Irish. If the Conservatives were able, on a division, to beat both the Irish and the Liberals, it would be bad for Ireland, for there would then be no proposals for reform. This is what took place in the last Parliament, when the Beaconsfield Ministry passed a life of six years without giving Ireland any particular measure of reform. This would be a bad state of things to recur; but it is, in the first place, impossible,—as will be shown presently,—and, secondly, even if possible, an overwhelming Tory majority has not dangers as grave as an overwhelming Liberal majority. For,—as has already been seen,—any coercive proposals by a Conservative administration would be certain to meet with strong hostility from a Liberal opposition, and so would be reduced in severity, and a Liberal opposition would also join an Irish party in putting pressure upon the Conservative government to introduce measures of reform.

But a strong Conservative government, independent alike of the Irish and the Radical party in the House of Commons, is a very improbable ' contingency. It would want to be very powerful indeed, for it would have to displace a majority of 100 which the Liberals at present have, and, besides, to be able to beat the Irish reinforcement of 80 men. The Liberals have this majority of 100 in the present Parliament over the Tories alone, and all the probabilities of the case point to their having as great, if not a greater, majority after the next general election. Two million voters have been enfranchised; the first impulse of these voters is to vote for the men who gave them the franchise, and the Liberals, of course, gave them the franchise. Then, times have been bad in the rural districts, and the agricultural laborer has been an ill-treated serf for centuries; ill-treated alike by the farmer and the squire. It is not unnatural to suppose that the first impulse of the laborer will be to go against the politics both of the squire and the farmer; and the farmer and the squire have been Conservatives from time immemorial. Hitherto the counties have been the strongholds of the Conservatives, as the great towns have been their weakness. If a number of the counties turn against them, the Liberals must have a majority in excess of any they have hitherto won. The probabilities, then, point to a large Liberal majority, and the last five years have conclusively shown what a Liberal majority means. It means coercion of a savagery that a Conservative administration could not even dream of, and the reforms cut and pared down to such proportions as the Conservative opposition in the House of Commons and the Conservative majority in the House of Lords may be willing to accept. The national question will have to be dealt with soon. If a Conservative administration, dependent on the Irish vote, were in power, the scheme proposed might not be originally large, but it would be broadened by a combined Irish and Liberal opposition. If a Liberal government propose a home rule measure, it will not be large in the start, and before it is carried it will have to be brought to the irreducible minimum which will be taken by the Conservatives in the two Houses of Parliament.

These are the reasons, and not the childish spirit of mischief, or the idiotic spirit of pure and uncalculating vindictiveness, that have lain at the root of the hostility of the Irish party to the Liberal Ministry, and of the comparative satisfaction with which Irish Nationalists received the intelligence that a Conservative administration was likely to be called into power. Much of this satisfaction was due to the prominent place which Lord Randolph Churchill was made to occupy in all the combinations suggested. Less satisfaction could, of course, be felt with the Premiership of the Marquis of Salisbury. The Marquis of Salisbury and Lord Randolph Churchill are potent figures in English politics, whether they come into office now or at any future time, and 'a sketch of their character and tendencies will not be without its uses.

The Marquis of Salisbury is a tall, thick-set, and very ungainly man. He has a heavy stoop; his face, which is unhealthily pale, is surrounded by a very black and stubbly beard; his eyes are deep-set; and, on the whole, the look of the face is not attractive. His speeches read very well, but they are not pleasant to listen to. He has a bad voice, a hesitant delivery, and in speaking he has a habit of lolling, which detracts very much from his forcibleness. He was a younger son when he began life, and not very well provided for. Falling in love with a very brilliant woman—the daughter of a judge—he insisted on marrying her in spite of the vehement opposition of his father and family, who regarded the match as a *mésalliance;* and as a result he was almost cut off and left to his own resources. Fortunately his brother-in-law, Mr. Beresford Hope, a wealthy *dilettante,* conceived the idea of starting the *Saturday Review,* and Lord Robert Cecil, as the Marquis of Salisbury was then known, was one of its first and most frequent writers. He has in his writings, and to some extent in his speaking, the qualities which provoked at once the admiration and hostility for the *Saturday Review* in its earlier and better days. He is antithetical, has a biting, sardonic humor, and coins magnificent phrases. He writes better than he speaks, and even during the last few years an article from his pen in the *Quarterly Review* was a literary as well as a political event. His earlier years are defaced by some of the most brutal as well as some of the most stupid things said by any public man against Ireland and against democracy. He probably wrote some of the vile sentences of brutal rejoicing over Irish expatriation which were among the many parents of such offspring as the dynamite policy and the Invincibles. Against any share of the masses in the government of their country, he raged, after a fashion somewhat similar to the ravings of Prince Bismarck's earlier parliamentary outbursts. His quarrel with the late Lord Beaconsfield was due to the resolve of the latter to give the working-classes a share in the franchise. But he has grown out of some of these prejudices with the advance of years and of the power of the masses. Since the death of Lord Beaconsfield he has been the acknowledged head of the Tory party, and has taken his turn on the stump after the manner of the most plebeian courtier of the electorate. His great cry a couple of years ago was, "Appeal to the People,"—a cry more worthy of a democratic Cæsar than an aristocratic scholar consumed with contempt for the judgment and ideals of the profane crowd. He has shown the first symptoms of repentance and enlightenment on the Irish question by dropping all thought or mention of coercion ; and, like other politicians, he will have to do as the times and the great political forces demand, and these two factors are on the side of Ireland.

His hostility will probably be transformed into at least a seeming of friendship.

Lord Randolph Churchill has fewer foolish things to forget and fewer convictions to give up. It may be doubted, indeed, if he have any very strong convictions on any subject. He is well described in a Liberal paper as an electioneerer before all things. He is a curious example of the kind of man that can come to the front and to a position of extraordinary power and popularity in English politics. The son of a needy duke, he was several years in Parliament without attracting any notice. He did speak about once in a year, but his speeches were remarkable above all things for audacity, and for a certain irreverent habit of laughing at his own side that made him the despair of his own family and the dread of the politically orthodox. Everybody took him for a young man of fashion, who sauntered into the House of Commons in search of some fun that might stimulate an appetite jaded with the inanities of the theatres or the flirtations of the ball-room. On one occasion he committed an indiscretion even more serious than his exploits in Parliament. At the very moment when his father was Lord-Lieutenant of Ireland and when Mr. Parnell and Mr. Biggar were starting out amid a tempest of British execration on the policy known as Obstruction, Lord Randolph, at a meeting in Dublin, entered on something like a defence of the universally loathed Irishmen.

It was not till the downfall of the Conservative government and the return of a great Liberal majority that Lord Randolph's opportunity came. The fight he had to undertake might well have appalled any but a very brave spirit. The Liberals were in the very insolence of their extraordinary triumph. They had over a hundred majority, while the Conservatives were broken in numbers and still more in spirits. Terror-stricken sheep, they were left without their shepherds, for after their expulsion from office the Tory leaders took a disgust to public life, and many of the most prominent among them ceased to attend the House of Commons at all. It was then that Lord Randolph Churchill organized the little party section known as the " Fourth Party." The idea was borrowed from Mr. Parnell and Mr. Biggar, and the tactics employed were pretty much the same. The proposals of the Ministry were met at every point. They were fought wholesale and in detail, and an incessant guerilla warfare was thus kept up, which had the effect of deranging the best-laid schemes and of defeating the most portentous combinations. This kind of warfare naturally did not recommend itself to the Ministerialists. They found that after their immense victory at the polls, with all their overwhelming majority, and with a Ministry with all the talents, they were being brought to nullity and futility by this little band of four determined and resolute and tireless talkers. An attempt was made to put Churchill down by terror, and he was bracketed with some of the Irish members who had made themselves most conspicuous and most unpopular—unpopular in England, *bien entendu*—by the activity of their opposition to the government. Then, when terror failed, ridicule was tried, and the Fourth Party became one of the jokes of Parliament. Finally, an even greater danger menaced Churchill and his party. The leaders of the Conservatives looked with no great favor on this servile imitation by members of their own party of the tactics associated with the hated Irish, and there were collisions between Lord Randolph Churchill and Sir Stafford Northcote and the other orthodox leaders of the party. Several times Churchill flouted his seniors and superiors, and soon he made no concealment of a feeling of utter contempt for the whole official hierarchy of his party. To be one of four men, or of three, for the party had come down to this, owing to the secession of Mr. Arthur Balfour; and to oppose the whole party and all its time-honored leaders, was one of the boldest enterprises that a young man of thirty-six ever entered upon. Most people, even those who had a sneaking liking for him, voted Churchill imbecile or mad. But he went on, and the final result is seen now. He has driven North-cote, the leader of the party, from the House of Commons; has put his own nominee, Sir Michal Hicks Beach, in his place, and has forced the Marquis of Salisbury to eat his own words and to take back his own insults. In fact, he has shown a firmness of purpose that makes him a potent force for good or for ill in the future of England.

It is hard to say what his official career will be in case he takes office. He has committed some great and almost unintelligible blunders; and one of the many blunders he has committed in opposition would be enough to damn him as a Minister. In any case, whether in office or out of office, he has shown an independent spirit about Ireland that distinguishes him from the rank and file of the Tory party. There is no use in going into the motives of politicians, especially of English politicians, dealing with Irish affairs. Lord Randolph Churchill may have good motives or bad. The essential fact is that he fully appreciates the enormous power of Mr. Parnell and his party, and that he has good sense enough to recognize strength when he sees it, and boldness enough to carry out any policy which he believes to be made inevitable by the circumstances of the time.

THE CATHOLIC DOCTRINE OF BAPTISM.

De Baptismo. P. Alberto a Bulsano. Taurini, 1857.

De Baptismo. Honoratus Turnelius. Parisiis, 1841.

The Westminster Catechism. Philadelphia: Presbyterian Board of Publication.

IN the Presbyterian Assembly, held at Cincinnati, on May 22d, a delegate, said to be a judge from Washington, D. C., offered the following strange resolution:

> *Resolved,* That it is the deliberate decision and decided judgment of this assembly, that the Roman Catholic Church has essentially apostatized from the religion of our Lord and Saviour Jesus Christ, and, therefore, cannot be recognized as a Christian Church; and as we do not recognize it as a portion of the visible Church, we cannot consistently view its priesthood as other than usurpers of the sacred functions of the ministry, its ordinances unscriptural, and its baptism as totally invalid.[1]

Fortunately this stupid and bitter attack upon the Catholic Church found sympathy with only a small minority of the Presbyterian body. The sane majority saw how impolitic and ridiculous it would be to give to the world as Presbyterian doctrine, that the largest and oldest of the Christian churches is pagan and to be put below even the Mormons in the scale of orthodoxy; that a church whose members, even in this country, far outnumber the Presbyterians, is no longer "to be recognized as Christian," although engaged in converting and sanctifying mankind for fifteen centuries before the birth of the Geneva autocrat, who caused Michael Servetus to be burned alive for denying Presbyterian articles of faith. The more distinguished of the clergy saw this man's mistake. Drs. Schaff and Nevin, of Pennsylvania, men of solid learning, opposed the resolution, and prevented the assembly from making itself "the laughing-stock of the world," to borrow the words of Dr. Alexander, a distinguished Calvinistic divine from the Pacific coast. The Presbyterians of the United States may thank these gentlemen for preventing the judge from appending to the head of their church a longer pair of ears than were ever worn by a Calvinist condemned to the stocks in the days of cavalier persecution. Had the resolution passed, it would have been an admission that Presbyterianism was founded by a pagan

---

[1] The Philadelphia Press of May 23d, 1885.

who had never been validly baptized, for John Calvin never received any other than Catholic baptism. We shall see, however, later on, that the judge's great error in regard to the validity of baptism administered by persons not considered orthodox, is only a flitting reminiscence of a heresy as old as the third century, and repeatedly condemned by the Catholic Church. But in order that all men like him, whose sincerity and whose ignorance we do not question, may have an easy opportunity of knowing what Catholics believe regarding the first of the sacraments in the order of time, we proceed to explain briefly the matter, form, minister, subject, necessity, and some of the ceremonies of baptism as now administered in the Catholic Church. Let us first see, however, by way of preface, what the Presbyterians hold in regard to this sacrament, and in what their teaching differs from Catholic truth.

The Presbyterian catechism defines baptism as "a sacrament, wherein the washing with water, in the name of the Father and of the Son and of the Holy Ghost, doth signify and seal our ingrafting into Christ, and partaking of the benefits of the covenant of grace and our engagement to be the Lord's."[1] The catechism of the last Catholic Council of Baltimore defines baptism as "a sacrament which cleanses us from original sin, makes us Christians, children of God, and heirs of heaven;" and adds: "Actual sins and all the punishment due to them are remitted by baptism, if the person baptized be guilty of any."[2] It will be observed that both catechisms call baptism a sacrament; but by a sacrament the Presbyterian means "a holy ordinance instituted by Christ; wherein, by sensible signs, Christ and the benefits of the new covenant are represented, sealed, and applied to believers."[3] Disrobing this thought of its theological garment, a sacrament is a mere outward sign, which confers no inward grace; it does not cleanse from sin; it does not justify, "faith alone" being the cause of justification; and it is a mere ceremony of initiation like those necessary to become a member of a lodge of Free Masons. The Catholic catechism defines a sacrament to be "an outward sign instituted by Christ to give grace." According to St. Thomas and all other Catholic theologians, three things may be distinguished in baptism: firstly, the external sign, which is the water applied with the proper form; secondly, the thing signified, which is the interior ablution of the soul by sanctifying grace; thirdly, the thing signified in all of the sacraments but three is, sanctifying grace; but in baptism, confirmation, and holy orders, there is, in addition, an indelible

---

[1] Westminster Catechism, Philadelphia, p. 47.
[2] Catechism of Third Plenary Council, Baltimore, p. 26.
[3] Westminster Catechism, p. 46.

character impressed on the soul. This character in baptism gives a right to the reception of the other sacraments. (3 pars Summæ, quæst. 66, art. 1)

Adam sinned and thus forfeited the rights and privileges of the supernatural citizenship with which he was endowed by his Maker. His posterity are all born disfranchised outlaws. Baptism restores them to citizenship. Or to use a comparison familiar to American ears, baptism is the Christian's naturalization. The Church is our Lord's republic. To become a citizen of it, the infidel, the pagan, must become naturalized, and baptism is the means to that end. The baptized person becomes at once a member of the visible church, sharing all its rights and duties. He becomes capable of receiving the other sacraments. While the external result of this sacrament is to make him a member of the body of the Church, the internal effect is to cleanse him from original and actual sin, sanctify him, and unite him to the soul of the church. The Catholic doctrine of original sin throws light on the Catholic doctrine of baptism.

In the Catholic Church there are two extreme schools as to the nature of original sin. The one which we may call the Augustinian, represented by Berti, and also seemingly by the theologians who made the catechism of the third Plenary Council of Baltimore, teaches that by the sin of our first parents " our nature was corrupted"; and that "this corruption of our nature and other punishments remain in us after original sin is forgiven." (Cat. Third Council of Baltimore.) The opinion of the other school is expressed by Father Perrone, S. J., who teaches that original sin consists in the mere " *privation* of sanctifying grace, and that justice which ought to be in us according to the order established by God," and that "death, concupiscence, diseases, etc., are only effects, or punishments of original sin." (Perrone, *De Homine*, c. iv., ed. Migne, Paris, 1841.) Between these two opinions the Thomists hold their course, although Perrone quotes a text of St. Thomas which seems to favor his view : " Thus, therefore, the *privation* of original justice, by which the human will was subject to God, is the *formal* part of original sin." (S. Th., 1a. 2æ, q. 82.)

The Presbyterian doctrine of justification by faith alone, of the impotency of human nature to do good works, of the destruction of free will by the fall of our first parents, must be all taken into account in judging the Calvinian theory of baptism. Calvin writes:[1] " It is clear that the teaching" (Catholic) "is false, which holds that baptism cleanses us from original sin, and from the corruption

---

[1] Instit., lib. 4, cap. 15.

which was propagated by Adam into his whole posterity." Other errors of the Presbyterians regarding baptism will be noted in their place.[1]

The Council of Trent summarized the Catholic doctrine on this sacrament in fourteen decrees, passed in the seventh session. In them, among other things, it was defined that water is the matter of the sacrament; that baptism conferred by heretics in the name of the Father and of the Son and of the Holy Ghost, with the intention of doing what the Church does, is valid; that baptism is necessary to salvation; that a person once validly baptized, and afterwards apostatizing, should not be rebaptized after conversion from apostasy; and that children should not be rebaptized when they come to the use of reason.

I. Luther, in his " Table Talk," holds that anything which serves to wash in, may be used as matter for baptism, consequently baptism in milk or wine would be valid. Theodore Beza held the same opinion. The second canon of the Council of Trent on

---

[1] The following is an authentic explanation of the actual teaching of the Presbyterian church regarding original sin :

In the Confession of Faith, which is the formula to which all clergymen of the Presbyterian church are required to subscribe before ordination, chapter vi treats of "the fall of man, of sin, and of the punishment thereof," in the following words :

" (1.) Our first parents, being seduced by the subtility and temptation of Satan, sinned in eating the forbidden fruit. This, their sin, God was pleased, according to His wise and holy counsel, to permit, having purposed to order it to His own glory.

" (2.) By this sin they fell from their original righteousness and communion with God, and so became dead in sin, and wholly defiled in all the faculties and parts of soul and body.

" (3.) They being the root of all mankind, the guilt of this sin was imputed, and the same death in sin and corrupted nature conveyed to all their posterity descending from them by ordinary generation.

" (4.) From this original corruption, whereby we are utterly indisposed, disabled, and made opposite to all good, and wholly inclined to all evil, do proceed all actual transgressions.

" (5.) This corruption of our nature, during this life, doth remain in those that are regenerated ; and, although it be through Christ pardoned and mortified, yet both itself, and all the motions thereof, are truly and properly sin.

" (6.) Every sin, both original and actual, being a transgression of the righteous law of God, and contrary thereunto, doth, in its own nature, bring guilt upon the sinner, whereby he is bound over to the wrath of God, and curse of the law, and so made subject to death, with all miseries spiritual, temporal, and eternal."

The same doctrine is differently phrased in the answer to the eighteenth question of the shorter catechism, also an authoritative standard of the Presbyterian church. The question is : " Wherein consists the sinfulness of that state whereinto man fell ?" And the answer reads : " The sinfulness of that state whereinto man fell, consists in the guilt of Adam's first sin, the want of original righteousness, and the corruption of his whole nature, which is commonly called original sin, together with all actual transgressions which proceed from it."

These doctrines are quite strictly interpreted by the majority of the clergymen now officiating in the Presbyterian church. Some may be more lax than others, but the majority would doubtless maintain these two statements with great emphasis.

baptism is against this error, and that of Calvin, who held that by water in the text, "unless a man be born again of water and the Holy Ghost, he cannot enter into the kingdom of God,"[1] is meant the blood of Christ, on account of the similarity of water and blood in cleansing and purifying.[2] A branch of the Manicheans of the twelfth century, called Cathari or Puritans, baptized in fire. "They place many candles around the wretch who is to be baptized or puritanized (*catharizandus*), and the archpuritan, holding a book in his hand, assists him, and puts the book on his head; the rest praying aloud, and thus is baptism performed."[3] So writes Eckbert, a priest, against them about A.D. 1160.

Thus, instead of pouring water on the head or immersing the catechumen, the ancient Puritans half roasted him. The Socinians and the Quakers also deny the necessity of water in baptism; as did the ancient Marcosians and the Beguards of the Middle Ages.

That natural water is the remote matter of baptism has been universally held in the Catholic Church, which has ever interpreted the text, "Teach all nations, baptizing them in the name of the Father and of the Son and of the Holy Ghost,"[4] and the verse already quoted from St. John, "Unless a man," etc., as implying the necessity of water in baptism. Indeed the text "Unless a man," etc., is one of the few which have received a dogmatic explanation from a general council. The second canon of the Council of Trent on Baptism embodies it in the doctrinal decree defining water as the necessary matter of the sacrament. The text, Acts viii., 36, "And the eunuch said: See, here is water, what doth hinder me from being baptized? . . . . and they went down into the water, both Philip and the eunuch, and he baptized him," shows the usage of the apostles and their immediate successors.

We need not quote the authority of the Fathers, who are unanimous on this point. Their testimony is summed up in the words of St. Augustine: "Take away water and there is no baptism."[5]

The Catholic Church, however, has been accustomed, from the remotest antiquity, to bless the water to be used in baptism, and to put into it a small quantity of blessed oil and consecrated chrism. St. Thomas gives the reason of this when he says: "The blessing of the water is not of necessity for baptism, but adds to it a certain solemnity by which the devotion of the faithful is excited."[6] Tertullian, in the fourth book of his work on Baptism, speaks of this blessing of the water as a very ancient custom. So does St. Cyprian in his seventieth letter to Januarius: "It is necessary," says

---

[1] St. John, chapter iii., v. 5.   [2] Calvin's Inst., lib. iv., c. 15.
[3] Quoted by Turnelius, p. 305.   [4] St. Matt. xxviii., v. 19.
[5] "Tolle aquam, non est baptismus." Tract. 15 in Joan.
[6] Summæ, 3a pars, q. 66, art. 3.

he, "that the water should be first purified and sanctified by the priest," before being used to baptize. St. Ambrose and St. Augustine both speak of the consecration of the baptismal font. The text of St. Basil,[1] "We bless the water of baptism, and the oil of unction, yes, even the very one who receives baptism. By what scriptural authority? Is it not from long-continued and secret tradition?" clearly shows the usage of the early church on this point. But perhaps the authority of these doctors will have no weight with Presbyterians of the Washington judge type; for the holy fathers belonged to that Church which, according to him, "has essentially apostatized from the religion of our Lord and Saviour Jesus Christ." Which of the two is more likely to be right, St. Basil and the Catholic Church, or this judge and his gradually evanescing minority in his own evanescing sect?

Although natural water is the remote matter of baptism, its application, either by immersion, infusion or aspersion, is the proximate matter of the sacrament. Up to the thirteenth century both the Greek and the Latin Churches used immersion in the solemn administration of baptism. In fact, our Lord and His apostles baptized with this rite. Christ Himself was baptized in this way by St. John, for in St. Matthew, iii., 16, we read: "And Jesus, being baptized, forthwith came out of the water." Why, then, do Presbyterians baptize by aspersion, since our Lord's practice is against it? Will the judge tell us why his sect has given up the scriptural mode of baptism, which the Baptists logically preserve? The Catholic Church, as the infallible custodiarr of the matter and form of the sacraments, claims the right to interpret them, and modify them with accidental conditions. No such claim is made by the Presbyterians. May we not justly, therefore, tax Presbyterian baptism with being invalid, judged by this judge himself, since it is not administered as St. John the Baptist, as our Lord and His apostles, and as the whole Christian Church generally administered it up to the thirteenth century, that is, by immersion? Is there not apostasy here?

A change in the mode of baptizing was made in the Latin Church in the thirteenth century. St. Thomas, who died on March 7th, A.D. 1274, writes: "It is safer to baptize by the mode of immersion, because such is the common usage."[2] St. Bonaventure, his contemporary, bears similar testimony.

As we have already hinted, the Catholic Church claims the right to modify in accidentals the matter and form of the sacraments. When good order and the common weal of Christians require it, she makes such modifications in her discipline. She is the inter-

---

[1] De spiritu Sancto, cap. 27.   [2] 3a pars, Sum. q. 66, art. 7.

preter of Christ's law, and the visible judge of His doctrine and precepts.   In virtue of her supreme authority, she changed the day of rest from the Sabbath prescribed on Mount Sinai to Sunday; and the Presbyterians in this humbly follow her example.   She took away the cup from the laity in the administration of the Blessed Eucharist, because she judged it better to do so; and using the same authority, she gradually substituted the rite of infusion and aspersion for immersion in the public and ordinary administration of the sacrament of baptism.

Infusion or aspersion was, however, always considered a valid mode of baptizing, although licit only in certain cases.

Thus, in the baptism of invalids unable to leave their beds, St. Cyprian tells us that aspersion was used; and he quotes in justification of it the words of Ezekiel (ch. xxxvi., v. 25), which are interpreted as a prophecy of Christian baptism : " And I will pour (*aspergam*) upon you clean water, and you shall be cleansed from all your filthiness."[1]   In various parts of the Church and on various occasions from the earliest times, infusion or aspersion was used in case of necessity, although immersion was the ordinary public ceremony.   We refer the reader for facts in proof of this assertion to any text-book of Catholic theology.[2]

II. The Catholic Church specifies and formulates the form of baptism : " I baptize thee in the name of the Father and of the Son and of the Holy Ghost."   The Presbyterians use the same form.   Where do they get it ?   From the Church which the poor judge and a number òf Presbyterians call an "apostasy."   Our Lord never used these words in baptizing.   He told His apostles to go and baptize in " the name of the Father and of the Son and of the Holy Ghost;" but He left it to the infallible Church to formulate the words.   The Greek Church baptizes with these words : " The servant of God N—— is baptized in the name of the Father and of the Son and of the Holy Ghost."   Why do not the Presbyterians use this form ?   One would think that their dislike of the Roman Catholic " apostate " Church, whose baptism some of them consider invalid, would prompt them to reject her form, and accept that of their more congenial schismatic sister.   But consistency is not a characteristic of error.   The Greek form is recognized as valid by the Roman Church.   We may remark here that the form and matter of the sacrament of baptism must be applied simultaneously.   There must be a moral union between them. The words, " I baptize thee, etc.," must be used while the party is being dipped or aspersed.   Further, there should be a real lotion

---

[1] St. Cyprian, epist. 69.

[2] Tournely, pp 324, 325, 326, gives numerous historical proofs of the truth of this statement.

in the sprinkling. A drop of water would not suffice. It must wash and flow to be matter of baptism. In this point many of the sects confer baptism invalidly. The Baptists, although they immerse properly, yet sometimes separate the form from the words so as to make their baptism doubtful. Our friends the Presbyterians are also very slovenly in this respect. Not believing in the sacramental character[1] of baptism, they sprinkle so carelessly that hardly a drop touches the head of the person baptized; and baptism administered by them is therefore doubtful.[2] This is the consequence of their "apostasy" from the mode in which our Lord was baptized, *i. e.*, by immersion. John Calvin's belief in fire was much stronger than his trust in water. Yet his followers ought to be strong champions of immersion, for he held, contrary to the Catholic Church, that the baptism of St. John and of Christ are the same in effect,[3] and no one can dispute the fact that St. John's baptism was by immersion. Those who were baptized by him went into the river Jordan.

III. In the early ages, for a long time, when the bishops were more numerous than now, they alone baptized. By degrees, however, when the Christians multiplied, priests and deacons were deputed to perform the duty. It is but proper that the sacrament of naturalization, which confers spiritual citizenship, should be conferred by those only who are officers in the spiritual Republic of Christ. But in His mercy, which embraces all men, He conferred the power on all mankind to administer this sacrament of regeneration in case of necessity. The Church has always held this clement and merciful view of the subject, and in this contrasts favorably with the bigoted limitations and restrictions of heresy.

She has ever taught that although the usual minister of baptism is a priest or a bishop, yet in case of necessity any lay person, man, woman, or child, even a heretic, or an infidel, or a civil judge, may validly and lawfully administer it. The reason for this broad doctrine is found in the necessity of this sacrament for salvation. One of the reasons given by St. Thomas for the institution of water as the matter of baptism is also applicable to the extension of the ministerial power for this sacrament to every human being in case of

---

[1] "The sacraments become effectual means of salvation, not *from any virtue in them*." Westminster Catechism, p. 45.

[2] On the 17th of September, 1830, an answer was given by the Pope to the following question: "Whether Calvinists and Lutherans, living in regions in which their baptism is doubtful and suspected, should be considered infidels, so that between them and Catholics the diriment impediment of marriage, *disparitatis cultus*, should be held to exist?" To this the authoritative reply was that in case of doubt, the baptism is to be held valid in order to the validity of marriage—*in ordine ad validitatem matrimonii*—(Roman Ritual, Baltimore, 1880).

[3] Calvin's Institutes, lib. 4, cap. 15, n. 7.

necessity. " Because water is common and universal, it is a matter adapted to the necessity of this sacrament ; for wáter can be found easily everywhere."[1]

Calvin[2] denied that a layman could administer this sacrament, even when the person to be baptized was in danger of death. The reason of this denial was because he denied the necessity of baptism. Thus Calvin denies to the Washington champion of his doctrines a privilege which the Catholic Church liberally concedes to him. All of the followers of the Geneva autocrat are not, however, of the same opinion on this subject.

We have no clear Scriptural text to prove that laymen can baptize in case of necessity. It is true that some hermeneutists say that Ananias, who baptized Saul,[3] was a layman. But this is doubtful. Tradition, however, is clear as to the custom and the obligation of laymen baptizing in certain cases. Tertullian[4] teaches that bishops, priests, and deacons can baptize ; bishops as primary, priests as secondary ministers, with permission of the bishops ; and deacons, with the same permission, if specially deputed ; and that laymen in case of necessity not only can baptize freely, validly and licitly ; but that they are bound to do so or be held responsible for the fate of those who die without the sacrament.

St. Jerome pithily puts this doctrine against the Luciferians in these words : " If necessity compels, we know that lay persons can baptize." The fourth council of Carthage, at which St. Augustine was present, decreed : " Let no woman baptize, unless necessity compels."[5]

Pope Eugene IV., in his instruction to the Armenians, decrees : " In case of necessity, not only a priest or a deacon, but even a layman or a woman, even a pagan or a heretic, can baptize, provided he uses the proper form, and intends to do what the Church does."[6]

The Church condemned even the great St Cyprian and his followers for teaching that the baptism of heretics and of unbaptised laymen was invalid because conferred by heretics or by unbaptized laymen. The error of our judge, who would insist on rebaptizing " papists," is only a travesty on the error of St. Cyprian.

IV. The Presbyterian doctrine regarding the subject of baptism is laid down in the Westminster Catechism as follows : " Baptism is not to be administered to any that are out of the visible Church till they profess their faith in Christ, and obedience to him ; but the infants of such as are members of the visible Church are to be

---

[1] Sum., 3a pars, quaest. 66, art. 3.   [2] Lib. iv., Instit. c., 15 par., 20 *et seq.*

[3] Acts of the Apostles, ch. ix., v. 18.   [4] De Baptismo, cap. 17.

[5] Turnelius, p. 469.   [6] Idem.

baptized."[1]   According to the judge, the two hundred millions of Catholics now in the world are all outside of the " visible Church," and they and their children are not even Christians ; yes, all the Catholics that ever lived, both before and since John Calvin, were invalidly baptized ! The Catechism considers children of members of the " visible Church " as capable of baptism ; but it does not tell us what or where the " visible Church " is, or how to find it, or whether the children of those who do not belong to it are capable of baptism or not ?   The theological judge, or the physician who seconded his stupid " resolution," would be sadly puzzled to answer these questions.

The Catholic Church teaches that baptism is to be given to all human beings, not excepting children.   Her custom is to baptize them very soon after their birth, and her theologians hold that it would be a grave sin for parents to neglect, for a considerable time, to have their children christened. '

The Waldenses taught that baptism need not be given to children, as it could do them no good.   The Petrobrusians, another sect of the Middle Ages, taught the same thing.   The learned Peter, Abbot of Cluny, refuted them in two letters.   The Cathari, or mediæval Puritans, denied the necessity and attacked the use of infant baptism, as did the Anabaptists of the 16th century, who rebaptized in adult age all those who had been christened in infancy.

Theodore Beza, with all the old Lutherans and Calvinists, held that only the children of believers should be baptized.   What the present opinion of the different sects on this subject is, it is hard to tell, for the new sectaries have slipped from the old moorings. There is no unanimity of teaching among them either regarding baptism or anything else.

The whole history of the Christian Church shows that infant baptism was practiced even in the earliest days.   In the sixteenth chapter of the Acts of the Apostles (v. 14 and 15) we read that Lydia and her whole household were baptized by St. Paul—the children included.   In Corinthians I., chap. xvi., v. 15, St. Paul intimates that he had baptized the whole household of Stephanas, the children not excluded. Just as the Jews circumcised their children, Christians baptize theirs, baptism being the fulfilment of the type circumcision : " In whom (Christ) also you are circumcised with circumcision not made by hand in the despoiling of the body of the flesh, but in the circumcision of Christ, buried with him in baptism."[2]

In the Council of Carthage, held A.D. 253, under St. Cyprian,

---

[1] P. 47, Philadelphia edition.   [2] Coloss., chap. ii., v. 11 and 12.

Bishop Fidus held that the baptism of children should be delayed till the eighth day after their birth, as was usual in the case of Hebrew circumcision. His opinion was rejected. " No one agreed with your opinion," writes St. Cyprian,[1] " and all held that the mercy and grace of God should be withheld from no one, especially not from children, who, recently born, have no sin except that of Adam." St. Augustine strengthens this testimony :[2] " Blessed Cyprian made no new decree in this case, but kept the faith of the Church against those who thought that no babe should be baptized until after the eighth day after its birth ; he and his fellow bishops holding that babes just born should be baptized."

The strongest reason, however, for insisting on the necessity of infant baptism is its necessity for salvation.

V. From the earliest date there were sectaries who denied the necessity of baptism. The Caians and Quintilians, in the second century, held that faith alone saves, and that consequently baptism is unnecessary. A similar heresy of the Wiclifites was condemned in the fifteenth session of the Council of Constance. Calvin, the founder of the Presbyterian religion, distinctly teaches, in a passage already quoted, that baptism is not necessary for salvation ; that the children of the faithful are saved by the " covenant " made between Christ and Christians, in virtue of which original sin is not imputed to them. Baptism does not purify children from original sin, but is only a sign of the divine promise. Nor is this sacrament necessary to adults, since they are justified by faith alone, and baptism is given to them only to nourish and strengthen their faith.[3]

In order to understand Catholic doctrine on the necessity of baptism, we must distinguish with the scholastics between necessity of means and necessity of precept. A thing is necessary as means when it is indispensable to attain the end ; necessary as precept when, although commanded, yet, if it is inculpably omitted, the end may still be attained. Thus, to illustrate from well-known Catholic doctrine, contrition or heart felt sorrow is indispensable in adults to obtain the remission of their sins ; the sorrow is necessary as means to the end ; while confession to a priest is only necessary of precept, for, if the sinner has no opportunity to confess, his heart felt sorrow and love of God will save him.[4]

We must also distinguish three forms of baptism, two of which are improperly so called. There is baptism of love, and baptism of blood.[5] Baptism of love is perfect charity, and contrition for

---

[1] Letter 59, to Fidus.   [2] Letter 166, to St. Jerome.

[3] *Quatenus erigendæ, alendæ, confirmandæque fidei nostræ datur, sumendu sest.*" Calvin's Instit., cap. xv., n. 14.

[4] Bulsano, p. 318.

[5] " Baptismus *flaminis, fluminis, et sanguinis,*" Theologi, *passim.*

sin, including the desire of baptism by water. Baptism of love can exist in adults alone, for babes are incapable of contrition, or the desire of baptism by water. To have baptism of love, perfect charity or love of God is required, so that the adult loves God above all things, and is ready to observe all the divine precepts. Imperfect contrition will not suffice. There must be also, in baptism of love, a disposition and explicit desire to receive baptism by water in him who knows that it has been instituted and commanded by Christ. An instance of baptism by love is the penitent thief on the cross, to whom, on account of his contrition, Christ promised paradise.[1]

The Council of Trent (sess. vi., de justif., cap. 4) decreed that since the promulgation of the Gospel there is "no translation from the state of old Adam to the state of grace without the laver of regeneration or the desire of it." Thus, then, in case of necessity, baptism in desire with the requisite conditions suffices for salvation. The practice of the Church from the sixth century has been according to this doctrine, for since that time she has said mass and offered prayers for catechumens dying before receiving baptism by water.

Baptism by blood, or by martyrdom, is another substitute for baptism by water. Even unbaptized babes, murdered out of hatred of the Christian religion, or of Christ, have always been considered saints in the Church;[2] hence the feast of the "Holy Innocents" in Christmas week. Martyrdom in the case of adults must be voluntary and accepted from supernatural motives. Hence, soldiers killed in a religious war are not considered martyrs. "Whosoever shall lose his life for My sake and the Gospel shall save it." These words of our Lord[3] justify Catholic teaching as to the efficacy of baptism by blood. St. Thomas epitomizes the faith of the Church on this point in these words:[4] "The shedding

---

[1] St. Luke xxiii., v. 43.

[2] What is the fate of children dying without baptism? Some Catholic theologians, like Pighius and Catharinus quoted by Bellarmine, teach that they enjoy a certain natural felicity, a species of terrestrial paradise. Cardinal Sfondratius, towards the end of the 17th century, taught that they are indeed excluded from the kingdom of heaven and the beatific vision, but not from the possession of natural good, nor are they condemned to everlasting punishment, nor liable to sin. He was denounced to Pope Innocent XII., A.D. 1697, for holding this opinion, but the Pope never condemned him. Bishop Frayssinous, in his celebrated *Conférences*, t. 3, writes: "We know that some theologians teach that children dying without baptism suffer on account of original sin not only the privation of eternal happiness, but also the sensible pain of fire; but the great majority of doctors, as St. Gregory Nazianzen, St. Thomas, and St. Bernard, deny this, and their benign opinion has never been condemned." It is the opinion of Frayssinous himself that these children are like "dethroned kings, deprived of a kingdom to the possession of which they could have aspired; like exiles, who grieve for a country which they shall never see again." They are happy, but their happiness is not without alloy.

[3] Mark viii., v. 35.　　　　　　　　[4] 3a pars Sum., q. 66, art. 11.

of blood for Christ, and the interior operation of the Holy Ghost,
are called baptisms because they have the same effect as baptism
by water."

Baptism by water is properly the sacrament. It is the gate of
the Church. It is necessary both of precept and of means, subject to the qualifications already specified. The text in St. John iii.,
v. 5, proves this: " Unless a man be born again of water and the
Holy Ghost, he cannot enter into the kingdom of God." Our Lord
commissioned His Apostles to teach and baptize all nations; but
the command to the Apostles to baptize has its correlative in the
duty of the nations to be baptized. If the former must preach because they are ordered to do so, the others must listen; if the
Apostles have the office to baptize, the nations have the duty to
receive the baptism. He that only believes is not the one who is
to be saved. Faith alone suffices not. He must also be baptized.
" He that believeth and is baptized shall be saved."[1]

The Presbyterian Assembly and its judge admit, as John
Calvin did, that faith is necessary to salvation. But our Lord puts
baptism in the same category as faith. He says that both are
necessary to salvation. By what authority do the Presbyterians
separate them? Are they not the "apostate" church instead of the
Catholic, since they rebel against the teaching of Christ, and refuse
to acknowledge the necessity of a sacrament which He declares to
be indispensable to salvation? " He that believeth and is baptized
shall be saved." These words of Christ stamp Presbyterian doctrine as a rebellion against the meaning of a self-evident text of
Scripture.

The condemnation of the Pelagians, who denied the necessity of
the sacrament of baptism in the early centuries, and the fifth canon
of the seventh session of the Council of Trent, clearly show how
the Catholic Church has always thought and taught on this subject.

VI. This matter becomes considerably clearer if we consider
what are the effects of the sacrament of baptism. The Calvinists
hold, with their founder, that sin remains in us even after baptism.
The Catholic Church teaches that it cleanses from original sin, as
well as from actual sin previously committed, destroys even the
temporal punishment due to it, confers grace by its own intrinsic
efficacy (*ex opere operato*), and imprints on the soul a spiritual character which can never be destroyed. St. Peter teaches that baptism obliterates sin, for he said to his hearers in his great sermon,
recorded in Acts ii. (v. 38), " Do penance and be baptized, every one
of you, in the name of Jesus Christ, for the remission of your sins."
In this text no distinction is made between original and actual sins;

----

[1] St. Mark xvi., v. 16.

all are remitted by baptism. Ananias told St. Paul (Acts xxii., v. 16), after his conversion, to " rise up and be baptized, and wash away thy sins." This indicates a real action, an internal purification, not a mere covering up or hiding of the foulness of the sinner. " But you are washed, but you are sanctified," writes St. Paul to the Corinthians,[1] thus indicating the inner efficacy of baptism by comparing its action on the soul to the action of water on the body. If baptism were a mere ceremony of initiation, the language of the Scripture regarding its cleansing powers would not be so strong. St. Justin[2] thus addresses the Jews in the second century of the Christian era : " There is no other way for the remission of sins,"—he includes both original and actual,—" except to acknowledge Christ, and to be washed by baptism." The fifth canon of the fifth session of the Council of Trent, treating of original sin, expresses the teaching of the whole Church in these words : " If any one denies that by the grace of our Lord Jesus Christ, conferred in baptism, the guilt of original sin is not remitted, or asserts that the whole of that which constitutes the true and proper reason of sin is not taken away, but only not imputed, let him be anathema." The meaning of these words is illustrated by the Catholic doctrine that justification consists in the interior purification of the soul by sanctifying grace, and that in the case of adults the coöperation of their own free will is essential to it. In order that a grown sinner should be justified, he must have the supernatural virtues of faith, hope, love of God above all things, sorrow for sin committed, and a purpose of amendment ; and besides these dispositions he must receive baptism, the instrumental cause of justification.[3]

The terms employed in holy Scripture, "to be born again," to be " regenerated," and " renewed," when speaking of the effects of baptism, show that it takes away all penalty, even temporal, due to sin. St. John Chrysostom, who certainly represents the early Greek Church in this matter, writes :[4] " Why is it " (baptism) " called the laver of regeneration ? Because it not only remits our sins and cleanses us from them, but acts on us, as if to make us be born again. It creates us anew, not making us out of the earth, but from another element—water. It does not simply wash the race, it moulds it anew ; for things that are only washed retain some vestiges of foulness ; but things recast in the furnace, and renewed by fire, come forth without spot or stain, and assume all their first splendor."

In consequence of the belief thus expressed, the Catholic Church has never imposed canonical penance on baptized adults for crimes

---

[1] 1 Cor. cviv., v. 11.   [2] Dial. contra Tryphon, n. 44.

[3] Bulsano, p. 302, and Catholic theologians passim.

[4] Catech. 1., ad Illum, n. 3.

committed before baptism. In all the early canons for public penance for those who were obliged to suffer temporal punishment in this world for sins confessed, and remitted in the sacrament of penance, there is not one for converted pagans, unless their sin was subsequent to their baptism. If catechumens were sometimes forced to do works of penance, it was only to prepare them better for the great sacrament of regeneration. Contrition, confession, and satisfaction are the parts of the sacrament of penance. A temporal punishment always accompanies it under the head of "satisfaction." But baptism is more sweeping in its effects, and washes away all penalty as well as all guilt.[1]

Each and every one of the Presbyterians holds that baptism justifies or sanctifies no one. The imputation of the merits of Christ does this. The mantle of Christ's redemption is thrown over the sins of the predestined, a paltry few out of the whole human race, so that their sins are hidden from the eyes of God. But their sins are there, nevertheless. Even the elect are foul and unclean, and nothing but sin. Even the elect are totally depraved, incapable of good or of merit. They have no free will; and certainly no will at all that can help them in the work of salvation. The elect, the handful of saints, are saved without any merit of theirs; and the immense majority of mankind are foreordained to hell's eternal realms of fire without any fault of theirs. God elects the few for His glory; and damns all the rest for His glory. Baptism is only a ceremony of initiation; it is no sign of grace, nor even of election; for even the majority of the Presbyterians are most likely to be damned, according to the judge's belief. The only ones sure of salvation are those who, like the learned judge, feel certain that they are confirmed in grace; and that all the hundreds of millions of the "apostate" Church are to be roasted for all eternity. This doctrine of blind predestination is abhorred and detested by the Catholic Church. She asserts the necessity of free will in adults for salvation; and proclaims the grand and ennobling truth that no man is damned without his own personal fault; and that it is possible for every member of the human race to work out his salvation by using the natural light of his intelligence, and the natural powers of his free will, in coöperation with grace, which is denied to no one. " *Facientibus quod in se est Deus non denegat gratiam*," is a well-known axiom of Catholic theology.[2] Baptism is not only the gate of initiation into the Church. It is also a sacrament which gives to the one who receives it a right to the other sacraments, and sanctifies the soul upon which it has been conferred. It washes, it justifies, and it

---

[1] Council of Trent, sess. vi., cap. 14, says in penance " not always is the whole penalty remitted, *as it is in baptism*."

[2] " Do your best and God will help you," is a free translation.

sanctifies.[1] "For as many of you as have been baptized in Christ, have put on Christ."[2] "He saved us by the laver of regeneration, and renovation of the Holy Ghost."[3] This putting on of Christ, what is it but the donning of the white robes of sanctifying grace? And this salvation by the laver of regeneration, what is it but justification through the waters of baptism, which washes away all sin and pours sanctifying grace into the soul? By baptism we put off the old man, and put on the new, who was created according to God; we become innocent, immaculate, pure, guiltless, beloved of God, heirs of God, and co-heirs of Christ.[4]

Baptism is one of the three sacraments which imprint an indelible character on the soul. This character is defined by St. Thomas as "a mark by which one of the faithful is deputed to receive or to give to others those things which pertain to divine worship."[5] Baptism imprints a character which entitles the baptized to receive the other sacraments; confirmation, in addition, is a mark of spiritual strength; while Holy Order imprints a character entitling the recipient to administer the sacraments to others. John Wiclef, in the fifteenth century, denied that any of the sacraments impressed a character on the soul; and so did the founder of the Presbyterians. These are his words:[6] "What they babble about an indelible character was unknown to the ancients, and savors more of magical incantations than of evangelical doctrine." But while the heresiarch thus ridiculed the teaching of the Church and refused to admit the existence of the character impressed on the soul by baptism, he invented a character of his own, and stamped it alike on the souls of elect and reprobate. He held that the "elect" are so confirmed in grace that they can never lose it; that "election" is ineffaceable and indelible; and that all the crimes, murder, adultery, or sodomy committed by the "elect" count for nothing. A Calvinistic "saint" is so confirmed in grace that he might sell himself to the devil, and yet never lose his "election"; while a Calvinistic reprobate might perform the most heroic acts of virtue and work miracles, and yet never be anything but a "reprobate." The character of "reprobation," as well as the character of "election," is indelible. Thus do men deny the reasonableness of what is divine, and substitute for it what is shocking to reason and common sense. St. Paul, according to St. Thomas and other great commentators, speaks of the character impressed by baptism in his Second Epistle to the Corinthians, chap. i., v. 21: "Now he that confirmeth us with you in Christ, and that hath anointed us, is God; who also hath sealed us." The Greek word

[1] I Cor. vi., v. 11; Ephes. v., v. 25.   [2] Gal. iii., v. 26.   [3] Tit. iii., v. 5.
[4] Council of Trent, sess. v., can. 5.   [5] Sum., 3d part, q. 63, art. 3.
[6] Calvin's Antidote, Concil Trid., Sess. VII., Can. 9.

for sealed, σφραγισαμενος, is very expressive. It signifies stamping, or imprinting a mark. The mark of circumcision, which certainly left a character, is called by St. Paul σφραγιδα—the seal of justice;[1] and circumcision was a most striking type of baptism. St. Jerome, speaking of baptism, says that by it God imprints a character on the soul.[2] So speak all the fathers and the councils, and thus teaches the infallible Church regarding the spiritual and indelible mark impressed by this sacrament. The sacraments which impress a character can be received only once. This doctrine was clearly vindicated in the celebrated controversy between Pope St. Stephen and St. Cyprian regarding the validity of baptism given by heretics. The Catholic Church rejected St. Cyprian's error.

In that controversy, however, St. Cyprian, Firmilian, and the other rebaptizers, did not insist on their practice, because they doubted that baptism imprints a character, but because they denied the validity of heretical baptism.[3] The indelible character and unity of this sacrament, according to the Fathers, is clearly intimated in the text: "It is impossible for those who were once illuminated"—a term frequently applied to the newly baptized in early Church history— ". . . . to be renewed again."[4] As circumcision, the figure, cannot be repeated, neither can baptism. Thus argues all Catholic antiquity; for, as there is but one Lord and one faith, so must there be but one baptism.[5]

The Presbyterians and others object also to the ceremonies used by the Catholic Church in administering baptism. They say we mix oil with the water, and thus destroy the matter of the sacrament. But since they attribute so little efficacy to it, deny its necessity, and consider it a mere sign of initiation, why strain at so slight a modification of the matter of it as is effected by the infusion of a drop of blessed oil or chrism? Fire swallowers who have such iron-clad throats as to gulp down John Calvin's eviscerating doctrine of total depravity and predestination, ought not to gag at a little oil infused into the water of baptism. Indeed, oil is what Presbyterianism wants, for the whole system is too acid for any ordinary man's digestion. The use of blessed oil, as we have already seen, is spoken of by St. Basil. St. Justin and Tertullian mention the exorcisms. St. Augustine speaks of the breathing on the head of the child by the priest. Origen speaks of the salt to be put on the tongue of the Catechumen. St. Ambrose writes about the spittle with which the ears and nose of the person to be baptized were touched. The use of this ceremony is sanctioned by

---

[1] Rom. vi., v. 11.   [2] Bulsano, p. 151.   [3] Turnelius, p. 526.
[4] Epis. to Heb. vi., v. 4.   [5] Ephes. iv., v. 5.

the example and by the very words of Christ Himself.[1] The anointing of the Catechumen with oil on the breast and shoulders before baptism, and with chrism afterwards, is mentioned by St. Clement, St. Chrysostom, and St. Ambrose. The proofs of the antiquity and universality of these ceremonies in the whole Christian Church may be found in Tournely, or in any Catholic theology treating of this subject. With these ceremonies was John Calvin christened ; with these was the devil expelled from him that afterwards returned, bringing seven others with him ; with oil and chrism was Calvin blessed by the Catholic priest of Noyon, in the north of France, A.D. 1509; and if that baptism was invalid, as our misguided friend, in the Presbyterian Convention, would have us believe, then, we repeat, the founder of the Presbyterian sect was a pagan.

---

[1] St. John ix., v. 6: " He spat on the ground, and made clay of the spittle, and spread the clay upon his eyes." " And spitting, he touched his tongue . . . . and said to him, Ephetha, which is, Be thou opened." St. Mark vii., v. 35.

THE NEW VERSION OF THE ENGLISH PROTESTANT BIBLE.

The Holy Bible containing the Old and New Testaments. Translated out of the original tongues : Being the version set forth A.D. 1611, compared with the most ancient authorities and revised. Cambridge : University Press, 1885.

MORE than fifteen years ago, in February, 1870, the Convocation of the Church of England, in its province of Canterbury, took action for a work that had long been felt to be sorely needed, a thorough revision of the English translation of the Bible published in 1611 with a fulsome address to King James I. That version is often called "the authorized version," although it was never directly authorized by any competent person or body. In fact, the term seems to have crept in from the mention on the title page of the lessons "appointed to be read in churches." And it would be curious indeed that the selection by the Catholic Church of portions of scripture could become in time a supposed approval of a Protestant version condemned by the Church. Certainly, though King James appointed translators, and the Convocation of Canterbury instituted companies for revision, this does not officially adopt in advance the work to be done. The revision of 1885 appears, like the edition of 1611, without any official authorization by the Head of the English Church, or by the Church of England convened in council. Yet though the revisers in their preface to the New Testament first guardedly speak of the 1611 Bible as "commonly known by the name of the Authorized Version," they constantly after that call it definitely the "Authorized Version."

The basis of the English Protestant Bible which has for the last two centuries been in general use is to be found in those published by Tyndale, 1526, and Coverdale, 1535, both ostensibly translated from the Hebrew and Greek, but really, to a great extent, mere versions of Luther's German Bible, which thus becomes the real parent of all the English Protestant versions. In regard to Tyndale Dr. Mombert in his recent work, issued by Bagster, leaves no manner of doubt. He is represented as a fair Greek scholar in 1523. "Yet any one who will impartially compare Tyndale's New Testament with Luther's will see," says the London *Athenæum*, "that our English translator is as much indebted, to say the least, to the German as to the Latin of Erasmus and to the Greek original."

" Luther's and Tyndale's New Testaments exhibit more than simple translations of the Greek. They contain introductions to the respective books, as well as marginal notes. As without a direct miracle the two translators could not write in two different languages exactly the same introductions and give literally the same comments upon the same passages, it will readily be conceded that Tyndale, who published his New Testament in 1525–6, copied Luther, whose Testament appeared in 1522." Tyndale copied nearly half of Luther's introduction, and 190 of 210 marginal references, without correcting errors in them. Of 69 glosses on St. Matthew, Tyndale transfers 59, often copying Luther so slavishly that at times we must go back to Luther to find what Tyndale means. In the translation, where Luther is free, Tyndale follows him. Where Tyndale left Luther he frequently went astray, and in the marginal notes which are clearly his own his violent abuse of the Pope, bishops and clergy exceeds even the virulence of Luther. So much for Tyndale's New Testament and its German origin.

As for Coverdale's, the case is equally clear. The original title as set up by Van Meteren at Antwerp in 1535 reads : " Biblia. That is, the holy scripture of the Old and New Testament faithfully and truly translated out of Douche and Latyn in to Englishe MDXXXV. Printed in the yeare of our Lord MDXXXV and fynished the fourth daye of October." A copy of this volume was lent by the Earl of Leicester to the Caxton celebration in 1877. When the sheets reached England, Nicholson set up a new title page, omitting the words from "and truly" down to " Latyn"; but the book as printed at Antwerp tells the story. The source was not the Hebrew and Greek, but Luther's " Douche," modified here and there by reference to the Latin, and, as Henry Stevens claims, the translation was made by Van Meteren, a Hollander.

The original English Protestant Bible was not made from the Hebrew and Greek, but from Luther's "Douche." The subsequent revisions were made to approximate it to the original languages; but as every reviser needed revision, the attempt has not been very successful.

Yet this is the volume so long held up as a model of English undefiled ! In no literature but English could a work if so mongrel and motley a character have ever attained the position of a standard for purity and elegance. In other tongues works that attain such eminence are the work of one individual full of his genius, representing the language in all its highest purity and elegance. Yet here a work made from a *Douche* original, with foreign ideas protruding at every pore, becomes a standard not only for matters religious but even for purity, elegance and symmetry!

As a knowledge of Greek and Hebrew increased, revisions were made to try and bring the current versions into greater conformity with the original languages. This gave rise to Matthews, in 1537. Taverner's, 1539, Cranmer's, 1540, the Geneva, 1557–60, the Bishops' Bible, 1568. These last two represented two diverse schools, the Bishops' that of the Church of England, while the Geneva was the work of the followers of Calvin. The last early revision, that made under the direction of King James, was an attempt to reconcile these two, but the Bible issued in 1611 did not supersede the Geneva or " Breeches " Bible, which was that adopted by all the Puritans, Presbyterians, and Independents in England and New England. The Geneva held its own till the time of Charles II., when the printing of the Bible was vested in the Universities of Oxford and Cambridge, which issued only the King James version. The Geneva thus ceased to be printed, and the non-conformist bodies had no alternative but to adopt the version which they disliked. If the Puritans in Old and New England accepted the King James at last, it was only as a matter of necessity; it was as repugnant to their feelings as it is to those of Catholics, on whom of late they delight in forcing it.

It has been the fashion to extol the King James Bible as a model of English, but the German Luther influence from the outset gave the Protestant versions a foreign tinge, and the violence of Tyndale against the Pope and the Bishops, against the Church and all connected with it, made him avoid, as much as he could, the terms and expressions which seemed to recall devotional use in the Church; this required the adoption of new, local, or antiquated words. The same spirit prevailed in all the revisions, and after a time, by constant reprinting, the new words came into general use. But the Bible of 1611 is not the English of any part of England at any particular time. Philologically it has no real value. Its influence for the last two centuries has undoubtedly been great, its very errors and misprints being so ingrained in the minds of the people that the revision, though adopted, will scarcely in a century consign them to oblivion.

The original Rheims-Douay (1583–1609), which we Catholics have unwisely discarded for Bishop Challoner's, is, on the contrary, the work of one man of acknowledged learning, in the best English of his time, not avoiding but embodying all devotional language to which the faithful had long been accustomed. It is, moreover, universally recognized as extremely faithful, while not one of the Protestant versions, from the Tyndale to the King James, has escaped severe censure for unfaithfulness, and the constant revisions are an acknowledgment of the charge. That the King James revisers were influenced by the Catholic version has long been known, and the present revisers acknowledge it frankly.

Indeed Catholic labors in translating the Scriptures and presenting them to the people seem never to be matters of indifference. If the revisers and translators of King James' day awaited the appearance of the complete labors of the Catholic scholar, Gregory Martin, as his volumes successively issued from the foreign presses to which penal laws had compelled him to resort, the translators of the Victorian era seem to have been no less observant. Besides the weightier matters of substance which occupied the minds of the latter, there were considerations of form engaging their attention, and to two of these they refer especially. One of these, the consecutive printing of the verses with the figures not breaking in on the sentence, but ranged in the margin, brings the new Protestant Bible to the wholesome look of the grand old version issued from the presses of Fogny at Rheims in 1582, and of Lawrence Kellam at Douay in 1609-10—those noble volumes of our forefathers which it was a penal matter unto death for them to possess in the days when Protestantism denied the authentic scriptures to the Catholics, who could read them only by stealth and in secret. Another point is the presenting of the poetical portions of the Holy Scriptures in the form in which poetry is habitually given, and in this they follow the idea of the learned but most erratic Catholic priest, Rev. Alexander Geddes, two volumes of whose very curious version of the Bible appeared at London in 1792, dedicated to Lord Petre, whose present successor sits in the House of Lords in his priestly garb.

In their version of the New Testament the present revisers follow no printed Greek text, and no one ancient manuscript; but formed a text of their own, which they translated. In regard to the Old Testament they made no such attempt to create a text. "The Massoretic text of the Old Testament Scriptures," they admit, "has come down to us in manuscripts which are of no very great antiquity, and which all belong to the same family or recension." The most ancient Hebrew manuscript at the time of Luther was only about six hundred years old, and was penned nearly a thousand years after the birth of our Lord. But Protestants are committed to the Hebrew, and the revisers "have thought it most prudent to adopt the Massoretic text as the basis of their work." The text used by the Septuagint translators no longer exists; that employed by St. Jerome is lost. The earlier Protestant translators and revisers rejected the aid of the Septuagint and of St. Jerome, who translated in Egypt and Palestine, with older Hebrew manuscripts and greater aids to secure accuracy than scholars in England, where Hebrew studies were then in their infancy, could possibly enjoy. Nothing could exceed the arrogant presumption of the small body of scholars who had acquired a smattering of Hebrew, and could thus refuse to profit by the labors of far better scholars, who translated with far superior advantages and with deep reverence, translating as faithfully as possible into Greek and Latin the Hebrew Scriptures, as they stood before and soon after the Christian era, when the original text had not been manipulated in the anti-Christian school of Massorah.

Independent of the sanction given to the Septuagint by the habitual use which our Lord and His disciples made of it, its value as an early rendering of an uncorrupted text by competent scholars must, even to an agnostic, be of great weight.

The Hebrew language, from the time in which Moses wrote the Pentateuch, to that when Esdras wrote, a period of more than a thousand years, must have undergone great vicissitudes in its vocabulary, grammatical forms, and expressions. The literature of no country covering such a period could be read as one work, the earlier writings would be archaic and obsolete to those who could read fluently those of the later period. A nation which had been in bondage to Chanaanite, Philistine, Egyptian, and Assyrian, must have adopted, from time to time, many terms from their conquerors, and we know that their proper language was, in the end, virtually superseded by the Greek, in the ordinary intercourse of life. More than a general knowledge of the Hebrew of any one period is requisite for the understanding of the Old Testament, while the New Testament demands merely a competent knowledge of the Greek spoken in one district for a period of fifty years, and for the intelligence of that dialect of Greek, the language of the deutero-canonical books, and of the Septuagint, habitually used by the sacred writers of the New Testament, affords immense aid.

For the intelligence of the Hebrew scriptures, there are no contemporaneous literature for any period, no codes of laws, no royal proclamations, no history, biography, poem, or tale. This renders such adventitious aid as that afforded by the Septuagint translators of the highest value. The dictionary to be formed from their work is the basis of our knowledge of the Hebrew.

The Hebrew text was not made the corner-stone of Christian teaching, but the Septuagint version was. With that and the deutero-canonical books, and the New Testament in Greek, the Church carried her teaching throughout the Roman Empire, and from them in time made her Latin translation. She multiplied her manuscripts in Greek and Latin. When the various heresies arose, not one of them attempted to justify its error by setting up the superiority of the Hebrew text. It was not till the 16th century that this idea was put forward, and it was then no longer possible to revert to the Hebrew text as it stood in the time of our Lord. All that the heresiarchs of that time could rely upon was the Massoretic text adopted after the Christian era, and as a Jewish safeguard against Christianity. The school of Massorah rejected all the books in Greek as having led to Christianity, and rejected the New Testament. Ben Sira or Ecclesiasticus, which existed in Hebrew, this school rejected because it favored the doctrine of the Holy Trinity. If Protestants reject the book, it must be on the same ground as will justify any one of them in rejecting the New Testament. The Hebrew school at Massorah, influenced by such feelings, necessarily adopted every reading unfavorable to Christian claims, just as Protestant scholars do every one unfavorable to Catholic doctrines. Thus the Hebrew text as it stands is imperfect, biassed, modern, and we possess no authorities to effect the restoration of the true text. How, then, can the current Hebrew text be a safer basis for translation than the version which the Apostles and their successors employed when converting the world to Christ?

In no part of the Scriptures was the presumptuous ignorance of the King James translators more manifest than in their rendering of the terms relating to the natural history of the Holy Land. It is inconceivable how men, living in England, utterly ignorant of the fauna of that portion of the world where the events described in the sacred pages took place, could assume to be better able to give a proper equivalent for a Hebrew term than men living in Egypt and Palestine while Hebrew was yet spoken and Greek in daily use, and who knew every animal and bird, as well as the learned and ordinary terms for each of them, the names yet in use as well as the names that had ceased to obtain.

Probably the most absurd error in the King James version was in Gen. 36: 24. " This was that Anah that found the mules in the wilderness." Discovering herds of wild mules would certainly have been worthy of note. But in the Revised Version the animals disappear, and for " mules " we read " hot springs," recognizing the accuracy of the Vulgate, " aquas calidas," rendered " hot waters" by Gregory Martin and Challoner. Almost as gross an error occurs in Isaias 14: 23. " I will also make it a possession for the bittern;" this last word occurring again in 34: 11. Now the bittern is a bird, and belongs to the heron family, but the revisers translate the Hebrew word *kippôd*, not bittern, but "porcupine," admitting that the vaunted translators whose work had been held up to us as almost divine confounded a quadruped with a bird, and did it as an exercise of the right of private judgment, for the Septuagint and Vulgate were there to caution them, rendering kippôd by εχίνος in Greek, and *ericius* in Latin, which Gregory Martin, in the original Douay, translated plainly " hedgehog," though Bishop Challoner, apparently fearing to hurt the feelings of our separated brethren, left untranslated " ericius." Another instance of confounding creatures totally different occurs in Proverbs 30 : 28, where the King James version reads: "The spider taketh hold with her hands." The Revised Version introduces us to an animal of another genus, and gives: " The lizard taketh hold with her hands," recognizing the fidelity of the Vulgate, which reads: " Stellio manibus nititur," our English translators retaining the name of that species of lizard. In Leviticus 11 : 16, the King James translated " bathaya'nah" by the word owl, and "shachaph " by cuckoo. The revisers render these words by ostrich and sea-mew, recognizing the accuracy of the Latin terms " struthio "and " larus " of the Vulgate, rendered ostrich and larus or stern by the Douay and Challoner.

In a similar manner, the ferret becomes the gecko, and the tortoise a great lizard, and the snail a sand-lizard. The badger-skins which cover the tabernacle become sealskins, neither being likely to be found in sufficient quantity in the desert. As to the term " tô " or " teô," which the King James translators rendered wild bull, and the Vulgate gave as oryx, the revisers follow the Vulgate, and translate antelope. The old Douay retained the word oryx, correct and now intelligible ; but Challoner, deferring, as he often did, to the Protestant version, gave " wild goat" in one place (Deut. 14: 5), and "wild ox" in another (Isaias 51 : 20). " Dayah," translated formerly vulture (Lev. 11 : 14 ; Deut. 14 : 13 ; Isaias 34 : 15), is now rendered kite, as in our Catholic Bibles. In the same way, " dukipath," instead of lapwing, becomes, as in the Douay and Challoner, the hoopoe (Lev. 11 : Deut. 14).

In Gen. 11 : 3 and kindred passages the utterly indefinite word " slime " is now aided by " bitumen " in the margin, the word used in our old Douay, though Bishop Challoner substituted " slime " for it.

The gnat recalls a blunder not in the original King James of 1611, but in later editions, which has given rise to a proverb in common use that will not readily give way to the true rendering. In Matt. 23 : 24, " Strain out a gnat and swallow a camel," was misprinted : " Strain at a gnat and swallow a camel," and the erroneous reading became general, although it never crept into our Catholic Bibles. The revisers restore the correct reading, " strain out."

The " linen yarn " which the translators of King James' day contrived to find in 3 Kings 10 : 28, has disappeared with the peacocks in Job 39 : 13.

These glaring errors have long been recognized among Protestants, but in popular works on the Bible, in order apparently to avoid shocking the unbounded confidence of the ignorant masses in this faulty and corrupt translation, the attempt was made to throw the fault on the Scriptures themselves and the holy men inspired by God who penned them. Thus they would speak of the porcupine as the "bittern of scripture," of other animals as "the ferret of scripture," "the wild ox of scripture," etc., making the Word of God and the inspired writers responsible for the presumptuous and self-willed ignorance of the men who under the direction of King James and his regulations gave the edition to English readers. A more honest feeling, compelled in no small degree by the movement for a purer translation, begun in this country among the Baptists, has at last forced authorities in the Church of England to make this tardy effort to present the Word of God in a better form, more conformable to the original.

Ignorance of Oriental customs was profound in England after the Reformation, while among Catholics, in consequence of pilgrimages to the Holy Land and the constant residence there of Franciscan Fathers, more general knowledge prevailed. The King James translators knew nothing of the use by Eastern women of kohl or antimony to make the eye look large and lustrous. They knew, however, that English ladies painted their faces. Hence they rendered 2 Kings 9: 30, "she painted her face;" and Jerem. 4: 30, "thou rendest thy face with painting," certainly a very curious performance. But the revisers translate "eyes" "eyes," and not "face," and give us "she painted her eyes" in the first text, and in the second "thou enlargest thine eyes with paint." Here the last word is very vague, while our old Douay was definite, "shalt paint thine eyes with stibick stone." The name of one of Job's daughters alludes to this cosmetic, Kerenhappuch (horn for antimony).

In the perversions of the Scriptures against which Catholics have constantly protested, the revisers have been evidently afraid to do right. Most of them remain. The spurious additions to the Lord's Prayer in St. Matthew and St. Luke have, indeed, been abandoned, and 1 Cor. 11 : 27 they at last give honestly, " eat this bread *or* drink this cup," instead of " and " as the translators have hitherto persistently done. In Jeremias 11 : 19 they admit "bread" to be the real translation of the Hebrew, though they do not put it in the text. The passage in 1 Cor. 9: 5 undergoes a curious change. The revisers will not translate ἀδελφὴν γυναῖκα, "a sister, a woman," or "a sister, a wife," as in the King James, but "a wife that is a believer," with "Gr. sister" in the margin! A Mormon elder will probably find authority here for leaving some wives at home on account of their scepticism. " Marriage is honorable in all" (Heb. 13 : 4) reads now : "Let marriage be in honor among all." In St. James 5 : 16 they at last "confess their sins"; good works are allowed to appear in Apoc. 19 : 8 as "righteous acts," the Blessed Virgin is "endued with grace" in the margin (Luke 1 : 28). As in the New Testament the pagan God Hades, whose name in the possessive case was used in Greek for hell, is used directly for hell, so in the Old Testament "sheol," the Hebrew term, is retained and replaces hell in some texts and "grave" in others. In the Concordance of the Revised Version the word hell will disappear in a host of passages. "In Isaiah xiv.," we are told, "where 'hell' is used in more of its original sense, and is less liable to be misunderstood .... the revisers have contented themselves with leaving 'hell' in the text, and have connected with other passages by putting 'sheol' in the margin." The word is, therefore, not uniformly rendered, and this involves great confusion.

The American revisers urged the introduction of Jehovah throughout for the ineffable name, but the English revisers adhered to the old version, printing Lord or God in small capitals to express it. As Jehovah is a word of very doubtful accuracy, they certainly acted wisely in not filling their volume with a word for others to alter hereafter. The uniform usage of Jew and Christian, in expressing the ineffable name by Adonai, or Lord and God, ought to prevail against any rash change at this late day to a word which many hold to be utterly incorrect.

"Abaddon," for destroyer, and "ashêrah," for grave, are, like "sheol," instances where they now follow what the Douay translators were condemned for, that is, retaining words of the original untranslated.

The language of the King James has not been generally modernized, although the American revisers called for very sweeping changes in this respect. The substitution of "plough" for "ear" is one of the few. "Bolled," in the sense of "podded for seed," is retained, and its use in the cotton districts of this country makes it sufficiently intelligible.

The suggestions of the American Old Testament Revision Company fill nearly sixteen pages of close type, and show that had their counsel been followed a radically new translation would have been the result. When we remember the persistence with which Protestants in this country have insisted on forcing the King James Bible on Catholics in schools, courts, and institutions, it seems strange to find a learned company from among them insisting on such sweeping changes and corrections, to which the English revisers hesitated to agree.

On the whole, the new revision of the oft-amended English Protestant version is far from meeting the wants of the intelligent and honest Christian. The Protestant expected a translation of the Word of God, on which he could ground his salvation as a Rule of Faith. The English-speaking Catholic expected, at least, as the nineteenth century was drawing to a close, that a body of English Protestant scholars, selected as the ablest in knowledge of Hebrew and Greek, most profound in all studies regarding the weight and critical value of the earliest known manuscripts of the Sacred Volume or parts thereof, well versed in all the secular learning that contributes to a due intelligence and comprehension of the time and places in which the Sacred Writers lived,—expected from such an array of Protestant learning a translation which on the selection of the text and the fidelity, clearness, and harmony of the Version given would, for purposes of study, replace to the general reader the original texts, and give the reader, with good editions of those texts before him, a reflex of it which he could respect and to some extent rely upon in occasional and incidental studies of his own. Both these classes have been sadly disappointed.

It may be said that the revisers were not free, that they were limited by rules, and that these rules or principles kept up the fable that the King James Bible was authorized, and was something so sacred that it must not be touched by rude or profane hands, when in fact its shortcomings were so notorious.

"The text to be adopted," they were told, was to "be that for which the evidence is decidedly preponderatory." Now the text of the Hebrew used by the King James translators was certainly not a critical one for which any great merit could be claimed. Yet here the learning of Protestant scholars was required to adhere to that text as translated in the seventeenth century, unless they had decidedly preponderating evidence against it. Such evidence was almost unattainable. As they themselves say: "The Received, or, as it is commonly called, the Massoretic Text of the Old Testament Scriptures, has come down to us in manuscripts which are of no very great antiquity, and which all belong to the same family or recension. That other recensions were at one time in existence is probable from the variations in the Ancient Versions, the oldest of which, namely the Greek or Septuagint, was made, at least in part, some two centuries before the Christain era." It is astounding to hear this collected learning term the existence of other Hebrew texts rather than the present recension of the Massoretic merely and only "probable," for if they concede that the Septuagint was made two centuries before the Christian era, they must not proba-' bly, but most certainly and assuredly, have had something premassoretic; and that at that time other recensions were in existence is certain, not probable.

The revisers were required " to introduce as few alterations as possible into the text of the *Authorized* Version consistently with such faithfulness," and " to limit, as far as possible, the expression of alterations to the language of the Authorized and earlier English Versions."

Compelled thus to render a kind of cultus to the King James, "which," they say, "for more than two centuries and a half had held the position of an English classic," they departed from it only " where they disagreed with the translators of 1611 as to the meaning or construction of a word or sentence ; or when, for the sake of uniformity, to render such parallel passages as were in identical Hebrew by the same English words, so that an English reader might know at once by comparison the difference in the translation corresponded to a difference in the original ; or where the language of the Authorized Version was liable to be misunderstood by reason of its being archaic or obscure ; or finally, where the rendering of an earlier English Version seemed preferable; or where by an apparently slight change it was possible to bring out more fully the meaning of a passage."

Thus terms of natural history were changed " only where it was certain that they were incorrect and there was sufficient evidence for the substituted reading."

In this department, as in many others, the doubtful and unauthorized renderings were left, simply because they could not find preponderating evidence that the rendering was wrong, and that some other rendering was right. Yet if Jehovah was to be introduced as a supposed Hebrew word, and Sheol, and Abaddon, and Asherah, Asherim, Asheroth, why could not Hebrew names of certain animals be retained where the English equivalent was uncertain or did not exist ?

To adhere to error merely because it is old can never be justified ; truth is older than the oldest error, and in mere point of time is more respectable. So, too, in regard to proper names. The translators of 1611 adopted a system of transliteration of their own for giving Hebrew names in English. They cut away from the names used in Catholic works in their own country from the early times, and were apparently guided to no little extent by Luther's " Douche" Bible. The names as they gave them were in many cases neither Hebrew nor accepted English, and with that freedom which they assumed unto themselves they did not follow out their own system. Here was another difficulty for the revisers. They accordingly tell us that they " endeavored to ascertain the system of transliteration adopted by the translators of the Authorized Version, and to carry it out with somewhat greater consistency. They have not, however, attempted anything like rigid uniformity, and have left unchanged all those names which by usage have become English; as, for instance, Moses, Aaron, Jeremiah, Ezekiel, and the like." The unauthorized translators of 1611 had no such respect for names which by usage had become English; why should those of 1885 be bound to follow their errors? Is not this deliberately preferring darkness to light, and clinging to error simply because it is old?

One point they do not mention at all, and it is a curious one. The Reformers rejected the Septuagint, the version of the Old Testament which, with the deutero-canonical books, was borne by the envoys of Christ throughout the world as they announced the Gospel and established the Church. They rejected this and went back to pick up a Hebrew text formed to preserve the unbelieving remnant of the house of Israel from becoming influenced by faith in Christ as the Messias. They made this anti-Christian recension the basis of their retrograde Christianity, but Providence permitted that they should retain the Septuagint names for most of the books of the Old Testament, as they do to this day. The revisers do the same, apparently without a thought—certainly without a line of apology. Translating the opening book of the Scriptures, why do they say, " The First Book of Moses, commonly called *Genesis*," and ignore entirely its Hebrew name? Why do they retain the Greek term Genesis, when they discard the Greek version? They do not even in any note or otherwise give the Hebrew, while our Catholic Bibles do, and tell us that " The Hebrews call it *Beresith*, from the word with which it begins," following the Vulgate, " Liber Genesis, Hebraice Beresith," in which, as on the Cross, the Hebrew, Greek, and Latin combine.

The Revised Version is after all only a cramped revision of a faulty and patched translation, made originally from the bold German rendering of Luther, altered by reference to the Latin, and then repeatedly by such Hebrew as they could get. The English Protestant Bible is presented to its unfortunate adherents as their religion, to quote Chillingworth's saying. If it is to be their religion, ought it not to be made from the best possible text, with the utmost sincerity, and entirely free from any subserviency to errors, no matter how respectable they had grown by age? If man's salvation is to depend on a translation, if man's damnation may be the result of wrong rendering, why should the opinions of fallible men of other days, or their ignorance, or their prejudice, or the commands of princes or popular opinion stand for a moment to sway translators, who if they touch the Sacred Volume at all, should do it only to present God's eternal truth to men in an intelligible language?

In the words of a book they reject (Wisdom, v. 6), they may well exclaim: Ergo erravimus! "Ergo erravimus a via veritatis, et justitiæ lumen non luxit nobis, et Sol intelligentiæ non est ortus nobis."

THE SCHOOL QUESTION IN BELGIUM.

BELGIUM is a country in which we are readily interested. The kingdom is new, but the country and people are old friends of ours. We separate Fleming and Walloon from Hollander as easily in the past as in the present. Flanders, Brabant, Namur, Liége, Hainaut, Limburg are grouped in our mind quite as well under Austrian or Spanish, as under Burgundian rule. To disunite the united Netherlands costs us no effort. Around Bruges, Ghent, Brussels, Antwerp, Liége, we gather historical associations that are quite independent of Utrecht or of Amsterdam. Two centuries and a half of a beautiful art, of painting, of architecture, and of engraving, make us intimate with our Belgium, rather than with the Netherlands. From the story of the so-called Reformation we have become especially familiar with the people who are Belgians to-day. The French Revolution, the Napoleonic wars, fatal Waterloo, the constrained union with Holland, have served to keep alive an interest, not abated by the revolution and separation.

A peaceful nation for fifty years back, Belgium has attracted little notice. The wonderful political changes of the last half-century have not affected her. In Germany, France, Austria, Russia, Italy, more active forces have been at work. With the internal and external movements in these powerful nations the daily press keeps us acquainted. Each morning brings 'its telegrams about their government policy, diplomatic moves, economic conditions. Thus informed in the daily history of the greater nations, we are prepared to frame intelligent opinions concerning their rulers and affairs. But Belgium has dropped out of notice. We are unable to follow her history day by day. For long spaces of time it seems as though the country had ceased to make history. Suddenly, however, the foreign correspondent telegraphs of an election, a riot, or a ministerial change. He not only states facts, but expresses judgments. Having but one version of the facts, unable to assure ourselves of its truth or falsehood, we are compelled either to take the judgment of the correspondent or the editor, or to suspend our own. If we accept the facts as stated, we are as likely as not to be misled. The facts generally have to do with the action of a Liberal party and of a Conservative party. Whatever is called " liberal " finds favor with Americans ; wherefore the American editor willingly sees the facts with a Liberal eye, and out-liberals Liberals in the expression of Liberal judgments. Having us at a disadvantage, he seems determined to keep us where he puts us. We have but one side of the story ; he sees that we get no other.

The events of the last twelve months forcibly illustrate our position in regard to Belgian affairs. In June, 1884, a Conservative replaced a Radical ministry, and in the following August a bill concerning primary education was carried through both houses of the Belgian parliament. Of these two facts the press informed us, at the same time giving us to understand that the school-bill was an especially iniquitous and inexcusable measure. Nothing more was heard about Belgian affairs until the 20th of October, when we learned from the cable of a great Liberal victory in the elections, and of a popular condemnation of the school-law. Later dispatches reported slight disorders, and a few arrests, and then came a story of mobs, rioting, the smashing of convent windows, and the interference of the civic guard. On the 24th the news was that the Premier, Malou, had resigned, and that the king had requested the withdrawal of two of the ministry. From Paris, on the 25th, it was telegraphed that an attempt had been made on the king's life. Brussels dispatches of the 27th stated that a new ministry had been formed, and had received the king's approval ; while the telegrams of the 28th assured us of Liberal disapproval. After this date the wires ceased working, and we have since heard little or nothing of Belgian politics.

From the dispatches here quoted, and they include all that were published, no one could gain a correct view of the real course of events, and, much less, of the questions at issue. The facts are hinted at, rather than completely and fairly stated. Most of the editorials on Belgian affairs, written at the time, are excusable on the supposition that the writers had no closer acquaintance with the internal politics of the country than the telegrams gave them. But an intelligent view of Belgian parties and issues, and more especially of the school question, can be had only by one who is fairly acquainted with the political history of Belgium since the allied powers handed over the country to Dutch rule. The issues that have so recently agitated the country are not to be judged by a superficial consideration of the immediate circumstances.

They are bound up with the history of Belgium, and with the life of the people. The dividing line between Liberal and Conservative has long been the religious question. But it was not always so.

Under the Dutch government the people of Belgium were a unit on the religious question. Inasmuch as there were Belgian Liberals, as distinguished from Belgian Catholics, the Liberal was not so much anti-Orange as pro-Catholic. The liberality he proclaimed found its chief and practical argument in the government's illiberal treatment of Catholics. The freedom of the Catholic press was hampered by the law and the ministry; the Catholic religion was aimed at, when religious education in the schools was forbidden, the policy of the Dutch government being to Protestantize Belgium. Against Catholic, more than against Liberal writers and speakers, was the law directed which made public criticism of the acts of the king, or of his officials, punishable with fine and imprisonment.

What made a Belgian Liberal was opposition to anti-Catholic laws. The Liberal wanted a constitution, so did the Catholic; the Liberal wanted relief from Dutch official preponderance, so did every Belgian. Practically, the Liberal was neither more nor less than a Catholic, and the Catholic was a Liberal.

So united in aim were Liberals and Catholics that in 1825 they combined their forces for the attainment of Belgian rights, emphasizing their unity of aim in the name they chose for their organization—" The Union." For three years the Union labored through the press—almost wholly a Catholic press,—to create a public opinion; and it was only in 1828, when this public opinion had been formed and in some degree unified, that the Union began to act as a real political body, with the announced purpose of obtaining an enlargement of the liberties of the citizen and religious toleration. Zealously did the Union now pursue its patriotic aims. The able men of the country were all of one mind, and all ready and determined to speak that mind.

Non-Catholics are not apt in any wise to associate the Jesuits with so-called Liberalism; and therefore it may somewhat surprise the non-Catholic to hear that the Jesuits gave the first great impulse to the Union, and to the cause of Belgian independence. Giving this impulse, the Jesuits do not appear in the time-honored rôle of adroit political schemers; unfortunately for themselves, they were playing the part so many modern governments have found it convenient to cast them for,—that of political scapegoats. To the Belgian of the Union, this was intolerable; he rallied to the cause of the Jesuits. De Potter, that Liberal of Liberals, took up his bold and biting pen. In the *Niederlandische Courier* he sharply rebuked the ministry for its treatment of the Order. The Jesuit was a man like other men, and De Potter claimed for him the same liberty and the same rights that other men claimed or enjoyed. He taunted the ministry with playing the transparent, but effective, trick—as transparent and unfortunately as effective in our day,—of dubbing all honest men who opposed its policy as Jesuits. Arrested for this, De Potter was tried on December 20th, 1828, fined a thousand guilders, and condemned to imprisonment for eighteen months. His condemnation moved the whole Belgian people, and, more than any other single act, prepared the revolution.

What question did the Belgian leaders now choose to unite and assure the country, and to gain its confidence? The question of the State monopoly of education. Through the press, and through a systematic publication and distribution of pamphlets, this monopoly was bitterly attacked during the year 1829. At the same time the Catholics, through committees, drew up and signed petitions, asking guarantees of liberty; and the Liberals, in the same organized way, presented petitions, asking guarantees for the Catholics. The representatives of the people gave official expression to the popular demands; the Liberals De Celles and De Brouckère, and the Catholic De Gerlache, claiming from the Chambers, in December, 1829, freedom of instruction, of speech, and of the press.

De Potter's condemnation for his defence of the Jesuits had unexpected consequences. The tyranny of the condemnation excited all men against a government that seemed to acknowledge no rights in the governed. Secretly, societies were formed with a view of drawing up a constitution, and of preparing the people for its acceptance. However peaceable the intentions of the Union, and of the constitution societies, a new and stringent press-law, De Gerlache's daring speech against it in the Chamber of Deputies, and the wholesale prosecutions under this law, supplied material to those who looked to a forcible separation from Holland.

The king's birthday (August 24th, 1830) saw Brussels barricaded; by the 8th of September a "Committee of Safety" had been elected. On the 29th of the same month this committee pronounced itself the "Provisional Government of Belgium"; on the 4th of October the independence of Belgium was proclaimed; and on November 24th the freely elected representatives of the people assembled at Brussels as a "National Congress," and declared the Orange-Nassau family forever deprived of authority in Belgium. A draft of a constitution was submitted on the next day. The three great guarantees of this constitution were freedom of the press, freedom of education, and freedom of association. Whatever differences of opinion were disclosed during the debates as to the modes of election, the division of powers, and the character of the government, there was unanimity as to these three principles, for which the whole country had so long and so patiently worked, and for which, in the end, it shed its blood.

On the matter of education, the constitution, adopted without dissent on the 7th of February, 1831, spoke with no uncertain tone : " Education is free ; every measure impeding its freedom is forbidden." The large interest that Catholics had in this freedom may be judged from the fact that out of a population of 4,000,000 there were not 10,000 who did not profess the Roman Catholic faith. Evidently the liberties that Belgium enjoys are liberties won by Catholics; without the support of Catholics, who were the nation, those calling themselves distinctively " Liberals " were powerless to gain for themselves one single right they now enjoy.

De Gerlache, De Theux, De Mérode, Deschamps, the Abbé de Foere, Vilain XIV.,—behind these Catholic leaders were the clergy and the people. They organized the country for liberty of speech, of the press, of worship, of education. These rights they had determined to compel from the Dutch government, but not by revolution. There they stopped. But when the people moved, and the Orange army threatened the land, they went forward in the field and in the council. With a large and generous patriotism they gave the honors of office to Liberals, not distinguishing religious profession, and freely sacrificing the personal to the great aims of freedom and political unity. By Catholic votes the Liberal leaders were placed in office, intrusted with the Presidency of the Congress, the Regentship, and the first Ministry, in which not a single representative Catholic name appears ; but through the Catholic leaders the negotiations with the intervening powers were carried on, through them were effected the transactions with the candidates for the new throne. The great names were Catholic, the great families were Catholic, the wealth of the country was Catholic, the producing power of the country was Catholic, all the great forces and interests were Catholic. The freedom fought for, and won, was not the freedom for ten thousand who did not profess Catholicity, but freedom for the country, and the country was Catholic.

When there was question of nominating the Duc de Nemours to the throne, it was not De Gerlache alone that opposed his election, but, with him, the Liberals Lebeau and Devaux ; and their joint opposition was based on the ground, that close relations with France might endanger the freedom of religion and education, which Belgium had so dearly gained. Prince Leopold, who was elected king July 7th, 1831, understood the country. When De Mérode, De Brouckère, Vilain XIV., and the Abbé de Foere went to London to consult with him, in the April before his election, he showed his knowledge and his wisdom, saying to them: " I am especially pleased to see that the Belgians are a truly religious-minded people ; a country that lovingly holds to its religious convictions is usually moral, and on that account more easily governed." Now, the religious mind that Leopold saw in the Belgians was a Catholic mind; and nothing can be truer than that Catholic-mindedness and Catholic convictions make a moral country, and one easily governed.

The clause of the constitution which established freedom of instruction, and forbade any measure impeding that freedom, provided that public instruction given at the expense of the State should be regulated by the law. Not till 1834 did the government take up the question of State-aided schools; then the ministry presented a draft of a law concerning elementary education, whereby the State would have an influence over elementary schools in communes where the schools were founded and supported by State funds. This bill was thrown out, and the whole school system placed in the hands of the communes.

There it lay undisturbed until 1840 when the ministry announced its intention of bringing in the regulating law suggested by the constitution. This law, the ministers proclaimed, should be drawn in the spirit of the constitution, and should guarantee to the youth of the country the fullest liberty of moral and religious instruction in all schools dependent on the commune, the province, or the State. However, it was not until 1842, and under a new ministry that a school-law was passed. How well this law met the wishes of the country is apparent from the vote by which it was carried. The Senate was unanimous, while in the Chamber of Deputies there were but three opposing votes. An examination of the measure will show that this remarkable agreement of the Liberal and Catholic members of the two Houses was due to the fact that the law was drawn in the spirit of the Union, of the political traditions before and since the revolution, of the revolution itself, in fine, in the spirit of the Belgian people. The law aimed to give them that liberty of which they had been so long deprived, and to obtain which they had gone to the length of making a new nation.

The education of the people was left with the people, where it had been placed in 1834. There were, in 1840, some 2600 communes in Belgium, with 5189 schools. Of the schools, 2109 were communal schools. The State, having no means, had thus far contributed little or nothing to primary education. But it is apparent that the people had not been idle. They desired that their children should enjoy the benefits of education.

The purpose of the law of 1842 was to assure the further extension of primary education, and to systematize the management of the schools. It provided that every commune should have at least one primary school. The commune, however, was not required to build a school; it might arrange with a private school, within the commune limits, to furnish its children the primary education specified by the law. Such private schools were to be known as "adopted schools." Equally reasonable and liberal was the further provision, that any commune which could show that its private schools sufficed for the primary instruction of the children, should not be required to found a communal school, or to "adopt" a school.

Article VI. of the law made clear what was meant by primary instruction. This "comprises, *necessarily*, instruction in religion and morals, reading, writing, arithmetic, the elements of history, etc. The instruction in religion and morals shall be given under the direction of the minister of that denomination to which the majority of the pupils of the school belong." The religious instruction is to be given in the school by the teacher, before or after class hours; but in no case in presence of those of another belief. The curé has the right to enter the school to supervise this instruction. The bishop is authorized to appoint priests, whose duty it shall be to visit the schools within his diocese, at certain times, and to report the results of their inspection as regards the religious instruction. Any denomination sufficiently numerous to maintain a school has the right to establish a school of its own. The communal authorities are to fix the class hours, time and period of vacations, and the school-tax. Gratuitous primary instruction has never been admitted by Belgian legislation. All who are able to pay must pay. Those who are unable to pay are admitted free, but it rests with the communal and provincial authorities to designate those who are relieved of the tax. The law likewise places the appointment of the teacher in the hands of the communal authorities. The teacher may be selected from among the pupils of State normal schools, or of private normal schools accepted by the State. A special council, wherein the clergy are represented, passes on the class-books, but the books having to do especially with religious and moral instruction are subject to the approbation of the bishops. Where the resources of the communes are not sufficient to meet the school expenses, the provincial councils are authorized to grant subsidies out of the provincial funds.

This law of 1842 will impress any thoughtful man as the work of true statesmen. It is a law made for a living people, made to meet real conditions, made to contribute to the welfare and peace of all the citizens. There is in it no touch of the doctrinaire's hand, trying to cast a whole nation in one mould. Our own republic, which we are pleased to hold up as the model of true liberality, can point to no school-law conceived in so democratic and so liberal a spirit.

To the people is left the organization and control of the school. The State imposes no direct charge on the people, beyond that of supplying needed instruction. The commune has to see that its children are provided with this instruction ; it can effect this in its own way. If it prefers to build schools, it may do so; if it finds it more to its advantage to make use of existing schools, it may do so. The aim is, properly, to instruct the youth of the nation ; let the commune take the readiest means to effect this desirable end, provided only that the means be fitting. The country is a religious country ; it has suffered for religion's sake ; it has fought for freedom of religion ; it must be protected in that freedom. Still, no one form of religion shall be protected, but all forms. The constitution—the first of European constitutions—has separated Church from State, wherefore the State has not to control religion, much less make war upon it, but to secure it in its rights. Primary instruction means not only the teaching of reading, writing, history ; it is, first of all, the teaching of moral and religious truths. The youth, then, according to the beliefs of their parents, shall be instructed in the moral and religious truths which go to make up those beliefs, and the correctness of this instruction shall be assured by placing its control in the hands of the recognized teachers of religion. Paying the expenses of the instruction of its own children, the commune shall select the teachers and direct the school. The commune having the greatest interest, who can better do the work ? To assure that the law is faithfully carried out, the executive of the nation, the king, shall, by selected officers, under the control of the State, supervise the whole system. No link is wanting in the logical chain.

For thirty-seven years, from 1842 to 1879, the Belgian school system was governed by this same law. The development of the system, during that time, seems to be an unanswerable argument in favor of the law. We have seen that, in 1840, there were 5189 schools in the whole country; there were 5857 in 1875. The communal schools numbered only 2109 in 1840; in 1875 they numbered 4157, and there were in addition 457 adopted schools. The whole number of children receiving primary instruction in 1830 was 293,000; by 1845 the number had increased to 426,000, while in 1875 the total was 669,195. Between 1830 and 1875 the increase of population was rather less than 25 per cent., while the increase in school attendance was more than 125 per cent.

To the impartial inquirer these figures give the strongest proof that the school law of 1842 had effected its purpose—the spread of primary instruction; and consequently that it must have met the wishes of the people, that it must have been a popular law.

However, in 1879 this law was radically changed; or rather, it was obliterated from the statute-book, and in its place was substituted a wholly new law, whose provisions were based on far other views of education, of the rights of the State, and of the people, of liberty, of justice, of religious freedom. Before giving our attention to the details of this second law, it will be helpful to us to have some further insight into the development of political parties in Belgium.

From 1830 to 1846 the traditions of the Union were in force. Liberal leaders and Catholic leaders worked for the unity of Liberals and Catholics, and for mutual concessions on dividing questions. All the ministries, within these sixteen years, depended on a combination of Liberal and Catholic votes. Liberal members were elected to either house by Catholic votes and influence. We have seen that, up to the election of the king, the Catholics freely gave the political leadership to the Liberals. Indeed, the Catholics had no representative in the ministry until 1834. In that year two of their ablest men, De Theux and De Muelenaere, went in. The ministry of 1842 gave the Catholics four portfolios; and in 1846 the king called upon De Theux to form the first Catholic Ministry. The Catholics had not held the premiership in any of the previous ministries.

De Theux's government was short-lived. It fell in 1847, when the Liberals under Rogier took control of affairs. Rogier remained in office until 1852. The French revolution of 1848 had disturbed the country but slightly. The Catholics patriotically declined to hamper the government by any active opposition; and a few companies of soldiers sufficed to repress the impotent uprisings of March 25th and 29th. However, the Liberal party became more and more divided year after year, and Rogier, to retain a working majority, was again and again obliged to adapt himself to Radical views. In 1851 the party divisions led to a ministerial crisis; the Senate was dissolved, and an appeal was made to the country. Though the elections left Rogier in a minority, he continued to hold office until the temper of the deputies compelled him to resign. He was succeeded (Oct. 31st, 1852) by De Brouckère, a moderate, who was supported by the Catholics and moderate Liberals. Under Rogier the country had passed through five years of continuous and increasing political excitement. De Brouckère's administration was wholly in the interest of internal peace. Dependent on the opposition for a majority, his position was difficult and uncertain. The Conservatives making considerable gains in the elections of 1854, the Ministry resigned, and, for the second time the Conservative-Catholic party came into power under the leadership óf De Decker and Vilain XIV.

The Catholics were not in a majority, but the ministerial majority was secure, and so remained until 1857. In that year the ministry proposed a law enabling religious corporations to acquire the right to receive donations and legacies; and recognizing the right of a citizen to dispose of his fortune in favor of the poor, and to choose at his will special administrators for the purpose. Not satisfied with a parliamentary opposition, the Liberals organized a system of mobs and riots in the large cities. These revolutionary proceedings being long continued, the king advised the majority to suspend the discussion of the law. The ministry, protesting against the disgraceful means by which the opposition sought to overturn them,—a minority appealing to force to overcome a majority,— closed the chamber and appealed to the country. The elections gave a Liberal gain, and the Conservatives resigned.

Rogier now took office, with Frère-Orban as his most prominent co-worker; and, though there were occasional changes of premier and portfolio, each change being in the direction of Radicalism, the Liberals governed the country continuously up to 1870. Then, for the first time in thirteen years, the Conservatives regained power, under the leadership of Baron d'Anethan and Malou, and they held the control of affairs until June 12th, 1878, when Malou was succeeded by Frère-Orban, the father of the new school law.

As early as 1839 a fraction of the Liberals had separated themselves from the Union and combined to control the ministry; but the leaders of the Union were as yet too strong for them. However, the first step had been made in the way of a new political movement. Defacqz, grand master of the Freemasons, made a second step in the same direction in 1841. He formed a political society called "The Alliance," whose membership was restricted to Masons, and whose object was to control the elections in the Liberal interest. In 1842 membership was extended to non-Masons. Even then its members did not exceed a thousand. Still the Alliance played an active part in the elections, carrying on a bitter anti-Catholic canvass. De Theux had been but a short time in power when Defacqz called a "congress" at Brussels, to consider the best means to insure the overthrow of the ministry. A plan of Liberal action was adopted; Liberal clubs were established in all the large centres, and the party was fully organized for political action. A split in the Alliance did not undo its work, Verhaegen, another active Mason, combining all the Liberal forces in the " Liberal Association."

At once the liberality of the Belgian Liberals assumed a new face. The ministry of 1847 adopted an advanced policy. Rogier, the success of whose early career was largely due to the clergy, announced this policy: "The clergy were to have nothing more to say in State affairs." Simple as this sounded, it meant neither more nor less than opposition to Catholics as Catholics. The Belgian Liberal who had started out as the defender of the Jesuits, the champion of religious liberty, and of freedom of association, had become, in 1857, a Radical incendiary, who stirred the country with the contemptible cry of " Down with the convents." To satisfy their large aspirations after liberty, the Liberals of 1858 were compelled to take an old leaf from the statute book of the House of Orange. The liberal measure whereby the Dutch government made criticism of king or ministry a misdemeanor, was now offered to Belgian citizens by Belgian citizens. A truly "liberal" spirit, however, confined the law to a class. To criticize, *from the pulpit*, the ministry, any law, or any act of the king, was made punishable with fine and imprisonment. Religious associations also felt the generous influences of the Liberal policy. They were deprived of all bequests, and compelled to hand over to the State those whose use they were enjoying. The graveyards were made a living Liberal question. Hereafter Christian and infidel must be buried side by side. The illiberal custom of burying Christians among Christians shall give way to the Liberal system of promiscuous burial. Electoral laws were carried with the avowed object of weakening and impeding the non-Liberal vote; while every attempt to enlarge the franchise was speciously opposed, for the reason that enlargement of the franchise meant increase of the non-Liberal vote.

This hasty review of the growth of the Liberal party and of Liberal legislation, may help us to realize the difference between the Liberal of 1825 and of 1875. The one is the negative of the other. If the former deserved the name " Liberal," what shall we call the latter? We have seen the Liberal of 1849 barring out the clergy from state affairs; the Liberal of thirty years later seeks to bar out the Catholic layman. From anti-clerical to anti-Catholic is short—if there be any step. The political action of the party was clearly anti-Catholic, unmistakably so. If we could be mistaken about the meaning of this action, the leaders took care that their words should quickly and wholly correct our error.

The Liberal leaders have further disclosed to us, indeed impressed upon us, the interesting and curious fact that in Belgium Liberalism means Masonry. We remember that it was a Mason,

Defacqz, who first organized the Liberals on a new basis, and another Mason, Verhaegen, who completed the work. From 1847 onward, Masonry controlled the party and its policy; indeed it is rare to find a Liberal minister not a high Mason. But let us hear representative Liberals and Masons on the relations of Liberalism and Masonry, the principles of the Liberal party, the principles of Belgian Masonry, more especially with a view to an understanding of the school question.

Said Brother Goblet, in 1877, when laying the corner-stone of a temple at Brussels : " Masonry is traditional, progressive, local, cosmopolite. She labors in the cause of freedom and reason. She has a beauteous and mystic symbolism, and a ceremonial intended to consecrate all the festal occasions of life. The completeness of her organization makes her a fitting rival to her greatest enemy, the Church ; and, at the same time, the natural, nay necessary, complement of the Liberal party. Masonry is the philosophy of Liberalism, and the Free-thinkers' church."

"What are the weapons to be used by a Democratic State against Ultramontanism ?" This is a "prize-subject," proposed by the Grand Orient in its sitting of March 18th, 1877.

"Catholicism," said Van Humbreck, an active Mason and active Liberal, more than once minister, on March 4th, 1879, "the Catholic religion is, in my eyes, a corpse; the Catholic religion, in its dogmas, is dead; these dogmas nullify conscience. We must fight it, and drive it out from elementary education."

Verhaegen, the Mason who reformed the Liberal party, had more moderately expressed the Masonic-Liberal ideas as early as 1856: "The intervention of religion in teaching is the abdication of the prerogative of the State."

" In demanding that the Church cease to be a power, we demand the abdication of the Church," writes M. Laurent, the Liberal authority on the relations of "Church and State." "There is but one way of freeing the people ; it is to secularize heaven as well as the earth. And the great means of this emancipation is, to take away education from the Church." Again, the first condition of this emancipation is "to do away with Christian spiritualism, the terrors of a future life, the preoccupation with an imaginary salvation." Belgian Masonry and Liberalism are not to be distinguished by any difference in the breadth of their views ; but it is remarkable how united they are on the subject of education. In 1863 the Grand Orient placed the question of obligatory instruction before all the lodges for study. The results of this study have been made public.

"The intervention of the clergy in instruction, under the title of authority, completely nullifies the action of the teacher, paralyzes it, and robs the children of all moral, logical, and rational instruction. The teaching of the catechism is the greatest hindrance to the development of all the faculties of the child. If freed from these things, the mind of the man would become normal and moral." Thus answered the Antwerp lodge.

"Morality," said the Namur brethren, "has nothing in common with the catechism. The characteristic of obligatory instruction consists in this: that it does not at all concern itself with religion, and, *perhaps*, not even with morals."

Louvain is more original, elegant, and philosophical, as one would expect a university town to be. "It is saddening to have to remark the negative influence of Catholicity on the progress of the masses. Protestanism has understood better than Catholicity what a moral and utilitarian religion ought to be. Pauperism and ignorance find their support in the gospels."

At Liége, the lodge expressed dissatisfaction with the existing laws on education, "inasmuch as they gave an unwholesome influence to the members of a *positive religion*, whose objects were diametrically opposite to those of liberalism."

These men may wear the same dress as did the Liberals of 1830; they may affect the same poses, interlard their wild speeches and cunning phrases with some of the ringing, honest words of the men of the Union,—but they are no Liberals. Haters of the Gospel, spurners of all religion, despisers of morality, declared enemies of the Church, men whose aim is to free the people from the yoke of spirituality, to release them from their foolish preoccupation with an imaginary salvation, *to secularize heaven*,—what a portrait of a "Liberal"!

In the Belgium of to-day, then, we see a party with a double organization, the one politico-Liberal, the other Masonic, fighting boldly, openly, studiedly, to injure a majority of its fellow-citizens. The warfare is bitter beyond our conception. From the hustings, the lecture platform, the legislative desk, the morning journal, the pamphlet, a constant stream of anti Catholic abuse flows, odorous and bountiful. As the worshipper leaves the church door on a Sunday morning, his ears are split by the loud cry of an "emancipated" boor, excited by offering some scandalous uncatechetical song, or broadside, or caricature, insulting to those to whom it is offered. The Cathedral "Place" affords the choicest advantages to these disciples of Van Humbreck, who would have a Sabbath kick at the "corpse." The "Freethinkers' church" is the "place"; his worship-ribaldry, insult. There may be mysticism and beauty in all this, but only the philosophical mind of Brother Goblet could discover and expose it.

Such was the party that brought in the new school bill in 1879.

Frère-Orban was at the head of the ministry; he had been connected with every Liberal ministry since 1849. Radical of the Radicals, Mason of Masons, he had ever been ready to press onward in the path marked out by the Grand Orient. Indeed Frère owes a great deal to Belgian Masonry; he may be called a born Mason. His mother, who was portress of the Masonic lodge at Liége, concealed his father's name, or did not know it, so that the lodge there adopted the boy as "brother," and brought him up. Rogier always seemed to be greatly attached to him, and introduced him to political life. In good time he replaced his patron, and soon left him behind. But we shall know Frère-Orban when we have made ourselves acquainted with the law of 1879.

The Malou cabinet had resigned on June 12th, 1878. On June 20th the new cabinet was formed. Its members besides Frère, were Van Humbreck, Rollin-Jacquemeyns, Sainctelette, Bara, Graux, Renard. Four of these, Frère, Bara, Van Humbreck, and Rollin-Jacquemeyns, had for years stirred the country with bitter anti-Catholic speeches. Indeed, the sum and substance of their policy can be best conveyed by the well-worn motto "Down with the Church." It is not surprising, then, to hear the speech from the throne setting forth as a fundamental truth the proposition that "public instruction should depend on the civil power exclusively." The ministry forthwith announced the creation of a new portfolio, that of public instruction, which was committed to Van Humbreck, the gentleman who has so bluntly told us that his great object is "to kick the corpse." The new minister, in the name of the government, outlined its policy in the Senate on the 21st of August. It is impossible to misunderstand Van Humbreck: "The teaching contained in the ten commandments of God, and in the laws of the Church, is the absolute negation of liberty of conscience, the teaching of a sect; on this account, from this time forward, this teaching would not be put before the pupils by the teacher, it would be excluded from elementary education."

The project for the revision of the law of 1842 was not presented until the 21st of January, 1879. The debate on the measure was a long and excited one, opening on April 22d, and closing only on the 6th of June, when the bill was carried by the small majorities of seven in the House and two in the Senate.

The new law made it obligatory on every commune in the kingdom to establish at least one communal school. This school should be "*neutre*"; which means, without religion, or, if you please, "Liberal." The commune could no longer "adopt" a school. Article IV. provided that religious instruction was to be left to the care of the family. In the schools religious instruction was replaced by the teaching of "universal morality"—*la morale universelle.* The priest might give religious instruction to such as desired it, either before or after class, in a room to be set apart for the purpose. The curé's right of inspection was withdrawn. No inspectors, other than those appointed by the state or municipal authorities, were recognized. The clergy were no longer represented in the matter of the examination of school books. While every commune was obliged to have and to maintain at its own expense a primary school, the government determined the minimum number of schools in each commune. The government also fixed the number of classes in each school. The communal councils, as of old, nominated the teachers, but the councils could choose no person not a pupil of a State normal school. Religious instruction no longer formed a part of the course of studies in the State normal schools. The supervision of the schools was divided between the communal councils and certain principal inspectors, cantonal inspectors, and school committees. The principal and cantonal inspectors were appointed and removed at pleasure by the king. The territory each one supervised was fixed by government decree. Over each territory or circumscription there was, in addition to these inspectors, a special school committee. Where the schools of a commune were all within one circumscription the communal council appointed the special committee; but where this was not the case, the minister named the committee, subject to an appeal to the king. The communal councils still had the right to determine all questions as to admission of pupils, school discipline, days and hours of work, and vacations. Attendance at school was not obligatory.

Compare this law with that of 1842, and it will be seen how completely the old law has been overturned. The family receives a beautiful tribute in the fourth article, wherein religious instruction is committed to its tender care; but throughout the rest of the bill there is consideration only for the paternal Liberal government. The " religious country " of Leopold the First is dealt with as though it had become an irreligious country under his son. The country wherein, less than fifty years before, Liberals had objected to a candidate for its throne because there was a possibility that freedom of religion and of instruction might be jeopardized under him, is now subjected to a law which practically denies the one and effectually minimizes the other.

Primary instruction, which in 1842 "comprised *necessarily* instruction in religion and morals," comprises now and as necessarily instruction in no religion, with the unknown morals of " universal morality." Logically, the teacher of religion has gone with religion; logically, he is not to supervise " neutre " books. Difference of denomination is no longer recognized. The children are the children of the government, and in this government the differences are not of sect, as they say, but rather of degree, of a mad hatred of religion. The teacher must logically be "neutre." To be "neutre," he must logically come out of the "neutre" normal school. The commune may choose the teacher; not the teacher the people want, but the teacher the ministry prescribe. Thus, the rights of the commune are respected! In return, the commune is obliged to provide schools whose number and expense is to be fixed by the government, and by a very skilful maneuvre the measure of the control that the commune shall exercise over the simplest details of the school is placed in the hands of the government. The system of inspection has been designed with this purpose. By the king are appointed the principal and cantonal inspectors, whose circumscription the ministry fixes. There is also a special school committee in each circumscription, and this committee is chosen by the communal council, but only when all the communal schools are within the one circumscription. The government, which fixes the circumscriptions, thus controls the school-committee. The communes are not liberal; the schools are divided between two circumscriptions. Now steps in the law; the government appoints the school committee. The communes may not be Liberal, but the school committees shall be. We of the States have no patent in our own native-born political trick of gerrymandering.

The law of 1879 was, like the law of 1842, well-suited to effect its purpose. The purpose of the law of 1842 was to spread education; that of the law of 1879 was to impede the spread of a certain kind of education, and to assure the diffusion of another kind of education.

This law was effectually carried out in so far as it depended on the government. New school buildings beautified the communes at the expense of the exchequer. Within five years the budget of public instruction was doubled; and though new loans were issued to the amount of eighty millions of dollars, and five millions of new taxes were laid on the country, Frère-Orban went out of office with a deficit of two millions.

The communal treasuries were compelled to honor requisitions over which the communes had no control. The inspectors and committees appointed by the government rigorously carried out the ministry's instructions. Where the organic law of the province or commune interfered with the school-law, as the ministry interpreted it, the ministry boldly superseded or modified the communal laws. Where communal magistrates declined to violate their oaths in order to give effect to the illegal orders of the ministry, special commissioners were appointed to do its bidding. All difficulties, all obstacles, were overcome by means of these special commissioners, who were multiplied in the land. Every local liberty was violated. The law accorded subventions to the communes to aid them in building and carrying on the schools. In the hands of the ministry this provision became a powerful political weapon. It was not the needs of a commune that were considered, but its political influence and its Liberalism.

We have read the answers of the lodges to the question of the Grand-Orient in 1863. After studying these answers, the Grand-Orient worked up the sketch of a law. According to the Orient, "it is the parents' duty to send their children to State schools, and if the parents cannot be *forced* to do their duty by means of fines and imprisonment, then the children shall be simply taken away from them." Force is evidently a principle of that "universal morality" which has suspended ordinary morality in the conscience of the Belgian Liberal. By force the law of 1879 was executed; and had it not been for the courageous action of a Christian people, to that force would speedily have been added the Masonic force to drag the child from the fined and imprisoned parent in order that conscience might be freed from the slavery of the Ten Commandments.

As the law of 1842 fitted the country, so the law of 1879 did not fit the country; and as the people worked with a will under the old law, so they would have none of the new law. The bill had hardly passed when the country was in revolution. The spirit of 1825 was still living and strong. From 1879 to 1884 the revolution grew in power. Throughout the five years it was constant, open, bold, peaceful. Let us see what it did.

It left the "neutre" schools to those who were neutral. For itself it wanted religious schools, and these it made. Committees were established throughout the country: parish committees, provincial committees, cantonal committees. The parish committee built a school, found the teachers and the pupils. The cantonal committees, made up of delegates from each parish, supervised in a general way the free schools of a circumscription, and dealt with all the difficulties in the way of the establishment of the schools. The provincial committee, a committee of "select men," under the bishop, was made up of clergymen, lawyers, business-men, farmers. Divided into sub-committees, these attended to matters of law and finance, arranged public meetings and lectures, and organized a propaganda of good books and conservative journals. A "Free Schools Pence Society" was formed throughout the country; contribution-boxes, wherein might be dropped the weekly subscription of a sou, were placed in the churches, shops, restaurants, even in private houses. Special collections were taken up at the church-doors, at concerts, at lectures, at private social gatherings. To help on the good work some gave lands, others buildings. Wealthy families built schools at their own expense. Many persons bound themselves to pay an annual sum into the provincial or parochial school-treasury. Laborers and mechanics gave donations in money, or in kind. Teachers were wanting, especially male teachers; the curé or the vicaire became the teacher. Fresh work was put into the existing Catholic normal schools, and new ones were forwarded.

How zealously, determinedly, intelligently the Catholics worked, is best told by a few figures. The new school-law was promulgated on July 1st, 1879. The government report of December 31, 1878, showed that the total number of children in the primary schools was 687,749, of whom 597,624 were in schools subject to state inspection. On the 15th of December, 1880, within less than eighteen months after the passage of the new law, the figures stood thus: Total number in primary schools, 749,535; of this number 455,179 were in Catholic schools, and but 294,356 in government schools. In the province of Antwerp 75 per cent. of the children were in the Catholic schools; in that of West Flanders, 83 per cent; East Flanders, 80 per cent.; Limburg, 84 per cent.; Brabant, 56 per cent.; Luxemburg, 52 per cent. In only three provinces was the percentage less than one-half: these were Namur, with 47 per cent.; Hainault, with 41 per cent.; and Liége with 39 per cent.

By the 31st of December, 1881, the Catholics had erected 2064 new school buildings for primary instruction. In 1884 the number of Catholic schools had increased to 3885, with 8715 teachers. Was not this a revolution? Surely; and one whose rapidity of action and complete success should not be lost on other people and other governments of the day.

" *La Loi de Malheur*," so the Belgian Catholics named the Frère-Orban law. Still, out of it came good to them. Their organization in the cause of religious education united them against Liberal tyranny, bound them together for the re-acquirement of their rights under the constitution, and rallied to them all fair and liberal-minded men. What liberty, whose liberty was secure when the law of the land was the crazy whim of a Frère, a Van Humbreck, or a Bara?

The majority by which the law had been carried would have made a ministry having at heart the interests of a whole country hesitate before committing itself to a policy of prejudice, of passion, above all, of ignorance. But no; the ministry was blind and reckless. We have seen how it executed the law; mark now how it labored to embitter and excite the country, to assure its power, to complete its illiberal work, and to " drive out the Catholic religion from elementary education " !

Having tried, by artful schemes, to divide the people, bishops, and Pope, on the very question of the school-law, and having failed, diplomatic relations with the Holy See were broken off, in a rude, undignified way. Through modifications in the electoral law, some six thousand electors were excluded from voting for senators and representatives. The electors so excluded were principally landholders, farmers, curés, classes notably conservative. Uniformly opposed as the party had been to an extension of the franchise, a law was brought in to increase the Liberal vote. In Belgium the right of franchise had been determined by the measure of taxation. The ministry's law gave a vote to specified employés and officials, regardless of the payment of taxes ; and further, authorized certain persons to vote who, after examination, should receive a diploma.

But these measures to reduce the Conservative and to increase the Radical vote were vain. The temper of the country was shown at the elections for provincial councils, held on May 25th, 1884. The Radicals lost 47 seats. In the provinces of Antwerp and Limburg, they did not elect a' single representative; while in Brabant, Hainault, Namur, old strongholds of Liberalism, the Conservatives made notable gains.

On June 10th the country was relieved of the incubus of the Frère-Orban ministry. The elections for deputies on that day proved disastrous to the anti-Catholics. All the ministerial deputies who presented themselves for re-election, excepting only two, were defeated. Even Brussels did not return a single supporter of the ministry. The Conservative majority in the lower Chamber was 34.

Frère resigned on the 11th of June. On the next day the king called in Malou to form a ministry. The Senate holding over, and having a Radical majority of five, Malou at once dissolved it, and appealed to the country. The senatorial elections were held on the 8th of July, with the result of a Conservative majority of seventeen.

The Catholic victory was complete, but it was not a victory gained by Catholics alone. The strain of the men of the Union had not exhausted itself; the intelligent youth of the country had rallied to the cause of liberty. Brussels elected its sixteen deputies, not as Catholics, but as Independents. The temper of the people is well shown by an incident that occurred shortly after the meeting of the chambers. " You claim to form a group," said the Liberal ex-minister Bara, addressing the Independents, " and yet you have no common platform." " We had one," answered Van der Smissen, the leader of the Independents, "it was to 'disembarrass the country of your government; on that point we were one."

The Chambers were convoked on the 22d of July. Two subjects were at once placed on the order of the day: 1st, renewal of diplomatic relations with the Holy See; 2d, a new school-law. The first measure was carried without discussion; not so the second.

Malou's cabinet was made up of able men,—Jacobs, Bernaert, Woeste, Pauters, Moreau d'Audray, and Vandenpeereboom. Jacobs, Bernaert, and Woeste were men of large experience in affairs. Like Malou, they had long been active in the cause of freedom and religion; and like him, they had been leaders in the opposition to the Radical policy, and in the work of establishing Catholic free-schools. Frère-Orban's creation, the separate ministry of public instruction, was abolished, and the portfolio again combined with that of the interior. To Jacobs, the minister of the interior, was given in charge the new school-bill which the Cabinet presented to the Chambers on July 25th. We shall examine this law.

Each commune shall have a communal school. The commune may adopt, or subsidize, one or more private schools. Where it does this, the king, on the advice of the permanent deputation of the provincial council, may dispense the commune from the obligation of establishing a communal school. This dispensation cannot be granted, however, if twenty heads of families, having children of school age, demand a school for the instruction of their children. As to religious instruction, the commune may place it at the head of the school programme. It shall be given at the beginning or at the end of class. Children whose parents make the request are to be dispensed from assisting at it. Should twenty fathers of families request it, the king may oblige the commune to organize a special class for their children. In case the commune refuses to give religious instruction, and twenty Catholic heads of families demand it for their children, the commune is not compelled to grant it; but the government may adopt and subsidize a free-school agreeable to the parents, provided that the school adopted meet the requirements for a communal school. In adopted schools the religious instruction shall be given at the beginning or at the end of the class, as in communal schools; and in the one, as in the other, pupils may be dispensed from attending the religious instruction at the request of the parents. The communal primary schools are subject to the direction of the commune. In all normal schools, absolute respect for liberty of conscience is guaranteed to each pupil. To the communal council the old power of appointing and suspending the teacher is restored. The teacher must have a diploma from a normal school, but normal schools inspected by the State are put on a footing with State schools. Should any teacher of an official school, appointed under the law of 1879, lose his position by the operation of the present law, he shall receive a stipend of not less than one-half, nor more than three-quarters, of his former salary, until such time as some fitting place has been provided for him, the expense to be divided between the commune and the State.

The bill was passed on the 22d of August, by a majority of 32 in the House, and of 15 in the Senate, two deputies and two senators being absent.

"You are going back fifty years," cried a member of the Left, on the last day of the debate. "You are right," answered M. Woeste, "and we are proud of it. It is of the very essence of our politics to bring back into their old place of honor the real principles of the constitution. One of the bases of the constitution is complete respect for the communal prerogatives. We have faith in the communal liberties and in their workings."

In one sense the ministry had gone back fifty years, in another sense it had not. The foundation of this law, said M. Jacobs, "is respect for the liberty of the communes, for liberty of instruction, for the free will of fathers of families. Not that there is ever unlimited liberty, any more than complete constraint. It is a question of limit. We propose a considerable *recoil on the side of liberty.*" The expression is happy. Progression is one thing, liberty another; they are not inseparable. The ministry had gone back fifty years for liberty's sake.

Is the law of 1884 a just law? After careful perusal, it is hard to find a flaw in it. We qualified the law of 1842 as a law of statesmen; the same qualification is even more applicable to this of 1884. The old law of 1842 was formed in times of political peace, when the aim of all was to satisfy all, when no passions had been aroused. Then, it was not hard to be just. But now, circumstances were very different. The Catholics had seen their rights taken from them by the law of 1879; they had been made to feel the harsh hand of a government whose avowed aim was to destroy their faith, to wrest their children from their religion; they had been forced, for five years, to suffer injustice, and to make rare sacrifices. It is not often that a party, victorious over oppression, lifts itself above itself. The natural impulse is to retaliate. But in the law of 1884 we find no trace of a retaliatory spirit. The makers of the law seem to have aimed solely at a practical application of the Christian maxims of liberty, fraternity, equality. There is a return to the principles of the constitution, and to that law of 1842 which had effected its purpose by encouraging education, while leaving the country at peace. Going back fifty years for their principles, the Conservatives had not gone back a day for their practice. The law of 1842 had been devised for the existing conditions; and so the law of 1884 was devised for other existing conditions. Though the "Loi de Malheur" was a bad law, and the law of a narrow majority, not backed by the country, still it had inaugurated a system, binding in some respects on an honorable people, and satisfactory to a minority. By the new law the rights of this minority are protected, and the moral obligations of the State are admitted. Take the matter of the teachers. When Frère-Orban passed his law in 1879, he declined to make any provision for those who would be thrown out of employment by the enforcement of the section by which all teachers were required to be graduates of State normal schools. Men long in the service, and yet not long enough to be entitled to the legal pension, were sent adrift, as though they had no claims on the State. Not so under the Malou law; they are made a charge against the State and Commune until they have found other employment.

Freedom of instruction is again assured, not only freedom of non-religious or irreligious instruction, but freedom of religious instruction as well. The 500,000 children who wish to study the catechism, the ten commandments, and the laws of the Church, are placed on an equality with the 300,000 that seem not to wish any of these things. No one religion is protected or persecuted by the law which, recognizing no particular form of religion, still recognizes differences, and guarantees to each citizen his constitutional right to freedom of conscience.

The family is acknowledged as the foundation of the State, and protected in its natural rights. To the family, not to the State, belongs the education of the children. The collection of families most closely united to form a society, and a body politic,—the commune,—is recognized as being, after the family, the chief factor in the constitution of the State. To the commune is given its rights, its liberties. The State assumes its proper rôle of overseer, of helper, of protector of the citizens. In as much as control is necessary, in order that all the families and all the communes shall work harmoniously, yet freely, according to their lawfully free opinions, in so much the State controls, but no farther. The State preserves order, encourages and protects the citizens, fosters education, and assures the utmost constitutional liberty.

One would imagine that the Radical, the Grand-Orient, the Liberal, could grant no less than this. But they did grant less. They were not satisfied with the protection of all rights, and the largest liberty for all. Belgian Liberalism, as we have seen, meant liberty for a sect, a class, to impose its views on a majority that differed from it. In the debates on the law, Frère-Orban himself had voiced the Radical idea. He protested against the liberty which the bill accorded; to him such liberty was a contradiction. "You detest the State-instruction," he cried out, "you oppose the principle of the ' neutre' school, you look upon it as pestilential, and yet you propose to leave to the commune the right to establish such a school, if it please." To have lived eighty years, and suckled Liberalism in the lodge itself, and still to be unable to understand true liberality! Liberty, in the estimation of Frère and his party, was the Liberal's, the Radical's will. Wherefore this law, which recognized the equality of the citizens before the law, and granted to all the fullest freedom, was obnoxious to the Radical-Liberal.

It was "a law of the convents"; "a Jesuit *coup d'état*"; "a return to the Spanish epoch." It gave rights to the communes which did not belong to them. Not to the commune, but to the State belonged the control of primary education. Were we not right in saying that the "Liberal" wanted less liberty than the law allowed? Here are the convents, the Jesuits, Alva's ghost, charged with the un-Liberal aim of treating all the citizens as equals, and the government reproached because its lack of anti-Liberal spirit led it to refuse to seize the communal liberties, in order that the vain and variable thing, Liberal liberty, might be the better assured.

No sooner had the bill been passed than an organized agitation against it was begun. Were school committees formed throughout the country to assure the diffusion of irreligious education? Were contribution boxes for the "Non-Catechetical-Schools-Pence" set up in the Lodges and the places of public resort? Was a literary propaganda organized? No, there was no occasion to do any of these things. The opposition was better protected under this law than under the law of 1879. An agitation of the kind would have been ridiculous, more than all, it would have been moral. Besides, the Radical-Liberals had their own peculiar and established system of agitation. This system was based on the same idea as was their system of government, on force. They resorted to riot.

In the use of this as a political contrivance they were adepts; and by its use they had again and again attained their ends. The riot, as a means of overturning a ministry, frightening a weak majority, strengthening a minority, intimidating a king, forcing a dissolution, carrying an election, was introduced with the Rogier-Frère-Orban ministry of 1857. In that year, as well as in 1870, '71, '72, '75, '77, '78, the larger cities had been again and again scenes of violence and of bloodshed. The " uncatechized" city rough was well trained in the business of window-breaking, threatening, assaulting. Why waste time on committees and books, when means of action so powerful and progressive were ready at hand ?

While the Chambers were discussing the school-law, intimidation was attempted. The streets about the parliament houses were day after day filled with a crowd of students, idlers, and roughs, who hooted and abused the members, and above all the ministers, as they passed. The police of Brussels, controlled by the Liberal burgomaster, M. Buls, an eminent Mason, made no attempt to repress the disorder. Finally, the Conservative deputies called upon the ministry to protect their dignity and independence ; and Jacobs, the minister of the interior, determined to place the keeping of public order in the hands of the governor of the province. However, as the burgomaster begged that the communal council might be spared such a humiliation, and promised to preserve the peace for the future, Jacobs did not carry out his purpose.

What had heretofore been done by crowds, was now done by groups and individuals. Insulting cries against the king were not uncommon. The Radical press encouraged the excitement, its columns were filled with threats and calumnies. Soon, the street disturbances were renewed.

Meanwhile, the bill had passed; and the Radical leaders, neglecting ministers and deputies for the time being, turned their attention to the king, in whose hands the bill lay. The agitation was kept up, in the hope of intimidating the king, and so extorting from him a refusal to sign the law. Processions were organized; violent speeches were made by the leaders ; there were bands of music, flags, mottoes. The 31st of August was selected for a final demonstration. On that day, 33,095 Liberals marched to the palace, carrying to the king a petition against the law.

The Conservatives, excited by this unseemly opposition, determined to give the king support, and to show the popularity of the new law. They therefore arranged to present, on the same day, a petition favoring the bill. This the burgomaster forbade them to do, giving as a reason that he feared *lest the public peace might be disturbed.* He agreed, however, to permit them to select some other day. Thereupon they chose the 7th of September, and on that day mustered to the number of 94,500. While marching through the streets, they were attacked at a favorable point by crowds of men, armed with clubs. The way was barred; they were beaten, battered, and eighty of them being seriously injured, their ranks were broken, and the procession compelled to disband.

M. Buls had evidently not provided against the disturbance of the public peace.

There was but one more card to play. Forty-eight Liberal burgomasters were gathered together, and in a body they went to the king, begging him not to sanction the law. When we remember that there are twenty-six hundred communes in Belgium, the forty-eight burgomasters will recall the Tooly street tailors. Still, the tailors were for popular rights, while the forty-eight burgomasters, the official representatives of their communes, were opposing a measure by which thousands of communes were to regain their stolen liberties.

What answer was the king to make to such a petition? The burgomasters' appeal was to an autocrat; Leopold was only a constitutional king. There was but one answer for him to give : "He had promulgated the law of 1879 in accordance with the wish of the Chambers ; he could not but do the same in the case of the new law; it was not for him to make distinctions between Belgians. If he accepted the address they presented, it was only fair to tell them that he had received addresses from a great number of communes expressing the very contrary wish." The king might have said to them: I signed the law of 1879, which was carried by a majority of seven in the Chamber of Deputies, and of two in the Senate. By what reason can a Belgian ask me to refuse my signature to this law, which has been carried by a majority of thirty-two in the one house, and of fifteen in the other?

The bill was signed, but the agitation did not cease. In October the communal elections were to be held; the new law must serve party purposes. It might be made of use to rally the drooping spirits of the Liberal organization, for the organization was in danger. An always malicious press became violent: "The law was infamous;" "it put the treasury of the State in the hands of brotherlets and nunlets;" "it was a law favoring public ignorance, a law reducing Belgium to the lowest rank among nations." On the ministry and the king insults were heaped.

Again were the streets resorted to : "Long live the Republic," "Down with the King," were not uncommon cries. A permanent committee was appointed, whose charge it was openly to unfurl the republican flag. Manifestoes, pamphlets, exciting and abusive, were scattered broadcast. "Monsiuer Cobourg" was the king, and, sorry joke, "Madame Co-bourgeoise" was the queen, or, more seriously, "the Austrian woman."

The effect of all this demagogy was apparent when the results of the communal elections of the 19th of October came in. "Ce n'est pas une défaite, c'est une désastre," said one of the most

prominent Radicals. Malou was vindicated; the people had set
their seal upon the school-law, and rejected Radicalism and the
mob. While the Radicals held their own in Brussels, Antwerp,
Ghent, Liége, Namur, and Ypres, the Conservatives carried Bruges,
Courtrai, Nivelles, Grammont, Alost, Termonde, Saint Nicolas,
Audenarde, Thielt, Roulers, Malines, Furnes, Tongres, Bastoyne;
the four last being gains from Radical rule. Of 2585 communes
in which elections were held, the Conservatives were victorious in
1658; 261 were divided, and only 642 were left to the Radicals.
Two hundred and forty-four communes had put out Radical administrations, and gone over to the Conservatives. If we take the
popular vote, the Conservative victory was no less decisive. The
Radical vote amounted to 2,473,960, while the Conservatives polled
2,872,459 votes, having a majority of about 400,000.

Toujours l'Audace! The Radicals claimed a victory. They
telegraphed us that the country had rejected the school-law and
the ministry, and our daily papers forthwith printed editorials on
the " unmixed blessing of the Liberal triumph," and on wicked
clericalism, which had been " following the paths that lead to civil
war "; and whose " meddling with the question of education drove
the people to revolt." Now and then it looks as though some
Van Humbreck or Bara tapped the keys in foreign news-bureaus at
odd hours. However, we are easily fooled when we wish to be,
and, no doubt, the Van Humbrecks know us. So we need not be
surprised at the telegrams; nor at the well-meaning but mistaken
editorials; and yet we cannot but wonder at the audacity which
could claim, before Belgians themselves, that this sound drubbing
was a victory so substantial for Radicalism that there was nothing
left for the king to do but to dismiss the ministry and to order
new elections. This was the claim of Radical leaders and press,
iterated and reiterated. The machinery of the riot was again put
in motion; the mob was gathered; the ministers were hooted;
the king and queen were hissed at a public distribution of prizes,
where, too, the cry of " Vive la République " was applauded. This
cry, and other cries more insulting, were repeated under the very
palace windows.

Thus far Leopold had acted like a man and a constitutional
king. Now he privately sent for two of the old Frère-Orban ministers, Bara and Rollin-Jacquemeyns, to consider the situation with
them. Learning of this consultation from the journals, Malou
called upon the king, represented to him that his action was opposed to the usages of a parliamentary government, and asked an
explanation. The king answered that the manifestation of opinion
in the communal elections seemed to require that something should
be done to calm the popular excitement. To this Malou rejoined

that the excitement was temporary, and without consistence; that, besides, the communal councils were not political bodies, that only the two chambers had a political character, and that their opinion was not doubtful; that no law had ever been carried by a larger majority than had this school-law; that to bend before the present clamor would be subversive of all constitutional ideas; and that he, the Premier, was ready to assume the responsibility. Still the king insisted, and finally disclosed his plans, saying that he considered it indispensable that Jacobs and Woeste should resign. Malou protested, and tried to make the king understand the gravity of his request and the difficulty of justifying it on any ground whatsoever. The king being obstinate, Malou withdrew to consult with his colleagues. The first resolve of the ministry was to stand or fall together, but at a second meeting Jacobs and Woeste asked permission to resign, *under the king's injunction.* Their view was, that the ministers owed it to the majority, to the electors who had so recently sent them to the chambers, to the Conservative party, to the great interests engaged in the contest, and to respect for the constitution, not to hand over the country to the Radical party and a new dissolution. Finally these views prevailed, but Malou announced that, having formed the ministry, and being responsible for it, he would go out with his two colleagues. It was then determined that Bernaert should take Malou's place in the new ministry. Having informed the king of this action, Malou called a meeting of the Conservative senators and deputies, and acquainted them with the position of affairs. Naturally the meeting was an excited one; the tendency was to resent the king's interference; but, in the end, the ministry's policy was agreed to, and a request was made to the king to reconstitute a Conservative cabinet, under the premiership of Bernaert.

This was not what the king had been aiming at; his purpose was to get a mixed or compromise ministry. But the Conservative position was too strong for him; he took all he could get, and accepted Bernaert, who completed his ministry by the appointment of MM. Volder, Thonissen, and Chimay to the vacant portfolios.

There was no further pretext for rioting, though it did not cease at once. The Radical leaders had reached the end of their tether. Either they had to accept the situation or to proceed to revolution.

To explain the king's action is not difficult; to defend it, not easy. The riots, the violence of the Radical press, the open insults to himself and the queen, the threats against the throne, implied by the cries of the roughs favoring a republic, had intimidated the king. He feared for himself and his dynasty. The political education he had received from his father had made him a man of peace and of compromises. When he came to the throne, in December, 1865, the Liberal leaders had tried to strengthen their party and to prejudice the king by charging him with Catholic leanings. His policy for many years has proved the very contrary, unless he be one of those whose love is shown by chastisement. In 1871 he had played the same part with Baron d'Anethan that he now played with Malou. Then, as now, the riot had been used as an argument, and by it the king had been convinced.

Practically the action of the king in 1884 altered nothing. It removed all excuse for disorder, but there was no excuse for it; to the law belonged the maintenance of order, to the law its maintenance should have been left. The ministry was the choice of the country; the king had no constitutional right to interfere with that choice. Fresh from the people, with a large and secure majority, the ministry was in its right. The communal elections were not political, as Malou had fairly stated; but, in as much as they voiced the popular will, they only served to strengthen the position and policy of the ministry. To concede, in the face of sedition, was to weaken the crown and to encourage sedition; to concede, at the expense of the constitution, was to offer a premium to anarchy and to make a claim for despotism. Time will tell the consequences of the king's action; but, if the logical consequences do not follow, it will be for the reason that a Conservative ministry, better than the king, loves and knows the country, and by wise and courageous means determines to preserve it to him and his heirs for its own happiness.

What did the Radicals gain? Nothing, but to endanger the constitution and their own party. The school-law remains the law; a Conservative ministry still holds a Conservative majority; the king is on the throne; but in what position are the Radical-Liberals? Hardly had the political difficulties been resolved when the less radical Radicals undertook to reform the party. Their defeat by the people they attributed to the adoption of the policy of the irreconcilables. None were more irreconcilable than the Masons, yet it is Brother Van Humbreck who leads the movement against the extremists.

Did the Conservatives lose anything? No, not politically. The crown invaded their rights, infringed upon their powers, hurt their dignity. Their loss was a moral one. Wise politicians, they accepted it, holding to the real things they had, and trusting to time and the country to repair the indignity which the king had so inexcusably placed on them.

The ten commandments and the laws of the Church are good for a country: they make a religious people, and that means, as the first Leopold so well said, " a people easily governed "; but they are bad for a party. They limit the means of political action to honest means, while the party that has advanced so far in the way of progress as to have relieved itself of them, enjoys the beautiful freedom of conscience which permits men to adapt the means to the end. Unfortunately for the Belgian Conservative, he is, and is likely to continue to be, a " nullifier " of this kind of progress, and he is face to face with an opposition whose conscience is freed from the bonds of commandment and law. The contest is not over, the issue is not certain. But no one who values religion and liberty can withhold his admiration from the Belgian Conservative Catholic. Intelligence, courage, patience, sacrifice, pluck,—these manly qualities he has shown for sixty years. The men of to-day are true sons of the fathers of 1825. Conservatives throughout the world, while admiring them, encouraging them, and hoping for them, may at the same time learn from them a lesson—in prudence as well as zeal, in patience as well as action, in toleration, in courage, above all, in moderation.

ANNE CATHERINE EMMERICH.

Life of Anne Catherine Emmerich. From the German of V. Rev. K. E. Schmoeger, C.SS.R. New York : Fr. Pustet & Co. Two vols., 8vo.

THE only account of Sister Anne Catherine Emmerich given to the public, previous to F. Schmoeger's Life, was a brief biographical sketch prefixed to her revelations on the " Dolorous Passion of Our Lord," published by Clement Brentano, in 1833, and not long after translated into French. But this scanty notice of the holy nun only increased the desire of pious Catholics for a fuller account of the virtues and wonderful life of this privileged servant of God. This longing was not gratified until the year 1870, when F. Schmoeger published his work, with the approbation of the Bishop of Limburg. He had meanwhile had access to many documents connected with the civil and ecclesiastical commissions that had been appointed to investigate the alleged preternatural state of the holy sister, also to the copious notes of Brentano's diary, who had spent six years in daily attendance upon her and had been the amanuensis to whom she dictated her revelations.

F. Schmoeger's book is as thorough and complete as could be desired, though sometimes lacking in order and precision, where precision is most necessary. Thus we have occasional accounts from Sr. Emmerich's own mouth of her interior life and of the invisible world, given in quotation marks; but to whom uttered or by whom reported, the author has forgotten to tell the reader. The English translator, who is understood to be a Religious of the Visitation Order in a neighboring State, has done her share of the work very commendably.

The great sanctity of Sister Emmerich, her love of holy poverty, of mortification and suffering, her profound humility in the midst of so many divine favors,—most touching and beautiful in its child-like simplicity,—with her many other virtues, are amply set forth in these volumes. Though not a model of biographical style, we have no doubt that they will interest and charm the Catholic reader to such an extent that he will find it difficult to lay down the book once it is taken up for perusal. Her expiatory sufferings for the persecutions and scandals that troubled the Church in her day, for ecclesiastics in high position or in immediate charge of souls, for her own enemies and persecutors, for sinners, for the sick and dying, form quite a prominent chapter in Sister Emmerich's history. This peculiar development of lively faith and ardent charity is not found in the lives of many saints, though analogous cases occur in the accounts that have come down to us of several sainted heroines of the Middle Ages. So intense was her faith that God rewarded it by a special privilege. He bestowed upon her soul, while yet surrounded by its bodily veil, not only the most vivid conceptions, but what may be called the actual sight of grace in its mysterious workings upon the human soul. She beheld and felt, more clearly than the senses do physical objects, the regenerative power of the Sacraments and the efficacy likewise of those things that are merely external helps to the Christian soul during its earthly sojourn, such as the priest's blessing, holy water, the sanctity, beauty, and power of relics, etc. In a reliquary she could discern instantly any relic that was not genuine; and where they were authentic, she felt sensibly their presence, though not exposed to view, and saw in-tuitively to what saints they belonged, their first gathering, their translation, and other subsequent vicissitudes.

But what is peculiar to this humble virgin of Dulmen is the fre-quency and wonderful character of the visions and revelations vouchsafed to her, even, it would seem, from infancy. These will strike the fancy and gratify, perhaps, the curiosity of some readers; but Catholic theologians, as did the saint herself, consider them as trivial and insignificant by the side of the solid virtues, as charity, obedience, humility, and others. They are but *gratiæ gratis datæ*, that is spiritual favors given by God gratuitously out of the super-abundance of His goodness. No one can claim them as his right, and the true saint, instead of desiring them, dreads them as a burden, a possible snare and source of temptation. So it was with Sister Emmerich. Besides, these visions and revelations rest solely on the authority of the one who receives or relates them. Hence, though they breathe nothing but the most exquisite piety, and can have no other result than to promote edification amongst Christian readers; though we know that this holy, guileless, simple-minded servant of God was absolutely incapable of wishing or attempting to deceive others, yet her visions and revelations can only command such belief as is commensurate with the authority on which they are based. This is only human; such, consequently, is the only faith which we are allowed to place in them. They are by no means to be received with that infallible certainty of divine faith with which we receive the truths revealed to us by God through His holy Church.

This is the explicit teaching of all Catholic theologians. It will be enough to quote Benedict XIV., in his magnificent work on the Beatification and Canonization of Saints: " Resolvitur ergo in humanum testimonium ejus qui refert aliis suam privatam revela-tionem; quare, cum illis desit objectum formale fidei divinæ, assensus non potest esse nisi solius fidei humanæ " (*Prati*, 1839, vol. iii., p. 609). " The truth of any such alleged heavenly com-munication resolves itself into the human testimony of him (or her) who relates to others his (or her) private revelation ; hence, since they have no formal object of divine faith, their assent can only be that of human faith."

We would not have added this remark unless we judged it nec-essary. For we have known some good Catholics innocently to entertain the opinion that the revelations of Saints Bridget and Catherine of Sienna, Blessed Hildegard and Colette have, by the fact of their canonization, the sanction of Church authority and must be believed accordingly ; and so too those of Sister Emmerich, were she admitted to the honors of the altar, would stand on the same footing. Nothing could be more unfounded, nothing more at variance with the teachings of sound theology.

Even when such revelations have been examined and approved by the Holy See, the term "approbation " is only used in a tech-nical forensic sense. It implies no added weight of sanction, no witnessing on the part of the Church to their truth. It is simply a "permission to publish them for the instruction and advantage of the faithful " (Benedict XIV., De Beatif. and Canoniz. SS., vol. ii., p. 300). " Sciendum est approbationem istam nihil aliud esse quam permissionem ut edantur ad fidelium institutionem et utilitatem." He adds that to revelations thus approved the assent of Catholic faith cannot and ought not to be given (Ibid.). Again, speaking of such revelations, he says "that it is lawful for any one to withhold his assent from them, provided it be done with becoming modesty, not unreasonably nor contemptuously" (vol. iii., p. 610.) And he notices the fact that Cardinal Torquemada, who gave his official approbation to the revelations of St. Bridget, afterwards wrote a book to refute a theological position contained in those very revelations (Ibid.).

Many who are conversant with the history and hagiology of the Church, and other branches of sacred and profane science, will see in the visions and revelations of Sister Anne Catherine certain opinions and statements from which they cannot but strongly dissent. Out of many we select one example. It is stated (vol. i., p. 349) that St. Anne had several children long before the birth of the Blessed Virgin. This opinion, drawn from apocryphal or uncertain sources, was held by some in the Middle Ages. But it has been reproved and refuted by the illustrious Cardinals Bellarmin and Baronius, Salmeron, Suarez, and the Bollandists; and in our day the *consensus fidelium* has made it offensive to pious ears. Doubtless she had imbibed this notion from old Lives of the Saints, which, in her youth, she was ever in the habit of reading and relating to others for their instruction (see vol. i., p. 108 and 109), and the subjective impressions lent their color to her objective visions. (See the great Bollandist, Papebrochius, in his answer to F. Sebastian à S. Paulo, quoted by F. Cuperus in the Acta Sanctorum, sixth vol. of July, p. 242, where he explains the vision of B. Colette, in which she relates having seen St. Anne with her three children, each the child of a different husband.) No Catholic reader need be disturbed by these visions, or frightened by them into renouncing his previous opinions, if he will only bear in mind the sensible conclusion of the same Papebrochius. "In talibus (sanctarum mulierum visionibus) nihil esse præsidii ad quæstiones pure historicas, seu sacræ illæ seu profanæ sunt, prudenter dirimendas; proinde nihil ipsis sanctis detrahi cum talium veritas citra ullum ad illas respectum, vocatur in controversiam, aliunde probanda vel infirmanda" (Ibid.). "Such (visions of holy women) can be of no help in deciding with prudence on merely historical questions, whether sacred or profane. Hence no wrong is done the saints themselves when the truth of such opinions is controverted, and decided on other ground, without any regard whatsoever to aught that has been said by these holy women."

One word more (and we think it seasonable, if not necessary) as to the visions and revelations of Sister Emmerich. They teem with denunciations of the lax disedifying life led by so many ecclesiastics. And for these denunciations there was abundant reason. The Church in Germany was slowly going back to that state of corruption and degradation in which it was sunk at the era of the " Reformation." Its condition in our day would have been the same, or worse, if possible, had it not pleased God to remember His former mercies, and for the sake of His servants Aphra, Boniface, Henry, Elizabeth, Gertrude, and other saints, to rescue from utter ruin the land watered by their blood and tears. In His infinite wisdom He made use of His enemies to accomplish His purpose. It was done step by step. The tyrannical oppression of the Church by Joseph II. was seemingly the beginning of better days, and still more, the unscrupulous despotism of Bonaparte, whose imperial sway extended to the left bank of the Rhine. But the dawn of quite a new era for Catholic Germany dates from 1837, when the Prussian government so signally outraged liberty and justice by the imprisonment of the Archbishops of Cologne and Posen. This high-handed measure awakened a feeling not only in Prussia, but throughout the whole of Germany, that of itself alone would have led gradually to the entire redemption of the German Church. But Divine Providence, wishing mercifully to hasten the completion of the good work, sent Bismarck to give the finishing stroke to whatever of evil yet lingered in the clergy and laity of Germany. No Attila, nor other divinely commissioned rod of iron, ever did the Great Master's work more successfully. By his cruel, brutal injustice, masked under forms of law, his attempts to annihilate free speech at home and abroad, his wicked, systematic persecution of the clergy by imprisonment, fines, and banishment, he has succeeded in creating a united Catholic Germany, of orthodox faith, of exemplary life, of heroic courage, as thoroughly devoted to the Holy See as Ireland or the Tyrol—in a word, a body that may well be a source of pride and envy to the whole Catholic world.

In the days of Anne Catherine Emmerich, however, it was far otherwise. Indifferentism, which had grown up with rationalism and false philanthropy amongst the sects, had penetrated the Catholic body and found adherents amongst churchmen and the more learned of the laity. Catholic princes grew tired of Rome's supremacy, and had no difficulty in finding ecclesiastical scribes whose pride or venality made them willing enough to aid their rulers in making war upon what they called Rome's pretensions. The mean, beggarly spirit that led Protestant men of letters in Germany to despise their own noble language, and strive to bring to perfection their literature by thoroughly Gallicizing it, made its way into Catholic theology. The true meaning of revealed doctrine, of discipline and Church jurisprudence, was no longer sought for in their true sources, but in the muddy streams of Pierre d'Ailly, Launoy, Fleury, Richer, and, still worse, of Nicole, Gerberon, and Quesnel. Thus originality, national pride, and self-respect fared no better than orthodoxy.

Where Catholic faith is wantonly abandoned, or treated with contemptuous indifference, a corresponding decline in good morals is sure to follow. Luther had often complained bitterly, that whereas he had expelled one devil by changing the old faith of Germany, seven other devils worse than the first had come in with his new gospel to occupy the ground he had won by his labors. So it was with these reformed Catholic ecclesiastics of the last century. They had got rid of all reverence for the Pope and his supremacy; they had brought themselves to believe that Protestants, and especially the Pietists, were as good as Catholics, if not much better; but they had not the honesty to leave the Church which they had ceased to respect. They retained its wealth, and dishonored it by their shameful lives. To use Luther's style, the devil of the Pope's pretensions was gone, only to give place to other devils, dishonesty, covetousness, rapacity, unbridled lust, and, in some cases, total unbelief. The ecclesiastical principalities, Cologne, Mayence, Treves, Salzburg, and others (Würzburg formed a noble exception), as they were first in dignity, held also the first place in worldliness and immorality. To give one instance out of many, the Elector and Prince-Bishop of Mayence, Frederic Charles, Baron von Erthal, was an enlightened hater of Rome and its primatial rights; but he was a liberal patron of the arts, of the chase, and of the theatres, one of which he supported out of his princely revenues, and where he frequently appeared with the *ladies* of his court (Hofdamen). He ground his subjects to almost starvation by his exactions to keep up his state and magnificence as a worldly ruler, forgetting all the while that they were his spiritual flock, and he their consecrated, divinely appointed shepherd. Whilst in public he affected the role of a Mecænas, or Augustus, or Leo X. in his patronage of art and science, and framed novel plans of education by the advice chiefly of Protestant counsellors,[1] in private life he was the slave of his titled harlots, whom he kept in his palace and paraded before the public so unblushingly that the whole city caught the infection and became the prey of im-

---

[1] In justice, however, we must add what Karl Adolf Menzel says of one of these Protestants, Nicholas Vogt, afterwards Professor of History in the projected University, that in his lectures, like John von Müller, he showed what Europe owes to the Catholic hierarchy in a more favorable light than has been done by Catholic writers of that day or of later times : " Doch hat gerade dieser protestantische Geschichtslehrer, wie Johannes von Müller, die Verdienste der Hierarchie um dis europäische Menschheit günstiger als viele der damaligen und der späteren Katholischen Historiker beurtheilt." Neuere Geschichte der Deutschen, Breslau, 1847, vol. xii., p. 300.

morality.[1] When Heinse published a filthy obscene novel, he received twenty Louis d'or as a gratuity from the prince-bishop. A rascally Jew, who kept a circulating library of the dirtiest, vilest literature in Mayence, was safe under the protection of the prince-bishop's police. And while all this was going on, as if to show his utter contempt for Catholic doctrine and morals, he sneeringly offered a prize to authors for the best essay on the excellence of celibacy.[2] But enough of this detestable prince-bishop of Mayence; we have only mentioned him that the others may be judged accordingly. *Ab uno disce omnes.*[3]

While corruption was so rampant in these high places and amongst the great dignitaries of the Church, what wonder is it that their demoralizing influence was felt throughout all Germany, in bishoprics, parishes, convents, monasteries, and amongst the laity, for whom all religious and devout confraternities and associations of piety and benevolence had been forbidden by so-called Catholic reforming princes, as savoring of superstition.[4] This was the state of things in Germany, though partially modified, when Sister Anne Catherine received her revelations.[5] We cannot be surprised to find from her Life by F. Schmoeger, that when the condition of the Church in Germany was revealed to her, this holy nun should be filled with just indignation in seeing God's ministers rebelling against Him and serving in the ranks of His enemies. That she received such revelation we have not a shadow of doubt; but we cannot bring ourselves to believe that the revelation came in the shape in which it is presented by Brentano and F. Schmoeger. The poet and the Redemptorist, though most excellent men, like all children of Adam have their human weakness, and without detriment to their character and reputation may be suspected of occasionally allowing their zeal to outrun their judgment; but nothing of the kind can be suspected of a pure, holy soul that communes with the invisible world, and stands face to face, as it were, with angels and saints and Deity itself. In that

---

[1] " Er spielte Leo X. begünstigte Wissenschaften und Künste, unterhielt aber seine Maitressen so öffentlich, dass vom Beispiele des Hofes angesteckt ganz Mainz liederlich wurde." Wolfgang Menzel, Geschichte der Deutschen bis auf die neuesten Tage. Stuttgart, 1855, vol. iv., p. 232.

[2] Ibid.

[3] These " sacred principalities," sinks of moral and social corruption, and bitterly hostile to the Holy See, were in the year 1803 swept out of existence by God's avenging justice, and their territories handed over to Protestant rulers.

[4] Yet so strong is the human mind that these pious associations, when driven out of existence, soon revived in a human or pagan form, as societies for the promotion of worldly gayeties and profane amusements. See J. Burton Robinson in Memoir of Moehler, prefixed to his Symbolism. New York, 1844, p. 48.

[5] Anne Catherine Emmerich was born in 1774, the very year in which Baron von Erthal was elected to the bishopric of Mayence.

presence she could never forget the precepts of Christian charity, nor lose sight of God's commandment to Israel, " *Principi populi tui ne maledixeris.*" [1]

There may be nothing very uncharitable in her mention by name of the priest Wessenberg, the leader of the anti-celibataire party in Baden ; but what good was to come of it, unless her warnings were published in Baden rather than in Münster, we cannot imagine. But what is most atrocious is the contumely heaped on the head of Cardinal Consalvi, who is almost invariably mentioned by name. In these alleged revelations he is a good-for-nothing (Taugenichts); "he does much harm, he hates his Father (Pope Pius VII.), but he is so mixed up in affairs that they cannot get rid of him. He is perfectly entangled by the secret society (the Carbonari or Weishaupt's Illuminati), that wide-spread association which works more quickly and still more superficially than even the Freemasons" (vol. ii., p. 346). She saw him "seizing her by the shoulders and endeavoring to prevent her from adoring the Blessed Sacrament" (Ibid., p. 350). She struggled to free herself and by physical force dragged him before the altar. He tried to burn down the old "Nuptial house" (the Church founded by Christ our Lord) in order to build up a new Church "which was to embrace all creeds with equal rights, Evangelicals, Catholics, and all denominations, a true communion of the unholy" (Ibid., p. 352, 353). Even the Pope is not spared, and his weakness is referred to in a way that no good Catholic likes to hear. Besides his want of firmness in the discharge of his Apostolic office, he is charged also with undue attachment to earthly ties (Ibid., p. 302). This is simply abominable. Pius VII. was an illustrious Confessor of the Faith, for which he suffered years of hardship and imprisonment. If in an unguarded moment, deprived of all counsel and deceived by false representations, he unhappily yielded to the pressing demands of his imperial jailer, it was the only fault of his life, and he nobly repaired it.[2] His memory is venerated by the whole world as that of a saint and confessor of the faith. As to Cardinal Consalvi, of whom this pious nun is alleged to have spoken so bitterly, he lived and died respected and highly esteemed by both Catholics and Protestants. From his first entrance into public life

---

[1] " Thou shalt not speak ill of the Angels, and the prince of thy people thou shalt not revile." Exodus, xxii., 28. For *angels* the Vulgate, Anglican, and Douay Bibles read *Diis, the Gods*. The Revised Version has God, and very correctly in the margin *judges*. We see no harm in adopting the euphemism (Angels for Elohim) of the LXX. in Psalm viii., 6, found likewise in the Vulgate, Anglican, and Douay Versions. The meaning, as we learn from our Lord's own interpretation (John x., 35), is "judges divinely appointed."

[2] For a full and most interesting account of the Pope's error and his glorious avowal and reparation of the same, see Cardinal Pacca's Memorie Storiche, Roma, 1830; or its English translation by Sir Francis Head.

till his last hour, as long as Pius VII. lived, he was prized and honored by that Pontiff. And if the friendship and esteem of holy personages are proofs of a man's good character, so, too, is the hatred of the wicked and of the enemies of the Church. Napoleon hated Cardinals Pacca and Consalvi more than any other members of the sacred college, because he regarded them as the Pope's most trusty counsellors and authors of the energetic measures which he took to defend the rights of the Church. He used to say of the latter that, "though he did not look like a priest, yet he had more of the priest in him than any of his colleagues." His liberality to the poor, his truthfulness, so rare in personages renowned for diplomatic ability, his rigorous observance of all ecclesiastical duties, fasting and frequent confession, are mentioned by all his biographers.[1] Theiner, while condemning from a historical point of view the written memoirs of Cardinal Consalvi,[2] does justice to his character. He calls him "cet illustre prince de l' Eglise, non moins remarquable par les vertus privées que par son talent diplomatique."[3]

And it is of this holy and exalted personage, this illustrious churchman and "prince of God's people," that Sr. Emmerich is made to speak in the harsh language of reviling and contempt, denouncing him as an outcast from the Church, and to behold him in vision as "surrounded by a fog, cut off by a wall of separation, as if under the ban of excommunication."[4] If we really believed that Sister Emmerich had uttered such unchristian language, we should feel disposed to treat her words as the hysterical ravings of a pious, nonsensical woman. But we believe nothing of the kind. Sister Emmerich was a Saint, as is very evident from her life, and in her speech was not like one of the unbelieving foolish women[5] rebuked by Job and Tobias. The fact is, we have very little confidence in either Brentano or Schmoeger, as exponents of the holy woman's revelations. Brentano was a noble, poetic soul, but he

---

[1] Franz Werner, art. Consalvi, in Herder's new edition of Wetzer and Welte's Kirchenlexicon.

[2] Memoires du Cardinal Consalvi, Secretaire d'Etat du Pape Pie VII., avec une Introduction et des Notes par J. Crétineau-Joly, Paris (Plon), 1864. Two vols. in 8vo.

[3] Histoire des deux Concordats de la République Française et de la République Cisalpine, par Augustin Theiner, Préfet des Archives du Vatican. Bar-le-duc, L. Guerin et Co., 1869, vol. i., Preface, pp. ix., x. It is natural to inquire what motives can have induced Theiner to attack the accuracy (defective memory he politely calls it) of the Cardinal, to accuse him of prejudice and bitterness, to see in Napoleon a loyal and zealous son of the Church, and to cover up his wicked persecution of the Church and its Visible Head by the soft name of "fautes echappées à la faiblesse humaine" (Ibid., p. viii.). But we can discover none, unless it be antipathy to whatever was written or published by Crétineau-Joly.

[4] Schmoeger's Life of Sister Anne Catherine, vol. ii., p. 351.

[5] "Quasi una de stultis mulieribus locuta es." Job ii., 10, cf. Tobias, ii., 8, 15, 22, 23.

could not tie himself down to the plain prose of what she uttered. The gaps (or what he thought such) in her communications he filled up from his own imagination, and where personages, especially churchmen, were introduced, the same fertile source supplied their names. Though born in the Catholic Church, he had wandered off into the desert of unbelief, and when he came back to the Church of his baptism, his ardent temperament fired him with all " the fury of a convert's zeal." He was especially severe on the German ecclesiastics who favored novelties and on the remissness of the Roman authorities in not condemning them with the rigor he desired, as if the Roman Pontiff and his counsellors were not better judges of such matters than a layman who had been just saved by divine mercy from utter shipwreck of faith and morals.

This is partially admitted by Father Schmoeger. Here is his account of Brentano's committing to paper Sr. Emmerich's visions. " He had, it is true, planted diligently (that is, in beginning a new Christian life), but many weeds yet remained to be rooted out. His rich, lively imagination was as yet (when he began his task as her amanuensis in July, 1820) too undisciplined for the reproduction of Sister Emmerich's visions in their native simplicity, and it cost him a struggle (did he succeed? That is the question) not to embellish them with his own poetical ideas. The interpretations he gave them were infallible in his eyes, and he hesitated not to introduce them freely *without specifying their origin.* This happened *principally* during the first year, when Sister Emmerich's labors for the Church formed the greater part of her communications. He had repeatedly been told that the invalid had asked Almighty God as a special favor not to be informed for what special individual among the clergy she was called upon to pray and suffer; yet it was not without difficulty that Brentano could be dissuaded from introducing the names of persons to whom he fancied certain visions particularly applicable" (vol. i., pp. 427, 428). When he undertook afterwards to rewrite his miscellaneous notes and put them into a more orderly shape, his old habit got the better of him. He again indulged his inventive, poetical fancy ; and even F. Schmoeger has to confess that he could make no use of this " revised record," because it did not " faithfully accord with the original notes" (Preface to vol. ii., p. viii.)[1].

---

[1] We would not willingly say a word to detract from the merits of such a thorough Catholic as Clement Brentano, nor appear to lend a voice to the chorus of his Lutheran, Evangelical, and infidel haters. As long as he was estranged from the Church of his baptism, he had numerous admirers everywhere amongst the literati of Germany. But as soon as he came back repentant to the faith of his fathers, a wild howl of execration, as if hell were groaning over a rescued soul, was heard from all quarters. Foremost among them was the Lutheran, Voss, a pompous old bigot who, without a spark of Christian faith, had outraged in the same way the return to the faith of such noble

Of Father Schmoeger's share in recording these visions, we cannot speak very highly. He has done credit to the saint's memory by giving the substance of her examinations, by commissions civil and ecclesiastical, which redounded to her honor, and covered her infidel enemies (Catholics, so called, and Protestants) with shame and ignominy. But as to her visions and revelations, he has only drawn from Brentano's notes, " selecting what he deemed necessary for the present biography" (vol. ii., Preface, p. vii.). We are thus driven back on Brentano's authority; and in his Life of the Saint (we use this word in a technical sense, and with all due reverence to the constitutions of the Holy Apostolic See) F. Schmoeger does not always let us know whether it is Brentano, Dean Overberg, or Father Limborg, or some one else, who received from her mouth the revelations. If the case of Sister Anne Catherine ever is referred to Rome, this will form an insuperable difficulty. She may be canonized, for her heroic virtues deserve the honor, but her visions and revelations will find no approbation, unless they rest on safer authority than that of Brentano or Schmoeger.

Far be it from us to disparage, by anything we have said, the value of what is good, useful, and authentic in Sister Emmerich's revelations. We think that clergy and laity can learn from them a great deal to their advantage. The sanctity and value of relics, the importance of priestly blessing, and the holiness of those fingers that handle daily the Holy of Holies, the advantage and necessity of prayer for the faithful departed, even for living heretics and schismatics, and for children yet unbaptized, with other matters that she treats of as one evidently "taught of God," cannot fail to edify all readers, lay and clerical, and encourage them to remember their Christian duties, and take their allotted share in what they daily profess to believe, the "Communion of Saints."

---

souls as Stolberg and Schlegel, and the beastly Jewish-Lutheran cynic Heinrich Heine. Here is a specimen of the way in which his conversion was ridiculed by Evangelicals, who would have preferred to see him become an Atheist rather than return to the Church of Christ. In the "Poetischer Hausschatz" (Leipzig, 1844), a thick and very interesting volume of more than 1300 pages, the editor, O. L. B. Wolff, a Jena professor (Evangelical or Infidel, or probably both), has the following spiteful, sneering notice of Brentano, some of whose poems are given in the volume. "Brentano Clemens, geb. 1777, zu Frankfurt a M., lebte einige zeit als thätiges mitglied der Propaganda zu Rom und privatisirt jetzt in Frankfurt a M." (Verzeichniss der Dichter, p. 1146.) This is a special, malicious notice accorded to no one else but Brentano. All other authors are merely set down as Catholic priests (Spee, Diepenbrock, etc.), Lutheran ministers, State counsellors, etc.; but the fiat had gone forth from Freemason headquarters to write down Brentano, and parsons, professors, and unbelievers of every kind obeyed it without scruple.

It must, however, be stated in fairness that Protestants like Bohmer and Wolfgang Menzel remained faithful in their admiration of the illustrious German poet, even after his conversion, and fearlessly expressed themselves in his favor.

BOOK NOTICES.

HISTORY OF THE UNITED STATES OF AMERICA FROM THE DISCOVERY OF THE CONTINENT. By *George Bancroft.* The Author's Last Revision. Volume III. 8vo. D. Appleton & Co. : New York.

The great history of the country is unequally divided. The picture of the earlier exploration of successive colonies, their settlement and growth, is unfolded to the reader in two volumes, yet here half that space, devoted to the annals of two centuries and a half, is given to a period of eleven years, extending from 1763 to 1774, a period not full of events or stirring transactions; in fact, a lull between two great wars. Eminently a philosophical historian, seeking to study the springs of action, and the successive phases of thought as schemes of statesmen grow, develop, modify, under the pressure of events or of public opinion or prejudice, Mr. Bancroft has in this period a task peculiarly suited to him, and for which he brings eminent qualities. A man who has himself borne his part in the highest councils of the nation, who in foreign embassies enjoyed the closest relations with the greatest statesmen of our time, with his mind stored with a mass of information bearing on his topic, the richness of which is almost incalculable, Mr. Bancroft in this volume traces with great skill and power, and with a vivid and clear narrative, the development of the anti-American action of the English ministries and the king, the apathy of the English people and the great mercantile community, which, too gross to look beneath the surface, beheld without alarm the progress of a policy which was to strike a deadly blow at the great commerce of England. Even self-interest, usually so keen of sight, was blind. On the other side Mr. Bancroft depicts the development of the sturdy opposition of the people of the British Colonies, clinging to their British liberties, still full of respect for the Crown and Constitution of England, but bolder even than their political leaders in their resolution to resist oppression in its very commencement. It is the period of the successive steps by which the English Government sought to tax the unrepresented Colonies, by the Act of a Parliament where even their representation would have been a mere ceremony, without power for good. It is the period of the Acts of Navigation, the Stamp Act, the establishment of military force in the Colonies, the Tea Duties. Step by step the purblind statesmen of England drove the people of each Colony to study, to question, to resist, and finally to unite with each other for deliberation and action in a representative body, which was the nucleus of a new government. The Stamp Riots, the Boston "Massacre," the Boston Tea Party, the Regulators' battle at Alamance, the burning of the Gaspee, were the few indications of the fierce volcanic fires burning beneath the surface. In the Colonies, themselves, there were few events not connected with the political question of the day,—the brief but tragic Pontiac War, the hard-fought battle with the Shawnees.

In the eloquent pages of Bancroft we can follow, too, the keen watch which the statesmen of France kept on the Colonies, and the accurate estimate which they formed of the temper, tendency, and determination of that British community which had grown up beyond the Atlantic. Shrewder than the English statesmen, the French Ministry sent its secret agents to America to traverse the Colonies, study and report. A Prime

Minister in France sat down from time to time to read, with experienced eyes, extracts from newspapers, sermons, political pamphlets, and letters received from America, and rose from his table better informed, by far, than the Prime Minister of the sovereign whose rule extended over those American Colonies.

The volume closes with less than a page devoted to the Quebec Act. In this, and a subsequent allusion to it, we think the great historian has misunderstood that legislative enactment. The Act was one to carry out the capitulation of New France,—a tardy but honest step. The Province of Quebec, created by it, was identical with the New France which capitulated, and which held by a line of forts from Du Quesne to Niagara the country northwest of the Ohio. It is fallacious to say : " In disregard of the charters and rights of Massachusetts, Connecticut, New York, and Virginia, it extended the boundaries of the new government of Quebec to the Ohio and the Mississippi, and over the region which included, besides Canada, the area of the present States of Ohio, Michigan, Indiana, Illinois, and Wisconsin." That territory, so far as its settlers went, had been part of New France ; its local government and officers were appointed by the French Governor of New France, its clergy by the Bishop of Quebec ; its laws, its ordinances, its tenure of real estate, all were those of New France. There was not in the territory any hamlet of English origin, any vestige of authority established by Massachusetts or Connecticut, New York and Virginia. It fell into the hands of the King as part of New France, and the Quebec Act did not include it " besides Canada," but as part of Canada or New France. Even after the recognition of our Independence, in 1783, the claims of Virginia, though reinforced by the occupation of that territory by Virginia troops, with the full consent of the inhabitants, were so little recognized by the other States, that one of the acts of the Continental Congress, after the war, was a substantial following up of the Quebec Act, after refusing to guarantee the claim of Virginia. The States yielded up their shadowy rights, and Congress, April 23d, 1784, adopted its " Ordinance for the government of the Northwestern Territory," an imperial act of the nation, like the Quebec Act, which had been in force unrepealed for ten years, and was necessarily adopted, except in so far as it was in conflict with the Ordinance.

The Quebec Act deserves more space than has been given to it. A storm of anti-Catholic prejudice was evoked by it, as may be seen in the newspapers and pamphlets of the day. More serious topics soon overshadowed it ; but the minds of the people and of some extremely narrow-minded public men, like John Jay, were influenced throughout by it. We see this in the Address Jay penned to the People of Great Britain, which, with the conduct that inspired New England troops in Canada, lost us that Colony. We see traces, too, in the errors of Jay, at Paris and Madrid ; and we see the influence of the bigotry even in the Declaration of Independence. In a study of the public mind the Quebec Act is necessarily an important element for consideration.

LIFE OF ANNE CATHERINE EMMERICH. From the German of Very Rev. *K. M. Schmoeger*, C.SS.R. New York: Fr. Pustet & Co. 1885.

The Life of Anne Catherine Emmerich is known to thousands in Germany, Italy, and France. On its first publication the late Pius IX., of blessed memory, ordered an Italian translation to be made from advance proof-sheets of the German. The French translation was in like manner made from proof-sheets furnished by the Very Rev. Author. The translation into English has been made from the German edition of 1870, under the conviction that a book which has proved highly useful to readers in other lands will not be less so to those of English-speaking countries.

The question of the reality of the supernatural ecstasies of Anne Catherine Emmerich, and of the visions with which she was favored during those ecstasies, has been subjected to successive rigid examinations, by eminent theologians and distinguished prelates, and are dealt with elsewhere in this number of the REVIEW.

In the light of faith there is nothing strange in the fact, that here and there there are chosen ones of God's children who are called to endure supernatural sufferings on earth, to endure in their persons the agony of the Cross and to be favored with special visions and revelations. Almighty God at all times selects certain souls who, either secluded from the world or amid the hurry of secular life, shall serve as instruments in suffering and combating for His Church, in testifying through their own experience, while still in the flesh, to the constant presence of the supernatural with us and to the realities of the spiritual world. The lives and sufferings of such chosen ones are often very different. Some appear as victims in the body, suffering excruciating physical torments, whilst others combat and suffer for the Church spiritually. Yet, as their lives are a perpetual sacrifice, a course of constant endurance in perfect abandonment to the will of God, they closely resemble one another.

But it is easy also to see that Anne Catherine Emmerich had also a special mission from God to fulfil. It was hers to bring before the German people the Gospel in its most minute details just at a time when the Divinity of Christ and other Gospel truths were most strenuously denied by the so-called philosophers of the day. These skeptics, "wise in their own conceits," could explain away, each to his own satisfaction, though not to the satisfaction even of other skeptics, the miracles and all the other evidences of the Divinity of our Blessed Redeemer, attributing them to natural or imaginary causes. But here was a poor, entirely uneducated girl, who without any natural means of knowledge endured over again in her own life His sufferings on the Cross, carried His wounds upon her own person, described even in their smallest details the various circumstances and situations in which the Sacred Person of our Divine Lord figures, at meals, at marriage-feasts, on journeys, etc.; and does it in a way in which not the least trace of anything unworthy of His Divinity can be found. Moreover, she describes the scenes she witnessed, the various places she visited in her ecstasies in the Holy Land and in different other far-off countries as regards the physical features of these countries, the various languages, manners, and customs of their people, and various other circumstances relating to the geography and archæology of those countries in times long past, and all with a minuteness of detail which the most observant travellers and distinguished scholars have never surpassed, if equalled, and with an accuracy that defies all their efforts to find a defect in.

Here is a fact which sets at defiance all the attempts of skeptics to resolve the supernatural into the natural, and to explain the former by the latter. Thus it is that God constantly chooses " the foolish things of the world to confound the wise, and the weak things of the world . . . . that He may confound the strong . . . . that no flesh should glory in His sight."

This to our mind is one of the lessons taught in this narrative of the sufferings and visions of Anne Catherine Emmerich. There are many other obvious lessons for the encouragement and edification of the fathful and devout which need not here be referred to.   .

A History of the People of the United States, from the Revolution to the Civil War. By *John Bach McMaster*, Wharton School, University of Pennsylvania. In Five Volumes. Vol. II. New York: D. Appleton & Co. 1885.

The second volume of Mr. McMaster's *History* embraces the period extending from 1790 to 1803; thus beginning after the organization of the Federal Government under Washington and extending to the fall of the Federal party and the election in which Jefferson, after a long struggle, defeated his fellow-candidate, Burr, and secured the presidency. It is the period when the influence of Revolutionary France was potent in forming a new set of political ideas, against which those who clung to the old system of English liberty strove manfully. The violence of partisans and of newspapers was excessive, and Washington lost his well-earned popularity, and received insults from Congress, from the press, and from individuals. The treaty with England, negotiated by Jay, aroused a storm of unpopularity against him, and drew upon the country the hostility of France, resulting in a brief war on the ocean; yet the treaty, with all its concessions, did not save us from a more serious war with England.

At home the necessity of direct taxation led to the Whiskey Insurrection and to a petty disturbance by Fries.

The author brings vividly before us, by his use of the newspapers of the day and the remarks of travellers, as well as letters and other sources, the social and domestic life, the amusements, dress, fashions, opinions, and ideas of the time. The political affairs, of course, in such excited times occupied no little of the public mind, but we can follow with interest the progress of the country, the decline of slavery at the North, the growth of the mail system, the increase of paper-mills and other manufactures, the invention of the cotton-gin and the impulse it gave to southern agriculture. It is curious to study here the decline of New England Puritanism, and the breaking away from the old strict rule, as well as the commencement of camp meetings and extravagant forms, the appeals to the feelings and the senses, instead of the old hard and dry system. Then began the tendency everywhere to make religious services more attractive. The old and conservative party in most denominations opposed it steadily, but the younger wished better music—the organ or other instruments. The Dutch and German began to give place to English in parts where new generations had grown up to whom the language of their fathers was a dead tongue.

The history of this period is familiar to few except professed historical students, but Mr. McMaster presents it in its most attractive form, and, what is not included in his scheme, the details of some important public events, is very generally familiar. The service rendered by the work is not confined to an entertaining picture of the past. It is full of instructive lessons, for it is impossible to look upon this picture of the past without feeling less complacency with our own times than self-love induces us to feel.

Summa Philosophica Juxta Scholasticorum Principia, Complectens Logicam et Metaphysicam. Auctore *P. Nicolao Russo*, S.J., in Bostoniensi Collegio Philosophiæ Lectore. Bostoniæ: Apud Thomam B. Noonan et Socium. 1885.

In this age of rampant error, when human thought is still running riot in the domain of philosophy, scattering its vagaries broadcast for the poisoning of men's minds, there is urgent need of orthodox thinkers and writers to supply the human intellect with healthy food. The name of the erroneous scribblers who undertake to make public the fancies of their disordered imaginations, is legion; and the majority of readers, unfortunately, are misled by the specious and hollow pretence of learning which they give to their ephemeral effusions. A great advantage which error has is, that it may be of infinite variety, and thus mislead the superficial by a pleasing novelty in its theories; while the truth is one and indivisible, capable of variation only in the peculiar manner one may assume in presenting it and the style of the language he may use. This is a strong reason why Catholic writers should take great pains to cultivate a good literary style, which is a garb always becoming to the truth and never too precious to clothe it with. In refuting error, Catholics must necessarily use arguments that have been availed of for ages; but they should not simply repeat the words of their predecessors. They must adapt themselves, in phraseology as in social customs, to the age in which they live, and meet on their own ground the propounders of erroneous interpretations of the latest discoveries in science.

As it is in our higher schools and colleges for the laity, as well as in ecclesiastical seminaries, that the future champions of the Church are trained, the text-books used here should meet the requirements referred to above. Works, therefore, that served as guides to a former generation cannot be expected to be entirely suitable to the present. New works on the same old subjects, or new editions if the old works be so recast as to suit the changed circumstances, should always be welcomed by Catholic scholars, teachers, and students, provided they possess the requisite amount of intrinsic merit.

It is with unfeigned pleasure that we find these conditions fulfilled in the octavo volume of 440 pages whose title appears at the head of this notice. The contents of this book Father Russo has taught for years to the graduating class of Boston College, where he is Professor of Philosophy. It is a thorough treatise on logic and metaphysics, written in a clear, elegant style, arranged in the most natural order, and with its parts properly proportioned. Armed with the knowledge of Logic, —both dialetical and critical,—Ontology, or General Metaphysics, Cosmology, Anthropology, and Natural Theology, or Special Metaphysics, contained in it, a student of ordinary intelligence should entertain no fear in the battle against error. A fit supplement to this work would be a treatise of like or even wider scope on Ethics or Morals, from the same practiced mind and hand. The paper, letter-press, and binding are of a very superior order,—in perfect keeping with the contents.

THE LIFE AROUND US: A Collection of Stories. By *Maurice Francis Egan*, Author of "Songs and Sonnets," "Preludes," etc., etc. Fr. Pustet & Co.: New York and Cincinnati. P. F. Cunningham & Son, 817 Arch Street, Philadelphia.

We sincerely wish that we had, and hope that we shall have, more volumes of such stories, not only from the pen of the writer, but from other pens cultivating the same field. For the field is large and there is abundant room in it for a number of workers.

The stories are fictions, so far as the persons and particular incidents are concerned, but in other respects are true descriptions of what is occurring every day around us; and true pictures of the lives and surroundings and characters of persons we are constantly meeting. Then, too, they are pure and healthful. While there is abundant action in them, it is not the action of imaginary men and women but that of everyday life, which is constantly weaving its web of mingled sorrow and enjoyment, adversity and prosperity, and is as full of all the elements which can stir deepest emotions in human hearts, as any incidents or scenes which the most powerful imagination can conceive.

Were writers of novels and stories to cultivate their powers of perception and observation more, and strain their inventive faculties less, their productions would be more interesting as well as less unreal and extravagant.

Consciously or unconsciously, Mr. Egan, we believe, has adopted this principle ; and this constitutes one of the excellences of his stories. He is a close observer of life around us, a keen analyst of character, and possesses large descriptive power. Along with this he has a vein of quiet humor which sometimes takes the form of keen satire, yet is without venom or malice.

The influence of his stories upon their readers is always good. There is a moral in them. But the moral is not lugged in nor preached to the reader, nor is the story written for the sake of the moral. It grows out of the story, and emanates from it as fragrance exhales from the flower.

We would be glad to see more Catholic stories from Mr. Egan's pen, and especially more such stories whose scenes and characters belong to this country. There is no need going abroad to find materials for tales of deepest interest. Those materials lie immediately around, in rich abundance, in the varying incidents and scenes of American life.

THE TRAINING OF THE APOSTLES. Part IV. By *Henry James Coleridge*, of the Society of Jesus. London: Burns & Oates. 1885.

This volume concludes the first half of the " Public Life of our Lord " by Father Coleridge, and forms the fourth part of " The Training of the Apostles." The title, " Training of the Apostles," which is given to the four volumes of which this is the last, is not intended to imply that our Lord did not begin to train His Apostles before the time at which these volumes begin, or that He did not continue their training afterwards. But it was during this period of time, especially, that that teaching of their souls by the Providential action of the Eternal Father, of which we hear so much in the Gospels, was at work in raising their minds to a recognition of the great truth of our Lord's Divinity. It is the Confession of that Divinity by St. Peter, which closes this period by the great promise made to him by our Lord in return for his faith. And it is the selection of St. Peter as the rock on which the Church is to be built, which makes the point at which this volume closes the very centre and pivot of the Gospel history.

Of these volumes of Father Coleridge's it is almost impossible to speak too highly. They are painstaking, critical and devout studies of the Life of our Divine Lord as recorded by the Sacred Evangelists, in the course of which Father Coleridge calls to his aid an extensive and profound knowledge of what the Church Fathers have said on the same subjects.

ASSYRIOLOGY : Its Use and Abuse. By *Francis Brown*, Associate Professor of Biblical Philology in the Union Theological Seminary, New York. New York : Charles Scribner's Sons. 1885.

This little volume has appeared none too soon. Long, indeed, before the address of which it is an expansion was delivered, now over nine months ago, the need of some such warning to and check on rash theorizers was felt. Quacks of all kinds do irreparable injury in their way, and much of the evil consequences of empiricism in the matter of Eastern archæology cannot be undone ; but yet the warning and advice here given should be heeded and taken, and repeated until all interested parties have heard it.

TO CLERGYMEN.

PLEASE READ.

It may seem a small matter, but it is nevertheles one of the most important, and at the same time most difficult questions for a clergyman to determine How shall I dress? A wide latitude is allowed to the laity on this subject, who may, if they please, indulge their own p culiar taste in the matter of dress, whether it accords with the prevailing style or not. But not so with the clergy. They must dress in a manner distinctive from other men, and in keeping with their sacred calling. And how to do this successfully, how to strike the happy medium between the secular and the ultra clerical in this matter of their dress, is where the difficulty lies.

Three things are necessary to a good clerical garment. First, the material should always be plain black goods of fine quality. Second, it should be cut in a style, modest, unpretentious, and gentlemanly, with just sufficient fulness in front, and length in the skirts, to indicate the wearer's profession. And Third, the fit should always be close and as near perfect as possible, for no matter how fine the goods, or how clerical the cut, if the garment is not a good fit it is an eyesore, and a cause of constant discomfiture to the wearer.

Now many years of experience in this branch of our business have given us a familiarity with the wants of clergymen in this matter of dress that has proved of great service to our patrons; and we shall be pleased to give to all who may favor us in the future the benefit of our best judgment on the subject.

Our large experience and extensive facilities enable us to give entire satisfaction, not only as regards the style and quality of the garments themselves, but also as to the reasonableness of the prices.

On application a set of samples will be forwarded to any Clergyman in the U. S., with full instructions for self-measurement. The samples will be of goods which will cost, when made up, from $20 to $50.

Address,

WANAMAKER & BROWN,

OAK HALL, SIXTH AND MARKET STREETS,

PHILADELPHIA.

The Largest Retail Clothing House in America.

P. S.—Samples also sent and orders received for all kinds of Gentlemen's Clothing at the lowest possible prices.

THE AMERICAN CATHOLIC

QUARTERLY REVIEW.

THE AMERICAN CATHOLIC QUARTERLY REVIEW is issued regu
larly in January, April, July, and October.

EACH NUMBER CONTAINS 192 pages, large octavo, printed from
legible type, on fine white paper.

SUBSCRIPTION, $5.00 per annum, payable in advance, or $1.25
a single copy. Postage free to all parts of the U. S.

The Editorial Department is conducted by Right Rev. James A.
Corcoran, D.D.

It is DESIGNED that the *American Catholic Quarterly Review*
shall be of the highest character that can be given it by the
educated Catholic mind of the United States and of Europe.

It is NOT PROPOSED that it shall be confined to the discussion
of theological subjects, but that it shall embrace within its scope
all subjects of interest to educated Catholics, whether philosophical, historical, scientific, literary, or political—using the latter term
in its original and proper meaning. Partisan politics, or politics
in the popular sense of the word, it is scarcely necessary to say,
will be rigidly excluded.

THE MOST LEARNED and scholarly writers that can be secured
will be enlisted in support of the *Review* as regular and
occasional contributors; and every effort will be made by its
conductors to render it an able and efficient auxiliary to the
Church in her warfare against modern error.

Subscriptions respectfully solicited.

Address, **HARDY & MAHONY,**

505 CHESTNUT STREET,

THE

AMERICAN

CATHOLIC QUARTERLY

REVIEW.

Bonum est homini ut eum veritas vincat volentem, quia malum est homini ut eum veritas vincat invitum. Nam ipsa vincat necesse est, sive negantem sive confitentem.

S. AUG. EPIST. ccxxxviii. AD PASCENT.

PHILADELPHIA:

HARDY AND MAHONY, PUBLISHERS AND PROPRIETORS,

505 CHESTNUT ST.,—P. O. BOX 1044,

York: D. & J. SADLIER & Co., F. PUSTET—*Boston:* THOS. B. NOONAN & Co., NICH. M. WILLIA
ltimore: JOHN MURPHY & Co., JOHN B. PIET & Co.—*Cincinnati:* BENZIGER BROS., F. PUSTET
St. Louis: P. FOX, BENZIGER BROS., B. HERDER—*San Francisco:* A. WALDTEUFEL.—*New Orleans:*
CHARLES D. ELDER—*Montreal:* D. & J. SADLIER & Co.—*St. John, N. B.:* T. O'BRIEN &
Co.—*London:* BURNS & OATES—*Dublin:* W. H. SMITH & SON, M. H. GILL & SON.

*NEWSDEALERS SUPPLIED BY THE AMERICAN NEWS COMPANY, NEW YORK—
NTRAL NEWS CO., PHILADELPHIA—NEW ENGLAND NEWS CO., BOSTON—CINCINNATI NEWS C
CINCINNATI, OHIO—WESTERN NEWS CO.. CHICAGO, ILL.*

Congress in the year 1879, by HARDY & MAHONY in the Office of the

THE AMERICAN CATHOLIC
QUARTERLY REVIEW.

VOL. X.—OCTOBER, 1885.—No. 40.

THE CAUSES OF THE JANSENIST HERESY.

Controversiarum de Divinæ Gratiæ Liberique Arbitrii Concordia, Initia et Progresssus enarravit Gerardus Schneemann, S. J. Friburgi Brisgoviæ: Sumptibus Herder.

GREAT historical facts are not the results of spontaneous causes, nor are they to be attributed to one man, with whose name they may be identified. The ideas, long before they take effect, lie, perhaps unconsciously, in the human mind; they gradually shine forth, change traditional views and belief, direct the desires and aspirations of the age, till one man is sent by God to open the new depths of the soul for the glory of the Most High and the joy of man, or is permitted by Divine Providence to let loose the tides of long-cherished and hidden errors as a new proof of human frailty and malice and a warning to coming generations. Three great powers move through the stream of human events: Divine Providence, which orders all things, never allowing chance, fate, or blind force; free will, unimpaired by the eternal decrees of the Almighty; and the ever active spirit of evil, permitted by God to entice and to seduce the soul by the unreal good. Without tracing the bright and dark periods of human history to the germs of their greatness or decline, historical understanding and knowledge are impossible.

Jansenism is the outgrowth of Protestantism, both in its spirit and in its doctrine. Great heresies, being favored by the spirit of the time,—for otherwise they could not succeed,—not only withdraw thousands of souls from the bosom of the Church, but also infect the remaining faithful, who too are children of the age, with their poison.   Thus Semipelagianism sprang from Pelagianism, thus modern Old Catholics from German rationalism in history and theology, thus Jansenism from the Reformation.   We see the same break with theological tradition, the same exclusive turning towards one author,—St. Augustine,—the same hatred of spiritual authority, the same courting of the mighty of this earth.   The Church then as now was stern and resolute, the heretics changeable and deceitful.   Jansenism is at the same time the precursor of the Encyclopedists and of the Revolution.   The names of Calvin, Jansenius, Arnauld, Quesnel, Voltaire, and Robespierre, only express the same idea in its different phases.   The long religious dissensions brought forth as a final result the infidelity which was ripening amid the religious strife.   " Few men to-day know the history of the Church during the seventeenth century, and yet it alone contains the key to all the religious events accomplished in the course of the following two centuries."[1]

Every heresy—Protestantism and Jansenism more than any other—subverts the true notion of the divine or human nature. Man either disappears before God, or he overrules God, but always the creature is either emancipated or deified.   " Either the objective truth is confounded with the subjective man, and then we have pantheism; or the soul is confounded with the body, and then we have materialism; or the image of God is rejected from the soul, and then God is declared unknown and unknowable."[2]   The two great dogmas of original sin and redemption, in their Catholic sense, form the balance against the intellectual, moral, and social disorder on earth.

The struggles of life, the restless aim towards an unknown end, the yearning of every soul after rest and peace, only prove the words of St. Augustine: " Thou hast made us for Thee, O God, and our heart is disturbed until it rests in Thee."[3]   To the ancients they were an enigma; we seek in vain for a certain hope of immortal life beyond the grave; despair is the gloomy picture of the thinking mind, pleasure the repose of the ignorant.   " There was wanting the consciousness of sanctity in God, and the need of sanctification in man."[4]   Christianity opened to man the true pathway to his glorious destiny.   The dualism staring from every pagan philosophy was overcome by the Incarnation, and the Incarnation had its reason in original sin, its term in the Redemption.   The creature was ele-

---

[1] Dom Guéranger: Inst. Lit., vol. ii., ch. 17, p. 43.
[2] Ullathorne: Endowments of Man, ch. i., p. 8.   [3] Confess., p. 1.
[4] Döllinger.: Heidenthum und Judenthum, p. 633.

vated to oneness with the Creator; the Church became the fruit of that union; the blessed Eucharist the source of grace. The "Reformers" and the Jansenists broke this bond of harmony. Exaggerating the fearful chastisements of the first man, they plunged human nature into an abyss of nothingness; God and humanity were separated by the denial of the Real Presence, for the wants of the soul could not be satisfied, because the Blessed Sacrament was no more the consolation of poor human life; the union of Christian nations was dissolved by the withdrawal from Rome, the centre of unity; the basis of the social order was shaken by loosening the sacred tie of marriage. Wavering and confusion became the marks of science, for reason lost its guide; nations were thrown into a chaos of intellectual and moral decay, the result of which is only known to God alone. In fine, the " Reformation" was a rebellion against the unity of faith and spiritual authority. "Elle était essentiellement révolutionnaire," says Guizot.[1] Jansenism fed this spirit of contempt and disregard during the following century, till its disciples embraced atheism and the worship of reason. "On vit ses adeptes passer de plain pied de la doctrine de Saint-Cyran et de Montgeron à l'athéisme et au culte de la raison."[2]

The essence of the conflict between the Church and the world is the combat of truth and error, of the spirit and the flesh. The weapons used by the world are always the same; "they have been, are, and always will be the civil power;"[3] the final end is its supremacy. Distrust and varying suspicion were kept alive against the Church of God from the beginning; they never could avert *her* from the path of her divine mission, but they often misled parts of her flock and of her pastors. Fraud and violence thwarted her earnest endeavors in selecting true guardians of faith; servility only too often stains the policy of the clergy; they join only too often the unscrupulous abettors of pride and ambition. Still the holders of one office in the Church never became the prey of human intrigue, never discarded a hair's-breadth of the heavenly treasure given to their trust; the Papacy is built on a rock, against which the gates of hell shall not prevail. Thither the enemy turns his zeal. What a joy, if he could overthrow that "stumbling block." "Christian faith and morals fall with the fall of Rome; Christianity without the Pope is only a human belief, unable to breathe into the heart the lofty ideas of eternal truth and wisdom."[4]

Jansenism could never have found its stronghold in French society without the league with Gallicanism, which summed up its tendency in this one idea, "to make the Pope the first of bishops,

---

[1] Civil. en Europe, leç. 12. [2] Guéranger: l. c., p. 45.
[3] Manning: Miscell. Essays, 17. [4] Maistre: Du Pape, p. 449, ed. 1821.

but to allow him nothing higher than that primacy of honor."[1] In the days of faith and piety the Church often allowed the clergy to choose their bishops, and conceded a wide influence to the secular power, because both were working in one spirit. But soon passion and private interest prevailed; the glory of God had to yield to the glory of man. This unfortunate spirit was manifested in the Pragmatic Sanction; monarch and parliament excluded Rome from the government of the Church. Dishonesty, simony, and violence penetrated the French clergy. The Church, complains Pius II., is like a hydra with many heads, and its unity is thereby totally destroyed—"si judex judicum Romanus Pontifex, judicio Parliamenti subjectus est; si hoc admittimus, monstruosam ecclesiam facimus et hydram multorum capitum introducimus et unitatem prorsus extinguimus."[2] Leo X. annulled the Pragmatic Sanction, yet its sting remained. The outcry against the Papacy arose on all sides: " Rome's tyranny has abolished a system long in force in the Church of France !" A lawless independence, the overthrow of the religious system of the Middle Ages, became the ideal dream of the intelligent throughout the kingdom. Their words were not, perhaps, as violent as those of the " Reformers;" they still professed an outward union with the head of the Church, but the disguised opposition was not less forcible in their hearts. This despotism of self-will afforded ample provision for Jansenistic insolence and haughtiness.

The world of letters furnished defenders of the fatal system. Mark Anthony de Dominis, archbishop of Spalatro, published in the year 1616 his work on the " Christian Republic," which, though not a product of Gallicanism, fully exhibits its doctrine and was eagerly used by the Jansenists as an armory against the Holy See. Dominis, refusing to pay a pension imposed on him by Paul V. with his consent before his election to the metropolitan see of Spalatro, went to England, where he published his work to take revenge on the Pope. It is a strange compound of Protestantism and Catholicity; above all, it annihilates the primacy and jurisdiction of St. Peter's chair. St. Paul is equal to the Prince of the Apostles; the Protestant theory of an ideal church without any outward manifestation of the essence of the Church, appears in the confusion of church taught and church teaching. Dominis called his work "Christian Republic," because the Pope should only be the minister, and in some sort the delegate of the Christian community.

When the condemnation of the book was to be passed by the Sorbonne, Richer,[3] formerly syndic of the theological faculty, refused to be present because five years before he himself had published

---

[1] Darras: Gen. Hist., vol. iv., p. 325, Eng. trans.
[2] Spalding: Reform., vol. i., p. 63, note.
[3] Cf. Baillet: Vie de Richer.

a similar work " on the ecclesiastical and civil power," wherein he pretended to expose the true sentiments of the Gallican church and the Sorbonne; he afterwards retracted his errors, but his writings remained. His reasonings are only the re-echo of the repeated charges made against Rome. The plea of foreign encroachments on the national church naturally led to the rejection of the universal authority of the Pope.

This hostility against Rome produced absolutism at home. The " Reformers" refused obedience to the Pope; they soon had to recognize the temporal prince as their spiritual head. The French bore divine authority unwillingly; they soon had to accept the dictum, "l'état, c'est moi." The sphere of the civil power now extended over man's will and conscience. The Catholic princes, especially the Bourbons, could not go as far as their Protestant neighbors, but they indemnified themselves by severing the state from the Church, making the former supreme and independent in its own domain.[1] It happened, in the beginning of the seventeenth century, that French jurists publicly burned the writings of Suarez and Bellarmin, because these two Jesuits maintained the grand principles of the Middle Ages, which favored neither despotism nor anarchy.[2] They taught that the sovereign power comes from God, but kings are liable to lose it, and their subjects may, under certain circumstances, be freed from the allegiance due to them.[3] The deputies of the States General of 1614 proposed to make it a national dogma that the king receives his authority immediately from God, and only death alone or free resignation can relieve him of his power. The clergy and nobility, under the leadership of Cardinal Duperron, opposed the presumptuous undertaking. The parliament, however, from the midst of which the motion originally came forth, approved the proceeding of the third estate, and many a difficulty had to be surmounted by the clergy to withhold the king's assent. Strange to say, the meeting of 1614 was the last before the French Revolution, before the regicides. Sad indeed was the state of affairs in France. The bishops opposed the Pope to maintain their supposed episcopal rights, the jurists made themselves the defenders of the Gallican liberties, both against the Pope and the bishops. " Protestant in the sixteenth century," says De Maistre,[4] " with the Fronde and Jansenism in the seventeenth, philosophical at length, and republican in the last years of its existence, the parliaments but too often appeared in antagonism to the true fundamental maxims of the state. The seeds of Calvinism, fostered in

---

[1] Ketteler: Freiheit, p. 156, 5599.
[2] Cf. Rohrbacher: General History, vol. 23, p. 247.
[3] Cf. Balmes' Civil., ch. 51, vol. 3.
[4] L'église Gallic., translation taken from Darras, l. c., p. 331.

that great body, became far more dangerous when its essence changed its name and was called Jansenism. Then conscience was set at ease by a heresy which proclaimed the principle, ' I do not exist.'" The poison reached even those illustrious names in the magistracy of which foreign nations envied France the possession. Then all errors, even errors hostile to each other, being always ready to unite against the truth, the new philosophy in the parliaments leagued with Jansenism against Rome. If we take into consideration the number of magistrates in all parts of France, that of the tribunals which made it a duty and a point of honor to walk in their footsteps, the many clients of the parliaments, and all that blood, friendship, or mere ascendency drew into the same gulf, we shall easily perceive that there was material enough to form in the heart of the Gallican Church a formidable party against the Holy See.

The religious wars and political disorders did not wield the best influence on the lower clergy. The wish of the Council of Trent, that each diocese should have its own seminary, remained an empty word. There are only three such institutions mentioned till 1600: Rheims, Bordeaux and Carpentras. The young theologians were deprived of the training necessary for ecclesiastical life. They lived in the world without any practical instructions in moral and mystical theology, without conferences and retreats. The admission to holy orders was granted without the necessary trials. The people were without religious instruction ; the sacraments were not sufficiently administered ; the preparation for them neglected ; sermons were rare, without zeal and effect; Christian charity had almost vanished ; to be called a priest was a sort of contempt and insult. "Selon la commune opinion du monde, c'était alors une espèce de contumélie et d'injure, que de dire à quelque ecclésiastique de qualité qui'il était un prêtre."[1] The grievous disorder of lukewarmness in the divine service increased the strength of heresy and indifference shooting forth from the spiritual lethargy in which so many lived.

Thus Arnauld's proclamations against frequent Communion had a deeper foundation than mere words. Dark clouds of error and weakness in faith had settled thickly around the throne of our Divine Saviour since the " Reformation."[2] To see the Holy Sacrament despised and trodden under foot, to behold ghastly shapes with priestly character, should fill every noble mind with horror and disgust. But unhappy the man who, wincing under the taunts of the enemy and overawed by that dread sanctity, turns away without hope of mercy. Such men were, or, what is more likely, pretended to be, Arnauld and his followers.

---

[1] Abelly: Vie de St. Vincent, p. 3.   [2] Müller: Mass, p. 14.

It was the design of Divine Providence to raise an Olier and a St. Vincent de Paul to restore the clerical life in France; the cancer, however, was too deep to be impeded at once in its fearful ravages.

"Een serpent in den eegen boezem"—a serpent in one's own bosom, was the title the Catholics received from the states of Zeeland in 1672. Holland was the bulwark of Protestantism on the continent of Europe, a formidable power sought and feared by every nation. The prestige Spain had held on the sea was ceded to the Dutch. Their cities became the asylums of all the Protestant refugees and malcontents of Europe; the Puritan and the Huguenot, the Socinian and the Bohemian found a hiding shelter on Dutch soil. Graswinckel and Salmasius defended there the rights of the kings; Ulrich Huber proclaimed democracy as the natural and only form of true government; Spinoza enjoyed in Leyden his gloomy and fantastic dreams of the eternal substance of all things. Amsterdam, Utrecht, and Leyden opened their presses for all pamphlets proscribed in other countries. Europe was full of the anonymous and pseudonymous writings of the firm of Cologne and Pierre Martineau. And strange, says Treitschke, an unsuspected author, the sectarian spirit of the people finally penetrated the old Church: the Jansenists of Utrecht rebelled against the infallible Pope—"und seltsam der sectirerische Geist des Volkes drang endlich sogar in die alte Kirche hinüber; die Jansenisten von Utrecht lehnten sich auf gegen den unfehlbaren Papst."[1] The bold disputers were sometimes stirred up by a thunderbolt from the Hague, but as long as the stomach and counting-house were safe, said Buzenval, there was no need of making great bustle about the matter. When Descartes' philosophy was threatening the peace of the university of Leyden, the wise counsellors commanded the arguments to be taken from law or medicine, and not from theology. It is but natural that the Jansenists looked upon Holland as their promised land, where the broad ideas "left room enough for their treachery and deceit." Their poisonous literature, prohibited in France, found ready publishers in the Dutch republic, and there linger till to-day the remnants of that sect.

The salvation of the faithful is the object so sublime for which God pours out His abundant graces. If the want is extraordinary, extraordinary means are employed to lead the faithful to truth and virtue. Thus the great fathers of the Church were sent against the numerous heresies of their times; thus the Benedictines to civilize the renewed west; thus the Jesuits to fight against the "Reformers." St. Ignatius, contemplating our Saviour's Incarnation, was convinced that it had no other object but his own perfection and the sanctification of man, and chose these two sublime intentions as the fitting

---

[1] Die Repub. der Niederlande, hist. polit. Aufsatze, vol. li. p. 593.

and only object of his institute.[1] To grow in virtue and to lead others to God, their eternal end, was the only desire of the saint and his followers. Seeing the Church filled with contemplative orders, he was inspired to found a society, as he said, "like a kind of flying camp, that should be ready at the least alarm."[2] To preserve the pure faith, to defend it against heresy, and to carry the Gospel into countries deprived of it, became its great task; perfect subordination to the superiors and unconditional obedience to the Pope its distinguishing marks. The spirit of the Society was entirely opposed to that of the "Reformers." Wherever their principles met one had to yield—the Jesuits to force, the Protestants to persuasion. No order ever endured more persecution than the sons of Loyola. They were accused of perverting the youth, of revolt, despotism, and regicide. Father Guignard expired on the scaffold, an innocent victim of blind fury. The whole Order was banished from France because the assassin, John Châtel, had studied for a short time in a Jesuit college. This was the masterpiece of the policy of the Huguenots; they called the day of the "arrêt" lucky —"il fut compté au nombre des jours heureux"[3]—and erected a monument to immortalize their glorious deed. Henry IV., however, took a decided stand in favor of the Society, which checked the violence of the Calvinists. Yet outward steps, how favorable soever, do not change so suddenly the minds of men; French society remained to a large extent as hostile to the Order as ever.

The *ratio studiorum*, causing a destructive contest between the Jesuits and Dominicans, roused the resentment still more. The sons of St. Dominic regarded St. Thomas as the absolute standard of theological science. St. Ignatius, on the contrary, allowed the members of the Society the use of authors treating *ex professo* on questions purely philosophical, scriptural, or canonical; and if in the course of time a theological work more appropriate to the wants of the age should be composed, the Order could accept it with the approbation of the General. "Legetur doctrina scholastica divi Thomæ, ... sed si videtur temporis decursu alius auctor studentibus utilior futurus, ut si aliqua summa vel liber theologiæ scholasticæ conficeretur, qui his nostris temporibus accommodatior videretur, gravi cum consilio et rebus diligenter expensis per viros, qui in universa societate aptissimi existimentur, cumque Præpositi Generalis approbatione prælegi poterit."[4] The learned Lainez was even commissioned to write such a work. St. Ignatius disliked two opinions of St. Thomas—those about the Immaculate Conception and the solemn vows. His views were afterwards, as we know,

---

[1] Cf. Bartoli: Life of St. Ignatius, vol. ii., p. 20.

[2] Rodriguez: Chr. Perf., vol. iii., p. 4.

[3] Duplessis: Mém., tome ii., p. 500.   [4] Const. IV., cap. 14.

confirmed by the Church. The bull "Ascendente Domino" did not require solemn vows as an essential condition of an Order, and the dogma of the Immaculate Conception must to-day be believed by every Catholic. St. Ignatius did not exclude the idea of a clearer understanding of theological problems in the course of time. Herefrom we shall trace the cause of the Thomistico-Molinistic controversy, which afterwards served the Jansenists as another pretext for exerting their ardor against the "subtle novelties" of the Jesuits, thereby propagating their own pernicious doctrine. Thus the hatred which the doctors, magistrates, and Dominicans caused to break forth against the Society was left to the rising Jansenists. Damped, but never extinguished, hardly appeased in one period when excited anew in another, it was made a kind of theological virtue for the higher classes of the French kingdom.[1]

It is well known how much the union of the Humanists with the "Reformers" contributed to the spread of Protestantism.[2] Both hurled the shaft of their ridicule at the scholastics, not so much for the barbarous Latin some of them used, as because the orthodox theologians often condemned the most elegant style for its spurious contexts. The whole scholastic theology was thrown overboard. St. Augustine had to hold forth as a shield of Protestant brawling. "I am the whole Augustine," said Calvin; the same boasted Luther. This partial and defective system soon entered into Catholic schools. Two young professors in Louvain, Michael de Bay (Baïus) and John van Löwen (Hessels), left the scholastic method, devoting themselves entirely to Scripture and St. Augustine; Protestant errors on grace and liberty were the result. Jesse Ravestein, Ruard Tapper, the chancellor of the university, and other distinguished doctors perceived the danger. Tapper, being himself well versed in St. Augustine's works, often disputed with Baïus, who was unable to answer the objections. "Read and study the scholastics, especially St. Thomas, and you shall easily understand me," usually replied the chancellor. Baïus was a man of learning and exemplary life. His authority was very great, both among professors and students. Philip the Second sent him as one of his theologians to the Council of Trent. After his return Baïus published his greater works, renewing his errors, known already before the council. They were condemned by Pius V. in the bull "Ex Omnibus Afflictionibus." Baïus's friends asserted that the propositions in their proper sense were erroneous, but could be sustained in the sense intended by the author. Baïus himself sent a long apology to the Pope, but the Pontiff, after a sufficient

---

[1] Cf. Daxes: Des Jesuites ligueurs, p. 36.
[2] Cf. Janssen: Geschichte des deutschen Volkes, vol. ii., p. 66.

deliberation, confirmed his former judgment, intimating to Baïus that he had incurred an irregularity by his proceeding. The professor then withdrew his heresy, but after the death of Pius V. he started his defence again, till he finally, in consequence of a repeated condemnation by Gregory XIII., abjured his errors at the feet of Francis Tolet, afterwards the first cardinal of the Society of Jesus.[1]

The hinge of the Baïan heresy is that two powers inevitably govern the freedom of man: theological charity, by which he loves God above all, and concupiscence, by which he turns towards creatures as his last end. There is a threefold state of human nature —innocent, fallen, and restored. The state of innocence displays nature in its perfect integrity, immortal and predestined to the intuitive vision of God; nay, it was but just and becoming that God should create angels and men to eternal happiness. Adam by his fall lost all gifts of the first grace; nature, now subject to concupiscence, had no other power but of committing sin. In the state of reparation every good work by its very nature merits eternal life; the justification of the sinner does not consist in the infusion of grace, but in the obedience to the commandments; the motions of sensitive pleasure, though not consented to, are transgressions in the just, yet God does not impute them; there are no venial sins; the penalty of sin is forgiven, not the fault. The act of absolution only affects the first; God alone, who suggests penance, can take away the guilt. The liberty sufficient for moral works is the freedom from constraint. In fine, Baïus, like Luther and Calvin, denies all free will, and misrepresents the true notion of the merits of Christ and the merciful providence of God. Jansenius embraced the same errors, trying to soften them by the name of his work, "Augustinus."

The Baïan troubles being hardly settled, another conflict arose intimately connected with them.[2] The Jesuits at Louvain were open rivals of the university. Their professors, Bellarmin, Lessius, and Hamelius, could not help warning the students against the errors openly proclaimed in the university. Their polemics, though not personal, roused the wrath of Baïus and his friends. The humiliation of abjuring his errors into the hands of a Jesuit increased the rancor. Besides this the Jesuits, having received the power of granting degrees, refused any fees for them, whilst the university imposed them. The contest between the two bodies broke out in the year 1587. In the week after Easter the professors of the university secretly collected several copies of Lessius's lectures on Scripture and theology. Three weeks after they showed him

---

[1] S. Liguori: Hist. of Heresies, p. 364.
[2] Cf. Duchesne: Hist. du Baïanisme, p. 195.

thirty-four propositions, asking whether he would acknowledge them as his own doctrine. Lessius declared them to be mutilated, offered thirty-four other propositions, and demanded a public dispute. This was refused, and Lessius was condemned. The Jesuits abstained from further quarrels till Rome would have decided the question. Their enemies in the meantime seized every opportunity to undermine the authority and reputation of the Order. Still many students remained faithful to the Society, which caused frequent rows between the academical youth. Baius, Jansen, and Cuccius were the chief promoters of the intrigue. They were especially "provoked" by the *scientia media*, then already proclaimed by Lessius. They charged the Jesuits with Pelagianism, but Rome disapproved their action.[1]

Let us remember that Jansen was the protector of Jansenius and DuVerger during their stay at Louvain. Both venerated Baius as a saint, adorned his picture with the aureola, and regarded his works as the infallible source of theological science. Under such circumstances, it is plain that the two founders of Jansenism were imbued with the spirit of the traditional errors, plots, and contrivances.[2] Here we enter into the famous Thomistico-Molinistic controversy.

Before we continue the subject, let us first state the question and ascertain the teaching of St. Augustine and St. Thomas, who frequently were misunderstood and misrepresented in the heat of the contest.

The work of man's regeneration was defined by the Council of Trent as being performed by the mutual co-operation of the human nature with divine grace. The fallen man retains moral and religious faculties, by which he becomes responsible for his actions. The Divine Spirit suffers human freedom, because an unconditional interference with that freedom would bring about the annihilation of the moral order of the world which Divine Wisdom had founded on liberty.[3] The gap between the two is infinite. The best use of our intellectual and moral force will not raise us to God nor merit grace unless God gives it freely; then both pervading each other accomplish the one "theandric" act of justification. The words of the Council are: "If any one maintains that the free will of man, inspired and excited by God, does not co-operate, by its consent, with God exciting and calling, whereby it disposes and prepares itself for receiving grace of justification; or if any one maintains that the will cannot refuse its consent when it pleases, but, like something lifeless, does not act at all, remaining merely passive, let him be anathema."[4]

---

[1] Cf. Schneemann's Thomistisch-Molinistische Controverse, i., 125.
[2] Tournelly: De Gr., i., 321. [3] Möhler: Symbolism, i., 122.
[4] Sess. vi., can. 4.

According with this doctrine, Catholic theologians distinguish different phases in the working of divine grace. The sinner, unable to merit, or even to desire, grace, is awakened by God (*gratia excitans*); giving his consent to the divine call, he gradually advances with assisting grace (*gratia adjuvans*), which, giving strength to his good intention, enables him to acquire a true and perfect power (*gratia sufficiens*); that he, finally, by efficacious grace (*gratia afficax*), may infallibly produce the justifying act. Herein all agree, though differing about the nature of the various graces. The question arises: Wherein consists the union of efficacious grace with the consent of man? How is it possible for this grace infallibly to produce the justifying act, whilst the human will is able to resist? Does the efficiency come from the *exterior* cause, namely, the foreknowledge of God that each created will, by the use of its liberty, will consent, when God should give the necessary grace—*scientia media*—or from the *interior* cause, namely, the irresistible power of efficacious grace itself? Is there any connecting link between the free will and that which precedes it?

The great controversy itself is a sufficient proof that neither St. Augustine nor St. Thomas has solved the problem. Great and saintly theologians, earnestly devoting their whole lives to the study of the two holy doctors, they nevertheless arrived at thoroughly contrary conclusions. This is certainly not derogatory to the greatness of the two saints; the essential point of the question was not stated with the same precision in their ages as in more modern times. St. Augustine's writings on grace, being chiefly directed against the Pelagians, who denied the necessity and gratuity of grace, principally dwell on these two qualities, and hence, by the nature of the combat, differ from the question stated above.

The words of the Apostle, "As by one man sin entered into this world, and by sin death, and so death passed upon all men, in whom all have sinned . . . so, also, by the obedience of one many shall be made just,"[1] sufficed for St. Augustine. This is the foundation of the Christian faith, one and One; one man by whom the ruin came, and another Man by whom the construction.[2] All men suffered by Adam's fall, but the essence of human nature remained. Who of us should say that by the sin of the first man free will perished from the human race? Freedom, indeed, perished, but that freedom, which was in paradise, of having full justice and immortality.[3] The essence and sufficiency of human liberty are two different things; the will often wishes what it cannot perform, and not always wishes what it can perform; liberty consists in the power of determining our mind to one thing or another; but from

---

[1] Rom., v., 12-19.   [2] Sermo 30, de verb. ap. n. 5.
[3] Cont. duas Ep. Pel., lib. i., cap. 2, n. 5.

the determination does not follow the ability of executing the intention.[1] This regards the act of justification. Our end is to see God face to face; human nature cannot, by its own force, reach the supernatural order. Hence arises the necessity of grace to enlighten the understanding, to inspire the will, to heal it, to prepare it, for even to desire grace is beyond human power; "provided," Pelagius concedes, "that God not only aids the natural strength in man; but when he (Pelagius) recognizes that the will itself and the action are assisted by God, and assisted in such a way that without His help we neither could wish nor do any good, there would be no reason for dissent between us."[2] The operation of grace is both physical and moral. The Pelagians and semi-Pelagians only admitted the extrinsic inducement on the part of God, abhorring the subjective elevation of man. Grace is the internal, hidden, wonderful, and ineffable power of God, whereby He not only operates true revelations, but also good wishes,[3] for God has a greater power over the human will than man himself.[4]

All theologians agree that, according to St. Augustine, efficacious grace properly is exciting grace itself. The Jansenists herefrom concluded that our will is forced by necessity either to do the good or to fall into sin, according to the greater or lesser degree of earthly or heavenly delectation. The Molinists prove from St. Augustine that man is perfectly free to give or to withdraw his consent. The other schools float, as it were, between these two extremes. There are, no doubt, many obscure passages in the saint's works which, taken by themselves, may lead to some misunderstanding. He says himself: "That question, where we dispute about free will and the grace of God, is so hard to understand that when free will is defended the grace of God seems to be denied, and when the grace of God is asserted free will is apparently taken away,[5] and yet both are true, but few are able to comprehend it."[6] The only way to understand St. Augustine is to discern the spirit breathing through all his writings, comparing the contested texts with others of the same kind.

Let us find out his definitions of delectation and efficacious grace, and we shall have the key to the most difficult passages in his works. " Quod amplius delectat id nos operemur necesse est— we necessarily perform what us more delights "—is the famous text on which Jansenius based his victorious delectation. This and similar texts do not prove the irresistible determination of the delight. St. Augustine always supposes the *deliberate* love of complacency actually predominating in our will. " C'est l'amour

---

[1] De Sp et Litt., n. 53.
[2] De Gr. Chr., c. 47, n. 52.
[3] De Gr. Chr., c. 24.
[4] De Corr. et Gr., c. 14.
[5] Lib. de Gr. Chr., c. 47.
[6] Lib. 2, contr. Litt. Pel., c. 84.

dominant de la volonté, laquelle commande suivant la disposition," says Fénelon.[1] Thus, when God draws us,[2] when He sometimes gives a victorious delectation to the saints, that they may know, it is not from themselves but from Him who is the light and truth,[3] the pleasure only precedes the consent. For what is concupiscence and pleasure, if not the willful assent to what we wish for; and what is fear and sadness if not the willful dissent from what we do not desire?[4] God delights by teaching, not by imposing the necessity.[5] St. Francis de Sales beautifully explains this thought. "We present nuts to a child," says St. Augustine, "and it feels itself attracted, not by an exterior force or a foreign violence which acts on the body, but by the attraction of the heart, or pleasure which never exists without some degree of love. Such is the conduct of God in our regard; He attracts by the delights which accompany His inspirations, not by the force of obligation or compulsion. He insinuates spiritual pleasures into our hearts, and these act as baits, inducing us to let ourselves be taken, and disposing us to receive and to relish His doctrine. Our will is not constrained by the omnipotent strength of the hand of God which touches it; grace urges, but does not compel, and notwithstanding its great power, we can yield or resist its influence as we please."[6]

God acts in the heart of man, performs the motion of his will, yet " I did not what, with an incomparable affection, pleased me more,"[7] says the holy bishop, and there is no contradiction in his words. " Facit ut faciamus, præbendo vires efficacissimas voluntati[8]—He acts that we may act, by offering a most efficacious power to the will"—is a general and most decisive key for the strongest texts in St. Augustine's works.[9]

The doctrine of *predestination* rests on the doctrine of grace. We have to distinguish between predestination to grace and to glory. The great mystery of the dogma consists in the predestination to grace. Though it is certain[10] and undeniable that God has reasons on which to act, yet it is far above our comprehension ; human speculation cannot dive into it. " If any one should bind me to scrutinize that depth why one is so charmed that he is persuaded, another not, I have only two things to answer: O the depth of the riches ! And is there iniquity in God ? "[11] All agree that the predestination to grace is wholly gratuitous, because free will cannot perform any meritorious works without and before

[1] Instr. sur la grace, tome i., lettre 5.   [2] In Joh., c. vi., v. 26.

[3] De Pec. Mer., c. 19, n. 32.   [4] De Civ. Dei, lib. xiv., c. 6.

[5] In Joh., c. vi., v. 27.   [6] Love of God, book ii., c. 12.

[7] Conf. i., 3, c. 8.   [8] De Lib. Arb., l. 3, c. 16.

[9] Fénelon says : " Voilà une clef générale et décisive des textes les plus forts de St. Augustin que ce Père presente de sa propre main." L. c., lettre 8.

[10] St. Francis of Sales, l. c.   [11] De Sp. et Litt , c. 34.

grace. This is the truth, for the defence of which St. Augustine so earnestly and successfully fought. Further, all agree that the predestination to glory necessarily supposes the merits flowing from grace, and, as such, on account of the gratuity of grace, is also a free gift. The dispute begins whether God, in the act of predestination, considers the meritorious works or not? Which, by its nature, precedes in the mind of God, the foresight of the good works or the simple predestinating act? Whether and how far is the foreknowledge an essential element in the eternal decree? " At non isto sensu disputatur inter theologos, an prædestinatio ad gloriam sit gratuita, sed alio, nempe utrum fiat ante vel post prævisa merita gratiæ." [1]

The thought of the Divine Providence so completely swayed in St. Augustine's mind that, on the slightest occasions, he perceived the incomprehensible wisdom and goodness of God. He looked upon the fall of the Roman Empire, but he was not crushed in the grasp of the conqueror. " As all human powers seemed dissolving visibly before him, his eyes fixed themselves more and more intently upon another vision, transitory, indeed, in one sense, in that it was passing in time, but springing from the council of God, ordained before time, and flowing on till the full tide of its waves is gathered into eternity " [2]—he wrote his *City of God*. There he traces the two commonwealths emerging into life from Adam, and passing away into an eternity they choose. God disposes of the minds of men; of the issues of their conduct; what they are responsible for, what will cause their reward is their good will. The moral worth of their actions is in their hands; their result is ordered by God as He finds best for His providential designs. God's foresight does not cause the thing foreseen. " He who fore-knew the causes of all things certainly could not ignore our will which He foreknew to be the cause of our actions." [3] " We do not sin because God foresees it, but because we sin God knows it." [4] Predestination and foreknowledge cannot be separated, though foreknowledge can exist without predestination, as, for instance, in every sin; [5] hence the definition: Predestination is the fore-knowledge and preparation of God's benefices, by which those are most certainly saved whosoever are saved. [6] We will now under-stand why St. Augustine calls God the Author of good and evil. " God delivers men to shameful passions, God sends the operation of error, that they may believe the lie; it is thus He operates in the hearts of men in any direction He pleases for the good or the

1 Tournelly: De Deo, vol. i., qu. 11, art. 1.
2 Allies: Formation of Christendom, vol. i., p. 209.
3 De Civ. Dei, lib. v., c. 9.   4 De Civ. Dei, lib. v., c. 10.
5 De Præd. 55, c. 10.   6 Lib. de Dono Persev., c. 14.

evil,[1] not because God is the author of sin, or withdraws sufficient grace, but because He permits sin." It is difficult to suppose that, after St. Augustine, the eternal decree concerning our salvation is made without any regard to human worthiness. God wishes all men to be saved and to come to the knowledge of truth, but not so that He should deprive them of their free will, for the good or bad use of which they shall be rightly judged.[2]

Many passages, indeed, seem to favor the opinion that grace efficaciously attracts our will, human consent seeming to be imperceptible; the rise of the one apparently overwhelms the other. The only reason for such and the like objections is that the saint had not yet determined the inmost relation between both. Besides, the difficulty is increased by the promiscuous use of predestination to grace and glory. The different schools quote the *same* texts in favor of their systems.[3]

It suffices for us to have shown that the downright predestination couched in the doctrine of Jansenius and the dangerous principles of the extreme Thomists have no foundation in St. Augustine's works. He nowhere upholds the constraining force of the spirit of good or evil in the vast scene of contending mankind; man has to wrestle with his heart; he is responsible for his freedom; the consent is neither extorted nor compelled. Disorders spring up from the perverse will, but are directed to a final order; eternal goodness is vindicated by eternal justice " until the loveliness of this whole temporal dispensation, of which the subordinate parts are those which suit each their own times, runs out like some grand composition of an unspeakably perfect artist, and from it those who, even in the time of faith, rightly worship God pass into the eternal contemplation of Him, face to face."[4]

There is a twofold order in every movement of God's providence; the primal cause, which is God's will itself, ordaining all things to their final end, the secondary causes implanted in His creatures. The irrational creatures are governed by the laws of necessity; the rational by the moral law of God, who never impedes the use of their free will. The operations are necessary, and fall upon God alone; when performed by the former, they are contingent; when enacted by the latter, the will necessarily tends towards beatitude, the universal good is its object.[5] The natural striving after happiness becomes the motor of all our actions, because it is natural that the immovable principle, namely, beatitude, on which the actions of the will are based, should become their cause.[6] Yet

---

1 De Gr. et Lib. Arb., c. 21, n 43.   2 De Sp et Litt., c. 33.

3 Cf. Hurter: Theological Dogma, vol. ii., p. 86; Scholion, numb. 2.

4 Cp. 1385, translated by Allies, l. c., p. 206.   5 I, 2 qu. 1, a. 3.

6 I, qu. 82, a. 1.

various may be the nature of the good we desire, good in its essence or only its appearance ; it may or may not have any connection with true happiness, and thus the will, though necessarily determined to the end, is not necessarily determined to the means.[1] To transfer the necessity of the irrational creation to human nature would pervert the whole character of the divine government; man would only act as he is acted upon by an unchangeable law. The dominion the will has over his acts, whereby it is in his power to wish or not to wish, excludes the determination to *one* thing.[2] It is, therefore, not repugnant to the goodness of God to allow evil, because, if sin should be debarred, divine providence would not govern man according to his nature,[3] and God does not destroy, but preserves, the nature of things ; His motion is appropriate to the being to be moved.[4] The divine goodness is one and single, and is the root of all the goodness that is to be found in created things. But, as individual creatures can but faintly represent the goodness of God, and each only in particular ways, it was needful that He should represent it in many different things, which, by their unity of relation with one another, should reflect in a certain sense the unity and simplicity of the Divine perfection, that each in that endless gradation of creatures might partake of it according to its own nature and capacity.[5] Thus the contingency on our part does not arise from the nature of the secondary cause itself, but from the efficiency of the divine will, by which we are created under such circumstances. God wishes that one thing should happen necessarily, another accidentally and voluntarily. His infallible foreknowledge and the contingency of human acts perfectly agree ; they are moved by God like instruments, their free choice being respected.[6] Even if God should infringe our deliberate determination, there is no reason why our will should not be influenced by Him who gives to it the power of determining itself.[7]

The indifference of the will is not an absolute one, the tendency towards the universal good being innate, but the election of the object, which seems best, is fully in its power. Ullathorne, reproducing St. Thomas, says : As the material and unreasonable creatures, devoid of free will, are governed by the laws of necessity, it is the noble plan of God that man, however divinely assisted, can accept that help, and work out his lot with the use of his freedom. For God has endowed him with a cause that must operate with the supreme cause in determining his course. He can choose the good that is offered to him, whilst the providence of God gives

---

[1] I, 2 qu. 10, a. 2.
[3] Comp. theol., c. 142.
[5] Comp. theol., c. 102.
[7] De Malo, qu. 3, a. 2.

[2] Contra Gent., i., 68.
[4] De Malo, qu. 3, a. 2.
[6] De Vero, qu. 21, a. 1.

him the means to achieve it.[1] The operation of God may be in a certain way determined or modified by the free creature. "Causa primaria plus dicitur influere in quantum ejus effectus est intimior et permanentior in causato, quam effectus causæ secundæ; tamen magis similatur causæ secundæ, quia per eam determinatur quodam modo actus causæ secundæ ad hunc effectum."[2] The whole creation exhibits a gradual progress of perfection, the lowest creature reflects the image of God, but the nearer the creature approaches the Creator, the greater becomes its power of determination and the less does God incline it.[3] The self-determination of man requires the non-determination of God.

St. Thomas accepts St. Augustine's definition of predestination.[4] It would be absurd to suppose that our merits *induce* God to raise us into the number of His elect. Whatever in human nature has any relation to the supernatural, belongs to the effects of predestination. Yet, if all our actions were only the result of God's motion, then one man were not better than another, and there could be no difference of reward on earth, nor of glory in heaven.[5] It is erroneous to say that human actions and events are not subject to the divine foreknowledge and predetermination; and not less erroneous is it that necessity is enjoined by them. God ordains things as they act; what is decreed from eternity happens in time according to the disposition of the proper cause.[6] The providence of God overrules that life, giving to everybody what he deserves; man's free will works out God's intention.

St. Thomas, like the great bishop of Hippo, defends human freedom, whenever in contact with divine grace, but where and why both join each other remains undecided.

We add this paragraph to complete the preceding one. The "Summa," written for beginners.—*ad conditionem incipientium*[7]—has been explained in its minutest details. Many and great are the names of the commentators, both among the Dominicans and other theologians. Till Francis Vittoria, however, and Dominic Bañez, the founders of the so-called Thomistic school, we do not find any deviation from St. Thomas's teaching on grace and liberty. Our Holy Father, Leo XIII., recommending in his grand Encyclical on St. Thomas the scholastic doctrine, ordered at the same time the edition of his works containing the commentaries of Cajetan and Ferrariensis. Both belong to the elder Thomistic school; and to avoid long and tiresome quotations, we only shall produce the opinions of these two authors.[8]

---

1 L. c., ch. iv.
3 De Vero, qu. 22, a. 4.
6 II dist., 25, qu. 1, a. 1.
7 Prologus.

2 De Vero, qu. 5, a. 9.
4 Lect. Pi. Rom. 8.
6 Decl. contra Græcos, c. 10.
8 Cf. Schneemann, l. c., Anhang.

Of Cajetan it was said that, if the works of St. Thomas could ever have been lost, they would have been found again in Cajetan's memory. He expressly says that the motion of the first cause undergoes a *modification* in the secondary cause. God does not operate by a previous motion; it suffices that He intrinsically co-operates in the choice and illumination of the intellect; man is free to use or to refuse God's influence.[1] God indeed gives power to the will, suggesting in every act the desire of the good, but the will determines itself to the particular good proposed by God.[2] Referring to our controversy, the cardinal says: "I have not found anything in St. Thomas concerning this doubt, for I do not recollect that he ever touched it, but he always was anxious to save the contingency of free-will."[3]

Ferrariensis, in his celebrated commentaries on the "Summa contra Gentiles," gives the same judgment. Distinguishing between *agi simpliciter*—to be simply moved—and *agi secundum quid*—to be moved indefinitely, he says, that whenever the inclination determines the hitherto indifferent power to a definite act, it simply moves; when the action is moved in such a way that it still remains free to act or not to act, it is moved without a determinate end. The operation of the Holy Ghost is of the second kind, because we have it in our power to follow or to withdraw.[4]

The same were the views of the theologians at the time of the Council of Trent. Schneemann says: " The universal doctrine was that God operates in us the consent through grace, provided we freely co-operate, and only in this manner the grace of God becomes efficacious."[5]

The *ratio studiorum* laying, as we have seen, great stress on theological tradition, gave a new impulse to theological studies. The Jesuits, accepting the fathers and scholastics, tried to shape the whole Catholic doctrine in one harmonious system. Their first great theologians and St. Ignatius himself were educated in the spirit of the older Thomistic school. They and their disciples regarded the *scientia media* as a necessary implement of St. Thomas's theology. We have seen that Lessius maintained it before Molina. Stapleton wrote to the Bishop of Middlebrough that he had heard all the propositions of Lessius twenty-five years before in the lectures of Father Toletus in Rome. The first Jesuit, however, who exhibited the whole doctrine of the order in its full extent was Louis Molina. Born in Cuença, he entered the Society at the age of eighteen, in the year 1555; having finished his studies

---

[1] In. i., qu. 14, a. 13.   [2] In. i., qu. 9, a. 3.
[3] In. i., qu. 22, a. 4 ads.   [4] In lib. 4, c. 22, lib. 3, c. 161.
[5] L. c., i., p. 102.   Father Kleutgen, in his great " Theologie der Vorzeit," maintains the same doctrine.

at Coimbra, he was made professor of theology at Evora.   He died in Madrid at the age of sixty-five, renowned for his modesty, piety, and learning.   His principal works are a Commentary on the first part of the "Summa," a treatise on right and justice, and the famous "Concordance of Grace and Free-will," published in 1588.

In order to solve the great question, Molina starts with the definition and minute description of human liberty, for the obscurer the subject the safer the way of choosing what is near at hand. Free will is certainly more known and better understood than the hidden working of grace.   Molina's definition is that of the scholastics: We are free, because we may do one thing or another; freedom formally lies in the will, but it supposes the judgment of reason, hence it is called "liberum arbitrium."   The grace given to the angels and the first man was not efficacious by itself, but changeable (*versatilis*).   It became efficacious in those angels who stood the trial; in man it remained inefficient, because he resisted it.   Still the essence of human nature was not injured by Adam's fall.   Man can perform good actions of the natural order, but neither can his intellect conceive nor his will desire anything proportionate to the supernatural.   The supernatural is to be taken in the strictest sense; it is above both angels and men.   The least meritorious act is impossible without an actual help of grace. The supernatural actions, though they are such not only by reason of their origin, but by virtue of their essence, retain, nevertheless, a close relation to the soul, because they come forth from its inmost depth and are performed by the faculties of human nature, many natural circumstances coinciding with their accomplishment.   Supernatural in their essence and completion, they notwithstanding totally belong to man and totally to God, not, indeed, as if the will had any influence on the supernatural, for anything meritorious attributed to the will requires the touch of grace, but because the human consent is the condition without which grace cannot start to act.   The foreseen consent is not by any means the reason or motive why God should pour out His blessings; His aid is entirely gratuitous; He may reserve His grace even if He foresees the consent of man. The *scientia media*, therefore, is the link between efficacious grace and human will.   It is necessary to understand fully the meaning of this word.

Molina and his followers distinguish a three-fold science in God: simple intelligence—*scientia simplicis intelligentiæ ;* visions—*scientia visionis*, by which He sees the things existing and to come; the science lying between both, *scientia media*, whereby he sees what would happen if certain conditions were fulfilled.   The question is not, whether *scientia media* can be reduced to one of the other two; that would be only a play of words, because the condition which the *scientia media* includes is merely possible, and thus known by the knowledge of simple intelligence; or the condition will be sometimes realized, and then the knowledge arises from vision. The centre of the controversy rests on the point, whether God in the formulation of His decrees is directed by the *scientia media*, that is, whether He predefines any actions of man without taking notice of human liberty.[1] With that knowledge, says Molina, God predestines the one to glory, the other to reprobation. He actually and sincerely desires the salvation of all men, provided they themselves correspond with the graces received. By reason of that will He sent His only begotten Son on earth to be the Saviour of mankind. He does not predestine by a decree efficacious of itself and antecedent to the prevision of the free consent of man; there is no predestination to glory before the prevision of the merits of man; no reprobation without the foreknowledge of the sins that will be committed. Yet there is no coördination of God and man. Whenever something supernatural is attributed to the human will, God is the principal, man only the subordinate cause. The efficiency of grace does not depend in its nature on the will, which cannot contribute anything to the supernatural power; the consent only is the condition that grace may unfold its wonderful works. God, however, can place the will under such circumstances and give such graces that the assent immediately follows, and on this ground Molina also accepts the predestination before the foreseen merits.

The fundamental principle of Molinism is: The nature of grace sufficient and grace efficacious is only one and the same thing. The grace takes effect through the consent of the human will; without it grace remains only sufficient, the same as the sacraments by themselves are channels of grace, but do not operate if the necessary conditions on the part of man are neglected. Molina distinguishes between efficacious grace in the first act (in *actu primo*), where the human consent is wanting; and in the second act (in *actu secundo*), where the consent is given. The difference between the first and inefficacious grace is this, that the first one is given to those whose assent God foresees, whilst the other is given to those who will refuse it. Thus, the *gratia efficax in actu primo* is a far greater benefit than the *gratia inefficax*, because the one will bring forth its fruit, whilst the other will remain barren. Of two men, therefore, who receive the same amount of grace under the same circumstances, the one may coöperate, the other resist; Bossuet, though not a Molinist, clearly showed the wide difference between Molinism and Semipelagianism. That heresy, he says,[2] objected that the necessity of grace ruined the freedom of man, extinguishing all zeal for virtue; the

---

[1] Tournelly: De Deo, qu. 7, c. 5.
[2] Second Avertissement aux Protestants.

Molinists admit the necessity and gratuity of grace, but deny the antecedent decree of predestination. Molina himself, answering the objections against *scientia media*, says that their opinion at first may seem probable; still, when we consider that God, having foreseen the disposition of our will, makes *this* the measure and rule of His choice, and thus confers the help and means for our salvation, fixed from all eternity, there is no cause for any prejudice against His omnipotence or foreknowledge.[1]

Great theologians like Maldonat, Stapleton, Lessius, Vasquez, Sfondrati, Franzelin, accept the Molinistic system, and St. Francis de Sales calls it old and of authority;[2] not less honorable is the enmity of the Jansenists against Molina's doctrine. When the Concordance was published, the Jesuits as a body never accepted the book, but they defended the *scientia media*, opposing the efficiency of grace by itself.

The *scientia media* met most vigorous adversaries in the Dominicans, who charged Molina with Pelagianism. Other reasons added to the animosity between the two orders. The Jesuits, though a new order, had gained an immense influence in Spain and other countries. Their constitution was entirely different from that of the older orders; the very name Jesuit intimated hypocrisy, if not blasphemy. Melchior Canus saw in them the coming Antichrist and preached in Salamanca against the associates of the devil. The bull "Ascendente Domino," and finally the Concordance brought on the fierce combat.

At the head of the Dominicans stood Dominic Bañez, professor *primarius* in the University of Salamanca, a man of great learning, virtue and energy, ready to carry his point to the extreme. The shield of the Louvain professors was St. Augustine, that of the Dominicans St. Thomas. The exclusive partiality for one author, and that propensity to attribute to St. Thomas what *they* thought to be his opinion, increased here as well as in Louvain the heat of the dispute. The original founder of the Thomistic school was Francis Vittoria, an intimate friend of St. Ignatius, Faber, and Toletus, whose teacher he was. His commentaries on the "Summa" are not printed. Schneemann used a copy of his lectures, preserved in the Vatican library. From these it appears that Vittoria forms a kind of transition from the older to the modern Thomists. Schneemann says, if we consider his doctrine, we see that he is completely opposed to Bañez, who rejected what with Vittoria all ancient and modern theologians accept. Yet there are at the same time certain propositions which, taken by themselves, directly lead to the system of Bañez.[3]

---

[1] Disp. I., qu. 23, a. 4, ct. 5.   [2] Letter to Lessius, 26 August, 1618.
[3] L. c., II., p. 223.

The fundamental principle of the Thomists is: God is the first cause of all things; He sustains the creature in its being and operation; it is repugnant to His dignity to await the determination of the creature, and make it the rule of His decrees. God Himself is the efficacious cause of everything good, and thus efficaciously wishes the end and the means leading to it, for no secondary cause can operate unless it is efficaciously moved by God. He not only wishes the act, but decrees it to be free, and thus His motion does not draw the will as something lifeless, but enlivens it and disperses the clouds from the intellect for the better choice of the object. Since God, together with the freedom of the act, determines its existence, His foreknowledge arises from its causality. The disposition of the creature cannot have any influence on Him, nor be the condition of His efficient gifts, *because that very disposition is the work of God.* Bañez's whole system will be best understood in his doctrine on Divine permission of sin. Denying the *scientia media*, he was compelled to say that the permission *precedes* the foresight of the refusal on the part of man. Thus going to the extreme, he maintained that God *probably* does not wish the salvation of all men.[1] He elected some for eternal life, some He disdained and despised, yet this contempt is nothing else than the will to allow them to fail in their last end. Bañez's followers, Billuart, Lemos, Alvarez, Bellarmin, and the others did not accept the harshness of this doctrine, which can hardly be excused from heresy. The Thomists rejected the severe conclusions of their master, but having the honest persuasion that Molina was renewing the Pelagian heresy, they followed the great Dominican in the struggle against the Jesuits.

The Inquisition found no fault in Molina's work. Bañez's complaints, brought before Rome, ended in prohibiting the mutual charges of heresy and imposing silence on both parties. The Dominicans, however, continued their attacks with a violence which even the ardor of dispute could not excuse. The Pope finally decided to bring the whole question before a tribunal, called the *Congregatio de Auxiliis.* The public sessions and disputes were without avail. Pope Paul V. dismissed both parties, advising them to wait till the Holy See should decide the problem at some future time. The general impression, however, the *congregatio* left was a condemnation *in petto* of Molina's system, which, in fact, was almost accomplished on two occasions. The first session took place January 2d, 1598; the last, August 28th, 1607. The question remained unsettled. The Jansenists pretended that their victorious delectation does not vary from the grace efficacious of

---

[1] Qu. 23, a. 23.

itself, taught by the Dominicans, but the difference between the two is great. The victorious *indeliberate* delectation of the Jansenists destroyed the freedom of the will; the efficacious grace of the Thomists means an enlightenment of the intellect and a strengthening of the will. The great controversy, and the Thomists above all, had to serve as a cover for the propagation of the subtlest heresy ever known in the Church.

Whether or not there was between St. Cyran, Jansenius and the others a secret association, a common plan of attack against the Church, drawn up by the sectaries at Bourg-Fontaine, is one of those problems which history has not solved satisfactorily.[1] Though from the evidence known thus far we are inclined to answer in the affirmative, the question is practically of not much importance, and beyond the scope of our essay. It is certain that all the causes enumerated met, like many strings tied in one knot, at Port Royal, the headquarters of Jansenism. The simple and solitary life of its inhabitants, the precision and elegance of their works, before unknown in the French language, generally increased the strength of that heresy. Nothing seduces more than a beautiful style combined with an apparently earnest doctrine and the fame of a virtuous and austere life led by its author. But foul ambition, conspicuous by its rigorism and contemptuous perseverance in errors repeatedly condemned by the Church, overshadow the glory of Port Royal. Its members proved themselves deplorably ignorant of the past and present of the religion they yet professed. They pretended to master and to exhaust the patrology and history of the Church. Whenever submission was required, they only admitted attenuated theories suiting their own frail system. The woe and misery brought on the Church by that heresy were great, but Jansenism to-day is, like the rest of the heresies, only a matter of history.

---

[1] Darras, vol. iv., p. 279.

THE QUEBEC ACT AND THE CHURCH IN CANADA.

A T the distinguished company assembled at Toronto last autumn in honor of Archbishop Lynch, many of the readers of this REVIEW who were present and heard the speeches will have remembered with what pardonable pride the venerable prelate from Quebec, Archbishop Taschereau, referred to the ancient boundaries of his diocese; to the time when his predecessors had jurisdiction not only over the province of his host, but westward to the valleys of the Ohio and the Mississippi. No one better than the illustrious speaker could have depicted the time when, in Canada, a long line of bishops traced the outlines of a great cross on this Continent, at once the symbol and limits of their jurisdiction, connecting the Atlantic with the Rocky Mountains, intersected by a belt of territory extending from Hudson's Bay to the waters of the Gulf of Mexico. This was the diocese of Quebec not only under the old French régime, but for many years after the cession of Canada to England in 1763—up, in fact, to the formation of the United States some years later. The early American Church, not owing allegiance to the French or Canadian bishops, comprised what was comparatively a small strip of Atlantic seaboard, with France to the north and west and Spain to the south. Probably the moderation of the speaker had been somewhat suggested by the cosmopolitan character of the assembly, fearing lest some representative of the Mexican Church might have arisen and asserted his claim, if not to the larger portion of the Continent, at least forestalling Quebec in priority by a good century and a quarter. Conceding this, there yet remained a respectable antiquity to Bishop Laval and his successors, and a jurisdiction of territory that now covers nearly a dozen ecclesiastical provinces.

But beyond this there are some unique things about the Church in Canada. We had a complete Church establishment prior to the cession, and we have had since the cession an attempted establishment, so to speak, under British law. Our bishops in French times were the choice of the king, and the diocese, convents and colleges were established by royal patent. In early English rule, since the cession, the King of England has been consulted in the choice of bishops, and the Downing Street authorities have time and again signified their disapproval or acceptance of nominees to the episcopal see of Quebec before they were preconized at Rome. In truth, we have had the representative of the Crown trying, by every means, to force the Church under the law, so that not only the bishop but every curé should seem to be appointed by the king's most excellent majesty. In former days, in England, a Catholic was thought to be good enough to be head of the Protestant Church; and as it was a poor rule that worked only one way, the flexibility of the constitution was thought to be sufficient to enable a Protestant king in return to become the head of the Catholic Church, at least good enough for the Church in a colony. We have had Protestants, legal luminaries amongst us at one time, arguing that Roman Catholics in Quebec or Lower Canada had no rights whatever, as compared with the Church of England, and at another arguing that the Catholic Church is the only Church there established by law. We have seen the one see of Quebec occupied by two titular Bishops—a Catholic and an Anglican—and the latter forced to give way. Learned judges and attorney-generals have wasted their time drafting *commissions* for Catholic bishops to be licensed as Chief Ecclesiastical Superintendents of the Church of Rome, with irremovable curés and state-erected parishes; and afterwards we have seen these officials sit, "cheek by jowl," with the self-same superintendents in the legislative councils of the province, not as superintendents but as recognized bishops of this favored Church. And to this day, in this same province, the parish, so erected by the Bishop, is equally as well known as is the township or county or ward under its municipal law, and the curé and church wardens are recognized in the public law of the land. The law apportions the tithes and its officers collect them. On the other hand, there is also on record within this country the refusal by Protestant rulers to grant Wesleyan Methodists any sort of legal recognition for their ministers, unless under a security of two hundred pounds sterling and the appearance of seven respectable members testifying before justices of the quarter sessions as to the genuineness of the minister in question, and the additional indignity of a violent protest against even this concession by a Protestant chief justice.[1]

We have had the Church of England established by law in one province and generally the attempted disregard everywhere of all who did not belong to that church. We have examples of a Catholic being in the position of O'Connell as to taking his seat in

---

[1] In order to show what a beautiful example this judicial dignitary bequeathed to his posterity, it is related that when the accounts of the Jesuits' estates were examined by the House of Assembly in Lower Canada it was found that one of the Church of England parsons, residing in Quebec, was in the habit of annually drawing a large income from the school funds on pretense of being "Chaplain to the Jesuits." "The Jesuits," says Wm. Lyon Mackenzie, who is authority for this story, "had been all dead many years before, and, besides, they were Roman Catholics. The parson's name was Sewell, a son of Jonathan, the Chief Justice."

the Commons. We have the sad story of the Acadians and the persecutions of religious, and by one of those curious retributions by which Providence makes a fool of people, we have a small province, into which no Catholic was allowed to emigrate, now numbering more Catholics than Protestants.

In our chief Protestant province we have had a committee of the legislature report that the Church of England is not the church by law established in Canada, and that no prayers from its chaplain would be tolerated. We have had governments make a choice of religions, and find them approving of four—the Catholic, the Anglican, the Presbyterian, and the Methodist—and following the example in Ireland of giving the most where it was least needed. We have had, however, within the last sixty years, a Catholic bishop and his clergy supported largely out of the public chest. In this same province we can turn up the estimates in blue books and find pounds upon pounds paid out of the public taxes for the building and repairing of Catholic churches. We have separate schools, and we have had large sums paid annually in this same Protestant province for the support of Catholic colleges. We have had tithes, as they still have them in Quebec. Here, too, may be found the name of a legislative councillor who was an Honorable and Right Reverend gentleman—the first Roman Catholic Bishop of Upper Canada—in receipt of a considerable pension from the state and of complimentary notices for his loyalty from his Prince Regent. We have had riots and mobs attacking processions, and we have in return a Protestant city turn out to honor its Archbishop, and the vice-regal, provincial, and civic dignitaries vieing with one another to honor this same rather outspoken churchman. There is, in fine, in Canada, an immense territory, with every assistance of nature, for a great nation, with the only serious drawback of a lack of anything like a proportionate population. There is need of fifty millions of people, but, in the meantime, things go on very well with a tenth of that number, one-half of whom are Catholics, holding their own fairly well. The Catholics believe that the form of government is one of the best in the world, and that the Church is as free and prosperous as the Church militant can expect to be.

When we speak of Canada some explanations must be made. Nowadays, every one must keep up his knowledge of geography, as the political changes are so numerous that what was true of boundaries and divisions yesterday may not be so to-day. Until the Dominion of Canada was created in 1867, the provinces of Upper and Lower Canada comprised what, for one hundred years, was included in the old Canadas, or in the older Province of Quebec. To-day Canada means, leaving out Newfoundland, all

British territory lying north of the United States. This includes everything on the map, except Alaska and Greenland, and is, indeed, as large as or larger than the States of the American Union. There are now seven provinces and several territories bound together by a central government in much the same way, politically, as are the American States. Two out of these seven provinces form the old Canadas, and these are the provinces of Ontario and Quebec, the latter returning to its old name in the Act of 1774. There are three provinces around the Gulf of St. Lawrence, and these retain their former names: Nova Scotia, New Brunswick, and Prince Edward Island. The first two of these were anciently known as Acadia, but they formed no part of Canada as ceded by France, belonging to the English for many years before Quebec fell. On the other hand, Prince Edward Island, called by the French St. John, and Cape Breton, were part of New France, and came to England under the Treaty of 1763. Newfoundland has never been fraternized, politically or ecclesiastically, with British Canada, and is no part of the Dominion. The other two provinces of Canada are British Columbia, on the Pacific coast, formerly owned by the Hudson Bay Company, and Manitoba, a new creation of the Dominion Government, carved out of the great Northwest, lying between Ontario and the Saskatchewan Valley, which runs westward to the Rocky Mountains. This latter valley and the great Lone Land to the north of it and Manitoba, extending east to Hudson Bay, is the Northwest Territory, and was formerly the seat of the posts and forts of the Hudson Bay Company and other great fur companies. The remainder of the map eastward to the Atlantic forms the Northeast Territory.

These provinces and territories have, of course, their own separate histories. They have their own local laws and, in general, the care of their own domestic concerns. Formerly they were separate colonies of Great Britain, now there is only one colony—rather one dependency—as no one now, except some newly-arrived Englishman, would talk of Canadians being colonists.

The new Dominion of Canada dates back only a few years, beginning in 1867 with four provinces and adding others since that date until the present dimensions have been attained. It is plain, therefore, that considerable limitation must be made in speaking of historical matters in Canada, as there are fully half a dozen or more places to be considered, each with a separate history of its own. However, the two Canadas, once the old Province of Quebec, and forming the bulk of what was New France, are very prominently before the mind of the reader of political and ecclesiastical history. They were divorced by the Act of 1791, to be united again in 1840, and seem to be marked out as political partners, strange enough though the partnership be. The present constitution is the fifth or sixth change under British rule within its first century.

During all these mutations in constitutions the Church has a history that, though naturally branching out in more recent times with the increase of its children and by force of political changes, nevertheless preserved for a long time one headquarters in one ecclesiastical province, having to deal entirely with the Crown of England as represented by the governors of Canada. As has been said, all of the other fragmentary possessions of Great Britain in America were separate colonies. But the Governor-General of Canada was, in an undefined way, their superior, was Captain-General of all the forces, and took precedence of other British governors. Living in Quebec with the Bishop, he seemed to represent the Crown, as did the latter the Church, for all the British provinces. The battle of the Church was fought between these two under British rule as it was fought there under the French rule. It was not until the last years of the reign of George the Third that the Bishop of Quebec got his immense diocese subdivided, but the rights of his Church were contested and decided long before this, though by the same heroic bishop. In 1819 Bishop Plessis, having obtained sanction in England and in Rome, established vicar-generals in Upper Canada, in New Brunswick, and in the Northwest. From that time a particular history in these places is necessary. It is to this period, within which Bishop Plessis (he was Archbishop, but prudently declined to style himself such) and his predecessors, as bishops of Quebec, held the Church in their own hands, that attention must be mainly directed at first. He and Bishop Laval stand at the end and beginning of the history of that Diocese.

Upper Canada was the resort of United Empire loyalists, and many others, to whom the rule in Lower Canada or Quebec was displeasing, and it will therefore come in for considerable notice, and is entitled to it, as now and always a part of old Canada.

In 1796 Newfoundland had been erected by the Holy Father into a Vicariate Apostolic, and the same condition of things obtained in Nova Scotia since the year 1817. The other portions of Canada were under the supervision of the Bishop of Quebec. Louisiana had passed out of French control to Spain soon after the middle of the last century, and, in 1793, had its bishop, who was suffragan of San Domingo; so that nothing remained to England south or west of the Great Lakes, though the mission in Detroit was still practically under the care of Bishop McDonell, auxiliary of the Bishop of Quebec and later the first Bishop of Kingston. As will be seen later, there is a certain analogy between the political and ecclesiastical divisions in Canada. What we call the Maritime Provinces, Nova Scotia, New Brunswick, and Prince Edward Island, now form one ecclesiastical province, and besides the popular name, the Constitution of Canada considers these as one division for purposes of representation in the Senate. Quebec and Ontario are also ecclesiastical provinces, and are separate political provinces, and the remainder of Canada goes to make up the fourth ecclesiastical province. It has a Senate representation with reference to its population, so that four divisions obtain in each, though as to the Northwest the analogy is not so complete as in the other three. There are still vicariates apostolic in Canada. Newfoundland stands aloof from the political combination of 1867, and is yet a colony of the empire. She also forms no part of any ecclesiastical province of Canada, being directly subject to the Holy See. The western portion of the island was made an Apostolic Prefecture in 1871, and is called St. George. The French islands in the Gulf of St. Lawrence form another Apostolic Prefecture.

Bearing this in mind, the reader will be better able to appreciate our past history and avoid some confusion in these matters that many Canadians have difficulty in avoiding. Many shufflings of constitutions have taken place since Canada passed under British rule. The Church alone, for two centuries and three-quarters, has pursued its unchanging way. "One great fact," says Parkman, "stands out conspicuous in Canadian history—the Church of Rome. More even than the royal power she shaped the character and the destinies of the colony. She was its nurse and almost its mother ; and, wayward and headstrong as it was, it never broke the ties of faith that held it to her. It was these ties which, in the absence of political franchises, formed under the old régime the only vital coherence in the population. The royal government was transient ; the Church was permanent. The English conquest shattered the whole apparatus of civil administration at a blow, but it left her untouched. Governors, intendants, councils, and commandants, all were gone, the principal seignors fled the colony, and a people who had never learned to control themselves or help themselves were suddenly left to their own devices. Confusion, if not anarchy, would have followed but for the parish priests, who, in a character of double paternity, half spiritual and half temporal, became more than ever the guardians of order throughout Canada."

Attention has been drawn to the extent of the Diocese of Quebec. That portion of it which now lies within the United States need not detain us. For twenty years after the cession the English owned north and south of the Great Lakes, and Quebec claimed jurisdiction, in the valley of the Mississippi, as far south as New Orleans. After the Treaty of Versailles, in 1783, only six years elapsed until the Catholics of the United States had a bishop of their own, and since that time the history of the Church in the United States would include that of the portion of Canada extending along the Mississippi. None of the territory south of Lake Erie or Ontario, or west of Lake Huron, though included in the boundaries of Quebec under the Quebec Act of 1774, need be taken into consideration, though for many years after it passed into the hands of the United States authorities the ecclesiastical limits were not the same as the political boundaries.[1]

So far as the Church in Canada is concerned, the extent of the Diocese of Quebec at the time of the Treaty of Paris, or in 1774, would not be a safe guide in estimating how far the guarantees of the treaty extend. It will be borne in mind that, while the French ceded Canada to the British, they stipulated for the free exercise of religion, but only as regards their own subjects. There was no compact entered into that all other Catholics under British rule in America should be secured in the same rights. The "new" Roman Catholic subjects were the subjects to be protected. Now, it is true that Acadia and Newfoundland and some of the Gulf islands changed masters very frequently, and that, in general, they were under the ecclesiastical jurisdiction of the Bishop of Quebec; but they were, excepting perhaps the Island of St. John (now Prince Edward Island), and Cape Breton, under the Crown of England before the date of the Treaty of Paris. These inhabitants were, therefore, not new subjects, nor has it been urged by any writer that any claim for the guarantees of the free exercise of religion was ever made outside of the territory actually known as Canada or New France in 1763. The terms of capitulation at Montreal, indeed, refer to the "Diocese" and to the "priests and people" in the "towns" and "country places" and "distant posts" and to the "missionaries," but under the usual construction put upon like documents the terms of capitulation would be binding only and until the definitive treaty was executed. They were binding, certainly, for three years, but then came the treaty in which "His Britannic Majesty on his side agrees to grant to the inhabitants of Canada the liberty of the Catholic religion. He will, in consequence, give the most exact and effectual orders that his new Roman Catholic subjects may profess the worship of their religion according to the rites of the Roman Church as far as the laws of Great Britain permit."

The writer, while stating his opinion that the treaty is now to be looked at rather than the terms of capitulation at Quebec and Montreal, is not unaware of the fact that almost every writer who

---

[1] The boundaries of Quebec were purposely set out in full in the Article on the Treaty of Paris in the April number of the REVIEW.

has dealt with this matter has read treaty and capitulations as forming one international bargain. It is difficult to reconcile this with the history of the treaty, and with the general principles applicable to the construction of agreements culminating in one considered and definite document. Of course, the capitulations are good enough evidence of the desire of the parties, and where they do not offend against the meaning of the treaty, but help to explain it, they ought to be admitted. But it is manifest that entirely new stipulations may have been finally settled by the treaty which were never entertained by the generals who drew up the capitulations. Indeed, these capitulations anticipate other terms.

Nearly every treaty between France and England in the seventeenth and eighteenth centuries adjusting European matters affected colonists in America, the Anglo-Americans and the Canadians, as the French inhabitants were called. In 1697 the Treaty of Ryswick was signed, and by it the French asserted the Kennebec to be the boundary between them and Massachusetts.[1] The entire eastern coast, Nova Scotia, Cape Breton, St. John (now Prince Edward Island), Newfoundland, Labrador, and Hudson's Bay remained to the French.

By the Treaty of Utrecht, 1713, Nova Scotia, then called Acadia, according to its ancient limits, with the whole of Newfoundland, was given up to England. The French retained some reservation as to the fisheries in Newfoundland, and the English secured the fur trade of Hudson Bay.

By the Treaty of Aix la Chapelle, in 1749, Cape Breton, with the islands of St. Pierre and Miquelon, was restored to France. Three years prior to this, Cape Breton had been taken by the English colonists. By a consideration of these treaties it will be seen at once who were and were not already British subjects in what is yet British territory before the Seven Years' War ending with the Treaty of Paris. The inhabitants of Acadia, afterwards two provinces of Canada, were, in 1763, not inhabitants of Canada, and consequently were not " new" subjects, as Acadia passed over to England in 1713 by the Treaty of Utrecht. In a court of law it would not be arguable on the documents and facts to say that the guarantees of the stipulation were coterminous with the boundaries of the diocese, or that New Brunswick or Nova Scotia come within the scope of its benefits. On the other hand, the people of St.

---

[1] Mr. Garneau says that soon after 1763 a slice of territory was detached from Canada and took the name of New Brunswick with an administration apart. Now Nova Scotia had a legislature of its own since 1758, and it then, and since 1731, included New Brunswick, but its western boundary was not easily defined. Acadia or New Brunswick, when it passed into the hands of the English in 1713, had for its western boundary the Kennebec River. Great Britain, since that time, lost the territory between the Kennebec and the present boundary, the St. Croix River.

John and Cape Breton may fairly be regarded as citizens of a part of New France, as " new" subjects of the Crown of Great Britain after the cession, though St. John was under British rule before the treaty and in 1758. However, it was part of the Seven Years' War; Quebec was in the same position, was under British rule since 1759, and Montreal since 1760.

There is no doubt at all but that the other provinces and territories in Canada, except probably British Columbia and some of the Hudson Bay territory, come within the treaty or the act. A reference to the words of the treaty will explain this. The territory ceded to England after the fall of Quebec and the capitulation is referred to in the treaty as follows:

" Sa Majesté Très-Chrétienne renonce à toutes prétentions qu' elle a jusqu' ici formées ou pourrait former sur la Nouvelle Ecosse ou Acadie, dans toutes ses parties, et en garantit le tout et toutes ses dépendances au Roi de la Grande Brétagne.

" De plus, Sa Majesté Très-Chrétienne cède et garantit à la dite Majesté Britannique, en plein droit, le Canada avec toutes ses dépendances, ainsi que l' Ile Cap Breton, et toutes les autres îles et côtes dans le golfe et le fleuve St. Laurent, et en général tout ce qui dépend des dits païs, terres, îles et côtes, avec la souveraineté, propriété, possession et tous droits acquis par traité ou autrement, que le Roi très-chrétien et la couronne de France ont eus jusqu' à présent sur les dits païs, iles, terres, places, côtes, et leurs habitants, de sorte que le Roi Très-Chrétien cède et transporte le tout au dit Roi et Couronne de la Grande Bretagne, et cela de la manière et forme les plus agréables, sans restriction et sans pouvoir d' écarter de la dite garantie, sous aucun prétexte, ou de pouvoir troubler la Grande-Bretagne dans les possessions sus-mentionnées."

The clauses to be construed with this are as follows, in the language in which they were written:

" Sa Majesté Britannique, de son côté, consent d' accorder la liberté de la religion Catholique aux habitants du Canada. Elle donnera en conséquence les ordres les plus efficaces pour que ses nouveaux sujets Catholiques Romains puissent professer le culte de leur religion selon les rites de l' Eglise de Rome, autant que les lois d' Angleterre le permettent.

" Sa Majesté Britannique consent de plus que les habitants Fran-çais ou autres, qui avaient été sujets du Roi Très-Chrétien en Canada, puissent se retirer en toute sûreté et liberté, ou ils jugeront à propos ; qu' ils vendent leurs biens, pourvu que ce soit à des sujets de Sa Majesté Britannique ; et qu' ils emportent leurs effets avec eux, sans être restreints dans leur émigration, sous aucun pré-texte quelconque, à l' exception de celui des dettes ou de poursuite criminelles ; le terme limité pour cette émigration sera fixé à l'espace de dix-huit mois, à compter du jour de l' éxchange de la ratification du présent traité."

Under this treaty there is, therefore, included the province ot Ontario and a part of the Northeast territory, along with the present Province of Quebec. These come within the operation of the Quebec Act as well.

What the western boundaries of New France may have been in 1763 is not now easy to determine. It was lately the subject of an appeal to the Privy Council between the Province of Ontario and the Dominion of Canada as to the western limits of this province. These were found to be more extensive than many supposed. But their extreme western limit does not reach into the province of Manitoba, and it would require a consideration of the Red River settlement and the wars of the traders to be able to offer any speculation as to whether treaty or act reached westward on the Saskatchewan. The country was explored by Verendrye, under French rule, in the early part of the eighteenth century, and large settlements made. The Hudson Bay charter goes back to the time of Charles II., but the French and English were alternately masters of the fur trade, and the settlements were largely made up of the traders and the half-breeds.

As regards the Hudson Bay settlement, there were very few Catholics, the inhabitants being nearly all from the Orkneys of Scotland or from Switzerland. In the Red River settlement and at Sault St. Marie there were flourishing French posts with missionaries and a prosperous body of settlers, all Catholics.

In a former article in this REVIEW it was pointed out how the Crown of England interpreted the treaty, and how, by means of the Quebec Act, the boundaries of Canada were defined and the benefit of a liberal interpretation of the religious guarantees extended to all Catholics within the large area of the new province of Quebec. Beyond this area the act does not go, but the treaty does, and to a considerable extent of territory. Under the Quebec Act there was Labrador, from St. John River to Hudson Bay, Anticosti, and the Magdalen Islands; under the treaty, the isles of St. John (now Prince Edward Island) and Cape Breton. The Canadas and parts of the territories are both in the treaty and in the act.

It will thus be seen that for a portion of British America the Treaty of Paris applied; for another portion the Quebec Act applied, and for the remainder there was no guarantee as far as the Church is concerned. Indeed, in Nova Scotia one of the early Acts of the Legislative Council was to establish there by law the Church of England.

Before discussing the question of the extent of the treaty as compared with the Quebec Act, or the benefits accorded by either, assuming that the former extends to the French territory now owned by Great Britain, by virtue of the law of nations, and that the latter (the act) is binding within whatever territory the Crown of England chose to extend it, it may be asked what difference would it make to claim under the treaty or under the act? There can be no great difference; the act is fuller, more liberal than the bare words in the treaty, and is not limited to the old French territory, may be within larger or smaller bounds, and may, like any other imperial statute, extend its provisions anywhere within the empire.

The treaty is limited to the old French territory, and cannot be extended beyond the ancient French possessions, nor does it include them all; on the other hand, it cannot be abridged as to that territory. There is no doubt also but that as long as the British Empire continues to exist and keep up its standing as a nation, it will be bound to keep faith with France as to the terms of the Treaty. The guarantees for these terms would extend to all Roman Catholics who, at any time subsequently, were British subjects in the ceded territory.[1] A treaty does not become effete, though it is otherwise with an Act of Parliament; but until the Quebec Act is repealed a mere non-user would not render it lifeless. As has been shown in a former article, this act has been expressly recognized for over a hundred years in Canada, and in every great political change has been referred to as the basis of all our constitutions. The effect of subsequent imperial and provincial legislation will be considered further on.

The treaty, it will be remembered, has one apparently inconsistent feature in it—the free exercise of the Roman Catholic religion is guaranteed to the new subjects, "so far as the laws of Great Britain permit." The Act of 1774 puts an interpretation upon these words, but the Act itself is not easy to construe. The ablest jurists in England and Canada gave it as their opinion at the time that these words, "so far as the laws of Great Britain permit," mean so far as the laws of Great Britain permit the exercise of the Roman Catholic religion in the colonies and outlying divisions of the Crown. Parliament adopted this construction. The statute books were then ransacked to discover what, if any, laws in force against the Catholics extended to the colonies. After a search,

---

[1] L' Abbé Ferland narrates that, when Monseigneur Plessis, Bishop of Quebec, was on a visit to Rome in 1819, an interview with Louis XVIII. was arranged for him at Paris. " The audience was private; the King spoke to Monseigneur Plessis with kindness, and put many questions relating to the state of religion in Canada, requested to be remembered in his prayers, and charged him to say to his diocesans that their former sovereign had not forgotten them, and that, if the conditions stipulated for in their favor by the Treaty of Peace were not observed by England, France would not neglect to claim them."

the most careful, as may be imagined, only one statute could be found. This was the Act of Supremacy of Queen Elizabeth, the first act in the first year of her reign. In the Quebec Act, as has been seen, they, accordingly, introduced the supremacy of the king, but greatly modified the oath, so that there was nothing very objectionable about it. Where the statute applies territorially, then this construction must obtain ; and without going into argument on the question, it may be assumed that, where the treaty extends beyond the boundaries of the old Quebec province, the same construction would be put upon it as upon the statute. To invoke the treaty would be to invoke the construction put upon it in the highest court of the realm. It was quite competent to the British Parliament to have made the Quebec limits coterminous· with the ceded territory, and if they fell short of part of it this would not affect the *ratio decidendi*, the purview and scope of the treaty generally.

If this be so, then the one construction suffices for treaty and statute, and reduces the question to this simply : How does the supremacy of the king of a Protestant country affect the free exercise of religion to his Roman Catholic subjects ? The Act of Supremacy was but a re-enactment by Elizabeth of a statute passed in the twenty-fifth year of Henry VIII., entitled : " *An Act for the submission of the clergie to the King's Majestie.*" The preamble of this act is painfully significant of the times : " Whereas, the King's humble and obedient servants, the clergy of this realm of England, etc.," and then it goes on to recite the desire of the King in matters ecclesiastical. The submission of the clergy is accounted for at this particular juncture by a Protestant writer, Short, in his " History of the Church of England." The clergy were then under a *præmunire* in regard to Wolsey. " In order to buy this off, the Convocation consented to a considerable subsidy, and in the bill which granted it the king's supremacy was asserted. It was, however, with much difficulty that this clause was passed, and so little with the good-will of the lower house that, after the acknowledgment, a proviso was inserted *quantum per Christum licet.*" This act made the King Primate of the Church of England, and by it the sovereign is regarded as being over all persons and over all causes, ecclesiastical as well as civil, supreme in the Church.

The author referred to very candidly admits the reason of the assumption of this supreme ecclesiastical power ; it was to procure a divorce for the King from Queen Catharine. " The existence of the Church of England," he adds, " as a distinct body and her final separation from Rome may be dated from the period of the divorce." To obtain this and yet remain a Catholic—a Defender of the Faith —it is by various authors contended, was the sole aim of the King, and it is certainly clear that whatever his motives may have been, the doctrine of the royal supremacy was not pushed to as great a degree as in the reign of Elizabeth. In the interval between the reigns of these two sovereigns the first statute of Philip and Mary repealed this act and established the Church in its former relations to Rome. Elizabeth, on her accession, passed an act reviving the supremacy of the Crown, and re-enacting nearly everything that her sister had repealed. Two short sections of the first act in the year 1558 will give all that is necessary. Section XVI. is as follows: "And to the intent that all usurped and foreign power and authority, spiritual and temporal, may, forever, be clearly extinguished, and never to be used or obeyed within these realms or any other of Your Majestie's dominions or countries. May it please Your Highness that it may be further enacted by the authority aforesaid, That no foreign prince, person, prelate, state, or potentate, spiritual or temporal, shall use, enjoy, or exercise any manner of power, jurisdiction, superiority, authority, pre-eminence, or privilege, spiritual or ecclesiastical, within this realm or any other of Her Majestie's dominions or countries, but the same shall be abolished thereout forever, any statute, ordinance, custom, constitution, or any other matter or cause whatever, to the contrary notwithstanding."

Section XVII.: "And that it may also please Your Highness that it may be established and enacted by the authority aforesaid, That such jurisdiction, privileges, superiority, and pre-eminence, spiritual and ecclesiastical, or by any spiritual or ecclesiastical power or authority, hath heretofore been, or may lawfully be, exercised or used for the visitation of the ecclesiastical state and persons, and for reformation, order, and correction of the same; and of all manner of errors, heresies, schisms, abuses, offences, contempts, and enormities shall, forever, by authority of this present Parliament, be united and annexed to the Imperial Crown of this realm."

Coke and Hale put constructions on this statute which, at all events, suited the royal pretensions. Coke says that, " By the ancient laws of this realm the kingdom of England is an absolute empire and monarchy, consisting of one head, which is the King, and of a body consisting of several members, which the law divideth into two parts. The clergy and the laity, both of them next and immediately under God, subject and obedient to the head, . . . such an authority as the Pope heretofore exercised, is now annexed to the Crown by the above-mentioned statute." And elsewhere it is laid down judicially that "all that power which the Pope ever exercised within this realm on spirituals is now vested in the King."

These opinions were certainly opposed to Magna Charta, the first chapter of which stipulates that the Church shall be free and have her whole rights and liberties inviolable. As to the statute being declaratory of the common law, that went for nothing, as the whole doctrine was novel, and without custom or precedent justifying it. The title of "Supreme Head of the Church and Clergy of England" appears for the first time in the Petition of Convocation to Henry VIII. to relieve them from the penalties·to which they were exposed.

If it were necessary to pursue this subject, there would be little difficulty in estimating how the members of the Church of England regarded the change from the Papal to the royal supremacy. It was well enough to inveigh against the supremacy of the Pope, but when the royal supremacy was found to be more intolerable, then it was time for a noted public man and writer to say that " pretensions of this sort, from whatever side they have come, have never found any permanent favor with the English people." This is very briefly the history of the passing of the Act of Supremacy—an act by which, in England, the King is supreme ordinary and who might, without any Act of Parliament, make ordinances for the government of the clergy, and if there be a controversy between spiritual persons concerning jurisdiction, he is arbitrator, and it is a right of his Crown to declare their bounds. The King in England, therefore, became head of the church, no matter what the church was and no matter what religion the King professed. He was King and Pope ; the church became a department of the state, quite subordinate to the Crown and to its judicial and executive officers. It exists with the Crown, and ceases when the Crown ceases. The Crown was the head of Episcopacy in England, and might have been head of Presbyterianism in Scotland that tolerates no Episcopacy. A Catholic Stuart was the head of this Protestant Church. With such precedents, what obstacle was there to the omnipotence of the Parliament of Great Britain to assume headship over the Church of Rome in Canada ? Under such a multiplication of recognized churches the Crown was likely to become an ecclesiastical hydra. If there was no great reason why that should be propagated in Canada which was regarded as damnable and idolatrous at home, then it was but a step further to have the viceroy in India proclaimed the head of the native church, as Lord Dalhousie thought he could be in Canada. Had the Act of Supremacy been held to be in full force in Canada, there is little doubt but that no Catholic could have assumed any office, or any clergyman become recognized before the law; but the statute itself was virtually repealed, especially as to the oath, and a new and simple one introduced. The words of the Quebec Act are, "may have, hold, and enjoy the free exercise of the religion of the Church of Rome, subject to the King's supremacy declared in the act, etc."

Now, as to the meaning put upon the statute by Lord Coke and referred to above, it is to this effect, that to the King of England there is now annexed such an authority as the Pope heretofore exercised. Suppose such power were annexed, it could vest only by some supposed transfer of it from the Pope himself; or that the King inherently was possessed of it. The latter was the only view possible. The statute affirming this inherent authority could not make it a fact or make it believed by Catholics, and the only course open to the Crown was by active coercive measures in the more modern form of persecution. The Crown then, in Canada, said in effect, we will assume control over the Church and be its head whether it wants another head or not. The Church in Scotland would have been satisfied with the Crown, and why should Rome be more particular?

It was evident that this was the only way out of the difficulty—to force the head on the body; but after sixty years of endeavor the Crown was utterly defeated in Canada, the Church rejecting the royal headship. The difficulty was settled by time, the Act of 1 Eliz., chap. i., was ignored, and the Catholic Church rendered independent of the Crown—neither its creature nor its slave. The details of this struggle form the most exciting part of the history of the Church in Canada, and will aid in discussing the present legal *status* of the Church.

The reader has had his attention directed sufficiently to those matters which lie at the foundation of the Church in Canada under British rule—the Articles of Capitulation, the Treaty of Paris, etc., and the Quebec Act. The Diocese of Quebec and its subdivisions have been adverted to and the extent within which the safeguards of the treaty extended. The acknowledged interpretation to be put upon the treaty as to the free exercise of the Roman Catholic religion has also been noticed, and the inconsistencies on the face of the guarantees endeavored to be explained. Wherever it was possible, reference was had only to authorized copies of state papers and Acts of Parliament and other official documents, so that the reader can draw his own conclusions. There still remains the question of the exact legal status of the Catholic Church in Canada, whether it occupies a position different from that of the other religious denominations. This was the question raised by the Privy Council in the Guibord case, but not decided there. It is not an easy question to approach, much less to attempt arriving at a definite opinion, but the writer will submit his evidences and authorities as to his own views, and the reader can form another opinion if he chooses to do so. This will be considered in the next article.

HUME'S THEORY OF CAUSE AND EFFECT THE BASIS OF HIS SKEPTICAL PHILOSOPHY.

HUME'S acuteness as a reasoner is generally admitted, and his influence upon philosophical ideas still continues. His professed followers, however, are few, perhaps because men see too plainly that his skeptical conclusions are false ; yet he contributed more than any other author to produce the systems of dubious thinking which have sprung up since his time, and which have terminated in the well-known skepticism and agnosticism of our own day. The influence he had and still has is owing not a little to the rare literary merit of his productions. A master of the language in its simplicity and beauty, and by nature a keen-witted Scotchman, he proposes his principles of doubt with fascinating subtlety, reasons from them in general consistently, and finally reaches conclusions that contradict universal experience, that are certainly false, and which Hume himself virtually admits to be erroneous when he confesses that the triumph of his doctrines is academical only, and therefore vanishes when put to the test of common experience and the practice of every-day life. For Hume is a skeptic, and, in his own words, " arguments are skeptical when they admit of no answer and produce no conviction ; their only effect is to cause that momentary amazement and irresolution and confusion which is the result of skepticism." As an argument by its definition consists of the truth supported by evident and demonstrative reasons, it is clear that an argument which is skeptical, according to the sentence just quoted, does not exist as a means of reaching rational and certain conclusions.

A survey of Hume's main principles will make manifest that the characteristic mark of his philosophy is doubt, though the doubt is not of so universal a kind as was Pyrrho's of old, for he admits at least one species of knowledge to be demonstratively certain, though he limits that species of knowledge, thus: " The only objects of the abstract sciences or of demonstration are quantity and number, and . . . . all attempts to extend this more perfect species of knowledge beyond these bounds are mere sophistry and illusion ; . . . . these may safely be pronounced the only proper objects of knowledge and of demonstration." This is the preliminary principle upon which his doctrines are based, but it supposes what is false, viz., that mathematical science alone is demonstrative, and that every other species of knowledge is only probable or doubtful.

Waiving for a moment the question how Hume could hope to demonstrate his assertion, since its demonstration could not pertain to mathematics, it is clear that if admitted it would prove all philosophy worthless, as philosophy has no real place in the circle of man's knowlege if its principles be not the most immutable and the most certain; yet philosophy is not specially concerned about mathematical quantity and numbers, although it is true that the sciences, respecting these objects, depend for their ultimate truth and certainty upon the superior truths of philosophy; there would be neither quantity nor numbers if there were not real natures and beings of which they are properties and of which they are predicated.

Metaphysics, or philosophy, comprises the absolutely first and most universal principles of human reason, together with all the necessary conclusions derived from them by demonstration. The first principles of every other science are only relatively first, because they presuppose other principles that are prior, and they regard only some particular being, or aspect of being, to which they are completely limited. Philosophy considers being comprehensively or under its aspect of most universal reality; it includes the intrinsic and most general properties of all things, its principles are the most evident and the most necessary, and they presuppose no other principles that are prior or to which they are subordinate. By consequence, the metaphysical is superior to all other truth in demonstrative perfection. Its supremacy in the order of purely human knowledge becomes apparent when we compare it with any other species of demonstrative knowledge. The science of geometry cannot take the first step in demonstration without presupposing many principles; *e.g.*, it assumes that the evident truth necessarily produces certainty, else its attempt to demonstrate would be vain; it assumes the objective reality of bodies and of quantity; it assumes that its own objects can truly affirm themselves to the mind, that the mind can read their essences, define them, and know that those objects which have the same definition are of the same essence. In short, the science of geometry assumes the whole body of metaphysical truths as the basis upon which it is ultimately grounded.

That this is only the usual teaching of the Christian schools, the following sentences clearly show.

" Nisi enim essent duo trianguli ejusdem speciei, frustra demonstraret geometræ aliquos triangulos esse similes; et similiter in aliis figuris." (St. Thom. in Arist. Met. Lib. 1, Lect. 10.) " If there were no two triangles of the same species, in vain would the geometrician prove certain triangles to be similar; and so for other figures."

And in Lib. 11, Lect. 4, he says: " Prima principia demonstrationis accipiuntur a mathematica et ab aliis particularibus scientiis particulariter tantum ; ergo eorum consideratio secundum quod sunt communia pertinet ad hanc scientiam [*i.e.*, metaphysicam] quæ considerat de ente in quantum est ens. . . . . Mathematica assumunt hujusmodi principia ad propriam considerationem. . . . . Non est aliqua mathematica scientia quæ consideret ea quæ sunt quantitatis communia in quantum est quantitas." " The first principles of demonstration are taken and employed by the mathematical and other sciences particularly only ; hence the consideration of them as common or general (principles) pertains to this science (metaphysics), which considers being precisely as being. Such principles are assumed by mathematics for its own consideration. . . . . No mathematical science considers what is common to quantity precisely as quantity."

Quantity as an object of mathematics is particular and limited, as an object of metaphysics it is universal and absolute ; its metaphysical consideration is prior to its mathematical. To a particular science a particular method is proper ; but to the universal science belongs a universal consideration of objects. The distinguished schoolman, Duns Scotus, following Aristotle, uses similar language: " Quæcumque communia a scientiis particularibus solum particulariter sumuntur, pertinent ad considerationem hujus scientiæ [*i.e.*, metaphysicæ] communiter et generaliter accepta." " All the common conceptions and principles of knowledge that special sciences employ according to a restricted application, pertain to this science [metaphysics], when they are employed according to their common and universal application." Metaphysical principles not being presupposed, magnitudes and dimensions could not be discovered, nor any of the relations of quantity and numbers ascertained, and reflexly tested by a final and absolute standard of truth. It is an axiom that no science proves its own first principles ; to do so it should prove them by other principles which are prior, and then the supposed first principles would not be really first. The first principles of any science are either self-evidently true, in which case they do not admit of proof, or else they are assumed from a superior science, and in this case they are not proved in the science of which they are first principles. Philosophy presupposes no other science whose principles or conclusions it takes for granted ; its own being simply first and those of every other science subordinate to them. It was on account of this real supremacy that the schoolmen, with Aristotle, considered philosophy the Queen of the Sciences.

Hume is not an advocate of universal skepticism.; but when his doctrines are consistently reasoned out, they tend in that direction.

When he asserts that none but mathematical science is demonstrative, the proof of his assertion, as just intimated, does not pertain to mathematics, but to metaphysics, an order of knowledge superior to mathematics and competent to declare the absolute requirements of demonstrative evidence. The assertion supposes two orders of knowledge, the non-mathematical and the mathematical. As to the first order, a principle is laid down despite the asserted impossibility of proving it, because the criterion of any demonstrative certainty, not mathematical, is rejected; and because demonstration, as distinguished from the particular science which employs it specially, and as containing the simply first principles of all proof, is proper to metaphysics, not to mathematics. On the other hand, why should mathematics itself be considered demonstrative, if the metaphysical and absolute tests of demonstration be arbitrarily set aside? The principles of mathematics have only a dependent necessity, for their objective certainty depends upon extra-mathematical and more absolute truths; and these being cast aside, by what inerrable process will you prove the demonstrative character of mathematical principles? And why may not mathematical certainty be denied, or at least questioned? It is upon evidence outside of mathematics, and clearer and more convincing, that we build securely the demonstrative certainty of mathematics. To deny or doubt the truth, then, of whatever is not mathematical science, would be to set at naught those principles which are primary and intrinsic in respect to all intellectual knowledge, and in reality to efface the certainty afforded by the sciences that regard quantity and number. The ultimate canon of all reasoning, "The Principle of Contradiction," it is almost needless to add, is not a principle of mathematics, and would be no principle at all if Hume's system, judged rigorously by his definitions, were true. When the conclusions of this philosopher are logically and completely drawn forth from his skeptical premises, it will be noticed that they seem to embody a skepticism which does not stop at the boundary of mathematical truth. And even for his reservation in favor of mathematical knowledge Hume is opposed by the more advanced skeptics of to-day, and notably by Professor Huxley, who attempts to show that whatever be the differences between mathematical and other truths, they do not justify Hume's statement. In proposing a system of philosophy, it is irrational to begin with what is doubtful; it is equally irrational to require proof of everything, though evidence is necessary for every assent of the intellect. Proof is justly required of any proposition or doctrine which is not self-evident, or which is not certified by adequate authority; then, until the proof be produced doubt may properly be entertained. To suppose that the self-evident first principles of philosophy can be proved, or that they need proof, would be as absurd as to imagine that the sun at midday requires some other luminary to make it visible.

Hume next develops his complete skepticism concerning the relation of cause and effect; this is brought out in the following sentences, which have been selected as most perfectly embodying his essential doctrines: "All the objects of human reason or inquiry may naturally be divided into two kinds, to wit, *Relations of Ideas* and *Matters of Fact*. Propositions of this kind (Relations of Ideas) are discoverable by the mere operation of thought without dependence on what is anywhere existent in the universe. Matters of Fact are not ascertained in the same manner.

" All reasonings concerning matters of fact seem to be founded on the relation of *Cause* and *Effect*. . . . . The knowledge of this relation is not in any instance attained by reasonings *a priori*, but arises entirely from experience when we find that any particular objects are constantly conjoined with each other.

" All inferences from experience are effects of custom, not of reasoning.

" All belief of matter of fact or real existence is derived merely from some object present to the memory or senses, and a customary conjunction between that and some other object. . . . . This belief is the necessary result of placing the mind in such circumstances.

" . . . Belief consists not in the peculiar nature or order of ideas, but in the *manner* of their conception, and in their feeling to the mind.

" . . . The sentiment of belief is nothing but a conception more intense and steady than what attends the mere fictions of the imagination, and this *manner* of conception arises from a customary conjunction of the object with something present to the memory or senses."[1]

These sentences contain the cardinal principles of Hume's speculative system; they contain also ideas prolific of modern skeptical philosophy, which advances beyond the limits set by Hume, and reduces all our intellectual knowledge to the kind which he intended only for cause and effect and matters of fact. To apprehend the unfitness of these principles for explaining the origin and real character of our knowledge, a few elementary distinctions are necessary.

Since our ideas are caused and measured by objects, all rational knowledge may, under this view, be divided into two kinds, viz.,

---

[1] Inquiry conc. Hum. Und., Sec. 4.

the knowledge of objects that are immutable and necessary, and the knowledge of objects which are mutable and contingent.

Judgments of the mind which regard objects of the first kind are called, especially since the days of Kant, analytical or *a priori* judgments; those which regard the latter kind of objects are termed "experimental" judgments. That "an effect requires a cause," that "the whole is greater than any of its parts," are instances of analytical judgments, all of which possess the characteristics of necessity and universality; that an effect requires a cause is necessarily true of every effect whatsoever, and the opposite of this truth is simply inconceivable, because it contradicts an evident definition based upon the objective and intrinsic nature of things. This judgment should also be distinguished from the positive truth, "This is an effect," which requires an inductive process to make it certain. All positive or experimental judgments, such as "bodies gravitate," "the sun will rise to-morrow," etc., are learned by observation and experience, and their certainty is proportioned to, and based upon, this species of evidence; they have that necessity which is proper to the physical laws of nature, but the mind perceives no evidence of an *a priori* necessity and universality, according to which the opposites of these truths are intrinsically impossible and inconceivable. It is conceivable that the law of gravitation might be suspended; but if it could be demonstrated that gravitation is of the intrinsic essence of bodies, or is a property necessarily resulting from their intrinsic essence, then to conceive a body which would not gravitate would be an impossibility and a contradiction in terms. Since the objects of analytical judgments possess necessity and universality, they are more adequately of the intelligible order, and hence more proportioned and congenial to our intellects. Mutable and contingent objects are less completely subject to the intellect than are those of the necessary and immutable order; though there is a species of necessity and at least a vague universality in all rational knowledge, since the intellect knows only by way of ideas that express a common essence of their objects whether such objects are of the necessary or contingent, abstract or concrete order.

Plato found it so difficult to account for rational knowledge of mutable objects that he invented his celebrated "*per se* intelligibles," by participating which material things acquired both real existence and an intelligibility. His error consisted in supposing an object's existence in reality to be identical with its ideal existence in the intellect, since that essence solely by which the intellect knows any object is in a true sense in that object. An aspect of the same difficulty seems to have induced Kant to propose his incongruous theory of "synthetical judgments *a priori*," according to which he explained the presence and union in our knowledge of the necessary element with the experimental. Necessary and positive truth being thus distinguished, Hume's skepticism concerning the latter becomes clear. Allowing demonstrative evidence only to mathematics, he professes to doubt whether we can know with certainty the cause of any real effect whatsoever. Our idea of natural causes, he argues, is not obtained by *a priori* reasoning according to which we would first know objects as causes and from this knowledge predict their effects before experience. This reasoning is true, for in the experimental sphere we first learn certain phenomena or facts, and of these we inquire the causes. But in the speculative and necessary order in which we abstract from concrete causes and effects, our reasoning concerning these objects is of an *a priori* character. The analytical principle, every effect must have a cause, is learned in early childhood after a very limited experience, which suffices to produce in the infant mind the idea of a cause, together with its necessary and immutable relation to the effect. A child may be unable to enunciate in the exact terms of metaphysics the proposition; every effect requires a cause, but its accustomed actions and language show that the judgment in its universality and necessity resides habitually in its mind from a very tender age, and is directive of its action in all those particulars which depend upon this principle. When we turn from the speculative to the positive order, Hume's principle is undeniable, for then we do not consider a cause under an *a priori* aspect, but whatever we know of it is learned *a posteriori*. Facts observed lead us to the knowledge of their causes, since there is an actual connection between any effect and its cause. The falling of the apple led Newton to know its proximate cause—gravitation; he did not know *a priori* the law of gravitation and from this law as a principle predict the falling of the apple as an effect. The human mind naturally inquires after causes, and from any real effect observed it can infer truly the existence of a cause; if the effect be such as adequately reproduces the perfection of the cause, and also if it be fully understood, then the nature of the cause may also be inferred, but from any effect whatsoever the mere existence of a cause may and must be concluded. It will be noticed that phenomena which are effects in the real order operate as causes in the order of our knowledge, since they determine the mind to know their real causes. When Hume professes to doubt whether we can know with certainty the cause of any real effect, he employs substantially the following argument: A cause is not learned by *a priori* reasoning, neither can it be learned by experience, and hence we have no certain knowledge of a cause at all; experience cannot furnish us with the idea of a cause, since it reveals only an unvarying sequence of certain facts and events, *e.g.*, that wax placed before the fire melts. Granted that we know as a fact that wax melts when placed before the fire, we do not know with certainty that the fire causes the melting of the wax, cause and effect as really such being unknowable. But though these philosophers profess to be certain of only so much respecting the conjunction of these two objects, mankind at large are certain of more, and they judge unhesitatingly that the fire is not merely adjacent to the wax, but *causes* it to melt. It must be allowed to Hume that we know natural causes only by way of an inference from their effects, and that the evidence, on account of which we infer the existence of any natural cause, depends upon observation and experience. Mankind know the fire as cause only by an inference from the melting of the wax, but all the requisites for the perfect certainty of experimental judgments are present in this instance, and the inference is evidently and inerrably drawn. The universal judgments of mankind are always true when they are the immediate inferences from matters of fact, and from primitive and self-evident truths. That the tree produces its fruit, that the animal is nourished by food—these and all similar instances of immediate conclusions from facts of universal experience are known by all men, inferentially indeed, but with complete certainty; so that in no system of philosophy can we rationally doubt such evident and familiar judgments. To reduce our knowledge of natural causes and effects to merely the knowledge of a customary conjunction between two objects does not distinguish it from the knowledge of a mere animal respecting the same objects. Animals can learn experimentally that one object always follows another, and can manifest by their action that they possess such knowledge; and if they do not know the customary conjunction as such, they at least know it by way of a concrete relation. Proofs of this will occur to every reader. Many proverbs are founded on the observation. The spider weaves and spreads its net with as much apparent skill as the fowler; and are we permitted to doubt that in its own sentient way it sees in the entrapped fly the effect of its gossamery cause? But when the human mind affirms by a judgment based upon a sufficient induction that one object is the cause of another, its act of knowing is of a higher order and it presents the cause precisely as such, or in its true and necessary relation to its effect. The power to know causes, as such and in their necessary relation to effects, is a distinctive mark of man's real superiority over mere animals. It would seem, then, that Hume does not clearly distinguish between the manner in which the mind knows causes and that in which causes are the objects of merely sensible cognition, for he allows certainty only to what is known as matter of fact and upon the testimony of the senses; whereas the mind does not know causes as matter of fact, but as conclusions from effects reported by the mind's ministers, the senses. It is an obvious and necessary inference or conclusion which reveals in the preceding example that the wax is not merely adjacent to the fire, but is really influenced by it. The evidence upon which the inference is based is complete, though inductive; and, like all inferences that are only physically true, it does not assert of the objects inferred any *a priori* and absolute necessity, but only such necessity as the physical laws of nature have, which is relative and is ultimately dependent upon the will of the author who conceived and produced these objects in accordance with such laws. When inferences pass by the limits of first and immediate deductions from matters of fact, or when they require some intricate reasoning to reach them, then they have not the same universal acceptance; they are then the subject matter of special sciences, and are known only by the learned.

The general tone of consistency and clearness with which Hume reasons from his skeptical principles shows the strength and subtlety of his intellect, and it is to be regretted that a mind so well fitted by nature and by culture for metaphysical pursuits should have adopted and advocated unsound and skeptical principles.

A primary object intended by Kant in his writings was the refutation of Hume's skepticism; in this attempt he not only was unsuccessful, but in addition he developed a theory of human knowledge which is, perhaps, more comprehensively unsound than that of any other celebrated philosopher. Towards the end of his elaborate system he is forced to admit that Hume's demand for the connection between cause and effect which enables us with certainty to conclude the one from the other has not yet been satisfied. Hume himself was influenced not a little by Locke; indeed, his theory seems to be in part a further application of Locke's principles. Locke holds that we know nothing of real essences nor of substance. He was, perhaps, led to this position by attending too exclusively to the declarations of the senses, substance not being thus declared but known only by an inference from its qualities. Qualities, we conclude, must have some subject in which they exist, and by which they are supported in existence, and this subject is substance. If inference cannot make us certain of the existence of substance, then Hume is not far wrong in declaring that it cannot disclose the existence of any real cause; for our knowledge in both cases is gained in the same way. The answer to both Locke and Hume, who here agree in principle, is that inference can disclose with certainty the existence as well of substance as of natural causes. It can, moreover, disclose the intrinsic nature as well as the existence of these objects, since causes and effects are proportional. Hume's succeeding chapter upon "The Idea of Necessary Connection" follows consequently from his skepticism concerning cause and effect, and the reply to his doubts upon this point is somewhat touched upon in what has been already said. As it is only by the necessary link between a given cause and its effect that we are enabled to know them as cause and effect, Hume, denying that we can know with certainty any causes at all, attempts to prove that we have no idea of a necessary connection between the one and the other. His argument is contained in these sentences: "The power or energy by which this [motion of our limbs] is effected, like that in other natural events, is unknown and inconceivable. . . . . It must be allowed that when we know a power we know that very circumstance in the cause by which it is enabled to produce the effect, for these are supposed to be synonymous. We must, therefore, know both the cause and effect and the relation between them."

An observation is here pertinent upon Hume's statement before given: "Arguments are skeptical when they admit of no answer and produce no conviction; their only effect is to cause that momentary amazement and irresolution and confusion which is the result of skepticism." We have here a proof how constantly and inseparably the link between cause and effect is fixed in the mind, whence it cannot be dislodged.

A cause may be viewed under two phases: First, merely to know whether it exists; and, secondly, to discover its exact and intrinsic nature, together with the power by which it produces its effect. In other words, we may know of a cause, "*an est,*" or we may know of it, "*quid est,*" that it is a cause, or how it is a cause. When it is said to be a matter of common experience that the command of our wills is the cause of motion in our limbs, it is not meant that mankind at large understand the exact and intrinsic nature of the will's causality over our bodily members, but that they perceive as a fact the motion of our limbs, and infer with truth the existence of its cause. In addition to this knowledge immediately inferred from facts common to all men and embodied in their familiar judgments, each person is directly conscious that his will has empire over his limbs, and that his limbs obey the command of his will; hence the direct consciousness of each person is a witness to the same truth that his will moves his limbs, although he knows not how. It is noways necessary for the multitude to know profoundly and psychologically the mode by which this process is accomplished in order to know that it is really accomplished. Mankind at large are incapable of following, or else have not the time and opportunity to follow, a long chain of reasoning; they stop with what is obvious and unmistakable. It is the province of psychology to give the philosophical explanation of the union and interaction of soul and body, but it is in the range of common experience to conclude, as it is also the office of direct consciousness to attest, that our wills cause the motion of our limbs. Hume's conclusion, then, is erroneous when he asserts that, because mankind do not understand how the motion of our limbs is caused, therefore they do not know that it is caused at all. Men often know the cause of a fact or event so imperfectly that they can only name the cause "something," but it is a want of logic to deduce from this that then they do not even know there is a cause. Complete certainty as to the existence of a cause is not incompatible with considerable ignorance of the cause's nature; to use the very obvious example of Boethius, we know there is a certain number of stars, but what that number is we do not know; we know also that the number is either odd or even. By what name soever we call that something in us which enables us to raise the hand, to walk, to sit, etc., whether we name it power, cause, or principle, its existence is none the less certain, even should our ignorance of its intrinsic nature and essential properties be equally evident. But in point of fact the science of Psychology enables us to know with demonstrative certainty the real essence of the human will, although we are not thereby enabled to perceive that essence intuitively. It is false to assert with Hume, Mill and others that the inmost nature or essence of things is unknowable and inconceivable. Definition manifests the essence of a thing, and while it is true that positive and mutable objects cannot be subjected to definition as readily as objects of the necessary order, still there are things positively and experimentally known whose essence we can apprehend and define with perfect certainty. The definition of man as a rational animal is a conclusion based upon induction, but it nevertheless expresses the inmost and immutable essence of man, that without which this being would be an impossibility. But in the domain of necessary truth the essences of things are perceived without a like difficulty, and their definitions are more readily expressed. A triangle is an object the intrinsic essence of which we perfectly comprehend and easily express by definition. The essence of a thing, or, as the schoolmen with Aristotle word it, the "*quidditas rei*," is really the proper term and object of intellectual operation; the quiddity, or conceived essence in its more rudimentary states, may be objectively vague and transcendental, but it is capable of being reflexly perfected and brought to express an object's intrinsic nature.[1]

---

[1] Τὸ τί ἦν εἶναι ὃν ὁ λογος ὁρισμός καὶ τὅντο ὁ οἰα λέγεται ἑκάστο ʼ, Arist. Met. Lib. 4, No. 2, ed. Bek.

"Quod quid erat esse cujus ratio definitio est, et hoc uniuscujusque essentia dicitur."

Scholastic phrases rendering Aristotle's ideas can always be relied on for accuracy in reproducing his thoughts, though not always for elegance. The schoolmen sought exact truth, even to the loss of elegance.

When Locke asserted that we know nothing of substance, which, in fact, we do not know intuitively but by inference, he, perhaps, did not foresee the erroneous consequences which logically result from his position. Hume, accepting this reasoning which invalidates our knowledge of substance, generalized the principle ·that none but *a priori* reasoning is demonstratively certain, and, therefore, that all inferences concerning matters of fact are doubtful and illusory: so that a species of reasoning which Locke intended only for actual substance and actual essence, Hume developed into a universal principle applicable to all reasoning that is grounded upon experience. Hume thus becomes the influential teacher of a skepticism which covers the whole field of knowledge gained inferentially from matters of fact. From this philosophy of restricted doubt to the more general skepticism of certain modern philosophers the transition is effected without much difficulty. The theory of the so-called "relativity of knowledge" seems to be a reproduction of Hume's skepticism, with modern skeptical additions. In this theory all of our knowledge is explained to be of a mutable character by the supposition of a superior order of truth which might essentially change, nay, even contradict, our *a priori* and most necessary truths. The theory is illustrated by the current example derived from the science of perspective. In this science objects are ranged in a picture, so that their situations in reality are exactly reproduced for the eye. It is an axiom in perspective that parallel lines meet, that two straight lines inclose a space, etc. Failing to note that an object, by its nature common to more than one sense, cannot be known perfectly by one sense alone, a philosopher might argue: If, instead of having five senses, man were endowed only with the sense of sight, then his knowledge of geometrical axioms would be such only as is declared by the science of perspective, which is under certain respects contradictory of real geometrical truths. In like manner, were that so, it might be possible that all our knowledge, which we now imagine to be objectively necessary and immutable, would be but "relative to the knowing mind" and subject to contradiction by a superior enlightenment, supposed to supplement our present limited conceptions and to contradict our primary axioms. Since all knowledge admitting this theory would be essentially relative, even this supposed additional and superior knowledge would be merely relative also, and the final consequence would be either that absolute certainty of anything is impossible, or that it could be reached only by passing through an infinite series of superior orders of knowledge, a process impossible to us, and possible, if at all, only to beings immeasurably superior intellectually to us. The really ultimate conclusion then would seem to be that absolute certainty of any-thing is impossible.[1]

Knowledge is the product of the object known and the faculty knowing, but of neither exclusively; hence, when it is said by Mill that all knowledge is relative to the knowing mind, a distinction is necessary; that the received influence from objects known exists in and is cognizable by the intellect, in a manner proportioned and natural to the intellect, is true; just as the mountain seen is received by the eye and perceived in a manner proportioned and natural to the eye itself. "Omne receptum per modum recipientis recipitur." In this sense it is true that all knowledge is relative to the knowing mind. But when the proposition is extended in meaning beyond this limit and made to imply that all knowledge is a merely subjective and mutable affection totally incapable of conjoining the intellect with the real intrinsic and immutable natures of things, then it is evidently false. For knowledge can and does truly express to the intellect the existence, nature and properties of objects. It can and does disclose that in an object which is necessary and immutable, *i.e.*, its essence.

In the usual acceptation of the terms, "all knowledge is relative to the knowing mind," it is intended briefly to embody a compre-hensive skeptical opinion which includes the theoretical uncertainty and mutability of axiomatic truths, together with Hume's specula-tive doubts concerning positive truths. The influence of Hume is clearly discernible in determining upon the subject of cause and effect the position of John Stuart Mill, an author who, one might suppose, would not be swayed by the authority of any philosopher whatever. "And how, or by what evidence," says this luminous writer, "does experience testify to it (the causation hypothesis)? Not by disclosing any *nexus* between the cause and effect, any sufficient reason in the cause itself why the effect should follow it.

---

[1] J. S. Mill, in his usual clear and direct language, thus states the theory: "But all this additional knowledge [conceivable in some future state of existence, or possessed by intelligences superior to us] would be like that which we now possess, merely phenomenal. We should not any more than at present know things as they are in themselves, but merely an increased number of relations between them and us. And in the only meaning which we are able to attach to the term, all knowledge, by how-ever exalted an intelligence, can only be relative to the knowing mind." An Exam. of Sir W. Hamilton's Philos., Chap. 2.

Again, in Chap. 3, he quotes with approval the following sentence from Sir William Hamilton: "Had we as many senses as the inhabitants of Sirius in the 'Micromegas' of Voltaire; were there, as there may well be, a thousand modes of real existence as definitely distinguished from one another as are those which manifest themselves to our present senses, and had we for each of these thousand modes a separate organ competent to make it known to us—still would our whole knowledge be, as it is at present, only of the relative." Mill thinks that "nothing can be truer or more clearly stated than this," an exposition of a doctrine which eliminates from rational knowledge all objective necessity and immutability.

No philosopher now makes this supposition, and Sir W. Hamilton positively disclaims it.   What experience makes known is the fact of an invariable sequence between every event and some special combination of antecedent conditions, in such sort that wherever and whenever that union of antecedents exists the event does not fail to occur." (Exam. of Sir W. Hamilton's Phil., Chap. xxvi.) That experience does not "disclose any *nexus*" between cause and effect may be admitted when it is understood by these terms that it is not the office of experience as such to disclose any *nexus*, but to furnish that complete evidence which enables the intellect to perceive a real *nexus* between an effect and its cause, so that the one may, with certainty, be inferred from the other.   Experience is rather limited to a declaration of facts, but reason is not so limited; reason can proceed from facts to their causes, perceiving by direct and certain inference that actual and intelligible relation which indissolubly connects causes and effects.   Experience reveals an unvarying sequence of certain objects or events, but the reason of man transcending mere experience discovers the real consequence and the necessary relation of effects to their causes.   It is worthy of note that the word "invariable" does not seem to express Mill's true meaning, because in that term is implied a real necessity to occur which Mill directly intends to exclude.   Although it is inference alone which discloses the causes of natural events, such as, *e.g.*, that the tree really produces its fruit, that the food which is eaten really nourishes us, yet such inference is a medium of certainty to the mind just as truly as the eye is a medium of certainty that the fruit really hangs from the tree.   There is as much reason to doubt the truth of the eye's testimony as there is to doubt the truth of a cause's existence duly revealed by inference, the only difference being as to the manner in which the intellect becomes certain ; immediately in the case of the eye's objects, mediately in the case of the objects inferred.   And if there is a difference in the intensity with which the intellect assents to each of the truths, it is a difference between two certainties, not a difference which leaves objects duly inferred only probable or doubtful, as Hume and his followers contend.   There is a certainty in both cases, and we can as readily make the irrational supposition that some optical illusion always frustrates normal vision, as we can imagine that just inference is untrustworthy in that sphere precisely in which it is the proper and only medium of certainty.   When inference reveals the existence of any cause without disclosing its intrinsic nature, as often happens, it would be as irrational then to reject its testimony entirely as to argue that the eye does not truly see because it does not discourse upon the medium through which it sees.   Inference or reasoning is not, however, in itself, so perfect a manner of knowing truth as is that of intuitive vision, the self-evidently true being more perfectly manifest than what is mediately evident. Evidence is the absolute criterion of certainty, and demonstrated conclusions concerning experimental matter afford that evidence which necessitates the firm assent of our understandings. The immediate and evident deductions from facts of experience can no more be denied than the facts of experience themselves.

Certainty is that condition of the mind in which there is an assent to the truth on account of a motive or principle which excludes all doubt and all fear of the opposite's being true; by consequence, it does not consist of any "feeling to the mind," be the feeling dull or lively. When the understanding acquiesces in the truth, it is possible that a certain feeling of satisfaction may result, but the feeling itself should be carefully distinguished from intellectual certainty. The species and degree of certainty we have of any object is proportioned to the evidence which such object affords, and evidence may be denominated that intelligible light which proceeds from an object and is shed upon the understanding so as to make the object visible. Certainty is proportioned to the species and degree of this light, and they are measured by the perfection of the object whence they proceed. What is made manifest by the light of metaphysical truth is received and possessed by the mind with the most perfect species of certainty. The intellect perceives in objects thus manifested a solidity and necessity of existence that it finds nowhere else. For example, when one judgment affirms precisely that which another denies, it is self-evident that both judgments cannot be true at the same time. This is a metaphysical truth which is known in such a manner that our intellect is rendered absolutely and infallibly certain upon understanding the terms; that this principle could admit of an exception, or be contradicted by any additional knowledge, is simply impossible and inconceivable. By this highest species of certainty objects are always known in a simply unchangeable character; but those of which we are only physically certain are not known in the like way; that bodies gravitate is, indeed, certain, but the mind does not yield the same kind of assent in this case that it does to metaphysical truths; for it is not simply impossible for gravitation to be suspended. When the mind possesses metaphysical certainty of a truth, the opposite of that truth is simply inconceivable.

The popular tendency to confuse inferred with merely conjectural knowledge, as well as the diverse intensity of assent proper respectively to physical and metaphysical certainty, was skilfully employed by Hume to prove our rational knowledge of physical objects merely doubtful, while allowing mathematical truths to be demonstratively evident. John Stuart Mill not only grants Hume's principle respecting objects of which we are physically certain, but, as will be seen presently, applies the principle also to mathe-·matical and necessary truths. Concerning the obvious relation between our wills and the motion of our limbs, Mill has the following observation: "I conceive that no more in this than in any other case of causation have we evidence of anything more than what experience informs us of, and it informs us of nothing except immediate, invariable and unconditional sequence."[1] In every known instance of real cause and effect we have evidence of something more than what mere experience informs us of; we have evidence of the relation between an effect and its cause, evidence of the actual influence of a cause upon its effect, and assumed also in support of the proof is the metaphysical axiom, every change has an adequate cause. The relation and the actual influence are neither of them intuitively evident, but they are both concluded with adequate and demonstrative certainty. Mutation is impossible without something which produces it, and when we observe any mutation in an object, we know with metaphysical certainty that such mutation has and must have a cause.

That our wills are the cause of motion in our limbs may be known in two ways: by consciousness, and by inference. By consciousness we directly perceive that our will moves our limbs, just as we directly perceive that we think, exist, etc. By inference the same truth may be known, but in an abstract way: we may reason from the evident fact of motion in our limbs to a cause of that motion; as we may also learn the nature of our own intellect in the same manner that we learn the nature of any other object; "intellectus intelligit seipsum sicut et alia." But this mode of reasoning employed to know merely the existence of an internal faculty is inferior to the intuitive and perfect knowledge which consciousness affords, although the sphere of consciousness on the other hand is limited and not discursive into the nature and properties of the faculty. Our wills, when discursively known as cause of the motion of our limbs, are a direct conclusion from facts universally attested; this conclusion is based upon the absolute need of a sufficient cause for the motion.

Mill professes to perceive no sufficient reason for distinguishing between that of which we are metaphysically certain and that of which we are only positively and relatively certain. His theory of "inseparable association" aims to reduce the metaphysical characteristics, necessity and universality, to merely physical properties of knowledge which denote no more than a uniform and constant

---

[1] An Exam. of Sir W. Hamilton, Chap. 16.

experience; he thus excludes from human knowledge any character by which it is objectively immutable and *a priori*. He is effectually and felicitously answered by Mr. Mansel, whatever theory the author of "The Limits of Religious Thought" may hold respecting "the relativity of knowledge." When Mr. Mansel asserts, and truly, that the experience upon which physical certainty is based is as uniform and habitual as that which we observe in connection with necessary truths, and when he, therefore, inquires why the results in the one case are to be regarded as "contingent and transgressible," while those obtained in the other must be regarded as "necessary and universal," Mill answers that the character of the experience with which the various truths are connected accounts for it all; that "nature, as known in our experience, is uniform in its laws, but extremely varied in its combinations;" that conflicting experience, as well as any other opposing circumstances whatsoever, prevents the formation of immutable certainty, and will always be found to exist in those cases in which only physical certainty is produced; that cases of so-called metaphysical certainty connote only a better known, a more invariable and universal experience than is obtainable in cases of physical certainty. In this answer it is falsely assumed that all certainty and truth are proportionate to and produced by experience alone; it is falsely assumed also that the experience pre-required for knowing mathematical axioms in their necessity and universality obtains as generally, and is as manifest, as that upon which our knowledge of physical truths is based. For perfection in mathematics is limited to the few.

Judged of in the light of mere experience and observation, physical truths are more manifest and better known than mathematical axioms; and, were necessity and universality mere properties of experience, physical truths would be in that case more necessary than mathematical axioms. Such axioms, moreover, refer to objects which do not even exist *in rerum natura*, much less are they matters of common experience. A circle, according to its mathematical definition, is an object which nobody has ever seen; so, also, a line and a point. Truths may be self-evident, but not in respect to all men; they may be so *"sapientibus tantum."* Physical truths, on the other hand, are not as abstract as are mathematical truths, and they connote objects which really exist and which belong more directly to the sphere of common life, sensible objects in general being more manifest to us than the supersensible. Mill's theory of "inseparable association" is totally insufficient to the purpose for which it is proposed, and mere experience, however constant and uniform, cannot account for the absolute and immutable characters of objects known with metaphysical certainty; such characters are really intrinsic to these objects, and are fundamentally contained in the declarations of experience; but it is eminently and essentially the office of the human intellect, as intuitive and discursive, to discover the absolute and immutable determinations of an object, and to elaborate from them propositions of necessary and unchangeable truth.

To conclude, the leading principles of this article may be re-stated briefly, as follows: Quantity and numbers are not, as Hume contends, the only objects of science and demonstration; they are, it is true, real and necessary properties of beings, and as such are just matters of rational investigation; but they are not the sole nor the most intrinsic properties of beings; they are only one branch of the Porphyrian Tree, which has other branches more robust and springing more immediately from its trunk.

Our knowledge of cause and effect is something more than the mere knowledge of a customary conjunction or of an invariable sequence between two objects or events; it is, in addition, the knowledge of the real and necessary relation between these objects, according to which an effect really depends for existence upon its cause. To deny that the relation exists is absurdly to suppose that an effect is self-sufficient for its own existence, or that a real production can take place without anything to produce it.

Inseparable association, proposed as a theory to account for the necessity and universality intrinsic to certain ideas and judgments, is logically destructive of metaphysical certainty; although these characteristics of ideas and judgments have an origin in sensible experience and an objective reality in common with all intellectual knowledge, nevertheless they are the result of intuition and *a priori* reasoning, which produces metaphysical certainty, such as transcends all experience and is based upon the immutable nature of things.

Reasoning, whether employed to determine positive truth from the data of experience, or to discover necessary truth based upon the inmost essence and properties of any object, is equally a medium of truth and certainty, but the certainty in each case is of a totally different species, being physical in the former instance, and in the latter metaphysical.

Finally, in Hume's theory the cause of every real effect is unknowable. It follows from this that the existence of a first cause cannot be proved, and when Hume, at times, distinctly asserts its existence, he does so at the expense of his theory and logic. Reason can demonstrate the existence of God only by a conclusion based upon the principle, every effect requires an adequate cause. Modern agnosticism, also, which accepts Hume's false theory of causation, cannot advance from his position of uncertainty respecting the Supreme Being. Opposed to this agnostic, skeptical, and erroneous philosophising are the plain truths of reason, asserted over two thousand years ago by the Sage of Stagira, that the visible universe is an effect requiring an absolutely first cause, that the first cause is God, an intellectual essence of eternal and infinite perfection.

AMERICAN CATHOLICS AND THE PROPOSED UNIVERSITY.

> " The thinge a work of praise,
> Her present shapp hereafter still to see :
> To keep length, bredth, and curving of the waise.
> Number, height, and forme of buildings as they be ;
> Eatch man to knowe his owne by just degree ;
> With all thinges else that maie adorn the same,
> And leave her praise unto eternal fame."
>
> *From an old map of Oxford (1578), preserved in the Bodleian Library.*

AN official announcement of the proposed Catholic University appeared a short time ago, in the form of an "appeal" under the name of the Board, "constituted by the Third Plenary Council of Baltimore." Though the document does not allow us to form any definite idea of the immediate prospects of the university itself as an active organization, enough is contained therein to arouse the intelligent interest of Catholics on the subject of its success. For who that loves our holy religion, and the beauty of that divine spirit, whose temples we were dedicated in baptism, will not rejoice at the prospect of having supplied to us a workshop whence may be brought forth fit adornments of mind and heart to grace the treasure of holy faith hidden within? Does not the fact bear with it the promise that the stifling and dark atmosphere of atheism and agnosticism around us will be cleared; that a true philosophy, a real science not resting on conjecture or hypothesis, but on a first cause and facts, will diffuse more widely a loyal spirit of faith; that a severe but sober and impartial criticism will give testimony to the truth wherever it may be found, so that wisdom may indeed supplant mere knowledge, and with her be brought to us all things good? And from the gradual intercourse with men of lofty aims, of high acquisitions, of a science that humbles because it is so far-sighted and true, can there come aught else but that thoughtful moderation, that regard for the rights of others, that charming urbanity of manners, sure company of true culture, bringing out more clearly the sweet notes of a simple charity, conquering clarion-like the brazen-voiced philanthropic cant that issues from society's great stage? Yes, surely, all this and much more that is lustrous and beneficent would be guaranteed by the establishment in our midst of a university worthy of its name.

If we realize this fact; if we are assured that the work is possible, and rejoicing in its promised accomplishment open our hands in generous material support of so grand a work—then let no man speak foul of our hearts. But though our men of wealth, keenly appreciating the needs of our time and the beneficent influence of education on our population, freely offer their treasures; though the poor add their mite to swell the blessing to the needful sum, and all this be placed into the hands of able men, intellectual architects and practical withal, who would wisely dispose of these means —is our task done and may we, basking in their wisdom and our munificence, stand idly by to watch the results? Able leaders are indispensable to a great work; the material means to carry out their plans are equally necessary—but this question of the erection of a university implies another need. Not our money alone will be wanted; our labor, too. Why and how, is our object to show.

It has been said, and a long experience has on the whole proved, that since first

> A University was reared,
> Ere yet the music of Messiah's name
> Had thrilled the world,

its strength has been the result of growth, of slow and simultaneous development. But we also know that centralization is frequently the fruit of some necessity. It supposes either foregone activity towards a definite end or else a struggle which by reason of some centripetal and incontrollable force quickly gathers the scattered powers around it into one energetic mass. Thus large cities have sprung into existence from one cause or the other of the two. We have in our own day and country built up great centres of industry and society in an incredibly short time. True, they bear somewhat the mark of their birth. They have neither the inherent strength nor the lasting air of Cæsar's Rome or the Minervan Acropolis. Still who will doubt that, if need be, we could raise old Rome precisely as it was in its best days in a much shorter space of time than it actually took its builders?

And what we say of great cities may be aptly said of universities.[1] Our own generation, undertaking such a work, is singularly

---

[1] Cardinal Newman makes an elaborate comparison of the two in his " Idea of a University."

favored with resources so abounding, so altogether new that in great measure they supply the long and systematic labor of a past age. We in our day are witnesses to the truth of Roger Bacon's prophecy in his " Opus Majus," 500 years ago, about the " chariots that will move with incredible rapidity without the aid of animals," and how " a little matter about the bigness of a man's thumb, making a horrible noise, producing a terrible corruscation, would de--stroy a city or an army in several ways." Yet in spite of all his wisdom the " Doctor mirabilis" had to make his journey from Paris to St. Ebbe's by the slow process of travel on foot, or by stage and sluggish sail, and the students who in his later days left Oxford to hear the new oracles of the Sorbonne, might still have listened to the old monk discoursing on astronomy and theology from Folly Bridge, had they but had our appliances of sound and thought transmitting wires. Thus time has shortened, and space contracted and labor quickened a thousandfold. But there is one element in this undertaking which no mechanism can supply. We said that centralization, if not the result of slow accretion, comes of a certain immediate necessity; we might say, of advantages paramount to such a necessity. There must be not only a need but a demand.

The inference is plain. The founding of a university, to be done safely, and at the same time so as to satisfy our eager search for telling results, cannot possibly rest exclusively on the zeal and devotion of the few, no matter how accurate their judgment, how large their experience, how prudent their enthusiasm, or how magnificent their material resources. For this is not indeed merely a question of farsighted legislation, or of complicated construction. It is a question essentially of coöperation, of connection of parts intellectual, moral, social, a question of proportion of basis and superstructure. And the Catholic educators of our community, whether they think well or ill, or not at all, of the project, should have to bear a share in the loss, if it happened to be a failure, as they should be participants of its success. Nor must we be understood to speak of a university here as a necessarily large or pretentious institution, at once fully equipped to dispense general knowledge or exerting that influence which is associated with the names of the ancient universities. We simply mean an institution which, aiming at that end, commands respect by reason of a well-sunk basis, of legitimate prospects of future success arising from the definite advantages which it offers, and from its ability to make these advantages understood and felt.

The strange comments which have been made from time to time in the general press and elsewhere with apparent good will towards the project, whilst they are not taken as authoritative statements, prove sufficiently that even in the circles of the better educated there is no clear understanding as to the precise aim and nature of such an institution. Beyond this, it must have struck anyone who has given the subject sufficient thought and has noted how other issues come to pass, that there has been a very limited amount of intelligent discussion given to this subject which touches so nearly our highest interests.[1] We are a large community. The youth who may expect at our hands a higher intellectual training count by thousands; the number of educators, clerical and lay, is legion. The mere possibility of improvement all-sided and high, such as the name of a university implies, should send a thrill of anxiety into the hearts of all such as, whilst not directly charged with the responsibility of carrying out, are yet to participate in the honorable task of sustaining an institution so far-reaching in its operation. Yet such anxiety is hardly apparent.

> "I saw a smith stand with his hammer—thus,
> The whilst his iron did upon his anvil cool,
> With open mouth swallowing a tailor's news."

And all this is the more striking when we recall the intense agitation —we can hardly call it anything else—which was exhibited precisely in this country some thirty years ago, on occasion of the founding of the Irish University. Not only were enormous sums raised for its support, exhibiting a generosity and appreciation which, considering the circumstances, has hardly been paralleled in any similar work since then,[2] but.the press and public men gave the project most spirited and intelligent support. They repeatedly set forth its aim and advantages. They created a keen anxiety in its behalf, by laying bare the difficulties besetting such a work, and thus enlisted the earnest solicitude and active sympathy of all classes of Catholics. Nay, as soon as the lists of the infant university were opened, Americans of the best society and highest literary accomplishments were among the first to have their names inscribed upon its books side by side with some of the most able European savants.[3] And so distinctly was this interest understood

---

[1] We cannot, of course, be understood to refer in any sense to the action of the prelates gathered in the late Council, whose deliberations must be considered as altogether private.

[2] We have not at hand a report of the total amount contributed in this country, but some estimate may be formed from the fact that New York and Albany alone subscribed above $25,000 within a very short time.

[3] Associated with the illustrious names of Cardinal Wiseman, the rector of Louvain University and others, we find upon that list the learned Dr. Kenrick, archbishop of St. Louis, the Hon. Enoch L. Lowe, LL.D. (ex-governor of Maryland), the Hon. S. R. Mallory (senator), Prof. S. S. Haldeman, Prof. George Allen, of the University of Pennsylvania, Rev. Sestini, S. J., of Georgetown College, Dr. John Bellinger, Esq. (Charleston); John Keating, Esq. (formerly Colonel in the French service), of Philadelphia, etc.

to be of the highest order, that Cardinal (then Dr.) Newman was anxious to have America represented among the faculty of the new university in the person of Dr. Brownson, then understood to be " about the first metaphysician and philosophical historian of the day in this country." [1]

It will hardly be denied that discussion on this subject is, under present circumstances, equally desirable if not absolutely necessary, in order to secure to the undertaking that amount and kind of popular sympathy which arises, as we have said, from a clear understanding of its usefulness and from a realization of the actual difficulties that attend its accomplishment. And this becomes very much more apparent when we note, as we have already said, how the most absurd statements made under the sound of great names, or such as we must respect, and that in reputable journals, not only gain credit but become the basis of further conjectures absolutely detrimental alike to the project as to the persons who have its furtherance in hand. At the same time, it is highly important that, as the machinery of this work has been actually set in motion, we may thoroughly understand what be our weakness and what our strength ; that they who are to feed its fire permanently be conversant with the labor which is expected of them, and that they be trained in good time to keep in line lest there be any confusion, any interruption in the work, and subsequent lack of power to carry on the labor begun.

We can hardly suppose, however, that in a matter of such vital consequence to our well-being, social as well as intellectual, there can be any positive apathy; and though there is a certain want of demonstrativeness rather uncommon in a community which is so easily roused into excitement on any question of public interest, whether in politics or trade, or education, or what not among the thousand questions which touch the common weal, it may be safely assumed that public opinion is in favor of a step so decidedly in advance. Indeed, it is hard to see why, at present, it should not be. But we must not attach too much importance to this condition of the popular atmosphere. Public opinion, even if strongly expressed, is a fickle thing, and no thinking man will be easily found to make himself responsible for it. Cardinal Newman, speaking of its value in this very matter of the founding of a university, says : " Public opinion is too often nothing else than what the whole world opines and no one in particular. Your neighbor assures you that every one is of one way of thinking ; that there is but one opinion on the subject, and while he claims not to be answerable for it, he does not hesitate to propound and spread it. In such

---

[1] See a controversy on the subject between the *Dublin Evening Mail* and the *Dublin Tablet*, April, 1854.

cases, every one is appealing to every one else, and the constituent members of a community, one by one, think it their duty to defer and succumb to the voice of that community as a whole."[1]

So if Catholics were hereafter to meet with any unexpected difficulties which to remove would rest with their readiness to make a personal sacrifice, and for which they were not prepared, public opinion might take another, though perhaps more unreasonable, turn. And this brings us to what we suppose is the real cause of that apparent lack of enthusiasm and energy which we are, at other times, so ready to expend, often by forerunning real needs, when there is a question of loss or gain, sympathy or resentment, or any good or ill affecting ourselves.

May it not arise from a want, on our part, of realizing the task which is, in truth, before the men who, seeing a great need, have generously set themselves to inaugurate and labor for its removal ? May it not be that we underestimate the difficulties and dangers that beset the accomplishment successfully of this work ? We have been so little thwarted of late, have been in many ways so successful materially, that it would be no surprise did we trust half blindly to our strength, and, without giving thought to a matter which must necessarily remain under the direction of a few, leave to them the task of its accomplishment. It is out of the question to presume that those who have generously undertaken the burden of carrying this scheme of the university into effect, having considered it in all its bearings, should not be aware, to the fullest extent, of all the harassing obstacles that beset it. But when we are assured that these difficulties can be overcome, it is necessarily expected that the Catholic community of these States give their all-sided support. And the zeal which prompts this support is not a thing which can be elicited at a very short notice, the more so as it is to arise out of convictions opposing, as we shall see, settled and rather comfortable prejudices. In commenting, therefore, on the subject, we simply desire to awaken that wider interest, that sense of responsibility among the educated of the clergy and laity, which we deem essential, now that we are committed to the work, to guarantee its ultimate success and prevent compromises, great and small, of our common cause and name.

In answer to some general objections urged against the practicability of at present establishing a university in this country, reference has been made to the later foundations of Louvain and Dublin. In the case of Louvain we hardly think the comparison is fair. The Dublin foundation, however, bears, in many respects, a close analogy to our own, and it may profit us to run over the phases

---

[1] Universities, Introductory, page 3.

of that work with reference to our own condition. As for the difficulties peculiar to our country and people, they naturally claim the first and greater share of our attention. They need to be realized in order to be removed. These obstacles, as they are stated, point to the remedies which will likely undo them. And even in this respect the case of the Irish University will help us to illustrate the reality of the former and the nature of the latter.

The main sources whence obstacles to the ready establishing of an American university will arise are two. The first is a predominance in us as a nation of the material or utilitarian principle. This carries with it a certain depreciation of all that is purely intellectual or ideal, unless it aid us at the same time to the accumulation of wealth. The second obstacle is found, and—*pace tua dicam*—in a certain incompleteness of our present educational system, both in extent and depth. And the fact that this incompleteness has been, in a manner, systematized in our non-Catholic institutions of learning, and has thus become adequate to the general demand, has forced us to aim at and adopt a standard of measurement in this direction which is vitally detrimental to the spirit that must support and emanate from a Catholic university.

As to the utilitarian tendency, it is quite pronounced in our leading American universities, of which it may be said: "Grand dans son genre, mais le genre est petit." We ask, what is the market value of the liberal education our children shall receive, and the theory which many years ago was vainly advocated in England by Locke and the Edinburgh reviewers, has, as it were, naturally grown up with our busy generation in these States. How far our Catholic youth, trained largely in the public schools and forced into competition for existence in all walks of daily life and profession, are imbued with such sentiments, will be readily testified to by the superiors of our Catholic colleges, who have, no doubt, often been obliged to go against their better convictions and yield a point in pedagogic science because they could not hope successfully to oppose the spirit of their time, unless it were done in a body by the united efforts of all, and, at the same time, on some prearranged plan.

Before we can realize the hindrances arising from this two-fold source, we must, of course, have a very clear understanding of what a university is; what are the essential elements of its existence; whether there is any, and, if so, what is the special work which must be the object separately of a university in this country.

"A university is a universal school in which are taught all branches of learning, or theology, medicine, law, and the sciences and arts."[1] This is its object and its profession. Its aim is of a

---

[1] Webster.

wider range : " A place where inquiry is pushed forward, and discoveries verified and perfected, and rashness rendered innocuous, and error exposed by the collision of mind with mind and knowledge with knowledge."[1] In its essential elements and character, " a university consists and has ever consisted in demand and supply, in wants which it alone can satisfy, and which it does satisfy, in the communication of knowledge, and the relation and bond which exist between the teacher and the taught. Its constituting, animating principle is the moral attraction of one class of persons to another, which is prior in its nature, nay, commonly in its history, to any other tie whatever ; so that, where this is wanting, a university is alive only in name, and has lost its true essence, whatever be the advantages, whether of position or affluence, etc."[2]

It will be noticed in this threefold definition that it implies three things, to wit : The capacity of attracting, together with the capability of being attracted. Further, the power of discernment (together with the liberty of using that power consistently), as to the particular kind of knowledge, complete in itself and defined in its relations to other knowledge, which is to be gained. This is commonly called academic freedom. And, lastly, as to its ultimate aim, the definition implies that a university, of its very nature, is entitled, nay, cannot but take position of authority, to correct and keep in proper balance the spirit of the age. In the case of a Catholic university for the United States this latter point involves application to circumstances altogether untried and very different from those found where the old honored universities hold sway. We do not live, as does Canada, or India, or Australia, largely on the time-honored traditions of our founders. The child has turned to make itself a man upon a new mode of self-training without pattern or tutelage. We are in our youth, in a state of metamorphosis, beautiful of itself and promising a beautiful maturity, but still with all the uncertainty of youth. European society, on the other hand, is settled ; it has its infallible signs and landmarks; it undergoes at times convulsions, but no changes. It is old in years, but still of the early habits. It may alter its temper, its attitude, its garment ; but it does not alter its character. Its best days are past. It does not look forward, as we do, but back upon its halcyon days. It speaks forever of the good old times of sober wisdom and propriety, and is scandalized at the bold sallies of this wanton youth, with his stars and stripes, shaking its hoary head and its finger ominously, for it is so new a thing to the old world, this substitution of quick attempt and elastic recovery for the safe lessons of patient experience.

---

[1] Newman, Universities, Chap. ii.   [2] Ibid., Chap. v.

And surely it were wrong to say that the new way has not proved an immense advantage over the old, and that, though our science be but the fruit of yesterday, it serves us quite as well as does on the whole the accumulated lore of years. Still, a university remains a university, that is, not merely a corporation dispensing knowledge of varied and excellent kind, but a high tribunal presiding over the spirit of its times; judging and fashioning thought and feeling; regulating public opinion; settling intellectual strifes; far above partiality or weakness or dependency of any kind.

We have said that our predominant tendency is towards the material, the practically useful, together with a proportionate under-valuing of the ideal, the purely intellectual for its own sake. Hence virtuosos have ever found it impossible to live amongst us, unless for a season, and with accompanying sound of trumpet which frequently pleased better than their own excellence This is demonstrated not only by the actual results of our efforts in the domain of education, by the character of our domestic literature and by the spirit of our press, but it has universally been the first and last impression upon foreign observers, who have attempted, under varying and more or less favorable circumstances, to make a diagnosis of our national character. Herbert Spencer came to us in friendly mood, and civilly told us that we needed a revised ideal of life; that not only the arts of peace but even "those of war had been supplanted by business as the purpose of existence"; that "even those who are not directly spurred on by this intensified struggle for wealth and honor, are indirectly spurred on by it." But he considers this a necessary result of our conditions, which it is hardly possible to correct, for, "where rapid material growth is going on and affords unlimited scope for the energies of all, little can be done by insisting that life has higher uses than work and accumulation."[1] Mr. Mathew Arnold, the acknowledged apostle of culture, warns us of the danger to which we are tending, viz., "hardness and materialism, exaggeration and boastfulness,"—"a false smartness, a want of soul and delicacy."[2] Few Americans will be inclined to accept the conclusions these and other observers of the same character draw from such premises. Nevertheless, we can hardly deny the premises themselves. They are facts so far, and will strike any one who does not choose to walk blindfold. Listen to the conversation of men in our railway-coaches, our hotels, and public places of resort. Stocks and bonds, rents and interest, property and investment, shares and percentage, profit and loss,—such are the sounds that repeat themselves *ad nauseam* from morn till night. The province of *belles-lettres*, such as it is, has been

---

[1] "The Americans," *Contemporary Review*, January, 1883.

[2] "Numbers," *Nineteenth Century*, April, 1884.

consigned, more or less, to woman. Hence, she has gained a peculiar intellectual ascendency. In the drawing-room, it is the lady who pronounces on the subject of art and letters. Our man is a different but in no way a superior being. He has almost less influence, unless it be in his own circle. If he goes to college or university, it is to prepare for a profession which he will not consider either a devotion or a distinction, but simply a means of gaining wealth. Of course, there are exceptions to this in a community so large as ours, yet they are still but the exceptions.

Is the university, then, a training-school for the professions, or a place where men receive what is commonly called a practical education? No more than an art gallery is a painter's studio or a sculptor's workshop. The one may be the other, but in their objects they are vastly different. To have studied with the best of masters could not dispense the most gifted pupil from going to Florence or the Vatican, Madrid or the Louvre. True, we may substitute a new aim for the old, we may paint china and buckets, and put it in a hall, and call it art gallery or school of design; but euphonious names will not give us the substance of things. Yet this is what we have largely done with our university education. We have opened professional schools and lecture-halls for specialists in science, and with a suitable admixture of what else may have been in demand here or there, they passed for universities. Certainly, these are thorough enough in their way. They are what we have wanted. But what we wanted was not a university, in the old and true sense of the word. If there has been any rise in the higher sphere of education, it lies in the abnormal increase of "schools of science." "These," says Professor Gilman, speaking of the growth of such schools during late years, "showed the desire for an advanced education founded upon some other basis than the literature of Greece and Rome; they showed the popular craving for what was vaguely termed, for want of a better word, a practical education." [1] The popular desire for this sort of advanced education, discarding the old basis of the Greek and Roman classics, has, of course, affected the curriculum of studies in our best American universities. But do they, in consequence, turn out really educated men, men conspicuous for breadth and depth and originality of thought? Do they not, rather, multiply the race of pettifoggers and schemers at law, quacks in medicine, talkers of cant or of sensation with the title of Reverend? Or, even granted that, out of so vast a number of youth frequenting these schools, we receive a fair average of excellent physicians and able lawyers, is the object of a university reached in this way? Let a student

---

[1] "Report of the Commissioner of Education," 1878, cviii.

spend, as is the case in our universities, one year of faithful labor in the laboratories of chemistry, pharmacy, osteology, histology, and in the dissecting-room ; another or two in attending clinical lectures in general medicine and surgery, a course of biology, physical diagnosis and gynæcology—and he will be able to handle a scalpel and make a good diagnosis and relieve many an individual and prolong some lives.   A good work, in sooth, but such work as is done by fresh air and pure water and good breadstuffs.   Has he the mental aptitude, the sweep of judgment with correctness and precision, and the various acquirements, such as they are obtained by the study of the classics, of intellectual philosophy, etc., which will make him, according to his value, a member of society, exerting a much wider influence and a deeper one than that of a patent medicine or a text-book on health?   This is the influence of a university through its members, whom it gives, preparatory to and together with the professional training, the " old-style liberal education."   Nor can this sort of education be supplied by the newspapers or general reading, as is commonly supposed.   Reason, prone to err, wants a corrective, found in the teaching of principles, and not of facts or views.   But facts and views are the only things which the press can teach, and education means quite a different thing from this storing-up in the memory.[1]   It has been customary of late to refer to the German universities as models.   Surveying the matriculation lists of these, we find invariably a large, sometimes the largest, contingent of students inscribed for attendance upon lectures in metaphysics and ethics.   Students of medicine, of jurisprudence, of philology, frequently take a full course of philosophy at one university, and then pursue their specialty at another or several others in succession.   It is no odd thing for any one to have spent ten years at the different universities, after having passed the examination of abiturients which, with its eight years of Latin and six of Greek, preparatory to it, qualifies the applicant to choose his academic course.   At an American university,[2] no such preparation is required, nor need philosophy always be chosen as the " principal branch " among those requisite for obtaining the doctorate in philosophy.   Quite in harmony with this tendency is the effort that has lately been made to replace the

---

[1] Cardinal Newman has an admirable chapter on " Knowledge and Professional Skill," which clearly sets forth the difference between both. (The Idea of a University.)

[2] It is impossible to make any satisfactory comparison, founded on statistics of attendance, as to the two systems.   We have attempted it, in order to show, what becomes at once evident, how very much practically our university education differs from that obtained at the European universities.   But the promiscuous and undefined manner in which titles and terms, such as university, college, literary, classical, scientific, modern, etc., are used in this connection, defeats any sustained attempt at fair analysis.

study of the ancient classics in our colleges by what are deemed more practical branches. What the German university authorities, who have made the test of utility, think of this tendency has been quoted often enough. Professor Haeckel, of Jena, believes it a great advantage to have the practical academic studies entirely separated and excluded from the university, and transferred to special high schools, in order that the university may remain in reality a *universitas litterarum*.[1] Dr. Zarncke, although he represents the modern languages and literature at the Leipzig university, writes to our Professor Adler: "I am fully convinced that the educated world would bitterly repent it some day, if it should ever cease for a time to consider the study of classical antiquity the main source of all higher intellectual culture."[2]

Now what is to the point here is this: That, as we wish to establish a real *universitas litterarum*, we shall encounter the prejudice of the popular educational party, whose standard, being more easily attainable by the student, will naturally carry with it a great deal of good-will. For this we must be prepared. Nor can we, what might be desirable, yield much to gain a footing at the start. Leo XIII. has taken pains to show how a sound philosophy—the only hope of the intellectual regeneration in our day—cannot easily be built, as we have nothing equivalent, unless upon the well-tried basis of the ancient systems of Greek and Roman thought, with which our lay world has naturally but little sympathy. It is plain, then, that unless we can make it an issue of conscience and convince parents that they are injuring themselves in following the current of their time, they that aim—as the majority do—at the emoluments of a profession for their sons, will prefer or leave to these the choice of a less laborious and shorter method by seeking our non-Catholic American universities. To produce this effect of inducing that class of parents who desire their sons to embrace a learned profession, to make a sacrifice in behalf of their souls, is a task that will not accomplish itself without serious and sustained labor. It will require the combined work of the clergy, the educated laity, and the press; we say the educated laity, for it is mainly the moneyed middle and half-educated class who aim at social distinction at the expense of religion. This danger needs hardly any proof. England and Ireland have, in reality, better facilities for furnishing Catholic students with a professional curriculum than we shall likely have for some time to come; yet for more than thirty-five years the hierarchy of those countries have incessantly had to appeal against those Catholics who, in spite of the advantages of a home university course and a university board conferring

---

[1] "Report of the Commissioner of Education," 1878, xcix.   [2] Ibid., ci.

degrees, would send their sons to Oxford, or Cambridge, or Queen's College, simply because it satisfied a certain hankering after social respectability. And with us the difficulty in this direction will inevitably grow the more we advocate a certain liberalism in the sphere of education. On the mere assumption of intellectual superiority, we should find it difficult to cope with Harvard or Yale or some other recognized institutions of the same character. For, whatever may be the true merit of the education these furnish, their degrees have a certain standing in the public estimation, and thus open more easily the coveted passages to social and professional advantages, and it is well known that:

" Il méglioe il nemico del bene."

In the matter of prestige we have nothing or very little to help us. The requirements of society and official life do not, in any sense, favor our project, as would be the case in Europe. In England, for example, a gentleman's son, unless he propose to enter the army or navy, must have passed through a certain amount of conventional education at a university before society opens to him its doors. In other countries, as in Germany, it is an absolute requisite for entering certain grades of the civil service. We, in this country, need nothing of the kind. A polished manner, a certain amount of *au courant* in topics of the day, practical good sense and power of adaptation, are qualities which will make their way through our social conditions to the highest offices of state. As for the European youth, bred for literary or other kind of leisure, we are rather inclined to look upon him with a sort of mild contempt, as lacking freshness, robust versatility, and practical good sense. He is utterly out of place in our land, and our opinion of the typical Oxford student is, with the *London Times:* "He is a cockney in the country ; a landlubber at sea ; in town, a greenhorn ; in business, a simpleton ; in pleasure, a milksop ;" which malappreciation certainly commends our good sense. Still we must remember that this character is not a necessary result of a university system, and that we might be no less practical and intellectually strong for the additional boon of a good university education. As it is, we supply such training by frequent contact with the world, and a world which, acknowledging no caste, is accessible to every one ; the omni-gathering character of our press does the rest, with its obtrusive multitude of sheets covering every field of thought and action. This suffices for the common purpose. Our mutual interests allow us at present no room for nice distinctions. We have business and contracts, which are an affair of chattels, not of persons. And so long as we are such, a *universitas litterarum* will have to battle and to educate its own members almost from the cradle up.

Nor can it be said with certainty that a higher seminary on the university plan would meet with none of these obstacles, at least for a considerable time. The practical views of our world of merchants, mechanics, professionals, and politicians have communicated themselves very naturally to the ecclesiastical sphere of education. It could hardly be otherwise. We must study the people, follow them in their individuality, and, in some sense, sustain their interests, in order to labor efficiently among them for their good. So we cannot blame ourselves for being such, but such as we are we must be content to be judged. To take an example: For a number of years facilities have been offered to ecclesiastical students in this country to avail themselves of a higher education at certain of our Catholic universities on the continent of Europe. Some of the most promising seminarians, after sufficient trial, are periodically selected and sent there with scarcely any expense to themselves, with the added attraction of foreign travel, or, what is nearly equivalent, the advantages of a peculiarly varied intellectual life, such as is found, for example, in Rome, where students meet from every part of the globe, with the common aim of gathering wisdom and stimulating their zeal for learning, whilst imbibing, at the same time, that correctness of religious feeling, that delicacy and penetration in matters of faith, which is naturally gained in the atmosphere of such centres. Nevertheless—and we may say it without giving umbrage—probably the greater number of those who, under the most favorable circumstances, and with no lack of ability, have been led into this sphere of higher education and intellectual distinction, prefer, on their return home, to devote themselves to the labor of the mission rather than seek positions as teachers and professors, which would naturally be open to them. Thus it happens that few of those among the clergy who lack neither talent nor opportunity, devote themselves to higher spheres of intellectual activity. This want of appreciation has the further disadvantage of habitually stifling any aspiration in the same direction among our younger students. They see no particular advantage derived from laboring in this field; and just as artists tell us that they find no encouragement in America unless they turn artisans, so our gifted young men set aside what they naturally consider an unprofitable employment.

This conviction of the weakness and want of appreciation of a distinctively Catholic intellectual life in our midst will strengthen when we take a glance at our literature and press. Catholic newspapers, like Catholic colleges, are struggling for support. Perhaps, when compared with sectarian influences, we seem to have the advantage. There are more Catholic readers of Catholic papers than there are, for instance, Episcopalian readers for Episcopalian papers. But statistics in this case are no standard by which to estimate religious life and activity. A Protestant may, without violence to his religious principles, endorse almost any doctrinal opinion of almost any sectarian journal. A Catholic cannot endorse any doctrinal opinion distinctly Protestant without thereby denying his own. But even with this distinguishing feature, Catholic opinion is hardly felt as exercising any adequate influence. In Europe Catholics are very much ahead of us in the matter of literary activity. The journalists on the continent fighting the war with infidelity and anarchy could teach us to wield that mighty weapon of the press so as to elicit respect and sometimes wholesome fear from those who wantonly and falsely attack our rights and truth. But there is a well-understood agreement on all sides that they must be supported. In England we see the same advance. Forty years ago Fred. Lucas set a current afloat, not turbulent but steady, which has worked in the interests of Catholic rights in that country perhaps as much as the united efforts of the hierarchy found it possible to do in the same direction. And so it has come to pass that Catholic intelligence commands this day in England a respect fully equal to that of its adversaries. Lilly, Wilfred Ward, following the paternal traces of the robust metaphysician, Harper, the Jesuit, St. George Mivart, Father Coleridge, S. J., Dr. Barry, and others, to say nothing of Cardinals Newman and Manning, chiefs of a larger tribe, are names which figure habitually in the best non-Catholic periodicals. They command attention from every quarter as—and this it is important to note—Catholic writers, Catholic leaders of thought. And yet they have to contend with prejudices far more unreasonable and possessing much more power of being enforced than could ever gain command amongst us. With us, whilst the press is a most efficient power in all other interests, Catholic thought does not impress one as being any marked feature in it; as like in most of our ephemeral literature we miss anything like a high or serious tone. Brilliancy and raciness and appeals to common prejudices largely supply the place of thoughtful editorials showing a philosophically trained mind. And all this is evidence that we care little, on the whole, for intellectual culture, unless it be ready-made. We like the facts and the pomp of it well enough when it comes in patent form, but to evolve, and shape, and make a sacrifice of ease or wealth for it, is not our general habit.

It has been said that, as to Catholics in America, there is no special need for a literary activity such as is forced upon Catholics abroad by the aggressive hostility of their adversaries, for Protestants in America are daily becoming more tolerant in proportion as they become acquainted with the real life and belief of Catholics. If this were true, all the more reason to work in behalf of the Kingdom of Heaven. Because the harvest is great, shall we put our hands into our lap and say: "There is no blight upon the crop; behold, we have plenty and can afford to lose a part of the reaping!" The Catholic Church is a living body, instituted not only to guard but to spread the true faith. Her Founder was ever consumed with zeal for the glory of that Church. And the legacy He has left us is: " Be zealous for that which is good in a good thing always." [1] Worldliness is far more dangerous to the Faith than heresy; it grows as quickly, and it grows within as without the fold, becoming the root of countless heresies.

But it is an error, both in fact and in principle, to suppose that the Catholic Church will ever cease to be an object of general aggression, whether from Protestantism or infidelity. Our Lord did not tell His disciples, who were messengers and lovers of peace, that the world would not mind them, but that it would hate them. They did not need to attack it. They were going among wolves, and that told them enough. If at any time the contrary appears to be the case, it is the greater sign of danger. It frequently implies that Catholics are on the point of settling down to a liberal sort of religionizing which is what lukewarmness is to the individual, a more hopeless state of the soul than any other. Whether the watchword outside of us be " no popery " or " liberalism " or " anarchy," or whatever else you will, it is quite the same to us in the end; the method only differs. Skepticism and infidelity only want to be systematized to find their sole and most serious enemy in the Catholic Church. And as a matter of fact, if we but take the trouble to attend to it, there is constantly alive against us a fearful and morbid activity. The various sects in this country publish in the gross about 400 papers [2] representing over two million subscribers. Run your eye over any one of them at random, and you will rarely fail to notice, more prominently than all its gospel cant, misrepresentations of the Catholic doctrine or imputations against Catholic morality which have their origin probably in the hatred of individual writers, but certainly also in a consciousness that such statements will find credit if not applause among the Protestant public. Even the unsectarian religious papers, of which we have nearly a hundred, teem, the best of them, with humiliating bits of gossip or false interpretations of facts, all laid to the charge of a religion as pure and consistent as its Divine Founder. The secular

---

[1] Gal. iv., 18.

[2] This does not include Sunday-school papers or tractarian publications issued periodically.

press, whilst it now and then gives a bone to Catholics, as befits it, since it feeds on their patronage, on the whole treats us with lofty condescension or mere toleration. Things are said of us in de-nunciation of our principles which would not be breathed against men of any other denomination on the score of their religious be-lief. And all this with a bland assurance in respectable and high-toned journals that makes one blush to think it could not have been written were there not some hope that it would be believed. If we realize the strength of our holy religion, what a boon it is to society, and what it might do through us as loyal members of either, then we must confess that we are sadly below the level that befits us in Catholic *esprit de corps*. Even as we glance in passing at one of our most energetic Catholic weeklies, we meet at the head of the editorial column the question put to the educators of our youth who have just left college : " Have they (the youth leaving college) been taught to take an interest in Catholic affairs ? A course of instruction on Catholic public spirit would not be a bad one for schools, colleges, pupils and teachers." True, the place where this spirit is to be infused is the school and the college. And this brings us to a second source of difficulties to be overcome in the erection successfully of a Catholic university. We mean the un-even character, the indefinite scope, and the incompleteness on the whole of what must become in one way or another the feeders of the university. As to the seminaries, a movement aiming at greater thoroughness and uniformity has, as is well-known, been already inaugurated by the late Council, and in spite of the materialistic atmosphere that surrounds us, some noticeable headway will un-doubtedly soon be made, to allow the University to continue and perfect the work. We cannot, without increasing beyond proper limits the bulk of this article, enter into the details of this question of our colleges as feeders of a university. The matter has, more-over, been amply and ably illustrated in these pages heretofore, by writers at once in position to judge and to influence. We may be permitted briefly to quote their testimony in corroboration of what we have stated. The first of these writers, though speaking anony-mously, is readily recognized as the author of various papers on the subject of education, a man devoted practically and wholly to the task of college and school-reform. He sees a main difficulty of our system in a combination of the college with the preparatory schools, which of itself tends to lower the grade of the former. Yet few of our colleges, he considers, are at once prepared to alter this state of things. For the rest he looks upon the condition of our colleges as hopeful;[1] "too hopeful," comments the Rev. F.

---

[1] "What is the Outlook for our Colleges ?" AMERICAN CATHOLIC QUARTERLY RE-VIEW, 1882, page 385.

Thébaud in an article written soon after, in which he supplements the paper of Brother Azarias by his own observations in the same field. The system of our colleges, he says, "is altogether faulty, and must be changed if there is to be any hope of a rise in the intellectual scale. The change must begin from the very studies which are preparatory to college."[1] A reform had been attempted, but failed. But, happily, he finds the cause of this failure, and offers a scheme by which it may be permanently remedied and by which at the same time a link would be supplied between our colleges such as they are and a complete university.[2] Dr. Gilmary Shea, who, though not in practice a schoolman, has had, we believe, more than ordinary opportunities of estimating the true merits of the educational question in this country, writes in the July number of the following year, complaining of the want of preparatory facilities: "But colleges and universities cannot thrive unless the preparatory schools exist in greater number." Similar complaints as to the insufficiency of the preparatory course for a university system upon the European principle are made by non-Catholic educators. A remedy is proposed, not in remodeling our system according to the German university plan, but by establishing more post-graduate courses, and thus, by carrying on the college system to a greater height, to give it a new development, whence will eventually issue an "American University."[3] If academic freedom is to be the prerogative and not an impediment and a disgrace to a university, then a rigid and sufficiently protracted college discipline, mental as well as moral, is absolutely essential. There is a tendency to introduce the elective system of studies in our principal colleges, which, if it obtain, must needs add to the difficulties in the way of a thorough university education.[4]

Nor can we wholly trust to the anticipation that excellent and even renowned professors will draw students around their chairs without any further effort on our part. Such professors—unless they be religious—cannot be expected to lose their time acting as tutors to unprepared collegians. Even if we were to assume that they would for a time lower their standard for the sake of profiting their hearers, much of the stimulus to original investigation, which should characterize a university professor, would inevitably be lost. It is to be supposed that these professors be not only prepared to give, but actually offer proof of their ability to keep apace in their respective departments and cope with the theologians, philosophers,

---

[1] "Superior Instruction in our Colleges." By Rev. Aug. J. Thébaud, S. J., AMERICAN CATHOLIC QUARTERLY REVIEW, 1882, page 681.

[2] Ibid., p. 696.

[3] See "The American College" in the *Independent* of May 21, 1885.

[4] See an admirable paper on the subject by Prof. West in *North American Review*, May, 1885.

scientists, and literati of their sister institutions.   Their names must
be before the public as among us are those of McCosh, Eliot, and
other representative men in their sphere.   To do this, to be able
to command the public ear, they need from us more than ordinary
co-operation.   Our professors, whatever their individual ability,
are necessarily without the thousand resources brought together
in the old universities by generations of toilers in the field of
knowledge and by the munificence of royal patrons.   In this way
European students have an immense advantage over us.   Even to
take merely a stroll through a place like Oxford adds to our education; the men we meet, the traditions which speak to us from
cornice and gate, invite inquiry and speculation, and all sorts of
knowledge, old and new, being accessible, we silently compare, and
our minds grow unconsciously.   The professor is drawn on at
once by the love for his work and by the honor and prestige that
attach to it.   His salary may be low enough in our estimation, but
it is proportioned to his needs, and amply compensated for by other
advantages.   He has not to provide special libraries for his purpose ; the periodical literature in his field of labor is at his hand
in the museums; experiments, travel, and such like, involve much
less expense than is the case with us.   A certain fitness of things
would demand that the professors at our university should be paid
on an equality with those of other institutions of the same order
in this country.   Some of our colleges without endowments pay
as high as Oxford divinity chairs, that is, between $7000 and $8000
per annum.   Johns Hopkins's regular professors receive, we understand, $5000.   The majority of institutions rate, of course, much
lower, but their influence is accordingly. , This implies that we
should be under considerable expense on the score of a respectable
faculty, a necessity which has been set forth in the document
referred to at the beginning of this paper.

    In all we have said so far, it must, of course, be borne in mind
that our university would have to be an "American university"
withal, that is, possess certain modifications necessitated by and
adapted to our national circumstances.   Its object is to be useful
to Americans, but still useful as a university.   There is enough,
then, to make us thoughtful, and whilst we may have cause for
confidence in so grand an interest, we must surely increase our
energy.   If it should happen that the university, no matter how
well equipped, should still attract but a limited number of students
in its beginning and for some years to come, those who have
pondered the subject will be in no wise surprised.   It is possible
that in times when we attach so much importance to numbers, this
turn of things might act as a discouragement to parents who think
of a great university only in connection with crowded halls of

students. This would be equivalent to abandoning a work in its most needy crisis. We must be prepared for drawbacks. If it turn out that these were groundless fears, so much the better.

For such reasons we may briefly refer, as said above, to the foundation of the Irish University. Not that the difficulties in particular which beset that undertaking were the same as would be in our own. We have hardly any downright opposition as had Ireland. Still an incubus is often as hindering, and requires as much labor to remove, as the aggressive attitude of an enemy who must be silenced. At all events, it will draw our attention to one aspect of the case, useful to us in forming an estimate of things to be tried for the first time. For there is one important feature which makes both cases alike. Among the modern foundations there is none that offers the analogous circumstance of an entirely new foundation except this one of the Dublin University. Louvain, Laval, the *École des Hautes Études,* even Salzburg just on the point of rising, are all either developments or revivals of older institutions. The old haunts of wisdom had, in most instances, retained their venerable air ; the honored traditions of better ages clung always about the places, and fired the student to unconscious ambition, and from the very ruins of tower and wall spoke the desire to be what they once had been :

> " Like the vase in which roses have once been distilled ;
> You may break, you may shatter the vase if you will,
> But the scent of the roses will hang round it still."

But the Irish University stands thus far alone. It was, as its founder says, " an anomaly in the history of universities. These had been the slow and steady growth of centuries out of a settled and uniform system of education, and, while expanding into their peculiar and perfect form, had, at the same time, been by anticipation educating subjects for its service, and had been creating and carrying along with them the national sympathies. But here was a great institution to take its place among us, without antecedent or precedent whether to recommend or explain it. It receives neither illustration nor augury from the history of the past, and requires to be brought into existence as well as into shape."[1] Such is also our case. For the rest, the Irish University had to encounter, besides the difficulties of raising sufficient funds, of finding able superiors and professors, and of obtaining a charter of incorporation, the opposition of public opinion. Even the bishops, to whom the thought of its realization was most dear, had serious

---

[1] Newman, Historical Sketches, Universities, chap. i.

misgivings as to its practicability.[1]　A negative opposition manifested itself in the reform movement going on at about this time
at Oxford and Cambridge, by which students were drawn thither,
inasmuch as it was proposed to modify the restrictions attaching to
college-fellowship and endowments, and tending to the general
increased efficiency and extent of study.　These were indeed diffi- ·
culties with hardly any of which we have, even in a modified degree, to contend.　But, not being in their nature insurmountable,
they tended to stimulate the zeal and activity of all concerned in
the success of the new university.　On the other hand, the then
condition of the Louvain University, which, though begun with a
certain prestige, had encountered many difficulties in its revival
similar to those which beset the Irish foundation, was very encouraging to the laborers in behalf of the latter.[2]　There was also
a sufficiently promising outlook that there would be no lack of
hearers.　Students were prepared and might be drawn from the
best colleges in England, such as St. Edmund's, Stonyhurst,
Ushaw, and others.　Ireland itself had, at that time, some twenty
respectable institutions, on a sound basis of classical instruction,
and under the supervision of the diocesan authorities.[3]　This advantage, however, was little understood and appreciated by those
who were not directly engaged in the interests of the university,
and in point of fact proved really less available than had been anticipated.

What was most necessary was funds; and to have them, public
opinion was to be gained over.　In this Cardinal Newman found
his main labor.[4]　And well did the " Old Lion of Oriel " do it for
the four years that preceded the actual opening of the university,
and ere any work had been done in it beyond his own appointment as rector of the proposed institution.　England soon handed
in her mite of over a million dollars.　We have already alluded to
what America did.　France, with the *Univers* as its interpreter,
supported the university scheme in Ireland (as it supported its
rector during the Achilli trial at the same time) by contributions
to its funds and to its staff of professors.　What Ireland herself
did we may readily surmise, when it is remembered that men such

---

[1] The then Bishop of Cloyne, Dr. Murphy, addressing a circular, dated Fermoy,
September 20, 1854, to his clergy, says : " About three years since, when the project
of founding the Catholic University was submitted by the Holy Father to the consideration of the Irish prelates, there were few indeed, even amongst the most strenuous advocates of the measure, who did not entertain serious doubts of its ultimate
success."

[2] After sixteen years of its new existence, Louvain had some forty professors, active
in the four faculties of law, medicine, letters and science.

[3] The Directory for Ireland, 1854, gives the number of regular colleges at twenty-
eight.

[4] *Vide* " The Idea of a University Defined and Illustrated," 1852.

as Dixon of Armagh, Cullen of Dublin, Dr. Vaughan, McHale of
Tuam, occupied the Episcopal chairs that supported the movement. And thus the enthusiasm increased from day to day until
the poorest laborer began to realize that the university was a work
which to sustain was a singular prerogative for every man that
bore the name of Catholic. The best powers of Catholic intelligence were engaged in the press to appeal to the sympathies of
the educated classes. The *Rambler* acted as a sort of university-
magazine so long as there was no other. The *Tablet*, then published in Dublin, then as now of a high tone and able to command
respect, constantly defended the interests and cheered the prospects
of the new university. And all through its crisis when actually at
work, this journal supported and popularized it in a consistent
manner, frequently publishing in detail the excellent lectures
delivered to a small body of students in the university hall by distinguished professors. Thus it kept the public informed and interested in the momentous enterprise, and warded off in a dignified
way sneers and discouragement, when the refusal of a charter
showed the displeasure from high places in government.[1] There
were other periodicals, such as the *Catholic School, Duffy's Magazine,* the *Lamp,* etc., which took at least an indirect part in the promotion of this cherished project.

On Whitsunday, 1854, Dr. Newman knelt before the Apostolic
Delegate in the Dublin Cathedral, to make his profession of faith
as Rector of the Irish University. Four years had passed since he
had accepted that office. That same week appeared, for the first
time, the *Catholic University Gazette,* the official organ of the new
institution. It was published every week[2] for about a year, when
it became a monthly magazine.[3] In it appeared successively the
well-known articles on the " Rise and Progress of Universities,"
which have since been collected and published in book form among
the Historical Sketches. They bore the title *prima facie* " Idea of a
University." The *Gazette* had the further object of familiarizing the
students in the various colleges with what the university expected
from its applicants. It gave specimens by which to direct the
studies of candidates for competition, and generally such information as is expected from a journal of that kind.

And what was the outcome of all this activity so prudently begun, so consistently carried out, benefited rather than injured by
unreasonable opposition, and by the existence of difficulties properly viewed and courageously handled? Let us extract the sub-

---

[1] Shortly after this time, Mr. Lucas handed over these to him sacred interests, involved in the principles of that paper, to Mr. Swift, saying : If you got £10,000 for it,
from the corruptionists, my wife would not touch a penny of the money.

[2] J. Duffy, Dublin.   [3] March, 1855.

stance of an account of its work and progress at the end of the first term after its formal inauguration :[1]

" The examinations for entrance were held, and above twenty passed successfully, and immediately afterwards commenced the university course.[2]   On Sunday following the examinations, Dr. Newman invited the University faculty, consisting of the Dean of Residence, the professors and lecturers, to a soirée in the Refectory by way of introducing the students to their academical career. There were fifteen students in all that evening.   Dr. Newman made a beautiful address on the subject of the career they were about to enter on.   He ended the same by alluding to their number, with which he was in no way disappointed, but rather " well pleased, though some might have expected more."

We see here many difficulties actually overcome by strenuous efforts.   The university was at last a reality.   If in subsequent days it had to change its outward form, owing to the hard policy of the government, which refused it a charter, it has neither lost its original aim nor ceased to grow in real efficiency.   We need not anticipate any such difficulty stunting the growth of an American Catholic university.   We enjoy full freedom of legitimate action, and our government would rather favor than narrowly oppose through political motives any real advance toward higher education. So far our university would not be prevented from being in truth a

> ——— Sacri domus hospita veri,
> Quam neque civiles potuerunt vertere motus,
> Bellorumque faces, nec conjurata revellant
> Secla.

Neither charter nor public favor would likely be wanting to us in this work.   Yet these are helps necessary to its well-being rather than its being.   What we mainly want is, it appears, a supply of properly qualified students, eager for knowledge for its own sake, clustering around their new Alma Mater, and *sicut novellæ olivarum in circuitu mensæ, sicut sagittæ in manu potentis*, becoming at once her support and her pride.   So long as a university is looked upon as a machine expected to turn out professional men merely, it must be a failure and a misnomer.   If the Irish University, with its corps of excellent professors,[3] with its uniformly

---

[1] Taken from a report in the *Catholic University Gazette*, of that date.

[2] Among the first students enrolled upon the examination list is found that of Daniel O'Connell, who, in consideration of his illustrious grandfather, was presented with an exhibition allowing him free residence.

[3] The *Catholic University Gazette*, October 19th, 1854, gives the list of professors and lecturers appointed up to that date.   They represent masters of Oxford, Cambridge, and the Dublin Universities.   Among the regular lecturers we have M. Pierre le Page Renouf, taken from the Chair of French Literature at Oxford (Pembroke College), Signor Marani, lecturer on Italian and Spanish Literature, from the University

graded colleges, with all its public-spirited activity, had so slender a beginning in this respect, as we have seen, we shall have to temper our grandiloquent expectations, lest disappointment paralyze that needful enthusiasm whence comes energy for the beginning of every arduous work.

An organized system of press work, the general and uniformly-directed co-operation of the clergy, lectures on the subject among our better educated classes, are means in our hands which might facilitate the work of creating a clear understanding and an active sympathy in behalf of the project. If we cannot have a university magazine at once, might not certain organs already in existence be officially set apart to bespeak plans and modes of action by which Catholic public spirit would be raised, the matter elucidated, discussed, and encouraged? This, even if it were necessary to pay, and pay adequately for such means, would probably prove a better investment of a university fund in the beginning than most others.

Next to this, an understanding with some of our reputable colleges and educational leaders seems a necessity of the situation. These also should have to make a sacrifice for the common good.

But we mean rather to suggest than to propose. More will unquestionably be done when the Holy See has made public its approval of the scheme, and then a blessing of peculiar weight would be added to our resources. Meanwhile, as this work is determined on, we must gather up and use our energies in every direction.

> ·Certare ingenio, contendere nobilitate,
> Noctes atque dies niti præstante labore
> Ad summas emergere opes, verumque potiri.

And this all the more deliberately because we have no direct opposition from interested persons or parties to urge us on and sharpen our sensibilities, or rouse our resentment into swift resolve and action for the gain of a noble end. The difficulties in the way of a higher seminary, though not quite the same as those of the remaining university faculties, are still sufficiently great to make us anxious. Less time would be required to remove them, because our clerics are generally under the control of a ten or twelve years' uniform discipline. In either case it is a task of building up from the foundation, of creating a somewhat different atmosphere from that which surrounds us on all sides. If there is need of a regeneration of society, those that are to do the work of regenerating must themselves be filled with the spirit of the Baptist. All must set to work on the task as if its fulfillment depended on each, or else bear the reproach of an unfinished tower.

---

of Modena, besides such familiar names as the poet D. F. McCarthy, Professor Robertson, Healy Thompson, Dr. Dunne (Irish College, Rome).

MARYLAND AND THE CONTROVERSIES AS TO HER EARLY HISTORY.

THE first view taken of the establishment and early history of the Province of Maryland was that its Patent had been solicited by a nobleman, liberal and tolerant in his views beyond the statesmen of his day, who left in the charter which he solicited the impress of his noble mind; that the Province was colonized by his Catholic son with gentlemen mainly of his own faith, who brought over settlers without regard to their religious opinions, making Maryland a home to all, opening its doors of refuge to men who fled from the persecution alike of those who upheld the Church of England and those who, while fugitives from that very persecution, were re-enacting it with fearful severity. Maryland not only established religious equality and an entire separation of church and state, but had officials, we were assured, bound by an oath prescribed by the Lord Próprietary, to vex no man on account of his religion. It crowned its career of religious equality by an act of its legislature, passed in 1649, while the dominant element was still Catholic.

The picture was a fair and goodly one. It was one of which Americans had reason to be proud. If it reflected credit on Catholics, it was not one drawn by men of that faith for their self-glorification; for, sooth to say, they have, as a body, shown little interest in their own part in American history. Writers drew the picture while the Georges were still honored as sovereigns in this land; other writers drew it after a republic was established. And nowhere does the picture appear in more glowing colors, or with nobler forms, than in the pages of Bancroft's "History of the United States," when the results of deep historic research were portrayed with a pen guided by the honest impulses of a generous nature. But, at last, some began to reckon with their Protestantism, and ask whether it was worth the while, necessary, politic or wise to give such credit to Catholics. As the Church, which, a century and a half ago, was but a handful of persecuted, oppressed people, developed as a religion with all its attributes, its definite creed and government and worship, there were some who felt that every claim in its behalf must be ignored, undermined, distorted and defeated. Protestantism, as Professor Fairbairn admits, is not a religion, but merely a phase of thought. It has no creed, no priesthood, no worship. It was in its origin, and must ever remain, a mere denial of something held by Catholics.

This negative quality of the mind led some to assail the early views of Maryland history, not with any noble aim of presenting the characters of the founders of Maryland in a nobler or more heroic light, but to lower them to the level of the most truculent and intolerant of their contemporaries. This school may be said to have originated with Bozman, author of a history of Maryland, been maintained by S. F. Streeter, and some other writers of the Maryland Historical Society, and more recently with intense and unscrupulous bitterness by Rev. Edward D. Neill. Their efforts have not been altogether unavailing; men of culture abroad, like Gladstone, have accepted these polemics as historic decisions, and at home we can trace the bias in the pages of the latest edition of Bancroft.

In defence of the earlier view, upholding it as correct, no Catholic has yet appeared, except McSherry, in his "History of Maryland," Colonel Bernard U. Campbell in his criticism of Honorable Brantz Mayer, and Richard H. Clarke in a reply to Gladstone; the Catholic interest in the early history of the province, evinced for some years in annual celebrations of the Maryland Pilgrims, having long since died away, leaving no monument but the printed addresses, in which even we look in vain for a manly and vigorous handling of the questions at issue.

The ablest upholders of the original view of Maryland history have been the honest, impartial investigators of early records, G. L. L. Davis, William Meade Addison, General T. Bradley Johnson, and, to some extent, J. Thomas Scharf, the latest historian of the State that still bears the blazon of the vanished house of Baltimore.

The first question raised was in regard to the charter for Maryland, issued by King Charles I. at the instance of the first Lord Baltimore, but, in consequence of Sir George Calvert's death, really made to his son Cecilius, the second Baron. The charter, vast as were the powers it conferred on the Lord Proprietary, guaranteed to the settlers and their descendants the rights of native-born subjects in England and Ireland, gave them freedom of trade, and assemblies in which in person or by representatives they should take part in enacting the laws of the province. Maryland was open to all British subjects who chose to settle there; notwithstanding the statute against fugitives and others of the kind, no man "except such to whom it shall be expressly forbidden" being debarred from embarking for it. The dissenter and the Catholic were thus secure in sailing for this favored colony.

Though a Catholic, the Lord Proprietary had the right of presenting to the churches of the established religion erected in the province, and the charter ended with this clause: " Provided always that no interpretation thereof be made whereby God's holy and true Christian religion or the allegiance due to us, our heirs and successors, may, in any wise, suffer by change, prejudice, or diminution."

" Representative government was indissolubly connected with the fundamental charter; and it was especially provided that the authority of the absolute Proprietary should not extend to the life, freehold, or estate of any emigrant. . . . Christianity, as professed by the Church of England, was protected; but beyond this silence left room for equality in religious rights not less than in civil freedom to be assured. . . . Calvert, in his charter, expressly renounced any claim " (to the fisheries). The king, " by an express stipulation, covenanted that neither he, nor his heirs, nor his successors, should ever, at any time thereafter, set any imposition, custom or tax whatsoever upon the inhabitants of the province. Thus was conferred on Maryland an exemption from English taxation forever." (Bancroft's "United States," 1861, i., pp. 242-3.)

Now, to whom is the credit due for the wise, tolerant and statesmanlike features that mark this charter, and prevented its being " as worthless as those of the London Company, of Warwick, of Gorges, or of Mason"?

It was from the outset asserted that the charter was drawn up by Lord Baltimore, who, as Assistant Secretary of State, and subsequently Secretary, and connected with the Virginia Company, and holder already of one patent, that of Avalon in Newfoundland, was perfectly familiar with all the details of charters granted for America.

Chalmers says: " He laid the foundation of his province upon the broad basis of security to property and freedom of religion." (" Annals," i., pp. 207-8.)

Bancroft says : " Calvert deserves to be ranked among the most wise and benevolent lawgivers of all ages. He was the first, in the history of the Christian world, to seek for religious security and peace, by the practice of justice, and not by the exercise of power." (" History of the United States," 1861, p. 244.)

The first to raise any other theory was the Honorable John P. Kennedy, who, in his discourse on Calvert, assumed the merit to the king: " There is more freedom of conscience, more real toleration a hundred-fold, in this charter of a Protestant prince to a Catholic nobleman than in that act so often called to our remembrance." This idea was taken up by Rev. Ethan Allen in a polemical tract entitled, " Maryland Toleration, or Sketches of the Early History of Maryland," to the year 1650 (Baltimore, 1855). Its virulence may be judged by the fact that on a single page it six times applies to Catholics the filthy and degrading nicknames, Romish, Romanist. The writer denied that the credit was due to Lord Baltimore. " What gave it its authority was the king's signature and seal. . . . The authority, then, which gave Protestants protection in the colony was the king's own authority, and he a Protestant." (p. 16.)[1]

This idea was soon taken up, and it was argued that, as a charter was the act of the king, the credit for any wise or liberal features in that of Maryland must be given to Charles I., because " whether this (or that) feature of the charter was the original conception of Lord Baltimore," says Allen, " is not material and cannot now be shown."

That the principles guiding Charles in England showed no such broad and liberal views as those contained in the charter, was to be overlooked, on the fallacious plea that because as he signed it, it must be regarded as, in its conception and detail, the work of the king. But on comparing this charter with that granted by King James I. to Lord Baltimore for Avalon, we find the same ruling ideas. These ideas are not found in other charters. The Avalon and Maryland charters stand alone in giving the people a share in the passage of the laws by which they were to be governed. These charters alone are free from a compulsory state church or the exclusion of particular faiths. If the credit of this political wisdom is to be given to a king, it must be given not to Charles I., but to his father, who gave the charter for Avalon, of which that for Maryland is in the main a copy !

As there is nothing in the character or policy of James or

---

[1] How utterly illogical or perverse this writer was, may be seen by a single example. The fourth section of the charter reads: " Also, we do grant and likewise confirm unto the said Baron of Baltimore, his heirs and assigns; . . . furthermore, the patronages and advowsons of all churches, which (with the increasing worship and religion of Christ), within the said region, islands, islets and limits aforesaid, hereafter shall happen to be built ; together with license and faculty of erecting and founding churches, chapels and places of worship in convenient and suitable places within the premises, and of causing the same to be dedicated and consecrated according to the ecclesiastical laws of our kingdom of England." This is perfectly clear and explicit. The king gave Lord Baltimore license and faculty to found churches of the Established Church, and nominate pastors, the latter right being enjoyed by great Catholic landholders in England till the reign of William and Mary, and which it is even now proposed to restore to them. Now, see how Rev. Mr. Allen perverts this: " This, it will be perceived, confined the erecting and founding of churches and chapels, and all places of worship, to his license and faculty. None, consequently, could be built but such as he should permit and authorize. It placed thus the erecting of Protestant churches, and Roman Catholic ones too, at his will and pleasure ; so that, if he saw fit, he could forbid and prevent any of either name being built." The charter simply gave Lord Baltimore permission to build and found. It has not a syllable about his permitting or preventing the colonists from doing so. A schoolboy would be ashamed of such an argument. If a schoolmaster gave one boy permission to go off for a day's fishing, could that boy argue that henceforward none of his fellow-scholars could go fishing without his leave ? Yet, such is Allen's argument, and grave writers follow him !

Charles to explain how or why such remarkable ideas of liberality in regard to civil government, and religious equality, manifested themselves in no other act or deed, except on the occasion of the granting of the two charters to Sir George Calvert, we must believe that they were like latent heat in a lump of ice, something theoretically existing there, but against which our senses bear testimony ; and that contact with Sir George Calvert was necessary to create the current by which these latent virtues became apparent. So that even under Allen's theory Calvert becomes the potent element by which popular assemblies and religious freedom could get into an American charter.

Against such fallacies men of sense will always coincide with the view of the judicious historian Chalmers. " Nothing can afford more decisive proof than these material omissions (that of subjecting the provincial laws to king or parliament, etc.), that Sir George Calvert was the chief penman of the grant. For the rights of the Proprietry were carefully attended to, but the prerogatives of the crown, the rights of the nation, were in a great measure overlooked or forgotten."

So much for the authorship of the charter, and the merit of the principles it embodies.

2. The next question that has been raised is, whether it really deserves any praise as having contributed to increase the welfare of mankind.

Anderson, in his "Colonial Church," condemned it because the supremacy of the Church of England was not established by it ; Brownson censured it as aristocratic and containing very little of any democratic element, and as inferior to the early New England plans of government, in that it did not recognize the Church as independent of the state ; George William Brown, addressing the Maryland Historical Society, maintained that " the people of Maryland are not mainly indebted to it for the freedom which they have always enjoyed." Others, to maintain that the charter really had no element favoring religious liberty, but simply guaranteed the maintenance and protection of the established church, resorted to a most comical expedient, and maintained that the Latin words of the charter, " Sacrosancta Dei et vera Christiana religio," which had from the time of the charter been rendered " God's holy and true Christian religion " should be translated " holy *service* of God and true Christian religion," as Streeter maintained ; or " God's holy rights and the true Christian religion," as Hon. Brantz Mayer translated. " The holy service of God and the true Christian religion could honestly and fairly mean," says Rev. Ethan Allen, " only that which was then established by law in England," that gentleman not recognizing any common Christianity or Christian religion, nor even admitting a common Protestant religion within the term.

Let us compare the charter with others. That of Avalon alone resembles it. The patent of Queen Elizabeth to Raleigh, in 1584, secured to those born in the colonies he might establish the rights of British subjects; but the power of making laws was reserved absolutely to Raleigh, and no provision made for the voice of the settlers in an Assembly: no liberty of trade was given, and no law was to conflict with the doctrines of the established church (Hakluyt, iii., p. 243).

The patents of the London and Plymouth Virginia Companies had no guarantee of the rights of colonists; and the royal charter for Massachusetts Bay gave the right of electing the governor and assistants and of making laws, not to the settlers, but to the freemen of the company. None of these gave any freedom of trade, nor did that of Virginia.

In the matter of religion the Virginia charter of 1606 required the doctrines of the Established Church to be preached to the settlers and the Indians; that of 1609 virtually excluded Catholics by authorizing the administration of the oath of supremacy to be tendered to all who wished to sail to that colony; and the New England charter granted to Sir Ferdinand Gorges in 1621 formally excluded Roman Catholics. The charter therefore granted to Lord Baltimore was in several points more liberal and enlightened, better calculated for the welfare of the colonists than any of the patents issued in that century. The latest historian of Maryland, who had all the views on the subject before him, gives his conclusion frankly and clearly: " And we cannot be far wrong in ascribing the peculiar independence of Marylanders, their unflinching maintenance of their rights, their stubborn resistance to wrong, their Spartan courage and endurance, and their ardent patriotism, to the extraordinary liberties of the charter, and the singularly excellent administration of a government under which they felt themselves to be truly freemen." (" History of Maryland," i., p. 62.)

But it has been advanced that the charter did not really secure religious freedom, because penal laws against Catholics were subsequently passed by both Puritan and Episcopalian. The answer to this view is simple. These laws were not passed under the charter, but when the charter and the government it established were suspended. The charter vested the lawmaking power in the Proprietary with the consent of the freemen. Clayborne and Bennet in the name of the Commonwealth deposed Lord Baltimore's governor, and appointed a board of ten commissioners to administer the government. They called an Assembly excluding all who had borne arms for the king, and all who " do profess the Roman Catholic religion." The Assembly thus called met in October, and in "An Act concerning Religion" declared "that none who profess and exercise the popish (commonly called the Roman Catholic) religion can be protected in this province;" and though it declares that "such as profess faith in God by Jesus Christ" "shall not be restrained from, but protected in, the profession of the faith and exercise of their religion," it concludes thus: "Provided such liberty be not extended to Popery or Prelacy."

The act was in direct contravention of the charter and passed by a government not authorized by the charter.

In 1691 Lord Baltimore was called upon to surrender his charter, and on his refusal his authority was set aside and a Governor sent over by William and Mary. From the Assembly called by Copley Catholic freemen were excluded, and were not even permitted to vote for members. The act, therefore, establishing the Church of England, and those subsequently enacted against Catholics, were not passed under the charter. Though the Crown pretended to continue the charter in force, it was virtually made a nullity. The descendants of Sir George Calvert recovered their authority only by renouncing the Catholic faith and accepting what had been done.

Both Puritan and Anglican recognized the charter as an impediment to intolerance, for they both deprived the Proprietary of his chartered rights, and without warrant of law deprived Catholics of rights as freemen in order to pass laws disfranchising them.

To give Sir George Calvert credit for the liberal provisions of the Maryland charter is galling to some, simply because Calvert was a Catholic. Since the Maryland charter is in the main a copy of that for Avalon, they discovered here matter for a new argument. The charter for Avalon was granted to Lord Baltimore when a member of the Church of England, and before he became a Catholic. Hence, they maintain, his statesman-like forecast, his care for the liberties, commercial rights, and religious equality of his colonists, was that of a Protestant—not of a Catholic.

The charter for Avalon, which Scharf gives in full ("History of Maryland," i., pp. 34–40), was issued April 7, 1623.

"The construction to be put upon its provisions, especially in regard to religion," says Streeter, "must depend upon the faith of Lord Baltimore at that period. If he was then a Protestant, as is generally asserted, the charter would be drawn in terms manifesting full confidence in the grantee as a member of the Established Church." This is not fairly stated. A Protestant does not become a Catholic by an instantaneous process. Periods of doubt, study, prayer, precede the final step. Even when conviction came, and instructions had been received preparatory to being admitted into the Catholic Church, a man in position would undergo a terrible mental trial that would often last for a long time. The step deprived him of official position, of a place at court, of social relations, subjected him to loss of property, heavy fines and a perpetual risk of loss of liberty under some of the ingeniously devised penal laws. A man in Sir George Calvert's position would naturally provide in advance before taking the step. He was already interested in American colonization, as a member of the Virginia Company and as a purchaser of Vaughn's grant in Newfoundland. To place his estate there in the safest possible position would be a step dictated by prudence, and he would frame its provisions, so far as he could, to meet his necessities as a Catholic, and what he solicited would be to meet the requirements of a Catholic.

When he signed as Secretary the order for the arrest of the Jesuit Father, John Sweet, November 29, 1621, we can regard him as still a Protestant by conviction. But when, on the 4th of March, 1622, we find him writing to endeavor to procure the release of two imprisoned Jesuits, for whom a foreign ambassador had interposed kindly offices, we can recognize a feeling friendly to Catholics. The interesting letter which he penned to Secretary Conway on the 26th of October, 1623, describing the terrible accident at Blackfriars, where a Catholic congregation with the priests were plunged down to death by the giving way of the floors, is written in such a strain that we can scarcely withhold our conviction that he must have been a Catholic at the time. His conversion has been ascribed to Count Gondemar and Sir Thomas Arundel of Wardour. Neill impeaches this on the ground that Gondemar was not then in England, but, after all, a good deal is effected in this world by correspondence.

Sir George Calvert certainly avowed himself a Catholic and resigned his offices before he was made Baron of Baltimore in Ireland, the patent for which issued February 16, 1624. This year, 1624, is that assigned by Wood ("Athenæ. Oxon." i., p. 565 ; Fuller and Archbishop Abbott) as the date of his conversion to the Catholic faith; but the transaction covered months, and he may have been received into the Catholic Church in 1623. At all events everything tends to show that in that year he was in conviction a Catholic, and was preparing for a step which was, in a worldly point of view, to make such a change for himself and his family.[1]

---

[1] Neill's "Founders of Maryland" asserts that he announced his conversion in 1625, but he gives no authority, and the date is not reconcilable with facts. Fuller, a contemporary, gives the year 1624. Wood says that when he was created Lord Baltimore (February 16, 1624) he was "then a Roman Catholic, or, at least, very much addicted to their religion." And Archbishop Abbott says : "since Charles's return from Spain (in 1623) Mr. Secretary Calvert apparently did turn Papist, which he now professeth."

3. The character of Lord Baltimore himself is the next point at issue. The earlier estimates were highly favorable. Bancroft wrote : " Before the patent could be finally adjusted and pass the great seal, Sir George Calvert died, leaving a name against which the breath of calumny has hardly whispered a reproach. The petulance of his adversaries could only taunt him with being ' an Hispaniolized Papist.' A man of such moderation that all parties were taken with him ; sincere in his character." (" History of the United States," i., pp. 241–2.)

John P. Kennedy, in a discourse before the Maryland Historical Society in 1845, made the first serious attack on Calvert's character by representing him as a religious hypocrite. He treated the statement of Fuller, Abbott, and others, that Calvert became a convert to the Catholic faith, as false. He arrayed arguments to "prove that Sir George Calvert was, if not actually nursed in the faith of Rome, no convert to that faith in his period of manhood; that if he ever was a Protestant there is no record of it within our knowledge. (" Discourse," p. 34.) " He thought it the part of prudence and wisdom to keep his religion as much as possible confined to the privacy of his own chamber." (p. 35.) Yet he speaks of his "deference to Calvert's high character, integrity, and honor." (p. 38.) His ideas of integrity and honor were strange. Could a Catholic of honor and integrity take the oath of supremacy to which Sir Thomas More preferred the block ? Could he be instrumental in sending Catholic priests to prison and the gallows for saying Mass? Could he, as a Catholic, have accepted the Longford grant in 1621, charged with conditions for the utmost severity against Catholics and schemes for their perversion ? That he accepted the grant as a Protestant in 1621, as in that year he was active against a Jesuit in England, tends to show that he was then sincerely a Protestant. When he became a Catholic he surrendered his grant and obtained a re-grant in fee simple, thus obtaining exemption from conditions which, as a Catholic, he could not conscientiously perform. The whole theory of Kennedy was at the time so thoroughly confuted by Bernard U. Campbell that few have since questioned the reality of Calvert's conversion, or asked us to admire him as a successful hypocrite.

Another mode of lowering Lord Baltimore in the general esteem of mankind is to impeach his moral character. From an expression in a letter of Stuyvesant, the Dutch Governor of New Netherlands, certainly no very high authority on a question of English family history, Hildreth assumed that Leonard Calvert, the first Governor of Maryland, the actual founder of the colony, who guided its destiny so ably, was the fruit of some disgraceful amour of Lord Baltimore. Even the cautious Davis in his "Day Star" accepted and repeated the charge. And yet in Hertingford-bury church a tablet to the memory of Lady Baltimore, first wife of Sir George, enumerates all her children, and second among them names Leonard. Even Neill ("Founders of Maryland," p. 41) admits that the charge is erroneous. Determined to sully Lord Baltimore's character, the charge was afterwards made that Philip Calvert, whom Cecil, the second Lord, styles "our very loving brother" (Bozman, ii., p. 699), was really illegitimate. But of this there is no proof. After the death of his first wife in 1622 Sir George married again, and the accounts of his residence in Newfoundland mention his wife and her children.

Scharf, whose very comprehensive "History of Maryland" has done so much to settle the annals of his State, gives (vol. i., p. 47) Leonard his due position, and adds: " Philip Calvert, who in 1656 was made Secretary of the Province of Maryland, afterwards Chancellor, and then Governor, was son of the second wife." This attempt to fix a stigma on the fair fame of Sir George Calvert fails.

4. Another mooted point in Maryland history is the position to be assigned to William Clayborne. Earlier historians represented him as the "evil genius of Maryland," the source of endless troubles. Streeter, Neill, and others, of late years, attempt to exalt him into a hero. Clayborne was one of those who refused to permit Lord Baltimore to remain in Virginia in 1629, unless he took the oath of supremacy. He was then an earnest upholder of the Church of England, and the king as head thereof. When Lord Baltimore obtained a grant south of the James, in 1631, he was active in opposing it, and the patent was revoked. In 1627, '28, and '29, he had obtained of the Governor of Virginia permission to trade to the Chesapeake, and, to confirm his privilege, in 1631 obtained of King Charles I. a license "to trade in all those seas, coasts, harbors, lands or territories, in or near about those parts of America for which there is not already a patent granted to others for sole trade." Governor Harvey subsequently gave him a license to trade to the Dutch. The only authority he had was to trade ; no power was given to settle ; no proprietary power given by the king or by the Colony of Virginia. He founded a settlement or trading post on Kent Island, and another on Palmer Island. When Lord Baltimore's colony arrived, he refused to recognize the authority of the Maryland charter, or the government established under it. But he surely had no valid title to the land, and the claim of a purchase from the Indians was one never recognized ; and even a lawful title to the land did not authorize him to resist a government created by royal charter. If the charter divided the territory of Virginia unconstitutionally, Virginia might, and did, raise the question,

but it was not competent for every citizen of Virginia to resort to violent acts against the Maryland government. He was finally driven out, and his little establishment brought under subjection. He returned to Virginia, and when the Commonwealth was established, the old adherent of the King and Church of England was sent out by Cromwell to reduce Virginia to Puritan rule, and assuming powers over Maryland also, overthrew the Proprietary government, defeated the Governor, Stone, and is responsible for the ensuing butchery in cold blood of the prisoners taken.

Writers who have attempted to belittle Lord Baltimore have endeavored to elevate this man. The fullest and fairest collection of material for forming a correct judgment of Clayborne, and assigning him his proper place in history, will be found in Scharf's recent "History," and it shows how utterly subversive of all sound ideas of government are the arguments by which his career has been justified.

5. The next point to be considered is the object which Lord Baltimore had in view in obtaining the Avalon, Southern, and Maryland charters. The older historians, all, without any equivocation, regarded and represented it as an attempt to found a colony to which Catholics might withdraw from the fierce persecution in England. But to let Maryland be presented to the minds of men as a colony for Catholics, in its inception, was galling to some minds, and they endeavored to evade. Hence Kennedy, in his "Discourse," says: "I find no reason whatever to suppose, as I have already intimated, that in the planting of either Avalon or Maryland, Lord Baltimore was moved by a special desire to provide an asylum for persecuted Catholics, as many have alleged. The charter of Maryland does not indicate such a purpose, nor do the proceedings under it." (p. 41.) "There is no evidence that his ardor in these undertakings was stimulated by any motive having reference to particular religious opinions. We are, on the contrary, bound to presume that his purpose was, in part, the advancement of his own reputation, the increase of the wealth of his family, and as the Maryland charter expresses it, 'a laudable and pious zeal for extending the Christian religion, and also the territories of our empire.'" (p. 25.)

This idea was at once caught up by a certain class of writers like Doyle, who, in his "English Colonies in America," everywhere seeks to belittle Calvert, and the assertion was boldly made that Lord Baltimore had no idea of founding a refuge for the persecuted Catholics of England. It is almost an insult to common sense thus to pervert the silence of the Avalon and Maryland charters, or to say, as Allen puts it, "the words Protestant or Roman Catholic, or their synonyms, are not found in the charter." A charter granting a refuge to Roman Catholics, in explicit terms, would have arrayed all the fanaticism of England against the king. The only thing was to word the grant so as to permit Catholics to proceed to the colony and live there in quiet. The penal laws were still enforced with unsparing rigor; priests were hanged, drawn, indecently mutilated, and quartered, for no crime but saying Mass as the English chaplains did on the field of Agincourt; laymen were punished by heavy fines and imprisonment for not attending the Anglican service, for harboring priests, for having a Catholic Bible; and we are gravely told that a document obtained from the king could not have been intended to benefit Catholics, because it does not say expressly: "And he is hereby authorized to convey to said land any of our Roman Catholic subjects, and freely to have the service of the Roman Catholic Church there." Calvert would have been a fool to ask such a clause, or Charles to allow it.

The period of Lord Baltimore's conversion shows a change in his plans. His grant from an individual in Newfoundland he merges in a proprietary government under a royal charter; other charters of that day, and from his interest in American colonization, and the office he held, he must have been familiar with them, pointedly excluded Catholic settlers; a law requiring the tendering of the oaths of supremacy and allegiance to Catholics seeking to pass to America, prevented them setting out. If Calvert had no wish to open his colony to Catholic emigration, why did he secure for Avalon, and afterwards for Maryland, the omission of the usual clause, and a proviso by which any one not specially forbidden could sail for those colonies? These points were not accidental, and if we are to presume at all, we are bound to presume that a trained statesman secured their omission with a motive, and the only motive for removing a restriction on Catholic emigration was the motive of making it possible.

The idea of a Catholic colony in America was nothing new. The voyage of Sir Humphrey Gilbert was part of a scheme of Catholic colonization, one of the projectors being the father of one of the earliest settlers in Maryland under Lord Baltimore's patent. The voyage of Weymouth to the coast of Maine was part of another project of Catholic settlement, projected by Thomas Lord Arundell of Wardour, who is said to have had so much influence in effecting Sir George's conversion, the two families being soon connected by intermarriage. Lady Anne Arundell's name is borne by a Maryland county to this day.

There were Catholics ready to emigrate; there were English Catholics on the continent of Europe who would readily join a colony where they could practice their religion, and live surrounded by those who spoke the language and followed the customs of old England.

That Lord Baltimore secured three priests in succession for Avalon, while affording his Protestant colonists means of practicing their religion, shows that he took out Catholics as settlers. He had scarcely secured his Maryland charter when fanatical efforts were made to thwart his sending out settlers, all showing a belief that many, if not all, would be Catholics. Streeter, who cannot be suspected of favoring this view, says: "Opposition was not wanting, also, from parties in England hostile to the plan of the new colony. False and exaggerated representations were made through the Attorney-General before the Star Chamber relative to the designs of Lord Baltimore; that he intended to carry nuns into Spain, and soldiers to serve the king; that his ships had left Gravesend without due authority from the custom-house; and that his people had abused the king's officers, and refused to take the oath of allegiance. But Calvert succeeded in showing the falsity of all the charges brought against him, and at the end of about eighteen months from the time the Charter passed the great seal all obstacles were overcome, and his ships, which had been detained in consequence of these false reports, were allowed to depart." ("Maryland Two Hundred Years Ago," p. 14.) The Jesuit Fathers, and evidently some others, did not join the vessels till after they reached the Isle of Wight ("Relatio Itineris," p. 9). Here is abundant evidence that a Catholic object was suspected, and means taken to defeat it.

That Lord Baltimore designed Maryland as a refuge for Catholics was asserted by Beverly in his "History of Virginia:" "Calvert, a Roman Catholic, thought for the more quiet exercise of his religion to retire with his family into this New World." ("History of Virginia," p. 46.) Wynne, in his "History of America," says: "His lordship was a Catholic, and had formed his design of making this settlement in order to enjoy a liberty of conscience." Douglass, in his "Summary," and "The Modern Universal History," expresses the same view; and the Maryland Catholics, in their petition in 1751, asserted it as an undisputed fact.

We have thus considered the main points in controversy, so far as Lord Baltimore is concerned. The latest historian of Maryland justly remarks: "Calumny has not shrunk from attacking his (Baltimore's) honored name. Detraction has been busy; and, as the facts could not be denied, Calvert's motives have been assailed; but empty assertion, conjecture, surmises, however ingeniously malevolent, have happily exercised very little influence over the minds of intelligent and candid men." ("History of Maryland," i., p. 52.) It must still, therefore, be recognized as historic truth that

Sir George Calvert was a man of integrity, ability, and unimpeached morality; that he was not a hypocrite, always a Catholic and concealing his faith, but a Protestant who from conviction became a Catholic; that he planned a refuge in America for those who, like himself, were the victims of penal laws, and obtained a charter for Maryland, which gave them an opportunity to settle there in comparative freedom; that this charter contained guarantees for the liberty and prosperity of the colonists unusual in charters, and that these beneficent features are due to the noble mind of Calvert.

. 6. Passing to the history of the Province, we encounter the great question in regard to the oath taken by the officers. According to Chalmers (" Political Annals," pp. 210, 235), the oath taken by the Governor and Council, between the years 1637 and 1657, was: " I will not, by myself or any other, directly or indirectly, trouble, molest or discountenance any person professing to believe in Jesus Christ, for or in respect of religion. I will make no difference of persons in conferring offices, favors, or rewards, for or in respect of religion; but merely as they shall be found faithful and well-deserving, and endued with moral virtues and abilities; my aim shall be public unity; and if any person or officer shall molest any person professing to believe in Jesus Christ, on account of his religion, I will protect the person molested and punish the offender."

We have this oath, as modified in 1648, and as it continued to 1657; but the question has been raised, whether the oath in the exact form given by Chalmers was in use from 1637 to 1648; whether, in fact, in the whole of that early period of eleven years this oath was taken. Streeter disregarded Chalmers, and maintained that the oath from 1639 to 1643 contained no allusion to religious matters. Yet, as Scharf reasonably argues, "Chalmers was too accurate a writer to use dates so loosely; and, as he was not only an experienced lawyer, but the custodian of the Maryland provincial papers, and had free access afterwards to all documents relating to the colony in the British State Paper Office, he could not have been in doubt as to the precise date, or ignorant of the exact language." ("History of Maryland," i., p. 171.) In fact, if Chalmers did not copy it, he must have invented it—a grave charge, indeed. Streeter does not give the form of the oath which he found, nor tell us where it can be seen. Scharf, who is the official custodian of the State archives, sustains Chalmers, and evidently has not in his keeping the form to which Mr. Streeter alludes. The volumes of the " Maryland Archives" ought to show the oath mentioned by Streeter, but it has not been our good fortune to secure a set, or even a reply to our application for one; and, in the examination we were able to give these volumes, in one of our public libraries, we did not find the oath referred to by Mr. Streeter, or any proof that any such oath was administered during the period he specifies.

Leaving this question, which can easily be decided by a reference to the archives, let us come to the Act of Toleration of 1649, and the oath prescribed at that time. Those who denied that Maryland was in its origin a Catholic colony; that Lord Baltimore had any religious motive in planting it; that religious freedom was intended or implied in the charter or early provincial rule, now come forward to maintain that the Legislature of 1649 was not a Catholic body, or that Catholics were in a majority in the Assembly. This strange set of writers seem to quake and tremble, from morn to dewy eve, for fear their fellow citizens should give Catholics credit for doing any praiseworthy act, from the first discovery and settlement of our coast to the present time.

In 1648 Lord Baltimore, evidently convinced that he must prepare for trouble in Maryland, affecting his own rights and those of the Catholic settlers, deemed it wiser to place a Protestant in the Governor's chair, and selected William Stone, a resident of Northampton County, Virginia. For the new Governor, and the officers under him, he drew up a new oath, in which the Maryland officials swore, in express terms, not to molest any Roman Catholic for or in respect of his or her religion.[1] In 1648 he also sent over a body of sixteen laws, which the Maryland Assembly were asked to pass and make perpetual. These laws are said by Johnson to have been proposed to Lord Baltimore, and he endeavors to show that they emanated from Father More, the superior of the Jesuits in Maryland. His arguments seem insufficient. There is nothing to show that the members of that Order had regained his goodwill and confidence to that extent that he would accept projects of laws from them to be imposed on the people of his province. In fact, it is known that at this time he was complaining at home of the Jesuits, and asking the Congregation *de Propaganda Fide* to send over other priests. It would seem much more probable that the contents of these laws were suggested by persons in Maryland versed in the actual condition of affairs. Be that as it may, they were sent by Lord Baltimore, as his act, to Governor Stone and the Assembly, to be made laws, under the charter which vested the making of laws in him, by and with the consent of the freemen. They were to be perpetual, and in token of their essential importance, as a kind of fundamental constitution of the province, they were engrossed on three sheets of parchment. In a session

---

[1] The oath is given in full by Scharf, i., p. 172-3.

held between April 2d and April 21st, 1649, the Legislature passed seven of the acts thus sent over, one of them being the Act concerning Religion. When the Assembly met again, in April, 1650, " they read and considered the sixteen laws sent over by his lordship to be assented to and enacted without alteration;" and then proceeded to pass the rest of the sixteen. These laws were confirmed by the Proprietary in one instrument, 20th April, 1650. The Act concerning Religion was thus passed by the Proprietary, Governor and Assembly, in 1649, and reconsidered in the Assembly in 1650 and confirmed by the Proprietary in that year. The "Short Account of ye State and Condition of ye Rom. Cath. in ye Province of Maryland," by Rev. George Hunter, notes this two-fold enactment, although in copying the figures have evidently suffered.

" In consequence of ye said declarations and promises in ye 1st Session of Assembly held in y^t Province in 1640 (9) a perpetual act passed entitled An Act concerning religion wch confirmed ye said declarations and promises concerning liberty of conscience." The same act was again reënacted in 1650, and confirmed in 1656 (9).

Now it was asserted that the majority of the inhabitants in 1649 were Protestant, that the majority of the Legislature were Protestant, the Governor, Stone, a Protestant, so that Catholics could make no pretence to the credit of passing the Act, which was purely Protestant and characteristic of that high sense of respect for the religious opinions of others which from the time of the Reformation they had invariably displayed.

Leaving the general question, however, as to the existence of any such tolerant spirit in the Reformers and their followers, which certainly the seizure of every Catholic church and convent in the British Isles, the disfranchisement of Catholics, their exclusion from emigrating to the colonies, and from abiding in them, do not permit us to see very clearly, we come to the explicit question whether the Maryland Assembly of 1649 was Catholic or Protestant in the majority of its votes.

The Lord Proprietary, from whom the law emanated and who confirmed it, was undeniably a Catholic. His Lieutenant Governor, Stone, if we consider him as an individual, was a Protestant, if as representing him whose agent he was, may not unreasonably be regarded as what his principal was, a Catholic. The Council of the Province, as is established by Mr. Davis, were Governor Stone, Secretary Thomas Hatton, Messrs. Thomas Greene, John Price, John Pile, and Robert Vaughn, as appears by their commission. Nine burgesses sat in that Assembly, Cuthbert Fenwick, Philip Conner, William Bretton, Richard Browne, George Manners, Richard Banks, John Maunsell, Thomas Thornborough and Walter Peake, their names being given in the Assembly committee's report on the bill of charges for that session, a document preserved in the Land Office.[1]

The councillors and burgesses on the day the Act passed sat together in one house. Including the Secretary, there were fourteen members besides the Governor. Of these Thomas Greene, afterwards well known as acting governor, John Pile, among whose descendants were a priest and a nun, Cuthbert Fenwick, ancestor of two Catholic Bishops, William Bretton, who gave land for a Catholic chapel, were undisputedly Catholics; Manners, Maunsell, Thornborough and Peake always acted with the Roman Catholics; the first two, though present at the signing of the Protestant declaration, did not affix their names; Maunsell and Peake's land grants bore Catholic titles; Thornborough was very·obnoxious to the Protestant party at a later day. From these and other incidental circumstances Mr. Davis makes these four gentlemen to have been Catholics. Messrs. Price and Vaughn were undoubtedly Protestants; Conner and Banks are inferred to be of the same faith, because in a will where the testator wished that his eldest son should reside with no Papist, he confides some of his children to Messrs. Conner and Banks. As to Browne's religion Mr. Davis could find no clue;[2] but assigning him to the Protestant side, it gives as the faith of the members of this famous Assembly eight Catholics and six Protestants. If Governor Stone voted as a member of the Assembly, it would not have made a tie; but there is no evidence that any Governor of Maryland acted as Lord Bellomont did when Governor of New York. When the penal law against the Jesuits and Catholic priests was brought before the council of New York, Governor Bellomont claimed to vote as councillor; this made a tie, and then by his casting vote as President of the Council it passed that body. After it had been passed through the lower house, Lord Bellomont signed it as Governor, having three times given his voice to place it on the Statute Book of the Colony of New York.

That Catholics were entitled to the credit of passing the Act of 1649 was called in doubt by John P. Kennedy, and by Bozman in his "History of Maryland": "There are strong grounds to believe that the majority of the members were Protestants, if 'not Protestants of the Puritanic order" (vol. ii., p. 349); by Streeter in his "Maryland Two Hundred Years Ago": "Because the laws were enacted by a Protestant Assembly" (p. 41); by Rev. Ethan Allen, quoting and endorsing Bozman ("Maryland Toleration," p. 55). But as their statement was based simply on conjecture, it was utterly demolished by the facts elicited by Davis in his patient and ex-

---

[1] Davis, Day Star, p. 129-131.
[2] See Mr. Davis' proofs at length in his Day Star, pp. 183-253.

haustive research. To this day no one has questioned the accuracy of the author of the "Day Star" in this matter.

But even this work did not prevent cavil. Rev. Mr. Neill at once endeavored to show that if Catholics voted for it, they did it as Protestants and not as Catholics. With the utmost serenity he tells us: "This Act was contrary to the teachings of the Church of Rome, since it was the recognition of Christians who rejected the Pope" ("Founders of Maryland," p. 122). For this astounding proposition he cites, as he of course could cite, no authority. The Catholics had from the first given the Protestants full liberty; from the settlement the Protestant had been free to practice his own religion. The Jesuit missionaries differed from Lord Baltimore on several points, but they nowhere assert that the Proprietary's recognition of Protestants was contrary to the doctrines of the Church; and it would certainly be very strange that Rev. Mr. Neill should be so much better versed in Catholic theology than the Jesuit Fathers who were in Maryland from 1634 to 1649. By confusing the Assembly of 1649 with that of 1650 Neill contrived to give so false an idea of the former, that Mr. Gladstone, at a moment when his mind was in a terribly illogical condition, following the guide of Allen and Neill, wrote: "Of the small legislative body which passed it, two-thirds appear to have been Protestant, the *recorded* numbers being sixteen and eight respectively."[1] Where he found the record does not appear. No record is known which shows any such state; and the unimpeached researches of Mr. Davis, and the "Bill of Charges," which is of record, give the names, and the certainty.

Mr. Scharf in his "History of Maryland," quoting the testimony of Spence in his "Early History of the Presbyterian Church," to the toleration established under the Lords Baltimore in Maryland, adds: "Would that all who have discussed the subject had done so in a like frank and honorable spirit." ("History of Maryland," i.,

---

[1] "Rome and the Newest Fashions in Religion," Preface. His illogical condition of mind may be seen. "The sinlessness of the Virgin Mary and the personal infallibility of the Pope are the characteristic dogmas of modern Romanism. . . . Both present a refined idolatry, by clothing a pure humble woman and a mortal sinful man with divine attributes." The doctrine of the Immaculate Conception declared Mary to have been from the first instant of her existence free from original sin. This he tells us is a divine attribute. Now, Adam and Eve, before they committed the first and original sin, must have been free from it, or it was not first and original. The devil told them that by eating a fruit they would become like gods. Gladstone would have gone further than the serpent: he would have told them that they were clothed with "divine attributes," in fact, gods; but how God could create gods, or how these created gods ever could incur sin, Mr. Gladstone does not explain; but full of this god-theory, he maintains that God cannot preserve those whom He makes judges of doctrine from error in giving their decision, without making them gods. Did He make the apostles gods when He empowered them to teach all nations?

p. 180.) He fully endorses the results attained and the documents cited by Davis.

Neill's next device to rob Catholics, and indeed Maryland, of the credit of passing this early act of religious freedom, was to maintain that it was copied from a Puritan model. " Although the House of Commons in 1645 had ordered liberty of conscience and worship in the plantations, the Independents of Somers Island and Virginia were oppressed by those in power. (" Founders of Maryland," p. 115, *n.*) The act was, as he himself admits (p. 111), one to protect a community of Independents under Rev. Patrick Copland, who had removed from Somers Island to Eleutheria. Then came the charge that Parliament had first established general toleration by an ordinance of 1647, which he styles " that golden apple." (" English Colonization," p. 280.) Following this unfaithful guide, Gladstone wrote : " The colonial act seems to have been an echo of the order of the House of Commons at home, on the 27th of October, 1645, that the inhabitants of the Summer Island, and such others as shall join themselves to them, shall, without any molestation or trouble, have and enjoy the liberty of their conscience in matters of God's worship; and of a British ordinance of 1647."

Mr. Gladstone ought to have been able to speak accurately of British acts and ordinances. The authorities were at his hand ; instead of consulting them he trusted to the garbled statements of a polemic. Bradley T. Johnson in his " Foundation of Maryland" says : " No order for general liberty of conscience, either in the colonies or in England, ever was passed by the Long Parliament. No such ordinance as that referred to by Mr. Gladstone was ever passed in 1647, or at any other time." None such is in Schobell's " Collection of the Statutes and Ordinances." Rushworth is given as authority for the alleged ordinances. Reference to his " Collection " shows that an ordinance for settling the government of the Church in a " Presbyterial way " was discussed in the Commons on the 6th of October, 1647, and an amendment was adopted for " giving ease to tender consciences of such as are godly, and make a conscience of their ways." (Rushworth, iii., p. 834.) On October 13th, 1647, the Lords resolved: " That the king be desired to give his consent, and that all who do not conform shall have libertie to meet for the service and worship of God, and so that nothing be done by them to the disturbance of the kingdom."

Here is an order passed by one House only. Mr. Johnson says : " It is the only order that can be found to support Mr. Gladstone." Of course, readers concluded from the assertion of Neill and Gladstone that it also passed the House of Commons. But what was the real fact ? " It was promptly repudiated the same day by the Commons," who " resolved " that liberty of conscience or worship granted shall extend to none that shall print, preach or publish contrary to the first 15 articles of the 39, except the eighth, which mentions the three Creeds, made many years after the Apostles; that *nothing contained in this ordinance shall extend to any Popish Recusants, or taking away any penal laws against them.*

And on the 15th the same House modified its resolution of the 6th so that it should not extend to tolerate the use of Common Prayer in any place whatsoever (Rushworth, vii., pp. 840–2).

Can any judgment be too severe on the writer who could give the action of the Lords, and suppress that of the Commons? The Summers Island act and the ordinance were conceived in the same spirit, they were passed by Puritans and Independents to give liberty solely to Puritans and Independents, it was a grand grant of toleration, freedom of conscience and of worship to all mankind who thought as they did. Not such was the idea of religious equality professed and practiced by Lord Baltimore and the Maryland Catholics, so long as they could sit in the Legislature of their Province.

We have thus taken up the main points of controversy as to Maryland history raised of late years, all aiming to detract from the claims put forward by or on behalf of the Catholics. The charges have been advocated with skill, research, and it is a pity we cannot say with impartiality and fairness. But every one has been met with clear and unimpeachable documents. The old theories and views of Maryland history have been triumphantly established, and it is most creditable to the historic students of America that the defence of the view favorable to Catholics has been maintained not by Catholics, but by scholars as Protestant as those whose arguments they so ably refuted.

CHRISTIAN BURIAL AND CREMATION.

Nouvelles Études sur les Catacombes Romaines. Par De Richemont. Paris, Poussielgue, 1870.

De Angelis. Jus Canonicum, Romæ. 1879.

Le Cimetière au Dix-Neuvième Siècle. Par Mgr. Gaume. Paris.

THE fundamental reason for the discipline of the Catholic Church regarding the disposition of the dead is the dogma of the Apostles' Creed: "I believe in the resurrection of the body." Her philosophy is that the body is an essential part of the man, and that a religion which even partially ignores this fact is not universal, and, therefore, not true. Although she does not hold that there is nothing in the intellect which was not first in the senses, yet she recognizes the fact that they are necessary in the order of natural cognition as well as in the order of religious belief. Through the senses men's minds are corrupted, and through them they may be improved morally and elevated spiritually. Unphilosophic Protestantism began by ignoring the important role which the body and its senses play in the work of salvation. It made war on the religious pictures and statues through which spiritual ideas are conveyed to the mind, and attacked the old sacramental symbolism which, by the action of sensible signs and ceremonies on the body, conveys invisible grace to the invisible soul. To ignore the material and sensible in divine worship, to deny the sacramental system established by Christ, is indirectly to weaken faith in the mystery of the Word made flesh. To try to establish a purely spiritual system of religion for beings who have a mixed nature, a physical body as well as an immaterial soul connected with it, and dependent on it for reflex cognition as well as for outward expression of religious worship, is to attempt to build a steeple in the air without a church to put it on. Yet this is what Protestantism has tried to do in warring on the sensible devotions of the Catholic Church and abolishing her sacraments, in diminishing the number of religious ceremonies and the impressiveness of the Christian ritual. A Catholic has only to attend a Protestant funeral to feel the chill produced by the curtailing of the Catholic ritual. The Protestant dead is put away in a dark room; the corpse is shunned; it is carried in silence to the church, where pagan symbols in flowers, wreaths, and broken columns surround the coffin, where a few dry words of Scripture are read; and thence to a graveyard, beautifully laid out, indeed, with gravelled walks, weeping willows, and evergreen trees, for there is sentiment still even where faith has ceased to exist, but a graveyard, almost without a cross and without the figure of the kneeling widow, or father, or child,—so often seen in the Catholic cemetery,—praying at the tomb for the repose of the soul departed. There is no heart in the Protestant funeral. There is a hurry to put the offensive corpse out of sight, and then forget all about it. The old Church holds on to her dead with eternal affection. The dead body is the body of her child. It is sacred flesh. It has been the temple of a regenerated soul. She blessed it in baptism, poured the saving waters on its head, anointed it with holy oil on breast and back, put the blessed salt on its lips, and touched its nose and ears in benediction when it was only the flesh of a babe; and then, in growing youth, reconsecrated it by confirmation; and, before its dissolution in death, she again blessed and sanctified its organs, its hands and its feet, as well as its more important members. Even after death she blesses it with holy water, and incenses it before her altar, amid the solemnity of the great sacrifice of the New Law, and surrounded by mourners who rejoice even in their tears, for they believe in the communion of saints, and are united in prayer with the dead happy in heaven, as well as with those who are temporarily suffering in purgatory. The old Church, the kind old mother of regenerated humanity, follows the dead body of her child into the very grave. She will not throw it into the common ditch, or into unhallowed ground; no, it is the flesh of her son. She sanctifies and jealously guards from desecration the spot where it is to rest until the final resurrection; and day by day, until the end of the world, she thinks of her dead, and prays for them at every Mass that is celebrated; for, even amid the joys of Easter and of Christmas, the memento for the dead is never omitted from the Canon. She even holds annually a solemn feast of the dead, the day after " All Saints," in November, when the melancholy days are on the wane, the saddest of the year, and the fallen leaves and chilly blasts presage the season of nature's death. Then are the graveyards filled with the living who go thither, "not as those without hope " to read inscriptions and curiously inspect stately and gorgeously carved monuments, or gratify a vain and pagan sentiment by hanging a wreath of immortelles around some favorite's tomb, but to kneel and to pray that the souls of the beloved dead and of all "the faithful departed through the mercy of God may rest in peace." The intense belief of the Church in the resurrection of the body is seen in all this solicitude and love. They are the expression of her conviction that a body, which has been repeatedly united with the flesh and blood of Christ through the reception of the Eucharist, ought to be honored even in the grave, and that it will be a sharer in the glories of His resurrection.

"The resurrection of the dead gives confidence to all Christians,"[1] wrote Tertullian in the third century. Two general councils—that of Constantinople and the fourth Lateran—have defined the resurrection of the body as an article of faith. The Christian belief on this point is inherited from the Hebrews, for Job says : " I know that my Redeemer liveth, and in the last day I shall rise out of the earth. And I shall be clothed again with my skin, and in my flesh I shall see my God."[2]   Daniel[3] and the second book of Machabees[4] bear similar testimony.

Martha's words to our Lord showed what was the common belief of the Jews in her time : " I know that he (Lazarus) shall rise again in the resurrection at the last day."[5] Our Lord expressly taught this doctrine in refuting the Sadducees, a sect of Hebrew materialists, who denied both the immortality of the soul and the resurrection of the body : " And concerning the resurrection of the dead, have you not read that which was spoken by God, saying to you : I am the God of Abraham, and the God of Isaac, and the God of Jacob ? He is not the God of the dead, but of the living."[6] Although dead to men, they were alive to God, both body and soul. The central idea which runs through many of the epistles of St. Paul is that there are but two men in the world,— Adam and Christ. All our misfortunes come from the former, original sin and death, while from the latter come our restoration, our regeneration and resurrection. Christ is our spiritual head, who proved His divinity by His resurrection ; we are united to Him, both to His soul and to His body, and by this union we share in the graces and privileges both of His soul and of His body. "For if the dead rise not again, neither is Christ risen again. And if Christ be not risen again, your faith is vain."[7] Then again he writes, in a text so often quoted in the Ritual of the Church : " And we will not have you ignorant, brethren, concerning them that are asleep, that you be not sorrowful, even as others who have no hope. For, if we believe that Jesus died and rose again, even so them who have slept through Jesus will God bring with Him."[8] Again, in words that remind one of Plato's arguments for the immortality of the soul, in " Phædo," the apostle writes : "So, also, is the resurrection of the dead. It is sown in corruption, it shall rise in incorruption. It is sown in dishonor, it

---

[1] Lib. de Resurrect. Carnis, n. I.
[3] Daniel xii., v. 2.
[5] John xi., v. 24.
[7] I Cor. xv., v. 16, 17.

[2] Job xix., v. 25, 26.
[4] 2 Mach. vii., v. 9-14.
[6] Matth. xxii., v. 31, 32.
[8] I Thess. iv., v. 12, 13.

shall rise in glory. It is sown in weakness, it shall rise in power. It is sown a natural body, it shall rise a spiritual body."[1]

This dogma of revelation is intimated even by the law of nature and its analogies. Nothing is annihilated. "Our bodies die to us, but not to God," says Tertullian in his treatise on this subject. "God is able to remake what He made. He gave life and can give it a second time."[2] There is restoration of all that perishes around us; life comes out of death. The winter is followed by the spring; the living bud and blossom come again on the same branch upon which they perished; and the green grass grows again where the frost and snow killed it. The juicy stalk and ripened ear spring from the soil in which the planted seed lies rotten and dead.

This is not only the argument of Tertullian, but even of the pagan Seneca.[3] And why should not the body live again, since the soul lives forever? Why should not the partner of the soul's toils, the instrument of its mortifications, of its abstinence and fasting, as well as of its sensuality, rise again to share its bliss or its misery? The whole man, not merely a part of him, is destined for eternity; and man is not complete without his body, either in this life or in the next. St. Ambrose puts this argument as follows: "Since the association of soul and body is continual during this life, and the resurrection implies a reward for well-doing or a punishment for wickedness, it is necessary that the body should rise to receive its due. For how can the soul be called into judgment without the body, since the account to be rendered concerns the relations of the soul with the body?"[4] The objections against this doctrine made by certain rationalists are all answered by the simple but profound philosophy expressed in the words of the *Catechism:* "Nothing is hard or impossible to God."[5]

---

[1] 1 Cor. xv., v. 42, 43, 44.

[2] De Resur. Carnis, C. 68, *et seq.* Here is the passage from Plato which expresses a thought similar to that of St. Paul and Tertullian:

"Οὐκ ἐναντίον μὲν φὴς τῷ ζῆν τὸ τεθνάναι εἶναι; ἔγωγέ." γίγνεσθαι δὲ ἐξ ἀλλήλων; ναί. Ἐξ οὖν τοῦ ζῶντος τί τὸ γιγνόμενον; τὸ τεθνηκός, ἔφη. Τί δέ, ἢ διός, ἐκ τοῦ τεθν.ʾωτος; ἀναγκαῖον, ἔφη, ὁμολογεῖν, ὅτι τὸ ζῶν. Ἐκ τῶν τεθνεώτων ἄρα, ὦ κέβης, τά ζῶντὰ τε καὶ οἱ ζῶντες γίγνονται Φαίνεται, ἔφη. τερνεῶτος. Teubner's edition, Leipsic, 1879. (Cap. 16, line 24th, *et seq.*)

[3] Ep. 36, v. ii., " *Videbis nihil in hoc mundo extingui, sed vicibus descendere ac surgere.*" This is but an echo of Plato.

[4] Lib. de fide resurrect., n. 52, *et seq.*

[5] As no theological question is completely discussed without the authority of St. Thomas, we quote what he says:

"The gift of Christ is greater than the sin of Adam. But death was brought into the world by sin, for if there had been no sin there would have been no death. (Rom. v.) Therefore by the gift of Christ man will be restored to life from death. Moreover, the members ought to be conformable to the head. But our head lives, and will live forever in soul and body, because 'Christ, rising again from the dead, dieth now no more.' (Rom. vi., 9.) Therefore men who are his members will live in soul and

Therefore the Church claims the corpse. It has once been a holy tabernacle of the body and blood of Jesus Christ. She orders the civil power away from the bier and the graveyard. The funeral and requiem mass are hers. Her jurisdiction over them is supreme; and although it may not be always respected, it nevertheless exists, for the dead man was a Christian and has a right to Christian burial; and Christian burial is not a subject within the province of the civil magistrate. The Church, indeed, recognizes the right of the State to make sanitary regulations and order things of a purely civil character regarding funerals and cemeteries; but she considers interference with her ritual, or with property owned and consecrated by her, as intrusion and usurpation. Hence her Canon Law—and it holds good wherever the Church is untrammelled by the State—gives the right of burying the dead to the priest alone, and descends into the most minute details regarding funerals. It dictates the place and manner in which bishops, priests, novices, and monks, as well as laymen, should be buried; tells who should bury those who die in hospitals; gives to the pastor of a parish the right even to choose the road which the funeral procession should take in going to the grave, and leaves nothing to doubt from the very death to the inhumation of the faithful.[1] Indeed, if we follow the letter of the old Canon Law, the authority of the relatives over the funeral is confined to inviting the guests to the ceremony and determining the expense of the funeral. All other matters pertain to the clergy.

Nor is this legislation recent or arbitrary. Its reason is found in the Old Testament and in the writings of the Fathers. Tobias is repeatedly praised for his care in burying the dead,[2] and St. Augustine[3] quotes the example of the Hebrew patriarchs to urge Christians to decency in funerals and care of the dead. "We should not despise nor reject the bodies of the dead," he writes; " especially should we respect the corpses of the just and faithful, which the Spirit hath piously used as instruments and vessels in the doing of good works. ·For if the coat of arms and ancestral ring are dear to children in proportion to their love of their ancestors, how much more are our bodies to be respected, which are nearer and dearer to us than any garments; for these bodies are not mere ornaments, but pertain to the very nature of man. Hence the funerals and burying of the patriarchs of old were cared for with officious

---

body; and therefore resurrection of the flesh is necessary." (3d part Sum., quest. 75, art. I., *et seq.*)

[1] See any Canonist, *e. g.*, Craisson, Jus Canonicum, tom. II., p. 48, *et seq.*, or Grandclaude in Lib. ter. Decret. tom. II. (Paris, 1882), p. 387.

[2] 1 Tob., 20, 21, xiii , v. 12.

[3] De Civ. Dei Cap. xiii., p. 27, tom. 41 of Migne's Patrologia.

piety. (Gen. xxv., 9;[1] xxxv., 29;[2] l., 2, 13, etc.[3]); and even while living they made provision for the burial or translation of their bodies. (Gen. xlvii., 29, 30; l., 24.) Our Lord Himself, about to rise on the third day, praises the good work of the woman who anoints His head, and says it will be told to future ages, because she poured ointment over His body;[4] and those who took care to have His body properly buried are praised. (John xix., 38–42.) But these authorities do not mean or intimate that there is any feeling or sense in corpses, but that they live to God, and such offices of piety are acceptable to His providence as confirming faith in the resurrection of the dead."

Any one who desires to see at a glance the riches of patristic literature regarding funerals, cemeteries, and care of the dead, has only to read the Index of Migne's "Patrology," under the head of "Sepulture." Tertullian, Lactantius and Jerome, Chrysostom, Ambrose and Augustine treat of it; and tell us of the Requiem Masses, and the prayers offered for the souls of the departed; the hymns and psalms sung at funerals; the solicitude of the faithful to be buried in consecrated ground; and the avoidance of all vain pomp, or display, or extravagance in the funeral. Prudentius, the Christian poet, speaks of the custom of decorating the martyrs' tombs with flowers; St. Ambrose, in his funeral oration on the death of Valentinian, alludes to the same custom: "I shall not strew flowers on his tomb, but incense his spirit with the odor of Christ." St. Jerome[5] also refers to the use of flowers at funerals. "Other husbands," says he, "scatter on the tombs of their wives violets, roses, lilies, and purple flowers."[6] Baruffaldi[7] also, treating of the rubric on the burial of children, speaks of the ancient usage of putting a crown of flowers, artificial, if natural ones could not conveniently be found, on the head, not only of dead children, but of all persons who died unmarried, no matter how old they might be, as a sign of their innocence and purity, real or supposed. This soon begot an abuse. Not satisfied with strewing flowers on the tombs of the dead, Christians began to bring them into the Church, and crown the coffin, not only of the child, whose well-known innocence deserved the tribute, but even of sinners who barely escaped damnation by a death-bed repentance. Some

---

[1] The burial of Abraham.   [2] The burial of Isaac.

[3] The burial of Jacob. He was carried away from Egypt and buried in his own selected sepulchre in the land of Chanaan.

[4] "For she in pouring this ointment upon my body, hath done it for my burial." (Matth. xxvi, v. 12.)

[5] Ad Pammach. de obitu uxoris.

[6] It will be noticed that these authorities speak of putting flowers on the graves, not of using them in the Church at funeral Masses.

[7] Commentaria ad Rituale Romanum, p. 275. Venice, 1792.

of the early fathers, like Lactantius, reproved this abuse; and by degrees bishops were obliged to condemn it by diocesan laws.[1] It is indeed very bad taste to crowd the church aisle and load down the coffin with garlands and crowns, and enormous bouquets, symbols of joy, which are out of place among the dirge, the mourning altar, and the sombre vestments of the Requiem Mass.

It would be long to tell of the influence of this Christian respect for the dead, and of Catholic belief in Purgatory, upon the art-life of modern peoples. Dante's " Purgatorio " could never have been penned by a pagan or a Protestant. The requiems of Donizetti, Mozart, and Rossini, and the plaintive wail of the Gregorian dirge, as well as the words and music of the " Dies Irae," are blossoms of Catholic teaching regarding the fate of the dead and the cult that is due to them. Over the tombs of the martyrs were built some of the finest Christian churches. The crypt, often a masterpiece of art, in Romanesque and Gothic architecture, finds its reason of existence in the Christian tomb. The beautifully decorated sarcophagi of the Middle Ages; the " brasses " and enamels on the tombs of the great and illustrious buried in the walls, or under the pavement of the mediæval church, the cenotaphs of marble, of stone, or wood, with angels swinging censers, surrounding the sculptured figure of the deceased, reposing on the marble pillow; tombs like those of the dukes of Brabant, in Louvain, or of Bishop Evrard de Fouillay, in Amiens Cathedral, which he founded; or of Philippe le Hardi, and Jean *Sans Peur*, at Dijon; the tombs at St. Denis, in France, and of Edward III., at Westminster, and of the Black Prince, at Canterbury, England, as well as countless others throughout Christian Europe, attest the piety of the living, and the influence of the doctrine of the resurrection of the flesh, and the communion of saints, upon the art-life of the people. The beautiful chantries, or little chapels, built in the cemetery, or near the tomb, to insure the saying of masses for the souls of the departed, is another fruit of belief in purgatory.

No one who has seen these splendid evidences of Catholic faith on the other side of the Atlantic, and who has examined the beauty of their design and execution, can fail to recognize their superiority to the broken shafts, draped shafts, the senseless columns, topped with capitals and with statues of rich and vulgar nobodies, the pagan nymphs, half nude, modeled by inartistic hands, and the other pagan symbols which characterize the modern cemetery, since the " Reformation." Nor has the hand of the botcher always spared in modern Catholic cemeteries the tomb from the desecrating travesty of the

---

[1] The fourth diocesan synod of New York, held in 1882, condemns the custom of decorating the coffins of adults with flowers, and urges its abolition, as contrary to the spirit of the Church.

Madonna or the Saviour. The invading spirit of revived paganism and its morganatic sister, Protestantism, has intruded, with its pagan symbolism, even into the Catholic " *Campo santo.*" Pagan vanity, a vulgar love of display, show themselves too often in the modern funeral and the modern cemetery, instead of the simple faith and modest hope of the Christian believer.

> " Blest are they
> That earth to earth entrust; for they may know
> And tend the dwelling whence the slumberer's clay
> Shall rise at last, and bid the young flowers bloom,
> That waft a breath of hope around the tomb,
> And kneel upon the dewy turf and pray! "[1]

II. The ground in which the bodies of the faithful are to repose has ever been an object of the Church's special legislation. She has given it the sweet name of cemetery,[2] or dormitory, because, as St. Jerome says, "the bodies sleeping in it are one day to rise."[3] " Lazarus, our friend, sleepeth; but I go that I may awake him out of sleep."[4] So said our Lord of His dead friend; and, imitating her divine Founder, the Church employs the word "sleep" to designate the death of her children. " He fell asleep in the Lord," instead of " he died," is a common form of expression in her liturgy.

In the early ages, any decent place served for the burial of Christians; and during the ages of persecution it was difficult to set apart and bless special cemeteries for them. Yet, even when the cemetery was not specially consecrated, the early Christians, as indeed even the pagans, looked upon the place of burial with religious reverence, and put it beyond the pale of human commerce.[5] But now, and for centuries, a Catholic cemetery is that place alone set apart, and solemnly blessed by the authority of the bishop, for the burial of the pious faithful.[6] This blessing distinguishes and separates the graves of Catholics from the graves of heretics, infidels, and others specifically excluded by ecclesiastical law from the right of Christian burial. " No Christian," says the Roman Ritual, " dying in the communion of the faithful should be buried out of the Church, or cemetery properly blessed; but, if necessity compel, and for some reason the body should be temporarily buried elsewhere, care must be taken to have it transferred to a holy place as soon as possible ' (quamprimum)'; and, in the

---

[1] Mrs. Hemans.

[2] From κοιμάω, to sleep. We have the word and the idea in Homer: " Ενθα τάρος κοιμαθ', ὅτε μιν γλυκὺς ὕπνος ικάνοι." Il., book I., l. 610.

[3] Ferraris' Biblioth., tom. ix., p. 27, Venice, A.D. 1770.

[4] John xi., v. 11.   [5] Grandclaude, tom. ii., p. 387.

[6] " Cæmeteria sunt loca, auctoritate Episcopi benedicta in quibus cadavera Catholicorum pie decedentium sepeliuntur." Reiffenstuel, Jus Can., lib. iii., tit. 28, No. 3.

mean time, a cross should be erected at the head of the grave to signify that the departed rests in Christ."[1] Up to the ninth century, except in very rare cases, no one except bishops, abbots, priests, or pious laymen, could be buried in the church; but gradually this privilege was granted to others, as the clergy saw fit.[2] The ancient place of burial was in the yard or porch of the church, or in ground adjoining it.[3] Most of the civil governments of Europe now forbid burials within the church. Hence, in France, even a bishop cannot be buried in his cathedral without permission of the government. Nor does the Roman Ritual favor the promiscuous burial of bodies in the church,[4] for it says: "Where the ancient custom of burying the dead in the cemetery exists, let it be retained; and where it can be done, let it be re-established." Everything which canonically desecrates a church will desecrate the cemetery, if it be adjoining, and therefore no one should be buried in it after desecration until it has been "reconciled" by a new blessing. But if the cemetery be apart from the church, the desecration of the church does not carry with it the desecration of the cemetery; nor does the desecration of the cemetery, even when it adjoins the church, imply the desecration of the church, "for the less worthy, or the accessory, does not carry with it the principal."[5] Where the same piece of blessed ground is divided into two parts by a wall, the desecration of one part does not carry with it the desecration of the other; the two parts, even though connected by a gate, are canonically considered separate and distinct cemeteries. In many Catholic cemeteries, however, there is no hedge or wall separating the consecrated portion from that set apart for the burial of the unbaptized children of Catholics.

The very important question now arises, who are excluded from Christian burial? The answer is clear in ecclesiastical legislation. Infidels, apostates, heretics, publicly and notoriously excommunicated or interdicted persons, suicides, duellists, public sinners who die impenitent, and sinners who die in the act of committing a crime, if the crime be certain and public. The words of the canon are as follows:[6] "It is decreed in the sacred canons that we cannot

---

[1] St. Cyprian makes it a crime in Martial, a Spanish bishop, to have buried Christian children in profane sepulchres. Ep. 68.

[2] Grandclaude, tom. ii., p. 388. [3] Ferraris, tom. ix., p. 27.

[4] Constantine was buried, according to his own wish, in the vestibule of the Church of the Holy Apostles, at Constantinople. This was contrary to the general usage of the Christians to be buried in catacombs or in cemeteries out of town (Eusebius in Vita Const., l. iv., 60). Theodosius and Honorius followed his example, and were buried close to churches; so that, in the 6th and 7th centuries, the custom of being buried near the church had become common. Hence the meaning of " church-yard."—Dictionnaire des Antiquités Chretiennes—Martigny, Paris, Hachette, 1865, p. 610.

[5] Cap. de Consecr. eccles., in 60 (Decretalium).

[6] Cap. Sacris, 12 de Sepulturis (Libr. tertio Decret.).

hold communion with those dead with whom we could hold no communion while they were living, and that those who have been cut off from the unity of the Church, nor reconciled to her in the hour of death, should be deprived of ecclesiastical sepulture." The Roman Ritual enumerates those who must be excluded from Christian burial: "Pagans, Jews, and all infidels, heretics and their abettors, apostates from Christian faith, schismatics and persons publicly stricken with major excommunication, persons interdicted by name and those living in an interdicted place, while the interdict lasts; suicides, unless it can be shown that they were insane, or unless they give signs of repentance before death; duellists, even if they give signs of repentance;[1] public sinners who die unrepentant, children dying without baptism, and those who are publicly known to have neglected to receive the sacraments of penance and the Eucharist once a year, and who have given no signs of contrition before death." Where there is doubt the bishop or his representative should always be consulted.

There is no part of Church legislation which has been more bitterly attacked in modern times than this regarding the sanctity and exclusiveness of the cemetery. Monseigneur Gaume's pious and earnest book, the title of which is at the head of this article, was prompted by the bitter onslaughts made by French freethinkers on the sacred character of Christian burial. Modern French law, in great part, ignores it. The present " statesmen " of France, instead of trying to bring their country back to the greatness which it lost through infidelity and the last war with Germany, are degrading the name of liberty and of republic, by using them to minimize the influence of, if not actually to destroy, the Church, and are seeking every opportunity to trample on her laws concerning the sanctity of the cemetery. They have secularized and desecrated it everywhere, as they have the school. To such extent has this desecration gone that now, in French cities, it has become a practical necessity for the bishops to leave cemeteries unconsecrated, and for the priests to bless each individual Christian grave when made. In Belgium, also, the so-called "Liberals" have nullified canonical legislation on the subject. Any Belgian magistrate now, ordering a person unworthy of Christian burial to be interred in the unconsecrated part of a cemetery, is liable to be brought before the Civil Court, and fined or imprisoned. "Promiscuous burial" is the freethinker's cry, "and no exclusiveness;" *no "coin des reprouvés."*

It is but a short time since Baron Kervyn de Volkaersheke,

---

[1] The French theologians, following Gousset (Theol. Morale, tom. 2d, 636), permit ecclesiastical burial to the duellist who, before his death, publicly asks for the sacraments. This teaching, however, would be hardly approved at Rome.

burgomaster of Nazareth, near Ghent, for having ordered the corpse of a suicide to be buried in the unconsecratèd part of the grave-yard, was fined and imprisoned for eight days. But the Belgian Catholics, among the most gallant in Europe to fight for their religious rights, are organizing to abolish the present odious law and restore the ancient custom of Christian burial to its proper conditions.

It is with pleasure that an American Catholic turns away from these self-styled liberal governments in Europe,—not excepting England, whose judges in the Guibord case in Montreal gave a decision which overrides all canonical legislation regarding cemeteries,—to admire the good sense and natural equity which breathe through our State laws on this subject. The leading spirits who founded our republic were true rationalists, and believed in the natural law and the natural rights of man. No bitter hatred against Christianity characterized them. Even Paine, although a mere Deist, respected the belief of Christians, and was totally opposed to any interference with the rights and liberties of the churches. A European "Liberal" or "Rationalist" seems to become a demoniac the moment he finds a chance to persecute the Church. Not so with the fair-minded American rationalist. He respects Christianity, and of all the churches he respects most the one which holds to the supernatural in its entirety, and which is alone uncompromising in teaching and practice. It is hard to find a European liberal or rationalist who is not a priest-hater, while the most bitter American rationalist bows to the Catholic priest.[1] The reason of this is, perhaps, because the European freethinker is an apostate, while the American rationalist is simply in a state of negation; he never knew the truth. Be this as it may, American legislation is not anti-Catholic, although it may be sometimes un-Catholic. The rights of American Catholics are respected; their property put on a level with that of other denominations. The greatest amount of personal and corporate liberty is allowed; for it is the true American idea of government that the state shall interfere in nothing which is not absolutely necessary for the common weal.[2] To leave to citizens the largest individual liberty, civil and religious, to trust to their good sense and spirit of obedience to law, not to make them feel that a large-standing army is necessary to keep them in order—this is the American way of ruling. This is clearly seen in the laws regarding cemeteries in nearly all the States of the Republic. Take those of the State of New York, for instance: "Every associa-

---

[1] We know that this is true of "Bob" Ingersoll. It was notoriously true of William Lloyd Garrison, "Thad." Stevens, and is so of nearly all the "Transcendentalists."

[2] There is one exception to this rule, and that is in education. The usurpation of the State in this matter is un-American.

tion (religious or other) incorporated may, from time to time, by its trustees, make such rules and regulations as it shall deem proper for the care, management, and protection of the cemetery lands and property, . . . the conduct of persons while within the cemetery-grounds, to exclude improper persons therefrom and improper assemblages therein, etc., ... to prevent improper monuments, effigies, structures and inscriptions within the cemetery grounds." Further, the rules and regulations of the trustees bind the lot-owners.[1]

Again, "the trustees shall from time to time make such ordinances as they shall think proper . . . . . and may enforce such ordinances by penalties not exceeding $25."[2] Sanction is even given to the custom in Catholic cemeteries, of reserving a portion for unbaptized children, "the trustees shall reserve a reasonable portion of such ground (cemetery) for the interment of strangers and other persons."[3] Such scandals as daily occur in Belgium and France, under sanction of law, in the burial of Freemasons, or persons otherwise under the ban of the Church, in consecrated ground against the will of the Church authorities, could not take place in the State of New York. No burial could be forced in a church here without the consent of its pastor. The scandal of Victor Hugo's funeral, and the consequent desecration of the Church of St. Genevieve, could not take place here. It was laid down as the law by the New York Court of Appeals, in the case of the Buffalo City Cemetery *v.* the City of Buffalo,[4] "that a conveyance for burial purposes only confers upon the grantee a right to use for the purpose of interment. No such estate is granted as makes him an owner in such sense as to exclude the general proprietorship of the association. The association remains the owner in general, and holds that relation to the public. While subject to this, the individual has a right, exclusive of any other person, to bury upon the subdivided plot assigned to him. He holds a position analogous to that of a pew-holder in a house of public worship." He has a privilege, but is not absolute owner.

It was decided by the Supreme Court of New York, that the certificate of ownership of a plot or grave gives a right to use it for burial purposes "subject to and in conformity with the established rules and by-laws of the corporation;" and, "that where a party applies for a burial lot at a cemetery distinctively Roman Catholic, it is with the tacit understanding that he is either a Roman Catholic, and as such eligible to burial therein, or that he applies on behalf of those who are in communion with that

[1] Laws, 1874, chap. 245, § 4.
[3] Id., § 5.
[2] Laws 1874, chap. 209, § 4.
[4] 46 New York Reports, p. 505.

Church."[1]   Thus the State will not force the Church to bury in her cemetery any one whom she considers unworthy.   Now contrast this legislation with that of France.   " When the minister of religion, *for any pretext whatsoever*, refuses to bury a body, the civil authority, either as of right or upon the requisition of the family of the deceased, will call in a minister of the same religion, to fulfil those functions.   In every case the civil authority is charged with the transfer and burial of bodies."[2]   Thus, if a conscientious priest refuses to violate the laws of the Church, French liberty calls in some pliant tool to break them both at the funeral and in the burying-ground.   This is a despotism of which even the most absolute and odious of the Bourbons was never guilty, and of which even Bismarck is not capable.

But although it would be a sin to bury in Catholic cemeteries any of those excluded by canon law, it does not follow that they are desecrated, and require " reconciliation " in the case of every such illegal burial.   Those who knowingly bury in consecrated ground a person nominally excommunicated or interdicted, or a notorious heretic, are excommunicated.   (Bull "*Apostolicæ Sedis.*") By burying others unworthy of Christian burial, sin is committed, but excommunication is not incurred.

If the party buried be excommunicated by name, the cemetery is desecrated.

But the burial of persons not excommunicated by name, or of heretics not denounced by name, does not desecrate a Catholic cemetery.   The law is the same for the desecration of a cemetery as for the desecration of a church.   " If notorious heretics be buried in the church, it is not considered to be desecrated, nor does it need reconciliation "[3]—reblessing or reconsecration.   Notoriety no longer suffices to induce all the effects of excommunication. Since the Bull of Martin V., " *Ad evitanda scandala*," denunciation is necessary for that purpose.   Hence, in places where Protestants and Catholics live together, the burial of the former in Catholic cemeteries, although illicit, does not desecrate them.[4]   Canonists

---

[1] Case of Coppers *v.* The Trustees of St. Patrick's Cathedral, reported in 21 Hun's Reports, page 184, etc.

[2] Art. 19 of 23d Decree of Prairial, year XII.

[3] Ferraris, quoted by Craissón, Jus Can., vol. iii., p. 481.

[4] Grandclaude, vol. ii., p. 397.   In the United States, the Second Plenary Council of Baltimore legislates, that where Catholic converts who own plots in non-Catholic cemeteries die, they may be buried ecclesiastically, and with a Requiem Mass, if their surviving relatives be non-Catholics.   If the surviving relatives be Catholics, and have owned a plot in a Protestant or other non-Catholic cemetery, from the year 1853, their dead may be lawfully buried in it after a private burial service in the house; but no Requiem can be said for them without episcopal permission.   Where Catholics own a family vault, they can bury their Protestant relations in it.   (Dec. S. Cong. Inq., 30th March, 1859, quoted in the decrees of II. Balt. Plenary Council, edition 1875, pp. 202, 203.)

are not agreed as to whether certain other persons, excluded by law from Christian burial, desecrate the cemetery so as to require its reconsecration. In this matter much must be left, especially in this country, to the judgment of the head of the diocese. If, even in the Catholic countries of Europe, it has been found necessary to modify very materially the old canonical requirements in regard to sepulture, as well as to many other subjects, certainly in a new country like the United States, where the Church has never had a true canonical status, much should be left discretionary with the bishop. For experience begins to show that the more of the old canonical legislation we introduce, the less does it agree with our surroundings, or prevent scandals from becoming public.

In concluding this part of the subject we call the reader's attention to the solution of two moral cases in Gury's "Casus Conscientiæ."[1] In the first, a priest goes to the death-bed of a man who for years had refused to receive the sacraments, and who dies unrepenting. No one knows it but the priest. Yet he acts wisely in permitting ecclesiastical sepulture in this case to avoid scandal, for we should not refuse Christian burial to an impenitent sinner unless his impenitence is publicly known.

In the second case, a pious man, but prone to melancholy, is found one morning hanging by the neck, dead. The priest is called in. He hides the fact of suicide, and gives the body Christian burial. He does well, because, as the suicide was secret, it should not be published to the detriment of the man's fame and that of his family. For the law of the Church does not bind in such cases. Besides, as the man was known to be a practical Christian before his death, his taking-off should be attributed to insanity; and when such is the fact, the Church does not exclude suicides from Christian burial.[2]

III. But how stands the Catholic Church in regard to the revival of the pagan system of disposing of the dead—cremation? Can she tolerate it? Is there anything in it contrary to Catholic dogma or the essential discipline of the Church? The answer to these questions is, that the Church could tolerate cremation if she wished. She has the right of eminent domain over her own discipline. There is, indeed, a portion of that discipline of divine origin, and it she cannot change; but all things purely ecclesiastical, having been made by the Church, and those things in which our Lord has not forbidden alteration, can be by the Church modified or abrogated. She has abolished the old system of public penances,

---

[1] Tom. ii., p. 471, Paris edition, 1881. Gury quotes Cardinal Gousset as sustaining his decision in the first case.

[2] Does the private burial of a freemason or of an unbaptized child in a Catholic cemetery necessitate its reconsecration? R. *Scinduntur theologi.*

which prevailed for centuries, and the " Discipline of the Secret," which was the direct opposite of her present mode of dealing with certain portions of the sacred deposit of truth. While the discipline of the secret lasted, the text continually on her lips was, " Neither cast ye your pearls before swine,"[1] while now she says, " that which you hear in the ear preach ye upon the housetops."[2] She repeatedly dispenses in vows, and in impediments of marriage arising from consanguinity. She has abolished the custom of baptism by immersion, which was common even up to the time of St. Thomas Aquinas; and has withdrawn the use of the cup from the laity, and again in certain cases conceded it, in the administration of the Holy Eucharist. In these changes she adapts herself to circumstances, and is prompted always by what is best for the salvation of souls.

As to modifications of the custom and law of inhumation, there are not lacking instances. In the Capuchin cemetery at Rome and at Einsiedeln, the desiccated bodies of the holy fathers are placed above ground and in plain view of whoever wishes to look at them. Is not this an infraction of the custom of inhumation? Again, in Catholic Naples the practice of putting the corpses each day into one of three hundred and sixty-five pits in the old " Campo Santo," and then throwing quicklime on them to burn away the flesh, does not seem to be a literal following-out of the law of inhumation. In case, therefore, a great epidemic should occur, or some extraordinary case might arise which would justify cremation, the Church could and might permit it. When a Catholic dies at sea, he is buried in the water; necessity sometimes abrogates a human law; and great difficulty in carrying them out is always a cause for which the Church grants dispensation from her enactments.

But, having said so much as to the right or power of the Church to permit cremation, the moral question now arises whether, if a dying Catholic wished to be cremated instead of inhumed, and insisted upon *post-mortem* incineration, a priest could give him the sacraments? No! Such a man would not have the proper dispositions for receiving them. He would be in a condition of wilful insubordination to Church law and discipline. He would be asking what the Church refuses to grant. He would be disobeying or asking some one else to disobey the requirements of her sacred liturgy in a very important matter. In a word, although the Church may modify her burial service in certain extraordinary contingencies, it is certain that cremation is contrary to all her traditions and to all her legislation regarding Christian burial.

---

[1] Matth. vii., v. 6.	[2] Matth. x., v. 27.

"The Christians never gave in," says Alban Butler,[1] "to the customs either of preserving the bodies of their dead, like the Egyptians, or of burning them with the Romans, or of casting them to wild beasts with the Persians; but, in imitation of the people of God from the beginning of the world, buried them with decency and respect in the earth where, according to the sentence pronounced by God, they return to dust till the general resurrection."

With the single exception of the cremation of the body of Saul and his sons by the men of Jabes Galaad,[2] to prevent them from further contumely by the Philistines, all the burials of Jewish history, most of which are alluded to in the text of St. Augustine, already quoted from the " City of God," expressly imply inhumation. Even after the cremation spoken of in the first book of " Kings," the men of Jabes Galaad inhumed the bones in the wood of Jabes.

Eusebius gives a reason for the Christian aversion to cremation, which still holds good, because " they (the Pagans) did this (cremated) to show that they could conquer God and destroy the resurrection of the bodies, saying, now let us see if they will arise."[3] It is notorious that the modern revival of cremation as a mode of burial is due to pantheists, materialists and other unbelievers in the resurrection of the flesh.

Even when the pagan Greeks cremated, they deposited the ashes of the dead in a grave, and over it " heaped a high earth mound."[4] Schliemann found at Mycenæ graves of the heroic age, with complete skeletons of both adults and children, showing that cremation was not universal. In early times inhumation was the rule. The grave was dug by the nearest relatives, and the corpse buried in it.[5] Thucydides[6] tells us that the bodies of Athenians who had fallen in battle were put in coffins and buried.

According to Cicero, inhumation was older in Rome than cremation.[7] Some noble Roman families never permitted their bodies to be burned, and Sulla is said to have been the first Roman who ordered his body to be cremated after death, lest his bones should be scattered by his enemies.[8] The pontiffs of pagan Rome would not acknowledge a funeral to be complete unless at least a single bone cut off from the corpse, or rescued from the flames, had been deposited in the earth.[9] It was a pagan superstition that those whose

---

[1] *Lives of Saints*, vol. ii., note to life of St. Callixtus, pope and martyr. London edition, 1833.

[2] 1 Kings, xxxi., v. 12. [3] Hist. Eccl , v. 1.

[4] Guhl and Koner's *Life of the Greeks and Romans*, p. 288, speaking of Homer's description of the burial of Patroklos.

[5] *Ibid.*, p. 289. [6] Book ii., chap. 34.

[7] *De Leg.*, ii., c. 22. [8] Pliny, *Hist.*, lib. vii., c. 54.

[9] *Roma Sotterranea*, Northcote, vol. i., book 2, c. 1.

bodies were left unburied had to wander about for a hundred years. Horace alludes to this belief in the twenty-eighth ode of his first book of songs, in which he represents Archytas as begging the passing sailor for a few handfuls of sand for his unburied corpse.

> "At tu, nauta, vagæ ne parce malignus arenæ
> Ossibus et capiti inhumato
> Particulam dare."

Virgil's lines on the subject are familiar.[1]

The early Christians, like the ancient Jewish patriarchs, ever showed their anxiety to be inhumed according to the Christian liturgy. Sometimes the living Christians tore the bodies of the martyrs from the flames in order to give them proper burial. St. Fortunata gave twenty pieces of gold to the executioner for rescuing her body from the flames and having it put in the earth.[2] The Catacombs were specially dug out by the Christians for burial purposes;. although they had also many graveyards in the open air, set apart from the pagan burying-grounds. The ritual of funerals and the consecration of cemeteries all suppose that the corpse is to be inhumed. All the Fathers, in explaining the resurrection of the dead, speak of inhumation as the only proper Christian mode of sepulture, as it was, in fact, the mode in which Our Lord Himself was buried.[3] Boniface VIII. (in C. I., tit. Sep., Extrav. Comm.) forbade all violent modes of disposing of the dead as savoring of barbarism. "The respect due to the human body requires that it should be allowed to decay naturally, without having recourse to any violent system;" so says Grandclaude, but this reason would seem to hold good against the Neapolitan custom of using quicklime as well as against cremation. A forcible argument against cremation is also found in the Catholic custom of preserving and honoring the relics of the Saints and putting their bodies or portions of them in the altar. It would be no longer possible to have the most important relics of future Saints if their flesh were to be consumed by fire.

The chief arguments in favor of cremation are from sanitary considerations. The cremationists say that inhumation poisons the air, and that cemeteries injure the healthfulness of the neighborhood in which they exist. But if proper precautions are taken, if the bodies are buried deep enough in the soil, as they must be, no danger can arise to the public health from the practice of inhuming the dead. The immense sewers which run through our

---

[1] "Centum errant annos, volitantque hæc littora circum,
Tum demum admissi stagna exoptata revisunt."
—*Æneid*, 6th Book, v. 325, *et seq.*

[2] Dictionnaire des Antiquités Chrétiennes (Martigny, Paris), p. 608.

[3] See Commentaries on I. Ep. ad Cor. xv.

populous cities do not injure health if they are properly built, although decaying refuse and poisonous vapors fill them. Neither can cemeteries properly managed, in which the graves are deep, and which are generally remote from the town or city. Would not the public health be far more endangered if the reeking stench of burning bodies, arising out of crematories on every side, were to pollute the atmosphere? On a moist summer's day, when the winds are still, how long would it take to get the smell of the crematory out of the nostrils of the community? You may put the crematory in the country; but you have no more right to afflict the rustic than you had to incommode the citizen with your nuisance.

De Cavagnis, a Professor of Canon Law in Rome, gives against cremation another argument which is rather striking. "Humation," he writes, "renders it possible to inspect the corpse long after it has been buried, if suspicion of foul play should arise; whilst cremation would give testimony, and then only when carefully done, as to death by poison alone."[1]

This affords, undoubtedly, a good legal argument against the new mode of disposing of the dead, but no such exceptional reason motives the Church's opposition to cremation. It is under her ban, because it is contrary to the letter and the spirit of her Liturgy, and to the universal custom of the Hebrew and Christian dispensation. "*Nihil innovetur nisi quod traditum sit.*"

---

[1] "Crematio ad summum venenii residua ostendit si rite fiat." Institutiones Juris Canonici—Can. Felix Cavagnis, Romæ, 1883, lib. iv., p. 162. As the difference between a medicine and a poison is frequently a mere question of dose, it is not always possible to detect criminal poisoning. Therefore De Cavagnis' exception is not medically correct. Many alkaloids are fatal in such exceedingly small doses that their separation by any process is frequently impossible.

RELATIVE INFLUENCE OF PAGANISM AND CHRISTIANITY UPON MORALS.

History of European Morals. By W. E. H. Lecky, M.A. New York. Appleton & Co. 1879.
The Gentile and the Jew. By J. I. Döllinger. London. Longman & Green. 1862.

M R. LECKY'S work is marked by much erudition. He sincerely aims at being impartial, but is somewhat tinctured with the traditional anti-Catholic prejudices of his country. Like Gibbon, he often betrays an ill-concealed predilection for Paganism.

Dr. Döllinger is a mine of historic wealth. He always exhibits a calm, judicious mind, which commands the admiration and confidence of the reader.

Although unable to close our eyes to the deplorable decadence of morals in this, our day—a decadence over which preceding generations have been equally called to mourn in their own age, —yet the contrast of Pagan with Christian morality cannot fail to result in the triumph of the latter. This thought has led us to place the two in juxtaposition, that the comparison may afford consolation to those who, with only too just reason, grieve for the evils of the times.

I.

We may form some idea of the moral degradation of the Pagan world when we reflect that they had no heavenly ideal of exalted virtue to follow.

The heathen gods and goddesses were monsters of iniquity. Jupiter and Bacchus, Mars and Mercury, Venus and Circe, were the patrons of some particular passion. Every vice was canonized in the person of some divinity. Lust and drunkenness, war and theft, had each its respective patron deity.

The Pagans had a religious worship; but, unlike the Christian worship, it was not intended to exercise, nor did it exercise, any influence on the morals of the people.[1] They had their priests. But what could be expected of a priesthood that offered sacrifice to divinities whose crimes they avowed? The disciples could not be expected to excel their masters; water does not rise above its level. Moreover, moral teaching was not included among the priestly functions. To make man virtuous was no more the business of the priest than

---

[1] Lecky, *History of European Morals*, vol. i., p. 161.

of the physician or the tax-gatherer. The priest was a mere state official.

They had festival days, but they were devoted to debauchery and not to moral growth. They had numerous temples, but they were haunts of licentiousness; the voice of exhortation to virtue never resounded within their walls. They offered sacrifices to Mercury from gratitude for his having made known the knavery and artifices of their slaves, and the slaves offered him the first-fruits of their pilferings.[1] On the festivals of Bacchus prizes were given to the deepest drinkers.[2] In Greece and Rome the worship of Aphrodite was characterized by shameless impurity and unnatural crimes. Shrines consecrated to Venus were maintained at the expense of notorious courtesans. Ovid advises women to shun the temples of the gods, that they might not be there reminded of the lasciviousness of Jupiter.[3]

" It is a matter of general notoriety," says Tertullian, " that the temples are the very places where adulteries are arranged, and procuresses pursue their victims between the altars."[4] In the chambers of the priests and ministers of the temple impurity was committed amid clouds of incense, and this more frequently than in the privileged haunts of sin.[5] Prostitution was practiced as a religious rite in many countries, notably in Syria, Armenia, Babylonia, and Lydia.[6]

If such scenes were enacted in the temples, we may judge of the obscenities of the theatres. The quarrels of the gods, their adulterous gallantries, their robberies and their deeds of violence, were the favorite themes of the plays. The effects of these exhibitions on the impressible hearts of the spectators are vividly described by Juvenal.[7] These representations were witnessed not only by the masses, but also by the Senate and Consuls, and even by the augurs and Vestal virgins, who had special seats assigned to them.

It should also be borne in mind that these popular amusements were regarded as religious acts, forming a part of the public worship. They were intended to appease the wrath of the gods and to propitiate their favor.

What mimic art presented in the theatre was reproduced in paintings on the walls of temples and private houses. Art was made the handmaid of vice. At every step the Greek and the Roman were confronted by lascivious portraits of their divinities. Religion became associated with lewdness in the mind of youth,

---

[1] Pausanias, v. 24, 1.
[2] Trist., 2.
[5] Minutius Octavus, c. 25.
[7] *Sat.* vi., 67.
[3] Döllinger, *The Gentile and the Jew*, ii., 191.
[4] Apol., c. 15.
[6] *Gentile and Jew*, vol. i., passim.

and the impure image was stamped upon the imagination, even before the heart was conscious of the poison it was imbibing.

We need not the pen of a Juvenal or a Tertullian to depict the abomination of Pagan art. A glance at the indecent pictures that have been unearthed from the ruins of Pompeii, reveals a moral depravity which the most prurient imagination can scarcely conceive.

If such were the gods, what must the mortals that worshipped them have been? If such crimes were represented as having been committed in heaven, what infamous deeds must have polluted the earth? If man, by his corrupt nature, has so strong a tendency to glide down the slippery path of vice, what momentum must have been given to his passions by the examples of the gods, of whose excesses he was constantly reminded?" "What means," says Seneca, "this appeal to the precedent of the gods, but to inflame our lusts, and to furnish a license and excuse for the corrupt act under shelter of its divine prototype?"[1]

After having feasted their eyes on wanton spectacles in the temples and theatres, the people hastened to the arena to slake their thirst for human blood. The gladiators must show no mercy to their antagonists; the sooner they dispatch one another, the more they delight the eager and impatient spectators. As soon as one victim has fallen, a fresh combatant enters the lists, till the amphitheatre runs with human blood. Cæsar once brought six hundred and forty gladiators into the arena.[2] Trajan, on one occasion, had ten thousand slaves engaged in mortal combat, and prolonged the spectacle for one hundred and twenty-three days.[3] At another time, Agrippa caused fourteen hundred men to fight in the amphitheatre of Berytus in Syria. These sanguinary contests extended over the empire; they were witnessed by multitudes of both sexes and every grade of society; they served to stifle all sentiments of compassion and to inflame the most fierce and brutal instincts of the human breast. It was the special delight of Claudius to watch the countenance of the dying, for he took an artistic pleasure in observing the variations of their agony.

The revolting practice of disgorging food by artificial means, in order to gratify the appetite anew, was quite general among the upper classes in Rome. Cicero, in defending King Dejotarus from the charge of having attempted to poison Cæsar while he was his guest, incidentally reminds Cæsar, who was presiding on the bench, of having expressed a wish to dispose of his last meal on a certain occasion. Cicero's remark was not intended as a reproach any more

---

[1] *De Vita Brevi*, 16.   [2] Suet. *Dom.*, 4.
[3] Dio Cass. lxviii., 15.

than if he had alluded to Cæsar's having taken a bath or a nap; for he was too dexterous an advocate to irritate the judge.

Juvenal lashes Domitian's gluttony by making the fisherman advise him:

> " Haste to unload your stomach and devour
> A turbot destined for this happy hour."—(*Sat.* IV.)

The same poet thus describes the Roman matrons:

> " All glowing, all athirst
> For wine, whole flasks of wine, and swallows first
> Two quarts *to clear* her stomach and excite
> A ravenous, an unbounded appetite.'' —(*Sat.* VI., Gifford's Trans.)

No president or lady of the land, if known to indulge in excesses so unnatural, could retain the respect of the American people.

The only teachers who might be supposed to have the capacity and authority to instruct the people and to check the current of immorality, were the philosophers. Some of them, indeed, guided by the light of reason, inculcated beautiful and sublime moral maxims; but many causes rendered their influence for good scarcely perceptible among the people.

Their audience was generally composed of a narrow circle of literary men. They shrank from proclaiming their doctrines to the masses for fear of exciting public odium against themselves.

They had no well-defined and uniform moral code, and they were often vague and contradictory in their ethical teachings. They suggested no adequate incentives to the practice of virtue. They never employed the great argument of the Apostle: "This is the will of God, your sanctification." The chief, indeed the only motive they had to offer for rectitude of conduct, was the intrinsic excellence of virtue and the deformity of vice.[1] But experience proves that the beauty of virtue and the hideousness of vice, unless fortified by higher considerations, afford a weak barrier against the encroachments of passion. If love, as they say, is blind to the defects of the lawful object of its affections, wanton love will little heed the repulsive character of the siren charmer.

There was no sanction attached to their moral precepts. They could not say, with the Christian teacher: " The wicked shall go into everlasting punishment, but the just into life everlasting," for they were in a state of lamentable uncertainty regarding a future life. The ablest moralists among them connived at, and even sanctioned by their example, certain violations of temperance, chastity, and humanity that Christianity reprobates.

Plato, "the Divine," condemned drunkenness, but tolerated it

---

[1] Cicero, in his admirable moral treatise, *De Officiis*, has no other inducement to offer for the practice of virtue.

on the feasts of Bacchus.[1]　In his ideal republic he recommends infanticide and community of wives, and declares contempt for slaves to be the mark of a gentleman.　He advocates the merging of the individual life into the public life of the state, by which personal liberty is lost and man becomes but a part of the great machinery of the state.[2]　He congratulates the Athenians on their hatred of foreigners.

The leading philosophers were so much addicted to those unnatural crimes denounced by St. Paul,[3] that parents generally forbade their children to have intercourse with them.[4]　And so low was the standard of morals that the indulgence of this passion was not regarded as reflecting any disgrace on the transgressor.

Aristotle was not free from this vice.　He also approved abortion and infanticide.　He advised the legal destruction of weak and deformed children.　While denouncing obscene pictures, he makes an exception in favor of the images of such gods as wished to be honored by indelicate representations.[5]　He taught that Greeks had no more duties to barbarians (foreigners) than to wild beasts.[6]

Even the wise Socrates, if he is correctly reported by his apologist Xenophon, indulges in a license of speech and conduct that would be tolerated by no Christian teacher of our day.[7]

The elder Cato was noted for his inhumanity to his slaves.[8]　Sallust, who advocated with eloquence an austere simplicity of life, was conspicuous for his rapacity.[9]

Seneca uttered sentiments worthy of the Apostle to the Gentiles.　But, unlike St. Paul, " his life was deeply marked by the taint of flattery, and not free from the taint of avarice; and it is unhappily certain that he lent his pen to conceal or varnish one of the worst crimes of Nero."[10]

To sum up: The standard of pagan morals was essentially low, because the pagans had no divine model held up to them; they had no uniform criterion of right and wrong; the motives presented to them for the practice of virtue were insufficient; no sanction was appended to their moral law; their teachers were limited in their sphere of action; they were often inconsistent in their ethical instructions, and the best of them were stained by some gross vice.

II.

The superior excellence of Christian over Pagan morals is due, first, to the peerless life and example of the Founder of the Chris-

---

[1] *De Leg.*, Lib. VI.
[2] Rep. iv., v., vi.
[3] Rom. viii.
[4] Plutarch, *De Educ. Puer.*, 15.
[5] Pol. vii.
[6] Lecky, *European Morals*, i., 229.
[7] *Mem. Socr.* iii., 13.
[8] Plutarch, *Cato Major.*
[9] Lecky, vol. i., p. 194.
[10] *Ibid.*

tian religion. Our Saviour never inculcates any duty that He does not Himself practice in an eminent degree. No matter how fast we may run on the road of perfection, He is ever before us. No matter how high we may soar, He is still above us, inviting us to ascend higher, as the eagle entices her young to fly. No matter how much we may endure in the cause of righteousness, we find Him laden with a still heavier cross and bearing deeper wounds. He sweetens the most unpalatable ordinances by the seasoning of His example. The beautiful maxims of Plato, Seneca, and Zeno lose much of their savor because their lives were not always conformable to their words. But we have no apology to offer for our Master. He alone is above reproach. He alone can say of Himself: "Which of you shall convict Me of sin?"[1]

"It was reserved for Christianity to present to the world an ideal character, which, through all the changes of eighteen centuries, has shown itself capable of acting on all ages, nations, temperaments, and conditions; has been not only the highest pattern of virtue, but the strongest incentive to its practice, and has exercised so deep an influence that it may truly be said that the simple record of three short years of active life has done more to regenerate and soften mankind than all the disquisitions of philosophers and all the exhortations of moralists."[2]

Jesus taught by example before He taught by words. We are drawn toward Him more by the charm of His life than by the sublimity of His doctrine and the eloquence of His words. The sermons of our Saviour inspire us indeed with esteem for virtue, but His conduct stimulates us to the practice of it. Never did any man speak as Jesus spoke. The most admired discourse that He ever delivered was the Sermon on the Mount. But even the Sermon on the Mount yields in force to the Sermon from the Cross. And if, like the Scribes and Pharisees, our Lord had restricted His mission to the preaching of the word, without illustrating that word by His glorious example, He never would have wrought that mighty moral revolution which has regenerated the world, nor would He be adored to-day by millions of disciples from the rising to the setting of the sun. When asked by the disciples of John whether He was the true Messiah, He laid more stress on His deeds than on His preaching. "Go," He says, "and relate to John what you have heard and seen. The blind see, the lame walk, the lepers are cleansed, . . . the poor have the Gospel preached to them."[3]

When we hear our Saviour saying on the Mount: "Blessed are the poor in spirit: for theirs is the kingdom of heaven,"[4] we are

---

[1] John vii., 46.   [2] Lecky, *European Morals,* ii., 8-9.

[3] Matt. xi., 4, 5.   [4] Matt. v., 3.

impressed with the sublimity of His teaching. But when we *see* Him acting out His words: " The foxes have holes, and the birds of the air nests: but the Son of Man hath not where to lay His head,"[1]—oh, then, we are made to feel the blessedness of voluntary poverty, we cherish and embrace our Teacher, who, when He was rich, became poor for our sake! When we hear Him say: " He that exalteth himself shall be humbled, and he that humbleth himself shall be exalted," we admire the virtue of humility. But when we *see* Him at the Last Supper laying aside His upper garment, girding Himself with a towel, pouring water into a basin, and washing the feet of His disciples, then that virtue assumes for us special attractions. When we hear Him say: " Blessed are the merciful: for they shall obtain mercy," we are delighted with His doctrine. But we are more profoundly moved when we *witness* His compassion for the hungering multitude in the desert, and His mercy shown to the erring Magdalen. When He says: " If you will not forgive men, neither will your Father forgive you," He is clothing an old commandment in new words.[2] But when He prays from the cross for His executioners: " Father, forgive them, for they know not what they do," He gives a sublime lesson of forgiveness never before exhibited by sage or prophet.

When we listen to these words: " Blessed are they that suffer persecution for justice's sake: for theirs is the kingdom of heaven. Blessed are ye when they shall revile you, and persecute you, and speak all that is evil against you, untruly, for My sake," we are in admiration at His doctrine. But when we behold the innocent Lamb Himself accused of being a blasphemer, a seditious man, and a disturber of the public peace, we are consoled in our trials and calumny loses its sting.

Beautiful above the sons of men was Jesus in His glorious transfiguration; but far more beautiful is He to us when suspended from the Cross. The crown of thorns is more comforting to us than the halo that encircles His brow on Mount Tabor.

Our Saviour excels the philosophers as well in His moral teaching as in His personal virtues.

There is not a single principle of the natural law, there is not a healthy moral precept of sages or legislators, nor any commandment of the Decalogue, that is not engrafted on the Evangelical Code; for Christ came not to destroy, but to fulfil the law.[3] The Christian religion appropriates all that is good, preserving the gold and eliminating the dross.

The moral teachings of our Saviour are as much superior to the Jewish law as the Jewish law itself surpassed all the Gentile

---

[1] Matt. viii., 20.   [3] See Ecclus. xxviii., 3, 4.
[2] Matt. v., 17.

moral codes. The Christian religion is more searching, more exacting, more specific in its obligations than the Mosaic legislation. The latter regulated chiefly the exterior conduct, the former guides the movements of the heart; the one forbids the overt act, the other the evil intention; the one condemned the crime of bloodshed, the other prohibits the sin of anger; the one demanded retaliation for injuries received, the other enjoins forgiveness of injuries; the one required us to love our friends, the other bids us love our enemies. "You have heard that it was said to them of old: Thou shalt not kill. And whosoever shall kill, shall be in danger of the judgment. But I say to you, that whosoever is angry with his brother shall be in danger of the judgment. . . . ."

"You have heard that it was said to them of old: Thou shalt not commit adultery. But I say to you, that whosoever shall look on a woman to lust after her, hath already committed adultery with her in his heart. . . . ."

"You have heard that it hath been said: An eye for an eye, and a tooth for a tooth. But I say to you not to resist evil: but if one strike thee on thy right cheek, turn to him also the other. . . . ."

"You have heard that it hath been said: Thou shalt love thy neighbor and hate thy enemy. But I say to you: Love your enemies, do good to them that hate you; and pray for them that persecute and calumniate you:

"That you may be the children of your Father who is in heaven, who maketh His sun to rise upon the good and the bad, and raineth upon the just and the unjust. For if you love them that love you, what reward shall you have? Do not even the tax-gatherers the same? And if you salute your brethren only, what do you more? Do not also the heathen this? Be ye, therefore, perfect, as also your heavenly Father is perfect."[1]

The intrinsic excellence of the Christian moral code is enhanced by its broad and comprehensive spirit adapting itself to all times and circumstances, to all races and forms of government, and sympathizing with every class of society.

Unlike the *national* religion of the Jews, the Christian religion proclaims the law of universal brotherhood. Unlike the sanguinary religion of Mohammed, which subsists only under despotic rule, and which demands the surrender of one's faith as the highwayman demands the traveller's purse, at the point of the sword, the Christian religion flourishes under every system of government, from an absolute monarchy to the freest republic. Unlike the school of the Pagan philosophers, which was restricted to a narrow circle of disciples, the Gospel of Christ is proclaimed to Jew

---

[1] Matt. v., 21–48.

and Gentile, Greek and barbarian, to bond and free. Like the air of heaven, which ascends the highest mountain and descends into the deepest valley, vivifying the face of nature, so has the Christian religion permeated every stratum of society, purifying and invigorating the moral world.

It has a message for the capitalist and the laborer, for the master and the servant, for the rich and for the poor. In the words of St. James, she warns the capitalist against the sin of labor-oppression: "Behold the hire of your laborers who have reaped down your fields, which by fraud has been kept back by you, crieth: and the cry of them hath entered into the ears of the Lord of Sabaoth."[1] She admonishes the laborer to perform his work with fidelity, "not serving to the eye, as it were pleasing men, but doing the will of God from the heart."[2] The most enlightened political economist never formulated a sentence so simple, so comprehensive, so effectual, as is contained in these words: "Thou shalt love thy neighbor as thyself." This principle, if properly applied, would solve every labor problem that perplexes the minds of statesmen.

The Church of God has always admonished the master, wherever slavery exists, to be kind and humane to his slave, reminding him that the Master of both is in heaven, and that He has no respect of persons.[3]

She has brought comfort and sunshine to the wretched home of the slave. She proclaimed his manhood when he was treated as a chattel. She told him there was no dishonor in his chains; that by baptism he was incorporated into the Christian family, and was delivered from the bondage of corruption into the glorious liberty of a child of God.[4]

She charges "the rich of this world not to be highminded nor to trust to uncertain riches, but in the living God who giveth us all abundantly to enjoy. To do good, to become rich in good works, to give easily, to communicate to others, to lay up for themselves a good foundation for the time to come, that they may lay hold on eternal life."[5]

She preaches words of comfort to the poor man. She has exploded the false maxim of the world that estimates a man's dignity by his dollars and his degradation by his poverty. She has declared that a man may be scant in this world's goods, and yet be rich and honorable in the sight of God.[6] She cheers him with the old and familiar but always refreshing story of our Lord Jesus Christ, who, being rich, became poor for our sake, that through His poverty we might be rich.[7]

---

[1] St. James v., 4.   [2] Eph. vi., 6.   [3] Eph. vi., 9.
[4] Rom. viii.   [5] I. Tim. vi., 17-19.   [6] James ii.
[7] II. Cor. viii., 9.

The exposition of practical duty, as we have seen in the fore-going pages, was wholly unconnected with the life of the Pagan priest and the religious ceremonies of the Pagan temple. Happily, the same cannot be affirmed of our Christian priests and temples. As Mr. Lecky justly observes: "To amalgamate these two spheres (of worship and morals), to incorporate moral culture with re-ligion .... was among the most important achievements of Chris-tianity..... Unlike all Pagan religions, it made moral teaching a main feature of its clergy, moral discipline the leading object of its services, moral dispositions the necessary condition of the due performance of its rites."[1] The one great aim of our Christian ceremonial worship, of our Sacraments and Sacrifice, our preach-ing and our priesthood, is the advancement of personal holiness.

The moral power exercised by a good priest in his parish is incalculable. The priest is always a mysterious being in the eyes of the world. Like his Divine Master, he "is set for the fall and for the resurrection of many in Israel, and for a sign which shall be contradicted."[2] Various opinions are formed of him. Some say of him as was said of our Saviour: "He is a good man. And others say: no, but he seduceth the people."[3] He is loved most by those who know him best. Hated or despised he may be by many that are strangers to him and to his sacred character; but he has been too prominent a factor in the civilization of mankind and the advancement of morality ever to be ignored.

The life of a missionary priest is never written, nor can it be. He has nô Boswell. His biographer may record the priest's public and official acts. He may recount the churches he erected, the schools he founded, the works of religion and charity he inaugu-rated and fostered, the sermons he preached, the children he catechised; the converts he received into the fold; and this is already a great deal. But it only touches upon the surface of that devoted life. There is no memoir of his private daily life of use-fulness and of his sacred and confidential relations with his flock. All this is hidden with Christ in God, and is registered only by His recording angel.

"The civilizing and moralizing influence of the clergyman in his parish," says Mr. Lecky, "the simple, unostentatious, unselfish zeal with which he educates the ignorant, guides the erring, com-forts the sorrowing, braves the horrors of pestilence, and sheds a hallowing influence over the dying hour, the countless ways in which, in his little sphere, he allays evil passions and softens manners, and elevates and purifies those around him; all these things, though very evident to the detailed observer, do not stand

---

[1] *Hist. of European Morals*, ii., 2.   [2] Luke ii., 34.   [3] John vii., 12.

out in the same vivid prominence in historical records, and are continually forgotten by historians." [1]

The priest is Christ's unarmed officer of the law. He is more potent in repressing vice than a band of constables. His only weapon is his voice; his only badge of authority his sacred office. Like the fabled Neptune putting Eolus to flight and calming the troubled waves, the priest quiets many a domestic storm, subduing the winds of passion, reconciling the jarring elements of strife, healing dissensions, preventing divorce, and arresting bloodshed.

He is the daily depository of his parishioners' cares and trials, anxieties and fears, afflictions and temptations, and even of their sins. They come to him for counsel in doubt, for spiritual and even temporal aid. If he cannot suppress, he has at least the consolation of mitigating the moral evil around him.

We must not overlook the strong inducements that the Christian teacher holds out to his disciples for the practice of virtue in the pressing motives he offers for its due fulfilment. In this respect Christianity has a great advantage over all other systems of religion. The Stoic was incited to a moral life by a sentiment of duty; the Epicurean, by pleasure and self-interest; the Mohammedan, by the hope of sensual delights; the Jew, by servile fear; but the Christian is drawn chiefly by filial love. He is far, indeed, from excluding other motives. He, as well as the Stoic, is influenced by the intrinsic beauty of virtue and by the enormity of sin which he knows could be atoned for only by the blood of his Saviour. He is actuated in the pursuit of virtue by an enlightened self-interest; for he is taught that "Godliness is profitable to all things, having the promise of the life that now is, and of that which is to come." [2] He is moved by a salutary fear of future retribution. But his predominant motive for the practice of piety is love for his Heavenly Father, and love is the strongest of all moral forces. No one can deny that the devotedness of a child to a father is more tender, more profound, more disinterested, and more enduring than the devotedness of a servant to a master, or of a hireling to an employer. A son obeys his father with more alacrity than a servant does his master; and in disobeying his father, he not only transgresses parental authority, but does violence to the instincts of filial affection.

Now, the Christian Church is represented to us as a family whose *Father* is God, and whose members are His adopted children. "You are no more strangers and foreigners," says St. Paul, "but you are fellow-citizens of the saints and of the household of God." [3] It is only in the Christian Church that God is habitu-

---

[1] *European Morals*, i., 152.   [2] I. Tim. iv., 8.   [3] Eph. ii.

ally appealed to as Father, and that He admonishes us as His children. We never find the ancient Gentile religions nor the Mohammedan people addressing God by the title of Father. And the same can be affirmed of the Hebrew people. We may search the Old Testament from Genesis to Machabees, and we shall not find the name of Father applied to God a half dozen times. He is called Lord, Omnipotent, Master, King, Judge, and Ruler, titles suggesting the reciprocal relations of authority and fear; not in a solitary instance is a prayer addressed to Him under the endearing name of Father.

Not so you, says the Apostle to the Christians of his time, " for you have not received the spirit of bondage again in fear, but you have received the spirit of adoption of sons, whereby we cry Abba, Father. For the Spirit Himself giveth testimony to our spirit that we are the sons of God, and if sons, heirs also." [1] " Behold," says St. John, " what manner of charity the Father hath bestowed upon us that we should be called and should be the sons of God." [2] In addressing our prayers to heaven, what name is more common on our lips than the name of Father, and what prayer is more familiar to us than that most touching and comprehensive of all prayers, the *Our Father?* The name of Father is applied to God upwards of one hundred times in the New Testament, brightening every page and cheering every heart.

What an incentive to virtue is presented to the Christian that recognizes in the moral precepts not only the injunction of his Creator, but also the voice of his loving Father, the Archetype of all sanctity! And what peculiar malice sin should have in his eyes since it is not only an infraction of the law, but also a straining or snapping of those tender ties that bound him to his Father in heaven.

We shall conclude this article by briefly reviewing the moral influence of Christianity on the world at the two extreme stages of its existence—in the first and in the nineteenth century. " It is not surprising," says Mr. Lecky, " that a religious system which made it a main object to inculcate moral excellence, and which, by its doctrine of future retribution, by its organization, and by its capacity of producing a disinterested enthusiasm, acquired an unexampled supremacy over the human mind, should have raised its disciples to a very high condition of sanctity. There can, indeed, be little doubt that for nearly two hundred years after its establishment in Europe, the Christian community exhibited a moral purity which, if it has been equalled, has never for any long period been surpassed." [3]

The primitive Church was not without its blemishes. There

---

[1] Rom. viii., 15-17. [2] I. John iii., 1.
[3] Lecky, *Hist. of European Morals,* ii., 11.

were occasional scandals, divisions, rivalries, envyings, strifes, acts of intemperance, and outbursts of litigious spirit, as is evident chiefly from the first epistle of St. Paul to the Corinthians.[1] The luminous picture of Christian holiness had its shadows, but these shadows were few and far between. They were transient clouds flitting across the moral horizon. Far from dimming, they brought out in bolder relief the brilliant constellation of saints and martyrs that illumined the world.

The Pagans saw with admiration that the Christians, amid the licentiousness and sensuality that surrounded them, preserved their chastity. Like the three children in the fiery furnace, their robes of innocence were not scorched by the impure flames of wantonness that enveloped them. Amid drunkenness and dissipation, they remained temperate and mortified. Amid injustice, rapine, and general self-seeking, they were not only strictly honest and fair-dealing, but they also distributed their goods with a ready hand to their suffering brethren.

While the Pagans fled with horror from the breath of pestilence, the Christians buried their plague-stricken friends, and even their enemies. They surrendered their liberties and their lives that they might ransom or relieve their captive brethren.[2] No wonder that the Pagans exclaimed on witnessing such evidences of heroic charity: "See how these men love one another, how they are ready to die for one another, while we are consumed by mutual hate."[3]

In a word, amidst calumnies, contempt, insults, and persecutions, they were calm, patient, and self-possessed. They extorted praise from their enemies by laying down their lives for their faith not only with sublime fortitude, but with unutterable peace.

This peace was not the stern composure of the Stoic philosopher, nor the cold impassibility of the Mohammedan fatalist, nor the intoxicating delirium of the Epicure, but the serene joy of the Christian believer.

The exemplary lives of the primitive Christians served as a powerful auxiliary to the Apostles and their successors in the conversion of souls to Christ, and in swelling the ranks of the Christian family. The observing public were sensible that a religion which bore such celestial fruits must have been planted by the hand of God. They saw and they believed. The preëminent piety of the early Christians and their influence in drawing men to the Christian fold, are attested by one who cannot be suspected of blind partiality toward the Christian religion. "There has probably never existed upon earth," says Mr. Lecky, "a community

---

[1] I. Cor. i. and vi.   [2] St. Clem. i., Ep. to Corinthians, St. Cypr. Ep., 51.
[3] Tertull., c. 39.

whose members were bound to one another by a deeper or purer affection than the Christians in the days of persecution. There has probably never existed a community which exhibited in its dealings with crime a gentler or a more judicious kindness, which combined more happily an unflinching opposition to sin with a boundless charity to the sinner, and which was in consequence more successful in reclaiming and transforming the most vicious of mankind."[1]

But does Christianity retain its hold on the public conscience? Most assuredly it does. The name of Christ in the nineteenth century, as well as in the first, is the great battle cry of moral reformation. He has stamped His seal on the laws, the literature, the fine arts of the civilization of Europe and America. His voice is ever ringing among the nations of the earth. He has leavened the social mass. His spirit circulates through the veins of modern society. The precepts of His Gospel continue to regulate public morals. He is the Standard by which we approve or condemn our moral conduct. The number of those whose life is influenced by the teachings of Christ has increased a thousand-fold since the days of the Apostles; and though many have ceased to believe His doctrines of faith, they never cease to admire and praise His transcendent ethical precepts and counsels. The aroma of His sweet life still lingers among many who live outside the pale of the Church.

I have no desire to extenuate the gross vices prevailing among us, which are the more reprehensible, committed as they are in the face of an enlightened conscience. But after making every allowance for this moral depravity, it must be conceded by the most ardent admirer of Gentile civilization that the average morals of a Christian community are of a higher standard than were those of pagan Greece or Rome. The obscenities compelled among us to lurk in dark places, were perpetrated by them openly and without shame. The homage that public opinion pays to virtue is such that vice is not permitted to stalk abroad. Cæsar during his campaigns committed, without detriment to his reputation, unnatural excesses of gluttony and lust that would have consigned any American general to public infamy.[2]

Chastity is held in public esteem in Christendom; it was religiously prostituted in Pagandom.

Lascivious paintings and statues that would not be tolerated in any public hall, and still less in a church in this country, were dutifully exposed in Pagan temples as an homage to the gods.

Unnatural crimes which are severely punished among us, were rarely prohibited by law in ancient Greece.

---

[1] *Hist. of European Morals*, i., 424.   [2] Sueton., *Cæsar*, 49.

The profanation of our Christian temples by acts of lasciviousness is unheard of among us; with the Pagans the temples were favorite haunts of lust.

Lascivious dancing is reprobated by Christian ethics; it formed a part of the religious rites among Pagans.

Lucretia was *their* highest type of female chastity. Christianity furnishes innumerable examples of women who suffered tortures and death rather than yield to the aggressor.

The augurs and Vestal virgins could publicly witness the most lascivious plays on the stage, and the butchery of the gladiators in the Flavian amphitheatre, without detriment to their sacred calling.

Imagine our Christian clergy and consecrated virgins frequenting the ballets and low theatres! Could they do so without shocking the moral sense of the people and forfeiting all respect in the community?

It is true, indeed, that the revelations of systematic crime in London, recently made by the *Pall Mall Gazette*, exhibit a state of moral turpitude hardly surpassed by Rome in the days of Nero. But Paganism was helpless to repair the evil. It had no remedial agencies at its disposal, nor any recuperative power to rise from the slough of sin. Its priests were silent. Its purest philosopher, Seneca, connived at, if he did not participate in, the corruptions of the court, and it sank under the superincumbent weight of its iniquity. The scandal of London, on the contrary, is exposed by the press; it is denounced from hundreds of pulpits, and condemned by a healthy public opinion, so that members of Parliament, to screen themselves from public odium, are compelled to vie with one another in enacting laws for the repressing of immorality.

IRELAND'S NEW PROGRAMME.

THE stages of national advance in Ireland are as rapid and interesting as the convalescence of a patient with immense vitality. Perceptibly the voice grows deep and strong, the movements free and deliberate instead of fitful and feverish.

From a manacled rebel in. the dock, defying his. English judge with hopeless heroism, to a national leader of eighty or ninety organized members of Parliament, calmly treating for legislative independence for Ireland, is surely progress enough for twenty years.

The Nationalist Party of to-day represents Ireland—and much more; it is not only national, but strongly international. The foundation stones are the peasants, farmers, laborers,—the natural base; its ranks are filled with mechanics, shopkeepers, merchants, and professional men. It is led by a landlord and a Protestant, who is earnestly supported by the entire Catholic hierarchy and priesthood. It is all that a national movement ought to be in aim, sentiment, and practicality.

For the first time since 1782 all political parties and social classes that are truly Irish are facing in the same direction. The exceptions are the British officials and their dependents, with the Tory and Whig landlords, and the Orangemen. The position of this small but potential minority resembles that of the Northern officials in the Southern States—the "carpet-baggers"—a few years ago; and the resemblance continues when their stability and significance are examined.

There are radicals and irreconcilables in Ireland, of course; but they no longer stand away from and condemn the majority of their more conservative or less hasty countrymen. The revolutionary societies may still keep their organizations intact; but their members are learning a larger and healthier lesson by co-operating in the open agitations under the safe and natural leaders of the country. Michael Davitt has not abandoned his dazzling theory of the nationalization of the land; but he supports it as a proposition in social equity rather than a practical Irish remedy; and his full support is given to the Parliamentary party.

The stages resulting in this condition are peculiarly interesting. The first, and, perhaps, the hardest, thing to be done, was "to compel John Bull to listen." Reason was futile; therefore Ireland invented her odd and audacious means of "parliamentary obstruction," "boycotting," and "no rent;" and England met these tactics with coercion, dragoon-rule, wholesale imprisonment of leading

Irishmen, unceasing police vigilance, arbitrary power in the hands of stipendiary magistrates, and arbitrary power over debate in the hands of the Speaker of the House of Commons.

But while England shook the sword with one hand, she had to offer concessions with the other. Cromwell's method of making silence and quiet in Ireland would hardly do for the nineteenth century—at least, any farther west than India or Egypt. Ireland has an extensive kindred in other countries; and the moral shield of the children probably saved the material head of the mother.

The milestones of Irish agitation are the concessions offered by England within twenty years. She has disestablished and disendowed the Irish Church; she has compelled landlords to make compensation to evicted tenants; she has enacted a law against rack-rents, and appointed commissioners to settle fair rents; she has struck off back rents by the Arrears Act; she has provided employment for the people in time of famine by the Public Works Act; she has offered a sop to the tenant farmers in the Land Purchase Act; she has largely increased the popular vote by the Franchise Act; and retained the full parliamentary representation under the Redistribution Act.

Every one of these reforms was bitterly opposed at first by the English majority; and it is amusing and instructive to turn over the files of the English papers and read the emphatic " Never !" with which each new Irish reform was received.

There was danger a few years ago of Ireland walking into a trap on the land question. It was urged by some honest Irishmen that the land question ought to be settled before the national issue was raised; that peasant proprietors already established would be the strongest supporters of the agitation for a Home Parliament. But the stream of events has been fortunately strong enough to carry the popular will past this seductive opening to the marsh— and the Irish farmers have not mortgaged themselves for life to the English Treasury. The only class now in favor of immediate peasant purchase are the landlords; and in their interest the English Parliament has passed the Irish Land Purchase Act, offering farmers three-fourths, and in some cases the whole of the purchase-money, on a Treasury loan secured by the holding. But the voice of warning has been heard and heeded, telling the farmers that the price of land in Ireland cannot be settled by the arbitrary will of the landlords who want to sell for fifteen or twenty years' rental, but that it has, like all other commodities, a fluctuating market value, the measure of which is the price per acre of American, Canadian, Austrian, and Russian wheat lands, *plus* the cost of freight to British markets. And the farmers are doing what wise men do when they want to get a fair bargain—waiting.

Step by step, through these morasses of local need, Ireland has advanced toward the national issue of Home Rule, successively attaching to the central line all kinds of interests and forces, until it has been recently said that " the Irish parliamentary leader is now, for the first time, also the leader of the whole people "; and that " he is the parliamentary leader only because he leads the people."

On the 24th of August, therefore, when Mr. Parnell announced in Dublin that Ireland had a " New Programme," the utterance was one of profound importance. " A programme and a platform with only one plank," said Mr. Parnell, " and that one, the plank of NATIONAL INDEPENDENCE."

The first question that the world will ask is : What is the meaning of " National Independence," as the Irish leader used, and as Ireland understands the word ? Does it mean absolute separation from Great Britain, and the establishment of a new European nation ?

In one word, the answer is : *No ; it means a union with the British empire, such as Canada and Australia have, or somewhat similar to that which Ireland herself had from 1782 to 1800.*

Ireland's new programme is a demand for true union, instead of subjection. But at the start, it is met by English statesmen, politicians, and demagogues, who desire to prejudice the English masses against it, with cries of " Treason !" " Secession !" and " Dismemberment of the Empire !"

" It would establish within thirty miles of our shores another foreign country," said one of the most powerful Liberal leaders, if not the most powerful, the other day, in a public speech, " a foreign country animated from outside with unfriendly intentions toward ourselves." And he added these remarkable words : " I cannot admit that five million Irishmen have any greater inherent right to govern themselves than would have the five million persons who inhabit the city of London."

In the excitement of this answer the truth was inadvertently told, at least so far as the speaker was concerned : Ireland must either be a subject province or a " foreign country." The pretence of natural sisterhood and fair union is dropped.

If Ireland did want to be " a foreign country," surely " thirty miles from our shores " is a safe and respectable distance—farther than from England to France, and not to be compared to the mere river-and-mountain divisions of contiguous continental nations.

To any but an unprincipled special pleader it is obvious that " five million Irishmen " have the true " inherent right to govern themselves," which the " five million people who inhabit London " have not. The Irishmen have the " inherent right " of a separate country, race, traditions, aspirations. God gave them Ireland, and it is theirs; the English people built London, and it is England's. Such an argument from an English statesman indicates two things: that the English opposition to Home Rule has not a fair arrow in its quiver, or it would fire it at the first attack; and that it will oppose the Irish demand with a malignity equal to its indefensibility.

Not a word has been said by the Irish representatives on which this charge of utter separation could be based. Even radical Irishmen, who would willingly fight for complete independence, have subsided with a self-control that is extraordinary, and to those who know them, pathetic. They acknowledge that it is the will of the majority of the Irish people to test the constitutional method of securing legislative independence, and, this secured, that they are willing to give it a fair trial. The most conservative and the most radical nationalists agree in this.

" The main end for which Ireland needs a native parliament," says Sir Charles Gavan Duffy, " is not to gratify the longing for autonomy, though no wise man will undervalue that sentiment; nor to engage in new political conflicts, but to administer national interests, which have long gone to wreck and ruin. Our resources are wasted, our trade and commerce in decay, and our people, after an exodus extending over forty years, still fly from the country for want of the guardian care of a legislature with adequate knowledge and sympathy."[1]

" With me it is no new theory of to-day or yesterday," said the new Archbishop of Dublin, Dr. Walsh, " but a settled and deeply-rooted conviction that for a remedy of the many grievances for the removal of which the people of this island have so long labored, there is but one effectual remedy—the restoration to Ireland of that right of which we were deprived now nigh a century ago by means as shameful as any that the records of national infamy can disclose."[2]

" Supposing," says Michael Davitt, " that we had an Irish Parliament or National Assembly, say a year, or two years hence, what would be the probable state of parties in such a native legislature? Beyond all doubt, as present indications go, Mr. Parnell would be sent for (let us say, by a new-departure Governor-General of Ireland, like Sir C. Gavan Duffy, for instance) to form a ministry for the rule of the country. Behind such a ministry as the Irish leader would organize there would be all the conservative interests and influences in Ireland—if not in active alliance, at least in friendly opposition, as against any revolutionary party, Socialist or-Separatist, that might possibly have representation. . . . . Mr.

---

[1] Recent letter to the Earl of Canarvon, Viceroy of Ireland.
[2] Speech in response to the address of the Corporation of Dublin.

Parnell was never a revolutionist, while he probably hates socialism as much as any other man bred in the atmosphere of aristocracy. The Catholic Church, which is essentially conservative and opposed to revolution, would be a powerful factor on the side of real law and order, when a state of things should disappear which now compels its bishops and priests to support an agitation policy by which alone justice can be won for their country. The commercial and professional [and landlord] classes might also be counted upon as Nationalist Conservative, while the ' territorial proprietors' and their following would, of course, swell the [conservative] parliamentary forces." [1]

These are the expressions of three Irishmen representing the three chief elements of the national life—the educated upper class, the clergy, and the working people.

Mr. Parnell's outline of the functions and powers of the Irish Parliament distinctly indicates its union with the British Empire. " We shall require," he said, in his speech on August 24th, " *that power shall be given to our Parliament* to do those things which we have been asking the English Parliament to do for us." And he proceeded to enumerate the internal reforms which he had in mind.

Ireland can go before England on this record, and appeal to the popular sense of fair play against the misrepresentations of her enemies.

But there is danger visible ahead in the already half-formed resolution of the Liberal leaders to abrogate all law in Ireland, and answer the national agitation with a brutal "" No!" They recognize the necessity of doing this in time, or of yielding. Ireland holds the winning cards, and must win, if the constitutional game be allowed to proceed. To avert further concern, the Irish representatives will have to " outsail and outpoint " the governmental statesmen, and carry their case directly to the English people. They will be listened to by the millions; and they will be supported by some of the ablest and best men in England. They need not use their own words even; let them cry out in the burning sentences of noble Englishmen like William Howitt: " From age to age they [the Irish people] have been insulted, trodden on, thrust out of their own soil and their own offices, and taunted with being ' alien in blood, language, and religion.' Great God!" continues this Englishman, " what business had we there? What business had we with their lands, their churches, their endowments? If we went as Christians to convert them, were violence and robbery and injustice the means? If we went to rule them, was it to be only by insult and slaughter? If we went to bind Ireland to Britain as a sister, was it to be only as

---

[1] In Dublin University Review for September, 1885.

an erring sister, whose fortune is to be flung into the streets and frowned on in her misery? In whatever character we *pretended* to go there, our eyes full of vengeance and our hands full of chains and plunder, betrayed us to the whole world as thieves and hypocrites." [1]

No Irishman has ever told the shocking truth about the " Irish " Parliament that voted the Union, in 1800, more fully than the latest English historian, Walpole, who calls it "the Parliament of the English Colony in Ireland." " It was never," he says, " in any sense, representative of the nation. It was the corrupt embodiment of a dominant race. It sold the birthright of a nation for its own selfish end." [2]

But the vote of this " corrupt embodiment " will be the base of the English statesmen's argument against the Irish party in the coming struggle. They have no other ground to stand on. The tactics practiced to carry the Union by Castlereagh will, in all probability, be used again. Appeals will be made—we see them already begun—to the selfishness and timidity of the English trading, shipping, mining, and manufacturing classes. As before, these will be told that Irish competition means ruin. Cowardly and wicked though this statesmanship be, its practical success may be read with disgust in the history of the Irish penal and anti-trade laws as told by Lecky and other historians of the eighteenth century.

The outlook is this: There will be an immediate demand of the landlords and officials in Ireland for a renewal of the Crimes Act; they are already organizing for this end. The Liberal party, in retaliation for Parnell's support of the Tories, will favor this movement, or at least appear to do so. There is little doubt that the Liberals will carry Great Britain at the coming general elections: the two million new voters will settle it. But, regardless of English parties, Ireland will have at least 80 Home Rule members in the next Parliament. Ireland's struggle is going to be with the Liberal party, and the business interests of the middle class is the stone in the sling of the leaders. The Tories have done their work; they are on quicksands for their own land-owning aristocratic existence. If Ireland can get any help from them as she climbs the hill, she may use them; but she would be fatuous to depend on them, except for a breathing spell.

Should the Liberal party meet the Irish demand in the spirit of Mr. Joseph Chamberlain's words, above quoted, and should that policy be adopted by the Government, Irish representatives will be face to face with a great danger.

---

[1] *The Aristocracy of England*, pages 272-3.
[2] *A Short History of the Kingdom of Ireland.* By Charles George Walpole, M.A.

Now, as in '98, the question would be settled for England if Ireland could be provoked or excited into violence. O'Connell, in 1843, declared that he had it on the authority of Lord Chief Justice Bushe and Plunket, and on that of the Parliamentary Committee's report in 1798, that the rebellion of that year "had been fomented by the English Government to hasten the Union." Could Ireland be goaded into such another outburst of despair, the trouble would be laid, for a generation at least, by a brief and bloody repression and a long period of disfranchisement. But there is not the least fear of general violence in Ireland. There is no need even for threats of organization for violent ends. This is what exasperation and injustice are meant to evoke. Ireland has a strong position at home, and she has representatives enough abroad to "see fair play" among the outside observers of the contest. She knows from experience that while England fights, tooth-and-nail and insolence, she knows when to yield. No country ever recognized the limit of her own interests more clearly.

In 1782, under an Irish pressure less than one-tenth of that now in movement, England granted to Ireland precisely what that country now demands—legislative independence. The scornful speeches of English leaders up to the moment of that yielding might have been stereotyped for such men as Mr. Chamberlain. Yet all the scorn and opposition vanished or were withdrawn when the Duke of Portland announced that the Government intended to concede the Irish demand of Parliamentary Independence. That announcement was far more unexpected then than would be Mr. Gladstone's or even Mr. Chamberlain's to the same effect two or five years hence.

"I understand," said Henry Grattan, when the announcement was made in the Irish House of Commons by the Viceroy, "that Great Britain gives up, *in toto*, every claim to authority over Ireland—everything is given up unconditionally."

"Great Britain in 1782," said Burke, "rose above the vulgar ideas of policy, the ordinary jealousies of State, and all the sentiments of national pride and national ambition."

Grattan and Burke admitted too much, but the Irishmen of the present day are standing on their experience. Disfranchised Ireland under the Protestant Parliament of '82 was one thing; the Ireland of to-day, with its far-reaching moral force affecting England from all sides, is quite another. What Ireland gained in 1782, her Government held; what she gains now, her people will hold, and without fear of losing. Ireland has measured and recorded the English statesman's "Impossible!" and she knows that Lord North's in 1781 had at least as much significance as Mr. Chamberlain's in 1885.

Ireland's winning policy will be still one of agitation, peace and patience. Her enemies will play for passion; they will inflame the pride, prejudice, and cupidity of the English business element. But if Ireland's dispassionate answer be always ready—that she does not propose to dismember but to strengthen the Empire; that she only demands a chance to be loyal instead of disloyal; that she only wants to take care of her own neglected and ruined internal interests, like an American State in relation to the Federal Government; that she wants peace, prosperity, and friendship instead of revolution, poverty, and hatred.

That Ireland will have to pass under the rod once more before she succeeds, we greatly fear. That the Crimes Act or some such form of coercion will be passed by the next Parliament seems more than probable. It will be the last clutch of the dominant faction—the convulsion of the landlord class. But if Ireland can be hopeful and steadfast in this last trial, if she will not look upon this concluding evil as the first of a hopeless series, the end of her unhappiness is not far off.

The past twenty years ought to encourage her for future exertion and patience. She has come heart-whole to the present emergency. At the head of her forces to-day, as in the 12th century, shine the mitre and crozier; and no other struggling Catholic country but has sent its wise guides to the rear. A thousand years ago, when King Malachi defeated the Northmen, the faith of Ireland was not purer nor more fervid than to-day—yet those thousand years have been for Ireland a gulf of war, conquest, pillage, ceaseless rebellion and outrageous re-conquest.

Ireland to-day is stronger than ever. A marvellous political if not ethnological problem is the moral unity and devotion of her exiled children and their descendants to the third and fourth generation. A century ago, England had reduced the Irish to about 4,000,000 people, and they were nearly all in Ireland, disfranchised, disinherited, unrepresented, friendless, voiceless. To-day, it is safe to say that between 30 and 40 millions of people respond to the rise or fall of the Irish barometer—a force as great in number as England's own, and greater in its scattered moral influence. Organization has its opposing and mastering force in disintegration, when the atoms contain and continue the argument for justice. In Great Britain, the United States, Canada, South America, Australia, Africa, New Zealand and other British Colonies, there are millions of native citizens who feel and acknowledge their Irish blood and sympathies. The English statesman who would ignore this fact is shortsighted. The Irish race, bound by its traditions, beliefs and hopes, has at present a singular strength, and for the British Empire a tremendous progressive significance.

THE TRUE IDEA OF THE BEAUTIFUL.

Sancti Thomae *Opera*. Migne, Paris.
Æsthetik. By Reverend Joseph Jungmann, S. J. Herder, Freiburg.
1884.

TO our knowledge, all who can justly claim the title of æstheticians agree that the object of the fine arts is the *beautiful*.
Every true work of art, whether it presents itself to us in solid
matter, in color, in sound, or in language, is a representation of the
beautiful in external form. The first question of the critic, therefore, must always be: Is the object which pretends to be a work
of art really beautiful; and, if so, why is it beautiful? The most
fundamental question in æsthetics, then, is: *What is beauty; or,
what constitutes an object beautiful?* This question is not new.
It is as old as philosophy. It occupied the minds of Aristotle,
the prince of Greek philosophers, and of the "divine" Plato;
and with it Socrates delighted to puzzle his flippant friends.
Taking for our guide the few principles which can be gleaned
from St. Thomas as bearing on the subject, and the excellent
work of Father Jungmann, referred to at the head of this paper,
we shall endeavor, if not to give a fully satisfactory answer, at
least to establish some principles, from which a sufficiently probable solution may be obtained for the vexed and vexing question
of the definition of beauty.

First, however, we may be allowed to make a passing remark
on the learned work before us. Among the numerous monu-
mental works of eminent Catholic writers published in Germany
for the last twenty years Father Jungmann's *Æsthetik*, in our
opinion, deserves a very high place, as it cultivates a field so far
little explored by Catholic writers. And while the eccentric
theories of German pseudo-æsthetics are being plagiarized and
gradually carried into English and American literature and
thought, it would be very desirable that learned Catholics of
English tongue, who would have reliable information on the
subject, should turn their attention to this truly classical work, in
which the wild dreams of extravagant æsthetes are not only
solidly refuted, but a sound system of criticism is established on
the unshaken principles of true philosophy and the great models
of Christian as well as pagan art. The author, who combines an
exquisite taste formed by the prolonged observation of the best

works of art at Rome and elsewhere, with the most extensive reading of ancient and modern literature, has been for more than twenty years professor of Æsthetics and Sacred Eloquence at the University of Innspruck, Austria; so that few might be said to have had such an opportunity of gaining a complete knowledge of the subject he treats. We will not, however, make the learned author responsible for all the opinions proposed in this paper, but we wish them to be taken for what they are worth from the evidences on which they are based. We shall even venture to differ from him in details of some importance.

Before attempting to build up a definition of the beautiful we shall make a brief review of those theories which, in our opinion, are utterly untenable. Though the science of *æsthetics* or *criticism* is of comparatively recent date, it has already, like the mother science of philosophy, undergone a complete series of metamorphoses, until at last it is presented to us as a philosophical structure reared upon the very unæsthetic basis of that melody wherewith our saurian grand-dams of old were wont to woo our semi-human grandsires in the primeval forests of the tropics. To such a degree have men "become vain in their thoughts."

The first among modern writers who has given a full treatise on the beautiful was *Edmund Burke*, the great orator and statesman, who in philosophy was a pronounced sensualist. In his juvenile essay on the "Sublime and Beautiful" he develops a theory, incidentally sketched by Addison in the *Spectator*, regarding the beauty of species, and extends it to beauty generally. According to Burke's views "beauty is some quality in bodies acting mechanically on the human mind by the intervention of the senses"; hence a material and sensible quality. "Beauty acts," he says, "by relaxing the solids of the whole body." "A beautiful object presented to the sense, by causing a relaxation of the body, produces the passion of love in the mind." We refrain from quoting the descriptions and illustrations of this process of relaxation, which are plastic almost to obscenity. From all his reflections on the beautiful it is manifest that he considered it as something merely *material*, that acted only *materially* on *material* organs and produced merely sensual effects, the sensual passion of love. The reader is much disappointed when he comes to a section headed, "Of Beauty," in which he expects to find the subject defined, but is only informed that beauty is the exterior quality of the sex which determines sexual love to one in preference to another—a denotion which would have amused Socrates no less than that given by his friend, Hippias, when in his perplexity he answered that "a fair maiden was beauty." In fact, every intelligent admirer of the truly great Edmund Burke must sincerely regret that he ever wrote the treatise on the "Sublime and Beautiful." However, if we may judge from his other works, and particularly from a brilliant and affective tribute which he paid to a fair but unfortunate queen, we may justly conclude that his better feelings corrected in practice those perverse principles which false philosophical theories had taught him. Had he clung in practice to his sensual theory of beauty, he never would have uttered the oft repeated sublime and thrilling complaint that the "days of chivalry are gone."

The English sensualistic theory of Burke was soon after introduced into Germany by *Baumgarten* and built up into a science, by him first called *Æsthetics* (Æsthetica). The very name itself (αἰσϑάνομαι, αἴσϑησις, αἰσϑητικός) signifies sensitive impression, and Baumgarten defines "æsthetics, or the theory of the liberal arts: the science of sensitive perception." His disciple, *G. Friederich Meier*, true to his master's teaching, declares that every "perfection perceived by the senses is *a beauty*, and every sensible imperfection in like manner is *an ugliness*." And for illustration he adds: "Wine tastes *beautifully* and flowers smell *beautifully;* music sounds *beautifully* and a handsome face looks *beautifully*." In the same sense Burke makes smoothness an essential element of beauty, and informs us that "sweetness is *beauty to the taste*." The German æsthetician *Lemcke*, building on the same principles, goes still farther in the development of this sensualistic theory and identifies the beautiful simply with the sensual, the immoral, in its grossest manifestations. In reference to the degeneracy of paganism he says in his "Popular Æsthetics": "The decline of *moral life* began to make itself conspicuous. *Æsthetic life* stifled it by its *sensual* influence (*sinnliches treiben*). Sensuality suffocated morality. All dreamt only of pleasure and *æsthetic* enjoyment." He then goes on to describe the struggle of Christianity against "*æsthetic* enjoyment, the world of the beautiful and sensual pleasure," treating these three antagonists of Christianity as synonymous, and winds up with the complaint that in Christianity the beautiful was disparaged or even transferred to the supernatural and the Deity—a complaint which is both unhistorical and, as we shall have occasion to show, unphilosophical.

This sensualistic theory of the beautiful comes very convenient to modern evolutionism. For, if beauty is and always was a mere object of sense, they are freed from the difficulty of explaining why we have a sense of beauty while our undeveloped ancestors had none. Æstheticians of the sensist school, on the other hand, gave a hearty welcome to the theory of the ape as a firm basis for their sensual system. *Berg*, the most recent of German æstheticians, tells us in all seriousness that "the theories of Darwin have thrown a clear light on the origin of beauty." "Through the results obtained by Darwin," he says, "we have finally arrived at a scientific theory of the beautiful." One flash of this "clear light" may suffice to enlighten the reader of its marvellous character. Berg, speaking of the æsthetic pleasure of music, informs us that the first object of vocal notes was to facilitate the association of the sexes. "Musical notes and melody have been applied by our semi-human ancestors at the time of mating. Now, as this musical courtship had been instinctively practiced for many generations, so the singing and hearing of musical sounds have been subsequently associated with now gentler, now more violent, pleasurable feeling, always arising from the passion of love." "The melody peculiar to some species of female apes has been more recently invented(?) as a means of decoying the male of the species." When we read such sublime nonsense uttered with the greatest composure in the name of science, philosophy and good taste, we feel disposed to exclaim with the prophet: "Woe to you that call evil good and good evil; that put darkness for light and light for darkness; that put bitter for sweet and sweet for bitter. Woe to you that are wise in your own eyes and prudent in your own conceits." While such theories find favor with critics we need not wonder that the bulk of our modern so-called polite literature is not only amatory in its character, but sentimental and sensual in the worst sense. So far have we come that the prejudice is almost universal that no literary composition written for entertainment, be it tragedy, comedy, or tale, can put any claim to artistic beauty unless it have an amatory plot.

Thus our English sensism and evolutionism have been exported and distilled in the alembic of German philosophy and are again contrabanded and vended in spicy doses for our æsthetic edification. A reaction, though not a healthy one, against those sensualistic theories has been brought about by the *idealistic and pantheistic* schools. "Schelling," we are told by an admirer, "has taken a new departure in æsthetics. For him it was reserved to give to the science of the beautiful an absolute basis. According to him we are to define beauty: The identity of the infinite and the finite, of the ideal and the real, of necessity and freedom, contemplated in sensible form." He throws a new incubus of impenetrable speculation on the subject, when he tells us that "wherever the individual (the real) is so congruous with the idea that the idea itself enters the real and is contemplated in the concrete, there beauty is to be found." These terms, we are told, contain a truth which deserves to be "treasured up" for the science of æsthetics. They are, doubtless, a valuable keepsake in a philosophical curiosity-shop. They have been "treasured up" by the followers of

Schelling, have obtained currency in text-books, encylopædias and other ponderous works. They have been admired even by Catholic authors and adopted after being stripped of some of their pantheism. One of the latter formulates (Schelling's idea) thus : " The beautiful is the manifestation of God in His creatures"—the Divine idea "expressed, made visible or audible in a work of art." This proposition enunciates truth, though somewhat vaguely.

Peculiar is the theory of *Schiller*, and it seems to have been a favorite idea of Herder, Lessing, Goethe, and other German poets and æsthetes of that humanistic school. According to Schiller, beauty is the combination of the *ideal* and the *real*, or the harmony between matter and form. Whence, as this harmony is to be found preëminently in man, he concludes: " The beautiful is identical with the *human.*" Therefore, *man alone* is truly beautiful; all inferior objects and the pure spirits are beautiful only metaphorically or by the appropriation of human qualities. *The human,* therefore, is not only *a* beautiful (object), but *the* beautiful. The ideal of the beautiful is woman. Thus we see that while the pantheism of Schelling changes the infinite God into finite sensible nature, the idealism of Schiller idolizes finite man and transforms him into the infinite God.

While sensualism, pantheism, and idealism have been thus indulging their morbid and phantastic reveries, there were not wanting Catholic philosophers who, following the principles of Plato, Aristotle and St. Thomas, and the doctrines of the Fathers of the Church, taught and wrote more correctly on the subject of the beautiful. Our great theologians, treating of the attributes of God, did not fail to enter fully into the nature of beauty as far as it was necessary to illustrate the beauty of Him who is the fountain of all beauty.

Cardinal Toledo, in his commentary on the "Summa" of St. Thomas, says : " Beauty, generally speaking, consists in a certain order and interior arrangement of the perfections of an object. Hence an object is called beautiful in reference to the intellect and to our perception ; for it is the function of the intellect to delight in order, as it is the function of the will to delight in good."

St. Francis of Sales, in his treatise on the " Love of God," almost adopts the words of the Angelic Doctor, St. Thomas: " Though beauty and goodness," he says, " coincide to a certain extent, they are, nevertheless, not quite identical, for the good is that which appeases the appetite and the will, the beautiful that which pleases the understanding and the mind."

Cardinal Pallavicini, in his work entitled " Del Bene," writes: " The beautiful, in my opinion, is nothing else in reality than a special kind of the good, which in virtue of its intrinsic excellence produces an agreeable apprehension of itself in the eye of the intellect."

Father Rogacci, on the "One Thing Necessary," defines beauty as a quality which renders the object in which it resides agreeable and delightful to the cognoscitive faculties.

Leibniz, who, though a Protestant, was eminently Catholic in his philosophic principles, gives a similar definition. According to him, beauty is the perfection of things which, inasmuch as it is apprehended, affects us with pleasure. This pleasure produced by the perception is its distinctive mark.

Another definition very popular among Catholic writers, attributed by some to Plato, by others to St. Augustine, is " *Splendor veri.*" It appears, however, that this definition is not to be found in the works of either of these authors. And though it were genuine, we think it would not throw much light on the subject in question. Others love to define beauty as " *multiplicity or variety in unity and unity in multiplicity;* " but this definition, too, is vague, and, at most, enunciates some attributes of the beautiful.

The first Catholic writer (abstracting from those Germans who have based their theories on pantheistic and idealistic principles) who has written an exhaustive treatise on the beautiful was *Father Taparelli, S. J.,* one of the shrewdest and profoundest thinkers of modern times, who, in the years 1859 and 1860, contributed a series of masterly articles on the Beautiful to the *Civilta Cattolica,* which were subsequently published in book form. Proceeding from the definition of St. Thomas, *Pulchra sunt quæ visa placent,* he conceives beauty primarily as the object of the cognoscitive faculties; and the beautiful as that the perception of which generates satisfaction, pleasure, delight in the same faculties. He then goes on to inquire into the causes of this pleasure and comes to the result that it is produced by the *conformity* of the objects with our various cognoscitive faculties, intellectual and sensitive.

He sums up his theory as follows: " Beautiful is that the contemplation of which delights, gives pleasure. Now, human perception is complex and comprises four grades. The first is sensitive perception. The various sensations are then concentrated in the interior sense; thence the imagination receives its representations, and from the imagination reason by its peculiar activity abstracts general ideas. The combination of these four degrees of perception forms the complete cognoscitive faculty of man. This latter complex faculty will consequently obtain complete satisfaction when each of the partial faculties finds its adequate share in the contemplation of the object, and when, moreover, each separate faculty contributes to give the supreme act of the intellect its completion, enabling it to move the will to proper action. Whence it is manifest that beauty, though its natural end is the repose of the cognoscitive faculties, is destined by the Creator to facilitate right action.

" From these considerations it is not hard to define the proper essence and nature of that beauty in which the cognoscitive faculty may find its satisfaction. We have only to consult reason and experience as to what objects are congenial to each of these faculties, on the one hand, and, on the other hand, how these four grades of perception act in harmony to produce that complete satisfaction in the apprehending subject.

" With regard to the tendency of the perceptive faculties, the *exterior sense* requires beauty of tone (whether in color or sound), clearness of manifestation, variety and order of form in the object as to space and time (symmetry and rhythm). The *interior sense* is the more delighted the more numerous are the sensations which the exterior senses supply from the individual objects. The *imagination* creates new representations by combining and disposing the impressions received according to the wants of the percipient subject, and gives form and life to the complex beautiful object. Finally, *reason* is satisfied when all these mutual relations, taken together, and the order of their mutual relations to each other, present it convenient matter from which to form true, definite, affective, and touching representations.

" Beauty, then, is nothing else than the relation of the object to the sensitive perceptive faculties, and of these faculties again to the intellect. . . . . Beauty in nature, as in art, consists always in this: *that the perceptive faculties find satisfaction both by the right relation of the object to them and their relation to one another, with a view to the end of perception, i.e., rational action.*"

The doctrine of Taparelli, which we could not give briefer or clearer than in his own words, has been adopted by most of the subsequent Catholic philosophers. Father Jungmann, however, feels himself obliged to depart from the teaching of the Roman philosopher, insomuch as the former maintains that the pleasure derived from the contemplation of the beautiful has its seat not in the cognoscitive faculties but in the will, and consists in *perfect love* or, as he prefers to call it, *love properly so-called* (eigentliche Liebe) in contradistinction to love improperly so-called (uneigentliche Liebe) or imperfect love. This is a distinction common in theology between *amor rei propter seipsam* and *amor rei propter aliud;* the love of an object for its own sake and the love of a thing for the sake of something else. Thus we love health for its own sake (love properly so-called), medicine for the sake of health (love improperly so-called). Taking pleasure in this sense of love properly so-called, Father Jungmann defines beauty " *the intrinsic goodness*

*of things, inasmuch as it renders them fit to be the object of compla-
cency to the rational mind* (Geist)."

Father Taparelli and his adherents, as we have seen, admit that
the contemplation of the beautiful is productive of love, and thus
" facilitates rational action"; but they deny that this love constitutes the essence of that pleasure produced by the beautiful. This
pleasure is perfected in the cognoscitive faculties; the attraction of
the will, or the love which thence arises, is only concomitant or
consecutive, the fruit of the intellectual complacency.

This great variety of discordant definitions, even among the profoundest Catholic philosophers, is an evidence of the difficulty of
the enterprise. The reason of this difficulty is obvious. First,
beauty, like truth and goodness, being a transcendental quality
and an analogous notion, does not admit of a *strict* definition *per
genus proximum et differentiam specificam*, as philosophers term it;
as there is no *genus* in which it can be said to be contained as a
species. Like truth and goodness, therefore, it can only be described in its relation to the faculties of rational nature. Here
again a new difficulty arises. While truth is defined in relation to
the perceptive faculties, and goodness in relation to the appetitive,
of which faculties they respectively form the proper object, the
question is, to which of those faculties shall we refer that attribute
or relation which we call beauty? To the rational or to the sensitive faculties? To the perceptive or appetitive? Or to the
partial or entire assemblage of the faculties of rational nature?
And if the latter obtain, whether coördinately or with a certain
subordination of the inferior to the superior? Of what faculty or
faculties is beauty the proper object? This question "makes
cowards of us all." And yet this is the gist of the cause, in our
opinion. He who will answer this question to evidence will, we
think, have obtained the necessary results for a satisfactory definition of beauty. We cannot here attempt a final solution of this
question, but will give it due consideration in the course of our
brief analysis of the idea of beauty.

All are agreed that beauty is that quality of objects which *pleases
the contemplator,* or, put more universally, *the apprehending subject.*
" The fact that *the beautiful pleases* us," says St. Chrysostom, " has
been, ever since the creation of the world, the cause why we distinguish the beautiful from the vulgar or ugly." And St. Augustine says: " Are you not seized with *pleasure* when you behold
the universe? *Why?* Because the universe is *beautiful.*" The
same has been the teaching of the stoic school of philosophy, as
well as of Socrates, Plato, and Aristotle, whose doctrine St. Thomas
reproduces in various places, when he declares those things to be

beautiful which please the contemplator (*quæ visa placent*).[1] The same, as we have shown, is the teaching of Toledo, Pallavicini, St. Francis of Sales, Leibniz, Rogacci, and Taparelli, as well as of the sensualists and evolutionists, and it is admitted by modern æstheticians generally, however they may differ among themselves. The effect produced by the contemplation of the beautiful is well illustrated by the conduct of St. Peter, when, after beholding the glory of the Saviour in the transfiguration on Tabor, he in his ecstasy exclaimed: "*It is well to be here;* here let us build three tents." Now, that quality of objects which produces this pleasure is called beauty.

But may not this quality be something merely apparent, subjective? The variety of contradicting tastes would seem to indicate this. What one calls beautiful another calls ugly; and what is an object of delight and love to one, is the cause of disgust and abomination to another. As little as the eye creates, extenuates, or modifies the brightness of sun, moon, and stars, so little do subjective views and tastes add to or detract from the beauty of objects. Whether it is realized and appreciated or not, it continues all the same to be a *constant, real, inherent* quality, which will not fail to be rightly perceived and justly apprized as soon as it is brought to bear on sound and well-disposed cognoscitive faculties. The denial of the objective reality of beauty would imply the negation of the objectivity of all perceptive qualities. Beauty, therefore, is *something real*, part and portion of the objects to which it is attributed.

If we further inquire whether this quality which we call beauty is a sensible or an intelligible one, we must come to the conclusion that it is *intelligible only*, i. e., a simple quality that can be apprehended not by sense, but only by reason or intelligence. Sense perceives a material object that is beautiful, but the perception of beauty *as such* is the exclusive function of the intellect. This is the teaching of St. Thomas. In his commentary on the work of Dionysius, "De Divinis Nominibus," discussing the proposition of the Areopagite that beauty is the same as goodness, the Angelic Doctor distinguishes as follows: "Though goodness and beauty are the same in the subject (the same reality), they are, nevertheless, different in their relations; for beauty adds something to goodness, to wit, the relation to a faculty cognoscitive of beauty *as such*." But the perception of a quality *as such*, according to the terminology of St. Thomas, is the peculiar function of the intellect, not of sense. Besides, an essential feature of beauty in external objects, according to Aristotle and St. Thomas, is order and symmetry. Now, according to all sound philosophy and familiar

---

[1] See *Sum.*, P. I, q. 5, a. 4, ad I.

experience, these are qualities that can be perceived only by the understanding or reason. The same conclusion follows from the fact that things spiritual and moral, which transcend all sensitive perception, and are the object only of reason and intelligence, as well as material things, are termed, and, as we shall show, actually are, beautiful. Therefore St. Augustine concludes: "Though many beautiful objects are *visible, yet that beauty itself whereby they are beautiful is by no means visible.*" Cicero, the Roman interpreter of Greek philosophy, says: "No other animal (but man) perceives the beauty, grace, and symmetry of sensible objects."

Though beauty as such is an intellectual quality, yet, like truth and goodness, *it is also an attribute proper to sensible objects.* For who has not been struck with the beauty of the starry firmament, or the glory of the sun, when he goes forth at morning as the "bridegroom from his bridal-chamber," or goes down at evening into his golden couch? Who can contemplate the sea, whether it dashes its crested waves on the hollow-sounding beach, or reflects the azure sky from its glassy surface, without being enraptured by its beauty and grandeur? Who is insensible to the beauty of the landscape, varied with the numberless tints and hues of blossom, flower, and foliage, now expanding its rich waving fields to the eye, now furrowed with hill and dale, enlivened with the music of the rippling brook and the sweet carols of a thousand vying song-sters? Who can resist the power of music, when it rushes in solemn sweeping accords from the "deep-laboring" organ or the rich human voice, and rolls in mighty volumes along the vaults and aisles of some sacred edifice? Then we forget ourselves, and seem to be rapt into some earthly paradise and say: "It is well to be here."

Yet the beauty of sun, moon, and stars, of heaven and earth, sea and land, with the gracefulness of the human frame, that masterpiece of divine workmanship, the sweet notes of music, and the charming imagery and rhythm of poetry, all the ideal creations of plastic art, are only a dim reflection, a shadow or an echo, of the beauty of the unseen, the spiritual, and supernatural. *The unseen is the proper region of the beautiful.* All the beauty of this visible world, and all those forms which human imagination can create, are, as it were, a handful of pearls taken out of the treasury of the spiritual and supernatural world, and strewn by the Creator's hand into a world of tears. This was the teaching even of pagan philosophy. "He who wishes to proceed rationally," says Plato, "must consider the beauty of the soul more excellent than that of the body." And again, Socrates prays: "O Pan, and all ye other gods of the place, grant that my soul may be beautiful and that my exterior may accord with my soul!" Plotinus, after summing up the various objects that are considered beautiful in the visible world, adds: "The beauty of the soul, which consists of all manner of virtue, is a more real beauty than that of the objects above mentioned." And Cicero asserts that the wise man is truly beautiful, "for," he says, "the features of the soul are more beautiful than those of the body." "Could we but see the soul of the virtuous man," says Seneca, "how beautiful, how venerable, how resplendent with majesty and gracefulness would she appear to us!" The same is the teaching of the Holy Ghost, when He exclaims: "How beautiful is a chaste generation with glory!" We might quote the grandest passages from the Holy Fathers, who never cease to impress upon the faithful that all true beauty is "from within," has its seat in the soul and not in the exterior form; and exhort them to appreciate, cultivate, enhance this true interior spiritual beauty. "If a man wishes to be beautiful," says St. Clement of Alexandria, "let him adorn the soul, which is the most beautiful of man, and make it wax more beautiful from day to day." This argument the Fathers are wont to urge most frequently and forcibly on the fairer sex. "Not with the tints of delusive art should they embellish their faces," says the same Holy Father. "We will teach them another more rational art of decorating themselves. The hightest beauty is the interior, as we have often said, when the Holy Ghost adorns the soul and diffuses His light upon it. Justice, prudence, self-control, love of whatever is good, modesty—the loveliest tint ever beheld—these are true ornaments. In their hearts they should wear their ornaments; by the beauty of the inward man they should commend themselves; for *in the soul alone is the seat of beauty and ugliness.* Therefore the virtuous man alone is truly beautiful and good."

Such is the teaching of philosophy and faith on inward beauty; and, in fact, it requires a considerable amount of degeneracy to make a man insensible of its attractions. The look of innocence, though residing in the most ordinary exterior, without the slightest ornament of art, is more attractive than the most fascinating exterior form; while outward graces, whether natural or affected, shrouding inward corruption, are alike abominable to God and man. Nay, we do not hesitate to say that material objects can be called truly beautiful *only inasmuch as they are capable, through the instrumentality of the senses, to lift up the mind to the contemplation of h gher spiritual beauty*, to transport it into the proper region of beauty, the unseen. It is not the exterior delineations, the various hues and shades of color, that the true critic considers in a work of art; it is rather what is implied than what is expressed; the invisible and untouchable, not what can be seen, heard, and grasped; the *idea* rather than the material *form*.

Not all the objects of sense, however, are capable of effecting this intellectual elevation, but only the objects of the more perfect of the senses, which approach nearer to the immaterial—*sight* and *hearing.* Though the objects of smell, taste, and touch are sometimes qualified in language as beautiful, yet this must be pronounced as either an abuse of the term or, at least, an analogical or metaphorical use; for the organic affections produced by such objects of sense are little or nowise subservient to higher ideas, but are merely animal both in nature and tendency. Wherefore St. Thomas rightly considers it unphilosophical to call tastes and smells (to say nothing of the grosser sense of touch) beautiful.[1] Hence, if we speak of a beautiful viand, we must attribute beauty to the skill displayed in dressing it; if of a beautiful perfume, we speak from the analogy of the sensation to that produced by really beautiful objects; while to the object of touch, as such, we never give the predicate of beautiful, no matter how smooth and soft it may be. In this regard Edmund Burke fails not only against sound philosophy, but also against good taste, when he makes smoothness an essential element of beauty, and calls sweetness beauty to the taste.

We do not deny, however, that these inferior, sensible qualities, smoothness, sweetness, etc., in some cases add intensity to the effects of beauty, inasmuch as they give *agreeableness* and sometimes gracefulness to really beautiful objects; but those qualities do not enter the strict notion of beauty, and, if abounding to any great extent, they will only obscure and mar the effects of real beauty by appealing too strongly to sensuality, and thus impeding the free operation of the higher faculties, whose proper function it is to apprehend, and contemplate the beautiful. It is this intensity of sensation, to which nature is viciously inclined, which makes so many mistake the sensually agreeable for the beautiful, and mere animal passion for genuine sentiment and true love. This error has always been and still is the most powerful agent for the perversion of good taste, and the most prolific source of false sentimentality, in the writing and reading world, and, we might say, in the whole domain of art.

Though the proper seat of the beautiful is the unseen and spiritual, yet in our present composite state it is the sensible that makes most impression on us. Our knowledge of things proceeds from the senses. These are the portals through which truth is brought home to the higher faculties. The intellect, though independent of the imagination in its nature and existence, is, in our present state, dependent upon it in its operations. Hence, our minds can

---

[1] See *Sum.,* P. 1–2 ae., q. 27, a. 1, ad. 3.

rest with ease only upon such truths as have corresponding or kindred representations in the imagination. Therefore there can be no poetry without imagery, and all the arts consist in representing ideas, intellectual or moral, in sensible form. Poetry and art, in general, are only an expediency invented by nature herself to bring truth and goodness home to us in a way suited to our natural imperfection. The pure, separate spirits do not require the medium of exterior form for the contemplation of spiritual objects. They apprehend and contemplate them directly, and yet there is no doubt but they realize and enjoy the beautiful in a much higher degree than we do, with all the parade of imagery and sensible representation. The fact, therefore, that we cannot rest with pleasure on mere speculative or transcendental objects is only incidental to our present composite nature, and *does not argue*, as some think, *that only the sensible is beautiful.* On the contrary, the more truth and goodness recede from the material, the more perfect they are, and, consequently, the more beautiful. The apparent lack of beauty is in our manner of apprehending them. Nay, as we shall see, it is a canon of æsthetics as well as metaphysics, that the more simple, immaterial, spiritual, an object is, other conditions being equal, the more beautiful it must be pronounced. On this principle might be based the scale of beauty as well as that of perfection.

From the considerations thus far made, it may be established that *beauty is a simple, intelligible quality, which, though residing in sensible and intellectual things, has its principal seat in the latter as in its proper subject.* If we now further inquire into the cause of that pleasure which is produced by the contemplation of the beautiful, the only reason which can be assigned for it is *the special conformity* of those objects which are called beautiful *with rational nature.* Wherever the mind is brought to bear on an object that reflects its own perfections in a greater or lesser degree, it will be found to rest upon that object with a complacency proportioned to the degree in which its own perfection is expressed in the object, provided it be presented to it in a manner congenial to its nature.

With regard to sensible objects, it is a common experience that the mind rests with pleasure on such as exhibit life, activity, movement, regularity, order, aptitude, completeness, simplicity, unity with variety combined, symmetry, harmony, durability, strength, firmness, light, brightness, perspicuity, etc. The more these qualities are combined in due order and proportion, and presented in any object, the greater will be the complacency with which the mind will rest in its contemplation. Now, what is the cause of this complacency? We can find no other than the special conformity of such objects with the mind, or with rational nature. The living, simple, spiritual, intellectual, ever-active, imperishable mind sees in such an object its own image and likeness.   And, if ever, surely here the axiom attains : *Simile simili gaudet.*

It would lead us too far if we endeavored to show in detail the special analogy of those objects which are considered beautiful with rational nature.   That our views on this point, however, may not seem new, we may be permitted to give some authorities from ancient philosophy in confirmation of our assertion.   " The beauty of exterior objects," says Plotinus, " strikes us at first glance.   Our minds, as soon as they perceive them, are affected with pleasure. They embrace them as something they recognize.   The mind becomes, as it were, one with beauty ; but, if it perceives some-thing ugly, it shrinks from it, disowns it, refuses to recognize it ; because *an ugly object does not harmonise with it*, is foreign to it.   This fact," he continues, " we explain as follows : The mind is, of all things, the most perfect.   Now, if it perceives some-thing which is *akin to*, or has even a trace of *kindred* with, itself, it is filled with joy and rapture."   Thus, the same philosopher explains the beauty of light, color, brightness, from their like-ness to the spiritual mind of man.   *Gold* was considered by the ancients as a natural symbol of the spiritual soul and its perfections and moral excellence, on account of its simplicity, purity, and durability.   Hence, the Neo-Platonist, Hierocles, says : " Gold is something pure, not mixed with dross, as other bodies.   Where-fore we justly attribute to the holy, pure and innocent soul the name of *golden.*"   In fact, the more the spiritual is exhibited or symbolized In material objects, the more beautiful they are and the greater intellectual enjoyment they afford, a circumstance which can be attributed only to their special conformity with rational na-ture.   We may add that the same doctrine is set forth by St. Thomas.[1]

Let us further examine in what this conformity of the beautiful with rational nature consists.   There is only a two-fold relation of conformity possible—with the understanding and the will.   There is no third imaginable.   Now, to which of these two faculties does the beautiful, as such, address itself ?   Notwithstanding the author-ity and arguments of the learned author before us, we are still in-clined to the opinion that this conformity of the beautiful to rational nature, primarily at least, consists in its relation to the intellect. Our reasons are the following :

First, St. Thomas, as often as he speaks of beauty in its relation to rational nature, clearly intimates that it is the object of the cog-noscitive faculty, not of the appetitive, and thus draws the distinc-

---

[1] See *Sum.*, P. I a, q. 5, a. 4, ad 1.

tion between beauty and goodness, that a thing *is called beautiful in order to perception; good, in order to appetite or desire.*[1]

Secondly, many of those qualities which we call beautiful, though they belong to the objective constitution of beings and form part of their intrinsic goodness, yet, in that precise regard in which they are beautiful, seem to be the objects of the understanding, not of the will. Such, for instance, are order, proportion, rhythm, harmony, variety, etc. We are unable to perceive how the sound of music, or the rhythm of poetry, or the exterior proportions of an edifice, or a certain blending of colors, can be the object of love or desire, except as far as their perception affords *delight to the understanding*.

Thirdly, it is a common experience that very many are charmed by the intuition of beauty, without being to any degree ethically affected. Thus, the voluptuary admires the beauty of virtue and innocence, but is not drawn beyond their fruitless contemplation. The infidel cannot but appreciate the beauty of the Christian Religion and Christ's Church, while he reviles and persecutes both. In fact, it is a characteristic phase of modern infidelity that many who would flatter themselves that they are Christians, are satisfied with the mere æsthetic aspect of Christianity, without embracing the substance; whose Christianity, in other words, is merely intellectual or speculative, not practical; a matter of taste, not an object of the will or desire. Hence, we find infidel poets and artists not rarely seeking their inspirations from Catholic subjects and ideals, while they openly profess their disaffection to the principles and practices which they cannot help admiring from an æsthetic standpoint. Now, if æsthetic pleasure had its seat in the will, and beauty addressed itself mainly to this faculty, such æsthetes, of whom there is a considerable number, who are deliberately disaffected to almost all that essentially constitutes the beautiful, could never be said to realize the pleasures of the beautiful. Their will would be continually at war with itself, " a house divided against itself, a Beelzebub casting out Beelzebub." Such a contradiction exists, indeed, in many, but not to the extent of excluding the essential enjoyment of the beautiful, which would be the case if beauty were the object of the will.

We do not, however, maintain that beauty affects the intellect only. It is, primarily, the object of the understanding, but, *secondarily, the object of the will*. The will is naturally moved to desire or abhorrence, to love or hatred, of every object that is brought home to the intellect, and, as the intellect apprehends a special conformity in every beautiful object, the will cannot but be

---

[1] See *Sum*, P. 1 a, q. 95, a. 4, ad 1; P. 1–2 ae, q. 27, a. 1, ad 3; P. 2–2 ae, q. 125, a. 2, ad 1; *In lib. Sent.* 1, d 31; q. 2, ad 4; *In Dion.*, cap. 4, lect. 5.

more or less strongly affected, according to the degree of conformity apprehended, and the degree of intensity with which it is apprehended by the understanding. Beauty is, therefore, preëminently a *cause* and a most powerful *motive of love;* and the enjoyment of the beautiful is but very imperfect, if the will cannot adhere to it while the mind contemplates it. It is only when the will, as well as the understanding, finds its rest in the beautiful object, that the measure of æsthetic pleasure is full. Every beautiful object, then, we must conclude, is lovable ; but it is not its lovableness that renders it beautiful in the first instance, but its special conformity with the intellect, whereby its lovableness is more forcibly brought home to the will.

If we proceed to inquire into the *ultimate cause* of this special conformity of beautiful objects with rational nature, we must needs come to the Divine Intellect and Essence Itself. Things are conformable to rational nature inasmuch as they are conformable to their prototypes in the Divine Intellect. These divine ideas have different degrees of conformity, according to the various grades of perfection with which they represent the Divine Essence. The more perfectly, therefore, an object represents the divine perfections or shadows forth the image of the Creator, the more conformable it is to rational nature, the most perfect likeness of God's own Essence ; and, consequently, the more beautiful it must be said to be. This consideration led Father Patavius, one of the sublimest intellects of his time, to define beauty simply " the conformity of an object with its ideal or prototype." " Beautiful," he says, " is that the perfection of which gives us pleasure because of its close conformity with its ideal or prototype." Though this definition is deficient in precision, it expresses a truth which leads us to the very fountain and ultimate cause of true beauty—the conformity of objects proximately with the divine ideas, and ultimately with the Divine Essence. The Divine Essence is the last and highest norm of beauty as of truth and goodness. It was the image and likeness of His Essence that God saw in His creatures when, contemplating them after the creation, He pronounced them to be good (καλά). Hence St. Thomas says : " The beauty of the creature is nothing else than the likeness of divine beauty communicated to things."[1] If we then discover a conformity with our rational nature in beautiful objects, and rest with pleasure in their intuition, it is because they bear the likeness of Him to whose " image and likeness " we have been moulded in creation as the most perfect expression of His Divine Essence.

From this conformity of beautiful objects with the Divine

---

[1] In *Dion.* cap. 4, lect. 5.

Essence we may determine the *scale of beauty ;* the source and fountain of all beauty—substantive beauty without mixture of imperfection—is *God,* the incomprehensible Truth and Goodness. From Him emanates, as from its exemplar and efficient cause, all beauty in the material and spiritual, natural and supernatural order. Must not He Himself, then, possess in an infinite degree that beauty which He has so liberally communicated to His creatures ? And as beauty is an unmixed perfection, which implies no imperfection, must not God possess it in its truest sense ? As God is infinite truth and goodness, therefore, so He is unspeakable beauty—that only beauty which can fill every understanding, and satiate every will; and that not only for a brief instant, but for all eternity. In Him alone rational nature can find absolute and perpetual rest, never-ending enjoyment and consummate happiness.

"No man is so stupid," says St. Gregory Nyssen, "as not to perceive as a self-evident truth, that the substantial, primordial, and only true *beauty,* splendor, and goodness is no other than God, the Lord of all things." We might also largely quote Pagan philosophy in proof of this statement.

Equal to God in beauty as in substance is His *Only begotten Son,* the true "figure of His substance and splendor of His glory," who, clothed with our humanity, was "fair above the children of men." "Our Redeemer," says Clement of Alexandria, "is so beautiful that He alone deserves to be loved by us who can love nothing but true beauty. He is the true beauty, for He is the light." "The prophet calls the Redeemer glorious in His beauty," says St. Basil, "considering His Godhead. It is not His external beauty that he celebrates, for we have seen Him, and there was no comeliness or beauty in Him. His exterior was without charms and unnoticeable before the children of men. It was manifestly by the divine love of the invisible glory that the prophet was charmed when he contemplated its splendor, when its rays were shed upon him and its beauty enraptured his soul. Whenever this beauty is revealed to the heart of man, it finds everything that it has hitherto loved ugly and contemptible. For did not the Apostle reckon everything as dirt to gain Christ after he had contemplated Him glorious in His beauty ? "

Next to the Son of God in beauty stands that woman whom He had chosen before all ages to be *His mother.* She is the blessed among women, full of grace, the first fruit of creation, the mother of beauteous love, all fair without spot or stain. She who goeth forth like the rising dawn, fair as the moon and beautiful as the sun ; the woman clothed with the sun, and the moon under her feet, and on her head a crown of twelve stars ; the great ideal to whom all true artists have looked up for inspiration. Need we wonder that she has been for eighteen hundred years the constant and inexhaustible theme of song and the grandest object of painting, sculpture, and architecture? Where is the true master-poet, painter, or sculptor, who has not plied his genius to glorify her beauty?

Second to Mary, the mother of God, and Queen of Heaven, are those holy *Angels and Spirits* who have been admitted to the presence of God in His heavenly courts, and who are " like to Him because they see Him as He is."

If we turn from the mansions of glory, the heavenly Jerusalem, and descend to our own orb, there we find highest in beauty the *Church of Christ,* His mystical body, the perfect image of the heavenly Jerusalem, that city built on unshaken foundations on the holy mount, His immaculate spouse, whom He has " cleansed to Himself in the laver of water in the word of life, that He might present her to Himself a glorious Church, not having spot nor wrinkle nor any such thing, but that she might be holy and without blemish." Here we find all the elements of true beauty, unity, multiplicity, harmony, brightness, purity, spirituality, supernatural and divine life, etc., a heavenly beauty which consists not in, but is only symbolized by, marble structures and golden and silver vessels, and rich apparel, and sweet incense, and gorgeous ceremony.

In the beauty of the visible world, *man,* created to the image and likeness of God, doubtless occupies the first place. In him we distinguish two different species of beauty: the one exterior, common in kind with that of other animals, though of a much higher order; the other internal or spiritual, which, as we have shown, far transcends the former. The exterior beauty of man consists in form, stature, symmetry, complexion, life, activity, gracefulness, etc.; the interior, in his intellectual and moral endowments and accomplishments, especially in the supernatural array of the sanctified and virtuous soul. Both these species of beauty, as the whole composite nature of man, coalesce into one. Ordinarily speaking, the exterior of man, if taken in its entirety, gives a fair picture of the interior, intellectual and moral character. The Holy Ghost Himself gives testimony of this fact. " A glad heart maketh a cheerful countenance." " The heart of the wise man shall instruct his mouth and shall give grace to his lips." " The wisdom of man shineth in his countenance." " The attire of the body and the laughter of the teeth and the gait of the man show what he is." St. Clement of Alexandria on this point says: " Even the beauty of the body is nothing else but virtue, which is visible in the features, and pours out its grace upon them; it is nothing else than the loveliness of innocence, the goodness of the heart, which transfigures the face of man. No one doubts that the beauty of animals consists in that perfection which their nature requires. What makes man perfect is justice, wisdom, fortitude, and the fear of God. *Beautiful,* then, is the wise, the just, in short, the good man." These sublime qualities of the soul once manifested, and they cannot remain long concealed, will throw a halo of beauty over the most ordinary form that will far transcend any degree of outward charms; while a fair exterior cannot long cloak the hideousness of a corrupt heart, which, when once revealed, will only be the more disgusting from its contrast with the pleasing exterior form. Nothing creates a more implacable disgust than outward tinsel, especially when it makes pretensions to reality.

From this view of personal beauty it will be evident to the reader how grossly the majority of our novel writers err against good taste when, pandering to passion and vanity, they luxuriate in hair-splitting descriptions of the female form. The truest description of real beauty we have met, we believe, has been that traced by the genial pen of Cardinal Wiseman in his " Fabiola." The subject of the picture is the angelic figure of St. Agnes. " When Lyra turned to leave the room, she was almost startled at seeing, standing in bright relief before the deep crimson door-curtain, a figure which she immediately recognized, but which we must briefly describe. It was that of a lady, or rather a child, not more than twelve or thirteen years old, dressed in pure and spotless white, without a single ornament about her person. In her countenance might be seen united the simplicity of childhood with the intelligence of maturer age. There not merely dwelt in her eyes that dove-like innocence which the sacred poet describes, but often there beamed from them rather an intensity of pure affection, as though they were looking beyond all surrounding objects, and rested upon One, unseen by all else, but to her really present and exquisitely dear. Her forehead was the seat of candor, open and bright with undisguising truthfulness ; a kindly smile played about her lips, and the fresh, youthful features varied their sensitive expression with guileless earnestness, passing rapidly from one feeling to the other as her warm and tender heart received it. Those who knew her believed that she never thought of herself, but was divided entirely between kindness to those about her and affection for her unseen love."

Tracing the image of the Creator in nature, we find three degrees of perfection, and consequently three grades of beauty. The highest of these is the animal kingdom, in which life, spontaneous locomotion, and sensation are added to material organism and vegetation. The second is the vegetable world, which is endowed with organic structure and the inferior functions of life, but bereft of sense. The lowest in the line of beauty, as well as perfection, is brute nature or matter. We do not contend that in nature always the degree of beauty coincides with that of perfection ; but that, other conditions being equal, the greater their perfection the greater their beauty, *i.e.*, if they possess in a prominent manner those attributes which render them conformable to rational nature, or more expressly bear the imprint of the likeness of the Creator. Anything that disturbs this conformity, or obscures this imprint, renders them less beautiful, however perfect they may otherwise be. This fact may be illustrated by comparing the horse and the lion with the elephant and the bear. Every one will pronounce the horse more beautiful than the elephant, and the lion more beautiful than the bear, not because one is more perfect than the other (for each is perfect in its own species), but because the one has those qualities which assimilate it to rational nature, the other lacks them. For this very reason many objects are standing symbols of certain mental and moral excellences or defects, according as they show forth a conformity or difformity with perfect rational nature. Thus the dove symbolizes simplicity ; the lamb, innocence ; the eagle, nobility of soul ; the lion, magnanimity ; the violet, modesty ; the lily, purity ; while, on the other hand, the peacock is the representation of vanity, the owl and the ape the symbols of intellectual and moral deformity. This symbolism may also be traced in the material world, as in gold, iron, fire, water, oil, salt ; various figures, colors, and sounds. It is well known how extensively the Church in her liturgy makes use of these allegorical significations of objects and actions ; and even Christ has availed Himself of this natural symbolism in His teaching and miracles, as well as in the institution of His sacraments. This symbolic meaning of things is by no means arbitrary or conventional, but is altogether based on the conformity or difformity of material or visible things with spiritual or rational nature, which is the foundation on which beauty and ugliness are based.

From what we have so far said the reader will perceive that we do not admit any *real*, but only a *logical distinction*, grounded in subject, however, *between beauty, truth, and goodness.* Beauty is nothing else than truth and goodness so presented to rational nature that it may discover in them a special conformity to itself, and thus rest upon them with a pleasure worthy of, and congenial to, a rational being. Hence truth, metaphysical, logical, and moral (where there is question of a historical fact), as well as goodness, physical and moral, form the necessary substratum of the beautiful ; for rational nature, if acting rationally, must necessarily shrink from anything that lacks these fundamental attributes. Whence it follows that whatever is untrue, unreal, inconsistent, unsubstantial ;

whatever is immoral in itself, in its adjuncts, or consequences, no matter how gorgeous, imposing, and attractive the garb may be in which it is clothed, cannot be called beautiful. It is only ignorance, prejudice, or passion that can attribute beauty to mere outward show without substance, or with a vicious substance.

If we now finally try to establish a *definition* of the beautiful, or of beauty, on the principles thus far established, we must say that *the beautiful is the true and the good so constituted as to bear a special conformity to rational nature, and thus afford congenial pleasure to the higher rational faculties.* The abstract quality of beauty may accordingly be defined : *The objective truth and goodness (or reality) of things so constituted as to render them in a special manner conformable to rational nature, and thus apt to afford congenial delight to the superior faculties of the rational contemplator.*

The patient reader, who has so far accompanied us in our investigation, may now ask : Is, then, everything beautiful ? Shall we call the ape and the toad and the bat and the grasshopper and the rattlesnake and the crocodile, and the many species of noisome vermin that creep and swim on our globe, beautiful ? All these have their objective reality, truth and goodness; are conformable as well with their prototypes as with rational nature, and may, consequently, according to our definition, claim to be beautiful. The same difficulty urges itself upon the young novice in metaphysics, when he is first surprised with the proposition : *omne ens est bonum.* The first thing he asks himself in blank amazement will be : " Is, then, Old Nick himself good ? Are the mosquitoes *good ?* " To this question we answer that everything, inasmuch as it has objective truth and goodness, has some real beauty, if we could only perceive in it all its bearings. Were we not restricted to the use of organic faculties in the perception of material objects, we would, undoubtedly, apprehend some beauty in all God's creatures proportioned to their objective reality, and reap a corresponding pleasure from their contemplation. God, when He created them, " saw that they were good," and was well pleased. Could we but see them in that same divine intellectual light, we would willingly, and without repugnance, indorse the judgment of the All-wise Creator, and say that they are good. The reason why we pronounce some things simply ugly is, that their conformity to our rational nature, though actually existing, is so obscured by seeming or real difformity, that it is feebly, if at all, brought home to our minds. The conformity of beautiful objects with our rational nature must be such that we can easily apprehend it without laboring to abstract it from numerous imperfections or difformities. If the difformity of an object with our rational nature, whether real or apparent, is preponderant or striking, so as to overcast its beauty, we call it simply ugly, or not beautiful, no matter how much objective perfection it may conceal beneath its repulsive form. Another reason why we call many objects ugly, is the fact of their being disagreeable to sense. But disagreeableness is by no means incompatible with true beauty. The practice of virtue, or death for a noble cause, is naturally disagreeable to sense, though, doubtless, beautiful and sublime.

A further fact that seems to militate against our explanation of the beautiful is the natural aversion of most men to the contemplation of metaphysical or abstract truths. This fact, as we have already hinted, has its cause in our composite nature, and consequent imperfect manner of apprehension through the instrumentality of sense. Hence we contemplate abstract truths of the sublimest character without being in the least æsthetically affected; but let the magic pen of Dante, Shakespeare, or Milton, only touch them and clothe them in the imagery of poetry, and we rest upon them with unspeakable delight. And yet, if we ask ourselves what the poet has added to those truths, which seem to us to be " airy nothings," we find that it is only " a local habitation and a name "—a " habitation" but too narrow to contain their substance, and a " name " that expresses but half their meaning. The poet lends nothing to truth by his imagery, but only subtracts from it through his inability to give it full expression. His sole work is to bring truth home to us in a way that is more congenial to our imperfect nature, by a direct appeal to the senses and the passions. Truth itself eminently contains all the beauty and charms of poetry, as soon as it is brought to bear on a mind which, in its perfection, can dispense with the expedient of imagery. Hence all goodness and perfection are beautiful, and that in the same degree as they approach the infinite goodness and perfection.

As beauty consists in a conformity with rational nature, so *ugliness*, which is the contrary of beauty, consists in a difformity with the same. • Ugliness may, therefore, be defined : *The imperfection of an object, so constituted as to exhibit a difformity with rational nature, and thus produce a disagreeable impression on the contemplating mind.* Ugly, then, is everything that is untrue, *i. e.*, inconsistent in its attributes, illogical, discordant with truth in theory or fact; ugly is everything that lacks the moral or physical perfection due to its nature. Besides, all those things that are connected with disagreeable associations, moral or intellectual; all those things that symbolize moral or mental depravity or imperfection, are, for the reasons stated above, termed ugly, though they may be objectively true and perfect in their species.

Akin to the ugly is the *comical or ridiculous.* Wherein this attribute properly consists has puzzled the greatest intellects to determine. Cicero says that he is not ashamed to confess his ignorance on this point. Aristotle, however, maintains that the ridiculous consists in a certain imperfection or ugliness, but harmless and inoffensive. And, in fact, these elements will be found in everything that is truly comical. In every really laughable object, character or manifestation, an imperfection, incongruity, or oddity, must be forthcoming; but as soon as this defect becomes painful, hurtful, or offensive, in any degree, to the contemplator, the subject in which it resides, or a third party, it thereby ceases to be ridiculous. The comical or ridiculous, therefore, may be defined: *A deformity or inconsistency with right reason, so harmless and inoffensive, however, as not to produce any disagreeable impression on the mind of the contemplator.* The sensation that arises from the contemplation of the ridiculous is generated by its striking contrast with right reason, which shocks us without making us grieve. The nature of that pleasure which results from this sensation seems to be mainly, if not wholly, organic or sensitive; for it is not easy to perceive how the higher faculties could rest with any degree of pleasure on such objects as are strikingly repugnant to them. It is interesting to read St. Thomas on this question. "As bodily labor," he says, "brings on bodily fatigue, so mental labor produces fatigue of the animal faculties (*fatigatio animalis*). Now, as the fatigue of the body is dispelled by bodily repose, so this fatigue of the animal faculties is dispelled by repose of the soul. But the repose of the soul is pleasure. . . . . Therefore a remedy must be applied against the fatigue of the animal faculties by means of some pleasure from the cessation of rational exertion." And after illustrating his principle by the trite example of the bow that's always bent, he concludes: "Such words and actions (indifferent, of course, as to morality) in which *only delight (repose) of the animal faculties is sought, are termed ridiculous or jocose.* And, therefore, it is necessary to indulge in them sometimes for the repose of the mind."[1]

In these words the Angelic Doctor seems clearly to intimate that the pleasure derived from the ridiculous has its seat in the animal faculties, the nervous system; while the operations of the higher faculties are, as it were, suspended. He also assigns the object and limits of the ridiculous or comic. They serve, and should be indulged in, only as a necessary or expedient relaxation from more serious studies or pursuits. As soon as the comical exceeds those bounds, it ceases to be rational in its tendency, and leads to dissipation and frivolity.

There remains for us to say a few words on the *sublime*, which is wont to be considered in connection with the beautiful. From

---

[1] *Summa*, 2-2 ae., q. 168, a. 2.

our explanation of the beautiful it will be seen that it does not exclude the sublime, but rather includes it as a special kind. The sublime is the highest species of the beautiful. Those objects or phenomena are considered sublime which manifest in a special manner the greatness, power, infinity of the Creator, and thus fill the contemplating mind with admiration and awe. To this class of things belong, first of all, God Himself and His attributes; in the second place, extraordinary manifestations of moral and supernatural power in His rational creatures; and, lastly, the more powerful and striking phenomena of nature. The impression produced by the sublime is caused by the contrast of our own littleness and weakness with the infinite greatness and power of God, whether manifested directly, by immediate Divine interference, or indirectly, when communicated, and manifested in a higher degree in His creatures. This impression, however, is far from being always the sentiment of fear, as was the opinion of Edmund Burke. It is, as we have said, admiration, arrangement, awe, reverence, and even love, towards the Supreme Goodness, Greatness, and Omnipotence; while fear is always a sentiment that arises from the apprehension of impending evil. A sea storm is no less sublime to him who, from the shore, contemplates the mountains of water breaking upon the cliffs, than it is to him who is tossed upon the heaving bosom of the deep; though the latter is naturally affected with fear, while the former is perfectly secure from danger. All agree that the opening verses of Genesis are sublime; yet one's conscience must be ill at ease to read those words with fear and not with reverential awe of the great Creator of heaven and earth. So also the words of the beginning of the Gospel of St. John are justly considered sublime; but, far from affecting with fear, the sublime effusion of the Evangelist is eminently calculated to inspire the devout reader with confidence, gratitude, and love.

It might be further asked here, *whether evil can be called sublime.* Modern infidel æstheticians answer in the affirmative. Satan in Milton, Prometheus and other Titanic characters are, in their estimation, eminently sublime. Nay, some, as Schiller, go so far as to say that the highest degree of sublimity is despair and its too frequent attendant, suicide; while others, as Vischer and Krug, pronounce rebellion against God—blasphemy—the summit of sublimity. That such theories are propounded in the name of philosophy and good taste, and find credit in educated spheres, is a sad sign of the times. Need we wonder to meet so much morbid weariness of life even in the better circles of society? Need we be astonished to see suicides multiplying from day to day?

" Who then would bear the whips and scorns of time ?"

Who should hesitate to sink into the highly' æsthetic virtue of despair and then seek relief in the sublime tragedy of suicide? Who would not then become the disciple of the blustering blasphemer, Bob Ingersoll, the sublimest figure of them all?

From our definition of the sublime it may easily be seen that evil, as such, cannot fall within its compass. Evil is not strength, but weakness; creates not admiration and awe, but disgust and horror; it cannot, therefore, be considered beautiful. If a morally evil character have some sublime traits, great strength or mental penetration, these attributes become only the less sublime the more they are bent on evil. Thus they only manifest their weakness, and cease to claim our admiration, though they may awaken our compassion. The impression of the sublime, however, may be produced by such fiendish and blasphemous creations as Milton's Satan, not from any strength or greatness that is manifested in their blasphemy and malice, but by the contrast of their impotent rage and hatred with the infinite power and unchangeable happiness of the Almighty. But in despair and its offspring, suicide, no one who has learned to analyze the motives of the human heart can see anything but blank cowardice or insanity, the cloak in which they are generally shrouded from public infamy.

A well-known species of the sublime is the *tragical*. It consists, on the one hand, in the manifestations of extraordinary moral strength and resignation in bearing the scourges of adverse fate, or, rather, the deserved visitations and chastisements of Divine Providence, in bowing in submission under the all-powerful hand of God; on the other hand, in the justifications of Divine Providence, which avenges wrong with unswerving justice. Every tragic event is an illustration of the truth : Man proposes, God disposes; or, Revenge is Mine, and I will repay—truths which, if forcibly brought home to us, cannot fail to produce the impression of the sublime.

It would be a pleasant task to illustrate the sublime with examples from literature, sacred and profane; but, as we feel that this paper has already grown rather long, we resist the temptation and break off our considerations. Should our treatment of the beautiful seem little in keeping with the subject, we would ask the indulgent reader to remember that we had to deal with first principles of an abstruse nature, rendered doubly obscure by the airy speculations of undisciplined philosophy—principles which do not lie within the flowery field of the beautiful, but which, in our judgment, form the only unerring way to the region of true beauty. What with the wanton aberrations of human genius, the fundamental principles of æsthetics in their present state might be compared to the impenetrable thicket that surrounds Milton's " Paradise."

" As one continued brake, the undergrowth
  Of shrubs and tangled bushes had perplexed
  All the path of man and beast that passed that way."

But if the student has once threaded his way to the Orient gate,

" Before him with new wonder now he views,
  To all delight of human sight exposed
  In narrow room, Nature's whole wealth, yea more,
  A Heaven on earth."

IN MEMORIAM.

CARDINAL McCLOSKEY.

JUST as the present number of the REVIEW was about to be published, the sad announcement reaches us of the death of John, Cardinal McCloskey, Archbishop of New York, in the seventy-sixth year of his age.

Born in Brooklyn on the 10th of March, 1810, and called to his rest on the 10th of October, 1885, his long period of ministerial life and ecclesiastical dignity forms an important link between the early days of American Catholicity, then just emerging from its previous state of weakness and childhood, and her present condition of matured growth, robust health, and vigorous strength. In his boyhood he could not find in his native city a church wherein he could assist at the Holy Sacrifice, nor a priest at whose hands he could receive the Sacraments, but had to cross over the river, frequently with great inconvenience and some risk, to hear mass in one of New York's two churches, or enjoy the blessings of confession and Communion. God signally rewarded the fidelity with which the young Samuel and his fervent family, who had destined him for the ministry, maintained their faith and cherished its pious obligations in spite of all obstacles. The life of this holy child, as he grew up to man's estate and to venerable age, ran parallel with the prosperous growth of the American Church. Brooklyn has now within her precincts a bishop, with more than a hundred priests, and nearly as many churches and chapels; New York has replaced her two insignificent churches by an archiepiscopal see, two hundred priests, and over a hundred magnificent temples of the True Faith. If in his youth he knew and felt the trials and privations to which the Church amongst us was subjected, his last days were cheered by the splendor to which she had attained, adorned and honored by the ecclesiastical dignities which she had it in her power to confer.

His sacred studies, which were begun in the Seminary of Mount St. Mary's, that has given so many bishops to the American Church, and completed in Rome at a riper age, by a two years' course of theological study at the Gregorian University, commonly known as the Roman College, and by daily intercourse with the illustrious theologians of the Eternal City. If his proficiency in sacred science was not given generally the prominence it might well have commanded, we must attribute this rather to the prelate's modesty and humility, that delighted to conceal gifts which, if allowed a chance to display themselves, would have secured the admiration of all. His natural powers and cultured mind were most clearly visible in his discourses, written or extemporized, in which he showed to the best advantage. The dignity and grace of manner, the quiet, gentle, but most persuasive style of oratory that carries conviction to every hearer, were peculiarly his, as all who had the good fortune to hear him can bear witness.

But all these gifts and endowments were as nothing compared to the beauty of his noble soul, which was the seat of all those virtues that render a man acceptable before God and dear to his fellow-men. If we had to mention only one trait of his character, we should select what perhaps was the most conspicuous, certainly the most edifying—the admirable blending in him of dignity, which repelled none, with a sweetness and charity that attracted all. The poet deemed these two things incompatible:

> " Non bene conveniunt nec in una sede morantur
> Majestas et amor,"

and perhaps with his heathen notions he could not well think otherwise. But in the soul of our deceased prelate, where Christian virtue had solid roots, they coexisted in wonderful union. In him were coupled the majesty of a prince, which inspired no fear, but exacted reverence of all, with the simplicity and amiableness of a child. So that we may justly style him, in the words of Holy Writ, "beloved of God and of man"—" *dilectus Deo et hominibus.*"

The watchful, provident eye of Rome could not long overlook the merits of the young ecclesiastic, whom it had first learned to know within the portals of the Holy City. He was gradually raised to her honors. He was first Bishop of Albany, then Coadjutor and subsequently Archbishop of New York, and finally Cardinal of the Holy Roman Church, the next dignity to that of Vicar of Christ. All, Catholic and Protestant, applauded his exaltation ; for all felt that in no worthier representative could the American Church receive honor at the hands of the Father of the Faithful. The meek way in which he bore his honors disarmed even prejudice itself; and the unanimity of the non-Catholic press in praising the record of his life and extolling his memory, is perhaps without precedent in our ecclesiastical annals.

He is gone, full of years and of merits ; but his work lives after him, and his name will be a blessing to generations yet unborn. " ETERNAL REST GIVE UNTO HIM, O LORD, AND LET PERPETUAL LIGHT SHINE UPON HIM !"

BOOK NOTICES.

CHRIST AND CHRISTIANITY. Studies on Christology, Creeds and Confessions, Protestantism and Romanism, Reformation Principles, Sunday Observance, Religious Freedom and Christian Union. By *Philip Schaff.* New York: Scribner's Sons. 1885.

This is a strange and, in some respects, very interesting volume. Its title is a misnomer. It might just as well have been almost anything else. It is made up of essays, lectures, and discourses, read or delivered through a series of years, on different occasions and various topics connected with the religion of Christ. But, instead of being "studies," they would more truthfully be characterized as dreams, or essays designed to conceal the real position of Protestantism, and apologies for heresy and error.

Indeed, according to the notion which runs through every paper and essay of the volume, there is no such thing as heresy on the part of persons who profess and love Jesus Christ. No existing religious society or organization, according to the ruling idea of the author of these papers, has the true faith, that is, the Christian faith, in its entirety, yet each one, holding some Christian truth, or one-sided aspect of a divinely revealed truth, is entitled to call itself a church, and has a right to recognition as a member of the happy family of warring, jarring "Christian denominations."

This, according to the author, is a great advantage. For no one man, and no one Christian denomination, nor, indeed, all the various "churches" taken together, of any one age, have in their belief the whole truth of divine revelation. Each one, consequently, is defective, and to a greater or less extent erroneous. But "the church," being made up of the aggregate of all who profess to believe in and love the Lord Jesus Christ, never has possessed the Christian faith in its entirety, and consequently has never taught it, and never will until the consummation of all things. For "there is nothing perfect under the sun," and never will be till the end of time.

Each division of the "church," therefore, represents a "distinct type of one Christian religion." Each has "characteristic excellences and defects." Thus, "the Greek Church represents ancient Christianity in repose; the Roman Church, mediæval Christianity in conflict with liberal progress; Protestantism, modern Christianity in motion." The Protestantism "is subdivided into three main divisions, the Lutheran, the Anglican, and the Reformed. These are again subdivided into a large number of separate organizations, and to these must be added "several large and influential evangelical associations, as the Independents, the Methodists, the Baptists, which are offshoots of the Reformation of the sixteenth century, and especially of the Church of England since the Toleration Act of 1689."

All these different and differing "churches," each affirming what others deny, and each denying what others affirm, "are branches of Christendom." They "are the growth of history, and embody the results of centuries of intellectual and spiritual labor."

We pause here for a moment to direct attention to the significant phrase, "the growth of history!" These few words furnish the clue to all the contradictory lucubrations of this volume. Following its author to the strict logical conclusion of his argument, every form and phase of religious opinion that has ever been broached is legitimate and good, because it was or is the outgrowth " of history," and embodied, however imperfectly, and however fragmentarily, some aspect or other " of Christian truth."

We pass this by, however, and return to our exhibit of the author's ideas. It is worth while to set forth a condensed statement of his expressed estimates of " the Greek Church" and of " the Latin Church," in one of his discourses, by way of contrast with his well-known anti-Catholic bigotry, and with his other declarations in this volume respecting the Catholic Church, on the one hand, and Protestantism on the other:

" The Greek Church," says the writer of this volume, " produced most of the ancient fathers, from the apostles (with an uncapitalized *A*) down to John of Damascus, and elaborated the œcumenical doctrines of the Holy Trinity, and the Incarnation, with a vast body of invaluable literature which must be studied, even to this day, in every school of theological learning. Hers are the apostolical fathers, the apologists, exegetes, divines, historians, and orators of the early church ; hers a long line of martyrs and saints ; in her language the apostles and evangelists wrote the inspired records of our religion ; to her we owe nearly all the manuscripts of the Greek Testament and the Septuagint," etc. She is "stationary, immoveable," but Dr. Schaff fails to tell us that she is so, so far as she is so, because she has sundered herself from the only true centre and ruling source of Christian life and progress, the Holy Roman See. Nor does he note the fact, that though seemingly "immoveable," and actually petrified, yet there has been motion within her, as within an iceberg, or a mass of silex when exposed to changes of temperature, disintegrating into fragments. Thus we have the so-called "ancient Greek Church" severed and separated into independent antagonistic "communions" in Russia, and Greece, and Turkey, and subject to the dictation of the secular sovereigns of each of these countries, and even of the separate semi-Turkish and semi-independent countries of what until recently was known as "European Turkey." All this the writer of the papers comprised in this volume overlooks. He tells us that "the Eastern Church held fast to her traditions during the dark centuries of Saracen and Turkish oppression" (forgetting, strangely, the countless heresies she has fostered, and ignoring her present slavery to the secular powers of each country in which she exists), and that "she looks forward (of which there is not the slightest evidence) to a day of freedom and resurrection, which may God grant."

As for " the Latin Church," it gave us " the works of the great African father, Augustin, which inspired the thinking of schoolmen, mystics, and reformers, and the Latin Bible of Jerome, which, for many centuries, interpreted the Word of God to the Western nations. She saved Christianity and the Roman classics through the chaotic confusion of the migration of nations ; she christianized and civilized, by her missionaries, the barbarian races, which overthrew the old Roman empire, and she built up a new and better society on the ruins of the old. She converted [to what ? If to Christianity, then she was and is the true and sole Church of Christ] the Anglo-Saxons, the Franks, the Germans, the Scandinavians ; she built the Gothic cathedrals, founded the mediæval universities, and educated such schoolmen as Anselm and Thomas Aquinas, and such mystics as Bernard and the author of the inimitable *Imitation of Christ.*"

And this, be it remembered, amid the disorders and confusion of the so-called "dark ages."

But the writer has not yet reached his climax. "Even the Reformers of the sixteenth century," he adds, "are her children, baptized, confirmed, and ordained in her bosom, though she cast them out as heretics with terrible curses, as the Synagogue had cast out the apostles." It would have been the simple truth, had he added, as the *Apostles* denounced and cast out heretics in *their* day. She dates from that congregation to which St. Paul wrote his most important epistle. Why did not the writer add, from "that congregation" which St. Peter founded and ruled? He admits this in his Church History. "She stretches in unbroken succession through all ages and countries; she once ruled nearly the whole of Europe; and, though deprived of her former power in just punishment for its abuse (?), she still guides for weal or woe millions of consciences, and is full of zeal and energy for the maintenance and spread of her doctrine and discipline in all parts of the globe."

After all this, declared with proper rhetorical emphasis to "the Eighth General Conference of the Evangelical Alliance, held at Copenhagen, September 2d, 1884," and now republished, it would seem hard to understand how the speaker and author of the volume before us (a Protestant, speaking and writing for Protestants) could vindicate Protestantism satisfactorily to himself and his fellow Protestants. Yet he has done it to his own professed self-approval, and according to his statement, eliciting "enthusiastic" expressions of "cordial approval," "oral and written," from "the distinguished (Protestant) ministers and scholars before whom his discourse was delivered." Of Protestantism, he says:

"The *various* Protestant churches have the unspeakable advantage of evangelical freedom (!); of direct access to the fountain of God's grace; of unobstructed personal union and communion with Christ," etc. "The Reformation emancipated a large portion of Christendom from the yoke of human traditions and spiritual tyranny, made God's book the book of the people, secured the rights of nationality and private judgment in the sphere of religion, and gave a mighty impulse to every department of intellectual and moral activity. Protestantism pervades and directs the freest and strongest nations in both hemispheres; it carries the open Bible to all heathen lands; it is cultivating with untiring zeal every branch of sacred literature, and popularizes the results of scientific research for the benefit of the masses; it favors every legitimate progress in science, art, politics, and commerce; it promotes every enterprise of Christian philanthropy; and it is identified with the cause of civil and religious liberty throughout the world."

If this characterization of Christianity be correct, it effectually shuts out the recognition which Dr. Schaff accords to the Greek Church and the Roman Catholic Church as severally representing distinct and genuine types of Christianity. If the eulogium he has pronounced upon Protestantism be well founded, then his commendations, even with the qualifications he has made, of the Greek Church and "the Latin" have no foundation. Whatever they did in the past, they have no mission to-day. They are but obstacles in the way of the spread of Christian truth and Christian freedom, and of "the emancipation of their adherents from the yoke of human traditions and spiritual tyranny." If Protestantism alone gives "unobstructed personal union and communion with Christ," then the "Greek" and the "Latin" Churches are obstructions to that union and communion, and, as obstructions, should be torn down and destroyed. Yet Dr. Schaff professes to "look hopefully for a reunion of 'the three sections of Christendom,' and a feast of reconciliation of the churches." A reunion and reconciliation of what ? Of " spiritual tyranny " with "evangelical freedom," of " human traditions " with " the open Bible," of " direct access to the fountain of God's word and of God's grace " with " human traditions" and " obstructions to personal union and communion with Christ" !

How Dr. Schaff can look forward to such a monstrous combination, to a "reconciliation " of what it is impossible to reconcile, is hard to understand. And how could he hope for it, were it possible ?

There is only one way in which this could become possible—if we may speak of an impossibility becoming possible—and that is by the utter sacrifice of truth and of true faith. Herod and Pilate became "friends." But it was because each of them, to gratify his pride and ambition, consented to crucify our Divine Lord. And much in the same way Dr. Schaff professes to "look hopefully for a reunion of Christendom." He professes to expect that one common belief among all who call themselves Christians will be brought about by an indiscriminate destruction of all antagonisms between truth and error, by an entire elimination, in fact, of all real, moral differences between them. Instead of "*one faith*," there will be a countless host of beliefs, and each belief will be as true as the others ; that is, none of them will be entirely true. In other words, there will be no true belief and no real faith.

"Every church," according to Dr. Schaff, " has its ' characteristic excellences and also its characteristic defects.' " " Nor need one wonder at it ; there is nothing perfect under the sun." " Every church has the right and duty to defend its own belief and practice, and everybody should belong to that denomination which he conscientiously prefers." " Denominationalism or Confessionalism has, no doubt, its evils and dangers, and is apt to breed narrowness, bigotry and uncharitableness. But the worst we can say of it is that, in the present state of Christendom, it is a *necessary* evil, and is overruled by God for the multiplication of regenerating and converting agencies."

"Denominationalism" and "Confessionalism" are the terms Dr. Schaff employs to designate the existence of countless sects and schisms, each maintaining a separate organization, and each professedly holding to its own declared creed over against all others. In one sense, the existence of " Denominationalism " is, indeed, a *necessary* evil. It is necessary as verifying the declaration of our Divine Lord that " false teachers " would arise, who would preach false Christs, and deceive, were it possible, " the very elect." But Christ also adds the warning, " follow ye *not* after them." It is " *necessary*," as Christ declared, " that it must *needs* be " that "scandals should arise." But *this necessity* does not diminish the force of the *woe* HE pronounced upon those through whom they might arise.

Dr. Schaff continues his double-faced apology for " Denominationalism," by declaring that " it is not the best state, but it is far better than a dead or tyrannical and monotonous uniformity." And yet the unity of the Church, which he styles " dead or tyrannical and monotonous uniformity," Christ prayed should ever exist and the Apostles enjoined those to whom they wrote never to depart from, and sects and schisms, which Dr. Schaff styles Denominations, the Apostles denounced as attempts to rend the Body of Christ.

Dr. Schaff's liberality, in recognizing various sects as Christian denominations, and heresies as only different " aspects " of the same truth, is so broad as to include Lutheranism, Calvinism, Arminianism, Socinianism, Arianism, and all their countless progeny of sects. But there is one religion for which he can find no room in his happy family

—that of "*Romanism.*" " Protestantism," he says, "stands or falls with the Bible. Romanism stands or falls with the Papacy. . . . We must, therefore, maintain the true infallibility of God's Word against the pretended infallibility of the Vatican, which, like Phariseeism, obscures and paralyzes the Bible by human additions. A union with Popery is as impossible as a union of apostolic Christianity with the Jewish hierarchy which crucified the Saviour under the plea of orthodoxy and zeal for the ancestral religion."

THE HISTORY OF ST. MONICA. By *M. l'Abbé Bannard*, Vicar-General of Orleans. Translated from the French by Rev. Anthony Farley, St. Monica's Church, Jamaica, L. I. New York: D. & J. Sadlier & Co.

At first thought it seems very strange that the life of this great saint should have remained unwritten until our own times. A model Christian wife and mother, one whose heart was wrung with agony through long years by a faithless, licentious, brutal heathen husband and a sensual, erring, though affectionate son, as only a pure wife's and loving mother's heart could be wrung, yet her trust in God, her faith and patience, her fortitude and devotion never failed. Through them and her unceasing prayers she snatched both husband and son from sin, and, even in her own lifetime, was rewarded with the joy of witnessing the conversion of the one from the unbelief and vices of heathenism, and of the other from the blinding influence of pernicious errors, skepticism, intellectual pride and sensuality to the Christian faith. Living, as she did, in the same age with St. Athanasius, St. Cyril of Jerusalem, St. Jerome, St. Gregory of Nazianzen, St. Gregory of Nyssa, St. Basil, St. Ambrose, St. Damasus, St. Ephraim, St. Hilary of Poitiers, St. Martin of Tours, and a host of other holy saints, a catalogue of whose names, even, would crowd this page, it seems strange that more than a thousand years should have been allowed to elapse before her name was solemnly enrolled in the Church's Calendar of Saints, and altars arose in her honor in the Church's cathedrals. It was not because her name and virtues were forgotten, and her memory had passed away with her departure from earth. They had all been imperishably embalmed in the copious references made to her in the writings of her illustrious son, in sacred tradition and in the frequent encomiums passed upon her by other distinguished saints, doctors, and ecclesiastical writers. Deep love and veneration for St. Monica have ever existed in the hearts of the Church's faithful children. Yet, as we have already said, more than a thousand years elapsed between her death and canonization, and upwards of four hundred years more passed away before her Life was written.

But God's ways are not the ways of men, and the Church, guided and directed by Him, knows how to wait as well as how and when to act. As a wise master of a house she guards and preserves her treasures, not displaying or employing them indiscriminately, but bringing them forth and putting them to use at the proper times for so doing.

St. Monica's remains were destined to be left in the tomb prepared for her on the seashore at Ostia, marked by a small marble monument, for some centuries,—her name and memory cherished and venerated there and soon throughout the Christian world,—yet no public cultus was rendered to her. Then they were quietly transferred, from fear of desecration during the invasions of the Lombards to the Church of St. Andrea at Ostia, and buried beneath the altar in a deep vault whose existence was known only to the priests of the church. There they lay undisturbed for a still longer period of time, until the sore needs of subsequent ages should lead the Church, guided by the Holy Spirit, to search for and open the closed tomb, place the sacred relics upon her altars, and assign to Monica her place in the ranks of the Saints.

This great work was reserved in the Providence of God for Pope Martin V. Nor is it now difficult to discover the reason why. Few Popes have suffered as did this Pontiff. True, his exaltation to the Holy See put an end to the great schism of the West. But he also beheld the painful scenes of the Council of Constance, which paved the way for the scandals of that of Basle. He saw Wycliff, and John Huss, and Jerome of Prague appearing, and the horrors of the Hussite war. Doubtless, too, from the height of St. Peter's throne, and with the luminous assistance of the Spirit of God, he perceived the evil days which, despite God and His Church, were coming upon the world through the apostasy miscalled the "Reformation," which was then rapidly approaching. It was at this critical time that, guided by one of those divine inspirations which are frequently communicated to Sovereign Pontiffs of the Church, Pope Martin V. ordered a search for the relics of St. Monica and their translation to Rome.

Miracles of the highest order accompanied and followed this translation. Simultaneously with the translation of her remains, Pope Martin V. issued the Bull of her canonization, April 27th, 1430. But another hundred years or more were destined to pass away before St. Monica had either church or chapel, though devotion to her was constantly increasing. Then, when Martin Luther had passed away, and his pernicious doctrines were threatening to defile and corrupt all Christendom, another seal, as it were, was added to the glorification of St. Monica by the erection of a grand basilica in her honor. Since then love and devotion to her have spread, deepened, intensified.

In all this the hand of God is evident. During the Middle Ages the sanctity of the marriage relation, and the reciprocal obligations of husbands and wives, of parents and children, were acknowledged, even though the obligations themselves were not always faithfully observed. But after Luther and Calvin and Henry VIII. had, each in his own way, sowed the seeds of heresy, schism, and lust, and Christian wives trembled for their husbands, and Christian mothers for their sons, thinking of the dangers that beset them, then God, in His Church, placed conspicuously before Christians the glorious memory and example of St. Monica, to increase their faith, strengthen their hope, and encourage them to be earnest, and constant, and believing in prayer.

In like manner we can trace the Providence of God in reserving for our own age a compiling of the Life of St. Monica distinct from, though not independent of or separate from, the Life of St. Augustine; for that were impossible. Heretofore her name and memory, her virtues and life have been chiefly associated with him. But even had he never attained the eminence he reached as one of the greatest Doctors of the Church and most glorious Saints, there would be lessons, highly significant, important, and salutary, for Christian wives and mothers to learn from St. Monica's life; lessons, too, especially suggestive and encouraging to them in our present age; lessons that come directly home to Christian wives of faithless husbands, and to Christian mothers of wayward sons; lessons of patience and suffering; of earnest, constant prayer; of abiding faith and hope, and tearful, tireless supplication to God; of trust in Him even in the darkest gloom, and of the power of a perfect Christian example and a mother's undying love.

All these lessons the volume before us sets forth in strong light. It is written in charming style, and cannot fail to interest and benefit all who read its pages. Would that it might find its way into every family in our land.

PARADISE FOUND: The Cradle of the Human Race at the North Pole. A Study of the Prehistoric World. By *William F. Warren*, S.T.D., LL.D , President of Boston University, Member of the American Oriental Society, etc., etc., etc. With Original Illustrations. Boston: Houghton, Mifflin & Company. 1885.

In his preface the author of this work anticipates' and endeavors to guard against preconceptions which the title of his book might easily give rise to. He says: "The book is not the work of a dreamer. Neither has it proceeded from a love of learned paradox. Nor yet is it a cunningly devised fable, aimed at particular tendencies in current science, philosophy, or religion. It is a thoroughly serious and sincere attempt to present what is to the author's mind the true and final solution of one of the greatest and most fascinating of all problems connected with the history of mankind."

The author acknowledges that the suggestion that primitive Eden was at the Arctic Pole "seems at first sight the most incredible of all wild and wilful paradoxes." On the other hand he contends that " within the lifetime of our own generation the progress of geological study has relieved the hypothesis of a fatal antecedent improbability." He believes, too, that "many of the most striking " of his alleged proofs, both in the physical and anthropological domain, are precisely the latest of the conclusions of the most modern of all sciences.

The question of the location of Eden has, in his opinion, a high practical importance, and to the "believer in Revelation, or even in the most ancient and venerable Ethnic Traditions," his volume "will be found to possess uncommon interest." This opinion he supports with the following remarks, which, regarded as a statement of the direction in which Non-Catholic opinion has been and still is steadily moving, are certainly true: .

"For many years the public mind has been schooled in a narrow naturalism, which in its world-view has as little room for the extraordinary as it has for the supernatural. Decade after decade the representatives of this teaching have been measuring the natural phenomena of every age and place ·by the petty measuring-rod of their own local and temporary experience. So long and so successfully have they dogmatized on the constancy of Nature's laws and the uniformity of Nature's forces that of late it has required no small degree of courage to enable an intelligent man to stand up in the face of his generation and avow his personal faith in the early existence of men of gigantic stature and of almost millenarian longevity. Especially have clergymen and Christian teachers and writers upon Biblical history been embarrassed by the popular incredulity on these subjects, and not infrequently by a consciousness that this incredulity was in some measure shared by themselves."

"To all such," the author believes, "and indeed to all the broader-minded among the naturalists themselves, a new philosophy of primeval history—a philosophy which for all the alleged extraordinary effects provides the adequate extraordinary causes—cannot fail to prove most welcome."

In this spirit the author sets himself to the performance of his self-assumed task. In his attempts to accomplish it he sweeps over a wide range of subjects and brings together and arranges under distinct heads an amount of antiquarian erudition, as well as of knowledge of the latest results of modern scientific investigations, which makes his work highly interesting, apart from its immediate object. For the Darwinian school of thought, and the advocates of the theory that primitive man was a savage, he has nothing but contempt, declaring that in their mutual contradictions they have effectually refuted their own theories, and "have shattered their own party into an indefinite number of mutually antagonistic factions. . . . . The modern Babel is worse than the ancient. To one surveying at the present time the different departments of science which relate to Man, it would seem as though in each the breakdown of the theory of primitive human brutishness were complete, though not yet publicly proclaimed and acknowledged."

Whatever may be thought of the author's theory, and whether any interest whatever be felt in the question he discusses and endeavors to solve, the book itself, from the style in which it is written and the materials for thought upon various subjects which it contains, is highly interesting.

THE WORKS OF ORESTES A. BROWNSON; Collected and Arranged by *Henry F. Brownson.* Vol. XVIII. Containing the Fourth Part of the Political Writings. Detroit: Thorndike Nourse, Publisher. 1885.

The political writings of Orestes A. Brownson are of great and permanent value. Even in those which contain his ideas when he was a rationalist groping in the dark, and with eyes shut to the clear light thrown by Divine Revelation upon social and political questions, there is an evident simplicity of purpose, a sincerity of intention, an earnestness of desire to discover and set forth truth, and truth only, conjoined with a clearness, directness, and power of argument which make those writings worthy of careful examination by those who desire to understand the principles on which human society and civil government are based, and the manner in which they influence the welfare of peoples according to their correct or incorrect application to the various interests and relations which human society comprehends.

That there are errors, some of them dangerous and pernicious, in some of these writings,—we mean particularly those which were put forth when Dr. Brownson was a rationalist,—is to be expected. But these errors are the result not of false logic but of the false premises upon which the author built his conclusions. And even these writings are valuable for the incisive, exhaustive criticisms and refutations they contain, of the sophistry and false reasoning of other writers on the same subjects which the writer exposes and refutes. But what Dr. Brownson wrote on political questions after he became a Catholic (such as are contained in the volume now before us) have a still higher value. They are lucid and acute logical discussions on the basis of Christian principles of various questions, which are inseparably connected with social economy, civil government, its institutions, its relations to the social, industrial, moral, and spiritual interests of mankind, the mutual comity of nations, and other questions of primary importance. For in them are found the results of long and careful reading and research and reflection by a mind naturally acute, penetrating, and severely logical, guided in its reasonings by the Christian faith.

The volume before us contains a part of these latter writings. The first two hundred and twenty pages of it are occupied by a treatise on "The American Republic, its Constitution, Tendencies, and Destiny." In this treatise Dr. Brownson first discusses, from the Christian point of view, the origin of good government, its basis, constitution, and development. In the course of this discussion he successively examines the following theories. First, government "originates in the right of the father to govern his child;" second, "in convention, and is a social compact;" third, "in the people, who collectively taken are sovereign;" fourth, "government springs from the spontaneous development of nature;" fifth, "it derives its right from the immediate and express appointment of God;" sixth, "from God through the Pope, or visible head of the spiritual society;" seventh, "from God through the people;" and eighth, "from God through the natural law."

After this preliminary discussion Dr. Brownson proceeds to examine the origin of political power in the United States, the Constitution of the United States, the relation of the several States to the United States, the doctrine of secession, the reconstruction of the States that seceded from the Union, the chief political tendencies of the people of the United States and their destiny, political and religious.

Following this treatise the volume contains twenty articles on political topics of direct concern to our own country, or on questions growing out of events in Europe, and particularly those connected with the revolutionary movements in Europe during the last fifteen or twenty years. These articles are interesting and valuable, both as historical studies and also on account of the philosophic acuteness and logical precision with which the subjects treated are examined and commented on.

THE WAR OF ANTICHRIST WITH THE CHURCH AND CHRISTIAN CIVILIZATION. A Review of the Rise and Progress of Atheism : Its Extension through Voltaire ; Its Use of Freemasonry and other Kindred Secret Societies for Anti-Christian War ; The Union and the " Illuminism " of Masonry by Weishaupt ; Its Progress under the Leaders of the First French Revolution, and under Nubius, Palmerston and Mazzini ; the Control of its hidden " Inner Circle " over all Revolutionary Organizations ; Its Influence over British Freemasonry ; Its Attempts upon Ireland ; Oaths, Signs and Passwords of the Three Degrees, etc   The Spoliation of the Propaganda. Lectures delivered in Edinburgh, in October, 1884, by *Monsignor George F. Dillon, D.D.*, Missionary-Apostolic, Sydney (Australia). Dublin : M. H. Gile & Son. 1885.

We hope the reader will not be deterred from perusing this book by the length of its title,—as long as an ordinary preface,—for it contains most valuable information, imparted in a very lively and attractive style, and on a subject, too, with which Catholics are not at all as well acquainted as they ought to be. This is due not so much to their unwillingness to inform themselves as to the lack of suitable books in English for them to derive the information from. To the many of them who are familiar with the French language most excellent works are within reach,—the three octavo volumes on *Secret Societies*, compiled and edited by the Jesuit Father Deschamps and M. Claudio Jannet, and the abridgment of this, in one duodecimo volume, by MM. Jannet and Louis d'Estampes. But to the great mass of readers these works must long remain an unexplored field, unless, indeed, some enterprising publisher be found, who will assure more than the usual generosity (?) of remuneration to a competent translator.

Under these circumstances Monsignor Dillon's work is a great boon, timely by all means, if not too late to save many from the ways of error and social and religious wreck. The work, too, is for the most part well done, there being but few blemishes, and these insignificant and unimportant. The very length of the title is a recommendation, for it shows at a glance the main divisions of the subject treated ; a subject, than which there is none more important in the whole range of modern history, which it is impossible to understand thoroughly with a deep knowledge of the workings of secret societies.

The pages under consideration contain, as indicated, the substance of two lectures delivered in Edinburgh a year ago. One of these lectures is given almost as it was spoken, and the other, that on secret societies, has been greatly expanded, for it now fills 164 large octavo pages. "It was not," the author tells us, "so much in the hope of directing Prot: estants from Freemasonry as in the desire to show to Catholics that all kinds of secret societies were as bad as, if not worse than, Free-masonry,—were, in fact, united with and under the rule of the worst form of Freemasonry,—that the lecturer essayed to speak at all upon the subject." If Protestants heed his warning, so much the better; but he thought it his duty to warn Catholics, and so, in order to make his warning reach a larger audience than he could gather in any lecture-hall, he determined to put his labors in their present form. We notice, here and there, indications of hasty preparation ; but, in a new edition which we hope soon to see appear, and that, too, in a more convenient and cheaper form, these blemishes need not appear. Considering, however, that these lectures, notwithstanding the great subsequent expansion of one of them by the insertion of long quotations that were merely referred to in the delivery, are mere "casual discourses, not formal and ex-haustive treatises on the subjects upon which they touch," they are ad-mirably instructive productions. It is a great convenience that they are divided up into parts with separate headings for these subdivisions, and that copious notes have been added where they were necessary to illustrate the text. Thus a clear exposition is given of the whole matter treated. Far more ground is covered here than was gone over in his famous Dublin Catholic University lectures on Freemasonry by Professor James Burton Robertson, though he dealt far more exhaustively with as much of the subject as he undertook to elucidate ; but his work is now, we believe, out of print, and many of his views and theories have become antiquated.

In his first lecture Monsignor Dillon, under the title, *The War of Anti-christ with the Church and Christian Civilization*, treats " the whole ques-tion of secret atheistic organization, its origin and nature, its history in the last century and this, and its unity of satanic purpose in a wonderful di-versity of forms." Beginning with some general remarks on the Encyclical *Humanum Genus* and the present condition of secret societies, he pro-ceeds to give an account of the rise of Atheism in Europe, of Voltaire, Free-masonry in its origin and development, in the " Union " and the " Il-luminism " of Adam Weishaupt, the " Convent " of Wilhelmsbad, Cabalistic Masonry or Masonic Spiritism, the French Revolution, Na-poleon and Freemasonry, its condition after his fall, the kindred secret societies in Europe, the Carbonari, the permanent instruction of the " Alta Vendita," the famous letter of Piccolo Tigre, the intellectual and war party in Masonry, Lord Palmerston as a Freemason ruler, the war of the intellectual party, the war party under Palmerston, the " In-ternational," the Nihilists, the " Black Hand," etc., Freemasonry in England, Fenianism, the sad ending of the Irish conspirators, the tri-umph of Irish faith, and, lastly, Catholic organization, including the Total Abstinence societies. Here is an unusually rich supply of food for reflection, and any reader can digest it at leisure.

Seeing the work contains so much that is good, it may seem to some that we are hypercritical in pointing out the few faults, or rather what we consider to be such. In our judgment, the translations from the French are entirely too literal ; the value of the documents as evidence is neither enhanced nor preserved by putting them in indifferent or bad English.

Any one versed in two or three languages knows how often an idiom in one makes sheer nonsense when rendered, word for word, into another. Again, why not say Convention rather than "Convent" of Wilhelms-bad? for such the mischievous gathering was in the true sense of the word. It is misleading to say that Voltaire, "by position and educa-tion, should have been an excellent Catholic." On the contrary, it was his early Jansenist preceptor's training that spoiled him, bending his mind in a wrong direction, and blunting his moral sense, so much so that when he afterwards became a pupil of the Jesuits, all the professors in the college except one, an aged member of the Society, were soon convinced that he would develop into a dangerous character. Our author makes a slip in referring to the Bishop of Grenoble as Monseigneur Ségur; he should say Monseigneur Fava, who has written a most valuable pam-phlet on "Freemasonry"; the celebrated blind prelate's productions are of a different character. But these things weigh only as a feather against the rich mine of gold in the book.

We have room only for a mere mention of the second lecture in this volume,—that on the spoliation of the Propaganda, which is equally excellent and interesting. He elucidates the state of the question, tells the history of the institution from its beginning, describes the urban college, the library and the printing office, the former resources and the work of the Propaganda, the persecution it has suffered, the present state of the case, and measures to meet the difficulty. "Every fact stated has been carefully authenticated," and the reader is made "fully acquainted with a great wrong done to one of the most beneficent Chris-tian institutions in the world by the greed and anti-Christian hate of the Infidel Revolution."

FATHER HAND: Founder of All-Hallows Catholic College for the Foreign Missions. The Story of a Great Servant of God. By *Rev. John MacDevitt, D.D.*, Professor of Introduction to Scripture, Ecclesiastical History, etc., All-Hallows College, Dublin. Dublin: M. H. Gill & Son. New York: Fr. Pustet & Co. 1885.

All-Hallows College is the largest Foreign Missionary College in the world. Yet it was founded only about forty-two years ago by a priest who, as regards earthly resources, was one of the poorest of the poor, and in a country which, whatever its natural resources may be, is in-habited by a people who, though rich in faith, are poor as regards the wealth of this world, so that their very name is suggestive of extreme poverty and destitution.

These facts are surely significant in no slight degree. They prove that, in our times as in past times, the declaration of the Holy Ghost through St. Paul, that God continually exhibits to mankind a plain proof of the divine origin and continuance of His Church, in that He chooses "the weak things of this world" and those which the world regards as "mean" and "contemptible" to confound and overcome all its vainly imagined wisdom and might. They show, too, that the ardent zeal and self-sacrificing charity which characterized the Apostles and their imme-diate followers continue to-day in the Church of Christ and animate her faithful children as in days of old. Moreover, they prove that Ireland, the "isle of scholars" when all Europe was plunged in darkness, the "isle of saints" when faith was corrupt and zeal lukewarm and morals were lax in other countries, the "isle of martyrs" when elsewhere thou-sands became apostate to save their lives, their wealth, or their politi-cal or social positions, is still animated by the same spirit which won for her those glorious titles.

The story, therefore, of the founder of All-Hallows College in Ireland, an institution designed from its inception to send the message of salvation to all English-speaking peoples throughout the whole earth, cannot be too interesting in the highest degree to all who have any apprehension of the truth that the characteristic spirit of Christ's religion is that of self-sacrifice and divine charity, seeking to return good for evil and to bless especially those who are at enmity with us.

This is the story told in the volume before us, and well is it told by the learned and devout writer. It is the story of how a boy, discouraged by his father, though encouraged by his pious mother, struggled, despite poverty and seemingly insuperable difficulties, first to prepare himself for the sacred office of the priesthood; and how, when by dint of heroic perseverance the prospect of ecclesiastical distinction became bright before him, he turned his back upon it, and chose a life of poverty and self-denial instead. It is the story of how this poor, self-sacrificing priest, convinced that his design was approved of God, labored and strove, despite the seemingly prudential advice of almost all the then Bishops of Ireland, to give up what they regarded as an impracticable scheme, and they declining to support it, yet persevered with firm faith until his plans were crowned with success and those who at first opposed his undertaking become its warm supporters. It shows, too, what a faithful, devoted priest who labors in the spirit of his divine Lord and Master, and is willing to sacrifice himself entirely to the greater glory of God and the advancement of true religion, can accomplish in a very short time. For Father Hand, the founder of an institution which has sent and is still sending faithful, devoted missionaries of Christ into every country on earth in which English-speaking people are found, died in the thirty-ninth year of his age, in the eleventh of his sacred ministry, and after having presided over his Missionary College only four years.

But the interest of the volume before us even goes beyond all this. Incidentally yet clearly and strongly, it sometimes suggests, and sometimes graphically describes the condition of the Irish people, their previous history, the close relations existing between the Irish people still remaining in their native land and those who have migrated to other countries, and other kindred topics.

THE ART OF ORATORICAL COMPOSITION, BASED UPON THE PRECEPTS AND MODELS OF THE OLD MASTERS. By *Rev. Charles Coppens, S. J.*, Professor of St. Louis University. 1885. New York: The Cath. Pub. Society Co. London: Burns & Oates.

Great stress is necessarily laid in our schools, of every grade, upon perfection in oratorical composition. That art has always been understood to be, as Ennius called it, the *Flexanima omnium regina rerum*, and the precepts of the ancients have never been superseded as the soundest principles upon which to build a system of efficient training of mind and speech. The unbroken sway which the old classics have held in our higher schools is a proof of this, to which Leo XIII. has lately added the peculiar weight of his recommendation. If, therefore, there were no other reason than a recent tendency among us to drift away from these approved landmarks, we should heartily recommend the above work, founded on the teachings of the best among the old model orators and philosophers. It is a clear, didactic exposition, with such illustrations from modern sources as will make it practical under our circumstances.

But it is also a text-book, which is saying something apart from its general merits, as teachers will understand. The multiplicity of branches which are necessarily taught in our higher schools makes it desirable that the texts confine themselves, as far as is possible, to giving a skeleton, as it were, of the science to be taught in a judicious exposition of its principles, with such examples as are essential, but without any unnecessary speculations, or even such explanations as should be left to the teacher or the inductive reasoning of the pupil; and it is expected that the different parts of a course will, at the end, if rightly combined, supply one another to a complete whole. We cannot enter into the details of certain excellences of this book, though the subject itself might warrant our speaking of it at length if the space here allowed it. But we call attention to the Second Book, "On the Invention of Thought." Blair considered it impossible to reduce this branch of the oratorical art to any satisfactory system of precepts, and hence passes it by. Our author, following the indications of the ancient models, succeeds admirably.

There is one feature we would take exception to, though it does not in any perceptible way impair the usefulness of the book. We mean the apologetic tone which its author occasionally adopts throughout his work. Such expressions as, "if any one be inclined to find fault with us," etc. (page 52); "it is not here intended to write a treatise," etc. (page 194); "the precepts of this book are written for pupils," etc. (page 203), should, in our opinion, be avoided in a book which is intended as an authority for the young. Least of all has Father Coppens reason to guard himself against distrust, for he amply proves his strength by the grasp he has of the masters in his profession.

But these are trifles in comparison to what the book is as a real help to one of the most fruitful branches in our educational curriculum. For Seminaries, we find here the entire course from preparatory school to the class of sacred eloquence in theology. We understand, moreover, that the practical usefulness of the work has been tested in several of the Jesuit colleges before it appeared in print. This, together with the long experience of its author, is an additional guarantee of its merits.

THE PROTESTANT FAITH: or, Salvation by Belief. An Essay Upon the Errors of the Protestant Church. By *Dwight Hinkley Olmstead.* New York and London: G. P. Putnam's Sons. 1885.

If any evidence were wanting of the rapidity with which the Non-Catholic world is falling into utter disbelief, Protestantism leading the way, this book would furnish a striking proof of it. Nor does the force of this evidence by any means depend on the writer's personal position in the estimation of the Non-Catholic public. His essay was read substantially in its present form before the Young Men's Christian Union of New York in 1856, and afterwards, on two other occasions, in 1860. In 1874 it was published, and now it is republished. It is written avowedly for the purpose of proving that human opinion, which the writer confounds with faith, is involuntary, and consequently is neither meritorious nor the reverse, and that it matters not what an individual believes or disbelieves. Yet at the same time, with strange inconsistency, he expresses "the hope that his book will be of service to persons whose minds are disquieted by modern doubts." But why doubts should disquiet or can disquiet if an individual has no control over "his beliefs and opinions," it is not easy to understand.

In the author's exhibition of what the Protestant Faith is fundamentally, he naturally first refers to the "Reformation." It is interesting here to note how completely he sweeps away in a few sentences the current delusion and misrepresentation that Protestantism is a restoration of "primitive Christianity." He says boldly and unqualifiedly that the conflict between the Church and Protestantism was "a conflict between the authority of Councils and the individual judgment." According to his avowed opinion, "the Lutheran Reformation was an intellectual rather than a religious movement. From it nothing has been gained directly for religion; nothing except what has resulted from independence of thought, free speech, and the present heterogeneous character of the Christian world, for even this last is progress. . . . ." "That the occasion and essential feature of the Reformation was an assertion of the right, or rather the recognition of the necessity of private judgment and interpretation, as opposed to the authority and dictation of the Church, it will not be difficult to show from the writings and disputations of Luther himself."

The statements of the writer are unquestionably true, but he uses them as starting-points from which to go down into deeper depths of error. It it not worth while to follow him in his argument. Suffice it to say that the conclusion he reaches is that "the performance of duty consists in neither believing nor disbelieving, but in being true to one's self, in a continual advancement towards the highest ideal," which simply means in the end worship of self.

OUR OWN WILL, AND HOW TO DETECT IT IN OUR ACTIONS: Or Instructions Intended for Religicus, Applicable also to all who Aim at the Perfect Life. By the Rev *J. Allen*, D.D., Chaplain of the Dominican Convents of the Sacred Heart in King Williamstown and East London, South Africa. With a Preface by Right Rev. *J. D. Ricards*, D.D., Bishop of Retimo and Vicar Apostolic of the Eastern Vicariate of the Cape Colony. New York, Cincinnati, St. Louis: Benziger Brothers. 1885.

This little work, as its title-page says, is chiefly intended for Religious. At the same time all who desire to make progress in the spiritual life can read it with great profit. It is full of plain and practical lessons applicable to the every-day life of all who are in earnest in the service of God.

The author has had long and large experience in the direction of Religions and has evidently studied the subject he treats, closely and profoundly. Like a skilful physician he carefully diagnosticates the symptoms of the disease he seeks to cure and applies the remedies required for its eradication. As he tells us in his preface, he does not enter into the questions regarding grace that are freely disputed over by theologians, his sole desire being to help those who are striving for perfection to avoid and overcome the difficulties which arise from natural faults and weaknesses.

The number of books that have been written on the state of perfection and how to attain it is very great. Yet comparatively few of them are well-suited in all respects to English-speaking readers. Most of them are translations from different European languages. Of necessity, therefore, even their translations retain the coloring of the peculiar characteristic ideas and modes of thought of the peoples for whom they were primarily intended, and consequently are to a certain extent foreign to and diverse from those of English-speaking countries. Their style, also, is often too involved and too exalted, and, it may be, too polished and refined. The work before us is free from these defects. It is plain, simple, direct, and practical, and well calculated, as we have already said, to benefit the laity who peruse its pages, by pointing out the secret workings of self-will in their daily lives and showing them how to bring their wills into accordance with the holy will of God, as well as to guide Religious in their efforts to attain perfection.

A LITERARY AND BIOGRAPHICAL HISTORY, OR BIOGRAPHICAL DICTIONARY OF THE ENGLISH CATHOLICS. From the Breach with Rome in 1534 to the Present Time. By *Joseph Gillow.* Vol. I. London: Burns & Oates. New York: Catholic Publication Society Company.

The volume before us is the first of a projected series of five in which he intends to complete the work he has undertaken. His purpose is to present, in the most ready and convenient form for reference, a record of the literary efforts, the educational struggles, and the sufferings for religion's sake of the Catholics in England from Henry VIII.'s breach with Rome, and the beginning of the consequent English schism, down to the present time.

Since the publication, in 1737, 1739, and 1742, of the three volumes of Catholic biographical history known as Dodd's Church history, which is only brought down to 1688, no successful attempt has been made to publish a complete collection of biographies of eminent English Catholics. Yet during the intervening period an immense amount of valuable material has been collected, and many valuable works, restricted to particular periods of the interval, or particular classes of persons or places, have appeared.

The scope of a Biographical Dictionary, comprehending notices of so large a number of persons, necessarily admits of only abridged and condensed accounts of their lives. Yet the work before us proceeds on the plan of giving the most interesting and important details tending to exhibit the characters and actions of the individuals mentioned. The writer states in his preface that nearly every Catholic family in England will be mentioned, and that he will endeavor to "elucidate family history as much as the circumscribed character of the work will permit." To English Catholics and those in other countries of English Catholic descent the work will have a special interest in the genealogical information it contains. Antiquarians, too, will find in it much that will repay perusal. Apart from all this, however, the work is an important aid to the student of general English history, and valuable, also, for reference.

MOVEMENTS OF RELIGIOUS THOUGHT IN BRITAIN DURING THE NINETEENTH CENTURY. ST. GILES'S LECTURES. By *John Tulloch*, S.T.D., Senior Principal in the University of St. Andrews. New York: Charles Scribner's Sons. 1885.

This volume consists of eight lectures, in which the author undertakes to describe the chief movements of religious thought in England and Scotland during the first sixty years of the present century. He classifies these movements as follows: "Coleridge and His School;" "The Early Oriel School and Its Congeners;" "The Oxford or Anglo-Catholic Movement;" "Movement of Religious Thought in Scotland;" "Thomas Carlyle as a Religious Teacher;" "John Stuart Mill and His School;" "Broad Church: F. D. Maurice and Charles Kingsley;" "Broad Church (continued): F. W. Robertson and Bishop Ewing."

The subjects thus enumerated are treated in a historical rather than a critical manner. The author, it is true, attempts to show the relation of each movement and the leading ideas of the chief personages in each movement, with reference to the general religious thought of England and Scotland. But he is deficient in philosophical acumen, and, moreover, is unconsciously influenced by his own rationalistic turn of mind which brings him into close contact and sympathy with Liberalism and Broad Churchism. He labors in his account of the "Oxford Movement" to do full justice to Newman. Yet such remarks as the following show how entirely unable he is to appreciate him : "With all the *apparent* frankness of the *Apologia*, ... the full history of Newman's religious opinions will only be known when we know more of the steps of his transition from Evangelicanism to High Churchism, and how far he took Liberalism on his way;" and, "It would be far too long to discuss it [Newman's *Grammar of Assent*] here. I have elsewhere examined it, and found it at the root—as I think all who probe it critically will find it—to be only a process of make-belief."

The subjects which the author treats are interesting, but his treatment of them is confused and superficial.

MEDITATIONS ON THE MYSTERIES OF THE HOLY ROSARY. From the French of Father Monsabré, O.P., by *Very Rev. Stephen Byrne, O.P.* New York: The Catholic Publication Society Company. 1885.

The two names appearing on the title-page of this little volume are so well and favorably known, the one throughout the Universal Church, and the other to all American and Irish Catholics, that they, of themselves, should be recommendation enough of the book. It is unnecessary to say that a work from the pen of the greatest of living French preachers is well written. The translation, too, is both faithful and elegant.

We have not here, however; all of Father Monsabré's work on the *Holy Rosary*, which, in the original, has gone through twelve editions. He has published seven series of *Meditations*, only three of which are given at present to English readers. We hope the present venture will meet with enough success to insure the early translation and publication here of the remainder.

In the first two series of Meditations given here, entitled *Jesus in the Rosary*, and *Mary in the Rosary*, the eyes of the soul are opened to the contemplation of Jesus and Mary in the joyful, sorrowful and glorious phases of their blessed lives, while in the third series are gathered the fruits of each Mystery of the Rosary. Attached at the end of the little volume is a magnificent document relating to the Rosary, the Encyclical of our present Sovereign Pontiff, Leo XIII., given on the 1st of September, 1883, along with his other letters to the same effect. The publication of these, rightly remarks the translator, "may be said to constitute a new epoch in the history of this devotion."

SISTER SAINT PIERRE AND THE WORK OF REPARATION. A Brief History, by the *Very Rev. P. Janvier*, Director of the Priests of the Holy Face at Tours. Translated by *Miss Mary Hoffmann*. With a Preface, by the *Right Rev. Mgr. T. S. Preston, V.G., LL.D.* Published for the Benefit of the Discalced Carmelites of New Orleans. With an Appendix of Prayers and Devotions for the Confraternity of the Holy Face. New York: The Catholic Publication Society Company. 1885.

This work, as its title indicates, is a translation of the brief *Life of Sister Saint-Pierre*, which was published by the Rev. Father Janvier at Tours, in 1882, with the approbation of his Archbishop. It has the *imprimatur* of the Archbishop of Tours, and the translation is approved by the Archbishops of Baltimore and New Orleans, and by other Prelates. It gives the principal facts in the life of the saintly Carmelite, and it cannot fail, we think, to be read by pious Catholics with profit and edification.

The Confraternity of the Holy Face (to promote the growth and extension of which is one of the objects of this volume) was established at St. Dizier in 1847, and at Tours in 1876. It has been enriched by indulgences granted by Pius IX., of blessed memory, and Leo XIII., gloriously reigning. With this high sanction, the Confraternity has also been introduced and established in the United States.

Its chief objects are, first, to repair the outrages committed against the Divine Majesty of God by blasphemies, the profanation of Sunday, and the feasts of the Church ; second, to obtain the conversion and salvation of blasphemers and profaners ; third, to preserve youth and the family from the fatal effects of these scandals.

To obtain this threefold end, the Confraternity proposes to render a special *cultus* of prayer, adoration and love to the most Holy Face of our Divine Lord, outraged and disfigured in His Passion. The Confraternity is placed under the patronage of St. Michael and St. Louis. It takes for its models the Immaculate Virgin Mary, the Apostle St. Peter, and the pious Veronica. Trinity Sunday is its principal feast ; the second one is that of the Holy Name of Jesus ; and for particular those of the Saints above mentioned.

The latter part of the volume consists of a number of appendices which contain the rules of the Confraternity, and also a number of devotions admirably calculated to promote its special objects.

TRIBUTES OF PROTESTANT WRITERS TO THE TRUTH AND BEAUTY OF CATHO-LICITY. By *James J. Treacy*, Editor of " Catholic Flowers from Protestant Gardens," etc. New York : F. Pustet & Co.

It is surprising what a wealth of unwilling testimony the editor of this beautiful little volume has collected in these four hundred 12mo pages. Veritable Balaams he makes out of some of the most illustrious men in the whole wide range of modern literature. An admirable conception was this, of showing at a glance what a large share of praise, often grudgingly given, the Church has extorted from her enemies. Nearly all the extracts which Mr. Treacy has made are short, but all are directly to the point. The volume is characterized by great variety, both as to the author and subject ; here, indeed, it seems to us, the compiler has exercised the soundest judgment as well as the keenest critical acumen, for he could easily fill such a volume alone with articles on the same subject by various Protestant writers, or on a variety of subjects by the same author. But, in the work which he here presents to the public, thefe are not two extracts on the same topic ; and, for the sixty-four subjects treated, he gives us specimens of the best efforts of forty-nine writers, nearly all of them preëminent masters of style. Among them we find Lord Brougham, Edmund Burke, Carlyle, Cobbett, E. A. Freeman, James Anthony Froude, Grotius, Guizot, Laing, Lecky, Leibniez, Longfellow, Macaulay, Mackintosh, Maitland, Mallock, Prescott, Robertson, Ruskin, Smiles, and others of hardly less note. It is impossible to read this book without deriving great profit from the perusal.

We have been greatly pleased to notice, by an announcement in the public press, that it has received the highest recognition of Papal approval, and its editor the special blessing of the Holy Father, along with a material as well as the spiritual favor from the same source.

THE LIFE OF JEAN JACQUES OLIER, Founder of the Seminary of St. Sulpice: By *Edward Healy Thompson, M.A.* New and Enlarged Edition. London: Burns & Oates. 1885.

None of the great French ecclesiastical reformers has been so fortunate in his biographer as was M. Olier in the late M. Faillon, who, however, as his English adopter, Mr. Thompson, remarks in the preface of the volume under consideration, "enjoyed one inestimable advantage, as compared with M. Olier's previous biographers, in having access to the *Memoirs* which the servant of God composed in obedience to his director, the Père Bataille ; a task which he performed with all the simplicity and sincerity of a child." By the aid of these Memoirs, M. Faillon was enabled, just before his death, to make great improvement on the earlier editions of his work, which, by this means, has become a masterpiece. Unfortunately, its author did not live to see it published in its perfect form, in 1873, as he died shortly after he had completed the preparation for the press of its last pages. To almost exactly the same extent is the present edition of Mr. Thompson's biography, which is grounded almost entirely, as we have said, on the great work of the Abbé Faillon, now consisting of three volumes, an improvement on that by the same well-known writer with which English readers have heretofore been acquainted. Every sentence in these six hundred pages is worth careful perusal, and the whole narrative is a deeply engrossing episode of a most important period in Church history. We obtain here a clear idea of the evils of the time, the corruption of morals following in the wake of heresy and war, the obstacles to reform, and the heroic efforts with which it was at last effected. That was the age of St. Vincent de Paul, Cardinal de Berulle, Father de Condren, Father Bernard, called "the Poor Priest," the Abbé Bourdoise, and others scarcely less eminent. But, notwithstanding the immense labors of these Apostles, there were more than enough abuses left for the Abbé Olier to correct, and right nobly he performed the great and holy task set him by Divine Providence. How much one man, who earnestly sets himself to his task, and yet dies at the comparatively early age of forty-nine years, can do, may be learned, and with pleasure, by the perusal of the work here under notice. It tells not only how the Seminary of St. Sulpice at Paris, the fruitful mother of many a worthy offspring both in the old and in the new world, came into being and grew to maturity, but also how the Faubourg St. Germain of Paris was changed, by the exertions of one man, from one of the most immoral and disorderly places to a parish of model conduct and exemplary piety. Some other important events are incidentally narrated here, such as the story of Jansenism in the first period of its crooked career. But most directly interesting to Americans is the account of the foundation of the colony and Seminary at Montreal.

LECTURES DELIVERED AT A SPIRITUAL RETREAT. Edited by a Member of the Order of Mercy, Authoress of the Life of Catherine McAuley, Life of St. Alphonsus, etc., etc. New York: The Catholic Publication Society. London: Burns & Oates. 1885.

These lectures, as we learn from the preface, were written out from memory many years ago by a Sister of a convent in the South of Ireland, immediately after their delivery by a holy secular priest who spoke without notes or memoranda. Copies of them have been so frequently asked for from time to time that, acting on the advice of the late Archbishop of New Orleans and after having them carefully examined by a learned ecclesiastic, they are now published under the *Imprimatur* of His Eminence, the late Cardinal McCloskey.

NATURE AND THOUGHT. An Introduction to a Natural Philosophy. By *St. George Mivart*. Second Edition. London : Burns & Oates. New York : The Catholic Publication Society Co. 1885.

This book is intended to clear up some of the confusion that has gathered around the discussion of those deeper problems which underlie all science, and to establish a basis for a Natural Philosophy on the ground of the concord of the world of Nature with the world of Thought.

It deals chiefly with the problem of certainty, and refutes satisfactorily many of the sophisms of the skeptical philosophy of the age.

After an introductory chapter, in which the writer briefly reviews the different opinions entertained about the origin of ideas and the basis of human knowledge, the main subject of the book is discussed under the following questions :

1. " Can we have absolute certainty about anything, and if so, what is the criterion, and what are the grounds and motives of all certainty ?"

2. " Can we have a certain knowledge of an external world existing independently of ourselves such as physical science postulates ?"

3. " Can we know universal and necessary truths, and if so, what is the bearing of such knowledge on the questions of man's nature and origin ?"

4. " Can we learn the purpose of human life and attain to such a knowledge of a First Cause as may reconcile the existence of Nature, as we see it, with the declarations of Conscience ?"

THE WORKS OF THE RIGHT REV. JOHN ENGLAND, Bishop of Charleston, S. C. With Memoir, Memorials, Notes, and Full Index. By *Hugh P. McElrone*. In two Volumes. Vol. II. Baltimore : The Baltimore Publishing Company. 1884.

This second volume of this selection from the works of the late Bishop England is made up of addresses and papers written by him on Infallibility, Intention, Penance, Celibacy, Liberalism and Liberality, Calumnies on Catholics, Dispensation, The Bulls of the Crusades, Transubstantiation, American Catholicity, The Papacy and Feudalism, True Basis of Republicanism, and the Republic in Danger. Nearly all of them are controversial in form, as are indeed the greatest part of Bishop England's writings, owing to the times in which he lived and the circumstances in which he was placed. As such they throw a clear light upon those times, their occurrences and characteristic spirit. But apart from this, they have a high value in the clearness and ability with which the truths relating to the subjects treated are set forth.

The title chosen by the compiler of these volumes, " Works of the Right Rev. John England," etc., is delusive. For these volumes do not by any means contain all his works. Nor do they furnish a just or adequate idea of his personal character, the extent of his labors, or his ability as a writer and theologian.

ELEMENTS OF NATURAL PHILOSOPHY. A Text-book for High Schools and Academies. By *Elroy M. Avery, Ph.D.*, Author of a Series of Physical Science Textbooks. Illustrated by more than 400 Wood Engravings. Sheldon & Company, New York and Chicago.

This is a very well arranged text-book. The definitions and explanations are clear and concise ; the illustrations are well executed and distinct, and an unusual number of practical problems are given to test the knowledge of the pupil. The chapters upon the subjects of magnetism and electricity are particularly full and detailed.

ALETHEIA; OR, THE UNSPOKEN TRUTH ON THE ALL-IMPORTANT QUESTION OF DIVINE AUTHORITATIVE TEACHING. An Exposition of the Catholic Rule of Faith, Contrasted with the Various Theories of Private and Fallible Interpretation of the Sacred Scriptures. With a Full Explanation of the Whole Question of Infallibility, and Application of the Principles to the Development of Christian Doctrine according to the Needs of the Times. By the *Right Rev. J. D. Ricords, D.D.*, Bishop of Retimo, and Vicar Apostolic of the Eastern Vicariate of the Cape Colony. New York, Cincinnati, and St. Louis: Benziger Brothers. London: R. Washburne. Dublin: M. H. Gill & Son. 1885.

The copious title of this work, which we have copied, states so fully its scope and purpose that further explanation seems needless.

It seems somewhat strange that of the works recently published to combat the leading errors of our times, two of the very best as regards the form in which the arguments are put, the most readable and best adapted for popular use, come from South Africa, a region which, it might be supposed, is far removed from the general current of the world's thought. Yet this is the case. One of these books is comprised in the volume before us. The other, from the pen of the same author, —" Catholic Christianity and Modern Unbelief,"—we noticed in a previous number of the REVIEW.

The writer carefully avoids all display of scholastic learning and theology. He adapts himself, as far as possible, to the prevailing tastes as regards style and the methods of thought of our times. His statements of truths are clear, brief, and terse, intermingled with illustrations that may amuse while they also instruct, and genial anecdotes, incisive exposures of fallacies, and vigorous direct reasoning from acknowledged principles. His work is emphatically a work for the times, and we hope it will have a wide circulation.

MARY IN THE GOSPELS; OR, LECTURES ON THE HISTORY OF OUR BLESSED LADY AS RECORDED BY THE EVANGELISTS. By *Very Rev. J. Spencer Northcote, D.D.*, Provost of Birmingham. Second Edition. London: Burns & Oates. New York: The Catholic Publication Society Company. 1885.

Father Northcote's little work is so well known, and its merits are so fully acknowledged, that an extended notice of it is needless. It confines itself to but one part, and that a small but very important part, of Mary's history—the notices of her in the Gospels. Examining these one by one, he clearly shows that the fewness and brevity of the references made to her by the Evangelists and the seeming indifference to her of her Divine Son on several occasions are not only inconsistent with her exalted position and dignity; they bear a like relation to her and her exaltation, which the humiliation and passion of our Lord bear to His glorification.

WOMEN OF CATHOLICITY: Memoirs of Margaret O'Carroll, Isabella of Castile, Margaret Roper, Marie de L'Incarnation, Marguerite Bourgeoys, Ethan Allen's Daughter. By *Anna T. Sadlier*, Author of "Names that Live in Catholic Hearts," etc., etc. New York, Cincinnati, and St. Louis: Benziger Brothers. 1885.

Although published under a different title from that of "Names that Live in Catholic Hearts," this work forms a second volume of Miss Anna T. Sadlier's series of Catholic biographies. The persons whose lives and characters are sketched in it have been judiciously chosen. They were, each of them, in their respective spheres valiant women, and their names will live as long as the qualities which constitute goodness and greatness are admired. A study of their lives, too, reveals the fact that while they were richly endowed with rare natural gifts, yet that the secret of their preëminence was something beyond and above these natural gifts; that it was a supernatural element, divine grace ennobling and purifying all they did and said, which raises them far above all mere human eminence. This, as the admirable mother of the author says in her preface, is the "golden thread" that runs through the lives of all the biographical sketches contained in this volume, and distinguishes them from other women renowned in history.

Miss Sadlier unites in these sketches a careful study of her subjects and strict adherence to historic truth with an animated and attractive style. These qualities make her writings both interesting and instructive.

OUTLINES OF THE PHILOSOPHY OF RELIGION. Dictated Portions of the Lectures of *Hermann Lotze.*. Translated and edited by *George T. Ladd*, Professor of Philosophy in Yale College. Boston : Ginn, Heath & Co. 1885.

No good purpose is to be served by the publication of such a book as this. While professing to inculcate belief in God, the chief aim of the author seems to be to discredit the scholastic proofs of the existence of the Supreme Being and in favor of revealed religion. The natural and philosophical religion which he teaches is scarcely even Deism. Nor is it worth while for orthodox Christians to go to this volume for objections; they will find them set forth much more clearly in their own books, with the advantage of having the answers appended. It is well that his style is so obscure and his expression of ideas so vague that few will have the patience to read him very far. Better it were had not this stuff been translated; nay, even, had it been left in the note-books of the unfortunate students who had to take down from the lecturer's dictation.

THE BLOOD COVENANT ; A PRIMITIVE RITE AND ITS BEARINGS ON SCRIPTURE. By *H. Clay Trumbull, D.D.*, author.of " Kadesh Barnea." New York : Chas. Scribner's Sons. 1885.

The writer of this book is a great reader, but a very small thinker. He has made a collection of facts from the customs of the Jews, of barbarous Asiatic, African and American tribes, respecting their notions, customs, etc., as regards blood, but, as for any intellectual or moral purpose his volume subserves, we are entirely at a loss to understand.

THE CATHOLIC HOME ALMANAC FOR 1886. New York, Cincinnati and St. Louis : Benziger Brothers.

The third yearly issue of this publication is before us, and, from a cursory inspection of its contents and workmanship, we think it deserves even warmer praise than the two former issues previously received. Got up in convenient form, it contains an enormous amount of matter for the mere trifle that it costs. It is also profusely illustrated, and the cuts are nearly all excellent. Besides the usual calendar and the astronomical calculations for next year, we find in it some fine poetry and bits of prose fiction, with which biographical and historical sketches are judiciously mingled. At the end is a summary of the important events in American Church History, occurring between July, 1884, and July, 1885.

PRACTICAL REFLECTIONS ON THE SUFFERINGS OF OUR LORD; OR, LESSONS OF THE PASSION. From the French of Cardinal de la Luzerne. By *Very Rev. S. Byrne, O.P.* Boston, Mass.: Thomas B. Noonan & Co. 1885.

These reflections are not a superfluous addition to the large amount of what has been already written on the Sacred Passion of our Divine Redeemer. Cardinal de la Luzerne was one of the most solid and practical thinkers of modern times, and the volume before us possesses these characteristics. The meditations and reflections it contains will be of great profit to all who read them devoutly.

———

A TROUBLED HEART, AND HOW IT WAS COMFORTED AT LAST. Notre Dame, Ind.: Joseph P. Lyons. 1885.

This is a narrative, originally published in the *Ave Maria*, of the struggles and experiences, long and severe, of one who passed through different phases of Protestantism and Rationalism, and finally found peace in the true faith and the bosom of the Holy Church.

———

BRAVE BOYS OF FRANCE. A Story of the late War in Europe. Boston: Thomas B. Noonan & Co. 1885.

A volume of interesting stories suitable for boys.

———

BOOKS RECEIVED.

INSTRUCTIO SPONSORUM, lingua Anglica conscripta ad usum Parochorum; Auctore Sacerdote Missionario. Cum permissu Superiorum. St. Louis: B. Herder. 1885. 12mo., pp. 31.

ENGLMANN'S LATIN GRAMMAR. Improved and edited by *P. Augustine Schneider*, O.S.B. Cincinnati: Anton Bicker. 1885. 8vo., pp. 425.

IRENE OF CORINTH. An Historic Romance of the First Century. By *Rev. P. I. Harold*. Toronto: Hunter, Rose & Co. 1884. 12mo., pp. 298.

PROBLÈMES ET CONCLUSIONS DE L'HISTOIRE DES RELIGIONS Par *l'Abbé de Broglie*, Ancien Elève de l'Ecole Polytechnique, Professeur d'Apologétique à l'Institut Catholique de Paris. Paris: Putois-Cretté. 1885. 12mo., pp. 416.

INSTITUTIONES MORALES ALPHONSIANÆ, seu Doctoris Eccl. S. Alphonsi Mariæ de Ligorio Doctrina Moralis ad usum scholarum accommodata, cura et studio *P. Clementis Marc*, Congr. SS. Redempt. Romæ: Ex typographia Pacis. 1885. Large 8vo. Tom. I., pp. 911. Tom. II., pp. 837.

ELEMENTS OF PHILOSOPHY. Comprising Logic and Ontology, or General Metaphysics. By *Rev. Walter H. Hill, S.J.* Seventh Revised Edition. Baltimore: John Murphy & Co. 1885.

THE IRISH AND ANGLO-IRISH GENTRY WHEN CROMWELL CAME TO IRELAND; or, a Supplement to Irish Peerages. By *John O'Hart*. Dublin: M. H. Gill & Son. 1884.

THE TRUTH ABOUT JOHN WYCLIF. His Life, Writings, and Opinions, chiefly from Evidence of his Contemporaries. By *Joseph Stevenson, S.J.* London: Burns & Oates. 1885.

THE VIRGIN MOTHER OF GOOD COUNSEL. By *Mgr. G. F. Dillon, D.D.* New (cheap) edition, with illustrations. Dublin: M. H. Gill & Son. 1885.

LITTLE MONTH OF THE SOULS IN PURGATORY. Translated from the French of the author of "Golden Lands," by *Miss Ella McMahon*. New York, Cincinnati and St. Louis: Benziger Brothers. 1886.

TO. CLERGYMEN.

PLEASE READ.

It may seem a small matter, but it is nevertheless one of the most important, and at the same time most difficult questions for a clergyman to determine, How shall I dress? A wide latitude is allowed to the laity on this subject, who may, if they please, indulge their own peculiar taste in the matter of dress, whether it accords with the prevailing style or not. But not so with the clergy. They must dress in a manner distinctive from other men, and in keeping with their sacred calling. And how to do this successfully, how to strike the happy medium between the secular and the ultra clerical in this matter of their dress, is where the difficulty lies.

Three things are necessary to a good clerical garment. First, the material should always be plain black goods of fine quality. Second, it should be cut in a style, modest, unpretentious, and gentlemanly, with just sufficient fulness in front, and length in the skirts, to indicate the wearer's profession. And Third, the fit should always be close and as near perfect as possible, for no matter how fine the goods, or how clerical the cut, if the garment is not a good fit it is an eyesore, and a cause of constant discomfiture to the wearer.

Now many years of experience in this branch of our business have given us a familiarity with the wants of clergymen in this matter of dress that has proved of great service to our patrons; and we shall be pleased to give to all who may favor us in the future the benefit of our best judgment on the subject.

Our large experience and extensive facilities enable us to give entire satisfaction, not only as regards the style and quality of the garments themselves, but also as to the reasonableness of the prices.

On application a set of samples will be forwarded to any Clergyman in the U. S., with full instructions for self-measurement. The samples will be of goods which will cost, when made up, from $20 to $50.

Address,

WANAMAKER & BROWN,

OAK HALL, SIXTH AND MARKET STREETS,

PHILADELPHIA.

The Largest Retail Clothing House in America.

P. S.—Samples also sent and orders received for all kinds of Gentlemen's Clothing at the lowest possible prices.

THE AMERICAN CATHOLIC

QUARTERLY REVIEW.

THE AMERICAN CATHOLIC QUARTERLY REVIEW is issued regularly in January, April, July, and October.

EACH NUMBER CONTAINS 192 pages, large octavo, printed from legible type, on fine white paper.

SUBSCRIPTION, $5.00 per annum, payable in advance, or $1.25 a single copy. Postage free to all parts of the U. S.

The Editorial Department is conducted by Right Rev. James A. Corcoran, D.D.

It is DESIGNED that the *American Catholic Quarterly Review* shall be of the highest character that can be given it by the educated Catholic mind of the United States and of Europe.

It is NOT PROPOSED that it shall be confined to the discussion of theological subjects, but that it shall embrace within its scope all subjects of interest to educated Catholics, whether philosophical, historical, scientific, literary, or political—using the latter term in its original and proper meaning. Partisan politics, or politics in the popular sense of the word, it is scarcely necessary to say, will be rigidly excluded.

THE MOST LEARNED and scholarly writers that can be secured will be enlisted in support of the *Review* as regular and occasional contributors; and every effort will be made by its conductors to render it an able and efficient auxiliary to the Church in her warfare against modern error.

Subscriptions respectfully solicited.

Address,   *HARDY & MAHONY,*

505 CHESTNUT STREET,

POST-OFFICE BOX, 1044.   PHILADELPHIA.

Lightning Source UK Ltd.
Milton Keynes UK
UKHW021347100219
336936UK00006B/314/P